"Behold, I stand at the door . . ."
Jesus, Revelation 3:20
Y0-CZP-598

# Jimmy Swaggart Bible Commentary

# I Thessalonians
# II Thessalonians

# Jimmy Swaggart Bible Commentary

# I Thessalonians
# II Thessalonians

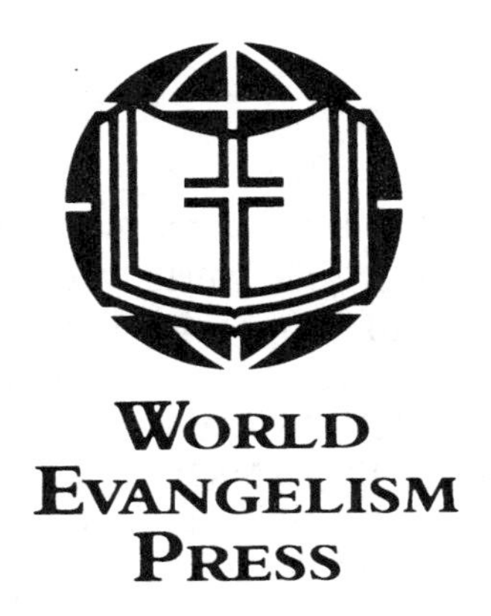

World Evangelism Press

ISBN 978-1-934655-16-0

P.O. Box 262550 • Baton Rouge, Louisiana 70826-2550
Website: www.jsm.org • E-mail: info@jsm.org
(225) 768-8300
12 13 14 15 16 17 18 19 20 21 22 23 24 25 26 27 28 29 / RRD / 20 19 18 17 16 15 14 13 12 11 10 9 8 7 6 5 4 3

# TABLE OF CONTENTS

# THE BOOK OF I THESSALONIANS

## THE INTRODUCTION TO THE FIRST EPISTLE OF PAUL THE APOSTLE TO THE THESSALONIANS

NOTES

Thessalonica was founded in 315 B.C. by the Macedonian King, Cassander, and was named after his wife, who was a sister of Alexander the Great. In later Roman times it was made a political capital and in 42 B.C. was given the status of a *"free city"* because it had sided with Antony and Octavius in the Second Civil War. As a free city, it appointed its own Magistrates, called *"Politarchs"* (*"rulers of the city,"* Acts 17:6).

Thessalonica was located on the Egnatian Road, the great highway which linked East and West. Possessing a famous harbor, it was in Paul's day a strategic converging point of culture and commerce, a great and thriving center. Cicero spoke of it as *"placed in the lap of the Empire."* In world trade, in Hellenistic culture, in Roman government, in Jewish influence, and subsequently in Christian Missionary strategy, it was a key center.

## THE FOUNDING OF THE CHURCH

Having been stopped by the Holy Spirit from going south into the Province of Asia and north into Bithynia (Acts 16:6-7), Paul arrived at Troas probably in late March or early April of A.D. 49. From Troas, the westernmost city of Asia Minor, he was directed in a Vision to cross the Aegean Sea into Macedonia and to take the Gospel there for the first time (Acts 16:9). That he did (Acts 16:10-11) was one of the crucial events in history because through it the Gospel moved to the west and the evangelization of Europe began. Arriving at the port of Neapolis after a two-day voyage, the Missionary party of Paul, Silas, Luke, and Timothy left almost immediately on a single-day journey of ten miles toward the largest city of Philippi to the north.

The successful mission at Philippi (Acts 16:12-40) lasted about two months. Then, leaving Luke and possibly Timothy behind, Paul and Silas left Philippi under pressure from the city officials and went westward toward Thessalonica, a major center about 100 miles or a five-day walk away. It must have been a painful journey because of what they had suffered while in prison at Philippi (Acts 16:22-24; I Thess. 2:2). In route they would no doubt have followed the famous Egnatian Way, which crossed Macedonia from east to west, and passed through Amphipolis and then through Apollonia (Acts 17:1). These two cities were apparently not suitable points for Evangelism at the time, so Paul and Silas continued to Thessalonica.

## PAUL'S METHOD

The Holy Spirit led Paul to plant his next Church in this city. The presence of a Synagogue offered an obvious place to begin (Acts 17:1-4), as was his custom. So he pursued his approach of proving from the Old Testament that the Messiah must suffer and be raised and that Jesus is this Messiah. In the meantime, he would readily follow his own trade of manufacturing the goat's hair cloth that was a prominent part of the local economy (Acts 18:3; I Thess. 2:9; II Thess. 3:8).

For three consecutive Sabbaths Paul spoke in the Synagogue, but met with the usual Jewish resistance. Luke's description of the events may be interpreted as meaning that the resistance forced him to leave the city immediately. However, to read it another way, it is possible that Paul may have remained in Thessalonica for a longer period of time, possibly even several months.

Three points make the latter alternative more probable:

1. Paul engaged in gainful employment at Thessalonica (I Thess. 2:9; II Thess. 3:8). Two to three weeks are not sufficient time for settling into a trade.

2. Upon his departure from Thessalonica, he left a thriving Church — not one still in the throes of separation from the local Synagogue. Indeed, by the time he left, this Church included many Gentiles, fresh from their heathen idolatry (I Thess. 1:9). It is highly unlikely that they had been won to the Lord in the two or three weeks that the Apostle was ministering in the Synagogue.

3. Before leaving, Paul had received at least two special gifts from Philippi a hundred miles or so away. It is difficult to crowd all of this into two or three weeks.

## THE SALVATION OF SOULS

A good number of Jews, God-fearing Gentiles, and prominent women responded to the Synagogue Ministry, including Jason at whose home Paul was entertained (Acts 17:4-9). Many others, principally Gentiles, became Christians in the weeks following (I Thess. 1:9). Numbered among the converts in this city were probably Aristarchus and Secundus (Acts 19:29; 20:4; 27:2), and perhaps Gaius (Acts 19:29) and Demas (II Tim. 4:10).

After approximately three months, the Church was of considerable size, and the Jews became unbearably jealous. So they instigated riots to force the Magistrates to rule against the Christians, whom they accused of upsetting society and opposing Caesar's decrees (Acts 17:5-9). Jason and several other Christians were brought in for a hearing. The city officials, however, stood firm under pressure, and eventually let Jason and the others go. Though not personally involved in this incident, Paul, Silas, and perhaps Timothy (if by now he had joined them from Philippi) knew it was time to leave so as to avoid bringing additional hardship on their new Brothers in Christ (Acts 17:10).

NOTES

## BEREA

From Thessalonica they traveled west for about two and a half days (about 50 miles) to Berea. Here, their Synagogue Ministry was favorably received for about seven weeks. It might have continued even longer if adversaries from Thessalonica had not heard of their success and come to disrupt their preaching. At this point Paul was forced to go on to Athens, but since Silas and Timothy had not been so conspicuous, they were able to remain for a time at Berea (Acts 17:11-15).

Some of the believing Brothers in Berea conducted Paul all the way to Athens, going first to the nearby coast (Acts 17:14) and then catching a ship for a one-week voyage to the city. A three hundred mile overland trip to Athens, is not probable. Paul's physical condition and his personal safety were too much a concern for his escorts to have taken this risk. The party probably arrived in Athens late in October, A.D. 49.

## ATHENS

Paul gave the returning Bereans instruction to have Silas and Timothy join him immediately at Athens (Acts 17:15), which they did (I Thess. 3:1). The two were then sent back to Macedonia, Timothy's responsibility being to encourage the Thessalonian Christians and bring back a report about them. If Timothy joined Paul at Athens by late November, it would have been about three months since Paul had left Thessalonica. He had become quite concerned about the converts there and at great personal sacrifice commissioned Timothy to strengthen them and find out how they were faring under persecution (I Thess. 3:1-5). Silas was probably sent on a similar mission to Philippi.

While the two men were away, Paul had some small results in Athens, but it seems not as successful as his other places of Ministry (Acts 17:16-34). Leaving there, he went to another Achaian city, Corinth, where he enjoyed a spiritually prosperous nearly two year Ministry. If the stay in Athens was about two months, his arrival in Corinth must have been in December, A.D. 49 or January, A.D. 50. If we allow time for Timothy's round trip to Thessalonica on foot and also time for his

NOTES

Ministry in Thessalonica, then he and Silas probably returned to Paul from Macedonia in the Spring of A.D. 50 (Acts 18:5; I Thess. 3:6-7). Timothy's report on Thessalonica was so encouraging that Paul wrote I Thessalonians almost immediately.

## THE DATE OF THE EPISTLE

Paul's initial visit to Corinth probably terminated shortly after Gallio became Proconsul in that city (Acts 18:11-18). An inscription at Delphi in central Greece dates a proclamation of Roman Emperor Claudius sometime early in A.D. 52. The inscription calls Gallio Proconsul of Asia at that time, probably meaning that he had begun his term in the summer of A.D. 51.

Paul's trial before Gallio appears to have come when he was new to the city, because his Jewish accusers tried to take advantage of his being a new arrival (Acts 18:12-13). His departure from Corinth was, therefore, in the late Summer or early Fall of A.D. 51. Since he spent nearly two years in Corinth (Acts 18:11, 18), we may reckon that he arrived there from Athens late A.D. 49 or early A.D. 50.

Timothy joined him from Thessalonica a few months later. After Paul's departure from the Thessalonian city, news about the Christians there had spread far and wide (I Thess. 1:8-9). Also, a number of converts to Christ had died, and Paul had been asked the question as to what was their destiny, which he answered by giving his great statement on the Rapture (I Thess. 4:13-18).

From the late summer of A.D. 49 till the Spring of A.D. 50 is enough time for these things to have happened, as well as for Timothy to have completed his mission. Hence, we may place Paul's writing of I Thessalonians sometime in the Spring of A.D. 50, although some have placed it three or four years later.

Incidently, I Thessalonians is probably the very first Epistle written by Paul.

As well, it is believed that Paul was at Corinth when he wrote I Thessalonians (Acts 18:5; I Thess. 3:6).

## THE PURPOSE OF THE EPISTLE

In response to Timothy's report, Paul had three chief aims it seems in writing the Epistle, even though there were, no doubt, other purposes:

1. To express satisfaction and thanks to God for the healthy spiritual condition of the Church (I Thess. 1:2-10).
2. To make a strong case against the false insinuations against himself and his associates (I Thess. 2:1-3:13).
3. To suggest specific ways in which already strongly Christian behavior of the Thessalonians could be improved as they continued to seek God — approved Holiness (I Thess. 4:1-5:24).

## THE SEVEN CHURCHES TO WHICH THE APOSTLE WROTE

I Thessalonians is the last in order, but the first in time, of the Epistles to the seven Churches to which the Apostle wrote. It is remarkable that in the more than 2,000 ancient Manuscripts of the New Testament the order of the Epistles from Romans to Thessalonians is always the same. Other Books vary in order, but these never. It is my thought that the Holy Spirit designed it this way, and hopefully the following lineup will prove the point:

Romans: The Gospel — Justification and Sanctification.

Corinthians: Failure as to practical Sanctification.

Galatians: Attempt to gain Sanctification by works.

Ephesians: The Church — Its Head and its members.

Philippians: Failure as to the unity of the members.

Colossians: Denial of the Supremacy of the Head.

Thessalonians: The Rapture of the Body into the air.

No Epistles by Paul to Churches followed Thessalonians because perfection will succeed to the Rapture. There cannot be then either failure or false doctrine.

Thus, Romans, Ephesians, and Thessalonians contain *"Doctrine"* and *"Instruction,"* and the remaining four, *"reproof,"* and *"correction"* (II Tim. 3:16).

Ephesians is the central Epistle of the seven. It corresponds to the central upright of the seven branch Lamp-stand of the Tabernacle.

THE THRUST OF THE EPISTLE

Even though I Thessalonians was not written as a major thrust of Doctrine, still, it is definite as it addresses certain particulars.

I speak of the supreme dignity of the Lord Jesus Christ, the Spiritual Kingdom which He has established in this world, the deliverance from the wrath to come effected by Him, the necessity of Holiness as a result of Salvation, the Reign of Christ in Heaven, the Resurrection of the Just, the Rapture of the Church, the Second Advent of Christ, the blessedness of the future state of the Righteous and the wrath which awaits the wicked, are all clearly made evident in this Epistle. In fact, the greatest treatment of the Rapture of the Church is found in I Thessalonians.

The great Plan of Redemption through the sufferings of Christ was clear to the Apostle from the beginning. We can hardly even affirm that there was a development, even at this early time, regarding the doctrinal stand of Paul, although he certainly continued to build on the foundation.

No doubt different doctrines are insisted on in the different Epistles, but this arose from the circumstances of the Churches to which the Apostle wrote. Thus, in this Epistle to the Thessalonians there is no mention of the great Pauline Doctrine of Justification, at least in the sense that it is found in Romans, because in that Church (Thessalonica) there was no controversy then with the Judaistic Christians, and, therefore, no necessity of defending the Doctrine of Justification against erroneous notions; whereas the errors of the Galatian Church caused the Apostle to dwell specially on that Doctrine.

So also at a still later period in the incipient Gnostic errors was the occasion which induced the Apostle to insist more fully on the nature of Christ's Person in the Epistles to the Colossians and Ephesians than in his earlier Epistles.

BISHOP LIGHTFOOT

Bishop Lightfoot, in his able article on the *"Epistles to the Thessalonians,"* notices three points of difference between these and Paul's later Epistles:

NOTES

1. First, in the general style of these earlier Letters there is greater simplicity and less exuberance of language.

2. The antagonism is different. Here, the opposition comes from the unconverted Jews; afterwards, Paul's opponents are Judaizing Christians.

3. The doctrinal teaching of the Apostle does not bear quite the same aspect as in the later Epistles. Many of the distinctive Doctrines of Christianity which are inseparably connected with Paul's name were not evolved and distinctly enunciated until the needs of the Church drew them out into prominence at a later date.

So far, then, it may be true that this First Epistle to the Thessalonians is not so doctrinal as the Epistles to the Romans, Galatians, and Ephesians. The circumstances of the Church determined the contents of the Epistle. The Doctrine most insisted on in this Letter explains the Rapture and the Second Advent, because erroneous views prevailed concerning it among the Thessalonians, giving rise to many disorders.

THE HEART OF THE APOSTLE

Paul, in writing to the Thessalonians, lays bare his heart; he speaks of his gentleness among them, even as a nursing mother cherished her children, and of his readiness to impart unto them, not the Gospel of God only, but his own soul by reason of the affection which he had for them.

The Epistle which it most closely resembles is that to the Philippians. The Macedonian Churches were peculiarly attached to the Apostle, and he to them; he writes to them in the fullness of his affection; and exhorts them, not so much with the authority of a spiritual Teacher, as with the love and tenderness of a parental affection, even as a father does his children.

PARTICULARS

It is Wednesday, October 5, 1999, as I begin this Commentary. I look forward to this effort for many and varied reasons. Each of Paul's Epistles are different in tone, in thrust, and of course, in content. And yet, they all tie together in a beautiful sense, weaving the fabric of the New Covenant, God's Gift to humanity through the Sacrifice and Resurrection of His Son, and our Savior, the Lord Jesus Christ.

I love the Word of God, actually more than I have vocabulary to express. It is truly *"a Lamp unto my feet, and a Light unto my path"* (Ps. 119:105). I find that the more I learn, the more I realize I do not yet know. The Bible is somewhat like a house which belies its interior, merely by an outward observation of the exterior. In other words, to merely observe the door which leads into the house, in no way portrays the treasures that lie within. The Word of God is absolutely inexhaustible, and because it is the Word of God.

When I was eight years old, I began to study the Bible. I remember asking my Dad at times the meaning of particular Scriptures, and with him at times telling me that he did not know, but would ask our Pastor. In those years, I kept a Bible with me at all times, actually one with very small print, and would read it during recess or our lunch hour at school.

Now the years have come and gone, and my love for the Word of God, I can say without any fear of contradiction, is greater today than ever before. I keep finding treasure after treasure, day after day; therefore, I look forward to the writing of the Commentary on this great Epistle of Paul the Apostle, to the Thessalonians.

## THE CROSS OF CHRIST

At a point of time in 1996, the Lord, in answer to much intercessory prayer, began to open up to me the great Revelation of the Cross. From that time, my Ministry has changed, my understanding of the Word has changed, at least in the sense that it has opened up to a greater degree, and I would like to believe that I have changed. Consequently, the Reader will observe that we take every opportunity presented to us to expound on the great Foundation of Christianity *"Jesus Christ and Him Crucified."* I personally feel that the Church in the last 50 or so years, has drifted from its moorings, and of course I speak of the Cross. In other words, there's been so little preaching and teaching on this all-important subject, that most Christians have little understanding as to the veracity of the Atonement.

NOTES

The Truth is, a thrice holy God cannot deal with sinful man, except through the premise of the Sacrifice of Calvary. Likewise, man cannot reach God, cannot have any communion with God, in fact, can have no contact with God whatsoever, unless he does so through the substitutionary Offering of Christ on the Cross. The Cross is the intersection of the ages, the foundation of the principles of Christ, the culmination of the great Plan of God for the Redemption of humanity, characterized so powerfully in the Old Testament, and brought to fruition in the New.

Regarding this great subject, I will attempt to not be overly repetitive, although repetition is needed and needed constantly as it refers to the absorption of any subject.

If one studies Paul at all, one quickly comes to this conclusion: the central theme of the Apostle's teaching is the Cross. Everything is based on the Finished Work of Christ. In fact, to properly understand Paul, one must read this into every statement he makes.

For instance, when he speaks of Faith, it is not merely a nebulous thing as believed by most, but always of Faith in the Cross of Christ. In other words, the Cross must ever be the object of one's Faith. If we do not understand this in reading him, we will not come to a proper conclusion regarding that which the Holy Spirit has given him. Consequently, the Word of God must be read through the many colors of the Cross. To do otherwise, is to miss the point altogether. Therefore, we will do our very best to not fail to address the subject matter of the great Apostle in this fashion.

## ROUTINE

I was asked the other day, if I had someone to write these Commentaries for me? To be frank, I was somewhat taken aback by the question.

No, I write every single word myself, even doing all of my research. I cannot imagine doing otherwise, considering that the love of my life is this study of the Word of God.

I generally get to the office each morning about 6:00, and sometimes earlier. I will work for about an hour on whatever portion of the Word of God I am at that time addressing. At 7:00 a.m. Tuesday through Friday, I have a daily 90 minute Radio Program. That period of time is devoted exclusively for teaching, which goes out over our *"SonLife Radio Network."* Actually, this Network features nothing but programming from Family Worship Center here in Baton Rouge, Louisiana. There are four teaching programs each day, seven days a week, other than Service times, going out over the Network, with the latter three being rebroadcasts of past teaching programs. The balance of the Programming consists of worship as it regards music, and of course, the preaching of the Word from the various Services of the Church.

The Lord instructed me to do this regarding Radio at the beginning of 1999. The Ministry only had two stations then, but the results have been, and are, absolutely astounding. People are being saved, Believers are being baptized with the Holy Spirit, the sick are being healed, and bondages of darkness are being broken in the hearts and lives of many people — all because of the Word of God, preached, proclaimed, taught, and sung under the Anointing of the Holy Spirit.

The Lord instructed me to install F.M. Radio Stations all over the nation, which we immediately set about to do, which will probably number several hundreds when we are finished, even possibly 1,000 or more, in an effort to cover the entirety of this nation. Of course, this is in conjunction with our Telecast which airs in about 31 countries of the world, translated into several languages.

After the morning program is finished, I start work again on the Commentaries about 9:00 a.m., and then stop again at 10:00 for our morning prayer meeting.

I put in another hour after prayer meeting before lunch, and several hours in the afternoon. This is done everyday, including Saturdays.

Of course, I have all the other duties as well, such as helping to Pastor Family Worship Center, editing all of our Telecasts, editing our monthly magazine, *"The Evangelist"*, which means I write all the copy for that as well, besides preaching Crusades all over the world.

This means that the writing of these Commentaries is done in the midst of the telephone constantly ringing, along with innumerable other interruptions, which means that our efforts are a constant start and stop, etc. Nevertheless, to be of any type of service in the great Work of God is the greatest privilege one could ever have. I so much thank the Lord that He has given me this opportunity, and I pray constantly, even soliciting your prayers, that we will always do exactly what the Lord desires.

NOTES

Of those over whom we might have some small amount of influence, our sole desire is that you grow in Grace and the Knowledge of the Lord. We want you to ever grow closer to Christ, to ever become more Christlike in your daily walk before God. That is our real reason for writing these Commentaries. I know that your study of the Word of God is an absolute necessity in your Christian life, that is if you are to experience growth. You have shown by your purchase of this Commentary that you love the Word of God, and that you desire to grow ever closer to your Lord. There is nothing more commendable than that.

Consequently, I pray that our efforts will help you in this, the single most important thing as it regards your heart, your life, and your family. Thank you for allowing us to be a part of this concerning you, which is so very, very special.

*"Furthermore then we beseech you, Brethren, and exhort you by the Lord Jesus, that as ye have received of us how ye ought to walk and to please God, so ye would abound more and more"* (I Thess. 4:1).

## CHAPTER 1

(1) "PAUL, AND SILVANUS, AND TIMOTHEUS, UNTO THE CHURCH OF THE THESSALONIANS WHICH IS IN GOD THE FATHER AND IN THE LORD JESUS CHRIST: GRACE BE UNTO YOU, AND PEACE, FROM GOD OUR FATHER, AND THE LORD JESUS CHRIST."

This salutation follows the form Paul used in all his Epistles and is in the same style as that of other Letters of his time. It contains three elements: the writer, the recipient, and the greeting or salutation proper.

Absent is the official title *"Apostle"* Paul used in all his other Epistles to the Churches except II Thessalonians and Philippians. A reasonable explanation of this is that no note of authority was necessary in Letters addressed to the Macedonian Churches, where his apostolic position never seems to have been questioned as it was elsewhere (Galatia, Corinth). This is not to say that there was no opposition to Paul in Thesssalonica. On the contrary, that there was opposition is evident from his self-vindication (I Thess. Chpts. 2-3). The opposition, however, never became overt as in other places and never specifically attacked his right to Apostleship.

PAUL, SILAS, AND TIMOTHY

The phrase, *"Paul, and Silvanus, and Timotheus,"* presents the Apostle associating Silas and Timothy with him in the writing of this Letter; however, the writing and its contents are all of Paul. Out of courtesy to them, and because they had shared with him the Thessalonian Ministry, he gives them this honor. However, I personally believe that his reason for including particular ones in the salutation in some of his Letters to various Churches, was of far higher motive.

As the Reader understands, the Church was then in its infancy. In fact, Paul was the Masterbuilder of the Church, meaning that the Lord had given him the responsibility of its foundation, even though others definitely contributed greatly (I Cor. 3:10).

Everything being brand-new, Paul was having to train all of these Brethren who felt the call to preach. As should be obvious, those who traveled with him would have had the greatest training of all. But there were those coming up in the Churches, as well, who actually were serving as the Pastors, even though not having been saved very long.

The only Bible they would have had then, other than the Old Testament, would have been what few Epistles Paul had written thus far, with I Thessalonians actually being the first one, with the exception possibly of James and the Gospel according to Matthew, both having been written, it is believed, several years before Paul's first Epistle. As well, and as is obvious, each Book of the Bible then was placed on a Scroll. So if anyone had all the Books of the Old Testament, plus any others, they would have had any number of Scrolls, which more than likely, most did not have, except for two or three. So, when Paul wrote his Epistles, no doubt many copies were made of them, with copies sent to all the Churches, and being eagerly received.

We take so much for granted today that they did not then have. Not only did they not have Bibles then, or at least they were hard to come by, there were no spiritual authorities they could refer to with the exception of Paul. In fact, Paul was the only one who knew and understood the New Covenant, because it was to him that the Covenant was given. While others greatly complemented his efforts, even the original Twelve; still, what knowledge they had concerning the New Covenant, they, as well, derived exclusively from Paul. Consequently, the responsibility on his shoulders was astronomical to say the least!

For instance, Paul's Epistle to the Romans, which is the Doctrinal Standard for the Church, was not written until the late 50's, with Paul's first Letter, this one to the Thessalonians, being written nearly ten years earlier. Consequently, Paul was furiously attempting to train these young Preachers, so they may be grounded and rooted in the Faith. He was careful to send only those who had been under his tutelage to the various Churches, men such as Timothy, Silas, etc. That's why he made the statement concerning the Philippians, *"But I trust in the Lord Jesus to send Timothy shortly unto you, that I also may be of good comfort, when I know your state.*

*"For I have no man likeminded, who will naturally care for your state.*

*"For all seek their own, not the things which are Jesus Christ's"* (Phil. 2:19-21).

Understanding these things, we now know that Paul including these Brethren in his Salutations, was for the purpose of making them recognizable in the various Churches, and to give them authority by linking them with himself, that people may heed what they say.

PAUL

If one studies and believes the Bible, and as a result the Bible Way, one must come to

NOTES

NOTES

the conclusion that the Apostle Paul has influenced humanity as no other human being. Being given the New Covenant by the Lord Jesus Christ, made him the Moses of the New Testament. It is not so much to say that Paul was a greater man than Moses or David, or Simon Peter, for that matter, etc., but the fact that he was given the New Covenant automatically places him in a position which he alone occupies. Consequently, and as stated, he was the only authority in the world of his day on the subject of the New Covenant, and what it all meant. Even the original Twelve had to learn from him, despite the fact that they had personally spent some three and one half years with Christ.

Looking at the New Covenant in spiritual, socioeconomic terms, Paul moreso than any other man is responsible for what we presently refer to as *"Western Civilization."* Despite the present unbelief and spiritual darkness, every iota of freedom and prosperity this particular Civilization has enjoyed, is anchored solely in the New Covenant as given to Paul and taught by Paul. Consequently, one cannot help but come to the conclusion, that this man Paul, has had the greatest influence on the world of any human being other than the Lord Jesus Christ, Who in reality was and is *"God."*

## PAUL'S THEOLOGY OF REDEMPTION

If one properly understands the New Covenant, which means to understand the gist of Paul's Message, one must come to the conclusion that his theology is, above all, a theology of Redemption. As well, this *"Redemption"* is centered up in *"union with Christ."* While imputed Righteousness is definitely a powerful factor, still, this Righteousness is fused to the Believer solely because of his identification with Christ. This means that Christ's Death and Resurrection along with His Ascension and Exaltation, have been recognized as the key to the meaning of *"union with Christ."*

Jesus Christ in His Death and Resurrection defeated for all time the *"powers"* of the old slavery of sin, death, and the demonic *"rulers of this darkness"* (Eph. 6:12; Col. 2:15). Now Christians are spiritually Crucified, Resurrected, Glorified (potentially), and placed at God's Right Hand with Christ (Gal. 2:20; Eph. 2:5). *"In Christ"* Christians have entered the Resurrection Age; the solidarity with the first Adam in sin and death has been replaced by the solidarity with the Second Adam, the Lord Jesus Christ, in Righteousness and immortal life.

## CORPORATE REDEMPTION

This corporate Redemption in and with Jesus Christ, this *"New Life"* reality, which the Believer enters at conversion (Rom. Chpt. 6), finds an individual actualization in the present and the future.

In the present life it means a transformation through the indwelling Spirit, the firstfruits of the New Resurrection Life (Rom. 8:23; II Cor. 5:5), of one's ethic (Col. 2:20; 3:1, 9, 12) and of one's total world view (Rom. 12:1). However, in the midst of moral-spiritual renewal the Christian remains, in his mortality, under the death claims of the old life. But this too is to be understood no longer in terms of *"in Adam,"* but as a part of the *"in Christ"* reality; for *"the sufferings of Christ abound to us"* (II Cor. 1:5; Phil. 3:10; Col. 1:24).

## TO DIE WITH CHRIST

The individual actualization of Christ's sufferings is, of course, in no way a self-redemptive process; rather, it means to be identified with Christ *"in the likeness of His Death"* (Rom. 6:5).

While the Believer died with Christ at His Crucifixion and in fact was buried also with Him, which refers to the *"old man,"* the old life, or old past, at the same time, there is a dying with Christ on a daily basis. One might say *"we <u>have</u> died with Him, and we <u>are</u> dying with Him."*

This is what Jesus was referring to in Luke 9:23, when He spoke of one denying himself, and taking up the Cross daily to follow Him (Christ).

The death we died with Him, or it might be better said *"in Him,"* guaranteed our *"Standing"* in Christ, which is *"Justification by Faith."* Our daily dying concerns our *"State,"* which we accomplish by a continued Faith in what Christ did at the Cross and His Resurrection.

The Believer is presently to walk in *"Resurrection Life"*; however, it is impossible to have the *"Resurrection Life"* (Rom. 6:5), unless we first have and understand the *"Crucifixion Death."*

As stated, *"we have died and we are dying."* Of course, we're speaking totally and completely of our spiritual experience.

*"Corporate Redemption"* means that our Redemption is totally and completely in Christ, in that which He has afforded through His Death and Resurrection. Outside of that there is no Redemption!

UNION WITH CHRIST AND IMPUTED RIGHTEOUSNESS

*"Union with Christ"* is the central core of Paul's Message respecting the New Covenant. I think that is obvious as it regards the writings of the Apostle.

However, as the Church slowly began to apostatize, ultimately going into a *"works religion,"* which characterizes the Catholic Church, emphasis gradually shifted from *"union with Christ"* to the *"imputed Righteousness"* doctrine.

This basically teaches that believing sinners come to God by Faith in Christ, with God then imputing to them a perfect, spotless, pure Righteousness, which is totally correct. However, the idea thereafter is, this righteous man, and because he is righteous, can now live this life of Holiness and Purity. This being unscriptural, led to a works righteousness effort which is bound to fail, with finally Salvation consisting of works altogether, which God can never honor. In this syndrome, the Cross is ignored as well as the Holy Spirit. In fact, the Book of Galatians addresses this very thing.

The Galatians had come in to the Gospel by believing in what Christ did at the Cross, but now due to false teaching, were attempting to sanctify themselves by other than the Cross, which referred to their own efforts by their own strength, etc. Paul addressed this by saying, *"Are ye so foolish? Having begun in the Spirit* (God's Way of the Cross), *are ye now made perfect by the flesh?* (Do you think you can sanctify yourselves by your own efforts?)" (Gal. 3:3).

Seeing and understanding the failure of this unscriptural doctrine, which could not help but bring grief to the Believer, the Nineteenth Century witnessed a growing emphasis on the present *"union with Christ,"* in other words, returning to that ultimately given by the Holy Spirit through Paul.

Most definitely, imputed Righteousness is one of the great foundations of the Faith. However, this Righteousness, which every true Christian has, is a *"position,"* and is not *"power."* Just because I'm Righteous, and made so by Christ, does not really give me any power to live a holy life. As a Christian, I am still in a body that's not glorified, which means it has been weakened by the Fall, and, therefore, subject to failure. So, I need power to help me live what I am — Righteous. That power comes from the Holy Spirit, and is derived by my continued Faith in the Cross of Christ (Rom. 8:1-2).

THE OLD PROBLEM

At about midpoint of the Twentieth Century, the old doctrine of *"imputed Righteousness"* being the great foundation of the Faith began to once again rear its ugly head. It has not been referred to in that capacity, but that's actually what it is.

This mostly came about through what is commonly referred to as the *"Faith Ministry."* The new, altogether Righteous man, was looked at as total and complete, with Faith in Faith being the great thruway. Once again, imputed Righteousness was looked at as power instead of position. Consequently, the *"union with Christ"* Doctrine was cast aside, which of course, means that the Cross has no place or value in that thinking. This new man infused with imputed Righteousness, is now the Resurrection man, and through Faith can do all sorts of great things, etc.

There is some Truth in this teaching, in that Believers definitely do have *"imputed Righteousness,"* for that's the only kind God will recognize, which incidently is Righteousness paid for entirely by the death of Christ on the Cross and His Resurrection. So, man cannot applaud himself at all as it regards this Righteousness, it totally being of Christ, and made possible by His great Sacrifice and that alone!

As well, all Believers are *"Resurrection Believers,"* meaning that we were raised with

Him in *"newness of life"* (Rom. 6:4). However, we must not forget, even as we've already stated, that the *"likeness of His Resurrection,"* which we now have, is predicated totally upon our properly understanding the *"likeness of His Death"* (Rom. 6:5).

Again we state, that it should be obvious that Resurrection Life cannot be enjoyed, until we first enter into His Crucifixion Death.

## THE BELIEVER'S PRESENT POSITION

Regarding *"union with Christ,"* the Believer's present position is that of being seated with Christ in Heavenly Places, which means that one is totally victorious over all the powers of darkness, etc. (Eph. 2:6). However, that position was gained and is maintained totally by what Christ did at the Cross. That must never be forgotten. If we fail to understand that, and attempt to ignore the daily demand by Christ that we take up the Cross, we will find ourselves living a life of spiritual failure. In other words, it will come to the place that sin will have dominion over us, even though we are Christians (Rom. 6:14).

The only way that the dominion of sin can be defeated in one's life, that our walk then be Holy and Righteous before God and the world, is that we properly understand that as Believers we are in Christ not only as it regards His Heavenly Places position but also His Crucifixion and Resurrection. To be frank, I think one can say without fear of contradiction, that the *"Crucifixion"* part is the most important of all. If we properly understand that, that we were baptized into His Death, understanding that the old life was completely obliterated with that and in His burial, we don't too much have to worry about the Resurrection part, that will automatically take care of itself.

Satan is a master at taking the Word of God and twisting it just enough in order to get us off track. Once we are in that debilitating position, he is then able to push us further and further away from the Cross, which alone is our Victory (Gal. 6:14).

If one institutes any doctrine other than that introduced by Paul, as it was given to him by the Holy Spirit, one has left the Gospel of Christ. In fact, the Apostle said, *"If any man preach any other gospel unto you than that ye have received, let him be accursed"* (Gal. 1:9).

NOTES

## SILAS

After the Great Council in Jerusalem as recorded in Acts Chapter 15, with Gentiles being given the right-hand of fellowship, Silas was sent back with Paul along with others, to Antioch, in order to carry the news.

When the others from Jerusalem returned, Silas remained in Antioch, where he was chosen by Paul as his companion for the second Missionary journey. Not much is said directly of Silas until he and Paul were beaten and imprisoned at Philippi, accused of causing a breach of the peace and preaching false doctrine, etc. (Acts 16:12-40). Undaunted, the two prisoners prayed and sang praises to God at midnight, with an earthquake then securing their miraculous release.

After the conversion of the jailor and his family, and the realization by the Magistrates that Paul and Silas were Roman citizens, they took leave of Philippi and the Brethren for Thessalonica and Berea, where Silas was left with Timothy, while Paul went to Athens to escape the riots (Acts 17:1-14).

Among other things, the membership of Silas in the Jerusalem Church may have been helpful to Paul. He is associated with the Apostle in the Letters written from Corinth to Thessalonica, and is not named again until the reference to him in I Peter. It is believed that he was also an Apostle, hence being included in the salutation of Paul.

## TIMOTHY

From the account in Acts and the mentions in Paul's Letters, Timothy seems to have been one of the most constant companions of the Apostle.

The first reference to this young man is found in Acts 16:1-3 at the beginning of Paul's second Missionary journey when he revisited Derbe and Lystra in Lycaonia. When he became a Christian is not specifically stated, but it is a reasonable inference that he was a convert of Paul's first Missionary journey, which included Lystra in its itinerary. This young man made a good impression upon Paul.

Timothy is not mentioned in connection with the experiences and imprisonment of

Paul and Silas in Philippi (Acts 16:12-40). Possibly because of his youth he was not imprisoned. Likewise, he is not mentioned in the account of Paul's Ministry at Thessalonica (Acts 17:1-9). However, Acts 17:14 indicates that Silas and Timothy remained in Berea after Paul's departure, although Paul requested that they join him as soon as possible (Acts 17:15). According to Acts 18:5, they rejoined Paul at Corinth.

However, I Thessalonians 3:1-3 indicates that Timothy at least was with Paul in Athens and that Paul, being anxious about the Believers at Thessalonica, sent Timothy to that city. Upon his return to Corinth where Paul was (Acts 18:5; I Thess. 3:6), he informed him about the situation in Thessalonica. In response Paul wrote this Epistle, I Thessalonians.

During his extended residence in Ephesus on his third Missionary journey, Paul sent Timothy to Corinth to deal with the vexing problems in that Church (I Cor. 4:17; 16:10). It appears that he was not successful in this mission and returned to Paul at Ephesus. Prior to Paul's departure from Ephesus, he sent Timothy and Erastus to Macedonia (Acts 19:22).

When Paul wrote his Letter to the Romans during the following winter while at Corinth, Timothy, identified as a *"fellow worker,"* was among those who sent their greetings (Rom. 16:21).

## ROME

Timothy accompanied Paul on his last journey to Jerusalem (Acts 20:4). It is not indicated that the young man accompanied Paul on his shipwreck voyage to Rome, but Philippians 2:19-20 suggests that Timothy was sharing Paul's first Roman imprisonment. Likewise, Timothy was included in the salutations of Philippians, Colossians, and Philemon, traditionally considered with Ephesians as the Prison Epistles, written from Rome.

Two of the Pastoral Epistles, written after Paul's first Roman imprisonment, were addressed to Timothy. The close relationship that existed between Paul and Timothy is very evident from these Letters. Paul refers to Timothy as *"my true child in the Faith"* (I Tim. 1:2), *"my son"* (I Tim. 1:18), *"my beloved child"* (II Tim. 1:2).

NOTES

In these two Epistles written directly to the young Evangelist, Paul uses a special term (found only in these two Epistles in the New Testament) to describe the responsible task or consignment that the Preacher has.

This term *"deposit," "consignment,"* is found in I Timothy 6:20; II Timothy 1:12, 14. Twice Paul urged Timothy to guard this *"consignment"* (I Tim. 6:20; II Tim. 1:14). In fact, this had also been entrusted or consigned to Paul (II Tim. 1:12).

This refers to the tremendous responsibility as we have previously mentioned, of the Church being founded correctly and that this great Gospel entrusted to Paul be handled responsibly by the young Evangelist. In fact, knowing that II Timothy would be the last Letter he would write, the Apostle, in effect, proclaims the fact that the continuation of his Ministry after he is gone, which would soon take place, must continue in the work of Timothy. The Holy Spirit had groomed him for this purpose.

## THE CHARGE TO THE YOUNG EVANGELIST

I Timothy was possibly written from Macedonia while Timothy was at Ephesus. A kind of legalism (I Tim. 1:6) and a kind of speculative theology based on myths and genealogies (I Tim. 1:4), were rising up in the Church. It was also in this period that ecclesiastical organization was developing, and Timothy was enjoined carefully to supervise the appointment of qualified Ministers. Personal Godliness was to be the necessary qualification of an effective Minister (I Tim. 6:11-16).

II Timothy was written while Paul was imprisoned in Rome, apparently the second time. The future looked very bleak for him and he wrote this Letter to Timothy to urge him to come to Rome for these last days.

Whether he reached Rome before Paul's death is not recorded. This Epistle (II Timothy) is the last Letter the great Apostle would write, at least as far as Epistles were concerned. It is the picture of a man passing the torch to his successor. Paul's confidence and trust in Timothy as a worthy successor are very evident.

It is not indicated where Timothy was at this time — apparently in western Asia, possibly at Ephesus, since he would be passing through Troas (II Tim. 4:13).

Although Paul was at the point of death (II Tim. 4:6) and had been abandoned by certain followers (Phygellus and Hermogenes) (II Tim. 1:15), nevertheless he expressed an assurance and Faith to Timothy which must have made a formative impression on this young Minister and have been an enduring inspiration to him.

The last reference to Timothy in the New Testament is found in Hebrews 13:23. The statement could mean that the young Evangelist had been in prison and was now released, or else Paul is speaking about him being released from his present responsibility and accordingly to begin another.

(It is believed that Hebrews was written only a short time, possibly two or three months, before II Timothy. Even though there is disagreement as to who the author of Hebrews actually was, it is my contention that the last few Verses of the last Chapter of that Book gives undeniable evidence that it was Paul.)

## THE CHURCH OF THE THESSALONIANS

The phrase, *"Unto the Church of the Thessalonians,"* presents this and the Second Epistle as the only ones so addressed.

The word *"Church"* denotes a select Assembly; here, Christians selected from the world. It does not denote in the New Testament, as with many presently, a building, but the congregation. In Paul's later Epistles, those addressed are called, not the Church, but Saints.

In other Epistles the address is to the city, as Rome, Philippi, Colosse; here, it is to the inhabitants.

This being the First Epistle of Paul, the salutation given here, *"to the Church of the Thessalonians,"* refers to the very first time in the history of the world that such was ever done. No such address had ever been written or read before, for the community to which it was directed was a new thing in the world.

The word translated *"Church"* was certainly familiar enough to all who knew Greek: it was the name given to the citizens of a Greek town assembled for public business; it is the name given in the Greek Bible either to the children of Israel as the congregation of Jehovah, or to any gathering of them for a special purpose; but here it obtains a new significance.

NOTES

First of all, this manner of address as given by Paul is not civic, as it would have been understood by the Greeks, but rather spiritual. As well, it is neither pagan nor Jewish; it is an original creation, new in its bond of union, in the law by which it lives, in the objects at which it aims; a Church in God the Father and the Lord Jesus Christ.

This newness and originality of Christianity could not fail to impress those who first received it. The Gospel made an immeasurable difference to them, a difference almost equally great whether they had been Jews or heathen before; and they were intensely conscious of the gulf which separated their new life from the old.

In fact, in another Epistle Paul describes the condition of Gentiles not yet evangelized. Once, he says, you were apart from Christ, without God, in the world. And of course, the world pertained to that great system of things and interests separated from God.

As the Word was given to them, the Gospel found them there, and translated them. When they received it, they ceased to be in the world at least in a spiritual sense; they were no longer apart from Christ, or without God: they were in God the Father and in the Lord Jesus Christ.

Nothing could be more revolutionary in those days than to become a Christian: old things passed away; all things became new; all things were determined by the new relation to God and His Son. The difference between the Christian and the non-Christians was as unmistakable and as clear to the Christian mind as the difference between the shipwrecked sailor who has reached the shore and him who is still fighting a hopeless fight with wind and waves.

## WHAT IS CHURCH?

First of all, Church is not an organization, a building, a Denomination, an institution, etc.

The word *"Church"* actually means *"called out ones,"* and refers to Believers being called out of the system of the world, in essence that which is of Satan, into the system of God, which is the Kingdom of Light. It is people who have been Born-Again, which means a spiritual birth, referring to having accepted Jesus Christ as one's Savior, which means that we believe in what He did at the Cross referring to His great Sacrifice.

The Church had its birth in the Cross of Christ. The Church is its product, which means that its origination was in Heaven. However, I want to emphasize the point that the Price that Jesus paid at the Cross, which was demanded, that is if man was to be redeemed, had as its natural outflow, the Redemption of humanity, i.e., *"the Church."* The Church is made up of redeemed souls, and those souls were redeemed because of what Jesus did at the Cross and the Resurrection.

Without the Cross, there would have been no Redemption; without Redemption there would have been no Salvation; without Salvation, there would have been no Church. So, one could say that the Church has as its Source, the Cross of Christ. There the sin debt was paid, which made it possible for man to be Justified by Faith. There the grip of Satan was broken, because all sin was atoned. Sin being the legal claim that Satan had on humanity, the reason or source of his claim being removed, left him with no claim at all, at least for those who will believe (Jn. 3:16).

The paying of the sin debt also satisfied the curse of the broken Law, which was death. Jesus paid this debt by the giving of His Life. So, the Master not only kept the Law perfectly in His earthly sojourn, and did so as a man filled with the Holy Spirit, but also suffered its full penalty on our behalf, even though He deserved no penalty Himself whatsoever.

Having satisfied the curse of the broken Law, and having atoned for all sin by the pouring out of His Life's Blood, which meant that no more sin remained, sin being the fuel of death, this monster death could no longer hold Him; therefore, He could legally be raised from the dead, which He was, which defeated death in totality.

All of this made possible the Church. Consequently, if we try to think of the Church apart from the Cross, the only definition one will come up with will be an earthly institution, which means it is a false impression.

NOTES

Satan seeks so strongly to subvert the True Church by inserting his own religious wares, and succeeds in many cases. Consequently, many so-called Religious Leaders will seek to imply that one is not a member of the True Church, unless they are a member of their earthly organization, etc. If even a semblance of that spirit is projected, the Believer should run from such attitude as fast as possible, because that being projected is of Satan. This is Satan's effort, and using religious individuals as his tools, to subvert the Cross of Christ, the true origin of the Church.

The Church is not a human institution, not of human devisings, not an earthly organization, and associating or not associating with any earthly organizations calling themselves *"Church,"* has no effect spiritually on anyone whatsoever.

This doesn't mean that it is spiritually wrong to have a Denomination, or to belong to a Denomination, or a certain Church, but that we should always understand what is actually the Church.

## JESUS CHRIST, THE TRUE CHURCH

As Jesus was the True Israel, and is the True Man, He is also the *"True Church."* As we have previously stated, Christianity is not a philosophy, it is rather a Man, the Man, Christ Jesus. More particularly, and to define the statement more carefully, the Church is Jesus Christ, and what He did at the Cross in order to bring about man's Redemption. We must never forget this, and must never look at the Church in any other light.

Entrance into this Church is by the *"born again"* experience (Jn. 3:3, 16; Rom. 10:9-10, 13; Eph. 2:8-9; Rev. 22:17).

This means that one joining the Baptist Church, or the Pentecostal Church, or the Holiness Church, or the Catholic Church, etc., has absolutely nothing to do with Salvation. While it may be good to belong to one of these particular Churches or Denominations, the fact of one becoming a part of these Churches, which are earthly institutions, has absolutely nothing to do with their spiritual condition. In fact, people should join a Church because they've already been saved. The idea, of joining one to be saved, is spiritually and Scripturally ludicrous!

Let us ever remember, that the Church is Jesus Christ, and as we have stated, more particularly what He did at the Cross and the Resurrection, out of which the Church sprang.

THE HOLY SPIRIT

The Holy Spirit is the Strength of the Church, the Power of the Church, the Leader of the Church, the protector of the Church, all under Christ (Acts 1:4, 8). And to be sure, the Holy Spirit could not come, at least in the dimension He has come, until Christ finished the work at Calvary's Cross. Only then could the Holy Spirit come, and abide within the hearts and lives of Believers (Jn. 14:17).

So, the Cross made possible the entrance of the Holy Spirit, at least in this fashion, which guarantees the veracity and power of the Church. Jesus is the Church, i.e., *"its Head,"* and the Holy Spirit is the Person of the Godhead, through Whom Christ works as it regards the Church.

But all of this is made possible by what Christ did at the Cross and the Resurrection. I'm afraid that we have a tendency to forget that, or ignore that. But if we do so, we do it at our peril. The Cross must ever be understood as the foundation of the Church, for it was there that Jesus made the Church possible.

WHAT THE CHURCH DID

In Thessalonica the Christian life was original enough to have formed a new society. In those days, and in the Roman Empire, there was not much room for the social instincts to expand.

Unions of all kinds were watched closely by the Government, and discouraged if the slightest infraction resulted. Local self-governments ceased to be interesting when all-important interests were withdrawn from Rome, which meant from its control; and even had it been otherwise, there was no part in it possible for that great mass of population from which the Church was so largely recruited, namely, the slaves. Any power that could bring men together, that could touch them deeply, and give them a common interest that engaged their hearts and bound them to each other, met the greatest want of the time, and was certain of a welcome. Such a power was the Gospel preached by Paul.

NOTES

It formed little communities of men and women wherever it was proclaimed; communities in which there was no law but that of love, in which heart, open to heart as nowhere else in all the world, in which there was fervor, hope, freedom, brotherly kindness, and all that makes life good and dear. We feel this very strongly in reading the New Testament, and it is one of the points on which, unhappily, we have drifted away it seems, from the primitive model. The bond ties of Christ are the strongest bonds of all, at least if people truly know Christ. A Church family, is exactly that, *"a family of united Believers, united in Christ, and glad servants of His."*

GOD THE FATHER AND THE LORD JESUS CHRIST

The phrase, *"Which is in God the Father and in the Lord Jesus Christ,"* proclaims what we have just been saying as it respects the origin of the Church. It is *"in God the Father"* because it is *"in the Lord Jesus Christ."*

To find out what it means to be *"in Christ,"* of course, we go to Romans 6:3-6. We are *"in Christ"* by virtue of being baptized into His Death, which refers to His Crucifixion, buried with Him, and raised with Him in Newness of Life.

In the Mind of God, the act of Crucifixion as it regards Christ, was Jesus serving as our Substitute and our Representative Man. As we have said in other Commentaries, as our Substitute, Jesus died *"for us,"* and as our *"Representative Man,"* i.e., *"The Second Adam,"* He died *"as us."*

Dying for someone is one thing; dying as someone, is something else altogether. In fact, while it is certainly possible for one human being to die for another human being, it is not possible for one human being to die as another human being. Only Christ could do that.

CHRIST OUR SUBSTITUTE AND OUR REPRESENTATIVE MAN

The Fifty-third Chapter of Isaiah, portrays Christ as our Substitute, inasmuch as He died *"for us."* Psalm 22 portrays Him as our *"Representative Man,"* as that Psalm graphically portrays Him dying *"as us."*

As total dominion was given to the first Adam (Gen. 1:28; Ps. 8:3-9), which he forfeited to Satan by the Fall, *"the last Adam,"* the Lord Jesus Christ (I Cor. 15:45), had to purchase back at great price, what the first had lost. Consequently, as the True Man, He had to keep the Law of God perfectly, which He did with the help of the Holy Spirit. Although He had not sinned, as our Substitute He had to go to the Cross on our behalf. But it had to be more than that! As our Representative Man He had to literally suffer exactly what we would have suffered had we been on that Cross. That means, even as we've already stated, that He had to suffer the penalty of the broken Law which was death, even though He had never Personally broken that Law. As us, He had to suffer that penalty, as us, He had to pour out His Life's Blood, and as us He had to be laid in the tomb; however, that's as far as the Representative Man went. The price was now paid, and Satan could not hold Him.

When He rose from the dead, He arose as the Son of God; however, He allowed us to be raised with Him in *"newness of life,"* which gives us *"Resurrection Life"* as Christians (Rom. 6:5).

The point I am attempting to make is, our Salvation is a completed affair, leaving no proverbial stones unturned, with every single thing that was lost in the Fall, being addressed in the Atonement. Admittedly, we do not yet have all the benefits of the Atonement, that coming at the Resurrection, but what we do have, is so absolutely miraculous and glorious that it defies all description. As the Scripture says, we have a *"great Salvation"* (Heb. 2:3).

## THE CROSS IS THE DOOR

The phrase, *"In God the Father and in the Lord Jesus Christ,"* has reference to the fact, that God cannot address fallen, sinful humanity, except through the Cross of Christ; likewise, man has no access to God whatsoever, except through the Cross.

Jesus said, *"Verily, verily, I say unto you, I am the Door of the sheep"* (Jn. 10:7).

To get a proper identification of that *"Door,"* we have to go to Egypt immediately before the deliverance of the Children of Israel. The Scripture says, *"And they shall take of the blood, and strike it on the two side posts and on the upper door post of the houses, wherein they shall eat it."*

NOTES

It then said, *"And the blood shall be to you for a token upon the houses where you are: and when I see the Blood, I will pass over you"* (Ex. 12:7, 13).

That *"Door"* is a Bloody Door!

From the very beginning, man has tried to dress up this situation, ignore it or even deny it, and I speak of the price that had to be paid for man's Redemption; nevertheless, the Cross is the only Way; there is no other!

This price, as gruesome as it was, was absolutely necessary, because man's sin was so awful, so terrible, so wicked, so destructive. Man does not want to admit that, thinking that his problem is only a slight maladjustment which can be changed by one means or the other. Despite trying to change the situation for some 6,000 years, man has made no headway at all, at least by his own efforts, and never will. The only solution for fallen humanity, for this terrible plague of sin, and a plague it is, is the Cross of Christ. Oh, I can sense the Presence of God even as I dictate these words, because this is the central Truth of the great Plan of God.

Man has access to God only through Jesus Christ, and more particularly, only by accepting what Jesus did at the Cross, and no other way. Let that never be forgotten!

## GRACE AND PEACE

The phrase, *"Grace be unto you, and Peace,"* presents the greeting in all the Apostle's Letters; it is not varied except by the addition of *"Mercy"* in the Epistles to Timothy and Titus.

In form, it has all the originality of the Christian Faith.

Grace is the Love of God, spontaneous, beautiful, unearned, at work in Jesus Christ for the Salvation of sinful men; Peace is the effect and fruit in man of the reception of Grace. It is easy to narrow unduly the significance of Peace; however, to do so, is to greatly misunderstand the tremendous value of this all-important product of Grace. First of all, let us address Grace:

Grace, as well, is a product of the Cross. In other words, God has always had Grace, not suddenly finding this great Blessing in this age and time. God cannot change, so that means He has always had the commodity which we refer to as *"Grace."* In other words, He had just as much Grace in Old Testament times, as He does now in the New.

It is the Cross through which Grace comes to sinful men, and the Cross Alone; consequently, the Lord has been able to open the spigot wider, so to speak, since Jesus paid the price at the Cross for man's Redemption.

Let not the Reader think that Grace just automatically comes. It doesn't! It comes to us as we place our Faith and Trust in the Cross of Christ, and in that manner exclusively.

If any Believer wants to shut down Grace, and it certainly can be done, all the Believer has to do, is to try or attempt to bring about Righteousness and Holiness in any other way than by depending on the Cross of Christ. He will find that spigot turned off, and turned off completely (Gal. 2:21).

To keep a plentiful supply of Grace coming to the Child of God, and on a continued basis, uninterrupted, all the Believer has to do, is to have Faith in the Cross of Christ, understanding that what needs to be done can only be done through that medium, and maintain one's Faith in that Finished Work. Everything we need comes from the Cross, what Jesus did there! Its benefits can never be exhausted, will never grow old, always remain present, are just as modern as tomorrow, etc.

Men have seemingly had difficulty in defining Grace, using one definition after the other. Personally, I think the abbreviated definition of *"undeserved favor,"* is probably the best that can be found.

Grace is not something mysterious. It simply means that God gives us all that we need, all good things, all blessings, even though we do not deserve them, and in fact, can never deserve them. However, He does demand one thing, and that is that we have Faith in the Finished Work of Christ, and maintain our Faith in that which Jesus has done. That's all He asks, and all these bountiful blessings which are Grace, will continue to come uninterrupted, to the Believer.

## PEACE

If you have studied any of our other Commentaries, you know there are two kinds of *"peace,"* one might say. The first is *"Justifying Peace,"* and we call it that, because it refers to the Peace of God which comes to the sinner, at the moment of Salvation, which means they have been justified (I Cor. 6:11). This *"Peace"* comes to all sinners upon Salvation. This means all the enmity between God and sinful man has been removed. Hostilities have ceased, and peace is now declared. It's called the *"Peace of God."*

Man does not feel this enmity nearly as much as God, because God is the One Who has been greatly offended by man's sin. In fact, He has been offended so much, that the Scripture says that *"God is angry with the wicked every day"* (Ps. 7:11). It also says, *"For the Wrath of God is revealed from Heaven against all ungodliness and unrighteousness of men, who hold the Truth in unrighteousness"* (Rom. 1:18).

Sin is the ruination of all that is good. And if one wants to know how bad sin is, one has to only look at the condition the world is in presently, considering all the murder, rape, war, hatred, etc. To be sure, every good thing that's in the world today, has been brought about all because of the Revelation of the Word of God into the world, and more particularly, the Death and Resurrection of the Lord Jesus Christ. Otherwise, sin is so horrible, so awful, so destructive, that this world would have been totally destroyed a long time ago. In fact, it became so bad after the Fall, with degeneration continuing day-by-day, until the Lord had to destroy it all with the exception of the family of Noah. The Scripture says, *"And God saw that the wickedness of man was great in the earth, and that every imagination of the thoughts of his heart was only evil continually"* (Gen. 6:5-10).

Man being spiritually dead, and, therefore, dead to all the things of God, which means he is as well dead to his true condition, doesn't know how bad the situation actually is with him, until he comes to Christ. And then he realizes just how awful his former life actually was, and how wonderful it is now in Christ, since this terrible enmity has been removed. That is Justifying Peace.

However, the *"Peace"* of which Paul speaks in this First Verse, is what we refer to as *"Sanctifying Peace."*

NOTES

This type of Peace is a growth process, just as Sanctification is a growth process. When one learns to trust the Lord, and to love Him with all one's heart, little by little, Sanctifying Peace takes over one's life, which makes Christianity a joy to behold and to have.

Just as *"Justifying Peace"* came about by the sinner accepting and trusting Christ, likewise, *"Sanctifying Peace"* comes about by the same method. The Believer is to place his Faith and confidence in the Cross, which will then guarantee the help of the Holy Spirit (Rom. 8:1-2), which will give the Believer all he needs and in every capacity. As Grace comes from, by, of, and through the Cross, likewise, Peace comes in the same way!

FROM GOD AND FROM CHRIST

The phrase, *"From God our Father, and the Lord Jesus Christ,"* specifies that this Grace and Peace can come from God our Father, only through and by the Sacrifice of Christ at the Cross. As the *"Church"* is *"in God . . . ,"* Grace and Peace comes *"from God. . . ."* However, all of this is predicated, on what Jesus did at the Cross and the Resurrection. The process is as follows:

1. Lord: This appellative identifies Christ as God.
2. Jesus: In the Greek, Jesus means *"Savior."* Therefore, the question must be asked, *"How did He save us?"*

He saved us by what He did at the Cross and the Resurrection, and our Faith in that.

3. Christ: In both the Hebrew and the Greek, Christ means *"Messiah," "the Anointed,"* or *"The Anointed One."* This means He is the One, the very One, predicted by the Prophets, thereby, fulfilling all prophecy. In fact, the Scripture says, *"The Testimony of Jesus is the spirit of prophecy"* (Rev. 19:10).

As well, the manner in which Paul uses these titles or appellatives, presents in bold relief, the Trinity of the Godhead. God the Father does everything through the Lord Jesus Christ, and the Holy Spirit inspires these words which are said, and, in fact, gave Christ the power to carry out these great works of Redemption; therefore, we have the Trinity.

(2) "WE GIVE THANKS TO GOD ALWAYS FOR YOU ALL, MAKING MENTION OF YOU IN OUR PRAYERS;"

NOTES

It was Paul's practice to begin his Letters by thanking God for his Readers. The only exception is the Letter to the Galatians, where indignation and disappointment ruled out gratitude. The Thessalonians, however, did not disappoint him. Paul found much in their lives for which to be grateful.

By thanking God at the beginning of the Epistle, Paul lifts the thought above the human level and rises above the conventional opening of letters of his time. He is not trying to win the Thessalonians over by flattery. On the contrary, he is sincerely trying to give the ultimate credit to the One from Whom spiritual progress comes. When Christians realize their complete dependence on God and keep this in clear focus, then and only then are they capable of moving on to greater spiritual exploits such as those spoken of later in this Epistle.

*"Mentioning you in our prayers"* tells how Paul expressed his thanks. *"Making mention"* is never used by Paul accept in conjunction with prayer. Making mention of them in his prayers enabled him not only to thank God for their progress, but also to intercede for their advancement in Christ (Thomas).

THANKS TO GOD

The phrase, *"We give thanks to God always for you all,"* presents more than politeness, but rather illustrates the warm, personal relationship which Paul had with his converts, and as well, exudes deep feeling, joy, and concern. This entire Passage is graphic Testimony from the primitive Church of the utterly transforming force of the Gospel in a pagan environment.

By Paul using the pronoun *"we,"* tells us that the Apostle had trained the ones mentioned above with him, to pray in the same manner. Paul's prayer for the Thessalonians took the form of thanksgiving, as did much of his prayer, and as should much of our prayer as well.

Every Believer has much for which to be thankful. The Lord has been so good to us, and in many and varied ways. In fact, His goodness knows no bounds. So, the Believer should be grateful enough, thankful enough, appreciative enough, of this which the Lord continually does for us, to thank Him constantly in our daily seeking of His Face. This means that every Believer should have a daily time of prayer. In this prayer, a great part should be given over to thanksgiving to the Lord.

The Psalmist said, *"Enter into His gates with thanksgiving, and into His courts with praise: be thankful unto Him, and bless His Name"* (Ps. 100:4).

He then said, *"For the Lord is good; His Mercy is everlasting; and His Truth endureth to all generations"* (Ps. 100:5).

That's it in brief: *"The Lord is good!"* He is good in every way, He is good in every manner, He is good at all times, in fact, His goodness knows no end. Any Believer who doesn't know that, who doesn't understand that, has to be in very poor shape spiritually. In fact, the blessings of God are so abundant, that it's impossible to even enumerate them. Consequently, we should never cease thanking Him, doing so constantly in our prayers, and even on a continuing basis, having a spirit of thanksgiving at all times.

How would you feel, if you were very, very good to someone, and they expressed little appreciation for your kindness? This one thing is certain, we simply cannot thank the Lord enough; and there's another thing that is certain, the Lord delights in our thanksgiving.

In no way does this mean that God is on an ego trip. God is not a man; consequently, He doesn't function as we do. He desires thanksgiving on our part for one purpose and reason:

Thanksgiving on our part to the Lord, which of course comes from a sincere heart, shows that we understand our dependence on Him, and as well, our inability to provide what we need on our own. Thanksgiving to the Lord portrays the spiritual barometer of the Believer, shows the spiritual aptitude, and perhaps above all of that, shows humility. Viewed in this light, we understand how important all of this actually is.

PRAYERS

The phrase, *"Making mention of you in our prayers,"* is so linked with the next phrase, *"remembering without ceasing,"* as to suggest that prayer was the atmosphere of this man's life. I'm sure that would have included, as well, Silas and Timothy.

NOTES

We ought not to lessen the force of these words, as if they were mere exaggerations, idle extravagances of a man who habitually said more than he meant. Paul's life was concentrated and intense, to a degree of which we probably have little conception. He lived for Christ, and for the Churches which were in Christ.

Other men's minds might surge with various interests; new ambitions or affections might displace old ones; fickleness or disappointments might change their whole career, but it was not so with him. His thoughts and affections never changed their object for the same conditions appealed constantly to the same susceptibility; if he grieved over the unbelief of the Jews, he had unceasing pain in his heart; if he gave thanks for the Thessalonians, he remembered without ceasing the Graces with which they had been adorned by God.

As we've already stated, I think it is obvious from Paul's writings, that he was definitely a man of prayer.

WHAT DOES THAT MEAN,
A MAN OF PRAYER?

First of all, it means that he understood his total dependence on the Lord, constantly needing leading, guidance, and direction by the Holy Spirit. This can only be derived by prayer. This man knew and understood that all his help came from the Lord; consequently, it was to the Lord he must constantly speak.

As well, he wanted, i.e., *"he must have,"* the Mind of the Lord in all things. Consequently, he sought leading and direction regarding every move that was made, every step that was taken, every direction posed, and every action carried out. He knew he couldn't make it unless the Lord helped him to do this thing; consequently, he sought the Lord about everything.

We make a great mistake, if we think such a prayer life should be the prerogative of someone only as Paul. Prayer is the greatest privilege any Believer could ever have. To be able to speak to someone Who is almighty, which means He is all powerful, and especially considering that He loves us very much, is the greatest privilege that one could ever have. But yet, so few Christians take advantage of

NOTES

this most important aspect of their Christian life.

As well, Paul believed God! He believed that everything should be taken to the Lord; he believed that God heard prayer; he believed that God answered prayer; he believed that God delighted in us bringing our petitions and needs to Him. So, he was a man of prayer, just as we should be a man or woman of prayer.

(3) "REMEMBERING WITHOUT CEASING YOUR WORK OF FAITH, AND LABOUR OF LOVE, AND PATIENCE OF HOPE IN OUR LORD JESUS CHRIST, IN THE SIGHT OF GOD AND OUR FATHER;"

Paul's Thessalonian Readers had fulfilled every spiritual expectation regarding everyday experience. Upon every remembrance of this success, he and his companions were moved to express gratitude to God.

The words *"before our God and Father"* show the sincerity of this remembrance in prayer.

## REMEMBERING

The phrase, *"Remembering without ceasing,"* concerns several things:

1. Paul's mind was always on the things of God. Such is the foundation of a healthy mind, attitude, and spirit. It is the key to victory over all worry, anxiety, and fear. A person's thought should be on the Lord only, being the last thought before going to sleep at night, and the first thought upon awakening.

Man is a spiritual being, and as such, must feed his spiritual man, which can be done only by communion with the Lord, and on a constant basis.

One may think that to do such all the time, exactly as Paul says here, *"without ceasing,"* to be a rather boring way to go; however, it is the very opposite! The sense of well-being, joy, even euphoria, are the result, which to be sure, the world cannot at all give.

2. In Paul's constant thoughts about the Lord, many were on what God had done, which in this case pertained to the Thessalonians. There were certain things he remembered about them, and even on a constant basis, which characterized their lives, and for the good we might quickly add, which had been done for them by the Lord. In other words, he had seen Spiritual Growth in them, and was confident that the growth was continuing.

3. Everything the Lord does is eternal in consequence. It is meant to be a lesson to us, and many times the lessons derived are filled out in our thought processes.

On a personal basis, many times I will think about some certain thing the Lord has done for me, sometimes many years past, and the Holy Spirit will quicken something to my spirit, concerning that very thing that happened years ago, and then give me added Light. In fact, the Holy Spirit means for us to think about these things over and over, in which He will enlarge upon, if we will only lend our minds totally and completely to this which the Lord is doing.

## WORK OF FAITH

The phrase, *"Your work of Faith,"* presents work which is a consequence of true Faith. The idea is, he who works little has little Faith, and conversely, he who works much has much Faith.

On this conception of Faith, our Lord's words are brought to mind. When the Jews asked, *"What shall we do, that we may work the works of God?"* Jesus answers, with an emphatic transition from the plural to the singular, *"This is the work of God, that ye believe on Him Whom He hath sent"* (Jn. 6:28-29).

As we have stated, true Faith will be evidenced by corresponding works; but mere *"good works"* which do not spring from Faith will lack Spiritual Fruit.

First of all, when Paul mentions Faith, exactly what is he speaking about?

Of course, most would instantly retort by saying, *"He is speaking of having Faith in God,"* or *"Faith in the Word,"* etc.

While that is certainly true, that really doesn't tell us much, but yet that's about as far as most Christians are in their understanding of Faith.

## THE DEFINITION OF FAITH

To best understand what Faith actually is, one must first of all understand what the proper object of Faith must be. When we say *"Faith,"* everybody in the world has Faith in something; however, that's not the type of Faith of which we speak here.

NOTES

Whenever we speak of Faith as it regards the Word of God, or having Faith in God, or trusting Christ, etc., it always means, and without exception, *"Faith in the Finished Work of Christ."*

The Believer must understand that every single thing we receive from the Lord, and that means in totality, comes to us totally and absolutely through and by the Finished Work of Christ, which pertains to what He did on the Cross and in His Resurrection. This is where the battle was fought and won, the price was paid, the door was opened, and all things that the Child of God needs and in every capacity, were carried out. So, when we speak of Faith, we must understand that it is Faith in the great Sacrifice of Christ. If we leave that premise, that principle, we have left the great Plan of God, which will not garner us anything.

This means that the Believer at all times, must have in his mind the origin of all things he receives from the Lord, which is the Cross. If we fail in that, we fail in everything. The Cross is where the whole thing was carried out, and it must ever be the object of our Faith. Then there will be fruit, glorious and wonderful as only the Lord can give! Then, you will have Faith that *"works,"* translating into a *"work of Faith."*

Sometime in 1996, in answer to prayer, the Lord began to give me a Revelation of the Cross, which has wondrously and gloriously changed my life. Even though that Revelation has greatly been enlarged since its beginning, and I trust will continue to be enlarged, even from the very first moment that this door was opened, my life began to change. I now know what Jesus was speaking about when he said, *"Come unto Me, all ye who labor and are heavy laden, and I will give you rest"* (Mat. 11:28-30). I also know what He was speaking about when He said, *"I am come that they might have life, and that they might have it more abundantly"* (Jn. 10:10).

In very simple terminology, the Lord patiently and graciously explained to me, that everything for which I was seeking, every question I had, all blessings in totality, all sprang totally and completely from the Cross. Consequently, this is where I was to place my Faith, keep my Faith there, not allow my Faith to be moved in any other direction, and then the Holy Spirit would work on my behalf, doing all the things that need to be done.

THE HOLY SPIRIT

In fact, there is absolutely nothing that we receive from the Lord, but that the Holy Spirit has to bring these things about. The Believer should understand that and understand it fully. It is the Spirit of God Who abides in us, Who guarantees all of the great Blessings for which Jesus purchased in the Atonement. He Alone can make us holy, righteous, Godly, and Christlike. He Alone can guarantee us access to God in prayer, and guarantee the answers. He is sent for this very purpose, and all that comes from God must in totality come through Him (Jn. 16:7-16; Acts 1:4, 8).

However, all of these things we have just stated, are not automatic at all. In other words, the Holy Spirit doesn't just do them, even though we may need them desperately. He demands first of all, and foremost, that our Faith be in the Cross. He will not bypass in any capacity, that which Jesus did at the Cross and the Resurrection. He works exclusively from that basis, and demands that we have a continuing Faith in the great Sacrificial Offering of Christ (Rom. 8:1-2).

When Jesus said, and speaking of the Holy Spirit regarding Himself, *"He shall glorify Me"* (Jn. 16:14), He was speaking of the Holy Spirit working exclusively from what Christ would do on the Cross. That's the manner in which He glorifies Christ, and that's the manner in which we glorify Christ. We are to understand, and to act upon the principle of what Jesus did at the Cross. Then the Holy Spirit will work for us, and do great and mighty things.

LABOR OF LOVE

The phrase, *"And labor of love,"* presents the *"work"* which comes by our Faith, but yet is not toil, because it is done out of *"Love."*

If one loves somebody or something, it is not difficult to do things for them, to work for them, or to do whatever needs to be done. As Paul said, it is a *"labor of love."*

It is the same with the Lord! We love Him so very much, and thereby, do not look at what we do for Him as wearisome toil, never, but rather a privilege and a pleasure.

The idea is, if we really love the Lord as we ought to, and as we say we do, then we will gladly work for Him, doing all that we can do to further His cause, and because He has done so much for us. The idea here, is not that we can pay Him for all of these wonderful things He has done on our behalf, for such is not possible. Actually, Love does not try to *"pay,"* because Love knows that the things given, were given out of love anyway. I speak of that which comes from God, which in totality are gifts.

We go back to the little story of the man who saw a boy physically carrying another boy, which obviously presented itself as a heavy load. He spoke to the young man saying, *"Isn't he heavy?"*

The answer was immediate, *"He's not heavy, he's my brother!"*

I know that I could never repay the Lord for what He's done for me, not in a million lifetimes; consequently, I do what I do, knowing that first of all, He needs nothing, and as well, what I do for Him is inconsequential. Yet, I do what little I can for Him because I love Him, and He holds what I do for Him, as inconsequential as it is, as something very precious, because He loves me.

We don't have to worry about God loving us. God is love; therefore, that is a given.

The problem always resides in our love for the Lord. If we really love Him, several things will happen:

1. He said, *"If ye love Me, keep My Commandments"* (Jn. 14:15).

2. If we truly love the Lord, we will at the same time, love our neighbor (Mat. 22:37-40).

3. Paul said, *"Abound in this Grace also* (of giving to the Lord respecting money) . . . *to prove the sincerity of your love"* (II Cor. 8:7-8). In other words, if we truly love the Lord, we will give generously and liberally to the Work of God.

## PATIENCE OF HOPE

The phrase, *"And patience of hope,"* concerns something which is guaranteed to come, but not exactly known when. Consequently, we are to have *"patience."* That means we keep believing (having Faith), and keep loving.

NOTES

Lightfoot said, *"Faith rests on the past; love works in the present; hope looks to the future."*

Whether this distribution of the Graces is accurate or not, it suggests the Truth that they cover and fill up the whole Christian life. They are the sum and substance of it, whether it looks back, looks around, or looks forward. The germ of all perfection is implanted in the soul which is the dwelling place of *"these three."*

## PROMISES OF GOD

When one thinks of *"patience of hope,"* one automatically looks to the future, and I speak of the Coming of the Lord, etc. However, even though this meaning definitely characterizes this phrase, the present is involved also.

When the Lord promises us something, it generally does not come immediately. Many times He will not even tell us when it is coming. During the intervening time, we must have patience and look forward with hope.

As well, Biblical hope is different than the way we presently use the word. When we think of hope presently, it refers to something that may or may not happen. However, hope as used in the Bible, has a totally different meaning. It refers to that which is guaranteed of fulfillment, but not exactly known as to when the fulfillment will come. We are to have patience, as stated, during the meantime.

In late 1991, I began to importune the Lord to give me the answer to some particular questions. These questions concerned the victorious life of the Child of God. How can a Christian walk in perpetual victory over all the powers of darkness? In other words, how can a Believer have total victory over the world, the flesh, and the Devil?

These questions were not asked out of mere curiosity, but actually out of desperation. A true Christian abhors any type of failure on his part as it respects the Lord. So, the true Christian wants to know how he can walk in perpetual victory?

With burning tears, even on a daily basis, I began to seek the Lord for answers to these questions.

The Lord almost immediately gave me particular Passages in the Word of God, which, in fact, told me that He would answer my petition; however, He did not say when. He continued to do that quite often.

The time period was approximately five years. I will admit that during this time I grew very discouraged. Five years is a long time, but yet, 25 years was an even longer period of time in which Abraham and Sarah had to keep believing, before Isaac would finally be born.

And then, as stated, sometime in 1996, the answer began to come. And to be sure, it was well worth the wait 1,000 times over.

WHAT IF I HAD QUIT SEEKING?

If the Lord had not helped me to have *"patience of hope,"* which means to wait until the answer came, and in the meantime to keep seeking, the answer would not have come. That being the case, catastrophe would have been the result.

How many Christians ignore these three simple words *"patience of hope,"* and fail to receive from the Lord that for which they are asking? The Reader must understand, that all three of these attributes are brought into play in the Christian experience. Faith must be involved, for this *"patience of hope,"* to succeed, and love must be the undergirding factor of all, knowing that a loving God will not disappoint us.

We live in a very strange society, made strange I might quickly add by many contributing factors.

We are not presently taught to wait on anything. Fast food has become the model of our patience, which means we don't have much patience. So we want everything else in the same manner. If God doesn't move on cue, *"I'm outta here,"* is the thought of most!

In fact, most Christians want some Preacher to lay hands on them, and thereby handle their problem whatever it might be, and for it to be done instantly. If it doesn't happen, and to be sure it actually never does in that manner, we're quick to seek out another Preacher. We want the instant blessing, the instant deliverance, the instant victory! However, we should consider the following:

First of all, when we ask the Lord for something, many times before that certain something can be given to us, there are many other things which need to be worked out in our lives, things I might quickly add, many times of which we're not even aware. To be sure, it doesn't take the Lord any time at all to do anything; however, unfortunately, it takes much time for most of us.

NOTES

The Holy Spirit has to work on us, layer by layer, to finally bring us to the place He wants us, before the answer to our petition can be given. As I've stated, the modern Christian is not too much in sympathy with this of which I have spoken. Nevertheless, God will not work on our timetable, but only on His. Consequently, that requires on our part, *"patience of hope."*

Having said that, we must understand the following also:

The delay is never unprofitable. It is never wasted time. Anything the Lord does for us, is always to our benefit, and to be sure, whatever time He requires that we wait, during which He is performing spiritual surgery on us, there are great blessings all along the way. Let not the Believer think, that the *"meantime"* is empty. In fact, nothing with God is ever empty, and if it is, that means we have drifted away from where the Lord actually is. Anytime we are in line with Him, wonderful and glorious things are constantly happening. And the closer we get to Him, the more we will see these things and understand what He is doing.

IN CHRIST

The phrase, *"In our Lord Jesus Christ,"* refers to these three great Graces, as coming from Him, as He is always the Source.

However, we should ask the question as to how all of this is *"in our Lord Jesus Christ"*?

As with Faith, when Paul uses this phrase in one fashion or the other, *"in Christ,"* he is always speaking of the Cross and Christ's Resurrection, and our part in that which He has done. Christ cannot be obtained any other way, cannot be had any other way, cannot be received any other way. So, all of these things of which Paul speaks, is due to our position in Christ, and our understanding of that position in that it came out of the Finished Work of Christ.

Everything is *"in Christ,"* and to be *"in Christ,"* means to be in what He did at the Cross and His Resurrection. The entirety of every Blessing, every benefit, every gift, and every Grace, given to the Child of God, comes through this Source, and this Source Alone.

IN THE SIGHT OF GOD

The phrase, *"In the sight of God and our Father,"* refers to the fact that all are under the scrutiny of His eye. This eye beholds all, but in what manner we might ask?

First of all, God is our *"Heavenly Father,"* which presupposes us as members of the family, meaning that He has nothing for us but good. He wants these Graces developed in us.

However, the general idea is, that He watches us, i.e., *"we are kept in His sight,"* as it regards the Finished Work of Christ. In other words, His Son has paid a terrible price for all this we presently have; consequently, He will not tolerate us going outside of the parameters of that Finished Work attempting to bring about these things which we must have. And whether the Believer understands it or not, much of the time we have attempted to go outside of those parameters.

What does that mean?

Let me repeat myself again and say it very carefully:

It means that everything we need is found in the Finished Work of Christ, i.e., *"the Cross."*

It means that we are to place our Faith in that Finished Work, and for it to remain there.

Third, once this is done, the Holy Spirit will work on our behalf, bringing about all that is necessary.

The Heavenly Father watches to see if in fact our Faith is properly placed, because what was done at the Cross was at such price, that it must not be ignored or set aside. Therefore, the Believer must understand, that every effort he makes, every direction he takes, that all are in the *"Sight of God."*

(4) "KNOWING, BRETHREN BELOVED, YOUR ELECTION OF GOD."

Even though this Verse is very short, it contains a wealth of meaning. And yet, many false doctrines have risen out of a misinterpretation of the word *"election."*

As we've said previously, Scripture interprets Scripture. That means, that on any given subject, we must see what the entirety of the Word of God says regarding that subject, before we can arrive at a proper conclusion. To pull one Scripture out of context, is not proper. If all that the Bible says on any given subject, is correlated, then the true interpretation becomes obvious.

NOTES

KNOWING

What is it that we are to know?

Concerning everything as it pertains to God, the Word of God is that which we should know. Everything that God has for us, which pertains to every subject, the answer is given in His Word. Understanding that, we should study His Word, should know His Word, should make His Word the criteria for all that we do.

Considering how important this is, and that it has eternal consequences, the study and learning of the Word of God, in order that we might *"know,"* should be the primary objective of every single Believer. In other words, knowing the Word, should be the most important thing in every Believer's life.

We know what we know, only because of what the Word of God tells us.

Unfortunately, too many Believers allow other people to do their interpretation of the Bible for them. While the fivefold Ministry (Eph. 4:11), is certainly given by the Lord to help the Body understand the Word, and apply it to our lives, still, that is only in the realm of helps (Eph. 4:12). This in no way absolves any Believer from their own personal understanding and knowledge of the Word. In fact, you as a Believer do not *"know"* the Word, unless you have personal knowledge. If you are accepting what someone else has said, then you really do not know.

OUTSIDE OF THE WORD

As we have stated, the Word of God addresses every spiritual problem that one might ever think of having. In other words, the Bible holds the answer, which is the answer that should be believed and acted upon. Unfortunately, much of the Church world operates on an entirely different basis. Many, if not most, form conclusions, and act upon those conclusions, even base their lives upon those conclusions, when in reality those conclusions have absolutely no bearing whatsoever on the Word of God. Many so-called Religious

Leaders make decisions which affect many people, with very few seemingly, checking to see if what is being said and done is Scriptural? Naturally, anyone of this stripe will always loudly claim that what they're doing is Scriptural, but when Chapter and Verse are requested, they have no Chapter or Verse, or else they attempt to make something fit which has no bearing on what is being done.

## PEOPLE DO WHAT THEY DO BECAUSE THEY BELIEVE WHAT THEY BELIEVE

A dear friend of mine, the Pastor of a Baptist Church made this statement in my presence, *"People do what they do because they believe what they believe."* I don't know if he originated the statement or not, but whether he did or someone else, the statement is absolutely correct.

All of us do certain things because we believe certain things. If we believe wrong things, we're going to do wrong things. It is just that simple! That means that what we're doing is based upon a lie. In other words, it means that we do not *"know!"* We think we do, but we don't!

You as the Reader should read carefully the words of the above heading. They are extremely important, and whether we realize it or not, they actually guide our lives.

If it is true that people do what they do because they believe what they believe, then it should stand to reason that we should be very careful about what we believe.

When Paul uses the word *"knowing,"* he knows exactly what he is talking about. None of this is happenchance or suppositional to him. It is Truth, and as such, he has based his life and his eternity on that Truth. So, he does what he does, because he believes what he believes.

## BRETHREN, BELOVED OF GOD

The phrase, *"Brethren Beloved,"* refers to the basis on which the entire Plan of God rests, which is *"Love."*

When God originally created man, it was not out of need, for God needs nothing, but rather out of love. Consequently, Redemption of man is based on the same premise. God is Love!

Inasmuch as that is true, all of God's dealings with us, and in every capacity, are based on Love. As stated, it is not out of need, or any other motive, only Love.

Understanding that, we know that this manner of dealing stands alone in its uniqueness. In other words, there's absolutely nothing that pertains to man, that is born or carried out, strictly from the basis and principle of Love. God stands alone in that capacity. Unfortunately, the world doesn't understand that and judges God very harshly, accusing Him of all type of negative things. However, none of that is true, with the fact remaining that God deals only in love.

That means that even when He is forced to use judgment, which He often does, that it is always for the good of all concerned.

For instance, if a Doctor performs major surgery on a patient to remove a cancer, even though it causes the patient pain and suffering, the Doctor is performing his task in order to save the patient's life. In other words, it is for the good of the patient. God works in the same manner:

He has to perform major surgery at times, but it is for our good, or the world's good in general. We may not think of it as such, simply because we only see in part, while the Lord knows all things.

## ELECTION

The phrase, *"Your election of God,"* gives us a clue as to the Plan of God.

In this case, the word *"election"* refers to the Gentiles, as Paul puts it, taking the place of Israel, with this nation being rejected, because of their rejection of Jesus Christ.

The Lord chose Abraham and Sarah, and proposed, from Abraham's loins and Sarah's womb, to raise up a people who would be called Israelites, who would love Him and trust Him. Through them was to come the Messiah, the Redeemer of the world; this was, in fact, the purpose for which they were raised up. Consequently, as would be obvious, they were *"elected."*

However, Israel forfeited all of this, and in fact crucified the very One they were raised up to bring forth. As a result, God had to set them aside, and thereby elect the Gentiles to take their place.

In addressing this subject, Peter plainly

NOTES

said, *"Wherefore the rather, Brethren, give diligence to make your calling and election sure: for if ye do these things, ye shall never fall"* (II Pet. 1:10).

NOTES

## THE FALSE TEACHING ON ELECTION

The teaching of *"election"* which claims that some are elected by God to be saved and some are elected by God to be lost, and there is nothing they can say or do in the matter that can change the situation, is patently false. There's nothing in the Word of God that even remotely substantiates such thinking. But yet, there are millions who have believed this error. Consequently, they take the position that if they are elected to be lost, there's nothing they can do about it, and if they're elected to be saved, they ultimately will somehow be saved. Consequently, they die eternally lost without God.

The truth is, the entirety of the world, and for all time, has been elected to be saved, if they will only choose the Lord of their own free will. It is always a matter of *"free will"* (Mat. 11:28-30; 20:16; Jn. 1:12; 3:16-20; I Tim. 2:4; Rev. 17:14; 22:17).

Man is a free moral agent, and at no time in his life does he ever cease to be a free moral agent. That means he has the power of choice as it regards God and Salvation.

It is possible for a person's will to be so overtaken by Satan, that they no longer have the power to choose whether they will drink or not drink, take drugs or not take drugs, etc. However, irrespective as to how far gone that individual might be, if they so desire, they still have the freedom and power of choice to accept or reject God. In fact, millions in the worst shape that anyone could ever imagine, have exercised that freedom, made the Lord their Savior, which brought about a miraculous change within their lives, and there was absolutely nothing Satan could do about the situation.

Let me emphasize it again: Man does have the power of choice, but the choice of which we speak, is the ability to accept the Lord and His Ways, or to reject the Lord and His Ways. That's where the choice actually is.

## ERRONEOUS TEACHING BY THE CHURCH

For the most part, the Church teaches that *"sin is a choice."* That is true, but only up to a point. In fact, even as we've just mentioned, there are millions of alcoholics right now, who no longer have a choice as to whether they will drink or not. The same would go for drug addicts, and many other problems that one could name.

Sin is a choice only in the realm of the individual choosing to go God's Way or not going God's Way. That and that alone is where the choice is.

Concerning that which we've said thus far, most in the Church would agree; however, the Church mostly teaches that after one comes to Christ, then they can simply choose to sin or not choose to sin. They reason that all sin is a choice, and, therefore, if a Christian sins, that means he has chosen to sin, and consequently he must be punished.

That teaching is blatantly wrong.

While the Believer definitely has a choice in the matter, the choice is whether to abide by God's prescribed order of victory or not to do so. If the Believer attempts to function outside of this prescribed order, which is, of course, the Cross of Christ, then he will quickly find himself unable to resist the Powers of Darkness. Simply because this is so very important, let us say it again.

There are millions of Believers right now who are living in Romans, Chapter 7. They are trying with all their strength not to commit some act of sin which they have committed many times, and seemingly have been unable to stop. It is not a matter of choice with these individuals. They don't want to do what they're doing, and are trying with all their strength not to do what they're doing (Rom. 7:18).

So what is actually happening with these people?

They are operating outside of the sphere of God's prescribed order of victory, which guarantees their failure irrespective of how hard they try to do otherwise.

When we get right down to the bottom line, the Christian actually has to make the same choice as the unsaved individual. If the unsaved person attempts to make his life what it ought to be outside of God's Salvation, as is obvious, he will fail. He simply cannot succeed! In a sense, the Christian is in the same position.

Even though the Christian is saved, he still has to make the choice of accepting God's Way of victory within his life. If not, whether through ignorance or otherwise, he will still fail. And to be sure, he is just as responsible for the failure, irrespective of how hard he tries to do otherwise.

So for the Church to take the position, that all Believers are committing some type of sin, because they desire to do such a thing, is false. While there certainly may be some few who would fall into such a category, that number would be few indeed! Any individual who truly knows Christ, abhors sin. So if they fall into sin, the far greater majority of the times, it is because they do not know God's prescribed order of Victory.

Now as we've already stated, that in no way means that the person is not culpable. They're just as guilty of sin, as if they desired to do the thing; however, guilt and motive are two different things.

The motive of the Believer is not to sin. And I'll say it again, if they do not go God's Way, which is the Way of the Cross, irrespective as to what they want to do or desire to do, and no matter how hard they may fight against the problem, whatever it might be, ultimately that individual is going to fail. Victory is obtained and maintained only by our Faith in the Cross.

So, it does no good to punish someone of that nature, as should be obvious! In such a case what should be done, is that it should be explained to them as to why they have gone wrong, and then the way of the Cross kindly and graciously shown to them, which is proper restoration (Gal. 6:1).

The Church has drifted so far away from the Cross, that now it just simply makes up its own rules, completely ignoring the Word of God, which brings disaster to all concerned.

(5) "FOR OUR GOSPEL CAME NOT UNTO YOU IN WORD ONLY, BUT ALSO IN POWER, AND IN THE HOLY SPIRIT, AND IN MUCH ASSURANCE; AS YE KNOW WHAT MANNER OF MEN WE WERE AMONG YOU FOR YOUR SAKE."

This particular Verse of Scripture is so very important, because the Holy Spirit through the Apostle will tell us what is the criteria for a Biblical Ministry and a Christlike life. While men may come up with all types of other particulars, and which they constantly do, in fact, with this by Paul given little credence at all; still the Truth of what the Apostle says here, nevertheless remains the criteria for that which is truly of God.

NOTES

## THE GOSPEL

The phrase, *"For our Gospel came not unto you in word only,"* tells us several things:

1. When Paul used the words *"our Gospel,"* he was referring to the New Covenant, and which was given to him by the Lord Jesus Christ (Gal. 1:11-12). Again, the words *"our Gospel"* by the very fact of its specification, tells us that there were other gospels also, but which were spurious. Satan, of course, feeds all types of gospels out to the public, and uses the Church to propagate his message. His gospels sound very much like the original, but with a variation here and there, and I think more particularly, as to how we deal with the Holy Spirit and with the Cross. The problem is no less presently than it was those days of long ago.

2. *"In Word only,"* pertains to the Bible being preached, but without the power of the Holy Spirit. Even though many contend that if the Word of God, i.e., *"the Truth,"* is preached, irrespective that there is no Anointing or power of the Holy Spirit, that it will still have its positive affect. I disagree!

I think this Scripture completely refutes such thinking. Anything and everything that comes from God, must have the Moving and Operation of the Holy Spirit, irrespective as to what it is, and if not, there can be no positive results (Acts 1:4, 8). The problem we have now, is untold thousands of Churches where the Bible is preached in some fashion each and every week, but with no Anointing of the Spirit, no Moving of the Spirit, no convicting power of the Spirit, which in that case, presents nothing but a *"dead letter."* Even though the Word of God is preached, and even though it is preached in Truth, which means that the Doctrine is correct, at least up to a point, still, there must be the Moving and Operation of the Spirit upon the Word for it to have any type of positive effect.

In fact, there must be an amalgamation or union of the Messenger, the Message, and the

Spirit, for the Gospel to be properly presented. That demands consecration on the part of the Preacher, which the Holy Spirit intends!

3. The Gospel that came to the Thessalonians was the True Gospel, and came in power and assurance. That is the only Gospel that will have its intended, positive affect.

The Gospel came to our family in 1939. I was only four years old, but thank God it was the Gospel of Jesus Christ empowered by the Spirit. It changed our lives totally and completely, because it brought Jesus to us.

Satan will fight this type of Gospel as he fights nothing else, even as is evidenced in the life and Ministry of Paul. If one is to notice, the Judaizers, who caused Paul such problems, are not mentioned as being subject to beatings and imprisonments, as was the Apostle. The reasons should be obvious, irrespective of their claims, they were doing Satan's work. And he does not oppose his own. What held true then, holds true now!

## POWER

The phrase, *"But also in power,"* proclaims that which is absolutely necessary if people are to be saved and delivered.

The kingdom of darkness headed up by Satan and all his fallen angels and demon spirits, are greatly opposed to God, and all of the Kingdom of God, which certainly includes the Church. In fact, Satanic forces in the spirit world, constantly steal, kill, and destroy. They do so, by possessing people who do not know God, or else, greatly controlling them, which the latter is always the case. It's a strong thing to say that all unsaved people are more or less controlled by demon spirits; however, that is the case.

When these people come to God, which has always been the case, there has to be a power stronger than the power which grips them and holds them in bondage. That's what Jesus was speaking about when He said, *"Or else how can one enter into a strong man's house* (Satan's house), *and spoil his goods, except He first bind the strong man? And then He will spoil his house"* (Mat. 12:29).

While Satan is definitely strong, he is not all-powerful, as Christ. As well, our Lord *"having spoiled principalities and powers, He made a show of them openly, triumphing over them in it"* (Col. 2:15). He did it all at the Cross (Col. 2:14).

So, the Power of God can set men free, and it is the Power of God alone, which can set men free.

That means that it takes more than intellectualism, more than mere instruction, more than verbal presentation! The Gospel must be presented with power, and only then can the soul be set free. We're not dealing here with an intellectual problem or an educational problem; we're dealing with the powers of darkness, and only a stronger power can deliver the person from that bondage. That stronger power is God.

## THE HOLY SPIRIT

The phrase, *"And in the Holy Spirit,"* tells us where the power is. The Reader must remember that. The Power solely resides in the Spirit. Without the Holy Spirit, there is no power. Without the Holy Spirit, there is no deliverance. Without the Holy Spirit, the Word of God has no effect. Let us say it again, *"all the power comes from the Holy Spirit."*

The Early Church was a Spirit Baptized Church. Paul preached Salvation by Faith, and the Baptism with the Holy Spirit with the evidence of speaking with other Tongues (Acts 2:4; 19:1-7).

While the Holy Spirit definitely does come into the heart and life of every Believer at Salvation, that is different than one being Baptized with the Holy Spirit. In fact, the Holy Spirit cannot come in to abide, until the individual has been washed by the Blood of Jesus (I Cor. 6:11).

The Baptism with the Holy Spirit is always received after conversion, whether moments later or months later, etc. He is never received instantaneously and automatically at conversion. Once again, I'm reminding the Reader, that I'm speaking of the Baptism with the Holy Spirit, which Believers were commanded by Christ to receive (Acts 1:4). I'm not speaking of Regeneration which is also a work of the Holy Spirit, which takes place at the moment of conversion. Even though that is definitely the Holy Spirit, and His great work; still, that is not the Baptism with the Holy Spirit, in which the latter will always be accompanied

NOTES

by the speaking with other Tongues (Acts 2:4; 10:46; 11:15; 19:1-7).

When one studies the Church in the Book of Acts, one must come to the conclusion that this was a Spirit Baptized Church. They preached the Gospel of Salvation, and invited men to accept Christ. They prayed for the sick to be healed and for those in bondage to be delivered. They also preached that Believers should go on and be baptized with the Holy Spirit, which is a Gift of God, and is always received after conversion (Acts 8:4-8, 14-17).

Even at the risk of being overly blunt, I maintain that the segment of the Church presently, which does not believe in the Baptism with the Holy Spirit with the evidence of speaking with other Tongues, is a powerless Church. Consequently, while there may be much religious machinery, there is little or nothing done for the Lord.

I also maintain, that Churches which claim to believe in the Baptism with the Holy Spirit, but yet have pushed Him aside, to where He has little latitude to move, work, and operate, is likewise, a powerless Church. In fact, I am not so certain that if the latter is not worse than the former. Regrettably, and even at the risk of sounding critical, I'm afraid that most Pentecostal and Charismatic Churches fall into this category. There simply aren't many Churches which have a true Moving and Operation of the Spirit. There are many who claim the Spirit, and because of all type of weird so-called manifestations; still, if what is claimed to be of the Spirit is not Biblical, then despite the claims, it is not of the Holy Spirit. The Spirit of God will never violate, contradict, or carry out anything that's not exactly according to the Word.

## ASSURANCE

The phrase, *"And in much assurance,"* proclaims the result which accrue as a result of the Gospel being properly presented.

So once again, we emphasize the fact, if the Holy Spirit is present, there will be power, and souls will be saved, Believers will be filled with the Spirit, the sick will be healed, and people will be delivered. We have that *"assurance!"* Otherwise, we have nothing!

NOTES

## THE CRITERIA

Unfortunately, that listed in this particular Verse, as stated, is little the criteria for modern Ministry. The modern criteria pretty well is summed up in approval by men. In other words, the true *"assurances"* of the Spirit are pretty well ignored. In fact, they are not only ignored, but mostly rejected.

The criteria presently is the approval by particular Denominations, or Churches, or a certain amount of education, etc.

While these things mentioned may carry weight with men, they carry no weight at all with God. Once again, if the Spirit of God moves, which will result in people being saved and lives being changed, that and that alone is the criteria for Ministry.

However, the Believer must look through the claims even of these spectaculars. Claims are easy to make; however, if truly the Holy Spirit is moving, there will be fruit that remains. I speak of souls being saved and lives being changed, which will have a lasting effect, for all to see.

## WHO PAUL WAS

The phrase, *"As ye know what manner of men we were among you for your sake,"* speaks of the fact, that the Gospel the Apostle preached, and those with him, was evident in their lives as well. In other words, the husbandmen had been partakers of the fruit.

If the Gospel I preach doesn't work in my own life, then something is wrong with my Gospel. What Paul and those with him preached, worked in their own lives, and was obvious for all to see.

I'm thrilled and thankful that I can say, as well, that the Gospel I preach today, works in my life, and will work in all who will accept its proposal.

In fact, Jesus is the Gospel. The whole thing is wrapped up in Him, and Him Alone. Even more than that, it's wrapped up in what He did at the Cross and through His Resurrection. It is that alone on which the Holy Spirit works, and I speak of the Finished Work of Christ.

If one accepts what Christ did at the Cross, one will be saved, and one will also walk in perpetual victory (Rom. 6:11, 14). As well, Jesus is not only the Savior, but He is also the

Baptizer with the Holy Spirit. To accept Him for one without the other, is a travesty! However, it must all be remembered, that Salvation in totality comes through the Cross, and the Baptism with the Holy Spirit comes as a result of the Cross.

(6) "AND YE BECAME FOLLOWERS OF US, AND OF THE LORD, HAVING RECEIVED THE WORD IN MUCH AFFLICTION, WITH JOY OF THE HOLY SPIRIT:"

This Verse, as the last, opens up other Truths to us.

We must remember that when Paul brought the Gospel to Thessalonica, the Gentiles had never heard of Jesus Christ. How much the Jews there of the Synagogue knew of Him, is anyone's guess. However, what little they knew, if anything, they probably had said little or nothing, so that what few Gentiles attended the Synagogue, would have had no knowledge of Christ.

What a joy it would have been to have been an observer of the founding of this Church. And yet, the Gospel we preach today, should be the identical Gospel as preached then by Paul, and should accrue the same results.

## FOLLOWERS OF US

The phrase, *"And ye became followers of us,"* presents the simple fact, that if the Messenger is disliked, the Message will be little received. In fact, every Believer in the world, is going to follow some Preacher. That's not wrong, even as described here, and in fact is right, that is if it's the right Preacher.

The intimation is, that these Gentiles, and what few Jews received Christ, at first were taken with Paul and those with him. In other words, they liked the Messenger.

They saw something in their lives that was so different than what they had, so outstanding, that they were instantly attracted to these Evangelists. That's the way it ought to be!

Jesus should so shine within our hearts, so live within our lives, that when men see us, they actually see Jesus.

Here, first of all, we're speaking of men (Paul and his associates) who had a relationship with Christ that was exceptional to say the least. In fact, one could probably say without much fear of exaggeration, that there were few, if any, in the world of that day, who were closer to the Lord than Paul, and those with him as well. These were the Godliest of the Godly!

NOTES

As such, there was a spirit of humility that enveloped them, which as stated, made them totally unlike any other human beings that these pagans had ever seen, observed, or witnessed. Now that's quite a statement, but it is true.

When Paul or the others preached, the Presence of the Lord was instantly felt by the listeners. They would not have known what it was, would not have known its origin, at least not at first; however, they knew it was unlike anything they had ever experienced in their lives. This was their introduction to the Gospel and what an introduction!

Every time I preach anywhere in the world, I ask the Lord, even plead with Him, that His Spirit will so fill me, so move through me, so have His way in my life, that when people see me, they really don't see Jimmy Swaggart, but rather the Lord. If the Presence of God doesn't characterize my efforts, then what little I'm able to do will by and large, be in vain.

When these people first heard Paul, they soon came under great conviction by the Holy Spirit, which would have been brand-new to them also. Of course, it is new to most all presently as well.

Then when they gave their hearts to the Lord, a transformation would have taken place, that would have been miraculous to say the least! With the great weight of sin rolled away, they would have experienced a joy and a peace that would have passed all understanding.

## FOLLOWERS OF THE LORD

The phrase, *"And of the Lord,"* could only be the case after they'd given their hearts to Christ. Paul and his associates introduced Jesus to these Gentiles, and now after having come to know Him, they've become His followers.

This was the greatest time of their lives, they had found Christ and they would never be the same again. Everything has changed. Whereas they had formerly been idol worshippers, no doubt, that was the case no longer. Old things had passed away, with all things becoming new. A love fills their heart now that they had never previously known. As well, they now have a peace in their hearts they had not previously known. Everything has changed!

Before accepting Christ, the sinner knows absolutely nothing about the Lord. In fact, even though most in modern times have heard of Jesus Christ, still, they would know little more now than those Pagans did then. However, the moment they were saved, all of that began to change. Now, the Satanic nature in their lives is smothered, with the Divine Nature taking its place. Their thoughts change! Their attitude changes! In fact, everything changes, which is indicative of the Gospel.

They find out that the Gospel and Christ are for all practical purposes, one in the same. In fact, the Gospel is Jesus Christ. They are aware of this constant presence in their hearts and lives, which is the Holy Spirit. They are cognizant of His help, which gives them a power they have never had before.

These Gentile Pagans have now become Children of God, by virtue of their acceptance of Christ and what He did at the Cross, and now, gloriously and wondrously, they are no longer pagans. And so was the Church at Thessalonica.

AFFLICTION

The phrase, *"Having received the Word in much affliction,"* proclaims the opposition of former friends or even relatives, etc.

Not only does the presentation of the True Gospel bring great joy, but, as well, it generally always tenders opposition. Quite possibly, that when Paul began to minister, not only were people saved, but others greatly rejected his word, even violently so. In other words, they could have even been threatening harm to both the Apostles and these new converts. Despite that, these people had accepted Christ.

As well, after they'd given their hearts to Christ, no doubt, much opposition came against them, as is generally the case also. As stated, it could well have been former friends and their relatives.

*"Affliction"* in the Greek is *"thlipsei,"* and means *"crushing pressure."* Consequently, the opposition must have been fierce, as it no doubt was.

Why is this so?

NOTES

Paul answers that question as well. He said, *"For we wrestle not against flesh and blood, but against principalities, against powers, against the rulers of the darkness of this world, against spiritual wickedness in high places"* (Eph. 6:12).

People reject Christ for ulterior reasons. Satan appeals to them in one way or the other, whether they realize it or not, and they yield to his pressure. Once they yield, he begins to stir them up against those who are attempting to live for the Lord. They don't realize that it's evil spirits in them or working on them, causing this opposition, but that's what it is. So, the Believer is to understand that the opposition is not so much *"flesh and blood,"* as it is the demon powers of darkness. Satan hates the person who has accepted Christ, and will attempt to hinder and hurt by working through other people who have rejected Christ.

The Believer is to understand what is happening, realizing that the same person who is causing the affliction can, in fact, be saved and changed immediately and completely. While such doesn't happen all the time, it definitely does happen some of the time. In fact, Paul was one of these very people, actually the very worst, and I speak of his before conversion experience. He hated followers of Christ, doing all within his power to hinder and hurt, with some possibly even paying with their lives. And then wonder of wonders, and miracle of miracles, the Lord on the road to Damascus grandly and gloriously changed the life of this former persecutor, with him now strangely enough, becoming the persecuted (Acts Chpt. 9).

THE JOY OF THE HOLY SPIRIT

The phrase, *"With joy of the Holy Spirit,"* proclaims several things:

1. The Baptism with the Holy Spirit brings a perpetual joy. It is totally unlike anything that one could ever begin to imagine. It is what the world, the flesh, and the Devil attempt to imitate, but fall light years short. This is joy produced by the Holy Spirit, which means a type of joy that the world does not have and cannot produce.

2. The affliction which Paul mentioned here, has absolutely no bearing whatsoever on

this *"joy of the Holy Spirit."* All the affliction is generated outwardly, while this joy is generated inwardly. So, let the Devil do his worst, it will not affect the joy of the true Christian.

3. The Thessalonians first of all became followers of Paul, which in essence means that they accepted the Message of the Cross which he preached. This is the foundation of all that they are, all they have, all they can have in Christ Jesus.

4. After accepting the great Message of the Cross, they are now followers of Christ, Who instituted all of these great things as it regards Eternal Life, the infilling of the Spirit, etc., and did so by His Death and Resurrection.

Inasmuch as Paul briefly alludes here to the persecution or affliction, i.e., *"suffering,"* that the Thessalonians endured because of their Testimony of Christ, perhaps it would be good to look at the word *"affliction"* or *"suffering"* to a greater degree.

## SUFFERING AND ANGUISH

Some 12 Hebrew words and 21 Greek terms (too many to list here), convey such ideas as: to suffer, to endure suffering, distress, anguish, pain, to cause pain, to be distressed, to be hard pressed, to torment, to permit, to leave, or to let alone. Generally, suffering is mental distress which may or may not include physical pain. Anguish is intense suffering.

The Biblical contexts suggest some answers to the extremely difficult question as to why there is so much suffering in the world. Suffering may be an effect of:

1. Divine judgment for sin.
2. Empathy for another's misery.
3. The vicarious bearing of another's penalty.
4. Authentic repentance and Faith in the Lord.
5. A warning to prevent a greater evil.
6. Discipline for training in Christlikeness.

The appropriate response to each kind of suffering is as different as the reason for the suffering. Such significant differences make generalizations about the purpose of all suffering improper and misleading. In an attempt to avoid the error of generalization as far as possible, each type of suffering is considered separately in the following order:

NOTES

1. Judgmental suffering.
2. Emphatic suffering.
3. Vicarious suffering.
4. Testimonial suffering.
5. Preventative suffering.
6. Educational suffering.

More than one of these purposes may be operative in any given instance of suffering. When that is the case, however, the reasons may be more readily recognized if first clearly distinguished.

1. JUDGMENTAL SUFFERING

How did mankind become subject to suffering in the first place? As created, men and nature were *"very good"* (Gen. 1:31). What made life on Earth a *"veil of tears"*? Neither a capricious act of God nor fate. It was man's pretentious and unbelieving violation of God's Will. The pains of childbirth and of hard labor may be traced to Divine judgment upon the first sin (Gen. 3:16-19).

In a fallen world we may bring suffering upon ourselves by failure to employ our God-given resources in accord with wisdom. For instance, an *"idle person will suffer hunger"* (Prov. 19:15).

*"He who walks with wise men becomes wise, but the companion of fools will suffer harm"* (Prov. 13:20).

*"A prudent man sees danger and hides himself; but the simple go on, and suffer for it"* (Prov. 22:3; 27:12).

*"One man gives freely, yet grows all the richer; another withholds what he should give, and only suffers want"* (Prov. 11:24).

Apparently God sustains a providential order in which people are judged for laziness, lack of foresight, companionship of fools, and greed. Furthermore, distress may result from social pressures to condemn an innocent man. Pilate's wife sent word to him, *"Have nothing to do with that Righteous man, for I have suffered much over Him today in a dream"* (Mat. 27:19). Of course, no Christian ought to suffer for wrongdoing (II Pet. 2:13).

## SIN

Judgmental suffering also follows for sins against God's Revelation through Prophets and Apostles. Israel's adults, so wonderfully delivered from Egypt, nevertheless continually murmured against Moses and God. For

NOTES

their *"faithlessness"* they suffered and died in the wilderness. Their children also suffered (Num. 14:31-33).

Awareness of family and national solidarity was explicit in the culture. However, the children suffered only temporarily; they entered the Promised Land, whereas their parents didn't!

FAMILY CURSE

It is taught quite strongly in some circles, that the reason for people's problems, at least in many cases, is that they carry with them a *"family curse."* What does this mean?

First of all there is some Truth in the statement, but not in the way it is mostly being taught.

Is there, in fact, a curse upon people and/or even families?

There are all types of curses on the human race because of sin and the Fall (Gen. 3:14-19; 27:12; Num. 5:27; Deut. 11:26; 27:15-26; 28:16-19; Prov. 3:33; 26:2; Jer. 26:6; Mal. 2:2; Gal. 3:10, 13).

In fact, the entirety of the human race which does not know God is cursed. This means that things will not come out right, cannot come out right, no matter which direction the individual may take, no matter how much money they may possess or power, etc., they are cursed, which speaks of wreckage and destruction in one form or the other.

The basic Scriptural Passage used to teach the *"family curse,"* is Deuteronomy 5:9. It says, *"Thou shalt not bow down thyself unto them, nor serve them* (idol gods)*: for I the Lord thy God am a jealous God, visiting the iniquity of the fathers upon the children unto the third and fourth generation of them that hate Me."*

So if there's a problem in the family of some nature, some Preachers are telling these people that the reason for the problem is because of something that their Father or Grandfather or Great-Grandfather did which was very evil, etc., allowing a curse to be brought upon the family.

They teach that it can come down to the third or even the fourth generation, and is now the cause of their problem. Consequently, they are told to come forward for prayer, where hands are laid on them, and this family curse rebuked, etc., and then they are free.

That's not Scriptural!

WHAT DOES THE BIBLE SAY?

First of all, the Ninth Verse which we have just quoted, ends by saying *"them that hate Me."*

There are exactly as the Bible says, curses upon particular families because of something that was done in the past which was very evil, and it has passed down now even to the third or fourth generation. The last thing I intend to do in this statement is to be unkind; however, I personally believe that the Kennedy's are cursed, hence the reason for all of their tragedies. Let me explain:

Just before prohibition ended, Joseph Kennedy, Sr., purchased the great Haig and Haig Scotch Whiskey industries in England. Knowing that the prohibition laws would be stricken from the books, making liquor legal once again in America, his tankers were sitting in New York harbor at the very moment the ban was lifted, with him supplying much of this nation with Scotch Whiskey, which he did for a period of time. He made untold millions of dollars out of this effort. However, what does the Bible say about the traffic in intoxicating liquor?

*"Woe unto him that giveth his neighbor drink, that puttest thy bottle to him, and makest him drunken also, that thou mayest look upon their nakedness!*

*"Thou art filled with shame for glory . . . the cup of the Lord's right hand shall be turned unto thee, and shameful spewing shall be on thy glory.*

*"For the violence of Lebanon shall cover thee, and the spoil of beasts, which made them afraid, because of men's blood, and for the violence of the land, of the city, and of all that dwell therein"* (Hab. 2:15-17).

These Passages plainly tell us that a curse will come upon all who traffic in the liquor business. I might quickly add, this not only includes the family of Joe Kennedy, but also every other person who makes the stuff or sells it. Plain and simple, they are *"cursed,"* which means that difficulties and violence will follow them. We may not hear near as much about all the hundreds of thousands of others who traffic in this business as it regards judgment, for the simple reason that they are not as famous as the Kennedy's; however, to be sure, God is no respecter of persons, and all who violate His Word, and do so with impunity, come under the same judgment.

## SALVATION

However, the moment any person in that family comes to God, that curse is broken as it regards the entirety of the family. In fact, the curse can continue unto the third or fourth generation, only as it regards those who *"hate the Lord"* (Deut. 5:9).

In the very next Verse, the Lord plainly states, *"And showing mercy unto thousands of them that love Me and keep My Commandments"* (Deut. 5:10).

So, the idea that a person can come to Christ and have a curse continue to hang over them, and that curse have to be rebuked, etc., before they can find relief, is not Scriptural, and in fact, is blatantly unscriptural!

The Word of God plainly says as it regards Salvation, *"old things pass away, behold, all things become new"* (II Cor. 5:17).

Now, either *"old things pass away and all things become new,"* or else they don't! I happen to believe they do!

So, the moment any individual in any family comes to Christ, all curses on that particular family are instantly stopped. David said, *"God setteth the solitary in families: He bringeth out those which are bound with chains"* (Ps. 68:6).

This means that even one person in a family coming to Christ, does glorious things for the entirety of that family, even though there may be no others in that family living for God. All judgment is stopped, even on the unsaved, at least as far as possible, with every opportunity for all chains of bondage to be broken. Regrettably, all in every family generally don't accept the Lord; still, even the ones who do not accept are greatly blessed by the one or more who do.

What kind of Salvation would it be, for a person to come to Christ, and all type of curses allowed to remain on that person? That would not be Salvation, but rather a joke! So, Preachers do a terrible disservice to Believers, when they tell them that the cause of their problems, whatever those problems might be, is a *"family curse."* Such only tends to breed fear, and to be sure, no matter how much they are prayed for with hands laid on them, no true help will come.

NOTES

## SO WHAT IS WRONG WITH THESE PEOPLE?

That these Believers are having problems, of that I do not doubt; however, the reason for those problems is, that they do not properly understand their place and position in the Finished Work of Christ. Therefore, Satan plays havoc with them, which in fact he does with most of Christendom, because the Message of the Cross is little known.

The Believer, even as we've said many times, and in fact, will continue to say it many times, must understand, that all blessings, all victory, all deliverance, everything we might need, is in the Finished Work of Christ. It's not so much something for us to obtain, but in fact, it has already been obtained for us by Christ. The problem is, even as I've just stated, most Believers have no knowledge whatsoever of Who they are, and what they are in Christ.

Knowing and understanding that all solutions are found in the Cross of Christ (what Jesus did there), the Believer must put his Faith in that Finished Work, and keep his Faith there.

Once Faith is properly placed in the Cross, which means that the Believer's Faith now has the proper object, the Holy Spirit will then guarantee all the benefits of the great Sacrifice of Christ to the Believer, which is intended all along (Rom. 6:2-6, 11, 14; 8:1-2).

How so many Christians suffer so needlessly, simply because we do not know the Truth of our great Redemption. So, we cast about in every direction trying to find relief, with this *"family curse thing"* being but one of the many erroneous paths.

No, your problem as a Believer is not a *"family curse,"* it's you not rightly knowing your proper place in the Finished Work of Christ. In fact, if the family curse thing were true, that would mean that Jesus didn't finish it all at the Cross, thereby leaving certain things undone. The proponents of this false doctrine may not understand that, but that's exactly what they're doing. By their very actions, they are saying that Jesus didn't do it all at the Cross, and there are things which were not addressed, and, consequently, must be addressed presently. To be frank, such thinking borders on blasphemy, even as the Reader begins to see and understand presently.

The Lord does not take kindly to the great Sacrifice of Christ being insulted and ridiculed, even though the people may be doing it ignorantly.

It makes no difference as to who the Believer might be, whether he's the biggest Preacher in the world, or the weakest Christian on the face of the Earth. If, in fact, that individual does not understand their proper place in Christ, as it regards His great redemptive work, problems will abound in these lives, with that Christian being a failure in one way or the other, and I speak of sin, despite all he can do to the contrary trying to have victory.

If what I'm saying is right, and it definitely is, then it is extremely important, as should be obvious. So, we should learn what the Word of God says about this most important subject of the Finished Work of Christ, and our part and place in that Work. To be sure, it extends all the way from us having been baptized into His Death (not Water Baptism, but rather a baptism into His Crucifixion), to being buried with Him, which refers to all of our old sins, iniquities, ungodliness, etc., and then being raised with Him in *"newness of life"*; however, it doesn't stop there, we are also seated with Him in Heavenly Places, which speaks of total victory, but all because of the Cross (Rom. 6:2-14; 8:1-2; Eph. 2:6).

## THE FINISHED WORK, FAITH, AND THE HOLY SPIRIT

Every single thing the Believer needs, and that means in every capacity, was addressed at the Cross. The Cross was not incidental or accidental, but planned, even before the foundation of this world (I Pet. 1:18-20).

There every sin debt was paid, the curse of the broken law was satisfied, with the total penalty taken by Christ, with all sin atoned, through the Death of the Savior. Because all sin was atoned, every claim that Satan and his cohorts had on humanity, was voided. That means Satan and every demon spirit are defeated, with the power of darkness broken.

NOTES

Out of this which Jesus did, Justification by Faith was made possible, Eternal Life was granted, Sanctification was guaranteed, victory over every power of darkness was guaranteed, Divine Healing was guaranteed, and even financial prosperity, and in fact, blessings of every sort. So, what Jesus did there, not only addressed the negatives, but brought forth the positives as well.

Understanding that, we must realize that everything we need is there, which refers to what Jesus did at the Cross and in His Resurrection.

Considering that every Believer is *"in Christ,"* which means, that when Jesus died, in the Mind of God, we died literally in Him, this means that all that He did was for us, and is, in fact, ours. Inasmuch as every Believer is *"in Christ,"* then all that we need is ours. All we have to do, is to exhibit Faith in that Finished Work. In other words, every Christian already has Faith. *So, it's the object of Faith which is so important.* The object of your Faith must be the Cross, must be what Christ did there, must be in His Finished Work. That's where your Faith must be anchored, and in fact, must never be moved.

To have all of these great things, one doesn't have to do anything else except simply believe. In fact, if we try to do something else, such as having hands laid on us to rebuke a family curse, or to try to fast away the problem, whatever the problem is, while some of these things plus others we have not named, in their own right can be very beneficial and helpful, they will help not at all in regards to this of which we speak. Because if we attempt to use these other things, and that list is long, we turn them into works, which God looks at as *"the flesh,"* which He will not honor. In fact, it grieves Him and even angers Him, for Believers to attempt to receive what we need, or be what we ought to be, etc., by means of the flesh (Rom. 8:8).

## KNOWING

In fact, the Holy Spirit through Paul, some nine times referred to the Believer *"knowing"* these things of which we speak (Rom. 6:3, 6, 9, 16, 19; 7:1, 14, 18; 8:22, 28). As well, there are other words or phrases in these three Chapters of Romans that refer to our understanding or knowledge of this subject. So I should think, that the Believer would understand, that when the Lord uses the word *"knowing"* or one of its derivatives this many times, that He is trying to tell us something.

This means that you as a Believer of all things, ought to *"know"* these things of which we say. You ought to *"know"* the Source of your victory, which is the Cross of Christ; you ought to *"know"* the place of all Blessings, which is the Cross of Christ; you ought to *"know"* your place and position in Christ, which guarantees all of these things; you ought to *"know"* all of this, which makes possible the work and administration of the Holy Spirit in your heart and life; you ought to *"know"* all these things, that pertain to your Sanctification.

DAILY

In fact, the Lord has so designed this manner of victory, that we will never forget the True Source. We are commanded to *"deny ourselves,"* which means not to trust in ourself for all of these things but rather that which Jesus has done for us, and to *"take up the Cross daily in our following Christ"* (Lk. 9:23-24).

Many Christians misunderstand taking up the Cross, thinking that it speaks of suffering. Actually it does, but in the suffering which Christ suffered for us, in order that we would not have to suffer. In fact, bearing the Cross daily, is the most glorious, wonderful life that one could ever know.

It refers to the Believer trusting solely in what the Cross produced, and doing so on a daily basis. That's all that it means; however, Satan has been very successful in perverting the Word of God as it regards the Cross, which has caused most Christians to run away from the Cross, instead of to the Cross where we rightly belong.

Let's go back to our subject as to why suffering is in the world today, and, in fact, the types of suffering which men experience.

ISRAEL

Repeatedly Israel faced judgmental suffering for her iniquities (Ps. 107:17) and her guilt (Isa. 24:5-6). As well, Jeremiah cried out, *"My anguish, my anguish! I writhe in pain! Oh, the walls of my heart! My heart is beating wildly; I cannot keep silent; for I hear the sound of the trumpet, the alarm of war"* (Jer. 4:19).

NOTES

Judah was destroyed because of the greatness of her iniquity (Jer. 13:22). Jerusalem lay in ruins and Zion suffered bitterly for *"the multitude of her transgressions"* (Lam. 1:5). Later Nehemiah confessed, *"They were disobedient and rebelled against Thee, and cast Thy Law behind their backs, and killed Thy Prophets, who had warned them in order to turn them back to Thee, and they committed great blasphemies. Therefore Thou didst give them into the hands of their enemies, who made them suffer"* (Neh. 9:26-27).

THE NEW TESTAMENT

The New Testament portrayal of judgmental suffering is equally severe. For premeditated lying to the Apostles and the Holy Spirit, Ananias and Sapphira suddenly died (Acts 5:1-11). Those who profane the Lord's body and blood at the Communion Table also face judgment. *"For anyone who eats and drinks without properly discerning the Body of the Lord eats and drinks judgment upon himself. That is why many of you are weak and ill, and some have died"* (I Cor. 11:29-30). As a result of sin the creation is subjected to futility and in bondage to decay until the revealing of the sons of God (Rom. 8:18-21).

In the Judgment the Believer's works of *"wood, hay, stubble"* will be burned up and *"He will suffer loss"* (I Cor. 3:12-15).

At death Lazarus went to Abraham's bosom, but the rich man in Hell called out *"I am in anguish! I am in anguish in this flame"* (Lk. 16:24). When the Lord Jesus is revealed from Heaven in flaming fire, taking vengeance on those who do not know God and do not obey the Gospel, *"They shall suffer the punishment of eternal destruction and exclusion from the Presence of the Lord"* (II Thess. 1:9).

2. EMPHATIC SUFFERING

In the face of intense suffering the Prophets were appalled. Concerned for the Church at Corinth, Paul wrote *"out of much affliction and anguish of heart and with many tears"* (II Cor. 2:4). All of us are to weep with those who weep (Rom. 12:15). Some suffering arises, not from sin, but love. We may enter fully through imagination and concern into another's feelings. Empathy with others who suffer produces suffering.

Does God experience emphatic suffering?

In the days of Noah when the Lord saw that the imaginations of man's heart were only evil continually, *"the Lord was sorry that He had made man on the earth, and it grieved Him to His heart"* (Gen. 6:6). In man's sin God takes no pleasure.

Robinson said, *"The only way in which moral evil can enter into the consciousness of the morally good, is as suffering."* God is not an impersonal principle, but the Living Lord of Abraham, Isaac, and Jacob. With loving empathy He entered fully into the sufferings of Israel.

*"In all their affliction He was afflicted, and the Angel of His Presence saved them; in His love and in His pity He redeemed them; He lifted them up and carried them all the days of old"* (Isa. 63:9).

### PERMISSION IS NOT PLEASURE

Some misunderstanding of God's relation to suffering arises from a failure to do justice to His place and position.

In Christ God suffered all that man suffers. God in Christ suffered intensely during the Passion Week right up to the Cross. Even though God was in Christ when Jesus died on the Cross, God did not die, for God cannot die. In fact, God had to literally become man in order to die, hence the Incarnation. Nevertheless, one must understand, that all that Jesus suffered, God the Father suffered as well (II Cor. 5:19).

Belief in a God Who permits suffering, others think, destroys human freedom to alleviate it. One must remember, however, that permission is not pleasure. The God Who suffers with the suffering encourages removal of the cause.

*"Why will you die, O house of Israel? For I have no pleasure in the death of anyone, says the Lord God, so turn and live"* (Ezek. 18:31-32). Although God permits suffering, He has acted at inestimable cost to provide a just ground on which to justify the ungodly, which will one day put all suffering away.

3. VICARIOUS SUFFERING

Jesus Christ became incarnate *"that through death He might destroy him who had the power of death, that is, the Devil, and deliver all those who through fear of death were subject to lifelong bondage"* (Heb. 2:14-15).

NOTES

The Lord did not simply permit sin; He came into the world to totally destroy this monster, which is the ruination of all the creation of God, at least in this world. The following steps presents the manner of this destruction:

A. The Cross was the first step in this destruction of sin, and the most important.

B. The Rapture of the Church will be the second step, which will give every Believer who has ever lived a Glorified Body, which will then make the Believer totally immune to all sin (I Cor. 15:53-57).

C. The third step will be the Second Coming of the Lord with all the Saints, which will at that time see Satan and all his demon spirits and fallen angels, thrown into the bottomless pit, where they will remain for 1,000 years (Rev. 20:1-3).

D. The fourth and final step, will be the cleansing of the heavens and the Earth by fire, with the New Jerusalem being transferred from Heaven to Earth, which means that God will move His Headquarters from Heaven to planet Earth (II Pet. 3:10-13; Rev. Chpts. 21-22).

### THE DEFEAT OF SATAN

The decisive defeat of Satan at the Cross inspires sacrifice to remove the deepest causes of suffering. To accomplish His purpose, Jesus had *"to suffer many things, and be rejected by the elders and Chief Priests and scribes, and be killed, and on the third day be raised"* (Mat. 16:21; Mk. 8:31; Lk. 9:22; 17:25; 24:26).

The battle with evil necessitated suffering on the part of Christ, which should be obvious. Furthermore, the Messianic predictions called for it. The risen Lord explained, *"Thus it is written, that Christ should suffer and on the third day rise from the dead"* (Lk. 24:46). Peter declared that God had foretold by the mouth of all the Prophets that His Christ should suffer. Some of Peter's hearers had, in ignorance, contributed to the fulfillment of that prophecy (Acts 3:18). The Prophets themselves had been curious about the time and the Sufferer of Whom they wrote (I Pet. 1:11). Peter goes on record as a witness to the sufferings of Christ, as well as to the glory to be revealed (I Pet. 5:1).

PAUL

Paul explained and proved from the Jewish Scriptures (the Old Testament) that it was necessary for Christ to suffer and to rise from the dead (Acts 17:3; 26:23). He also stressed in Hebrews that the vicarious nature of Christ's agony in that Jesus suffered death for (in behalf of) everyone (Heb. 2:9). Christ's substitutionary Atonement is frequently mentioned in the New Testament. Furthermore, Jesus, as the pioneer of Salvation, was made perfect through suffering (Heb. 2:10).

He suffered temptations so that He could help the tempted (Heb. 2:18). He did not suffer death repeatedly, but once for all (Heb. 9:26). Just as Sacrifices had been burned outside the camp, Jesus *"suffered outside the gate in order to sanctify the people through His Own Blood"* (Heb. 13:12).

Through Faith in the One Who suffered in their place men are delivered from eternal anguish. No Stoic denial of suffering will change our sinfulness. Resentment does not help. To alleviate the suffering which is bound up with judgment on our sin, we must repent and trust Christ.

4. TESTIMONIAL SUFFERING

Inner distress, however, may result from genuine commitment to a Christlike life. Although Believers receive a new nature, their old nature, as we quickly find out, is not annihilated. Daily the Christian must combat temptations to serve the flesh. Genuine Christian living is not merely for pleasure. It is not a mere existence, stumbling from defeat to repentance, defeat to repentance, and neither is it a life of hypocritical Law-keeping. As well, a merely ethical existence is not a Christian existence.

The genuinely Spiritual Life is one of continuous looking to the Cross, for there every need was met.

Also, every Christian must always be aware, that we are not living up to the perfect ideal, and also, that we are nothing apart from the Grace of God; consequently, the Christian must ever cast himself upon God's Grace.

Whether we like it or not, inner suffering is a doorway to all the Blessings of the Christian Life. In fact, the real satisfactions of life lie in the area of suffering, not indulgence and pleasure. So this type of suffering may testify, not to judgment on sin, but to an authentic Christian commitment.

NOTES

This completely negates the erroneous teaching of the so-called *"Faith Ministry,"* which teaches that a proper confession will do away with all suffering, etc. This misguided effort also claims, at least some of its devotees claim, that if Paul would have had their Faith, he would not have had to have suffered all of the difficulties which he faced.

The absolute crassness of such thinking defies all description. These individuals could not stand a hundred miles back in Paul's shadow, much less claiming that his Faith was inferior to theirs. Some error is sophisticated error; however, this error runs pell mell into stupidity.

People who choose to live for Righteousness in an evil world must expect suffering also from external sources. Service for the Savior runs counter to the aspirations of this world's powers. Followers of Christ may suffer *"for His sake"* (Phil. 1:29), *"for Righteousness' sake"* (I Pet. 3:14), *"for the Kingdom of God"* (II Thess. 1:5), *"for the Gospel"* (II Tim. 2:9), for resisting Satan (I Pet. 2:19), *"as a Christian"* (I Pet. 4:16), and *"for the Name"* (Acts 5:41). Such persecution indicates that the Believer shares or partakes of Christ's sufferings (II Cor. 1:5; I Pet. 4:13).

JOB

Through intense suffering Job gave testimony to the integrity of his trust in God. Satan charged that Job's Faith depended upon temporal benefits received. Thereupon, God allowed the Devil to test Job's allegiance by taking away all that he possessed (Job 1:9-12), and even his health (Job 2:4-6).

Calamity in Job's case was not judgmental for certain sins. To his *"comforters"* it seemed that Job must have been a hypocrite or a liar, but his plight was not penal. It was a test of his integrity as a testimony to others.

Jesus' Disciples also fell into the error of thinking that all sickness was the result of sin. Upon seeing the man born blind, they asked, *"Rabbi, who sinned, this man or his parents, that he was born blind?"* Jesus answered, *"It was not that this man sinned or his parents, but that the works of God might be made manifest in him"* (Jn. 9:2-3). The healing of the man born blind ended a life of suffering, when the works of God were manifested in him by the opening of his eyes which had never seen the light of day.

What response is appropriate when we experience suffering as a testimony to our Trust in the Lord?

Remembering Christ's example of endurance under stress, we should follow in His steps (I Pet. 2:21).

One should not forget the heros of Faith who *"suffered mocking and scourging, and even chains and imprisonment. They were stoned, they were sawed in two, they were killed with the sword, they went about in skins of sheep and goats, destitute, afflicted, ill-treated"* (Heb. 11:36-38).

Like Moses, one may consider suffering abuse for Christ greater wealth than the treasures of Egypt (Heb. 11:26). So Believers shall complete the suffering necessary for the building of the Church (Col. 1:24), knowing that it assures future glory (I Pet. 4:13). In comparison with that eternal glory, the present momentary affliction is slight (Rom. 8:18; II Cor. 4:17).

5. PREVENTATIVE SUFFERING

God may allow physical suffering to keep one from more serious spiritual problems. Paul found it so.

He said, *"To keep me from being too elated by the abundance of Revelations, a thorn was given me in the flesh, a messenger of Satan, to harass me, to keep me from being too elated"* (II Cor. 12:7). Because of this weakness, Paul had to rely more completely upon God's Grace. In the midst of energetic service under most difficult conditions he found that Grace sufficient. When weak in himself, he was strong in the Lord, which I might quickly add, is the manner of the Lord (II Cor. 12:8-10).

Some suffering in a fallen world is a beneficial warning of the danger of more tragic possibilities. A medical Doctor writing on psychosomatic illnesses says, *"Pain is a sign that action should be taken; it implies that if action is not taken, the survival chances of the organism are going to decrease."*

NOTES

For such signs one may indeed be thankful. Sometimes physical suffering becomes a sign of spiritual need. If a person flat on his back begins to look up to the Savior, there is also room for gratitude, that even though it took this, better this than miss the Lord.

6. EDUCATIONAL SUFFERING

The greatest good of the Christian life is not freedom from pain; it is Christlikeness. God works all things together for good by surrounding us with conditions which help us conform to the image of His Son (Rom. 8:28-29). Christ's life was one of total conflict with the forces of evil. As His followers, then, *"we are afflicted in every way, but not crushed; perplexed, but not driven to despair; persecuted, but not forsaken; struck down, but not destroyed; always carrying in the body the death of Jesus, so that the life of Jesus may be manifested in our bodies"* (II Cor. 4:8-10).

## CHARACTER

God is far less concerned with the comfort than with the character of His people. What produces character? Suffering produces endurance, and endurance produces character (Rom. 5:3-4). When we fail to endure, we may require discipline as does any child.

God disciplines *"for our good, that we may share His Holiness. For the moment all discipline seems painful rather than pleasant; later it yields the peaceful fruit of Righteousness to those who have been trained by it"* (Heb. 12:10-11).

Anyone who does not experience the Heavenly Father's discipline is an illegitimate child. *"My son, do not regard lightly the discipline of the Lord, nor lose courage when you are punished by Him. For the Lord disciplines him whom He loves, and chastises every son whom He receives"* (Heb. 12:5-6).

## DISCIPLINE

The follower of the Lord not only passively accepts discipline, but actively disciplines himself. Like an athlete in training, Paul exercised self-control. To keep from being disqualified after preaching to others, he brought his body into subjection, meaning that he would not succumb to temptation (I Cor. 9:25-27).

The Bible does not support asceticism or self-flagellation as virtuous in themselves; neither does it underwrite self-indulgence as Christian liberty. There is freedom from the domination of sin in order to develop a Christlike character. Respecting that liberty, many count all else refuse in order that they *"may know Him and the power of His Resurrection, and may share His sufferings, becoming like Him in His death"* (Phil. 3:10).

C.S. Lewis observed that purification normally involves suffering. Looking back over his life he mused, *"Most real good that has been done me in this life has involved suffering."* To achieve the higher values in a fallen world requires disciplinary suffering. The immature may complain and cry; the mature will accept the fact and by God's Grace discipline themselves.

THE WISDOM OF GOD

In summary, we need the Wisdom of God to determine whether a given experience is judgmental, emphatic, vicarious, testimonial, preventative, or educational. The very possibility of condemnation and eternal anguish for persistent pride, unbelief and disobedience present a Divine summons to repent. To wait until judgment begins to fall is sheer folly. Today is the day of Salvation.

Whoever suffers a conviction of sin can count on Divine empathy. God takes no delight in the necessity of judging the ungodly. He so desires their deliverance that He gave His Son to suffer their penalty at Calvary. For that vicarious suffering all Believers give praise.

Furthermore, we are grateful to be counted worthy of suffering with Him in the battle against unrighteousness. With rejoicing we testify in the midst of suffering to the integrity of our commitment. We accept the warnings of physical pain and act to avoid the danger signals. We discipline ourselves and readily accept that of our Heavenly Father.

Some experiences may not fit in any of these categories, alone or in combination. From the present limited perspective, no one can obtain all the answers. But the unknowns do not render meaningless that which we do know.

As someone has said, *"We may know little, but the little that we do know is more valid for our interpretation of the world than the much that we do not know."*

NOTES

(We acknowledge our gratitude and indebtness to G.R. Lewis for some of the material above, regarding suffering and anguish.)

(7) "SO THAT YE WERE ENSAMPLES TO ALL THAT BELIEVE IN MACEDONIA AND ACHAIA."

The Thessalonians had experienced spiritual advancement, so much so, in fact, that they were an example to the entirety of the region. It is because they had received Paul's Message of the Cross which brought them into Redemption, and they continued in that Message of the Cross which gave them liberty to live a holy life. The evidence is, that they had not resorted to the flesh in their attempt to gain Sanctification, as had the Galatians (Gal. 3:2-3), which in fact, brings the very opposite results.

Part of the problem of the Galatians had been that the Judaizers came in, attempting to subvert Paul's Message of the Cross by inserting Law, which if embraced, would bring spiritual catastrophe, which it was doing with many Galatians.

The flesh is such, even in the Redeemed man, that if given the slightest opportunity, it will seek to exert authority, which without fail causes untold problems. Even though the Church at Thessalonica was by no means the first Church founded by the Apostle, still, it was the first Church to which he wrote; therefore, at the time of the writing of this Letter, evidently the Judaizers had not made their way to Thessalonica as of yet, which means that these good people had been spared that blight thus far.

EXAMPLES

The phrase, *"So that ye were examples,"* speaks of many things.

They were examples of evidencing the joy of the Lord despite persecution. They were examples of properly following Paul and most of all the Lord. However, the two, following Paul and following the Lord go hand in hand. They were examples of heeding the Message of the Cross to its fullest extent, and, therefore, reaping the excellent results. They were examples of Righteousness, as a result of this.

Of no other Church is it said that it became a pattern or a model Church. High praise indeed!

## ALL THAT BELIEVE

The phrase, *"To all that believe,"* automatically begs the question, *"believe what?"*

The average Christian reading this, would automatically presuppose that it refers to believing in the Lord Jesus Christ, having accepted Him as Savior, etc.

Most definitely that is correct; however, to properly understand the word *"believe,"* at least as Paul uses it, the following must be noted:

First of all, we must understand that the manner in which Paul uses words like *"Faith,"* or *"believe,"* or *"Righteousness,"* or *"Grace,"* or *"in Christ,"* or *"Salvation,"* etc., all have a particular object in view. That object was and is the Cross of Christ.

In other words, whenever Paul preached the Gospel, whether it was to pagans who had never heard the Message, or whether it was to established Churches, he always preached the Cross (I Cor. 1:18; 2:2). Therefore, if he spoke about *"Faith,"* it was *"the Faith,"* which referred to what Jesus did at the Cross and the Resurrection, and our part in that great, Finished Work. When he spoke of *"believing,"* as here, he is referring to believing in this which Jesus carried out on our part. Irrespective as to what word he used, it always had *that view* in mind. So, when the Reader reads these words as given by the Apostle in all of his Epistles, those words must be read with the viewpoint of the Cross in mind, and our part in that great Sacrifice of Christ. If the Reader does not understand that, does not subscribe to that, in fact, does not do that, then the Reader comes out with an improper understanding of what the Apostle is saying. However, if that is understood, then the Scriptures will take on a brand-new meaning, and everything will suddenly begin to come clear.

## DOES THE MODERN CHURCH THINK IN THESE TERMS?

For the most part, no! Of course, there are some exceptions, but only a few.

As we've said many times, the modern Church has drifted so far away from the Cross, that it has actually forgotten its foundation. Consequently, it casts about trying to find the solution to victory in other means, which is a fruitless effort. As a result, we have Christians running all over the world, trying to get some Preacher to lay hands on them in order to solve their problems, and then with many entering into ridiculous manifestations, such as *"barking like dogs,"* or *"crowing like roosters,"* and then claiming that such foolishness is of the Holy Spirit. And to be sure, foolishness is exactly what it is!

The answer to all things, as it pertains to the Child of God, is the Cross of Christ and what He did there. That speaks not only of Salvation for the soul, but, as well, for victory over sin and every type of sin. It speaks of *"more abundant life"* (Jn. 10:10), and, *"rest"* from the struggle of trying to be Righteous and Holy by one's own efforts (Mat. 11:28-30). It speaks of Divine Healing, financial prosperity, joy in the Lord, peace of mind, power to do the works of Christ, liberty to live a holy life, etc.

When the Lord began to give me this Revelation of the Cross in 1996, it immediately brought about a change in my life; a change so profound, so all-encompassing, so total in its completion, so victorious in its conclusion, that I have difficulty even attempting to express the feelings of my heart. As I've said several times in these Commentaries, it's like I have been *"born again!"*

However, that Revelation did not stop there, but continues unto this hour, and I personally believe will ever continue. In fact, it's impossible to exhaust the potential of the Finished Work of Christ. Once one understands this, the Word of God takes on a brand-new complexion. Pieces begin to fall into place. The Words of Jesus in the four Gospels take on a brand-new meaning, because now they've become clear as to what He is talking about. As this Revelation has continued, and will continue, it affects every part of my life, every part of my thinking, with each day opening another door.

In fact, if I could get every Believer in the world to read and believe this Commentary, or the last two or three we have written, it would change their lives to such an extent, as they never thought possible. Christianity

NOTES

would become what Jesus promised it to be. Each morning will present a joyous occasion. Now knowing the Source of all victory, all joy, all power, all life, all understanding, in other words, now knowing Christ as one ought to know Him, each new day becomes a pleasure of serving Him. All fear is gone! It is truly what Peter said, *"Joy unspeakable and full of Glory"* (I Pet. 1:8).

COME TO THE CROSS!

Over our daily Radio Program, *"A Study In The Word,"* I made a particular statement, which I want to repeat: *"If I stood behind the pulpit at Family Worship Center, and announced that the Lord had shown me a particular type of holy water, which sprinkled on Believers would bring forth amazing results, the place would be packed out with people. But if I tell the Church, and by using the word 'Church,' I'm speaking of all Believers everywhere, that I have the answer given to me by the Lord, and it is the Cross of Christ, the response is almost nonexistent."*

Why?

There are many reasons, but perhaps the following will give us a little added light.

Flesh attracts flesh, and Spirit attracts Spirit. And what do we mean by that?

The flesh is that which is carnal, not of the Lord and no matter how religious it might be, in other words, not of the Cross. With most of Christendom operating in the flesh, and sadly that's exactly what is happening, the flesh in them will respond to the flesh in the Preacher, no matter how absurd it might be, such as *"barking like dogs,"* etc., claiming such to be of the Holy Spirit. I trust that I'm saying this clear enough to where it is understandable by the Reader.

The Holy Spirit in the Preacher of the Gospel appeals to the Holy Spirit in Believers. While, of course, as a position, the Holy Spirit is in all Believers. But inasmuch as most Believers are little functioning after the Spirit, but rather the flesh, the flesh is what responds — and to be sure, the flesh doesn't want any part of the Cross.

So, and as stated, this means that most of the modern Church is functioning in the realm of the flesh, or that which is other than the Cross of Christ. In fact, it is so obvious

NOTES

that this is what is happening, that it cannot be denied.

About the only way that most Christians will properly respond to the Cross, is that they are very consecrated to begin with, and sincerely want all that the Lord has. So when they hear this great Message, they will respond accordingly. However, that number sadly and regrettably, is few and far between.

The other group who will respond to the Cross, at least some of them, are the ones who are desperate. In other words, they've just about bottomed out, meaning that the domination of sin is getting worse and worse, and unless there is an answer soon, they face total wreckage. Regrettably, that number is astronomically large.

Regarding these people, the Church has recommended *"psychology!"* In one of the issues of the *"Pentecostal Evangel,"* the weekly voice of the Assemblies of God, they devoted a whole page (if I remember correctly the size of the article), to the recommendation of a *"good twelve step program,"* as they addressed the situation. To be frank, this is tantamount to rank blasphemy.

The world of psychology holds absolutely no answer for hurting humanity. As well, and worse yet, this means that the Leadership of this particular Denomination, has abandoned the Word of God as the answer and the solution to hurting souls. You can't have it both ways! We either believe the Lord, or we don't believe the Lord. In fact, at least as I dictate these words in October of 1999, the Leader of the Church of God, the second largest Pentecostal Denomination in the world, is a practicing Psychologist.

The words of Jeremiah come to mind:

*"For my people have committed two evils; they have forsaken Me the fountain of living waters, and hewed them out cisterns, broken cisterns, that can hold no water"* (Jer. 2:13).

Now you know why that most modern Religious Leaders do not like Jimmy Swaggart.

Let's look at psychology for a moment.

PSYCHOLOGY

What do you the Reader think that psychology can present as a help for the problems of sin, aberrations, etc.? Stop and think a moment. Psychology offers no particular medicine of any nature as it regards wonder drugs, antibiotics, etc. They don't offer such of course, simply because the problem is not physical and, therefore, doesn't respond to such. As well, there is no medicine, at least as we think of such, which will apply, at least that which is devised by man. So, what does the Psychologist do in order to help someone?

Talk!

Yes, that's all they can do for the individual, is talk to him or her.

What do they say?

Take your choice! About any and every ridiculous thing that one could ever begin to imagine. In fact, there are hundreds of *"psychological methods,"* many of them worthy of a Roman Circus.

For instance, one of the modern techniques is *"scream therapy!"* The individual who is having problems of whatever nature, is advised to scream as loud as he or she can, for a particular period of time, and this is supposed to bring help.

Then I might suggest *"touch therapy,"* which calls for individuals, both men and women together, sitting in a circle naked (yes, I said naked), closing their eyes, reaching out and feeling of each other.

Or what about *"frustration therapy,"* which suggests the person taking a pillow and beating it over and over, in order to vent his frustrations and anger. Oh yes, they also recommend that this person, imagine that the pillow he is hitting, is the person with whom he is angry. This is supposed to relieve him of his anger and frustration, etc.

And then there is *"fantasy therapy,"* with the individual fantasizing all type of beautiful things, which is supposed to bring relief.

I could go on and on, with almost no end in sight, with each recommendation more ludicrous than the other.

Sometime back, I was sitting in an office in a major city waiting for some particular legal work to be done, and I noticed a bookcase by the wall. I walked over and selected a book at random, and it was a book on psychology, etc. I opened it and began to scan its pages, and noted the Chapter which was giving an account of a recent (recent then) convention of Psychologists.

NOTES

In giving the account, the writer went on to mention how that different Seminars were being conducted at this particular convention, headed up incidently by some of the worlds leading Psychologists, and this is what the man said:

One Psychologist addressing a group of people was promoting his theory, and at the same time, denigrating the theories being promoted by others, who were also giving Seminars at the same time.

The Reader must remember, that the book I was holding in my hand, was not written by a Christian, but rather a secular writer, who had no interest whatsoever in the Bible. It's a mystery that many in the world can see the absolute absurdity of this foolishness, but those in the Church can't!

Why?

I think Paul's answer is the most appropriate of all. He said:

*"Examine yourselves, whether ye be in the Faith; prove your own selves. Know ye not your own selves, how that Jesus Christ is in you, except you be reprobates?"* (II Cor. 13:5).

## IMAGINATIONS AND HIGH THINGS

Paul also said, *"For though we walk in the flesh, we do not war after the flesh:*

*"(For the weapons of our warfare are not carnal, but mighty through God to the pulling down of strong holds;)*

*"Casting down imaginations, and every high thing that exalteth itself against the Knowledge of God, and bringing into captivity every thought to the obedience of Christ"* (II Cor. 10:3-5).

What are these *"imaginations"* and *"high things"*?

*"Imaginations"* in the Greek is *"logismos,"* and means *"reasonings and conceit."*

*"High thing"* in the Greek is *"hupsoma,"* and means *"an elevated place or thing, a barrier."*

Imaginations and high things refer to the reasonings of men as it regards the solutions to man's need, which *"exalts itself against the Knowledge of God."*

What is the Knowledge of God?

*"Knowledge"* in the Greek is *"gnosis,"* and means *"knowing or true science."*

So, the Knowledge of God, is the Cross of Christ, which is the Plan of Redemption for the human race. It is the Finished Work of Christ, the great Sacrifice, the Atonement. Anything that opposes that, claims that there is another way, holds up something as the answer other than the Cross, pertains to these *"imaginations and high things."*

It pertains to all philosophy, which is a search for Truth. True Christianity is not a philosophy, but rather a Man, the Man, Christ Jesus. All search for Truth outside of Christ, is a fruitless search, and is a *"high thing."*

It pertains to all religions, which refer to man attempting to reach God in other ways than the Cross, or attempting to better himself in some way outside of the Cross.

It includes psychology, which is the answer of the world for the aberrations of man, which regrettably, much of the Church has adopted. All of these things *"exalt themselves against the Knowledge of God,"* and can bring no favorable results, as should be obvious. As well, they incur the Wrath of God (Rom. 1:18).

There is no answer to the ills of man, except Jesus Christ. And as well, the question must be asked, as to what kind of Jesus is being promoted by the Church.

## ANOTHER JESUS

Paul said, *"For if he that cometh preacheth another Jesus, whom we have not preached . . ."* (II Cor. 11:4).

What did the Apostle mean by that statement?

First of all, he said, *"Whom we have not preached,"* meaning that someone was preaching a *"Jesus"* other than the Jesus of the Cross and the Resurrection. In this case, the Judaizers were recognizing Jesus in many ways, but minimizing His Work at the Cross, making that great Sacrifice a mere incident, etc. Their thrust was the Law of Moses. They were teaching that one must accept Christ in order to be saved, but as well, must also keep at least a part of the Law of Moses, such as Circumcision and Sabbath keeping. To be frank, the emphasis was on the latter (Acts 15:1-2). It is the same problem presently:

We now have the *"entertainment Jesus,"* with the ways of the world regarding music being adopted. Jesus is somewhat held up, but only in passing, with the greater thrust being on rock-'n'-roll. Then we have the *"faith Jesus,"* with Faith being the great thruway, but not exactly in Jesus. Actually, it's Faith in Faith, or else what is claimed as the Word. Scriptures are pulled out of context, using them as a means to get all type of things, etc. Jesus and Him Crucified, in these particular circles, is little promoted, with many of these *"word people,"* as they sometimes refer to themselves, referring to the Cross as *"past miseries."* Then we have *"Jesus the Psychologist,"* with once again humanistic psychology, and that's the only kind there is, being promoted, with Jesus serving only as a symbolic figure. The Christ of the Cross is ignored altogether as the only hope of the world. Then we have the *"money Jesus!"* Money is the object here as should be obvious, with once again, Jesus promoted only as some type of glorified *"bell boy."*

It doesn't really matter what it is, what direction it takes, what it promotes, if it's not *"Jesus Christ and Him Crucified,"* then it's not the Jesus of the Bible, which means it's an *"angel of light"* (II Cor. 11:12-15). So, the Reader should understand the following:

The Believer must keep his eye on the Christ of the Cross. If the Message does not emphasize the Finished Work of Christ as the great Source of all that we receive from the Lord, then it must be rejected out of hand. To do otherwise, is to invite spiritual destruction.

To be sure, Satan as an *"angel of light,"* will dress up his wares in order that they look like the real thing; however, while he will promote Christ in some erroneous ways, even as we have mentioned, if it's the Devil one can be sure, that he will not promote *"Jesus Christ and Him Crucified."* The Believer must examine that which he is following. Is it another Jesus or is it the Jesus that Paul preached, i.e., *"the Crucified, Risen, Exalted Lord"*?

## THE CROSS OF CHRIST

The tragedy is, the Cross has been so little preached in the last few decades, that even the Preachers who strive with all of their ability to preach the Truth, little know or understand the veracity of the Cross as it pertains to the life and living of Believers. These Preachers of the Truth definitely do hold up the Cross as it pertains to the initial Salvation experience; however, their knowledge of the Cross thereafter, leaves much to be desired.

As a result, Christians far too often, are living lives of defeat, while striving with all of their strength to do otherwise. That's at least one of the reasons, for the mad rush to embrace particular fads, whatever they might be. As we've stated several times, while there are many and varied proposed solutions to Victory in the life of the Saint, perhaps the one most promoted presently is, *"being slain in the Spirit,"* etc. While this is Biblical, that is if it's truly from the Lord, it is not the answer to a victorious, Christian life. If that is in what the person is trusting, they will get off the floor in the same condition they fell, despite having been truly touched by God.

We must ever understand, that the way and manner that we receive all of these great things which Jesus did at the Cross, is to simply have Faith in that which He did.

## WHAT THE LORD EXPECTS!

When you came to Christ as an unsaved soul, of course, you had no knowledge whatsoever of God or His Word. You heard a Gospel Message, whether it was preached, or witnessed to you somehow. You came under conviction by the Holy Spirit, and gave your heart to the Lord.

All you did was to admit that you were a sinner, and that you wanted to accept Christ. That's all the Lord requires, and you were saved (Rom. 10:9-10, 13). However, now that you have come to Christ, which means that you are a new creation, with old things having passed away and all things becoming new, the Lord now expects you to learn some things about this great Salvation which you now possess. Even though there is much to learn, the basic foundation is found in Romans Chapters 6, 7 and 8. In fact, there is absolutely nothing more important than this as it regards your Christian experience. And yet, most Christians have absolutely no knowledge whatsoever as to what these three Chapters teach, even though more is at stake here than one could ever begin to imagine.

NOTES

Of course, the major cause of this huge lack of understanding, which brings about all type of problems for the Christian, is that most Preachers, as we have just stated, have little knowledge themselves of this all-important Truth. Consequently, if the pulpit is silent, the pew is going to be ignorant, if you will permit my bluntness.

I'm not saying there aren't any Preachers who understand this great Truth of the Cross as it refers to the Child of God, but I am stating that those who do have understanding are few and far between.

I am positive that the reason the Lord has given me this great Revelation is not only for my own personal benefit, but as well that I proclaim this Message far and wide. And that's exactly what I'm attempting to do, using every means I might quickly add, at my disposal.

Having said that, and considering how important all of this is, I'm asking you the Reader, to help us do this great thing as well.

These Commentaries we are writing, especially from Galatians forward, must be read and studied by all Christians, irrespective as to what Church they might attend. The Truths contained therein, will change the lives of all who believe and practice their concepts. So, it is imperative that all Believers know these great Truths of the Cross.

## MACEDONIA AND ACHAIA

The phrase, *"In Macedonia and Achaia,"* refers to modern day Greece and part of Albania.

Thessalonica was an important city of Macedonia, and of course its influence would be felt on the whole of the surrounding region.

This is a striking instance of the effect which a Church in a city may have on the entirety of the area.

Achaia proper was the part of Greece of which Corinth was the capital. The word, Achaia, however, was sometimes so used as to comprehend the whole of Greece, and in this sense it seems to be employed here.

It is to be observed that Macedonia and Achaia were the two Provinces into which all Greece was divided when it was brought under the Roman yoke, the former of which comprehended Macedonians proper, Illyricum,

Eprius, and Thessaly, which comprises much of modern Bosnia and Yugoslavia. Therefore, the meaning here is that the influence of the Church in Thessalonica was felt on all the parts of Greece; that their piety was spoken of, and the effect of the conversion of those in that area had been felt in all those places.

Thessalonica was a commercial city, and a Seaport. It had intercourse with all the other parts of Macedonia, with Greece, and with Asia Minor. It was partly owing to the advantages of its situation that its influence was thus felt.

It is impossible to overestimate the importance of such places in regard to the spread of the Gospel; and Christians who attend such Churches, wherever they might be, be they merchants, mechanics, lawyers, physicians, day laborers, etc., should feel that on them God has placed the responsibility of using a vast influence in sending the Gospel to other lands.

## FAMILY WORSHIP CENTER

Please forgive me if I boast somewhat, of our Church located in South Louisiana. To be sure, this region in no way carries the commercial and communications significance of other great cities and areas in the nation; however, times have changed somewhat regarding Paul's day and now.

With the advent of modern transportation and communication, any Church anywhere in the world, if evidencing a Move of God, can at this time have a worldwide influence.

For instance, our Church is a part of the Television Program which we send out all over the world, translated into several languages. It's also a part of the Videos that go into untold areas of the world, as well as the Radio work in the United States. In fact, Family Worship Center, in Baton Rouge, Louisiana, is one of the most Missions conscious Churches in the world. In fact, due to the Call of God that the Lord has placed on my heart and life respecting World Evangelism, I know I can say without fear of contradiction, that this Church is one of the most influential in the world today. Of course, we give the Lord all the praise and glory for that which we have said, understanding that we are only mere instruments in His Hands, and I fear poor instruments at that!

NOTES

Our people have a spirit of World Evangelism, having been imbued with this spirit from the very beginning.

Even as I dictate these notes (Oct. 11, 1999), we are gearing up for the greatest thrust of World Evangelism in which we have ever been engaged.

Even though our Telecast is now aired in approximately 30 countries of the world, translated into several languages, still, we must, in fact, place the Telecast in every city in the world, where it is possible to do so. That's what God in unmistakable terms has called us to do. As well, He has told us to cover the United States with Radio, which in fact, contains some of the most unique programming we think, in the world.

As previously stated, we have set out to secure F.M. Stations all over this nation, and at the time of this writing, have 170 applications before the Federal Communications Commission. We plan to put one of these small F.M. Stations in every town and city in America, which in fact, could number several thousands at least where there are frequency availabilities. This is what the Lord has told us to do, and this is what we are setting out to do.

The Gospel over Radio has been around for a long, long time; however, the type of programming we present is totally different than anything I have previously heard. Everything aired over our stations, 24 hours a day, comes entirely from Family Worship Center. I speak of the music, worship, and of course, the Messages. However, what makes this programming so effective, is the Anointing of the Holy Spirit which is upon the efforts.

Our business, and our total business, is twofold:

1. The Lord has called us to help bring in the harvest, which refers to lost souls being saved.

2. He has called us, as well, to strongly address the Spiritual Growth of the Saints. Consequently, as the Church at Thessalonica was widely influential, I want that spirit to continue in Family Worship Center, and even to increase which I definitely believe that it is.

## THE BELIEVER

Of course, when we say *"Church,"* we are actually speaking of the Believers in that respective Church. Jesus referred to Himself as the Light of the world (Jn. 8:12). He also said, *"Ye are the light of the world,"* referring to the Saints of God (Mat. 5:14). Of course, we must ever understand, that we as Believers are not the Source of that Light, that being Christ. We are merely His reflection, or at least, that's what we are supposed to be!

The Believer is loved and elected of God from all eternity. His existence began in the Will and Love of God, and all the attributes and emotions of God being eternal, the Believer has had, therefore, an eternal existence in the past in the *Mind* of God, as he will have an eternal existence in the future in the *Presence* of God.

His brief existence in time is comprised within Verses 5-9 of this Chapter. The Believer hears the Gospel (vs. 5); he becomes a follower of the Lord, thus evidencing true conversion; his life is an example to his fellow Christians; he boldly preaches the Word of the Lord, as we will see in Verse 8; he separates from all evil, which we will see in Verse 9; and in Verse 10 he is caught up in the clouds to meet the Lord in the air and so returns, so to speak, to that Divine bosom from whence he issued (Williams).

Going back to the significance of Thessalonica, Barclay observes: *"It is impossible to overstress the importance of the arrival of Christianity in Thessalonica. If Christianity was settled in Thessalonica, it was bound to spread East along the Egnatian Road until all Asia was conquered, and West until it stormed even the city of Rome. This means that the coming of Christianity to Thessalonica was a crucial day in the making of Christianity into a world influence."*

Consequently, as proper *"examples"* the Thessalonians served their Lord well, taking to heart the great Message of the Cross preached by Paul, and allowing it to become a molder of Christlikeness in their lives.

(8) "FOR FROM YOU SOUNDED OUT THE WORD OF THE LORD NOT ONLY IN MACEDONIA AND ACHAIA, BUT ALSO IN EVERY PLACE YOUR FAITH TO GOD-WARD IS SPREAD ABROAD; SO THAT WE NEED NOT SPEAK ANY THING."

NOTES

In describing how the Thessalonians were a model Christian community and giving further proof of the effect of the Gospel on them, Paul gives another indication of their consecration. It was their vigorous propagation of the Faith.

Their progress was remarkable in that what Paul and his associates had preached and the Thessalonians had received, they were now sharing on the widest scale possible. Here, Paul affirms that these converts were playing a substantial part in this ever-widening scope of Christian witness.

THE WORD OF THE LORD

The phrase, *"For from you sounded out the Word of the Lord not only in Macedonia and Achaia,"* pertains to the Message of the Cross which had changed their lives.

The inference in all of this is, that the way they lived spoke even louder than what they said.

These Thessalonians had been brought out of rank heathenism, just as the next Verse proclaims. Their lives had been so gloriously and wondrously changed, that it was noticeable to all.

*"Sounded out"* in the Greek is *"execheomai,"* and means, *"to sound forth as a trumpet."* The idea is, that the Gospel was proclaimed like the sonorous voice of a trumpet echoing from place to place.

In all of this, there is no improbability in the supposition that they sent out members of their Church — Messengers of Salvation — to other parts of Macedonia and Greece, that they might communicate the same Gospel to others.

What did they sound out? What was their Message?

Paul plainly says it was *"the Word of the Lord."*

Without a doubt, it would have been the Message of the Cross, for that is the only Source which has the power to change lives. So, they could have been ministering nothing else!

This means that we must understand *"the Word of the Lord,"* in this fashion. It is, unequivocally, and without a doubt, the Message of *"Jesus Christ and Him Crucified."* Anything else which does not have the Cross as its foundation, is spurious, and, therefore, not the Word of the Lord.

### WHAT WORD IS THE CHURCH SENDING OUT PRESENTLY?

For the most part regrettably, it's not the Word of the Lord; consequently, despite the untold thousands of Churches which dot the landscape, even all around the world, there are precious few which are actually seeing lives changed. Thank God for the few which are having miraculous results, but that number is small indeed!

Far too many are sending out the word of *"psychology"*; far too many are sending out the word of *"money,"* or some other foolishness. It is the business of the Church to preach the Cross, and the Cross exclusively.

What is the story of the Bible?

It is the story of the Fall of man and his Redemption.

How was man redeemed?

As is obvious, man was redeemed by what Jesus did at the Cross, and that exclusively! Actually, the first three Chapters of Genesis proclaim the story of the Fall of man, with the story of Redemption beginning in the Fourth Chapter, and continuing through the entirety of the Bible. In fact, it begins with the story of Cain and Abel, with their two respective but yet different, sacrifices. Abel's sacrifice was that of an innocent victim, which was the command of God, and portrayed the coming Christ. That of Cain was the work of his own hands, which God could never accept. Consequently, these two efforts have been the major thrust of humanity from then until now. Unfortunately, only a few look to the *"Slain Lamb"* (Jn. 1:29), while the far greater majority, offer up to God that of their own making, which God can never accept.

In fact, that has ever been Satan's greatest effort, the attempt to substitute something else in the place of the Crucified, Risen Christ.

In view of this, Satan fights the Cross, as he fights nothing else. So, if we understand the *"Word of the Lord"* apart from the Cross, it is really not the Word of God we have embraced, but something else altogether. The Believer must ever understand that, must base everything on that.

NOTES

If we recall the trials of Paul in Macedonia and his early anxiety for this Church, we can understand his deep satisfaction in its providential and strategic Ministry. One senses in this language an exultant, even defiant, note. The worst of circumstances cannot muzzle the Word of the Lord. Rather, they serve to amplify the note of Victory!

Another meaning of the phrase *"sounded out,"* is, as the blast of a trumpet can little be concealed, likewise, the lives of true Christians will be so changed, that it will be as obvious as a trumpet blast.

### FAITH IN GOD

The phrase, *"But also in every place your Faith to God-ward is spread abroad,"* presents the fact that nothing advertises the Gospel or the Church quite like the life-changing conversion of sinners to God. From Thessalonica the news was *"gossiped"* by the streams of travelers until it penetrated far-off places.

The words, *"in every place,"* are not to be taken in their full literal sense, but are merely a strong expression for the wide diffusion of the Faith of the Thessalonians. In fact, Paul uses similar statements in other places, as when he speaks of the Faith of the Romans being spoken of throughout the whole world (Rom. 1:8), and of the Gospel having come into all the world (Col. 1:6).

It has also been suggested that Aquila and Priscilla, who had lately come from Rome (Acts 18:2), must in their journey have passed through Thessalonica, and would bring with them to Paul at Corinth such a report of the Faith of the Thessalonians.

The phrase *"Faith to God-ward,"* actually should have been translated *"Faith in God."* The Faith of which he speaks, of course, is *"the Faith,"* which once again, speaks of the Finished Work of Christ. As we explained further back, when Paul uses words such as this, he is always, and without exception, I think I can say, referring to the Cross, and what Jesus did there. Therefore, we can properly understand his terminology only as we understand it in that fashion, and when we understand it in that fashion, everything he says becomes much more clear.

To turn this thing around, instead of Paul telling others what had happened in Thessalonica, others were giving him a twofold report about this Macedonian city. As would be obvious, this greatly encouraged the heart of the Apostle, as it would any Preacher. Other than a person coming to Christ, that person's Spiritual Growth is the single most important thing there is. And to be sure, unless the Believer has the proper Message of the Cross, their growth, of necessity, will be stunted. Only when they understand this Message, and act upon this Message, can true Spiritual Growth be accelerated, as God intends.

NO CORRECTION NEEDED

The phrase, *"So that we need not to speak any thing,"* harks back to Verse 7.

The Thessalonians were so conspicuously Christian, so unmistakably exhibited the new Divine type of character, that they became a model to all the Believers in Macedonia and Achaia. They were so much this, that Paul did not have to reprimand them at all, as he had been forced to do so with others. Again, what a joy this was to the heart of the Apostle.

(9) "FOR THEY THEMSELVES SHEW OF US WHAT MANNER OF ENTERING IN WE HAD UNTO YOU, AND HOW YE TURNED TO GOD FROM IDOLS TO SERVE THE LIVING AND TRUE GOD;"

Someone erroneously said, *"The only difference between the Believer and the nonbeliever is the Blood of Christ."* While the Blood of Jesus is definitely a major difference, and that which characterizes the great Christian Faith, still, if the Blood of Jesus has actually been applied to the heart and life of the believing sinner, there will definitely be a change in one's life — even a miraculous change! Those who claim the Blood as being the only difference, insinuating that there is no real change in the lives of Believers, with Believers continuing to sin just as much as unbelievers, the Truth is, those people aren't actually saved.

If the Blood has really been applied by Faith, even as this Verse proclaims, there will be an obvious change in the life of the person. This is one of the great hallmarks of Christianity. So, to divorce the Blood of Christ from the Power of God, is to blaspheme.

THE MANNER

The phrase, *"For they themselves show of us what manner of entering in we had unto you,"* proclaims the fact that the energy of the Christian life in the Thessalonians proved how successful was the preaching among them of Paul, Silas, and Timothy. In Grace, as in nature, if the parent is strong and healthy the children will be strong also. So here the Spiritual Fruit of Thessalonica testified to the character of the laborers.

The *"manner"* of which Paul speaks here, amounts to several things. It concerns the Apostle's life and Ministry, and above all the Doctrine of the New Covenant.

For a period of time after his conversion, the Apostle had lived a life of defeat. Romans, Chapter 7 records the fact.

I realize that many Preachers claim that Romans, Chapter 7 merely depicts Paul's preconversion experience of him trying to live for God and not being able to, etc.; however, there is no validity to that whatsoever. In the first place, before his conversion, he thought he was doing exactly what he should have done, even though in reality, he wasn't saved. As well, the language of Romans, Chapter 7 portrays a hatred for sin, despite the fact of not being able to overcome that monster. No sinner, hates sin. They may hate the effects of sin, but they don't hate sin, rather enjoying its pleasures. In fact, an unsaved person, no matter how religious they are, has no capacity for hating sin. They are a sinner and function as a sinner because it's all they know.

No! Romans, Chapter 7 is Paul's experience immediately after conversion. However, the Lord gave him the answer to this dilemma of sin, which the Apostle gave to us in Romans, Chapters 6 and 8.

He learned that every victory is found in what Christ did at the Cross, the price that was paid, the Sacrifice offered, the great victory won in the Finished Work. As well, he portrayed to us in those first few Verses of Romans, Chapter 6, how that the Believer fits into this situation, actually being baptized into Christ's Death, buried with Him, and raised with Him in newness of life (Rom. 6:2-6).

The Lord having shown the Apostle this great Truth of Romans, Chapter 6, He then showed him the manner in which the Holy Spirit works in bringing about the great benefits of the Cross in the Believer's life, as Paul gave us in Romans, Chapter 8.

NOTES

The idea is, as I have repeatedly stated:

1. All victory, in fact, everything the Believer needs is found in the Cross, i.e., *"the Finished Work of Christ."*

2. Inasmuch as all that we need is found in the Cross, the Cross must ever be the object of our Faith.

3. As out Faith is anchored in the Cross, and remains in the Cross, understanding that this is where the victory was won, the Holy Spirit then helps us obtain all the benefits of the Cross, which includes many things, the least of them surely not being, a victorious, overcoming, Christian walk. The Believer must understand, that the Holy Spirit will not function at all outside of the Finished Work of Christ. As well, He demands that our Faith be in that exclusively and in nothing else. The moment we try to bring about the desired results by resorting to anything other than simple Faith in the Cross, the Holy Spirit will not help us, which guarantees our defeat.

Paul had learned the secret of victorious, overcoming, Christian living, was now walking in that victory, and that's the Message and the manner of that Message which he took to Thessalonica, plus every other city. It worked in his life, and as the Thessalonians heard him preach this great Message, they accepted it, and it worked in their lives as well, even as it has worked in the lives of untold millions of others from then until now. It is God's provision for victory, paid for at great price, and He has no other, because no other is needed.

## A FINISHED WORK

I have just left Prayer meeting a few minutes ago, and while addressing our small group, even as I do every morning, some remarks were made in the short discussion, which we always have, that proved very interesting.

In this particular gathering there was a Preacher present, some housewives, an accountant, a financial advisor, a lawyer, and a businessman if I remember correctly.

For a few minutes we began to discuss the tremendous effect of this Message of the Cross and how it was affecting their lives, and in a very positive way.

One of the Brethren made the statement that he had studied after quite a few of the

NOTES

Preachers of the past and present, whom God had used, and while they definitely believed in the Cross and preached the Cross, all of them stopped short of proclaiming the totality of the Finished Work of Christ. In adding to what the Brother said, I can say the same thing.

In my years of serving the Lord and Ministry, I have studied behind hundreds of Preachers, and I can recall only two or three, who had the understanding of which I speak, and who brought it out in detail, even as Paul did in Romans, Chapter 6 and elsewhere. As a result, we have seen two or three generations of Christians who for the most part, have not lived lives of spiritual victory. Of course they were saved, and some were mightily used of God, and, as well, some surely did walk in victory, but not many. Actually, I don't think it's possible to walk in victory without a proper understanding of the Source of that Victory, which is the Cross and how it works in the hearts and lives of Believers respecting our everyday walk before God.

## THAT WHICH FAITH IN THE FINISHED WORK OF CHRIST ACTUALLY DOES

We are actually speaking of two things relative to the Child of God.

First of all, we're speaking of the Sanctification process, which actually gives the Believer victory over sin. We're not teaching sinless perfection, for the Bible does not teach such. We are, however, teaching that sin shall not have dominion over the Believer (Rom. 6:11).

Many Christians pride themselves in the fact that they have not committed some certain type of sins, etc. It is certainly good that they haven't done such things, whatever those things might be; in fact, our answer to sins of passion, etc., is *"God forbid!"*

Nevertheless, just not doing these things, whatever they might be, is not enough. That's not what we're speaking about. Again I emphasize, thank the Lord that you haven't succumbed to temptation in that fashion, that is if you actually haven't; however, if that is as far as your victory goes, in the eyes of God, such cannot really be labeled as victory.

In fact, the world has methods of shifting things around, making man think that

NOTES

progress is being made, with even the possibility existing that those particular methods can stop a few people from drinking, or gambling, or taking drugs, etc. Thank the Lord for that; however, even that, as few as they are, are not that of which we speak.

As I've said many times, if a Believer is fighting and winning, after awhile that Believer is going to fight and lose. And I might quickly add, I'm speaking of every single type of sin of the flesh of which one could begin to think from uncontrollable temper, on to jealousy and envy, and everything in-between.

The victory given by the Lord, furnished by the Finished Work of Christ, and the Believer's Faith in that great Work, completely blocks out the power of darkness altogether, which is brought about by the Holy Spirit, which leaves absolutely no semblance of fleshly desire. Consequently, such a Believer is no longer that which he once was. It is totally and completely gone, with no semblance of the thing left in thought, word, or deed. *Now that's what Christ does! However, He does such only, through the Holy Spirit, Who carries out His Work totally and completely, within the parameters of the Finished Work of Christ, and our Faith in that great Work.*

That's what the great Prophet Jeremiah was talking about when he said, *"Heal me, O Lord, and I shall be healed; save me, and I shall be saved: for Thou art my praise"* (Jer. 17:14).

In addressing the efforts of man, he had also said, *"They have healed also the hurt of the daughter of My people slightly, saying, Peace, peace; when there is no peace"* (Jer. 6:14).

There is no power on Earth that can completely rid one of every vestige of the sins of the flesh, except the Power of God. To have that Power manifested in our lives, we have to subscribe to God's Way, which is the Way of the Cross. As stated, there is no other.

## THE WHOLENESS OF THE FINISHED WORK OF CHRIST

The second factor or blessing of what Christ did at the Cross for lost humanity, is the wholeness of this lifestyle in Christ. What I'm saying is, that millions of Christians are not whole as far as their condition is concerned. Consequently, even though they love Christ very much, they don't really have all that Christ can do for them, simply because they are trying to live this life, in the wrong way.

Unfortunately, when we speak of the Cross, many Christians have the idea that what we're talking about might be needed for some poor Christian who has some terrible bondage of sorts, etc. But in their thinking, that would be the only type person who would need this of which we speak.

If that is the case, such thinking shows a total ignorance of the entirety of the Plan of God, which I'm afraid is the case with most Christians. While the Message of the Cross is definitely for the type of individual I have just mentioned, still, that is only a tiny part of all that Christ did in His great Victory at Calvary.

The point I am attempting to make is, that every single thing the Believer needs and that God wants to give us, is found in the Finished Work of Christ, and in that Work alone. And to make this point clear, the moment that the Believer begins to walk according to this direction as laid down by the Holy Spirit through Paul in Romans, Chapter 6, the Believer will then begin to enjoy the wholeness of this Christian experience, as he or she has never known before.

As I have repeatedly stated, most Christians I think are living in Romans, Chapter 7, and if the Truth be known, their condition is the same as it was with Paul at that stage in his life, *"O wretched man that I am! Who shall deliver me from the body of this death?"* (Rom. 7:24).

Unfortunately, due to the modern spiritual climate, much of the modern Church has been forced into a state of hypocrisy. It's not intentional, but nevertheless that's what it amounts to.

Christians who know absolutely nothing about the victory afforded by the Cross, and the Cross alone, which regrettably make up the vast majority, are running around talking about how wonderful things are, because they think that's what they're supposed to say.

## IS IT REALLY WONDERFUL?

Of course, just the fact of being saved is definitely wonderful! However, that's not what I'm addressing. I'm speaking of the reality of Christ, and how that He can be so real to one, that living becomes a pure joy, and surrounding circumstances as negative at times as they might be, have no effect whatsoever on this of which I speak. I'm speaking of living without condemnation, exactly as Paul said in Romans 8:1. In fact, condemnation is a terrible thing, and to be frank, most Christians I think, live under that cloud. It is that way because they are *"walking after the flesh,"* even though they think they're walking after the Spirit. And how can one know the difference?

If you're failing in any respect, such is always the result of *"walking after the flesh."*

Someone asked me the other day as to how one could know that one is walking after the Spirit and not after the flesh?

The answer to that is simple: If you have to ask that question, you're not walking after the Spirit. It is just that simple!

How does one know the difference in daylight and midnight?

When the Believer is walking totally *"after the Spirit,"* no one will have to tell him he's doing so, he will know beyond the shadow of a doubt. And as stated, if you don't know, that means you aren't!

## WHAT DOES IT MEAN TO WALK AFTER THE SPIRIT?

Walking after the Spirit is the greatest life that one can live because, in effect, God is doing for us, for the Holy Spirit is God, what we cannot do for ourselves. And the Believer should understand and address that statement very carefully.

Even though you are saved and possibly Baptized with the Holy Spirit, still, within yourself, you cannot live the life you ought to live, and will fall terribly short, if, in fact, you attempt to do so outside of the boundaries laid down by the Lord. This is the big mistake made by many Christians. The particular spiritual climate in which we presently live, which actually is mostly wrong, elevates the Believer instead of Christ. And that's the road to disaster. In fact, the so-called Faith Ministry has probably been more responsible for this erroneous direction than any other form of Doctrine. That direction

NOTES

is pride, and in one way or the other can lead to nothing but spiritual wreckage.

I'll say it again, the Believer can in no way live the life he ought to live, or even have the benefits paid for by Christ at the Cross, unless the Holy Spirit does these things within our hearts and lives.

To follow after the Spirit, means to follow the way the Spirit is leading. And how is He leading?

As we've said over and over again, the Holy Spirit works within a set of parameters, and in no other way. Those parameters are the Finished Work of Christ, in other words, what He did at the Cross and in His Resurrection. This is so ironclad, that it is called *"the Law* (that which cannot be broken) *of the Spirit of Life* (the Holy Spirit) *in Christ Jesus* (in what Jesus did at the Cross and the Resurrection). *Adherence to this Law has made me free from the Law of sin and death"* (Rom. 8:2). Actually, this is the only manner of victory. There is no other!

What does it mean?

In simple terminology, it means that the great victory that Jesus won at the Cross, is the confines in which the Holy Spirit works. Consequently, as a Believer I am to place my Faith in that totally and completely. I am to do nothing else, engage in no other type of activity, trust in nothing else, believe in nothing else, just simply have Faith in what Jesus did there, understanding that it's a Finished Work, and that nothing can be added to it, and nothing must be taken away. When I as a Believer function accordingly in that, keeping my Faith in that capacity, that is *"following after the Spirit,"* which will guarantee all the things the Holy Spirit can do, which guarantees total and complete victory for the Child of God, and in every capacity.

We just simply trust in what has already been done, believing that it was for mankind and mankind alone, which includes you and me, and that God wants me to have this for which such a price has been paid. My Faith in that, will guarantee me all of this which Jesus has done, at least all that we can now have.

## THE PRICE

It is impossible for any human being, no matter how close to God we might be, to fully understand the tremendous price that Jesus paid at the Cross in order that we might have Salvation. There is nothing in human thinking to even remotely resemble that which Heaven did on our behalf. We can skirt the edges, but by no means can we plumb the depths. Perhaps man, even redeemed man, even glorified man, will never fully be able to do so.

In the first place we cannot even begin to comprehend such love. We have an idea, but only an idea! The Fall has left too many clinging vines on us, for us to fully understand all of this for which Jesus has given Himself for us.

When God became a Man in order for this thing to be done, in essence the Creator became the created. That within itself, is totally beyond our comprehension. But that's exactly what happened!

Irrespective, we at least understand that the price He paid, was beyond magnitude. As well, we are to understand, that all that He did, was done totally and completely for sinners, i.e., *"the human race."* It was not at all done for Heaven or any part of Heaven, or any part of Himself. All that was done, He needed not at all! So now the question is:

Considering that He paid such a price for our Redemption and for our Victory, doesn't it stand to reason that He would want us to have all for which He has paid such a price? I think that should go without saying.

How it must grieve His heart for us to ignore, or even reject, this for which He has paid such a price, and, of course, He knows such erroneous direction will bring us untold sorrow and heartache. Does not the Believer understand, that the heart of our Lord is grieved greatly when we miss His Way! Anyone who could love as He loves, is grieved greatly, when the full benefit is not enjoyed, especially considering all that He has done that we might have this benefit. So what am I talking about?

I think all Christians know and understand the part the Cross plays as it regards our initial Salvation experience. But for most Christians, their knowledge of the Cross ends then and there. When it comes to living a victorious, Christian life thereafter, it's pretty much every man for himself. The results are catastrophic.

NOTES

No, the Cross of Christ, plays just as much a part in our everyday living for God, our constant Victory, and our Spiritual Growth, as it did in our initial Salvation experience. But most Christians don't know that; consequently, they stumble from one failure to the next.

### TO PLEASE THE LORD

Looking at my own life, my heart grieves when I look back and see my own efforts at attempting to walk after the Spirit, when all the time I was walking after the flesh. Admittedly, I did not know better, which means that my actions were not intentional; nevertheless, the results were the same, as such results can only be the same. I speak of hurt, pain, and failure.

Looking back now, I realize that all this of which I was doing, and the type of efforts are too numerous to mention, were not at all pleasing the Lord, but rather having the very opposite effect. I was trying to do something that I couldn't do in the first place, and to add insult to injury, I was attempting to do what He had already done. One can see how this must anger the Lord.

Paul plainly said, and because he had learned it the hard way, *"So then they that are in the flesh cannot please God"* (Rom. 8:8).

As we've explained, *"the flesh"* simply refers to trying to do what only He can do.

I look back at my frustration, my tremendous efforts, trying harder and harder, but not at all making the matter better, but rather worse. How many Christians are presently following that same course?

Of course, the Lord Alone would know the answer to that; however, I think the majority fall into that category.

This means they are trying very hard, but failing just the same, which leaves them very confused; or else, with many, I think they are now just sort of drifting as far as their Christian experience is concerned. Either way is a road to disaster.

In fact, I think if one addressed many people who once knew the Lord, but are no longer living for Him, if the Truth be known, they would say, *"It's too hard. I tried to live right and I just can't do it."*

The sad Truth is, this cannot be done within one's own abilities.

One can only live the life they need to live and must live, if they allow Christ to live in and through them, which He does by the power of the Holy Spirit (Gal. 2:20-21).

As should be obvious to the Reader, I'm doing my best to address this subject from every single point of the compass in which it can be addressed, even at the risk of being overly repetitive. I feel if I keep saying the same thing in several different ways, after awhile it will get down into your spirit, that is if it hasn't done so already, which I pray it has. I know how important this is, and the Lord has told me to relate this great Truth as succinctly, as forthrightly, as clearly as I can, and in every respect. There is nothing more important to your Christian Life than this. Consequently, you ought to want to know every single thing there is to be known about this, which has to do with everything you are and everything you do.

## TURN TO GOD FROM IDOLS

The phrase, *"And how ye turned to God from idols,"* pertains not only to those of that time, but is just as pertinent presently.

An idol is anything which comes in-between the individual and Christ, irrespective as to what it is.

Why do you think John wrote, *"Little children, keep yourselves from idols"*? (I Jn. 5:21).

He wasn't speaking of little figurines made out of wood or precious metal, but something else entirely. While it very well may have been true that those addressed by Paul would, in fact, have been worshipping idols made with hands; nevertheless, the actual figure itself is only the result of a state of being, which comes from the heart. It's the worship of anything other than God, or that which takes the place of God.

To untold millions of Americans, and which would actually include the entirety of the world, football is their idol, or baseball, the movies, money, or even their family, etc. With others, it's alcohol, gambling, nicotine, drugs, immorality of every stripe, etc.

Some of these things we have mentioned are not wrong within themselves; however, we make them wrong by undue attention, which if addressed correctly, can be construed as none other than *"idol worship!"*

NOTES

Modern man thinks that the idol worship of old, which referred to men and women bowing down to strange looking figures designed by men, and claimed to be some type of god, was brought about by ignorance and superstition. Actually, that is true! However, while the modern variety may not be so blatant, the principle is the same. Anything that comes between the person and God, which characterizes every single person in the world who is unredeemed, refers to idol worship, whether the individual understands such or not. It is the major problem in the lives of Christians as well. In fact, if the person does not understand the Message of the Cross, in one way or the other, idol worship will be the result. The reason is simple!

Not following God's prescribed order of victory, Satan is going to be able to lead the individual into bondage of one type or the other, with the results being *"idol worship,"* whether the person desires to do such or not. In fact, I think I can safely say that no Christian desires to do such; nevertheless, that's what the result will be, if we walk after the flesh.

## IDOLATRY IN ANCIENT TIMES

Inasmuch as this subject is of such significance, and covers a wide spectrum of human thought, even greater than we can imagine, perhaps it would be helpful to investigate more fully this of which we speak.

Ancient man believed that the image was the dwelling place of a superhuman force or being, or was the Deity itself. Idols were made of wood, stone, or clay, and sometimes of gold or silver.

For the Hebrews, idolatry included the worship of anything other than Jehovah. Of course, that was correct. As well, Rabbinic writers considered idolaters as enemies of Israel.

The Talmud says that the three cardinal sins were *"idolatry," "unchastity,"* and *"bloodshed."* Idolatry was given precedence because it implied a denial of Revelation, thus shattering the entire basis of Salvation and ethics. In the New Testament, the term was extended to mean obsession with anything to the degree that it took the place of devotion to God.

For instance, a short time ago I watched a documentary on India which portrayed the Ganges River as being worshipped by many as a *"god."* Millions I suppose, think that washing in its filthy waters, will make one holy, etc. Consequently, untold numbers of human corpses are floated out into the River, because the loved ones think that such action will provide eternal life for the deceased. As a result, the River is unspeakably filthy. As well, in India there are temples built to the rat god, with untold numbers of rats having the run of the place, and actually worshipped, etc. In fact, the list is long of gods in India, and in many other places as well. One's heart breaks at this superstitious idolatry, which is fostered by Satan himself.

## MAN'S PRIDE

Idolatry is the embodiment of human desire and thought. Idols of old, though made in many shapes and sizes, really represented the image of man, for they expressed his thoughts, desires, and purposes. Man's pride caused him to trust in himself rather than in God, hence his idols were and are, really expressions of self-worship (Isa. 2:8-22). The Bible repeatedly depicts man as debasing himself when he worships that which he made with his own hands.

Idolatry has been practiced from primitive times. The ancient oriental world was thoroughly polytheistic — the worship of many gods. Everything that occurred, whether good or bad, was attributed to the gods; for life was not separated into religious and secular categories. Nature and its unexplained forces were probably the earliest deities worshiped by primitive man.

The Sun, Moon, Stars, Fire, and Lightening were objects of worship; for man could not explain them, and they seemed more powerful than he.

## VARIOUS IDOLS

The various gods of Mesopotamia, Egypt, and Canaan were known to the Israelites. Babylon exercised greater formative influence upon Hebrew spirituality than either Egypt or Canaan. Even the father of Abraham worshipped other gods (Josh. 24:2). Abraham must have been acquainted with the cult of the moon god Sin. His contemporaries built impressive temples and ziggurates in honor of the moon god. It is not inconceivable that

NOTES

Abraham himself was a worshipper of the Babylonian deities before God called him to leave his home and land. In fact, every evidence is that Abraham was an idol worshipper before the great Revelation given to him by Jehovah.

The ancient Sumerians believed that the universe was directed by a pantheon of gods, the chief ones being *"An, Ki, Enlil, and Enki,"* who controlled, respectively, Heaven, Earth, air, and water.

The Mesopotamian pantheon was composed of more than 1,500 gods, some of the better known ones being Shamash, Marduk, Sin, and Ishtar. The fertility gods were especially honored. Ishtar, goddess of love, descended to the underworld to seek her husband Tammuz. Nabu was the patron of science and learning. Nergal was the god of war and hunting.

## EGYPT

Ancient Egyptian religion was polytheistic (the worship of many gods) and complex. Though the chief gods were represented in human form, most of the numerous deities were depicted in animal form, such as the crocodile god Sobek and Anubis with the head of a jackal.

There were also cosmic deities, such as Re, the sun god. Osiris (the patron of agriculture) and Isis (counterpart of Astarte) associated with regeneration. There were triads of gods such as Osiris, Isis, and their son Horus. Hieroglyphic inscriptions on obelisks on the tombs give the impression that the Egyptians had thousands of deities. Every aspect of nature, animate and inanimate, was thought to be inhabited by a deity. There was even a merger of gods, such as Amon with Re. The ruler himself was considered to be the incarnation of a god; each one while living assumed the name Horus, the deity who avenged the death of Osiris, supposedly.

## THE CANAANITES

Of particular interest for Biblical studies are the gods of the Canaanites because of the mixing of the Israelite way of worship with the Canaanite fertility cult.

The fertility cults were common to Mesopotamia, Egypt, and Canaan, but exerted their strongest influence on the Israelites in Canaan, being the chief complaint held by Jehovah against Israel.

The chief Canaanite deities were El, the creator of the Earth and controller of storms, and *"Baal"* (both symbolized by the bull as indicative of their procreative powers), and the fertility goddess Astarte (Biblical Ashtaroth). She was immensely popular at the temples, and prostitution was a legalized part of the cult, which drew in Israel as well.

There were many other Canaanite deities, such as Melkart, Koshar (the Vulcan of the Canaanites), and Hauron, the shepherd god. Mot was the god of death and sterility.

The Canaanite religion was particularly dangerous for the Israelites because of its appeal to carnal human desires, especially of the sexual nature. Baal and Astarte were associated with fornication and drunkenness. Sacred prostitution and various orgiastic rites characterized the religion. Amos charged that Hebrew participation in these rites profaned the Name of God (Amos 2:7).

Canaanite religion was a debasing form of paganism. Deuteronomy 7:4 and 20:18 warn against the dangers of Canaanite influence. Moses instructed the Israelites to destroy all the inhabitants of the land so that they would not be tempted to follow their gods (Deut. 7:1-5). They were also instructed to destroy the high places, the wooden pillars, and graven images (Deut. 12:2-3), which were associated with the sexual aspects of Canaanite worship practices.

## IDOLATRY IN THE OLD TESTAMENT

The worship of idols was an abomination to the Hebrew way of worship. In fact, Israel in her day, was the only monotheistic people on the face of the Earth, which means they were the only ones to worship one God. All other nations, even as we have stated, worshipped many gods. Consequently, any Israelite who adopted the Canaanite way of worship, or any of the other surrounding nations, was roundly condemned. The Old Testament emphasizes that the worst sin was to acknowledge other gods besides Jehovah and to make an image or likeness of that so-called deity.

In fact, these gods worshipped by the surrounding nations, were actually no gods at all. However, there was an element of power involved, simply because demon spirits were behind all of this idol worship. So, there was some action, even though it would have been minor, etc. In fact, the Old Testament emphasizes the powerlessness of idols and the gods of the Canaanites. A recurring theme in the Old Testament is the ridicule heaped upon those who would make an idol with their hands and then bow down and worship it (Isa. 44:9-20; Jer. 10:2-10; Hos. 8:5; 13:2; Hab. 2:18).

An example of this is Elijah who mocked the priests of Baal in the contest on Mount Carmel (I Ki. 18:27). There were many other examples also!

However, despite this, the influence, even as the text bears out, of other religions upon Israel was very great.

## THE TEN COMMANDMENTS

The prohibition against idolatry found expression in the Ten Commandments (Ex. 20:4), which forbade the representation of God in any form. The Commandment was not an attack on artists or sculptors, but on idolaters. To worship idols was to go whoring after other gods; therefore, idolatry was described as spiritual adultery (Ezek. 16:15-17; 23; Hos. 1:2; 9:1, 10).

Regrettably, there is no period in Hebrew history when the people were free from the attraction of idols. Rachel took the Teraphim (household gods represented by clay figurines) with her when Jacob and his family fled from Laban (Gen. 31:34). The Israelites worshipped the idols of Egypt during their sojourn there and did not give them up even when led by Moses out of bondage (Josh. 24:14; Ezek. 20:8-18; 23:3-8).

They made a molten calf which they worshiped when Moses tarried in the mountain receiving the Law from God (Ex. Chpt. 32). God would have destroyed them for their idolatries had not Moses interceded for them. Even as they neared the end of the wilderness wanderings, they joined with the Moabites in the worship of Baal (Num. 25:1-3; 31:16). Just before they entered the Promised Land, Moses warned them not to make any images or to worship other gods (Deut. 4:15-19; 7:1-5), or they would perish (Deut.

NOTES

8:19). The one who would entice his fellow Hebrew to worship other gods was to be put to death (Deut. 13:6-16). Deuteronomy 17:2-5 actually required the stoning of the person who worshipped other gods.

The Israelites did not obey the injunctions given by Moses to destroy the heathen completely, but settled down among them. They continued to worship the foreign gods they had brought from Egypt (Josh. 24:14-15, 23) and also were enticed by the gods of the Canaanites after they settled in the land (Judg. 2:11-13; 6:25-32).

The Ephod made by Gideon became an object of worship (Judg. 8:24-27). The exact nature of the Ephod in early Israel is not certain. It was apparently a garment (I Sam. 2:18) worn or carried by the Priest (I Sam. 14:3) and used in divination (I Sam. 30:7-18).

### SAMUEL THE PROPHET

Samuel the Prophet said the subjugation of the people to the Philistines was due to their idolatry and promised that they would be delivered if they would put away their false gods (I Sam. 7:3-4). The Teraphim placed in David's bed by Michal when he fled from Saul (I Sam. 19:11-17) has been interpreted as a household idol. However, others have said that it represented something else.

At any rate, we do know that the Teraphim were used in divination (Ezek. 21:21; Zech. 10:2), though such use was condemned (I Sam. 15:23). The Old Testament says little about idolatry during the reign of David, but it must have flourished during the reign of Solomon for he permitted his foreign wives to worship their gods and was, in his old age, enticed to worship them also, including the abominable Chemosh and Molech (I Ki. 11:1-8). His sin prompted God to divide the kingdom upon his death (I Ki. 11:9-13).

### JEROBOAM

Jeroboam, who became ruler of the Northern tribes that seceded upon the death of Solomon, placed golden calves at Dan and Bethel so that the people would not desire to return to Jerusalem to worship (I Ki. 12:25-33). These calves were either images of the Canaanite deities or pedestals symbolizing

NOTES

their presence, as the Ark was the symbol of the Presence of God.

This act brought God's Wrath upon the house of Jeroboam (I Ki. 14:7-11). Matters were no better in Judah at this time. Idolatrous practices flourished there also, during the reign of Rehoboam, Solomon's son (I Ki. 14:21-24). During the reign of Solomon's grandson Asa, an *"abominable image"* for Asherah was destroyed, which had been set up by the Queen mother Maachah (I Ki. 15:13).

### AHAB

A hundred years later, following the succession of kings who *"walked in the way of Jeroboam,"* Ahab came to the throne of Israel and established the cult of Baal of Sidon at Samaria under the influence of his heathen wife Jezebel (I Ki. 16:32). Elijah denounced Ahab and challenged the power of Baal (I Ki. Chpt. 18).

The principal struggle in which Elijah and Elisha were engaged was to see whether God or Baal would be acknowledged as God.

Jehu, who succeeded the Omri dynasty, made an attempt to uproot Baalism by the wholesale destruction of the temple, priests, and worshippers of Baal (II Ki. 10:18-28) but was not wholly successful in stamping out idolatry, for he did not *"turn from the sins of Jeroboam"* (II Ki. 10:29-31).

### THE PROPHETS

Beginning with the Prophets of the Eighth Century B.C., was an emphatic rejection of any material representations of God. Amos protested against the Canaanite high places and the images of their gods (Amos 5:26). Hosea denounced the stubborn harlotry of Israel (Hos. 2:16-17; 8:4-6; 13:2). Isaiah, looking upon the appalling apostasy of the age, grieved over the golden images, the work of men's own hands, and the sins of the new moon festivals (Isa. 2:8; 40:18-20; 41:6-7; 44:9-20; 45:20; 46:1-2, 5-7).

I Kings 17:7-18 contains a stinging indictment against Israel as justification for God's destruction of the Northern Kingdom in 722 B.C. Among the charges made were that they'd built high places and pillars, served idols, burned their children as offerings, and refused to obey the Commandments of God.

NOTES

## HEZEKIAH

Conditions were not much better in Judah as evidenced by the idolatrous practices when Hezekiah came to the throne. The people were worshipping the bronze serpent that Moses had made, so Hezekiah destroyed it (II Ki. 18:4). All the great reforms of Hezekiah were undone, however, by his successor, his son Manasseh, whose idolatries are among the most shocking in all the Old Testament (II Ki. 21:1-18).

He revived Baal worship and built altars to astrological gods within the very Temple at Jerusalem. He offered his own son as a human sacrifice. An interesting reference to human sacrifice is found in Psalm 106 where the pagan influences upon Israel were denounced.

In the period before the end of the kingdom of Judah, the Prophets struggled against the widespread idolatry that filled the land. Zephaniah warned against the worship of astral deities, against Milcom, and against pagan superstitions (Zeph. 1:2-9).

Habakkuk pronounced woes upon those who would worship a god made with their own hands (Hab. 2:18-19).

## JEREMIAH

No prophet fought the apostasies of Judah more vehemently than Jeremiah. He preached against the sacrifices to Molech, the worship of the Baalim, the offering of cakes to the Queen of Heaven, and against the gods that were as many as their cities (Jer. 2:23-25; 8:1-2; 10:2-10; 11:13; 23:13-14).

Even the sweeping reforms of Josiah, which included the destruction of a Sanctuary of Chemosh and Milcom built by Solomon (I Ki. 11:7; II Ki. 23:13), could not save the nation that was so polluted by her idolatries (II Ki. 23:4-20), for the people immediately returned to their old ways under his successors.

## EZEKIEL

Ezekiel revealed that worship of animals, of the vegetation god Tammuz, and of the Sun were taking place within the Temple, in the final years before the destruction of Jerusalem (Ezek. 8:7-16). He also denounced the sacrifice of children to the gods (Ezek. 16:20-21).

## DANIEL

During the period of the Babylonian captivity, Nebuchadnezzar built a great image and demanded that the people worship it. The refusal of Daniel's three friends to worship the image would have cost them their lives except for Divine intervention (Dan. Chpt. 3).

## WHY IS THE STUDY OF THE OLD TESTAMENT IN THIS FASHION IMPORTANT?

When one reads the Old Testament, one should understand that one is reading more than mere Biblical history. Even though it is certainly that, it is far more.

Every single illustration and happening in the Old Testament can be constituted as another step along this long road that ultimately led to the Redemption of mankind.

Israel was raised up by God for the very purpose of giving the world the Word of God, and more important if possible, to bring the Messiah, the Redeemer of all mankind into the world. Consequently, anything which happened to these people was of the utmost importance.

So, when we read these stories, these illustrations, these happenings, we should never read them with a detached interest, but realize first of all, that this is the Word of God. And, as well, everything given in the Old Testament presents the story, even the struggle, to bring Redemption ultimately into the world through Jesus Christ and the great Sacrifice of Himself on the Cross of Calvary.

So when the Old Testament is read, it should be read with the understanding that each one of these happenings, whatever they may have been, is slowly leading up to you the Reader, and your Salvation, which it ultimately did. As a result, and as should be obvious, nothing is of greater significance. So, when you read the Old Testament from now on, read it with these things in mind. The illustrations given are not only the portrayal of what happened then, but is really a portrayal of the struggle to bring Redemption to you and me. All of these people figured in this great scenario, whether in opposition, or whether attempting to serve God. Therefore, looking at it in that light, that it is not only the Word of God, but in a sense, the story of our Salvation as well, gives it supreme importance.

### IDOLATRY IN THE NEW TESTAMENT

Idolatry is not mentioned as frequently in the New Testament as in the Old Testament. In the New Testament, idolatry includes the worship of any gods other than the Living and True God. The Christian Church arose in a world given to idolatry, but also out of a Jewish background that maintained a stubborn protest against image worship of any kind.

Paul pictures the widespread idolatry of the pagan world (Rom. 1:18-25). He observed that idol worship was so widespread that the Athenians had even erected an altar to an unknown god (Acts 17:23). He never intimated an interpretation widely held today that idolatry represents a primitive phase of religious development. Paul considered it a perversion, a turning away from the knowledge of the True God. Paul called idolatry a work of the flesh (Gal. 5:20), and warned the Christians to shun the worship of idols (I Cor. 10:14).

Believers were warned to be careful not to compromise themselves with idolatry (Acts 15:29). One problem for early Christians was the eating of meat that had been offered to idols. Paul said that idols had no real existence, so eating meat offered to them would not be wrong, but he added that a Christian should do nothing that would cause a weaker brother to stumble (I Cor. 8:1-13; 10:14-33).

Paul warned that one may abhor idols but commit other sins (Rom. 2:22). He emphatically denied that idols have any real existence (I Cor. 12:2; Gal. 4:8; I Thess. 1:9), actually the same Message as preached by the Prophets of old.

His protest against idolatry was so effective in Ephesus that it hurt the business of those engaged in making silver images of Diana (Acts 19:23-27). Idolatry is used figuratively by Paul to include covetousness (Eph. 5:5; Col. 3:5) and gluttony (Phil. 3:19).

### EMPEROR WORSHIP

Mystery religions, where the individual or the community sought to appropriate the experiences of dying or resurrected nature gods such as Osiris, were widespread in the Greco-Roman world of Paul's time. As well, Emperor worship was an accepted practice.

Herod the Great established the cult of Augusta at Samaria. Caligula (A.D. 37-41) ordered his image to be set up in the Temple at Jerusalem.

Christians suffered severely at the hands of Domitian (A.D. 81-96) who insisted that he be worshipped as *"God"* and *"Lord."*

The Book of Revelation appeared at such a time with its warning against the danger of idolatry (Rev. 2:14, 20). It affirms the powerlessness of idols (Rev. 9:20) and warns against worshipping an image of the beast which will be set up in the last days (Rev. 13:14-15; 14:9-11), and promises the exaltation of those who refuse to worship the beast or its image (Rev. 20:4).

### WHY IDOLATRY IS CONDEMNED IN THE BIBLE

Idolatry is vigorously condemned both in the Old Testament and New Testament because it degrades both God and man. It denies the existence of the True God Who created the world and mankind, and Whose Glory cannot be adequately captured in any tangible form. It is absurd that a person could carve an idol with his own hands and then be afraid of what he has made.

Some religions claim that an image is an aid to worship, though not an object of worship. The danger of such reasoning is that two people may have a different idea of what the image signifies. One person may look upon it as a representation and void of value or power in itself, but another may regard it as the abode of the god and fraught with power, and, therefore, he will worship the image.

A visible representation of the deity tends to restrict a person's concept of God, for he will base his concept of God, consciously or unconsciously, upon the image or picture.

Finally, man becomes like that which he worships (Hos. 9:10).

Only the True and Living God can fulfill the hope of eternal life.

### PRESENT IDOLS

As we've already stated, anything that comes in-between a person and Christ is an idol (I Jn. 5:21).

NOTES

In fact, religion is probably the biggest idol in the world at this present time. I speak of people looking to particular Churches or Denominations for their Salvation. In that case, such devotion is idolatry. That means that all of Catholicism is idolatry with its worship of the Church and of Mary and of various Saints, etc. Unfortunately, many Protestants fall into the same mode or category.

They give certain allegiance to their Church or Denomination, which should go only to Christ. Consequently, it becomes an idol.

That means that if any Baptist, or anyone who is associated with the Assemblies of God or the Church of God, or any Denomination or local Church for that matter, who thinks that their association with such, contributes anything toward their Salvation, it has then become an idol.

In fact, much of the Christian world has made idols out of sports, entertainment, money, power, position, even family. Many of these things are not wrong within themselves, but if we allow them to come in-between us and Christ, or I should say, they fill the place in our lives which Christ Alone should fill, then that thing has become an idol.

Our identification with all things, as it pertains to our life, our livelihood, our joy, our peace of mind, our happiness, our past, present, and future, our security, our enjoyment, our pleasure, etc., must be identified totally in Christ. He alone can meet all of these needs, but regrettably, Satan can make other things seem more than they are, even those things which are innocent within themselves.

In fact, Satan is a master at taking the sacred Ordinances of the Church, such as Water Baptism, or the Lord's Supper, and making an idol out of those things, by causing the people to think that Salvation resides in participation. It doesn't! In fact, even mere association with Christ, even as Judas had, contains no Salvation.

Total identification with Christ, first of all demands making Him one's Saviour. Then one accepts His role as Baptizer with the Holy Spirit. Now being *"in Christ,"* which is the position of the Believer upon coming to Christ, the Believer must understand that everything that is needed or desired is found totally in Christ. If that seems not to be so, it is not the fault of Christ, but rather the problem of self-will, or a misunderstanding or lack of knowledge, as it regards our position in Christ.

NOTES

## THE ROLE OF THE CROSS

In fact, the Cross is central in all of this. One being *"in Christ,"* and understanding what it means to be in Christ, means that they understand the Finished Work of Christ, which was done exclusively for us and not at all for Christ Himself. The *"in Christ"* position, which pertains to the Death, Burial, and Resurrection of Christ, plus His Exaltation, identifies that position. Understanding that the Cross and the Resurrection of Christ in the central point in all of this, brings about two things:

1. Humility: The Cross within itself is the greatest example of humility there is and ever shall be. In fact, the Believer cannot know real humility unless he properly understands the Cross and his place and position in that great Sacrifice.
2. All the Blessings of God: Everything comes through the Cross in totality. Without the Cross, there is no Salvation! Without the Cross, there is no Baptism with the Holy Spirit; without the Cross, there is no forgiveness; without the Cross, there is no Sanctification; without the Cross, there is no power; without the Cross, there is no Justification; without the Cross, there is no Faith; without the Cross, there is no access to God; without the Cross, there is no love; without the Cross, there is no joy; without the Cross, there is no peace; without the Cross, there is no understanding of the Scriptures; without the Cross, there is no Grace; without the Cross, there is no Christlikeness; without the Cross, there is no prosperity; without the Cross, there is no Divine Healing; without the Cross, there is no Eternal Life; without the Cross, there is no fellowship with the Lord; without the Cross, there is no coming Glorification; in fact, without the Cross, there are no Blessings from God whatsoever; actually, without the Cross, there is no way to reach God in any capacity!

I maintain, that if the Believer doesn't have a proper understanding of the Cross, that somehow and in some way, idols will be the result!

THE LIVING AND TRUE GOD

The phrase, *"To serve the Living and True God,"* here presents God called *"Living,"* in contrast to lifeless idols; *"True,"* in contrast to the whole system of idolatry which is based totally on a lie.

The turning toward God by the Thessalonians, or any Believers for that matter, at once excluded all lesser and contrary loyalties. In fact, this was a decisive act of the whole man in whom intellect, emotions, and will, move together in a sublime act of Faith and trust in the True and Living God. That is genuine repentance!

Salvation for the Thessalonian Believers manifestly involved a radical change in belief and in conduct, a change which henceforth effected all of life and its relationships. Indeed, there can be no real beginning in the Christian life without a genuine turning about, known as repentance.

These young Believers broke with their ancestral past and with their pagan environment, a classic example for all time of the Gospel's power to transform both heredity and environment.

Life henceforth was spent in the service of God and in anticipation of the return of Him through Whom they were redeemed. He who is truly born of God will work while he watches and waits!

(10) "AND TO WAIT FOR HIS SON FROM HEAVEN, WHOM HE RAISED FROM THE DEAD, EVEN JESUS, WHICH DELIVERED US FROM THE WRATH TO COME."

Three points are made in describing the conversion of the Thessalonians:

1. They turned to God from idols.
2. They began to serve the Living and True God.
3. They began to wait for His Son from Heaven, i.e., *"to live in the light of the Coming of Christ."*

The word translated *"turned"* is the characteristic expression in Acts for conversion (Acts 11:21; 14:15; 15:19; 26:18, 20).

To God from idols expresses repentance. (Repentance means a total turning about.)

NOTES

In order to face toward God they must turn their backs on idols. A radical change both outwardly and inwardly is meant; a change in conduct — but also in thought, attitude, and will. Destiny is involved. Without true repentance there is no real conversion.

Paul did not share the half-admiring attitude of some toward pagan culture. He associated idols with uncleanness and demonism (I Cor. 10:14-21; II Cor. 6:16-17; Rev. 9:20).

It is impossible to derive from Paul's statements other than the following:

We are to have no illusions about what it meant to be a pagan . . . for the ordinary man and woman, bewildered by a multiplicity of temples and shrines to innumerable gods and goddesses, astrology, and demonology provided the normal background to life. Eroticism (sexual immorality) was synonymous with worship. Expediency (what was deemed necessary) dictated behavior. Life was a gamble with fate and ended in extinction.

When one remembers that Paul's converts had abandoned as vain the heritage of paganism that had permeated their whole way of life, the epithet of his persecutors becomes justifiable: *"They have turned the world upside down . . . "* (Acts 17:6).

But further, conversion involved turning to God; that is, facing into the light of personal, moral accountability to the one God, Creator, Redeemer, and Judge. Truly, the Word had come *"in power, and in the Holy Spirit."*

TO SERVE AND TO WAIT

Such repentance issued positively in a twofold way: *"to serve"* and *"to wait."* To serve suggests total surrender, the service (although loving) of a slave.

In the expression *"to serve the Living and True God"* there is contrast with the dead, counterfeit, *"nothing"* idols (Isa. Chpt. 40; I Cor. 8:4; 12:2; Gal. 4:8). God is real to human experience.

Trench points out that *"true"* as used of God means that God fulfills not only the Promise of His lips but *"the wider Promise of His Name."*

He concludes, *"Whatever that Name imports, taken in its highest, deepest, widest sense, whatever according to that He ought to be, that He is to the full."*

## TO WAIT FOR HIS SON FROM HEAVEN

The phrase, *"And to wait for His Son from Heaven,"* presupposes preparation and readiness (I Jn. 3:3).

Paul is here briefly alluding to the Rapture of the Church, or what we might refer to as the Resurrection, both being the same.

Paul portrays two Comings of the Lord in his writings, as given by the Holy Spirit. The First Coming which we refer to as the *"Rapture,"* or it could be called the *"Resurrection,"* as I've already stated, is referred to in I Thessalonians 4:13-18.

The Second Coming is referred to in II Thessalonians 2:8.

These two Comings should not be confused. The Scriptures that apply to one do not apply to the other. Not one Passage refers to both events as if they were one. These two distinct Comings are separated by several years, and so are not two stages or phases of one Coming.

## THE RAPTURE OF THE CHURCH

The Rapture is the first of the two Comings, not a coming to Earth but in the air. It could not be the Second Advent because Christ does not come to the Earth to live here and fulfill a mission as He did at the First Advent.

When Christ meets the Saints in the air He takes us back to Heaven with Him and presents us before the Father's Throne where we remain during the time the Tribulation is running its course on the Earth (Jn. 14:1-3; I Thess. 3:13).

Christ does not remain in the air with the Saints when we meet Him as in I Thessalonians 4:13-17. The Marriage Supper and the Judgment of Saints take place in Heaven, then at the Second Advent after the Tribulation, Christ and the Saints leave Heaven together to come down to the Earth (II Cor. 5:10; Rev. Chpt. 19).

The Rapture is the time Christ comes *for* the Saints to take them to Heaven.

## THE SECOND COMING

The Second Advent, or Second Coming, is the time that Christ comes to the Earth to live here and fulfill a mission. This is the time He comes from Heaven *with* the Saints, having raptured us at least seven years before.

NOTES

The Second Advent cannot take place until all of Revelation 1:1-19:21 is fulfilled while the Rapture can take place any moment without anything being fulfilled.

## THE RESURRECTION OF CHRIST

The phrase, *"Whom He raised from the dead, even Jesus,"* pertains as is obvious, to the Resurrection of Christ, Who was raised from the dead three days after His Crucifixion.

God's Son is identified as Jesus, the historical Person, and further as the One Whom He raised from the dead. The Resurrection, always in the foreground of Apostolic preaching, was the supreme proof of Jesus' Divine Sonship (Rom. 1:4).

Here also was the chief argument for the certainty of Judgment (Acts 17:31), certifying as it did the defeat of Satan and the ultimate overthrow of evil. He Who ascended into Heaven will come again from Heaven.

The Resurrection of Christ ratified His Death on the Cross. Inasmuch as the wages of sin is death, had there been one sin left unatoned, past, present, or future, Christ could not have been raised from the dead. In other words, Satan would have had a legal right to have held Him in the death chambers, and to have held Him there forever, even though He was the Son of God. Inasmuch as all sin was atoned, Satan's legal claim on humanity was forever broken, at least for those who will believe (Jn. 3:16). Death now has no claim; sin has no claim; eternal judgment now has no claim.

The debt to God has been paid, for that's what happened when Jesus died on the Cross. He paid the debt for man, which man could not pay for himself. In doing this, He acted as our Substitute and our Representative Man.

This means that when He died, He died as a sinner by taking the penalty of sin which was death. He was not a sinner, and in fact had never sinned, but took the penalty of sin on our behalf. When He was buried, He was buried accordingly, which refers to all transgressions, sin singular, sin plural, all iniquity, all disobedience, and all rebellion, being buried with Him, which refers to every sinner who has ever lived or ever shall live — at least for those who will believe.

However, when He was raised from the dead, He was not raised as our Substitute or Representative Man as such, but rather as the Son of God. All the debts had been paid. All the claims had been settled. God is satisfied, and Satan is a defeated foe, all carried out at the Cross.

With no claim left, Satan is defeated and helpless, and now Jesus as the Son of the Living God, came forth from the tomb, completely victorious over Death, Hell, and the Grave. However, inasmuch, as we were baptized into His Death, buried with Him, which means, that all the Victory He purchased with His Own Blood, became ours in totality, we now have the right to be Resurrected with Him, which we were (Rom. 6:2-6).

However, as He was raised as the Son of God, we, as well, were raised in *"newness of life"* (Rom. 6:4).

NOTES

## THE GREATEST DISPLAY OF POWER IN HUMAN HISTORY

Before the Resurrection of Christ, and I speak of the time of the Old Testament, creation was offered as the greatest display of the Power of God ever recorded, with the deliverance of the Children of Israel placed as a close second.

However, in the New Testament, the Resurrection of Christ is placed in demonstration as the greatest display of power that humanity has ever known. While a few had been raised from the dead previously, there were several differences:

First of all, the raising of these few souls was not a Resurrection, for they would die again. The raising of Jesus Christ was a Resurrection, for He will never die again. And furthermore, all who believe in Him will never die as well, and of course we speak of spiritual death (Jn. 11:26).

Second, the Resurrection of Christ, guarantees the Resurrection of every Saint of God who has ever lived and died, which, of course, the raising of others from the dead had no such meaning. So, in a sense, the Resurrection of Christ, was the Resurrection of all who believe in Him, which gives it preponderant proportions.

Third, the raising of others from the dead, as few as they were, did not signify any victory over death. Conversely, the Resurrection of Christ signified victory over Death, Hell, and the Grave. Consequently, its significance is absolutely beyond our comprehension.

Therefore, the Resurrection of Christ, was more than One being raised from the dead, as wonderful as that would have been, but was rather, a victory of astounding, eternal proportions. As stated, the Resurrection of Christ, completely ratified everything that Jesus did at the Cross. Consequently, Redemption is complete, now signified as the *"Finished Work of Christ."* Hence, He is presently *"sat down on the Right Hand of the Majesty on high"* (Heb. 1:3).

He is *"sat down"* because His mission is complete, His victory is total, and there is nothing else to be accomplished.

## DELIVERED US FROM THE WRATH TO COME

The phrase, *"Which delivered us from the Wrath to come,"* refers to rejected Grace. In other words, if Grace is now rejected, Wrath is sure to come.

In Paul's teaching, Divine Retribution occupied a somewhat complementary relationship to the Doctrine of Grace (Rom. 1:16-18; 2:1-11; Eph. 5:6-8). Moral law is grounded in the nature of God, involving both love of Righteousness and hatred of all unrighteousness.

The Greek word for *"wrath"* is *"orge."* In other Passages it is used in *"Wrath of God"* (Jn. 3:36; Col. 3:6).

Trench, commenting on this word, says it indicates an abiding and settled habit of mind with the purpose of retribution, rather than mere temporary agitation of feeling. It is the necessary complement of God's love.

If one is to love good, one at the same time must hate evil, the two being so inseparable, that either He must do both or neither.

It is, then, the personal Wrath of God, not an impersonal process by which evil produces disaster. Nor can it be divorced from *"feeling,"* without God at the same time making His love an unfeeling thing. But God's Wrath is without the flaws which characterize that of men.

## WRATH TO COME

It is *"Wrath to come,"* an inevitable, approaching *"Day of Wrath"* (Rom. 2:5; Rev.

6:17), in terrible contrast with the present day of Grace. The idea is not exhausted by the day-by-day consequences which are always *"coming"* because of sin.

From this Wrath upon sin, it is *"Jesus, which delivered us,"* (literally, Who delivers us, or Jesus, our Deliverer).

Vincent says that the verb means literally *"to draw to one's self."* Jesus is rescuing, drawing from danger, those who are committing themselves, their past, their present, and their future, wholly to Him.

This *"Wrath to come"* is portrayed as certain as the Grace which is now present. It pertains to the coming *"Great White Throne Judgment"* outlined in Revelation 20:11-15.

At this Judgment, will be every unsaved person who has ever lived, no Believers will be there. God will then open the Books, which outlines everything ever done by all individuals. In other words, man will have no excuse, with the record made clear before him in proverbial black and white.

The conclusion of that Judgment is foreknown. It is, *"Depart from Me, ye cursed, into everlasting fire, prepared for the Devil and his angels"* (Mat. 25:41).

### IN WHAT MANNER WERE WE DELIVERED?

The word *"deliver"* or *"deliverance,"* refers to *"rescue or being rescued."* It implies that one is being held captive by someone or something. In this case, it speaks of the individual being delivered from the powers of darkness, the clutch of Satan, the power of sin. Every unsaved person in the world is more or less, under the control of Satan and his legion of demon spirits. The unsaved do not understand that; nevertheless, it is true! As a result there are untold millions of alcoholics, drug addicts who cannot stop, gamblers who cannot quit, and a host of other vices which controls men and women more or less. Then there are fear, doubt, unbelief, greed, covetousness, lust, etc., in other words, a host of evil passions, which grip fallen humanity in a vice, all fueled by the kingdom of darkness.

Being *"spiritually dead,"* the unsaved do not have the capacity to understand their lot, their dilemma or their position. Instinctively, they know that something is wrong; however, they think it can be solved by a simple readjustment, or proper education, or a change of environment, etc. So, like an endless treadmill, the world keeps swirling and turning in its vortex of evil, only able to produce cosmetic changes, if that!

NOTES

As stated, being spiritually dead, the unredeemed do not know what they don't have as it refers to God, what He can be to their hearts and lives. In fact, even though they may correctly mouth some proper words, the unsaved have absolutely no idea as to who God is, what God is, or anything about God. What they think they know is all wrong, totally skewed, a completely erroneous concept, all because a spiritual death grips them, which makes it impossible for them to have any type of understanding as it regards their Creator. While many unsaved believe that God exists, beyond that they have absolutely no conception of His Being, and what He can be to them.

Held in this clutch of darkness, they can no more extricate themselves than they can turn back time. In fact, despite all of man's efforts, designs, education, so-called abilities, the Truth is, unredeemed man is helpless as it regards his spiritual condition.

### JESUS

Out of this darkness into Light, there is only One Deliverer. His Name is Jesus. Now please let me emphasize that:

There aren't ten, five, even two deliverers, there is only One, and that is the Lord of Glory, The Lord Jesus Christ. That means that Mohammed cannot deliver anyone! Buddha has never delivered anyone! Confucius has never delivered anyone! Joseph Smith has never delivered anyone, neither has the Pope.

Conversely, it means that every single person in this world who has ever experienced deliverance from darkness to light, from slavery to freedom, from bondage to Salvation, all and without exception, have been carried out through and by the Person of the Lord Jesus Christ. There are no exceptions to that, and there will never be any exceptions to that. He Alone is the Deliverer.

First of all, Jesus is God. Even though He became man in order to deliver the human race, which we will address momentarily, still, in this Incarnation, He never ceased to be God.

NOTES

As someone has well said, while He did lose the expression of Deity in the Incarnation, He never for a moment lost the possession of Deity. This means that man's condition was so bad and, in fact, is so bad, that it took a monumental Plan of Redemption to liberate fallen humanity. When we consider that God had the power to speak everything into existence as it regards creation, and that in fact He is Omnipotent, which means all-powerful, but yet, He could not speak Redemption into existence, from that it becomes clear just how bad this situation really was.

In fact, this is one of the great arguing points of mankind. Man does not admit, will not admit, that his situation is that bad, i.e., *"hopeless!"* If in fact it is that hopeless, then he doesn't have a prayer of delivering himself, which he absolutely refuses to admit.

The idea is, he refuses to admit that he is *"spiritually dead,"* with all the affects that death brings. If someone is sick that is one thing; however, if one is dead, that is something else altogether. If someone is dead, no amount of medicine can help that corpse, no amount of surgery can help that corpse, in fact, there's absolutely nothing that can be done to change the situation of a corpse. It is the same with man in his spiritual death.

Spiritually speaking, man is a corpse. He is dead while he lives, which means that he has absolutely no contact with his Creator in this condition, and can hope to have none in this condition.

So, to address this terrible problem which besets humanity, the problem of spiritual death which was incurred at the Fall, something has to be done that is different than the application of medicine or even radical surgery. In fact, spiritually speaking, every unsaved person, at least if they are to change, has to literally be raised from the dead. So, understanding that, one can now see the dilemma that man is actually in.

This means that if any deliverance is affected, only God can carry out this great, this miraculous, this momentous work. To do this, one of the Members of the Godhead, would have to step down from His lofty position of Glory and Honor, a position of such magnitude that it is impossible for us to comprehend, which Paul describes in Philippians 2:5-11, at least the manner in which it was done. He did not describe the Glory that Christ previously had with the Father, because such would be impossible to describe. As one Theologian has properly said, when it comes to Redemption, and the manner in which it was done, we human beings can understand or grasp some part of this great work, but only part! We soon reach a barrier, beyond which we cannot travel, simply because it is beyond the human ability to grasp such.

So, God would become man, *"And thou shalt call His Name JESUS: for He shall save His people from their sins"* (Mat. 1:21). Actually, the very Name *"Jesus"* means *"Saviour."*

Understanding that, this means that the entirety of the human race must deal with Jesus Christ. Now please allow me to say that again:

I said that every human being who has ever lived, must deal in one way or the other with Jesus Christ. You will either deal with Him now by accepting Him as your Saviour, or else you will deal with Him at the Great White Throne Judgment (Rev. 20:11-15). One way or the other, you will deal with Him!

## THE CROSS OF CHRIST

To which we have already inferred, God could speak worlds into existence, in fact all of creation; however, He could not speak Redemption into existence, which shows how terrible, how awful that sin actually is. He would have to become man and for a particular purpose.

Inasmuch as God cannot die, and inasmuch as the broken Law demanded the penalty of death, God would have to become man in order to carry out this great Plan of Redemption. In other words, man could not do this thing for himself, so God would have to do all of it for him.

Consequently, what God did in the Redemption of humanity, by literally becoming man, and then above even that, suffering the penalty that man should have suffered, by dying a horrible death on the Cross, was the greatest act of Love that humanity will ever know.

Could God have delivered man another way?

There is some indication in the Scriptures that He could have. In the Garden, Jesus just hours before the Crucifixion prayed, *"Father, all things are possible unto Thee; take away this cup from Me: nevertheless not what I will, but what Thou wilt"* (Mk. 14:36).

From this statement by Christ, we deduce that possibly there may have been another way; however, we must assume this was the best way; therefore, it was the way that Christ would suffer.

Understanding that, we must come to the conclusion, that the Cross of Christ was the destination of the Saviour, the manner and the way in which He would carry out the Redemption of humanity. This means that the Cross was not an incident or an accident. It was a design; in other words, it was purposed by God, and in the words of Simon Peter, *"was foreordained before the foundation of the world"* (I Pet. 1:20).

WHY DID REDEMPTION DEMAND DEATH?

In the Garden, Eternal Life was forfeited by Adam and Eve due to them purposely cutting themselves off from the Life of God, their Creator. All life is found in God, which means that if one is to have life, and we speak of Spiritual Life which, of course, affects everything else as well, it must be obtained from our Creator.

The disobedience of Adam and Eve was much more than a mere transgression. Adam had been given dominion over all the creation of God, which tells us how monumental the first man actually was (Gen. 1:28; Ps. 8:3-9). Being deceived by Satan, the archenemy of God, Adam and Eve gave this glorious dominion to the Evil One (Gen. Chpt. 3). In effect, they changed Lords, i.e., *"Masters."* Whereas God had been their Lord, now Satan is their Lord. It was a sad trade! In this change, life from God was forfeited, because Adam and Eve were now fallen creatures, with which a Thrice Holy God, could not associate, at least with the life-giving properties of communion.

Man has now committed a preposterous crime against God. He has forsaken God and gone over completely into the camp of Satan, which is 180 degrees opposite of the Righteousness of God. While it is true that Adam did not at all know or realize what he was actually doing in the sense of how it would turn out,

NOTES

nevertheless, the results were the same. Due to the dominion which he previously had being forfeited, everything is now lost.

This crime against God demands payment, as does any crime. Furthermore, it was a monstrous crime, a crime of such magnitude as to defy all description. To know and understand just how bad it was, we need only look at the world which God originally created as *"very good,"* now turned into a slaughterhouse. All the sorrow, war, heartache, hatred, pain, sickness, suffering, and death, have been the result of this crime.

So, how can man pay this monstrous debt to his Creator? We must understand that God in creation has set up a system of laws, meaning that creation is all based on laws, laws incidently devised by God. Those laws cannot be broken, and if they are broken, which Adam and Eve did in the Garden of Eden, the crime must be addressed, and the debt must be paid. That's the reason that Government is so very important.

However, man's problem is, that he seeks to devise Government which is not of God, instead of functioning according to God's Government, which is His Word.

So this crime must be addressed, and the debt must be paid. Inasmuch, as it is a capital crime, there will have to be capital punishment. In fact, it is the same way with man's laws.

In essence, man actually did pay for this crime by having spiritual death laid upon him, which ultimately resulted in physical death as well.

Knowing and understanding this, how can a dead man be brought back to life. In fact, it will require a Resurrection. Now we come to the manner in which this debt can be paid, and man not be totally destroyed.

WHY THE CROSS?

The manner in which God would address this terrible problem is to become man Himself, and do for man what man could not do for himself. So, Jesus would be man's Substitute, actually his Representative Man, with Paul referring to Him as the *"Second or Last Adam"* (I Cor. 15:45-47).

To pay for this terrible crime, as life was forfeited by the first Adam, a perfect life would have to be offered in Sacrifice by the Last Adam.

Death was required, because a capital crime had been committed; consequently, capital punishment would have to be administered.

The seed of this found in the Noahic Covenant, which in essence was the first portrayal of human government, was devised by God. However, just because it was only then given, did not mean that it originated there. God has always had Government.

The Scripture says, *"And surely your blood of your lives will I require; at the hand of every beast will I require it, and at the hand of man; at the hand of every man's brother will I require the life of man.*

*"Whoso sheddeth man's blood, by man shall his blood be shed: for in the Image of God made He man"* (Gen. 9:5-6).

When Adam forfeited the Life of God, he became all that darkness is. Hence, he became a murderer, which immediately shows up in the first brother, Cain, killing the second brother, Abel (Gen. 4:1-8).

Inasmuch as the crime committed was the most awful crime that one could begin to imagine, which, in effect, was total rebellion against God, the worst type of punishment would have to be administered. The type was death, and the form was the Cross.

I think one could say without any fear of contradiction, that taking all things into consideration, there is no worse form of death than Crucifixion on a Cross. The victim hung naked on the Cross, oftentimes for days, dying in humiliation and shame, and finally succumbing through shock. It was the most torturous manner of dying that one could imagine. With spikes through the hands and the feet, the muscles of the body would soon begin to contort, with breathing becoming more and more laborious. Many victims went out of their mind with thirst, sheer pain, and agony, until the body finally succumbed in convulsions of agony.

This law of execution was so awful, that if a person under the Mosaic Law committed a crime that was of a hideous nature, he was to be stoned to death, and then his body hung on a tree, at least for a short period of time. This was to portray the fact of the hideousness of his crime, and the Curse of God upon such action (Deut. 21:22-23).

Even though this spectacle was in the Law of Moses, it really did not specify death by Crucifixion, that having originated somewhere it is believed in the East. Alexander the Great seems to have learned of it from the Persians. Rome borrowed the idea from the Phoenicians through Carthage, and perfected it as a means of capital punishment.

The Romans reserved Crucifixion, however, for slaves, robbers, assassins, and the like, or for rebellious provencials. Only rarely were Roman citizens subjected to this kind of treatment.

NOTES

## THE MANNER OF THIS DEATH

Upon receiving the sentence of death the condemned person was flogged with a leather whip loaded with metal or bones so cruelly that it became known as the intermediate death. Christ suffered this as well!

He was then required to shoulder the crossbar upon which he was to be extended and carry it to the place of his Crucifixion. He also wore about his neck a placard naming his crime (King of the Jews).

At the execution site he was stripped and tied or nailed to the crossbar, which then was fastened to an upright post. (Jesus was nailed to the Cross.)

As stated, death was slow in coming, except when it was hurried by soldiers breaking the crucified man's legs (Jn. 19:31). This was not done with Christ, as He had already died.

According to Josephus Crucifixion in Israel was a most common sight. The fact that two robbers were crucified with Jesus in Jerusalem tends to confirm this claim.

The Jewish nation, unlike the Romans, even as we have stated, did not crucify living persons. Frequently, however, they did suspend the bodies of the executed upon a tree to intensify their punishment and to expose them to public shame (Num. 25:4; Josh. 10:26; I Sam. 31:10). Men thus hanged were considered accursed by God (Deut. 21:22-23).

## WHAT THE CRUCIFIXION OF CHRIST ACCOMPLISHED

The first thing we must always remember is, that Jesus was not crucified because of crimes He had committed, but because of crimes we had committed. We were the ones under the sentence of death, which includes every single human being who has ever lived other than Christ. So, the thing we want to know is, how could this Crucifixion of Christ aid or help the criminal, and especially in a figurative sense, to literally raise him from the dead. The sinner being spiritually dead, there must be a Resurrection to life, if man is to be brought back to his rightful place.

The crime was a capital crime, so the punishment would be capital punishment, which is the only thing God would accept. It would do man no good to die on the Cross, because his death would be a polluted sacrifice, which would not pay the debt. That which died, and more particularly, the One Who died, must give up a perfect life, which could only be done by God becoming man and perfectly keeping the Law in every respect, etc., which Jesus did.

When He died, pouring out His Life's Blood, for the life of the flesh is in the blood, it was a perfect life that was poured out, which God accepted in payment.

Some may claim that God demanded too much; however, God did not demand too much, especially considering that He paid the price Himself. Having to pay it Himself, we should understand that if the price could have been lessened, He surely would have done so.

Inasmuch as the penalty for breaking the Laws of God was death, and because the crime was so monstrous, when Jesus died on the Cross, this debt was paid, being accepted by God in full. This means also, that it was a debt paid for every single human being who has ever lived and who will ever live, at least if they will believe.

The payment for this debt, atoned for all sin, which destroyed Satan's claim on mankind, because his claim is sin, which we've already stated earlier in Commentary on this Chapter. Jesus was then buried, and because there was no sin left, Satan could not legally hold Him in the tomb; therefore, He was raised from the dead. If there had been one single sin unatoned, Satan would have still had a claim; however, there was no sin left, Jesus had atoned for it all.

## THE MANNER IN WHICH MAN ENTERS INTO THE DEATH AND RESURRECTION OF CHRIST

Inasmuch as Jesus was our Substitute and Representative Man, meaning that He did all of this *for* us and *as* us, He literally took our place. However, as our Representative Man He did more than take our place, He as the True Man, Christ Jesus, in a sense, became us. Actually, this is what the entirety of the Incarnation and Crucifixion were all about. He as the Last Adam, did what the first Adam failed to do. Jesus purchased back by perfect obedience, in the giving up of His Own Life, the dominion that Adam had forfeited in the Garden.

When the believing sinner hears the Word of God, which is moved upon by the Holy Spirit, he is placed under conviction for his sin and for being a sinner, which is actually one of the great Office Works of the Spirit (Jn. 16:7-11).

Placed under conviction, which means he is then made aware of his terrible, lost condition, and that the only Saviour is Christ, he then trusts in Christ and what Christ did at the Cross, which brings him Salvation (Jn. 3:16; Rom. 10:9-10, 13; Eph. 2:8-9; Rev. 22:17). He does not understand very much about what he has done, he just knows that he has simply believed, which means to believe in Christ, and the Lord does the rest. It is called *"Justification by Faith"* (I Cor. 6:9-11).

However, even though the exhibition of Faith is all that man does, in the Mind of God, the sinner was actually in Christ when Jesus died, with the terminology being used, *"Baptized into His Death"* (Rom. 6:3). So, God looks at the Death of Christ, as the death of the sinner which paid the terrible debt, even though the sinner was not actually there.

As well, the sinner is also buried with Christ, which speaks of all the old life, the transgressions, iniquities, sins, actually every single thing the sinner was before conversion, with all of its attendant evil, literally being buried with Christ. That's what the Burial of Christ was actually all about.

Dying, Christ suffered the penalty of the broken Law, which was death, which we should have suffered, but which He suffered in our place. He never sinned, so He deserved no punishment, so He took the punishment we should have taken.

When He was buried, this signified, as would be obvious, that He had died. It also signified, that we had died — died to the old

NOTES

life, the old existence, the old person we used to be.

However, had He remained dead, even though the debt would have been paid, had it stopped there, man would have had no new life. Consequently, He *"Who was delivered for our offenses . . . was raised again for our Justification"* (Rom. 4:25).

When He died, He did so as a sinner, even though He was not a sinner. When He was raised, however, He was raised not as a sinner, but as the Son of the Living God. The debt had been paid, so that problem no longer remained. As well, when He was raised, we were raised with Him (Rom. 6:4-6), which means we could not have been justified without His Resurrection.

While a dead man can be pardoned, only a living man can be justified. As I say these words, I greatly sense the Presence of God, and must shout *"Hallelujah!"*

God does not justify dead men, because there is no need for Justification for a dead man. It is only the one who is alive, which we have been made so by Christ, who can be Justified. That means that God declares this new man, this new creation *"not guilty, totally innocent,"* which is a legal work. There is no way that God could legally justify a sinner, but He definitely can justify a new man, which every person is, who trusts Christ (II Cor. 5:17).

This is how that God can justify one who previously was not just, and not violate His Own Righteousness. In Truth, He is not justifying the sinner, or the old man, or the person we once were, but rather the new man in Christ Jesus, and made that way, by what Christ did at the Cross and the Resurrection, and our Faith in that.

Now, this new man can walk in Righteousness and Holiness, becoming more and more Christlike, as he is now a habitation of the Holy Spirit (Eph. 2:21-22).

RIGHTEOUSNESS AND HOLINESS

We wonder in our minds, how that God can honestly declare a guilty man not guilty, an unrighteous man as one who is righteous, a man who is unholy, declared holy? In effect, He is not declaring a guilty party *"not guilty!"* Jesus has taken the guilt, suffered its penalty, and the person whom God addresses, declaring not guilty, is, in fact, exactly that way — not guilty, all because of his Faith in what Christ has done on our behalf, as our Substitute and Representative Man. Identification with Him, grants us all that He did at the Cross.

Regarding mankind, the Crucifixion and Burial pertained to his lost condition, as the Resurrection pertained to his new condition in Christ. It is all *"in Christ,"* hence that term or one of its derivatives being used well over a hundred times in the New Testament.

ALL ARE IN THE CROSS AND
THE RESURRECTION

The Cross and the Resurrection are the foundation of Christianity. To this everything pointed, and from this everything comes. Everything the Believer receives is through and by the Death and Resurrection of Christ, and our Faith in that. We must not leave that thought, that Truth! We must ever understand that if we depart from that, we have, in fact, departed from the Gospel Message. It is all the Cross, it is ever the Cross!

That is the manner in which man was delivered, and what a deliverance it was and is.

Now I do not have to fear the *"wrath to come,"* which speaks of the coming *"Great White Throne Judgment,"* with its attendant results being the Lake of Fire, forever and forever, because I allowed Jesus to take that wrath for me on the Cross. As previously stated, it is Jesus to Whom all of mankind will answer. You can answer to Him now as it refers to the great Salvation Message, or you will answer to Him at the Great White Throne Judgment (Rev. 20:11-15), but answer you will!

*"Free from the Law, O happy condition!*
*"Jesus hath bled, and there is remission;*
*"Cursed by the Law and bruised by the Fall,*
*"Grace hath redeemed us once for all."*

*"Now are we free, there's no condemnation!*
*"Jesus provides a perfect Salvation;*

NOTES

*"Come unto Me, O hear His sweet call!*
*"Come and He saves us once for all."*

*"Children of God, O glorious calling!*
*"Surely His Grace will keep us from falling;*
*"Passing from death to life at His call,*
*"Blessed Salvation, once for all."*

*"Once for all, O sinner, receive it;*
*"Once for all, O brother, believe it!*
*"Cling to the Cross, the burden will fall,*
*"Christ hath redeemed us once for all!"*

## CHAPTER 2

(1) "FOR YOURSELVES, BRETHREN, KNOW OUR ENTRANCE IN UNTO YOU, THAT IT WAS NOT IN VAIN:"

In a slight way, and because of the manner in which Paul addresses himself in this Chapter, we gather that there had been some criticism of his person and Ministry. From whom such would have come, we have no way of knowing. The phrase, *"warn them that are unruly,"* in I Thessalonians 5:14, gives us some small clue. In I Thessalonians Chapter 1, the Apostle proclaims the great and glorious entrance of the Gospel into Thessalonica, but in Chapter 2 the same themes establish Paul's defense against insinuations about his alleged ulterior motives.

The identity of these Thessalonian opponents is a puzzle difficult to piece together. Suggestions have included heretical pseudo-apostles as found in Corinth and Galatia, who could have been Judaizers. Also whether they were within the Church or outside remains a mystery. A possible reconstruction seized the Jews as continuing adversaries of Paul, even after he left Thessalonica, for they were so intent on destroying the work he had started that they persistently hurled accusations at him and labeled him another self-seeking religious propagandist. How they distorted his teaching to accuse him of treason while he was yet in the city (Acts 17:7) shows an abiding animosity toward him. Subjected to a constant barrage of accusations, Thessalonian Christians may easily have begun to question Paul's sincerity.

NOTES

There is no evidence of organized opposition within the Church, yet Timothy apparently brought back news (I Thess. 3:6) that some uncertainty had arisen within it as to whether Paul's concern for it was genuine.

### BRETHREN

The phrase, *"For yourselves, Brethren, know our entrance in unto you,"* presents his defense, a justifiable defense of his personal Ministry for the sake of Truth and the preservation of the Church. Probably, to which we have briefly alluded, the slanderers were fanatical Jews who, if they could not strike him physically, attempted savage character assassination. It seems the opposition was not from inside, but outside the congregation.

By using the word *"Brethren"* Paul turns from the witness of outsiders (I Thess. 1:9), to the witness of the Church itself respecting his Ministry.

The opposition from the Jews without had been fierce, and continued to be so until the day of his death. When they had opportunity they used open violence; they roused the Gentile mob against him; they had him scourged and stoned, and would have killed him had it been within their power.

When he personally was out of reach, they assailed him through his character and affections. They crept, it seems, into the Churches where his love and zeal had gathered here and there, and scattered injurious suspicions against him among his followers.

He was not, they hinted, all that he seemed to be. They could tell stories about his early days, and advise those who did not know him so well to be on their guard. Evangelizing paid him quite well, they insinuated, and his ambition was gratified by lording it over his ignorant converts.

Such messengers of Satan had apparently made their appearance in Thessalonica since Paul left, and this Chapter is his reply to their insinuations.

### THE HEART OF THE APOSTLE

There is something painful in the situation thus created. It would have been like a sword piercing the Apostle's heart, had his enemies succeeded in their attempt to breed distrust in the Thessalonians toward him. He could not have borne to think that those whom he loved so utterly should entertain the faintest suspicion of the integrity of his love. Happily he is spared that pain.

He writes, indeed, as one who has felt the indignity of the charges brought against him, but with the frankness and heartiness of a man who is confident that his defense will be well received. From baseless insinuations he can appeal to facts which are well-known to all. From the false character in which he has been dressed by his adversaries he can appeal to the Truth, in which he lived and moved among them (MacLaren).

OPPOSITION

I empathize with the Apostle, even as many Preachers can. However, it seems presently, that the opposition comes from both without and within. The Media never ceases its efforts to steal, kill, and destroy. As I have previously stated, I learned the hard way, that the far greater majority of those in this profession little regard the Truth, at least as it pertains to the Gospel. Their minds are made up, and irrespective as to how honest and true the effort may be, they seek to twist all that happens, to make it appear something it isn't.

However, that is the world, and we expect no less. When it comes from within, the hurt is keenly felt, and because we're supposed to be pulling for the same thing, working for the same Lord, striving for the same purpose; therefore, it is very difficult to experience the opposition, sometimes even worse than that of the world, from those who should be pulling in the same direction.

One wants to ask, *"Why?"*

In years of suffering this type of abuse, I have been forced to come to certain conclusions.

First of all, all who say *"Lord, Lord,"* really aren't serving Him. That number to be sure, is far larger than one realizes. This means that despite their claims, these people actually aren't saved, so what else can one expect from them than opposition!

Second, many Christians little think for themselves. They simply play *"follow the leader."* If their leaders, and I speak of their Pastors and Denominational heads, oppose a particular Ministry, they follow suit. They ask few questions, if any at all, and are content to just follow, irrespective as to where it leads.

NOTES

So-called leaders generally oppose that which they cannot control. Of course, all do not fall into that category, but I think the majority do. The moment they cannot control it, is the moment they begin to oppose it. It really doesn't matter how many people are being saved, how many lives are being changed, in fact, if those individuals are the kind who demand blind obedience, they really care little about the real purpose of the Ministry, but something else altogether.

And there are some who love to hold past failures over someone's head. They seem to delight in that, forever consigning that individual to a place of spiritual oblivion, at least in their own minds. They seem to think that failure of some sort, no matter how long past, gives them the right to take any position they need to take. They actually feel, they can say anything about the person in question they so desire, do anything to him or her they so desire, and all is sanctioned by the Lord, they think. They seem to feel they have some type of license for this type of behavior.

These type of individuals have absolutely no concept of the Word of God, what it teaches and what it demands. In fact, the Word of God never enters into their thinking. They have automatically conjured up their own scenario, and they, consequently, feel justified in all that they do.

There's very little that hurts more, than to have fellow Christians think very evil thoughts about you, actually in their minds, feeling that you're something very degrading, which is not the case at all. Until one has been on that side of the fence, one has no conception as to how such feels.

Unfortunately, gossip is one of the great pastimes of the Church. And to be frank, with many so-called Christians it is not pastime at all, but rather full-time.

PERCEPTION

The other day I either heard or read (I forget which), a statement made by a particular reporter who was quite familiar with Washington, D.C. His major thought, was that the entire political structure of Washington functioned on the premise of perception. In other words, people base their thinking and their decisions on the way things seem to be, and seem to be such because of appearance, etc.

He then went on to make the statement, that things are seldom as they seem to be. Surface appearance generally lets us know little as to what actually is beneath.

Regrettably, the political structure in Washington is not the only ones guilty of such, if in fact they actually are! The Church need take a back seat to no one in this regard.

Almost all judging, which our Lord strongly warned against, is based on perception, at least what somebody thinks something is without really knowing the Truth. This is so serious, that Jesus plainly said:

*"Judge not, that ye be not judged.*

*"For with what judgment ye judge, ye shall be judged: and with what measure ye meet, it shall be measured to you again"* (Mat. 7:1-2).

Let not the Reader think that our Lord was merely using empty words in regard to this statement. It is a very serious business, so serious in fact, that before we form judgments, especially considering that we don't know the Truth of the matter, we are placing ourselves on very dangerous footing. Whatever we say and do, is going to come back to us, exactly as we have dished it out. Don't think that the Words of our Lord can be taken lightly. He said what He meant, and He meant what He said!

And yet, it seems that many Christians flout this warning with impudence. They seem to think it does not apply to them, or in some manner or way, they are justified in what they do. In fact, Christians constantly try to justify themselves in this capacity.

## SELF JUSTIFICATION

A lady wrote me sometime back and said, *"Yes I'll admit that we have done you wrong, but it's your fault!"*

That's an interesting observation, but it is held by many, if not most.

In other words, she was claiming, that one is justified in doing wrong, if the one to whom the wrong is being done, has committed some type of wrong himself or herself.

I'm sorry, but that's not in the Bible. We are never justified in doing wrong, irrespective as to what someone else does. As well, how in the world could anyone think they are morally qualified to punish another? That's an interesting question that should be thought out very carefully.

We must think very highly of ourselves, if we think we are so superior from a moral position, that this gives us the right to hurt someone else. If we think such, that shows that we do not truly know ourselves, do not really understand what Christianity actually is, and have no idea as to what the Bible says.

James addressed this very strongly when he said, *"There is one Lawgiver, Who is able to save and to destroy: who art thou that judgest another?"* (James 4:12).

He is actually saying, *"Who do you think you are, thinking you are morally qualified to judge someone else?"*

It's a question we should look at very carefully!

## A PERSONAL STATEMENT

Taking a cue from Paul, I feel it is satisfactory to make the following statement:

I am a man of God. I have a Call of God upon my life. That Call by the Goodness and Grace of God, has helped me to see hundreds of thousands brought to a saving knowledge of Jesus Christ. It has helped me to see many thousands Baptized with the Holy Spirit. It has helped me to see untold numbers of lives gloriously and wondrously changed by the Power of God. I give the Lord all the praise and the glory for that, and I am most grateful to Him, that He has used this unworthy vessel to carry out this very important task.

As well, there is absolutely nothing in my life of which I am aware that would be displeasing to the Lord. By the Grace of God I can say that, and I say it gladly and I say it thankfully! My life is clean and my Ministry is clean. I say that loudly, boldly and to the point, because it is true.

The Gospel I preach, is anointed by the Holy Spirit, which no one can deny, at least if they will be honest with themselves. And I will quickly add to that, the Holy Spirit does not anoint error and He does not anoint sin. In fact, the highest acclamation of all, the highest accord of all, the highest acceptance of all, is the Presence of God upon a Ministry. I thank

NOTES

the Lord, that His Presence is upon this Ministry, and it is upon my person.

If the things I have said are true, and they definitely are, then those who would oppose this ministry, can be concluded as doing nothing but opposing the Lord. One cannot have it both ways. One cannot be for the Lord, and opposing that which is of the Lord. Such is not possible! If one opposes that which belongs to God, which is of God, and which is being used of God, one at the same time is opposing God.

To do such a thing, as is made abundantly clear in the Word of God, is a serious offense indeed! In fact, nothing could be more serious for the Believer. And yet, sadly and regrettably, that's where many Believers find themselves.

With Paul, I'm glad I can say, *"For I am the least of the Apostles, that am not meet to be called an Apostle, because I persecuted* (failed) *the Church of God.*

*"But by the Grace of God I am what I am: and His Grace which was bestowed upon me was not in vain; but I labored more abundantly than they all: yet not I, but the Grace of God which was with me"* (I Cor. 15:9-10).

### TO LABOR IN VAIN

The phrase, *"That it was not in vain,"* refers to something being fruitless, or without success. Paul makes this statement not so much to show that his Ministry was successful, as to meet a charge of his adversaries that he was an imposter. Paul tells them that, from their own observation, they knew that this was not so.

The Lord had sent Paul and those with him to Thessalonica. He did not go according to his own volition or will, but was definitely led by the Holy Spirit.

Even though meeting severe opposition, the Lord helped the Apostle to establish a great Church (Acts Chpt. 17). The Gospel he preached, was definitely not in vain, reaping its eternal rewards in seeing lives gloriously and wondrously changed by the Power of God. Quite a number of people were brought out of paganistic bondage into the glorious light of the Gospel.

I might quickly add, that this is the proof of Ministry. Unfortunately, as we begin this Twenty-first Century, something else entirely seems to serve as the proof presently. I speak of the plaudits of men, and acceptance by the institutionalized religious structure, neither one is recognized by God. Irrespective, the proof that Paul had, is that which I seek, and only that which I seek, and only that which I will accept. I care nothing for the other!

NOTES

### IS IT POSSIBLE FOR THE GOSPEL TO EVER BE MINISTERED IN VAIN?

The Scripture tells us, *"So shall My Word be that goeth forth out of My Mouth: it shall not return unto Me void, but it shall accomplish that which I please, and it shall prosper in the thing whereto I sent it"* (Isa. 55:11).

However, we should understand exactly what is being said here.

The Word of God, like rain and snow that water the Earth and cause it to produce fruit, will be sowed in the hearts of men and produce fruit in the moral world (Deut. 32:2).

As the rain and snow fall on various kinds of ground, so does the Word of God (Mat. 13:3-8, 20-23). Like rain and snow, it will accomplish its best good in the Eternal Reign of the Messiah, when the Knowledge of the Lord will cover the Earth (Isa. 11:9). Thus, the final fulfillment of this Scripture will be in the future; there is only a partial fulfillment at present in the preaching of the Gospel.

In fact, the presentation of the Word does not guarantee success, but rather only provides the opportunity for success. The Truth is, some accept the Word, and some reject the Word. In a sense, that's what the Word of God is designed to do — to force individuals to a decision, one way or the other. Of course, it greatly grieves the heart of God, when men refuse; nevertheless, they must be given the opportunity to do one or the other.

Therefore, even if they refuse, in a strict sense of the word, the presentation of the Word has not been in vain.

(2) "BUT EVEN AFTER THAT WE HAD SUFFERED BEFORE, AND WERE SHAMEFULLY ENTREATED, AS YE KNOW, AT PHILIPPI, WE WERE BOLD IN OUR GOD TO SPEAK UNTO YOU THE GOSPEL OF GOD WITH MUCH CONTENTION."

The opposite of the empty Ministry denied in Verse 1 is one where no obstacle or threat is sufficient to deter the speaker of God's Gospel. In Philippi, Paul and Silas had been beaten and severely flogged; they had been put in prison with their feet in stocks (Acts 16:22-24), and possibly otherwise cruelly mistreated because they had rescued a slave girl in the Name of Jesus Christ.

They had also been insulted by being arrested unjustly, stripped of their clothes, and treated like dangerous fugitives. Their Roman citizenship had been violated (Acts 16:37).

Still staggering from these injuries and indignities, the two came to Thessalonica. Under such conditions, most people would have refrained from repeating a Message that had led to such violent treatment, but not these men. With God's help, they mustered sufficient courage to declare in this new city their Gospel from God, and it compromised not at all!

The words *"we were bold"* ritually describes how they spoke out despite the same potential dangers as faced in Philippi.

## SUFFERING

The phrase, *"But even after that we had suffered before, and were shamefully entreated, as ye know, at Philippi,"* proclaims several particulars which should be addressed:

1. High motives are required for men to continue a true, and, therefore, costly, Gospel Ministry. To suffer so, and then continue to proclaim the Message, with the possibility that such suffering could happen again, proclaims the determined dedication of these men of God. Such treatment quickly separates the insincere from the sincere.

How many presently would be willing to undergo such treatment, and continue on despite that treatment, even with the possibility of it continuing, and actually in all likelihood that it will continue?

2. Paul and Silas definitely were shamefully entreated at Philippi. Knowing that God can do anything, why would He allow such?

Without going into detail as to why, the Truth I propose to bring out presently is, that Paul and Silas both knew that God did not have to allow this severe treatment. The thing is, they did not question what He did, but suffered it without complaint, and actually rejoiced that they were counted worthy to suffer so for the sake of Christ.

NOTES

This is one of the greatest lessons we can learn from this experience.

3. We know that everything that happens to a Believer, is either caused by the Lord or allowed by the Lord. We know that He doesn't cause sin or failure, etc., but He definitely does allow such things, but always with the understanding that such direction will always bring chastisement (Heb. 12:5-11).

We know that Paul and Silas had not done anything wrong, so why would the Lord allow such punishment to come their way, when He could have easily stopped it?

All the reasons we do not know, and all the reasons Paul and Silas did not know. It was enough that they trusted God, that what He did was right. They let it go at that, and praised His Name instead.

The flesh is always a problem for the Child of God, and for one who is used as Paul and Silas were used by the Lord, the flesh no doubt is even a greater danger.

When we speak of the *"flesh,"* we're speaking of self-will, self-effort, dependence on self, etc. The only real way that these things can be throttled, is by the administration of suffering in some way, even as with Paul and Silas. I guess the statement could be made, if Paul and Silas needed such, and I think we have to come to the conclusion that they did or else the Lord would not have allowed such, where does that leave us?

All of us want blessings, the more the better! But all blessings, actually nothing but blessings, may teach us a lot about God, but it doesn't teach us much about ourselves. While we definitely need to learn just how good and wonderful that God is, which we do continually as He continually blesses us, at the same time, we need to learn some things about ourselves. Unfortunately, that can only come by way of *"suffering."* Then we learn how to depend on the Lord, how to look to the Lord, how to trust the Lord, which we seemingly, cannot learn any other way.

4. The present approach to the Gospel, in many ways is directly backwards from that of the Early Church. Then, the idea was, *"what will it take to stop Preachers of the Gospel?"* Satan must have asked himself that many

times. The Truth is, nothing can stop a true Preacher of the Gospel.

At the present time, the idea is, what will it take to get a Preacher started? The modern Gospel dangles carrots of every description, promising benefits galore, until the modern Preacher has an entirely different conception of what the Gospel and its presentation actually is than during the times of the Early Church.

The present crowd wants to know how plush the hotels are, while Paul and his associates wanted to know how the jails were, because they knew that's probably where they would end up.

Too many modern Preachers boast about the amount of money they are making, while Paul's boast, if one could call it that, was in his infirmities, which he listed in II Corinthians 11:23-27.

To be completely honest with you the Reader, I don't have much respect for much of the modern variety, which you probably have already detected concerning the flavor of my statements.

If we preach the same Gospel that Paul preached, and serve the same Christ that Paul served, and have the same call that Paul had, we will be as Paul. If we serve *"another Jesus,"* which is the case with most, then it will be something else altogether (II Cor. 11:4).

I haven't suffered physically as the great Apostle of earlier days suffered, but I have suffered mentally and spiritually. I know what it is for every effort to be made by both the world and the apostate Church, to stop us from preaching the Gospel. They have not succeeded, and by the Grace of God they will not succeed. I say with the Great Apostle of old, *"For though I preach the Gospel, I have nothing to glory of: for necessity is laid upon me; yea, woe is unto me, if I preach not the Gospel!"* (I Cor. 9:16).

## BOLDNESS

The phrase, *"We were bold in our God to speak unto you the Gospel of God,"* proclaims the fact that far from being intimidated by events, Paul and his associates, rather determined even more to proclaim the Message. The courage, Paul insists, was *"in our God"*; that is, it came from God, in Whom they lived.

NOTES

In declaring that he spoke *"the Gospel of God,"* Paul, in refuting the Jews, takes the position of ultimate authority for his Message.

The Apostle is saying that it is only with God's powerful aid that could have enabled them to persevere with ardor and zeal in such a work after such treatment.

The meaning here is, that they were not deterred from preaching the Gospel by the treatment which they had received, but at the very next important town, and on the first opportunity, they proclaimed the same Truth, though there was no security that they might not meet with the same persecution there. Paul evidently appeals to this in order to show that they were not impostors, and that they were not influenced by the hope of ease or of selfish gains. To be sure, men who were not sincere and earnest in their purposes, would have been deterred by such treatment as they had received at Philippi, to say the least! It should be overly obvious, that anyone who would suffer as these men suffered, and then continue on in the same manner, had to be doing so for a deeper reason than merely some surface attraction. No, as we've already said, nothing could stop these men from preaching the Gospel, as nothing did stop them from preaching the Gospel. The only way they could be silenced, was their life being taken, which could not happen, until the Lord would allow it to happen.

## WHY DID THE JEWS HATE PAUL SO MUCH?

There were two reasons:

First of all, they looked at him as a traitor, a turncoat if you will! He had once been their fair-haired boy. In fact, Paul before his conversion on the road to Damascus, had been the hope of Phariseeism. Having studied under the great Gamaliel, Paul, then called by his Hebrew name of Saul, was looked at as one of the great authorities at that time on Mosaic Law. The Truth is, he really did not know Mosaic Law, for the simple reason, that no one unsaved could properly understand it, and Paul was unsaved at that time.

As well as being the great hope of Phariseeism, he was also the strongest opponent at that time against followers of Christ, Who the leaders of Israel had crucified a short time earlier. So, Paul was a comer. In other words, he was climbing the ladder fast, even to which he alluded in Galatians 1:13-14. And now, this one who had been their champion was instead, the champion of the Christians. So they hated him, and with a passion.

And yet, the situation at Philippi to which Paul here alludes, had not been fomented or educated by the Jews, but rather by Gentiles who had made a lot of profit from a girl in the fortune telling business, who had been set free by the Power of God. The source of their ill-gotten gains cut off, they became very angry at Paul and Silas, which resulted in the Magistrates beating them severely, etc.

## CONTENTION

The phrase, *"With much contention,"* refers to conflict. The idea is, the triumph of the Gospel was secured only by an effort of the highest kind, and by overcoming the most formidable opposition.

The Reader must understand that there *is* an animosity against the True Gospel of Jesus Christ. That animosity comes from both the world and the apostate Church, one might say. It is fueled by the powers of darkness.

As I've already stated, it is understandable as it regards the world, simply because they are actually controlled by Satan. It is not so understandable as it refers to the Church, but yet this is from where the greatest opposition springs. In fact, Satan uses this method moreso than any, simply because he can be far more successful there. He seeks to pervert the Gospel, subdue the Gospel, compromise the Gospel, and hinder the Gospel anyway he can. To do such through those who claim to be Believers, and especially through so-called religious leadership, presents his greatest effort of all. Millions erroneously think if Denominational heads say something, then it must be right. In fact it might be right, but not necessarily so!

This short statement by Paul, *"with much contention,"* blows to pieces the claims of many Christians who think that if God has called someone to do something, then every problem will instantly be solved, with plenty of money to get it done, along with all other resources. Nothing could be further from the Truth. In fact, those who claim to be Christians who would advocate such foolishness, either aren't really saved, or else, they feel guilty about not giving or helping in some way, therefore, they try to justify themselves by claiming that whatever is being done is not of God, etc.

The Truth is, that when God calls someone to do something, that Satan will immediately begin to hinder the effort in every way possible. And how does he do that?

The ways are too numerous to list; however, to name just a few, he will try to make fellow Christians believe that what is being proposed is not of God. Or it is not of my Denomination, so I cannot support it. Or our leaders tell us that we should not support that effort, therefore, I will not support the effort.

The idea is this. When the Lord gives a Preacher of the Gospel direction as it regards a work which He desires to be carried out, any Believer who comes under the hearing of that appeal for help, is obligated in some way to be of help. It may only be prayer, but whatever it is, the Believer is to be of service. It is impossible for any Preacher to carry out a work, unless he has the help of other Believers in some manner. That's why Paul thanked the Philippians so profusely for helping him by them sending an offering, etc. (Phil. 4:16).

In fact, the Philippians helped Paul in the founding of the Church at Thessalonica, which Philippians 4:16 brings out. The Holy Spirit was so pleased with this, that He had the Apostle to mention it, which would be read by untold millions down through the centuries, which is meant to serve as an example.

## A PERSONAL EXPERIENCE

Even though I have mentioned this, I believe it was, in our Commentary on Colossians, due to its great significance, let me briefly allude to it again:

To be brief, at the beginning of 1999, the Lord laid it on my heart to change the programming entirely on the two Radio Stations owned by the Ministry. We did this immediately, doing what we feel the Lord told us to do, in originating all programming from Family Worship Center, in one way or the other. The results almost instantly, were fantastic, with people being saved, lives being changed, the sick being healed, etc.

The Lord then told me to obtain small F.M. Radio Stations all over the United States, covering this nation as best I can, in order that the Message we preach be heralded to as many people as possible. This we immediately set out to do. Actually, as I dictate these notes on October 14, 1999, we have 174 applications before the F.C.C. for approval, which we will of course have hopefully received by the time you read this. We actually plan to obtain many hundreds of these, if not thousands.

Of course, as should be obvious, it will cost quite a sum of money to do this, money incidently which we do not have, and which the Lord will have to provide. How will He provide it?

He will do so as He has always done, through the Body of Christ.

The Lord spoke to my heart in one of our morning Prayer meetings, telling me, *"Tell the People, if they will help you carry out this Work which I have called you to do, that I will see to it that their barrel of meal does not waste and their cruse of oil does not fail."*

Now that's a powerful statement, but I know the Lord gave me that Word.

Did He mean what He said? In fact, if He really spoke that to my heart, and I know He did, then most definitely, He meant exactly what He said.

God will always bless those who help Preachers do that which God has truly called them to do. However, the following must be noted as well:

COUNTERFEITS

Satan always has individuals who claim to be of God, even claiming all kinds of great things, which demand support as well. In other words, Satan is very successful in drawing away support that should go for the True Gospel of Jesus Christ, but instead goes to charlatans, or those who really have not heard from the Lord. Only God knows the amount of money and effort wasted on that which claims to be of God, but isn't. I would dare say, that probably about 90% of all money spent for that which claims to be of God, is really not for the Lord at all, but rather a clever ploy by Satan to deceive. He is very successful at his efforts!

NOTES

The Judaizers opposed Paul greatly in his Ministry. They claimed to be of God, and in fact, pulled away many people after them, who, as should be obvious, were supporting them with their money, etc. No one in their right mind could even begin to think that these people were of God, especially considering that the Holy Spirit through Paul referred to them as *"Satan's ministers"* (II Cor. 11:15).

It's going to be a terrible thing for many Christians when they stand at the Judgment Seat of Christ, where all of us will definitely stand, and find to their dismay that they had actually helped support the work of Satan in some cases, if not many cases. While they won't lose their souls, they will definitely lose reward, which will be an eternal loss.

(3) "FOR OUR EXHORTATION WAS NOT OF DECEIT, NOR OF UNCLEANNESS, NOR IN GUILE:"

Not only was the preaching of Paul and those with him filled with power and earnestness when they evangelized Thessalonica, but wherever they went it was above suspicion, despite the accusations of the detractors, which always seemed to be in plentiful supply.

Paul had apparently been accused of appealing on wrong grounds. The damage from this accusation he is quite anxious to repair.

EXHORTATION

The phrase, *"For our exhortation,"* refers to an attempt to get men to take a particular line of action.

Actually, the word has a twofold signification, denoting both *"exhortation"* and *"consolation"*; when it refers to the moral conduct it denotes exhortation, but when it is an address to a sufferer it denotes consolation. In the Gospel these two meanings are blended together. The idea here seems to include preaching in general.

Paul and those with him had a definite thought in mind when going to Thessalonica, and in fact, any other area where the Holy Spirit would send them.

Their purpose was to preach the Gospel, and for the Holy Spirit to move upon that which had been preached, and do so on the hearts of men, with the motive of bringing them out of spiritual darkness into light.

They wanted to bring them to Christ Jesus, Who Alone could save their souls.

While the Message was moreso a *"come to Jesus,"* rather than a leaving of idol worship, still it did entail the latter. It's impossible to come to Christ, without leaving these other things. Consequently, when individuals leave their former lifestyles, Satan suffers loss, which translates into loss for particular efforts of men, as it regarded heathen temples, or whatever! Satan doesn't give up his dupes easily, and neither does he do so without a fight.

If he cannot keep the individual from responding favorably to Christ, he will then seek to arouse anger against the Preacher of the Gospel, even as he did Paul and those with him.

## DECEIT

The phrase, *"Was not of deceit,"* refers to the fact that Paul had no ulterior motives in mind. He had only one purpose, and that was the well-being of the people to whom he preached, which well-being could be arrived at only in Christ.

Deceit can function in two ways: A. First of all, in the manner of the Preacher purposely setting out to deceive people with false doctrine, in order to obtain a desired end, mostly money; or, B. The Preacher himself being deceived, meaning that he believes that he is preaching Truth, when in reality it is error. Probably the latter is the most common. Irrespective as to what manner deception takes, it will still reap its bitter fruit. The Preacher who sincerely believes that what he is preaching is Truth, even though it is error, is probably the most dangerous. Believing as he does, he delivers his message with conviction, which of course has some impact upon the hearers. So, we come down to the fact, that if a person doesn't know the Word of God as they should, they are easy marks for deception.

As would be obvious, most of the people to whom Paul preached, at least as it regarded Gentiles, had no knowledge of the Word of God whatsoever. In fact, they didn't even know there was a Word of God, much less having some understanding of its precepts. So, that type of person is very blessed, if they have the privilege of first hearing the Gospel by someone as Paul. Unfortunately, many do not have that privilege, thereby, first hearing the message which contains only part Truth. Many of these people are thereby hindered for life.

NOTES

As an example, many people first hear the Gospel by someone who preaches Truth as it regards Salvation, but preaches error as it regards the Baptism with the Holy Spirit. If the individual accepts the message, even as many do, due to what their father in the Lord has taught them concerning the Holy Spirit, they will be heavily impacted toward continuing in that error. Some few climb out over it and receive what God has for them, but not many!

Of course, it is better for the unsaved to hear that message, although only partly correct, than to not hear the Message at all.

I'm trying to say that deception is a powerful thing, and comes in many forms. In fact, I think it can probably be said that every single Believer who has ever lived, including Paul, has been deceived about something regarding the Gospel, at one time or the other. Paul gives his own experience in Romans, Chapter 7, which in reality was deception. The idea is, that every Believer earnestly seek the Lord as it regards all the Light of the Gospel. In other words, they who hunger and thirst after Righteousness will be filled (Mat. 5:6). That is the Promise of God. Regrettably, there are many Christians who do not have the spiritual hunger and thirst that they should have. Consequently, they do not receive much from the Lord, meaning that they remain in error. Actually, the very fact of a lack of desire for growth in the Lord, proclaims a state of error, i.e., *"deception."*

## UNCLEANNESS

The phrase, *"Nor of uncleanness,"* refers I think to immorality, although it could have the meaning of impure motives as well.

I lean toward the former, because most all of the religions of that day in the Gentile world, were soaked with immorality in one way or the other. Their temples were filled with both male and female prostitutes, with certain types of sexual acts demanded upon initiation. In fact, the purity of the Gospel as it related to Christianity concerning morals, is what finally made such an impact on the Roman Empire. Immorality of any nature is like leaven, which only tends to get worse and worse in its depravity. Due to this *"law of immorality,"* one might say, the Empire steadily declined, slowly sinking into a quagmire of filth. In Paul's day, it was Christianity alone, which held up a standard of purity. To be frank, it is the same presently! While particular religions presently might advocate purity in one form or the other, there is no power to back up their stipulations; consequently, immorality is rampant, even as it is in one way or the other, with most who do not know the Lord.

So, the Apostle reminds the Believers in Thessalonica as to the purity of not only what he preached, but the pure lives which it produced.

This is the manner in which I think the Apostle is using the word *"uncleanness."* There doesn't seem to be much indication, at least here, that he personally was being accused of some type of immorality. That definitely could have been the case, but not likely, at least at this particular time. If so, I think he would have been much more bold in his denunciation of the accusation, had it regarded him personally.

GUILE

The phrase, *"Nor in guile,"* refers to trickery or cunning.

It is said of our Lord, *"Who did no sin, neither was guile found in His mouth"* (I Pet. 2:22).

*"No guile"* refers to no point being carried by art, cunning, or stratagem. Everything is done on the most honorable and fair principles. It is much when a man can say that he has never endeavored to accomplish anything by mere trick, craft, or cunning. Guile, craft, cunning, imply deception, and can never be reconciled with that entire honesty which a Minister of the Gospel and all Christians for that matter, must possess.

In all things Paul was the servant of those to whom he preached. And as his motives were pure, so were the means he used. His exhortation was not in guile. He did not manipulate his Message, or the people. He was never found using words of flattery. The Gospel was not his own to do with as he pleased. It belonged to God, and, therefore, must be handled every moment in that capacity.

NOTES

(4) "BUT AS WE WERE ALLOWED OF GOD TO BE PUT IN TRUST WITH THE GOSPEL, EVEN SO WE SPEAK; NOT AS PLEASING MEN, BUT GOD, WHICH TRIETH OUR HEARTS."

To be *"approved by God"* entails a process of testing, success in completing the tests, and a consequent state of endorsement by God, which is pronounced by the anointing of the Holy Spirit upon the efforts of the Minister.

After calling Paul on the Damascus road, God subjected him to necessary rigors to demonstrate his capability for his assigned task. Having thus prepared him, He committed to him the Gospel Message for Proclamation among Gentiles such as these Readers.

Paul always sought God's approval, and never that of men. The scrutiny of God, Who is able to sound the depths of every thought, was Paul's ultimate court of appeal, as it should be of all men.

TO BE PUT IN TRUST
WITH THE GOSPEL

The phrase, *"But as we were allowed of God to be put in trust with the Gospel,"* proclaims several things:

1. *"Allowed"* in the Greek is *"dokimazo,"* and means *"to be put to the test."* For those who are truly called of God, to be sure, the test is severe.
2. *"To be put in trust"* refers to the fact that the test has been passed. The manner in which Paul makes this statement, tells us that the testing has been completed, and thus signifies an approval by God.
3. *"The Gospel"* originates in God, and is ours only as a sacred trust, and, therefore, is not a delusion.

Paul and Silas knew in their hearts that they were approved of God, no matter what people might say about them. God, in fact, showed His approval by the very tests He put them through. By approving them in testing and finding them worthy He allowed them to be entrusted with the Gospel.

It is God Who calls men and women to preach. As well, those whom He calls, He also qualifies. While men may or may not recognize the qualifications, such has little to do with the actual fact of the matter.

The idea of all of this is, that we must please God and not men. While we love our Brothers and Sisters in the Lord, and actively seek their fellowship, it is God Whom we must please. That which is approved by man does not at all mean that it is necessarily approved by God. As well, that which is approved by God, will not always be approved by man, and in fact, the closer we get to the Endtime, those whom God approves, will be less and less approved by men, if at all!

THE MANNER IN WHICH WE SPEAK

The phrase, *"Even so we speak,"* tells us volumes.

First of all, it must be noticed that Paul submitted his Ministry to no man. In other words, while he loved all the Brethren, no one told him what to preach, when to preach, how to preach, or where to preach. He would not even subject his Ministry to the original Twelve, and that should tell us something. It was not the case that he was a lone ranger, who *"did his own thing,"* but rather, that he was to do the Lord's thing, and that only. One cannot answer to both men and God. The Preacher of the Gospel, at least the one who is truly called of God, must answer only to God; consequently, *"even so we speak."*

The things I'm saying will not gain much approval in most modern Church circles. However, that's not my concern; my concern is to please God, and if I please Him, and displease all others, I will be sorry about the displeasure, but not enough to cease making every effort to please God only.

As Paul, I am not a lone ranger. I love my Brothers and Sisters in the Lord. I seek their counsel and advice; however, the Gospel which has been entrusted to me, I consider to be of such significance, of such import, of such value, that I must never allow myself or it to be placed in a position to where it can be compromised. I'm sorry if that offends some; however, that's the way it has to be.

PLEASING MEN

The phrase, *"Not as pleasing men,"* presents the greatest problem in the Ministry. It was a problem then, or the Holy Spirit would not have made such a point as He did here through the Apostle, and it is a problem now!

This is at least one of the greatest problems regarding religious Denominations. To be accepted in the Denomination, to receive approval, Preachers far too often, seek to please men at the expense of the Gospel of Christ. Of course, most all would deny such, but in fact, this is no doubt the largest problem in the Church world presently, and maybe in some way, always has been.

In the strict sense of the word there's nothing wrong with a Denomination, and there's nothing wrong with belonging to a Denomination. It is only when pressure is applied in one way or the other, especially in the manner of which we speak, which then causes difficulties. That's at least one of the reasons, that there were no Denominations or Denominational Structures in the Early Church. The Holy Spirit is the One Who set up the Government of the Early Church, as recorded in Acts and the Epistles, and it was set up in the form of a fellowship, with each Local Church being autonomous as far as its own particular authority was concerned, of course, all under Christ Who was and is the Head. When authority is moved from the Local Church to some designated Headquarters, as it is in most Denominations, the door is then open for this problem to present itself. When the Local Church loses its spiritual autonomy, that means it must answer to some authority figure other than God. As a result, the Message oftentimes is compromised.

As well, Paul always handled the money situation at an extreme distance. In many of these places, he supported himself in order that his effort for the Cause of Christ, would not be similar in any way to the pagan temples which gouged their devotees for money constantly. And then again, he must never be subject to particular individuals in the Church who might possibly be wealthy, and maybe wouldn't like what he preached, with the threat of withdrawing their support. In fact, it is doubtful that this would have happened with Paul, but it certainly has happened in many modern Churches.

The Preacher of the Gospel has to make up his mind early as to whether he is seeking to please men or God. As stated, he cannot please both. If he pleases God, he's going to displease many men. If he pleases men, it is guaranteed that he will not please God. That's the struggle, even as it has always been the struggle.

At the same time, we must not think that pleasing men and pleasing God are opposites in the sense that we welcome men's disapproval as evidence of God's approval. Not at all! I think I can say without any fear of contradiction that any true Preacher wants and desires men's approval. I think that Paul did, with every evidence pointing in that direction; however, desiring and having that approval, must never be at the expense of compromising the Gospel. To purposely antagonize men only hurts our cause, so we should do everything we can, everything at least that is right, to not antagonize those over whom we might have some influence.

CHRIST AND PAUL

Using both Christ and Paul as our models, with of course, Christ being the perfect example, I think we should take our cue. While Christ of course is the perfect example, the one who would most closely resemble Christ, at least in my opinion, is Paul.

Both always treated everyone with the utmost kindness and respect. In fact, they went out of their way to be conciliatorial, agreeable, kind, and helpful, and in every respect that was right. However, not one time did Christ or Paul ever compromise their Message, not even in the slightest degree. That made some people angry, even very angry; nevertheless, the Message was always of utmost importance, even at the risk of jeopardizing themselves, even their very lives.

GOD WHO TRIES OUR HEARTS

The phrase, *"But God, which trieth our hearts,"* flatly contradicts the charge that he used guile. Paul is saying that God, Who has tested and approved them, is also continually (present tense) testing their hearts. This examination of the heart (the whole inner life, including motives), this constant scrutiny by Omniscience, is a great comfort to those whose aim is to please God rather than men. Man even at his best *"looketh* (merely) *on the outward appearance"*; but God, from Whom nothing is hid, *"looketh on the heart"* (I Sam. 16:7).

NOTES

COVERING

In the decade of the '90's the word *"covering"* has become big in Church circles. It is speaking of the covering of man and not God.

In other words, the idea is, that if you are a part of a particular Denomination, or else you have certain men to act as your *"covering,"* which means to vouch for you, etc., that means that you are a man or woman of integrity. Otherwise, the idea is put forth, you are trying to hide something, and, therefore, not a person of integrity. Let's address this idea:

First of all, it is wicked, and I'll tell you why:

1. Looking to men for covering, is denying God.

The Lord addressed this a long time ago, when He said, *"Woe to the rebellious children, saith the Lord, that take counsel, but not of Me; and that cover with a covering, but not of My Spirit, that they may add sin to sin"* (Isa. 30:1).

In fact, when Christians go outside of the Lord for a *"covering,"* they're doing the same thing the world does. The Lord Alone is our covering. We are covered by His Blood, His Spirit, and His Power. If we seek any other type of covering in any other manner, we sin.

2. The very reason for seeking the covering of men, is the very opposite of what is claimed. It is claimed that this denotes integrity; however, the Scripture which I have just quoted from Isaiah, says that men seek the covering of other men that they may hide their sin.

3. Even as Paul says here, how can men be a covering for other men, when men can only look at the externals and not even that very well?

4. Anyone who has to have other men to watch him all the time, must not be very trustworthy anyway. What kind of organization is it, that must spy on each other all the time?

5. These individuals who act as a so-called covering, many times live hundreds of miles away from the individual they are supposed to cover, seeing him perhaps once or twice a year, if that. So even if such were desired, there could be no effectiveness in such a covering.

6. Men can lie to other men, but they can't lie to God. And in the first place, if a person is doing something wrong, that's the first thing they're going to do, is to lie! That's at least one of the many reasons why such is absurd!

7. This is just another scheme devised by religious men, in order to play *"big shot."* In the first place, what man is worthy enough to act as a covering for another? The answer is quickly obvious, none! Consequently, it is very pompous for one to claim that they are qualified to serve as the covering of another man or woman.

8. God is the only proper covering, and the only One Who must be looked to and in totality. He alone can search the hearts of men and know exactly what is there. So, if men would rather have other men as a covering, it shows they are trying to hide something from God, which of course is impossible anyway. Changing coverings, does not change the all-seeing eye of God.

9. One cannot have the covering of men and the covering of God at the same time. If you have one you cannot have the other.

## WHAT DOES IT MEAN FOR GOD TO TRY OUR HEARTS?

First of all, it is something, as stated, which He does constantly. Every single thing we do as Believers, our motives are constantly being judged, our intent is being judged, in other words, every single thing we are and every single thing we do. The Holy Spirit is in the hearts of all Believers, constantly evaluating, and then pointing out our weaknesses and errors.

God being God He already knows all about us, but the trying of our hearts is done that we may know. That means that we cannot even properly judge our own selves and motives. We do the best we can, but as common sense would dictate, our thinking is heavily weighted in our own favor. In other words, we are very prone to classify impure motives as spiritual concern, etc.

The idea is, that the Holy Spirit try our hearts constantly, and then convict us of whatever is wrong (Jn. 16:7-15).

In fact, the more the Holy Spirit checks us, corrects us, even chastises us, portrays the fact that we are closer to the Lord, and in fact getting ever closer. The further away from the Light, the less obvious are the flaws. The closer to the Light, the more obvious the flaws.

NOTES

(5) "FOR NEITHER AT ANY TIME USED WE FLATTERING WORDS, AS YE KNOW, NOR A CLOAK OF COVETOUSNESS; GOD IS WITNESS:"

In Verses 5 and 6, Paul flatly denies allegations against his character.

In the first of three denials, he calls his Readers to verify his complete abstinence from any word used for flattering purposes. The insidious practice of saying nice things to gain influence over others for selfish reasons, which is the method of false Apostles, is roundly condemned here.

Second, he denies putting on the kind of mask that greed wears.

In fact, only God can verify inner freedom from greed. So Paul calls on God as witness. The greed of which he was accused includes more than just avarice or love of money, but is rather a self-seeking greed of all types, a quest for anything that brings self-satisfaction. It grows out of complete disinterest regarding the rights of others — an attitude foreign to Paul and his associates.

## FLATTERY

The phrase, *"For neither at any time used we flattering words, as ye know,"* refers to the attempt to gain selfish ends by insincere speech. This means that flattery is more than the attempt to give pleasure to another person by fair words.

As well, in this case, it could have referred to the accusation against Paul concerning the Jewish charge that he was preaching an easy Gospel of Grace in contradistinction to Jewish Legalism.

The meaning here is, that the Apostle did not deal in the language of adulation; he did not praise them for their beauty, wealth, talent, or accomplishments, and conceal from them the painful truths about their guilt and danger. He stated simple Truth — not refusing to commend men if Truth would admit of it, and never hesitating to declare his honest convictions about their guilt and danger.

One of the principal arts of the deceiver on all subjects is flattery; and Paul says, that

NOTES

when preaching to the Thessalonians he had carefully avoided it. He now appeals to that fact as a proof of his own integrity. They knew that he had been faithful to their souls.

By these statements, the Apostle is not meaning to say, and we are not meaning to say, that it is wrong to be kind and gracious to people. If they have good points we should readily praise those good points, but never at the expense of their true need, whatever it is. The flatterer has no regard or concern for the soul of the individual or their Spiritual Growth. He is concerned only about winning the favor of that person, in order to obtain some desired end, mostly money! Irrespective as to what it might be, that desired end is not the spiritual welfare of the individual. Of that, one can be certain.

## COVETOUSNESS

The phrase, *"Nor a cloak of covetousness,"* refers to a pretense, which is what the word *"cloaked"* means, of helping the person, but in reality only to get personal gain in some manner.

*"Eros"* is a Greek work for *"love."* It is not used once in the Bible. And yet, it probably characterizes most all of the *"love"* that is in the world among the unredeemed, and can be even among Believers, and in fact often is!

One might say that the *"eros"* type of love and *"covetousness"* are twins. In effect, *"eros"* says, *"I love you, as long as you are useful to me in some way."* In other words, if a person has something worthwhile, covetousness wants that, and in the most ungodly way. Consequently, Churches welcome people who make the Church and the Pastor look good, while others of lesser stature are not so welcome – sometimes not welcome at all! People are friends only as long as they can contribute something that is needed, which, in reality, is no friendship at all.

But regrettably, and as stated, the world is filled with such *"covetousness,"* and also the Church.

Covetousness is a sin mentioned frequently in both the Old Testament and the New Testament. It is considered a root of other serious and moral iniquities. In fact, *"Thou shalt not covet,"* is the tenth and final Commandment, and which in a manner, addresses the previous nine Commandments relative to intent and desire.

*"Covet"* in Scripture has in view the intense love and desire for any object or person, which becomes a substitute for the devotion and love due only to God. Because of the intensity of this desire it tends to overshadow the moral demands of the Law and to allow the end, the possession of the coveted object, to justify any means for its achievement.

Covetousness is the epitome of *"greed."* It has its seedbed in materialism, which refers to the belief that the highest values or objectives lie in material well-being and in the furtherance of material progress. It is a preoccupation with material rather than spiritual things, at least as it is used here.

## THE MODERN MONEY GOSPEL

This particular message, which is *"another gospel"* pure and simple (II Cor. 11:4), is without a doubt, at least one of the worst blights on the present Church scene. It appeals to pure greed. Of course, it is cloaked with all type of high sounding Scriptural phraseology, but the Truth is, it is *"covetousness."*

People are made to believe if they give so much money to these particular individuals, whomever they might be, that they're going to get astounding sums in return. The Gospel of Jesus Christ is reduced to *"things,"* when Christ pointedly said, *"Take heed, and beware of covetousness: for a man's life consisteth not in the abundance of the things which he possesseth"* (Lk. 12:15).

He also said, *"Take no thought for your life, what ye shall eat, or what ye shall drink; nor yet for your body, what ye shall put on. Is not the life more than meat, and the body than raiment?"* (Mat. 6:25).

As is overly obvious here, the Lord told us to really take no thought about money matters, etc., which is a far cry from virtually every message being on money, and the entirety of the thrust of these particular Ministries, in fact, being on money.

He then said, *"Wherefore, if God so clothed the grass of the field, which today is, and tomorrow is cast into the oven, shall He not much more clothe you, O ye of little Faith?"* (Mat. 6:30).

Once again as is very obvious, the Lord says

NOTES

here, that if we spend all of our thought and attention on that aspect of our Christian experience, instead of it being a portrayal of great Faith, it shows that we don't have any Faith at all, which means that we're not really leaving it up to the Lord to meet our needs.

And finally, the Lord said, *"But seek ye first the Kingdom of God, and His Righteousness; and all these things shall be added unto you"* (Mat. 6:33).

The Lord is not denying our need for material things, but He plainly tells us here, that if we would seek His Kingdom first of all, He would then see to it that we are cared for as well. In fact, when a person comes to Christ, they literally enter into God's Economy, with its Promises given to us in these Passages and elsewhere.

The only ones who are going to get money, and a lot of it, in this *"money gospel,"* are the Preachers. The people are not going to get anything, because they are responding to an unscriptural message, which God cannot bless.

THE WORK OF THE HOLY SPIRIT

How any Preacher who claims to believe the Gospel, can at the same time claim that the Work of the Holy Spirit in our lives is to make us rich, and give us things, is beyond me. The work of the Spirit in our lives is to make us Christlike. He is there to develop Righteousness and Holiness within us, because the opposite of those things is the real problem of mankind. That and that alone is the business of the Spirit. He is in our hearts and lives to make us into the Image of the Heavenly.

Now at the same time, does God also bless in a material sense?

I think we have just given you Scriptures that plainly tells us that He does. He told us if we'll just trust Him, that He will do all these things which need to be done. So it's not the idea that God will not bless, or that He is not interested in our material welfare. In fact, the Lord is interested in every single thing we do; however, His greatest interest is that which is the most important, which is our spiritual welfare.

There is no way that one can define these so-called Ministries except as *"Ministries of covetousness."* That's a strong statement, but it is true! Even though the message is dressed up with Scriptures, Scriptures incidently which are twisted and perverted, such in no way justifies the action. Whatever the trappings, whatever the claims, these are *"Ministries of covetousness."* Any time that people are attracted to a Church or Ministry, with the idea in mind, that they're going to get rich, etc., that is a dead giveaway.

In fact, it has come to the place that the purveyors of this false message are pulling off all the covering, actually revealing it for what it is — a grab for money. And yet, the greed factor is so powerful in the hearts and lives of many so-called Christians, that when it becomes overly obvious as to actually what it really is, they still pour the results of their hard earned labor into this covetousness. What I'm about to say is strong, but it needs to be said:

Flesh appeals to flesh; therefore, covetousness appeals to covetousness! The interpretation of that is, that the covetousness in the Preacher appeals to the covetousness in the hearer. Ultimately, they will both fall in the ditch, because they are both *"blind!"*

A SPIRIT OF DARKNESS

There is an evil spirit of darkness behind all greed, behind all covetousness. It is not merely a matter of particular thoughts, or a feeling, or even a principle. It is far more than that. The reason these sins are so strong, that they have such a drawing power, is because spirits of darkness (evil spirits), are providing the impotence for this erroneous direction. That means that this money message was instituted by demon spirits, and demon spirits actually help these Preachers deliver the message, with demon spirits making the message attractive to the hearers, and demon spirits generating the response factor from the hearers.

I didn't say these individuals are demon possessed; however, I am saying that they are energized by demon spirits. If in fact it is covetousness, and it is, then it can be no other way.

God definitely blesses people who give to Him, i.e., *"His Work."* But He never responds to greed or to covetousness, as should be obvious!

I once referred to this as the *"prosperity message,"* however, that is really incorrect. It is moreso the *"greed message,"* or the *"covetousness message."* In fact, the True Gospel of Jesus Christ is really the prosperity Message, because it causes one to prosper in every capacity beginning with the most important, which is the spiritual. Again, that's what Jesus was speaking about when He said, *"Seek ye first the Kingdom of God. . . ."*

NOTES

## THE ULTIMATE WITNESS

The phrase, *"God is witness,"* means exactly what it says.

Any of us, and in fact, all of us, can claim whatever we desire; however, it is God Who is the witness, and His testimony or witness is impeccable, as should be obvious. This is the One to Whom we shall answer, not man, but God!

So, what we live, what we preach, what we believe, how we act, what we do, in fact, every single thing we are and hope to be, is all done before God. He alone is the witness, at least the One Who counts, and of that we should ever be cognizant.

Paul is appealing here to the highest authority of all, to God as his witness, that his motives were impeccable, that his desire was Scriptural, and his work that of the Holy Spirit. There was no flattery, covetousness, or seeking for personal glory, etc.

The question must be asked of all Preachers, *"Can you call God to witness that in preaching and in His service, you have had no end in view by your Ministry, but His Glory in the Salvation of souls and the spiritual upbuilding of the Saints?"*

The ministry was once referred to as *"a cure of souls"*; consequently, what actual care do you really have for the souls of them by whose labors you are, in general, more than sufficiently supported?

Is God witnessing that, in all these things, you have no cloak of covetousness? Happy is the man who can say so, and God help the man who cannot say so. Woe to that man who enters into this labor, or turns this labor into *"hire!"* He doesn't really know Christ, so how can he preach Him?

## THE POWER OF DECEPTION

When Preachers go into deception, or in fact, any Believer, this spirit, and a spirit it is, has so much power, that without the Holy Spirit helping, it's impossible for that individual to extricate themselves. In the first place, they don't even believe they are wrong. And second, Satan, as an angel of light, is constantly promoting the wrong way, but always dressing it up in such religious garb, that it looks right to the one deceived. So it takes a miracle, and I mean a literal miracle, to get such an individual out from under such direction. The facts are, that many of these people, if not most, actually believe what they are saying, and that is because the deception is so deep.

Understanding that, one must quickly ask the question as to how deception can be avoided?

Inasmuch as we're speaking here of the single most important thing there is, and I'm speaking of one's relationship with Christ, we should give due diligence to this of which we are saying.

The only manner in which the Believer can be protected from deception, which Satan is constantly attempting to promote, and using the Church to do so, is by the Believer having a heart that is constantly open to God, constantly seeking His Face in the sense of asking Him to keep us on the right road. We have to be aware that we can lose our way, that it is possible, and especially so if we do not correctly follow the Lord. However, if a proper hunger and thirst after Righteousness is present in the heart and life of the Believer, which means they will be constantly seeking after the Lord, thereby seeking only His will and not at all operating in the capacity of self-will, that Believer then need have no fear.

Paul plainly said, *"For ye have not received the spirit of bondage again to fear; but ye have received the Spirit of adoption, whereby we cry, Abba, Father"* (Rom. 8:15).

## THE CROSS IS THE SURE PLACE OF SAFETY

I am persuaded, that the real reason for deception, the real reason for Believers going astray, whether Preachers or otherwise, is that they have little knowledge of their true position in Christ, which speaks of the safety of the Cross.

What do we mean by that?

If one is trusting totally and completely in what Jesus has done at the Cross and in

His Resurrection, understanding that He did all of this for us, and that in the Mind of God, we were actually in Christ when He died, was buried, and Resurrected, one will then properly understand from where all the Blessings actually come.

In its entirety, the Cross was and is for sinners and, as well, for Believers. In other words, the sinner cannot be saved unless he believes in what Jesus did there, even though he may understand precious little at the outset. As well, Believers cannot enjoy Sanctification, meaning that they are overcomers regarding the world, the flesh, and the Devil, unless they understand their place and part in the Cross.

Most of the Church understands the part the Cross plays as it regards sinners coming to Christ, but they have little or no understanding whatsoever regarding the significance of the Cross for Believers. In fact, this is the great tragedy in the modern Church. We leave the Cross at the Salvation experience, and then proceed with the effort of trying to sanctify ourselves. In other words, most of the Church believes in Salvation by Faith, and then practice Sanctification by works, which Paul addressed very pointedly in his Epistle to the Galatians.

The Believer can no more sanctify himself, than the sinner can save himself. I'm not exaggerating when I say that; the Believer will have absolutely no more success in trying to sanctify himself, no matter how hard he tries, no matter how he loads up his efforts with Scriptures, than the sinner does in attempting to come to Salvation through the merit of good works. Either way presents a hopeless scenario. And yet that's where most Christians are.

## WHAT IS THE RESULT OF THE CROSSLESS CHRISTIAN LIFE?

Notice what I said! I said *"the Crossless Christian life,"* not the Crossless unsaved life. I'm speaking of the Believer who is attempting to live this Christian life, to have this more abundant life which Jesus promised, to be the overcomer he must be, outside of the parameters of the Finished Work of Christ. There is only one conclusion to that effort, no matter how hard one tries, no matter what direction one takes, and that conclusion is total failure.

NOTES

And that's where the modern Church for the most part, presently is!

Consequently, several things happen: Untold thousands just simply after a time of trying and failing, trying and failing, just give up and quit. In other words, they make no more effort to live for God. In fact, the shores of Christianity are littered with these Christian wrecks.

Others take the position that some were taking in Paul's day, that they tried and failed so much, that now they just simply take sin in stride, hoping that Grace covers it. Paul answered that with a *"God forbid!"* (Rom. 6:1-2).

Others put on a false front, claiming something that's not there, in other words shouting victory at the top of their lungs, while they are in reality living in failure. They don't really call it lying or think of themselves as lying or even hypocrisy. They've been taught that if they confess something long enough that it will ultimately come to pass, so they are loudly confessing their victory and their triumph, etc., when in reality, no such thing actually exists.

Others are running from one fad to the other, thinking that if they can get some type of spiritual experience, whatever it might be, that they will then find victory. In fact, even as we've already stated, the world is full of Christians at this particular moment doing just that.

Despite the fact, that some of these things are actually Scriptural, still, they actually become unscriptural when used in the wrong way; irrespective, there will be no help from any of these type of efforts, whatever they might be.

Anyone who's not functioning in the Finished Work of Christ, which speaks of the Cross of Christ and what He did there, which of course also includes His Resurrection and Exaltation (Rom. 6:2-6; 8:1-2; Eph. 2:6), cannot know true freedom in Christ. The Lord doesn't have several ways or even two ways, only one way, and that is the way of the Cross. If we fail to understand that, we will simply fail!

The only avenue of victory over the world and its allurements, over the flesh, which speaks of self-effort, over all the wiles of the Devil, is that we understand the following:

1. Every single thing we need as Believers, is found in totality in the Cross of Christ. He paid the sin debt there, atoned for all sin, all which destroyed Satan's legal right to dominate humanity. He then gave us Resurrection Life (Rom. 6:4-6).

2. Understanding that, my Faith in totality, must ever be in the Cross of Christ, understanding that it is there that all victory was won, and all victory is given. In other words, the Cross of Christ must ever be the object of my Faith, or else it is not Faith which God will recognize (Rom. 8:1-2; I Cor. 1:18; 2:2).

3. Once my Faith is properly placed, the Holy Spirit will then help me, and since He is God, there is nothing He cannot do (Gen. 1:1-2; Rom. 8:1-2).

The Holy Spirit works only as it regards the parameters of the Finished Work of Christ, and what does that mean?

THE PARAMETERS OF THE HOLY SPIRIT

*"Parameter"* in the Greek is *"metron,"* and means *"measure."* It refers to boundaries, which means there is something inside those boundaries, and something else entirely outside of the boundaries.

When Jesus died on the Cross, He carried out a particular work which benefits go to all who will believe Him. In fact, the only requirement is Faith, Faith in this which He has done.

What Jesus did was a legal work, and the Holy Spirit operates in the confines of that legal work. He will not go outside of those parameters, because it would be illegal to do so. That's the reason it is referred to as, *"the Law of the Spirit of Life in Christ Jesus."* It is the Holy Spirit giving Life, on the basis of what Jesus did at the Cross and in His Resurrection (Rom. 8:1-2).

Now the question may be asked as to exactly what benefits are inside these parameters, constituting the legal work of Christ?

To make it very brief so that all of us can understand, this great Finished Work of Christ provides everything the sinner needs to be saved, and the Christian needs to be victorious. And I mean everything!

If you need victory, it's there! If you need financial help, it's there! If you need the Fruit of the Spirit or the Gifts of the Spirit, it's all there!

NOTES

Due to what Jesus did there at the Cross, the Holy Spirit can now come to abide forever in the hearts and lives of all Believers, which He does at conversion. His abiding in us, and work in us, is then made possible by two things:

1. The Baptism with the Holy Spirit (Acts 2:4), which will always be accompanied by the speaking with other Tongues.

2. Our Faith in the Finished Work of Christ, which gives Him the latitude to do what He desires.

As we have repeatedly stated, He will not function outside of the Finished Work of Christ, which means if we go outside of those parameters, we are on our own. The results are not going to be pretty! To get everything we need, all we have to do is simply believe in what Jesus did there, understanding that this is the Source of all victory, and the Holy Spirit will see to it that this victory is ours (Acts 1:4, 8).

A PENTECOSTAL ERROR

I have just mentioned the Baptism with the Holy Spirit, with the evidence of speaking with other Tongues, which all Pentecostals believe, or certainly should! However, there's an error in our thinking, at least some, as it concerns the Baptism with the Spirit.

Many have been led to believe, that once they are Baptized with the Holy Spirit, that the Holy Spirit just automatically carries out all of these things in our lives, bringing about victory, etc. That is totally incorrect!

While the potential is definitely there, it is never automatic. Stop and think about this for a moment:

If victory was guaranteed and automatic merely as a result of one being Baptized with the Holy Spirit, then there would never be a single failure again in the heart and life of any Believer who has been Baptized with the Holy Spirit. However, we know that this is not the case. So what is the problem? Is the Baptism with the Holy Spirit as necessary then as we have been taught to believe?

Yes it is! But not in the fashion many of us have been taught.

As stated, the Baptism with the Holy Spirit definitely proclaims the potential for anything and everything which needs to be done in the

Believer's life; however, it is potential only, unless certain things are brought to bear.

In the first place, the Holy Spirit is not the One Who hung on that Cross and died for lost humanity and then rose from the dead, all on behalf of sinners and Saints. It was the Lord Jesus Christ Who did that. In fact, the Holy Spirit plainly tells us, that it is His business to *"glorify Christ"* (Jn. 16:13-14).

It is the business of the Holy Spirit to guarantee the Believer all the benefits which Jesus purchased by the offering up of Himself on the Cross. Those benefits are great, grand, glorious, and of such abundance, that actually they defy all description. However, the Truth is, that most Christians are little availing themselves of all that Christ has done (Acts 1:4, 8).

While we should definitely have Faith in the Holy Spirit to get these things done within our hearts and lives, still, as for the reason and the way they are done, our Faith must be properly in the Cross. If we have Faith in Him only, ignoring the Cross, the Holy Spirit will not respond to such Faith, because to do so, would be an insult to Christ, which the Holy Spirit will never honor.

Think about the following for a moment:

## A HYPOTHETICAL SITUATION

Let's say that John Doe is saved and Baptized with the Holy Spirit. He wants to live for God, in fact, he wants to be a good Christian.

Let's also say, that John has not been taught anything about the Cross of Christ, which refers to his correct position in Christ, which lack of knowledge opens him up to onslaughts by Satan, and which he is having trouble overcoming, whatever those onslaughts might be. In fact, it seems like the harder he tries, the worse the situation becomes.

He then goes to his Pastor, and somewhat divulges to him, most of the time without telling the whole story, that he's having problems, and doesn't quite understand how to overcome as he should.

The Pastor, who let's say is also a Godly Brother, listens to him patiently, as he has listened to many. He doesn't know the way of the Cross either, so he gives the Brother a stock answer.

NOTES

*"You must try harder!"* or *"You must pray harder!"* or *"You must increase your Faith!"*

All of that sounds good, and the Brother nods his head in the affirmative, but leaves puzzled and even more confused than ever. How can he try any harder than he's already trying? What is meant by *"praying harder"*? Also, how does he get more Faith?

The Truth is, the Brother has not been helped at all, because the advice given him, is not Scriptural.

He then hears about a particular Preacher whom God is using, and he feels in his heart that if he can just get there, and have this man lay hands on him, this will be his answer.

He goes to the meeting, gets in the prayer line, hands are laid on him, and the Spirit of God in some cases, comes down mightily, and he is *"slain in the Spirit,"* etc.

It has been a wonderful experience, and he finally gets up from the floor, knowing now that his problem is solved. However, a few days later, or even a few hours later, to his shocking dismay, he finds out that the problem is still there. Now he's more confused than ever.

He knows that the Lord touched him in that meeting, he has no doubt that it was the Holy Spirit, but why isn't he free from this difficulty which has plagued him for so long?

The scenario I have just devised is hypothetical, but yet it is true in millions of cases. Christians are trying, trying, ever harder, ever harder, in some particular way, but their situation doesn't grow better, but rather worse.

The Devil takes advantage of all of this, telling them anything he can get them to believe. Maybe they are Demon possessed! Maybe it's the Family Curse! Maybe all of it is just a big joke anyway!

Some wearily resign themselves to the struggle, and keep trying, but never succeeding. Many others, as we said sometime back, just simply quit. And that's where most of Christianity is presently.

## THE CHURCH AND THE CROSS

The Church in the latter half of the Twentieth Century, has drifted so far away from the Cross, that it little knows anymore where it has been, where it is, or where it's going! It's like a big ship that has no rudder, with its steering gone, but which doesn't really matter too much, because it doesn't even know where the harbor is anymore. So it drifts, and is at the mercy of rocks, reefs, and anything else that might be lurking around.

The Preachers don't know what to tell the people to do, so many of them have succumbed to the ways of the world. They simply recommend a Psychologist, for the worst cases, and muddle along with the rest! There isn't much victory in most Christian lives.

I don't want to leave the impression that no one is walking in victory, for some few actually are; however, if the Truth be known, that number is very small.

Why?

The Truth of the Cross is not presently known by most in the modern Church. If anyone asks if it is understood, most will shake their head in the affirmative, probably actually believing they really do know; however, they don't know!

If any Christian will read these Truths which the Lord has given unto us concerning the Cross, and which we have placed in our Commentaries, but really beginning with the Commentary on Galatians, and going forward, but also including Romans, they can be totally and completely free in the Lord. In fact, it will be like they are *"born again!"*

The Lord gave me these great Truths as a result of seeking His Face incessantly for over five years, and maybe for a lifetime. To be sure, He gave them to me for my benefit, but not for me alone, but for the entirety of the Body of Christ.

If you will understand the things we have said, and make the Cross the proper object of your Faith, the Holy Spirit will then do great and wonderful things for you. Your whole world will change! This *"more abundant life"* of which Jesus spoke (Jn. 10:10), will now be yours, and in a way that you never dreamed possible.

I'm going to say it exactly as Paul said it; this of which I say *"God is witness."*

NOTES

## FAITH

I've already stated several times, that the Believer's Faith must be in the Finished Work of Christ, understanding that this is from where all the Blessings come; however, we need to look at the very word *"Faith"* for a few moments.

There will be many people who will read these Commentaries, and the Spirit of God will bear witness with their spirit that what we're saying is right. They'll say in their minds, *"I'll try this!"*

However, that manner of approach, which many will do, and in fact, many do with God in many things, is really not Faith. It is really only experimentation, which God never really honors.

The Scripture plainly tells us that *"Faith is the substance of things hoped for, the evidence of things not seen"* (Heb. 11:1).

Four things are said here:

1. *"Substance,"*
2. *"Things hoped for,"*
3. *"Evidence,"*
4. *"Things not seen."*

Two and Four tell us that we do not yet have the things for which we are having Faith. One and three tell us we will have these things.

The two words *"substance"* and *"evidence,"* tell us that true Faith means that it is locked into that for which it believes. There is no turning back, no quitting, no stopping, no flagging, but only that which goes forward, only that which keeps believing.

This means that those who experiment really don't have Faith. Those who face difficulties and problems don't quit. Some erroneously think that proper Faith guarantees the absence of all problems. On the contrary, Satan will greatly test our Faith, of which we will speak more about momentarily. The idea is this:

You as a Believer, at least if you want to have the benefits of the great Finished Work of Christ, must believe this of which we say, i.e., *"actually, what the Bible says."* It's not a question of trying it, but rather of putting the entirety of your past, present, and future into the Cross of Christ.

A man hinted to me the other day that he wasn't so sure he wanted to do that. Here's the ironical thing about his statement!

When he accepted Christ as his Saviour, he put every single thing in his life, past, present, and future, into the Cross of Christ. He could not have been saved had he done otherwise. So, we are to continue to do that.

That means as stated, *"No turning back."* The idea of *"I'll try it, and if it works well and good, and if not, I'll try something else,"* is not Faith, and I can save you the trouble right now. Just forget what we are saying, because such experimentation will not bring any positive results.

You must reason in your mind, that live, die, sink, or swim, to use an earthly vernacular, you are going God's Way. In other words, you're putting all your eggs in this basket. This means that you won't stop when the difficulties come. You are committed! That's real Faith.

## THE TESTING OF FAITH

I've had many to say to me, *"I've put my Faith in the Cross of Christ, but the situation is no better,"* or words to that effect. In this case, one of two things are happening:

First of all, if they haven't really sold out all the way, it's really not Faith.

However, even if they really have placed their Faith in this of which we speak, and in totality, and are determined to not look back, Satan is going to try your Faith. And the Lord will allow him to do that.

What does that mean?

It means that just because you actually evidence true Faith, and it's in the right object of the Cross of Christ, that doesn't mean that all the battle is going to cease. Satan will still hinder. There might even be a failure or two along the way. If so, you are to ask the Lord's forgiveness (I Jn. 1:9), and keep your Faith right where it is, continuing to believe God.

Little by little, whether in the course of a month, or even a year, etc., you will find yourself getting stronger and stronger, with the attacks of Satan becoming less and less severe, with the ultimate destination guaranteed, that sin will no longer have dominion over you (Rom. 6:14). This is called *"the good fight of Faith"* (I Tim. 6:12). While it is a fight, it is a good fight, because victory is assured.

## WHAT THE LORD SPOKE TO MY HEART ABOUT FAITH

In addressing this problem, and seeking the Face of the Lord, He gave me this answer:

When the Christian begins to understand some things about the Cross, and His part in the Finished Work of Christ, and places his Faith in that great Work, he must first of all understand, that at this stage his Faith is very, very weak. In fact, not having had Faith in the Cross, and probably because of simply not knowing these great Truths, what little Faith he has had, is mostly that which helped him to come to Christ as it regards his initial Salvation. In fact, without continued Faith in the Cross, there's not much way that Faith can grow.

The Scripture plainly tells us that *"Faith cometh by hearing, and hearing by the Word of God"*; however, if we do not properly understand the Word of God as it relates to the Cross, and the Cross as it relates to the Word of God, we really cannot even properly understand the Word; consequently, the study of the Word in that capacity, although somewhat helpful, is not nearly what it can be, and in fact, will be, once one's Faith is properly placed.

So, the Believer who now learns and understands this great Truth of the Cross, as the Holy Spirit makes it real to his heart, has very little more at this stage than elementary Faith. Consequently, it is still full of flaws, of which Satan takes full advantage.

Even though that's not the only reason for Satan's attacks, it is definitely one of the greatest reasons. However, as we continue to believe the Lord, refusing to give up, refusing to allow our Faith to be moved from this Finished Work of Christ, we will sense our Faith getting stronger and stronger, and the failures less and less. As our Faith gets stronger, which it definitely will, and because it is now properly placed, we will find everything changing, and in a way we never thought possible.

This means that the fight we are encountering is the fight of Faith, but it is a good fight, because, as stated, victory is guaranteed. The Holy Spirit through the Apostle plainly said, *"Sin shall not have dominion over you"* (Rom. 6:14). If you keep believing, this is exactly what will happen, along with *"more abundant life,"* and the great *"rest,"* which Jesus gives (Jn. 10:10; Mat. 11:28-30). We're speaking here of the key to everything, and that's the reason that once a Christian has his Faith properly placed in the Cross, which gives the Holy Spirit great

NOTES

latitude in which to work, that things begin to happen fast — good things. This is the most glorious life there is, in fact, so glorious that it defies description, but only if we go God's Way. He has a Way, and that Way is the Cross, i.e., *"the Finished Work of Christ,"* i.e., *"The Atonement,"* i.e., *"His Vicarious Offering and Sacrifice."*

Going back to what we have originally said, once this stage is reached, which in fact will never cease to expand, the Lord will continue to allow Satan to attack in various different ways. He does this to keep us trusting Him, depending on Him, leaning on Him, and looking to Him. That's why He told us to *"deny ourselves, taking up the Cross daily in order to follow Him"* (Lk. 9:23). The Christian will be bothered with the flesh, the world, and the Devil until Jesus comes; however, we need not fear, if we stay in the Cross, continuing to believe God in this capacity, which the Holy Spirit intends. Just stay hidden in Christ, which presupposes the Cross and the Resurrection, and even the Exaltation, then victory is assured (Col. 3:3).

(6) "NOR OF MEN SOUGHT WE GLORY, NEITHER OF YOU, NOR YET OF OTHERS, WHEN WE MIGHT HAVE BEEN BURDENSOME, AS THE APOSTLES OF CHRIST."

The world of Paul's time was filled with wandering philosophers, prophets of other religions, magicians, false prophets, and others seeking not only financial gain, but also the prestige of a good reputation.

However, Paul and his associates did not fall into this category at all. Divine approval, not public esteem, was what motivated Paul and his companions, whether in Thessalonica or elsewhere.

## GLORY

The phrase, *"Nor of men sought we glory, neither of you, nor yet of others,"* refers to conduct designed to elicit or extract praise, honor, or expressions of esteem from men. The idea here is, that such is sought in order to gain something from people, whether control or money.

Self-promotion, self-gain, self-glory — how subtle are these temptations in the life of the Christian who is fired with ambition to achieve for Christ and His Kingdom! The *"pure in heart"* may, however, be conscious of purity of motives, as Paul attests.

NOTES

The idea is, that no man will profess himself covetous, but of course, God knows the heart. In this, however, we can see the sign of covetousness.

If the Preacher, or anyone for that matter, seeks glory from other men, in other words, if things are done to draw attention away from Christ to self, that is a sure sign of covetousness. The individual, will attempt to put on a cloak of *"glory,"* thinking this hides the real intent. While such may do so from the carnal mind, it definitely does not do so from the spiritual heart.

## FLESH AND SPIRIT — CARNALITY AND SPIRITUALITY

Flesh attracts flesh, while the Holy Spirit attracts the Holy Spirit. Carnality attracts carnality, while spirituality attracts spirituality.

What do we mean by that?

We have already addressed this, but due to its vast significance, please allow me to make a few more observations.

When the spiritual heart observes the Preacher who is obviously operating in *"the flesh,"* or *"carnality,"* one might say, but still draws great crowds, etc., one might wonder as to how that Christians could be deceived by such?

Such Christians, who incidently are always in the majority, have very little spirituality. In other words, there is very little spiritual depth in their heart. They function almost altogether according to *"the flesh,"* with very little of the Holy Spirit. As well, these individuals, are so weak in the Lord, that they are on the verge of spiritual death.

Nevertheless, when they observe a Preacher who is operating in the flesh, which speaks of self-glory, etc., the flesh or carnality in them, will respond favorably to the carnality in the Preacher. They will mistake it for spirituality, when it is no such thing. As a result, they will not be spiritually helped, in fact, this added push toward greater carnality, could even cause them to lose their way altogether.

Along with the *"flesh,"* being attracted to the *"flesh,"* it also at the same time, rebuffs true spirituality. In other words, like a baby selecting a little toy rattle in preference to a hundred dollar bill which is before it, the worldly Christian will do the same.

In fact, a worldly Christian, and I speak of one who is operating primarily in the flesh, which as stated characterizes most, will fight out against the true moving of the Holy Spirit, sometimes even more than the unsaved. That's the reason that spiritual declension is so dangerous. It carries with it its own seed of destruction, as should be obvious.

Is there hope for these carnal Christians?

Of course there is hope, and when shown the true moving and operation of the Holy Spirit, some will turn. But the Truth is, not many!

One need only look at the Ministry of Christ, which of course, far eclipsed any other Ministry that has ever been and ever will be. And yet, despite all the miracles of healings and His great Words of Life, which as stated, were so absolutely overwhelmingly of the Spirit of God that it defies description, still, the crowds were thin at the conclusion of the Master's Ministry, and that despite the fact that almost all of Israel concluded herself to be close to God.

## IN SUMMARY

In conclusion, the Believer must be very careful as it regards following Preachers. While it is certainly true that all Christians follow Preachers in some manner or the other, and which is intended by the Holy Spirit. He has given these particular Ministers to the Church for edification and Spiritual Growth (Eph. 4:11-12). However, if the Believer observes the Preacher attempting to draw attention to self, in other words, to glorify self in some manner instead of Christ, the Believer should think again, and be very careful as to what is to be received and accepted.

The Holy Spirit here through Paul attests to the fact that self-glory is never permissible in any fashion or form. Such is reserved only for Christ. No man is worthy of any glory whatsoever. All men are weak and frail, and if by chance, they do have Gifts from God, it is never through any merit of their own, but always because of the Grace of God. Paul dealt with this very succinctly in I Corinthians Chapter 1.

NOTES

It was Jesus Who died upon that Cross, purchasing Redemption for mankind, and no one else. He Alone deserves all Praise, Glory, and accolades. And the Truth is, the more that a person knows themselves, the more they will know that they deserve nothing that is good. As well, the more that one knows Christ, the more they will know and realize that Christ Alone deserves the glory.

## BURDENSOME

The phrase, *"When we might have been burdensome, as the Apostles of Christ,"* refers to the fact that as Apostles, they might have demanded certain things, as one Expositor said, *"We might have made our weight felt,"* but Paul never did such a thing. Just because he was an Apostle of Christ, which in effect, constitutes the highest calling and position on the face of the Earth, still, he made no demands on anyone, sought no privileges, asked for no ease of burden, in effect, sought nothing in return. The greater the calling, the greater such humility must characterize the man or woman of God.

## MODERN APOSTLES?

In many of the Charismatic Churches, as well as some Pentecostal Churches, the Preacher too often is looked at as some type of demigod. Someone is always there to carry his coat, to open the door for him, to carry his briefcase, etc., because of course, he is too high and mighty, too important, to do such mundane things.

If I sound as though I am sarcastic, that is exactly the way I am attempting to sound. Such individuals are not Apostles, they are in fact, much of nothing, at least as far as God is concerned. Consequently, any time one observes such, one can be dead certain that one is not observing the Spirit of God, but rather *"the flesh,"* and it is screaming so loud that it deafens all who are truly Spiritual. The idea of such, is repulsive to the true man of God. It is repulsive to the Holy Spirit as well, and of that, one can be certain!

This is not to mean, that Preachers are not to be loved, respected, and appreciated. In fact, all true Christians will give *"honor to whom honor is due"*; however, such honor will never be in the spirit of *"fawning!"* And as an aside, the true man of God will carry his own coat and open his own doors, etc.

A LESSON!

I am attempting to relate the following by memory, having read it some years ago. I trust that what I relate will be at least somewhat close to what actually happened.

At one of the major Universities, either Harvard or Yale, etc., some four United States Court Justices were to appear at one time, for some type of symposium. Of course, as the Reader knows, the Supreme Court of the United States, is the highest Court of Appeal in the land.

When the symposium was over, for some reason, the transportation which was supposed to convey the Justices to the Airport, was not there. In fact, there was no vehicle present except that of a young man, and it was no more than an old rattletrap of a car.

Due to the fact that they had no time to spare, the young man was asked by the Master of Ceremonies if he could convey the Justices to their destination? Of course, he immediately conceded, and at the same time apologizing for his car.

The four Justices (if I remember the number correctly), piled into the old vehicle, with the young man proceeding toward their destination.

A few minutes later, to his embarrassment, the car had a flat. All four Justices got out of the car, each one pulling off his coat, rolling up his sleeves, proceeding to help the young man change the tire, etc.

Inasmuch as they were still on the University grounds, and it was past curfew, one of the security policeman saw the stopped car and the people around it, and went to investigate.

He immediately asked as to who owned the car, and why they were out that late?

The young man spoke up allowing that the car was his, and that the men with him were Supreme Court Justices of the United States, and he was taking them to the Airport. He pointed to the flat tire, and related as to how they were putting on the spare.

The security guard glanced at the old rattletrap of a car, and at the men, and quickly retorted, *"Yeah, and my Mother is the Queen of England."*

NOTES

The four Justices standing there with their sleeves rolled up, and hands dirty, having been trying to change the tire, one by one began to introduce themselves.

The guard shined the light in their faces, and then quickly realized that they actually were who the boy said they were.

Of course, his embarrassment was rather acute, but the point I want to make is this:

I wonder if some Preachers are so lifted up within themselves, that they wouldn't think of dirtying their hands as these Supreme Court Justices did!

In fact, I'm afraid that it is the case with some, and what a shame!

Humility and unpretentiousness should characterize the man and woman of God, and I wonder if all of us who refer to ourselves as such, should not look at ourselves and our situation again.

(7) "BUT WE WERE GENTLE AMONG YOU, EVEN AS A NURSE CHERISHETH HER CHILDREN:"

The important position of Paul and his colleagues as Christ's representatives earned for them the right to receive special respect, but they did not stand on this right. So this is further evidence that they were not prompted at all by lower motives.

While intermingling with these Macedonians as equals, Paul and his helpers were gentle, not authoritarian. They put aside their rights of being respected and playing a dominating part and demonstrated the utmost tenderness, comparable to that of a mother nursing her own children.

The figure as used here by Paul, implies a special effort to protect and to provide for every need, even to the extent of great sacrifice. In other words, Paul and those with him, were the very opposite of being burdensome.

GENTLE

The phrase, *"But we were gentle among you,"* presents remarkable words, especially considering that they come from one once known as Saul of Tarsus, the harsh and implacable persecutor. Only from his Lord could he have received and learned this gentleness as a *"new creature,"* indeed, *"in Christ"* (II Cor. 5:17).

Consequently, the line is drawn here between the charlatan, licentious, sophistical, fawning, greedy, vainglorious teachers, to whom Greeks were well accustomed, and the Apostles, presenting that which was the total opposite. What an example! And again, how the Thessalonians must have noticed the great difference.

Instead of selfishness there is love, and nothing but love. We are all familiar with the great Passage in the Epistle to the Philippians where the Apostle depicts the mind which was in Christ Jesus.

The contrast in that Passage between the disposition which grasps at eminence and that which makes itself of no reputation, is reproduced here.

Paul had learned of Christ; and instead of seeking in his Apostolic work opportunities for self-exaltation, he shrank from no service which was not imposed by love.

Paul does not indulge in boasting but on compulsion; he would never have sought to justify himself, unless he had first been accused. And now, over against this picture, drawn by his enemies, we can see the true likeness which is held up before God and man.

## A NURSE

The phrase, *"Even as a nurse cherisheth her children,"* refers to a mother feeding her children.

The high standard of pastoral care is exemplified here.

The idea is, that Paul and those with him, did not in any way do anything, that could cause these new converts to stumble. They watched over them, guarded them, even protected them, even like a mother nursing and protecting an infant baby.

This is the very opposite of using people, as should be obvious. In fact, the Apostle and his associates, were in fact, used themselves. In other words, instead of asking from these converts, they gave of themselves, and unreservedly, even sacrificially.

This is the true Christlike attitude, the true Christlike Spirit! It is a far cry from the pridefully bloated, vainglorious, egotistical, pompous stuffed shirt, which characterizes far too often, some parts of the Ministry.

NOTES

## SERVANTS

Over and over again, Jesus taught the servant principle to His Disciples. He said, *"Whosoever will be chief among you, let him be your servant:*

*"Even as the Son of Man came not to be ministered unto, but to minister, and to give His life a ransom for many"* (Mat. 20:27-28).

Even at the Last Supper, the Scripture says, *"And there was also strife among them* (the Disciples), *which of them should be accounted the greatest"* (Lk. 22:24).

He was able to cure this in them only by the foot washing example (Jn. 13:4-17).

This, the foot washing example, which typifies the servant mentality, is what Paul had and what we must have, whether Preachers or the laity, but especially, Preachers.

(8) "SO BEING AFFECTIONATELY DESIROUS OF YOU, WE WERE WILLING TO HAVE IMPARTED UNTO YOU, NOT THE GOSPEL OF GOD ONLY, BUT ALSO OUR OWN SOULS, BECAUSE YE WERE DEAR UNTO US."

This Scripture teaches us, that sharing the Gospel of God means sharing our lives as well.

This means that even a stronger relationship of love developed as their Ministry continued — a relationship like that of a nursing mother with her child.

## LOVE

The phrase, *"So being affectionately desirous of you,"* refers to *"having a longing after, or a strong affection for."* The sense here is, that Paul was so strongly attached to these Thessalonians, that he would have been willing to lay down his life for them. In fact, *"being affectionately desirous"* is a single Greek word found only here in the New Testament.

Paul had been accused of seeking gain and glory when he came among them; but his sole desire had been not to get but to give.

## WORDS USED BY PAUL

It has been suggested by some Greek Scholars, that the Greek word used by Paul and translated *"being affectionately desirous,"* was in fact, coined by him. Actually, at times, Paul did coin words.

But we may be sure, these same Scholars say, that whenever this is done, the word is always formed fairly, according to the general rules of the Greek language, which Paul religiously observed.

In other words, the Holy Spirit helped him to form this word, whatever the word might have been, and which no Greek Scholar of his day would have refuted. The idea is, we can be doubly certain of the text that it is correct and right.

OUR VERY LIVES

The phrase, *"We were willing to have imparted unto you, not the Gospel of God only, but also our own souls* (lives)," tells us two great things:

1. The mere fact of being able to share the Gospel with others, is a tremendous privilege; however, with that privilege comes at times, great opposition. Satan is not at all happy with the Gospel of God, as would be obvious, and, therefore, the Satanic nature in unredeemed men, rises up at times against those who bring this great and wonderful *"good news."*

While we know it to be *"good news,"* it is impossible for the unredeemed to see such, at least at the outset, considering that they are *"spiritually dead."*

So, Paul is in effect saying, that to bring you the *"Gospel of God,"* requires a commitment on our part, to subject ourselves to whatever dangers might be imposed.

2. If one properly shares and offers the Gospel of God, they will at the same time, have to give of themselves. In other words, we must be willing to lay our lives on the line at all times. As well, we must be willing to live a selfless life, which means that others come first.

Airhart says, *"Is it possible, after all, to really share the Gospel of the Love of God without at the same time giving one's own self also?"* This heart-and-soul involvement is costly; but is there an easier way? No, there isn't!

All of this refers to the fact that Paul kept back from the Thessalonians nothing of the whole purpose of God; he kept back no part of himself. His daily toil, his toil by night, his prayers, his preaching, his spiritual ardor, his very soul, were theirs. They knew his labor and travail; they were witnesses, and God also, how holy and righteously and unblamably he had behaved toward them.

NOTES

DEAR UNTO US

The phrase, *"Because ye were dear unto us,"* is literally in the Greek, *"Because you became beloved ones to us."* In other words, the Apostle had the God kind of love (agape), for these Thessalonians.

The very Greek word *"agape,"* which means *"the God kind of love,"* refers to a self-giving love. In other words, its very nature is self-giving, with the example being that of God Who so loved the world, that He gave His only begotten Son, that whosoever believeth in Him, should not perish, but have everlasting life (Jn. 3:16).

This love comes only from God, which means it's love that the world does not have, does not understand, and in fact, cannot have, without coming to the Lord. The idea is also, that every Believer, who in fact does have this love, at the same time, show this love to all others.

As we have stated, but allow us to emphasize, this love is always self-giving love, which means to pour out to others, and not at all means to take unto ourselves. If it's not self-giving love, then it's not agape love.

WHAT DOES SELF-GIVING EXACTLY MEAN?

The only way that one could come to a proper definition, is to observe Christ. He Alone is the perfect example, although Paul might be in turn the best example of Christ.

First of all let's see what this agape love actually isn't, instead of what it actually is.

If we are to notice Christ, while He was always kind toward his enemies, who seemed to be in abundant supply, He at the same time, was firm with them. He always defended the Gospel to the utmost. He would not allow accusations or erroneous interpretations to go unchallenged. And to be sure, His challenge always silenced the critics.

So let not one think, that if the Preacher of the Gospel, or any Christian for that matter, stands up boldly for the Gospel, that he is not evidencing love. In fact, that type of position is definitely the Love of God.

The Medical Doctor cannot stand by silent, when he knows that medicine is being given which will not only not help the patient, but will actually hurt the patient, and in fact could kill the patient. Is he not evidencing love when he steps in and demands that the right thing be given? I think the answer to that is obvious.

On the other hand, Christ dealt with all individuals alike, when it came to healing, help, Salvation, etc. The beggar was treated exactly as the Nobleman. No favoritism was shown, with love being extended to all.

How perfect His life was; how much of an example He set for the entirety of the world. He was the True Man, and as such, is to be the example of all mankind. That's why Paul bluntly said, *"That I may know Him"* (Phil. 3:10).

(9) "FOR YE REMEMBER, BRETHREN, OUR LABOUR AND TRAVAIL: FOR LABOURING NIGHT AND DAY, BECAUSE WE WOULD NOT BE CHARGEABLE UNTO ANY OF YOU, WE PREACHED UNTO YOU THE GOSPEL OF GOD."

Paul's work was probably tent-making (Acts 18:3), or tent repairing, though it may have been the production of tent material from animal hair or skins. Part of a Jewish child's upbringing was learning a trade, and Paul was no exception to this.

He received some financial help from the Philippian Church while he was in Thessalonica (Phil. 4:15-16), but it seems not enough to permit him to stop working.

## LABOR AND TRAVAIL

The phrase, *"For you remember, Brethren, our labor and travail,"* refers to his self-sacrificing as it concerns the Gospel.

The narrative in the Acts, if very strictly pressed, might lead us to suppose that Paul had only spent at Thessalonica about 27 days at the utmost, or perhaps only 21 or 22 (Acts 17:1-2, 10).

The narrative in Acts, however, does not absolutely demand such narrow limits of time. And two circumstances seem to require its extension — the conversion of many idolaters (I Thess. 1:9), and his own express statement, that he remained long enough in Thessalonica to receive assistance, *"once and again"* from Philippi (Phil. 4:16). Paul probably stayed several months in Thessalonica.

*"Labor"* indicates the kind of work; it was wearisome toil or costly exertion.

*"Travail"* either indicated the hardship, difficulty, and intensity of the work, or else it speaks of the spiritual travail in prayer, which is probably the case.

## THE POLICY OF THE APOSTLE

The phrase, *"For laboring night and day, because we would not be chargeable unto any of you,"* probably refers to a mixture of preaching the Gospel and the repairing of tents, etc.

It seems that Paul ministered only three Sabbaths in the Synagogue in Thessalonica, before having to seek other quarters for preaching (Acts 17:1-5). That may have been the house of Jason. Luke is not specific at all in writing the account in Acts, but the manner in which he worded his statements, does not preclude the possibility of Paul ministering from that house for several weeks or even elsewhere for that matter. As well, there is a good possibility, that if in fact he did stay several weeks or even months in the city, that he ministered in other houses at night, or even at times during the day. The manner in which Luke words his account, lets us know that quite a few people had accepted the Lord, even some of higher position. So, it is doubtless correct that houses were opened to him for Ministry.

Irrespective, the point I desire to make is, that the Apostle it seems, labored every available hour he could as it regarded his menial job of making a little money to support himself, and then constantly preaching and teaching as well. This seemed to have been his policy in many places in establishing Churches.

## WHY DID THE APOSTLE ADOPT THIS POLICY?

First of all, I'm sure he prayed about this thing much, and was impressed by the Lord to conduct himself accordingly. We do know, that he was not at all adverse to receiving offerings from the people, even making heavy appeals, as II Corinthians Chapters 8 and 9 record; however, this was for other situations and not at all for himself.

NOTES

When he went into a new city to plant a Church, while he deeply appreciated and even solicited help from other Churches he had founded, he little sought any sustenance at all from the local effort. All of his reasons we do not know; however, perhaps the following will shed some light on the subject.

In all of these cities of the Roman Empire, there were temples to many and varied gods. The Priests in these heathen temples, sought every means to extract money from the devotees to the particular god or gods. In fact, the people were drained in every conceivable way possible, with every effort being made to extract funds.

Paul no doubt, wanted to show new converts in each of these areas, that his purpose was not money, and that the Gospel was not for sale. Consequently, to keep down any talk or gossip, and to show the utter difference between Christianity and heathenism, the Apostle would make no demands whatsoever on the people regarding money, in order to set a proper example. To keep down talk, and to show the people that his intent was not at all mercenary, he would labor *"night and day,"* to support himself, in order to better lift up Christ.

He was not at all opposed to receiving funds for himself from established Churches, which is obvious; however, regarding the initial planting of Churches, he took great pains to use much wisdom to keep down potential gossip.

And then again, in establishing these Churches, Paul had to deal with every type of problem that one could begin to imagine. I speak of problems in the lives of these new converts. In this, he wanted to be free to deal with each and every problem as he Scripturally saw fit, and not be pressured by someone who had perhaps given him sums of money, etc. While it was different with mature Christians, it was something else altogether with those who had just come to Christ. As is obvious, and even as he said, he was *"gentle among them, even as a nurse cherisheth her children"* (vs. 7).

NOTES

### THE GOSPEL OF GOD

The phrase, *"We preached unto you the Gospel of God,"* seems to lend much credence to the last thought suggested. The Apostle must be free to expound the Gospel exactly as he saw fit, and not be swayed one way or the other by *"gifts,"* etc.

There is absolutely nothing more important than the Gospel of Jesus Christ. It is the only answer for suffering souls, for hurting hearts, and in fact, for anyone. One can be assured that what Paul preached to the people, was the pure, undiluted, uncompromised Gospel. It must be this way, if people are to receive from God what they should receive.

The word *"Gospel"* means *"good news"*; however, it is good news only as it is presented undiluted. If compromised at all, which it is, sadly and regrettably in most cases, it ceases to be *"good news."*

In brief, the Gospel can be summed up as follows:

1. Salvation by Faith: This refers to the fact that Jesus died on the Cross in order to pay the sin debt and in fact, to atone for all sin. He suffered the penalty of the broken Law (God's Law), which was death, even though He had never sinned. In other words, He did all of this on our behalf. When He atoned for all sin, this destroyed Satan's legal right to place humanity in bondage, for sin provided that right. With sin gone, he has no more rights. Of course, this applies only to those who believe Christ (Jn. 3:16).

When the sinner evidences simple Faith in this which Christ has done, he instantly receives Salvation. He doesn't have to work for this Salvation, or try to earn it in any way, just simply *"believe."* Actually, if he attempts to earn Salvation in any manner, even as much of the world does, such efforts totally and completely nullify Salvation in any and all degrees. As stated, it is all by Faith, and that refers to having Faith in what Jesus did at the Cross.

2. After the believing sinner comes to Christ, he then should be Baptized with the Holy Spirit, which in fact, cannot take place until one has first been saved (Acts 19:1-7). As well, all recipients of this Spirit Baptism, will without exception speak with other Tongues, as the Spirit of God gives the utterance (Acts 2:4; 10:46; 19:1-7; I Cor. 14:18, 21-22).

In fact, the Baptism with the Holy Spirit is so necessary as it regards a full Christian life, and the development of Christlikeness, that without this experience, I think these tremendous qualities are not possible. In other words, without the Baptism with the Holy Spirit, there can be precious little true Christian growth.

3. Divine Healing according to Faith in Christ, is a definite part of the Gospel of Jesus Christ. This means that Jesus Christ, is not only the Saviour, and the Baptizer with the Holy Spirit (Mat. 3:11), but as well, He is our Healer. In fact, He is everything to the Child of God.

4. The Gospel also includes provision for our material needs. In other words, Jesus Christ is the great Provider. As we believe Him for spiritual things, we should also believe Him for material things. God has promised to *"supply all your need according to His riches in Glory by Christ Jesus"* (Phil. 4:19).

That didn't say part of our needs, but *"all our needs."*

Some Preachers argue over what is included in the Atonement. Some claim Divine Healing is not in the Atonement, with many claiming that financial prosperity is not in the Atonement.

To be sure, every single thing that man lost in the Fall, was addressed in the Atonement, which refers to what Jesus did at the Cross and His Resurrection. That means everything from *"A"* to *"Z."*

While it is true that we do not yet have all the benefits of the Atonement, which will not come in totality until the Resurrection of Life; still, the benefits we presently have, are in fact so over abundant, that every single need of the Child of God can be met, whether it be spiritual, physical, or financial. The Christian has only to believe, understanding that all of these great benefits come from the Cross of Christ, which always must be the object of our Faith.

It is regrettable, but the greatest problem in the modern Church, is *"Believers who won't believe!"* The Scripture plainly says:

*"But without Faith it is impossible to please Him* (to please God)*: for he that cometh to God must believe that He is, and that He is a rewarder of them who diligently seek Him"* (Heb. 11:6).

NOTES

## A PERSONAL EXPERIENCE

Years ago, when we began to conduct citywide Crusades in major cities of the world, and I speak mostly of Third World countries, the Lord told me to *"preach Jesus"* to these multitudes. I was to preach Jesus as the Saviour, as the Baptizer with the Holy Spirit, as the Healer, and as the Provider.

In other words, I was to tell the people that they must not look to man for help, because precious little will be forthcoming from that sector. They are to look to Christ, Who supplieth our every need.

In obeying the Lord in this regard, time and time again, as we would bear down on this particular Message, exactly as the Lord told me to do, I would sense a swell of Faith rising up in the tens upon tens of thousands of people who had gathered for Service. It was easy to sense that what was being said was right. The Lord is our Provider, our Sustainer, and every single thing we need, excluding nothing, is found in totality, in Jesus Christ. He is our sufficiency, and above even that, He is our all sufficiency.

That means that the Believer does not have to look to the world for anything as it regards soul satisfaction. The Lord has it all, and in fact, the world has nothing at all, at least in this regard.

While Satan is a master at dressing up his lies, making them seem to be something desired, the Truth is, he has nothing that the soul of man needs.

In fact, God is a *"Blesser,"* meaning, that He longs to bless His people, longs to make Himself real to us, longs to open up the windows of Heaven on our behalf. All of this was bought and paid for by what Jesus did at the Cross. We are to never forget that, relying on this great Finished Work for all our needs.

I am saved because of what He did at the Cross; I am baptized with the Holy Spirit solely because of what He did at the Cross; I have been healed several times, even gloriously, because of what he did at the Cross; I have been blessed financially over and over again, because of what He did at the Cross; I have the Peace of God, solely because of what He did at the Cross; I am Sanctified, simply because of what he did at the Cross; I have all the Fruit of the Spirit, because of what He did at the Cross; I have Gifts of the Spirit, because of what He did at the Cross; I have leading and guidance by the Holy Spirit, because of what He did at the Cross! In fact, I could go on in this vein page after page, with all that is provided, made possible by what Jesus did at the Cross. We must never forget that; never lay that aside; never ignore that; never move our Faith from that.

In fact, the word *"Gospel"* and *"Cross"* are synonymous!

(10) "YE ARE WITNESSES, AND GOD ALSO, HOW HOLILY AND JUSTLY AND UNBLAMEABLY WE BEHAVED OURSELVES AMONG YOU THAT BELIEVE:"

The Apostle appeals to the Thessalonians as witnesses as to their conduct.

Evidently, as we have already stated, some, no doubt the Jews, were making all type of accusations against the Apostle. When one lies, one can tell anything. And regrettably, lies are often believed, which is the intent of the Evil One to begin with.

In fact, there is no defense against a lie. One can only allude to that which is obvious, even as Paul is doing here. But as far as an ironclad defense is concerned, such is almost impossible!

The following should be read very closely and adhered to by all means:

1. When a Christian hears gossip about a fellow Christian, they must treat it exactly as that, which means to place no confidence whatsoever in that which is being told. The Believer must ever remember, that Satan is the great accuser of the Brethren; and, regrettably, he oftentimes uses Christians to peddle his accusations, of which some, regrettably do an excellent job.

2. Even if we think we have firsthand knowledge regarding the situation, whatever the situation might be, we must remember at the same time, that we have little knowledge at all as to the spiritual warfare involved. Reckoning that, there should be no accusation or judgment which should fall from our lips.

3. If we were placed in the same situation as the individual in question, would we have done any better, or even as well? We should ask ourselves that question, and in fact, do so over and over again.

WITNESSES

The phrase, *"Ye are witnesses, and God also,"* presents the fact that it is important

NOTES

that conduct should appear right in the eyes of men; however, only God's Judgment is infallible.

Only one who is totally conscious of his own integrity could make this type of statement, and rightly so! No hypocrite, or none who did the work of the Lord carelessly, could make such an appeal both to God and man.

Looked at as a whole this Passage warns us against slander. it probably could be said, that it is a given that slander will be spoken and believed; but woe to the man or woman by whom it is either believed or spoken! None are good enough to escape it.

Christ was slandered; they called Him a glutton and a drunkard, and said He was in league with the Devil.

Paul was slandered; they said he was a very smart man, who looked well to his own interest, and made dupes of simple people. The deliberate wickedness of such falsehoods is diabolical, but it is not so very rare. Numbers of people who would not invent such stories are glad to hear them. They are not very particular whether they are true or false. To sympathize with such, is to have the spirit of the Devil, and not of Christ.

The Believer should never give utterance to a suspicious thought. One should never repeat what would discredit a man, if you have only heard it and are not sure it is true; even if you are sure of its truth, be afraid of yourself if it gives you any pleasure to think of it. Love thinketh no evil; love rejoiceth not in iniquity (MacLaren).

SLANDER

Slander in fact, is one of, if not Satan's greatest weapon against the Child of God.

Slander is the utterance of false charges or misrepresentations which defame and damage another's reputation. Even if something is true, it is almost certain, that a part of what is being heard is not true. The point I'm making is this:

Even as we have stated, this is something that Satan will definitely continue; however, for a Believer to be a part of this evil scheme, to join in with Satan, to peddle his wares, is wicked beyond compare.

One can certainly understand the world repeating anything and everything, but when

NOTES

it comes to a Child of God doing such, it is unthinkable! And yet, Christians seem to be worse about this even than the world.

To do so, enters into Satan's efforts to steal, kill, and to destroy. It makes the peddler of such, in far worse spiritual condition, than the one he is accusing.

That's the reason I warn Christians to not be a party to the efforts by the Media to destroy those in the Ministry, even if what they are saying contains some Truth! In fact, I think it is impossible for a Believer to watch such over Television, or to read such in a book or publication, without being adversely affected in a great way. In other words, this spirit of darkness, which is a spirit of destruction, gets down into one's spirit, and is almost impossible to dislodge. That's the reason we are told to avoid the very *"appearance of evil"* (I Thess. 5:22).

## HOW WOULD YOU FEEL?

To have the most evil things told about you by those who claim to be Christians, and things incidently which are not true, and then to have other Christians to believe them, is an extremely hurtful situation. How would you feel if such happened to you? In fact, I'm certain that it has to some of you.

Some Christians seem to take the position that if a fellow Christian has in fact, done something wrong, that this gives them the license to do or say about anything negative they so desire. Nothing could be further from the Truth! Please allow me to say it again:

Even if we do know something that is true about a fellow Christian which is very debilitating, still, we only know in part. In other words, part of what we know, or think we know, is untrue. A little common sense should tell one that.

Let the Reader look at the following very carefully:

It really doesn't matter who it is as it regards such situations; however, if we're talking about a man or woman of God, then it becomes even more serious. So what am I saying?

If we as Christians lend a voice of gossip as it regards slander against a man or woman of God, in other words, one who is truly called of God, irrespective as to whether what is said is true or not, we have just placed ourselves on very dangerous ground.

The Lord has said two things about this, and we should heed them very carefully:

1. First of all, He said, *"Touch not Mine Anointed, and do My Prophets no harm"* (I Chron. 16:22).

He meant that then, and He means it now!

Concerning that, it is said, *"He suffered no man to do them wrong: yea, He reproved kings for their sakes"* (I Chron. 16:21).

Jesus said, *"And whosoever shall give to drink unto one of these little ones a cup of cold water only in the name of a Disciple, verily I say unto you, he shall in no wise lose his reward"* (Mat. 10:42).

If in fact such a reward will be given for such a small gift, doesn't it make sense, that judgment will also come if harm is attempted?

2. Jesus also said, and plainly, *"Judge not, that ye be not judged."*

He then said, *"For with what judgment ye judge, ye shall be judged: and with what measure ye mete, it shall be measured to you again."*

And finally He said, *"And why beholdest thou the mote that is in thy Brother's eye, but considerest not the beam that is in thine own eye?"* (Mat. 7:1-3).

One should be assured that Jesus meant exactly what He said; and if we believe that, and we certainly had better, it should give us pause before helping Satan with his accusations.

Whenever the Jews in Thessalonica began to slander Paul and those with him, and then some Christians started to believe what they were hearing, making necessary Paul defending himself accordingly, what do you think the Holy Spirit thought?

Inasmuch as these were new converts one might say, I'm sure the Holy Spirit had great patience with them; however, where does that leave those who are supposed to be mature in the Lord, who believe such things?

## HOLY, JUST, AND UNBLAMEABLE

The phrase, *"How holily and justly and unblameably we behaved ourselves among you that believe,"* concerns the lifestyle of the Apostle, plus Silas and Timothy, and anyone else who may have been laboring with him.

There are several Greek words which are translated *"holy."* It has been suggested that the word used here (hosios) indicates reverence for and pious obedience to moral obligations as everlasting Ordinances, and as coming from God.

*"Justly"* in the Greek is *"dikaios,"* and means *"one who comes up to a specific standard of Righteousness."*

*"Unblameably,"* in the Greek is *"amemptos,"* and means *"one who is walking in all the Light he has been given and in that regard, is without reproach."*

Paul's situation here is somewhat different than it would be with most Preachers presently. The only Gospel these Thessalonians had ever known was that preached by Paul. As well, he was the only Preacher of the Gospel they had ever known. Consequently, if they perchance believed the accusations against him, they would in fact, turn their back on the entirety of the Gospel altogether.

Most presently, if they don't like a particular Preacher and for whatever reason, simply go to another Church. What they are doing may be right or wrong; nevertheless, they do have another recourse, at least after a fashion.

But in Paul's day, if they didn't hear him, or rather refuse to hear him, there was no one else to turn to, so the loss of everything was definitely possible.

And yet, the seed of that is applicable even now, despite the fact that there are Preachers galore. If in fact, a Christian believes something about a Godly Preacher which is not true, or else if they misread something which is actually true, consequently, turning away, they do so to their detriment. In fact, it is impossible to be otherwise.

The Truth is, there aren't many God called, anointed Preachers. In fact, they are few and far between, and as someone said, as scarce as the proverbial hen's teeth. If in fact, you the Reader have been blessed by the Lord to have found such a Minister of the Gospel, you should think long and hard, and pray much, before such a one is rejected. It is very unlikely, that you will find another!

Preachers who truly care for your soul, who truly care for your Spiritual Growth, and who are truly called of God, and have the evidence to prove such, just as Paul did, are few and far between. Preachers fall into one of three categories:

1. Those who are in the Ministry for all the wrong reasons, and are not truly called of God. They're really going to be of little service to anyone. Unfortunately, a great percentage of the Ministry is made up of this kind.

2. Those who have been truly called by God, but have long since forsaken the True Way of the Lord. They seek to please men, and have, therefore, compromised the Gospel. This number is very, very large! This group exploits the people instead of developing them.

3. The few who are truly called of God, have not compromised the Message, who are close to God, and anointed by the Holy Spirit. These are the instruments used by the Holy Spirit, who can change lives. They follow in the line of Paul.

(11) "AS YE KNOW HOW WE EXHORTED AND COMFORTED AND CHARGED EVERY ONE OF YOU, AS A FATHER DOTH HIS CHILDREN,"

Changing from a Mother's tender care in Verse 8 to a new metaphor, Paul is now a Father dealing with his own children individually. Christians need fatherly teaching and advice as well as motherly care.

What a privilege it was for these people to have had Paul as their Pastor, their Instructor, their Evangelist, etc. I'm sure at the time that they didn't understand how fortunate they actually were. But perhaps as time went on, and their Christian experience deepened, I'm sure that at least many of them realized how blessed they had been. The Lord had made it possible for them to have the very best teaching and instruction available in the world of that day.

## EXHORTATION

The phrase, *"As ye know how we exhorted,"* pertains to dealing with the Thessalonians with encouragement, as well as by solemn injunctions.

*"Exhorted"* in the Greek is *"parakleton,"* which means *"comforter,"* and can carry the meanings of *"exhorting, consoling, encouraging, instructing"* (Jn. 14:16).

NOTES

The idea is, that Paul and those with him, were continually teaching and instructing the objects of their charge. This was their general work. As well, there is some implication, that specific time was spent with each person in the Church.

No doubt, the Church at this time was small, with it being possible to devote time and attention to each.

## COMFORT

The phrase, *"And comforted,"* in the Greek is, *"paramythoumenoi,"* and also means addressing for the purpose of persuading, consoling, or encouraging. Both *"exhorted"* and *"comforted,"* are very similar in meaning.

## CHARGE

The phrase, *"And charged every one of you,"* is the same as a military command.

*"Charged"* in the Greek is, *"martyromenoi,"* and means *"the idea of declaring solemnly, protesting, beseeching as in God's Name, exhorting solemnly."*

## FATHERLY DIRECTION

The phrase, *"As a father doth his children,"* presents the image being changed from that of motherly tenderness to that of fatherly direction.

The sight of the great Apostle so carefully seeking out the individual person provides an important insight into his Ministry, and indeed an example for our own. It is a practical commentary on Paul's concern for individual worth in the sight of God, on persons as individual members of Christ's Body, and on the Holy Spirit's individual Ministry to each Christian man and woman. In fact, the concept of the infinite value of every soul came supremely through the Gospel of Jesus Christ.

The idea was revolutionary in most of Paul's world, but was never more relevant than in ours. Within the Church there is no true evangelism or Pastoral care which does not follow this example.

As a Mother the Apostle nourished their Spiritual Life, and as a Father he superintended their spiritual education.

*"Exhorting and comforting and charging"*; representing three modes of the Apostle's instruction: *"Exhorting"* denotes

NOTES

also encouraging and consoling; *"Comforting"* denotes supporting and sustaining; and *"charging"* denotes testifying or protesting — a solemn pressing home of the exhortation to the hearers.

The translation of this Verse is somewhat clumsy; it probably would be better translated according to the following:

*"As ye know how we dealt with each one of you, as a father with his own children, exhorting you, and encouraging you, and testifying."*

(12) "THAT YE WOULD WALK WORTHY OF GOD, WHO HATH CALLED YOU UNTO HIS KINGDOM AND GLORY."

The *"walk"* refers to lifestyle, and *"worthy"* relates primarily to the moral sphere. Conduct should be on the plain of God's standards.

The Call of God into His Kingdom and Glory is an incentive to a high quality of life.

In one sense God's Kingdom is already present (Mat. 12:28; 13:1-52; Rom. 14:17; I Cor. 4:20; Col. 1:13), but ultimate realization of the Messianic Kingdom with its future glory is in view here (Acts 17:7). Frequently in this Thessalonian Letter, Paul points ahead to the glory which is coming, as an incentive to live Godly now. *"Glory"* is that unhindered manifestation of God's Presence in which Believer's will share (Rom. 5:2; 8:18).

## WALK WORTHY

The phrase, *"That ye would walk worthy of God,"* represents several things:

1. This *"walk,"* as stated, has to do with our daily living before God and the world.
2. The Christian walks today in the light of tomorrow's sure hope.
3. The Standard is that given by God and not man, and is found in the Word of God.
4. Christians are to live *"worthy of the calling"* (Eph. 4:1) we have received in Christ, in harmony with His Person and Teaching.

As well, a Believer is considered *"worthy,"* not on the basis of talent or position, but by how well his or her actions display Christian character.

## THE ONLY MANNER IN WHICH THIS CAN BE DONE

First of all, when the believing sinner comes to Christ, the *"sin nature,"* which has ruled and guided his life up until now, has had its fire put out. It is not taken away, because the Believer can still sin, and as well, if the Believer does not conduct himself according to God's prescribed method of Faith in the Cross, the sin nature will once again become predominant, with sin dominating the Believer. Were this not so, Paul would not have given all the instructions which he did concerning this subject, in Romans, Chapters 6 and 8. He said, *"Sin shall not have dominion over you"* (Rom. 6:14). If it were not possible for sin to have dominion in the life of a Christian, for it is to Christians to whom Paul is speaking, then the Apostle would not have made this statement. The Truth is, unless the Believer understands the Cross, and has Faith in that which Jesus has already done, in some manner, some way, sin will dominate the Child of God. It may not be one of the vices such as alcohol, drugs, immorality, etc., but it will definitely manifest itself in some fashion, such as pride, self-will, stubbornness, covetousness, etc.

Upon the believing sinner coming to Christ, the Divine Nature comes into the Believer, which now gives him God-consciousness. Before he was spiritually dead, and now he is spiritually alive.

As a result, the Believer wants to live for God, abhors sin, and desires to do this of which Paul spoke *"walk worthy of God."*

Unfortunately, most Christians, due to a lack of teaching on this all-important subject, set about to do this in all the wrong way.

It is not a contrived thing on the part of the Christian, just a matter of not knowing God's prescribed order of victory.

After conversion, Satan attacks, as he always does. In this effort of the Evil One, we must remember that every attack by Satan, irrespective as to the form it takes, is for but one purpose, that is to destroy or at least, seriously weaken our Faith. Always, that is his goal, his destination, his ambition. He very well knows that the Believer's Faith is the single most important ingredient. He knows that this is the manner in which God works; however, his effort is not so much to rob you of your Faith in that you would deny the Lord, for in most cases that is unlikely, as it is for you to make as the object of your

NOTES

Faith that which is unscriptural. That's his target, the object of your Faith.

## THE OBJECT OF YOUR FAITH

Having little or no teaching whatsoever on this tremendously important subject, upon an attack by Satan, if there is failure involved, the Believer is left confused and bewildered. And sooner or later, there will be failure of some sort.

Due to now having the God Nature in one's spirit, sin is a terribly, debilitating thing. When the Believer sins, fellowship with the Lord is broken, at least until repentance is enjoined, and fellowship restored, which it always is upon confession of the sin to the Lord (I Jn. 1:9).

Not wanting this to happen again, and I speak of failure, the Believer sets about to ensure victory. Probably at the time, he does little or nothing but resolve that he will not fall into this trap again; however, what he doesn't know is, that mere resolve, as important as it is, is not enough. The Believer now finds himself as having failed again, and we speak of whatever manner in which Satan has chosen to attack.

Unfortunately, most Christians have been taught, or else they have been taught nothing on the subject, and have come to their own erroneous conclusions, that when we speak of sin, we're speaking basically of the vices, such as immorality, drugs, gambling, etc. While those things definitely are sin, and gross sin at that, still, there are many more types of sin, such as apathy, covetousness, pride, etc., as we've already stated. These latter sins, are much more difficult to identify, than the vices. But they are still sin in the eyes of God, and at times, even worse than the vices. However, if the Believer is doing his best to walk close to the Lord, the Holy Spirit will definitely warn the Child of God of any erroneous direction. The problem is, that too often, the Believer doesn't heed the still, small voice of the Holy Spirit, which guarantees the problem, whatever it might be, getting worse and worse.

In one way or the other, every Believer fights these battles. There are no exceptions. Satan is ever walking about as a roaring lion, seeking whom he may devour (I Pet. 5:8). So, no Believer is immune!

Not knowing what to do, the Believer now begins to formulate in his own mind means and ways to obtain victory. He will be more faithful to Church. He will read his Bible more. He will try to pray more. He might even fast once in awhile.

All of these things are good, plus even many we have not addressed, and the Believer to be sure, definitely should do these things and even be diligent about the doing; however, if Faith is placed in that whatever it might be, to help us be an overcomer or to be victorious in any manner, as good as these things might be in their own way, our doing of them to our chagrin will bring no victory.

And this is what confuses many Christians. These things they are doing are very spiritual, but the problem, whatever the problem might be, is not only not helped, but it rather gets worse.

It is all because the Believer has his Faith misplaced. To be sure, the things we have mentioned, in which he places his Faith, are good things, but what he's doing is all wrong. Let's see why!

### THE CROSS OF CHRIST

The modern Church has very little understanding of the Atonement of Christ, and what it all means. While it will little agree to what I've just said, still, its knowledge of the Cross is pretty well confined to the initial Salvation experience. In other words, if the Church claims to be fundamental, that is, it believes all the Bible, it believes that the sinner must have Faith in what Christ did on the Cross in order to be saved. While the sinner may not understand much about this, still in some manner, he must know that Jesus died for him, and Faith in that, brings Salvation, as he makes the Lord his Saviour.

Of course, that is correct; however, most Believers then leave the Cross at their initial Salvation experience, thinking it plays no further part in their everyday living, as Paul mentions here. It's a case of Salvation by Faith, and Sanctification by works, which of course, the latter cannot succeed. But that's where the Church mostly is.

To say it another way, it is mostly *"Salvation by Faith, and Sanctification by self."* Now that the person has come to Christ, he believes that he can do all of these things which need to be done, simply because he is now a Christian.

NOTES

In fact, a Brother said to me just the other day, *"Now that I'm a Christian, I have the power to choose what I desire to choose."*

He's right, and at the same time, he's wrong!

As a Believer he definitely does have the power now to choose that which is right; however, it is only if he has chosen God's Way, which is the Way of the Cross. If he chooses to go in another direction, whether ignorantly or not, he will soon find his will power being eroded by the powers of darkness. In other words, if he doesn't choose God's Way which is the Cross, he will find himself unable at some future time to make the choice he knows he needs to make. Paul addressed this very succinctly in Romans, Chapter 7. You, see, he fought this same battle that we fight. He tried to gain victory through the flesh, which refers to his own ability and machinations, and found that he could not do so. Consequently, he said, *"For I know that in me* (that is, in my flesh,) *dwelleth no good thing: for to will is present with me; but how to perform that which is good I find not"* (Rom. 7:18).

He plainly says here that his will is not strong enough to do the things he knows he needs to do, and that's exactly where most Christians now find themselves.

They have been taught by Preachers that inasmuch as they are now a Christian, this guarantees them the strength of willpower to do whatever needs to be done. Consequently, in this erroneous teaching, if the Believer fails, which he is most certainly going to do, that is if he attempts to overcome in this manner, then he is judged as having *"willed"* to sin. In other words, he just wanted to do this vile thing, whatever it was, and made the choice to do so.

Such thinking is completely wrong! While there certainly may be some Christians who want to sin, that number would be few and far between. The very nature of a Christian militates against sin of any nature.

However, in this erroneous thinking, with the Church completely misunderstanding the Believer's position in Christ, it automatically assumes that sin is a choice; therefore, if failure happens, then that Christian willingly and maliciously chose to do this thing; therefore, they should be punished, etc. Unfortunately, this is the thinking of the modern Church.

### HAS THE CHRISTIAN MALICIOUSLY CHOSEN TO FAIL?

If they are truly Born-Again, most definitely not!

I am persuaded that there are many people who go under the name *"Christian,"* who actually have never been Born-Again. As a result, those people definitely do want to sin, and because of their very nature. In fact, Churches are filled with people of this nature. They've never really come to Christ, although being very religious. So, sin is going to be their lot!

However, if a person is truly Born-Again, that person doesn't want to sin. If they do sin, it is because of having an improper understanding of their position in Christ, and, therefore, because of that, being overcome.

In fact, there are millions of Christians at this very moment, who Satan has placed in bondage. They're living lives of sinning and repenting, sinning and repenting, sinning and repenting! They don't want to do whatever they're doing, whatever that might be, and are trying with all their strength and power not to yield; however, they find themselves powerless in the hands of Satan, which Paul plainly addresses in Romans, Chapters 6, 7, and 8, even as we've already stated.

In fact, this is at least one of the reasons that tens of thousands of Christians are running all over the world, trying to find a Preacher who they have heard is being used of God, who will lay hands on them and rid them of their problem. In the 1990's, that effort has taken on two or three different directions.

In the early 1990's Christians by the thousands were flocking to places where they were told that the spirit of *"Holy Ghost laughter"* would come upon them, and they would then be victorious, etc. That gradually faded into Christians crawling around over the floor crowing like roosters, or roaring like lions, claiming that this was the Holy Spirit. It then went to being *"slain in the Spirit,"* which really has been in vogue all along.

NOTES

In many Churches, the people were led to believe, if they did not have one or more of these particular manifestations, then that meant they were not spiritual, etc.

While some little of this was definitely of the Lord, most of it wasn't! While the Lord may definitely knock people off of their feet at times, and bless them greatly, which we all desire; still, as a Believer I do not need that to fulfill my Christian experience. My experience with the Lord is due solely and completely, through my Faith in what Jesus did at the Cross and His Resurrection. If I seek to add anything to that, or take from that, I have abrogated the great Plan of God, which can bring me nothing but trouble.

Once again, I emphasize the fact that the Lord definitely does do things at times to greatly bless His people. But this is strictly a *"handful on purpose,"* and has absolutely nothing to do with whether I am spiritual or not. As stated, my spirituality is in the Finished Work of Christ, and my Faith in that Work.

However, the point I wish again to emphasize is, that Christians are doing these things, at least for the most part, because they're trying to find victory in their lives. If the Truth be known, that's at least the major reason for all of this particular activity regarding manifestations, etc.

### WHAT IS THE SOURCE OF VICTORY?

The Source of Victory for all Christians, which does not change and because it cannot change, is the Finished Work of Christ at the Cross and His Resurrection. Of course, this would also include His Exaltation (Eph. 2:6).

This means that the Believer is to understand that everything he needs in the Lord, is found in the Atonement, which refers to what Jesus did at the Cross. In fact, terms like *"Atonement," "the Finished Work of Christ,"* or *"the Cross,"* are all synonymous. They mean the same thing. Actually, and to which we have already referred in earlier Commentary, words like *"Faith," "Gospel," "Justification," "Sanctification," "Righteousness," "Holiness,"* etc., are as well, in one way or the other, all synonymous with the *"Cross."* In other words, when you say one you've said the other as well! Actually, if you do not understand what I've just said, and understand it in that fashion, you will cause yourself great problems, which we are discussing here.

Understanding that everything you need is in what Jesus did at the Cross, you are to place your Faith in that great Work, which the Lord intends for you to do. This is what the Lord showed Paul (I Cor. 1:18; 2:2; Eph. 2:8-9).

As we have previously stated, the great Apostle after his conversion, found himself not able to live the life he knew he had to live, and in fact, wanted to live. He tried to have Righteousness and Holiness, in other words, to walk in these great Attributes of God with all his strength, but found he simply could not do so.

The Lord then showed him the correct way of Victory, which is in the Cross, which Paul very succinctly and graciously, gave to us in Romans, Chapter 6. And there is one thing I want to shout from the housetops, *"It works!"*

The Believer is *"in Christ,"* meaning, that he was in Christ when Christ died on the Cross, was buried with Christ, and was raised with Christ in His Resurrection (Rom. 6:2-6). In fact, even as we've already stated, the Believer continues to be in Christ in all of these things, and even presently as Christ is seated on the Throne at the Right Hand of God (Eph. 2:6).

As a result of being *"in Christ,"* I have all of the victory that Christ purchased. It is mine simply by Faith. This means that I am to believe that what Jesus did there, grants me all that I need to live the victorious life. In fact, every single Believer in this world is already an overcomer. They may not be acting that way or living that way, primarily because of not knowing their proper place in Christ; however, irrespective of that, their position is actually one of Righteousness and Holiness. We are all of that, because of what Jesus did there. As stated, He did it all for us, and certainly desires that we have all of that for which He paid such a price. In fact, that is a gross understatement!

## VICTORY

The only thing the Saint needs to do in order to have total and complete Victory in his or her life, is to simply have Faith in what Jesus did at the Cross, understanding that this is the only Source of Victory.

This is what Satan doesn't want you to have. In fact, he doesn't really care where you put your Faith, whether in prayer, fasting, manifestations, or whatever, and again, even as good as those things might be in their own right, Satan knows that you will find no victory in your Christian experience in this manner. I've said it many times, it's like trying to use a hammer for a handsaw. And that's exactly what many Christians are trying to do. They're trying to use prayer or manifestations, etc., in a manner in which the Lord never intended. While all of these things are very good in their own right, if we try to use them wrongly, we turn them into works, which God can never bless, and because it insults the Finished Work of Christ.

I have said it over and over again, that Faith is the vehicle through which the Lord works (Heb. 11:6); however, it is Faith exclusively in the Cross and in nothing else. Our Faith must not be divided, must not be placed elsewhere, but always in the Cross of Christ (I Cor. 1:18; 2:2).

## THE HOLY SPIRIT

Once our Faith is properly placed in the Cross, and we keep our Faith in that Finished Work, the Holy Spirit will then work on our behalf, guaranteeing us all the great Benefits of the Finished Work of Christ. To be sure, what I cannot hope to do, the Holy Spirit can do. Let me ask you a question!

Have you as a Christian ever thought in your mind, that the Lord was allowing Satan too much latitude with you? Have you ever felt that Satan was pressing you harder than you could bear? You knew that the Scripture says that the Lord wouldn't allow that (I Cor. 10:13), but whatever was happening, you knew that Satan was pushing you so hard, that you could not seem to overcome.

Have you ever wondered as to why the Holy Spirit didn't help you more? You know that He is present in your heart and life, and of that there is no doubt; however, something is wrong, in that He is not doing all the great things you have been led to believe that He would do.

NOTES

NOTES

The Truth is, He in such circumstances is *not* helping you. That may come as a shock, but the reality is exactly that of which I've said.

Yes, He definitely is present within your heart and life, and He is there, to do great and mighty things. So what's stopping Him from doing these things?

Irrespective of all the side issues and other things that may be happening, the real reason that the Holy Spirit is not helping you as He desires to, that is if in fact He isn't, is because your Faith is improperly placed. He works exclusively within the parameters of the Finished Work of Christ, which speaks of what Jesus did at the Cross and the Resurrection. He will not go outside of those boundaries, which means that He will not help you to sanctify yourself. He will not help you to be righteous by your own machinations! He will not help you to be holy by your own devices! In fact, for Him to do such a thing would be illegal (Rom. 8:2). He will not break His Own Laws, and to deliver you by any means other than what Christ has already done on the Cross, that He will not do.

He will not do it for many reasons: First of all, what you're trying to do, Jesus has already done at the Cross. Consequently, there is no point in fighting that battle all over again. I speak of Righteousness, Holiness, and Victory, etc. The Lord by the shedding of His Own Precious Blood, has already purchased all of these things for us. He did it as our Substitute and as our Representative Man. We couldn't do it for ourselves, so He had to do these things for us.

The way we obtain all of these things, in other words, to actually be what our position actually is, is to simply have Faith in that which He has done, and rely totally and completely on that. Whenever we do this, and not allow our Faith to be moved to other things, then the Holy Spirit will begin to work mightily on our behalf, and we will see things we've never seen before, and have things we've never had before, in other words, begin to live this *"more abundant life"* (Jn. 10:10).

This and this alone, is God's prescribed order of Victory. As well, it is the only order of Victory that He has, and because none other is needed.

That is the only way that you as a Believer can *"walk worthy of God."* You do this through what Jesus did at the Cross, and by no other manner.

## WHAT IF THE WAY OF THE CROSS IS REJECTED?

As I've already stated, God, as should be overly obvious, has no other method of Victory or Salvation. We either believe what the Scripture tells us as it regards this of what we're saying, or there is no Victory, or anything for that matter from the Lord. In fact, the entirety of the Bible concerns this very subject. And I speak of everything from Genesis through the Book of Revelation.

This has been the age-old struggle, whether to accept God's prescribed order which is the Cross, or attempt to devise our own means. In fact, all of this began in the Fourth Chapter of Genesis, with Cain and Abel. It has raged ever since!

God says that man cannot do this thing for himself; therefore, He had to do it for us, which He did do at the Cross and the Resurrection of Christ. If one reads the Old Testament, it becomes immensely obvious that the Cross is the destination of all that is done. Everything speaks of Jesus and what He would do at the Cross. Every Sacrifice pointed to that; all the Jewish Feast Days pointed to that in some manner. In fact, the Old Covenant was meant only as a stopgap measure, always pointing to the New Covenant which was to come, and which is called *"an Everlasting Covenant,"* meaning that it will never be replaced (Heb. 13:20). The Lord has no other way, because no other way is needed.

Unfortunately, the Church has been subtly maneuvered by Satan into a position at least for the most part, that is outside of the Cross. It looks today to Psychology, or to other things, whatever it might be. The result is failure on every hand.

In fact, I personally believe that the modern Church is weaker today than it's ever been before. While it is big, it is big only in the sense of being sloppy fat. While a 500 pound man might be big, he is definitely not healthy!

The Church as well boasts that it is rich, and in fact, it is. It has more money than ever before; however, I hear the Words of

Jesus as He says, *"Because thou sayest, I am rich, and increased with goods, and have need of nothing; and knowest not that thou art wretched, and miserable, and poor, and blind, and naked"* (Rev. 3:17).

Regrettably, that is the condition of the modern Church!

It is all because of having left the Cross, having placed the Cross in a subordinate position, or in some sad cases, even denying the Cross.

A DENIAL OF THE CROSS!

When we speak of *"denial,"* we're speaking of an actual repudiation of the Cross, whether in practice or outright denial. We'll look at the latter first.

As is obvious, the Modernists deny the Cross, and much of everything else about the Bible. Many of these individuals do not believe that Jesus is the Son of God, or that He was raised from the dead, etc. And of course, they in no way believe that the Cross of Christ has anything to do with one's Salvation, that is, if they actually believe in any type of Salvation at all.

Regarding this group, and they are quite large, even though at times somewhat religious, they're quite easily identified.

There is another group, however, which embodies the Charismatic community, which is not so obvious. What I'm about to say does not at all include all Charismatics, but it does include many in the so-called *"Faith Community."*

They openly repudiate the Cross, even refusing to sing any songs about the Blood or the Cross in their Services, etc. Some of them claim that while the Cross is possibly necessary as it regards the initial experience of Salvation, that the Believer is to leave the Cross at that point going on to greater and higher things, etc.

They teach that the Cross epitomizes weakness, and as such does not belong in the Christian's belief system. Their system they claim, specializes in *"Faith,"* but it's definitely not Faith in the Finished Work of Christ.

This is very subtle, and ensnares many people, with many not realizing the terrible danger of what is being said and done, simply because this group claims to be Spirit-filled, operating in the Gifts of the Spirit, etc. So, most of the adherents, simply draw a blank when it comes to this part of their teaching, not really realizing how serious, in a negative sense, it actually is what they are hearing.

NOTES

In the first place, while it is true that Jesus did die in weakness (II Cor. 13:4), it was a contrived weakness. In other words, the Lord did not save Himself from this Sacrificial Offering, even though He had the power to do so. That is all that is meant by weakness. The very fact that Jesus died constitutes weakness, as should be obvious; however, it was a weakness not of lack of power, but simply referring to the fact that He willingly laid down His life. That's all that it means.

The way these people explain *"weakness,"* is that He had no choice but to die, and that somehow, He merely ran afoul of Roman law, etc. That is blatantly unscriptural!

Jesus did not run afoul of Roman law or Jewish law. He plainly said of Himself and concerning His Life, *"No man taketh it from Me, but I lay it down of Myself. I have power to lay it down, and I have power to take it again. This Commandment have I received of My Father"* (Jn. 10:18).

So, these people reason that if Jesus died through weakness, that songs and sermons about the Blood and about the Cross, constitute weakness as well, and of course, these great Faith people, do not have any type of weakness, so such Songs and Messages are rejected.

Outside of the Cross, the only strength one has is his own personal strength, which is nothing! All strength is found in the Cross, because out of that came the Atonement, which gained total victory over all the powers of darkness. The bottom line is this:

These people, that is if they in fact do believe this of which I've said, actually have no Faith, at least that which God will recognize. He only recognizes Faith that's tied to the Cross, i.e., *"the Finished Work of Christ."* As well, they have no power, because all power comes from the Cross. Paul plainly said, *"For the preaching of the Cross is to them that perish foolishness; but unto us which are saved it is the Power of God"* (I Cor. 1:18).

Beyond all of this, those who would believe this fallacious doctrine, are tampering with their very souls. It's one thing to be wrong about some things in the Bible, but something else again to be wrong about the Cross.

That's like a person in the physical sense who might have a problem with his foot. That's one thing; however, if he has a problem with his heart, that's something else again. In other words, the heart problem can kill him!

To be sure, having a problem with the Cross and not interpreting it rightly, can cause one to lose their soul.

## PSYCHOLOGY

Another large segment of the Church denies the Cross by their practice. They do not openly come out as the so-called *"Faith people,"* and deny the Cross, but they definitely do in practice. I speak of humanistic psychology!

For Preachers of the Gospel (once again, so-called), to recommend psychology as an answer to the ills of humanity, is at the same time a repudiation of the Cross of Christ, whether they mean such to be that or not. There is no other way that one can arrive at any other conclusion. Either Jesus Christ and what He did at the Cross is the answer to the sin problem of humanity, and the aberrations of mankind, and anything spiritual that might be wrong with anyone, or else the Bible is a lie. One cannot have it both ways!

I maintain that what Jesus did at the Cross and in His Resurrection, addressed every single thing that man lost in the Fall. While it is true that we do not yet have all the benefits of the Atonement, that awaiting the coming Resurrection; still, what we do have concerning that which Jesus did, definitely addresses the sin problem in every capacity, and in fact, is the only answer. So, when man recommends psychology which in fact holds no answers whatsoever, and is actually the dementation of a warped, sinful, wicked mind, and that's exactly what it is, they are at the same time, saying that what Christ did at the Cross is of no benefit. Such direction can be constituted as none other than *"blasphemy!"*

The sadness is, I think that many Preachers have followed this course simply because they don't know any better. Possibly I'm being too lenient on them, but I would rather think they're doing such through ignorance than through maliciousness. If anyone maliciously ignores the Cross, they can only do so through unbelief, which is spiritual disaster. Consequently, I would rather believe that with most of these Preachers it is *"Scriptural ignorance,"* rather than *"unbelief!"*

Either way, however, it is a repudiation of the Cross, which cannot fall out to any help for those who are ensnared, but rather the opposite.

I know from experience, and so do untold millions of others, that the Cross of Christ works. It is the answer, and it is there that Jesus defeated every power of darkness. I have experienced it in my life, so I know what this great Finished Work of Christ can and will do. And to be sure, it does not need any help from the Devil and the world.

## DIVIDING FAITH FROM THE CROSS

The great sin of the Church at least presently, is severing Faith from the Cross. Let me first of all address the subject as it should be.

When we think of Faith, of believing God, of trusting Christ, we must always think of these terms in relationship to the Cross of Christ. If we think of it otherwise, we are nullifying the great Work of Redemption. So, Faith in our thinking, and in our practice, must ever be linked totally and completely with the Cross. Actually, even that is an understatement.

Faith in the Cross should be so intertwined in our thinking, that when we say one, we actually say both. That's how closely aligned that the Believer's Faith must be in the Cross. He must understand both as one in the same, in other words, that no Faith can be recognized by God which is not anchored firmly in the Cross.

When the Scripture says, *"Abraham believed God"* (Gen. 15:6; Rom. 5:4), it didn't mean that he merely believed there was a God. Much of the world believes that, and it does them no good whatsoever.

It rather means, that he believed that God would provide a Redeemer for mankind. That was the core of his Faith, the core of his believing. As well, it must be the core of our believing!

NOTES

If we sever Faith from the Cross, we have Faith which God will not recognize. In fact, this is what much of the modern Faith movement has done. It has Faith in Faith. In other words, Faith itself is the object, which in reality, is no different than the Faith the world has.

It doesn't matter if one uses the Word of God as it regards Faith, if it's not Faith in the Cross, such use of the Word amounts to no more than what Satan did in the wilderness in the temptation of Christ. The Evil One used the Word as well, but he used it wrongly! (Mat. 4:1-11). I'll say it again:

Satan doesn't care what we have our Faith in, or how much we claim to use the Word of God, or how much we claim that our Faith is based on the Word, if it's not Faith in the Cross, he knows that it's Faith that God will not recognize.

And I think one can look at the modern Faith Movement, observing the fruit it has produced, and if one is honest with themselves, one will have to come to the conclusion that it's not been the right kind of Faith. In fact, it has degenerated presently into little more than a *"money gospel!"*

When Faith is removed from the Cross, in other words, when the Cross is no longer the object of Faith, then it is no more, as stated, than the type of Faith the world has. While that may do some certain things, it will not be Faith which God will recognize (Heb. 11:6).

THE CALLING

The phrase, *"Who hath called you unto His Kingdom and Glory,"* should have been translated, *"Who is calling you into His Kingdom and Glory."*

The Greek is using the present tense, which *"is calling,"* rather than *"called."* It suggests that the Call of God to Salvation in the sense of final glory, although heeded in a crisis of Repentance and Faith, is yet not a once-for-all event in the past. Just as God is always calling, so Believers are to always be responding. So, the urgency expressed in Verse 12 is not to be construed as concern for conduct alone, but also for personal Salvation.

The *"Kingdom"* is in one sense come, a present possession, but is in another sense coming, a future inheritance. The Kingdom or Reign of God, through the indwelling Holy Spirit, and the economy of Divine Grace, which the Lord has given us through the Cross, is already present in the hearts of Believers. It exists where His sovereignty is owned and His will is done. But its consummation and completeness are yet future — at Christ's Coming. In fact, it is this future aspect which is stressed here.

*"Glory"* signifies splendor, magnificence, and brightness.

Verse 12 suggests *"The two Sides of Christian Living"*:

A. What God does for us; and, B. What we ought to do for God.

In matchless love He calls us, offering both Grace and Glory. He does this through the Cross of Christ, and our Faith in that Finished Work.

How shall we respond to this infinite mercy? We may accept His offer and through Grace seek to live lives worthy of God. Is it not a paradox, especially considering that man within himself cannot actually do this? The suggestion then seems staggering.

Indeed, the whole concept of Divine Grace finds its meeting ground in man's utter unworthiness. However, man must admit his unworthiness, which means he is trusting totally in what the Cross provides, before Grace can be admitted. In fact, to be qualified for Grace, one might say that one has to be disqualified and know it.

THE BASIS ON WHICH GOD CALLS MANKIND

In effect, the Call of God is extended to the entirety of the human race. The Scripture plainly tells us that it is *"whosoever will . . ."* (Rev. 22:17; Jn. 3:16). However, the basis on which God calls humanity, is on the basis of the Finished Work of His Son, and our Saviour, The Lord Jesus Christ. Other than through the Cross, God will not call anyone, in fact, cannot call anyone.

A thrice holy God cannot meet with sinful men, except on the basis of a Mediator or go-between, Who is Jesus Christ. As well, He is a Mediator only on the basis of His Cross.

Likewise, man cannot respond to the Call of God, except he does so through the Finished Work of Christ. If he tries to approach God in any other manner except the Cross,

NOTES

NOTES

God will not recognize his approach, and in fact, will ultimately bring judgment. God speaks to us through the Cross, and we respond to Him through the Cross.

So, to obtain this *"Kingdom and Glory,"* it can only be done through the Sacrificial, Atoning, Death of the Lord Jesus Christ, and His Resurrection.

To be sure, the *"Kingdom and the Glory,"* are great and magnificent things. So great in fact, that it's difficult for us as human beings to even remotely comprehend what is actually being said; nevertheless, it is true. But the Believer must ever remember, must ever understand, that all of this comes to us, as great as it is, at great price. That price is what Jesus did at the Cross. If we forget that, or attempt to go around the Cross of Christ, which we have just dealt with, to be sure, such effort will meet with very serious disapproval from God, even judgment.

(13) "FOR THIS CAUSE ALSO THANK WE GOD WITHOUT CEASING, BECAUSE, WHEN YE RECEIVED THE WORD OF GOD WHICH YE HEARD OF US, YE RECEIVED IT NOT AS THE WORD OF MEN, BUT AS IT IS IN TRUTH, THE WORD OF GOD, WHICH EFFECTUALLY WORKETH ALSO IN YOU THAT BELIEVE."

To accentuate the Word's ultimate Source, Paul bluntly states that they were not accepting *"the word of men,"* but what it actually was — *"the Word of God."* Their appraisal of what they heard was accurate. Here is indication of Paul's consciousness of his own Divinely imparted authority (I Cor. 14:37).

His preaching and delivery of this Word, was not the outgrowth of personal philosophical meanderings, but was deeply rooted in a Message given by God Himself.

Once received, this Word of God becomes an active power operating continually in the Believer's life. When it is at work in those *"who believe,"* there is a change in behavior and constant fruitfulness. This is what makes the Word of God different than anything else in the world today, or in fact ever has been. It changes people's lives.

THANKFULNESS TO GOD

The phrase, *"For this cause also thank we God without ceasing,"* refers to the manner in which the Thessalonians had received the Word, which is evidenced in the balance of this Scripture. Paul was thanking God, that the Word had been rightly presented and rightly received.

We learn many things from Paul's statements. We learn the worth of souls, the Grace of God, the rightness of the Message, and how the Holy Spirit works in helping men to receive Christ, and then to be what they ought to be in Christ.

As a result, the attitude of the Apostle was one of unceasing thanksgiving to the Lord in respect to the fruit that was evident regarding the lives of these Thessalonians, as it regarded the Word of God.

This of which we see here, is what the Gospel is all about. It is about men and women, boys and girls, who accept Christ, and have their lives gloriously changed. Unfortunately, many in the modern Church have made other things the criteria, mostly the approval of other men. Paul has one interest, and that is souls, and their progress in the Lord. Everything else is of little consequence.

THE WORD OF GOD

The phrase, *"Because, when ye received the Word of God which ye heard of us, ye received it not as the word of men, but as it is in Truth, the Word of God,"* proclaims several great Truths:

1. What Paul was giving them was the Word of God, which means it was not the philosophy of men.

What is the Word of God?

In brief, it is that men are spiritually lost, without God. If they remain this way, they will literally burn in Hell forever (Mat. 5:22, 29; 10:28). That sounds awful blunt, but whether men believe it or not, that's exactly the way it is.

To remedy this situation, God sent His Only Son to die on Calvary, in order to pay the terrible sin debt owed by man, which man could not pay. In effect, Jesus became our Substitute.

Faith in that, this which Christ has done, grants the believing sinner Salvation, forgiveness of all sin, and Eternal Life (Jn. 3:16; Rom. 10:9-10, 13; Eph. 2:8-9).

As the Believer continues to have Faith in the Cross of Christ, which pertains to the Finished Work, Christlikeness will be developed in the Believer, as he grows in Grace and the Knowledge of the Lord. In brief, as stated, this is the *"Word of the Lord."*

2. These Thessalonians received this Word, which means they received it with all their heart. When they heard the Word, the Holy Spirit convicted them of sin, and at the same time gave them Faith to believe, which they did.

3. The Word of God is *"Truth,"* meaning that it is the only Truth in the world today, and in fact, ever has been.

These people had formerly been idol worshippers; consequently, they had been under the domain of Satan, with all of its kingdom of darkness, subterfuge, bondage, and shame. Admittedly, the unredeemed do not know that, because they have no way of knowing Who and What God is actually like; nevertheless, once the person comes to Christ, then the difference between the kingdom of darkness and the Kingdom of Light becomes very apparent.

In the Greek, the two words translated *"received"* are not the same; the first means simply an outward reception by the mind, while the second means to welcome with approval. The meaning seems to be that when the Thessalonians received or heard the Word of God with their ears, they accepted or welcomed it inwardly in their hearts. They did not, as others did in unbelief, consider it to be the mere words of men (Heb. 4:2).

## THE ANOINTING OF THE HOLY SPIRIT UPON THE MESSENGER

Paul is making a claim here to the unction and Anointing of the Holy Spirit upon the Preacher of the Gospel, giving him power to preach the Word. This means that God speaks with authority and power through His qualified Messengers.

Unfortunately, Preachers proclaiming the Gospel under the Anointing of the Holy Spirit are not as common as one would think. Actually, it is quite rare. However, when this does happen, as it certainly should with every Preacher, the Message delivered takes on a brand-new perspective.

NOTES

If the Message is delivered in the power of the Holy Spirit, it is then extremely important that the hearer hear the Message right! *"Take heed therefore,"* said Jesus, *"how ye hear"* (Lk. 8:18).

Solemn responsibility rests upon those who hear the Word of God mediated through Spirit-filled Preachers. It is tragically possible to be so preoccupied with the person of the Preacher, or so prejudiced by proud and obstinate thoughts, that the Word becomes only words.

The preaching of the Gospel is to be *"with authority."* It does not come to us to solicit our approval, submitting itself, as a system of ideas for our scrutiny, and courting approval. It rather speaks with authority . . . its decisive appeal is made to the conscience, the heart, and the will; and to respond to it is to give up will and heart and conscience to God.

In speaking of Paul, his theology was the sum of the Divine Truth he held, and he did preach it — he did not submit it to men as a theme for discussion. He put it above discussion . . . he published it . . . as the Word of God, for the obedience of Faith.

The proclamation of the Word of God under the Anointing of the Holy Spirit, is the most powerful and moving factor on the face of the Earth, as it regards persuasive power toward men.

## HOW CAN THE PREACHER HAVE THE ANOINTING OF THE HOLY SPIRIT?

The following may be of some help:

1. The Preacher must be Baptized with the Holy Spirit with the evidence of speaking with other Tongues (Acts 2:4).

2. He must actively desire that the Holy Spirit control him in all things; however, this is control he must give to the Holy Spirit, for the Spirit will not take it otherwise.

3. The Preacher must understand that he is preaching the Word of God, and that it must be done without fear or favor, in other words, no compromise.

4. The Preacher must have a strong prayer life. In fact, without such a prayer life it is impossible to have the Anointing of the Holy Spirit as one desires. He must seek the Lord that God would use him, and that the right Word would be given to him. The Lord has a Word for each and every congregation, in

effect, for every person. It remains for the Preacher to find the Mind of the Lord, as it regards this which he will minister.

5. Humility must be the hallmark of the Preacher of the Gospel. There must never be any lifting up in pride, or egotistical attitudes. The true man of God must always imitate the Master as far as possible, Who was always *"meek and lowly in heart"* (Mat. 11:28-30).

6. The true Preacher of the Gospel must ever seek to please God. This must be his overriding compulsion. He is to have no concern whatsoever as it regards pleasing men. He has been called by the Lord, he ministers for the Lord, and it is to the Lord to Whom he must answer.

7. In all of this, he must be a Preacher of the Cross, understanding that the Cross is the very foundation of the Faith. When we speak of *"preaching the Cross,"* we are meaning that this should be the foundation of every Message, understanding that anything and everything that comes to the seeking soul, must come through and by the Finished Work of Christ. While there are many subjects as it regards the Word of God, and all are very important, the Truth is, that each subject must have as its anchor, its foundation, the Cross of Christ.

This is not meaning that the Cross is first; in fact, the Word is first (Gen. 1:1; Jn. 1:1). However, one cannot know the Word, cannot understand the Word, and cannot apply the Word, unless it is filtered through the Cross of Christ. In Truth, the Word is Jesus and Jesus is the Word (Jn. 1:1). Actually, the very Name *"Jesus,"* means *"Saviour."* And of course, He saves by what He did at the Cross, and man's Faith in that Finished Work.

## THE ANIMOSITY AGAINST THE ANOINTING

As we've already stated, there are very few Preachers who actually have the Anointing of the Holy Spirit upon their Ministry. But for the few who do, they touch the world, exactly as Paul of old. In this, however, the following should be noted:

There is a special animosity against those who are truly Anointed by the Holy Spirit. And to be sure, the far greater animosity will come from inside the Church, rather than without. It comes from those who do not have the Anointing, and for whatever reason. In fact, any Preacher of the Gospel can be anointed by the Holy Spirit, if that Preacher will only go God's Way.

The problem is, many Preachers seek to please men instead of God. They serve their Denomination instead of the Lord. As well, it takes a tremendous consecration for a Preacher of the Gospel to have a touch of God upon his or her life. Many are not willing to make that consecration.

Joseph's *"coat of many colors,"* is a perfect example. It typified the *"Blessing,"* and in a limited way, the Anointing of the Holy Spirit. His Brothers hated him for this, even desiring to kill him, which they would have done, had it not been for the intervention of the Lord. It was all because of the *"coat!"*

Even though the original coat was taken from him by his Brothers, that which the coat represented, the Blessings of God, i.e., *"the Anointing of the Holy Spirit,"* remained. Consequently, Potiphar's wife acted this time as Satan's agent. It resulted in Joseph going to prison (Gen. Chpt. 39).

Irrespective as to the animosity, which to be frank is a given, it ultimately led to Joseph becoming the Viceroy of Egypt, then the most powerful nation in the world. However, there was a price to pay, as there always will be a price to pay. I think that is very evident in the life of Paul.

## EFFECTUAL WORKING

The phrase, *"Which effectually worketh also in you that believe,"* refers to the fact that the Word *"is working"* only in those who *"are believing."* It follows that the operation ceases when Faith ceases. As one Expositor said, *"We cannot live today on the spiritual capital of yesterday."* The energy of the Word is released by Faith! God Himself is at work through His Word (Heb. 4:12; I Pet. 1:23-25).

Every single Believer I suppose, wants the Word to effectually work within their hearts and lives. When this happens, mighty things are done, with wonderful growth taking place in the heart and life of the Believer.

## HOW CAN WE GET THIS EFFECTUAL WORD TO WORK WITHIN OUR LIVES?

We are told here to believe, and of course, that is exactly right; however, as it regards the

NOTES

Christian who doesn't know the Word as one should, his first reaction is that he is already believing, but still this mighty power is not working through him as it should.

The Truth is, while the Power of God definitely works in the hearts and lives of every Christian to a certain extent, most Christians are experiencing this miracle working power within their own lives only to a small degree by comparison as to what they could have.

Why?

No doubt, there are several reasons; however, the greatest reason of all, is because most modern Christians do not understand how this power originates, how it works, and what causes it to work.

In fact, there has been all type of teaching on this subject in the last several decades. Untold numbers of books have been written on this very principle, with almost none of them being Scripturally correct.

For the most part, people are being told that they must have more Faith. And to receive more Faith, they are told to memorize Scriptures, or to listen to certain Faith tapes, etc.

In Truth, it's not more Faith that the Believer needs, but rather how to use the Faith he presently has.

This is a subject over which I have sought the Lord for years, with Him in 1996 giving me the answer to this for which I had so long sought. Actually, for some five years, or even longer, I sought the Lord earnestly about this very thing. And when I say *"sought the Lord,"* I don't mean only once in awhile, but rather on a daily basis, even with tears.

When the answer came, it totally revolutionized my heart and life. It revolutionized my Ministry, the way I live, and actually every single thing with which I have to do.

I have always known the Power of God in my life, but until the Lord gave me the Revelation of the Cross, I did not know it to the extent of which Paul speaks here.

In an abbreviated manner, the following is what the Lord gave me:

1. He told me that everything I needed, and without exception, is to be found in the Cross of Christ.

2. In view of that, my Faith is to be in the Cross at all times. That's what Paul is speaking about here when he talks about *"believing."*

NOTES

We are to believe exactly that which I have stated, which means to have Faith in the Finished Work of Christ.

3. Having Faith in the Cross of Christ, which at the same time presupposes His Resurrection and Exaltation, the Holy Spirit will then work on our behalf doing great and mighty things for us. This is where the power comes from. The power is always in the Spirit, but we cannot have that power manifested in our lives, if we do not place our Faith properly in the Cross. All of this is found in Romans Chapters, 6 and 8.

When the Holy Spirit revealed this to me, my life began to instantly change; however, the change became more and more pronounced, as my Faith became stronger and stronger, which it always will when it is properly placed. Little by little, the Holy Spirit began to *"effectually work"* even in a fashion that I have never known Him to work in my life. So, what I'm telling you meets the test on the two fronts that really counts:

1. There's nothing more Scriptural than what I've said about the Cross. Actually, the entirety of the Word of God points completely and totally toward the Cross of Christ. In fact, that is its story.

2. The power manifested, changes one's life. It's changed mine, and in fact, it has changed the lives of untold millions.

But due to the fact that there has been so little preaching and teaching on the Cross in the last several decades, most Christians have no idea as to where their Faith should be, and what really constitutes a victorious, overcoming, Christian life. Many have the idea that all of this is automatic, and then they find it isn't, they don't know what to say or do. Others, in the Pentecostal and Charismatic camps (and I am Pentecostal), think that once they're Baptized with the Holy Spirit, the process is automatic from then on. As well, they find that it isn't, and become more confused than ever.

## NOTHING IS AUTOMATIC WITH THE LORD

The Christian should get that in his mind. The Lord always requires something, and that something is Faith, and more particularly, Faith in the Finished Work of Christ.

NOTES

All Christians know about Faith, but they don't know what the proper object should be, which is the Cross. So, they keep trying to increase their Faith, having been taught that their *"Faith level"* determines all things, etc.

It's not one's *"Faith level"* that determines anything. While it is certainly true that there is such a thing as *"weak Faith"* or *"strong Faith"*; still, it's the object of one's Faith that makes all the difference. That object must ever be the Cross.

Even then, this is Faith that must be evidenced even on a *"daily"* basis. Jesus plainly said this in Luke 9:23.

The Lord has designed this in this manner, in order that we may continue to evidence Faith in Him. That's what He means by taking up the Cross daily.

That means the Faith we had in the Cross yesterday, will not suffice for today. There must be a fresh enduement of the placing of our Faith, even as there is a fresh enduement of power.

Faith does not really go up and down. It's just that we need to renew on a daily basis, the placement of the Faith we already have, which in essence means that we start each day understanding that our benefits in every capacity come from the Cross, i.e., *"what Christ did there!"* The Lord has designed it in this fashion, that we never forget that which the Lord has done.

## THE CROSS AND THE PERFECT AGE TO COME

The last two Chapters of Revelation proclaim the perfect age to come. Satan will be locked away forever in the Lake of Fire, along with all of his demon spirits and fallen angels (Rev. 20:11-15). God will actually transfer His Headquarters from Heaven to Earth. There will be no more sin, neither any of the results of sin, which are death, suffering, pain, sickness, crime, etc. The former things are truly *"passed away."*

But yet even in this environment, a perfect environment incidently, in order that the eternal generations to come never forget the price that was paid to make all of this possible, the Holy Spirit in those last two Chapters of Revelation, refers seven times to the *"Lamb,"* referring to Christ Jesus (Rev. 21:9, 14, 22-23, 27; 22:1, 3).

*"Seven"* is God's number of perfection, and in this case, refers to all that Christ has done.

*"Lamb"* as it refers to Christ, points to what He did for fallen humanity, by becoming the *"Lamb of God Who taketh away the sin of the world"* (Jn. 1:29).

The Holy Spirit in proclaiming these things in this manner, wants us to never forget this which was done, and which was done at such a price, and in fact, Who did this great thing. It was the One Whose Name is above every name, and yet, He is referred to here as *"the Lamb."*

## IN YOU

The statement made by Paul, *"Which effectually worketh also in you that believe,"* refers to the Holy Spirit Who abides within. This is the only answer for man!

The world of psychology attempts to address the problems of man by dealing with externals. That's all it can do, which of course is no help whatsoever.

To the contrary, the Lord goes to the heart of the problem, that which is inside of man, and does so by the power of the Holy Spirit. It is only the Spirit of God Who can make one what one ought to be. He can change one's personality, one's passions, in effect, everything! That's His business, and He knows exactly how it should be done. He demands only one thing on our part:

That our Faith be in the Finished Work of Christ. That being the case, humility will be our lot also, for the Cross is the very epitome of humility. We are to have Faith in that, and we can be assured, that the Holy Spirit Who is God, and Who resides in us, is there to stay forever, and in fact is there to perform a task, will in fact, perform that task. The only thing that hinders Him, is our misplaced Faith. Again I emphasize, it's not so much lack of Faith, as it is misplaced Faith (Jn. 16:14).

If we place our Faith properly in the great Sacrifice of the Redeemer, we can be assured that the Holy Spirit will do great and mighty things with us because He is *"in us."*

(14) "FOR YE, BRETHREN, BECAME FOLLOWERS OF THE CHURCHES OF GOD

WHICH IN JUDAEA ARE IN CHRIST JESUS: FOR YE ALSO HAVE SUFFERED LIKE THINGS OF YOUR OWN COUNTRYMEN, EVEN AS THEY HAVE OF THE JEWS:"

The moral of this particular Scripture is, that persecution inevitably arises from the outside when a Christian patterns his life after the Lord.

Paul tenderly reminds these Brothers that they were not the first to be afflicted. The Churches in Judea, which are in Christ Jesus had been the first and through faithful endurance had become an example of what Jesus had predicted about the suffering entailed in Discipleship.

Apparently the way these earliest Jewish Christians handled themselves had become widely known, even before Luke wrote Acts about A.D. 62. Paul's sympathy toward and harmony with Judean Christianity, whose bitter opponent he had been before conversion, is hereby assured, and the unity of all Christians, no matter what ethnic background or geographical locality, underlies this description of their common experience regarding persecution. Hearty acceptance of the Word, which is so often accompanied by adversity, is the very thing that insures one against falling away when adversity arises (Mat. 13:20-21; Lk. 8:13).

Both the Thessalonian Churches and the Churches in Judea suffered persecution from fellow-countrymen. For the Thessalonians these were predominantly Gentiles, though Jews also had been instrumental in stirring up opposition in that city (Acts 17:5-9). For the Judean Churches, opposition had come from those of a Jewish background who, of course, were also strong advocates of Jewish religion that Christianity so strongly threatened (Thomas).

## THE CHURCH

The phrase, *"For ye, Brethren, became followers of the Churches of God which in Judaea are in Christ Jesus,"* identifies all as being True Churches, because they *"are in Christ Jesus."* They are founded on His Truth, which pertains to His Finished Work. This does not mean that the Church at Thessalonica was founded on the same model, for actually it wasn't; or that they professed to be the followers of those Churches, but that they had been treated in the same way, and thus were like them.

NOTES

The object of this is, to comfort in the same manner, and that it was to be expected that a True Church would be persecuted.

By Paul using the first Jewish Christians as examples, is probably because they had first suffered for Christ, were the oldest part of the Christian Church, and had endured the fiercest trials. Ironically enough, even as we mentioned earlier, these were the very Churches in Judea which Paul had tried to literally put out of business. In fact, he would have gone to any lengths to have blotted out their memory from the Earth. He hated Christ that much.

However, there had been the great Damascus Road experience, which changed this man in a moment's time, and changed him forever. Consequently, the persecutor now becomes the persecuted. How ironical!

Therefore, Paul knows both sides of this fence so to speak, as no other man in the world of his day.

Even though the Church would become splintered a little later, the Early Church was in fact, one Church. They were one, because they were one in Faith and in fact, one in persecution. In other words, all of them suffered persecution to one degree or the other.

There were no religious Denominations of that day, and as well, there was really no Headquarters Church. As the Holy Spirit began in Jerusalem, some few years later, He moved His sphere of operation to Antioch. However, Antioch somewhat became a Headquarters Church, not so much by popular acclaim, but rather because of the action taking place in this Church.

It seems that this Church first of all, had very successfully mixed the two types of people, Jews and Gentiles. This was not done in Jerusalem, with any Gentile belonging to that Church, doing so by becoming a Jewish proselyte. But it was Antioch which soon became the major thrust in the Church of the world of that day, and because of the Missionary activity which went out from that Assembly (Acts 13:1-5).

As well, there was no titular leader of the Church of that time. Once again, had the

Holy Spirit desired such, Simon Peter certainly could have been, or Paul, etc.; however, such did not exist, and was really not intended to exist.

All of these men, and I speak of the original Twelve, plus others, played a great part in the Early Church, with Paul without a doubt, playing the most important part of all. He was given the New Covenant by the Lord, and actually was given the responsibility of being the Masterbuilder of the Church, which referred to the fact, that the New Covenant must be the foundation of the Church, and it was his responsibility to see to it that nothing else intruded (I Cor. 3:10).

Christ was the Head of the Church, and a very active Head at that! He worked exclusively through the Holy Spirit, as the Holy Spirit worked through the various Disciples and Apostles, etc.

Regrettably, the Church began to apostatize after the death of Paul and the other Apostles. From this apostasy, it took some 13 centuries to bring it back, which began with the Reformation.

Since the turn of the Twentieth Century, the Church has experienced the great outpouring of the Holy Spirit, exactly as prophesied by Joel, who referred to it somewhat as the *"Latter Rain"* (Joel 2:23).

Personally, I do not feel the Latter Rain is over. I feel the greatest outpouring is yet ahead!

## PERSECUTION

The phrase, *"For ye also have suffered like things of your own countrymen, even as they have of the Jews,"* pertaining to persecution, was mostly instigated by the Jews.

While both Jews and Gentiles suffered persecution from their own countrymen, still, in many places it was the Jews who stirred up the Gentiles against the Churches. In Israel proper, the Jews persecuted the Churches directly; in other parts of the Roman Empire, they did it by means of others. They were the real authors of it, as they were in Judea; but they usually accomplished it by producing an excitement among the heathen, and by the plea that the Apostles were making war on Civil institutions, which of course, was basely false. This was the case in fact, in Thessalonica.

NOTES

*"The Jews which believed not, moved with envy . . . set all the city on an uproar.*

*"They drew Jason and certain Brethren unto the rulers of the city, crying, these that have turned the world upside down have come hither also"* (Acts 17:5-6). The same thing occurred a short time after at Berea.

*"When the Jews of Thessalonica had knowledge that the Word of God was preached of Paul at Berea, they came thither also, and stirred up the people"* (Acts 17:13).

And then, *"The unbelieving Jews stirred up the Gentiles, and made their minds evil-affected against the Brethren"* (Acts 14:2).

The Epistle, as Paul gives the information here, represents the case accurately as the history states it. It was the Jews mostly who set on foot the persecutions against the Apostles and their followers.

## PERSECUTION OF TRUE CHRISTIANITY

On the other hand, Paul sees the persecution as proof of genuineness (Jn. 15:20). To suffer for Christ's sake, to endure the inevitable antagonism and persecution of the world, is to be found in the holy succession of the True Church from the beginning. However, when the Gospel is received as God's Word and not man's invention, it is effectual in the moral realm. It produces holy living, and is not overthrown by persecution, but actually thrives in that atmosphere.

Why the persecution?

The Message that Paul preached, which was the very Word of the Living God, supreme and authoritative for time and for eternity, was and is different than any other message or philosophy in the world. In fact, this is the character in which the Gospel challenges men for all time, and unto today. The Word of God, unlike the word of mere men, does not solicit our approval or court our approbation. It confronts us with the authority of Heaven and, as Paul declared on another occasion at Athens, now *"commandeth all men every where to repent"* (Acts 17:30).

It is this confrontation which brings out the animosity in men. They are confronted with their lost state, their rebellion against God, their sinful condition and even their present sins. Nothing else confronts them in this fashion, only the Gospel.

However, if it is to be noticed, the Jews who in fact, professed God, and in a great way one might quickly add, were far more fierce in their antagonism toward the Gospel than the Gentiles.

Why?

It is the same presently with those who claim to be of God, but really aren't. In other words, we're speaking here of the Apostate Church, which would have characterized the Jews of Paul's day, and characterizes great parts of the modern Church presently, actually, the far greater majority.

In a sense, there have always been two Churches, which goes all the way back to the very beginning of the Jewish people. While they did not refer to themselves as *"Church,"* still, the nation of Israel was God's representative in the world; however, there were always two Israel's so to speak! Such is very obvious as one reads the account of Israel in the Old Testament. There was always a small segment which loved God and served Him faithfully, while the greater part of the nation, although still claiming Righteousness, in fact served idols, etc.

It is the same today with the modern Church, as it was then with Israel. There have always been two Churches, and both are usually intermingled. The apostate Church is far larger than the True Church, and almost altogether instigates persecution against the True Church.

## HOW CAN ONE TELL THE DIFFERENCE?

As should be obvious, Satan dresses up his wares very religiously. This thrust is generally always as an *"angel of light"* (II Cor. 11:12-15). In other words, it looks like God, acts like God, and on the surface seems like God. But in reality, it is the very opposite.

Those who are shallow in the Lord, mostly ignorant of God's Word, cannot tell the difference. In fact, almost altogether, they will opt for this false way, or I should say *"false ways,"* for there are many.

Almost without exception, the false way promises its dupes something which appeals to their flesh. It might be pride, it might be money, it might be other things; nevertheless, the *"flesh"* in the apostate Church appeals to the *"flesh"* in the shallow Christian,

NOTES

and simply because there is no Holy Spirit in the apostate Church.

As we stated in previous Commentary regarding this Chapter, there was a time that religious apostasy abided mostly in modernistic Churches; however, that day has long since passed. Apostasy is in the Fundamentalist Churches grandly, in their denial of the Baptism with the Holy Spirit; as well, it is in many Pentecostal and Charismatic Churches, with the respective Leadership in many of these Denominations completely apostatized.

To tell the difference in the two, the True Church and the Apostate Church, first of all, one must know the Word of God. That means they must check everything according to the Word, and if it doesn't match the Word, it must be discarded.

One need only turn on what is referred to as *"Christian Television,"* and in many cases, the flesh screams out so loud that it is deafening. And yet, many Christians not only cannot hear it or see it, but they readily accept its lure. In fact, the problem is so awful at the present time, even so blatant, that many, if not most, unsaved people can see this of which I speak, but many so-called Christians can't! In fact, it is so awful, so blatant, that one wonders why a blind man couldn't see what's being done, but regrettably most Christians don't, continuing to pour hundreds of millions of dollars into that which is not only worthless, but actually aids and abets the Devil.

As Paul said, *"Ye suffer fools gladly"* (II Cor. 11:19).

## A DEPARTURE FROM THE CROSS

Due to the fact that the modern Church has had almost no teaching and preaching on the Cross in the last several decades, the Church has lost its way, has lost its moorings. Without a proper understanding of the Cross, I personally believe that it's not possible for one to understand the Word of God as one should. I think it's very difficult to have very much leading of the Holy Spirit. Consequently, I place the cause of the condition of the modern Church at the doorsteps of a misunderstanding, or outright denial of the Cross of Christ, i.e., *"the Finished Work of Christ."* If one doesn't have this proper foundation, every structure built is consequently going to be somewhat wrong.

In fact, and to which we have already alluded, the situation has gotten so bad, that great segments of the modern Church are openly repudiating the Cross, even referring to it as *"past miseries,"* and telling Christians they do not want to have anything to do with the Cross.

Such teaching is not only wrong, but borders on the edge of rank blasphemy. But yet, millions of people are flocking to these particular teachers, and in many cases, in their heart of hearts, the people know this teaching is wrong, terribly wrong! So what is it that attracts them?

For the most part, these same so-called Teachers also proclaim grandly the *"money gospel."* In other words, everything has been reduced down to a dollar bill. Their gospel claims that if one gives so much money, one will receive ten times that amount back, or even a hundred times, etc. This message, although crass, appeals to greed, of which all of us seem to have some measure.

If the sinner rejects the Cross, there remains no other way for him to be saved. Likewise, if the Christian rejects the Cross, all Spiritual Growth stops, with the door being opened wide to the onslaughts of Satan, over which the Believer will have no defense. I wish to ask the Reader this question!

How long has it been since you've heard a Message on the Cross of Christ? Even in the Churches where the Pastor truly loves God, the Cross is by and large ignored. In those cases, it is not done maliciously or even intentionally, but rather because of spiritual blindness. As stated, the Church has drifted further and further away from its true foundation.

## THAT WHICH THE LORD HAS INSTRUCTED ME TO DO

The great Revelation which the Lord has given me on the Cross, and in fact, continues to give to me, which has changed my life, is not intended to be kept in my heart alone. That should be obvious! The Lord has instructed me to proclaim this Message of the Cross loud and clear, that all may have an opportunity to hear and receive. That's at least one of the reasons, He is opening up Radio Stations all over the nation, that we may air this Message 24 hours a day, seven days a week. Already, the results have been absolutely phenomenal, for which we give the Lord all the Praise and all the Glory.

In fact, in these Commentaries, and I speak primarily of Romans forward, I have done my best to do exactly what I feel like the Lord has instructed me to do as it regards the teaching of this all-important subject concerning the Cross of Christ, the great foundation of Christianity. I've tried my best to make it as understandable as possible, and I believe the Lord has helped me to do that.

One of the greatest favors that you the Reader could do anyone, is to give them at least one of these Commentaries, which could change their lives. In fact, if it's at all possible, you ought to try to give away one a week, or at least one a month. While all Christians should be included, if possible, you should target Preachers most of all, and for the obvious reasons.

In speaking to a Pastor by telephone in a distant city day before yesterday (October 18, 1999), he made mention to me of one of the Commentaries I had given to him regarding this very subject of *"the Cross."* He said, or words to this effect: *"Brother Swaggart, the teaching contained in that Commentary has changed my life."* He went on to say many other things, which let me know that he had been studying this which was written, and it had gotten down into his spirit, and definitely was in the process of gloriously changing his life.

This is a Pastor who loves God, but his knowledge of the Cross, as it is with many Preachers, was very limited. As a result, the lack of knowledge as it regards this all-important subject, the most important of all, had caused him great problems, as it does with all who love God. There is no victory outside of the Cross; there is no overcoming power outside of the Cross; there is no real closeness to Christ outside of the Cross!

## WHAT IS APOSTASY?

Apostasy is a departure from Truth. Pure and simple, it is a dilution of the Word of God in some manner, whether denying it altogether, or mixing man's ideas with the Word, which is generally the case.

NOTES

Apostasy in one form or the other, has always existed; however, the apostasy of the last days, in which we have already entered, will be the worst of all. Paul plainly said, *"Now the Spirit speaketh expressly, that in the latter times* (the day in which we now live) *some shall depart from the Faith, giving heed to seducing spirits, and doctrines of devils;*

*"Speaking lies in hypocrisy; having their conscience seared with a hot iron"* (I Tim. 4:1-2).

If it is to be noticed, Paul spoke of a *"departure from the Faith."* This plainly and simply speaks of the foundation of Biblical Christianity, which is the Vicarious, Offering of Christ of Himself on the Cross as a Sacrifice to atone for all sin (Jn. 1:29; 3:16). A departure from anything in the Word of God is bad enough, but a departure from the Cross spells doom to those who would go in that perfidious direction! *And that's the great apostasy, a departure from the Cross.*

I personally feel in these days, and especially those soon to come, that is if the Lord tarries at all, that the dividing line is going to be more and more the Cross. Against the onslaughts of Satan, and the allurements of this world, the Cross is the only refuge (Rom. 6:2-6; Gal. 6:14). For those who reject that, they will go into apostasy, and ever deeper I might quickly add! For those who accept the Cross of Christ as the great foundation of all that we have in Christ, they will know victory beyond compare.

I believe one of the reasons the Lord has given me this great Revelation, and believing that He at the same time is giving it to others, is that this great Truth of Truths, can be abundantly known. That's one of the reasons, as stated, that the Lord has instructed me, I believe, to install Radio Stations all over this nation, which we have already begun doing. The Message of the Cross, is *"the Message."* Everything must spring from the Cross, and means everything. Of course, I'm speaking of all that comes from God.

The Church has been inundated with teaching on Faith in the last several decades, but it's not been Faith in the Cross, but rather *"faith in faith,"* or *"faith in ourselves,"* etc. Either way, it is not the type of Faith which is taught in the Word of God, which always has as its object the Cross of Christ. In fact, that's what the term *"the Faith"* actually means (Gal. 1:23; 2:16, 20; 3:14; Eph. 2:8; 3:12, 17; 4:13; Phil. 1:27; 3:9, etc.)

I know I'm right about this of what I say, because the Lord has given me this Truth; consequently, it would behoove you to study the things we've said concerning the Cross in these Commentaries. This is not something I've made up out of my mind, but rather the Word of the Lord which was given to me by Revelation. In fact, in the doing of this, the Lord led me directly to the Word, showing me in the Word where this great Truth is, which when seen, becomes the entirety of the Word so to speak.

First of all, He took me to the Sixth Chapter of Romans and showed me what it meant. He then took me to the Eighth Chapter of Romans, showing me how the Holy Spirit works. He then enlightened me on Romans, Chapter Seven, showing me that most Christians, even most Preachers, misunderstand this Chapter, which brings upon themselves tremendous problems. In other words, I know of what I say; consequently, I'm asking you to study these words very carefully, because they are very important in more ways than one.

(15) "WHO BOTH KILLED THE LORD JESUS, AND THEIR OWN PROPHETS, AND HAVE PERSECUTED US; AND THEY PLEASE NOT GOD, AND ARE CONTRARY TO ALL MEN:"

Mention of *"the Jews"* furnishes Paul an occasion to digress slightly and deliver a violent criticism of this persecuting element among them. Some have said that such harsh language is markedly out of character for Paul as we know him from his other writings. I do not necessarily think so!

While it is true that he really never repeated himself in this fashion again in his other Epistles, still, the undertone is there, especially in Romans. As well, the Apostle was led by the Holy Spirit in these things that he said, meaning, that the Spirit of God desired that they be said, and in this manner.

We must never forget this as we read the Scriptures, the things said by all the writers, are exactly what the Holy Spirit wanted said, and said in the manner in which they were said.

NOTES

NOTES

Paul had been chased out of Damascus (Acts 9:23-25) and Jerusalem (Acts 9:29-30) by his own people not very long after his conversion. His Message was rejected and his party driven out of Pisidian Antioch as well (Acts 13:45-46, 50). At Iconium the Jews poisoned people's minds against Paul and Barnabus and ultimately forced them out (Acts 14:2, 5-6).

The Jews made a special journey to Lystra to instigate an uprising that produced Paul's stoning and being left for dead (Acts 14:19). Jewish opposition continued to hound this Gospel band well into the second journey, specifically at Thessalonica, again producing Paul's exit (Acts 17:5, 10).

Even now as Paul pens these words from Corinth, a united attack has been mounted against him by the city's Jewish residents (Acts 18:6, 12-13). Coupled with this, the present plight of the Thessalonian Christians (I Thess. 3:3), is ultimately traceable to Jewish opponents. It is no wonder that Paul uses the occasion to recount their consistent opposition to the Lord Jesus.

## THE GREAT CRIME OF ISRAEL

The acme of the Jews' opposition is their part in the death of the Lord Jesus. Hence, Paul places this crime first among their offenses. By persuasion of the Jewish Leaders, the Roman authorities crucified Jesus (Jn. 19:16; I Cor. 2:8). Though joint responsibility was shared by Gentiles and Jews (Acts 4:27), at this point Paul lays guilt for the crime on Israel. The aggravated nature of the injustice is implied by the way Paul uses the Name *"Lord Jesus."* It was none less than the Exalted Lord of Glory against Whom this heinous crime was committed.

*"The Prophets"* are grouped with *"the Lord Jesus"* as murder victims of the Jews. This is a possible interpretation in that many, though not all, the Old Testament Prophets died in this way. Also, it is an oft-sounded note in Biblical writings (I Ki. 19:10; Mat. 23:31, 35, 37; Lk. 13:34; Acts 7:52; Rom. 11:3).

More important in this connection is Jesus' Parable of the Vineyard in which killing some of the servants (Prophets) is preliminary to killing the Son (Mat. 21:35-39; Mk. 12:5-8).

Paul concludes Verse 15 by listing two more characteristics of the Jewish antagonists. *"They displease God and are hostile to all men."* The former is clearly an understatement, since they were militantly opposed to God as well. Their zeal for God was not guided by knowledge (Rom. 10:2). So by opposing God's Messiah so strenuously, they became God's adversaries. This could not help but produce hostility to all men — a hostility arising not from a supposed racial superiority, but one manifested in stubborn resistance to admitting Jesus' Messiahship, which continues unto this very day (Thomas).

## MURDERERS

The phrase, *"Who both killed the Lord Jesus, and their own Prophets,"* presents the crime of the ages. To kill the Prophets was bad enough, evil enough, more terrible than words could imagine, but to murder the Lord of Glory, their own Messiah, was a crime which has no equal, and a crime which can have no equal.

Of course, Christ allowed Himself to be killed, for He could have stopped the situation at any time. He plainly said concerning His life, *"No man taketh it from Me, but I lay it down of Myself. I have power to lay it down, and I have power to take it again"* (Jn. 10:18).

Nevertheless, this in no way lessened the murderous intent of the Jews nor the evil of their black hearts. Even though the Lord allowed them to do this, that in no way lessened their guilt. In the eyes of God and man, they *"killed the Lord Jesus!"*

No, I am not anti-Semitic because I say that, as Paul certainly was not anti-Semitic, being Jewish himself. I love the Jews, even as Paul did; however, for me to deny what they did, or for Paul to have done so, would in no way have done them a favor. To be sure, they have suffered down through history as few people have ever suffered, and their darkest days are just ahead.

Paul was proud with no common pride of his Jewish descent; it was better in his eyes than any patent of nobility. His heart swelled as he thought of the nation to which the adoption pertained, the Glory, the Covenants, the giving of the Law, the service of God, and the Promises; whose were the fathers, and of whom, as concerning the flesh, Christ came. Apostle of the Gentiles though he was, he had great sorrow and unceasing pain in his heart, when he remembered the antagonism of the Jews to the Gospel.

However, irrespective of that, only in the character of bitter enemies has he been in contact with them in recent years. They have hunted him from city to city in Asia and Europe; they have raised the populace against his converts, even as we have already said. They have sought to poison the minds of his Disciples against him. He knows that this policy is that with which his countrymen as a whole have identified themselves; and as he looks steadily at it, he sees that in doing so they have only acted in consistency with all their past history.

THE CROWNING SIN

The crowning sin of the race is put in the forefront; they slew the Lord Jesus; but before the Lord came, they had slain His Prophets; and after He had gone, they expelled His Apostles. God had put them in a position of privilege, but only for a time; they were the depositaries, or trustees, of the knowledge of God as the Saviour of men; and now, when the time had come for that knowledge to be diffused throughout all the world, they clung proudly and stubbornly to the old position. They pleased not God and were contrary to all men, in forbidding the Apostles to preach Salvation to the heathen.

The words of Paul are but an echo, all through this Passage, of the words of Stephen, whom Paul remembered greatly: *"Ye stiffnecked and uncircumcised in heart and ears, ye do always resist the Holy Spirit as your Fathers did so do ye."*

And yet, what we have here on the part of Paul is not a burst of temper, though there is undoubtedly strong feeling in it; it is the vehement condemnation, by a man in thorough sympathy with the Mind and Spirit of God, of the principles on which the Jews as a nation had acted at every period of their history. In other words, even though Paul writes these words, it is the Holy Spirit Who is the actual Author.

NOTES

Down through the years their cup of iniquity was filling all the time. Every generation did something to raise the level within.

The men who bade Amos begone, and eat his bread at home, raised it a little; the men who sought Hosea's life in the Sanctuary raised it further; so did those who put Jeremiah in the dungeon, and those who murdered Zechariah between the Temple and the Altar.

When Jesus was nailed to the Cross, the cup was full to the brim. When those whom He left behind to be His witnesses, and to preach repentance and remission of sins to all men, beginning at Jerusalem, were expelled or put to death, it then ran over. God could bear no more.

Side by side with the cup of iniquity the cup of judgment had been filling also; and they overflowed together. In fact, Paul will say in the next Verse, *"The wrath is come upon them to the uttermost"* (MacLaren).

THE PERSECUTION OF PAUL

The phrase, *"And have persecuted us,"* presents in both statements a strong denunciation of sin coupled with prophetic insight into the consequences which are following.

The Jews thirsted for Paul's life, and tried in every manner to find a way to kill him. Their hatred of him was bitter to say the least!

Without a doubt, they hated Paul as they hated no other man. As we said previously, they considered him a turncoat. The one who had bitterly opposed the Church, was now the great builder of the Church. The one who had hated Christ, was now His greatest promoter.

How they accounted for this, is anyone's guess. They knew Paul, and knowing him, they knew that he had no leanings whatsoever toward followers of Christ, rather hating them. So, how in the world could he have been changed so dramatically?

No doubt, they heard of the Damascus Road experience, with Christ appearing to him. Paul was quick to relate this experience and no doubt it had come to the ears of the Religious Leaders of Israel. However, they took that, even as they had taken everything else, and turned it into something devious and licentious. They evidently did not at all stop and think, as to what power must have been manifested in this appearance of

Christ, to turn one as strong-headed as Paul, who was then called *"Saul!"*

In a sense, this tremendous occasion of Paul on the Damascus Road, was as well offered to national Israel. But they treated that as they had treated all else, as it pertained to God. They did not seek Him out at all, asking as to what had happened, allowing it to be a visitation to them as well! They rather attempted to kill him, and probably was greatly instrumental in that terrible act finally being brought to bear when Paul was ultimately executed by Nero.

As the statement was made, their cup of iniquity was constantly filling and was now running over.

## THE ATTITUDE OF PAUL TOWARD THE JEWS

Some may take umbrage, as some have taken umbrage at Paul's statements here, as being too harsh. As stated, they were not!

To judge because of these statements, that the Apostle did not love his own countrymen, despite their cruel persecution of him, is reading too much into the Text. In fact, Paul loved them dearly. The Reader must realize, that love does not overlook sin, even though it continues to love the sinner. As well, the Apostle was not speaking of all Jews, or speaking to them as a particular people, only against those who were guilty of the terrible crimes which he mentioned, and those who had continued in their paths.

I remind the Reader, that Jesus referred to the Pharisees as *"snakes"* (Mat. 23:33), and that's exactly what they were!

There are few people in the world more cruel than the self-righteous. They will do absolutely anything, no matter how negative or wicked it might be, and feel justified in doing so. In fact, they do it all in the Name of the Lord. Of course, these people do not really know the Lord, as the Pharisees of old did not know the Lord. Regrettably, that includes the far greater majority of those who call themselves *"Christians."*

## WHY DID PAUL HAVE TO BE SO PLAIN AND CLEAR IN HIS STATEMENTS?

As stated, this is what the Holy Spirit wanted him to say.

NOTES

It is regrettable but true, that many people who sincerely love the Lord, still have to have someone to spell it out for them very clearly, before they know what you're talking about. They don't have enough spiritual discernment to see the situation as it really is; unfortunately, only a few have such discernment.

For instance, occasionally we get letters into our office, and the writer will mention that they support our Ministry and then they will name another Ministry which they also support, which is so contrary to what we teach and believe, that it's almost laughable. One has to wonder as to how in the world some Christians could entertain such thinking? It would be about like someone supporting Paul and the Judaizers at the same time. How in the world could they come to such a conclusion?

Don't misunderstand, I am very grateful for the support, irrespective as to the thinking of the individual; however, my first and foremost business with every Christian is not their financial support, but rather their Spiritual Growth.

It is definitely not pleasant for the Preacher to have to make very strong, negative statements. I'm sure it grieved Paul to have to say the things that he did; however, the main thrust of any Preacher of the Gospel, or any Believer for that matter, is to hear from the Lord, and then to deliver undiluted and uncompromised that which he has heard.

## PLEASING GOD

The phrase, *"And they please not God,"* in fact, presents a monumental understatement.

As should be obvious, they did not please God, nor seek to please Him; though they pretended that their opposition to the Gospel was through their zeal for God's Glory, they were in fact, hypocrites of the worst kind.

God's Plan is to save the world, or at least as many as will believe, through Jesus Christ, His Son. The Jews greatly displeased Him, and were contrary to all men by hindering, at every turn, God's program to save men. In their outrageous perverseness, exclusiveness, and willful blindness, they not only refused Christ themselves, but tried to prevent the Good News of Salvation from reaching the Gentiles.

CONTRARY TO MANKIND

The phrase, *"And are contrary to all men,"* refers to their sectarian, self-righteous spirit and attitude.

The hatred and contempt which the Jews had for other nations is noticed by Tacitus, Juvenal, and other heathen writers. Thus, Tacitus writes of them:

*"They are faithful to obstinacy, and merciful toward themselves, but toward all others are actuated by the most irreconcilable hatred."*

And Juvenal says, *"They will not show the road to one who was not of their religion, nor lead the thirsty person if uncircumcised to the common spring."*

How had they come to this?

The Truth is, when people make up their own religion, even as the Jews had come to do, which meant they had forsaken the Word of God for their own fabrications, this is always the result. While every single one does not come out to this description, I think I can say without fear of contradiction, that most do.

For instance, the *"religious right"* in this country, is in fact the worst thing that ever happened to this country, or any other country for that matter. Don't misunderstand, I'm not a political liberal, but neither do I consider myself a conservative. I am a Christian, and that should state the case.

If the crowd which I have mentioned had their way, they would shut the doors of every Church in this nation and the world that did not agree exactly with them. They would stop every single Ministry that did not see eye to eye with their doctrines, whatever those doctrines might be. They put on such a front and claim to be so pious, but in reality, they have the same spirit as those who crucified Christ.

The following is hypothetical and somewhat humorous, but perhaps at least to some degree it proves my point:

The story goes like this: I was walking across a bridge recently. I spied this man who looked like he was ready to jump from the bridge into the water. So, I thought I'd try to stall him until the authorities showed up (or at least until I had time to put film in my camera).

*"Don't jump,"* I said.

*"Why not?"* he said, *"nobody loves me."*

*"God loves you,"* I said. *"You believe in God, don't you?"*

*"Yes, I believe in God,"* he said.

*"Good,"* I said, *"Are you Christian or Jewish?"*

*"Christian,"* he replied!

*"Me, too!"* I said. *"Protestant or Catholic?"*

*"Protestant,"* he said.

*"Me, too!"* I said. *"What kind of Protestant?"*

*"Baptist,"* he said.

*"Baptist?"*

*"Me, too!"* I said. *"Independent Baptist or Southern?"*

*"Independent Baptist,"* he said.

*"Me, too!"* I said. *"New Evangelical/Moderate Independent Baptist or Conservative Independent Baptist?"*

*"Conservative Independent Baptist,"* he said.

*"Me, too!"* I said. *"Calvinistic Conservative Independent Baptist or Lose-Your-Salvation Armenian Conservative Independent Baptist?"*

*"Calvinistic Conservative Independent Baptist,"* he said.

*"Me, too!"* I said. *"Dispensational Premillennial Calvinistic Conservative Independent Baptist or Historical Premillennial Calvinistic Conservative Independent Baptist?"*

*"Dispensational Premillennial Calvinistic Conservative Independent Baptist,"* he said.

*"Me, too!"* I said. *"Against Women in Ministry Dispensational Premillennial Calvinistic Conservative Independent Baptist or For Women in Ministry Dispensational Premillennial Calvinistic Conservative Independent Baptist?"*

*"Against Women in Ministry Dispensational Premillennial Calvinistic Conservative Independent Baptist,"* he said.

*"Me, too!"* I said. *"Unashamed Fundamentalist Against Women in Ministry Dispensational Premillennial Calvinistic Conservative Independent Baptist or Strict Separation of Church and State Against Women in Ministry Dispensational Premillennial Calvinistic Conservative Independent Baptist?"*

*"Unashamed Fundamentalist Against Women in Ministry Dispensational Premillennial Calvinistic Conservative Independent Baptist,"* he said.

*"Me, too!"* I said. *"Pro-Disney Boycott Pro-Life Unashamed Fundamentalist Against Women in Ministry Dispensational Premillennial Calvinistic Conservative Independent Baptist or Anti-Disney Boycott Pro-Choice Unashamed Fundamentalist Against Women in Ministry Dispensational Premillennial Calvinistic Conservative Independent Baptist?"*

*"Pro-Disney Boycott Pro-Life Unashamed Fundamentalist Against Women in Ministry Dispensational Premillennial Calvinistic Conservative Independent Baptist,"* he said.

*"Me, too!"* I said. *"KJV Only Pro-Disney Boycott Pro-Life Unashamed Fundamentalist Against Women in Ministry Dispensational Premillennial Calvinistic Conservative Independent Baptist or Modern Versions Pro-Disney Boycott Pro-Life Unashamed Fundamentalist Against Women in Ministry Dispensational Premillennial Calvinistic Conservative Independent Baptist?"*

*"Modern Versions Pro-Disney Boycott Pro-Life Unashamed Fundamentalist Against Women in Ministry Dispensational Premillennial Calvinistic Conservative Independent Baptist"* he said.

*"You heretic!"* I said . . . and pushed him over!

If you want a definition of *"religion,"* I've just given you one!

(16) "FORBIDDING US TO SPEAK TO THE GENTILES THAT THEY MIGHT BE SAVED, TO FILL UP THEIR SINS ALWAY: FOR THE WRATH IS COME UPON THEM TO THE UTTERMOST."

The Jews hated Jesus Christ, even with a hatred that goes beyond the normal animosity. As well, Paul's Gentile Mission provoked even more indignation, because it implied God's forsaking of Israel (Acts 13:46, 48-50; 17:4-5; Rom. 11:11, 25). The saving purpose of Gentile preaching was what the Jews sought to eliminate.

They filled up the cup, until Divine chastisement became inevitable. After generations of repeated apostasies and rebellion, Israel had arrived. The climax had come especially with the rejection of the Messiah Himself, and their already fixed Judgment was biding its time till its direct consequences were released, which they were a short time later.

NOTES

MINISTRY TO THE GENTILES

The phrase, *"Forbidding us to speak to the Gentiles that they might be saved,"* does not mean that the Jews were averse to the proselytism of the Gentiles, provided they were circumcised and kept the Law of Moses, in other words, becoming proselyte Jews. What they hated so much fell into two categories:

1. They hated Jesus Christ and all who followed Him, irrespective as to who they were.
2. Paul maintained, that the Jews and Gentiles were now on a level with regard to Salvation; that the wall of partition was broken down; that the Jew had no real advantages over the rest of mankind in this respect, and that the heathen might be saved without becoming Jews, or being circumcised (Rom. 2:25-29; 3:22-31). As stated, Jews did not hold it unlawful *"to speak to the Gentiles,"* and even to offer them eternal life (Mat. 23:15), but it was only on condition that they should become proselytes to their religion, and should observe the institutions of Moses. If saved, they held that it would be as Jews — either originally such, or such by becoming proselytes.

Paul maintained the very opposite direction, that heathens might be saved without becoming proselytes to the Jewish system, and that, in fact, Salvation was as freely offered to them as to the children of Abraham. And the Apostle taught of course, that all of this had been made possible by the Life, Death, and Resurrection of the Lord Jesus Christ. So, as stated, this was a double-barreled threat to Israel, at least in their present direction. Had they accepted the Lord, they would in fact in a sense, have been the premiere people. That would need explanation which I will not now take the time to do, but it will come to pass in the coming Millennium, when in fact, Israel will finally accept Christ Jesus, not only as Saviour, but as Messiah as well (Zech. 12:10-14; 13:1). In fact, almost all the Prophets of the Old Testament proclaimed this coming glad day. But with Israel setting themselves against the Plan of

God, which had always been the Lord Jesus Christ, in other words, everything for which God had proposed and the very reason that Israel had been raised up, there was nothing left but Judgment. God cannot abide anyone standing in His way, at least indefinitely. He will deal with people graciously and kindly, even though the people are very stubborn, and he will show mercy and grace for a long, long time; however, at some point, Judgment will come, if the person, or even an entire people such as Israel continue in their rebellion and rejection.

NOTES

### THE FILLING UP OF SINS

The phrase, *"To fill up their sins alway,"* proclaims the fact, and in glaring terminology, that there is a limit beyond which God will not go. Whatever that level is, and perhaps it changes or is different with different people and circumstances, barring repentance, which is a complete turnaround, Judgment will come.

The world can scoff at this or even the Church for that matter. None of that makes any difference, there is a measure of sin beyond which the Lord will not allow. That measure may be different as I have stated for some people because of the present light they have; nevertheless, it is a measure. We must never forget that.

To give you an example, the Lord spoke to Abraham about the Promised Land, and He mentioned the Amorites who occupied a part of that land, and who were idol worshippers, saying, *"For the iniquity of the Amorites is not yet full"* (Gen. 15:16). In other words, when they reached a certain limit, the Lord would destroy them, which in fact He did.

One can look at the nations and empires of the world all the way back to Adam, and this story is repeated over and over. There is a limit beyond which God will not allow. The reasons should be obvious. Sin is the most destructive force in the world. That means that if God did not step in with Judgment at some point, that man would ultimately destroy himself in totality.

Going back to the first phrase of this Verse, one of the characteristics of wrong direction, wrong doctrine, wrong thinking, in other words that which is the opposite of the Lord, is that such who hold these views, even as the Jews of old, are not satisfied to merely reject that which they oppose, they feel it is their duty to stop the Message *and* the Messenger regarding that of which they do not approve. And they will go to any lengths to stop the Message. In fact, it is no different now than then.

Even at the present time, if particular Religious Denominations are crossed in some way, or else they think they are, they will do the same as the Jews of old as it regarded Paul. They were trying to stop Paul from preaching, and, therefore, would kill him if they could. They felt they had to stop his voice. Their modern counterparts are identical in their viciousness.

They're not satisfied to no longer have that person in their particular Denomination, they feel that they must stop the man or woman from preaching, and as stated, they will use any tactics to do so. They will attempt to close every door, in other words, they feel they must silence the voice. The idea is this:

If one does not obey them in every capacity as to what they demand, and irrespective as to how unscriptural it might be, they feel this gives them the license to do whatever it is they desire. The individual in question becomes *"fair game,"* meaning, that anything goes.

I actually believe that if the law of the land allowed it, that these religious leaders, even as the Jewish leaders of old, would hire someone to murder the person in question.

First of all, they have a God-like complex. They actually believe, that whatever they say must be obeyed, and irrespective as to what it is. They believe they have spiritual authority and was granted this spiritual authority, when they were elected on the eighth or ninth ballot, etc. Of course, even an elementary knowledge of the Word of God debunks such foolishness; however, believe it or not, that's the manner in which the leadership of most Pentecostal Denominations operate. I certainly wouldn't say that all do that, but I do feel that most fall into that category.

The amazing thing is, they do not at all see the wickedness in what they're doing. They justify themselves irrespective as to what is done. Lying, cheating, slander, destruction, stealing, etc., are commonplace, all done in the Name of the Lord.

I think one could say without any fear of exaggeration, that the single most evil thing in the world of Paul's day, was the Religious Leaders of Israel. Because of the light they had, or were supposed to have, they were held much more responsible than Nero, or anyone of that ilk. It is the same presently.

I personally believe that the greatest evil in the world of this hour, is not the drug business, or any of the vices, as evil and wicked as those things actually are, but rather, much of organized religion, and even that which is not organized. There is no evil like religious evil, no wickedness like religious wickedness!

## THE WRATH OF GOD

The phrase, *"For the wrath is come upon them to the uttermost,"* is used somewhat in the past tense, simply because it is so sure of fulfillment. It is the certain climax of a long process. The idea is, that Paul saw in the signs of the times that the nation's day of grace had come to an end. What exactly he felt in his spirit, we do not know. Did the Lord give him a premonition as it regards what would actually happen to Jerusalem some 15 to 20 years later? In A.D. 70, Titus would completely destroy the city, with over a million Jews dying, and other hundreds of thousands sold as slaves all over the world of that day. At that time, Israel would in effect cease to exist as a nation, which condition would actually last for nearly 1900 years.

## PRESENT CIRCUMSTANCES

As I dictate these words, I am looking at a Commentary written by a British Preacher of the Gospel before the turn of the Twentieth Century. Speaking of his own country then, he said, *"Many observers tell us that the character* (of the nation) *has degenerated into a mere instinct for trade; and that it has begotten a vast unscrupulousness in dealing with the weak."*

He went on to speak about the opium trade with China, the liquor trade with the natives of Africa, the labor trade in the South Seas, etc.

He went on to say, *"All these are matters in regard to which the nation is in danger of settling into permanent hostility to God."*

NOTES

He then said, *"The wrath which is the due and inevitable accompaniment of such hostility, when persisted in, has not yet come on us to the very end; God has given us opportunity to rectify what is amiss, and to deal with all our interests in the spirit of the New Testament."*

And finally, *"The heritage of sin accumulates if it is not put away by well doing; and with sin, judgment. It is for us to learn by the Word of God and the examples of history that the nation and kingdom that will not serve Him shall perish."*

As stated, he said that before the turn of the Twentieth Century. And what happened?

England did not heed that word. In fact, at that particular time, England was the most powerful nation on the face of the Earth. Economically and militarily it was the strongest. But then came World War I, which saw a bloodletting of such proportions among British soldiers that it defies all description. Then some 20 years later, World War II exploded, which further diminished the nation. Consequently, Great Britain is only a shadow of what it once was.

## THE UNITED STATES

I have to wonder how close to Judgment is this nation? The terrible degree of wickedness is taking its deadly toll. This generation of children has been raised on MTV (Music Television). This particular network literally mocks every Standard of the Word of God, with kids paying the bitter price. It is a price of drunkenness, immorality, drug addiction, and now murder, with even the Public Schools becoming one of the most dangerous places in the country. When God is taken out, Hell is let in. Of that one can be certain!

The Judgment now is spotty, with the elements seemingly going berserk! What will it be tomorrow?

The Insurance Companies of America according to historical evidence, estimate that so many billions of dollars will be spent as it regards adverse weather conditions, whether earthquakes, Hurricanes, etc. In the last five years, that number has increased almost five-fold. In fact, the entirety of the world falls under the same adverse conditions. Whether it be the elements, war, pestilence, or disease, it is the Judgment of God upon a nation because of its sinfulness and wickedness. The United States has been given much Light as it regards the Gospel; consequently, much more is required of this nation than most. For the most part, what it has been required to do it has not done; consequently, the iniquity level is climbing higher and higher, and to be sure, there is a stopping point.

One of the most dangerous signs of all presently is, the lack of World Evangelism as it regards the Gospel.

Mark Buntain, the great Missionary to India, and who is now with the Lord made this statement, *"As long as America's greatest export is the Gospel of Jesus Christ, this soil will never know the jackbooted heel of an invader."*

Once the Gospel was America's greatest export, but now just as in England at the turn of the Twentieth Century, there is very little effort being made in this respect presently. Regrettably, with some few exceptions, most of the Missionaries being sent out now, are for the most part, amateur Psychologists. In other words, most of them have no touch of God within their lives whatsoever. I know what I'm talking about, because I've been there. There is an exception, as stated, here and there, and thank God for that; however, those exceptions are few and far between. This I think, is America's greatest danger.

Last week I was speaking with an Evangelist who is a product of one of the great youth programs in this nation, at least it was once great, who mentioned to me that most of these programs are nowhere as they once were. He went on to say, *"Brother Swaggart, where once their forte was prayer and dependence on the Holy Spirit, it is now psychology. Many of them,"* he went on to say, *"are now accepting Government aid, which means they must subscribe totally to the psychological way, which means at the same time, a repudiation of God's Word."*

THE FAULT OF ALL THIS IS THE CHURCH

As the Church goes, so goes the nation. Only the Church can set the moral tone, and the Church for the most part in the United States has abandoned the Word of God. This means they have abandoned God's Way, which is the Way of the Cross, opting for the things of the world instead. Man's wisdom has replaced God's Wisdom.

NOTES

The old-line Religious Denominations have for the most part denied the Baptism with the Holy Spirit. As a result, there is almost nothing of any spiritual content going on in these respective Denominations. To be sure, there is much religious activity, with such activity fooling many people into thinking that it is spiritual, when it really isn't. Without the Holy Spirit nothing is going to be done for God, and to be sure, the Holy Spirit has been denied. Of course, they will not agree to what I've just said, but it is the Truth.

The Pentecostal Denominations which once filled the world with Missionaries, have not so much denied the Holy Spirit, as rather ignored Him. Almost entirely, these Denominations have opted for the psychological way, and they are spiritually speaking, but a shadow of what they once were.

Of the tens of thousands of Charismatic Churches, many, if not most, of these have opted for the *"money gospel,"* which is actually in the category of rank heresy.

One Missionary with one of the leading Pentecostal Denominations after being out of the country for some years, came back a short time ago on furlough. According to his words, he was shocked at what he saw in the Churches. People were crawling around over the floor barking like dogs or roaring like lions, claiming that such stupidity is the moving of the Holy Spirit. Others were *"blowing on people,"* claiming that was the Spirit of God, with them falling over, etc. In other words, this particular Denomination had gone *"manifestation crazy!"*

There definitely are some few exceptions to all of these things I've said, but not many. As well, and to be sure, I take no delight in saying these things; however, I feel they must be said in hope that some Christians will wake up.

The Church needs to repent and get back to the Word of God. I realize, that I'm not liked at all among the Denominations. And this is the reason why. They do not like attention being called to these things which are being done, and above all, they don't like it being spelled out exactly as I have done so. But the question is, is what I'm saying the Truth?

As stated, the Church has entered into the last great apostasy. The line is being drawn, and that line is the Cross of Christ. Those who embrace the Cross will draw ever closer to the Lord, while those who repudiate the Cross, will go in the other direction.

(17) "BUT WE, BRETHREN, BEING TAKEN FROM YOU FOR A SHORT TIME IN PRESENCE, NOT IN HEART, ENDEAVOURED THE MORE ABUNDANTLY TO SEE YOUR FACE WITH GREAT DESIRE."

Paul's warm words about his feeling for the Thessalonians may reflect rumors that he did not really care for them. Apparently some had said he had no interest in coming back to them and had come the first time only to satisfy selfish ambition.

## TAKEN FROM YOU

The phrase, *"But we, Brethren, being taken from you for a short time in presence, not in heart,"* refers to the Apostle having to leave the city before he desired to do so, because of the action of the Jews against him (Acts 17:1-10). Here, he represents himself as feeling what an affectionate father must feel when torn from his children. He cannot find words strong enough to describe the pain of separation. It was a bereavement, although he hoped it would only last for a short time. His heart was with them as truly as if he were still bodily present in Thessalonica. His strongest desire was to look upon their faces once more.

Here we ought to notice again the power of the Gospel to create new relations and the corresponding affections. A few months before Paul had not known a single soul in Thessalonica; if he had been only a traveling tentmaker he might have stayed there as long as he did, and then moved on with as little emotion as troubles anyone in similar circumstances.

But coming as an Evangelist, preaching the Gospel, which changed lives, he finds or rather makes Brothers, and feels his enforced parting from them like a bereavement. This is one of the ways in which the Gospel enriches life; hearts that would otherwise be empty and isolated are brought by it into living contact with a great circle whose nature and needs are like their own; and capacities, that would otherwise have been unsuspected, have free course for development. What I'm saying is this:

NOTES

No one knows what is in him; and, in particular, no one knows of what love, of what expansion of heart he is capable, till Christ has made real to him those relations to others by which his duties are determined, and all his powers of thought and feeling called forth. Only a Child of God can have all of these emotions, which is part and parcel of the Gospel of Christ. That's the reason the Family of God is exactly that, *"a family."*

In fact, people who are saved are closer to each other in relationship than they are to blood relatives who aren't saved. All of that is because of the bond ties of Jesus Christ.

## THE WORDS OF CHRIST

Such an experience as shines through the words of the Apostle in this Passage furnishes the key to one of the best known but least understood words of our Saviour. *"Verily I say unto you,"* said Jesus to the Twelve, *"There is no man that hath left house, or wife, or Brethren, or parents, or children, for the Kingdom of God's sake, who shall not receive manifold more in this time, and in the world to come Eternal Life."*

These words might also stand for a description of Paul. He had given up everything for Christ's sake. He had no home, no wife, no child; as far as we can see, no Brother or friend among all his old acquaintances. Yet we may be sure that not one of those who were most richly blessed with all these natural relations and natural affections knew better than he what love is. Consequently, no father ever loved his children more tenderly, fervently, austerely, and unchangeably than Paul loved those whom he had begotten in the Gospel.

Christ had fulfilled to him the Promise just quoted; He had given him a hundredfold in this life, houses, Brothers, Sisters, Mothers, and Children.

Paul is anxious that the Thessalonians should understand the strength of his feeling. In fact, from his writings, I have to believe that the Apostle was a very warm-hearted individual. I believe at times that his feelings were very evident, which would almost be a necessity for him to be as effective as he was in the Cause of Christ. A cold, aloof, withdrawn, unfeeling personality, could never share the emotions that this man shares with all who read his Epistles. And the beautiful thing about all of this is, the Holy Spirit approves totally of his statements, which at least should tell us something.

### TO SEE YOUR FACE

The phrase, *"Endeavored the more abundantly to see your face with great desire,"* presents no want of affection, but from causes beyond control. His separation from them did not destroy his parental feelings, and the manner in which he was obliged to leave them increased his desire to visit them as soon as possible.

The word translated *"desire"* indicates strong feeling or passion. *"You have been torn,"* Paul says, *"not from our hearts, but only from our presence. And, although the separation has been for only a short time, our affection for you is so great that we are filled with intense desire to see you face-to-face again."*

(18) "WHEREFORE WE WOULD HAVE COME UNTO YOU, EVEN I PAUL, ONCE AND AGAIN; BUT SATAN HINDERED US."

The tug on his heart is manifest in the words *"certainly I, Paul."* Though Timothy and Silas had already returned to Thessalonica, Paul's failure to do so did not come from lack of intention; he had attempted another visit several times.

How Satan hindered, the Apostle did not say.

### PAUL

The phrase, *"Wherefore we would have come unto you, even I Paul, once and again,"* presents the fact that he had already sent Timothy and Silas to them, but he himself was anxious to see them, and had purposed this once and again, but Satan hindered.

### SATAN

The phrase, *"But Satan hindered us,"* proclaims the fact that the Evil One is a real personality, and not a mere figure of speech.

NOTES

*"Hindered"* in the Greek is *"egkoptein,"* and is the technical for *"putting up a roadblock calculated to stop an expedition on the march."* It is Satan's work to throw obstacles into the Christian's way — and it is our work to surmount them, in other words to overcome them, for roadblocks were made to be circumvented.

To attempt to say how Satan hindered the Apostle's return would be an exercise in speculation. But while Satan might hinder the action of a Believer, he cannot defeat the Divine purpose for these Believers, as the succeeding Verses imply.

Paul recognized that Satan (the adversary) is the real enemy behind all opposition to the Gospel. As the adversary, Satan's purpose is to hinder the Work of God and stop the forward march of the Church. As the god of this world, he blinds the minds of unbelievers, trying to keep out the Light of the Glorious Gospel of Christ (II Cor. 4:4). As the prince or ruler of the power or domain of the air, he is the spirit that works in those who are disobedient to God (Eph. 2:2).

Believers are warned not to give any chance or opportunity to the Devil to exert his influence (Eph. 4:27). Though the shield of Faith is sufficient to quench all the fiery darts he throws at us (Eph. 6:16), he can still hinder. In spite of our intention, purpose, and desire, Satan can sometimes cause a setback for God's people, as is obvious here with Paul (Horton).

### THERE ARE SEVERAL QUESTIONS WHICH POSE THEMSELVES AS A RESULT OF THIS SHORT STATEMENT BY PAUL

1. We find here the kingdom of darkness and the Kingdom of Light, the one bitterly opposed to the other. The kingdom of darkness, as is obvious, is headed up by Satan, once known as *"Lucifer."* Satan is actually an Angel, originally created by God, and possibly the most powerful Angel ever created, or at least among the most powerful. He served God for a period of time in Righteousness and Holiness, and then at some point in eternity past, he rebelled against God. That rebellion carried over into the Earth and the creation of Adam and Eve, which has resulted in all the sorrow this last nearly 6,000 years.

How long ago was Satan's Rebellion, we are not told. The Bible is the story of the Fall and Redemption of man, and not that of Satan and his fallen Angels, etc. So what we learn about Satan, we only learn in passing. While Jesus totally defeated Satan at the Cross of Calvary, still, for reasons known to God, he has been allowed to continue; however, not so very long from now, he will be removed from the scene, and finally, banished forever in the Lake of Fire (Rev. 20:1-3, 7-15).

2. This was not a bad confession by Paul as many in the modern Gospel would claim. To tell the Truth is never a bad confession. Despite what some presently teach, the Gospel of Christ does not promise an event free life, or a life without opposition from the powers of darkness.

3. We know that Satan cannot do anything, unless God allows him to do so. In other words, he is on a leash, so to speak (Job Chpts. 1-2).

Anyone who doesn't understand that, then makes God subservient to Satan, which of course, is ridiculous. In the second place, God Who is powerful enough to note each sparrow's fall, and to number the hairs of every head in the world, would surely not allow one as destructive as Satan to have free run. No, Satan must answer to God on all counts.

4. Why then would God allow Satan to hinder Paul in this manner, or in fact, allow him to do a lot of things which causes difficulties for Believers?

I think our lack of Faith, or the allowance of sin in our lives, can in fact give Satan much latitude, or one might say, that God allows him more latitude, due to our failure in whatever capacity; however, I don't think this could be said at all of Paul. And neither can it be said of many Christians.

The only answer we can give, barring those things we've just mentioned, is that the Lord allows Satan certain latitude as it regards hinderance of our efforts, etc., in order that we might understand our adversary a little better, which will cause us to lean more and more on the Lord, which is the intention of the Lord all along. He uses Satan constantly as His tool, etc. Of course, Satan means everything for our destruction, but the reasons of the Lord of course, are the total opposite — all for our good.

NOTES

5. The intention of the Holy Spirit I think, is that we not spend too much time lamenting the fact of hindrances caused by Satan, but rather to believe God for victory despite whatever efforts the Evil One might make. Satan is our adversary, and as such, he is going to do everything within his power to hurt and to hinder. Even though we recognize him, we do not fear him, and because *"He Who is within us* (the Holy Spirit), *is greater than he that's within the world"* (I Jn. 4:4).

As well, if God does in fact allow Satan enough latitude that he might be able to stop us from doing some things, even as he did here with Paul, we must realize that the Will of God is going to come out in the end, that is if we will continue to believe the Lord. If we try with all of our effort, even as Paul no doubt did, and continue to be thwarted in our efforts, we must not be chagrined over the fact of delay, but rather believe that God has something in mind that we cannot presently see, and that it will ultimately work out to our good.

This was not a defeat for Paul, only a different direction. Likewise, such momentary setbacks must never be looked at on our part as defeats as well. If in fact we are the cause of the problem because of misplaced Faith, or unconfessed sin within our lives, we should allow the situation to be the instrument which God intends — to help us see ourselves. If that is not the case, we should believe that God is going to work out the situation, irrespective of the present circumstances.

## THE LONG VIEW

Paul no doubt, had many things he wanted to yet teach the Thessalonians. Also, his special love for them caused him to want their fellowship.

But despite all of this, from the tone of his Letter, they had progressed fairly well in their spiritual experience. In other words, it didn't fall apart because he could not make the trip when he desired.

We must always remember that the Work is the Lord's. That means that even as much as we are concerned and feel our responsibility, still, the Lord is far more concerned than we could ever be. While in fact He definitely does give us great responsibility, which means that a lot is riding on our actions; still, He reserves the right to oversee and overrule all things. He is still God, and there is nothing He cannot do. While all of us would like for Him to make our way easier, or to give us more of which we only have a little; still, that should not be our chief concern. Our overwhelming desire should be to become more and more Christlike. Righteousness and Holiness should be the hallmarks of our desires. If we will see to that, we can also feel assured that He will take care of the other. While Satan does hinder, that's really all he can do. He cannot stop the process, that is if we don't allow him to do so.

Of course, his intention is that we get discouraged and quit. If we won't quit, there's really nothing he can do to stop us. Victory is ours! We must never forget, and always remember, that we serve God, Who is almighty and all-knowing; consequently, whatever hindrances the enemy may attempt, they will only be that, just hindrances and no more!

(19) "FOR WHAT IS OUR HOPE, OR JOY, OR CROWN OF REJOICING? ARE NOT EVEN YE IN THE PRESENCE OF OUR LORD JESUS CHRIST AT HIS COMING?"

The idea is, if the Apostle is hindered completely from seeing the Thessalonians again, which he wasn't incidently, his heart rested in the sure hope and joy of meeting them at the Parousia (the Rapture of the Church) and Satan could not hinder that meeting.

To see them in that day of glory, and to be with them, would be both glory and joy to Paul, as such will be to all of us as well; and the greater joy of being forever with the Lord would enrich and not destroy the lesser joy of being forever with them.

The Parousia animates the heart; Believers wait for it; it assures the Communion of Saints and the reward of labor; it satisfies longings after Holiness; it comforts in sorrow and it enriches prayer.

NOTES

## THE GREAT QUESTION

The question, *"For what is our hope, or joy, or crown of rejoicing?"*, presents the Apostle pointing beyond, far beyond, the minor annoyances now, to the great coming time, when there will be no more separation and no more hindrances by Satan. It will be the time of the Rapture of the Church, when we will go to be with the Lord forever and forever.

In other words, the Holy Spirit through the Apostle is saying to the Thessalonians, and to us as well, that we must not become distracted over difficulties and problems at this present time. So Satan does hinder! So other situations do not go as we would like for them to go! Soon and very soon, as the songwriter said, all of this will be past.

The idea is, don't get bogged down in trivia, and miss the big picture. Everything is working toward the moment when the Trump of God shall sound. We should keep our eyes on that, our mind on that, our understanding on that! Whatever problems we now have are temporal at best, with our eyes ever to be on the coming great event. That above all must be our *"hope,"* our *"joy,"* and our *"crown of rejoicing."*

The *"crown of rejoicing,"* incidently is *"the crown of victory."*

The idea is, Satan is a defeated foe! A whipped adversary! Not possible of victory. This means that victory is assured for the Child of God who keeps his eye on the long view, which means, he has an understanding of the big picture.

## THE RAPTURE OF THE CHURCH

The question, *"Are not even ye in the presence of our Lord Jesus Christ at His Coming?"*, points to the coming Rapture of the Church.

It is unfortunate that many in the modern Church do not any more believe in the Rapture. What they do not seem to realize is, that the Rapture and the Resurrection are one and the same. In other words, if they believe in the coming Resurrection, which every Christian must, then at the same time, they're believing in the Rapture.

Now while we may disagree as to the time of this coming event, there cannot be any disagreement as to the actual event itself. This which Paul explains so vividly in I Corinthians Chapter 15, is actually the Rapture of the Church, which he will also deal with briefly in the Fourth Chapter of this Epistle.

Another strong thrust is presented here by the Apostle. The true Christian, in other words the Christian who pleases his Lord, will always have in his mind and heart, this glorious Coming of Christ. If not, something is vitally wrong!

The sad Truth is, that many, if not most, in the modern Church, have little regard or concern for this coming event. As stated, many do not even believe it. Such only shows a spiritual declension of terrible proportions.

Incidently, the title *"Lord Jesus Christ,"* is the Resurrection Name of our Lord. His Resurrection guarantees the Resurrection of all Saints, hence the Holy Spirit having the Apostle to use this Title or Name here.

(20) "FOR YE ARE OUR GLORY AND JOY."

The meaning is, that the source of happiness to a Minister of the Gospel in that coming day, is the conversion and the Salvation of souls.

GLORY

The phrase, *"For ye are our glory,"* reflects what should be the purpose of every Child of God. By that I mean the Salvation and spiritual nurture of souls. That's why Jesus died.

He didn't come down here to die on a Cross, in order for men to hold religious positions or some such like foolishness. Neither did He do all of this in order that we might trade our Pinto for a Cadillac, in other words, *"the money gospel."* People who would teach such foolishness, sell the Lord mighty short.

The purpose of the entirety of the Body of Christ, is to tell this grand story of Jesus Christ to a hurting world. Every single person in the world must have an opportunity to hear, whether they accept or reject.

When we all stand before God, and give account for this life that He has given unto us at such price, the *"Glory"* which we will receive, will have to do totally and completely with our participation or lack thereof, as it regards the Salvation of souls, i.e., *"World Evangelism."* In other words, what did we do? What part did we play? Did we look at Christ as someone to be used for our own selfish purposes?

NOTES

The *"Glory"* will be in this, and this alone! Everything else will be, *"wood, hay, and stubble."* This should give us room for pause!

JOY

If we have done what we could; if we have understood the real purpose and reason for our Salvation; if we have properly understood why Jesus came, suffered and died; maybe we could do nothing but pray, but whatever it is we could do, if we did it with the idea in mind, that every person in this world must have an opportunity to know about Christ, then, we will have *"joy!"* Otherwise, I don't think so!

Without saying it, Paul is actually speaking here of the coming *"Judgment Seat of Christ."* There we will answer and there we will be answered. We had best not forget that.

*"Hear the Lord of harvest sweetly calling,*
*"Who will go and work for Me today?*
*"Who will bring to Me the lost and dying?*
*"Who will point them to the narrow way?"*

*"When the coal of fire touched the Prophet,*
*"Making him as pure, as pure can be,*
*"When the voice of God said, 'Who'll go for us?'*
*"Then he answered, 'Here I am, send me.'"*

*"Millions now in sin and shame are dying,*
*"Listen to their sad and bitter cry;*
*"Hasten, Brother, hasten to the rescue;*
*"Quickly answer, 'Master, here am I.'"*

*"Soon the time for reaping will be over;*
*"Soon we'll gather for the harvest home;*
*"May the Lord of harvest smile upon us,*
*"May we hear His blessed, 'Child, well done.'"*

CHAPTER 3

(1) "WHEREFORE WHEN WE COULD NO LONGER FORBEAR, WE THOUGHT IT GOOD TO BE LEFT AT ATHENS ALONE;"

Even though Paul used the pronoun *"we"* it seems he was actually referring to the singular, for he would remain in Athens alone, having sent Timothy to Thessalonica.

Our duty here is to reconstruct the situation as it is portrayed in Luke's record in Acts. Paul had left Silas and Timothy behind in Berea, and had been escorted by Brethren to Athens. On their return to Berea they carried a request from Paul that Silas and Timothy should join him at once (Acts 17:14-15). From Acts 17:16 and 18:5 it would seem that by the time Silas and Timothy joined him he had gone on to Corinth, inasmuch as these three were reunited there. Luke simply omits any mention of Timothy or Silas being in Athens at all. His condensed story in Acts contains only as much detail as was necessary to his purpose.

Whether both Timothy and Silas actually came to Athens we are not told. We know that Timothy came to Athens from what Paul says here, but we are not sure about Silas. Quite possibly, Silas did get to Athens with Timothy, but was immediately sent elsewhere by Paul, with Timothy remaining there, which was probably the case. Timothy was then sent to Thessalonica, with both men later joining Paul at Corinth (Acts 18:5).

## THE SITUATION AT THESSALONICA

The phrase, *"Wherefore when we could no longer forbear,"* refers to Paul strongly desiring to know the situation back at Thessalonica. As we have already commented, the unbelieving Jews had created quite a scene which necessitated Paul leaving the city. Naturally, he was very concerned about the state of affairs. What had transpired after he left? What was the state of the Church presently?

As we said at the outset, it is not known exactly as to how long Paul was there before he was forced to leave; irrespective, it could not have been very long. The Lord had done a tremendous work, but as the account shows, Satan had opposed greatly.

Would the new converts stand up in the face of strong persecution? However, as we shall see in this Chapter, Timothy would bring back *"good tidings,"* concerning the situation there.

NOTES

As I've mentioned previously, Paul felt a responsibility regarding all Churches at that time, and especially among the Gentiles, due to the fact that the Lord had placed this responsibility in his hands. This is not to say that the original Twelve, or others, did not share that responsibility, for they certainly did; however, I believe that Paul felt all of this far more keenly. This was the beginning of something that would cover the entirety of the Earth. The great price that Jesus paid for man's Redemption, in fact, that to which all had been pointed through the past centuries, could only be made real in the hearts and lives of dying men and women through the *"Church."*

Jesus had said, *"Upon this Rock I will build My Church; and the gates of Hell shall not prevail against it"* (Mat. 16:18).

This is the manner in which it was to be built, and in fact, the manner in which it was being built. To be sure, Satan would try his hardest to stop the embryo Church even as we read the account in the Acts of the Apostles, but the Words of Christ continue to ring out, that the Evil One would not be successful.

After the passing of the Apostles off the scene, it would look, however, as if Satan would succeed. The Church gradually went into apostasy, ultimately becoming what would be known as the *"Catholic Church,"* completely ruled by men, i.e., *"Satan."* The Reformation began in the 1500's under Martin Luther and others, with the ringing declaration, *"The just shall live by Faith,"* once again started the Church on its right destination. Even though the gates of Hell would try, and how hard they did try, the Words of Christ would continue to ring ever true, *"They would not prevail!"*

## ATHENS

The phrase, *"We thought it good to be left at Athens alone,"* refers to Timothy being sent back to Thessalonica, with no mention of Silas. As stated, quite possibly Silas did not come to begin with, or if he did, Paul had already sent him elsewhere. At any rate, Paul it seems, was left in Athens without any of his associates, but which he felt the Lord wanted.

Of all the places that Paul visited, Athens was the most trying I think, to his ardent temperament. It was covered with idols and exceedingly religious; yet it was more hopelessly away from God than any city possibly in the world of that day.

One could probably say, that Paul had never been in a place so unsympathetic with the Gospel; never had he felt so great a gulf fixed between others' minds and his own.

About 500 years before this time, Athens was famous for its culture, and the home of the great Philosophers like Plato and Aristotle. After the Roman conquest of Greece, Athens became a city linked to Rome by treaty, but entirely independent of the Governor of Achaia, and paying no taxes to Rome. They had internal judicial autonomy.

Of the three great university cities Athens, Tarsus, and Alexandria, Athens was the most famous. Philo the Alexandrian said that the Athenians were the keenest-sighted mentally of the Greeks.

It was also famous for its temples, statues, and monuments.

Though the Athenians were religious and eager to discuss religion, the truth was, they did not know God at all. In fact, Apollonius the Philosopher, a contemporary incidentally of Paul, rebuked them for their lascivious jigs at the festival of Dionysus and for their love of human slaughter in the Gladiatorial games.

There are some who think that a Church came out of Paul's short visit there, and some who think otherwise. At any rate, Paul's stay there was short.

(2) "AND SENT TIMOTHEUS, OUR BROTHER, AND MINISTER OF GOD, AND OUR FELLOWLABOURER IN THE GOSPEL OF CHRIST, TO ESTABLISH YOU, AND TO COMFORT YOU CONCERNING YOUR FAITH:"

Some have claimed that it is impossible to harmonize Paul's account here with those recorded by Luke concerning the same incident, in Acts Chapters 17 and 18. However, there is no contradiction whatsoever.

Luke just didn't bother to relate the incident regarding Timothy in Athens, it not being necessary to his account. He does, however, tell of both Timothy and Silas joining Paul after him leaving Athens and going to Corinth (Acts 18:5).

NOTES

Luke omitting that part of the incident, in no way means that it didn't happen. He just didn't relate it, it not being necessary for the things he wanted to say.

It is amazing how that some people will attempt to take a perfectly logical account, easily explained, actually something which happens constantly in everyday life, and just because it's in the Bible, try to turn it into an error regarding the Text.

What the Holy Spirit wanted to bring out in Luke's account in Acts, had nothing to do with Timothy or Silas at that particular time. So, he had Luke to just omit whatever part they did play in Athens, if any at all. As well, Paul no doubt did many other things that Luke did not record, but that doesn't mean they didn't happen.

TIMOTHY

The phrase, *"And sent Timotheus,"* implies that Paul sent Timothy from Athens to Macedonia. The evidence is that Paul placed great trust in this young man, and I think that Paul's second Epistle to Timothy, which incidentally was his last, makes it clear that the Holy Spirit had chosen Timothy to bear the torch after Paul had been called home to Glory. And yet, I don't really think that anyone could fill Paul's shoes, and there is no record that Timothy even claimed to have such capabilities. Nevertheless, the evidence is that this is what the Spirit of God wanted and desired, hence the manner in which Paul phrased the wording of the last Epistle.

Paul no doubt needed Timothy with him very much in Athens, yet his anxiety for the Thessalonians overcame all motives of personal convenience.

Of all things going on in the world of that time, in the Eyes of God, this was the single most important. The Holy Spirit didn't mention the doings of Nero, or the great Roman Senate, or the march of armies, or the state of business activities, only about a fledgling Church in Thessalonica, plus Paul's concern. The point is this:

If this was the single most important thing in the world of that time as far as the Holy Spirit was concerned, and it definitely was, well then it should have been the single most important thing regarding every Believer.

The idea is, that we as Believers should think like the Lord, should place our interest as to where is His interest, should have His concern! It is not that some of the things of the world aren't important, for they are; however, as should be obvious, it is the things of God which interest Heaven, and little else!

Due to the fact that all Believers have the Holy Spirit abiding within them, there is no reason as to why our attitude, interest, love, and concern, should not be exactly as that of the Lord. While of course, we may not know everything that goes on in the world as it regards the Work of God, it is certain that we are aware of some things. Whatever it is that the Holy Spirit calls to our attention, in essence in some way making us a part of that which is being done, should be our primary interest.

It is a shame, when Christians have more concern for the things of the world than they do the things of God. While we do live in this world, and consequently have to make a living, still, it is the Lord actually Who takes care of us and no one else. Let me ask, please, you the Reader, a very important question!

In all honesty, how interested are you in the Work of God? And of course, I am speaking of that of which you are a part, in essence, of which the Holy Spirit has made you a part. How much do you pray about this and for this, of which is at least some part of your responsibility? How much do you give of your resources?

THE COMMENDATION OF TIMOTHY

The phrase, *"Our Brother, and Minister of God, and our fellowlabourer in the Gospel of Christ,"* presents an obvious emphasis upon Timothy's status and valued service. As well, the Holy Spirit sanctioned these words as written by Paul, placing his seal of approval upon that spoken about this young man, by the Apostle.

Different reasons have been assigned for this eulogy pronounced by Paul regarding Timothy. Some suppose that it was to show how eagerly the Apostle valued the welfare of the Thessalonians, by sending to them a person of such importance and of such use to himself as Timothy; others think that it was to recommend Timothy to the favorable regard of the Thessalonians in the absence of himself; others claim it was just a natural outburst of affection for the young man.

NOTES

However, I think none of that properly explains Paul's statement. While he certainly did regard this young man highly, as is obvious; still, it was more to it than that.

First of all, the Holy Spirit had placed Timothy with Paul for a Divine purpose. Even though I Thessalonians was more than likely the first Epistle written by Paul, still, this young man had already proven himself to the great Apostle.

To which we have already briefly alluded, I personally believe that the Holy Spirit even then was grooming him to take the torch, as stated, when Paul would leave the scene of action. Although that would be some years away, still, the preparation had already begun.

THE GOSPEL OF CHRIST

As Paul uses the phrase, *"The Gospel of Christ,"* it carries more meaning than a mere catch word. This was the New Covenant. Its significance was and is beyond the comprehension of anyone, even Paul. Actually, the fate of the entirety of mankind rests upon those few words. The Gospel of Christ is a summation of the entirety of the great Plan of God as it involved this world, and the Redemption of mankind. The price paid for this all-important work, was and is literally beyond comprehension. God would literally become man, and offer up Himself on the Cross of Calvary, which was necessary, that is if humanity was to be saved.

And now this great Message has to be taken to the entirety of the world. Every man must hear! All must have an opportunity to either accept or reject!

At this time, due to the fact that Paul had been given the ingredients of the New Covenant, he knew more about this all-important Work of God than any other human being in the world of that day, even the original Twelve. To be frank, what they knew, they would have to learn from Paul. Consequently, those who would carry the torch after Paul was gone, would have to be prepared.

GOD'S WAY

We should take a lesson from this which is so easily observed. The Lord did not entrust this all-important task of selection to the original Twelve, or even to Paul. He did the selecting Himself.

He brought these men to Paul's attention, and by providence put them with him, whether Timothy, Silas, or others. It was all planned by the Holy Spirit, and not at all by man. Please allow me to venture this statement:

If man had selected these individuals, even the Godliest of men, the choice would not have been right. Only God can do such a thing; consequently, He has to make a way, and He will definitely do so, if men will simply trust Him.

Unfortunately at this present time, and it has mostly been this way following the Early Church, man has too much attempted to do the selecting and do the calling. Consequently, the Church totally apostatized beginning in the latter part of the Second Century, and by the Fifth Century had reached total apostasy, where it remained for many centuries.

Even in the Church, even among those who should know better, God's choice is little accepted, but mostly opposed. In other words, man will little approve what man has not selected! And God will never approve what man has selected; and that's the state of much of the Church, which the Holy Spirit has to break through in order to send Revival.

So, Timothy, plus others, was being groomed in this great *"Gospel of Christ"*; and he could not have had a better teacher than Paul, and God, the Holy Spirit.

## TO ESTABLISH

The short phrase, *"To establish you,"* refers to the fact that due to Paul having to leave before his work was completed, the Thessalonians needed more teaching. Especially considering, they were facing heavy persecution, one can tell that the Apostle is greatly concerned that they be given all the great Truths of the Word of God. For this to be done, there must be qualified teaching, which must come from a qualified Teacher; one who was Spirit-filled and Spirit-led! Paul was confident that Timothy could fit this bill.

We learn from this just how important the Teaching of the Word actually is. In fact, there is absolutely nothing more important in the life of the Believer. The reason there are so many problems, so many difficulties among Christians, is simply because many have not been *"established in the Faith."* Sometimes it's a lack of proper Teaching, and sometimes it's a lack of proper interest on the part of the Believer.

As many of you are aware, this Ministry (JSM) has a network of Radio Stations spanning over a great part of this nation and even growing daily. These stations are for the total purpose of the presentation of the Gospel of Jesus Christ.

Every morning, seven days a week, at 7 a.m. CST, we have a 90-minute program set aside exclusively for the teaching of the Word of God, which is rebroadcast at 7:00 p.m. — actually, the entirety of the 24-hour day, seven days a week, is taken up with the Gospel and nothing else. (Four of the mornings are live, with the other three airing rebroadcasts.) As I dictate these notes, for the last two or more years, we have been teaching primarily on the Cross of Christ. If every Christian would avail themselves of studying with us each and every day, or at least when possible, the change that would be effected in their lives would absolutely know no bounds. In fact, that is what we are seeing for those who do avail themselves of this opportunity.

The Lord has opened up these Stations for us as it regards this very task. As well, He has instructed me as it regards this teaching program every day, even to its content, and especially its content. So, understanding that the Lord is the Author of this, and He definitely is, we should certainly come to the conclusion that He desires for His Children to take advantage of that which He has done and is doing. All of this is prepared by the Holy Spirit in order to *"establish"* the people of God. In fact, this is what the fivefold Calling is all about (Eph. 4:11-13). Unfortunately, all Preachers aren't of God, which means they are not sent by the Lord, which means the message they are preaching is not the Word of God, although it may closely resemble the Word of God. If the Believer is properly led by the Holy Spirit, they will find the right one. If they are led by the flesh, unfortunately, they will gravitate toward that which is also of *"the flesh!"*

NOTES

### YOUR FAITH

The phrase, *"And to comfort you concerning your Faith,"* suggests encouragement.

*"To establish"* in the Greek is *"sterixai,"* and carries the idea of buttressing. *"To comfort"* in the Greek is *"parakalesai,"* and speaks of *"holding one up."* The idea is, a barrier is to be built around the Child of God, which within itself will bring a tremendous comfort or encouragement.

What is that barrier?

It is *"the Faith!"*

And what is *"the Faith"*?

In brief, it is *"Jesus Christ and Him Crucified"* (I Cor. 2:2).

The Cross of Christ is the *"saving place"*; it is the *"hiding place"*; it is the *"victory place"*; it is the place for everything which comes from the Lord.

It was there that Jesus paid the price, defeated Satan, satisfied the claims of Heavenly Justice, atoned for all sin, and made it possible for human beings to be redeemed, and to be given new life in Christ. This is where the Believer is to ever be.

### FAITH IN THE CROSS

The manner in which we arrive there first as described in Romans 6:2-6, is simply by Faith. In other words, the believing sinner places his trust in Christ and what Christ did at the Cross. That's all he has to do, and he is saved (Rom. 10:9-10, 13; Eph. 2:8-9).

Here is what that Faith does, at least in the Mind of God!

When the believing sinner exhibits Faith, in the Mind of God he is placed literally into the dying form of Christ, literally baptized into His Death. There could be no closer connection than that, for the word *"baptize"* literally means *"to dip under,"* or *"to be in something, and that something to be in you."* As stated, there is no word that would more properly describe a total union than *"baptize."* A perfect illustration is a ship which has been sunk in the ocean. The water is in it, and it is in the water.

In that same posture we are buried with Christ, which refers to all of our old life, the past sins, all that we once were which refers to sinfulness, wickedness, disobedience, and rebellion against God. It is all buried with Him, never to be resurrected again, for this is why Christ died.

Christ was then raised from the dead, and the believing sinner is raised with Him, but in *"newness of life,"* which refers to a *"new Creation"* (Rom. 6:4-6; II Cor. 5:17).

In the Mind of God this is what happens when the sinner exhibits Faith.

Now that we are a new creation in Christ, actually a brand-new person, with *"old things having passed away, and all things now having become new,"* we are to understand, that all else that we receive from the Lord, such as the leading of the Holy Spirit, the power of the Holy Spirit, actually all that the Holy Spirit does, which brings about Victory in our everyday walk before the Lord, continues to come to us through the Finished Work of Christ. In other words, exactly as we placed our Faith in that great *"Work,"* when we were saved, we are to keep our Faith in that great Work. The reason is, that's where all the benefits are, and that means there are no benefits outside of this Finished Work of Christ. So, the Believer's Faith is to remain in the Cross of Christ at all times. It must never go outside of those parameters, for the Holy Spirit works in those parameters only (Rom. 8:1-2).

### THE HOLY SPIRIT

It is a tragedy, when we understand that all of these things which we receive as Believers, come to us totally and completely by the power and work of the Holy Spirit, and yet as Christians we know so little about Him. In fact, most of the old-line Denominations have completely rejected the Holy Spirit, which leaves them with nothing from the Lord; consequently, almost all they do is man-originated, which means it is man-led and man-directed. While there may be much religious machinery in operation which fools a lot of people, in actuality, there is nothing truly done for the Lord.

Unfortunately, we Pentecostals and Charismatics who claim to believe in the Baptism with the Holy Spirit with the evidence of speaking with other Tongues, too often go little beyond the initial experience of being filled. In other words, if we are baptized with the Holy Spirit, and speak with

NOTES

other Tongues, we somehow think that's all it is. Consequently, we go no further!

As I've said many times, the Baptism with the Holy Spirit, is not a goal toward which one strives, but rather a *"gateway,"* to the great and glorious things of God.

In fact, the Holy Spirit couldn't come into the hearts and lives of Believers to abide until the Cross was an accomplished fact (Jn. 14:17). That's how important the Cross was and is. Believers before the Cross, as Godly as they might have been, still had the sin debt hanging over their heads, simply because the blood of bulls and goats could not take away sin. They were saved, and saved by Faith, exactly as we are presently; however, Satan in effect, still had a claim on them, so at death they were taken down into Paradise, actually held captive by Satan, with only a gulf between them and the burning side of Hell (Lk. 16:26; Eph. 4:8-10).

When Christ died on the Cross, forever settling the sin debt, which destroyed Satan's claim, He then delivered them from the captivity of Satan, taking all those righteous souls to Heaven. Now, and ever since the Cross, when a Believer dies, their soul and spirit instantly go to be with the Lord Jesus Christ (Phil. 1:21-23).

Due to the Cross, and all that it means, which refers to the fact that it performed a legal work so to speak, as well as a spiritual work, the Holy Spirit can now come and abide in the hearts and lives of Believers. That's what Paul was talking about when he said, *"Christ hath redeemed us from the curse of the Law . . . that the Blessing of Abraham* (Justification by Faith) *might come on the Gentiles, through Jesus Christ* (what He did at the Cross and His Resurrection)*; that we might receive the Promise of the Spirit through Faith"* (Gal. 3:13-14).

As well, this is what Jesus was talking about just before His Ascension, when He *"commanded them that they should not depart from Jerusalem, but wait for the Promise of the Father"* (Acts 1:4).

While the Holy Spirit definitely helped Believers before the Cross, even coming into them on special occasions for a period of time, He could not abide then as He does now. That means that the weakest Christian now, has greater access to the Holy Spirit than the strongest Believer before the Cross. Actually, that's what Jesus was talking about when He spoke of John the Baptist, saying, *"Among those that are born of women there is not a greater Prophet than John the Baptist: but he that is least in the Kingdom of God is greater than he"* (Lk. 7:28).

He wasn't meaning that people now are greater than John the Baptist, but rather that the Dispensation in which we now live, gives us far greater privileges than those enjoyed by the greatest Prophet of all, John the Baptist. That refers to what Jesus did at the Cross, which makes it possible for the mighty Holy Spirit to come into the hearts and lives of Believers and abide, and to do so eternally.

NOTES

## TO UNDERSTAND THE WORKING OF THE HOLY SPIRIT

As stated, most Pentecostals and Charismatics little understand the working of the Holy Spirit after conversion. They sort of think that it concludes with us speaking in Tongues, with maybe some few having one or more of the Gifts of the Spirit. As well, we have equated manifestations with the Holy Spirit, and in some cases that is correct. But that's about as far as we've gone respecting this all-important work within our lives. In other words, we are receiving only a small percentage of what the Spirit of God can do with us, and in fact, desires to do.

Years ago I can remember many times weeping before the Lord, seeing the Holy Spirit work within my heart and life resulting in hundreds of thousands being brought to a saving knowledge of Jesus Christ, understanding that this was a mighty work, but at the same time, not seeing victory in my own life. I would weep and ask the Lord as to why the Holy Spirit wasn't helping me?

In fact, He was helping me in many ways, but not in the way of which I speak; however, at that time I did not know the reason why.

The sadness is, precious few Christians know the answer to that question even now.

As it regards walking in victory before the Lord, which means to be an overcomer in every respect, I think most Preachers don't have a clue as to how this is done. In the past two or more years, I have started noticing the answers given by Preachers as it regards this very question:

How can a Christian walk victoriously before the Lord?

How can a Believer have victory over every type of sin?

In fact, one could easily ask that question in many and varied ways, but the meaning is the same. The very fact that the question is being asked and discussed, portrays the fact that the answer is not forthcoming.

The reason the answer is not forthcoming, is because most Preachers do not know or understand how the Holy Spirit works within our hearts and lives as it regards this very question. Actually, He Alone, can bring about the victory which we need. Paul plainly said it: *"But if the Spirit of Him that raised up Jesus from the dead dwell in you, He that raised up Christ from the dead shall also quicken your mortal bodies by His Spirit that dwelleth in you"* (Rom. 8:11).

To be sure, Paul is not speaking here of the coming Resurrection, but actually, of us living victoriously in this Christian Life, in other words, *"living the Resurrection Life"* (Rom. 6:2-6).

So, the question must be asked, how do we get the Holy Spirit to *"quicken our mortal bodies,"* which means to give us power over the flesh?

THE CROSS AND THE HOLY SPIRIT

The answer is found in Romans 8:2. It says, *"For the Law* (this presents a Law of God which the Spirit of God will not break) *of the Spirit* (the Holy Spirit) *of Life* (the Spiritual Life which quickens our mortal bodies) *in Christ Jesus* (referring to what Jesus did at the Cross and His Resurrection) *hath made me free from the law of sin and death."*

The Holy Spirit works within the confines of this particular *"Law,"* which refers to what Jesus did at the Cross and the Resurrection. It is somewhat like the Constitution of the United States. The President, Congress, and the Supreme Court, plus every other Judge and Law Enforcement Officer in this nation, are all supposed to abide within the framework of the Constitution. The entirety of this nation is built upon that.

NOTES

Using that as an example, one could call the great New Covenant, the *"Constitution of Heaven."* This Constitution one might say, is based totally and completely on what Jesus did at the Cross and His Resurrection. Jesus plainly said this at the Last Supper when He took bread, gave thanks, broke the bread, and said, *"Take, eat: this is My Body, which is broken for you, this do in remembrance of me."*

In the same manner He took the cup, and when He had supped, He said, *"This cup is the New Testament* (New Covenant) *in My Blood: this do ye, as oft as you drink it, in remembrance of Me."*

And then, *"For as often as you eat this bread, and drink this cup, ye do shew the Lord's Death till He come"* (I Cor. 11:23-26).

The New Testament or New Covenant, is what Jesus gave us by what He did at the Cross and the Resurrection. In other words, through His Death and Resurrection He established a New Covenant.

The Old Covenant of Law was based on performance, which man could never keep, but this New Covenant is based on Promise, which means it cannot be broken.

And why is it that it cannot be broken?

A Covenant to be a Covenant, has to be between two people or two nations, etc. In this case, it is between two, *"God and man."*

Looking at that, we have no fear when it comes to God, but when it comes to man, we wonder how is it that the Covenant can be guaranteed as to not be broken, considering that man is not very reliable?

That would be true were we speaking of just any man; however, we are talking about *"The Man, Christ Jesus."* The manner and way in which this Covenant was carried out, guarantees its infallibility. The reason is simple:

Jesus is *both* God and Man. He is Very God and Very Man. As our Representative Man, in essence, the Second or Last Adam, He stands in our place, and guarantees the Covenant on our behalf. Consequently, it cannot be broken. And what does that mean?

That means, as long as the Believer continues to trust Christ, he cannot be lost, he cannot be defeated, and that he is guaranteed of one day crossing the threshold of the New Jerusalem. His trust in Christ, guarantees that!

In this great and glorious Covenant, this great Finished Work, this Constitution one might say, the Holy Spirit works and moves. He will not go outside of this Covenant, will not work outside of this Covenant, which means that if any Believer tries to function outside of the Covenant, he will have to do so without the help of the Holy Spirit, and that's where the problem comes in. That's why the Holy Spirit those years ago was not helping me, and it is the reason He is not helping most Christians. I was operating outside of the Covenant, trying to walk in victory by my own strength, which was impossible, and so are most Christians presently.

## WHAT DOES IT MEAN TO WALK OUTSIDE THE COVENANT?

In the most simplistic way in which I can make this statement, it refers to anything we might do, irrespective as to what it might be, or how holy it might seem on the surface, or how right it might seem to be, which is other than simply having Faith in what Christ has already done. Now study that statement very carefully.

The only thing the Lord requires of us as Believers in order to have a victorious, overcoming, consistent Christian life, is to just simply have Faith in what Christ did at the Cross. In other words, the Cross is to ever be the object of our Faith. That's all the Lord requires, that's all that He asks! So why don't we do that?

The answer to that question is not as simple as it might seem. As I've said countless times in the last several Commentaries we have written, the Church has moved so far away from the Cross, which means that it's had so little teaching on the subject, that most Christians don't have the slightest idea as to what I'm talking about, when I speak of our Faith remaining in the Finished Work of Christ. They've never been taught that; they've never heard that; consequently, most Christians are living in the state that Paul was in, when he said, *"O wretched man that I am! Who shall deliver me from the body of this death?"* (Rom. 7:24).

In attempting to gain deliverance, and we're speaking of all types of problems, Christians not knowing the manner in which the

NOTES

Holy Spirit works, which is totally and completely through Faith in the Cross, we set about to devise other means. To be sure, the other means we devise look good in our sight, because most of these things are right and good in their own way. And what am I talking about?

Once again, I'm speaking of anything that we might do in an attempt to find victory, other than simply having Faith in the Cross of Christ. It might be, that we think we can pray thirty minutes a day, and that will solve our problem. It won't! While prayer will definitely do you good, will bless you, and give you fellowship with the Lord, all which definitely are essential in the Christian walk; still, you won't find victory over sin by that route. Neither can you *"fast"* this problem away! As well, you can journey to the ends of the Earth, and find the Preacher whom God is using, and have him lay hands on you, and even with the Power of God flooding your heart and life at that time, and you being *"slain in the Spirit,"* while all of that is great and good, and definitely of God, that is if it actually is of God, while you will be blessed, you won't be delivered.

Stop and think a moment!

If it takes anything other than what Christ did at the Cross and in His Resurrection, to guarantee total and complete victory for the Believer, then that means that Jesus did not accomplish the task at the Cross, and in fact, His Work is not a Finished Work, but rather an incomplete work. We know that is wrong, and in fact, for us to conduct ourselves in any manner or way, which even remotely lends credence to the idea that He didn't do it all at the Cross, considering the price that He paid, our action can do nothing but anger Him, which should be obvious! In fact, I personally believe that one of the greatest sins of all, is for the Believer to attempt to find in his own ways and mechanisms, that which can only be found in Christ. The tragedy is, we think what we're doing is in Christ, and by Faith, and according to the Spirit of God, when it is no such thing!

Again I state, once we place our Faith in the Cross, understanding that all Blessings come from that Source, the Holy Spirit will then go to work in our lives, and do great and mighty things with us, through us and for us. Other than that, He will do very little, at least in this regard (Rom. 8:1-2).

## THE BAPTISM WITH THE HOLY SPIRIT

The greatest thing that can happen to a sinner is finding Christ in the realm of Salvation. The greatest thing that can happen to a Believer who is already in Christ, is to be baptized with the Holy Spirit (Acts 2:4).

While it is certainly true that the Holy Spirit comes into the heart and life of every person immediately upon conversion, still, that is totally different than being Baptized with the Holy Spirit, which every Believer should receive immediately after Salvation. In fact, one cannot receive this experience of the Spirit Baptism, until one is first saved. Jesus said this very succinctly when He said, *"Even the Spirit of Truth* (the Holy Spirit)*; Whom the world cannot receive, because it seeth Him not, neither knoweth Him"* (Jn. 14:17).

While the sinner can definitely receive Salvation, which is brought to him by the Holy Spirit in the realm of Regeneration, which is all done by the Spirit of God, in which the Holy Spirit actually comes into the believing sinner's heart and life to abide; still, there is a great difference in being *"born of the Spirit,"* which takes place with every sinner coming to Christ, than being *"Baptized with the Spirit,"* which always takes place after one has come to Christ (Acts 19:1-7).

In studying the Bible ever since I have been eight years old, and trying to live this life for that many years, I've learned a few things about the Holy Spirit. Regrettably, I had to learn some of them the hard way.

It is my belief, that the Believer, although definitely saved, is still not going to do very much for God, and is not going to grow very much in Grace, unless that Believer is first Baptized with the Holy Spirit, which will always be accompanied by the speaking with other Tongues (Acts 2:4). As I stated previously, the Holy Spirit is not a goal at which we arrive, but rather a *"gateway,"* to all the great things of God. In other words, every single thing we receive from the Lord, is all done within the Person, Office, Ministry, and Work of the Holy Spirit. To overestimate Him would be very difficult, and to underestimate Him, which is the great sin of the modern Church, is one of the worst things we can do.

NOTES

Since the Lord began to give me the Revelation of the Cross, I have noticed a total change of the Work and Ministry of the Holy Spirit within my heart and life. Now I understand that the Holy Spirit demands that I have Faith in the Cross, always understanding that the Lord did this all for me, and that He definitely wants me to have the benefits of what He has done at such great price. I am to have Faith in that, and the Holy Spirit will then do for me great and mighty things. That's all that He asks, that I have Faith in the Cross, and the Cross totally.

That's what Paul was talking about when he said, *"The preaching of the Cross is to them that perish foolishness; but to we who are saved it is the Power of God"* (I Cor. 1:18).

In fact, the Cross within itself, contains no power. Nor in a sense does the Resurrection, at least as far as we are concerned. The Power in totality is in the Holy Spirit. That's what Paul was speaking about in Romans 8:11. And please believe me, the Holy Spirit, Who is God, has almighty Power, meaning there is nothing He cannot do.

My pitiful efforts amount to nothing in the face of Satan. He merely shrugs them off, and causes me untold problems, that is, if I am depending on that. And please believe me, I've been down that road, and I don't want to travel that path anymore.

In years past, how many times have I wept, wondering if it was possible for a human being to stand such onslaughts of Satan! In fact, there are millions of Christians, even as we've already stated, who are in that same boat presently, so to speak. Satan is coming against them so hard that they can't stand it. They are afraid to say anything, especially in this present Church climate, because if they do, precious few have the answer anyway, and besides that, they will be tarred and feathered and run out of town, proverbially speaking. Self-righteousness is an evil thing, and that's where most of the modern Church actually is, and because it has forsaken the Cross!

So the individual Christian suffers in silence, not knowing what to do, and in fact, every single thing he does, not only not helping the problem, but the problem, whatever it might be, seemingly getting worse.

However, what is impossible for us, and impossible it is, is not impossible at all for the Holy Spirit, in fact, it is not even hard for Him.

Satan will take us on any day in the week, but he doesn't want to have anything whatsoever to do with the Holy Spirit. And I sense the Presence of God even as I dictate these words. He is waiting for you, the Believer, for whom Jesus has paid such a price, to simply exhibit your Faith in what our Lord has done, and when you do that, and not allow Preachers or anyone else for that matter, to move your Faith elsewhere, you will find the Holy Spirit beginning to work in your life, a work incidentally, which will never end, and will take you to such raptured heights as you have never known before. Yes, it is *"more abundant life,"* but only in the manner in which the Lord has directed.

### THE MANNER IN WHICH THIS WAS SHOWN TO THE PATRIARCHS OF OLD

The Lord told Abraham in essence, what He was going to do, at least up to a point (Gen. 12:1-3); however, He didn't tell him at that time exactly the *"way"* in which it would be done. I am speaking of the Redemption of humanity.

In Genesis Chapter 22, the Lord showed Abraham the way it would be done. He used the most graphic illustration that one could ever begin to use, telling Abraham to offer up his son Isaac in Sacrifice (Gen. 22:1-2).

To the credit of the Patriarch, Abraham obeyed the Lord, and moments before the knife was to be driven into Isaac's breast, the Lord stopped him, showing him a Ram caught in the thicket, which was to be offered instead.

The Scripture says, *"And Abraham called the name of that place 'Jehovah-Jireh,'"* which means, *"the Lord will provide!"* (Gen. 22:12-14).

Provide what?

The Lord would provide a Redeemer in the form of His Only Son, Who would die for lost humanity, thereby redeeming mankind. Abraham now knew the *"way"* in which God would do this thing.

NOTES

As it regards this, Jesus said of the Patriarch, and speaking to the Jews, *"Your father Abraham rejoiced to see My day: and he saw it, and was glad"* (Jn. 8:56).

However, even though Abraham now knew the *"way"* in which God would do this thing, he really did not know the *"means"* by which it would be done. That information would be given to Moses.

Not long before the Children of Israel were to leave the wilderness and go into the Promised Land, they sinned greatly against the Lord, murmuring against Him, finding fault, etc. (Num. 21:4-5). As a result, *"The Lord sent fiery serpents among the people, and they bit the people; and much people of Israel died"* (Num. 21:6).

As it regards this terrible thing brought on by their sin, they begin to cry to Moses, even admitting, *"We have sinned, for we have spoken against the Lord"* (Num. 21:7).

Moses prayed for the people, and *"The Lord said unto Moses, Make thee a fiery serpent, and set it upon a pole: and it shall come to pass, that every one that is bitten, when he looketh upon it, shall live"* (Num. 21:8).

There, the Lord showed Moses the *"means"* by which He would redeem fallen humanity, bitten by the serpent of sin. His Only Son which He had showed Abraham, would hang on a Cross and die for lost humanity. This is the manner in which it was to be done.

As the first Revelation sobered Abraham, this no doubt sobered Moses greatly as well!

In referring to this, Jesus spoke to Nicodemus, telling him the manner in which man was to be redeemed, and said, *"And as Moses lifted up the serpent in the wilderness, even so must the Son of Man be lifted up:*

*"That whosoever believeth in Him should not perish, but have Eternal Life"* (Jn. 3:1, 14-15).

And then Jesus also said, *"And I, if I be lifted up from the earth, will draw all men unto Me"* (Jn. 12:32).

He was referring to being lifted up on the Cross, which was necessary for men to be saved, and that we are to Preach the Cross, i.e., *"Him lifted up, which draws men to Himself,"* and which alone will draw men to Himself.

In other words, we are to preach the Cross, live the Cross, sing the Cross, believe the

Cross, because it was there where the Prince of Glory died. And when He died upon that Cross, His Death judged the world, and in effect, *"did cast out the prince of this world,"* i.e., *"Satan."*

In other words, through and by the Cross of Christ, Satan was totally and completely defeated.

(3) "THAT NO MAN SHOULD BE MOVED BY THESE AFFLICTIONS: FOR YOURSELVES KNOW THAT WE ARE APPOINTED THEREUNTO."

At Paul's instruction, Timothy was to tell the Thessalonians, that they were not to be *"unsettled by these trials."* In fact, such is the lot of Christ's followers (Jn. 16:33).

However, it is to be understood, that irrespective of the afflictions or trials, they cannot in any way dim the glory and the luster of this Christian experience. The latter so far outweighs the former, that there is no contest. In other words, to live for God, is the greatest life that anyone could ever live, in fact, the only real life there actually is. We should brush these afflictions aside, and go on in Christ, ever looking forth toward the coming glad day, when we shall be with Him forever and forever.

## MOVED BY THESE AFFLICTIONS?

The phrase, *"That no man should be moved by these afflictions,"* refers to the fact that we should not allow these things to discourage us, hinder us, or in the slightest to turn our heads away from Christ.

*"To be moved"* in the Greek is *"sainesthai,"* and means *"to move or waiver in mind, as from fear; to dread, to tremble."* Here the sense is, to be so moved or agitated by fear, or by the terror of persecution, as to forsake the Lord.

*"Afflictions"* in the Greek is *"thlipsesin,"* and means *"anguish, persecution, tribulation, trouble."*

If it were not possible for Believers to be moved away from the Lord by these things, then Paul would not have admonished the Thessalonians as he did. In fact, Jesus addressed this in His Parable of the Sower. He said, *"He that received the seed* (the Word of God) *into stony places, the same is he that heareth the Word, and anon with joy receiveth it;*

NOTES

*"Yet hath he not root in himself, but dureth for awhile: for when tribulation or persecution ariseth because of the Word, by and by he is offended"* (Mat. 13:20-21).

The word *"offended"* means that he *"trips up, stumbles, is enticed to sin, and goes back into apostasy."*

The Church at Thessalonica was suffering; suffering a trial which not everyone can bear; and Paul was anxious to have someone with them who had learned the elementary Christian lesson, that such is inevitable.

The Believers at Thessalonica had not, indeed, been taken by surprise. The Apostle had told them before, that to this lot Christians were appointed; we are destined, he says, to suffer affliction. Nevertheless, it is one thing to know this by being told, and another to know it, as the Thessalonians now did, by experience.

So, the afflictions are going to come. That is a given, and the next phrase tells us why.

## APPOINTED THEREUNTO

The phrase, *"For yourselves know that we are appointed thereunto,"* means, *"We are destined for such."*

Moffatt said, *"Troubles are our lot, you know that well. It was necessary to counteract the Satanic suggestion* (used by Satan only when it fits his purpose) *that peacefulness and prosperity are evidence of Righteousness or true spirituality, and that conversely pain and trouble indicate God's displeasure."*

The Truth is, Christians are to face trouble, not as an appointment with blind fate, but as something included in God's Good and Perfect Plan.

Christian's suffering or trouble are not the consequence of a Divine penal decree, but is rather the unavoidable result of Godliness at work in a wicked world. The Cross of Christ is itself an offense and a stumblingblock. It is an intolerable rebuke to pride, selfishness, and self-will.

To be true to our commission, Christians must in love attack the corruption and the false gods of society. Deeper still, we must find our life's meaning by identifying ourselves with Him Who could not avoid Gethsemane's bitter cup, and Who bore the world's transgressions on the Cross.

There is no suggestion here of suffering for suffering's sake. This is no self-induced torture. As Christians, we are destined for holy character and for eternal values; therefore, in a world like this, we are destined also for tribulation. But there is nothing meaningless in such suffering: God uses it in His Redemptive purpose, both for His Glory and for our spiritual refinement.

## THE BLESSINGS OF GOD AND THE TRIALS OF THE CHRISTIAN

For the last half of the 20th Century, Christians were led to believe that if they had enough Faith, they could ward off all tribulations, etc. In fact, people were told if they had problems or difficulties of any kind, this was a sign that their Faith was weak, etc. Some of these Teachers even suggested, that if Paul had obtained to their level of Faith, he would never have had to suffer the difficulties which he encountered.

In fact, there could be nothing more preposterous than such drivel, and drivel it is!

While all of us want the Blessings of God, and rightly so, and simply because God is a Blesser. Through and by His many Blessings, we learn many things about Him. We learn how good He is, how wonderful He is, how beneficial He is, etc. That's a wonderful thing, in which every Believer must know and understand. God is a good God!

However, even though we learn from Blessings how good and wonderful that God is, we in fact, learn precious little about ourselves, at least in that capacity.

Unfortunately, we don't learn very much about ourselves, until we face trials and tribulations; hence, the Lord must allow such to come our way at times, hence Paul using the word *"appointed thereunto."*

The suffering of the good because they are good is mysterious, and in part because it has the two aspects made so manifest here. On the one hand, it comes by Divine appointment: it is the Law under which the Son of God Himself and all His followers live. But on the other hand, it is capable of a double issue.

It may perfect those who endure it as ordained by God; it may bring out the solidity of our character, and redound to the glory of our Saviour; or it may give an opening to the tempter to seduce us from a path so full of difficulties.

The one thing of which Paul is certain is, that the Salvation of Christ is cheaply purchased at any price of affliction. Christ's life here and hereafter is the supreme good; the one thing needful, for which all else may be counted loss.

## THE DOUBLE ISSUE

This possible double issue of suffering — in higher goodness, or in the abandonment of the narrow way — explains the difference of tone with which Scripture speaks of it in different places.

With the happy issue in view, it bids us to count it all joy when we fall into divers temptation; blessed, it explains, is the man who endures; for when he has found proof, he shall receive the Crown of Life.

But with human weakness in view, and the terrible consequences of failure, it bids us pray, *"Lead us not into temptation, but deliver us from the Evil One."* The true Christian will seek, in all the afflictions of life, to combine the courage and hope of the one view with the humility and fear of the other (MacLaren).

(4) "FOR VERILY, WHEN WE WERE WITH YOU, WE TOLD YOU BEFORE THAT WE SHOULD SUFFER TRIBULATION; EVEN AS IT CAME TO PASS, AND YE KNOW."

This doesn't sound very much like some of modern Christianity. In fact, much of modern Christianity plainly says that if we have the right kind of Faith, we will have no tribulations, or problems of any nature. If in fact these difficulties do come, we are told that our confession is not what it ought to be, and if we will straighten up our confession, then we can get rid of all the problems.

Well of course, it is obvious that there is a conflict here. Either the Word of God is right, or else the modern Gospel is right. Both cannot be correct, as should be obvious!

Of course, I am being somewhat sarcastic, for the Word of God cannot be wrong, which means that much of the modern Gospel definitely is wrong!

## THE MESSAGE PAUL PREACHED

The phrase, *"For verily, when we were with you, we told you before that we should*

NOTES

*suffer tribulation,"* proclaims the Apostle preaching an entirely different type of Message than is mostly preached presently.

Today, the carrot of riches, guaranteed health, and a trouble-free existence, are held up as a portrayal of one who lives for Jesus. Consequently, inasmuch as the Message is unscriptural, i.e., *"untrue,"* it appeals to greed, selfishness, and a totally improper view of Christ. In fact, in this genre Christ is looked at as some type of glorified bellhop, etc.

The Message as preached by Paul, didn't pull any punches, plainly telling these new converts, that without a doubt, they would suffer tribulation.

Now we might quickly ask, if this wasn't a wrong approach?

Well of course, we know it wasn't wrong, because the Holy Spirit sanctioned that of the Apostle.

With this other way, the Church has filled its buildings and its coffers, but mostly with people who actually have never been saved. They are religious, but wrong! They are alive in the flesh but dead in the spirit. In fact, most of modern Christendom is a crossless Christianity, which in effect, presents *"another Jesus"* (II Cor. 11:4). This means that Christianity has been reduced to mere ethics, which makes it no better than Islam, etc.

There are two things that make Bible Christianity different than any of the religions of the world. Those two things are: A. Christ; and, B. The Cross!

If Christ is divorced from the Cross, which by and large the modern Church has done, then we are left with a Christ which is not the Christ of the Bible. And if we divorce the Cross from Christ, we have a Christ Who can no longer save, because all Salvation comes from the Cross.

It is a strange thing, the Early Church suffered terrible persecution, but for everyone who was snatched out of its ranks and went to their death, ten more stepped in and took their place.

How? Why?

In the Early Church, Christ was properly presented, as should be obvious. As a result, people obtained from Him what the heart had long sought. I speak of peace such as the world cannot give, of joy unspeakable and full of glory, of a Resurrection Life that far exceeded any problems or difficulties which might arise.

NOTES

Presently, the type of Christ held up, is merely a promise of money, or some such foolishness! Consequently, the poor seeker doesn't get Christ or the money, so he is a loser all the way around. All of this because of greedy Preachers!

IT CAME TO PASS

The phrase, *"Even as it came to pass, and ye know,"* means that it will come to pass presently as well!

If one gets to the bottom of all persecution, all tribulation, etc., one will find that the Cross of Christ is primarily that which attracts such. Satan hates the Cross and for all the obvious reasons!

Even in Thessalonica, the Cross is what caused the persecution. The Pagans were stirred up by the unbelieving Jews, who had rejected Christ and the Cross. They did not at all believe in Jesus, and they certainly didn't believe in the Cross, so they persecuted the entire way. They could not really do much themselves, so they stirred up the Gentiles against Paul and the Church.

At the present time, one will find the Cross as the greatest lightning rod of all. But most of the lightning will come not from the world per se, but rather from the apostate Church, which is always far larger than the True Church.

As far as the Church is concerned, this thing started back with Cain and Abel. Because of the Cross, Cain persecuted his brother, and even killed him. The spirit of animosity toward the Cross in its portrayal, began there, and has continued ever since.

Beginning in 1996, even as I have stated, the Lord began to give me a Revelation of the Cross, which has completely revolutionized my life. He has shown me the answer to the victorious, overcoming, Christian life. In other words, as to how it can be done and as to how it is to be done.

Even though most Christians know very little about this of which I speak, and as a consequence are living in defeat, still, the response to this of which I am saying, will be very weak.

Why?

One would think that a Believer would want total victory in the Lord, and if they didn't have that victory, which most don't have, that if that door was open they would surely take advantage of this wonderful opportunity; however, most won't!

Man does not like to admit he is wrong, and Christians most of all don't like to admit they are wrong. Consequently, we are speaking here of pride and stubbornness. Others do not want to abandon the false crutches on which they are leaning, continuing to think they are going to get that million dollars that the Preacher has promised them.

The whole thing is an offence to the Cross.

The Holy Spirit through Paul plainly said there was (Gal. 5:11). As well, the Apostle said that Jesus would be *"a stumblingstone and Rock of offence"* (Rom. 9:33).

How is He that?

THE OFFENCE OF THE CROSS

It all centered up in His Cross. Had He been only a Healer and Miracle-Worker, it would have been different. It was the Cross which made Him this of which we speak.

The Cross tells man how bad he is, and how good that God is. He doesn't want to believe either one!

He wants to think that he can solve his problems himself, hence the advent of psychology, and all the self-improvement efforts made by man. Regrettably, the Church falls into the same trap.

Man does not want to admit that he cannot save himself, so he will not trust in the Cross. The Church does not want to admit that it cannot sanctify itself, so it refuses to trust the Cross. They are both the same!

That and that alone is the real cause of the *"tribulation and persecution"* of the Saints of God, at least as it concerns the world and the apostate Church.

So, on the surface it would seem that I'm not helping the Cause of Christ very much, by writing in this Commentary how much people are going to have to face trouble and tribulation, if they accept Christ and the Cross.

That's not true, I will definitely be helping the Cause of Christ, and because I'm telling the Truth, just as Paul did so long ago.

Jesus further addressed this when He gave the requirements for being His Disciple. He said, *"If any man come to Me, and hate not his father, and mother, and wife, and children, and brethren, and sisters, yea, and his own life also, he cannot be My Disciple.*

*"And whosoever doth not bear his Cross, and come after Me, cannot be My Disciple."*

He then said, *"For which of you, intending to build a tower, sitteth not down first, and counteth the cost, whether he have sufficient to finish it?"* (Lk. 14:26-28).

He is telling us here, exactly what bearing the Cross entails. It will draw the animosity of the world and the apostate Church. So, before one says *"Yes,"* one should evaluate his situation, in other words, *"Count the cost."*

That doesn't sound like many of the modern invitations, does it!

It is best to have one who truly accepts the Lord, and will live for Him irrespective of what comes or goes, than to have a Church filled with people who actually are unsaved. And regrettably, the latter is the condition of the modern Church.

(5) "FOR THIS CAUSE, WHEN I COULD NO LONGER FORBEAR, I SENT TO KNOW YOUR FAITH, LEST BY SOME MEANS THE TEMPTER HAVE TEMPTED YOU, AND OUR LABOUR BE IN VAIN."

Considering the persecution, Paul was constrained to find out through Timothy the state of their Faith. He knew that *"the tempter* (Satan)*"* (Mat. 4:3) had been at work among them and that God had permitted the enemy this activity.

What Paul did not know about the Thessalonians, however, was whether or not the tempter's solicitations had been successful, which would have meant that his work in Thessalonica (Paul's) had been in vain.

THIS CAUSE

The phrase, *"For this cause,"* speaks as stated, of the persecution, and their response. Considering that these were new converts, only having come to Christ in recent days, the Apostle as would be understandable, was very concerned about their spiritual welfare. Exactly what form this persecution took we are not exactly told, but the uproar had been severe enough, that Paul and Silas had to be spirited out of the city by night. The rulers of the city, as Acts Chapter 17 proclaims, had become involved due to the state of the

NOTES

uproar caused by the Jews. Paul knew these people were capable of any thing, any lie, any action, any subterfuge, any form of violence for that matter. In fact, he had once been of the same spirit, so if anybody in the world understood what was happening, this man did.

## A NEED FOR INFORMATION

The phrase, *"When I could no longer forbear,"* presents the Apostle repeating for emphasis what has already been said in Verses 1 and 2.

Some may claim here that the Apostle was not evidencing Faith as a result of his anxiety; however, only those who have no knowledge whatsoever of the Word of God would say such a thing. The Holy Spirit sanctions the Apostle's concern.

I'm quite certain that Paul was seeking the Lord earnestly as it regards the spiritual welfare of the Thessalonians; however, it seems that the Lord had given him no direct answer which would have settled his spirit; consequently, he feels he must have firsthand information concerning their present status; therefore, he sends Timothy.

Should the Apostle have left the care of the thing with the Lord, and gone about his business?

If the matter had been such that he could not have done anything, that would have been what he should have done, and no doubt would have done; however, his concern was far greater than merely the need for information. He knew that the Thessalonians in their infant spiritual state, needed a strong hand at this time to give them encouragement, and as he had said, to establish them in the Faith. In other words, at this particular moment, and especially now, they needed a strong Leader. He could not go back himself for all the obvious reasons, so he did the next best thing and sent Timothy.

While the Lord will definitely uphold His part in the work, it is up to us to uphold our part as well. Consequently, we want to make doubly certain that we carry out our task with responsibility and forethought.

## YOUR FAITH

The phrase, *"I sent to know your Faith,"* presents volumes to us.

NOTES

This Christian experience, is an experience of *"Faith!"* And what do we mean by that?

It actually refers to one placing his Faith and Trust in the Lord Jesus Christ and what the Lord did at the Cross and the Resurrection on our behalf, in order that we might be redeemed. It is not faith in a philosophy, but rather in a Man, The Man, Christ Jesus. But more particularly, and as stated, it is Faith in what He did at the Cross on our behalf.

Faith includes the idea that the Believer knows that he was lost without God, and that the only way to God is through His Son, The Lord Jesus Christ. In brief, that is the sum total of *"Faith."*

Regarding these former Pagans, they had previously had no knowledge of God whatsoever, unless some of them had been going to the Jewish Synagogue, which no doubt some had done. Although they would not have learned the way to Salvation at all by doing this, still, they would have learned many valuable things.

The Greek/Roman world, even as we have previously addressed, was a world of idol worship, etc. Consequently, these individuals would have believed there were many gods. What they were taught at the Synagogue, at least for the few who did actually attend, would have debunked this paganism. They would have learned that there was only one God, the God of Abraham, Isaac, and Jacob. In other words, that God nearly 2,000 years before had revealed Himself to these men, with a people, the Jews, born out of this Revelation. They would have learned some things about the Law of Moses as it regards the right way of living. Some few of them may have even become proselyte Jews, but more than likely, those would have been few and far between, if any at all! Actually, in every Jewish Synagogue, they had a place reserved for Gentiles who had not become proselytes, and were, therefore, called *"God-fearers."* Consequently, when Paul went into any new city to bring the Gospel, if there was a Synagogue, which there was in most, he would first of all go there. He would have an opportunity to bring the Words of Life to the Jews and to what Gentiles who were there as well. In fact, this is the way that most of his Churches were begun, including Thessalonica (Acts 17:1-4).

SALVATION?

Even though what the Gentiles would have learned attending a Synagogue would have been mostly good as far as it went, in fact, a tremendous enlightenment over their paganism, still, no way of Salvation was actually offered. The Jews believed that their Salvation consisted of keeping the Law, etc., which of course did not provide Salvation, as it was never intended to provide Salvation. The Jews had long since lost the actual intention of the Law, which was originally meant to bring them to Christ. As stated, they had attempted to make Salvation out of the Law, just as many presently attempt to make Salvation out of the Church. Salvation, exclusively, has always been in Christ, to Whom the Sacrifices were always meant to point. The Jews lost sight of that, attempting to make Salvation out of the ritual.

When Paul and his associates began to preach Jesus Christ as a fulfillment of all the prophecies and the Law, etc., and considering that his words would have contained the Anointing of the Holy Spirit, many Gentiles and even some few Jews, eagerly accepted the Message brought by the Apostle. Jesus Christ and Him Crucified was the theme.

FAITH AS THE VEHICLE

Whereas the Jews would have taught a tremendous array of religious doings, which concerned all their rituals, Paul reduced the whole thing down to a matter of simple *"Faith."* In other words, all Believers, whether Jews or Gentiles, were to simply believe in what Jesus Christ had done at the Cross on their behalf, and they would be saved. There were no sacrifices needed, for the simple matter, that Jesus Christ had been the great Sacrifice, in fact, the One Sacrifice of which all the others were merely symbolic. No Circumcision on males was required, no keeping of Feast days, no rituals regarding the many washings, no Sabbath-keeping, in fact, no law whatsoever.

Due to the fact, that Jesus Christ had been crucified by the Jews as an imposter, and that Paul was teaching that the Law of Moses had served its purpose in introducing Christ, and was now at an end, all in Christ, many of the Jews in these local Synagogues, would become very angry, even violent. That's what happened at Thessalonica, and that's what happened in many other places as well.

NOTES

At any rate, Paul preached and preached strongly, that the only requirement to be saved, the only requirement to know God, the only requirement to have Salvation, was to simply believe on the Lord Jesus Christ, which means to accept what He did for us on our behalf (Jn. 3:16; Rom. 10:9-10, 13; Eph. 2:8-9; Rev. 22:17).

When true Faith was registered, an immediate work of Regeneration took place in the hearts and lives of these Pagans, which gave them a joy that they had heretofore not known. They had been *"Born-Again"* (Jn. 3:3, 16). Of course, this was light-years ahead of their old paganism, and as well, far ahead even of Judaism. It was a *"know-so"* Salvation, all by *"Faith!"*

So that's why Paul said, *"I sent to know your Faith!"* Were they still believing? Out of fear, had they abandoned their Faith?

ONCE SAVED ALWAYS SAVED?

Commentators who espouse a *"once in Grace, always in Grace"* view have some problems with this Passage. They argue that what Paul sought to learn was whether or not the Thessalonians had originally had true Faith and a real conversion, or had merely experienced a spurious, emotional change on the occasion of his preaching the Gospel to them.

But it is obvious that Paul's knowledge of their election based on evidence derived from the event cited in I Thessalonians 1:4-10, debunked this idea.

Paul wished to know whether or not their Faith, which had been genuine in the beginning, meaning that they had truly given their hearts and lives to Christ, had been extinguished as a result of their temptations. He succeeds in conveying his underlying confidence in them even while expressing the tragic possibility of their spiritual failure, in which case his labor with them would prove to be *"in vain."* The purpose of Satan was to destroy the Faith of the converts. God uses permitted sufferings to strengthen Faith and build holy character; Satan uses the same sufferings to seduce from the path of trust and obedience.

In our probation the issue is in doubt only until by our choice and attitude we either humbly receive or willfully frustrate God's sufficient Grace.

No, this Passage as stated by Paul, clearly proves that a Believer who has evidenced Faith in Christ, or he couldn't be a Believer, meaning that he has been *"Born-Again,"* can indeed abandon Faith, and do so for many and varied reasons. Irrespective of the problems, if a Believer continues to trust Christ, that person is not lost; however, if they abandon their Faith, cease to believe, which in fact can happen, then the person is no longer a Believer, no longer trusting Christ, which means they are no longer saved (Heb. 6:4-6; 10:26-31).

Some are fond of asking the question, *"Can a Believer in Christ ever be lost?"*

Of course not!

However, a Believer can cease to believe, even as many have done, and then they are no longer a Believer, and are definitely lost. A person comes to Christ by his own free will, which is the only way a person can come (Jn. 3:16; Rev. 22:17). God does not force people to be saved. He moves upon their hearts as the Word of God is presented to them, but still, it is the individual who has to make the choice themselves to accept Christ.

When this is done, the free moral agency of the person does not cease to be. They continue to be a free moral agent, which means, even as we have just stated, that they can humbly continue to receive the Grace of God, or willfully frustrate God's sufficient Grace. In other words, the same *"will"* that brought a person into Grace, can at the same time, if they so desire, take a person out of Grace. Were that not the case, examples and illustrations such as these Thessalonians, which abound in the Word of God, would make no sense.

Were it not possible for these Thessalonians to quit believing, while Paul surely would have continued to be concerned about their welfare, he would have had no concern about their Faith. But he did have concern about their Faith, simply because that was actually what was at stake. While he was definitely concerned about their physical welfare, their economic welfare, and their mental welfare, still, it was their *"Faith"* of which he was greatly concerned, and for the obvious reasons.

NOTES

## THE TEMPTER

The phrase, *"Lest by some means the tempter have tempted you,"* refers to the temptation to forsake their Faith, to forsake their trust in Christ, to forsake their Salvation.

Years ago I heard the great Preacher A.N. Trotter say, *"Every attack by Satan is for but one purpose, and that is to destroy our Faith, or at least for it to be seriously weakened."* I never forgot what he said!

That means that whatever course the Evil One takes, whether an attack upon our physical body, on our finances, on our family, or on us personally and in some way through discouragement, etc., all present an attack upon our Faith, attempting to get us to quit. He wants you to grow discouraged and quit, or else become disillusioned and quit, or become bitter and quit, or to lose heart and quit. In fact, millions have and millions do.

The *"tempter"* is Satan, with the same title given to him in Matthew 4:3.

However, temptation falls into several categories. If Satan cannot get you as a Believer to quit believing and, therefore, cease your trust in Christ, he will attempt to pull you from the True Gospel, into error. Either way he has succeeded, whether to get you to quit believing, or to have you believe error. In fact, the latter method is his most successful way.

If one's Faith is not true, then it is the same as not having Faith at all.

For instance, nearly a billion Catholics have faith in the Church, in the Virgin Mary, in their Priests, etc. While that might be Faith, it is not True Faith; consequently, they are not saved. As well, untold thousands of Mormons believe that Salvation consists of belonging to the Mormon Church. They fall into the same category.

The same can be said for untold numbers of Churches of Christ who believe that Water Baptism saves, and many others of different particular persuasions, etc. The idea is, Satan really doesn't care what you believe, or how dedicated you are to what you believe, just so it is not simple Faith in Christ. He doesn't mind people *"using Christ,"* as a part of the mix, or even accepting Him in some historical way, or even a philosophical way. He knows that none of that, as religious as it might be, contains any Salvation.

What he hates and hates with a passion, is the Message of *"Jesus Christ and Him Crucified"* (I Cor. 2:2).

He doesn't mind so much a person accepting Christ, if they do so apart from the Cross. It's the Cross he hates, and, therefore, the Cross he greatly opposes.

Jesus as the Healer, Jesus as the Miracle-Worker, Jesus as the great Teacher and Preacher, Jesus as the great Prophet, etc., although necessary, Satan knows in those modes only can bring no Salvation. It is Jesus and Him crucified which affords Redemption for lost mankind; consequently, it is that which the Evil One opposes to such degree.

TO LABOR IN VAIN

The phrase, *"And our labour be in vain,"* proves that such can be, or else the Apostle would not have made mention of such. So, as stated, this among a host of other Passages debunks the theory of *"Once in Grace, always in Grace,"* irrespective of what one might do.

The principal figure in this scenario of course, is Satan, who Paul addresses as *"the tempter,"* and who always seeks to drag down the Child of God. Considering how important all of this is, let's take a closer look at this Evil One called *"Satan."*

SATAN

The name *"Satan"* means *"Adversary,"* which means *"to lie in wait as an adversary, to oppose."* In fact, *"the Adversary"* becomes a proper name for Satan and denotes his personality. It is so used in Job Chapters 1 and 2 and in Zechariah 3:1-2 where it clearly designates a Celestial being, i.e., *"fallen Angel."*

It is sometimes said that in the Old Testament the figure of Satan is not portrayed in all his evil posture, at least as bad as he actually is; however, even though the full picture of his evil character is not given totally in the few Old Testament references to him, clearly though, his evil nature is recorded in unmistakable terms. And yet, it is a remarkable feature of the theology of the Old Testament that so little mention is made of Satan as the great Adversary of God and His people, that awaiting the Revelation of the New Testament.

NOTES

SATAN IN THE NEW TESTAMENT

It is in the New Testament that the picture of Satan receives its full unfolding. Here he is given particular names, which portray his evil character and work.

He is called *"Abaddon"* and *"Apollyon"* (Rev. 9:11), both meaning *"the destroyer"*; *"the accuser of our Brethren"* (Rev. 12:10); *"the adversary"* (I Pet. 5:8); *"Beelzebub"* (Mat. 12:24); *"Belial"* (II Cor. 6:15); *"the deceiver of the whole world"* (Rev. 12:9); *"the great dragon"* (Rev. 12:9); *"an enemy"* (Mat. 13:28-39); *"the Evil One"* (Mat. 13:19, 38); *"the father of lies"* (Jn. 8:44); *"the god of this world"* (II Cor. 4:4); *"a liar"* (Jn. 8:44); *"a murderer"* (Jn. 8:44); *"the prince of the power of the air"* (Eph. 2:2); *"the ruler of this world"* (Jn. 12:31; 14:30; 16:11); *"the ancient serpent"* (Rev. 12:9); *"the tempter"* (Mat. 4:3; I Thess. 3:5).

HIS POSITION

Satan holds a position of great power and dignity in the spiritual world. Actually, he is an Angel originally created by God, who served God in Righteousness and Holiness for an undetermined period of time. As well, there is some indication, that he was at least one of the most powerful beings ever created by God, if not the most powerful. He was known then as *"Lucifer,"* with his name meaning *"brightness or morning star"* (Isa. 14:12-15; Ezek. 28:11-19).

At some point he led a revolution against God, with one-third of the Angels throwing in their lot with him, which revolution spilled over into the creation of man, as recorded in Genesis Chapter 3.

In Job Chapters 1 and 2 he is pictured as numbered among *"the sons of God,"* although by his moral nature not one of them. He has personal access to the Presence of God, a privilege that will be taken from him in a future day (Rev. 12:9). So exalted is his position that Michael the Archangel found him a formidable foe and *"did not presume to pronounce a reviling judgment upon him"* (Jude vs. 9).

NOTES

The New Testament reveals that Satan is the ruler over a powerful kingdom of evil which he rules with intelligent consistency. In refuting the charge that he was casting out demons by the power of Beelzebub, Jesus pointed out the absurdity of the charge since it meant that Satan, that is if such a charge were true, *"is divided against himself; how then will his kingdom stand?"* (Mat. 12:26).

Satan does not operate in isolation but is the head of a well-organized kingdom in which his subjects exercise delegated responsibility under his direction. He is the leader of a vast, compact organization of spirit beings, *"his angels"* (Mat. 25:41; Rev. 12:7), and demon spirits.

As *"the prince of the power of the air"* (Eph. 2:2), he skillfully directs an organized host of wicked spirits in the heavenlies and on this Earth, who do his bidding (Eph. 6:12). The fallen Angels who gave their allegiance to Satan when he rebelled against God some time in eternity past (Rev. 12:4, 7, 9) apparently retained their ranks, dignities, and titles which were Divinely given them when they were originally created by God as righteous and pure.

DEMON SPIRITS

Even though the Bible is abundant with mention of Demon Spirits who operate under the command of Satan, and especially in the four Gospels, still, there is no concrete proof as to the origin of demons; however, it is clear that they render willing and wholehearted obedience to the rule of Satan (Mat. 12:28-29). Acts 10:38 makes it clear that the outburst of demonic activity during the Ministry of Jesus was Satan-inspired. Actually, Satan, who is not omnipresent (present everywhere as God), through the work of his numerous subordinates, however, makes his influence worldwide. In fact, the Book of Revelation reveals that at the close of this age and in the Great Tribulation there will be another fearful outburst of demonic activity (Rev. 9:1-11; 18:2).

Demon Spirits are not fallen Angels as some have claimed. All Angels, fallen or otherwise, have spirit bodies, with Demon Spirits not having such. Actually, they seek a body to inhabit whether man or beast. There is no record of any Angel ever seeking someone to inhabit, etc.

This we do know, the Lord did not originally create Demon Spirits in the capacity in which they now operate. In other words, they became this way because of rebellion against God, which no doubt took place in Satan's original rebellion. Some Bible Scholars believe that they were formerly a creation on this Earth, and we speak of the time before the creation of man. There is some evidence, especially in Isaiah Chapter 14, that Lucifer, before the creation of man, may have ruled this Earth in Righteousness and Holiness under God. If in fact that was the case, there would have been some type of creation for him to rule. As well, there is indication of this in what is referred to as the *"gap theory"* between Genesis 1:1 and 1:2. We do know that when God originally created this planet called Earth, He did not create it a chaotic wreckage as is recorded in Genesis 1:2. So, something must have happened to have brought it to this state, which many Scholars believe was actually the revolution of Satan against God. If that happened, and there is I think an overwhelming amount of evidence that it did, whatever type of creation was then on Earth threw in their lot with Lucifer, with the result being those we now know as *"Demon Spirits."*

THE RULER OF THIS WORLD

Satan is also described as *"the ruler of this world"* (Jn. 12:31). The *"world"* which he rules is the present world system organized according to his own principles, methods, and aims, which he obtained by forfeit upon the Fall of Adam and Eve (II Cor. 4:3-4; Eph. 2:2; Col. 1:13; I Jn. 2:15-17).

The greed and self-centered ambitions of the nations, the deceptive diplomacy of the political world, the bitter hatred and rivalry in the sphere of commerce, the godless ideologies of the masses of humanity, all spring out and are fostered by Satanic influence. Satan exercises his domination over *"the sons of disobedience"* (Eph. 2:2).

The statement that *"the whole world lies in the Evil One"* (I Jn. 5:19) indicates that the world of unregenerate humanity lies in the grip of Satan and supinely yields to his power. Satan has gained his power over mankind by trickery and usurpation. As the instigator of human sin, whose punishment is spiritual death, Satan gained *"the power of death"* and uses the power of deception as a means to keep men under his domination (Heb. 2:14-15).

The statement that he is *"a murderer from the beginning"* (Jn. 8:44) does not mean that he can inflict death at will, but that through the Fall of Adam and Eve he brought about the death of the human race. In His Death Christ broke the power of Satan over death and took the prey (humanity) from under his control, at least for those who will believe (Jn. 3:16; Rev. 1:18).

During the wilderness temptation Satan displayed to Jesus all the kingdoms of the world, asserted that all had been delivered to him, and claimed that he could give them to whom he wished (Lk. 4:5-6). Significantly Jesus did not dispute Satan's claim to sovereignty over this world. However, Christ categorically rejected the Satanic offer to invest Him with sovereignty over this world, but that offer will in fact be accepted in the near future by *"the man of lawlessness,"* i.e., *"the Antichrist"* (II Thess. 2:3-9; Rev. 13:4).

## HIS ACTIVITIES

In Job 1:7; 2:2 Satan himself described his restless activity of consisting in *"going to and fro on the earth"* and *"walking up and down in it."* He is engaged in a worldwide and unremitting conflict against God and His people. In other words, the revolution continues! This stamps him as *"the enemy"* of God and Truth (Mat. 13:28, 39; II Thess. 2:9-12). His activities are associated with the realm of moral darkness (Acts 26:18).

The phrase, *"The tempter"* as used by both Matthew and Paul (Mat. 4:3; I Thess. 3:5), designates Satan by his characteristic activity. His intention is ever to lead those tempted to fall into sin. The people of God are always the objects of his fierce hatred.

The Church of Smyrna was informed that they would be the subjects of Satan's special onslaughts (Rev. 2:10). As well, the Lord informed Peter that Satan had *"demanded to have you, that he might sift you like wheat"* (Lk. 22:31).

NOTES

Satan uses the weaknesses and limitations of men to entice them to sin (I Cor. 7:5). He also employs the allurements of the world (I Jn. 2:15-17; 4:4). He commonly tempts men to evil by the falsehood that they can attain a desired good through the doing of wrong. His mode of operation is vividly demonstrated in the account of the Fall in Genesis Chapter 3. Deception is a universal feature of his activities, justifying his description as *"the deceiver of the whole world"* (Rev. 12:9).

He constantly lays *"snares"* for men to make them his captives (I Tim. 3:7; II Tim. 2:26). A fundamental temptation employed is pride (I Tim. 3:6).

## COUNTERFEITS

Satan opposes the Work of God through his counterfeiting activities. He over-sows the wheat with tares, placing counterfeit believers among *"the sons of the kingdom"* (Mat. 13:25, 38-39). These counterfeit believers form *"a synagogue of Satan"* (Rev. 2:9; 3:9). In fact, Satan often disguises himself as *"an angel of light"* by presenting his messengers of falsehood as messengers of truth (II Cor. 11:13-15). Thus, those who give themselves over to evil and become agents of Satan to persuade to do evil are the children and servants of the Devil (Jn. 6:70; 8:44; Acts 13:10).

Apostate workers may engage in great religious activity without accepting the power of God's Truth (II Tim. 3:1-9). Satan blinds the minds of men to the Light of the Gospel (II Cor. 4:2-4) and induces them to accept his lie (II Thess. 2:9-10).

He also induces men to give heed to *"deceitful spirits and doctrines of demons"* through the pretensions of religious liars who have their conscience seared (I Tim. 4:1-2). He hates the Word of God and eagerly acts to snatch it out of the hearts of the unsaved (Mat. 13:19). He actively hinders workers concerned to further the welfare of the Saints (I Thess. 2:17-18).

Satan also opposes the Work of God through open and fierce opposition. The act of betrayal by Judas was instigated by the Devil (Lk. 22:3; Jn. 13:2, 27). Peter pictures Satan's ferocious activity in warning Believers that *"The Devil prowls around like a roaring lion, seeking someone to devour"* (I Pet. 5:8). His violent attacks manifest themselves in the persecutions experienced by God's people (II Tim. 3:11-13; Rev. 12:13-17).

HIS LIMITATIONS

Although a mighty and determined enemy of God, the Scriptures make it clear that Satan is a limited being. While it is true that he is a super being, he is in no way coequal with God. The power of Satan is derived (Lk. 4:6) and he is free to act only within the limits laid upon him by God. Satan was able to inflict loss and suffering upon Job only to the extent that God permitted (Job 1:12; 2:6).

The Church of Smyrna was assured that their tribulation would last only *"ten days"* (Rev. 2:10).

The length of their period of testing was set by the Lord, and Satan would not be able to go beyond it. At present the efforts of Satan on Earth are restrained and frustrated by the operation of the Divine Restrainer; with the removal of the restraint, Satan will be able to achieve the full outburst of evil in the end time in the manifestation of the man of lawlessness (the Antichrist) (II Thess. 2:7-8).

Believers are assured that God is greater than the forces of Satanic evil and that these evil forces will never be able to defeat God and separate Believers from the Love of God, that is if they keep trusting and believing in Christ (Jn. 3:16; 10:28; Rom. 8:38-39; I Jn. 4:4). Satan is permitted to afflict God's people but we are assured he will never experience complete victory over us (Jn. 14:30-31; 16:33). In fact, Satan can only hinder; he cannot defeat a Child of God, that is if the person continues to believe the Lord.

God at times even uses Satan as His instrument to chasten and correct erring Saints (Lk. 22:31-32; I Cor. 5:5; I Tim. 1:20).

Satan is not Divine; he is neither omnipotent (all-powerful), omniscient (all-knowing), nor omnipresent (everywhere). He has vast power, but that power is definitely limited. He is not omniscient, as is evident from his blunders during the course of history, as seen for example, in his futile efforts to destroy the Child Jesus.

Satan is not omnipresent but makes his power felt worldwide through the operations of his many evil spirits and fallen Angels.

NOTES

Satan acknowledged his limitations in his conversation with Jehovah concerning Job (1:7-11).

HIS ORIGIN

Satan is not eternal or self-existent, as God. Scriptural monotheism (one God) leaves no room for any view of an eternal dualism of good and evil — in other words, that Satan has always existed. His limitations are consistent with his nature as a created being.

The Words of Jesus in John 8:44 indicate that Satan is a fallen being. The assertion that he *"standeth not in the truth"* indicates not only his past fall but his resultant apostate character. Satan fell under God's condemnation through ambitious pride (I Tim. 3:6). In fact, Ezekiel 28:11-19 proclaims pride as the cause of his downfall.

Even though this Passage begins by addressing the human king of Tyre, we quickly understand that it is the one behind this king, who is Satan, who is really being addressed as the source of all such pomp and pride. Thus viewed, the Passage clearly sets forth the origin of Satan as a created being, his original position of power and dignity over the created universe under God, or at least over this Earth, and his fall through pride. As stated, Isaiah 14:12-14 is also a complimentary Passage.

Addressed to *"Lucifer,"* which means *"morning star,"* this Passage likewise is understood to go beyond the king of Babylon and to refer to Satan, the prince of this godless world system of which Babylon was the type. Thus viewed, the fivefold *"I will"* of Lucifer in this Passage portrays Satan's rebellious exaltation, marking the beginning of the conflict between the Will of God and Satan's own will.

In fact, Ezekiel 28:12-15 and Isaiah 14:12-14 throws much light on the question of Satan's origin and is in harmony with the Scriptural picture of Satan's close relations with world governments (Dan. 10:13; Jn. 12:31; Eph. 6:12).

HIS MOTIVE

With Satan's substitution of his own will for that of his Maker there began the protracted conflict between good and evil which has extended through the ages. God has permitted the effort of Satan to establish his own will in opposition to the Divine Will to be thoroughly tested. The unrelenting conflict between the Kingdom of God and the kingdom of evil is the direct result of Satan's determination to establish his claim.

The presence of sin, suffering, and death reveal the inevitable consequences of the Satanic claim. Through his seduction of Adam and Eve (Gen. 3:1-7; II Cor. 11:3) Satan succeeded in establishing his domination over mankind. Through the work of the Incarnate Christ that power was broken at the Cross (Heb. 2:14-15).

In his efforts to establish his own will Satan relentlessly works to thwart the Purpose and Work of God (Acts 13:10). In his ambition to assure the place of God Satan is mastered by a consuming passion to receive worship as God. That master passion was revealed in Satan's bald offer to invest Jesus with authority over the kingdoms of this world on condition that Jesus would worship him. This passion for worship will be gratified through his empowerment of the man of sin who is soon to make his appearance (II Thess. 2:9-11; Rev. 13:4).

Idolatry, with its diversion of worship from the True God, is another example of this of which we speak, and is motivated by demonic forces (Ps. 106:34-38; I Cor. 10:20).

In other words, idolatry is the worship of Satan, irrespective as to what form it takes.

## HIS JUDGMENT

The crucial battle between the Kingdom of God and the kingdom of evil took place in the conflict between Christ and Satan. The explicit purpose of the coming of Christ into the world was *"to destroy* (render inoperative) *the works of the Devil"* (I Jn. 3:8). Satan's initial defeat came in the wilderness temptation at the beginning of Jesus' Messianic Ministry (Mat. 4:1-11; Lk. 4:1-12). Because of that victory Jesus was able during His Ministry to enter *"a strong man's house and plunder his goods"* (Mk. 3:27).

The decisive defeat of Satan came in the Cross of Christ (Jn. 12:31; 16:11). There Satan was judged as an usurper and cast out as the legitimate ruler of this world. In the Cross and the Resurrection Christ broke the power of Satan over mankind (Col. 2:14-15; Heb. 2:14-15) and potentially delivered every soul from Satan's power.

Those who in Faith accept that deliverance are rescued from the dominion of darkness and transplanted into the Kingdom of God's beloved Son (Col. 1:13).

## THE CROSS AND THE RESURRECTION

Sin and transgression, in other words disobedience to God, are Satan's legal claim upon humanity. He has the legal right to this claim as a result of the sin and transgression of man. This all came about at the Fall of Adam and Eve in the Garden of Eden. Even though they were both deceived and fell by trickery, still, the results were the same. As we have previously mentioned, there is some slight evidence that Lucifer once had dominion over all of God's creation, which speaks of the time that he ruled under God in Righteousness and Holiness. When he rebelled against God, this dominion it seems was taken from him, and now given to God's greatest creation, man. There is even evidence, that Adam and Eve as originally created, were higher in rank than even the Angelic creation, including Lucifer. Psalms 8:5 as much as says that. The King James translates it, *"For Thou* (God) *hast made him* (man) *a little lower than the Angels."* However, the word *"Angels"* is actually in the Hebrew, *"Elohim,"* which means *"God."* So it should have been translated, *"For Thou hast made him a little lower than God, and hast crowned him with glory and honor."*

And then it says, *"Thou madest him to have dominion over the works of thy hands; thou hast put all things under his feet"* (Ps. 8:6).

This dominion which Satan once had, and was now given to Adam and to his posterity, infuriated Satan, with him determining to spoil this excellent creation by God. Hence, we have the Fall in the Garden of Eden (Gen. Chpt. 3).

However, God knew all of this would happen, and had already planned the Redemption of mankind through the Cross of Christ (I Pet. 1:18-20).

Dominion of this world and even of mankind now in his control, we find here the

NOTES

reason for all of the war, suffering, sickness, disaster, plagues, and trouble which inhabits and infests the Earth.

Because Satan's claim was legal, God could not merely by decree make null and void that claim. Its cause would have to be addressed, which would necessitate the sending of a Second Adam into the world, the Lord Jesus Christ. As man had forfeited dominion, man would have to purchase back dominion. Due to the fact that all of mankind born of woman would be born in sin, there was no way that man could redeem himself; consequently, Satan's claim was secure, at least if it remained in this fashion. However, God would remedy the situation, by becoming Man, and doing for man what man could not do for himself.

Inasmuch as Jesus was born of the Virgin Mary, which means He was not conceived by man, but rather conceived by the decree of the Holy Spirit, He was not born in original sin as all other men are born (Mat. 1:18-25). This could be done in this fashion and not destroy the type, because Adam was created in somewhat the same manner.

To win back dominion, which would defeat the claims of Satan, this Second or Last Adam (I Cor. 15:45-50), would have to do what the First Adam failed to do, but under an entirely different set of circumstances.

The First Adam had the privilege of functioning in a perfect environment, while the Second Adam, the Lord Jesus Christ, was forced to function in a very polluted environment.

First of all, He would have to perfectly keep the Law of God, which the First Adam did not do. In other words, He would have to live a perfect, moral life, in thought, in word, and in deed. If He failed even once, He would fail altogether.

Some have argued that inasmuch as He was Very God as well as Very Man, it was not possible for Him to fail. That is totally incorrect, inasmuch as He had to function exactly as the first Adam. He did have the Power of the Holy Spirit to help Him, which the first Adam also had, but that was all. That means He did not function at all as Deity. To have done so, would have violated the type. Someone who cannot fail, at the same time cannot succeed.

Therefore, at this particular juncture in the history of eternity, God placed everything into the hands of His Only Son, the Lord Jesus Christ, and in the form of human Incarnation. In other words, had He failed, the entirety of the Kingdom of Heaven would have failed as well. In other words, Satan would have won his revolution.

But Jesus did not fail, not even in the slightest, coming down to the end and able to say, *"For the prince of this world cometh* (Satan), *and hath nothing in Me"* (Jn. 14:30).

However, even though all of this was absolutely necessary, it was at the Cross where Satan was totally defeated.

NOTES

## WHAT HAPPENED AT THE CROSS?

Jesus perfectly kept the Law of God, but at the same time, in order to redeem fallen humanity, He would at the same time, have to take the penalty of the broken Law which was death, even though He had not broken the Law at all. He did this as our Substitute and Representative Man.

In other words, the original Adam acted as the Representative Man for all of humanity, which condemned men to death because of his failure, Jesus acted as our Representative Man, and purchased back what the original Adam had lost (I Cor. 15:21-22). Once again, He could do this without destroying the type.

As I've said several times, as our Substitute, He died *"for us,"* and as our Representative Man, He died *"as us."*

*"For us"* He purchased back what we had lost, and *"as us"* He paid the penalty we should have paid, but couldn't pay. However, it must be understood, that while He died *"as a sinner,"* He did not die a sinner, for He had never sinned. This means that He could take the penalty for our sin, which He did, which was the pouring out of His Precious Blood, which gave up His Life, and thereby satisfied the demands of Heavenly Justice.

The Reader must understand, that this debt was owed to God and not Satan. In other words, the terrible crime against God must be addressed, in which it was addressed in Christ, with the debt fully paid.

On the Cross, Jesus not only paid the sin debt in full, in the doing of this, He also atoned for all sin, past, present, and future, at least for those who will believe (Jn. 3:16).

With all sin atoned, Satan has lost his grip and claim on the human race. When Jesus died, that paid the debt, and when He was buried, that totally erased the debt from the Books of God, laying it all to rest, taking it away, even as the *"Scapegoat"* as a symbol, took the sins of Israel away into the wilderness.

This death that He died, destroyed all of Satan's claims, which at the same time defeated Satan, every fallen Angel, and Demon Spirits.

It must be understood, that the defeat that Satan suffered, was his claim of sin on the human race. When it came to defeating the Devil and all his minions of darkness, that was never in question. God is all-powerful, while Satan is a mere creation of God; therefore, his defeat has never been the question as far as defeat is concerned. The defeat we are speaking of here, actually has to do with the legal claims of Satan, which were sin and transgression on the part of man. That's what Jesus had to address, and what He did address, and which was settled at the Cross.

That's why the Cross is so very, very important! To fail to understand the Cross and all its implications, is to fail to understand the Plan of God in its entirety.

As well, the Believer must understand, that the great victory there won by Jesus Christ not only made it possible for the sinner to be saved, but also for the Saint to be sanctified, i.e., *"to live a victorious, overcoming, Christian life in front of God and men."* It's all found in the Cross, because it was all done in the Cross. One might say, that it's a matter of Substitution and Identification. Jesus was our Substitute and our Identification with Him, grants to us all the great victories which He won at the Cross, and in fact did on our behalf.

## ALL FOR THE SAKE OF MANKIND

It must ever be understood, that Jesus did all of this, on behalf of fallen humanity. He did not need such, and neither did Heaven in any capacity. In totality, in completion, in all things, Jesus Christ came into this world for one purpose, and that was to die on a Cross, in order to redeem humanity. This means that the Cross was not merely an incident or accident. It was a designed conclusion even before the foundation of the world (I Pet. 1:18-20).

NOTES

Considering the price that Jesus paid here, which is so staggering that it is beyond the imagination of man, doesn't it stand to reason that God wants us to have all for which such a price was paid! I think it's obvious that He does!

The information I have just given concerning the Cross of Christ, has been given several times in our other Commentaries, and no doubt will be given again. I'm addressing this in this fashion, even going into detail, even being repetitive, simply because of the outsized significance to all of this. In fact, if one is wrong as it regards the Cross, in other words, if one doesn't properly understand the Cross, then one cannot properly understand any part of the Plan of God. To say it in another way, to the degree that one is misinformed as it regards the Cross, to that degree will one suffer defeat in one's life. Everything hinges on the Cross, because everything comes from the Cross. This is the Plan of God, and to fail to understand this, is to fail to understand His Plan.

Due to the fact that the Church has drifted so far away from the Cross in these last several decades, which has caused untold difficulty and harm for Believers, I have felt it necessary to proclaim this Truth again and again, and from every angle which I believe the Spirit of the Lord directs me. Nothing could be more important to your spiritual welfare, as nothing could be more important to the sinner who needs to be saved. The Cross of Christ is the focal point, the intersection, the foundation of all the Work of God. It is from the Cross that all Salvation springs, that all Victory and in every capacity comes to the Child of God.

It is through this great Finished Work of Christ, that the Holy Spirit works in His entirety. In other words, He will not work outside of the parameters of the Cross of Christ, which includes His Resurrection and Exaltation (Rom. 6:2-6; 8:1-2; Eph. 2:6).

As well, the Holy Spirit, Who the Believer must have in order to live this victorious life, demands Faith on our part as it regards His Work. And when we speak of Faith, we are meaning that the object of our Faith, must always be the Cross of Christ. That is where the Victory is, and that is where our Faith must be directed.

This is the same as having Faith in the Word, because the Word and the Cross are synonymous.

SAINT JOHN CHAPTER ONE

Saint John 1:1 says, *"In the beginning was the Word, and the Word was with God, and the Word was God."* Of course, this tells us that Jesus and the Word are One and the Same.

And then it tells us that *"the Word was made flesh, and dwelt among us"* (Jn. 1:14).

Of course, He was made flesh in order to die on a Cross. That was His only purpose and reason.

And then it says that John said of Him, *"Behold the Lamb of God, which taketh away the sin of the world"* (Jn. 1:29).

Jesus is referred to as *"the Lamb of God,"* for a purpose and reason. It referred to Him becoming a Sacrificial Offering on the Cross, of which all the slain millions of lambs before Him, were symbols. This would *"take away the sin of the world"* which the blood of lambs could never do.

So we see from this, that the Word of God, which in fact is Jesus, and the Cross are all synonymous. Therefore, when we speak of having Faith in the Cross, we are at the same time, saying to have Faith in the Word.

As well, if we do not understand the Word in this capacity, as it relates to the Cross, then we really do not understand the Word. To properly understand the Word, one must properly understand the Cross, and to properly understand the Cross, one must properly understand the Word.

While Jesus has defeated Satan at the Cross, and Judgment has already been pronounced upon him, the Evil One is still permitted to operate as a usurper until the time of his final imprisonment (Rev. Chpt. 20).

As a dethroned Monarch he is still allowed to rule over those who accept his authority while he persecutes those who have declared their allegiance to Christ.

HIS DOOM

Scripture reveals the certain outcome of the conflict between good and evil and the inevitable doom of Satan and his hosts. Jesus saw a picture of that final defeat of Satan in the victory of the 70 over the forces of evil (Lk. 10:18). Christ asserted that *"the eternal fire"* had been prepared *"for the Devil and his Angels"* (Mat. 25:41).

NOTES

The Book of Revelation portrays the final judgment carried out on the Devil. At the return of Christ in glory Satan will be confined to the sealed bottomless pit for 1,000 years, during which time the Earth will be free from his deceptive and seductive influences (Rev. 20:1-3).

At the end of the 1,000 years Satan will again be loosed from his prison and will again resume his deception of the inhabitants with great success, but only for a very short period of time. This final rebellion will be summarily crushed by Divine action and the Devil will be thrown into *"the Lake of Fire and Brimstone"* where with the Beast and the False Prophet he *"will be tormented day and night forever and ever"* (Rev. 20:7-10). His doom will be to share the eternal punishment of those whom he deceived (Rev. 20:12-14).

BELIEVERS AND SATAN

Having been rescued from the kingdom of darkness, Believers are assured of victory over the malicious activities of the Devil. We are promised that *"the God of Peace will soon crush Satan under our feet"* (Rom. 16:20). We find our security in the keeping power of Christ, which is derived by what He did at the Cross (Rom. 8:31-39; I Jn. 5:18).

For effective victory over Satan, Believers must recognize that on the basis of the Work of Christ at the Cross, Satan is a defeated foe. Consequently, we are called upon to take a firm stand against the Devil. *"Resist the Devil and he will flee from you"* (James 4:7).

Any attempt to flee from the Devil which many Christians attempt, is useless, but in claiming the Victory of Christ, Believers can put the Devil to flight.

In order to experience victory over Satan, Believers cannot remain *"ignorant of his designs"* (II Cor. 2:11). Recognizing that he is a powerful and crafty foe, we must *"give no opportunity to the Devil"* by allowing sin in our lives (Eph. 4:25-27). Instead, we must *"be sober, be watchful,"* alert to the danger from the Devil, and firmly resist him in Faith (I Pet. 5:8-9). Ephesians 6:10-17 repeatedly stresses the need to take a firm stand against the Satanic enemy.

## HOW IS THE BELIEVER TO DO ALL OF THIS?

In fact, a way has been made for the Child of God to walk in perpetual victory over all the powers of darkness, and to live a life of Godliness, in order that sin not have dominion over us in any capacity, bearing fruit for the Lord Jesus Christ (Rom. 6:14).

The great question is, *"How?"*

God has a prescribed order of Victory, and if we follow that prescribed order, we will have the Victory which is promised. If we attempt to go in any other direction, no matter how sincere we may be, there will not be victory in our lives, but the very opposite.

The Believer must understand, that Victory is not automatic, which should be very obvious. As well, the Believer who is Baptized with the Holy Spirit, by that mere fact alone, is not guaranteed of victory.

None of this is automatic for the Believer, but the following is the way laid out by the Holy Spirit:

1. The answer to the overcoming, victorious life, is found totally and only in the Cross of Christ. Of course, the Cross also presupposes the Resurrection and Exaltation of Christ. This is where the victory is, because this is where the victory was purchased by the Shed Blood of Christ.

So, the Believer must look exclusively to the Cross, i.e., *"the Finished Work of Christ,"* for all victory, and in fact, anything and everything which comes from God to the Believer.

2. Understanding that, the Believer is to make the Cross, even as we've already stated, the total and complete object of his Faith. In fact, whenever Paul uses the word *"Faith,"* he is speaking exclusively of Faith in the Cross, in one way or the other. If we do not understand that, then we really do not properly understand Faith.

In fact, everybody in the world has Faith of some sort, but it's only Faith in the Finished Work of Christ, which of course pertains to the Cross, which God will recognize. Therefore, when Believers claim that they have Faith in the Word, they had better understand that the Word and the Cross are actually synonymous (Jn. 1:1, 14, 29).

So, our Faith at all times, must be registered in the Cross of Christ, understanding, that this is where our victory is, and because it is where our victory was won.

3. When our Faith is properly placed in the Cross, and remains in the Cross, the Holy Spirit will then go to work on our behalf, and do whatever needs to be done to give us victory (Rom. 8:1-2). As we've stated over and over again, it is the parameters of the Finished Work of Christ, in which the Holy Spirit works. Consequently, in our Faith we must not go outside of those parameters. If we do, the Holy Spirit will not work. In that case, we are doomed to failure. In other words, we will live less than a victorious, Christian life.

Consequently, Satan directs his greatest attacks against the Cross of Christ. And when we speak of Satan coming against our Faith, which in fact every one of his attacks actually do, it is against our Faith in the Cross. He will try to sidetrack our Faith to other things, and if successful, he's perfectly content for us to continue in that capacity. He knows, that no matter how much we might quote Scriptures, or might bolster our nerve in the flesh, that none of it is going to bring any victory. So he is perfectly satisfied for us to be very religious if we so desire, just as long as our Faith is in other than the Cross.

## WHAT DOES IT MEAN TO HAVE FAITH OTHER THAN THE CROSS?

This confuses many Believers, because most of the time the very thing in which we place our Faith is very Scriptural in its own right. Inasmuch as it is Scriptural, and I speak of things like *"prayer, fasting, laying on of hands, spiritual manifestations, the giving of money to the Lord's Work, proper confession, faithfulness to Church, reading so many Chapters in the Bible each day, witnessing to souls,"* etc., it deceives us into making us believe that this is the right way. As stated, these things are very right in their own place, so in no way, are we minimizing these great qualities. But if we put our Faith in those things, thinking they will give us victory, it won't happen.

NOTES

And yet at the same time, those things do play a part in our victory, but only a part. It was in prayer that the Lord showed me the right Way. And it was certainly in the Scriptures that the Way was found. So, in that capacity, they do provide tremendous help; however, they must be understood correctly or else we will turn them into works, and we will be disappointed to be sure.

In order that the Reader may hopefully understand exactly what I'm saying, let's look at a hypothetical scenario.

Let's say that John Doe does not know or understand the Way of the Cross, even as most Christians don't, nor even most Preachers. As a result, he becomes even more of a target for Satan.

In some way, he begins to fail the Lord. As a Christian who loves the Lord, and hates sin, whatever it is that is giving him problems is repugnant to him, which he knows must cease, whatever it might be. And I might quickly add, the manner and ways in which the Devil attacks Christians are multitudinous in number and design.

Knowing that this problem in his life must be conquered, he reasons in his mind as to how it can be done. Inasmuch as prayer is extremely necessary in the life of the Child of God, he reasons that if he will faithfully pray 30 minutes a day, or whatever, that this will bring victory. Consequently, he sets about on this course, and in fact, is greatly blessed by the Lord regarding his prayer time each day.

But he finds to his dismay, that his problem is not any better, but really getting worse. Now at this stage, he can add anything he desires to his prayer time each day, and even though these things, providing they are Scriptural, will definitely be a blessing to him, he still will not find the relief that he needs. In other words, there will be no victory.

At times, he will congratulate himself that he has gone for several weeks or even months without a reoccurrence of this problem, but he also finds that it always comes back. At times he congratulates himself that he is fighting and winning, but then he comes to the sickening result, that after awhile he's going to fight and lose.

NOTES

What is wrong?

That's what he asks himself, and if he dares to talk to anyone about the situation, chances are he will be given the wrong advice, simply because most do not know God's prescribed order of Victory. That's tragic, but it is true!

His problem is, even as it is with untold millions of Christians, that he doesn't know God's Way. The things he is doing, are good in their own right, even very helpful and beneficial, but they will not bring victory. The reason is because he doesn't know the way of victory; therefore, he has his Faith placed in the wrong thing.

He needs to understand this which we've already stated, that all the answers are found in the Cross, and it is there where he must place his Faith. When he does that, the Holy Spirit will suddenly begin to work on his behalf, and he will find that the things which were impossible to him, now become so very easy, because in effect, it is Christ living within him, which was meant to be all the time. Christ works through the Holy Spirit Who abides within us, and guarantees all the benefits of the Cross (I Cor. 3:16; Gal. 2:20-21).

Upon Faith placed in the Cross, and Faith remaining in the Cross, even on a daily basis (Lk. 9:23), he will find himself walking in victory, with sin not at all having dominion over him, actually having this *"more abundant life"* promised by Christ (Jn. 10:10).

He will find that this is the greatest life in the world, because the struggle and the fight are over, at least as it refers to trying to carry out this victorious walk himself. To be sure, the fight actually continues, but it's a fight of Faith, and a good fight at that, because it is guaranteed of victory (Rom. 8:1-2).

### WHAT DOES IT ACTUALLY MEAN TO HAVE FAITH IN THE CROSS?

Of course, the entirety of the Bible is the story of the Cross of Christ, which is the story of man's Redemption. All of history strains toward the Cross in one way or the other. Every Sacrifice of the Old Testament pointed to the Cross. In fact, every prediction and prophecy in some way, points toward the Cross.

The Cross of Christ is actually the New Covenant which Christ proclaimed at what we refer to as the *"Last Supper"* (I Cor. 11:23-30).

In this great New Covenant carried out on the Cross, and ratified by the Resurrection, of course, the entirety of the New Testament is its proclamation. And yet, Romans, Chapters 6 and 8, pinpoint the details of the New Covenant, as it concerns what Christ did on the Cross, and the Believer's part in all of this, which gives us the help of the Holy Spirit.

To not be so awfully repetitive, I will be brief:

The Believer must understand that when Jesus died on the Cross, that we in effect were literally baptized into His death (Rom. 6:3). At any rate, this is how it is seen in the Mind of God, and which is guaranteed by our Faith. This is Jesus dying as our Representative Man, in other words, *"as us."*

This means that when He suffered the curse of the broken Law, which is death, as our Substitute, the Lord allowed its benefit to accrue to our behalf. Once again, our Faith in that gives us this benefit.

Christ was then buried, and we were literally buried with (in) Him, which refers to all the old life, old sins, old way, etc. (Rom. 6:4). In fact, Paul uses the term *"in Christ,"* over and over again in one way or the other. Actually, that phrase or one of its derivatives such as *"in Him,"* or *"in Whom,"* etc., is used about 160 times in the Epistles. It refers totally and completely to this of which we speak.

When Christ was raised from the dead, the believing sinner is raised with Him, in fact *"in Him,"* to *"newness of life"* (Rom. 6:4-6).

As our Representative Man, we are *"in Christ,"* and we are to ever remain *"in Christ,"* even as we are seated with Him in Heavenly Places at this moment (Eph. 2:6).

The Believer being *"in Christ,"* guarantees all the benefits of what was done at the Cross and the Resurrection. Inasmuch as it was all done there, and that means victory in every capacity and for everything, the Believer, of necessity, must make that the object of his Faith. To place Faith otherwise, no matter what the otherwise might be, or even how Scriptural it might be in its own way, in effect, says that what Christ did at the Cross and the Resurrection was not sufficient. In other words, it's an insult to Him, as should be obvious!

NOTES

## THE MAJOR PROBLEM IN THE MODERN CHURCH

Paul's Message, which should be obvious, is the Message of the Cross. In fact, the great Apostle learned this exactly as we do.

Romans, Chapter 7 proclaims his efforts at attempting to live a victorious, Christian life before he knew and understood the great victory of the Cross. He failed as fail he must, even concluding by saying, *"O wretched man that I am, who shall deliver me from the body of this death?"* (Rom. 7:24).

But then, Paul was given the details of the great Finished Work of Christ, which in effect is the heart of the *"New Covenant,"* given to us in Romans, Chapters 6 and 8. In fact, all the other teaching and instruction given in all the Epistles, point to this exclusively in one way or the other.

As stated, Satan fights this and does so extensively. In the last several decades, the Church has drifted from the Cross, until it presently knows little as to its source of victory. Consequently, it flounders about like a fish out of water, not quite knowing where it is or what it is. Its present condition, is primarily because of not understanding the Cross, not knowing about the Cross, and trusting in things other than the Cross. Consequently, it has built up a theology which for the most part is totally unscriptural, and the blame can be laid at the doorstep of not understanding the fundamentals of the Cross of Christ, i.e., *"the Finished Work of Christ."*

In fact, Israel did the same identical thing with the Law. They misinterpreted the Law, not understanding, or refusing to understand, that in totality it pointed toward the Cross as the Salvation of mankind, and more particularly, what Jesus would do on the Cross. Instead, it attempted to make Salvation out of the Law, which of course, was impossible, and only succeeded in making them self-righteous, which concluded with them crucifying Christ, the very One Who had come to save them.

The Body of Christ is too much and too often doing the same thing with the Church. In one way or the other, it is treating the

Church as Israel treated the Law. While the Law was of God, just as the Church is of God, still, taken out of their proper context, they cease to be what God originally intended.

In fact, this is not new at all, with Satan making this great attempt even in the Early Church, with it gradually going into apostasy, resulting in the Catholic Church. Openly and blatantly, the Catholic Church claims that the *"Church saves."* Of course, that is a total repudiation of Christ and what he did at the Cross.

Regrettably and sadly, much of the Protestant Church world is in one way or the other, doing the same identical thing. The spirit of *"Church Salvation"* permeates the Protestant Denominations. And what do I mean by that?

In many Denominations, the idea is put forth, that if one is to be saved, one has to belong to their particular Denomination. As it was with the one with which I was formerly associated, their idea was and is, that if one is truly right with God, they will belong to that particular Denomination. And while they might be a Christian outside of that Denomination, the very fact of them being outside, means that something is wrong with them.

This spirit pervades most Protestant Denominations, and is what I mean by *"Church Salvation!"*

All of this is a departure from the Cross, which makes the Work of Christ secondary, if given any place at all. In fact, in many Church circles presently, what Jesus did on the Cross is in no way held up as the answer for dying, hurting humanity, but is paid lip service only, if that. In fact, many in the modern Charismatic Churches, openly repudiate the Cross, calling it the greatest defeat in human history, etc.

Such proclaims a total misunderstanding of the Word of God, in fact, a gross ignorance of its meaning. To be sure, anyone who would sit under such teaching and preaching, cannot help but be seriously deformed in a spiritual sense, if not outright losing their soul.

## OBJECTIONS TO THE DOCTRINE

Closing out this scenario on Satan, which of course is the reason for the Cross, the New Testament clearly pictures the Evil One as a malignant, super-angelic personality. However, the concept of a personal Devil is unacceptable to many minds today. The objection is raised that the existence of a personal Devil is incapable of scientific proof, yet with the world drowning in Satan's wares, i.e., *"wickedness and sin, etc."*

Admittedly spiritual realities cannot be proved by means of naturalistic scientific criteria, and consistency would require that the Biblical Revelation of a Personal God also be rejected.

At any rate, humanistic psychology, and, incidently, there is no other type of psychology except that which is humanistic, while admitting there is a problem, claims it to be minor, is outside of man, and can be solved with rehabilitation.

The Bible of course, claims that man's problem is within him, actually a sinful, wicked heart, which can only be changed by the Power of God, hence the *"born again"* experience (Jn. 3:3, 16).

In fact, the Bible does not teach rehabilitation, which actually means that a person regains their ability to do things in a right way. But of course, the *"right way"* spoken of is a way devised by man and not at all by God. In other words, unredeemed man has never been able to do the right thing. His worsened condition in many cases, only means he does things more and more wrong. In fact, rehabilitation is like trying to put lipstick on a hog. Irrespective as to how much he is dressed up, the hog will seek a mudhole just as soon as possible. So it is with unredeemed man!

Psychology denies any need for the Cross of Christ, because it denies the actual condition of man, which only the Cross can cure, claiming that it alone holds the answers. Regrettably, the Church for the most part, has bought into this travesty in a wholesale way.

I should warn the Reader, that to accept humanistic psychology, means a rejection of the Cross. One cannot have it both ways. It is either one or the other.

It is also claimed by some that the Devil is in reality man's invention to account for his own sinfulness. This view seems laudable in its attempt to make man responsible for his

NOTES

own problems, claiming that man can actually solve these problems whatever they might be.

Such thinking, leads to a shallow view of the reality of sin in the world. It is due to a failure to take sin seriously. Such thinking, which is actually an offshoot of psychology, cannot adequately account for the depths of iniquity in the world.

An objective evaluation of the reality of sin reveals that it is *"too masterly marshalled, too subtly planned, too skillfully directed, too logically remorseless, for any such simple explanation."* There is a design in sin; there is a certain type of weird diplomacy in sin; there is a cunning in sin; there are stratagems and campaigns. Consequently, there must be a mastermind behind these activities.

The Biblical view of a personal Devil who is a limited being under the control of Divine sovereignty best explains the awful realities of sin and fits the correct world-view — at least as things really are. And actually, that's what the Ways of God actually are, a right and balanced view. It is Satan who skews and misaligns everything, meaning that his entire kingdom is built on a lie. The Bible gives the correct and only view that can be acceptable.

These references are woven into the very warp and woof of the Biblical Revelation, and cannot be consistently demythologized without serious damage to the fabric as a whole. The recorded utterances of Jesus in the Gospels clearly assert the existence of a personal Devil. In this He agreed with the views of the Jewish leaders of His day. His acceptance of the view cannot be explained simply on the basis of accommodation to prevailing views, since Jesus did not hesitate to expose the erroneous views of the Jewish leaders wherever He found such.

The Biblical picture of Satan is not dualistic, meaning both to be eternal. Good and evil are not presented as distinct and coeternal principles.

While Satan is seen as a mighty being who is totally evil, his kingdom is viewed as having a definite beginning and will have a definite end. Consequently, the operation of evil is always viewed as being under the sovereign permission of the Eternal God. God allows Satan to continue his work in order to give a cosmic demonstration of the bankruptcy of the Satanic lie.

NOTES

As we have previously stated, the entirety of the creation of God is built on a system of Laws — Laws incidently, laid down in respect to order. As it concerns Satan and evil, the Lord has addressed this, and continues to address this according to His Laws, hence the necessity of the Cross.

Bibliography:

F.C. Jennings, *"Satan: His Person, Work, Place, and Destiny."*
D.L. Cooper, *"What Men Must Believe."*
D.G. Barnhouse, *"The Invisible War."*
F.A. Tatford, *"The Prince of Darkness."*

(6) "BUT NOW WHEN TIMOTHEUS CAME FROM YOU UNTO US, AND BROUGHT US GOOD TIDINGS OF YOUR FAITH AND CHARITY, AND THAT YE HAVE GOOD REMEMBRANCE OF US ALWAYS, DESIRING GREATLY TO SEE US, AS WE ALSO TO SEE YOU:"

The way that Paul frames his words in this particular Passage, shows us that Timothy's arrival from Thessalonica immediately preceded the composition of the Epistle and probably provided its chief motivation. This arrival is the same as that in Acts 18:5, when Timothy and Silas came to Corinth where Paul was, at approximately the same time. This substantiates the earlier conclusion that Paul was actually separated from both Timothy and Silas for a time.

The report that Timothy gave him was both spiritual and personal. Spiritually, the Thessalonians had progressed in Faith and love, and that despite the persecution. Their trust in God had been sufficient for their difficulties. Yet room for improvement remained.

Timothy's report of the kindly feelings of the Thessalonians toward him assured Paul that they loved him dearly, and had not listened to the detracting reports of his enemies.

## TIMOTHY

The phrase, *"But now when Timotheus came from you unto us,"* refers as stated, to Corinth, where Paul now was. The young Evangelist had been sent to Thessalonica to ascertain the condition of the situation there, and now brings back his report to Paul. As also stated, this is probably the account given in Acts 18:5. Although Paul does not mention Silas' return here, this is probably because Silas had not been in Thessalonica but in some other part of Macedonia.

The Letter again takes on an exuberant tone as Paul recalls how Timothy's tidings changed his anxiety to joyful thanksgiving. As a true Pastor with his flock, or a true Teacher with his pupils, he had not been able to rest until he had learned of their situation and steadfastness. The expression, *"came from you unto us"* suggests that Timothy had in fact become their messenger to Paul, not simply a reporter of his own observations, although I'm certain he did add that as well.

GOOD TIDINGS

The phrase, *"And brought us good tidings of your Faith and charity,"* refers to an excellent report on their Faith and love.

The concept of *"Faith,"* mentioned again in the next Verse, is the most definitive term used in describing a Christian. It involves his beliefs, the basic values by which he lives, his most profound choices, his grasp on God and unseen realties, the hopes he cherishes, the basis and source of his very life in Christ, and his steadfastness in all of this. It is his Faith that distinguishes the Christian from all non-Christians.

If the Believer's Faith in the Cross is as it ought to be, in other words, if he properly understands the Finished Work of Christ as it concerns his Salvation and Victory, Faith in all else will fall into place. The biggest problem with Faith as it concerns a Christian, which in reality, is the greatest problem of all, is him not having the Cross as his proper object of Faith. That being wrong, if in fact it is, everything else is going to be somewhat skewed.

That doesn't mean the individual isn't saved, it just means he's not having all that the Finished Work of Christ provides, and to whatever degree his Faith is lacking in this most important principle.

If the Faith of the Believer is correct, love, which is the universal hallmark of genuine Christian Faith, will be correct as well.

NOTES

In fact, these two graces of Faith and Love are the very soul of the Christian life.

The word translated *"good tidings"* is the one Paul normally reserves for describing the Gospel itself, i.e., *"good news."* Such was the measure of his joy.

A GOOD REMEMBRANCE OF US

The phrase, *"And that ye have good remembrance of us always, desiring greatly to see us, as we also to see you,"* actually presents a test of their Faith which had come out well.

Had they been going back on their Faith in either heart or life, they would have preferred Paul's absence. And the joy this news brought to Paul was also a very personal thing, as the Verses which follow indicate. It meant a great deal to him to have a place in the hearts of his children in the Faith, and in this we see something of the greatness of the man, this shepherd of souls (II Cor. 6:11; 12:15; Phil. 1:7).

A PROPER UNDERSTANDING OF FAITH

Due to the great significance of Paul's statement, as it regarded the *"Faith and charity"* of the Thessalonians, it would be good to address this further.

As we have stated, these two words *"Faith"* and *"Love"* (that's what charity means here), characterize the Christian experience moreso than any other explanation.

Once again as we have stated, if the Faith is proper, there will be a natural outgrowth of the proper kind of Love, i.e., *"the God kind of Love."* So, the problem is not so much in *"Love"* as it is in *"Faith."* Regrettably, there are many Christians who are praying for more love, when their Faith is not properly addressed, which automatically precludes proper love and its advancement.

In fact, I think one can say without fear of Scriptural contradiction, that every other Biblical Grace falls into the same category. It is impossible for Sanctification to be what it ought to be without one's Faith being properly placed, i.e., *"placed in the Cross."* The same goes for the Grace of God, patience, hope, trust, etc. Everything hinges on Faith, hence Paul stressing the point.

(7) "THEREFORE, BRETHREN, WE WERE COMFORTED OVER YOU IN ALL

OUR AFFLICTION AND DISTRESS BY YOUR FAITH:"

One can hold up under affliction and distress much better, if one knows and understands that one's work has been accepted and is bringing forth fruit, even as Paul proclaims here. The Apostle was human like the rest of us, and to know that your efforts are not in vain, is a tremendous encouragement. If one knows that one's efforts are bringing forth fruit for the Lord, whatever one is called upon to undergo, such then becomes secondary. But to labor, and to labor under these circumstances, and then to see your efforts made void, is extremely discouraging.

COMFORT

The phrase, *"Therefore, Brethren, we were comforted over you,"* presents the steadfastness of these Thessalonians as a great source of comfort to him at this particular time.

The news that Timothy has brought from Thessalonica is a veritable Gospel of good news to him. It has comforted him in all his necessities and distresses; it has brought him new life; it has been an indescribable joy.

If he had not written this Epistle for several weeks, we should have missed this burst of exuberance and gladness; and what is more serious, the Thessalonians would have missed it also.

Who can doubt that, when this Letter was read in the little congregation at Thessalonica, the hearts of the people warmed again to the great Teacher who had been among them, and to the Message of Love which he had preached? The Gospel is wonderfully commended by the manifestation of its own spirit in its Ministers, and the love of Paul to the Thessalonians no doubt made it easier for them to believe in the Love of God, and to love one another.

To the Christian who is not very spiritual, he may not quite understand the reason for Paul's outburst of joy, or why so much should be made over this matter!

VALUES

The entire situation is summed up in one's values. As a Christian, what is it that is dear to you? What brings you joy or distress for that matter? What saddens your heart? Or what gladdens your heart?

NOTES

Paul lived, breathed, ate, slept, and dreamed, the Lord Jesus Christ. Christ was his life and that in every capacity. As such, the Work of God was of supreme importance.

The idea is, if Jesus Christ is made Lord, if He is the Captain of one's Salvation, if He is our all in all, if He is our sufficiency, then everything else for Christ is going to fall into place.

Many Pastors are constantly attempting to get the people in their respective Churches to perform certain tasks, to be busy for the Lord, etc. To be frank, that's going about the situation backwards.

If a person, be he Preacher or laity, really has a proper experience with Christ, in other words, Christ is everything to him, everything else will take care of itself. The labor for the Lord will come easily, because it is a labor of love. Our problem is, when we attempt to be busy for the Lord without having a proper relationship with the Lord, then it becomes drudgery and work, and ceases to be that which Paul makes evident — our very life.

The key is Christ! If our love and devotion to Him is what it ought to be, then everything else will fall into its proper place.

AFFLICTION AND DISTRESS

The phrase, *"In all our affliction and distress,"* is looked at by the armchair Generals, as a bad confession on the part of the Apostle. They claim if one has a proper confession, that one will never have any afflictions or distress. Poor Paul! If he only had been able to listen to their tapes, how so much trouble he could have saved himself.

In the first place, anyone who would think that Paul didn't have proper Faith, has to be so swelled up with their ego on one side, and so absolutely dense with their ignorance on the other, that putting both of these together, one comes up with a spiritual dolt! I don't really know how to explain it with any more tact than that.

There is some *"affliction and distress"* in the Gospel, and at times there is very much — that is, if one is truly preaching and living the Gospel. I think some of these people experience very little of this, simply because they are giving Satan no problem at all. The True Gospel of Christ, depopulates Hell, and drives back Satanic darkness. Satan is opposed to that, and will do everything within his power to bring it to a halt, even as he attempted in every manner to stop Paul.

However, as we have previously said in Commentary on the preceding Chapter, irrespective as to what Satan might do, he can only *"hinder,"* he cannot stop the Child of God — not unless the Believer simply quits. The Believer should comfort himself with these words. Satan can go just so far and no farther.

YOUR FAITH

The phrase, *"By your Faith,"* presents that of which its exhibition gladdened the heart of the Apostle.

*"Faith"* is that on which the entirety of the Work of God rests. In eternity past, Faith was chosen by God as the vehicle through which he would deal with the human race, and the human race would deal with Him, and which makes the playing field level for all concerned.

I do not think the Church properly understands how important this is of which we speak. When one understands that God can be reached only by Faith, and that He deals with us on the same identical method, and in no other way, then we begin to realize the great significance of this of which we speak. And even at the risk of being overly repetitive, it is Faith in the Finished Work of Christ which constitutes true Biblical Faith. This was pointed out immediately with the first family at the very beginning of the ages, when they were told to offer up a Sacrifice as it respected a clean animal (Lamb), which would be a symbol of the Redeemer, Who was to come. They were to have Faith in what the Sacrifice represented. Now we have Faith in the Sacrifice which has come. However, the point I want to make is, the object of Faith has not changed from then until now, and in fact, never will change.

The problem with most Faith as it's been taught in the last several decades, is that it's not Faith in the Cross, but rather Faith in Faith, or in other words, Faith for the sake of Faith. The Church has been taught almost not at all as it regards the correct object of one's Faith.

It has been taught that when a problem presents itself, that a Scripture should be found that applies to that particular problem, with proper confession bringing about that which we seek.

To be frank, even though in this scenario the Word of God is used, it is only as a side attraction, or in other words, we use it to try to get what we want. The Will of God is not considered, with God's Word more than often, being used against God, or else, the effort made just the same, even though God will not allow such.

This is a most improper use of the Word of God. In this manner, it is used as little more than some type of magic talisman, which of course, God will never honor. So, the Truth is, that most of the teaching on Faith in the last several decades, has been actually without any Scriptural foundation; consequently, it has been Faith in name only, and that which God will never honor.

THE CORRECT OBJECT OF ONE'S FAITH

This is so very, very important, actually the very center or core of one's belief system. The object of our Faith, is to be always and without exception, the Cross of Christ. Of course when we say *"the Cross of Christ,"* we are actually speaking of the *"Finished Work of Christ."* We must ever understand, that all that we need, all that we must have, every blessing, every Promise, every prophecy of old, everything given to us by the Lord, in its totality and completion, comes to us solely through what Christ did at the Cross.

Even though I've said these things repeatedly, I want the Reader to get it in his or her mind. I want you to understand this without fail. I want there to be no doubt in your heart as to what we're saying.

I suppose the most oft quoted Scripture in the Bible is John 3:16: *"For God so loved the world, that He gave His only Begotten Son, that whosoever believeth in Him should not perish, but have everlasting life."*

So what does that Scripture actually say?

Any time in the Bible that God speaks of giving His Son for us, or the *"Gift of God,"* without fail, it is always speaking of giving Him as a Sacrifice on the Cross of Calvary, which would atone for all sin. The person is to believe in that, place his Faith in that, understand that this is the key to all victory, and eternal life will be granted. So, as clear and as plain as it can be, this is given to us, and leaves no room for misunderstanding.

NOTES

### NOT A PROBLEM THAT THIS CANNOT SOLVE

Inasmuch as everything is found in the Cross of Christ, which at the same time presupposes the Resurrection and Exaltation, then we should understand that all victory is found here, and that means for every problem, irrespective of what it is, be it physical, domestical, financial, or spiritual.

If the individual, irrespective as to what his situation might be, will understand these things we are saying, and place his Faith squarely in the Cross of Christ, understanding that all victory and blessings and leading of the Spirit, are found here, and because this is where Jesus paid the price for everything, then that Believer is well on his way to total victory. This is the answer to all blessings, all depression, all healing, all fruitfulness in Christ, all leading and guidance by the Holy Spirit, in other words, everything.

At this time we are having a New Testament reprinted for the Ministry, which we have carried for some time called *"The Counselor's Edition of the New Testament And Psalms."* It is designed to deal with particular problems in the hearts and lives of individuals, whether saved or unsaved. And of course, the Word of God alone holds the answer to the ills and aberrations of mankind.

As it regards the instructions given in this New Testament, I am going to offer two bits of information.

First of all for the unsaved, we're going to tell them how to come to Christ with the short article, *"What must I do to be saved?"*

For the Believer, we're going to direct them totally and completely to the Cross of Christ. It doesn't matter if the problem is alcohol, uncontrollable temper, depression, jealousy, gambling, drugs, immorality of any stripe, envy, etc., the answer is the Cross on all counts.

### WHAT HAPPENS WHEN ONE BEGINS TO PUT ONE'S FAITH IN THE CROSS?

First of all, Satan will attack, and will be allowed to do so by the Lord. As someone has well said, *"Faith must be tested, and great Faith must be tested greatly."*

Immediately upon our initial understanding of the Cross and what it means, our Faith is weak. Consequently, attacks by the Evil One, and allowed by the Lord we might quickly add, as stated, will bring out the weaknesses in our Faith.

When this happens, the Child of God might even experience failure in some manner, but you are not to be discouraged. Ask the Lord to forgive you, and to show you how your Faith is weak, because that's the problem!

However, the longer you keep your Faith in the Cross of Christ, and that means for all things, the stronger your Faith will become, and it will do so rather speedily. Now you are embarking upon the greatest life that anyone could ever live. As Peter said, it will truly be *"joy unspeakable and full of glory."*

Now you will start to enjoy Christ, as He is meant to be enjoyed. This Christian life will become a pleasure instead of a pain. In fact, if you will do this of which we say, making the Cross of Christ the total object of your Faith, you will begin to experience Spiritual Growth as you have never previously known. The joy of the Lord will truly become your strength. You will find yourself understanding the Scriptures far better, and your prayer life will change also. In fact, every single thing will change in your Christian experience.

### THE HOLY SPIRIT

The reason for all of this change, and please understand that the changes will come and quickly, is because the Holy Spirit can now do great and mighty things for you. Your Faith is properly placed, and inasmuch as He works on this basis, and I speak of the parameters of the Finished Work of Christ, you will see Him begin to function in your life as you have never experienced previously (Rom. 8:1-2, 11). To have the help of the Holy Spirit, is to have the help of God, for the Holy Spirit is God. This is the *"Comforter"* of which Jesus promised (Jn. Chpt. 16).

This is true Christianity! This is Bible Christianity! This is the way Christianity ought to be! And this is what Jesus suffered on the Cross in order that we might have.

So, when Paul speaks of *"Faith,"* this is the Faith of which he speaks.

(8) "FOR NOW WE LIVE, IF YE STAND FAST IN THE LORD."

The Apostle actually says two things here in this short Verse:

1. He once again refers to his encouragement as a result of the victory maintained be the Thessalonians.

2. Their Faith had produced their *"firm stand,"* which should be a lesson to all Believers.

NOW WE LIVE

The phrase, *"For now we live,"* presents the idea of someone who has feared the worst, but instead has received the very opposite news, the very best news!

The entirety of Paul's life was the Work of the Lord. And don't think by any means that this was a dreary existence. Despite the *"afflictions and distresses,"* the Apostle was probably one of, if not the happiest man on the face of the Earth. Whenever one is in the direct center of God's Will, which most certainly Paul was, there is a joy that constantly fills one's soul — a joy incidently, of which the world knows nothing about, cannot produce, and in fact, doesn't understand! However, in the midst of all of this, there could be consternation, even as evidenced here, as it regards the Work of the Lord and how it was going. If one truly cares about something, one truly cares; and even though, total trust is implicit in the Lord, still, being human Paul felt things keenly.

From studying the Apostle as I have, I would like to think to some small degree that I know him.

I think that it's very obvious that the man was extremely courageous. I also feel that once he felt he had the Mind of the Lord, he was resolute in his determination. Opposition did not deter him, did not slow him, even to the point of the possibility of him losing his life, which he ultimately did. He was that committed to the Lord.

As should be obvious, it takes an extremely courageous individual, even a strong-willed person, to function as the Apostle functioned.

Also, I feel that he was very emotional. I think he felt things very keenly, and responded, even as we see here, to what he felt. Consequently, I don't think anyone had any trouble knowing where Paul stood.

NOTES

I think he wept easily and I think he laughed easily. I personally feel that when he preached, he felt what he preached, and felt it strongly. As one man said, I think he shouted with the redeemed and wept with the lost.

Paul was controversial, extremely so! However, the controversy was not because of things he did which produced such, but because of the Message he preached. He would not compromise the Message, he would not bend in any capacity. So, people either loved him very dearly or hated him in like capacity.

He attracted followers, and most of them were extremely loyal to him, so loyal, that they would even, it seems, lay down their lives for him, if they had to do so. They were attracted to him, no doubt, because of the tremendous Move of God within his heart and life, and they wanted to be close to that.

I personally think that Paul was somewhat compulsive, but never to the point that he didn't know what he was doing. He seemed to always have things under control, at least as best he could, but over that which he seemingly could not control, even as the experience concerning Thessalonica, he could give way to grave concern.

Many have claimed that the Apostle had some type of bodily illness due to some of the things he said. I think not! To keep the rigorous schedule which he kept, and understanding the rigors of travel in those days, this man had to have an iron-willed constitution to be able to stand what he stood. He took beatings, several of them, that would have killed lesser men. He was nearly stoned to death one time, beside all the other problems which constantly came upon him in both the physical and the spiritual sense. No, I don't really think that Paul had any physical disability. I don't see how he could have, and labor as he did. Not only was he constantly preaching and teaching, but in many places, even as in Thessalonica, he had to earn his living by repairing tents, or whatever it is they did. At any rate, the evidence is, that it was bone grinding work, not easy at all on the flesh.

I think it is obvious that Paul was a man's man. He never started a fight, but he never backed down from one if the need arose. He would stand up for what was right, and it didn't matter who the other person was, even as with the situation concerning Simon Peter (Gal. Chpt. 2).

This was the man who no doubt contributed more to Western Civilization than any human being on the face of the Earth. I believe it was George W. Truett who said, *"Paul was the greatest example for Christ that Christianity ever produced."* Perhaps it would be better to say, *"Paul was the greatest example for Christianity, that Christ ever produced!"* Either way, few have left their mark on history as the Jew from Tarsus.

NOTES

## STANDING FAST IN THE LORD

The phrase, *"If ye stand fast in the Lord,"* presents that which was produced by their Faith.

*"Stand fast"* in the Greek is *"stekete,"* and means *"to stand firmly."* Notice also that the common but important Pauline theme of a Believer's position *"in Christ"* is seen in the phrase *"in the Lord."* This means, that though they were new converts, that Christ was the basis, the center, the soul of their life. Their Faith is mentioned twice, because that is the most comprehensive word to describe the new life in its root; despite the persecution, whatever it may have been, instead of it weakening their Faith, it rather strengthened their Faith, which the Holy Spirit of course intended.

As we've said repeatedly, every attack by Satan is meant to destroy or at least to weaken our Faith; however, if our Faith is properly placed, which refers to being placed in the Cross, it will have the opposite affect, i.e., *"strengthen one's Faith in the Lord."* In other words, one will come out of the test stronger than when one went in, which is the intention of the Spirit of God, and which can be the lot of every single Believer.

## WHAT STANDING FAST ACTUALLY MEANS

Even though I Thessalonians was written some 10 to 15 years before Ephesians, we can see in this statement given by Paul, the seed of the great Truth he will give to the Ephesians in that particular Epistle. He said, *"Put on the whole armor of God, that ye may be able to stand against the wiles of the Devil"* (Eph. 6:11).

The word *"stand"* as it is used here, has the same idea of *"standing firm."* However, it doesn't mean what most people think:

It is not referring to being backed into a corner as some think, and now being told to *"stand!"* It has the opposite meaning.

It actually refers to the inheritance that God has given the Saint, and in whatever capacity that might be. The Saint is to serve notice on the Devil and all the powers of darkness, whatever they might be, that he will not give up one iota of that which God has given to him. He will stand his ground, refusing to budge one inch, claiming every single thing that belongs to him. That refers to his family, his business, his work, his health, his life, his joy, his talent, his ability, in fact, every single thing that God has given unto us.

We are to defend every ounce of our inheritance, giving no place to Satan whatsoever, not allowing him one foot of our inheritance so to speak, standing firm like the proverbial Rock of Gibraltar, unmoved by the onslaughts of the enemy, whatever those onslaughts might be.

The Reader must remember, that it is only Faith in the Cross which can produce that type of courage and strength. The reason is simple!

Jesus has defeated every single power of darkness at the Cross. Consequently, as long as we remain in Christ, even as Paul states here, there is absolutely nothing that Satan can do about the situation. The spirit of this world may belong to him, but that on which we stand belongs to us, bought and paid for by Jesus Christ, and here we will *"stand,"* and *"stand firm!"*

(9) "FOR WHAT THANKS CAN WE RENDER TO GOD AGAIN FOR YOU, FOR ALL THE JOY WHEREWITH WE JOY FOR YOUR SAKES BEFORE OUR GOD;"

The result was thanksgiving to God. Paul found words inadequate to express his appreciation for what had happened in their lives. In fact, the change in Paul's mood could be described as radical; *"all our distress and persecution"* has now become *"all the joy we have"* because of the steadfastness of the Thessalonians. This was no superficial happiness, but rather heartfelt and sincere joy *"in the presence of our God"* (Thomas).

THANKSGIVING TO GOD

The beginning of the question, *"For what thanks can we render to God again for you,"* in essence says, *"How can we thank our God enough concerning you!"*

While the Salvation of souls and even the Salvation of a Church are always cause for rejoicing, and even extensive rejoicing; still, as important as that is, I think there is more behind this situation than this of which we have mentioned.

Even though the Apostle does not reveal any more than we see here, I personally think that the Holy Spirit had revealed to him far more than meets the eye here. I'm almost certain that there was a grand strategy as it regards Evangelism for this part of the world. And of course, what was done here in Europe, would ultimately spread to all of Europe, and ultimately to the Americas. Of course, we know that the Holy Spirit always has a grand strategy. Nothing is happenchance with Him. How much of this He had revealed to the Apostle we are not told, but I suspect that Paul had at least some idea of what was happening here, hence the reason for his tremendous exuberance regarding the situation at Thessalonica.

Being an extremely important port city, to fail here, could well jeopardize the Work of God elsewhere, which no doubt it would have.

Once again, I realize that the armchair strategists would smile broadly at Paul's consternation, claiming that he should have evidenced more Faith, etc. There's only one thing wrong with that. These individuals, whomever they might be, have never built a Church, have never pioneered a work anywhere, and in fact, many, if not most, of them have never even seen anyone saved, despite all their boastful claims! Understanding that, I think we can dismiss their prattle; however, it seems like a boastful, egotistical, supposed superiority, always has a ready audience.

Even though Paul goes into no detail at all, I think one can say that the fear in the Apostle's heart had nothing to do with a lack of Faith in God. The consternation regarding

NOTES

the outcome of this situation, was at least in part I think, as it regards himself. Did he do right by leaving Thessalonica when he did? Should he have stayed irrespective of what the advice had been for him to leave?

I have no doubt that the questions flew thick and fast in his mind, which is human, and which plays its part in the minds of all. However, only one who is doing something for God, would have the cause and capacity to have such questions.

Inasmuch as Timothy has brought back great news, the Apostle is quick with his thanksgiving to the Lord, that the situation is in fact, as he had hoped it would be. And I think the thanksgiving to the Lord, is as much for himself, in other words that he had made the right choices, as it was for the Thessalonians.

JOY

The phrase, *"For all the joy wherewith we joy for your sakes before our God,"* presents that which produces joy in the heart of the Apostle, which is success in the Work of God.

His *"joy"* was not the result of some gladiator winning some particular match in the Roman Arenas; it was not in some Senator who had just been reelected to public office; it was not in the increase in the price of some commodities, which made some people instantly rich; in fact it was in nothing that had to do with this world's system.

Paul's life was Christ, even as we have already said; consequently, his joy was altogether from that Source.

Perhaps I should ask you the Reader, as to how important the great Work of God is to you? How much do you pray about its extension, which in fact, is the single most important thing in the world? Or possibly I should ask as to how open your heart is in order that the Holy Spirit might be able to properly intercede for and through you regarding these all-important consequences?

One day we will all stand before the Lord, and then we will realize that the only thing that really counted, the only thing that really mattered, the only thing that was of any consequence whatsoever, was that which was done for Christ. All else pales into nothingness. In fact, the things that we get so excited about here, will not even be remembered there — only what's done for Christ!

If it is to be noticed, the Apostle expressed the fact that his joy was *"for your sakes before our God."* The idea is, if the situation had gone the other way, these people could have, and in all probability, would have lost their souls. That's what he meant by the statement, *"lest by some means the tempter have tempted you, and our labor be in vain"* (I Thess. 3:5). And of course, there is nothing more important than the eternal souls of men. In fact, that's what it's all about!

(10) "NIGHT AND DAY PRAYING EXCEEDINGLY THAT WE MIGHT SEE YOUR FACE, AND MIGHT PERFECT THAT WHICH IS LACKING IN YOUR FAITH?"

Along with his rejoicing, Paul prayed extensively for the Thessalonians. Of course, as we see over and over again, the Apostle was a man of prayer.

As well, having weathered this first test one might say, the Apostle is eager that their Faith can now grow, which it certainly shall. He knows that if he can have the opportunity to visit them again for even a short period of time, he can greatly instruct them more perfectly in the Word of God, which he longs to do, and which they desperately need.

PRAYER

The phrase, *"Night and day praying exceedingly,"* records the one great weapon that any Christian has, but regrettably and sadly, of which so few take advantage.

Any and every Believer has access to God through prayer. This avenue is open to all, none excluded! Of course, there are some qualifications.

When the Believer goes before the Lord, first of all he must be willing to have the Holy Spirit search his heart, that any and all wrongdoing, especially as it regards self-will, may be laid aside, or in effect laid upon the Altar. The business of the Holy Spirit in our hearts and lives, Who greatly helps us pray, and without Him there will really not be any praying done, at least that will amount to anything, is to carry out the Will of God and that alone (Rom. 8:26-27).

As well, much if not most of Prayer, should be made up of thanksgiving to the Lord for all the things He has done for us, is doing for us, and shall do for us. Most of all, I speak of the great Spiritual benefits, such as Salvation and the Baptism with the Holy Spirit, which concerns the greatest attribute a Believer can have, the Holy Spirit to lead, guide, and help.

NOTES

THE WORK OF THE HOLY SPIRIT

Do you realize as a Saint of God, that of all the things the Holy Spirit does for us, and does with us, that His greatest Work by far, is the help He gives us in our prayer life?

The Scripture plainly says, *"Likewise the Spirit also helpeth our infirmities* (physical, mental, or moral weaknesses or flaws)*: for we know not what we should pray for as we ought: but the Spirit itself* (Himself) *maketh intercession for us with groanings* (unutterable gushings of the heart) *which cannot be uttered."*

And then it says, *"And He* (Christ) *that* (Who) *searcheth the hearts knoweth what is the Mind of the Spirit, because He* (the Holy Spirit) *maketh intercession for the Saints according to the Will of God"* (Rom. 8:26-27).

Of all the things He does for us, and those things are many and varied, it is His help which He gives us in prayer, which I think the Scripture bears out, that is the most important. When we consider that most Christians little pray at all, we are left aghast at what is being missed. When we consider, that the leading of the Spirit, the guidance of the Spirit, the help of the Spirit, is all wrapped up in this as well, we are left with the understanding, that if the Christian doesn't have a prayer life, then the hands of the Holy Spirit are pretty well tied so to speak. Considering as well, that He works exclusively according to the Finished Work of Christ, and our Faith in that Work, which regrettably, most Christians little understand as well, leaves the Holy Spirit as almost a dormant force within our lives. What a travesty! What a loss!

WHAT IS INTERCESSION?

*"Intercession"* comes from two Greek words, the first being *"huperentugehano,"* which means *"to intercede in behalf of, to make intercession for."* The other is, *"entugehano,"* which means *"to entreat in*

*favor of, to deal with."* It also means *"to give self wholly to."*

The Greek Scholars also state that the word *"intercession"* as used here by Paul, pertains to *"protocol."* In fact, the Scripture plainly says, *"For we know not what we should pray for as we ought,"* and then it speaks of *"groanings which cannot be uttered."*

This means that our approach to the Lord as should be obvious is somewhat less than satisfactory. Consequently, we must have the Holy Spirit as a go-between so to speak. In other words, He takes this which He has given to us in our hearts, and for which we are praying and seeking God, and presents it to the Father in a fashion appropriate for such an audience.

Years ago I was invited to the White House in Washington, for a short meeting with the President of the United States. To explain protocol, perhaps the following would be of some small help.

When I arrived there, I had to sign in at the gate. A call was made to security at the White House, they found my name on the list, and I was given admittance.

If I remember correctly, there were two or three others with me. We walked down a long drive from the gate to the White House entrance. Along the drive, just before getting to the entrance, there were representatives of all the Armed Forces in their dress uniforms standing at flank attention.

Several people met us at the entrance, and then showed us into a room with a long table and chairs. It was filled with Photographers, Television Cameras, and Reporters, etc. We were even told where to sit.

A few minutes later, the President and the Vice President walked in, in which we all instantly stood, with flash bulbs going off and cameras whirling. One by one we were introduced to the President of the United States, and when he and the Vice President sat down, then we sat down, but not until then.

I'm trying to say that protocol was observed, especially considering that the United States is the most powerful nation in the world. As well, I have met many World Leaders in other Countries, and without exception, there was always protocol observed in some manner.

NOTES

Perhaps that is a poor example of this of which I speak respecting the Holy Spirit regarding the Throne of God; however, in some manner, the Holy Spirit Who is God Himself, makes our entrance to the Father as it should be, in other words, makes it presentable.

I think if Christians knew and understood just how important prayer is, just how much it is expected of us, that there would be much more praying.

### THE CROSS AND PRAYER

I am not at all meaning to say that one has to have a proper understanding of the Cross in order to pray. In fact, one of the very benefits of prayer is for us to be able to seek God, simply because we don't have the answers and we know that He does!

Nevertheless, having said that, if the Believer has a proper understanding of the Cross of Christ and what it all means, at least as far as we can understand such, prayer I think, takes on a brand-new meaning. At least it did for me.

I think a proper understanding of the Cross, gives the Holy Spirit greater latitude within our hearts and lives in every capacity. In fact, I know that it does! This being the case, the Holy Spirit, can function I think, with greater latitude within our hearts and lives, and especially as it regards prayer.

As I have mentioned quite a number of times in these Volumes, in the Fall of 1991, the Lord instructed me to begin two prayer meetings a day, which we instituted immediately. The idea is not that one can earn something from the Lord as it regards this of which I speak, for such is impossible. The idea is communion and fellowship with the Lord. The idea is presenting our needs to Him, knowing that He has all the answers and can do all things. The idea is, that the Holy Spirit will have a greater time and opportunity to probe in our lives, which only He can do, thereby bringing us to a place of consecration, which is the idea all along. Above all of this, the Work of the Spirit is to make us Christlike! This is not done easily and neither is it done quickly. And to be sure, without a proper prayer life, I don't think that such can be done at all.

As I dictate these notes on October 27, 1999, it has been eight years, in which we have done our best to faithfully obey that which the Lord instructed us to do. To be frank, I don't think we could have made it without these prayer times. We meet every morning at the Office at 10:00, and every evening at 6:30, with the exception of Service times, and Saturday Morning.

During this time, the Lord has given me many Promises, and now I'm seeing some of those Promises begin to come to fulfillment. In fact, what's been happening in the past two years, which steadily increases with each day, has been the most wonderful thing that I've ever experienced in all my life. Of course, I'm speaking of the Revelation of the Cross which the Lord began to open up to me in 1997. And yet, I don't think any of this would have happened, had we failed to follow what the Lord told us to do as it regards prayer. The only way this Ministry could survive was and is by a miracle from the Lord. In fact, we have had to have a miracle each day, and the Lord has faithfully provided. But once again, I don't think any of this would have happened, had this strong prayer life not existed.

So, when the Apostle speaks of *"praying night and day,"* I know a little bit of what he's talking about.

## MIGHT SEE YOUR FACE

The phrase, *"That we might see your face,"* has to do with the desire of the Apostle to once again visit this fledgling Church, which he did some time later (Acts 20:1-2).

It was Paul's practice to revisit the Churches he had established and for all the obvious reasons. They desperately needed his teaching.

Preachers were at a premium in those days. In fact, most of these Churches planted by the Apostle and others as well, had to depend for the most part, on Preachers being raised up out of the local body. While the Lord definitely did do this, still, as would be obvious, their instruction and understanding of the Word of God would have left some things to be desired.

For instance, the Bible in those days consisted of Genesis through Malachi. As well, copies had to be laboriously printed by hand, which made them somewhat expensive for most people. Also, whenever Paul wrote his Epistles, they were eagerly received by the Churches, and many copies made, with them being passed around it seems from Church to Church. Of course, these Epistles were the Word of God.

NOTES

At any rate, these Letters, such as I Thessalonians which we are now studying, were the greatest means of instruction which the Church in that day had. Inasmuch as these are the Word of God, they still serve the same purpose presently and always will.

Still, these Churches were greatly blessed, when the Apostle had the opportunity to visit them personally, which he tried to do as often as possible.

## LACKING IN YOUR FAITH?

The conclusion of the question, *"And might perfect that which is lacking in your Faith?"*, presents a thought which should be heeded most carefully.

We should ask ourselves the question, *"Is anything lacking in our Faith?"*

While it's impossible for one to exhaust the potential of what Faith in Christ really means, still, one can definitely have a firm grasp and understanding on the great fundamentals of the Faith, which are definitely required.

First of all, it is obvious that some things were definitely lacking in the Faith of the Thessalonians. Timothy had probably enlarged on this with Paul; nevertheless, these converts were young in the Lord, and considering that Paul's stay there had been greatly shortened, gives us a reason for their *"lack."*

So, what is our excuse?

As I've said over and over again, when Paul mentions Faith, the far greater majority of the times, he is speaking of Faith in the Cross. Actually, in the Greek, this phrase says *"the Faith."* When Faith is used in this manner, and even times when it's not used in this manner, it always refers to Faith in what Jesus did at the Cross and His Resurrection. In other words, it speaks of what that great Work produced, referred to as *"the Finished Work of Christ."* And to be sure, regrettably, most of the modern Church world is deficient in their understanding of this *"Faith."* Much is lacking in their Faith in this respect.

## WHAT DOES THE FAITH MEAN?

First of all, the single most important thing in the world, and I literally mean the most important thing, is your understanding of *"the Faith."* Misunderstanding about other things will definitely have an effect; however, to misunderstand this, is to incur upon ourselves grave difficulties to say the least. So, it's incumbent upon you to fully understand this of which we speak. Inasmuch as you have purchased this Commentary, and you have studied thus far regarding its contents, I have to believe that you are one of the few who really take these matters as serious as you should. *"Congratulations"* may seem to be a trite word as it regards this, but I will use it for the want of one better at present.

The Truth is, even to which we have already alluded, most of the modern Church is greatly deficient as it regards understanding of this all-important means of Redemption and Victory. As a result, the Church is suffering extensively so, with not nearly as many believers walking in victory as they should. In fact, every Believer should walk in victory. Due to this lack of understanding *"the Faith,"* the Church has built up a facade, all based on unscriptural ideas and directions. In other words, the matter is not getting better, but worse, for that's the nature of *"leaven."*

Let's look at this all-important subject:

## WHAT IS THE FAITH?

It is Faith exclusively in what Christ did at the Cross and the Resurrection. This great Work is referred to as *"the Finished Work of Christ."* It included every single thing that man needs, leaving out nothing.

The death of Christ on the Cross is not a mere historical fact, but rather a happening in history, that was planned by God from before the foundation of the world (I Pet. 1:18-20). Consequently, it is the intersection of all time. All history strains toward the Cross. It and it alone is the focal point of man's Redemption, which of necessity, makes it the single most important thing there is.

## WHY WAS THE FAITH NECESSARY?

To better understand the question, we could ask, *"Why was the Cross necessary?"*

NOTES

The terrible Fall by Adam in the Garden of Eden was because of the first man's disobedience to God. In other words, he committed a grave crime against the Lord in that he literally gave his dominion given to him by the Lord, to Satan himself, which brought about all the sorrow and heartache into the world (Gen. 1:26-27; Ps. 8).

It would be the same as you giving someone a very valuable object, and them turning around and giving it to your worst enemy, which would cause untold problems.

This means that the sin of Adam and Eve was of far greater degree than merely eating forbidden fruit. They took that which was extremely precious, Eternal Life, communion with God, dominion over all of God's Creation, and gave it to Satan. Admittedly, they were tricked out of it and deceived. But still they didn't have to do what they did, and what they did, doomed the human race for all time, with the exception of God's intervention.

Considering the magnitude of the crime, and it was of such a magnitude as to defy all description, the price demanded for payment, was of such staggering proportions that it also beggars all description.

To understand how bad the crime was, one need only look at the condition of the world, which has resulted in so much death, war, sorrow, heartache, hunger, loneliness, sickness, and disease, etc. That's what the crime caused!

It was love that created man, and it was love that must redeem man. So, irrespective of the price, it must be paid.

Man couldn't pay the price, and neither could Angels. So the only One Who could pay the price, was God Himself, which He did, by becoming man and dying on a Cross.

The worst form of death, the most humiliating, the most shameful, and reserved for the worst criminals, was death by Crucifixion. Due to the magnitude of the crime, this was the punishment demanded, and this is what made the Cross a necessity.

## WHO MADE POSSIBLE THE FAITH?

Man unable to do this thing, because he couldn't provide a suitable Sacrifice due to being sinful, God would have to provide the Sacrifice, even as He had promised Abraham

(Gen. 22:13-14). That Sacrifice was His Only Son, The Lord Jesus Christ (Jn. 3:16).

Even though the Cross was an absolute necessity, the Cross within itself as should be obvious, contained no saving Grace, or anything good for that matter. In fact, on the day that Jesus died on the Cross, at least two others died with Him, and probably throughout the Roman Empire, there were innumerable others also who died that day on Crosses.

So, the mere fact of dying on a Cross, even though that was necessary, would not suffice for anything. It was the One Who died on that Cross, which made Redemption possible.

The Sacrifice prepared, and that's exactly what Jesus was, and the very reason for which He came, had to be perfect. Consequently, He was born of the Virgin Mary, meaning that His birth was not brought about by natural procreation, but rather by a miraculous conception. Had He been born as other babies, He would have been born *"in sin,"* just like all others, because Adam's failure passed down to all. But being born of the Virgin Mary, He was not born in Adam's likeness, as are all other babies (Gen. 5:1-3).

However, even though He never ceased to be God, He was 100% Man as well.

As a Man He must face all the onslaughts of the Tempter. This means that He could not use His Powers of Deity. But yet, He could do so with the Holy Spirit, which the original Adam had as well.

With the Power of the Holy Spirit, the same Power made available to us presently, He faced every onslaught of Satan. The first Adam faced Satan in a Garden, in a perfect environment, while the Last Adam faced Satan in a wilderness in a totally imperfect environment.

He lived this life as a perfect human being, tempted in all points as we are, but yet without sin. So, when He went to the Cross, He was perfect in spirit, soul, and body; consequently, acceptable to God as a perfect Sacrifice.

As our Substitute He took our place, and as our Representative Man He in essence, became us. As the first Adam disobeyed and wrecked all of us, the Last Adam obeyed, thereby purchasing back what the first Adam lost.

Due to being a perfect Sacrifice which God would accept, and in fact did accept, His death atoned for all sin, past, present, and future — at least for those who will believe (Jn. 3:16).

His death paid the debt which was owed to God, satisfying the claims of the broken Law.

So, it was the One Who hung on that Cross, Who made *"the Faith"* possible!

NOTES

### WHEN DID THE FAITH HAPPEN?

It happened when Jesus died on the Cross, was buried, and rose from the dead on the third day. Whenever the believing sinner exhibits Faith in this which Jesus did, he has entered into *"the Faith"* and is now saved. To have Faith, literally means and simply means, to believe in what Jesus did there. It refers to the fact that one must believe that Jesus Christ is the Son of God, and that He died on the Cross, taking our place, doing all of this on our behalf. Accepting Him and what He did, gives us the benefit of all of His Finished Work.

Before the Cross, all were saved by looking forward to that coming event. Since the Cross, all are saved by looking back to that accomplished event. So, *"when it happened,"* provides the time frame for the greatest event in human history. It is there that *"the Faith"* commences, and it is in that which the person must believe. This is when the Redemption of man was consummated.

Placing man's Redemption any other place or any other time, is completely unscriptural, and a serious tampering with the Atonement. The Cross is when Redemption happened, because it was there that the sin debt was paid, and the curse of the broken Law was taken by Christ. This must never be forgotten, and it must ever be held up as the only way of Salvation. There is no other!

To fully answer the question as to *"When?"*, the simple answer is that it was nearly 2,000 years ago.

### WHERE THE FAITH WAS BROUGHT ABOUT!

Once again, it was the Cross and alone the Cross! That's the reason the Cross is so very, very important. And of course, when we speak of the Cross, we're not actually speaking of a wooden gibbet, but the fact that Jesus died there, and the fact of Who He was.

Concerning *"the Faith,"* we've touched on *"What?" "Why?" "Who?" "When?"* and now, *"Where?"*

The actual site was the city of Jerusalem, in essence its suburbs. But it was the Cross which was necessary, and thereby, the Cross where it all happened.

So, the Holy Spirit through the Apostle, tells us to *"preach the Cross"* (I Cor. 1:18, 21). In fact, this is the only way that man can be saved. The Cross must be preached, and man must believe in what transpired on the Cross.

The Cross is not only a necessity as it regards Salvation, and of course we speak of the One Who died on that Cross, but as well, belief in the Cross is necessary for the victorious, overcoming, Christian life, as it regards the Believer. As necessary as the Cross was for the initial Salvation experience, as necessary it is for our victorious walk before God and man.

Therefore, when we say *"the Faith,"* that's what we're speaking about. It constitutes what Christ did on our behalf at the Cross, and our belief and Faith in that which He did.

Every religion in the world specializes in what man can do or should do. Bible Christianity specializes in what Christ did on man's behalf. Simple Faith in what He did, and minus all works, guarantees Salvation. It is all of Christ and none of man.

To make it very brief, one must believe the following:

1. The Cross of Christ holds the answer to every question that man might have, as well as the solution to every problem. From this Source all blessings flow.
2. Understanding that, the Believer must exhibit Faith in that which Christ has done, and do so at all times.
3. When this is done, the exhibition of Faith in the Finished Work of Christ, the Holy Spirit then helps us greatly, doing for us all the things we need to have done, which He Alone can do (Rom. 6:2-6; 8:1-2, 11).

(11) "NOW GOD HIMSELF AND OUR FATHER, AND OUR LORD JESUS CHRIST, DIRECT OUR WAY UNTO YOU."

Paul recognizes that unless the Lord opens up the way, that it will be very difficult, if not impossible, for him to see the Thessalonians any way soon. In fact, even as we have stated, it would be six to eight years before he would actually be able to visit this Church. Due to many particulars, the Lord will have to open these doors, in which He ultimately would!

NOTES

If it is to be noticed, everything that Paul does is predicated on the Will of God, and the Lord opening doors, etc. Every plan he made, every direction he sought, was always according to the Will of God, at least as best as he could ascertain that Will. Sometimes that's not easy, but even during the times that things seem cloudy, the Lord will ultimately reveal His way.

## GOD OUR FATHER

The phrase, *"Now God Himself and our Father,"* presents privileges which are absolutely unexcelled. Some of them are as follows:

1. The privilege we have of going to God about every need.
2. The privilege of having Him to lead us, guide us, and to do for us what is needed (Rom. 8:14).
3. The privilege of being an heir of God, a joint heir with Jesus Christ, which means that we are now part of the Family of God (Rom. 8:16).
4. The privilege of referring to God as our Heavenly Father (Rom. 8:15).
5. The privilege of Him directing our way, even as this Eleventh Verse proclaims.

All of this is made possible solely and totally by what Jesus did at the Cross. That's why I keep saying that the Cross is so very, very important! This type of relationship was not possible before the Cross, by even the greatest men and women of God. It took the Cross to open up the way to Heaven's Gate.

## OUR LORD JESUS CHRIST

The phrase, *"And our Lord Jesus Christ,"* refers to the One Who has made all of this possible, and as well refers to the Trinity. Inasmuch as the Holy Spirit is the One Who is inspiring Paul to write these words, we have here the Trinity in bold relief, *"God the Father," "God the Son,"* and *"God the Holy Spirit."*

Incidently, *"Lord Jesus Christ,"* is the Resurrection Name of our Lord.

*"Lord"* refers to Him as God, *"Jesus"* refers to Him as Saviour, and *"Christ"* refers to Him as the Anointed Messiah.

DIRECT OUR WAY

The phrase, *"Direct our way unto you,"* presents the Will of God being sought, and the way being made as the Will of God comes to the fore.

*"May direct"* in the Greek is *"kateuthunai,"* and means *"the making of a straight path and the removal of obstacles."*

Solomon said, *"In all thy ways acknowledge Him, and He shall direct thy paths"* (Prov. 3:6).

(12) "AND THE LORD MAKE YOU TO INCREASE AND ABOUND IN LOVE ONE TOWARD ANOTHER, AND TOWARD ALL MEN, EVEN AS WE DO TOWARD YOU:"

This which the Apostle says is not mere rhetoric. It is actually that which the Believer can be, can have, if the Holy Spirit is allowed to have His way. While Paul could teach them, only God through Christ could cause them to increase and abound in these great qualities.

TO INCREASE IN LOVE

The phrase, *"And the Lord make you to increase and abound in love,"* pertains to that which ever increases, and in this case *"love."* It is Divine love (agape).

*"Increase"* and *"abound,"* are nearly synonymous. The former signifies spiritual *"enlargement,"* the second spiritual *"abundance."*

Regarding the great Graces which come exclusively from the Lord, I think it would be impossible for one to have too much. I speak of Faith, Love, Peace, Grace, etc. It is the Will of God that we continue to ever increase in these tremendous qualities. Actually, these are *"Fruit of the Spirit."* In respect to my own personal life, my prayer is that God will answer this petition as given by Paul. Whatever the Lord has, I want to *"increase and abound"* in these tremendous Graces.

TOWARD ALL

The phrase, *"One toward another, and toward all men,"* refers to the saved and the unsaved. In fact, Love is not really Love, until it is shown to others. This is always the acid test of Love. How do we treat others? What do we do toward others? How concerned are we about others?

NOTES

To properly understand the God kind of Love, and this is the type of which he speaks, we have to go to the great treatment given this subject by Paul in I Corinthians Chapter 13.

If it is to be noticed, Paul speaks first of their Faith, and then their love. If the Faith is proper, it will always produce love, and when I say *"proper,"* I'm speaking of Faith in the Cross of Christ and not at all in ourselves. Faith in anything other than the Cross, always breeds self-righteousness, which to be sure, has no love whatsoever. So, once again, we see how utterly important the Cross of Christ actually is, and our Faith in that Finished Work.

TOWARD YOU

The phrase, *"Even as we do toward you,"* proclaims two things:

First of all, the Apostle had a burning love for these people even before he knew them, which in fact brought him to this place in order that a Church might be planted. It was love that brought him there, love that kept him there even in the face of dire persecution, until it was no longer possible to stay, love that underwent any hardship that the Gospel might be given to these people. In fact, I think the Apostle Paul is the perfect example of the Love of God, other than Christ Jesus, Who of course, is the epitome of this of which we speak.

Now that they have accepted the Lord, his love shows again in his concern for them. It was like a Mother concerned for her children.

In fact, the Holy Spirit is using him as an example to the Thessalonians. As they had seen the Love of God manifested in and through him toward themselves, they were likewise, to allow this to be an example for them, that they might evidence love among themselves and toward the unsaved.

The Love of God produces kind Christians; it produces patient Christians; it also produces gracious Christians.

The Child of God is to always bear in mind, that as God has shown us love, and as well in the manner in which it was shown, we are to do the same for others. As the Lord has been gracious to us, we are in turn to be gracious to others — irrespective as to how they might act. The same would go for patience and kindness, etc.

A PERSONAL EXAMPLE

Sometime back, I was attempting to pray for a Reporter who had tried his best to hurt me and this Ministry, in fact, doing all within his power to do so, even using resources that spanned the entirety of the globe; consequently, one can well imagine the power of such an effort.

Soon after this effort I was in prayer, and I knew in my heart that I should pray for him. I will confess, it wasn't easy.

Finally I stopped and said to the Lord, *"How do I pray for this man?"*

The answer was almost instant in coming, *"Ask Me to show him the same type of Grace, that I have shown you."*

The moment the Lord said that to me, everything changed. I recalled instantly, an abundance of Grace which He had lavished upon me, and in fact, was continuing to do so. As I thought upon that for a few moments, all of a sudden the complexion of the entirety of the situation changed.

In a moment's time, the Lord gave me a love in my heart for this man, with me then beginning to call out his name before God, asking the Lord to help him and to bless him. What had been hard, even impossible, now became very easy.

(13) "TO THE END HE MAY STABLISH YOUR HEARTS UNBLAMEABLE IN HOLINESS BEFORE GOD, EVEN OUR FATHER, AT THE COMING OF OUR LORD JESUS CHRIST WITH ALL HIS SAINTS."

First of all, I want you to notice that Paul concludes every train of thought, which actually ends each Chapter, with a statement regarding the Coming of the Lord.

At the end of Chapter 1 he said, *"And to wait for His Son from Heaven, Whom He raised from the dead, even Jesus, which delivered us from the wrath to come"* (I Thess. 1:10).

At the end of Chapter 2 he said, *"For what is our hope, or joy, or crown of rejoicing? Are not even ye in the presence of our Lord Jesus Christ at His Coming?"* (I Thess. 2:19).

And now at the end of the Third Chapter, he gives that which is the Text of our present study.

NOTES

At the end of the Fourth Chapter he says, *"Then we which are alive and remain shall be caught up together with them in the clouds, to meet the Lord in the air: and so shall we ever be with the Lord"* (I Thess. 4:17).

At the end of the Fifth and final Chapter he says, *"And the very God of Peace sanctify you wholly; and I pray God your whole spirit and soul and body be preserved blameless unto the Coming of our Lord Jesus Christ"* (I Thess. 5:23).

THE ESTABLISHING OF OUR HEARTS

The phrase, *"To the end He may stablish your hearts,"* presents the idea, *"May the Lord cause you to increase in love, in order that you may be established, and be without blame at the Judgment Seat of Christ."* Without love to God and man, there can be no establishment in the way of Christ. It is love that produces both solidity and continuance. And, as love is the fulfilling of the Law, he who is filled with love is unblamable in Holiness; for he who has the Love of God in him is a partaker of the Divine Nature, for God is Love. In fact, this statement should be substantially investigated.

When the believing sinner comes to Christ, the sin nature in him (or her) which heretofore has propelled the individual toward sin in every capacity, in other words, it was the sinner's very nature to sin, now has this terrible liability throttled so to speak, but not entirely removed. It is replaced by the Divine Nature. As the sinful nature formerly propelled the individual toward transgression and disobedience, the Divine Nature now pushes the individual toward God, and in every respect. Before conversion, the sinner, although able to keep from committing some sins, is not able at all to stop the process, and many can not stop it at all, going deeper and deeper into the worst quagmire of sin; it is somewhat the same in the Believer after coming to Christ as it regards the Divine Nature, but in reverse.

In other words, the Believer can fail to obey the Divine Nature as one should, in other words, not pushing on toward a greater union with the Lord, even as Paul is speaking here. As the sin nature can push the unbeliever into the deepest of sin, which of course is death, the Divine Nature if properly heeded, can push the Believer closer and closer to God, which is Life.

Unfortunately, most Christians do not push on toward God as they should, rather missing out on so much they could have. Inasmuch as this Divine Nature is expressed most in love, even as God is Love, this is to be the yardstick of the Believer's position in Christ. We can say all type of things, and do all type of things, but as Paul also said, *"If I have not Love, it profiteth me nothing"* (I Cor. 13:1-3). So, while men point to the Gifts of the Spirit, or that which they think is sensational, etc., the Holy Spirit rather points to *"Love."* And if love is truly there and truly growing in the heart and life of the Believer, it will manifest itself toward man and God. There is no such thing as love doing anything else but that (I Cor. 13:1-3).

As well, whenever the Holy Spirit uses the word *"heart,"* as it refers to the individual, He is speaking of the very seat of one's being, one's passions, one's will, etc.

## UNBLAMABLE IN HOLINESS BEFORE GOD

The phrase, *"Unblameable in Holiness before God, even our Father,"* refers to the fact that it is God Who is the Judge of these things. Constantly, religious men come up with a pseudo-holiness, which means a holiness of their own contrivance, which God will never recognize. Unfortunately, men do recognize the holiness contrived by other men, actually, far more than they do that developed by the Lord. This has to do with self-righteousness, etc.

The whole emphasis of this which Paul says, is upon the inwardness of personal character, of which Holiness actually is. It is implied that the character required to make the Thessalonians and every Believer for that matter, ready to stand before Christ at His Coming is more than a certain blamelessness of outward behavior or service. God's requirement is rather a blamelessness in inward devotion to God, and inward moral purity. In other words, the heart, the whole personality, inwardly as well as outwardly, must be pure before God. As stated, not man's judgment, but God's Judgment will be the Standard. The true quality of our love and our motives is known only to Him.

NOTES

The manner in which this Holiness (Sanctification) is bestowed is described here as an *"increase,"* an abounding infusion of the pure love of God which *"is shed abroad in our hearts by the Holy Spirit which is given unto us"* (Rom. 5:5). It is the Lord Who will make you to *"abound in love."* Holiness is a gift of God's Grace; not the result of human effort, but the answer to Faith in Christ. Since this love is from God, it is pure and holy, corresponding with the Nature of God. Such love is *"the fulfilling of the Law"* (Rom. 13:10).

This love is the Spirit's instrument for the expulsion of that which is impure and incompatible from the heart; its necessary outcome is full obedience to the Will of God. A *"Holiness"* which comes some other way than by a Baptism of Divine love will be spurious — sanctimonious, censorious, legal, which God can never recognize.

Divine love is *"the bond of perfectness"* (Col. 3:14), and will manifest itself toward one another and for all men. It is the energy of all true Holiness. It is the means to spiritual stability, since all else is transient (Airhart).

## HOW HOLINESS IS DEVELOPED IN THE HEARTS AND LIVES OF BELIEVERS

I heard A.N. Trotter say once, *"The definition of Holiness is, that we allow the Holy Spirit to have His perfect Work within our lives. In other words, that He has total control of us."* Of course, if one would use such terminology, the very first Name of the Holy Spirit is obviously *"Holy!"* So, what the man said is right.

However, the only way in which the Holy Spirit can have proper control in our lives in order to do the things which only He can do, is that the Believer's Faith be totally and completely in the Cross of Christ, which means that it's in the Finished Work of Christ. As we have said over and over again, the Believer must understand that everything which the Saint has from Salvation on, and that means everything, and of course I'm speaking of that which comes from God, is found in the Finished Work of Christ. That and that alone is the basis from which the Holy Spirit works.

As well, the writer of Hebrews, who I believe was Paul, said, that all of this is *"through the Blood of the Everlasting Covenant* (of which), *makes you perfect in every good work to do His Will, working in you that which is wellpleasing in His sight, through Jesus Christ"* (Heb. 13:20-21).

Several things are said here:

1. This Covenant is an Everlasting Covenant, which means that it will never be changed, and because it doesn't need to be changed. It is all in Christ, and, therefore, perfect.

2. We're plainly told in this Passage in Hebrews, that what the Holy Spirit wants to do within our hearts and lives, comes clearly and totally through the Finished Work of Christ. This means that we must have Faith in that Finished Work, always making that the object of our Faith, and never anything else.

3. Inasmuch as this is an Everlasting Covenant, if we go beyond this Covenant, which in reality one cannot do, but still if we try to do so, we forfeit the Covenant, which means that we're going to receive nothing from the Lord. In essence, such an effort is an insult to Christ, saying that what He did even at such price, was only a stopgap measure, with something else to come later. That is either rank ignorance or raw blasphemy. And yet, that's where much of the Church presently is.

Some think that the Cross is necessary for the Salvation experience, but once that is accomplished, then we are to go on and leave the Cross, going on to other things, etc. Has anyone ever noticed, there are no *"other things!"* And the reason for that is, because everything is in the Cross, and nothing is outside of the Cross, at least as it refers to the Lord.

## RIGHTEOUSNESS IS A POSITION AND NOT AN ACTIVITY

The Reader should read that heading very, very carefully. Because most people do not understand Righteousness, or Holiness, or any of these great attributes of God as a position, but rather an activity. And what do we mean by that?

We mean that many Christians think that Righteousness or Holiness are arrived at by certain religious activity on our part. In other words, that we are Righteous because we do certain good things or don't do certain bad things. That's what we mean by *"activity."* It all translates into works, which God will never recognize.

Righteousness and Holiness are never an activity, but rather a *"position,"* and we speak of a position *"in Christ."* It actually means that one is Righteous or Holy simply because they have trusted in what Christ did at the Cross, understanding that He was and is totally perfect, thereby offering up Himself as a Perfect Sacrifice, which paid the terrible sin debt of man and satisfied the curse of the broken Law, which God could and did accept, and Faith in that which Christ did, and did incidently as our Representative Man, awards us instantaneously, a perfect, spotless Righteousness, the Righteousness of Christ. It is all gained by Faith in what He did there, and by no other means. That is the position that one has in Christ, and it is a position that's gained totally by Faith in the Finished Work of Christ. If we try to obtain it in any other way, that is what I mean by activity, it is an activity which God cannot accept. The only activity God will accept is the activity of Christ — never the activity of man.

## THE EARLY CHURCH AND APOSTASY

This problem of which we speak did not begin yesterday. In fact, it began with Cain and Abel at the very dawn of time, which account is given in the Fourth Chapter of Genesis. So, the problem of Righteousness and Holiness by *"position"* or by *"activity,"* has always been the great controversy. Of course, it doesn't have to be a controversy, because the Bible is very clear on the subject. These great qualities and attributes of God are all freely given, and are really a *"position"* in Christ, and in Christ totally and completely, and are gained without exception by our Faith in the Substitutionary Offering of Christ on the Cross.

Looking at the Early Church, which record is given in the Book of Acts and the Epistles, after the passing of those particular Apostles, little by little the Church began to go into apostasy. It was not a quick thing, actually gradually declining over several centuries. Man began to take the Government of God out of the hands of God, thereby, devising

NOTES

their own government, which has plagued the Church from then until now.

Not long after Paul was taken home to Glory, the Church began to be persecuted very heavily by the Roman Government. These persecutions were more extensive in some places of the Roman Empire than others, and broke out at times very severely and then would subside for awhile. At any rate, tens of thousands of Christians paid with their lives during this time.

These great persecutions pretty well could be summed up in the demand by Rome that Christians pay homage to Caesar, recognizing him as a god, hence proclaiming *"Caesar is Lord,"* which of course most Christians would not do, and paid with their lives. But yet, there were quite a few who when faced with this terrible choice, would yield to the demands of Rome and proclaim Caesar as Lord. While their lives would be spared, they were then faced with the terrible problem of what they had done. In effect, they had denied Christ.

So, the Church during those times had to face this difficulty and answer this question. Many of these people who had truly accepted Christ, but now had committed this terrible sin, would repent of what they had done, and wanted to be then given fellowship again in the Church. So now we have the great controversy. There were three schools of thought on this subject which transpired at that time, and really carried over down through the centuries, and plagues us even unto this hour. Those three schools of thought were:

1. Never allow them back into the Church (Fellowship) again irrespective that they have repented.
2. Let them back into the Church after they have gone through a period of penance, which would be prescribed by the powers that be.
3. Accept repentance before God as the criteria alone, and admit these individuals back into the Church immediately.

Of course, the only one of these schools of thought which is Scriptural, is number three. One must understand the following about the Early Church.

First of all, it wasn't perfect. Even during the time of Paul, there were strong, strong efforts being made to compromise the great Gospel of Grace. Even Peter and Barnabas were carried away with this error, even as Paul addressed in Galatians, Chapter Two. And, when the great Apostles like Paul passed from the scene, lesser men took their place, with the Church gradually deteriorating regarding spirituality.

NOTES

The temptation has always been to depart from the Scriptures, with man making up his own rules as he goes along. In fact, religious men love to make up rules and love to make other men obey them.

Of course, as bad as this terrible sin was of these people denying Christ, after doing such a thing, if they truly repented before the Lord, which no doubt many did, the Bible plainly declares that all sin is forgiven, washed, and cleansed (I Jn. 1:9). According to the Bible, the matter stops then and there.

For anyone then to attempt to ladle more punishment upon the individual, or any punishment at all for that matter, presents a travesty on the Word of God. The Lord either forgives totally and completely, or He doesn't forgive at all. In fact, there is no such thing as a 50% or 75% Justification. Such thinking is silly! But yet, that's what many were advocating in those days, and that's what many are advocating presently.

When men begin to make up their own rules, these are rules that God will not accept, no matter how religious they might be. The Word of God is clear and plain on the subject. *"The Blood of Jesus Christ, God's Own Son, cleanses from all sin"* (I Jn. 1:7). Now either it does, or it doesn't! I happen to believe that it does, and you had better believe that way also.

When anyone tries to add anything to repentance, they are insulting the Finished Work of Christ, thereby setting themselves up as Judge and Jury, in effect, claiming moral superiority. By the very fact of them doing such, they have placed themselves in a worse spiritual condition than the one they are trying to punish.

Penance is punishment, anyway you look at it. It is never sanctioned by God, because it, in effect, says that man can cleanse himself, and that Jesus didn't finish the Work at the Cross. And beside that, what Christian would dare to think of himself as morally qualified to judge someone else? I can assure you, that no Christian is. James plainly said that:

*"There is One Law-Giver, Who is able to save and to destroy: who art thou that judgest another?"* (James 4:12).

In other words, who do you think you are, thinking you are qualified to judge someone else?

Paul also said, *"He that spared not His Own Son, but delivered Him up for us all, how shall He not with Him also freely give us all things?*

*"Who shall lay any thing to the charge of God's elect? It is God that justifieth.*

*"Who is he that condemneth? It is Christ that died, yea rather, that is risen again, Who is even at the Right Hand of God, Who also maketh intercession for us"* (Rom. 8:32-34).

All of this means that it's a very serious thing to find fault with God's Justification, which is brought about solely and completely by the Finished Work of Christ. So what am I saying?

I am saying that many in the modern Church, are still attempting to put forth the same religious foolishness as those of long ago. They are passing sentence which God can never ordain or justify. Many are claiming that if someone does something wrong, whatever it is, and especially if for any reason they don't like that person, that individual can never function in Ministry again.

Others are saying, that such a one can function again, but only if they go through a prescribed regimen of penance. They may not call it *"penance,"* but one can label it as nothing else.

This is not only error, it is a slap in the Face of Jesus Christ. It is a total repudiation of the Word of God! It is an insult to the Finished Work of Christ. It is men setting themselves up as God, which means they are in far worse spiritual condition than the ones they are attempting to judge.

It is in effect, the *"Cain and Abel controversy."* We can either accept the Sacrifice of Christ, or we can offer God the work of our own hands, which He will never accept. Of course, as Cain murdered Abel, the modern variety are still attempting to do the same.

Whereas the law of the land doesn't allow actual killing and murder, which incidently they would do if the law did allow such, they do the next worst thing, by attempting to murder one's character, Ministry, and reputation. And to be sure, God labels it as *"murder"* even though they do not actually take the person's life.

It comes down to accepting God's Way, or devising ways of our own. To be sure, Satan works far best inside the Church, than he does outside. Refusing God's Way as given in His Word, which is the Way of the Cross, and instituting one's own way, no matter how religious it might seem, is the height of rebellion against God, and is in reality, the worst sin that one can commit, other than blaspheming the Holy Spirit.

NOTES

## THE RAPTURE OF THE CHURCH

The phrase, *"At the Coming of our Lord Jesus Christ with all His Saints,"* refers not to the Second Coming as many believe, but rather the Rapture, or the Resurrection, to which it can also be referred. This refers to the Lord Jesus Christ coming from Heaven, and then going back to Heaven with all the Saints, which includes all who will be a part of the First Resurrection of Life, which refers to every Born-Again Believer who has ever lived up to that time. In fact, there will be several phases to this First Resurrection, extending to those who will be martyred during the Great Tribulation which of necessity, will take place after the initial Resurrection, and as well to the 144,000 Jews who will accept the Lord during that time, along with the two witnesses at the very end of the Great Tribulation, who will be Elijah and Enoch (Isa. 66:7-8; I Thess. 4:16-17; Rev. 7:1-17; 11:7-11; 12:5; 14:1-5; 15:2-4; 20:4-6).

As we have previously stated, the Rapture of the Church and the Resurrection of the Church, are one and the same. So, for anyone to claim they don't believe in the Rapture, whether they understand it or not, they are at the same time saying that they don't believe in the Resurrection. I don't believe any Christian would knowingly say such a thing.

While we may differ as to the time of the Rapture, we cannot differ as to the fact of the Rapture. If we do so, it shows a gross misunderstanding of the Scriptures, which in effect is a denial of the Resurrection.

We teach and believe from the Scriptures, that the Trump of God could sound at any time, which will signal the beginning of the First Resurrection, which means that every Saint of God, both those dead and those alive, is going to be instantly changed by the Power of God. Then, all Saints will be given Glorified Bodies, which will in effect complete the Salvation process. As Believers we are now Sanctified, we are now Justified, but we are not yet Glorified. The latter will come at the Rapture of the Church.

*"My heart has come to the place of rest,*
*"Leaving it all with Jesus;*
*"The cares of life doth no more molest,*
*"I'm leaving it all with Jesus."*

*"I've brought the guilt of my weary soul,*
*"Leaving it all with Jesus;*
*"I've brought not part of it, but the whole,*
*"I'm leaving it all with Jesus."*

*"I'm walking safe in a path unknown,*
*"Leaving it all with Jesus;*
*"I find the path with His blessings strewn,*
*"I'm leaving it all with Jesus;"*

*"O wounded soul, here in Heavenly balm,*
*"Leave it all with Jesus;*
*"Then change thy sadness to joyous Psalms.*
*"In leaving it all with Jesus."*

## CHAPTER 4

(1) "FURTHERMORE THEN WE BESEECH YOU, BRETHREN, AND EXHORT YOU BY THE LORD JESUS, THAT AS YE HAVE RECEIVED OF US HOW YE OUGHT TO WALK AND TO PLEASE GOD, SO YE WOULD ABOUND MORE AND MORE."

The Thessalonians had already been given instructions about how they must *"live in order to please God."* Paul again views the Christian life as a *"walk."* The Apostle might have immediately requested compliance with earlier instruction, but in the Greek word *"order"* he interrupts himself before doing so, lest he appear to be condemnatory. As always he gives credit where it is due, in this case recognizing the substantial progress that has been made.

Yet the realization of the ultimate goal of pleasing God and receiving His commendation entailed continual improvement. *"Do this more and more,"* though referring to the overflow of love Paul had prayed for and was to urge, here relates to other dimensions of the Christian life as well (Thomas).

### THE MANNER OF PAUL

The phrase, *"Furthermore then we beseech you, Brethren, and exhort you by the Lord Jesus,"* presents the beginning of a change in the tone and subject matter of the Letter. Paul passes from thanksgiving, defense of his Ministry, and reminiscences to practical exhortations on the Christian life. In this section the Apostle is no doubt dealing with matters on which Timothy's report indicated that instruction was needed. Consequently, the section contains two Passages on practical Holiness, which goes into the next Chapter, which are separated by one on Doctrine, which also goes into the next Chapter. The whole section, however, including Doctrine, is intensely practical.

The word *"Furthermore"* is an expression marking the transition in subject matter. The double expression *"beseech . . . and exhort,"* indicates the great seriousness of the writer. The Apostle does not threaten or command these persecuted Christians. The earnest exhortation matches the fervent prayer which precedes it. The idea is, God's Grace must be matched by human response.

The entreaty is *"by* (in) *the Lord Jesus."* These ethical requirements follow from union with Christ, and are grounded in and inspired by the authority of Christ.

If it is to be noticed, basically everything which Paul outlines, at least that which is received from God, is always *"by"* or *"in"* the Lord Jesus. And as well, this always refers to His Finished Work. In other words, we have these things, or else, we are able to do certain things, only because of what Jesus did at the Cross. His Sacrifice of Himself is what made everything possible.

As by now the Reader recognizes, I will take every opportunity given to proclaim this great foundation principle of Christianity. I do so because it is so very, very important, and because the Church has been pushed so far away from the Cross these last few decades, that it hardly knows its true place anymore. Consequently, Believers are living lives of failure, certainly not all, but I definitely think most! Consequently, the Salvation proposed by most in the modern Church, leaves something to be desired. It is not the trumpet blowing with a sure and certain sound, but rather a discord. The Christian Bookstores for the most part, are filled with psychological mishmash instead of the Word of God. We now have Christian Comics, who turn the whole thing into a joke. Entertainment in Christianity has become a best seller, with music having degenerated to the place that it is entertainment at best, and Satanic at its worst. Another segment of the Church is busy telling people how to get rich, when in reality, it's only those particular Preachers who are getting rich. Many Leaders of Denominations care little for souls, but rather how to perpetuate the organization. Of course, all do not follow in these categories, but far too many do!

Whatever the reasons, much of it can be laid at the doorstep of a departure from the Cross. Consequently, Christians no longer know where their true help comes from, and are, therefore, casting about in every direction possible, trying to find victory.

As we have previously said, the great fad at present is *"manifestations."* Christians are looking for Preachers who can lay hands on them, with some type of sensation experienced, which is supposed to deliver them from all their problems. While God definitely uses Preachers, and while the laying on of hands is definitely Scriptural, and while certain manifestations are definitely Scriptural as well, still, these things provide no answer. While some are good and right in their own way, they are not God's prescription for Victory. If we'll think about it for just a moment, it will quickly become obvious why not!

Our victory totally and completely, comes solely from the Cross of Christ, and our Faith in that Finished Work. That and that alone is God's criteria for all that we need from Him, which was provided by Christ. Simple Faith in that, and simple Faith remaining in that, ensures the help of the Holy Spirit (Rom. 8:1-2). The victory is then ours, and in fact, this is the only way that victory can be ours.

NOTES

This means that the Believer can travel halfway around the world, and after arriving at their destination receiving everything for which they had come, at least as far as the manifestations are concerned, a few days later say, *"O wretched man that I am, who shall deliver me from the body of this death?"* (Rom. 7:24).

While those things mentioned are good in their own right, and my statements here are in no way meant to demean anything that God does; however, one cannot take a hammer and make a handsaw out of it. And that's what Christians often try to do in the spiritual realm.

Those things have their purpose, but they do not pertain to the great Sacrifice of Christ on the Cross. In fact, if we could receive victory in any one of a hundred ways that Preachers propose, Jesus would not have had to come down here and die on that Cross. He had to do that, simply because all of these things of which we speak would not perform the task, simply because they could not perform the task.

Our victory was purchased by the Shed Blood of Jesus Christ when He hung on the Cross. He died there in our place, paying the sin debt, satisfying the curse of the broken Law, which atoned for every sin. Satan thereby lost his claim on humanity, because his claim is sin. And with all sin atoned for, he has no more claim. One must shout *"Hallelujah!"*

That is where the victory for the Child of God is found, simply because when Jesus died there and was buried and even raised from the dead, you by your Faith were actually in Him, and that's what it means to be *"in Christ."* That's where the victory was; that's where the victory is!

## THIS GREAT SALVATION

The Holy Spirit says, *"How shall we escape, if we neglect so great Salvation"* (Heb. 2:3).

It is a *"great Salvation!"*

The problem with most Christians, is that we really do not quite comprehend how great it actually is. Just this morning I was telling our College Chapel Service, that even though God could speak worlds into existence, and that's exactly how they were created (Heb. 11:3), He could not speak our Redemption into existence. He had to become a man and die on a Cross in order that we might be saved. This should tell us something.

It should tell us how awful that sin really is, how terrible the Fall actually was, in fact, to a far greater degree than any of us ever dare realize.

When we consider, that it took some 2,000 years before the world was ready even for the first stage, and I speak of Abraham. For the first 1,600 years after the Fall, the spiritual deterioration was so awful, with the entirety of the world agonizing in violence at that time, that God even repented that He had made man (Gen. 6:5-7). He salvaged the entire situation by performing major surgery, which refers to the entirety of the world and mankind being drowned in the Flood, with the exception of Noah and his family. That's how bad the situation was.

From Noah to Abraham was about 400 years, with the Lord calling this man out of idolatry in order to prepare a people who would receive His Word, and ultimately bring the Redeemer into the world; consequently, from the loins of Abraham and the womb of Sarah, the Incarnation was finally prepared, at least in its initial stages, even though it had been promised some 2,000 years earlier in the Garden of Eden, immediately after the Fall (Gen. 3:15).

From Abraham and Sarah would come Isaac, and then Jacob, from whom the great family of Israel would ultimately come forth. Hence, the Old Testament over and over again refers to the *"God of Abraham, Isaac, and Jacob."*

This has reference totally to their Faith. In other words, they believed God respecting what He said concerning the Redeemer He was going to bring into this world, which would be through their lineage.

Israel became a great nation, raised up strictly for the purpose of giving the world the Word of God in order that some spiritual light may come into this darkness, which it did. They also were to be the womb of the Messiah, which was the ultimate plan as stated, promised in the Garden.

It took some 2,000 years from the time of Abraham to the Birth of Christ, for this great Work to be carried out, and the world to be made ready for the Advent of the Son of God. So, we're speaking here of approximately 4,000 years from the time of the Promise in the Garden, at least if one could refer to this statement by the Lord as such. In Truth, the Promise and all of its golden glory was not realized, until it was actually given to Abraham. So, we ask the question as to why it took so long, nearly 4,000 years, before the Advent of Christ?

The great length of time tells us of the terrible seriousness of the situation. With the Fall man was plunged into spiritual darkness, i.e., *"spiritual death."* And when the Lord said that man would die if he did a certain thing, He meant exactly what He said. When something is dead, that means there is no life there whatsoever, which means there is no understanding or comprehension whatsoever.

At the Fall, Adam who was the father of us all, lost in totality the God Consciousness which he had, with instead, sin consciousness taking him over. Consequently, not only Adam, but all who were born thereafter, for all theoretically speaking, were in his loins, came into this world spiritually dead, which means no comprehension of God whatsoever.

Man was left with nothing but self-consciousness and a sin nature which controlled him entirely, and does unto this hour, at least for those who have not been Born-Again. To be sure, sin is the most destructive force that this world and the universe has ever known. As stated, it is so destructive, that God could not merely speak it out of existence, but a very intricate Plan had to be put in operation, which as stated, took some 4,000 years. From this fact alone, and understanding that it is God Who is doing this, and understanding that He is Omniscient (all-knowing), Omnipotent (all-powerful), and Omnipresent (His Presence is everywhere), then we know how awful this thing must have been. Consequently, as the lostness of man was very great, it took a great Salvation for man to be saved. That's the reason the Cross was demanded and actually required. There was no other way for this

NOTES

thing to be done, or at least this was the best way for Redemption to be carried out.

NOTES

## SHOULD NOT BELIEVERS UNDERSTAND THIS?

It is understandable as to why the unredeemed do not know the extent of their lost condition or the power of the Grace of God. As stated, they are *"spiritually dead"*; however, it is not quite so understandable as to why Believers do not realize the fact of the power of sin, and the greatness of their Salvation. By that I mean this:

If it took God Almighty some 4,000 years to bring the Redeemer into this world, and the Cross to pay the sin debt and to redeem mankind, how in the world do we as Believers think that we can effect our own Salvation or Sanctification? Surely we ought to know better! And if we don't, why don't we know better?

Let's say all of this again, and because it's so very important.

The believing sinner comes to Christ and receives this great and glorious Salvation. He is *"born again."* He understands that he was saved by simply having Faith in Christ and accepting Him as his Saviour. He believed that Jesus is the Son of God, and that He died on a Cross for our sins.

However, after coming to Christ, somehow we think that we can effect our own Sanctification. In other words, we think we can become Christlike, overcome sin, have victory over all the powers of darkness, by our own machinations. Consequently, we become very religious, very heavily embroiled in religious works, and we think somehow this affects something within our lives, at least as far as Righteousness and Holiness are concerned.

As previously stated, it is Salvation by Faith and Sanctification by self. What we don't realize is, that we can no more Sanctify ourselves, even though we are now new creatures in Christ Jesus, than we could save ourselves when we were unredeemed. But yet we try, and oh how we try! We should know better, but it seems we don't!

Why?

I think it's still the clinging vines of the Fall, to which we are still subject that causes us our problems. Man likes to believe he can save himself, he can straighten himself out, he can pick himself up, he can lift up himself, he can heal himself, he can redeem himself! The world is filled with that, even as Christians know and understand; however, that same problem bleeds over into our lives as Christians.

As it's difficult for the sinner to understand that he can do nothing to save himself and must depend totally upon Christ, it is likewise hard for the Christian to admit that he cannot in any way Sanctify himself, and must depend totally upon Christ. As stated, the clinging vines of the Fall continue in some way to attach themselves to us.

The Christian cannot Sanctify himself, and all his religious works will not do the job either. In fact, the following is what will happen when he engages in this particular pursuit in this fashion and regrettably, which affects almost all of Christendom:

1. First of all, Righteousness is not developed within his heart and life, but rather self-righteousness, which is the worst blight that can take place in the life of a Christian.
2. Despite all his efforts to do otherwise, he will find himself being overtaken by sin of some sort. In other words, sin will begin to have dominion over him, which will confuse him greatly, especially considering that he's doing many things which he thinks will solve this problem (Rom. 6:14).
3. The problem, whatever direction it might take, does not get better, but rather worse.

He doesn't realize that the course on which he has embarked, which constitutes almost all of the modern Church, is a course of rebellion against God's Way, which within itself is gross sin (Rom. 4:15). In other words, it is in effect saying, *"I can do this thing myself!"* This is so important I want to say it again:

The great sin that Christians commit, is failing to avail themselves of the great Plan of God as it regards the Cross of Christ and all the victory it brings, and, instead, attempting to do this thing on our own, and I speak of our Sanctification, etc.

## FUNCTIONING OUTSIDE OF THE CROSS

Anything outside of the Cross, and I speak of our Faith in the Cross, constitutes the flesh, which cannot please God (Rom. 8:8). Now let's look at that again, because it's very important.

I said anything and everything, and irrespective as to what it might be, and irrespective as to how Scriptural it might be in its own right, if we attempt to take these things and make victory out of them, instead of the Cross, we are in effect turning them into works, which God can never bless, and which will only bring us grief.

Any Christian who doesn't understand the great Victory posed in the Cross of Christ, and irrespective as to who he is, whether the largest Ministry in the world, or otherwise, is going to live a life of spiritual failure in some way. It cannot be otherwise! God has only one Plan of Victory and that is the Cross. If as Believers, we do not understand that, and avail ourselves of its great potential, it is guaranteed that there will be failure. It may not result in one of the vices but something else entirely; irrespective, it will be failure, whether sins of passion or sins of pride. As stated, self-righteousness is the only result of anything and everything outside of the Cross.

In fact, at this very moment, untold millions of Christians are living a life of spiritual failure, and don't know what to do to have victory.

They go to their Pastor, and if he is like many, he will recommend a Psychologist! If he is sincere with the Lord, and loves God very much, he will recommend that they *"get in the Altars,"* or *"pray more,"* etc.

Others will tell him, *"your Faith is weak, you must build up your Faith,"* etc.

While some of these things may be right in their own place, the Truth is, that none of these things will help. In fact, such Preachers are having the same problem themselves in one way or the other, and don't know what to do. Understanding that, how can they help others if they cannot even help themselves?

I'm not saying these things sarcastically, if anything, I'm saying them with a broken heart. The reason is very simple:

The things I'm talking about, I've been there! I've been on both sides of the fence, not knowing what to tell someone, and not knowing what I should be told! And all the time, trying so hard, so very hard, but failing just the same!

So, these things I say, I have lived them, and lived them in glaring black and white, and in fact, as few people on Earth have ever lived them, at least as it refers to worldwide attention.

The Church has been pushed so far away from the Cross with erroneous teaching, or through sheer unbelief, that it little more knows the way of Victory. So, in one sense of the word, it lives a vast lie. It's not intentional, and in this great mix of untold millions, there are many who love the Lord with all their hearts, and actually they would die for Him if called upon to do so; irrespective, they're not walking in victory, because they don't know God's prescribed order of Victory, having been taught something else altogether.

NOTES

## MY OWN PERSONAL EXPERIENCE

As I've already stated in this Volume, I sought the Lord earnestly regarding this thing which is the single most important thing in the world as it regards a Christian. I speak of living a victorious, overcoming, Christian life. I speak of being victorious over sin in every shape, form, and fashion. I speak of being Christlike, in other words, living a life of Righteousness and Holiness, which means to be led by the Spirit of God in all things.

I sought the Lord with tears, for nearly five years, and perhaps for a lifetime. *"Lord, I know the answer is in Your Word, and I implore You to show me that answer!"*

We wonder why it takes so long, don't we! However, this thing is not easy, is not simple, and is not done quickly. It took some 25 years before the miracle child could be born to Abraham and Sarah, even though the Lord had given them the Promise at the very beginning.

Whatever the reason for the delay, for the time which seems so long, for the trial and error period which is extremely debilitating, the fault is ours and ours alone. It is never the fault of God! As one great English Preacher said, *"Before the Spirit can do His great work within our lives, all hope of the flesh must die."* That's quite a statement and exactly, what did he mean?

Man has to come to the end of himself, even Christian man. That's not easily or quickly done! However, this we can guarantee, if the person will hold on, and not despair, and believe the Lord, the answer will come. It did for me, and it will come for anyone who truly seeks the Lord.

As well, the Lord didn't give me this great Revelation on the Cross, showing and telling me that this great Finished Work of Christ contains the answer to all my questions, just for Jimmy Swaggart alone. He intended for me to give it to you, and to everyone else in this world, at least where my voice can reach. And by the help and Grace of God, that I intend to do.

What I'm talking about is not some fad that will pass with tomorrow. I'm speaking of the very foundation of the Church. In fact, that which the Holy Spirit gave to the Apostle Paul, which we refer to as the New Covenant, is actually this of which we speak. This is God's Way, and not man's way. It is all in Christ; 100% in Christ; totally in Christ, and all that He did at the Cross and the Resurrection. If we divorce Jesus from the Cross, we are preaching *"another Jesus!"* If we divorce the Gospel from the Cross, we are preaching *"another gospel!"* If we function by another spirit, other than the Spirit of God Who always leads men to the Cross, we are functioning in *"another spirit!"* (II Cor. 11:4). And that's where most of the Church presently is. They are promoting *"another Jesus," "another gospel,"* and *"another spirit."* To turn it around and say it another way:

If it's not the Jesus of the Cross, if it's not the Gospel of the Cross, if it's not the Holy Spirit Who always leads one to the Cross, then it's false! I realize that's blunt and to the point, but that's exactly what it is!

## TO WALK AND TO PLEASE GOD

The phrase, *"That as ye have received of us how ye ought to walk and to please God,"* pertains to the whole manner of living. *"Please God"* has to do once again with our walk, in other words our victory, and suggests that to glorify God and do His Will is the heart of Christian living. The little word *"ought"* reminds us that the Redeemed are men under obligation, and yet the *"yoke is easy"* and the *"burden is light"* (Mat. 11:28-30).

NOTES

Not found in the King James Version, but derived from the oldest and best Manuscripts we are told, immediately following *"please God"* are the words *"just as you are doing."* Paul is not suggesting that the Thessalonians had been failing to live the Christian life. Indeed, these words are a tactful bit of praise. The emphasis is on achieving, going forward, making faster progress.

## SANCTIFICATION AND OUR WALK

Actually, our *"walk"* is our Sanctification, whatever it might be. As stated, our *"walk"* has to do with the way we live, our manner of life, our lifestyle, whether we are Christlike or aren't!

As a Christian we want to live a holy life, and by that I mean, that the Fruit of the Spirit develops within our life, with us becoming more and more Christlike. Therefore, the great question is, how do we do this?

It can be done only one way, and I emphasize that point:

1. We must realize that the wherewithal for this, and I speak of a sanctified walk, is found totally and completely in the Cross of Christ (Rom. 6:2-4).

2. Our Faith is to always rest in the Finished Work of Christ, understanding that it is from here, that all Blessings flow.

3. Whenever this is properly done, which must be done even on a daily basis (Lk. 9:23), the Holy Spirit will then begin to do great and mighty things within our hearts and lives, helping us to walk this walk, even as we ought (Rom. 8:1-2).

The only way the Believer can *"please God"* is to function according to God's prescribed order of the Cross of Christ. This means to totally depend on that which Jesus has already done on our behalf. If we attempt any other way or manner, we cannot please God, as the Scripture emphatically says (Rom. 8:8).

To help us understand this thing a little better, let's use a hypothetical situation, but yet which is partially true:

A young man and his wife sat in my office, a young man incidently who felt the call to preach, but who was suffering failure in his Christian experience. In other words, he was committing a particular type of sin, of

NOTES

which I will not go into any detail, simply because the type of sin does not really matter that much.

This was a number of years ago, and to be frank, I really did not know how to deal with the situation, exactly as I have described Preachers some paragraphs earlier. I prayed with the young man and his wife, and told them both all I knew to tell them, which really was insufficient.

A short time later they were in my office again, with the wife exclaiming to me the great victory which had recently been won. She went on to tell how they had been in a service in a distant city, and she and her husband had gone forward, and the Power of God had come upon them, and he had actually been *"slain in the Spirit,"* with both now feeling that their problem was solved.. In fact, that's what both of them said!

I nodded my head in agreement, praying that it was so, but fearing that it wasn't. At that particular time, I knew what wouldn't work, but I was not exactly sure about what would work, at least as it referred to victory.

Sure enough, in a short time, the failure repeated itself. I wept with them again, prayed with them, with the young man sincerely repenting before the Lord; however, repentance and forgiveness is not deliverance. We need to read that very carefully and think about it a few moments.

While repentance and forgiveness are absolutely necessary, that is if relationship with the Lord is to be restored, we must not mistake the grand feeling that comes to us when forgiveness is enjoined, thinking that it is deliverance. As stated, it isn't!

As it regards what happened to the young man in the particular Church Service, and him being *"slain in the Spirit,"* was that not real?

I was not at the Service, so I personally have no idea as to what was happening there; however, from what he and his wife said, I would certainly believe that it was real. The Lord did move upon them, and in a great way. In other words, it was not mere flesh, or imagination, but actually the Lord. But still, he wasn't delivered of his problem, and neither is anyone else in such circumstances.

In fact, and as we have already stated, untold thousands of Christians are trying to bring about similar circumstances, even traveling thousands of miles to go to certain particular Services, where they think victory will be found. While the Lord might definitely bless them and bless them greatly, there will be little victory found in such circumstances, as real as it might be otherwise.

Once again I go back to the statement, that if victory could be found in that manner, and I speak of what we need to live a victorious, overcoming, Christian life, then Jesus didn't need to come down here and die on a Cross. All He would have to have done, is simply teach Preachers how to lay hands on people, with His Power touching them, etc.

No, the problem is far worse than that. In other words, it took the Cross to address this problem, and it takes the benefits of the Cross, to solve this problem.

So, what should that young man do?

He must do the same as all others who truly come to the Lord; he must understand first of all that this thing of victory is not at all of works, but altogether of Faith.

## WHAT DO WE MEAN, ALTOGETHER BY FAITH?

First of all, we mean that all of these other things as we have mentioned, as right as they might be in their own way, must be laid aside, with no dependence put in them whatsoever. Now please understand, we're not demeaning these manifestations, whatever they might be, but rather saying, that as helpful as they might be in their own way, they will provide no Victory in this capacity.

At this very moment as I dictate these words, there are untold numbers of Christians all over the world, who are being overcome by the powers of darkness in some way, and are thinking that if they can just pray 30 minutes a day, or an hour a day, and do so without fail, that this will bring them victory.

While prayer is one of the greatest privileges that a Christian has, and while the praying so much each day will definitely bless the person in other ways, he will not find any victory as it regards his problem. Once again, if such could bring about this for which we seek, then Jesus went needlessly to the Cross.

Now again, please understand, we're not demeaning prayer, not at all! We're simply saying, that if we try to use prayer in this manner, we are in effect turning it into works, which God cannot honor.

Please forgive my being overly repetitive; however, this is so important, that I feel I must address it every way I can, praying that you the Reader will catch this thing in your spirit, as the Holy Spirit reveals it to you, and will, therefore, embark upon a life of Victory as you've never known before.

So, when we speak of Faith, we are altogether referring to Faith in the Cross of Christ. That refers to what Jesus did there, which of course, is *"The Finished Work of Christ."*

You can have Faith in your prayer life, or in the manifestations we have just mentioned, and those things will definitely bless and help you, but it will not bring about that for which you seek. You must have Faith in the Cross, and in the Cross exclusively!

When you do this, understanding that all that you seek is in what Jesus did at the Cross, the Holy Spirit will then begin to do things for you that you never dreamed possible. Your days of sinning and repenting, sinning and repenting, etc., will be over. There might be a little struggle to begin with, as your Faith needs to be strengthened, but to be sure, that which Paul said will definitely come to pass in your life, *"sin will have dominion over you no more"* (Rom. 6:14).

That's why Paul said, *"But God forbid that I should glory, save in the Cross of our Lord Jesus Christ, by Whom the world is crucified unto me, and I unto the world"* (Gal. 6:14).

This which we have just related to you, is that which will *"please God,"* and guarantee your *"walk"* before the Lord. Nothing else will, because nothing else can.

### TO ABOUND MORE AND MORE

The phrase, *"So ye would abound more and more,"* proclaims the manner of Spiritual Growth.

This is what will happen to you, whenever you place your Faith properly where it belongs, in the Cross of Christ, which gives the Holy Spirit total access to your life. You will now begin to see proper, Spiritual Growth. Otherwise, your growth was stymied, which regrettably and sadly, is the state of most Christians.

NOTES

The Holy Spirit can do wonders for us. In fact, His very nature is that of *"abounding more and more"*; however, He can only do these things as we make the Cross of Christ our object of Faith. Otherwise, He is greatly hindered (Rom. 8:2).

(2) "FOR YE KNOW WHAT COMMANDMENTS WE GAVE YOU BY THE LORD JESUS."

Paul is now going to look at the practical aspects of Christianity, which has to do with the way we live and various different sins. He is especially going to deal with the moral aspect of our lives. And to be sure, this is exactly what the Holy Spirit always does.

It is His business, to clean us up, to give us purity, to give us victory over the sins of the flesh, etc. He can definitely do these things, but only if we function in the manner we are supposed to function, which is according to our Faith in the Finished Work of Christ.

### COMMANDMENTS

The phrase, *"For ye know what Commandments,"* refers to that which comes from the Lord, and which Christians are not to do. In other words, these are not suggestions, but rather *"Commandments."*

Someone has said that there are no Commandments in Christianity. In fact, in the manner in which they were making the statement, it is correct. The Ten Commandments, of which the Brother was actually speaking, have all been fulfilled in Christ. To be sure, they are incumbent upon Believers, but not in the manner of attempting to keep them, etc. As stated, they have already been kept in Christ, and as the Believer is *"in Christ,"* all of these Commandments will be kept very easily and very well.

However, if the Christian sets the Ten Commandments before him, and sets out to try to keep them, he will find himself failing. Everything must be understood as *"in Christ,"* meaning that Jesus has already done these things. We are to rest in Him, enjoying victory in Him, which simply requires Faith in the Cross, and that alone!

So, what type of Commandments is Paul addressing here?

It was not so much a list of Commandments, if at all, but rather a command to be

NOTES

holy. Of course, when we are holy, as it refers to our Sanctification, then all impurities are laid aside. It is not done as a matter of Law, but as a matter of being *"in Christ!"*

BY THE LORD JESUS

The phrase, *"We gave you by the Lord Jesus,"* proclaims the Son of God as being the authority behind these *"Commandments."*

As should be obvious, this destroys the idea of *"sinning a little bit everyday!"* The Believer should ever understand, that the Lord saves from sin, and not in sin. Even as we will study in the next Verse, the Lord demands Holiness and Righteousness, i.e., *"Sanctification,"* in all His followers. This is the aim of the Holy Spirit, the work of the Holy Spirit, and that which the Holy Spirit has been given instructions to bring about within our hearts and lives.

We had better take these words seriously, because if anything should be taken seriously, this certainly should. We are speaking of the effect of Salvation within our hearts and lives, which of course is *"Sanctification."* Inasmuch as it is demanded by the Lord, and it definitely is, then to not do this which the Lord has especially commanded, serves as a gross disobedience, and can do nothing but fall out to our moral ruin.

To carry out what the Lord has commanded, we can only do it one way, even as we've already discussed as it regards our particular *"walk."* It can only be done through the Cross and the Cross alone!

(3) "FOR THIS IS THE WILL OF GOD, EVEN YOUR SANCTIFICATION, THAT YE SHOULD ABSTAIN FROM FORNICATION:"

We would do well to carefully peruse all this which the Holy Spirit has given through the Apostle. To be sure, we're dealing here with the very heart of the great problem which besets humanity, even Christians.

To be sure, if immorality had not been a terrible problem, and in fact continues to be a terrible problem, then the Holy Spirit would not have spent this much time on the subject.

SANCTIFICATION

The phrase, *"For this is the Will of God, even your Sanctification,"* is primarily the work of making one holy, separating from sin unto God, making morally pure; but it is also the resulting state of Holiness. God wishes, says the Apostle, to sanctify (to consecrate to Himself, and purify inwardly) these Thessalonian converts in order that they shall be holy.

This is not, of course, a definition of God's Will, but the statement, within the context, of God's purpose for His redeemed children (Jn. 17:19; Eph. 5:25-27; Heb. 13:12). *"The Will of God"* may be seen as *"precept* (unalterable Law or Commandment, to which men must submit)"; as *"purpose* (Divine Wisdom and Love seeking their sublime ends)"; as *"power* (Divine efficiency working out what is purposed)"; and as *"promise* (utter dependability in the fulfillment of its purpose)" (Airhart).

THE WILL OF GOD

The phrase, *"The Will of God,"* has two significations in Scripture:

1. The determination of God — His Decree.

2. His Desire, that in which He delights.

However, the sad fact is, the Will of God is often frustrated by the perversity of His creatures. It is in this latter sense that the word is employed here. In other words, those who claim to serve the Lord, do not all the time subscribe to that which He desires, but rather function in self-will.

The Believer's heart should always and without fail, strive to carry out the Will of God in every respect. This is the way to blessing, happiness, joy, fulfillment, development, and everything that God has. In fact, the only way to that which the human soul truly craves is the carrying out of the Will of God in every respect. So, the Believer should actively seek the Will of God, should strive to carry out the Will of God, should seek the Lord for His help in this regard, and should understand how important all of this is.

First of all, God has a *"Will"* for every particular life. And when I say that, I'm not meaning a generalized concept, but actually a tailor-made plan for each particular person. God being God is capable of doing such.

The Believer is to find out what that Will is, which can easily be done by simply being sincere with the Lord, and seeking His Will for our lives.

Once the *"Will"* is ascertained, the Believer must seek the Lord incessantly, even for His help in carrying out that Will, which is the single most important thing in anyone's life. Let me say that again:

The carrying out of the Will of God in one's life, and down to the minute detail, is the single most important thing in the life of the Believer. Everything else takes a distant second. In Truth, one might say, that the carrying out of the Will of God is everything, with there being no second or third, etc. In other words, the Will of God, and the carrying out of that Will, must literally take up the entirety of one's life, which if carried out with consecration, will bring a peace and a joy that passes all understanding.

SANCTIFICATION

*"Sanctification"* in the Greek is *"hagiamos,"* and means *"consecration and holiness."* In its literal context it refers to *"being set apart to something, and in this case God, from something, in this case the world and self-will."* It refers to the fact, that all Believers have been bought at great price, and in essence are servants of the Lord, i.e., *"bond slaves,"* but such in a different sense than normal.

One is a bond slave to the Lord willingly and not by force. It carries the idea of one loving the Lord so much, being so grateful to Him, that one willingly gives oneself to Him in every capacity. The idea then is, to consecrate to Him in totality, doing His bidding in every manner of life.

There are actually two types of Sanctification one might say:

1. Positional Sanctification: This is the position that is granted the Believer automatically and instantly upon coming to Christ (I Cor. 6:11). This is a position granted to the Believer upon Faith, and because the Believer is *"in Christ."* By Faith the Believer has gained this distinct position, which means he was instantly cleansed by the Precious Blood of Jesus. In fact, Sanctification is *"making one clean,"* while Justification is *"declaring one clean."*

So, this positional Sanctification is brought about instantly upon conversion, and never varies regarding the degree of that position.

NOTES

2. Conditional Sanctification: This is the type of Sanctification which Paul is speaking about in this Third Verse. In other words, it is the Will of God that our *"condition"* be brought up to our *"position,"* which the Holy Spirit sets out to do.

Even though Paul tells us here it must be done, he really does not tell us how. He does that in the Sixth and Eighth Chapters of Romans. The Epistle to the Galatians is dedicated to the Sanctification of the Saint as well. In fact, this one subject of the Sanctification of the Believer, is the single most important subject of one's life. In fact, so much of Paul's teaching centers up on this all-important aspect. How is one to be holy? How is one to be consecrated? How is one to be Sanctified?

As well, this is where Satan fights the Saint more than all. He desires to hinder your Sanctification, or stop it altogether.

ONE CANNOT SANCTIFY ONESELF

This is the greatest struggle which the Child of God faces. At the moment of conversion, the Believer instantly gains the Divine Nature, which pushes one toward Sanctification and Holiness, which should be obvious. That becomes the natural instinct of the Child of God; however, in obeying that instinct, this wonderful Divine Nature, is the area in which we so often go wrong. In other words, we try to do this thing ourselves, and what do I mean by that?

We set about to carry out this task, by engaging in a regimen of works of some kind. Unfortunately, there is also a natural instinct in us to go in this direction, which is always a road to disaster. In fact, entire Religious Denominations fall into this trap.

Many claim that if you follow their rules, obey their Commandments, whatever they might be, which almost altogether deals with externals, then you will be *"Sanctified."* Nothing could be further from the Truth! In fact, not only will you not be Sanctified, you will actually go in the opposite direction. Once again, we come back to the premise that the Believer cannot Sanctify himself. It doesn't matter that the leadership of an entire Denomination functions in this capacity, their success will be no greater than you making the attempt yourself. Both are doomed to failure.

Several Holiness Denominations have claimed that Sanctification is some type of instantaneous work. In other words, the Believer comes to Christ, and then at a point in time whether soon or later, the individual is Sanctified, as the result of some experience at the Altar, etc.

That is patently unscriptural. There's nothing in the Word of God that evenly remotely points to such a situation. As stated, every Believer is instantly Sanctified upon conversion, and then the Holy Spirit sets about to bring us up to that which we actually are in Christ. It is a progressive work, and will continue in that fashion until we die or the Trump sounds.

So, the idea of going to an Altar somewhere in some Church, etc., and having an experience with the Lord which is called Sanctification, and then being free from sin from then on, is not taught in the Word of God. Once again, Sanctification is not an activity, but rather a position. It is that not only in our initial experience at Salvation, but it is the same in our everyday experience, and this is what confuses us at times.

We tend to think that Sanctification is something we can do ourselves, in other words, an activity of sorts, when it is nothing of the kind.

To say it in a different way, it is the thinking that we're sanctified simply because we do some certain good things, or we don't do some certain bad things. In fact, there's absolutely nothing one can do within oneself in order to sanctify oneself, but at the same time, there are many things one can do which will make one unsanctified and quick, even as we will study in the next phrase of this Verse.

So the Reader must understand, that there is nothing he can personally do to sanctify himself, which means that all of his faithfulness to Church, or the giving of money to the Work of the Lord, or prayer life, etc., does not at all sanctify one, as important as these things might be in their own right. We're not demeaning these things, as we've already said several times in Commentary regarding this particular Epistle. In fact, we should do these things, but as a *"result"* of our Sanctification, and not in any manner as the *"cause"* of our Sanctification.

NOTES

### THE SANCTIFICATION PROCESS IS ALONE IN THE REALM OF THE HOLY SPIRIT

Paul graphically brings this out in the Eighth Chapter of Romans. He says, *"There is therefore now no condemnation to them who are in Christ Jesus, who walk not after the flesh but after the Spirit"* (Rom. 8:1).

In fact, this is one of the great office works of the Holy Spirit, to sanctify the Believer. As stated, His purpose and Mission is to bring our actual condition up to our actual position. What we already are in Christ, He wants to bring about in our practical living. In other words, that we live what we actually are in Christ.

Therefore, it is the task of the Believer to cooperate with the Holy Spirit in this all-important task. In fact, He cannot do this thing unless He has our cooperation, and in totality. Unfortunately, we too often work against Him, which frustrates His purposes. We don't intend to do this thing in this manner, but oftentimes that's what we are actually doing, which always causes us tremendous problems.

This of which I say is something of which I know. In other words, I've been there. I was very sincere, and I mean as sincere as a human being could ever be before God, but at the same time sincerely going in the wrong direction. What do I mean by that?

I mean I was trying to sanctify myself. I was using very legitimate means of the Lord, but using them out of context.

For instance, I thought I could pray myself into Sanctification; therefore, I had a prayer regimen that was second to none I suppose. To be sure, the Lord blessed me in this and blessed me greatly, but not in that for which I sought. In fact, prayer is one of the greatest privileges of the Child of God, and the Believer cannot have a proper relationship with the Lord without having a prayer life. However, our prayer life is to be the result of Sanctification, and not the cause of Sanctification, which it can never do.

At the same time, I thought that great Faith would accomplish the task. And to be sure, the Lord gave me great Faith, for which to believe Him for great and mighty things, even for the Salvation of hundreds of thousands of souls, and I'm not exaggerating at all.

But when it came to Faith for personal Sanctification, I had it in the wrong thing. I had it in these other things I was doing, which were very important and very necessary in their own right, but not in this manner for which I sought.

So what is the right way?

## WHAT IS GOD'S WAY OF SANCTIFICATION?

To be sure, He has only one Way, and that is the Cross of Christ. And what do we mean by that?

The Believer is to understand that everything the Saint needs is found in what Jesus did at the Cross and in His Resurrection. This refers not only to Salvation from sin in the initial Salvation experience, but as well for Victory as it regards the daily living of the Child of God.

As we've said repeatedly, the problem with the Believer is that the object of his Faith is oftentimes wrong. It's not that he doesn't have Faith, or that he's not using his Faith, the problem is he's not using it in the right way.

The object of Faith on our part must always be the Cross of Christ. Now many Christians have never heard that before. They think that the Cross should be the object of Faith as it regards the sinner being initially saved; however, most have never heard the phrase that the object of their Faith must continue to be in the Cross, as it regards one's daily, victorious living (Rom. 6:2-14; 8:1-2, 11; I Cor. 1:18; 2:2; Gal. 6:14).

The Christian can no more sanctify himself by his own efforts, than the sinner can save himself by his own efforts. They are one and the same!

As it took the work of Christ on the Cross to bring the sinner to Salvation, it took the work of Christ on the Cross to bring Victory regarding daily living, to the Child of God. When Jesus died on the Cross, He addressed every single solitary problem that man could ever have as it regards his spiritual condition.

NOTES

So, to grow in the Grace of the Lord, to live a sanctified life, which the Lord demands here, as is quite obvious, all the Believer has to do, is to understand that all that he needs, all the victory, all the power, all the instruction, etc., is found in what Jesus did at the Cross. He is to put his Faith totally and completely in that, and not allow it to be moved from that.

When the Believer does this, then the Holy Spirit, whom we have been discussing, can then do His great office work of bringing about the Sanctification process in the Believer's heart and life.

This is what Paul was talking about in Romans 8:11. The same Spirit (the Holy Spirit) Who raised Jesus from the dead, will also quicken our mortal bodies. This means, that the flesh is very weak, which keeps us from bringing about this process by our own efforts, irrespective of the sincerity. However, when the Holy Spirit begins to energize our flesh, then whatever has been a terrible problem, is no longer a problem, because it's the Holy Spirit doing this thing, Who is God, and Who cannot fail. In other words, that which had proved such a terrible problem to you as a Saint, which has caused you so much grief and tears, over which you have repented time and time again, will suddenly fall off as if it never existed, and without any struggle or fight at all. It is because the Holy Spirit is doing the thing.

Most Christians know and understand that it's the Spirit of God Who must do this thing. But they don't know how He works, and in fact, if the Truth be known, He's not working very much in most Christian lives. He wants to, but we have clipped His wings, as A.W. Tozer said, due to our Faith being improperly placed.

The Lord doesn't require much as should be obvious. If He did, we would be shot down before we begin. He only requires that we know and understand the rudiments of the Cross and what it all means. This is plainly given to us in Romans, Chapter 6.

As already stated, He tells us there how the Believer is baptized into Christ's death. This is not speaking of Water Baptism, but actually the Crucifixion of Christ. Of course, we were not there when Jesus actually died;

nevertheless, the moment we have Faith in that, exhibit Faith in that, proclaim Faith in that, in the Mind of God we are literally in Christ, respecting all that He did regarding His Crucifixion, Burial, and Resurrection (Rom. 6:2-6).

### IN CHRIST

The secret of all of this, is our being *"in Christ"*; however, we must fully understand as to how we are *"in Christ."* This is not some nebulous thing that just sort of happened, or some will-o'-the-wisp, which many Christians seem to think. Neither is it something that's incomprehensible! In fact, it can be very well understood, and in fact, the Holy Spirit demands that we do understand this.

When you got saved, you didn't understand much of anything about the Lord, but now that you are a Child of God, the Holy Spirit demands that you know some things. The trouble is, we as Christians spend our time learning about ball teams, where the fish are biting, or how to make money, or a hundred and one other things, which may have some small significance, and give little attention, if any at all, to these things that really matter.

In Romans, Chapters 6, 7, and 8, some nine times, the Holy Spirit refers to the fact that we ought to know some things. Actually, there are other words in these three Chapters which mean the same thing, but I've only addressed the words *"know"* or *"knowing,"* etc. (Rom. 6:3, 6, 9, 16; 7:1, 14, 18; 8:22, 28).

*"In Christ"* refers to what Jesus did at the Cross and the Resurrection. When He died, as already stated, we were literally *"in Him."* I use the word *"literal,"* even though we were not actually there, because in the Mind of God this is actually what happened. Our Faith in this which He did, places us there.

When He died on the Cross, He did a great number of things, all pertaining to you and me.

First of all, He suffered the penalty of the broken Law, which was death. He did all of this in our place. The Bible says *"the wages of sin is death."* So Jesus died, in order to satisfy that demand.

As well, He did not die as anyone else has ever died. All other deaths are a cessation of life, as life is taken from the individual. No man took Jesus' life from Him, He laid it down of His Own accord. So it was a voluntary, sacrificial death. In other words, He offered up Himself as a Sacrifice, of which all the millions upon millions of offered lambs in the past had been but symbols.

Inasmuch as His Body and Life were Perfect, the offering up of His Life satisfied the terrible sin debt owed to God by man. Consequently, when the sin debt was paid, that means all sin was atoned, which means, that the record was cleared of all transgressions and infractions, at least for all those who will believe (Jn. 3:16).

This means that Satan lost his grip on the human race. Satan's legal claim upon man is sin; however, with the sin removed, he has no more legal claim, which means he is a defeated foe in every capacity.

Then Jesus was buried, with us continuing to be buried with or in Him. This refers to the old life, all the old transgressions, all the sin and iniquity, all that we were and had been before accepting Him as our Lord and Saviour. It's all buried, out of the sight of God and man, and can never again be brought up against us.

As well, when he was raised from the dead by the Holy Spirit, we were raised with Him and in fact *"in Him."* However, we were not raised as we had died. We were raised in *"newness of life"* (Rom. 6:2-4). That's what it means to be *"in Christ!"*

In fact, He died as our Substitute, which the Fifty-third Chapter of Isaiah amply proclaims, and as well, as our Representative Man, which the Twenty-second Psalm proclaims. This means that whatever He did, God looked at it as if we did this thing, which means that all the victories He won, and He won them all, are now ours. So, how do I get all of these victories?

### VICTORY!

I get them simply by having Faith in what He did. My Faith puts me *"in Christ,"* which has to do with all that He did, all the victories He won, which means He defeated every power of darkness, and now all of that is mine. As the first Adam threw it all away, Jesus as the Last Adam, purchased it all back.

NOTES

So, if I attempt to do anything, no matter how good it is, trying to find victory, other than my Faith in what Jesus has already done, whether I realize it or not, I am doing nothing but insulting Christ. I am saying that what He did was not enough, and that I have to add something to His great Work. Let the Believer ever understand, that the Work of Christ is a *"Finished Work."* In fact, it is so *"finished,"* that He today is *"sat down at the Right Hand of the Father,"* which means there is nothing else to be done. He has done it all (Heb. 1:3).

Inasmuch as He has done it all, that leaves nothing else for me to do. In fact, if there was something else to do, it wouldn't be possible for me to do it anyway. However, it is a Finished Work, and we are to think of it constantly in those terms.

Consequently, for me to receive all of these benefits, all of this largess, all of these great Blessings, in fact the Blessing of Abraham, which is Justification by Faith, which refers to total and complete victory, all I have to do is simply have Faith in this which Jesus has done. When I do that, making that the object of my Faith, and continuing to do it until I die or the Trump of God sounds, the Holy Spirit will guarantee me all the benefits of what Jesus has done.

## THE CROSS, THE OBJECT OF ONE'S FAITH

Even though I have said this over and over again; still, due to how important this is, how critically important it is, I want to make certain that you the Reader understand perfectly what is being said.

God works with humanity strictly from the premise of Faith. Paul said, *"For by Grace are ye saved through Faith; and that not of yourselves: it is the Gift of God* (which refers to the Sacrifice of Christ)*: not of works, lest any man should boast"* (Eph. 2:8-9).

Paul also said, *"For the Promise* (Promise of Salvation), *that he* (Abraham) *should be the heir of the world, was not to Abraham, or to his seed, through the Law* (the Law of Moses or any type of Law), *but through the Righteousness of Faith"* (Rom. 4:13).

Abraham is used here as an example, simply because it was to this Patriarch that God explained the obtaining of the great Promise of Salvation through Faith. As it was then, so it is now.

NOTES

Everything we receive from the Lord, and without exception, comes through Faith. It is never of works, but always through Faith!

However, that which I've just said, although right, is not quite sufficient regarding total understanding. When we say *"Faith,"* we must understand, that we're speaking of Faith in the Cross of Christ, always the Cross of Christ! That is what the Holy Spirit through Paul is saying.

The object of our Faith, and in every circumstance, must always be in the Cross of Christ, which of course also presupposes His Resurrection and Exaltation (Eph. 2:6).

Our Faith must be in the Cross, because it was here, even as we have already explained, that every victory was won, every demon and even Satan himself were defeated, and all things were made right. Let me give another example:

The United States is one of the greatest nations in the world. Its citizens, at least for the most part, have faith in this country. And what do we mean by that? We speak of its greatness, its glory, its riches, its prosperity, etc.

However, all these glorious rights and freedoms granted to Americans, have not come to us and in fact, do not come to us, simply because this nation is great, or rich, or prosperous, etc. All of these things come to us because of a little piece of paper called *"the Constitution of the United States."* It is on that piece of paper that our rights and freedoms are guaranteed. In fact, it is that if one wants to look at it in a strict legal sense, which has made this nation great.

It is the same with Christ. When we talk about Salvation, or in this case *"Sanctification,"* or anything else from the Lord, we're speaking of all of this being made possible by what He did at the Cross. We must never forget that, never ignore that, never place it in a subsidiary position, never take it lightly, never think of it in a lesser manner. It must always stand as the Foundation of Christianity and in every respect.

In fact, the entirety of the story of the Bible, is the story of the Redemption of humanity, which is the story of the Price paid by Christ on the Cross. All the millions of lambs, bullocks, heifers, and goats offered up under the Old Testament economy, pointed in totality to that coming Crucifixion, that One Sacrifice of Christ.

Even as that pointed to Christ, now, we have the Blessing which has been made possible by what Christ did. We must never forget where it comes from, and what made it all possible. But I'm afraid, that most of the Church has forgotten.

Today, much of the Church is trusting in humanistic psychology, which is one of the greatest travesties of the Twentieth Century. Such direction in effect says that Christ did not accomplish the task, or else, that which He did is no longer believed, which I'm afraid is the case with many.

And then others, as it regards the Sanctification process, are doing all types of things, all constituting works, which God can never accept, and which will never bring that for which we seek. As Paul says here, it is Sanctification which is the issue, and as far as the Saint is concerned, always the issue.

### FORNICATION

The phrase, *"That ye should abstain from fornication,"* refers, as is obvious, to all types of immorality.

Paul speaks here with great solemnity upon a Truth which at various times, even in the Church, has been, if not denied, yet half forgotten, that *"moral"* evils are always *"spiritual"* evils of the first magnitude.

It is certainly remarkable that here, and elsewhere repeatedly, the Apostle does not speak of this offense as of an evil scarcely known among, and little to be feared by, true Believers, but rather as of an evil not only widely spread but certain to assault them.

Prof. Jowett Finely says: *"What he seems to penetrate is the inward nature of sin, not its outward effects. Even its consequences in another state of being are but slightly touched upon in comparison with that living death which itself is. It is not merely a vice or a crime, or even an offense against the Law of God, to be punished here or hereafter. It is more than this. It is what men feel within; not what shall be, but what is; a terrible consciousness, a communion with unseen powers of evil."*

NOTES

Incidently, the way the original Greek uses the term, it is *"the fornication,"* which pertains to all types of immorality.

### A CLEAR AND PRESENT DANGER

Many commentators claim that Paul addressed this subject in this manner, because the heathen were notoriously involved in all types of immorality. While that was no doubt true, still, he was not merely addressing a problem which was prevalent then, and of little consequence presently. This matter of *"sexual immorality,"* is the crowning sin of humanity. It is Satan's greatest effort of evil in his pollution of mankind. It covers the gamut all the way from adultery to homosexuality, bestiality (humans having sex with animals), lewdness, impure thoughts, etc. This is not only the great sin of the world, and always has been, but it is also the great danger for the Child of God. This pollution, this filth, this uncleanness, this ungodliness, characterizes itself in many ways.

For instance, there are millions of Christians, both men and women, who are guilty of adultery, but have actually never committed the sin, at least as far as the physical act is concerned. They have committed it in their heart, which is the seedbed of all sin. In other words, the barrier is the fear of consequences or lack of opportunity.

To simply not do something, because consequences are feared, does not absolve one of guilt, at least in the Eyes of God. This is what Jesus was talking about when He said, *"Ye have heard that it was said by them of old time, thou shalt not commit adultery:*

*"But I say unto you, that whosoever looketh on a woman to lust after her hath committed adultery with her already in his heart"* (Mat. 5:27-28).

Jesus was going to the core of the problem here, by going to the heart of man, where all sin originates. While it's certainly good that a person doesn't actually commit the act, still, the Salvation afforded by Christ, takes away all desire, in other words, it addresses the heart. As we've already said, to not do something merely because one fears the consequences, is the way of the world. It is not to be the way of those who follow the Lord.

We do certain things, or don't do certain things, because our heart has been changed. In other words, there is no desire there for those things whatsoever. Once again, I go back to the Cross.

The only way this can be brought about, with all desire for that which is ungodly and unholy being taken away, and taken away completely, is by the Believer having total Faith in the Cross of Christ, understanding that it was there that all of these problems were addressed, with Jesus defeating all the powers of darkness.

It doesn't matter who the Christian is, or even whether he is one of the greatest Preachers in the world. If he doesn't have his Faith in the Cross of Christ, Satan will definitely try to pull him down in one way or the other, by immorality of some nature. Without Faith in the Cross of Christ, he will succeed in some manner. It is impossible otherwise! Others may not know, but God will know.

Again I wish to emphasize, that no human being is exempt from these attacks by Satan in some manner, and no Christian is exempt from trust in the Cross of Christ. If we attempt to go another way, we are painting a big target on our heart and inviting Satan to shoot, which to be certain, he shall do.

## PRESENT CIRCUMSTANCES

From what information which crosses my desk, I personally believe, that more Preachers are failing today than ever before. And these are the only ones we hear about. As well, many of these Preachers pastor some of the largest Churches in the land. Also, there are untold thousands of Preachers who fall into this category, but which are known only to themselves. Of course, Satan makes Preachers special targets, but the laity falls into the same category also.

This of which the Holy Spirit spoke through Paul, pertains to everyone, and not just one certain segment of Christian society.

In fact, even as I dictate these words, there are untold numbers of Christians, both of Preachers and the laity, who are fighting a battle in their own lives. In fact, it is a battle they are losing. And it concerns this very problem as mentioned by Paul, in one way or the other.

NOTES

Now here is what I want the Reader to understand:

As it regards the far greater majority of these people, irrespective of whether they are Preachers or otherwise, this thing happening to them, is not what they want or desire. That doesn't make them any less guilty or responsible, but it is a fact that ought to be known.

This situation has developed within their lives, not necessarily because they dabbled in something in which they had no business doing, but simply because of an attack by Satan. Unfortunately, the Believer does not have the choice as to how Satan attacks him or her. Satan can choose any method which the Lord allows him to take (Job Chpts. 1-2).

Satan has been successful in these lives, and will succeed in destroying some of them, simply because they are attempting to oppose him in all the wrong way. Their Faith is not in the Cross of Christ but something else altogether, of which Satan takes full advantage. In fact, until they understand the Cross of Christ, and that this is where all victory is found, and that their Faith must always have the Cross as its object, they are going to continue to fail, even with the situation getting worse and worse. It doesn't matter what else they do, what other tactics they may try, what other methods they may choose, or how much they exert their willpower, they are going to fail. In fact, it doesn't really matter how many times that you as a Believer fight and win, after a while you are going to fight and lose. It is just that simple!

The secret is in not having to fight at all, with the situation totally being taken away as if it never existed. This can be done by the Holy Spirit, and in fact will be done by the Holy Spirit, if the Believer will put his Faith in the Cross of Christ, understanding that it is there, where all victories were won, and, consequently, all victories are His — all by Faith.

As I dictate these notes, I have just left our morning prayer meeting. Just before going to prayer, we were discussing this very thing. One of the men present who has just begun to hear the teaching on the Cross, made the statement, which I have tried to address in one way or the other.

*"If a person will stay in prayer, and keep his mind on the Lord, and study the Word constantly, he will have victory,"* he said!

My answer to him was in this vein:

While those things mentioned are very Scriptural and very right and very helpful in their own way, no, the victory for which one seeks, is not found in that manner. If we think it is, we have turned these very valuable privileges into *"works,"* which God can never honor.

Total and complete victory is found exclusively in what Jesus did at the Cross, and our Faith in that. When I say total and complete Faith in that, I mean just that. Works in any fashion, even good things, are not to be added. If we do, we only seek in frustrating the Grace of God (Gal. 2:20-21).

The simple Gospel is simple Faith in the great work carried out by Christ on the Cross. When this is done, and done in totality, the Holy Spirit will then do great and mighty things for us, guaranteeing the victory for which we seek.

These things I've said in no way are meant to demean the great privileges of prayer and fasting, etc., of which we have previously mentioned. In fact, we have two prayer meetings a day here at the Ministry, with the exception of Service times and Saturday mornings. So from that, I would surely think that the Reader understands how much value we place on the privilege of prayer. But again I emphasize, if we try to use this, thinking that it brings us victory, we are then replacing that which Christ has done at the Cross with our own efforts. And irrespective as to how good those efforts may be in their own way and right, we then have turned them into works, which nullifies this of which Christ has done.

It is Faith in the Cross, and Faith alone in that Finished Work, which guarantees us total and complete victory. Nothing else is needed, because to be sure, what Jesus did there, is enough and then some.

(4) "THAT EVERY ONE OF YOU SHOULD KNOW HOW TO POSSESS HIS VESSEL IN SANCTIFICATION AND HONOUR;"

The meaning of the word *"vessel"* here is the key to this particular Scripture. The Greek word which Paul used, could refer to a person's own body, or to a wife, whom a man is privileged to possess in marriage relationship.

NOTES

From Verse 4, I feel that Paul is speaking here of the physical body, referred to as *"his vessel."*

HIS VESSEL

The phrase, *"That every one of you should know how to possess his vessel,"* pertains, as stated, to the physical body. Man is created spirit, soul, and body, with the weakest of this being the body.

Inasmuch as it is weak, due to the Fall, the physical body is used by Satan in all manner of moral uncleanliness. As a result of this, many people have thought that the physical body is wicked or at least unclean; however, the Bible teaches that the physical body is *"neutral,"* therefore, capable of being used also in the realm of Righteousness. Hence, Paul said, *"Let not sin therefore reign in your mortal body."*

He also said, *"Neither yield ye your members as instruments of unrighteousness unto sin: but yield yourselves unto God, as those that are alive from the dead* (raised with Christ in newness of life), *and your members* (eyes, tongue, hands, etc.) *as instruments of Righteousness unto God"* (Rom. 6:12-13).

If the physical body wasn't neutral, it would not be possible to *"yield"* it to anything. No, it's not the physical body that's at fault. The body is actually just a shell or tent, for the soul and the spirit.

As well, it must be realized that the New Testament in no wise adopts the scheme of good-soul vs. evil-body, as some authorities have proposed. In the New Testament the soul is not necessarily good or in antagonism to the body (II Pet. 2:8 in contrast to II Pet. 2:14). The soul like the body is justified through the imputation of Christ's Righteousness, by the new birth, at least for those who are saved (I Pet. 1:22). Actually, the Bible does not separate the spirit, soul, and body as it regards sin. In other words, sin equally affects the spirit, soul, and body, even as Chapter 5, Verse 23 of this Epistle proclaims.

Some have claimed that when a Christian sins, it is only his body that sins and not his soul and spirit. Others have stated that it is the soul and body which sin, but not the spirit.

The Bible doesn't teach any such thing. Sin affects the entirety of the human being, spirit, soul and body, irrespective as to whether the person is a Believer or not!

## THE ORIGIN OF SIN IN THE HUMAN HEART

When we say *"the origin of sin,"* we are not speaking of the beginning of sin, which no doubt began with Satan in eternity past, but rather, as it regards the human being and the fact of sinning.

To which we've already alluded, some have claimed that sin originates in the physical body, but it doesn't. As stated, the physical body is neutral, able to be swung either way.

Jesus said, *"For out of the heart proceed evil thoughts, murders, adulteries, fornications, thefts, false witness, blasphemies"* (Mat. 15:19).

When Jesus mentioned the heart, He was not talking about the physical organ in one's body, but rather the seat of one's being. He was actually speaking of the soul and the spirit, which combined together form the seat of sin or Righteousness, with Jesus describing it as *"the heart of the matter."*

The Bible says, *"The soul that sinneth it shall die,"* proving that the soul can and does sin (Ezek. 18:4).

Paul said, *"Having therefore these Promises, dearly beloved, let us cleanse ourselves from all filthiness of the flesh and spirit, perfecting holiness in the fear of God"* (II Cor. 7:1). This tells us of course, that the spirit of man as well can sin, and can even be *"filthy."*

The will of man originates the thought of sin, which is actually in the spirit of man, for the spirit of man is the part of man which among other things, *"knows."* Paul also said, *"For what man knoweth the things of a man, save the spirit of man which is in him?"* (I Cor. 2:11). As stated, this Passage defines the human spirit as that part of man which knows — *"the intellect, mind, and will."*

The moment the thought of sin originates in the spirit of man, generated by the will, the soul is also activated in this capacity. However, the Reader must understand that man *"is a soul,"* while he *"has a spirit."* They are two different things, but yet are indivisible, departing from the human body only at death.

NOTES

The spirit of man is that which corresponds with the spirit world, whether with Satan and demon spirits, or the Lord and the Holy Spirit.

The spirit of man, is the Breath of God, which gives life to the soul, hence the Scripture saying, *"And the Lord God formed man of the dust of the ground, and breathed into his nostrils the breath of life* (the spirit of man from God)*; and man became a living soul"* (Gen. 2:7).

The word *"living"* pertains here to far more than mere physical life. It refers to the Life of God. At the Fall, man lost this Spiritual Life, and is now *"dead while he lives"* (I Tim. 5:6).

Once the thought of the sin originates in the spirit and the soul, the soul then seeks to carry out the act through the physical body. As stated, the spirit of man is that which deals with the spirit world, while the soul deals with self through the physical body. The soul and the spirit through the physical body, deal with the world.

As we've already stated, many times the act of sin will not be carried out, because the person knows it's wrong to do the thing, whatever it might be, or else the person does want to do whatever it is, but fears the consequences, etc. Considering how sin operates, to assuage the problem God has to deal with the human heart, in other words, the very seat or origin of sin in the human being. Psychology, being able to only deal with externals, as should be obvious, can effect no positive result.

## PROPERLY ADDRESSING SIN

The mere fact of not carrying out the act of sin, while being totally acceptable with the world, is not at all acceptable with God. In fact, all the world can do is to try to stop the act, having no power at all to deal with the source. They can succeed only in a very limited way.

It's like a dog who has a habit of biting people. One can stop this problem by putting a muzzle on a dog; nevertheless, he is still a *"biter,"* restrained only by the muzzle. That's the best the world can do!

The Lord doesn't muzzle people, but continuing to speak in the same vein, He goes to the very heart of the problem and takes away the desire to bite. In other words, he effectively deals with sin in the heart and life of the Believer.

How does He deal with sin?

Actually, it is not a present tense situation, but rather one of *"past tense."* The Lord has already dealt with the sin problem, and did it at the Cross. In fact, all sin, past, present, and future, was dealt with in totality, meaning He paid the price for this monstrous crime of man against God, which removed the penalty which is death, i.e., *"spiritual death."* He did it by addressing the matter in the only way it could be addressed, by physically dying on the Cross, which atoned for all sin.

Consequently, the entirety of the matter of sin has been dealt with in totality, with nothing remaining to be done, which means that sin will not have dominion over the Believer (Rom. 6:14). And when the Lord gives victory over sin, He gives it over all sin and in totality. In other words, and as stated, He does not muzzle the individual, but rather removes even the desire, which means that the Believer is free to live a holy life. And once again, we are speaking of the dominion of sin.

No! The Bible does not teach sinless perfection, but rather the breaking of sin's dominion. In fact, the Believer can still sin, and in fact definitely will sin, if he does not avail himself the privilege of God's prescribed order of victory.

## GOD'S PRESCRIBED ORDER OF VICTORY

In brief, and which we have already addressed several times, the following is God's prescribed order:

1. All victory, all power, all overcoming grace, in fact the Grace of God in totality, all and without exception, comes through the Cross of Christ (Rom. 6:2-6).

2. Understanding this, the Believer must without fail, and even on a daily basis (Lk. 9:23-24), place his Faith in the Finished Work of Christ, i.e., *"the Cross."* Placing one's Faith there, means that one believes that Jesus paid it all here, and that everything that is needed is found in this great Finished Work. Consequently, one's Faith must not leave this of which we speak.

3. Upon doing this, the Holy Spirit will then work mightily on behalf of the Believer, doing great things, in fact whatever is needed. The Holy Spirit is the One, Who guarantees all the benefits of what Christ did at the Cross and in His Resurrection. However, we cannot have His help, if we do not evidence Faith in the Cross of Christ. The two, Faith in the Cross, and His Help, go hand in hand.

When one does this, and continues to do this, even on a daily basis, the sin problem is dealt with so effectively, that even the desire is gone. So, as stated, it is not a matter of muzzling one, or trying to stop a person from doing certain things, but rather dealing with the very heart of the problem, removing in totality its power. And to be sure, and even as every human being in this world can testify, sin is a powerful factor. That's the reason it took the Death of Christ on the Cross to address this horrible problem.

This is the only manner in which one can *"possess his vessel,"* i.e., *"walk in sanctification regarding the physical body."* It is all in Jesus and what He did at the Cross, and our Faith in that great, Finished Work.

## SANCTIFICATION AND HONOR

The phrase, *"In Sanctification and honor,"* refers to the physical body being made and kept morally clean. In fact, the physical body is described by Paul as *"the Temple of God,"* in which the *"Spirit of God dwells."* Of course, the Spirit of God occupies our spirit and soul also (I Cor. 3:16).

Due to the fact, that our bodies are temples of the Holy Spirit, they are to be treated *"with honor,"* which suggests the resulting reverence for the body, rather than in prostitution of its faculties and appetites. It is lifted up in the way to purity and to the fulfilling of the *"Will of God."*

A separated and holy life is God's norm for all Believers, whether they lived in the First Century or now in the Twenty-first. And this involves not only a resolute and conscious separation from sin in the abstract sense of the word, but also from sin in all of its concrete and essential forms (I Pet. 4:1-4). Jesus didn't die to save us in sin, but rather from sin.

This principle of separation must govern all the relationships of life, for these, too, can compromise our Christian Testimony and hinder our service for God (II Cor. 6:14-18).

NOTES

Such separation from all evil, and such entire dedication to God, which comprises Sanctification — nothing less — represents the Will of God for His people. God is absolutely holy and He can be satisfied with nothing less than a moral likeness in us that corresponds in kind to His Own Holy Nature.

The Will of God is admittedly *"good and perfect"* (Rom. 12:2), and must of necessity cover every department of the Christian life, and thus become the governing principle in every action and in every relationship. As we shall see in the next Chapter, the entire man — spirit, soul, and body — is to be *"Sanctified wholly,"* hence, every relationship of life, both natural and legal, must measurably manifest the spirit of Jesus Christ.

(5) "NOT IN THE LUST OF CONCUPISCENCE, EVEN AS THE GENTILES WHICH KNOW NOT GOD:"

The Gentiles, unlike the Jews, had no inkling of the Law of Moses or Christian practice; therefore, they know nothing of this holy and honorable behavior. Their guiding principle is *"passionate lust"* because they *"do not know God."*

Such reprehensible behavior is a consequence of their refusal to respond to God's Revelation of Himself (Rom. 1:18-32).

*"Who do not know God"* is a familiar expression of Paul's for the Gentile world (Ps. 79:6; Jer. 10:25; Gal. 4:8; II Thess. 1:8).

Once removed from that realm of spiritual ignorance and sin, the Believer is obligated to maintain much higher standards, and in fact, told how to maintain those higher standards (Rom. 6:2-6; 8:1-11).

## CONCUPISCENCE

The phrase, *"Not in the lust of concupiscence,"* reveals the very spirit in which those without God function and operate.

*"Concupiscence"* in the Greek is *"epithumia,"* and means *"a longing for that which is forbidden."* The idea is, that the physical body of the Believer is not to long for that which is unholy, which in fact, characterizes the ungodly.

Actually, the question should be asked, as to why a Christian would lust for anything ungodly, etc.?

NOTES

In the true sense of the word, a Christian doesn't long or lust for that which is ungodly, for the simple reason that the Divine Nature now dwells within him, which totally and completely changes the desires of the Believer. This is what is meant by a Believer being *"a new creature, with old things passing away, and with all things becoming new"* (II Cor. 5:17). And yet we know there is a danger here, or the Holy Spirit through Paul would not have broached the subject.

The idea is this:

If the Believer tries to function outside of Faith in the Cross, whether through ignorance or rebellion against God, failure in some manner is going to result, and we speak of moral failure. It may not be one of the vices as Paul mentions here, although that is prevalent and extremely so, but it will be a moral failure in some way, i.e., *"lying, stealing, self-will, self-righteousness,"* etc.

The Believer had better understand that, in fact, be very narrow in his thinking concerning this all-important Truth. Outside of the Cross there is no victory, irrespective as to who the person is, what the person is, or where the person is.

Whenever the Believer fails, the sin nature which has lain dormant, now springs to life. Operating outside of the Cross, the Holy Spirit will not help the individual, and the result is going to be sin domination, i.e., *"the lust of concupiscence."*

In reading this which Paul says, or rather the Holy Spirit says through Paul, one wonders how in the world that a Believer could be involved in such ungodly attitudes and direction, i.e., *"lusts of concupiscence"*? It happens the way I've just stated, and in fact, the problem is pandemic.

The Church has had so little teaching on the Cross in the last several decades, that it has absolutely little or no knowledge as to how to walk in victory before the Lord. Consequently, these problems rage within the Church, and of every description.

## WHAT POSITION DOES THE CHURCH TAKE?

Not knowing what causes the problem, and not having any solution for the problem, but refusing to admit such, the Church goes off in all types of directions, all wrong directions I might quickly add!

Much of the time, instead of admitting that something is wrong, and I speak of something being wrong with our thinking, the Church takes an even harder and harder position, resorting to punishment, banishment, all designed to make it look like it is hard on sin, etc. The Truth is this:

Christians, whether so-called Religious Leaders or not, who treat unkindly, and in fact, very unkindly, those who have failed, and especially Preachers, only show how guilty they are themselves. Consequently, being guilty of whatever, they somehow think that their hard-nosed attitude toward others who have been *"caught,"* somehow atones for their own terrible failures.

No, I'm not saying that every single Religious Leader who conducts himself accordingly, is hiding some sort of secret sin. Not at all! However, if the Truth be known, many are! But irrespective, by working outside of the Cross, which most of the Church is presently doing, constitutes the very direction of sin. Paul plainly said, *"For whatsoever is not of faith is sin"* (Rom. 14:23).

This speaks of *"The Faith,"* and is referring to the Finished Work of Christ. It means that anyone, who is not functioning entirely in that Finished Work, is following a sinful course, even by their very direction, whether they commit certain acts of sin or not.

In this case what you have is *"sinful men trying to punish sinful men!"* Anyway, punishment is totally unscriptural!

Jesus was punished severely on the Cross, suffering the punishment for sin in our place, and anyone who thinks that Believers should be punished further, is saying that Jesus wasn't punished enough, and more punishment needs to be added. I would trust that the Reader can see the absolute blasphemy of such action.

It's not punishment that's called for, but rather proper, Scriptural instruction as to how victory is to be found (Gal. 6:1).

## SCRIPTURAL IGNORANCE

In fact, most Christians, whether Preachers or otherwise, who fail, do not do so because of desire for such on their part, but rather because of not knowing how to function in the Cross of Christ. To be sure, an unholy desire has developed within their hearts and lives, but it has not come about through a willful direction of dabbling with sin, etc. It has come about in most Christians, simply because of the reasons I have said, which refers to their lack of Scriptural knowledge as it regards God's prescribed order of victory.

These particular people do not need punishment, or being ostracized, banished, or some such foolishness, but rather for someone to simply tell them the way of the Cross (Rom. Chpt. 6). In fact, to ladle punishment on top of the tremendous trauma the individual is already experiencing, is cruelty almost beyond compare. In fact, the Religious Leaders who inflict punishment on such individuals, are committing a far graver sin, than the sin for which the poor individual is being punished.

However, I personally believe that many, if not most, Religious Leaders no longer believe in the efficacy (sufficiency) of the Finished Work of Christ. I think if they did believe in this all-important Finished Work, they wouldn't recommend humanistic psychology. Any Preachers who would recommend such a thing, and especially those who conclude themselves to be spiritual leaders, can be concluded as nothing less than operating in unbelief. In other words, they simply do not believe that what Jesus did at the Cross, and one's Faith in that great Sacrifice, will bring positive results.

## THE QUESTION OF SANCTIFICATION

Sanctification, which by now is overly obvious, is the topic of discussion here. That refers to one's Godly, holy life, or else the lack thereof. As one of my associates said, and which I quoted some pages back, *"Most of Christendom,"* he said, *"believes in Salvation by Faith, but Sanctification by self."* He is exactly right!

The great Work that Christ carried out on the Cross, is a very simple work. It's not difficult at all to understand, and yet at the same time, it is extremely difficult. And no, I'm not contradicting myself.

The idea is, once the Holy Spirit reveals this to you, it then becomes very clear, plain

NOTES

and simple; however, otherwise, it is not so simple at all!

The problem is *"the flesh."* And what do we mean by that?

We fail to understand that religious flesh, and by that we speak of our own efforts, abilities, machinations, etc., is just as lacking in capability as nonreligious flesh.

And what do we mean by religious flesh?

Paul used the word *"flesh,"* quite often, and especially in Romans, Chapter 8. In this case, it is referring to our own personal ability or strength. The Holy Spirit through the Apostle said, *"So then they that are in the flesh cannot please God"* (Rom. 8:8).

In fact, in Romans, Chapter 8 Paul is speaking of Believers attempting to sanctify themselves by their own efforts, or rather trying to *"help"* the Holy Spirit in this all-important work. He labels this as *"flesh,"* which God cannot abide. And of course here, it is *"religious flesh."*

There is really no difference in *"secular flesh"* than *"religious flesh"*; however, it is hard for the Believer to see that. Let me explain:

Some days ago, as I dictate these notes, several very rich businessmen in the nation contributed large sums of money to charity, etc. I do not judge them as to their reason for giving this money, but most people do such, thinking it's helping them in some way. As is obvious, we are speaking of unbelievers. If they believe there is a God, they think this buys them something with Him, etc. If they don't believe there is a God, their attitude more than likely is, *"Whatever is out there after death, this which I've done will help in some way,"* or thoughts to that effect. In fact, almost all unredeemed people, function somewhat on what I refer to as the *"Brownie point system."* In other words, they measure their so-called good deeds up beside their bad deeds. In their minds, if the good deeds outweigh the bad, and they always do, that is their Salvation. As stated, that is *"secular flesh."*

The principle is the same with Christians, although now it is religious flesh.

As the unredeemed attempt to purchase something with God by their good deeds, we Christians try to attain something from the Lord, by our efforts. As a Christian we

NOTES

instinctively know that we should draw closer to the Lord. So how do we do that?

To draw closer to Him, our mind goes to particular things we can do, such as establishing a prayer life, reading so many Chapters in the Bible each day, being faithful to Church, being faithful with our giving and our witnessing, etc.

Now these things I've mentioned are very good, and in fact, should be the staple of every Believer; however, if we do them, or anything else for that matter that we could think of, thinking that it earns us something with the Lord, or that it will sanctify us, or make us holy, this it will not do. It then becomes *"religious flesh,"* which is extremely offensive to God.

## WHY IS THE FLESH OFFENSIVE TO THE LORD?

In reality, these things which I have labeled *"religious flesh,"* within themselves are not at all displeasing to Him, but actually the opposite. He delights in His Children seeking His Face, as should be obvious. In fact, no one can have a proper relationship with Christ outside of a proper prayer life. The same could go for all of these other things we've mentioned, plus many we have not mentioned.

So what is wrong?

If we do these things in this fashion, and I speak of trying to make ourselves holy, or acceptable to God, or approved by God, on the basis of these things we do, they present themselves wrong in two ways:

1. In the first place, it is not possible for Believers to make themselves holy or to sanctify themselves in this fashion. If one could do such, Jesus would not have had to come down here and die on the Cross. So, by the doing of such things, if we think they accrue us something with the Lord, we must be quick to learn they don't! In fact, the very doing of them in this fashion, and notice I said *"in this fashion,"* constitutes *"works,"* which God cannot accept, or *"flesh"* which always displeases Him.

2. We can only be holy, i.e., *"Sanctified,"* by trusting in what Christ did at the Cross, which alone can make us holy in the sight of God. In other words, to be sanctified, and that means to function in a sanctified life,

all the Believer has to do, and in fact, all the Believer can do, is to simply have Faith in what Christ did at the Cross on our behalf. Then you are trusting solely in what Jesus has done, and not at all in what you are doing, which is what the Lord demands.

The Believer has the same problem understanding his situation, as the unredeemed do in understanding theirs. And of what situation do we speak?

Man's problem is far worse than he realizes. That means that unredeemed man is much more lost than he could ever begin to comprehend. In fact, he is *"spiritually dead,"* and dead means *"dead!"* That means there is no Spiritual Life there whatsoever in any capacity. So, in order for any unbeliever to be saved, there has to be a monumental work which causes several things to be brought to pass, which were all done by Christ at the Cross. If the unsaved individual believes in what Christ has done for him, he will then be saved (Jn. 3:16; Rom. 10:9-10, 13; Eph. 2:8-9).

The things I've just said are understandable by most Christians; however, now that we are Believers, meaning that we are now new creations in Christ Jesus, we somehow think that due to this newfound position which we now hold in Christ, that we can effect some things for ourselves. We probably wouldn't label it that way, but in our heart that's exactly what is happening. We tend to think these things we do which I've just mentioned, which are very good in their own right, somehow draw us closer to God, etc. However, as good as they are in their own right, they do not draw us closer to God, and in no way make us acceptable with God.

Once again, we come back to this situation of sin, which the Christian has to face.

## THE CHRISTIAN AND SIN

As should be obvious, in this Epistle to the Thessalonians, Paul is speaking to Believers. And to be sure, he warns them (and us) of sin and all of its consequences. Unfortunately, many Believers have been taught, that inasmuch as they are now a Christian, that sin is no longer a problem. While many admit, that something might crop up once in a while, for the most part, sin is no problem, they say.

NOTES

Many of these Preachers, especially in the Charismatic community, teach that Preachers should not ever even preach about sin, etc. They claim that this causes a *"sin consciousness,"* and will cause Christians to get involved in sin in some way.

That is strange! If that is in fact true, I wonder why someone did not tell Paul? Is him telling Christians here not to get mixed up in any type of immorality going to create a *"sin consciousness"* in them?

To be frank, such teaching is silly!

The Truth is, the problem that every Christian faces in one way or the other, is sin. That's what *"Sanctification"* is all about. In fact, if one will follow Paul closely, one will find that he is the great Teacher and Preacher of Grace. But at the same time, he also warns strongly of the problems of sin in the life of the Christian. And he does so of course, for a reason (Rom. 13:9-14; Gal. 5:19-21, etc.).

The Holy Spirit mentioned these things, these works of the flesh, through Paul, simply because every Christian faces these problems in one way or the other. Just because you are a Believer, doesn't mean that Satan ceases all activity against you. In fact, this conflict is of such nature, such strength, and power, that the Holy Spirit refers to it as *"war"* (II Cor. 10:3; I Tim. 1:18; James 4:1; I Pet. 2:11). So, that should tell us we are not dealing here with just a minor thing, which happens only once in a while, and if we don't mention it, as many Charismatic Preachers claim, then it will go away. I am sorry, but that is not the case!

As a Believer, these things are going to war against you, and denial does not lessen their activity whatsoever. Second, the only way that you are going to have victory, to walk as you ought to walk before the Lord, is to completely place your trust in what Christ did at the Cross, and in nothing else, not even your own good works. As I've said previously, *true Faith in Christ, which refers to Faith in the Cross, will produce an abundance of good works, which is one of the signs of true Faith; however, good works will never produce Faith.* So, our problem is, we get it backwards.

In one way or the other, your problem as a Christian is sin. The Holy Spirit has shown us a way to have victory over sin, and in every capacity. That way is the Way of the Cross. We are to have Faith in what Jesus did there, and Faith in that exclusively. As well, our Faith is to remain in this Finished Work of Christ all the days of our life, or until the Trump sounds. Then the Holy Spirit will help us, work for us, do great and mighty things for us, in other words, do for us what we cannot do for ourselves, which refers to the Sanctification process.

## GREAT ATTACKS AGAINST THE CROSS

If the Church is not a Cross Church, then it is not in the Will of God, and will suffer commiserate consequences. If the religious Denomination is not a Cross Denomination, it will suffer like consequences, and irrespective as to how large or rich it might be. If the Believer doesn't have his Faith anchored squarely in the Cross of Christ, understanding that this is where all his blessings are derived, then that Christian is going to have problems.

There is only one way for all of this, only one Source of Victory, only one means and method of Salvation, only one strength, and that is the great Sacrifice of Christ. That and that alone, must be the base, the foundation, the very citadel of all that we do, have, and are in Christ. If the Cross is not our foundation, then we have built on sand, and to be sure the storms are coming, and great will be the wreckage of our efforts. It is only the house that is built on the rock that will stand, and that rock is Christ.

And who is Christ?

Of course, we know that He is God; nevertheless, whenever we read the Name *"Jesus,"* or *"Christ,"* or *"Saviour,"* or *"Lord Jesus,"* etc., we must always connect those names with the Cross and the Resurrection. If we don't, we miss the whole point of the Word of God altogether.

The attacks against the Cross presently, which I think are going to increase regarding intensity, come in two ways. One way is subtle and the other way is blatant and open.

The subtle way concerns the departure of the Church from the Cross to humanistic psychology. It is subtle because it is not a frontal attack upon the Cross, but rather a somewhat ignoring of its great capacities. One cannot entertain humanistic psychology and the Cross of Christ at the same time. The two are totally opposite of each other, and in fact, bitterly opposed to each other. One is man's way, and the other is God's Way.

Unfortunately, not only have all the Modernist Denominations gone in this direction, the direction of humanistic psychology, but as well, the Fundamentalists have also, at least for the most part. (Fundamentalists are those who claim to believe all the Bible.)

Unfortunately, most of the laity in the Churches do not understand the terrible implications of these things of which I speak. Most of them will never seek the services of a Psychologist, so it hardly affects them, or so they think!

Whenever the Leadership of anything goes in a certain direction, and I'm speaking of a doctrinal direction, then of necessity, those who are associated with that particular effort, whatever it might be, must go along as well whether they desire to do so or not, that is if they remain in that particular Denomination, etc. They may claim they are not in favor of such and have no part of such; however, if the Leadership is going in that direction, whatever that direction might be, they have no alternative but to follow suit. And regrettably, that's where most of the Leadership of most Religious Denominations have gone — the psychological route, which by its very definition, disavows the Finished Work of Christ. As stated, one cannot have it both ways. Either Jesus did, and we should trust Him, or He didn't, and we should seek the help of the likes of Freud, Maslow, Rogers, and Skinner, etc.

As Joshua of old, *"As for me and my house, we will serve the Lord"* (Josh. 24:15).

The other mode of attack is blatant and obvious, and I speak of many in the so-called *"Faith community."* I am certainly not saying that all fall into this category; however, many of their so-called bright lights definitely do.

They openly repudiate the Cross, claiming that it was the greatest defeat recorded in the Bible. Consequently, Believers should not have anything to do with the Cross in any fashion. As a result, they will not sing songs about the Blood in their Churches, or the Cross, or anything of that nature. To be

NOTES

NOTES

frank, such thinking is heresy pure and simple. In fact, it borders on rank blasphemy.

It shows a complete misunderstanding of the Plan of God, and to be sure, those who follow in this train will come to no conclusion but spiritual wreckage. As well, this same element functions in the *"money gospel,"* which is a travesty regarding the Word of God.

However, I personally feel that due to the fact that the Church is entering into the great apostasy, which will be the last apostasy before the Antichrist, that the attacks upon the Cross of Christ are going to intensify. Actually, I personally believe that the Cross of Christ is going to be the dividing line. I think the Holy Spirit is going to make it so clear, that one will have to come down on one side or the other. In Truth, that's really not something new. It has actually always been that way. But inasmuch, as these are the last of the last days, this of which I speak is going to intensify.

There was a day that people pretty well knew what was taught in respective Churches according to the name on the door. No longer! The criteria is no longer the name on the door, or the Denominational affiliation, but rather, *"The Cross of Christ."*

THOSE WHO KNOW NOT GOD

The phrase, *"Even as the Gentiles which know not God,"* finds the Apostle speaking of the Gentile world which walked in darkness before the advent of the Gospel.

Beginning with Abraham and those who were raised up from his loins and Sarah's womb, and we speak of the Jews, they alone had the Word of God. God gave a Covenant to Abraham, and followed that Covenant with the Covenant of the Law given to Moses, which in effect meant that the Jews were the illumination of the world, spiritually speaking. All, other than the Jews, had no knowledge of God whatsoever, and in fact were idol-worshipers, etc. Paul would later speak of them as *"aliens from the commonwealth of Israel, and strangers of the Covenants of Promise, having no hope, and without God in the world"* (Eph. 2:12).

But then the Holy Spirit through him said, *"But now* (in this time of the Gospel) *in Christ Jesus ye who sometimes were far off are made nigh by the Blood of Christ"* (Eph. 2:13).

The idea is, the Apostle is pointing out this fact to the Gentile Christians, which made up most of the Church at Thessalonica, that they didn't want to go back into the ways they had once known, the ways of darkness and bondage. The Gospel of Jesus Christ had now come to them, which was a blessing unparalleled, and they must take advantage of these great Blessings from the Lord, and not at all slip back into the old ways.

In the Old Testament, the world in the Eyes of God, Whose Eyes Alone matter, was divided into two parts: *"Jews and Gentiles."* Of course, as stated, the Jews alone knew God, at least those among them who did, with the Gentiles not knowing God at all.

Upon the advent of Christ, which pertains to His Crucifixion and Resurrection, that particular distinction was erased. In other words, in the Eyes of God the world is no longer divided between those of Israel and the Gentiles. The dividing line now comes between His Body, the Church, made up of all people, both Jews and Gentiles, who will come to Him, and those who do not know Him. In other words, the entirety of the world in the Eyes of God is divided up into two groups, *"the saved and the unsaved"* (Jn. 3:3).

We as followers of Christ are to be a distinct people. We are in the world, but we are to never be of the world. We do not march to its drum, or sing to its tune. We are followers of Christ, which means that we have left the culture of the world and entered into the culture of Christ, i.e., *"the Word of God."* People either *"know God,"* or they *"don't know God!"* There is no middle ground.

WHAT DOES IT MEAN TO KNOW GOD?

Paul said, *"They profess that they know God; but in works they deny Him, being abominable, and disobedient, and unto every good work reprobate"* (Titus 1:16).

Paul was speaking here of his own people, the Jews. He spoke of *"Jewish fables, and commandments of men, that turn from the Truth"* (Titus 1:14).

One can only know God through Jesus Christ. One cannot know God through the Church, through good works, through religious

NOTES

institutions, etc., only through Christ (Jn. 10:1, 7-9). Jesus plainly said, *"I am the Way, the Truth, and the Life: no man cometh unto the Father, but by Me"* (Jn. 14:6).

What did He mean by *"the Way, the Truth, and the Life"*?

The *"Way"* speaks of what He did at the Cross. He there purchased man's Redemption by the giving of His Own Life. Man must believe that in order to be saved (Jn. 3:16).

The *"Truth"* of which He speaks, is what He is. This means that everything He is, is Truth.

But its greatest reference is to what He did at the Cross. This embodies the Truth, the reason for which He came, the purpose which He carried out, the Salvation and Redemption of lost humanity, by the shedding of His Life's Blood on the Cross. If one doesn't believe this *"Truth"* one cannot be saved!

As well, all *"Life"* which comes to mankind, comes to him as a result of what Christ did at the Cross. Life could not be imparted other than by that means. If we think it can, we misread the Word of God and actually blaspheme.

Ironically enough, all life springs from the Death He died, which of course, includes His Resurrection, through which we have *"newness of life"* (Rom. 6:2-6).

So, if one is to truly know God, one can only know Him through the Cross of Christ, which portrays His Finished Work.

(6) "THAT NO MAN GO BEYOND AND DEFRAUD HIS BROTHER IN ANY MATTER: BECAUSE THAT THE LORD IS THE AVENGER OF ALL SUCH, AS WE ALSO HAVE FOREWARNED YOU AND TESTIFIED."

Paul is speaking here of conduct between Christians. While the primary emphasis is on sexual misconduct, i.e., *"referring to adultery and fornication, etc."*; however, due to the very nature of what Paul is saying, the admonition must include everything as it regards dealings with a Brother in the Lord, or anyone for that matter. The Christian at all times is to provide everything above board, which speaks of it being clean, moral, righteous, honest, and truthful.

## THE DEFRAUDING OF ONE'S BROTHER

The phrase, *"That no man go beyond and defraud his Brother in any matter,"* as stated, refers first of all to sexual misconduct between Christians. Of course, such is sinful and wicked even with the unsaved, but from what Paul says here, the sin is greater if committed between Christians.

The illegitimate or intemperate satisfaction of sensual appetite remains an area of temptation in all healthy and normal Christians, but the unsanctified Christian is perilously vulnerable to such appeals.

There is a resurgent paganism of our own time with its smutty entertainment, pornographic literature, laxity in marriage vows, promiscuity, overall obsession with sex, and general permissiveness in sex relationships. In times like these the New Testament teaching on sexual purity is desperately needed, and the New Testament experience of Sanctification, with its full devotion to the Will of God, is the real answer.

Sexual purity, self-mastery, and self-discipline, seen as characteristics of the sanctified life, and which can only be handled at the Cross, are under discussion here. The marriage relationship and all relationships between the sexes are to be *"in honour."* As well, reverence and honor for the human body is particularly a Christian concept.

This means that Christian Holiness redeems marriage from the degraded level of those who know not God, who regard the body *"as an instrument for self-gratification."* All kinds of immorality and sexual looseness constitute wrongs against innocent people who are, or will become, involved.

This means that for a Christian man to have relations with a Christian woman outside of marriage is not just a trespass against God's Law, but is also a defrauding of some fellow Christian, whether the husband of such a wife, or if the woman is not married, against the man who eventually will take this woman as his own wife.

This is an especially heinous sin, because the one robbed is a spiritual relative of the robber. Paul does not allude to the other injustice, which is quite obvious. The woman herself is an object of cruel abuse in such a situation, but is not held guiltless.

## ANY MATTER

Even though the general thrust of this statement as given by Paul, and to which we have already alluded, is toward immorality between Christians, the admonition does not stop there. It includes any matter in any situation.

It is possible to defraud another Believer, by gossip as it refers to the sullying of his or her reputation, of taking advantage in money matters, of attempting to usurp his position, whatever that might be, etc. In fact, the list is long!

That is why Jesus plainly said, *"Therefore all things whatsoever ye would that men should do to you, do ye even so to them"* (Mat. 7:12).

*"Defraud"* in the Greek is *"pleonekteo,"* and means *"to over reach, to get an advantage, to be covetous, to make a gain."*

To look at business dealings for a moment, any Christian who would cheat another Christian, or anyone for that matter, for it's just as wrong to cheat an unbeliever as a Believer, and in any capacity, such action shows that the person is not trusting God, but has resorted to the ways of the world.

If we trust God to provide for us, it certainly would preclude any covetousness on our part, and especially the defrauding of others. If I'm trusting in God, I'm certainly not trusting in stealing, etc. If I'm trusting God, I'm certainly going to give to the Lord. If I'm trusting God, instead of taking from my Brother, I am rather going to give to him. So, as we shall see in the next phrase, to defraud a Brother in the Lord, is going to ultimately pull down judgment on one's own head.

## GOD, THE AVENGER

The phrase, *"Because that the Lord is the avenger of all such,"* presents the fact that the Judgment of God upon all impurity is sure and terrible, irrespective as to what society may or may not say. While reckoning in the fullest sense must await the final judgment (and this is likely the primary reference here), there is a recompense exacted upon the bodies and the emotional, moral, and spiritual natures of those who have indulged in immoral conduct. The moral Laws of God are written in the constitution of human nature, and the disregard of these Laws brings with it a vengeance which is sometimes dramatic, sometimes quiet and stealthy, but always certain (Rom. 1:24-32; Gal. 6:7-8; Eph. 5:5-6).

The heathen and of course, all their religions, had no system of ethics which forbade abominations of immorality. The Christian Faith contrary to these systems, not only discountenances these things, but forbids them on the most awful penalties. The Holy Spirit through the Apostle brings it out succinctly and even dogmatically, that one of His great works in the heart and life of the Believer, is to address all types of immorality, and in every capacity. As stated, the Christian Faith is the only system on Earth, which does such, and because all other systems are man-devised in totality, whereas the Christian Faith is propelled and motivated by the Spirit of God, which in fact is the only means by which purity can be approached and obtained.

## FOREWARNED

The phrase, *"As we also have forewarned you and testified,"* presents the possibility, that this could have been a besetting temptation for the Thessalonians. This seems to have been especially stressed by the Apostle, due to the fact that paganism involved every type of immorality, from which these Thessalonians had been brought.

As well, the very words *"forewarned"* and *"testified"* proclaim the fact that the Apostle was quick to name sins, thereby emphatically pointing out wrongdoing. If the Holy Spirit had this Preacher of Righteousness to set such a course at that time, it stands to reason that the problem being the same presently, even as it always has been, the approach to the problem should be the same also. Preachers should point out that which is wrong and in no uncertain terms.

Of course, that little goes with much of the modern positive gospel, so-called; nevertheless, this is what the Lord says do, and this is what should be done, that is if a Preacher of the Gospel is going to be faithful to his calling.

This certainly doesn't mean that such preaching should make up the entirety of the Message. It is obvious that it doesn't; however, *"warnings"* should be included in the Message.

What kind of watchman is it who will not warn of potential or even approaching danger?

NOTES

The very purpose of the watchman is to function in this respect, and to be sure, all God-called Preachers are *"Watchmen."*

To be sure, to preach the Gospel as it should be preached, and even as the Holy Spirit demands that it be preached, will always strike fire in some circles. That is a given! So, for the *"hail-fellow well met"* type of Preacher, this doesn't set well. Nevertheless, if a Preacher is to be true to his calling, that is if he is truly called of God, he must *"warn"* as well as *"proclaim!"*

(7) "FOR GOD HATH NOT CALLED US UNTO UNCLEANNESS, BUT UNTO HOLINESS."

The Child of God has been called from something: ungodliness, spiritual rebellion, immorality, uncleanness, anger, wrath, impurity, and pollution of every form; to something: Godliness, Holiness, Purity, Righteousness, and Honesty in every form.

THE CALL OF GOD

The phrase, *"For God hath not called us unto uncleanness,"* concerns every single Believer, and emphatically states, that the Grace of God is given to Believers not that one may continue in sin, but that one may gain victory over sin, and of every stripe and nature.

No one can read the Word of God with any degree of honesty, and even remotely come up with the idea that God saves in sin rather than *"from sin."* The very idea, the very thrust of the Gospel, is to bring about a change in the lives of all Believers. So, the very Call of God in all its power and glory, totally militates against all immorality, whether in thought, word, or deed, and any other type of wrongdoing for that matter.

God is the Creator of male and female, and the institution of marriage, and He has called men and women to this state, which militates against all premarital sex, or immorality of any nature.

While all sin is forbidden, and while all types of sin characterize the world and its system, still, it is immorality of every stripe which overflows society like a disgorging cesspool. The whole thrust of unredeemed men and women, which includes all entertainment, all business activity, in other words every face and facet of life, contain at least the general undertone of immorality of every stripe. While some few who do not know God may not loosely engage in such, still, their restraint is because of consequences, at least for the most part, and certainly not from Righteousness.

NOTES

In fact, every moral Standard laid down in the Word of God, which incidentally is totally and completely for the betterment of humanity, is lampooned and ridiculed by Hollywood, and in fact the entertainment industry as a whole, which has the most negative effect on the youth of this nation and the world. Actually, this generation has been raised on the fare of Music Television (MTV), which of course appeals to the youth, and openly lambastes every Standard held up by the Word of God. And then the powers that be, wonder as to why our public schools have become animal-crawling jungles, with in fact, these institutions becoming some of the most dangerous places for anyone to be! It is like the man with an arrow protruding from his head, wondering why he has a headache?

*"Uncleanness"* in the Greek is, *"akatharsia,"* and means *"impure, lewd, demonic, foul."*

HOLINESS

The phrase, *"But unto Holiness,"* presents the second part of this Call. God has called us from *"uncleanness,"* unto *"Holiness."*

In this brief but vivid contrast, Paul states the whole sweep of God's high purpose for Believers. It is nothing less than Holiness, the restoration to man of the moral image of God which has been effaced by sin.

The thought returns to that of Verse 3, and to *"the Will of God,"* which is here connected with that wonderful day in their (our) lives when in Mercy and Grace God called them (us) out of a life of sin into fellowship with Himself.

The Call was God's initiative; it was God's Love in action. The Call is purposeful, and the purpose is nothing less than *"the most thorough purity"* — Holiness of both heart and life.

Since the Call is mediated by the preaching of the Gospel, the Church can have no other Message than this.

*"Holiness"* in the Greek is *"hegiasmos,"* and is the same word translated *"Sanctification"*

in Verses 3 and 4. It means *"to be set apart exclusively unto God."*

The argument here is that for a Christian to fall short of a life of Holiness is for him to deny the Divine Purpose in saving him in the first place.

UNCLEANNESS, HOLINESS, AND THE CROSS

Paul doesn't mention the Cross in this Epistle; however, the undertones are there from the beginning. As we have stated, whenever Paul mentions *"Holiness, Faith, Righteousness,"* etc., he is at the same time speaking of the *"Cross,"* for the simple reason, that none of these things can come about in the heart and life of the Believer, without what Jesus did at the Cross, and our Faith in that. This is the undertone and even the open proclamation of the entirety of the New Covenant as given by Paul. By the time of the writing of the Epistles to the Corinthians, which was approximately five to eight years later, the Apostle strongly advocates the preaching of the Cross, and the living of the Cross, one might say (I Cor. 1:18, 21; 2:2).

Knowing that Revelation from God is progressive, in other words we don't get it all at one time, but is rather given to us in stages, is it possible that Paul understood more fully with time, the total rudiments of the New Covenant, which of course is all centered up in the Cross? I think the answer to that question could be according to the following:

When the New Covenant was given to Paul by none other than Jesus Christ Himself (Gal. 1:11-12), it was given to the Apostle in totality; however, I think it is safe to say that the Apostle did not understand all of it immediately, but with time that understanding became more and more pronounced. I think this is obvious in his Epistles.

The Holy Spirit will seldom anoint us to write, or preach, or teach that of which we do not have proper understanding. He uses what we have and then enlarges upon that, even as we go forward. While prophecy is the exception to that rule, which definitely divulges information at times of which the individual as the instrument doesn't always fully understand, still that is different. In fact, the entirety of the Bible is filled with prophetic utterances, with the one who gave the prophecy not at all understanding in totality, or even perhaps very little, of what was given. While they might have some grasp of what is being said, it is only in part.

NOTES

But still, that is totally different than the normal Preaching and Teaching of the Word. As stated, the Holy Spirit will seldom go beyond our grasp of understanding as He uses us to deliver Truth to the people. So, I think the Holy Spirit worked with Paul exactly as he does all Believers, helping him to learn more and more of this great New Covenant which was given to him, as it was gradually fleshed out.

A PERSONAL EXAMPLE

In 1997 the Lord began to give to me the Revelation of the Cross. To be sure, at the very moment of the Revelation, this Truth was so striking, so powerful, that it instantly had a marked effect on my life; however, the Holy Spirit from that day forward began to enlarge upon this Revelation, opening it up wider and wider, even as He has continued to do unto this very hour. In fact, I don't think that the Revelation will ever come to a conclusion, with the Holy Spirit continuing to expand this great Truth within my heart and life. In fact, it would have to be that way, inasmuch as it is impossible to exhaust the potential of the great Finished Work of Christ. So, what am I saying?

I am saying that by the time Paul founded the Church at Corinth, which was a little later than when he founded the Church at Thessalonica, that he knew much more about this which the Lord had given unto him, hence, the strong proclamation of the Cross in the Epistles to the Corinthians. The idea is not at all a different revelation, but rather a building upon that which has already been given. The point is this:

All *"uncleanness"* is laid aside according to one's Faith in the Cross of Christ; and, as well, Holiness is attained in the same manner.

THE METHOD BY WHICH ALL OF THIS IS ATTAINED

We Christians are told to do all type of spiritual things by Preachers, but very seldom told how to do these things. And if we are told, we are most of the time told that which is wrong.

In the last several decades, the great manner of receiving from God, of being what one ought to be in God, has been by the throughway of *"Faith."* On the surface, that seems right, because it is definitely Faith which is the instrument through which God works, and entirely. But yet, most of the teaching has been on how to receive from the Lord, instead of how to be what one ought to be in the Lord. These are two different things altogether!

While Faith definitely does play its part in things we receive from the Lord, it also is the primary ingredient respecting what we ought to be in the Lord, which to be frank, is the major thrust of the Holy Spirit.

However, the Faith which has been taught, has by and large been *"faith in faith."* And what do we mean by that?

The idea has been to just simply get more Faith, and according to one's level of Faith, accordingly they will receive various things. The major means has been to take particular Scriptures as Promises, which they definitely are in their own way, and then claim these Promises according to whatever wants or desires we might have.

Unfortunately, almost all the teaching on this subject has been in the realm of *"works,"* which refers to the individual doing certain things, thereby increasing his Faith, which then is the medium of success, etc.

All of that is totally wrong:

While there definitely is such a thing as weak Faith or strong Faith, still, the ingredient of Faith on its own, is not what the Bible teaches. To be frank, that is no different than the Eastern religions, or that which is used by the world, which in fact, uses faith constantly, but not Faith in God.

Whenever Faith is mentioned, at least in the context of the Word of God, it must always be understood that it is Faith in the Finished Work of Christ. In other words, it is centered up in that great Sacrifice, that great Work of the Lord, in fact, that *"Finished Work."* It is the *object of Faith* which is in view, and not necessarily the amount of Faith, so-called.

In almost every breath, the Word of God teaches that our Faith must be anchored squarely in the Finished Work of Christ, which alone has guaranteed all of these great benefits from God. In fact, as we have stated repeatedly, Genesis, Chapter 4 succinctly bears this out. The Sacrifice of the Lamb from the flock which typified the coming Christ and what He would do to redeem fallen humanity, proclaimed in glaring detail, the very means and manner of God's dealings with men, and our Faith in that means and manner, i.e., *"the Cross of Christ."*

The power of sin is strong. In fact, it is so strong, that man cannot even begin to hope to overcome its driving thrust, and I speak of mankind in general. The world keeps trying, but it keeps failing, as fail it must.

The Christian too often falls into the same trap. We think because we are saved and even Spirit-filled, that now we can be what we ought to be in Christ, devising our own machinations, whatever they might be. However, the Truth is, we can no more effect Holiness in our lives, which means victory over *"uncleanness,"* at least by our own devices, than the poor sinner can get saved without trusting in Christ. The requirement for the unsaved, at least in order to be saved, is to trust Christ. The requirement for the Believer to walk in victory, is to trust Christ. They are identical! However, what exactly does it mean to trust Christ?

NOTES

## WHAT THE BELIEVER MUST DO

1. The Believer must understand that sin is the great problem. It is not a lack of money, or a hundred and one other things we might name. It is sin. Satan will do all within his power to drag us down.

2. The Believer must realize as well, as to exactly how bad that sin actually is. It is so bad in fact, that even though God could bring worlds into existence by His very Word, He for all His Omnipotence, could not speak Redemption into existence. That should tell us something! If sin is that bad, and it definitely is, then we should understand how helpless we are in the face of this monster, at least helpless in our own capacities.

3. The Christian must understand, that as dependent as he was on Christ in order to be initially saved, he is still just as dependent on Christ in order to walk in victory over

all sin. Him being a Christian, although changing many things, does not for one iota change this dependency on Christ. The Believer must understand that and realize that in no uncertain terms.

4. When we say *"dependent on Christ,"* we are actually meaning that we are to be dependent on what He did for us at the Cross and in His Resurrection. The great danger of Believers is to understand Christ in another fashion. Everything comes through what was done at the Cross! That refers to all Salvation which provides for us Justification, Sanctification, Divine Healing, Reconciliation, Blessings of every nature, Financial Prosperity, in other words everything.

5. Understanding that, our Faith must be totally in what Christ did at the Cross and in His Resurrection. If it is Faith in any other manner, it is Faith which God will not recognize. And this is what has been wrong with most of the teaching on Faith in the last several decades. It has not been Faith in the Cross, but rather something else. And no matter how much that *"something else"* may seem to be right, it is not right, if it is not Faith which is squarely in the Cross of Christ.

## THE ROLE OF THE HOLY SPIRIT

The Christian can live this holy life, which means a departure from all that the world has, only by the power and help of the Holy Spirit. That is why Paul mentioned this fact in describing the *"Blessing of Abraham,"* which was and is *"Justification by Faith."* This all came *"through Jesus Christ,"* which refers to what He did at the Cross, in other words, the great *"Finished Work of Christ."*

Because of that and through that, the Apostle says that it was all done, *"That we might receive the Promise of the Spirit through Faith"* (Gal. 3:14).

Faith how? Faith in what?

It refers to Faith in what Jesus did at the Cross, and in no other manner.

The idea is, due to this great Work of Christ, the Holy Spirit can now come in to abide in the hearts and lives of Believers, which He definitely does at conversion, and also promises the great *"Spirit Baptism"* (Acts 2:4). In fact, this is the great difference between the Old Covenant and the New Covenant.

NOTES

Under the Old Covenant, and due to the fact that the sin debt had not yet been paid because Christ had not yet gone to the Cross, the Holy Spirit, while with all Believers, could not come into their hearts and lives to abide forever as He now does (Jn. 14:17).

Consequently, this left Believers then at a great disadvantage. While they definitely had some help by the Holy Spirit, they in no way had the help we now have, all due to what Christ did at the Cross.

So, there is no excuse whatsoever at present, for any Believer not departing from all *"uncleanness"* and being *"holy,"* that is to live a Holy and Righteous Life before the Lord. If we had to do such strictly on our own, even though Christians, such would be impossible; however, we don't have to do these things on our own, and in fact, the only real thing we are asked to do, is to have Faith in what Christ has already done. Then the Holy Spirit will work mightily and greatly on our behalf, but only if our Faith is properly placed (Rom. 6:2-6; 8:1-2, 11).

In fact, the Role of the Holy Spirit in our hearts and lives, is absolutely indispensable. The secret is, in knowing how to have all of the great things He can do. Unfortunately, many Believers, and especially Pentecostals and Charismatics, sort of think it's all automatic. To be frank, the non-Pentecostals, just about completely ignore the Holy Spirit altogether, but which most Pentecostals and Charismatics have an erroneous view of His Work.

None of His Work is automatic, but requires on the part of all Believers, Faith in the Cross of Christ.

While the Holy Spirit will always do within our lives what He can do; the fact is, He will not break the Law. And to be sure, the Finished Work of Christ is definitely a *"Law"* (Rom. 8:2).

If we function within that Law, which means to have Faith strictly in Christ and what He has done for us at the Cross and in His Resurrection, we are guaranteed of the all-powerful help of the Holy Spirit, which then gives us power over all the powers of sin, and brings us into the place of Holiness and Righteousness in Christ. That is His Way, and His only Way!

(8) "HE THEREFORE THAT DESPISETH, DESPISETH NOT MAN, BUT GOD, WHO HATH ALSO GIVEN UNTO US HIS HOLY SPIRIT."

Rejection of this which the Apostle states, is not a rejection of man, but rather of God; consequently, in understanding that, we should as well comprehend and grasp the fact as to how serious all of this actually is.

Emphatically the Apostle states, that the Lord has given us the Holy Spirit to help us be what we ought to be, even as we have just been explaining. So, as stated, there is no excuse!

### THE DESPISING OF GOD

The phrase, *"He therefore that despiseth, despiseth not man, but God,"* refers to the fact, that these things that Paul gives are not mere words out of his own mind, but actually that which has been given to him by the Holy Spirit. Consequently, it is the Word of God, and meant to be obeyed. If anyone takes lightly these words, or twists or perverts them in any manner, it is not the same as treating lightly the words of men, but is looked at by God as despising His Word, which is a serious offense indeed!

There are three types of sins which are directly against God. They are:

1. The murder of a fellow human being (Gen. 9:6), whether by the actual killing of the person, or trying to destroy their reputation by clandestine gossip.
2. Hindering or hurting the least Believer (Mat. 18:10; 25:31-46; Lk. 10:16; I Thess. 4:8).
3. The rejection of Jesus Christ and what He has done for us at the Cross (Jn. 12:48).

### THE HOLY SPIRIT

The phrase, *"But God, Who hath also given unto us His Holy Spirit,"* pertains to two things:

1. This which Paul is giving the Thessalonians, and all other Believers as well, is a Revelation from God. The Lord had taught Paul that he may teach us. In fact, that is God's Way (Eph. 4:11-13).
2. As well, He has also given to us His Holy Spirit that we might understand and be enabled to practice these things. It is one thing to receive a Revelation from the Spirit of God; it is another thing to receive that Spirit to enable a man to live according to that Revelation.

NOTES

In other words, the mere hearing of a Truth, as important as that is, is not enough. For us to truly understand what the Truth entails, the Holy Spirit has to quicken it to our hearts.

Once again we go back to our Faith in the Cross. Inasmuch as that is the basis on which the Holy Spirit works, this means that even though we hear Truth, we will not necessarily understand it, unless our Faith is properly placed.

As I've said several times in this Commentary, we are addressing this all-important subject in every manner in which the Lord gives us opportunity. But yet, unless the Holy Spirit quickens it to your heart, you simply will not understand that of which I speak. You may understand all that is on the surface, but that alone will actually be of little help. To understand what is fully being said, the Holy Spirit must quicken it to our hearts, which demands our Faith in the Cross.

### WHY WOULDN'T A CHRISTIAN HAVE THIS TYPE OF FAITH?

As we've said many times, every Believer had to believe in Christ and what He did at the Cross for us, in order to be saved (Jn. 3:16). However, after that, most Christians simply do not know the part that the Cross plays in our daily living. They don't know, simply because it hasn't been taught from most pulpits. In fact, there has been almost a total silence regarding the Cross in the last several decades. Therefore, Christians have terrible problems, as all will have who do not understand God's prescribed order of victory.

However, that is a given:

What we really want to know is the reason that some Christians will read these words I'm saying, or hear them preached or taught, and then reject what is being said? Unfortunately, that is the case with some, which will guarantee their spiritual declension, and even maybe the eventual loss of their souls. As stated, this which is being said by Paul is not the mere words of men, but that which is of God. Consequently, to despise it, is to despise God!

With many Christians, the reason they reject something which is truly from God, is because they are prejudiced toward the Messenger. In other words, if they don't like the Messenger, and for whatever reason, they will not accept the Message. Unfortunately, we don't have the latitude as to whether we like or dislike those whom God has called and sent. These are prejudices which God will not recognize, which means that the Believer can suffer eternal loss, which in fact many do.

Others will reject Truth because of pride. They have embraced something which is error, but thinking it is Truth they have given it their all. And then to be faced with the possibility that what they have been believing is wrong, even dead wrong, presents more than many can handle. So they fight out against the Truth, while attempting to embrace the error all the more. That as well, is a sure road to destruction.

The Believer must understand, that when Light is given, that Light must be accepted. If it is rejected, not only is that which is given lost to us, but then we lose what little we have had. That is a principle of the Ways of the Lord, and must not be taken lightly (Mat. 25:28-29).

And then some Christians are led totally by other Christians, in other words, allowing them to do their thinking for them. That means if their Denomination approves of something, then they follow along, otherwise, they do the same.

So, the heart has to be right with God, before the Believer can have understanding of Truth. To be frank, that's the reason that most Believers do not advance very much; even though Truth is presented, they are in no spiritual condition to understand the Truth, simply because the Holy Spirit will not override the various wrong thinking and direction in their lives. That's the reason a lot of Christians desperately need to repent! In fact, until they do so, which Jesus graphically brought out in His Message to the Church at Laodicea, they will receive precious little from the Lord (Rev. 3:14-22).

(9) "BUT AS TOUCHING BROTHERLY LOVE YE NEED NOT THAT I WRITE UNTO YOU: FOR YE YOURSELVES ARE TAUGHT OF GOD TO LOVE ONE ANOTHER."

NOTES

To begin this Passage, *"now about"* surfaces in the original language, and is a frequent Pauline formula for introducing a new subject (I Cor. 7:1, 25; 8:1; 12:1; 16:1, 12; I Thess. 4:13; 5:1).

In Corinthians the formula indicates answers to written questions, but here Paul responds to different elements of Timothy's oral report about Thessalonica (I Thess. 3:6).

*"Brotherly love"* an expression for attachment to one's blood relatives in secular speech, was taken over by Christianity because of the close ties within the spiritual family of God. Paul views further writing on the subject as superfluous in that they are *"taught by God"* to have brotherly love.

*"Taught by God"* a rare term, does not refer to any single teaching such as an Old Testament Passage (Lev. 19:18), the teaching of Christ (Jn. 13:34), or a prophetic revelation to the Church through Paul or anyone else. It rather describes a Divine relationship through the indwelling Holy Spirit.

At conversion, Believers become lifelong pupils as the Spirit bears inner witness to the love within the Christian family (Rom. 5:5; Gal. 5:22). This means that no external stimulus is necessary. It also means that mutual love among Christians is an inbred quality (Thomas).

BROTHERLY LOVE

The phrase, *"But as touching brotherly love ye need not that I write unto you,"* presents Paul with customary tactfulness beginning in a complimentary manner and then proceeding to the admonition.

*"Brotherly love"* is in classical Greek the love of family members by birth, but in the New Testament it always means love of the Brother in Christ.

In fact, the Early Church was such a wonder to the heartless, pagan society of Paul's day, that they could only exclaim, *"Behold how they love one another!"* It ought to be thus presently.

In view of that, I guess the question must be asked, *"Is such love prevalent today in Christendom?"*

In view of what the next phrase tells us, which we will address momentarily, I would have to say that it's not prevalent in the hearts and lives of many Christians. While it certainly is in some, in the aggregate, which refers to all who claim Christ in one way or the other, one I think, has to come to a negative conclusion.

So what does that mean?

While the Lord Alone must judge the heart, He being the only One qualified for such a thing, still, the Scripture plainly tells us, *"By their fruits ye shall know them"* (Mat. 7:20).

About the only answer that could be given is, many people who claim Salvation really aren't saved; consequently, they do not have the Divine Nature within their hearts and lives; therefore, they aren't taught anything by the Holy Spirit, simply because He isn't present.

## WHAT DOES BROTHERLY LOVE MEAN?

John writes, *"We know that we have passed out of death into life, because we love the Brethren"* (I Jn. 3:14).

John also said, *"He that loveth not knoweth not God; for God is Love"* (I Jn. 4:7-8).

I think in our efforts to explain this question, the explanation given by Christ is the greatest of all. Let's see what He said:

First of all, He made *"Love"* the criteria for rightness with God. He said:

*"Thou shalt love the Lord thy God with all thy heart, and with all thy soul, and with all thy strength, and with all thy mind; and thy neighbor as thyself."*

The Lawyer then asked Jesus, *"And who is my neighbor?"*

Jesus then gave the Parable of the Good Samaritan (Lk. 10:25-37).

He told of a certain man who went down from Jerusalem to Jericho, and fell among thieves. They robbed him and left him half dead.

He then told of a certain Priest who saw the man in this deplorable condition, evidently laying on the road, or else at the side of the road, and instead of stopping to help him, rather *"passed by on the other side."*

Then Jesus told of a *"Levite,"* who did the same thing.

But then He told of a *"certain Samaritan,"* who *"came where he was: and when he saw him, he had compassion on him."*

He then went on to tell how the man helped him, and *"brought him to an inn, and took care of him,"* etc.

NOTES

Jesus then asked, *"Which now of these three, thinkest thou, was neighbor among him that fell among thieves?"*

The answer was quick in coming, *"He that shewed mercy on him."* Jesus then said, *"Go, and do thou likewise."*

The idea is this I think, at least as it regards brotherly love:

It is very easy to show love to those who are rich, have need of nothing, or are not in trouble, etc. However, I think from this graphic lesson given to us by Christ, that *"brotherly love"* is not truly expressed, until it is expressed to someone who has fallen on hard times, etc. In fact, the kind of love that most so-called Christians express, is the same kind the world expresses.

The world gladly loves its champions, its heros, those to whom it looks up to, the rich, the famous, the powerful, but it is another story altogether regarding those who do not fit those categories. If the Church follows suit, which most do, then that means the Love of God is not in them, and that means that despite all their profession, they are not even saved. Understanding, that the Holy Spirit has made love the criteria, then this is the only conclusion to which we can come. Let me put it another way:

When one is down and cannot defend oneself, and anyone can do any negative thing to him they so desire, and do so without any fear of reprisal or censure, but rather be applauded for their action, one finds out rather quickly just how much love there is. Regrettably there isn't much!

I would hope that the Reader would peruse very carefully this statement we have just made. If one has not been in that position, one hardly knows or understands what is being said; however, if one has been in that position, even as the *"certain man"* of Jesus' illustration, then one definitely does know.

Please allow me to make this statement again: If love is actually the criteria by which Christianity is to be judged, and to be sure it definitely is, then the modern Church is in serious trouble!

## TAUGHT OF GOD

The phrase, *"For ye yourselves are taught of God to love one another,"* presents brotherly

NOTES

love as a part of our regenerate nature, one of those spiritual instincts which comes with being truly Born-Again.

The Divine Nature is the Love of God, which of course speaks of *"Agape Love."* It is the type of love which the world doesn't have, and in fact cannot have, because such does not exist in that system. It is only those who are born from above, which carries with it the Divine Presence. So, if a person is truly Born-Again, that person truly loves his fellow Brothers and Sisters in the Lord. While some will definitely function in this capacity in a greater measure than others, still, all will have this Divine principle. It is impossible to be otherwise!

### HOW DOES GOD TO BELIEVERS TEACH A GREAT EXPRESSION OF THIS LOVE?

First of all, let us again reemphasize the fact that this Love, if truly possessed, will express itself toward those who are unlovely, or at least to those who cannot return the expression, at least for the time being. That is always the acid test, as portrayed by Christ. If that is not evident, at least in some way, the person professing Salvation really isn't saved.

Regarding those who are truly Born-Again, and, consequently, have Divine Love, the Lord mostly teaches by example and opportunity. In other words, He allows certain people to cross our paths, who are unlovely in deed or in person. To be sure, we will respond to them, with each experience teaching us more and more about the God kind of Love.

To serve as the foundation for that, is the overwhelming example of God giving His Only Son, Who in fact, gave Himself for those who hated Him.

(10) "AND INDEED YE DO IT TOWARD ALL THE BRETHREN WHICH ARE IN ALL MACEDONIA: BUT WE BESEECH YOU, BRETHREN, THAT YE INCREASE MORE AND MORE;"

Even though we are given no information, it seems that the Thessalonians had proven their Salvation by their love, and had done so in a way that had caught the attention of Paul. Even though the Text is sketchy, it seems they were busy taking the Gospel to other parts of their province, even though only having been saved a short time themselves. In fact, one of the greatest ways of all as it regards loving those who are unlovely, is the taking of the Gospel to such people. Nothing will help them more.

But at the same time, John said, *"Whoso hath this world's good, and seeth his brother have need, and shutteth up his bowels of compassion from him, how dwelleth the Love of God in him?"*

He then said, *"My little children, let us not love in word, neither in tongue; but in deed and in truth"* (I Jn. 3:17-18).

So, the two, the taking of the Gospel to others, and provision where we are able to do so, proclaims the criteria, I think!

### THE BRETHREN

The phrase, *"And indeed ye do it toward all the Brethren which are in all Macedonia,"* proclaims an excellent lesson.

Too oftentimes we set our sights on something half way around the world, when there are things we can do close to home, even as these Thessalonians. In fact, I think if we do not prove our love where we are, that we are seldom going to prove it elsewhere.

Whatever it is these Thessalonians did, it is actually the Holy Spirit Who commends them. Paul could have easily left out this little tidbit, but the Holy Spirit wanted it included.

The early Christian Churches were little companies of people where love was at a high temperature, where outward pressure very often tightened the inward bonds, and where mutual confidence spread about continual joy. Many times, persecution will have that tendency, which reared its head in the Early Church, and which even increased in intensity a few years after this particular time.

A little later Paul mentioned the poverty of the Churches in Macedonia, as it regarded worldly goods, and how they gave very generously despite that difficulty (II Cor. 8:1-5).

There is some history as it regards Macedonia and Roman involvement. There had been some type of political problem, with Rome taking stern measures, which brought serious economic hardship to the region. Consequently, Christians suffered along with those who were unbelievers, and yet, these people, even as we've just described, gave abundantly to the Work of God, even from the small amount they possessed. Consequently, the

Holy Spirit used them as an example of correct Christian giving to the Work of God.

TO INCREASE MORE AND MORE

The phrase, *"But we beseech you, Brethren, that ye increase more and more,"* presents the Apostle not admonishing them, but definitely exhorting them.

It is significant that this Church was not expending all of its affection and effort upon itself. It was reaching out to others, which is the very nature of true Christianity. The Truth is, the more that the Love of God is expressed by the Believer, the more it will grow, even more and more. If it is not expressed, it will not remain static, but rather diminish.

In fact, the whole of Christianity functions in this manner. We grow or die!

(11) "AND THAT YE STUDY TO BE QUIET, AND TO DO YOUR OWN BUSINESS, AND TO WORK WITH YOUR OWN HANDS, AS WE COMMANDED YOU;"

From the subject of love, Paul apparently changes to something quite different — the importance of industry and individual responsibility in Christian living. However, the two are not completely unrelated.

Paul having to address this situation regarding idleness, even as he does again in II Thessalonians 3:6-15, could very well have been caused by their misapplying truths about the Lord's return, thinking it was going to be very soon, so why make efforts otherwise. Hence, the Apostle deals with this extensively in the Second Epistle.

STUDY TO BE QUIET

The phrase, *"And that ye study to be quiet,"* presents a kind of paradox. It is literally *"Be ambitious to be tranquil."* It is the opposite of aspiring to be prominently seen and heard.

The idea is that the sin nature be controlled, which can only be done by the Believer evidencing Faith in Christ and the Cross, which gives the Holy Spirit latitude to develop His fruit within our hearts and lives.

The sin nature out of control is the very opposite of this which Paul addresses. Such a person is not *"quiet,"* but rather given to temper tantrums, which are works of the flesh (Gal. 5:19-21).

All of this of which the Apostle teaches us speaks of control over the flesh; a lack of such causes a resurrection of the sin nature, which is the last thing the Believer wants or desires. And to be sure, the flesh cannot be controlled, not at all, except by the Holy Spirit. And He does so, as we have just stated, by virtue of our Faith properly placed in Christ and the Cross (Rom. 6:3-14; 8:1-2, 11).

NOTES

That which we have just stated is the only manner that God has as it regards the Believer living a righteous life, thereby obeying the Word of the Lord as given here.

The manner in which Paul uses this terminology, is a strong use of the rhetorical figure called *"oxymoron."* It is a combining of words totally contrary in meaning, in order to give force and point to the style. So, the Holy Spirit through the Apostle tells us to diligently seek ways in order to calm ourselves in any and every distraction. Let's see if we can go a little deeper into his thought.

THE DISTRACTIONS OF CHRISTIAN LIVING

There are things which constantly crop up which have a tendency to disturb our peace, or else to do so if allowed. And this is what the Apostle means. While we cannot stop all of these annoyances, and some which are fairly severe, we can react toward them in a manner which proclaims Faith in the Lord.

To become agitated and disruptive in spirit, which all of us have done at one time or the other, because of situations and circumstances, shows a lack of Faith, or patience, or both!

There is absolutely nothing which should disturb the *"quiet spirit"* for this is what it means, of the Child of God. For us to allow ourselves to be disturbed, only shows that we are not properly trusting the Lord as we should. Anything that disturbs our Peace, presents the fact that our Faith is not properly placed, or our trust in the Lord is not what it ought to be.

In the first place, the Lord has everything under control. As we've said many times and will continue to say, Satan can do nothing to the Believer but that it is permitted by the Lord. While it is quite obvious that our actions in the realm of unbelief, doubt, or even unconfessed sin, will grant Satan more latitude; still, the alternative to that is to get things right with God.

The point is, the *"settled peace"* of the Child of God, which refers to peace under any and all circumstances, is that which alone the Lord can give, and which the world knows nothing about. But yet, even as the word *"study"* proves, this *"peace"* is something we must work at, in other words, we must *"practice peace,"* and then it will become second nature.

MIND YOUR OWN BUSINESS

The phrase, *"And to do your own business,"* is without a doubt, one of the greatest practical Commandments ever given by the Holy Spirit through anyone.

Some have conjectured as to why Paul gave these admonitions to the Thessalonians, thinking that there were problems of this nature in that particular Church. First of all, there are problems of that nature in every Church. And as well, the Holy Spirit gave this through the Apostle not only for the Thessalonians, but for every other Believer and Church which have ever existed.

To simply *"mind one's own business,"* may seem to be a very simple request. But yet, how many problems would it solve, how much strife would it stop, if Christians followed this admonition.

First of all, all gossip would come to an instant halt, and that alone, would perform miracles in the Church, this sin being one of the most prevalent sins of all and as well, one of the most destructive.

For this to be done, would mean that the mind is filled not with other people's business, or what we think other people's business might be, but rather with the Lord, which would present quite a change to say the least!

Second, if we did nothing but mind our own business, instead of trying to mind the business of others, that would mean we would have far more time to spend on things of the Lord. This alone would completely change our attitude, demeanor, direction, thinking, posture, and about anything else about which one could think.

As well, trying to tend to the business of others, gives one much less time to mind their own business, which upon investigation, proves to not be getting much attention itself, at least the right kind.

This which the Apostle is saying is what could be referred to as *"practical Christianity."* In other words, it is that which involves itself with us and us with it, every single minute of our lives. Consequently, it is something that we ought to heed very carefully, understanding, that the Holy Spirit is actually the One Who gave these admonitions.

TO WORK WITH OUR OWN HANDS

The phrase, *"And to work with your own hands,"* is thought by many to mean that most of the Believers in the Church in Thessalonica, were not professional people, but rather day laborers. In fact, most of the Churches then were made up of slaves, with some few of the opposite class mixed in. In fact, Christianity was the great leveler.

Christians who attempt to sponge off others, aren't really Christians at heart, or else they need to seriously look at themselves. Irrespective of one's age or physical condition, there is something that most people can do to earn their way. While it is certainly true, that some few are totally incapacitated, that number would be small. Most Christians claiming they can't work because of a bad back, etc., are mostly not telling the truth. Far too often, laziness is the problem, not a *"bad back,"* etc.

Growing up as a kid, my Mother and Dad raised me with the thought in mind, that laziness was at least one of the worst vices which could attach itself to anyone. I was raised, and rightly so, to believe, that honest labor, was not only a necessity, but even a privilege. From the time I was 11 or 12 years old, I worked at various odd jobs, purchasing all of my clothing, and much of anything else that I had.

In fact, my parents were middle class, but I was raised to show responsibility, even from a young boy, which was to be a tremendous boon to my efforts for the Cause of Christ in later years.

Pastoring a Church the size of Family Worship Center, we are besieged quite often with individuals who have an excellent sob story, attempting to bilk money out of our Church Members. Many of these people have honed their story down to a sharp edge, which is engineered to play upon one's sympathy. I have told our people many times, that when people come asking for money, they should

NOTES

NOTES

call our office and consult with us first. Of course, these are adults and they can do whatever they desire; however, many times if following my advice, they would save their hard-earned dollars from being given to someone who makes a practice at pilfering money out of soft-hearted Christians.

Mostly at this present time, when people ask for money we tell them, that if they would desire to work a few hours, we will be glad to help them. Mostly, this completely solves the problem. They suddenly have business elsewhere!

Every once in a while, we will have such people come into our Prayer Meetings which are conducted each morning and each night at the Church. I remember one in particular:

The individual who was a stranger to all of us, began to pray quite loud, telling the Lord (the Lord?) that he desperately needed a new transmission for his car. Of course, he was praying loudly so that the people there could hear him, and then they would shell out to get him the new transmission, or whatever it was he claimed to have needed.

After listening to that for a few moments, I walked over to where he was, and politely told him, that he would probably be happier elsewhere. He quickly got the message, and when he drove away, it seemed like to me that his transmission was working pretty well.

He wasn't there to pray or to seek God, but rather to pilfer money.

## OUR NEEDS BEFORE THE LORD

We are to take our needs to the Lord and not to man.

By that, I mean that we are not to be dropping hints here and there to friends or fellow Saints about our personal needs. This comes under the heading of *"sponging."* In other words, we are trying to wheedle money out of people with hard-luck stories, etc.

If one truly trusts the Lord, one takes his personal needs to the Lord and no place else. According to those needs, the Lord will do the things which only He can do, which will bring Glory to God, and at the same time be a blessing to all; however, whenever we personally attempt to manipulate the situation, we are really conducting ourselves in the same manner as *"con men"* of the world, who make it their business to con money out of people — in other words, to fraudulently obtain such money.

Concerning laziness, Paul addressed this situation elsewhere as here, by saying, *"For even when we were with you, this we commanded you, that if any would not work, neither should he eat"* (II Thess. 3:10).

That doesn't leave much wiggle room, does it!

## A COMMAND

The phrase, *"As we commanded you,"* pertains to strong terminology, showing there had been a problem in this capacity which had necessitated direction.

As well, one should understand that this is not a suggestion, but rather a *"command."* The word *"command"* in the Greek is, *"paraggello,"* and means *"to charge, to give a mandate, to enjoin, to declare."*

As we've said several times, Christianity has its own culture. It is the Bible culture, which of course, is given and ordained by the Holy Spirit. This means that every Believer, irrespective of their background, must lay aside old habits which do not conform to the Word of God, which also include particular directions and ways, in fact, anything and everything that impacts our lives. Everything must be measured according to the Word of God. If it doesn't measure up, we ought to lay it aside.

One of the surest ways to destroy the Work of God, which in effect is to destroy the Message, is to attempt to incorporate the culture of any given area into the Word of God. For instance, some claim that drinking alcoholic wine in France is common, because it's their culture, as drinking beer in Germany is their culture. To be frank, that's about the poorest excuse in the world.

Why not join witchcraft with the Word of God because in some parts of the world, it's their custom!

No! The very idea of the Born-Again experience, of following Christ, of allowing the Holy Spirit to align our lives according to the Word of God, is what Christianity is all about. In fact, that's what ultimately brought down the Roman Empire. They saw that the lives of Christians constituted a marked

NOTES

difference than theirs. That's the way it should be everywhere.

Again I emphasize, that the culture for the Child of God, irrespective as to what it has previously been, is the Word of God. And that's exactly what the Holy Spirit will do with our lives, if we allow Him the latitude and leeway which we certainly should do.

(12) "THAT YE MAY WALK HONESTLY TOWARD THEM THAT ARE WITHOUT, AND THAT YE MAY HAVE LACK OF NOTHING."

These exhortations find a twofold result. For their conduct to *"win the respect of outsiders,"* the Christians in Thessalonica, and everywhere else and for all time, for that matter, must eliminate restlessness, meddlesomeness, and idleness. Even so-called *"outsiders"* because they have no connection with Christ and hence are outside the Family of God (I Cor. 5:13; Col. 4:5; I Tim. 3:7), recognize winsome conduct.

On the other hand, they are repelled by those who do not carry their share of social responsibility. Closely associated with the importance of a good testimony is the need not to *"be dependent on anybody."* Of course, independence in an absolute sense is neither possible nor even desirable. We must understand Paul's admonitions not to be dependent in the light of the situation described in Verses 11 and 12 (Thomas).

## HONESTY

The phrase, *"That ye may walk honestly toward them that are without,"* in effect says, *"That you may command the respect of them that are without."* This of course, refers to non-Believers.

Barclay says, *"When we Christians prove that our Christianity makes us better workmen, truer friends, kinder men and women, then and only then are we really preaching. The important thing is not mere words but deeds, not preaching so much on our part, but life."* The humblest Christian has opportunity to reflect honor upon the Cause of Christ through the consistent and faithful performance of his duties, and nothing can really compensate for the discredit suffered through failure to do so.

In fact, the entirety of the Word of God, including both Old Testament and New Testament, demands honesty in all things, and in every respect. In other words, it is to be, at least in our terminology, *"12 inches to the foot," "16 ounces to the pound,"* etc. Nothing else will suffice!

Christian honesty demands that the Believer give an honest day's work for an honest day's pay. That means if you are hired to do hourly work, which many are, that eight hours a day belong to your employer. Consequently, other than the prescribed time for *"breaks,"* you are not to fool away your time by needlessly talking to people, or to attempt to conduct your own business during these hours. You are cheating the man for whom you are working, if you do such, in effect, *"stealing from him,"* which should never be the manner of the Child of God.

As well, your word should be your bond, meaning that before you promise something, you should think about it carefully. But if you do promise something, unless circumstances completely make it impossible for you to hold to that promise, it should be carried out, even to your hurt.

We are Christians; our words should mean something; our time should mean something; who we are and what we do, should mean something!

Does it?

*"Honestly"* in the Greek is, *"euschemonos,"* and means *"well-formed, honorable, decently, decorously."* Consequently, the word carries a greater meaning than merely referring to 100 cents to the dollar. It refers as well, to the manner and the way in which the transaction is carried out and done. There are many people who are honest as far as the strict dealings of their transactions are concerned, but if they have taken advantage of the other person, then their transaction has not been carried out *"honestly."* I'm sure the Reader understands what I mean.

The Christian is to go beyond the mere letter of the contract. He is to make every effort to conduct himself in a way as to be kind, gracious, and charitable to all concerned, even at the expense of himself, if necessary!

## A PERSONAL EXAMPLE

Our type of Ministry, which is Mass Evangelism, and which includes Television, Radio, and citywide Crusades, plus literature, etc., of necessity, brings us in contact with all types of people around the world. I speak of Television Station owners, managers, sales persons, etc.

In fact, Frances takes care of all of these particulars, which is a monumental task, especially considering that we seldom have enough money to pay all the bills.

I was very pleased some time ago, when one of the Television brokers with whom we do business, who incidently places our Program on various Stations all over the nation, made the following statement to someone who passed it along to us.

He said, *"I do business with many Preachers; however, Jimmy Swaggart Ministries is the only Ministry that I can honestly hold up and say, that whatever they tell you they will do. If perchance something intervenes that their word cannot be kept, they will be on the phone immediately, telling you what the situation is, and what to expect."* He went on to say, *"I cannot honestly say that about most others, if any!"*

This man is Jewish, not saved, not a follower of Christ. I'm very thankful that the Lord has helped us to be a testimony to him.

At the same time, I'm very sad that the word of all Ministers and Ministries is not at times what it ought to be. I have no idea, as to how many Preachers he deals with, or in fact, with whom he deals; however, that particular information is inconsequential. Whomever they are, they should do their best to carry forth that which their name as followers of Christ implies.

There are times I suppose, in the lives of all Believers, that things happen which hinders us from keeping our word. That being the case, we should call the people involved and explain to them the situation, and then tell them what to expect, and then do our very best to uphold that which we can do. To ignore a debt that is not in dispute, is the same thing as stealing the money, or even worse!

Those *"from without"* as Paul puts it, are many times turned off, by the attitude and actions of those who call themselves Believers, but are in reality, a very poor testimony. Perhaps all of us could take some lessons in this capacity; however, in everything we do,

NOTES

and with whom the thing is done, we must always understand that we are followers of Christ, and that He is observing every single transaction. *"Whatever measure we mete, will be measured to us again"* (Mat. 7:2).

## LACK OF NOTHING

The phrase, *"And that ye may have lack of nothing,"* proclaims the thought, that if one fully obeys the Lord, doing all that he can do to follow the admonitions of the Holy Spirit, even as given in the Word of God, that there will be no *"lack."*

*"Lack of what,"* some may ask?

*"Anything and everything"* is the answer!

When any individual comes to Christ, that person enters into what might be called *"God's economy"* (Lk. 12:22-32). That means that if he fully trusts the Lord, and obeys the Word the best he can, that he has the solemn Promise of God that he will be taken care of as it regards his needs, whether those needs be *"spiritual, domestical, financial, or physical."*

## WHAT IS EXPECTED OF THE BELIEVER AS IT REGARDS THE ECONOMY OF GOD?

1. We are to understand that God definitely has an economy, meaning that He has a way and a means of doing things, which are totally different than the ways of the world. As stated, this is found in Luke 12:22-32.

2. We are to understand that upon accepting Christ, that we enter into this grand and glorious economy.

3. In this economy, we are to *"seek ye first the Kingdom of God, and His Righteousness; and all these things shall be added unto you"* (Mat. 6:33). As should be obvious, that simply means to put the Kingdom of God, and our place in that Kingdom, first of all, and then, the necessary things of life will be added to us. We have that as a Promise of God! In other words, we take care of His business first, and then He promises to take care of ours. And friend please listen to me, that's a good trade!

As well, many Christians read these words, thinking they apply only to Preachers, etc. That is far from the Truth! They apply to all Believers.

4. We are to have Faith that God will carry out His end of the bargain, which we can be assured that He shall. In other words, the Child of God doesn't live by chance, the luck of the draw, or the variances of life; *"the just shall live by Faith."*

This means that we are not subject to the variations of this world, whether Wall Street, Congress, or local conditions, etc. While we might be momentarily affected by these things, the Lord will see to the situation, that provision is made for us. In fact, it has already been made!

5. We should earnestly search the Word of God, that we might know how to live, how to conduct ourselves, what we ought to do, the way we should act, etc. Tragically, most Christians know little about the Word of God; therefore, they trample all over its admonitions, and then wonder why this great economy doesn't work for them?

6. Every Christian should have a prayer life, and that means *"a daily prayer life."* In other words, we should set aside a little time each day, whatever time we think is right, and hold to that faithfully, which prayer time will prove to be very important to us.

During this time, we should first of all Praise the Lord for all the mighty, wonderful, and good things which He constantly does for us. After that time of praise, and only after that time of praise, should we approach Him with our various needs, which He encourages us to do (Lk. 11:9-13).

7. The Believer should ever understand, that all of these good things, all of these wonderful things, all of these grand things given to us by the Lord, whether they be spiritual, physical, financial, or domestical, come to us solely and completely through what Christ did at the Cross. In other words, He paid a terrible price for all of these things we have. As well, considering the great price He paid, we must at the same time understand, that the benefits which come from that tremendous Work, the Finished Work of Christ, is grand as well! It cannot be otherwise!

God has always greatly loved man. In other words, He didn't just suddenly start loving man 2,000 years ago, etc. As well, He has always wanted to give man great and wonderful things, which He alone can do; however, due to man's sinful condition, God was very limited as to what He could do with or for man. However, since the Cross, which incidently settled the account, the door was flung open wide, for God to do all the things He has always wanted to do. The Cross made it all possible. Oh, how I sense the Presence of God even as I say these words. What a wonderful God we have; and how wonderful He is to us! His Blessings are abundant and *"His Mercy endureth forever"* (Ps. 136).

NOTES

Reader I implore you to read carefully these words, for the Lord has given them to me. If you will heed Him, follow Him, love Him, and faithfully serve Him, as Paul said, *"you will have lack of nothing."* That means that everything is handled, everything is provided, everything is for you.

To be sure, the Cross of Christ did not change God at all, for God doesn't need to change. It did not add anything to Him or take anything from Him. The Cross, or rather what Jesus did on that Cross, made it possible for God to be to us what He has always wanted to be.

The Cross removed all the hindrances and obstacles which kept God from giving to us, and doing for us, all the things He Alone can do. And please believe me, there's nothing He cannot do.

## A PERSONAL EXAMPLE

Many years ago, when Frances and I were just beginning in the Ministry. If I remember, the year was 1956. Having not been married long, our living quarters at that time were very sparse, only a little, tiny, thirty-two foot long house trailer. I was just starting to preach, and to be frank, I did not see how in the world it would be possible for me to do anything for the Lord. I knew, and I knew greatly, that His Call was upon my life, and even in a strong and powerful way; however, we seemed to *"lack"* everything. We had no money, our car was several years old, and above that, I was entering into Evangelistic Work, and no one even knew I was alive, except the Lord. But I was to find out, that was enough!

One afternoon I was alone, Frances having gone someplace, and she had taken Donnie as well, who was then two years old.

I remember sitting down against the little bed at the back of the trailer, as I began to pray, and have a time of fellowship with the Lord. There were problems of some type, of which I do not now remember. I was taking those problems to the Lord, thinking in my mind, that they were insurmountable.

Isn't it strange, these things which were so big then, are not even remembered now!

As I began to pray, the Lord brought to my mind the words of a little chorus which we had just learned:

*"My Lord is able, He's able, I know that He is able,*
*"I know my Lord is able to carry me through.*
*"My Lord is able, He's able, I know that He is able,*
*"I know my Lord is able to carry me through.*

*"For He has healed the brokenhearted, set the captive free,*
*"He's healed the sick, raised the dead, and walked upon the Sea.*
*"My Lord is able, He's able, I know that He is able,*
*"I know my Lord is able to carry me through."*

As those words began to come to me, the Spirit of God began to move upon me mightily, telling me, *"I am Able!"* That's all it was, *"I am Able!" "I am Able!"*

For quite some time I sat there on the floor weeping and praising God, as the Spirit of God covered me, with that Word going through my heart and mind, over and over again, *"I am Able!"*

The Cross of Christ not only opened the door, but in fact, it blew the thing off the hinges. The Way to the Lord is wide open now, due to what Jesus did at the Cross. Reader can you not sense and feel the Spirit of what we are saying!

Concerning all things that pertain to the Lord, the Cross turned the light green, so to speak.

(13) "BUT I WOULD NOT HAVE YOU TO BE IGNORANT, BRETHREN, CONCERNING THEM WHICH ARE ASLEEP, THAT YE SORROW NOT, EVEN AS OTHERS WHICH HAVE NO HOPE."

NOTES

Paul's words *"we do not want you to be ignorant"* as usual mark what follows for special attention.

It seems that the Thessalonians had concluded that *"those who sleep"* would miss the victories and glory of the Lord's return. Of course, *"those who sleep"* is an expression chosen in lieu of *"the dead"* and because of death's temporary nature for Christians (Jn. 11:11; I Cor. 7:39; 11:30; 15:6, 18, 20, 51).

As a result, the Holy Spirit through the Apostle will give the clearest teaching on the coming Rapture of the Church, found in the entirety of the Word of God.

## SPIRITUAL AND SCRIPTURAL IGNORANCE

The phrase, *"But I would not have you to be ignorant, Brethren,"* proclaims one of Paul's oft used expressions. As we have just stated, the expression generally precedes a very important statement, or one might say, greater clarification of a particular Doctrine.

The Apostle had not been able to be with the Thessalonians long; therefore, he was not able to flesh out many things which he no doubt told them, and which they only had partial knowledge.

That is understandable as it regards the Thessalonians, and in fact, all of that particular day and time. There was no New Testament then, with understanding of the New Covenant being very sketchy to say the least. I Thessalonians was probably written sometime between A.D. 50 and A.D. 53. At this time, there had probably been only two Books or Epistles written, Matthew and James. I Thessalonians is thought to be Paul's First Epistle, with Peter not writing his until some years later, and John his, many years later. So, the point I'm attempting to make is, there was some excuse for these people being ignorant of the Word of the Lord. Only when these Epistles written by Paul began to make their presence felt, did the people begin to gather some understanding regarding these great Doctrines of the Word of God. We look at these things now after the fact; however, during Paul's time, all were in the making.

However, having said that, whereas one could say there was an excuse then, there is no excuse now. If Believers are ignorant now of the Word of God, it is strictly because of a lack of interest. No one could ascribe it to anything else. And the Truth is, most Christians are sadly and regrettably, ignorant of the Word.

This is sadder still, when one realizes that we're speaking of the single most important thing in the world. There is nothing more important to you as a Believer than your learning and understanding the Word of God. It has to do with your past, your present, and your future. In fact, as I've said many times, *"The Word of God is the only revealed Truth in the world today, and in fact, ever has been."*

Spiritual problems are the great problems of the human race. To be sure, these problems flow over into every other aspect of life. In other words, spiritual difficulties, which arise mostly because of a lack of understanding of the Word, have an impact on everything else. Other particulars may cause us problems, such as financial difficulties, etc., but those things cannot affect our spiritual standing, at least if we do not allow them such latitude. But spiritual problems impact every single thing we are and every single thing we do. So, if that is neglected, it affects all other things as well.

If I could get every Christian to get these Commentaries and read them, even study them, I think I can say without any fear of contradiction, that it would change the Church for the better, and I mean a great deal better! Naturally I'm prejudiced as it regards my own work; however, at the same time, if the Lord told me to do this, and I definitely know that He did, then the material is needed by the Body of Christ. It's just that simple!

In fact, I'm not personally aware of any Commentaries being written on the entirety of the Bible at this present time. While there certainly are other Commentaries, most of them were written from 50 to 100 years ago or longer. As well, the material on prophecy and/or the Holy Spirit in these particular efforts is very meager.

While proper instruction concerning the Cross of Christ is definitely portrayed in most Commentaries, with the exception of two or three, at least of which I am aware, the information given is extremely small by comparison to this which the Lord has given us, and which we have done our best to portray in these Volumes, especially in the Epistles of Paul. As well, I personally believe that the Lord has given us a Revelation as it regards the Cross, which I think portrays the veracity of the Finished Work of Christ, as has little previously been done.

NOTES

A Revelation from the Lord is a powerful happening. I think one can safely say without any fear of contradiction, that no instruction in the world can equal such. It's like the Holy Spirit imprints the subject matter on one's mind and in one's spirit, to such an extent, that it becomes crystal clear, and then He continues to add to what He has already given. At least that's the way it's been with me as it regards the Cross of Christ. I know what this Revelation has done for my life, and I know what it will do for anyone who will avail themselves of this given by the Holy Spirit, even as we have attempted to portray this information in this very Volume.

## THEM WHICH ARE ASLEEP

The phrase, *"Concerning them which are asleep,"* refers to the dead in Christ.

The Thessalonian Christians, so recently converted from paganism, were apparently deeply troubled. Paul had told them about the Rapture of the Church, but evidently he had not spent much time on the subject, which left the Thessalonians with many questions.

It seems that the two most pressing questions were:

1. Was the Rapture going to take place immediately?
2. What about the Believers who had died? Would dying keep them from having a part in this event?

The first question, Paul would not fully answer until his Second Letter; however, he will address the second question now.

## NEW REVELATIONS

The New Covenant, which was given to Paul, fleshed out greatly that which had only been in shadow in the Old Testament. These new Revelations concerning the Resurrection are as follows:

1. Every Believer who has died will come

NOTES

back with Christ in the Resurrection (Rapture), and will be given a Glorified Body (I Thess. 4:13-18; I Cor. 15:20-23, 35-58; Phil. 3:21).

2. All who are alive and redeemed at the time of the trump will be instantly changed (I Cor. 15:51-58; II Cor. 5:1-10; Phil. 3:21).

3. At the Rapture, the Lord will not come all the way back to the Earth, only somewhere at or below approximately 6,000 feet (I Thess. 4:13-18; II Thess. 2:7).

4. The Lord will not send an Angel at the Rapture, but rather will come Himself (I Thess. 4:13-18; I Cor. 15:23, 51-58).

5. The righteous dead will be changed first of all, and then the living will be changed (I Thess. 4:13-18; Phil. 3:21; I Cor. 15:23, 51-58).

6. Every Believer who has ever lived, from the time of Abel to those living at the time of the Rapture, will be instantly changed and given Glorified Bodies (II Cor. 5:1-10; II Thess. 2:7; Jn. 14:1-3).

## SORROW NOT

The phrase, *"That ye sorrow not,"* does not deny sorrow as it regards the passing of loved ones, but rather that it's not the type of sorrow expressed by those who do not know the Lord. Being human, we feel things and feel them keenly; however, that is a far cry from those who face things with despair and hopelessness. The following constitutes at least some of the reasons Christians have for looking at things differently.

## THE BELIEVER'S HOPES

The word *"hope,"* as used in the Bible, carries with it a slightly different connotation than the manner in which it is presently used. Now it means *"maybe,"* or *"possibly so,"* etc. However, the way it is expressed in the Bible does not pertain to guesswork. The Greek word for *"hope"* is *"elpis,"* which means *"to anticipate, usually with pleasure, to expect, and to do so with confidence."*

In other words, the outcome is not in doubt, but rather the date and time of fulfillment. What is promised by God, and we speak of good things, is definitely coming.

Incidently, Paul uses a gentle, euphemistic expression for the dead: *"them which are asleep."* The present tense may also suggest *"those who are* (from time to time) *falling asleep."* Since this figurative language for death was common in both Judaism and pagan Greek writers who had no concept of Resurrection, it is impossible to base any Doctrinal significance upon it. The ideas which it suggests, such as death without fear or sting (I Cor. 15:55-57), actually refers to the fact of dying, and not which follows death. It is no different, as Paul implies, than one falling asleep. Other than the act of dying, it carries no other implications. The idea is, which we will address more fully momentarily, there is no justification for the notion of *"soul sleep,"* as is taught by some.

As well, some claim from this Passage that Paul is saying that there should not be any sorrow at all. However, that is incorrect. The sorrow here prohibited is a despairing and an unbelieving sorrow; we are forbidden to sorrow as those who have no hope, no belief in a blessed Resurrection.

The tears of Jesus at the tomb of Lazarus have authorized and sanctified Christian sorrow, one might say.

*"Paul,"* observes Calvin, *"lifts up the minds of Believers to a consideration of the Resurrection, lest they should indulge excessive grief on occasion of the death of their relatives, for it were unseemingly that there should be no difference in them and unbelievers, who put no end or measure to their grief, for this reason, that in death they recognize nothing but destruction. Those who abuse this testimony so as to establish among Christians stoical indifference, that is, an iron hardness, will find nothing of this nature in Paul's words."*

## NO HOPE

The phrase, *"Even as others which have no hope,"* concerns those who do not know the Lord, who will not have part in the First Resurrection of Life, and, therefore, no hope for Heaven.

The pagans of old which of course, included those of Paul's day, had no hope whatsoever as it concerned life after death. In fact, they were bitterly opposed to a Resurrection, thinking that it meant somehow, to come back as they had previously been. Life being hard, even very hard in those times, they didn't want to do this all over again, which is somewhat understandable.

And yet they expressed terrible grief at parting, simply because so far as they had any evidence, they would never see their loved ones again. It was on this account, at least in part, that the heathens indulged in expressions of such excessive grief. When their friends died, they hired men to play in a mournful manner on a pipe or trumpet, or women to howl and lament in a dismal manner. They beat their breasts, uttered loud shrieks, rent their garments, tore off their hair, cast dust on their heads, or sat down in ashes.

Understanding that this is the culture in which the Thessalonians had been previously involved, it is not improbable that some among them, on the death of their pious friends, kept up these expressions of excessive sorrow.

To prevent this, and to mitigate their sorrow, the Apostle refers them to the bright hopes which Christianity had revealed, and points them to the future glories of reunion with the departed pious dead.

From this we must learn several things:

THE HOPELESSNESS OF A LIFE WITHOUT GOD

1. That the world without Christ is destitute of hope. It is just as true of the heathen world now as it was of the ancient pagans, that they have no hope of a future state. Please understand the following:

Those without Christ have no evidence that there is any such future state of blessedness; and without such evidence there can be no hope.

2. That the excessive grief of the children of this world, when they lose a friend is not to be wondered at. They bury their bones in the grave. They part, for all that they know or believe, with such a friend forever. The wife, the son, the daughter, they consign to silence — to decay — to dust, not expecting to meet them again.

They look forward to no glorious Resurrection, when that body shall rise, and when they shall be reunited to part no more. It is no wonder that they weep and excessively so — for who would not weep when he believes that he parts with his friends forever?

NOTES

3. It is only the hope of future blessedness that can mitigate this sorrow. An experience with Christ reveals a brighter world — a world where all the saved shall be reunited; where the bonds of love shall be made stronger than they were; where they shall never be severed again. It is only this hope that can soothe the pains of grief at parting; only when we can look forward to a better world, and feel that we shall see them again — love them again — love them forever, that our tears are made dry.

4. The Christian, therefore, when he loses a Christian friend, should not sorrow as others do. We do feel, indeed, as keenly as do those who do not know Christ, the loss of our loved ones; the absence of their well-known faces; the want of the sweet voice of friendship and love; for an experience with Christ does not blunt the sensibility of the soul, or make the heart unfeeling. As stated, Jesus wept at the grave of Lazarus; and Salvation in no way prevents the warm gushing expressions of sorrow when God comes into a family and removes a friend. But this sorrow should not be like that of the world.

It must not be: A. Such as arises from the feeling that there is no future union; B. It should not be accompanied with repining or complaining; and, C. It should not be excessive, or beyond that which God designs that we should feel. It should be calm, submissive, patient; it should be that which is connected with the steady confidence in God; and it should be mitigated by the hope of a future glorious union in Heaven. The eye of the weeper should look up through his tears to God. The heart of the sufferer should acquiesce in him, even in the unsearchable mysteries of his dealings, and feel that all is right.

5. It is a sad thing to die without hope — so to die as to have no hope for ourselves, and to leave none to our surviving friends that we have gone to a better place. Such is the condition of the whole heathen world; and such is the state of those who die even in so-called Christian lands, who have no evidence that their peace is made with God.

As I love my friends, my Father, my Mother, my Wife, my Children, I would not have them go forth and weep over my grave as those who have no hope in my death. I would have their sorrow for my departure alleviated by the belief that my soul is happy with the Lord, even when they commit my cold clay to the dust. And to be sure, were there no other reason for being a Child of God, this would be well worth all the effort which it requires to become one (Barnes).

NOTES

### THE TIME OF DEATH

As a Minister of the Gospel, I have preached many funerals. Almost all of these have been for those who have known the Lord, and have made Him their Saviour. Even though the passing of friends and loved ones, and any fellow Christian for that matter is grievous, still, there is at the same time a certain joy at their passing. You know beyond the shadow of a doubt, they have gone to a better place. At that moment they are with Christ, beyond the vale of tears and sorrow. As well, we also know and realize, that there will be a meeting some glad day, a meeting which will never end, a meeting which will never again know a parting.

So, in the midst of the sorrow, for as we have stated, there is sorrow, but still, at the same time there is a joy, all because of what Christ did at the Cross and the Resurrection. Because He lives, we shall live also!

And then again, I have preached the funeral of one who does not know God, who died without hope, who had made no profession of Faith, who was snatched out unexpectedly. The awfulness of such a time knows no bounds. What can one say? What can one do?

The words *"no hope"* which the Holy Spirit gave to Paul, adequately and terribly describe the situation.

The loved ones reach out for some kind of hope, but what kind of hope can be given them! They want some word that gives some sunlight in that darkness, but outside of Christ there is none. Let the Reader read those words slowly; *"outside of Christ there is no hope!"*

Christ has faced that dark void, and defeated that terrible enemy called death. He has gone before us, and as a result, the sting has been removed from death. But it's only those who know Him, who have accepted Him, who have made Him the Lord and Love of their lives, who have the *"blessed hope!"* As serious as it is, as troublesome as it is, even as dark as it is, I must say it again:

*"Without Christ, there is no hope!"*

(14) "FOR IF WE BELIEVE THAT JESUS DIED AND ROSE AGAIN, EVEN SO THEM ALSO WHICH SLEEP IN JESUS WILL GOD BRING WITH HIM."

For Christians, relief from sorrow is related to what the future holds. Just as *"Jesus died and rose again,"* so will *"those who sleep in Him"* be raised when God brings them to Heaven with Jesus at His Coming. The fact of Jesus' Death and Resurrection guarantees as its sequel the eventual Resurrection of the dead in Christ. This in effect, is the same as the guarantee of His return in I Thessalonians 1:10.

It is significant that Paul does not refer to Jesus' Death as *"sleep."* The difference between Jesus' experience and that of Believers is that He really endured actual separation from God at the time of His Death, for the world's sins. Because of His real death, Christian death has been transformed into sleep, and that refers to the actual act of one dying, and not what happens after death.

If it is to be noticed, Paul did not write *"God will raise"* as it refers to the Saints at that time who have died, but instead, *"God will bring with Jesus,"* referring to the Saints. He used this latter phrase for a particular reason. All Saints who have died, are with Jesus in Heaven, in their soul and spirit form, while their body has gone back to dust, with that body, however, being resurrected at the Rapture and glorified, and then reunited with the soul and the spirit.

### THE DEATH AND RESURRECTION OF CHRIST

The phrase, *"For if we believe that Jesus died and rose again,"* refers to the very foundation of Christianity. In fact, the Death and Resurrection of Christ, is the proof of life after death and a glorified state for all Saints in that life, which incidently will never end.

The very fundamental of Salvation, is that the Saint *"believe that Jesus died and rose again."* This is the key to all Christian hope.

The word *"if"* does not imply any question of that belief. In fact, it actually should have been translated *"since."*

The idea is, as surely as we believe, and believe in this which has been stated, so surely will the Believers who have died be with Jesus when He returns. However, the following fact must be noted:

The belief in Christ's Death and Resurrection is not a mere mental acceptance of these things. It as well, involves a personal identification with Jesus in His Death and Resurrection, even as He identified with us. The Death of Jesus Christ is the assurance of Salvation for all who will believe (Mat. 26:28; Rom. 5:6-11; I Pet. 2:24). The Resurrection of Jesus Christ is the assurance of Justification and Resurrection for all men, at least who believe (Jn. 14:19; Rom. 5:10; 6:5-8; I Cor. 15:4-23; II Tim. 2:11).

The Apostle's argument proceeds on the supposition that Christ and Believers are one body, of which Christ is the Head and Believers are the members; and that consequently what happens to the Head must happen also to the members. In fact, as stated, our knowledge and belief of a future state, and especially of the Resurrection, is founded on the proof of the Resurrection of Christ (I Cor. Chpt. 15) (Gloag).

Incidently, Paul using the human Name of our Lord, *"Jesus,"* links His Humanity with ours.

As well, the idea of believing as Paul mentions here the necessity, is not merely believing that Jesus rose, but that the Death and Resurrection of the Saviour is connected with the Resurrection of the Saints: that the one follows from the other, and that the one is as certain as the other. The Doctrine of the Resurrection of the Saints so certainly follows from that of the Resurrection of Christ, that, if the one is believed, the other must be believed as well.

## IDENTIFICATION WITH CHRIST

To which we alluded several paragraphs back, the word *"believe"* here presupposes the identification of the Saint with the Lord in His Death and Resurrection, that is if He is to identify with us in our death and resurrection. As should be obvious, this is extremely important.

There are millions of people who die, who have never accepted Christ as their Saviour, have never identified with Him in His Death and Resurrection, but yet want Him to identify with them in their death and resurrection. It is not to be!

We know that Jesus identified with us by the very fact that He came down to this world, actually for that very purpose. The Incarnation, which refers to God becoming man, was carried out for one purpose only, and that is to identify with lost humanity, in order that lost humanity might be saved. Whether God could have done this thing another way is a matter of conjecture; however, whatever that case, we know the way which it was done, which was through His Incarnation and Death on a Cross and Resurrection. This was the best way.

This which we have just said in a few words, still, is of such magnitude as to defy all description. That God would pay such a price to redeem those who in fact did not love Him at all, is beyond the ability of man to grasp.

When He died on the Cross, He identified with us in our lost condition. He became our Substitute, which is portrayed in the Fifty-third Chapter of Isaiah. However, as well, He was also our Representative Man, which Paul referred to as the *"Second"* or the *"Last Adam"* (I Cor. 15:45-47), which is also described in Psalm 22.

As we've said previously, as our Substitute He died *for* us; as our Representative Man, He died *as* us. In other words, He died as a sinner, suffering the full effect of the broken Law, which was death (Rom. 6:23). And yet, even though He died as a sinner, He was not a sinner, in fact never having sinned or failed in even the slightest aspect, to any degree. The Scripture plainly says of Him, *"Who is holy, harmless, undefiled, separate from sinners"* (Heb. 7:26).

So, when we say that He died as our Representative Man, even as a sinner, that doesn't mean as stated, that He was a sinner, because in fact, He was totally *"separate from sinners,"* having never sinned. Still, He suffered the terrible curse of sin on our behalf, in effect, doing for us what we could not do for ourselves. In other words, He took the full brunt of the penalty which we should have taken.

So, in totality He identified with us, which means that He came to this world for the very

NOTES

purpose and reason of this identification, which necessitated His Death on the Cross. The Cross was ever in view, ever a necessity, ever the means by which this great thing would be done (I Pet. 1:18-20).

OUR IDENTIFICATION WITH HIM

Inasmuch as He identified with us, for us to receive what He came to give, we must as well, totally and completely, identify with Him. In fact, as His identification with us was total and complete, our identification with Him must be in the same vein.

This is what constitutes real Salvation, and is an absolute necessity, that is if one is to be saved. There is no other way (Jn. 3:16).

So, what type of identification are we speaking about?

Are we speaking of identifying with Him regarding His perfect morals? What about His ethical example? What about His princely life? Are we to identify with Him in humility? In His kindness?

So, what exactly do we mean by identifying with Him?

In Truth, if the world recognizes Jesus at all, it is an identification in these things which we have mentioned, such as *"morals and ethics,"* etc. However, as noteworthy as that is, and as much as Jesus is definitely the perfect example in all things; still, identification with Him in that capacity will not save or deliver anyone. In fact, the identification which is demanded is mostly rejected by the world, and regrettably even by much of the Church.

The identification of which we speak, must be our identifying with Him in His Death and Resurrection, i.e., *"the Cross."* And that's what stops the world cold, and as stated, even much of the Church!

To identify with Him as a *"good man,"* or something of that nature, is perfectly acceptable by the world, but to identify with Him in His Death on the Cross, with all its attendant horror and humiliation, presents itself as a great barrier for most of the world.

WHAT DOES IDENTIFYING WITH HIM IN HIS DEATH ACTUALLY MEAN?

First of all, it means that one must definitely believe that Jesus Christ is God, and that His becoming man, was for the express purpose of redeeming mankind. He must believe that the Cross was God's Way of Redemption, i.e., *"the Death of Christ on the Cross."*

As well, he must believe that he is a sinner, lost, undone without God, with no way to save himself, and no means to do so, even if he had a way, which he doesn't!

The sinner must believe that Jesus Christ died for him, actually taking his place, and then accepting Him as Lord and Saviour.

In fact, this identification which God demands is of such magnitude, as stated, as to defy all description. It goes so far as to place the believing sinner literally, at least in the Mind of God, in the Death of Christ on the Cross (Rom. 6:3). Actually, this identification is so close, so total, so complete, that the Holy Spirit used the word *"Baptized into His Death,"* referring to believing sinners. Without the believing sinner dying himself on a Cross, which would have done him no good even if he had, this is the step or way that God provided in order for man to be saved.

As well, we must identify with Him, not only in His Crucifixion, but as well in His Burial (Rom. 6:4). In fact, this part of our identification is necessary, in order to complete the purpose of identification with Him in His Death.

Identifying with Him in His Death, proclaims us in the Eyes of God paying the penalty of the broken Law which is death. Incidently, this payment was owed to God because of man's terrible crimes against Him.

In being buried with Him, this refers to all the past life before conversion, all sins, all iniquities, all transgressions, all rebellion against God, in other words, every single thing that pertained to the unredeemed state. All and without exception, are buried with Him, which means, that it can never be charged to us again. Identification with Him in His Death, guarantees identification with Him in His burial, which puts the old life out of sight.

However, our Identification does not stop there, also including His Resurrection. As we died and were buried with Him, we were also Resurrected with Him, in fact *"in Him,"* in *"newness of life"* (Rom. 6:4-5).

Therefore, to believe on Christ, even as Paul states here, this is what it actually means. As He totally and completely identified with

NOTES

us, we are to totally and completely identify with Him.

Knowing this was not literally done, and knowing yet that it must be done, and in fact was done at our conversion, how was it all brought about?

## FAITH

The ingredient that does all of this, that puts us into His Death, Burial, and Resurrection, is Faith. And what exactly do we mean by that?

Of course, God knows that we could not literally die in Christ, as is obvious. So, the manner in which He allows us this benefit, this glorious Redemption, is strictly through Faith, which means that we simply believe in what Jesus did there on our behalf. That's all that God requires.

In fact, if we attempt to do anything else to earn this right or merit this right, instead of it having the desired effect, it will actually have the very opposite effect. Works on our behalf of any fashion, will nullify the Grace of God, which in effect stops our Faith (Gal. 2:20-21). Faith cannot operate at all in the position of works. As Paul says over and over again, if it's Faith it's not works, and if it's works it's not Faith (Rom. 4:4-6).

In fact, this is the problem with the world, and much of the Church. Man attempts to earn Salvation, which is impossible anyway, but of which there is no need, for Jesus has already paid it all. So, the Lord only asks that we have Faith in this which Christ has done, which means to believe fully in this, taking upon ourselves the Person of Christ in every respect. In other words, to properly believe on Christ, means to accept what He did at the Cross and the Resurrection on our behalf.

Paul said in respect to this, *"Who gave Himself for our sins, that He might deliver us from this present evil world, according to the Will of God and our Father"* (Gal. 1:4).

## SLEEP IN JESUS

The phrase, *"Even so them also which sleep in Jesus will God bring with Him,"* refers to the Rapture of the Church, or one might say, the Resurrection of all Believers, even as Paul describes in I Corinthians, Chapter 15.

Without going into detail, this phrase tells us what happens to Believers upon death. The moment the Christian dies, he instantly goes to be with Christ (Phil. 1:20-24). This is made possible by what Christ did at the Cross and in His Resurrection.

Before the Cross, when Believers died, they did not go to Heaven to be with Christ, but rather were taken down into Paradise, which in effect was a part of Hell, separated from the burning part only by a great gulf. Incidently, this is in the heart of the Earth, and is still there, but now empty (Lk. 16:19-31). In fact, all the righteous souls who went to Paradise, were held captive by the Devil against their wills (Heb. 2:14-15). Actually, he had hopes of keeping them there forever, and would have done so but for the Cross.

He could hold them there simply because a sin debt was still upon them. Actually they were saved, and because of Faith in Christ, but due to the fact that the blood of bulls and goats could not take away sin, the sin debt remained.

When Jesus died on the Cross, the sin debt was completely paid and settled, and that means for every single person who has ever lived who will believe (Jn. 3:16). Now Satan had no more claim on these righteous souls.

Consequently, Jesus had the legal right to go down there and liberate them, which He did, even as it tells us in Ephesians 4:8-10.

Now as stated, when Believers die, they instantly go to be with the Lord Jesus, at least as it regards their spirit and soul. The body is placed in the ground (or somewhere), there to await the Resurrection, when it will be joined in glorified form with the soul and the spirit, which will come back with Christ at the Resurrection. That's what Paul is meaning when he says, *"Even so them also which sleep in Jesus will God bring with Him."*

## SOUL SLEEP NOT TAUGHT IN SCRIPTURE

Some teach that the moment the Believer dies, his soul and spirit along with his body, go to the grave, where they sleep there until the coming Resurrection. Nothing like that is taught in Scripture.

All the Scriptures that speak of such, are referring to the body only, and not to the soul and the spirit of the individual. As we have stated, before the Cross, at death, the soul and

NOTES

NOTES

the spirit went down into Paradise, with the body going into the grave. As stated, these were liberated from that place by Christ after His Death on the Cross. Since the Cross, the soul and the spirit of all Believers go to be with the Lord at death, there awaiting the Resurrection of the body which in fact, does sleep.

While the Word of God definitely teaches that the flesh, or the human body, goes back to the dust of the Earth, and in effect sleeps in the dust of the Earth until the Resurrection, in no place does the Bible teach that the soul, or the soul and the spirit, sleep.

In fact, the soul and the spirit cannot die, and also cannot sleep. It is only the physical body of the human being, which incidentally is not yet redeemed, which can die, and in fact does die, thereby awaiting the Resurrection, whether of life or damnation (Gen. 3:19; Eccl. 3:19-21; Mat. 9:24; I Cor. 11:30; I Thess. 4:13-18).

In order to fully express what Paul is saying here, words must be supplied. Christ is alive forevermore in the unseen Glory; the Christian dead are in Him, and actively participating with Him; therefore, they cannot miss the *"Parousia,"* or Coming, since God will bring them with Christ when He returns.

(15) "FOR THIS WE SAY UNTO YOU BY THE WORD OF THE LORD, THAT WE WHICH ARE ALIVE AND REMAIN UNTO THE COMING OF THE LORD SHALL NOT PREVENT THEM WHICH ARE ASLEEP."

The authority that validates Paul's affirmation in Verse 14 is nothing less than *"the Lord's Own Word."*

Exactly as to how this *"Word of the Lord"* came to Paul, we are not exactly told; however, every evidence points to the Lord personally revealing this to Paul (Gal. 1:11-12).

## THE WORD OF THE LORD

The phrase, *"For this we say unto you by the Word of the Lord,"* presents the Doctrine of the Rapture of the Church, as the *"Word of the Lord,"* which all would do well to heed, as should be overly obvious! We're not speaking here of ideas or the mere thoughts of men, but rather that which has been given by the Lord of Glory. Consequently, irrespective as to what some say, or what some believe, the Rapture of the Church is going to happen, and in fact, it's going to happen very soon.

Part of the following has been given in another one of our Commentaries; however, due to the great significance of the Rapture of the Church, and understanding how Commentaries are normally studied, I felt it would be proper for this information to be given again.

As well, much of the following is from the material of Kenneth Wuest, to whom we are indebted.

## JESUS OF NAZARETH — HIS COMING FOR HIS CHURCH

The next great event on the prophetic calendar in the Bible is the Coming of Jesus of Nazareth for His Church. The event is imminent. In fact, there are no prophecies unfulfilled which would withhold His Coming. Briefly, its purpose is to raise the righteous dead from Adam to the time of this Coming, and to translate living Believers who are on Earth at that time. This will involve the bringing of the former with Him from Heaven, the transforming of their dead bodies which have moldered into dust, into perfect glorified bodies, and also the transformation of the living bodies of Believers then on Earth into like perfect, glorified bodies, and the transportation of both classes to Heaven.

This event is called in theological circles, *"The Rapture of the Church,"* in that the Church of Jesus Christ will be joined forever to her great Bridegroom, Jesus of Nazareth.

Our Lord speaks of His Coming for His Own in John 14:1-3, where He tells His Disciples that He is going to His Father's House to prepare a place for them, and that He will come again and receive them to Himself. In other words, He is coming from Heaven into the atmosphere of this Earth to take the Church with Him back to Heaven. And this event may take place at any moment. Believers will be taken to Heaven, and unbelievers will be left on Earth to undergo the terrible times of the Great Tribulation Period.

## WHERE IS HEAVEN, AND HOW FAR IS IT FROM EARTH?

We will address ourselves to the question as to what is involved in this great event. First of all, where is Heaven, how far is it

NOTES

from the Earth, how long will it take the Lord Jesus to travel that distance, and just how close to the Earth will He come?

As to the locality of Heaven, Isaiah gives us some hints. He reports the words of Lucifer, the mightiest Angel God created, who was His regent on the perfect Earth of Genesis 1:1 (Isa. 14:12-14), before his fall.

Lucifer said, *"I will ascend into Heaven."* This means that he was not in Heaven when he rebelled against God. *"I will exalt my throne above the stars of God."* This tells us that Lucifer had a throne below the stars of God, on this Earth, and having a throne, he reigned over a pre-Adamic race of beings, directing their worship to the God of Heaven.

This last utterance also teaches that God's Throne is beyond the stars of the universe. God's Throne, the place of His centralized authority, is in Heaven. Heaven is outside of the universe. Lucifer speaks again:

*"I will sit also upon the mount of the congregation, in the sides of the north."* This localizes Heaven as above the Earth in a line with the axis of the Earth, above the North Pole, and in a place beyond the farthest star. Heaven is not above the Earth in all directions. The inhabitants at the equator look up and see blue sky. But Heaven is not above them as they look directly up from where they stand. The explorers of Antarctica looked up and saw blue sky. But Heaven was not above them. Heaven has a fixed location above the North Pole, in a line with the axis of the Earth.

## WHAT IS THE DISTANCE TO HEAVEN?

How far is Heaven from the Earth?

By new and more powerful telescopes, Astronomers have recently discovered stars that are 500,000,000 light years from the Earth. That means that it has taken light from these stars, traveling at the speed of 186,000 miles per second, 500,000,000 years to reach this Earth. But how far are these stars from the Earth?

Multiply 500,000,000 by 60 (seconds), that number by 60 (minutes), that number by 24 (hours), that number by 365 (days), and that number by 186,000, and you will have the number of miles which these stars are from the Earth. The number is 2,932,848,000,000,000,000,000. Heaven is at least that many miles from the Earth.

These Astronomers say that beyond these stars, there is a thinning out of stars, indicating either that the material universe ends here, or that there may be a relatively empty space, after which stars may again appear. In fact, such figures stagger one's imagination.

Think of the great God Who could speak such a universe into existence by Divine fiat.

He spoke the Word, and a universe sprang into existence. Job says that the sons of God (Angels) shouted for joy when they saw the universe come into existence (Job 38:7). And we should be careful to note that they did not exclaim with joy over a chaos, but rather a cosmos, a perfect, ordered creation (Gen. 1:1). The chaos of Genesis 1:2 came as the result of Lucifer's Fall.

## THE SPEED OF THOUGHT

Our Lord then, when coming to take out His Church from the Earth, will travel a distance of 2,932,848,000,000,000,000,000 miles, or more!

If He traveled through space at the speed of light, 186,000 miles per second, it would take Him 500,000,000 years to reach the Earth. But a bird's eye view of Bible history and prophecy shows that the Divine program for the human race on Earth is only about 7,000 years, 6,000 of which have rolled around. No, this Jesus of Nazareth Who is Very God of Very God, will come with the *"speed of thought"* from Heaven, one moment in Heaven, the next, in the atmosphere of this Earth.

## HOW CLOSE TO THIS EARTH WILL HE COME?

Paul, in His classic account of the Rapture, which we are now studying (I Thess. 4:13-18) says that we will *"meet the Lord in the air."*

The Greeks have two words for *"air."* The first Greek word is *"aer,"* and refers to the lower, denser atmosphere, and the second Greek word is *"aither,"* which speaks of the rarefied, thinner atmosphere. A Greek would stand on the summit of Mt. Olympus which is 6,403 feet high, and pointing downward would say, *"aer,"* and pointing upward, would say *"aither."* Now, which word did Paul use?

A glance at the Greek text shows that he used the word *"aer."* All of which means that the Lord Jesus, when He comes for His Bride, the Church, will descend to a distance within 6,403 feet of the Earth, which is little more than a mile or less.

THE ASSURED HOPE

The great Apostle was writing to the Thessalonian Christians who were sorrowing over the loss of loved ones who had died. He tells them not to sorrow as others who have no hope.

The tombstones in the cemeteries of Thessalonica were inscribed with the words *"No Hope."* These pagan Greeks, striving to pierce the future through their philosophies, could never arrive at any positive assurance of a reunion with loved ones in the afterlife. They had no hope.

To these Christian Greeks, Paul holds out the assured hope of reunion with loved ones who were Believers, a reunion in the air, when Jesus comes for His Church. He says that since we believe that Jesus died and rose again, God will bring with Jesus from Heaven, our loved ones who have fallen asleep (euphemism for death) in Jesus. He states that we who are alive when Jesus comes, will not prevent (old English for *"precede"*) the dead in the order in which we will receive our glorified bodies. In fact, they will receive their new bodies first.

After receiving our new bodies, we who are alive when Jesus comes, will be caught up together with the dead who have been raised. We will be caught up in the clouds.

Actually, there is no definite article in the Greek Text before the word *"clouds."* There should not be one in the translation. We shall be caught up in clouds, which really refers to *"clouds of Believers."*

That is, the great masses of glorified Saints going up to Heaven, will have the appearance of clouds. The Greek word for *"clouds"* here is used in Hebrews 12:1 in the phrase, *"Wherefore seeing we also are compassed about with so great a cloud of witnesses,"* the inspired writer visualizing a Greek stadium with its thousands of onlookers occupying the tiers upon tiers of seats. The same word is used in the Greek classics of a large army of foot soldiers.

NOTES

Paul says that we will be caught up. The Greek word translated *"caught up"* has a number of meanings which give us some important information regarding the Rapture. The word is *"harpazo."* The following are its meanings:

TO CARRY OFF BY FORCE

The first meaning is the words of our heading *"to carry off by force."* This gives us the reason why the Lord Jesus will descend to at least 6,403 feet above the Earth. Satan and his kingdom of demons occupy this lower atmosphere. Paul speaks of him as *"the prince of the power of the air"* (Eph. 2:2), and uses the Greek word *"aer"* which speaks of the lower, denser atmosphere in which we live.

The demons inhabit this portion of the atmosphere around the Earth in order to carry on their work in the kingdom of darkness as it regards the human race, etc. They also attempt to prey upon Christian Believers. They attempt to disrupt the workings of the Church, spoil the testimony and service of Christians, and prevent the unsaved from receiving the Lord Jesus as Saviour. They are trying to insulate the Church one might say, from Heaven.

At the time of the Rapture they will attempt to keep the Church from going up to Heaven with the Lord Jesus. Jesus of Nazareth, however, will exert His Omnipotent Power in taking the Saints with Him to Heaven through the kingdoms of Satan, and against his power and that of his demons, hence *"to carry off by force."*

TO RESCUE FROM THE DANGER OF DESTRUCTION

The word *"harpazo"* also means *"to rescue from the danger of destruction,"* which means that the Church will be caught up to Heaven before the seven year period of great tribulation occurs on Earth.

By the Church here we do not mean the visible organized present-day Church composed of Believers and unbelievers, but only those in the visible Church whose Christian profession will stand the test of actual possession of Salvation. The nominal Christian, that person merely identified with the visible Church by membership, and not possessing a

Living Faith in the Lord Jesus as Saviour, will be left on Earth to go through the terrible times of the Great Tribulation.

As to the pre-Tribulation Rapture of the Church, more might be said. The Divine analysis of the Book of Revelation *"the things seen* (the Patmos Vision by John of the Lord Jesus)"; Chapter 1: *"the things that are* (the Church Age, which has lasted now for nearly 2,000 years)"; Chapters 2 and 3: *"the things which shall be after these things* (events happening after the Church Age)"; Chapters 4-22, found in Chapter 1, Verse 19 of the Book of Revelation, indicates that the Church will be caught up before the Tribulation Period begins.

Chapters 6 to 19 describe that period. These events take place after the Church Age. Again, the Promise given the Missionary Church (Philadelphia) which is in existence today and which blends with the last age of Church History, the Apostate Church (Laodicean), to the effect that God will keep that Church from the hour of *"the testing"* (Rev. 3:10), namely, the Tribulation Period, also indicates a pre-Tribulation Rapture.

Again, there is nothing in Scripture which indicates that the Church will either enter or pass through the Tribulation. Israel is given many signs which will warn her of the near approach of that Period (Mat. Chpt. 24), but the Gospels and the Epistles are entirely devoid of any sign given to the Church. The Epistles speak of the Day of Christ Jesus (Phil. 1:6), an expression not found in the Old Testament or the Gospels. This is a day to which the Church is to look forward with joy. It is the end of the pathway of the Christian Church. If this day does not occur before the Tribulation, then there is no place for it in the prophetic calendar of events which will take place during or after that period.

## THE GREAT TRIBULATION

The Great Tribulation Period is a time when the Divine Wrath is to be visited on Earth-dwellers, particularly upon Israel. But the Promise to the Church is that it has been delivered from the Wrath to come (Rom. 5:9; I Thess. 1:9-10; 5:8). The Bible expressly states who will be the objects of the Divine Wrath during the Tribulation Period, namely, Israel and the ungodly of the Gentile nations.

NOTES

If the Church were destined to suffer, surely, the Bible would make note of that fact along with the mention of the above two companies of individuals. The Biblical attitude of the Believer is one of waiting for the Glorification of His Body (Rom. 8:23), and of looking for the Saviour (Phil. 3:20-21; I Thess. 1:9-10). The language is clear that the Believer is to expect Him at any moment, not look for Him in connection with some predicted event for which signs have been given to Israel and not to the Church.

In fact, to teach that the Church will go through the Tribulation Period, is to nullify the Biblical teaching of the imminent Coming of the Lord Jesus for the Church. Events on Earth are not yet in readiness for the Great Tribulation. Indeed, at this writing (1999), that period, although very close, cannot begin immediately because of certain prophetic events which are yet to be fulfilled. But the Lord may return for His Church at any moment. Paul (Phil. 4:5), Peter (I Pet. 1:13-15), and John (I Jn. 3:2-3) all make the imminent Coming of the Lord for the Church a ground of appeal for holy living and diligent service.

## FOUR DAYS IN SCRIPTURE

Finally, Paul in II Thessalonians 2:1-12 states that the Day of the Lord (the Great Tribulation), cannot come until the departure of the Church from the Earth, which must precede the Great Tribulation. There are four Days in Scripture, which denotes specific time factors. They are as follows:

1. *"The Day of Man"*: This is referred to as *"man's judgment,"* (I Cor. 4:3), which Jesus referred to as the *"Times of the Gentiles"* (Lk. 21:24). Under the permissive Will of God, man has been allowed to have his day, which has lasted now for about 2,600 years — from the time Judah was taken over by Nebuchadnezzar, with the scepter of power passing from the faltering hands of the kings of Judah, to the Gentiles.
2. *"The Day of Christ"*: (Phil. 1:6), when Christ has His Day, the Rapture, when He comes for His Bride, one might say.
3. *"The Day of the Lord"*: (II Thess. 2:2), best Greek Texts, do not have Day of Christ, but *"Day of the Lord."* This is when the Lord

has His Day of Judgment, which will be the Great Tribulation Period.

4. *"The Day of God"*: (II Pet. 3:12), this presents the Millennium merging into eternity.

In the II Thessalonian Passage, Paul is speaking of the Great Tribulation. Someone had written a letter to the Thessalonian Church, stating that the period of the Great Tribulation was then present, and had forged Paul's name to the document. The great Apostle calms their fears by saying that this particular day cannot come until *"a falling away"* comes first. The Greek word translated *"falling away"* has as one of its meanings, *"a departure."*

The definite article in the Greek appears before it in the original Text. This word is used in other places in the New Testament, and in these places the context indicates that from which the departure is made. But here there is no such information.

Evidently, Paul had already covered this ground with them, and consequently was already known. The Apostle had taught them about the Rapture in I Thessalonians 4:13-18, the Passage of our study. Consequently, the II Thessalonians Text speaks of the Church leaving the Earth for Heaven (II Thess. 2:7). The word *"let,"* is old English for *"restrain."* Consequently, the Text should read:

*"For the mystery of iniquity doth already work: only he* (the Church) *who now restrains will restrain, until he be taken out of the way"* (II Thess. 2:7).

Thus, the departure of the Church precedes the Great Tribulation. The Church will thus be rescued from the danger of destruction.

## DIVINE POWER TRANSFERRING PEOPLE SWIFTLY FROM ONE PLACE TO ANOTHER

The Greek word *"harpazo"* is used of Divine power, in the act of the Lord Jesus taking with Him to Heaven all Believers from Adam's time to the Rapture.

How long will it take the Church to traverse that immense distance between Earth and Heaven? If the Church traveled 186,000 miles per second, as we've already stated, it would take 500,000,000 years to reach Heaven. The only solution to the problem is that we will go to Heaven with the speed of thought, again as we have stated.

NOTES

In fact, Believers will then have new powers of transport or one might say, *"super motion,"* forever in eternity. A settled thought will instantly transport the individual to the destination desired in an instant of time.

## TO CLAIM FOR ONE'S SELF EAGERLY

Again, the Greek word *"harpazo"* means *"to claim for one's self eagerly,"* and speaks here of the great Bridegroom of the Church, coming from Heaven to claim His Own, the Church, and take her to Himself.

From this meaning, we derive the idea that the Lord is very eager to wrap this thing up, one might say. And to be sure, that time is at hand. It cannot be long until the Trump of God sounds, which will usher in the appearance of our Lord and the Rapture of the Church.

It's a shame that many in the modern Church have little interest in the Rapture. In fact, I think I can say without any fear of exaggeration, that most don't even believe in a coming Rapture.

In the last several decades, most of the so-called Gospel which has been preached, has placed the emphasis in this present world, instead of in Heaven where it rightly belongs. The Holy Spirit is getting people ready for Heaven, actually ready for Christ, while many Preachers are attempting to get people ready for this present world. As should be obvious, the two don't go together.

Even as we've already stated, each one of these Chapters in this Epistle, concludes with Paul pointing toward the Rapture of the Church. If the Holy Spirit was this serious about this all-important matter, and He definitely was, then it stands to reason that we should follow suit.

I'm afraid, that the lack of interest in the Rapture, and in fact, the down right denial by many of this coming great event, is a part of the great Apostasy which will characterize the Church at the very end of this age. Even though Christ is very eager to come and claim His Own, many in the modern Church are not eager at all for Him to come.

Why?

## TO SNATCH OUT AND AWAY

Finally, the word *"harpazo"* means, *"to snatch out and away,"* which tells us that the Rapture will occur so suddenly that it will take many by surprise.

Some day soon this great event will take place. How soon? It cannot be far off.

Glance down Bible history for a moment. It is significant that God has been in the habit of doing some great thing with reference to Salvation, at the turn of a Millennium or of two Millenniums. The date of Adam is approximately 4000 B.C., now some 6,000 years ago. The Plan of Salvation in which God the Judge was to step down from His Judgment Throne to take upon Himself the guilt and penalty of human sin in order that He might satisfy His justice, maintain His Government, and at the same time open the floodgates of Mercy to lost sinners, was prefigured in the Sacrifices which He instituted when He made coats of skins and clothed Adam and Eve.

The initial step in the fulfillment of this Plan He took in 2000 B.C., when He called Abraham to be the progenitor of the Jewish nation from which would come the Saviour Who would die and pay for sin.

The next step He took in 1000 B.C., when He started the dynasty of David, from which line of kings the Messiah and Saviour would come.

The next step was taken in A.D. 1, when God, in the Person of His Son came to Earth, became Incarnate in the human race by Virgin Birth, and died on Calvary's Cross, the Substitutionary Atonement for sin. This was His First Advent.

The Second Advent of the Son of God is predicted in Scripture. All indications point to the fact that the Second Advent is near at hand.

The Church has been in existence almost 2,000 years. It would seem logical that God would repeat His custom of doing something of great importance at or near the turn of these two Millenniums, that is, within the next few years. That would be His Coming to Earth a second time. But the Rapture must take place before the Second Advent. All of which means that we are fast approaching the wind-up of things. In fact, the Rapture could occur at any moment.

## CHURCH HISTORY

Let's look at this matter from the standpoint of Church History. The Second and Third Chapters of Revelation, contain the history of the Church, divided into seven periods or ages. They are as follows:

1. The Apostolic Church: This period lasted to about the turn of the First Century.
2. The Martyr Church: This lasted to about A.D. 300, and saw tremendous persecutions of the Church by Rome.
3. The State Church: This lasted to about A.D. 500, which began with Constantine.
4. The Papal Church: This began about A.D. 500, and continues even unto the present. Actually, a so-called Church Leader was first referred to as *"Pope,"* in about A.D. 602.
5. The Reformation Church: This began in about A.D. 1500, and continues hopefully, unto the present. Of course, this speaks of the great Reformation under Martin Luther, and others, which in effect formed the Protestant Church, pulling it away from the Catholic Church.
6. The Missionary Church: This began in about A.D. 1800, with Missionaries being sent out over the world in an unprecedented fashion, which again continues unto this moment; however, at this particular time, 1999, the missions efforts of Churches are probably weaker than ever, especially considering, that most of those who go under the name of *"Missionary,"* are proponents rather of a social Gospel, which is hardly the Gospel of Jesus Christ.
7. The Apostate Church: The Church has already entered into the Apostasy, which will in effect ultimately usher in the Antichrist. This means we are very close to the Rapture, which will actually close the Church Age.

In view of that, I might ask the question, *"Are you ready for the Coming of the Lord Jesus to take His Church with Him to Heaven? Are you living for God now as you should, trusting Christ for all that you have in the Lord?"*

If you have never seen yourself as a lost sinner and Jesus Christ as the Saviour of sinners, and never by an act of heart-faith put your trust in Him as your Saviour from sin through His Precious Blood, you are not ready for His Coming. Should He come while you are in that state, you will be left on Earth to go through the terrible times of suffering and affliction. But you can be ready. The

NOTES

Day of Grace is not over. He will receive you if you will come to Him in Faith believing.

At the same time, we also should appeal to the individual who is saved. Are you also ready for His Coming? Is there anything between yourself and the Lord Jesus that would prevent communion with Him? Are you in the center of His Will? Living a life of constant yieldedness to the Holy Spirit?

These are very serious questions, which we all should ask ourselves, especially considering that the Trump of God could sound at any moment.

### THE NEW MILLENNIUM

This past year of 1999, I have watched scores of Preachers trying to stir up fear in the hearts of Christians by claiming all type of gloomy things, such as banks failing, all utilities shut off, no gasoline for sale, etc. Many have advised their followers to purchase dried food, ammunition, and guns, etc.

To be frank, all this which we have said, and a lot we have not said, can be construed as nothing but foolishness.

Of all people, Christians surely should be able to trust the Lord in something of this nature, which will not present itself as a problem anyway. In fact, if there is any problem whatsoever, it will primarily be because of Preachers who have stirred up fear in people's hearts, causing them to do certain things which will actually be the cause of the difficulty, at least if there is one. However, I said all of that to say this:

Preachers of the Gospel should be warning the people instead, to be ready for the Rapture of the Church. According to the things we have just said about certain particular events taking place on Earth at the change of Millenniums, as instituted by the Lord, at the change of this Millennium, we should certainly know that one of the greatest events of all is surely about to take place. It would seem that Preachers would be encouraging the people to be prepared for this momentous occasion; however, I don't think I've heard one single Message, one single word as it regards this of which I have said. Perhaps some few Preachers have surely broached this all-important subject, but it hasn't come to my ears. That tells me several things:

NOTES

First of all, I think that most Preachers simply don't know their Bibles very well. Also, even as we have previously stated, most of the preaching in the last few decades has attempted to prepare people for this Earth rather than for Heaven. What a travesty! So, it would stand to reason, that if people aren't ready, they will not too much be interested in broaching this subject.

I am dictating these notes on November 4, 1999, just 57 days before the new Millennium. Will the Rapture of the Church take place near this event?

Of course, I cannot answer that! However, there is one thing I can answer: Whatever time the Rapture of the Church will take place, which only the Lord knows, it cannot be very long.

### ISRAEL, THE GREATEST TIME CLOCK OF ALL

As we have previously mentioned, there are all types of signs regarding Israel as it pertains to these last days. In fact, the coming Great Tribulation will be about many things, but most of all about bringing Israel back to God. Jeremiah referred to this coming terrible time as *"the time of Jacob's trouble."* But he said, *"he shall be saved out of it"* (Jer. 30:7).

As well, Jesus pointed out this coming time graphically so in Matthew, Chapter 24.

As well, this will be the time of Satan's greatest effort, with his advent of the Antichrist. The Believer must understand, that Satan the great deceiver of mankind, is in fact, deceived himself. He actually believes that he can win this thing, hence his final great push.

So, this thing will come to a conclusion with the Antichrist making his big debut for world domination, which will close out the Times of the Gentiles (Lk. 21:24). Look at the order of events:

Knowing that the time is at hand, Satan put it in the heart of Adolph Hitler to annihilate the Jewish people, which terrible Holocaust began in the late 1930's, and carried through World War II. It resulted in the slaughter of some 6,000,000 Jews, the most horrible, systemized bloodletting that humanity has ever known. If enough Jews could be killed, they would not be able to form a

State, which Satan knew from Bible Prophecy was going to happen. In fact, this was the reason that Satan raised up Adolph Hitler, and deceived the German people to such an extent. They suffered for it horribly so, not realizing how they had been dupes in the hands of Satan, the arch enemy of God.

Satan failed in this effort, but it was not for a lack of trying.

After World War II, world Jewry set about to reclaim their ancient land, which they actually had not occupied for some 1,900 years — basically since A.D. 70, when Jerusalem was completely destroyed by Titus, the Roman General. During the intervening centuries they were scattered all over the world, and suffered persecution as few people have suffered. Their cry, *"We have no king but Caesar,"* proved to be a self-fulfilling prophecy (Jn. 19:15). But they found that Caesar proved to be a very hard taskmaster.

For Bible Prophecy to be brought to pass concerning the last days, Israel must reform her ancient State, which she did in 1948, with the Star of David for the first time in some 1,900 years, flying over Jerusalem. Her becoming a State, with the Arabs violently opposed to this action, was none other than a miracle within itself. But of course, despite every effort of the Evil One, the Lord worked this thing out, and brought it to pass. He put it in the heart of President Harry S. Truman to put the full weight of the Presidency of the United States behind this action. Shortly before he died, when Truman was asked by a Reporter, *"What do you consider to be your greatest achievement while in Office?"*

The former President thought only for a moment, and then replied, *"The help I gave in the forming of Israel as a State!"*

His answer somewhat shocked the Reporter, who was thinking of the Marshall Plan, or the ushering in of the world into the Atomic Age, of which Truman set the stage. In fact, there were any number of things he could have said, but instead he surprised this Reporter with his reply about Israel.

Perhaps the President, coming down to the closing days of his life, realized how extremely important this event actually was, as he thought upon spiritual things. He was right, that was the most important thing that he did.

NOTES

I had the occasion to hear an interview with Clark Clifford which took place not long before he died. He had been an Advisor to every Democratic President from Truman up to and including Jimmy Carter. However, most of his interview centered up on the State of Israel and President Truman.

Mr. Clifford went on to say how George C. Marshall Head of the Joint Chiefs of Staff, and one of President Truman's closest friends, was bitterly opposed to the forming of Israel as a State. He used all his persuasive powers upon the President, attempting to get him to go in the other direction.

Clark Clifford related as to how he wrote President Truman a short note, strongly urging him to seriously consider the forming of Israel as a State, and that it must be in their ancient geographical homeland, and that it must be called *"the State of Israel."*

Clifford was a young man at the time, and was surprised when President Truman sent for him. The President wanted to talk to him about his views regarding the formation of the State of Israel.

*"Why, should we do this?"* he asked Clifford.

The President knew, whichever way he went, would decide the fate of these people, at least as it regards their forming a nation. Without the Blessing of the United States, it would be virtually impossible for them to succeed.

Clark Clifford answered the President, *"Because it's right Mr. President, because it's right!"*

According to Clifford, the President gave no sign as to his feelings. The conversation ended in a few moments, and Clifford was excused from the Oval Office.

But then Clifford now gray in years, said, *"What impact my views had on the President I am not sure; however, he did exactly what I recommended. After 1,900 years, Israel was again a State."*

Once again, it is amazing that this Advisor to Presidents, when coming to the end of his life's span, would discuss Israel, and his part whatever that might have been, in the formation of this State, when he could have talked about any number of things!

I'm trying to say, if men of the world who make little claim on God, somehow realize the significance of this of which we speak, which was actually a powerful fulfillment of Bible Prophecy, whether they understood that or not, why is it that Preachers, who claim to know God, who claim to understand the Bible, cannot see the same thing?

At this present time Israel is struggling to try to find some type of accommodations with the Arabs. And yet, her darkest days are just ahead, even though at the moment she does not even remotely realize such. In fact, as the Antichrist deceives her, making her think that he is her saviour, who she will actually claim to be the Messiah, with a shocking finality, she will realize that he is not who he claims to be, which will result in her near destruction as a nation and a people. That is just ahead!

Actually, this coming dire time, even as prophesied so dramatically by Zechariah, will bring her to the edge of total destruction; however, Satan will not have his way, because her extremity, and it will be an extremity such as she has not known previously, will bring about the Coming of her True Messiah, The Lord Jesus Christ (Zech. Chpts. 12-14). This will be the Second Coming, which will be the most dramatic event in human history (Rev. Chpt. 19).

Then Israel will finally say *"yes"* to the King of kings and the Lord of lords.

Zechariah said, *"In that day there shall be a fountain opened to the House of David and to the inhabitants of Jerusalem for sin and for uncleanness"* (Zech. 13:1).

Then the world will be ushered into the Millennium, the thousand year Reign of Christ on this Earth, with all the Saints of God with Him, who will actually accompany Him back to Earth. The world will then know a peace and prosperity it has never previously known. Isaiah said:

*"They shall not hurt nor destroy in all My holy mountain: for the earth shall be full of the knowledge of the Lord, as the waters cover the Sea"* (Isa. 11:9).

Israel will then gain her place which she has so long sought, but in all the wrong ways. Now she will be, that which the Lord originally promised her, and which she could have had so much sooner, but sadly, and regrettably, rebelled against Christ. That night will now have ended, and ended forever, with the Daystar now dawning, in which it will shine forever!

NOTES

## SAINTS ALIVE

The phrase, *"That we which are alive and remain unto the Coming of the Lord,"* concerns the second segment who will go in the Rapture.

Some have attempted to take the pronoun *"we"* and make it seem as though Paul thought that he would be alive when the Rapture took place. That is not the case at all!

The Apostle plainly says in II Thessalonians 2:1-2, that certain things had to happen before *"the Day of Christ"* could come about. By Paul using the word *"we,"* he was merely referring to those who would be alive at Christ's return. That's all!

From the account given in II Thessalonians, Chapter 2, he knew this coming time concerning the Lord's return would not happen in his day. In fact, the Gospel according to Matthew had more than likely already been written, with the Twenty-fourth Chapter of that Book, even in the Words of Jesus Himself, giving an outline of futuristic events. To be sure, Paul had studied this Gospel very, very closely. I cannot even remotely see, that he would have done otherwise.

As we know, Luke who traveled with him for years, was used by the Lord to write the Gospel which bears his name, as well as the Book of Acts. Considering how much Luke knew and understood concerning the Life of Christ, one can well imagine the countless hours that both men spent together discussing this momentous event.

The Apostle knew that the Church must be expanded to cover the entirety of the Earth, which of necessity, would take some time. Unfortunately, after the demise of Paul and the original Twelve Apostles, along with other great men and women of God of that time, the Church began to apostatize, eventually going into a strictly man-devised organization, calling itself *"the Catholic Church."* This hindered the progress of the Work of God to such an extent, that it defies all description. Not until the Fifteenth Century, which ushered in the Reformation under Martin Luther, did this terrible situation begin to change.

Also, there have been very few Preachers in history, who have had the zeal of Paul and those with him, to spread this Gospel all over the world, which of course, is priority with God. So, the building of the Church, which Jesus mentioned in Matthew 16:18, has not come about nearly as fast as it should have; nevertheless, it ultimately has been carried out, at least to a great extent one might say!

As well, many other events in these last times must take place, such as the rise of the Antichrist, which will usher in a time of wickedness such as the world has never known. However, even as Paul said, this will not happen until the Church is taken out of the way (II Thess. 2:7).

Irrespective, the point I wish to make is, that even though that time was not at hand in Paul's day, it definitely is at hand presently. We're living in the very last of the last days. And how do I know that?

## THE LAST OF THE LAST DAYS

There are several earmarks given in the Bible as it regards this particular time. Some of them are as follows:

1. The outpouring of the Holy Spirit all over the world: The Prophet Joel told us of a *"former rain"* and a *"latter rain"* as it concerns the outpouring of the Holy Spirit (Joel 2:23). The former rain consisted of the great outpouring of the Holy Spirit recorded in the Book of Acts as it regards the Early Church. As we've already stated, there was a great spiritual declension after that, which hindered the Work and Moving of the Holy Spirit. In other words, the Church departed from the Word of God.

However, at about the turn of the Twentieth Century, the *"latter rain"* began to be poured out on this world, which has resulted in untold millions being Baptized with the Holy Spirit even as in Bible times, which refers to speaking with other Tongues as the Spirit of God gives the utterance (Acts 2:4). As well, a total and complete way of life was brought forth, as a result of this great Pentecostal experience, which is available to all.

So this sign, is one of the greatest of all that we're living in the very last of the last days. When we consider, that the Holy Spirit has been being poured out for nearly 100 years now, this should tell us that the *"Day of Christ"* is at hand!

2. The great falling away: Paul said this concerning these last days:

*"Now the Spirit speaketh expressly, that in the latter times* (the very times in which we now live) *some shall depart from the Faith, giving heed to seducing spirits, and doctrines of devils"* (I Tim. 4:1).

Notice that he said, *"some shall depart from the Faith,"* not all!

As well, what did he mean by *"the Faith"*?

To sum it up, the Apostle was speaking of the Cross of Christ. This is what *"the Faith"* is all about. It is what Jesus did at the Cross in order to redeem mankind, and man's Faith in that Finished Work.

As I've said previously, I believe *"the Cross"* is going to be the dividing line in these last days as it regards Truth. Those who ignore the Cross, or downplay its veracity, will *"depart from the Faith." "The Faith"* and *"the Cross"* being synonymous, it can be no other way. So let me say it again:

The Cross of Christ is going to be, and in fact has already begun to be, the dividing line as to what constitutes true Believers and otherwise.

## THIS REVELATION

If in fact that is correct, and I definitely believe it is, even to the extent, that I believe the Lord has revealed that to me, then this Revelation which the Lord has given us is of far greater significance than meets the eye. It means that this great thing the Lord has revealed to me, is not merely for me, even though it definitely is for this Evangelist, but as well for the entirety of the Church. That being the case, it takes on a completely new complexion.

Of course, no Truth as given by the Lord, which of course always coincides perfectly with the Word of God, because in fact, it is the Word, must ever be taken lightly; however, there are some things far more important, due to the fact of what it is intended to address. This of which I speak, is intended to address the entirety of the Church all over the world. I believe in what I say that strongly. In other

NOTES

words, to ignore what we are saying, or any other Preacher for that matter who proclaims this Message, is to do so at one's peril.

To be sure, that is in no way because of me, or any other Preacher, but because of the Message itself.

If the Lord is telling the Church to come back to the Cross, to understand the veracity of the Cross, or in other words what Jesus did there, understanding that every Victory comes from that Finished Work, and that Message is rejected or ignored, the consequences cannot be pleasant.

As well, for anyone to take the position that they already know these things, and, therefore, pass it off with a wave of the hand, is a dead giveaway that in Truth they do not know these things, and in fact, don't really know anything at all about these things. If one truly knows what we're teaching here as it regards the Cross of Christ, one will hunger to hear more, one will thirst for this great Revelation to be ever expanded, one will not be able to get enough of this Message, and for all the obvious reasons. Once you properly understand the Cross of Christ, i.e., *"the Finished Work of Christ,"* at least, as far as a poor human can understand it, it will change everything about you. It will change your understanding of the Word of God, the way you think about things, the way you look at the Lord and especially, the way you look at yourself. And when that happens, and it definitely will if your Faith is properly placed in the great Sacrifice of Christ, it will be the greatest day of your life, other than the day Jesus saved you.

The Lord is coming, and He to be sure, is coming soon. Consequently, He is getting His Church ready. And with all of my heart, I believe this is the way and the manner in which He is preparing His Church — bringing us back to the Cross.

## WHAT DETERMINES THE TIME OF THE LORD'S RETURN?

First of all, when we speak of *"the Lord's return,"* we are speaking here of the Rapture; I say that because the term can also be used for the Second Coming, which is totally different than the Rapture.

To help us understand it better, these two Comings of the Lord, are just that — two Comings. This means that these two appearances are not two stages of one Coming.

NOTES

At the First Coming one might say, Jesus comes back *"for"* the Saints; at the Second Coming, the Lord comes back *"with"* the Saints (I Thess. 4:13-18; Rev. Chpt. 19).

The question has surely been asked many times, as to what determines this First Coming? In other words, is there a definite date fixed in the Mind of the Lord, which in effect has been fixed forever one might say, or is this Coming predicated on the spiritual condition of the Church?

Both!

God Who knows all things, definitely knows the exact time when Christ is coming back for His Church.

As well, He is definitely preparing His Church, which will coincide with that time, and which I think is that which I've just said, the Message of the Cross. However, that doesn't mean that all Believers are going to accept this which we have said. In fact, if history is any teacher, I think that most will reject this which the Lord does; however, for those who do accept, and many will, they are going to be closer to the Lord than ever before. This is the preparation.

Now how long this preparation will continue, only the Lord knows that. But inasmuch as it has already begun, and I definitely believe it has, this should tell us that time is very short.

3. Israel: We've already dealt with Israel; however, we should again say, Israel is God's greatest, prophetic time clock. So, if Israel is being prepared for the coming rise of the man of sin, and the Great Tribulation which will be her most trying time, and she definitely is, this should tell us that the Rapture of the Church is very, very close!

## THE LIVING WILL NOT PREVENT THE DEAD IN CHRIST

The phrase, *"Shall not prevent them which are asleep,"* refers to the fact that the living Saints will not precede or go before the dead Saints. In fact, even as the next Verse portrays, the *"dead in Christ shall rise first."*

Without a doubt, the Rapture of the Church, which is in effect the Resurrection, will be the most stupendous event the world has ever known, other than the event which will closely follow, the Second Coming of the Lord to this Earth.

The idea of Paul's statement is, that since the Cross of Christ, death has no more hold on the Child of God. While this physical body does die, the soul and the spirit of the Saint automatically goes to be with Jesus, there to await the Resurrection, with untold millions waiting at this present time. Their wait is about over!

## PREVENT

The word *"prevent"* as used in this Verse means presently *"to so order or control circumstances that a certain proposed act will not take place."* But when the King James Version was translated in A.D. 1611, it meant what the Greek word from which it is translated means.

The word means *"to precede, to get the start of."* The teaching is that the Saints who are alive when our Lord comes, will not precede the Saints who died previous to the Rapture, in receiving their glorified bodies, for the dead in Christ shall take the precedence, being glorified first.

(16) "FOR THE LORD HIMSELF SHALL DESCEND FROM HEAVEN WITH A SHOUT, WITH THE VOICE OF THE ARCHANGEL, AND WITH THE TRUMP OF GOD: AND THE DEAD IN CHRIST SHALL RISE FIRST:"

This which Paul gives here, continues to be the *"Word of the Lord"* from the previous Verse, even as the entirety of this Passage. In other words, this which the Apostle is giving, is a Revelation from the Lord to Paul, which had not heretofore been given.

There was here and there in the Old Testament glimpses concerning this great event, but only a hint, and in fact, so dim, that unless one first knew this of which Paul has said, it is doubtful that the word given here and there concerning this occasion, would be recognizable. In fact, four great Truths are brought out in this one Verse. They are as follows:

## A SHOUT

The phrase, *"For the Lord Himself shall descend from Heaven with a shout,"* refers to *"this same Jesus"* of which the Angels proclaimed in Acts 1:11.

NOTES

It is sometimes supposed that the three attendant phenomena, the *"shout,"* the *"voice,"* and the *"trump,"* are three expressions of the same thing; each, however, may be seen as having a distinct meaning.

*"Shout"* in the Greek which is actually a *"cry of command"* is a word used to denote the cry of a Commander to his soldiers in combat, by a charioteer to his horses, or by a ship's master to his oarsmen. It is a loud, authoritative summons, exciting and stimulating.

It speaks here of Christ as the *"Victor,"* thereby *"a shout of Victory."*

It will be the signal for this great event of events, the Resurrection of the Saints, whether dead or alive, of the Living God. The power represented in this *"shout,"* which actually springs of course from Christ, is power beyond the comprehension of any man. It will be enough power not only to raise all the Sainted Dead, but as well to glorify the bodies of both the dead and the living, and to do so instantly. Incidently, the glorified body will be the same as that contained by Christ in His Glorified Form. John said, *"Beloved, now are we the sons of God, and it doth not yet appear what we shall be: but we know that, when He shall appear, we shall be like Him; for we shall see Him as He is"* (I Jn. 3:2).

John was speaking here of the Rapture of the Church, i.e., *"the Resurrection."*

## COMMAND

This *"shout"* will not only be a shout of power, but also it will be a *"command."* It is the same thing as a military order, the same as a General giving orders to his troops.

However, the difference is this: This General is the *"King of kings,"* and the *"Lord of lords,"* meaning that whatever His command is, it will be obeyed, and that without question. Satan obeys Him, fallen angels of every description obey Him, demon spirits obey Him, and in fact, everything obeys Him and in every respect.

This *"command"* will be the signal for the Glorification of every Saint who has ever lived up until that time. It will be the signal for a change that is absolutely unprecedented in human history, and that is a gross understatement! Whatever is incorporated in this *"shout,"* whatever it means, all that God intends, the totality and the completion of this intended by the Holy Spirit, will happen and without fail. It is the First Resurrection of Life, and that Life is in Christ Jesus.

That is partly what He meant when He said, *"I am the Way, the Truth, and the Life"* (Jn. 14:6).

The *"Life"* mentioned here, has to do not only with the Spiritual Life imparted to the believing sinner upon Salvation, which comes solely from the Son of God, and because of what He did at the Cross and His Resurrection, but also refers to that coming day when He will give this *"shout,"* which will impart *"Life"* to every single Saint whether dead or alive, which will result in their Glorified bodies. This speaks of Life of such magnitude, of such dimension, of such power, that it defies all description. It is an outflow of the Spiritual Life already given to the Child of God, but enlarged upon, and to a degree beyond our comprehension.

VICTORY

This *"shout"* not only will be a command, but also a *"shout of victory!"* This is victory unparalleled! It is victory unprecedented! It is victory total and complete!

It is as if to say, the long night is over, the Sun is now rising, which in effect says, *"The Son is now Coming!"*

Satan as a foe was defeated at the Cross, and that includes every fallen angel and demon spirit; however, he has been allowed to continue for nearly 2,000 years now. But it's about over! He has just a short time left, before he will be locked in the bottomless pit, where he will remain for 1,000 years (Rev. Chpt. 20). He will then be loosed for a little season (a very short period of time), and then will be locked in the Lake of Fire where he will remain forever and forever.

So, the shout which will be exhibited by our Lord, in effect proclaims that despite everything Satan could do, that this great number which are going to rise in the air to meet the Lord, will be of such staggering proportions, such vastness, that the Holy Spirit actually refers to it as *"clouds,"* i.e., *"clouds of Saints!"*

NOTES

Someone has said that this shout is going to be *"Hallelujah!"* Of course, that is merely conjecture, for the Scripture doesn't say; however, inasmuch as *"Hallelujah"* is the same in every language all over the world, quite possibly that could be the *"shout!"*

VOICE

The phrase, *"With the voice of the Archangel,"* actually refers to Michael, the only one referred to as such (Jude vs. 9).

Concerning Michael the mighty Archangel, Daniel notes him as the *"Prince of Israel"* (Dan. 10:21). This means that Michael is in some sense in charge of Israel, which refers to protection and leading in some way. Israel has been away from God for a long, long time. However, at the Rapture of the Church, the Great Tribulation which Jesus graphically spoke about in Matthew, Chapter 24, will commence. Even though there are many purposes for the coming Tribulation, the main purpose will be to bring Israel back to God. In fact, this will be the darkest time that these people will have ever faced, in which they will come very close to being totally destroyed by the Antichrist, saved only by the Second Coming of the Lord (Rev. Chpt. 19). Consequently, the commencement of the Great Tribulation will necessitate tremendous involvement by Michael the Archangel, due to Israel being the principal of this terrible time. Of course, it will come out to victory, although by a very laborious process. In other words, Israel will not bend easily, but bend she will!

Perhaps the *"voice"* of this Archangel, has to do with this. As the *"shout"* stipulates the conclusion or gathering of the Church, the *"voice"* will stipulate the beginning of the conversion of Israel, so to speak!

THE TRUMP

The phrase, *"And with the Trump of God,"* doesn't exactly say that God will Personally blow this Trumpet, but that it definitely does belong to Him, whoever does signal this blast.

When the *"Trump of God"* is mentioned, some people get it confused and mixed up with the Trumpets of the Book of Revelation, especially the Seventh Trumpet of Revelation 11:15-13:18.

The *"Trump"* which Paul mentions will signal the Rapture, or Resurrection, of the Church. The Seventh Trump which will sound, which will be in the middle of the Great Tribulation, will signal the Rapture of the 144,000, i.e., *"the man child"* (Rev. 11:15-13:18).

Consequently, one should not confuse the *"Trump of God"* with the *"Trump"* or *"Trumpets"* of the Book of Revelation. They are two different things entirely. In fact, the *"Trump of God"* of I Thessalonians speaks of great blessing, while the Trumpets of Revelation speak, in one way or the other, of judgment (Rev. 6:1-9:21).

## THE TRUMPETS OF ISRAEL

Under the Old Economy of God, the Lord gave instructions to Moses that he was to make *"two trumpets of silver"* (Num. 10:1-2).

When those Trumpets blew, all of Israel was to *"assemble themselves to thee at the door of the Tabernacle of the Congregation"* (Num. 10:3). Likewise, the *"Trump of God"* will signal the assembly of all the Saints.

If they were to go to war, the Trumpets were to be blown (Num. 10:9). The Saints of course will not go to war, but rather to be with Christ; however, this *"Trump of God"* may very well signal the beginning of the Great Tribulation, that is if it is to begin immediately, as well as the Rapture of the Church. Of course, the Great Tribulation is going to bring war such as this world has never known.

Also, the Trumpets were to be blown on *"days of gladness,"* and on *"solemn days,"* and *"in the beginnings of your months"* (Num. 10:10). Of course, the Rapture will in no wise be a solemn day, but rather a day of great gladness, which according to the proclamations of Israel of old were to be signaled by a trumpet blast. As well, the Rapture will be the beginning of the great Joy of Glory, which in fact will never end.

Whether those Trumpets of Israel of old were types and shadows of the great Trump of God, we're not exactly told. But they very well could have been.

## THE DEAD IN CHRIST, FIRST

The phrase, *"And the dead in Christ shall rise first,"* presents the fourth great Truth in this Verse.

NOTES

At the Resurrection, the *"shout,"* the *"Voice,"* and the *"Trumpet,"* will signal two great movements. The first response to this triumvirate will be the Sainted Dead. They will rise first. The second response will be of course, the Saints who are alive, and that refers to the entirety of the world. How long the time factor will be between the two groups, we are not told; however, it couldn't be long, possibly only a few moments, if that!

The short phrase *"the dead in Christ"* beautifully and compactly presents a precious Truth: The position of being in Christ never changes, whether one is alive or dead. The status remains the same, with one change. All the Sainted Dead not only continue to be *"in Christ,"* but as well they are *"with Christ"* (Phil. 1:23). At the Rapture of course, all, both those who have passed on, and all who are presently alive, will now be *"with Christ."*

This is what takes the sting out of death regarding all who have passed on. Even though the loved ones left behind naturally experience grief and sorrow, however, the one who is passed on is instantly with the Lord, and as far as they are concerned, as Paul also said, it is *"far better"* (Phil. 1:23). Only Believers in Christ can say such a thing.

(17) "THEN WE WHICH ARE ALIVE AND REMAIN SHALL BE CAUGHT UP TOGETHER WITH THEM IN THE CLOUDS, TO MEET THE LORD IN THE AIR: AND SO SHALL WE EVER BE WITH THE LORD."

As we have previously stated, the Rapture of the Church is going to be the greatest event in human history, at least as far as the attention of the world is concerned. It will be eclipsed only by the literal Second Coming of the Lord, which will take place about seven years later. As someone has said, if one desires to get the attention of the world, to be sure, the Rapture of the Church will get its attention.

The dead in Christ being given Glorified bodies and being reunited with the spirit and the soul, will attract no attention whatsoever, because they will not be seen, known, or understood; however, when every living Saint of God on the face of this Earth, instantly leaves this mortal coil, that is going to be the event of all events.

On one side of the world it will be night, while on the other side it will be the opposite. This means that Christian pilots who are at the time flying airplanes, whether airliners loaded with people or other kinds, will instantly leave the cockpit to go to be with the Lord. Consequently, that particular situation will spell real trouble for those in the planes who are left behind. Business transactions will be in process, with all of a sudden one or some of the participants instantly leaving the scene, actually vanishing before the very eyes of the other participants. An unsaved husband will be speaking to his redeemed wife, and she is no longer there.

Elementary classrooms of little children will instantly be emptied, as well as all other little children on the face of the Earth, because I personally believe, every baby and young child will go in the Rapture. Consequently, if I'm right in that, this will cause a mourning and lamentation all over the world, exactly as it did in Egypt upon the death of the firstborn. This means every single baby in the world will disappear, as well as all young children, whether their parents are saved or not!

There are some who claim that only the children of saved parents, or at least one parent in the family who is saved, will go in the Rapture, etc. Considering the manner in which Jesus spoke of little children, I cannot really see in my heart how that they would be left on this Earth at that particular time. If all babies and children who die go to Heaven, which I definitely believe they do, especially considering that they are below the age of accountability, at the same time I must believe that they will also go in the Rapture. Requirements for one, are requirements for the other (Mat. 19:13-15).

As stated, if one wants to get the attention of the world, it should be definitely understood that the Rapture will accomplish that fact. If we think this thing through, this will be something of earthshaking proportions, even far beyond what we can even begin to imagine. The idea of millions of people instantly disappearing, and most of these people doing so, right before the eyes of others, leaving only their clothing on the floor, has to be something of such proportions as to boggle the mind.

NOTES

Some have claimed that the news will be put out that this is some type of hoax; however, that is silly! How can one explain the instant disappearance of millions of people before untold millions of eye witnesses, and try to claim that it's a hoax! And that's exactly what's going to happen.

Two things will happen at that time:

1. There has been at least some preaching on the Rapture in many Churches, so that will be the instant observation as to what has happened.

2. There are going to be untold millions of people left in this world who claimed to know God, but really didn't, who will know enough about what has happened to be able to verify what has actually taken place.

No! The world is going to know and in no uncertain terms, that the Rapture of the Church has taken place.

### WHAT WILL THE WORLD DO AT THAT TIME?

It's not so much what the world will do, as to what the world will become. With all Believers taken out, which constitute salt (preservative) and light (illumination), Satan is pretty much left with free reign. So, the world will begin a vortex of evil, a cascade of evil, a niagara of evil, such as it has never known in all of its history. In this climate, the Antichrist will make his debut, and for awhile the world will think that he actually is the true Messiah, especially considering that the Jews will claim him as such. However, that will not be the case, but rather, the very opposite!

Jesus said of this seven years: *"For then shall be Great Tribulation, such as was not since the beginning of the world to this time, no, nor ever shall be."*

He then said, *"And except those days should be shortened, there should no flesh be saved: but for the elect's sake those days shall be shortened"* (Mat. 24:21-22).

The idea is, that the first part of this seven year period will be relatively peaceful, but with the second half or approximately so, witnessing the most horrifying evil and destruction the world has ever known. It is that time which He speaks of as being shortened. Otherwise, there would be no one left alive on the Earth; however, the real reason for this terrible time of bloodletting being shortened, is for Israel's sake, who is referred to here as *"the elect."*

WHY SEVEN YEARS?

The Angel Gabriel appeared to Daniel and told him that *"seventy weeks are determined upon thy people and upon the holy city"* (Dan. 9:24).

In the Hebrew language, seventy weeks literally means seventy-sevens, i.e., *"seventy sevens of years — 490 years."*

Without going into detail at this time as to what that means, suffice to say that sixty-nine of these weeks (483 years) have already been fulfilled. The only thing remaining to be fulfilled is the one week, or seven years, which is actually the time of which Jesus spoke in Matthew 24:21.

Concerning this one week of years, or seven years, Daniel also prophesied and said, *"And he* (referring to the Antichrist) *shall confirm the covenant with many* (this speaks of nations) *for one week* (seven years)*: and in the midst of the week* (after three and one half years) *he shall cause the sacrifice and the oblation to cease* (will stop the Jews from offering up their sacrifices in the newly reconstructed Temple in Jerusalem)," which actually refers to him declaring war on Israel at that time, which will then show his true colors, with Israel going into the worst time of conflict and trouble it has ever known, even as Jesus said (Dan. 9:27). They will be saved only by the Second Coming (Rev. Chpt. 19).

So, when we say *"seven years"* as it refers to the coming Great Tribulation, that is why the number seven is used.

(For a detailed explanation of these Prophecies, please obtain our Commentary on Ezekiel and Daniel, Volume 5. It will be well worth your time and study.)

ALIVE AND REMAIN

The phrase, *"Then we which are alive and remain,"* refers to the second phase of the Rapture, which will no doubt take place moments after the Resurrection of the dead bodies of Saints.

As we've already said, the sudden disappearance all over the world of millions of Believers, actually vanishing into thin air, and even before the eyes of untold numbers of onlookers, is going to create a spectacle, a sensation, an absolute phenomena such as the world has never known.

Due to the proliferation of the Gospel by Television and Radio, there are many in the world who have heard of the Rapture of the Church. In fact, just a short time ago I overheard part of a song (not a Christian song), which mentioned the Rapture, but in a very sarcastic and derogatory way. In other words, they were making fun of this which the Bible teaches. And so, that is the spirit of the world!

Concerning Believers, will there be any warning that this is about to take place?

Actually, the Bible doesn't say. We are rather told to expect this event at any time, and, thusly, to live close to the Lord. In fact, John said: *"And now, little children, abide in Him; that, when He shall appear, we may have confidence, and not be ashamed before Him at His Coming"* (I Jn. 2:28).

He then said, and speaking of the Rapture, *"And every man that hath this hope in Him purifieth himself, even as He is pure"* (I Jn. 3:3).

So, the very idea of the imminent return of the Lord Jesus Christ for His Saints, has a strong tendency, even as the Holy Spirit said through John, to keep one close to the Lord — that is, if one is truly watching and waiting for that coming, which in fact, few are!

In fact, much of the modern Church doesn't even believe in the Rapture. Worse yet, most in the Church are actually not even saved, so, what can be expected!

CAUGHT UP TOGETHER

The phrase, *"Shall be caught up together with them in the clouds,"* refers to the dead in Christ rising first, and then all those alive being instantly changed as well, and then catching up with them, *"to meet the Lord in the air."*

*"Caught up"* in the Greek is *"harpazo,"* and which we have already explained in previous Commentary on this Chapter.

The short phrase *"with them,"* implies a meeting of sorts, even before meeting Jesus.

The change which will take place in the Believer at the Resurrection, pertains first of all to the *"physical body"* being Glorified, with

NOTES

the Lord changing those who are alive (I Cor. 15:51-52), with the dead being given a new body as well as changed (I Cor. 15:38, 44).

However, this *"change"* which will take place, will not only be in the physical realm, but in the *"mental realm"* also. Paul said, concerning this present time, *"For we know in part, and we prophesy in part."*

He then said concerning the Rapture, *"But when that which is perfect is come* (the Resurrection), *then that which is in part* (the old way) *shall be done away.*

*"When I was a child, I spake as a child, I understood as a child, I thought as a child: but when I became a man, I put away childish things"* (I Cor. 13:10-11).

The Apostle is likening the difference in now and then (after we are Resurrected), as the difference in a child and an adult. That's how increased will be the mental ability of the Child of God at that time.

The Apostle went on to say, *"For now we see through a glass, darkly* (not clear at all)*; but then face to face* (we'll see clearly)*: now I know in part; but then shall I know even as also I am known,"* which implies, perfect knowledge (I Cor. 13:12).

As well, this great change also involves the *"spiritual."*

In our present state, the physical body pretty much dominates the human being, with the spirit of man answering to the physical body. In the coming Resurrection, this will no longer be the case. The spirit of man, then energized constantly by the Holy Spirit, will dominate the individual, giving man a complete new dimension. Jesus said, *"Watch and pray, that ye enter not into temptation: the spirit indeed is willing, but the flesh is weak"* (Mat. 26:41).

In other words, the Master is saying that the spirit of man cannot function as it ought to, due to the weaknesses of the flesh. As stated, that will all change in the Resurrection, where the spirit of man will then have dominion, even as God originally intended.

Before the Fall, in the Garden of Eden, Adam and Eve were controlled by their spirit, energized by the Holy Spirit. At the Fall, however, and because of that sickening degeneration, the flesh became the dominant factor. The reason was, the spirit of man is

NOTES

that which worships God. After the Fall, man being spiritually dead could not worship God, so the spirit became moribund.

After conversion (the Born-Again experience) the spirit of man of course, is no longer moribund (lifeless), but now can worship God; however, even though the Believer is Sanctified and Justified, he still isn't Glorified, and will not be such until the coming Resurrection. Therefore, the physical body although not now dominant, or else it's not supposed to be, still plays a great part in our existence, as is obvious, and due to it being the weak link, although spiritually neutral, still, presents the Believer with great problems. Thank the Lord, that will be changed at the Resurrection.

### A MEETING IN THE AIR

The phrase, *"To meet the Lord in the air,"* presents the greatest meeting that humanity has ever known; however, only those who are washed in the Blood of the Lamb, will participate in this meeting.

As we've already stated, the Greeks have two words for *"air."* The first is *"aer"* which refers to the lower, denser atmosphere, and the second is *"aither,"* which speaks of the atmosphere above the lower atmosphere. Actually, the Greeks, at least in their thinking, separated these two to the very foot.

They used the summit of Mt. Olympus which is 6,403 feet high, as the limit of the lower atmosphere, and referred to that as *"aer."* Anything above that, they referred to as *"aither."*

Paul used the Greek word *"aer,"* referring to the lower atmosphere, or from 6,403 feet down.

Consequently, knowing that the Holy Spirit inspired the Apostle to say these words, even giving him the exact word to say, we know that Jesus will come at least within 6,403 feet of this Earth, and perhaps even lower. At this particular height, whatever it will be (6,403 or lower), this great meeting will take place.

Those who go to meet Jesus, will be those for whom He died. Of course, He actually died for the entirety of the world (Jn. 3:16), but most of the world sadly and regrettably, has rejected Him. It was and is the most foolish decision they will have ever made.

For all who have accepted Him, and what He did at the Cross on our behalf, that was the greatest move we ever made. The absolute glory of it all, the splendor of it all, the wonder of it all, absolutely defies description! As someone has said, *"All of this and Heaven too!"*

## EVER BE WITH THE LORD

The phrase, *"And so shall we ever be with the Lord,"* presents unparalleled glory, a rapture absolutely beyond expression, the actual reason and purpose for all that we are and all that we hope to be — to be with the Lord.

As well, we will be with Him forever and forever.

This does not mean that the Saints will always remain with Christ in the air, but rather to be with Him wherever He is.

At that moment, all the Saints will go to Heaven with Jesus, with the *"Judgment Seat of Christ"* then taking place, as well as the *"Marriage Supper of the Lamb."*

Then the Lord, along with every Saint, will come back to this Earth, actually during the middle of the Battle of Armageddon, when He will defeat the Antichrist, and then set up His Millennial Kingdom. He will reign on the Earth for 1,000 years, with all the Saints of God reigning with Him. Israel will once again become prominent during this time.

At the end of the 1,000 years, Satan will be loosed from the Bottomless Pit for a short period of time, but will not be allowed to remain loose very long. He will then be consigned to the Lake of Fire, along with all of his fallen angels and demon spirits, plus every lost soul who has ever lived. He will remain there, locked away, forever and forever (Rev. Chpt. 20).

At that time, the end of the Millennial Reign, the Lord will renovate the heavens and the Earth with fire, cleansing it totally and completely from its defilement of the previous time, after which John said, *"And I saw a new heaven and a new earth* (refurbished)*: for the first heaven and the first earth were passed away; and there was no more Sea"* (Rev. 21:1).

John then said he saw the New Jerusalem coming down from God out of Heaven, then being relocated on planet Earth, where it will remain forever. In fact, God will transfer His Headquarters from Heaven to Earth (Rev. Chpts. 21-22).

John then describes what this New Jerusalem will look like, giving some information concerning that coming time, which presents it as glorious beyond compare.

## THE CROSS

However, I would remind the Reader, that even though Revelation Chapters 21 and 22 describe the perfect age to come, in fact, when there will be no more Satan, sin, or the effects of sin, still, the Holy Spirit through John the Apostle, reminds us as well, that all of this, all of its beauty and glory, all of its splendor and magnificence, has been made possible because of what Jesus did at the Cross. In these two Chapters the Holy Spirit refers to this of which I say, by using the Name *"Lamb"* seven times. This is done that future ages, even forever and forever, will never forget, that all of this was bought at a price, at such a great price, the Death of our Lord and Saviour, Jesus Christ, and His Resurrection (Rev. 21:9, 14, 23, 27; 22:1, 3).

(18) "WHEREFORE COMFORT ONE ANOTHER WITH THESE WORDS."

A little more than 300 years after the Epistle of Paul had arrived at its destination in Thessalonica, seven thousand people were put to death in the Circus in that city. This terrible slaughter was carried out within three hours, by order of the Emperor Theodosius (A.D. 389).

It is very much possible, that some of the Believers in Thessalonica, remembering so long before, the admonishment of the Apostle, *"Comfort one another with these words,"* did exactly that to the bereaved thousands at that horrible time.

## COMFORT

The phrase, *"Wherefore comfort one another,"* concerns two things:

At its best, life is hard. Even if a person has all the money they can spend, and even place and position, and there aren't many who fit this bill, considering the population of the entirety of the world; still, even with those things, perchance they would come one's way, the disappointments, frustrations, and heartbreaks of life, are present just the same, whether one is rich or poor.

Even with Believers, there are still frustrations and disappointments, despite the grand and glorious help of the Holy Spirit. The idea is this:

Preachers make grand mistakes, when they attempt to acclimate people to this present world, instead of the one which is to come. Regrettably, there is little interest presently in that which is to come, with almost all attention directed toward the present. People who follow such Preachers, are being led down a path of spiritual oblivion.

The Saint of God is to ever keep his eyes on the things of Heaven. His inheritance is above and his Lord is above. We look forward, even groan within ourselves, knowing that because of the Fall of man, things aren't right. So, we look for a better land, a better place, a better time, and to be sure, it is coming (Rom. 8:23).

The *"comfort"* we are to provide among ourselves and between ourselves, is the knowledge that this mortal coil is going to soon end. Jesus is coming back for His Church, and we will forever be with Him. What a glorious thought! What a glorious Promise! What a glorious Truth!

## THESE WORDS

The phrase, *"With these words,"* refers to that which Paul gave concerning the Rapture of the Church.

Some try to belittle the word *"Rapture,"* claiming that it should not be used because it's not in the Bible. In-depth study shows, however, there is justification for using it.

The Greek word used here means *"to seize."* Then, it came to mean *"to snatch up forcibly."*

The Greek word was translated into the Latin by *"raptus."* From this comes our English words *"rapt"* and *"rapture."* Today these words usually speak of being carried away emotionally or spiritually. But one meaning of *"rapt"* in current dictionaries is *"lifted up and carried away."*

Thus, it is perfectly good English to translate this Verse, *"Then we which are alive and remain shall be rapt* (raptured) *together with them in the clouds, to meet Jesus in the air."*

NOTES

As well, we should understand that *"these Words,"* are actually the Words of the Lord, and by all means, should be heeded to the utmost. Consequently, for those who claim there is no such thing as a *"Rapture,"* they would do well to read and study *"these words"* very carefully!

## THAT WHICH HAS BEEN AND THAT WHICH IS COMING

At no time in past history has the universal situation of the human race I think, been so desperate as it is today. The powers of evil seem to have intensified their activities to carry the human race on swiftly to a dreadful destruction. Juvenile delinquency is rampant, with morals long since gone, and because the Bible has been removed from the social position of mankind, resulting in schools becoming one of the most dangerous places in the city, with the home following a close second.

Teenage crime is frightening, with gangs ruling parts of great cities. Drunkenness is on the increase, in fact, there are some 20,000,000 alcoholics in America. Add to that the horrifying scourge of drug addiction, with prisons glutted, and we see the true condition of the nation, and in fact, the world.

However, we are lulled to sleep, because the great threat of atomic warfare has ended with the demise of the Soviet Union, leaving America alone as the world's Super-Power. In fact, as I write these words on November 6, 1999, the prosperity of the nation has never been higher. But at the same time, I think that the spiritual temperature has never been lower.

Why?

Apostasy is sweeping the Church, with it lulled to sleep as well, not seemingly realizing what is happening. Much of the Denominational world has rejected the Holy Spirit, and, consequently, has been left with nothing but an empty profession. Pentecostals and Charismatics are running after hucksters and religious con-men. However, the more they are conned, and their pockets picked, it seems like the more they enjoy what is happening.

This present darkness is subtle and, therefore, extremely dangerous. In fact, the Church has never been bigger and has never been richer; however, a 500 pound man, although big, is not healthy, as should be obvious. As well, even while the Church boasts of its gold and silver, the Lord says, *"Because thou sayest, I am rich, and increased with goods, and have need of nothing; and knowest not that thou art wretched, and miserable, and poor, and blind, and naked"* (Rev. 3:17).

What an indictment! The reason for much of this, is the Church abandoning the Word of God and in its place, inserting the wisdom of men.

With one act of disobedience, Adam dropped the entire human race into sin, with the result noted as we have just stated.

Actually, the entrance of sin into the human race produced two problems, an individual one, and an international one.

To meet the first, someone was needed who could pay the price for Redemption; to meet the second, a nation was needed.

Each individual, due to Adam's Fall, was and is constituted a sinner and needs a Saviour. The Promise of a Saviour was given in Genesis 3:21 where the type predicts a Substitute Who would bear that person's sins, pay the penalty, and thus make a way for a Righteous God to bestow Salvation upon the believing sinner and at the same time maintain His Righteousness by satisfying the just requirements of His Law which sinners broke.

But the aggregate of sinners resulted in the formation of nations, which, were composed of sinners, and became hostile to one another, which is the result of such, resulting in the international situation we have presently.

To meet that problem, a nation was needed, a Righteous nation that would form the nucleus around which the other nations might live in a state of Peace and Righteousness. To bring that nation into existence, which was of absolute necessity in God's Plan of Redemption, He called out a pagan living in Ur of Chaldea, a wealthy, sophisticated, self-sufficient man of the world, saved him in sovereign Grace, and gave him this unconditional Promise:

*"I will make of thee a great nation, and I will bless thee, and make thy name great; and thou shalt be a blessing.*

*"And I will bless them that bless thee, and curse him that curseth thee, and in thee shall all the families of the earth be blessed"* (Gen. 12:2-3). That man was Abraham, and that nation is Israel.

NOTES

UNCONDITIONAL PROMISES

It is important to note that these Promises are, *"first,"* a means to an end, the Blessing of the entire human race, and *"second,"* that they are unconditional, and are to be fulfilled irrespective of Abraham's conduct or that of the race descended from him. God could not afford to base the Blessing of all mankind upon the actions of a frail human being.

He promises to make the Jewish nation a great nation. By what standards could that be said of that nation up to the present moment?

Israel failed God despite His protection and blessing by persisting in idolatry, and He had to send the nation into a captivity in which the larger part still remained. The minority that returned to the land of Israel after the Babylonian captivity, were offered the restoration of the earthly kingdom with a Davidic king on the throne, which offer was actually made by Christ, the Messiah of Israel. However, the nation of Israel would not recognize Him as the Messiah, despite incontrovertible proofs, and the results were, they crucified their Messiah, actually, the very One Who made the offer. Because of that, Israel was sent into worldwide dispersion, which took place in A.D. 70, when Titus with the Roman tenth legion, completely destroyed Jerusalem, with over 1,000,000 Jews killed, and hundreds of thousands sold into slavery. In effect, the nation ceased to exist at that time, with the nation consequently being scattered all over the Earth.

This means that the Promise of God has not yet been fulfilled, which means that the time of Israel's greatness is yet future.

To preserve this people, even with the nation destroyed, for its future great history, God in a loose sense of the word, throws His Own protection around these people, as scattered as they might be!

Their rejection of Christ, submitted the world to a continued bloodletting, privation, misery, want, suffering, disease, and destruction, which Jesus could have handled forthwith, even as His short three and one half years of public Ministry proved. But Israel rejected Him!

In effect, Israel, and because of who they were and the Promises by God made to them, answered for the entirety of the human race. As Adam answered for individuals, Israel answered for the nations. Both answered wrongly, and the suffering which followed has been astonishingly awful to say the least.

The nations of the world in turmoil presently, is due to the fact that Israel is not totally in her rightful place in the Promised Land and under her covenanted King, the Son of God, her Messiah, and the world's Saviour.

Jonah, refusing to preach to Nineveh, was swallowed by the fish. The gastric juices of the fish could not digest Jonah. Since the presence of the undigested body of Jonah was a source of discomfort to the fish, it vomited him out on the shores of Israel.

Israel has not fulfilled her mission to the Gentiles, and failed because they thought they had a monopoly on God's Salvation, for which the Holy Spirit through Paul warned them over and over.

The Gentile nations have swallowed the Jewish nation, and not being able to assimilate it, are suffering the discomforts of international strife. All the Presidents from Harry Truman to the present time, have had to deal with Israel. Despite her comparatively small size, Israel along with her contenders, remain the great trouble spot in one way or the other of the world. The Truth is, not until Israel is ruled by her Messiah, the Lord Jesus Christ, from the loins of David so to speak, will real peace come. And not until then will that nation be a blessing to the entire human race. The Promise of Genesis 12:2-3 is still to be fulfilled in the future. Under Israel and by Israel, ultimately and eventually, all the families of the Earth will be blessed; however, that will not come, in fact, cannot come, until Israel finally accepts the One she rejected and even crucified, the Lord Jesus Christ, which she will do at the Second Coming (Zech. Chpts. 12-14).

## ISRAEL AS A NATION

In addition to the Promise that God would make of Abraham a great nation, there was given him the Promise of territory which the future nation would own and occupy. Here again the Covenant was unconditional, depending only upon the sovereign action of God, not at all upon Abraham.

Here is God's Promise, *"Unto thy seed have I given this land, from the River of Egypt unto the great River Euphrates"* (Gen. 15:18). Notice, if you will, the past tense of the verb, *"I have given."* The action had already been taken by God.

This land grant extends from the Nile River up to the western shore of the Mediterranean Sea to the upper reaches of the Euphrates, down the Euphrates to the Persian Gulf and west to the Nile River. In fact, the Jewish nation has never occupied this entire land section.

When Joshua conquered the land of Canaan, Israel occupied the land from the Mediterranean Sea to the Jordan River and a small stretch on the east side of the Jordan. Actually, this was the land section it occupied during our Lord's Ministry on Earth. However, David did push the borders to the Euphrates, actually extending the boundaries not so far from the original territory promised by God to Abraham.

To posses all that God promised, Egypt will have to give up the Sinai. Northern Arabia will be included, along with modern Jordan, parts of Iraq and Syria. This means that this enormous tract of land will yet be occupied by Israel in fulfillment of its great destiny as the nation which will bless the entire human race. This will take place in the coming Kingdom Age, and will begin at the Second Coming.

## A KING

A nation must have a king to rule over it, at least as we think in Old Testament terms. And so God in the process of time establishes a dynasty of kings to rule it forever. He brings David to the throne, who during his reign conceives the idea of building a Temple for the worship of God. But God had other plans for David.

Instead of allowing him to build a house for His worship, He tells David that He will build of him a house of kings. The Prophet Nathan was sent by God to inform David of this fact.

NOTES

The Prophet gives the king this message, *"The Lord telleth thee that He will build thee an house.*

*"And when thy days be fulfilled, and thou shalt sleep with thy fathers, I will set up thy Seed after thee, which shall proceed out of thy bowels, and I will establish His Kingdom.*

*"He shall build an house for My Name, and I will establish His Kingdom forever.*

*"I will be His Father, and He shall be My Son"* (II Sam. 7:11-14).

JESUS, THE FULFILLMENT OF THAT PROMISE

The writer to the Hebrews quotes the words *"I will be His Father, and He shall be My Son"* (Heb. 1:5) in proof of the fact that the Lord Jesus is better than Angels, applying them to the former.

In fact, Solomon, David's son, served as a type of this which is to come. During his reign there was peace and prosperity, such as Israel had never known — all a symbol or type of what will be in the coming Kingdom Age when the greater Solomon rules, the Lord Jesus Christ.

When Solomon died, His kingdom was divided, meaning that the kingdom referred to by God to David is yet future.

The Lord Jesus did not occupy the Throne of David, although He offered the Kingdom to Israel. They wanted the Kingdom, but they didn't want Christ, and it's impossible to have the Kingdom without having the King. Consequently, all that Israel could have then had, was forfeited, actually submitting the world to at least some 2,000 more years of bloodshed, war, privation, sickness, and want.

The Reader must understand, that the nations of the world cannot find peace, cannot find the rest they seek, until Israel accepts her proper place in the family of nations, which in effect, refers to her rulership in this capacity over the entirety of the world, but under Christ. That latter phrase is very important.

Israel can only be what she ought to be, do what she ought to do, if Christ is serving as her Head; otherwise, she would be no better than the other nations of the world. Jesus must be the Supreme Head, which He definitely shall be at the Second Coming, when Israel will then accept Him as Lord, Messiah, and Saviour (Zech. Chpts. 12-14).

NOTES

A PROMISE TO DAVID

The Promise to David by the Lord was that the dynasty of kings of which he was the founder, would reign forever; however, the Davidic line was taken captive by Nebuchadnezzar, about 600 years before Christ, and has never occupied the throne since. Therefore, for this Promise to be fulfilled, which it most definitely shall, there must be a restoration of the throne yet in the future. Furthermore, the Promise was that it would be an everlasting dynasty.

David questions the *"how"* of this in the words, *"Thou hast spoken also of Thy servant's house for a great while to come. And is this the manner of man, O Lord God?"* The implication being that a dynasty of merely human kings could not reign forever, but that it would require a human king who was also eternal in His Being to maintain an everlasting dynasty.

These considerations point to the fact that David's dynasty would terminate in One Person Who was both God and Man, Who in fact, would be and is, The Lord Jesus Christ. When He comes to the throne of Israel, then will the Promise be fulfilled, *"I will establish the Throne of His Kingdom forever"* (II Sam. 7:13).

ISRAEL IN DISPERSION

History reveals the fact that the Promises to Abraham, that he would be a great nation and that nation would possess a great land, and the Promise to David of an eternal King to rule on His Throne in an Everlasting Kingdom, have never been fulfilled. Israel is in worldwide dispersion today, and the greater part of that immense tract of land from the Nile to the Euphrates is in Gentile hands, and no king from David's line is reigning on the throne in Jerusalem. Since these Promises were unconditional, and unconditional because through their fulfillment God would bless the entire human race (He could not depend upon frail man), they are still to be fulfilled in the future.

(However, it must be understood, that even unconditional Promises of God can be delayed, because of sin and rebellion on the part of the party or parties in question, which in fact did happen with Israel.)

Not only can we see the necessity of their future fulfillment from the fact that they have not yet been fulfilled, the Prophets predict their final fulfillment as well. In fact, almost every Old Testament Prophet grandly predicts this fulfillment, with the following merely an example.

Ezekiel predicts the regathering of Israel from worldwide dispersion, *"Thus saith the Lord God; behold, I will take the Children of Israel from among the heathen, whether they be gone, and will gather them on every side, and bring them into their own land,*

*"And I will make them one nation in the land upon the mountains of Israel; and one king shall be king over them all"* (Ezek. 37:21-22).

Isaiah says, *"He shall set up an ensign for the nations, and shall assemble the outcasts of Israel, and gather together the dispersed of Judah from the four corners of the Earth"* (Isa. 11:12). At no time has God gathered the Jewish nation from all over the Earth back to its land. However, it should be quickly stated, that He has definitely begun this regathering even as we look at present Israel, but of course, its total fulfillment is yet future.

As to the occupancy of the land, Ezekiel has given us specific directions (Ezek. Chpt. 48). The land from the Nile on the west to the Euphrates on the east will be occupied in longitudinal, horizontal strips east and west by the individual Tribes. At no time has all this land been occupied by Israel, nor have the Tribes possessed it in the form outlined by Ezekiel. The occupation of this land is still future, at least in this manner, but will definitely take place in the coming Kingdom Age.

## THE LORD OUR RIGHTEOUSNESS

With reference to the occupancy of the Davidic throne by a king from David's dynasty who would reign forever, the Prophets spoke clearly:

Jeremiah says, *"Behold, the days come, saith the Lord, that I will raise unto David a Righteous Branch, and a King shall reign and prosper, and shall execute Judgment and Justice in the earth.*

*"In His days Judah shall be saved, and Israel shall dwell safely: and this is His Name whereby He shall be called, THE LORD OUR RIGHTEOUSNESS"* (Jer. 23:5-6).

Ezekiel, living long after David says, *"And David My servant shall be king over them; and they all shall have one shepherd: and shall also walk in My Judgments, and observe My Statutes, and do them.*

*"And they shall dwell in the land that I have given unto Jacob My servant, wherein your fathers have dwelt; and they shall dwell therein, even they, and their children, and their children's children forever: and David shall be their Prince forever"* (Ezek. 37:24-25). Here we have the prediction of the restoration of the Davidic dynasty ruling in the Promised Land forever.

## WHEN WILL THESE PROPHECIES BE FULFILLED?

The question could be asked in this manner: When will this regathering of Israel take place, and its restoration to the land, and the enthronement of the King from David's line?

We have the answer in one of the most important prophetic Passages in the New Testament. It was on the occasion of the Church Council at Jerusalem which was convened to decide the relation of the Gentile converts of Christianity to the Mosaic economy. After the discussion, James, the Moderator announced his judgment.

He quotes the Prophet Amos who in writing in a context of the dispersion of Israel, which actually took place in A.D. 70 with the destruction of Jerusalem by the Roman General, Titus which says, *"In that day will I raise up the Tabernacle of David that is fallen, and close up the breaches thereof; and I will raise up his ruins, and I will build it as in the days of old"* (Amos 9:11).

The Prophet is predicting the restoration of the Kingdom to Israel after the dispersion. James, speaking of the fact that for the first time God visited the Gentiles as a racial group with Salvation, recognizes that a new order of things has come in, following the Age of Law in which God dealt with His people Israel. James did not at that time know the full implications of this new order, the Truth of the Church of Jesus Christ, composed of Jew and Gentile, a mystery even then being given to the Apostle Paul. But he quotes

NOTES

NOTES

Amos, *"After this* (the Church Age) *I will return, and will build again the Tabernacle of David which is fallen down; and I will build again the ruins thereof, and I will set it up:*

*"That the residue of men might seek after the Lord, and all the Gentiles, upon whom My Name is called, saith the Lord, Who doeth all these things"* (Acts 15:16-17).

In Amos, the *"I"* Who is speaking is the Jehovah of the Old Testament. In the context in which James quotes Amos, the *"I"* can be none other than the Second Person of the Triune God, Jesus Christ, for a return to this Earth requires a first visit, namely, the Incarnation. And as the Son of God in His First Coming to Earth assumed a human body, so in His Second Coming, He will have the same human body glorified. It will be a personal return of the same Person of the Godhead Who came the first time.

In Amos, the return is predicted to be after the time of Israel's dispersion. In Acts the return is predicted after the Church Age closes. The dispersion of Israel and the Church Age run concurrently, and so there is no contradiction involved.

That is so important, that we must of necessity say it again: Israel's dispersion all over the world, which began in A.D. 70, and has continued unto this time, is the same period as the Church Age; however, since 1948 Israel has once again existed as a Nation. So, as stated, the regathering has already begun, with Israel, however, still yet to go through the great trial of the coming Great Tribulation. But yet, the point I wish to emphasize is, if Israel's dispersion is about over, and it definitely is, then that means that the Church Age is about over as well. In other words, the Rapture of the Church can take place at any time.

## I WILL

The Tabernacle of David is the Davidic dynasty, of which James spoke. It includes the Kingdom of Israel and the Temple Worship. In the Greek Text we have four *"I will"* statements.

*"I will return," "I will build," "I will build," "I will set it up."* It is the Personal return of our Great God and Saviour, Jesus Christ, Who will Himself at His return restore the Kingdom to Israel concerning which the Disciples were asking just before His Ascension when they said, *"Lord, wilt Thou at this time restore again the Kingdom to Israel?"* (Acts 1:6), and they were given to understand that a new order of things was to come in before that event, a period of witnessing to the ends of the Earth (Acts 1:8), which we now recognize as the Church Age.

As well, this means that Israel's efforts presently to bring about peace between herself and the Arabs, will not be a fruitful enterprise. Irrespective of America's involvement, Israel will not be able to make this thing work. In fact, the Antichrist will make his debut by seeming to settle this age old conflict between Israel and the world, which will cause Israel to think that He is the Messiah, actually accepting him as such. As we have previously stated, they will be rudely awakened to the fact that they have made a tremendous mistake, when he turns on them, with every intention of destroying them completely.

Israel will not have what she seeks, cannot have what she seeks, in fact, is impossible to have what she seeks, until she accepts her True King and Messiah, Who is none other than The Lord Jesus Christ.

To be sure, all of this is so very, very important, simply because of the part and place that Israel must play in the eternal future, as it regards the Plan of God. That's why this little nation, these people, are significant all out of proportion to their size and place. Consequently, when Preachers read Israel out of modern Prophecies, as many now are doing, they are completely misunderstanding Bible Prophecy, which means, they are completely misunderstanding the Plan of God.

Every single thing that happens to Israel presently, every effort made by America to solve her problem, everything which she does, is all in some way, in some manner, a part of the fulfillment of Bible Prophecy, which literally marks the happenings of the Endtime. So, if we take these things lightly concerning Israel, we are completely misreading the signs of the times, for in fact, Israel is the greatest prophetic sign of all!

## THE CHURCH

The important point to be grasped is that this Personal Reign of Jesus Christ over the Kingdom of Israel and thus also over the entire Earth will be brought in by the Son of God at His return, and not by the Church as is taught by some.

In the last few years, we have witnessed the Church attempting to do the very thing which is not meant for the Church to do. By political means, which refers to political involvement, the Church is trying to usher in the Kingdom Age, with some misguided Preachers even claiming that the Kingdom Age is about to begin. These Preachers disavow the Rapture of the Church, the Coming Great Tribulation spoken of by Christ (Mat. Chpt. 24), the Battle of Armageddon, etc., claiming that the Church itself will bring back Christ, and referring to the Second Coming. Some of these individuals refer to themselves as *"Kingdom now,"* or by various other names. However, I think it should be crystal clear that such is totally unscriptural.

In fact, when the Republicans swept into power in the early 1990's, many were claiming that this is the time. Of course we have seen that the Republicans fared no better than the Democrats, which means that the Church wasted its money which should have been spent on trying to win souls to Christ.

Nevertheless, pride which is a great part of this last day apostasy, loves to think that it's going to great things, which little by little figures Jesus Christ out, and itself in.

The business of the Church is not political; the business of the Church is spiritual. It is to herald the Message of Jesus Christ all over the world, which refers to the Message of the Cross. That is what the Church is called to do and nothing else (Mk. 16:15-18; Rom. 10:9-17; Rev. 22:17).

In this age of Apostasy, which means a departure from Truth, and which characterizes, regrettably, the final Church Age, pride is one of its great factors, which as always, leads into greed (Rev. 3:14-22). In fact, the *"money gospel"* which is pure and simple *"another gospel"* (II Cor. 11:4), is the rage of the present. The Church no longer looks up, but rather down! It no longer looks outward as an effort to bring lost humanity to Jesus, but rather looks inward, as it regards its own bloated greed. It is not looking for the Rapture, but rather riches! It is not looking for Christ, but rather the Antichrist.

NOTES

Most of so-called Christian Television presently, is such an abomination before God, that it is a joke of a joke. How is it possible that those who call themselves *"Christians,"* can pour hundreds of millions of dollars into that which is so obviously wrong? The only answer is, the flesh appeals to the flesh, and religious flesh appeals to religious flesh most of all!

As I've said previously, I personally feel that the Lord has spoken to my heart that the Cross is going to be the dividing line between the Apostate Church and the True Church. It will not be Denominational lines; it will not even be doctrinal lines as such; it will be the Cross!

To those who reject the Cross of Christ as the answer to the ills of man, they will go into apostasy. To those who accept God's Gift to this fallen human race, they will draw ever closer to Christ. The Cross is that dividing line.

## EARTH'S GOLDEN AGE

That for which John cried, as he closed out the Canon of Scripture on the island of Patmos, as he finished the Book of Revelation, *"Even so, come, Lord Jesus,"* will come to pass when the Lord actually does come, and which He most definitely will (Rev. 22:20). Earth's Golden Age will then begin, a period of universal Righteousness, Peace, and Prosperity, a time when there will be ideal conditions on Earth for the Salvation of Earth's multitudes.

James gives as the purpose of this Age, *"that the residue of men might seek after the Lord"* (Acts 15:17). In other words, the greatest Salvation, Divine Healing, Holy Spirit Baptized Revivals the world has ever known, will take place in the coming Kingdom Age. In fact, Israel will then fulfill her eternal destiny as Evangelists to the world (Isa. 66:18-21).

During this 1,000 year period of time, when Jesus will be ruling personally from Jerusalem, there will be no more wars, there will be plenty of food, clothing, and shelter for everyone. There will be no false religions, Satan and his demons being bound in the Bottomless Pit. There will be no extremes of climate, a greatly increased fertility of the soil, with the Son of God, as stated, reigning Personally on Earth. This is Earth's Golden Age which the Second Advent of the Son of God will bring in.

His Personal return to this Earth and that only, will be able to cope with the desperate situation in which the human race finds itself today. Only He can bring order out of chaos, peace instead of war, plenty instead of poverty, Righteousness instead of sin. This is the only hope of the human race. But it is a sure hope. For just as surely as He came Personally the first time will He do so a second time.

Until then, the Sovereign God of Heaven will restrain evil and hold things together. Before Earth's Golden Age there will come a mighty conflict between God and Satan, this Earth being the battlefield, a time of terrible Judgments upon sin and sinners; but the Church of Jesus Christ will be taken away from the scene before that time. And until that time comes, the Lord Jesus will watch over and care for His Bride in tender love. Such is the bright outlook which Prophecy affords for the future in the midst of this present darkness.

## WHAT TIME IS IT?

Even though the following has been given in bits and pieces in previous Commentary on this Epistle, due to the vast significance of the time in which we presently live, a placing of this material in chronological order, would perhaps be beneficial.

The question, *"What time is it?"* could probably be better asked in this manner; at what time in the Plan of God for human history, are we living today?

To gain a proper appreciation of the times in which we are living as they are related to what has gone before in human history and to that which is scheduled to come to pass in the future, we must span the time between the eternity before the universe came into existence by the Divine Fiat of God and the time when eternal conditions will begin in the future.

## THE CREATION

The Angels, at least as far as we know, were God's first creation. They existed before Genesis 1:1, for they shouted for joy at the beauty of the newly created universe (Job 38:4-7).

NOTES

Moses records the creation of the universe in the majestic statement, *"In the beginning God created the heavens and the earth"* (Gen. 1:1).

This universe left the creative hands of God in a perfect state. The inspired writers of the New Testament when alluding to its creation, call it a *"cosmos,"* which is *"an ordered system."* This means that something powerful, something very destructive took place, between Genesis 1:1 and Genesis 1:2. Genesis 1:2 describes a *"chaos,"* which means *"a rude, unformed mass,"* which became that way as the result of some form of catastrophe. We will see what that catastrophe was in a moment.

No date is given in the Bible for the creation of the universe. It is believed that the sciences of Geology and Astronomy both demonstrate that the universe is millions of years old. If in fact that is true, it would not violate the Scriptures in any way concerning Genesis 1:1.

## LUCIFER

On this perfect Earth of Genesis 1:1, God placed the mightiest, wisest, most beautiful Angel He had ever created, Lucifer, as priest and king over a race of beings, with the responsibility of ruling over them and directing their worship to God.

At a point in time, Lucifer rebelled against God, actually striking at God's Throne, drawing this race of free moral intelligences with him into rebellion and sin, as well as one third of the angels (Rev. 12:4). Actually, it is possible that this race of beings, whoever and whatever they were, over which Lucifer ruled before his rebellion, and who threw in their lot with him at that rebellion, are now those referred to as *"demon spirits."* This we do know, God definitely did not create demon spirits, so they had to come to this state in some manner.

Lucifer was deposed from his position, banished from the Earth, and due to this conflict, the Earth and its planetary heavens were rendered a chaos (Gen. 1:2; Isa. 14:12-17; Ezek. 28:12-19).

No one knows how many millions of years (if that long) this chaotic condition of the Earth lasted. We do know this:

In approximately 4000 B.C. God said, *"Let there be light,"* and the six-day work of reconstruction began, actually superintended by the Holy Spirit (Gen. 1:2), and after six days the chaos became a *"cosmos,"* an ordered system again. Upon this Earth made perfect again, God placed a man and a woman, the progenitors of the human race, actually believed to be of higher creation even than the Angels (Ps. 8).

We will now trace briefly the history of the human race as it relates to the program of God with respect to sin and Salvation, dividing this history into a period from Adam (4000 B.C.) to Abraham (2000 B.C.), from Abraham to David (1000 B.C.), from David to the Incarnation (A.D. 1), from the Incarnation to the present time (1999), and the yet future 1,000 year reign of the Son of God on Earth; approximately 7,000 years of human history.

## FROM ADAM TO ABRAHAM

From Adam to Abraham was a period of approximately 2,000 years.

Our first parents fell into sin as they succumbed to the temptation of the fallen Angel Lucifer, who with his demons had taken up their residence in the atmosphere of this Earth. Satan regained the position on Earth he had forfeited by sin and became the god of this world. Adam constituted the whole race as sinners by his one act of disobedience. Consequently, the Earth was cursed, and man was driven out of the Garden of Eden (Gen. Chpt. 3).

Cain, the son of Adam and Eve, developed a civilization which was godless (Gen. Chpt. 4). The human race being sinful and wicked, sank to an unimagined level of sin and depravity, which resulted in the Flood. In fact, the Flood was an absolute necessity, if God was to salvage the human race. Even then, only one family, that of Noah, was saved.

Beginning even with Adam, the Lord had provided Salvation for those who would believe in the Sacrifice for sin, He would someday offer. Of course, that Sacrifice would be the Lord Jesus Christ. Consequently, Salvation has always rested in the Sacrifice of Christ, and more particularly, Faith in that Sacrifice. There has never been any other way of Salvation, and there never will be another way of Salvation. That's the reason that

NOTES

we say that the Cross is the intersection of all humanity.

However, for this great thing to be done, God would literally have to become man, thereby purchasing back as the Last Adam, what the first Adam lost. As a result, and even from the beginning, Satan began to greatly persecute the line of Seth (another son of Adam and Eve), through whom the Redeemer would come.

In a great attempt to destroy this necessary line (the line of the Incarnation), Satan's fallen angels intermarried with the human race, resulting in offspring, part angel, part man, the purpose of which was to dehumanize the race, thus preventing the Incarnation, and thus the Substitutionary Atonement (Gen. Chpt. 6).

As stated, God met this threat by the Flood, saving only eight people to repopulate the Earth, the family of Noah, who evidently had not been sullied by this terrible effort of Satan (Gen. Chpts. 6-9).

After the Flood, which took place approximately 1,600 years after Adam, the family of Noah was told by God to replenish the Earth. However, as it began to multiply, instead of scattering over the face of the Earth, it concentrated at Babel, which was actually, at least as far as we know, Earth's first organized rebellion against God. To stifle the plans of evil men, God gave different groups different languages, forcing them to separate and thus populate the Earth. Thus, the nations were brought into existence (Gen. Chpt. 11).

## THE TIME OF ABRAHAM

This brings us to the time of Abraham, which was about 2000 B.C. — about 2,000 years from Adam. We will trace briefly the history of the race to 1000 B.C., the time of David.

Abraham was called to become the progenitor of the Jewish nation through which God proposed to send the Saviour to die for lost sinners, and through which He purposed finally to bring in everlasting Peace and Righteousness to the Earth (Gen. Chpt. 12).

The ancestry continues through Isaac, and his son, Jacob, the latter's 12 sons, the Twelve Tribes. The bondage in Egypt lasted about 400 years which was until the time of Moses, who in about 1500 B.C. led Israel out of Egypt to the land of Canaan. Under Joshua, Israel conquered Canaan. This is followed by the period of the Judges, who governed Israel until God was ready to bring into being the Davidic dynasty and make Israel a kingdom, which took place in about 1000 B.C.

The Reader must understand, as I'm certain you do, that all of this is extremely important, actually, every single thing that happened in the Old Testament, because it all was leading up to your eventual Salvation. That means that every single thing that happened as recorded in the Old Testament, were steps which led eventually and ultimately to the coming of Christ, Who would die on a Cross, making it possible for mankind to be saved. So, that's the reason that you as a Believer ought to learn the Bible in every capacity, understanding all that it says, at least as far as is humanly possible, realizing that this is the single most important thing in the world.

You ought to know the Bible a thousand times better than you know the activities of certain sports, or the variances of Wall Street, or anything else that one might name. But sadly, most Believers do not see the significance of this of which we speak.

If you the Reader will understand, that every single thing in the Bible pertains to that which ultimately led to *your* Salvation, which obviously is the single most important thing there is, then the Bible will take on a brand-new complexion. It is my prayer that upon reading these statements, that you will realize the necessity of learning the Word of God as possibly never before, consequently, applying yourself in a manner worthy of such a privilege — and a privilege it is!

DAVID

David comes to the throne, followed by Solomon who, in his latter days, is guilty of idolatry. God, at his death, divides the Kingdom: The Northern Kingdom of Israel with its capital at Samaria ruled by a succession of dynasties not of Davidic ancestry; the Southern Kingdom of Judah, with its capital at Jerusalem, ruled by a succession of Davidic kings. These Kingdoms sadly and regrettably, went from bad to worse until in 722 B.C., the Northern Kingdom was taken captive into Assyria, and the Southern Kingdom in 586 B.C. into Babylonia.

NOTES

Under the Medes and Persians, the Tribes of Israel returned to the land. This was about 500 years before Christ.

During this 500 years, Israel was ruled by a succession of Gentile powers, which consisted of the Medes and the Persians, the Greeks, and then the Romans, who were in power at the Birth of Christ.

THE INCARNATION

This brings us to the time of the Incarnation and the First Century. While Israel was under Roman domination, the Son of God came from Heaven and incorporated Himself with the human race through the Virgin Birth in the line of David, to offer Himself as Israel's Messiah and restore the earthly Kingdom taken away in the captivities, making it a righteous Kingdom. He was rejected and crucified, became the Substitutionary Sacrifice for sin, arose from the dead, and ascended to Heaven.

Of course, the Lord knew that Israel would reject her Messiah; therefore, He brought into existence a new channel through which He could reach Earth's multitudes for Salvation. At Pentecost, the Holy Spirit outpoured in fulfillment of Joel's Prophecy, rejected by national Israel, gathered into a nucleus individual Believers by placing (Baptizing) them into Christ, forming the Church, the mystical Body of Christ. Thus, began the Church Age which in Revelation Chapters 2 and 3 is divided into seven periods or ages. These we will trace briefly to the present day.

Please note: I once did not see the following as it is presently given concerning the Messages of Christ to the seven Churches of Asia, rather teaching that His Messages were for all time and all Churches. In fact, as far as it goes, that is correct; however, after doing a more detailed study of this subject, I have come to the conclusion that had this been the case, this which I have just said, the Lord would not have given seven distinct Messages, but rather just one Message, etc.

While each Message definitely does apply to all Churches and for all time, still, I now believe the Messages in the manner in which they were given, constitute also particular Church ages, with a particular word or warning given for each age. As well, the time factors given are approximate with, in fact, each age overlapping the other, and some ages continuing even to the present hour. They are as follows:

1. The Apostolic Church: This age began in A.D. 33, and concluded in about A.D. 100. The account of this time is given in the Book of Acts and the Epistles. One could say that it ended with the death of John the Beloved.

2. The Martyr Church: The age of this Church was about A.D. 100 to A.D. 300. During this time, Rome hurled some 10 bloody persecutions against the Church.

3. The State Church: This began in about A.D. 300 and extended to about A.D. 500. At the beginning of this particular time, Constantine the Great legalized Christianity, making it the state religion of the Roman Empire. During this time the State supported the Church financially, in which period hoards of pagans came into the visible Church unsaved.

4. The Papal Church: This age began one might say, in about 500, and continues to this hour. In the early 600's the Bishop of Rome assumed supreme authority over the entire Church and announced himself Pope. However, the Church which actually began to decline spiritually after the passing of the First Century Apostles, was working toward this for quite some time.

5. The Reformation Church: This began in about 1500, and continues unto this time. This age began under the leadership of Martin Luther, with him proclaiming the Doctrine of Justification by Faith which was again brought to light from under the blanket of false doctrine by which the Papacy had hidden it for about 1,000 years. This time was known as the *"Dark Ages."*

6. The Missionary Church: This age began in about 1800, and has continued unto this hour. It was the period when modern missions had its start. It also incorporates the great outpouring of the Holy Spirit which began at about the turn of the Twentieth Century, resulting in hundreds of millions being Baptized with the Holy Spirit, with the evidence of speaking with other Tongues

NOTES

(Acts 2:4). This was in fulfillment of Joel's Prophecies, as it concerned the former and the latter reign (Joel 2:23). The *"former reign"* was fulfilled with the Early Church, with the modern Church continuing to be in the *"latter reign,"* at least for those who will believe and accept the Word of God.

7. The Apostate Church: For the sake of clarification, we will put this date at the year 2000; however, the modern Church has been building toward this apostasy for quite some time. This period will wind-up Church history. In its totality, it will help usher in the Antichrist.

As I have previously stated, I believe that the dividing line between the Apostate Church and the True Church, is the Cross of Christ. For those who repudiate the Cross, or ignore its veracity, they will go into apostasy and I might quickly add, ever deeper into apostasy. For those who understand the merits of the Cross, proclaiming its veracity as it regards Salvation and a victorious life, through Faith in what Jesus did there, such Believers will grow ever closer to the Lord.

How long this period will last, no one knows. It will close with the Coming of the Lord Jesus into the atmosphere of this Earth to take out the True Church.

## EVERYTHING IS TOWARD THE SECOND COMING

The Church has been in existence for about 1,970 years. (I am dictating these notes in November of 1999.) However, even though the Church did technically begin in about A.D. 33 with the Advent of the Holy Spirit on the Day of Pentecost, one could say, and with some substantiation, that it actually began with the Birth of Christ. That being the case, this time span has been about 2,000 years.

From Adam to Christ was about 4,000 years. The Messianic Kingdom of 1,000 years is yet to come. This totals up to approximately 7,000 years of human history.

As we've already stated in previous Commentary, the Reader will have observed that God has done something of great importance with regard to Salvation at the end of two Millenniums or of one Millennium. 2,000 years after Adam's Fall, Abraham became the progenitor of the Jewish Nation through which God brings Salvation in the Work of His Son on the Cross, and gives the race the Bible, the Word of God, and through which He will yet bring universal Peace and Righteousness. 1,000 years after Abraham, He called David to become the first of a line of kings, in whose line the Messiah would come. 1,000 years after that He incarnates Himself in the Person of His Son to become the Sin-Offering. Now, some 2,000 years after that, the Ministry of the Church is almost finished, for the visible Church is rapidly becoming apostate.

When Israel failed God, He brought in the Church. When the Church fails God, as it is doing today, He will bring back Israel again. This refers to the Second Coming. A sweeping glance down the history of the human race, indicates that the return of the Son of God to this Earth must come very, very soon. This is the Second Advent. The Rapture must come before that, and can take place at any moment.

Six-sevenths of human history are behind us. The last 1,000 years are just ahead.

## WHEN WILL THE RAPTURE TAKE PLACE?

Two questions confront us with regard to the Rapture of the Church:

1. Will the Church go through any part of the coming seven year, Great Tribulation Period?
2. If the Church is in fact raptured out before this coming time of Great Tribulation, will there be a period of time from that event to the beginning of the seven year period, or will the seven year period begin immediately after the Rapture?

The Book of Revelation is obviously a Book of Prophecy. Of its 22 Chapters, three are historical in character. Chapter 1 speaks of John's Vision of our Lord on the island of Patmos. And yet, this Chapter is Prophetic in character in two respects:

1. There is definite prediction in the words, *"Behold, he cometh with clouds; and every eye shall see Him, and they also which pierced Him: and all kindreds of the earth shall wail because of Him"* (Rev. 1:7). Here we have the prediction of His Second Advent to a Christ-rejecting world.

NOTES

2. Then, the Vision which John had of our Lord was one in which He as the present High Priest in Heaven is prepared to come to Earth in Judgment.

Chapters 2 and 3 of Revelation are Messages from Christ addressed to seven historic Churches which were in existence in Asia Minor in John's day. Each as stated, had a definite characteristic. Since these seven Churches were not the only Churches in Asia Minor at that time, it is evident that they were purposely selected for these definite characteristics. Since that is so, it is clear that these definite characteristics are for the guidance of the Church during its earthly history. In fact, the number *"seven"* was not chosen at random, but with deliberation. Seven is God's number of completion; therefore, these seven Messages by Christ to these seven Churches are meant to take in the entirety of the Church Age. In other words, to complete the Church Age.

In a Book of Prophecy such as Revelation, which was written in the First Century to predict the future of Israel, the Second Advent, the Millennium, and the perfect age to come, it would seem strange should the inspired writer hurdle the intervening years from his time in history to the Millennium without taking note of the intervening years, especially since the Book was written for the guidance of the Church. Consequently, these definite and separate characteristics of these seven Churches must have some connection with the history of the Church during the interim between Israel dispersed in the First Century, and Israel restored for the Millennium.

As one compares these characteristics in their order with the history of the Church, one discovers a striking resemblance between them and that history, so striking and in such an order that this similarity cannot be a mere coincidence. This was occasioned in this manner by the Holy Spirit deliberately in order to portray the entirety of the Church Age.

In Chapters 2 and 3 of Revelation, the Church is seen on Earth. After Chapter 3 the Church is not mentioned again as being on Earth. In fact, in Chapter 19 it is seen in Heaven.

Chapters 6 through 19, portray the Great Tribulation Period which will take place on

Earth, of which Jesus spoke about graphically in Matthew Chapter 24. Now, if the Church is on the Earth during that particular time, or any part of that particular time, it seems strange doesn't it, for it not to be mentioned whatsoever by the Holy Spirit. No! The Church is not mentioned at all during that period, because the Church is not on Earth, having been Raptured away by the Lord before this seven year period begins.

THE ANALYSIS OF THE HOLY SPIRIT

Revelation is the only Book of the Bible which God has analyzed for us. His analysis is found in Revelation 1:19 in the words, *"Write the things which thou hast seen, and the things which are, and the things which shall be hereafter."*

It is clear that the things John *"has just seen"* refer to the Vision he had of the Lord Jesus, which is recorded in Chapter 1, and which is prophetic of the Second Advent.

*"The things which are"* must refer to that which follows, namely, the seven Churches in Asia Minor of Chapters 2 and 3, and which are prophetic of the Church Age, which we have already addressed.

Then he is to write the things *"which shall be hereafter."* This in the Greek Text is, *"ha mellei genesthai meta tauta,"* exactly — *"the things which are about to become after these things." "These things"* refer to the Church Age.

The third division of John's Prophecy, namely, everything predicted after Chapter 3, is to occur after the Church Age closes. That which terminates the Church Age can be nothing else but its removal from the Earth at the Rapture. Thus, all the predicted events of Chapters 4 to 22 of the Book of Revelation, will take place after the Church is caught out from the Earth to Heaven, namely, the Seventieth Week of Daniel (Rev. Chpts. 6-19), divided into the first half of the week — first three and one half years (Rev. 6:1-4), and the second half of the week — last three and one half years, referred to as the *"Great Tribulation"* (Rev. 6:4-19:21).

Revelation Chapter 19 proclaims the Coming of the Lord, with Chapter 20 proclaiming the Millennium, and Chapters 21 and 22, which close out the Book of Revelation, proclaiming the perfect age to come, which latter in fact will never end.

NOTES

THE GREAT TRIBULATION

Chapters 4 and 5 describe scenes in Heaven after the Church is removed from the Earth. Verse 1 of Chapter 4, correlates with Revelation 1:19. It begins with the words, *"After this,"* and closes with the words *"which must be hereafter."*

In the Greek both the beginning and the ending of the Verse are *"meta tauta,"* which means *"after these things."*

After what things?

He has just finished speaking about the Churches, so it is *"after the Churches."*

This confirms and settles the question as to the time of the fulfillment of all the events of Revelation Chapters 4-22. These things cannot take place until after the Churches, or after the Rapture of the Church. In other words, the Church is no longer on Earth when the events of Revelation Chapters 4-22 take place.

As stated, Chapters 4 and 5 describe scenes in Heaven after the Church is removed from the Earth; however, in Chapter 6 we are introduced to events to take place on the Earth after the Church is caught up to Heaven.

This Scripture says, *"And I saw when the Lamb opened one of the seals, and I heard, as it were the noise of thunder, one of the four beasts saying, come and see"* (Rev. 6:1).

The actual words in the Greek which John heard were, *"Be coming."* Actually, the words *"and see"* are not in the best Greek Texts. In fact, these words were not really addressed to John. He was standing there, and would have no need for such a thunderous voice. These words in fact, were addressed to the Rider on the White Horse, which of course, is symbolic (Rev. 6:2). This Rider on the White Horse is the Antichrist, and not Christ as some have claimed.

The words *"be coming"* signal the beginning of this seven year period, referred to as the Great Tribulation.

Revelation 6:2 says, *"And I saw, and behold a white horse: and he that sat on him had a bow; and a crown was given unto him: and he went forth conquering, and to conquer."*

If it is to be noticed in Verse 2, the Antichrist is portrayed as having a *"bow"* but no arrows are mentioned. This is stated in this manner for a purpose.

Concerning the beginning of this seven year period, Daniel says of the Antichrist, *"And through his policy also he shall cause craft* (deceit) *to prosper in his hands; and he shall magnify himself in his heart, and by peace shall destroy many"* (Dan. 8:25).

That's the reason that John saw him with no arrows. He will make his debut in the world on a platform of peace, when all the time he is planning war. During this time of peace, is when Israel will accept him as the Messiah, with much of the world falling into line. He will solve the problem, at least temporarily, between the Arabs and Israel, even making it possible for Israel to rebuild her Temple. In fact, this portrays the possibility that a period of time will be needed between the Rapture of the Church and the beginning of the seven year period, in order for all of these things to come about. Things do not begin, especially on a worldwide basis, instantly. Even though things take place presently at a much greater speed than years before, still, some time, as would be obvious, will be required. That's the reason I believe, which we will address more succinctly later on, that there will be a time period between the Rapture of the Church and the beginning of the seven year period of the Great Tribulation. In fact, the Great Tribulation cannot begin until the Antichrist signs a seven year pact with Israel, and other nations (Dan. 9:27; Mat. 24:15-31). It stands to reason, that the signing of this agreement, cannot take place the day after the Rapture occurs. Even though preparations for these things can definitely be going on and no doubt will, before the Rapture takes place; still, I think it is obvious, that a time period of some length will take place between the Rapture and the beginning of this seven year Tribulation Period!

The peace with which the Antichrist began his effort will now be broken, with war of terrible proportions being the result. This is proclaimed in Revelation 6:4, *"Power was given him to take the peace from the earth."* The original Greek has the definite article *"the peace"* here, which is very important. It points to a particular peace, in fact, the false peace instituted at the beginning of the reign of the Antichrist, which will now be broken.

NOTES

### THE CHURCH AND THE GREAT TRIBULATION

Considering all of these factors which point to a pre-Tribulation Rapture, Paul nails it down in II Thessalonians 2:1-12.

The Apostle does not deal with everything in this Passage, simply because he is addressing a particular question posed by the Thessalonians.

They had been told by false teachers that they were in the midst of the Day of the Lord, and they thought they had missed the Rapture and were destined to endure the sufferings of the Great Tribulation. Paul assures them that this Day will not come until after the departure of the Church and the revelation of the Antichrist. That would satisfy their hearts and banish their fears. Suffice to say, Paul in this Passage and also in I Thessalonians 4:13-5:9 teaches a pre-Tribulation Rapture of the Church.

The Church at Philadelphia (Rev. 3:7-13), representing the period of modern missions, the Sixth Church period, and in existence today, and concurrently with the Laodicean period, or the Apostate Church, is given the Promise, *"Because thou hast kept the word of My patience, I also will keep thee from the hour of temptation, which shall come upon all the world, to try them that dwell on the earth."*

The word *"temptation"* as used here by Christ is *"peirasmos,"* and means *"adversity, affliction, trouble."* The definite article *"the temptation"* appears in the Greek, pointing to a particular period of affliction. This is described as well, as affecting the whole inhabited Earth. This can be nothing else but the Great Tribulation.

The word *"keep"* as used in the phrase, *"I also will keep thee from the hour of temptation,"* is taken from the Greek word *"tereo,"* which means *"to attend to carefully, take care of."* The word also means *"to guard."*

The word *"from"* in the Greek is *"ek,"* which means in general usage, *"out of, from within."*

Some have attempted to take this word *"from"* to indicate that the Church will go into the Great Tribulation, but will be guarded and protected in it by the Lord, etc.

However, to fully understand what John is saying here, we have to go back to the manner in which people used that word in the First Century.

They did not then use it in the sense of being merely guarded and protected while remaining in the same place, but rather being removed altogether. For instance, the use of the word *"from"* in the First Century would have been, *"He has removed the material from my reach."* The word *"from"* being *"ek."* The material was placed out of the reach of the person spoken of. God promises to guard the Church from the reach of the Great Tribulation. He does this by removing it from its reach. This is accomplished by the Rapture.

The Church will be removed from the reach of the Great Tribulation by a distance of many billions of miles, for it will be in Heaven, outside of this universe, during that particular time.

This removal of the Church out of the reach of the Tribulation is spoken of also in the Greek word *"harpazo,"* translated *"caught up"* (I Thess. 4:17). One of the meanings of *"harpazo"* even as we've already stated, is *"to rescue from the danger of destruction."* The Church will not only be rescued from destruction, but from the very presence of destruction. In other words, it will not be subject to the dangers of the Great Tribulation.

In fact, there is nothing in Scripture which indicates that the Church will either enter or pass through the Tribulation. Israel is given many signs warning her of the near approach of that period (Mat. Chpt. 24), but the Gospels and Epistles are entirely devoid of any sign given to the Church.

The Epistles speak of the *"Day of Christ Jesus"* (Phil. 1:6), an expression not found in the Old Testament or the Gospels. This is a day to which the Church is to look forward with joy. It is the end of the pathway of the Christian Church. It is the time of the Rapture. If this day does not occur before the Tribulation, then there is no place for it in the Prophetic calendar of events which will take place during or after that period.

NOTES

DIVINE WRATH

The Great Tribulation Period is a time when the Divine Wrath is to be visited upon the Earth, particularly upon Israel. But the Promise to the Church is that it has been delivered from the wrath to come (Rom. 5:9; I Thess. 1:9-10; 5:8). The Bible expressly states who will be the objects of the Divine Wrath during the Tribulation Period, namely, Israel and the ungodly of the Gentile nations. If the Church were destined to suffer, surely, the Bible would make note of that fact along with the mention of the above two companies of individuals. The Biblical attitude of the Believer is one of waiting for the Glorification of his body (the Resurrection) (Rom. 8:23), and of looking for the Saviour (Phil. 3:20-21; I Thess. 1:9-10). The language is clear that the Believer is to expect Him at any moment, not look for Him in connection with some predicted event for which signs have been given to Israel and not to the Church.

As well, and even more important, to teach that the Church will go through the Tribulation Period is to nullify the Biblical teaching of the imminent Coming of the Lord Jesus for the Church.

At this moment, events on Earth are not yet in readiness for the Great Tribulation. But the Lord may return for His Church at any moment. Paul (Phil. 4:5), Peter (I Pet. 1:13-15), and John (I Jn. 3:2-3) all make the imminent Coming of the Lord for the Church a ground of appeal for holy living and diligent service.

*"We're looking for His Coming, in the clouds of Heaven,*
*"Coming back to Earth to catch away His Own,*
*"Then may we all be ready, when the midnight cry is given,*
*"To go and reign with Christ on His Throne."*

*"We're longing for the glory, that awaits the faithful,*
*"Who shall overcome and every conflict win,*

*"Press ever bravely onward, the prize is life eternal,*
*"To all who win the fight over sin."*

*"We're praying for the Advent, of our blessed Saviour,*
*"Who has promised life to all who trust His Grace,*
*"His Coming now is pending, the Message being given,*
*"And soon we'll see our Lord face to face."*

*"We see the signs appearing, of His blessed Coming,*
*"Lo, behold the fig leaves now becoming green,*
*"The Gospel of His Kingdom, has gone to every nation,*
*"That we are near can be seen."*

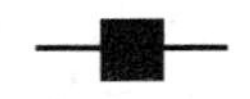

## CHAPTER 5

(1) "BUT OF THE TIMES AND THE SEASONS, BRETHREN, YE HAVE NO NEED THAT I WRITE UNTO YOU."

With the perplexity about the dead in Christ resolved, Paul turns to a new subject, yet not one completely distinct from the previous one. The proper interpretation recognizes a shift in thought, but not without some connection with the foregoing.

Despite their ignorance about the dead in Christ, the Thessalonians had received some instructions regarding other eschatological (Endtime) matters.

During his first visit Paul had effectively communicated the basic features of precise times and accompanying circumstances of future events. But due to the complexity of these matters, and especially considering that someone would later write a letter to the Thessalonians forging Paul's name, claiming certain erroneous things about the Endtime, the Apostle would be forced to give more instructions which he did in his Second Epistle.

Two false attitudes toward the Second Advent tend to be found among Christians: The one, a restless, speculative preoccupation with signs and dates; and the other, a busy absorption in worldly affairs to the exclusion of the hope.

NOTES

Paul's remedy for both these tendencies may be summarized under the following:

1. Preparation for the Rapture.
2. The unexpectedness of Christ's Coming.
3. The personal and moral responsibility of those who look for Christ's return.

### TIMES AND SEASONS

The phrase, *"But of the times and the seasons,"* introduces the recurring question of the curious and the anxious: How long before Christ comes? And at what point in history?

*"Times"* in the Greek is *"chronos,"* and suggests *"duration,"* while *"seasons,"* in the Greek is *"kairos,"* and suggests a suitable period.

Of these dates, Jesus said, *"It is not for you to know the times or the seasons, which the Father hath put in His Own power"* (Acts 1:7).

It is obvious that the Thessalonians expected an immediate advent. The Apostle, however, represses their curiosity on this point by reminding them of the uncertainty of the time of the Lord's Coming.

To better explain *"times"* and *"seasons,"* the word *"times"* denotes a time absolutely in disregard to circumstances. The word rendered *"seasons"* denotes a definite point of time; not merely the day, but actually the hour. Jesus said, *"But of that day and that hour knoweth no man, no, not the Angels which are in Heaven, neither the Son, but the Father"* (Mk. 13:32).

I'm sure that Christ at the present time knows the exact hour all of this will take place, but the record is clear that He did not know at the time that He was making the statement. In the Incarnation, Christ was stripped of His Omniscience (the ability to know all things, past, present, and future), then learning whatever it was the Father wanted Him to know.

I think it is obvious by now, that man has no say whatsoever, no control whatsoever, over the time factor regarding these last day events. Consequently, for the Church to think that it has the power to do something, in order to bring Christ back, which many claim, is facetious indeed! These *"times and seasons"* are not really dependent at all on anything the Church does or doesn't do.

Everything is dependent totally upon the Will of the Father. Consequently, as should be overly obvious, date setting regarding the Rapture or the Second Coming is foolish to say the least. While we can certainly look at particular times as it regards certain events, and thereby know that certain things are drawing near, that's the best that we can do.

NOTES

## INFORMATION

The phrase, *"Brethren, ye have no need that I write unto you,"* was not because he regarded the information for which they sought as to be unprofitable or superfluous, but because he had already informed them when at Thessalonica that the time of the Advent was beyond the sphere of his knowledge. The Apostle mentions this to repress that vain curiosity which is natural to man, and which was the occasion of so much disorder among the Thessalonians. Our duty is, not to pry into the times and seasons which the Father, as stated, has put in His Own power, but rather, to exercise constant watchfulness.

(2) "FOR YOURSELVES KNOW PERFECTLY THAT THE DAY OF THE LORD SO COMETH AS A THIEF IN THE NIGHT."

Paul is not sarcastically alluding to their own claim, but conceding that their previous learning on this subject had been adequate, definite, and specific, ultimately including even pertinent Teachings of Christ (Mat. 24:43; Lk. 12:39).

The focus is on *"the Day of the Lord,"* a theme for extensive Biblical attention. This *"Day"* has multiple characteristics. It is so associated with the ultimate overthrow of God's enemies (Isa. 2:12) and refers to *"Judgment"* (I Cor. 4:3).

## THE DAY OF THE LORD

The phrase, *"For yourselves know perfectly that the Day of the Lord so cometh,"* presents a technical term used by the Old Testament Prophets to designate a certain future period with regard to Israel (Isa. 2:12; 13:6, 9; 34:8; Jer. 46:10; Lam. 2:22; Ezek. 13:5; 30:3; Joel 1:15; 2:1; 3:14; Amos 5:18; Obad. vs. 15; Zeph. 1:7-8, 18; 2:2-3; Zech. 14:1; Mal. 4:5).

The character of this period is seen in the following: *"For the Day of the Lord of Hosts shall be upon everyone that is proud and lofty, and upon everyone that is lifted up; and he shall be brought low"* (Isa. 2:12).

As should be obvious, for the Jews *"the Day of the Lord"* was a familiar expression with a rather fixed meaning. As stated, it is a frequent theme with the Old Testament Prophets, where it is a catastrophic Day of Judgment on God's enemies, deliverance for God's people, final vindication of God's Righteousness, and the beginning of a new era of righteous peace.

It is the time between the present evil age and the coming Golden Age. It will begin with the Great Tribulation, and in a sense carry on through the Millennium. One might say that it ends with the final consummation of all things, which pertains to the new heavens and the new Earth.

## THE MODERN CHURCH

Many in the modern Church deny a coming Tribulation, claiming that all the prophecies of Daniel and those of John in the Book of Revelation, were fulfilled with the destruction of Jerusalem in A.D. 70. Of course, the foolishness of such thinking is obvious on the surface. How in the world that anyone could claim that the great Prophecies of the Book of Revelation were fulfilled at that time, is beyond me!

At the same time, this segment of the Church claims that things are getting better and better in the world, and that Christianity is going to ultimately take over everything, which incidently will be done by political means, and will usher in the Second Coming.

At the same time, this segment of the Church little believes in Evangelism which stems from the Preaching of the Gospel. In fact, they claim entire cities or areas won to the Lord, on the basis of one Government official being so-called saved.

The Truth is, this segment is a part of the Apostate Church, and as with all leaven, their false direction ultimately colors the whole.

The tragedy is, that many Christians have so little spiritual discernment, that they actually help support this effort financially. I refer elsewhere in our Commentaries to this segment as *"Kingdom now,"* etc.

As well, most in this particular belief system, which basically is totally unbiblical, repudiates Israel, claiming that they are no more, at least as far as Bible Prophecy is concerned. They claim that the Church is now Israel.

In a sense, the Church is Spiritual Israel, but it's in the spiritual sense only. In fact, the Promises of God to national Israel, cannot be fulfilled by the Church, and are not intended to be fulfilled by the Church. The Church is another segment altogether.

As we have previously stated, with Israel's rejection of Christ, the Church was ushered in to complete the witness of God in the world, which Israel failed to do, and which Paul addresses in Romans Chapter 11.

In fact, continuing from Abraham to Christ, Israel's existence lasted about 2,000 years. The Church took her place as stated, and the Church Age now has lasted about 2,000 years. Actually, the Church Age is about over, and will close out with the Resurrection of Life, which is referred to as the *"Rapture of the Church."* Israel will then pick back up where the Church left off, and will commence doing so at the Second Coming (Rev., Chpt. 19).

## A THIEF IN THE NIGHT

The phrase, *"As a thief in the night,"* refers as is obvious to something sudden. A thief never announces beforehand his intentions, but does everything by surprise. To be sure, he knows what he's going to do, but he goes to great pains to see to it that his plans are not known, and for all the obvious reasons.

Paul uses the term, *"as a thief in the night,"* and so do Peter and John (II Pet. 3:10; Rev. 3:3; 16:15). The term refers, in one way or the other, to Judgment, which, I might quickly add, is very close to breaking forth upon this Earth.

The *"Day of Christ"* refers to the Rapture of the Church, while the *"Day of the Lord"* refers to the Great Tribulation, and following!

As Paul writes to the Thessalonians, the idea is this:

## THE MANNER OF ITS APPROACH

The Great Tribulation will be ushered in by the Antichrist signing a seven year non-aggression pact with Israel and other nations.

NOTES

It is the beginning of what is referred to as *"Daniel's Seventieth Week"* (Dan. 9:24, 27). This time will be heralded as *"peace and safety,"* even as the next Verse of this Fifth Chapter proclaims. Consequently, it will seem as if the problems of the world are solved, with Israel claiming that her Messiah has now come, and with much of the world believing this lie.

To which we have already alluded, the Antichrist will usher in a false peace, which will lull the world to sleep as it regards his true intentions. Whenever he does show his hand, it will be sudden and without warning. He will strike in a flash, having deceived Israel and most of the world. Consequently, the *"Day of the Lord"* will be ushered in exactly as the Holy Spirit through Paul said, *"as a thief in the night."*

(3) "FOR WHEN THEY SHALL SAY, PEACE AND SAFETY; THEN SUDDEN DESTRUCTION COMETH UPON THEM, AS TRAVAIL UPON A WOMAN WITH CHILD; AND THEY SHALL NOT ESCAPE."

*"Peace"* characterizes inward repose, while *"safety"* reveals freedom from outward interference. Yet at the moment that tranquility seemingly reaches its peak, *"destruction will come on them suddenly."*

*"Destruction"* means utter and hopeless ruin, a loss of everything worthwhile, causing the victims to despair of life itself. Thus will begin the greatest time of terror the world has ever known. The Judgment will be twofold:

1. The Antichrist will set about to take over the entirety of the world, and by first of all attacking Israel. Some nations will throw in with him, but others will oppose him. Consequently, it will be war on a grand and horrible scale.

2. Coupled with that, the Wrath of God will be poured out on the world as it regards weather patterns, meteorites, and even demons being turned loose from the infernal regions. Actually, the Scripture defines this time as *"the great day of His Wrath is come; and who shall be able to stand?"* (Rev. 6:17).

## PEACE AND SAFETY

The phrase, *"For when they shall say, peace and safety,"* actually refers to Israel in its truest sense, but will as well characterize the feelings of the world.

With the Church raptured away, which will mean the disappearance of untold millions of people, along with every baby and child below the age of accountability, when the initial shock wears off, the world will say *"good riddance!"*

The Apostate Church will aid and abet the rise of the Antichrist, as he makes his debut on the greatest peace platform the world has ever known. He will propose to solve many problems, not the least of them being the thorny Israeli-Arab problem, which has plagued the world from the time of the formation of Israel as a state in 1948. In Truth, it has plagued the world since the time of Abraham, when Ishmael was brought into the world as a result of the carnal effort of Abraham and Sarah. From the time several years later when Isaac was born, the conflict between Isaac and Ishmael has raged. It will come to a head at the midpoint of the Great Tribulation.

The Antichrist will be totally different than any other world dictator, being very religious to begin with, all of which will have a tendency to lull the world to sleep. Daniel said, *"And by peace* (he) *shall destroy many"* (Dan. 8:25).

The world will think it has finally solved its problems, with this new Millennium ushering in a world of peace, prosperity, and plenty. The world Press, and the Television commentators will herald the fact that with these Jesus fanatics now gone, man can finally realize his true potential. It will be called the *"Golden Age,"* or *"the hope of mankind!"*

Little will the world know that it is being set up for the kill. Man without God and for all his technological advancement, can be described as none other than *"stupid!"* The fear of God is the beginning of wisdom; the opposite of that is stupidity!

NOTES

## SUDDEN DESTRUCTION

The phrase, *"Then sudden destruction cometh upon them,"* once again refers primarily to Israel, but as well will ultimately involve the entirety of the world.

Having signed a seven year, nonaggression pact with the Antichrist, and actually believing that he is their Messiah, and their Saviour, they will be lulled to sleep. They will have absolutely no inkling as to what the plans of the Antichrist actually are. Their Temple will be rebuilt, and now once again beginning to offer Sacrifices, even as they did in the days of long ago, they will give the Antichrist all the credit.

In fact, every evidence is, that this man will be a Jew, therefore, acceptable to his own people, but with other ideas in mind altogether.

He will have been arming all along, even at a ferocious rate, but claiming that all of this is merely for peaceful purposes. This is what is meant in Revelation 6:2 where it says, *"And I saw, and behold a white horse: and he that sat on him had a bow; and a crown was given unto him: and he went forth conquering and to conquer."*

If it is to be noticed, he is pictured here as on a white horse, which symbolizes peace, and as having only a *"bow,"* with no arrows mentioned. He evidently will be solving so many world problems, with the nations of the world at least at the beginning, seemingly enjoying great prosperity, that little attention is given to his rearmament program.

In fact, the rise of Hitler was very similar, although on a smaller scale. Hitler brought great prosperity to Germany, which caused most of the nation to turn its head as it regarded his anti-Semitism. While arming at a ferocious pace, he claimed all the while to the nations of the world, that he was doing so only for peaceful purposes.

In fact, World War II was brought about by Satan, and allowed by God, moreso because of Adolph Hitler than anyone else. His ambition was the conquering of the world, but the ambition of Satan through him, was the annihilation of the Jews. Satan knew that it was now time for the fulfillment of the Prophecies concerning Israel to begin. He also knew that for these prophecies to be fulfilled, Israel would once again have to establish herself as a nation, and in the same geographical area as always. If he could slaughter enough of them, this could be stopped; consequently, he raises up his champion, the monster from Germany to carry out this bloody task, which in fact, he pursued with great zeal! He did not succeed, but it was not from lack of trying, with some 6,000,000 Jews slaughtered in that horror.

The world doesn't understand the reason for his horrifying anti-Semitism, or the henchmen around him. It was the power of Satan, which is little understood, if at all, by the world.

With the Church gone, which means that all restraining of evil is gone, that which Hitler did, will only be a microcosm of what the Antichrist will attempt to do on a worldwide scale.

## REBUILT BABYLON

There is Scriptural evidence that Babylon in these last days will be rebuilt, and that the Antichrist will make his headquarters there, at least during the first half of the Great Tribulation (Isa. Chpts. 13-14; Jer. Chpts. 50-51; Zech. 5:5-11; Rev. 14:8; 16:19; 18:1-24).

From the Scriptures it seems that rebuilt Babylon will play a great part in latter-day events, not only as the political capital of the kingdom of the Antichrist but as the headquarters for a religious system called *"Mystery Babylon."*

It will be a great commercial center in the Earth in the last days as pictured in Revelation Chapter 18.

It seems that the man of sin will reign from Babylon during his rise to power over the ten kingdoms of the Middle East, which he will take over (Isa. Chpt. 14; Dan. 7:23-24; Rev. 17:12-17).

In New Testament times Babylon was still a city and even had a Christian Church (I Pet. 5:13). About 500 years later the Babylonian Talmud was written there. Since then it has not been destroyed as Revelation Chapter 18 says it will be destroyed.

Even today there is a city called Hilla of nearly a half million people built just south of the old site of ancient Babylon. The soil it is said, is exceedingly fertile and engineers estimate that the Euphrates and Tigris Rivers could irrigate 7,000,000 acres in winter and about 3,000,000 in summer to grow varied crops. In fact, the whole of the East is rich in oil and other minerals.

## THE ANTICHRIST SHOWS HIS TRUE COLORS

At about the mid-point of the Great Tribulation, the Antichrist will show his true colors, and invade Israel, thereby breaking his covenant with them. He will enter into Israel and actually take over that country, and make the newly built Jewish Temple his headquarters, at least his religious headquarters (Dan. 7:21-25; 8:9-14, 22-25; 9:27; 11:36-45; Mat. 24:15-24; II Thess. 2:3-4; Rev. 13:1-18; 17:8-17).

At that time, he will then do away with all Jewish Sacrifices in the Temple and set himself and his image in the Temple to be worshipped as God. This will continue for over three years.

## ISRAEL'S FLIGHT

At this juncture, the Antichrist could easily destroy Israel, but the Lord will divert His attention elsewhere. Actually, Israel at that time, at least for the most part, will flee into Jordan, which incidently of all the countries of the Middle East, this little country will not be controlled by the man of sin (Dan. 11:41).

As many Bible students know, Petra is located in Jordan. This very strange city is surrounded by mountains, and accessible only by a very narrow road located between two towering cliffs. It is now empty.

To this place many in Israel will flee upon the invasion of the Antichrist. The Beast could easily destroy these ancient people at that time, but the Scripture says that he will encounter problems in the North and the East, and will be forced to then deal with these problems (Dan. 11:44).

He will leave the Jews for the time being to go forth against these new enemies until he conquers them in the last three and one half years of this age. He will then come back into Israel to do what he formerly planned, only to be defeated by the Coming of the Lord.

During the last days of this three and one half years of the Great Tribulation, the Jews will have regained control of Jerusalem, because the Antichrist is away elsewhere. He will then come against Jerusalem intending to destroy Israel once and for all, in what is known as the Battle of Armageddon (Isa. 63:1-6; Ezek. Chpts. 38-39; Joel 3:13; Rev. 19:15).

To be sure, the Antichrist would at that time succeed, but for the Coming of the Lord.

NOTES

(The following Scriptures proclaim Petra as a place of refuge for Israel during that coming dark time: Ps. 60:6-12; Isa. 16:1-5; 26:20; 63:1; Ezek. 20:33; Dan. 11:41; Hos. 2:14; Mat. 24:16; Rev. Chpt. 12.)

TRAVAIL

The phrase, *"As travail upon a woman with child,"* presents a familiar Oriental simile. It carries the idea of the inevitability or unavoidability of Judgment, and that as well of suddenness.

Israel in her rejection of Christ some 2,000 years ago, carried them into a dark night of unbelief and rebellion against God. They have suffered much as all such position brings suffering and judgment. It is not so much that God has leveled Judgment against them, as much as them taking themselves out from under the protection of God, which has left them wide open to the powers of darkness, which steal, kill, and destroy (Jn. 10:10). In fact, Christ prophesied this very thing when He said, *"O Jerusalem, Jerusalem, thou that killest the Prophets, and stonest them which are sent unto thee, how often would I have gathered thy children together, even as a hen gathereth her chickens under her wings, and ye would not!*

*"Behold, your house is left unto you desolate.*

*"For I say unto you, ye shall not see Me henceforth, till ye shall say, blessed is He that cometh in the Name of the Lord"* (Mat. 23:37-39).

In fact, Jesus was in the Temple whenever this Prophecy was uttered. He then went to Olivet where He gave the great Matthew Chapter 24 discourse which spoke of the coming *"Great Tribulation,"* which for the most part, pertains to Israel (Mat. 24:21-22).

The simile used here by Paul, pertains to a woman who is experiencing birth pangs, knowing that the birth is imminent, but not knowing the time!

The difference in Israel and the example of the woman in travail is, that a woman knows when she is pregnant; however, Israel will have no knowledge whatsoever regarding her impending danger, and because she fully trusts the Antichrist. So, it will definitely be *"sudden destruction."*

NOTES

However, as it regards the *"travail,"* the Lord definitely knows what is happening, and how it's happening, because in fact, He will have allowed it to happen. Whatever the Antichrist may think, or try, he can only do what the Lord allows him to do. His ambition will be to take over the world and to destroy Israel; however, God will use him for another purpose altogether, and that is to bring Israel to a place to where she will sincerely call for the Messiah, having no one else to help her. This she will do, which will be during the Battle of Armageddon, and which looks like her total destruction as a people and as a nation. In fact, were it not for the Coming of the Lord, she would be totally and completely destroyed. But Jesus will come, and His Coming will be totally unlike anything the world has ever known before. Israel will then accept Him as Lord, as Saviour, and Redeemer!

NO ESCAPE

The phrase, *"And they shall not escape,"* refers to all of this of which we speak being inevitable. In other words, all of these things definitely are going to happen. There is a possibility as students of the Word, that we might misinterpret Bible Prophecy to a certain extent, but irrespective of the fine detail, it is guaranteed that the overall thrust of these Prophecies are definitely going to take place. I speak of the Rapture of the Church, the rise of the Antichrist, the coming Great Tribulation, and the anger of God against a world who has forgotten Him days without number. I speak of the Wrath of God being poured out on this world as it has never known before. While the area of the Middle East will be the greatest target, still, the entirety of the world is going to be affected, and in a way that it's never known before.

Preachers can claim that all of this has been fulfilled, with the world getting better and better, etc.; however, the Word of God plainly says, *"they shall not escape,"* i.e., *"the Great Tribulation is definitely coming upon this world."*

(4) "BUT YE, BRETHREN, ARE NOT IN DARKNESS, THAT THAT DAY SHOULD OVERTAKE YOU AS A THIEF."

The Word of the Lord is explicit here. Even though these things will overtake the world like a thief, and simply because they do not know the Word of God, or even believe the Word of God, for those who are truly following the Lord, from our understanding of the Word of God, we know what is coming upon this world.

As one knows the Word of God, one sees the absolute absurdity of the casting about of even those who are the most intellectual in the world as it concerns the future. In other words, they don't have a clue as to what is coming! In fact, the future as far as the world is concerned, is pretty much limited to what Hollywood produces as it regards *"Star Wars,"* etc.

The greatest pastime of the world one might say, is the delving into one's roots. Somehow, they seem to think that this holds some type of answer for them.

The great uncertainty among those who do not know God, is because of the terrible emptiness they have in their soul, and the absolute lack of purpose in their lives. In other words, the world has nothing but a dark past, a hurting present, and an unknown future!

ARE NOT IN DARKNESS

The phrase, *"But ye, Brethren, are not in darkness,"* refers to spiritual enlightenment, which comes only from the Word of God.

Even though the statement, *"Ye, Brethren, are not in darkness,"* is very simple, it speaks volumes!

*"Darkness"* in the Greek is *"skotos,"* and means *"shadow, error, shadiness, and obscurity."* In fact, the entirety of the world lies in terrible, spiritual darkness, other than those who know the Lord Jesus Christ. Actually, one cannot know God, unless one knows Christ. The way to the Father alone is by Christ (Jn. 10:9). As well, Jesus is *"the Way, the Truth, and the Life: no man cometh to the Father, but by Him"* (Jn. 14:6).

The intersection has always been the Lord Jesus Christ, and more particularly, *"Jesus Christ and Him Crucified"* (I Cor. 2:2).

The only way out of darkness is to accept Christ, and this speaks of the Crucified, Risen, Exalted Christ. Millions in the world, would like to accept Christ *"the good man," "the miracle worker," "the great Teacher,"* but they don't want the Christ of the Cross.

NOTES

However, to accept Christ in any other capacity, is not really to accept Christ.

MAN'S PROBLEM

Man's problem is sin! And when we say *"sin,"* we're not speaking of a mere mendacity, or a mere infraction. We're speaking of that which is of such power and strength, as to completely cut off an individual from God. In fact, the only thing that can separate man from God, and God from man, is *"sin."*

The only remedy for sin is the Cross of Christ. There is no other remedy, because no other remedy is needed. So, the whole idea of accepting Christ, is to accept what He did at the Cross on our behalf, and to accept that fully, totally, and completely. There is Salvation in no other way or source (Rom. 6:2-6).

NO EXCUSE

The phrase, *"That that day should overtake you as a thief,"* refers to the world being in that condition, because they are in darkness, but that the Child of God functions in a totally different capacity. There is no excuse for the Believer not knowing these things, even as Paul says to the Thessalonians who had not been saved very long.

I'm afraid the Truth in many cases is, that some Christians definitely are in *"darkness,"* at least as far as understanding the Word of God is concerned, simply because there is very little consecration to the Lord. Were this not so, Paul would not have given the admonishment which he did in the following Verses. In other words, it is possible for a Christian to be *"spiritually asleep!"*

(5) "YE ARE ALL THE CHILDREN OF LIGHT, AND THE CHILDREN OF THE DAY: WE ARE NOT OF THE NIGHT, NOR OF DARKNESS."

The word *"day"* as used here by Paul, has no reference to the coming eschatological Day of the Lord, which we studied in Verse 2. It is used metaphorically in association with spiritual Light.

This Verse guarantees the Readers' participation in a spiritual environment entirely different from that of non-Christians. I suppose the question should be, *"How much are we taking advantage of this position afforded us by Christ?"*

NOTES

CHILDREN OF LIGHT

The phrase, *"Ye are all the Children of Light,"* refers to knowing Jesus Christ, Who is *"the Light of the world"* (Jn. 8:12).

The Believer is to always understand that everything we have from the Lord comes from and through Christ, and more particularly, what He did for us at the Cross. The Cross of Christ made it possible for God to do wonderful and glorious things for those who would have Faith in Him. We are *"Children of the Light"* only in that capacity, and to be sure, that is a great capacity.

CHILDREN OF THE DAY

The phrase, *"And the Children of the day,"* is pretty much the same as the former phrase, but with some difference.

First of all, we walk in the *"day,"* simply because we have the *"Light."* The *"Light"* Who is Jesus Christ, affords the *"day!"* Otherwise, the individual walks in *"darkness."*

As we've said many times in these Volumes, the Bible is the only revealed Truth in the world today, and in fact ever has been. Only those who know their Bibles, have a grasp of the past, the present, and the future. Otherwise, and as stated, and no matter how much the education, the individual draws a blank. The Word of God tells us where we have been, where we are, and where we are going. There's nothing in the world other than the Bible, which can boast of such information and knowledge. To be frank, if a person knows their Bible, they are educated, at least in the things of life. Conversely, if they have degrees from the greatest universities in the world, and they do not know the Bible, as far as the things of life are concerned, they are ignorant! That's a blunt statement, but it is true.

That's the reason that millionaires and even billionaires, and even the most educated, oftentimes make fools of themselves, in fact living miserable lives, and I speak of those who do not know the Lord. They know many things, but they don't know how to live, simply because, it is the Lord Alone through His Word which tells us how to live. And if one doesn't know how to live, irrespective as to how much money one might have, or how much education, life, to say the least, is not what it ought to be. That's the reason that Jesus said, *"A man's life consisteth not in the abundance of things he possesseth"* (Lk. 12:15).

NOT OF THE NIGHT

The phrase, *"We are not of the night, nor of darkness,"* presents the fact, that the Child of God is in a totally different sphere of operation.

The Believer is in the world, but we are to never be of the world. This must always be clear in the thinking of the Believer. We have a distinct life to live, a distinct path to follow, in other words, *"the straight and narrow."* We do not march to the world's drum and neither do we function to its tune. Our excitement is elsewhere! Our joy and happiness are elsewhere! In other words, Christ in totality is our sufficiency. From Him, we derive all things, and *"In Him we live, and move, and have our being"* (Acts 17:28).

As well, all of this means, which should be crystal clear, that the great destruction that's coming upon this world, is coming upon the children of darkness, and not the children of Light. Behind all that's being said, the Holy Spirit through the Apostle is making this abundantly clear. The gist of all these statements, give credence to this Truth.

(6) "THEREFORE LET US NOT SLEEP, AS DO OTHERS; BUT LET US WATCH AND BE SOBER."

It is impossible for a Child of God who is consecrated to the Lord to not understand, at least in some measure, the coming *"Day of the Lord,"* which is going to burst upon this world. Of course, some know much more than others; nevertheless, the very fact of the Divine Nature being a part of the Child of God, guarantees at least some knowledge of these coming events.

However, from the manner in which Paul addresses himself here, I believe it is possible for a Christian to lose his way, until even these things proclaimed by the Apostle are denied. A Believer can lose his way, cease to believe, and go into apostasy. In that case, an erroneous interpretation of the Word follows suit, at least in most things.

As I have stated previously, and will continue to say, *I personally believe that the Cross of Christ is going to be the great dividing line in these Endtime days in which we live.* I have found that if a Believer understands the Cross of Christ, then most everything else falls into place as well. In other words, there is a more sure grasp of what the Holy Spirit is teaching through the Word of God.

If the Cross is denied or ignored, spiritual oblivion can be the only result. That's how serious I personally believe all of this is.

In fact, I believe the Lord has spoken that to my heart concerning the Cross being the criteria for our belief, the plumb line so to speak, by which everything is measured.

SPIRITUAL SLEEP

The phrase, *"Therefore let us not sleep, as do others,"* presents the Apostle continuing to use a metaphor regarding spiritual things, even as he did in the previous Verses.

*"Sleep"* suggests indifference or indolence. In Ephesians 5:14, in a similar context, it connotes spiritual death.

The point is, it is possible for a Believer to fall into such a spiritual stupor, and if continuing in that direction, to ultimately lose one's soul. In fact, I think that the *"sleep"* of which Paul here speaks, is possibly the greatest danger of all for the Child of God.

In a sense, *"sleep"* suggests apathy, which is somewhat like a person drifting with the current.

To do such, one really has to do nothing. To go against the current, as should be obvious, requires much effort on the part of the individual. It is not that we earn anything from the Lord, but it is the struggle against the very forces of evil which are in this world. Sin and Satan's way, are not limited to mere acts, but rather is a spirit. And by *"spirit"* we actually mean *"spirits of darkness,"* i.e., *"demon spirits."*

Even though demon spirits cannot possess a Child of God, they can definitely oppress Believers, and can cause their influence to be felt in about every capacity. In this struggle, and a struggle it is, if the Child of God doesn't keep up his prayer life, stay in the Word, and above all keep his Faith in the Cross of Christ, understanding that there all victory is found, *"spiritual sleep"* will be the result!

NOTES

WATCH AND BE SOBER

The phrase, *"But let us watch and be sober,"* actually pertains to the statement I have just made.

The exhortation given by Paul is actually not to backsliders, but to encourage Christians to sustain their relationship by continued watchfulness. As Christians we belong to a future Kingdom of Light where darkness will be forever banished, and although that day has not yet come, we are walking already in its Light. Consequently, all who walk with Christ in the Light will not be unprepared for the Rapture, nor lacking in understanding concerning end-day events, i.e., *"the Day of the Lord."* To be a Child of Light involves openhearted obedience to the Truth coupled with trust in Christ, and what He did for us at the Cross (Jn. 12:36; I Jn. 1:6-7).

As *"sleep"* suggests indifference or indolence, *"watch"* suggests a wide-awake alertness.

*"Sober"* carries the meaning of *"calm and collected in spirit, temperate, dispassionate, circumspect."* Together they imply that to be a Child of the Light is more than a formal relationship; there must be ethical connection with the Light, meaning that what we profess, has a bearing within our lives, which develops Righteousness.

(7) "FOR THEY THAT SLEEP SLEEP IN THE NIGHT; AND THEY THAT BE DRUNKEN ARE DRUNKEN IN THE NIGHT."

A particular direction is proposed in this Verse of Scripture. In fact, the Holy Spirit constantly gives us such instruction, that if heeded, will make our way much easier.

Consequently, this Passage serves as a barometer one might say!

THE NIGHT

The phrase, *"For they that sleep sleep in the night,"* in effect tells us, that those who walk in darkness are those who sleep. Consequently, this should not be the attitude or position of the Child of God. We are not of *"darkness,"* we are not of *"night,"* so why should we *"sleep"*? The idea is, that one will sleep only if one begins to walk in darkness.

What does it mean for a Christian to walk in darkness?

To do so means that one is not alert to what is happening, actually being in a spiritual stupor. This of which we speak is deception. Unfortunately, it characterizes many, many Christians. Before one goes completely to sleep, one first gets drowsy. Inasmuch as the Holy Spirit had the Apostle to use this metaphor, then this of which I have just said, continues to hold true as well.

A drowsy Christian, spiritually speaking, is not aware of danger, not aware of things which are happening all around him, which are a portend of great danger.

## HOW DOES A CHRISTIAN GET IN THIS CONDITION?

That is the great question!

The Lord saved me when I was eight years old, and Baptized me with the Holy Spirit a short time later. As I dictate these notes, that has been a time span of about 56 years.

During that time I've learned some things about working for the Lord and about living for the Lord. Except for a period of time in my early teens, I have done my very best to diligently serve the Lord and be what He wants me to be. I've always had a strong prayer life, as well as a strong love for the Word of God. Actually, I think I've read the Bible completely through, not too much short of 50 times, if not more!

Coming up in Church, and then preaching the Gospel, and doing so for many years, I found to my sorrow, that my knowledge of the Cross of Christ, actually the very foundation of the Faith, was somewhat deficient. I understood the Cross strongly so as it regarded the initial Salvation experience, preaching it boldly and powerfully, actually seeing hundreds of thousands brought to a saving knowledge of Jesus Christ. However, I had never been taught, nor did I know, the part that the Cross plays in our everyday living before God. I did not know or understand that the Holy Spirit functions and works entirely within the parameters of the Finished Work of Christ (Rom. 8:1-2). I did not understand Faith in the Cross for Sanctification, and if one doesn't understand Faith in this capacity, one automatically resorts to works. In fact, there is no alternative!

Resorting to works, even though doing so sincerely, and no matter how dedicated one might be, the end result is going to be failure.

NOTES

The Holy Spirit, Whose help is an absolute necessity, simply will not function in that capacity. In other words, when we resort to Law, whether ignorantly or otherwise, we are strictly on our own; consequently, failure will be the result, irrespective as to who we are or what type of Call of God might be on our lives. As a result, there was failure, and despite the fact of doing all I knew to do to oppose the powers of darkness in this arena.

As a result of that failure, I cried to the Lord as I had never cried to Him before. As I've stated, I have always had a very strong prayer life, but now, I cried to the Lord in acute desperation. This was the late Fall of 1991.

I didn't have the answer to a victorious, overcoming Christian life, but I knew the answer was in the Word of God. And I knew if I sought the Lord long enough, that He would hear and answer my plea. And that He did!

The answer didn't come as quick or as soon as I would have liked, but in looking back, I know that whatever delay there was, the fault was definitely not of the Lord, but rather mine. Also, I in no way blame failure on anything other than myself. But yet, there is a difference in one failing because of not knowing what the Word of God teaches regarding a certain matter, than to fail deliberately.

To be frank, I'm not sure if anyone of us knows our heart as we ought to. We think we do, but I'm not sure if what we think is always right!

Irrespective, if we're sincere before the Lord, and no matter the problem, He will always answer. In fact, I sought His Face earnestly for about five years, even with tears, and as Paul said *"day and night,"* before the answer finally came.

## PERCEPTION

It's not a very pleasant thing to have almost the entirety of the Church think of you in very debilitating terms. Especially, when you've tried so very hard, but failed just the same, and don't know the answer. And then above that, you don't really know anyone who does know the answer. I'm sure some few did, but not many!

In such a situation, the only thing that one can do is to take the matter to the Lord. One has no other recourse. I now know the reason, but then I did not know. So what could I say? When people call you a hypocrite, or at the very least look down on you as something to be pitied, you can say nothing. And then to make matters worse, if the Truth wasn't bad enough, lie upon lie is added to the Truth, and still, you have no defense whatsoever.

I should warn the Reader, that oftentimes what one perceives things to be, most of the time isn't! That's the reason that Jesus very succinctly told us *"Judge not!"* (Mat. 7:1-3).

One doesn't really know how it feels to be judged in such a negative way, until one has been in that position. It's a position in which I pray that you the Reader, never find yourself.

WHAT THE LORD TOLD ME

When the Lord answered my prayer, as stated, even after seeking His Face for several years, He answered me strictly from the Word of God. It was a Revelation of the Cross.

He took me to the Book of Romans, and explained to me the meaning of Chapters 6, 7, and 8, of that great Epistle. He showed me what it meant to be *"in Christ!"* In other words, He showed me my position as a Believer, a position incidently which never changes, and a position which is maintained by Faith and not by works.

As well, He told me that the Cross of Christ held the answer to every question I had, the solution to every problem, the resource for every need. Inasmuch as that is true, I was to place my Faith in the Finished Work of Christ, understanding that this is where all Salvation and Victory are.

The Lord then showed me the manner in which the Holy Spirit works. In fact I had cried to Him many, many times, asking as to why the Holy Spirit wasn't helping me? To be sure, He was helping me with many things, and I speak of Preaching the Gospel, winning men to Christ, seeing lives gloriously and wondrously changed by the Power of God; however, after the Lord showed me the manner in which the Holy Spirit works, He then began to help me in my own personal life, and in a way that I had never dreamed was possible. The victory that I preached, I now have, and in a way that is beyond anything I could ever begin to imagine. I now know what this *"more abundant life"* actually is (Jn. 10:10). I now know what this glorious *"rest"* in Jesus actually is (Mat. 11:28-30).

NOTES

Actually, this Revelation once it began, continues to come, ever enlarging upon that which the Lord had given me. In fact, I don't think it will ever stop.

It has completely revolutionized my life; completely changed my life in every respect. I now know what victory is, and in a way that I've never known before.

In this, there is a consuming desire that all other Believers know exactly this of which I say, and experience this of which I say. I realize that some few have, but I also know, that most haven't!

THE STATE OF THE CHURCH

From experience, I feel that the Church has by and large lost its moorings as it regards its true foundation. I speak of the Cross of Christ. There has been so little teaching and preaching in the last several decades on the Cross, that most Believers have little understanding as to their only Source of Victory. So, what am I saying?

I am saying that most of the Preachers, have no idea of this of which I speak. Many of them are Godly, and preach all the Light they have, but when it comes to the Cross of Christ, they have little knowledge as to its veracity, its place, and position as the very foundation of all that we are in Christ. In fact, their knowledge, at least for the most part, begins and ends with the initial Salvation experience.

Sometime ago in South Africa, I was addressing a group of Preachers, I suppose a hundred or so! I asked them the following question:

*"What do you tell your people when they come to you and they have experienced spiritual failure?"*

I then went on to ask, *"What do you tell them to do? What kind of advice do you give them?"*

Of course I knew the answer to the questions even before I asked them.

These Pastors would tell their people that they need to consecrate more to the Lord. They would tell them to *"get in the Altars,"* and seek God! They would tell them to be more faithful to Church, more faithful in their giving to the Work of the Lord, more faithful in witnessing to lost souls, etc.

If the Pastor is more spiritual than usual, he will tell his people that they need to *"pray more,"* or develop a greater study of the Word of God.

The only difference in the Preachers in the United States and South Africa, is that some Preachers in the States would probably recommend a Psychologist, which is worse than nothing, which would little be done by Africans.

Concerning all the other things we have said, they are good, and to be sure, Believers should be engaged in these things constantly. Nevertheless, these things that Pastors recommend, as right as they may be in their own way, will not give the Believer victory. In fact, they can *"stay in the Altars,"* and be so very sincere before God, and in fact be blessed greatly in many ways, but they will not find victory within their lives in this manner. That may come as a shock to many Christians, but it just happens to be true!

Consequently, most Christians are living an endless treadmill of extreme activity, but no visible results. Many are confused! Many are hurt! Most come to think that everyone else has victory; consequently, something must be personally wrong with them, they surmise!

The Truth is, most of the others aren't walking in victory either, and there's nothing any more wrong with you than there is with anyone else. The problem is, that most Christians don't know God's prescribed order of victory. Consequently, they fail and in fact, many, if not most, live lives of spiritual failure in some way. They try to hide the fact, try to tell themselves that it's not so, and confess loudly the very opposite, but the Truth is, most are not walking in victory.

When the Pastor, or anyone for that matter, at least those who know, begin to tell the individual how that the Cross is the answer to their Sanctification, for this is really what we're speaking about, just as it was for their initial Salvation experience, then they will be giving Truth to that individual, which will lift them up above the shadows, and plant their feet on higher ground. In fact, that's what Paul was talking about in Galatians 6:1.

NOTES

A Christian who is trying and failing, doesn't need someone to condemn him. He's already condemned! He needs someone to tell him the right way of Victory, and Victory to be sure, which is found only in the Cross.

The state of the Church is such presently, that I don't think most know this way of victory, in fact, the only way of victory! Regrettably, most Preachers don't know either, so that leaves most Christians in a very precarious condition. I know, I've been there!

## HOW CAN ONE TELL IF ONE IS WALKING AFTER THE FLESH OR AFTER THE SPIRIT?

Romans 8:1 says: *"There is therefore now no condemnation to them which are in Christ Jesus, who walk not after the flesh, but after the Spirit."*

To anyone who has studied the Eighth Chapter of Romans, it is obvious that Paul is giving here the secret to a victorious, Christian life, which is accomplished and brought about by *"walking after the Spirit."* The idea is this:

The Believer although saved and even a new creation in Christ Jesus, meaning that old things have passed away and all things have become new (II Cor. 5:17), still, cannot live the Christian life, at least in the manner in which it is incumbent upon us to live, without the help of the Holy Spirit. Therefore, understanding that, this which Paul says in this Chapter is crucial to our life in the Lord.

The key is *"walking after the Spirit,"* but how does one do that?

Many Pentecostals and Charismatics have the erroneous idea, that when one is Baptized with the Holy Spirit with the evidence of speaking with other Tongues, that the Work of the Spirit is then automatic in one's life.

If that were true, why do Spirit-filled Christians still fail? In fact, if all of this was automatic, there would be no Christians with problem areas in their lives, no failures, no carnality, no flesh, etc. But the Truth is, every single Christian in the world, even Spirit-baptized Christians, face this struggle of the flesh and the Spirit constantly. In other words, there's a war that's going on in the heart and life of the Believer, with the sin nature ever attempting to regain supremacy. The trouble is, in most Christian lives, the sin nature succeeds in some way.

The reason is, the Believer is not *"walking after the Spirit,"* i.e., *"the Holy Spirit."*

Therefore, the question should be asked, as to how one can know if one is walking after the Spirit or after the flesh?

If one has to ask that question, then one is not walking after the Spirit. It is just that simple! Believe me, when one is walking after the Spirit, there will be no doubt about it, no question about it, simply because the individual will be living victoriously. In other words, sin will not have dominion over him or her (Rom. 7:14). So, asking that type of question, is like asking whether it's daylight or midnight!

The Holy Spirit Who incidently, is in our hearts and lives because of what Jesus did at the Cross, works exclusively according to a particular *"Law!"*

### THE LAW OF THE SPIRIT OF LIFE IN CHRIST JESUS

Continuing in Verse 2 of the Eighth Chapter of Romans, Paul says, *"For the Law of the Spirit of Life in Christ Jesus hath made me free from the law of sin and death."*

Consequently, we have two powerful laws mentioned here in this Second Verse:

1. The Law of the Spirit of Life in Christ Jesus.
2. The law of sin and death.

The only way the Believer, for it is Believers to whom the Apostle is speaking, can have victory over *"the law of sin and death,"* is by *"the Law of the Spirit of Life in Christ Jesus."* To have Victory, and that means Victory in any and every capacity, we must *"walk after the Spirit,"* Who is functioning according to this Law.

What is this Law?

It's not the Law of Moses; it is the Law of the Spirit of Life in Christ Jesus.

First of all, as is obvious, it is the Holy Spirit of Whom is being spoken, and as well, He guarantees *"Life"* to the Believer.

Is this *"Life"* resident in the Spirit?

Of course, all Members of the Godhead are the Source of Life; however, the *"Life"* being spoken of here, is a Life all its own, in fact, that which comes from Jesus Christ exclusively, and more particularly, that which comes from Him as a result of what He did at the Cross and in His Resurrection.

NOTES

Months before His Crucifixion, Jesus was in Jerusalem to keep the Feast of Tabernacles. *"On that last day of the Feast, Jesus stood and cried, saying, if any man thirst, let him come unto Me, and drink."*

He then said, *"He that believeth on Me, as the Scripture hath said, out of his inmost being shall flow rivers of Living Water."*

John then explained this by saying, *"But this spake He of the Spirit, which they that believe on Him should receive"* (Jn. 7:37-39).

Jesus is pictured here as the Source of the Living Water, which speaks of Life Eternal as it regards those who believe on Him. This *"Living Water"* which of course is a metaphor for Spiritual Life which comes from Christ, comes to all Believers as a result of what Christ did at the Cross. It is imperative that we understand this.

Jesus has always been God, but the life He imparts to us, is that which He can give to us because of what He did at the Cross and the Resurrection, and our belief and Faith in that. Without the Cross, none of this would have been possible.

It is the Holy Spirit Who superintends the giving by Christ of this *"Living Water,"* i.e., *"Life,"* and the Holy Spirit Who superintends the receiving of it by the Believer, in effect, making all of this possible.

The idea is, this Life is not possible except through what Christ did at the Cross, and it cannot be received by the Believer without the Holy Spirit being the One Who makes this great benefit possible.

In all this that the Holy Spirit does, this giving of Life, which in effect comes totally from Christ, all are done strictly according to the parameters of what Christ did on the Cross. That's the reason it is said, the Law of the Spirit of Life *"in Christ Jesus!"*

This Law refers strictly to what Christ did at the Cross on our behalf and in His Resurrection.

### WHAT DID CHRIST DO AT THE CROSS?

Of course, the totality of what He did and I might quickly add, did for us, will probably never be fully known. Or I should say, one will never exhaust its potential; however, the following will hopefully give us a general idea:

1. Christ provided Himself as a Sacrifice to God on our behalf. In other words, what we could not do for ourselves in that we were sinful and wicked and as a consequence, could not serve as any type of Sacrifice, Jesus did for us. His perfect, sinless Body, Soul, and Spirit, was a Sacrifice which God could accept, and in fact, did accept.

2. Man had committed a monstrous crime against God, thereby, owing Him a debt that was so huge, so large, that man could not hope to pay such a debt. Jesus by the giving of Himself, paid the sin debt in full, at least for all who will believe (Jn. 3:16).

3. In the paying of this sin debt, He also atoned for all sin, which means that the record against man is cleared totally and completely of all transgressions against God, once again, for all who will believe.

4. With the sin debt paid and all sin atoned, Satan lost his claim on the human race, for sin and transgression is his claim, and a legal claim at that. However, with all such infractions removed, Satan now has no claim. Even though we're being overly repetitive, we must quickly add, still, it is only according to those who believe.

5. With all sin removed, and Satan having lost his claim on humanity, this means that he as well as every demon spirit and fallen angel, and in other words every power of darkness, are totally and completely defeated, and for all time.

6. In effect, this which Jesus did was and is a legal work, which means it satisfied the claims of Heavenly Justice, and which Satan must obey.

7. This which Jesus did, addressed every single thing that man lost at the Fall. This speaks of all spiritual problems, material problems, physical problems, mental problems, and domestic problems. This means that everything was included in the Atonement.

Now as the Reader should understand, even though everything was included in the Atonement (this legal Work of Christ), Believers do not yet have all the benefits of this great Work; however, at the coming Resurrection, the total balance of all that Jesus did, of which we now only have a down payment, will come in totality. Our coming Resurrection was and is guaranteed, by His Resurrection (I Cor., Chpt. 15).

8. This which Jesus did at the Cross, made it possible for the Holy Spirit to come into the heart and life of the Believer, to abide forever (Jn. 14:16-17; Gal. 3:14).

NOTES

To understand it even better, the Atonement, which refers to what Jesus did at the Cross and in His Resurrection, even including His Exaltation (Rom. 6:2-6; Eph. 2:6), is a legal work somewhat like the Constitution of the United States. Regarding the Constitution, all citizens of the United States are guaranteed certain rights. Consequently, every single Judge, Law Enforcement Officer, or legal representative of any kind, including Congress and the President of the United States, are supposed to function totally and completely within the binding precepts of the Constitution. It is the same with the Atonement.

The Lord works strictly within the confines of that which Jesus did at the Cross, and Satan must abide by that as well. As would be obvious, the Holy Spirit Who is God, functions completely within the confines of this great Work, this Substitutionary Sacrifice of Christ, all on our behalf. So, when it speaks of the *"Law of Life in Christ Jesus,"* this is the Law of which it speaks, and what Paul is talking about.

## HOW DOES THIS LAW AFFECT THE CHRISTIAN?

It affects the Christian in every single way. The reason is simple:

As the Lord, and in fact, the entirety of the spirit world, both good and bad, must function according to this Law, the Believer must function accordingly as well. And this is what most Christians don't know! And Satan knowing that we do not know this, takes full advantage of our Scriptural ignorance, causing us untold problems and difficulties.

Jesus plainly said, *"And ye shall know the Truth, and the Truth shall make you free"* (Jn. 8:32).

However, it is only the Truth one knows, which can affect this task. Truths not known, serve as no benefit whatsoever to the Believer. And the facts are, most Believers do not know

NOTES

or understand the benefits of the Finished Work of Christ. Actually, most Christians know and understand somewhat concerning the Cross as it involves their initial Salvation experience. In other words, they know that one has to believe on the Lord Jesus Christ and what He did at the Cross to be saved. Beyond that, most Christians draw a blank as it regards the effect of the Cross upon our daily living.

*"Walking after the Spirit"* involves allowing the Holy Spirit to perform the Work of Sanctification in our lives, and to do so in totality. In other words, He doesn't need any help, and in fact, other than our Faith, if we attempt to help Him, we only succeed in doing the very opposite, which is to frustrate the Grace of God (Gal. 2:20-21). This means that God will give us all kinds of good things, but He will do so only on one basis, the basis of what Jesus did at the Cross. The Holy Spirit guarantees us all of this, but only if He is allowed to do it undisturbed and uninterrupted by our own efforts.

How do we bring that about?

We bring all of these good things about, by simply understanding that first of all we cannot do it ourselves, and that the Holy Spirit Alone can accomplish this task, and that He does so strictly according to our Faith in the Cross of Christ.

## THE OBJECT OF OUR FAITH

Now this of which I will say is so very, very important! All that the Lord demands of us is Faith; however, just having Faith is one thing. In fact, all Christians have Faith, but it's the object of one's Faith which is the key.

What do I mean by the *"object of one's Faith"*?

I'm speaking of that in which we place our Faith, in which we place our confidence, that to which we look, that in which we believe. *The object of one's Faith must be in the Cross of Christ in totality, before the Holy Spirit will work and function on our behalf.* However, that needs some explanation.

There are many who will read these words, and will sense the Truth in what we say, but will only render a head Faith of sorts toward this of which we speak. That won't work!

One must understand, even as we have laboriously gone into detail, that everything one receives from the Lord is exclusively through and by, what Jesus did at the Cross and in His Resurrection. We must understand that, believe that, and not allow ourselves to be pulled away to other things. In fact, many Christians have what one might call *"divided Faith."* That won't work either!

This speaks of having Faith in the Cross for one's initial Salvation, which all must have, and then having Faith in self or something else other than the Cross, as it regards our Sanctification. That is divided Faith! As well, it's Faith that God cannot recognize.

James plainly said, *"But let him ask in Faith, nothing wavering. For he that wavereth is like a wave of the Sea driven with the wind and tossed.*

*"For let not that man think that he shall receive anything of the Lord.*

*"A double minded man is unstable in all his ways"* (James 1:6-8).

How much clearer can it be!

But yet that's where most Christians are, they are *"double minded,"* in that they have Faith in the Cross for their Salvation, and Faith in themselves for their Sanctification. Such won't work which is plainly evident in the failure rate regarding Christians.

The object of our Faith must be totally and completely in what Jesus did for us at the Cross, through which all blessings come. When our Faith is properly placed, properly understood, and there properly remains, the Holy Spirit will then work on our behalf in great and glorious ways.

Please understand, these things of which I say are not mere rhetoric. They are the Word of God. And as well, everything I'm telling you, every erroneous direction as well as every right direction, I have been down both paths. I know what it means to not have my Faith in the proper object for my Sanctification, and to suffer terrible failure, and I know what it means for my Faith to be properly placed, and to experience Victory, and Victory in such proportions that it defies all description.

## SALVATION BY FAITH AND SANCTIFICATION BY SELF

That heading I have just given you, is where most of Christianity presently is. Most are doing exactly as the Galatians of old.

We place our Faith in what Christ did at the Cross as it regards our Salvation, and then we shift our Faith to ourselves as it regards our Sanctification, which caused Paul to say to the Galatians, *"Are ye so foolish? Having begun in the Spirit* (Faith in the Cross in which the Spirit works), *are ye now made perfect by the flesh?* (attempting to sanctify yourselves by your own efforts?)" (Gal. 3:3).

*"Foolish"* is an apt word, exactly as the Holy Spirit through the Apostle said! We are so foolish to attempt this, but that's where most of us are.

Why? How?

Satan has been very, very successful in the last few decades, at steering the Church away from the Cross of Christ. He has done so through a series of manners and tactics.

More than likely, unbelief is one of the greatest facets of all. This means that many Christians, and especially so-called religious leaders, simply do not anymore believe in what Jesus did at the Cross as it regards Salvation and Sanctification. Hence they have gravitated toward humanistic psychology. In fact, this drift toward psychology, is one of the most awful signs of all, of the spiritual drift into unbelief. The very nature of this ungodly action, blatantly and openly states that what Christ did is not enough. In fact, one Pentecostal writer said (Pentecostal?), *"Man is facing problems today which were not prevalent in the past, and, therefore, needs the help of secular psychology."*

Such a statement is either gross ignorance of the Word of God, or actually a repudiation of the Cross of Christ. One cannot have it both ways!

Jesus addressed this very succinctly, when He spoke to the Sadducees, *"Ye do err, not knowing the Scriptures, nor the Power of God"* (Mat. 22:29).

I'll say it again: Either what Jesus did at the Cross and in His Resurrection suffices for every single need of suffering, hurting humanity, or else it doesn't! If it doesn't, then we need to abandon the Word of God and look to the likes of Freud and other Psychologists. However, I want it to be known, and I want to say it loud and clear, even as Joshua of old:

*"And if it seem evil unto you to serve the Lord, choose you this day whom you will serve; whether the gods which your fathers served that were on the other side of the flood, or the gods of the Amorites, in whose land ye dwell: but as for me and my house, we will serve the Lord"* (Josh. 24:15).

NOTES

Considering that the Leadership of almost all of the Pentecostal Denominations in the United States and Canada, have opted totally and completely for the psychological way, you now understand why they do not too very much like Jimmy Swaggart.

## FAITH?

Psychology is one way of Satan, but actually, he has many ways. The *"Faith way"* which sounds right and seems right and looks right, but in fact isn't right, is another one of his ways.

In the last several decades, the Church has been inundated with *"Faith teaching."* Some small amount of it has been very good, but the general direction of most of it has been totally false, i.e., *"unscriptural!"*

It fools people, because Faith in fact, is the very ingredient through which the Lord works with humanity, and that ingredient alone! So, understanding that, how could any teaching on Faith be wrong?

Most of the teaching given in these last few decades has been wrong, because the object of the Faith has been improper. The Faith that's been proclaimed has not been Faith in the Cross, not by any stretch of the imagination, but rather Faith in other things.

It is called *"Faith in the Word,"* but in actuality it is merely, Faith in Faith.

And what do we mean by that?

To be brief, it refers to an individual wanting or desiring something, and then looking up a particular Scripture that seems to go with their desire, and then using that particular Scripture to get what one wants. One is then to begin to confess what one wants, by confessing what the Word of God says, and do so over and over, attempting to wed the two.

As should be obvious, such Faith is not Faith in the Cross of Christ. Actually, it's not really even Faith in the Word of God. It is an attempt to use the Word of God according to one's own likes and dislikes, completely ignoring the Will of God in all matters. In other words, the teachers of this error claim that they automatically know the Will of God, and that the Will of God is always that they be rich, wealthy, great, strong, etc.

To be frank, it is heady stuff, simply because there is a lot of greed and self-will in all of us; consequently, it draws a large audience.

Such teaching completely ignores the Cross, which attempts to manipulate the Word of God, which as should be overly obvious, cannot be Scriptural. In other words, God will never allow His Word to be used against Himself.

While it is definitely true that His Word is His Will, it is just that, *"His Will,"* and not our will! There is a vast difference in the two. The secret of the Word of God, and all its great and wonderful Promises, is that our Will be brought totally and completely into the Will of God in all things. In fact, this is what the Cross does, and this is what alone can be done in the Cross.

The Cross, and I should say Faith in the Cross, breeds humility in the Child of God, which in fact, is the only manner in which humility can be gained. The other way of which we have been speaking which claims to be true Faith, but in reality is anything but true Faith, breeds the very opposite — arrogance and pride!

Coupled with psychology, the so-called Faith teaching, among other things, have steered the Church away from the Cross of Christ, until presently, it little knows where it's been, where it is, or where it's going, which brings us to the last phrase of this Scripture of our study, the Seventh Verse of this Fifth Chapter of I Thessalonians.

## DRUNK

The phrase, *"And they that be drunken are drunken in the night,"* as is obvious, refers to those who are controlled by another spirit, and in this case *"spirits."*

Even though Paul is not here actually speaking of alcoholic beverage, only using the word *"drunken"* as a metaphor, still, the following Verse I think will shed even more light on this subject.

The Apostle also said, *"And be not drunk* (controlled) *with wine, wherein is excess; but be filled* (controlled) *with* (by) *the Spirit"* (Eph. 5:18).

NOTES

If it were not possible for the Christian to be in this condition, the Apostle would not have broached the subject. Regarding that, I personally feel, that to whatever degree the Believer is deficient as it regards his understanding of the Cross, which is the Finished Work of Christ, to that degree will these admonishments of Paul affect him.

In almost every other Commentary which I consulted as it regards this phrase, the writer dealt with alcoholic beverage, and its evils, etc. While that is certainly true, that's not actually what the Apostle is speaking about here. As stated, he is using these words as metaphors, which refers to a figure of speech in which a word or phrase literally denoting one kind of object or idea is used in place of another to suggest a likeness or analogy between them. For instance, we say that computers have senses and a memory, which are metaphors. Computers are machines, so in effect, they cannot really sense anything or have a memory about anything.

So, *"sleep"* here speaks of *"spiritual stupor,"* while to be *"drunken,"* speaks of one not having complete control of themselves. As well, *"night"* is also a metaphor, speaking of the world walking in darkness, and of Christians who can also do the same, if they do not stir themselves from spiritual drowsiness.

(8) "BUT LET US, WHO ARE OF THE DAY, BE SOBER, PUTTING ON THE BREASTPLATE OF FAITH AND LOVE; AND FOR AN HELMET, THE HOPE OF SALVATION."

One Commentator said that it was a puzzle as to why Paul used the metaphor of a soldierly figure of speech, to address this issue. Well, it's not a puzzle at all.

As we will attempt to explain, the terminology used here by the Holy Spirit through the Apostle, leads the Believer straight and true to the Cross.

## SOBER

The phrase, *"But let us, who are of the day, be sober,"* refers to knowing who we are, what we are, and why we are what we are, all in Christ.

The word *"sober"* also speaks of *"assurance,"* which is within itself, a steadfast Rock.

Sober here does not speak of *"somber,"* which refers to that which is dull and morose, but actually the very opposite. It speaks of knowing one's ground, having one's Faith properly placed, which gives one an assurance of incalculable proportions. In fact, this is where the *"more abundant life"* actually is, where the *"rest"* in Jesus actually is. This type of *"sober"* produces a joy unspeakable and full of glory, of which the world knows nothing about, and in fact, cannot have or possess.

## THE BREASTPLATE OF FAITH

The phrase, *"Putting on the Breastplate of Faith,"* is said a little different in Ephesians 6:14. There Paul uses the phrase *"Breastplate of Righteousness."*

However, in the way the Apostle is using both words, they mean the same thing. The Righteousness spoken of in Ephesians 6:14, is produced by *"Faith."* Without Faith being properly placed, it is impossible to obtain Righteousness, at least the Righteousness of Christ. And if one has the Righteousness of Christ, it was obtained by Faith in the Finished Work of Christ, and by that means alone!

So how does this fit in with the Cross?

I'm sure that the Reader is ahead of me at this point. Faith properly placed in the Cross, where it always must be, produces the *"Breastplate of Faith."* Paul uses the term *"Shield of Faith"* in Ephesians 6:16. They are one and the same, inasmuch as one cannot have the proper Breastplate of Righteousness without Faith.

This *"Breastplate"* or *"Shield,"* which again is used as metaphors, furnish a Divine protection from the powers of darkness. This is what the Apostle is speaking about. He wants the Believer to be sober and vigilant in the Lord, in other words, alive in Christ, and at all times.

This is brought about by the Believer having a proper understanding of the Cross of Christ, and one's part and place in this which Jesus did on our behalf. The idea is this:

Whenever the Apostle mentions *"Faith," "Righteousness," "Love," "Hope,"* or any words of this nature, be they Salvation, Justification, Sanctification, etc., while they do definitely have different meanings, still, all spring totally and completely from the Cross of Christ. In other words, the only way that *"Faith, Love, and Hope,"* can be obtained by the Child of God, or anything else from the Lord for that matter, is through what Christ did at the Cross.

NOTES

The only way that God could commune with man, has always been through the Shed Blood of the Lamb; and the only way that man can approach God, is by the same manner.

All the millions of animal sacrifices of the Old Testament, were but symbols of that which Christ did on the Cross.

Man does not have to concern himself about the manner in which God reaches down to us, which is the Cross, because the Lord is never going to deviate from that way; however, man's problem is trying to reach God, trying to have things from God, trying to do things for God, outside of the Finished Work of Christ. It cannot be done!

So, the Faith of which Paul here speaks, is Faith that comes from the Word of God, which is anchored in the Cross of Christ, in other words, made possible altogether by what Jesus did at the Cross.

## LOVE

The phrase, *"And Love,"* places this great commodity from the Lord, one might say, in connection with Faith, which forms the *"Breastplate."*

In fact, all of these terms are so interlocked, so intertwined, that to say one, one automatically says the other. Actually, *"Faith and Love,"* are Fruit of the Spirit, which produces *"Hope."*

The *"Fruit of the Spirit"* produces nine attributes one might say. However, if one is to notice it is *"Fruit"* in the singular, instead of *"Fruits"* in the plural.

This means that this *"Fruit"* is so intertwined, that it all becomes one, which means that it's impossible for one to be possessed more than the other. This means if *"Faith"* is low, so is everything else! If meekness is low, so is everything else! etc. Conversely, if any one of the Fruit of the Spirit is high, so are all the others!

In fact, I think that one can say the same for all the other qualities and attributes of the Lord. If our Sanctification is weak, so is our Salvation, as well as our Justification, etc. In the strict sense of the word, however, it's impossible for Justification to vary to any degree; however, the Truth is, while Justification does not vary, and because it is in Christ, and cannot vary; still, potentially, it can. And by that I mean the following:

Due to a lack of knowledge of the Cross, or other problems, one's Sanctification can become so polluted, that one can go into unbelief, which if remaining in that capacity, can lose one's way with God, which destroys one's Justification.

The *"Love"* of which Paul speaks here, is agape Love, which of course is the Love of God. It is that which Saints alone can have, of which the world knows nothing.

## THE HELMET

The phrase, *"And for an helmet, the Hope of Salvation,"* carries a wealth of meaning.

First of all, the word *"hope"* does not refer to its present meaning of *"maybe so or maybe not,"* but rather, of a guaranteed fact, but not known exactly when as to completion.

The *"hope"* of which Paul here speaks, as it regards Salvation, is the coming Resurrection, when the totality of Salvation will be obtained by every Believer. All Believers are presently washed, Sanctified, and Justified (I Cor. 6:11), but no Believer is yet Glorified. This will be done at the coming Resurrection, thereby completing the Salvation process.

Even though all Believers are totally and completely saved, and will be no more saved at that coming time than presently, still, no Believer yet has all the rudiments of Salvation. In other words, none as of yet have all that Jesus paid for at the Cross. As Paul amply says, *"And not only they, but ourselves also, who have the firstfruits of the Spirit* (a down payment), *even we ourselves groan within ourselves, waiting for the adoption, to wit, the redemption of our body"* (Rom. 8:23).

Paul is speaking here of the coming Resurrection, when the Saints of God will then be Glorified (Rom. 8:18).

## SALVATION

*"Salvation"* in the Greek is *"soteria,"* and means *"to rescue, to deliver, to save, to bring one to safety, to bring one to health."* It carries the idea of a Saviour as well, Who is Christ, and Who Alone can save, i.e., *"to bring to Salvation."*

NOTES

In fact, this word incorporates every single thing the Lord does for the individual, and why the individual needs what the Lord does for him. It is in this manner that Paul uses this word here, and in fact, the manner in which it is almost always used.

According to the Genesis account, when God created man He entered into a Covenant with him, in which, by following the pathway of obedience, man might maintain his confirmed state of holiness; whereas, should he choose to disobey, he would then fall to enslavement under sin. Obedience would lead to Eternal Life and Communion with God; disobedience would bring death and slavery to Satan. The positive dimension of this Covenant is to be inferred from the Scripture, whereas the negative side is explicit.

As Genesis Chapter 3 makes clear, man chose to disobey his Creator. When confronted with the serpent, who was used as a tool of Satan, Eve succumbed to the challenge to assert her independency of God. And this is man's crowning sin, his effort to be independent of God, which of course, is impossible!

She endeavored to deify herself and dethrone God so to speak. Pride is the essence of sin! Sin is not only a lack of conformity to or any transgression of the Law of God; it is also, and perhaps even more fundamentally, a rending of one's personal relationship with his Creator. When man disobeys a Command of God he offends the loving and Holy One Who as the absolute Spirit Person sustains all life. So, in a sense, all sin is not only against God, but as well, against ourselves.

Inasmuch as the seed of all mankind was in Adam, in him all men sinned (Rom. 5:12). In other words, what he did negatively affected all men, as what Christ did positively affected all men, at least those who will believe.

The Apostle Paul establishes the universal condemnation of all men because of their sinful state. All, whether Gentile or Jew, have sinned and are failing to reflect the glory of that original Image of God (Rom. 3:23).

## MAN'S GUILT

Because of man's sin, his disobedience, he is deserving of God's judgment. We are to understand, that man's sin in Adam, was of far greater magnitude than our minds can even begin to comprehend. He not only disobeyed his Creator, from Whom he draws all life and sustenance, he as well gave the entirety of God's creation, over which he had been given dominion (Gen. 1:28; Ps. 8), to Satan and the powers of darkness. The magnitude of this actually knows no bounds.

After establishing from Psalm 14 that Jews and Gentiles are alike under the power of sin, Paul states, *"Now we know that whatever the Law says* (God's Standard of Righteousness) *it speaks to those who are under the Law, so that every mouth may be stopped, and the whole world may be held accountable to God"* (Rom. 3:19).

This means that all are guilty, which includes every human being who has ever been born, with the exception of the Lord Jesus Christ. In theological language guilt means liability to punishment on account of sin; it means to be answerable to God for contradicting His Holiness. Guilt must not be confused with moral pollution nor with mere demerit. For various reasons one may feel guilty when there is neither pollution nor personal demerit. Likewise one may not feel guilty where both exist.

This sense of guilt for disobeying God is immediately evident in the account of the Fall. After Adam and Eve had taken of the forbidden fruit we learn of their vain effort to hide from God. A sense of shame compelled them to flee from their Creator.

Man in his fallen condition has been doing this down through the entire course of human history. But all men exist in a responsible relationship to their Creator, and if they do not fulfill this responsibility in loving obedience to Him through Faith in Jesus Christ, then only judgment and the second death await them. There is no other alternative!

MAN'S ESTRANGEMENT

Because of sin man's predicament may be described as one in which he finds himself a victim of anxiety, dread, despair, frustration, alienation, absurdity, meaninglessness, and estrangement. He has cut himself off from God, his fellow man and himself.

In this situation man either seeks to make meaning for himself by deifying himself (humanism) or by admitting his failure to discover any meaning at all (nihilism).

NOTES

Evidences of man's estrangement from his God, his fellow man, and even himself, scream at us in every conceivable way, whether in contemporary art forms such as literature, music, painting, sculpture, architecture, drama, motion pictures, etc., or war, fighting, murder, crime, etc.

THE NATURE OF SALVATION

An Angel in a dream said to Joseph, the foster father of Christ, *"Fear not to take unto thee Mary thy wife: for that which is conceived in her is of the Holy Spirit.*

*"And she shall bring forth a Son, and thou shalt call His Name JESUS: for He shall save His people from their sins"* (Mat. 1:20-21).

An understanding of the Old Testament word group as it refers to Salvation, is necessary to understand what was implied in this statement concerning Jesus as *"Saviour."*

In the majority of Old Testament references Salvation is seen to be the work of a Sovereign God (Isa. 43:11). It is the Lord Who saves His people from Egypt (Ps. 106:7-10); from Babylon (Jer. 30:10); from trouble (Jer. 14:8), etc.

The first occurrence of the word *"Salvation"* is found in Exodus 14:30. In this reference there is the account of Israel's deliverance from Egyptian bondage: *"Thus the Lord saved Israel that day from the hand of the Egyptians."*

This national deliverance made the deepest impression on the Hebrew mind, an impression which was to be maintained by the annual Passover Feast (Deut. 16:1).

This deliverance of Israel from Egypt is the supreme Old Testament sign of God's Saving Grace. In fact, this great miracle performed by the Lord in saving Israel, pointed beyond itself, to that central saving event of history, the coming of Jesus Christ, and His Death on the Cross, which purchased Redemption for mankind.

It is most significant that Luke describes the decisive victory of Christ over Satan in terms of a new Exodus (Lk. 9:31).

DELIVERANCE

Salvation is deliverance from enemies. Among those enemies were death and its fear

(Ps. 6:4-5; 107:13-14); the lion's mouth (Ps. 22:21); the battlefield (Deut. 20:4); the wicked (Ps. 59:2); sickness (Isa. 38:21); trouble (Jer. 30:7); and sins (Ps. 51:14; 130:8; Ezek. 36:29). In Old Testament times God was conceived to be the Saviour from all foes, both spiritual and physical.

As well, Salvation is not only deliverance *from* enemies, but it is deliverance *to* the Lord. Jehovah not only delivered His people from that which would destroy them but He also brought them to Himself. His Salvation was not merely a rescue from a dangerous situation but it was also a rescue for a special purpose, that purpose being that those rescued should worship, praise, and glorify Him through lives dedicated to obeying Him in all of life (I Chron. 16:23; Isa. 43:11-12; 49:6-7; Zech. 8:13).

The order is well expressed by the Psalmist, *"Save me, that I may observe Thy Testimonies"* (Ps. 119:146). In fact, the entire Bible makes it very clear that the imperative of *"do"* for man is based upon the indicative of *"done"* by God.

## SALVATION HAS ALWAYS BEEN BY FAITH

Salvation is appropriated solely by Faith in God apart from any reliance upon supposed merit or human effort.

The whole initiative of Salvation is with God. *"For God has not destined us for wrath, but to obtain Salvation through our Lord Jesus Christ"* (I Thess. 5:9).

In this great Salvation process, Jesus is the center of God's saving work, and more particularly, what He did at the Cross and in His Resurrection. In no one else or by no other means is there Salvation (Acts 4:12; Heb. 2:10; 5:9).

Salvation in the New Testament sense of spiritual deliverance means a total Salvation. God saves fallen man — spirit, soul, and body. It is Salvation from sin (Mat. 1:21), from wrath (Rom. 5:9), from lostness (Mat. 18:11; Lk. 19:10), and from physical illness (Mat. 9:21; Lk. 8:36).

Salvation is also eschatological, meaning there is a future benefit as well. Although the Christian begins to enjoy his Salvation here and now, there is yet a time coming when he will realize it in all its fullness. That time will be at the Rapture of the Church, when we shall be changed, and then also at the Second Coming, when we will rule and reign with Christ (Rom. 13:11; I Cor. 5:5; II Tim. 4:18; Heb. 9:28; I Pet. 1:5; Rev. 12:10).

There are four great words or terms one might say which when taken together give a most comprehensive portrayal of the saving work of the Triune God. These are *"Sacrifice," "Propitiation," "Reconciliation,"* and *"Redemption." "Sacrifice"* views Salvation as the answer to man's guilt; *"Propitiation"* as the answer to God's Righteous Wrath; *"Reconciliation"* as the removal of the ground of God's alienation from fallen man; and *"Redemption"* as a release from bondage to sin.

## SACRIFICE

This word which is used approximately 35 times in the New Testament is squarely rooted in the Old Testament. The most frequent single occurrence of the term in the New Testament is found in the Book of Hebrews.

The primary though not exclusive meaning of the term in Scripture is that of an expiation (to pay the penalty) of guilt, Atonement (Heb. 5:1; 7:27; 8:3; 9:9, 23, 26; 10:1, 5, 8, 11-12, 26; 11:4; 13:15-16).

## PROPITIATION

This word is used only three times in the New Testament (Rom. 3:25; I Jn. 2:2; 4:10).

The particular stress of the word is probably best taken as indicating God's diverting of His Righteous Wrath from the sinner through the Atoning Work of His Son. Propitiation does not imply that the Son has to win over an incensed Father to an expression of love toward man; rather, it was precisely because of His eternal Love that the Father sent His Son to be the propitiation for our sins.

The idea is, that the Cross turned aside the Wrath of God. It was expended on His Son, rather than on the sinner.

## RECONCILIATION

This word is used four times, all by Paul (Rom. 5:10-11; II Cor. 5:18-20; Eph. 2:16; Col. 1:20-22).

NOTES

Reconciliation was a work of God in Christ whereby He removed the ground of His Holy alienation from the sinner and thus did not impute his sins against him.

The idea is, the Cross handled the sin problem which created enmity between God and man, thereby making it possible for man to be reconciled to God, and God to be reconciled to man.

## REDEMPTION

This word speaks the language of purchase and ransom. Redemption is the securing of a release by the payment of a price.

In the theological sense, Redemption means the release of the Shed Blood of Christ. Redemption from sin embraces the several aspects from which sin is to be viewed Scripturally:

1. Redemption from the guilt of sin (Rom. 3:24).
2. Redemption from the power of sin (Titus 2:14).
3. Redemption from the presence of sin (Rom. 8:23).

## REGENERATION IS THE EFFECT OF SALVATION

It is God the Father Who calls His Own out of the kingdom of darkness into the Kingdom of Light, but the sinner must do the coming. And yet, how can he?

Is he not dead in trespasses and sins? The spiritual dilemma of the Minister is analogous to the utter futility of a Doctor's efforts to revive the lifeless body of one of his patients. Whether we preach the terrors of Hell or the blessings of Heaven, whether we proclaim the Law or the Gospel, there can be no response apart from a miracle of Grace. But it is the Glory of God's sovereign Grace that it overcomes this dilemma.

God's call, when it is effectual, carries with it the operative Grace necessary to secure a response of Faith in Christ. This Grace is the Grace of Regeneration or quickening.

However, even though God calls, and even though the Grace of God makes it possible for the individual to respond favorably, still, they can say *"no,"* if they so desire. Man is a free moral agent, and God never abrogates the will of an individual. The Scripture lends the flavor of the spirit of *"whosoever will,"* from Genesis through the Book of Revelation (Rev. 22:17).

NOTES

## THE REALITY OF REGENERATION

Perhaps the most well-known figure is that of new birth. Jesus said to Nicodemus, *"Truly, truly, I say to you, lest one is born anew, he cannot see the Kingdom of God."* The language presupposes a first birth (born physically as a baby) to which regeneration is the second. Note the following contrasts between the two.

The first birth is of sinful parents, the second of God; the first is of corruptible seed, the second of incorruptible Seed; the first is of the flesh — carnal, the second of the Spirit — spiritual; the first marks one as Satan's slave, the second as Christ's free man; in the first man his spiritual condition is viewed as an objective of Divine Wrath; in the Second as an object of Divine Love. In John Chapter 3 one reads of the meeting of Nicodemus with Jesus. Nicodemus was a leader in the orthodox religious party of his day, undoubtedly a member of the Sanhedrin, but he was unregenerate, i.e., *"unsaved!"*

On this occasion he desired to see Jesus in order to discover the secret of entry into the Kingdom of God (the redemptive rule of God through Christ). But even before he had opportunity to express what was in his mind, Jesus provided the answer to his question: a man may not so much as see the Kingdom unless he is Born-Again. It is Divinely necessary that he be sovereignly regenerated by the Spirit of God.

## AN ACT OF GOD

In the most definitive sense Regeneration denotes that act of God whereby spiritually dead men are made alive through the Spirit. By this act God plants a new Spiritual Life in the soul; one is Born-Again from above. Regeneration in this restricted sense is solely a Work of God. Hence the Words of Christ to Nicodemus, *"You must be born again"* (Jn. 3:7), speak not of a moral obligation (we cannot beget ourselves) but of a Divine necessity.

As well, Regeneration is a passive work; man can no more contribute to his spiritual conception than an infant can to his natural conception. The very nature of the work clearly shows that it is not in the power of men to do it; it is represented in Scripture as a creation, a new creation, and only God can truly create (II Cor. 5:17).

Regeneration is an instantaneous Work of the Spirit; it is not like progressive Sanctification. As an infant is generated at once and not by degrees, so it is in spiritual generation. One does not gradually become alive. No man can be said to be more regenerated than another, though of course once regenerated one may be said to be more Sanctified than another.

This Work of Regeneration is a mysterious Work as Christ indicates in His Words to Nicodemus. The Work of the Spirit is like the wind; *"You do not know whence it comes or whither it goes"* (Jn. 3:8).

### THE ACT OF FAITH

Conversion means basically *"to turn"* and, in the spiritual sense, denote a change of outlook and a new direction in life and action. Conversion involves a turn both toward and away from something or someone.

Positively, the turn toward something or someone is what may be appropriately called Faith. In the spiritual sphere it is a turn *"toward God"* (Acts 9:35; 11:21; 15:19; 26:20; I Pet. 2:25).

This turn, or act of Faith, may be defined as an understanding and mental assent to certain basic facts concerning the Person and Work of Christ (I Cor. 3:14-15) culminating in a committal of one's entire being to the Person of Whom those facts testify. Three important elements are to be noted in this definition:

### KNOWLEDGE

The first indispensable element in saving Faith is information. We must know Who Christ is, what He has done, and what He is able to do. We are not called to put Faith in someone of whom we have no knowledge. In order to exercise Faith we must know about the Death, Burial, and Resurrection of Jesus Christ. Without such knowledge Faith would be but a foolish leap in the dark.

Admittedly, the unsaved person doesn't know much about these great and glorious

NOTES

things, but he must have a working knowledge that at least these things have happened. And in some way as the Spirit of God moves upon him, his Faith must be placed in Christ and what Christ did regarding His Death, Burial, and Resurrection — in other words, that all of this was done for sinners.

### ASSENT

The second element is that of conviction concerning the truthfulness of that which is known. In other words, one must believe in or have Faith in this small amount of knowledge that one has regarding the Person of Christ. It is possible, of course, to understand the import of certain propositions of Truth and yet not believe these propositions. In saving Faith, Truths known are also accepted as true.

In fact, this is where Faith begins to take hold. The Word of God is ministered in some way, which the Holy Spirit has anointed, and as well the Holy Spirit moves upon the heart of the sinner as he hears the Word, giving him the ability to believe, that is if he so desires. As stated, it is still *"whosoever will!"*

### TRUST

The third element is that of commitment. Knowledge of and assent to the Truth of the Gospel is not saving Faith. Millions have gone this far, and have not been saved.

These must be accompanied by trust in the person of Jesus Christ Himself. Christian Faith is not merely intellectual assent to the Divinely revealed Truths of Scripture; it must include a personal encounter with Christ, the One in Whom all Truth is summed up.

### REPENTANCE

All of this can be summed up in the one word *"repentance."* The Biblical term for repentance indicates a change of mind and conduct. It properly denotes a change for the better, a change of mind that is productive of good works. Repentance is the Gift of God, the purchase of Christ, and the Work of the Holy Spirit (Acts 11:18). It is produced by the Spirit at Regeneration.

As well, repentance is an abiding principle. The Scriptures teach that there is not only a necessity for an initial conversion of the sinner but also subsequent repentance at times of erring Saints. It is the latter which is probably stressed in Psalms 119:59-60.

Repentance is a turning from idols (I Thess. 1:9), from vain things (Acts 14:15), from darkness (Acts 26:18), and from the power of Satan (Acts 26:18). It is a turn from transgression (Isa. 59:20).

As for the means of conversion which incorporates repentance, Scripture clearly teaches that the efficient cause is God, not man. The drastic change wrought by conversion is not in man's power to effect. An Ethiopian might just as well try to change his skin or a leopard his spots (Jer. 13:23; Jn. 1:13; Rom. 9:16).

The instrumental cause of all of this is the Ministry of the Word. *"Faith comes from what is heard, and what is heard comes by someone preaching Christ, and more particularly, preaching the Cross."*

And yet, even the preaching of the Word is not sufficient of itself to produce the response of conversion. It is obvious that men may hear and yet not turn. To be effective the proclamation must be accompanied by the Power and Demonstration of the Spirit (I Cor. 2:1-5).

This is at least one of the reasons the Baptism with the Holy Spirit is desperately needed as it regards our Work for the Lord (Acts 2:4).

## JUSTIFICATION

In a fundamental sense, Justification is concerned not with our spiritual *"condition"* but with our spiritual *"relation"*; it is not a matter of our actual *"state"* but of our judicial *"standing."* One might say, that Justification is the result not of an *"activity"* on our part, but rather a *"position,"* made possible for all believing sinners, by simple Faith in Christ. It is a judicial position one has in Christ, which one gains by having Faith in Who Christ is, and What Christ has done.

Justification is the legal answer to the disrupted relationship between man and his God brought about through sin. As the result of sin all men stand before God as guilty, condemned, and separated from their Creator. Justification is the restoration of man to his original relation to God through the Work of Christ.

NOTES

Significantly it includes, according to Paul: removal of guilt by the imputation of Christ's Righteousness (Rom. 8:33), removal of condemnation by the gift of forgiveness (Rom. 8:34), and removal of separation by the restoration to fellowship (Rom. 8:35).

## THE RIGHTEOUSNESS OF CHRIST

Justification must be seen from a twofold perspective, actual and declarative. Actual Justification means that a sinner is *"constituted"* by having Christ's Righteousness imputed to him. This refers to Christ offering up Himself on the Cross as our Substitute, paying the terrible sin debt which man rightly owed to God, and could not pay, thereby atoning for all sin. Faith and Faith alone guarantees the believing sinner the Righteousness of Christ. Only in this way may a just God justify the ungodly.

Declarative Justification means that the one who has been *"constituted"* Righteous in Christ is also judged Righteous before Him. Justification is a forensic or legal term, and should be carefully distinguished in meaning from Sanctification which is experiential and progressive.

The distinction between the two concepts may be stated as follows:

Justification has to do with Christ *"for us"*; Sanctification with Christ *"in us."* Justification has to do with our *"position"*; Sanctification, with *"fellowship."* Justification has to do with out *"acceptance"*; Sanctification with our *"attainment."*

To turn it around, which it actually is in Scripture, Sanctification *"makes one clean,"* while Justification *"declares one clean."* As stated, it is a legal work!

## JUSTIFICATION BY FAITH

The foundation of Justification is God's Grace not man's works. Paul emphasizes that a man is justified by Faith apart from the works of the Law (Rom. 3:28). The Apostle is concerned to make unmistakably clear that God has accomplished in Christ what man is completely unable to do for himself. What God has done for the sinner in Christ is totally unmerited, unprompted, and unsought. This is the essence of Grace (Rom. 3:24). Our Justification depends wholly on God and not on anything in man.

Long ago Job asked *"How can a man be just before God?"* (Job 9:2). This most important question raises the matter of method. The only satisfactory answer is found in the Word of God.

The Justification of the sinner is pronounced in the Word of the Gospel. As near as the Word of Faith is to us, just so near is the Word of God's acquittal. The merit of our Lord becomes ours *"through Faith,"* which actually means, to have Faith in the Cross of Christ and what Jesus did there (Rom. 3:21-22; Eph. 2:18).

FAITH IS THE CHANNEL

It is imperative to understand that Faith is never the ground of Justification, but only its means or channel; it is the hand which simply reaches out to accept the Gift.

In the strict interpretation of the word, Faith is never portrayed as something meritorious; it is always and only instrumental. In other words, it is the instrument through which man reaches God, and the instrument through which God demands that He be reached.

When we consider the value of Justification certain things become immediately clear from the New Testament. Justification provides the ground of Peace with God (Rom. 5:1). When one stands before God as Righteous in Christ he may experience the Peace of God in his life and share this with others.

It is also the basis for freedom in Christ. This means freedom from bondage to sin and freedom to serve God in Righteousness and Holiness. When one is released from anxiety about himself, he is able to use his life for God and for others. It also means freedom to enjoy all the good things of life within the context of genuine love for God and others (Rom. Chpt. 14).

ADOPTION

When a believing sinner comes to Christ, he is instantly made a *"son of God."* However, the sonship referred to here is not to be confused with that which Christ sustains to the Father as the Only Son. Nor is it to be equated with the relationship which all men sustain to God as His subjects by creation (Mal. 2:10; Acts 17:25-29; Heb. 12:9; James 1:18).

NOTES

This great Doctrine of *"adoption"* is exclusively that of Paul, in fact given to him by the Holy Spirit. The Greek word rendered *"adoption"* occurs five times in Paul's Letters.

Once it is applied to Israel as a nation (Rom. 9:4); once to its full realization at the Rapture (Rom. 8:23); and three times as a present reality in the life of the Christian (Rom. 8:15-16; Gal. 4:5; Eph. 1:5).

In Romans 8:15 it is probably best to understand the Spirit of Adoption as the Holy Spirit.

In fact, the Holy Spirit is not the One Who adopts; this is more especially said to be the work of the Father — but He, the Spirit, is the One through Whom the Child of God is able to cry *"Abba Father"* and exercise the rights and privileges of God's Child.

In Galatians 4:5 Paul indicates that God's purpose is twofold: Redemption and Adoption; God purposed not simply to release slaves but rather to make sons. In Ephesians 1:5 Paul states that God *"destined* (marked us out in advance)*"* as those who were to receive the honored status of sons.

In fact, it seems that the Holy Spirit through the Apostle, used the Roman manner of adoption to explain His case.

In the act of Adoption of a child which was Roman Law, the child was taken by a man from a family not his own, introduced into a new family, and regarded as a true son, entitled to all the privileges and responsibilities belonging to this relation.

The reality of spiritual Adoption may be outlined as follows:

1. Fallen mankind are strangers to the Family of God. As enemies of God they are of their father, the Devil.

2. Yet despite this fact mankind are invited to enter God's Family; to take His Name upon them; to share in His Fatherly care and discipline.

3. Such as accept this invitation are received into His Family and care. From this point they are called the sons of God and are privileged to address Him as Father.

God as the Heavenly Father of Believers provides care (Lk. 11:11-13), sustenance (Ps. 23:1), protection (Ps. 114:1-2), instruction (through His Word and by His providence), correction (Heb. 12:7), and an inheritance (Rom. 8:17).

## SANCTIFICATION

When one is converted to God he must ask how his new life is to be lived out here on Earth. When such a question is faced, the subject of Biblical ethics becomes an important aspect of the Doctrine of Sanctification; the one cannot be properly considered without the other.

Sanctification has to do with the progressive outworking of the new life implanted by the Spirit in Regeneration (quickening). Christian ethics has to do with the study of the basis upon which, the power whereby, and the goal toward which the Believer's Life is lived.

In Paul's writings, expositions of the Doctrine of Justification are generally followed by exhortations to duty. It is not good works which make a good man, but a good man definitely does perform good works.

## WHY?

The distinctive feature of a Christian ethic is found in the matter of motivation. As our Lord made clear in the Sermon on the Mount (Mat. 5:7) more important than *"what"* one does is *"why"* one does it. Goodness is not merely a matter of outward action, but more fundamentally of inward attitude. Jesus makes the moral Law an inward thing.

Sanctification and ethics have to do fundamentally with what we *"are,"* and not so much as to what we *"do."* The idea is, we will do what we are! That's the reason that external changes can never bring about an inward result. It is only the inward result, which can bring about outward changes.

## HOLY

The basic meaning of *"holy"* is *"separated,"* or *"set apart."* In addition to God being holy as separate from His creatures, He is also separate from sin. It is this latter ethical aspect of God's Holiness that provides the basis of our understanding of the Doctrine of Sanctification; and yet, Sanctification is not only a separation *"from"* that which is sinful but also a separation *"unto"* a reflection of the Image of God. Sanctification is the progressive refashioning of our natures by the Holy Spirit, into the Image of God, through Jesus Christ (II Cor. 5:17).

NOTES

The Sanctified are the elect of God. All whom the Father chose in eternity, He Sanctifies in time in Christ.

Sanctification involves the totality of the Believer's being — spirit, soul, and body (I Thess. 5:23). In respect to the soul and spirit, Paul indicates the following:

1. The understanding is enlightened (Eph. 1:18).
2. The will of man is subservient to the Will of God (Phil. 2:13).
3. The affections are made holy (Rom. 12:10). In respect to the body and all its members the Apostle exhorts Believers to yield themselves *"to God as men who have been brought from death to life, and your members* (the members of your physical body) *to God as instruments of Righteousness"* (Rom. 6:13).

## THE POSITION OF SANCTIFICATION

Sanctification involves the Believer being *"positionally"* set apart unto God by virtue of his new life in Christ. This is done the moment the person comes to Christ, which means that the Believer is at that time sanctified, and because of being *"in Christ."* This position never varies; however, the true *"condition"* of our Sanctification is somewhat less than our *"position,"* which the Holy Spirit immediately sets about to correct.

Positional Sanctification is not a matter of the degree of one's spirituality. Concerning all the Christians at Corinth, Paul wrote, *"But ye were washed, ye were sanctified, ye were justified in the Name of the Lord Jesus Christ and in the Spirit of our God"* (I Cor. 6:11).

## PROGRESSIVE SANCTIFICATION

Even though the Believer is set apart unto God at conversion regarding his position (positional Sanctification), he is also *"experientially* (relating to experience)*"* set apart to God by reason of the Ministry of the indwelling Spirit. This aspect of Sanctification is progressive; it admits of degrees. Although no one can be more or less regenerate than another, one definitely may be more sanctified than another. Scripture frequently exhorts Believers to grow in Holiness. *"But grow in the Grace and Knowledge of our Lord and Saviour Jesus Christ"* (II Pet. 3:18; II Thess. 1:3).

The Bible speaks of *"growing"* in Grace, *"abounding"* in hope and love, and *"increasing"* in the knowledge of Divine things. There would be no reason for such terminology if experiential Sanctification were perfected at the moment of Regeneration.

Sanctification involves the Believer being completely set apart to God. Ultimately, the ideal is, that practice and position will be brought into perfect accord. Toward this, the Holy Spirit ever strives (Eph. 5:26-27; Jude vss. 24-25).

## EVERY CHRISTIAN

Sanctification is required of every Christian (I Thess. 4:3). It is not the responsibility of an elite group within the Church. There is no Scriptural basis for the adoption of a twofold standard of Christian commitment, one for *"full-time Christian workers"* and another for *"Christian laymen."* Scripture speaks of all Believers as Saints (I Cor. 1:1-2).

In Paul's Epistle to the Colossians, for example, he deals with personal ethics under the practice of *"putting off"* and *"putting on."* In Chapter 3, the Apostle first describes what is to be put to death (Col. 3:5, 8-9); namely, *"immorality, impurity, passion, evil desire, and covetousness, which is idolatry,"* and *"anger, wrath, malice, slander, foul talk, and lying."* He then speaks of what is to be put on; namely, *"compassion, kindness, lowliness, meekness, and patience,"* being forgiving and above all loving (Col. 3:12-14).

In Colossians 3:18-4:1, the Apostle then deals with ethics on a social level. He gives instruction concerning wives and husbands, parents and children, and slaves and masters. The latter area may find its functional equivalent today in the relationship of employee to employer.

In all the relationships of life, personal and social, Christians are to seek the Kingdom of God and His Righteousness. The dynamic for the realization of this goal is the Holy Spirit. The motivation is God-given agape love. The guidance is provided by the moral law, to be appropriately applied under the leading of the Holy Spirit in each and every situation. Since God is holy we are to be also.

NOTES

## THE MANNER IN WHICH SANCTIFICATION IS BROUGHT ABOUT

In all the preceding paragraphs we have related to you as to what the Believer ought to be. As well, I should think every Believer should desire to be this which the Holy Spirit has outlined in the Word of God. We are to be holy! We are to be righteous! We are to be Godly!

So, how do we do this?

As we've said many times, none of this is automatic. In other words, just because a person becomes a Christian, doesn't mean that they are automatically *"holy or righteous."* To be sure, the Divine Nature is definitely present within the hearts and lives of all Believers, which gives an incentive to be what God wants him to be, but that is only desire, and not power.

The Truth is, no Believer within himself, no matter how much he knows the Scripture, in other words, knows what he ought to do, can in fact, do these things, or be these things, within himself. Such is not possible!

As well, just because one is Baptized with the Holy Spirit, and is being used of God, even to the winning of many souls, or whatever, doesn't mean that individual is at the same time living a holy and righteous life. The two things, *"righteous works,"* and *"the work of Righteousness,"* are two different things altogether! Righteous works comes about because of a Call of God within our lives. The working of Righteousness is our Sanctification, exactly what we are speaking about here. Both are gifts; however, whereas we have a tendency to accept the former as a gift, we have problems accepting the latter as a gift.

This of which we are speaking, is the single most important thing in the life of the Believer. Irrespective of what we can do for Christ, if we don't know how to be *"in Christ,"* our *"work of Righteousness"* is not going to measure up.

Where do we go wrong?

Well there are so many places that we go wrong, that it's difficult to enumerate them all.

Perhaps our biggest problem is, that we think *"the work of Righteousness,"* is brought about by *"works!"* Righteousness is Christ-likeness carried out in our lives, and done so by the Holy Spirit. To be sure, it is a *"work,"* in fact, a *"definite work,"* and brought about, as stated, by the Holy Spirit; however, this *"work"* cannot be brought about by *"works."*

### WHAT DO WE MEAN *"WORKS"*?

To simplify the answer, *"works"* refers to anything which is other than our Faith in the Cross of Christ. And to be sure, that means anything!

Christians are very bad about turning good things into *"works,"* and by that, I speak of prayer, fasting, witnessing, giving money to the Work of the Lord, manifestations, etc. All of these things mentioned, are very good, and should be a part of the Christian life, and in every respect. However, when we think that the doing of these things brings about Righteousness and Holiness, i.e., *"Sanctification,"* then we turn them into works, which God can never honor. However, most Christians do this, and I especially speak of those who really love the Lord and want to be what He wants them to be, simply because they don't know any better. In other words, they don't know the right way, so they try to do the things which they do know, which do not bring victory, but actually the very opposite. Anything we turn into law, is always going to have the very opposite effect of what we intend, and no matter how hard we try. In fact, the harder we try, the worse things get. Let me give you an example:

### A WAY THAT SEEMS RIGHT

Let's say that the Christian is having problems with something of the flesh. It's wrong, and he knows that it's not pleasing to the Lord for the thing to continue, whatever it might be!

Knowing that this thing must stop, he sets about to bring to fruition the desired result. If he really loves the Lord and is spiritual, he thinks in his mind, that he will pray 15 minutes a day, be faithful to that, and surely this will bring about victory.

He sets about on this task, and is greatly blessed, because all prayer, at least that which is done sincerely before the Lord, always brings blessing. But the very thing he's praying about, thinking this 15 minutes a day will perform the task, he finds has not helped. So he reasons in his mind the following:

He extends his time before the Lord to 30 minutes a day. Once again he is blessed, but the problem is not solved. It's confusing, and he really doesn't understand why.

He reasons in his mind, I will pray an hour a day, and I will be faithful, and I know this will bring about the victory for which I seek. He sets about on this task, and again, is greatly blessed by the Lord, and helped in many ways; however, there is not only no victory in that for which he seeks, but the problem actually has gotten worse.

At this stage, he really doesn't know what to do; so, knowing that somehow he must have victory, and hearing everybody else talking about the great victory they have, he surmises that possibly something is worse with him than with others, whatever that might mean. Perhaps it's a *"family curse,"* as he's heard some Preachers say. It seems logical!

He then journeys the long distance to where the Preacher is who is laying hands on people as it regards the *"family curse,"* and after arriving, he feels certain in his heart that this will surely perform the task. He gets in line, is prayed for, and is greatly blessed by the Lord. Quite possibly he is even *"slain in the Spirit,"* and rejoices in the Lord greatly.

But then four or five days later, or sooner, he finds the same problem is with him again. In fact, it's really never left.

No, it wasn't a *"family curse,"* or anything else of that nature. To be sure, demon spirits always get involved in any type of wrongdoing; however, it's not demon possession, as some Preachers claim, with them attempting to *"cast out the Demon,"* or rebuking the Demon, etc.

The entirety of the problem, is simply because one doesn't know or understand the part the Cross plays in one's Sanctification. In fact, there's no dependence whatsoever on what Jesus did at the Cross as it regards Sanctification, which stops the Holy Spirit from working on our behalf. While He definitely helps us in other things, He will not help us in this capacity, because we're turning these things into works, which He cannot honor.

NOTES

As we've already stated several times, the Holy Spirit works exclusively according to the Finished Work of Christ. He demands that we have our Faith in that Work, and when that is done, and it continues in that fashion, He then helps us and helps us mightily, with the problem, whatever it is, being totally and completely defeated (Rom. 8:1-2, 11, 14). That's the way to victory, and by victory, I speak of Sanctification. There is no other way.

It doesn't matter who the Believer is, if he will understand the part the Cross plays in his Sanctification experience, even as it did his Salvation experience, he can walk in total and complete Victory before the Lord. The Holy Spirit will work on his behalf, bringing him into the Sanctification experience, actually perfecting Righteousness and Holiness within his life.

Please understand, that this is not one of several ways that this can be done, it is in fact, the only way!

NOTES

## GLORIFICATION

Glorification, which will take place at the Rapture of the Church, is the final climactic act in God's redeeming Work (Rom. 8:30). As stated, all Believers are now Sanctified, are now Justified, but then the body will be redeemed (Rom. 8:23). In fact, it will involve the perfecting of the entirety of the person, spirit, soul, and body. Although the New Testament represents Glorification as a complete legal exoneration, it also views it as a moral perfecting. A number of Scriptures make this clear (I Cor. 1:8; Eph. 5:27; Phil. 1:10; Col. 1:20; I Thess. 3:13; 5:23; etc.).

Glorification also means full participation in Eternal Life. By God's Grace Believers even now have Eternal Life (Jn. 5:24); but the fullness of this life is yet to be realized (Jn. 5:25-28).

John states, *"Beloved, we are God's Children now; it does not yet appear what we shall be, but we know that when He appears we shall be like Him, for we shall see Him as He is"* (I Jn. 3:2).

Eternal Life includes two ideas: a new quality of life and a never-ending life.

When the sinner is restored to his proper relationship with God through Christ he enters a new quality of life — a life in harmony with the Life of God Himself. This is a kind of life drastically different from that previously possessed; it is indeed an abundant life. Glorification then means the full bestowal of Eternal Life upon Believers — the final realization of Salvation, which refers to a perfect relationship with God as we are with Him forever.

Glorification will bring a full realization of freedom from sin and death (Jn. 8:33-36; Rom. Chpts. 6-8; Gal. 5:1, 13). Then we shall be what we truly are. While in this life we strive through the Spirit to be like our Lord; then our souls shall be perfectly conformed to His Image (Rom. 8:28-29). Glorification is the transformation of our manhood into the perfect manhood of the God-man Jesus Christ.

## THIS BODY WILL BE CHANGED

Glorification also includes the perfecting of the physical body (Rom. 8:23). Scripture attributes a dignity to the human body. Genesis teaches that man is not a soul merely inhabiting a body unity. It is the total man, spirit, soul, and body, who is said to have been created in the Image of God (Gen. 1:26-30; 2:4-8, 15-18).

It is the total man who is affected by sin. So, the foolishness of the teaching of some, who claim that it is the spirit only which is saved, with the soul being saved, or the soul and the spirit saved with the body being saved, holds no Scriptural validation. When the individual comes to Christ, the total man is Born-Again; likewise, when the individual sins, it's the total man who sins, spirit, soul, and body.

The focal point of Divine judgment is death and, although the death of the body does not exhaust the Biblical concept of death, it is nevertheless central to it. Physical death (separation of the soul and spirit from the body) is the outward sign of spiritual death (separation of the person from God).

Christ's Resurrection guarantees ours. According to the New Testament, Christ rose from the dead Bodily (Mat. 28:9; Lk. 24:31, 43, 50; Jn. 20:17, 22, 27; etc.) and this glorious body in which He arose is the pattern after which ours will be fashioned (II Cor. 5:1-5; Phil. 3:20-21).

Philippians 3:21 reads: *"Who shall change our vile body. . . ."* The word *"vile"* should be rendered *"lowly."*

Although the Greeks viewed the body as the prison of the soul, Paul viewed the body as designed by God for the abode of the Spirit (I Cor. 6:19). In our present state, because of the influence of sin, our body is in a state of humiliation, but at Christ's return it will be refashioned after the Glorious Body of our Lord (I Jn. 3:2). The details regarding the nature of this change is outlined in I Corinthians Chapter 15.

Glorification then, is the climax of God's saving work, a work which extends from eternity to eternity. Glorification involves the total man — spirit, soul, and body. In that day all will be complete; death will be swallowed up in victory and God will be everything to everyone.

## HOPE

Salvation is a hope and not actually an unforfeitable possession, at least until the Resurrection (Rom. 8:20-25; II Thess. 2:16; I Pet. 1:5, 9, 13). Eternal Life is also a hope now even though we possess it (Heb. 3:6; 6:11, 18-19; I Pet. 1:3, 13).

It will actually not be an unforfeitable and an eternal possession until the next life and at the end of a life of sowing to the Spirit (Dan. 12:2; Mat. 7:13-14; 18:8-9; 19:28-29; Mk. 10:29-30; Lk. 18:29-30; Jn. 5:28-29; Rom. 2:7; 6:21-23; Gal. 6:7-8; I Tim. 1:16; 4:8; 6:12, 19; I Pet. 1:5, 9, 13; 3:7; I Jn. 2:25; Jude vss. 20-24).

Concerning God's keeping power, Peter said, *"Who by God's power are guarded through Faith for a Salvation ready to be revealed in the last time"* (I Pet. 1:5). There are basically three ideas in this Text:

1. Believers are kept. The Greek term here is a military one. It means quite literally that our life is garrisoned by God; He stands over us as a sentinel all our days.

2. Believers are kept through Faith. The final preservation of Believers is never divorced from the use of means. Believers are preserved through a Faith that works. This refers to Faith in the Cross of Christ, referring to what He did for us regarding the Atonement.

3. Believers are kept unto Salvation. This undoubtedly refers to the final consummation or ultimate realization of our Salvation to be revealed in the last time (Rom. 13:11).

NOTES

And yet, it must be noted that a person's Faith in Christ, which is the ingredient of our Salvation so to speak, is generated by his will. It is *"whosoever will"* (Rev. 22:17).

Upon coming to Christ, an individual has to exercise his will, as should be obvious. After coming to Christ, one can definitely draw back from Faith, and cease to believe if one so desires. In fact, I think it can be said without any fear of contradiction, that millions have done this down through history (Heb. 6:4-6; 10:26-31).

The Bible does not teach a Salvation against someone's will. And the idea that no one will ever *"will"* to go back on God after conversion, is not taught in the Word either, and is not carried out in practice.

Unfortunately, there are millions at this present time who really do not know God, and whether they ever were saved or not only God knows. They are living a life of willful sin, making no attempt to do otherwise, but think they are saved, because they believe the unscriptural doctrine of unconditional eternal security. To be sure, there definitely is eternal security for the Believer; however, it definitely is not unconditional. Jesus plainly said, *"If ye continue in My Word, then are ye My Disciples indeed"* (Jn. 8:31).

I think this is about as clear as it can be. It's not a matter of beginning, but rather continuing and even finishing this race.

Any person who continues to trust Christ is saved, irrespective of the problems they might have; however, if they discontinue their trust in Christ, Salvation is forfeited.

## HELMET

Once again, Paul uses the word *"helmet"* as a metaphor, as it regards Salvation. Why did the Holy Spirit have him use this in this manner?

As is obvious, the helmet covers one's head. Naturally when we speak of the head, we're speaking of the brain and the thinking processes of the human being. Even though the *"will"* of an individual springs from his total being, it is the head which puts it in operation. This pertains to all guidance, leading, direction, decisions, etc. That is at least one reason, why Christ is referred to as the *"Head"* of the Church (Col. 1:18), and in fact, of all *"principality and power"* (Col. 2:10). So, what idea is the Holy Spirit presenting?

The Lord has provided for mankind through His Death on the Cross and His Resurrection, a total Salvation for the total man. Even though Salvation begins in the heart of man, which refers to his total being, it then affects the entirety of his thinking, decision making, attitude, etc., which now gives him the power for a completely new direction. This involves every part of his life and being.

As a result, Satan's attacks always enter first by the way of the mind, which of course has to do with the head, i.e., *"the brain."* This is where his suggestions, his temptations, his thoughts, his ideas of death and destruction begin. In other words, the terrible sin that is ultimately carried out, in fact if it is, begins with a suggestion to the mind, i.e., *"the brain!"*

The *"helmet"* as the Holy Spirit uses it through Paul, pertains as is obvious, to protection. As again would be obvious, this is crucial!

Down through the years, I have had untold letters, and especially from men, asking as to how they could control their thoughts. In other words, they did not want to think things which were ungodly, impure, unholy, etc. Those thoughts can lead to other things, which is of course what Satan intends.

The Holy Spirit through the Prophet Isaiah said, *"Thou wilt keep him in perfect peace, whose mind is stayed on Thee: because he trusteth in Thee"* (Isa. 26:3).

Paul also said, *"Casting down imaginations, and every high thing that exalteth itself against the Knowledge of God, and bringing into captivity every thought to the obedience of Christ"* (II Cor. 10:5).

## HOW DO WE BRING EVERY THOUGHT INTO CAPTIVITY?

God has one solution for everything, and that is the Cross of Christ. If the Believer can come to understand that, most of his battle has been won. And in fact, if he does understand this, the only fight he actually has is the *"good fight of Faith"* (I Tim. 6:12). While it is a fight, it is a good fight, because the end result is guaranteed — victory. So, the whole thing as far as Sanctification is concerned, victory is concerned, the Power of God is concerned, the working of the Holy Spirit is concerned, the Peace of God in our hearts is concerned, pure thoughts are concerned, etc., are wrapped up totally in three things one might say. They are as follows:

1. Whether it's pure thoughts, or anything else for that matter, even as we've already said, the solution to everything is in the Cross of Christ. In other words, the Atonement, which is what Jesus did on the Cross, addresses every single thing that man lost in the Fall, whatever that might be. The Reader can be assured, that this means everything. The Work of Christ is a Finished Work, which means He left nothing out.

In fact, this Covenant is so grand, so glorious, that it is referred to as an *"Everlasting Covenant,"* meaning that it will never have to be amended, never have to be replaced, but will in fact, last forever (Heb. 13:20).

So, if the Reader understands this, then the first part of your battle is already won.

2. Your Faith is to be in this which Christ has done. This simply means that you believe what we have said, or rather what the Word of God has said (I Cor. 1:18; 2:2; Gal. 6:14). As we've already said in this Volume, your Faith must not be divided. A double-minded man is not going to receive anything from the Lord (James 1:6-8).

If you have doubts about what we are saying, as should be obvious, doubt isn't Faith. I've had many questions along this line.

*"Brother Swaggart, I hear what you're saying, and I believe it, but it simply doesn't work for me!"*

First of all, I know it works, so I took this to the Lord asking Him, the reason for these supposed difficulties?

He spoke to my heart, saying, *"It's their Faith!"* In other words, as it regards many Christians, there is still much doubt in their hearts, and even with those where there is no doubt, their Faith is weak in other ways. The whole thing is hinged on Faith, and more particularly, Faith in what Christ did at the Cross. The tragedy is, most Christians little know or understand this, having been taught other things all their lives. Consequently, many think they have Faith in this of which we speak, but really don't, and when they analyze their situation as they should, it quickly becomes obvious that their Faith is not like it ought to be. In other words, even as we've just said, they have doubts! As a result, they're really not going to receive much of anything from the Lord. And to which I have already alluded, I have learned the following also:

Even when our Faith in the Cross is straight and pure, in other words we understand this is God's Way, and we believe it; still, as we begin this glorious way of the Cross, our Faith naturally is weak, and has to be developed.

During these times, there can be weakness and even failure of some sort. However, if that really does happen, the Believer is to seek the Lord's Mercy and Grace, which will always be extended to a sincere heart (I Jn. 1:9), and then renew his Faith in this great provision of the Cross. Little by little he will sense his Faith strengthening, and victory becoming more and more pronounced.

3. The Holy Spirit will then begin to help, because He works entirely on the premise of the Finished Work of Christ, and our Faith in that Work. This means He'll help us with impure thoughts, jealousy, uncontrollable temper, or whatever it might be. There's nothing He cannot do, and nothing He will not do, at least if it's in the boundaries of the Atonement, and according to our Faith in that Finished Work.

The Holy Spirit is the One Who has the power, and to be sure, He will definitely use His power on our behalf, providing we function according to Faith and Faith alone, and more particularly, that our Faith has as its object the Cross of Christ. This is absolutely imperative!

So I'll go back to my original statement: The Lord has a solution for everything, and that solution is the Cross of Christ. That is the way; however, the means by which it is all done, is our Faith in that Great Work, that Great Sacrifice of Christ.

Does the Reader understand what I'm saying? And please understand, this is the only way to victory, there is no other!

(9) "FOR GOD HATH NOT APPOINTED US TO WRATH, BUT TO OBTAIN SALVATION BY OUR LORD JESUS CHRIST,"

Paul now summarizes the reason for this guaranteed Salvation. *"God did not appoint us to suffer wrath."* Without question, this wrath is future and specific, being identified with the Messianic Era just prior to His reappearance (I Thess. 1:10; 2:16) and with the sudden destruction mentioned I Thessalonians 5:3.

The word *"appoint"* is used regularly for God's sovereign determination of events. The idea is, when God vents His anger against this Earth, which He most definitely shall (Rev. 6:16-17), the Body of Christ will be in Heaven as the result of the series of happenings outlined in I Thessalonians 4:13-18. This is God's purpose.

NOTES

## WRATH

The phrase, *"For God hath not appointed us to wrath,"* as we have already stated, refers back to Verse 3, where the Lord spoke about *"sudden destruction coming upon this world."* There is no way that one can look at this Passage and not immediately understand the Endtime implications. It ties to the Third Verse where it speaks of *"sudden destruction coming upon this world."* The idea is this:

Before the coming Great Tribulation which Jesus spoke about (Mat. 24:21), the Lord is going to rapture His Church away. It is regrettable that a great part of the modern Church no longer believes this, that is if they ever did. Irrespective, it's going to happen, and there is no reason as to why the Church should not be prepared. As we've already stated, Israel being restored in order to fulfill its prophetic predictions, is one of the greatest signs of all that things are changing — and fast. In fact, even as we've stated several times, Israel is God's greatest, prophetic time-clock. So, the Church has no excuse whatsoever, especially considering the tremendous things which are now happening, which speak of the fulfillment of Bible Prophecy, even as it relates to the Endtime.

Therefore, every Believer should be drawing closer to the Lord, preparing for this great event which is about to take place, the Rapture of the Church.

*"Wrath"* in the Greek is *"orge,"* and means *"violence, anger, indignation, vengeance."* The Scripture says, *"For the great day of His* (God's) *wrath is come; and who shall be able to stand?"* (Rev. 6:17).

The *"wrath"* spoken of in the Scripture of our study and Revelation 6:17, is not the same as that in Romans 2:5, 14-15; Rev. 20:11-15. This wrath begins with events of the Sixth Seal, which portray *"a great earthquake: and the sun becoming black as sackcloth of hair, and the moon becoming as blood."*

It also speaks of the *"stars of heaven falling unto the earth, even as a fig tree casting her untimely figs"* (Rev. 6:12-16).

This will take place during the first three and one half years of the Great Tribulation and will continue through the Trumpet and Vial Judgments, which will actually go to the end of the Great Tribulation.

DIVINE WRATH AND THE ATONEMENT

The Wrath of God works in two ways simultaneously, in that it delivers the oppressed (I Sam. 15:2) and condemns the wicked (Deut. 7:4-5). However, a basic part of the Biblical teaching concerning the Wrath of God is that an Atonement is offered to remove the wrath and justify the ungodly. This Atonement in the Old Testament is appropriated by the keeping of the Law and trust in God's Promises (Ezek. 36:22-32).

Since the nations of the world are required to come to the Covenant people of Israel for Grace, the Old Testament demands the Gentiles follow the Law of Israel for Mercy. The Wrath of God then acts as a warning and an encouragement to human obedience. One special factor of the Atonement in the Old Testament is that it is consistently futuristic. It presents the final removal of God's Wrath and the preservation of the atoned in terms of the great final day or days of God's Judgment. This eschatological (Endtime) aspect is associated with the Old Testament teaching about the culmination of history in the *"Day of the Lord."* The day of the Divine visitation is primarily a day of Wrath (Isa. 2:12), but the same Divine proclamation which shall bring damnation to the wicked will bring Salvation as well, upon God's people, Israel (Isa. 2:2-5).

The anger of God as it regards the last days, which will be poured out upon this world, will be unprecedented in human history. As should be obvious, the True Church of Jesus Christ has not been appointed to this wrath, even as the Holy Spirit proclaims through Paul. So, that means the Church will not be here then.

NOTES

With the True Church gone, which of necessity has been a powerful restraining force against evil, wickedness will then know no bounds. It will rise like a crescendo all over the world. With all restraining forces gone, the whole complexity of wickedness, iniquity, and sin will increase exponentially. It will be as if man will attempt to taunt God, which in fact he will. The Scripture plainly says several times in the Book of Revelation which outlines this terrible time, *"And they repented not"* (Rev. 2:21; 9:20-21; 16:9, 11). As the arrogance of man increases at that time, so will the Judgment of God. It will be a time such as the world has never seen before, and will never see again (Mat. 24:21). So, the idea of God demanding the Church be here at that particular time, carries no Scriptural support, or no Scriptural reason.

WHY ARE MANY IN THE CHURCH PRESENTLY DENYING THE RAPTURE AND THE COMING JUDGMENT?

A part of the Church among other things, claims it's going to bring Jesus back by its own machinations. Irrespective that such a viewpoint is totally unscriptural, in that Christ waits on no man as far as the fulfillment of Bible Prophecy is concerned; still, this is heady stuff, for one to think that whatever one does will bring back the Lord. Consequently, the pride factor enters in. I refer to this particular element in the Church as *"Kingdom now,"* or *"Kingdom agers,"* because of their viewpoint on the coming Kingdom Age.

Of the thinking of these people, whomever they might be, Jesus is little the focus of their attention, but rather the *"Kingdom."* Some even claim that we're already in the Kingdom, which will culminate with Christianity as the dominant religion, etc. Political means enter into this strongly as well. In other words, the Kingdom, according to these individuals, is going to be brought into the world by good men being elected to political office, etc.

This segment of the Church, which is quite large, puts little stock in the Preaching of the Gospel, and even though they claim to strongly believe in World Missions, their definition of the term is totally different than the orthodox view.

Evangelism to them is little the proclamation of the Message of Jesus Christ, but rather social work and the supposed Salvation of a political figure, in the particular city or country, etc. With the supposed Salvation of this individual, the entire city, or even country is concluded to be *"evangelized!"*

I hope the Reader can see the absolute absurdity of such thinking! When we leave the Word of God and resort to the wisdom of men, foolishness is the result. The tragedy is, tens of thousands of Christians send money to these Preachers or so-called religious leaders, which means they are in effect, supporting the work of the Devil. As we've previously stated, Satan as an *"angel of light,"* is the most dangerous of all (II Cor. 11:12-15).

The tragedy is, Christians who do not have enough spiritual discernment to know the difference!

## SALVATION

The phrase, *"But to obtain Salvation by our Lord Jesus Christ,"* presents the only manner in which Salvation can be obtained.

The word translated *"obtain"* carries the idea of personal effort in gaining Salvation. Thus the sentence contains an interesting tension between the idea of God's purpose and that of man's effort with respect to Salvation (Phil. 2:12-13; II Thess. 2:13). However, there is a difference in effort and merit. Salvation is by Grace without human merit, for it is by our Lord Jesus Christ. The effort itself, although of our own choice and free cooperation with Grace, is made possible through the indwelling Christ (Col. 1:27).

However, the greater thrust of this phrase pertains to the Person of Christ. The emphasis is not necessarily on the Doctrine of Christ, nor even Faith in Christ, at least as Paul states the case here, but rather through the Lord Jesus Christ Himself, through what He has done for us, and especially through His Atoning Death.

One might say that the appointment of God's Grace is here mentioned as the efficient cause of our Salvation; and the Lord Jesus Christ, as the Mediator through Whom Salvation is bestowed (Gloag).

## THE LORD JESUS CHRIST

A failure to properly understand Christ, is a failure to properly understand one's Salvation.

NOTES

The Reader must understand, that the entire purpose of God becoming man, being born of the Virgin Mary, His sinless, perfect Life, all and in totality, were for the purpose of going to the Cross. All the other was acutely necessary, but it was the Cross which effected the change of man's Redemption.

Consequently, the Believer makes a great mistake if the Cross is placed in a subsidiary position regarding the Salvation experience. And it should be noted, when we speak of Salvation, we are speaking of the entirety of all that we are in Christ, not merely the conversion experience.

If the Reader places the Cross in any position other than the very purpose for which Christ came, this shows a misunderstanding of what Redemption actually is, and what it costs to afford man Eternal Life.

The Truth is, much of the modern Church little understands the Cross, simply because it has by and large been ignored, or even denied in some circles, at least as far as its veracity is concerned. Consequently, many Believers have an improper view, and in an improper understanding of what Salvation really is, and how it comes about. As we've said repeatedly, about the limit of understanding as it regards the Cross among most Believers, is the initial Salvation experience. Thereafter, the Cross is not understood at all as having any significance regarding one's Sanctification, when in reality, it is the secret of all Victory. The Lord has only one way of victory, one way of overcoming Grace, and that is in fact, the Cross of Christ.

My point is, the Believer must understand the absolute significance of the Cross of Christ, that in reality it was and is the very purpose of God from all eternity past, with all history in fact straining toward the Cross or back to the Cross. This is the Atonement, the Substitutionary Work of Christ, the Great Sacrifice, the culminating event of all history, the fulfillment of the Prophecies, the very purpose of God. In what Jesus did at the Cross, we find the answer to every question, the solution to every problem, the victory for every defeat, the life for all death, the healing for all sickness, the Salvation for all sin.

(10) "WHO DIED FOR US, THAT, WHETHER WE WAKE OR SLEEP, WE SHOULD LIVE TOGETHER WITH HIM."

Inasmuch as I Thessalonians is Paul's first Epistle, here for the first time, he states the specific means by which Jesus Christ procures our Salvation: *"He died for us."* In four key Epistles (Romans, I and II Corinthians, and Galatians), the Apostle laid prime emphasis on the Cross of Christ, but here is the first mention in this Epistle.

So sufficient is Christ's Death that it brings assurance of future life with all obstacles removed. In fact, this was the very reason He died. He gained for us a full, total, and complete Salvation, which speaks of victory over every single problem in the Spiritual, mental, physical, domestical, and financial. This is truly a *"Full Gospel."*

The words *"wake or sleep,"* refer to being physically alive, or having died. Either way, living or dead, and we speak in the physical sense, for this is what Paul is dealing with as it regards the Resurrection, refers to that coming time.

## JESUS DIED FOR US

The phrase, *"Who died for us,"* presents the idea, that He died that we might live.

All Believers gain Salvation, not by what we do, but by what Christ has already done for us. He died for all, but only those who accept His Sacrifice will live together with Him forever.

The very Foundation of Christianity is built on the Doctrine of the Atonement of Christ, i.e., *"His Death on the Cross, which of course, presupposes His Resurrection, and even His Exaltation"* (Eph. 2:6).

Even though the Apostle doesn't go into detail here, the simple manner in which he says this, to which we have already briefly alluded, does not so much speak of our Faith in this Atoning Work, but rather the fact of that Atoning Work. In other words, this, the Sacrifice of Christ on the Cross, is the Foundation of the Faith. Everything revolves around the Cross of Christ.

If the Believer doesn't properly understand that, then everything else he believes will be somewhat skewed as well! Even though I am being repetitive, please read this carefully:

The Cross of Christ was not an incident or accident. In other words, Jesus did not die as a martyr. The very purpose of the Incarnation, the prediction of all the Prophets, and the very purpose for which He came, was the Cross. If we take that lightly, then we are taking lightly the single greatest thing that God ever did for lost and dying humanity. And if we think of it lightly, we do so at our peril, simply because, everything that we have from the Lord and in totality, from Salvation on, comes by, of, and through the Cross of Christ, i.e., *"that which He did in His Death and Resurrection, which was all on our behalf."*

NOTES

## THE EXTREME SIGNIFICANCE OF ALL THIS

At times I feel that I'm being too repetitive respecting the great Finished Work of Christ. But then the Lord brings across my path particular situations that lets me know the tremendous significance of all of this, and how that Satan attempts to hinder this Message, in fact, the Message of Redemption, Freedom, and Victory.

First of all, Satan fights this Message, the Message of the Cross, moreso than he does anything else. Knowing this is the place of all Salvation and of all victory, he tries to steer the Believer in other directions. If he succeeds, and to be sure, he has succeeded very, very well in these last few decades, the results are extremely hurtful to say the least, and catastrophic at worst.

To entertain or learn philosophic ideas, is a simple thing. One hears them and either accepts them or rejects them; however, when it comes to the Truth of the Gospel, of which the Cross is the Foundation, the Evil One seeks to hinder the reception of this Word. Consequently, demon spirits seek to deceive Christians, to dull their thinking, to fill them with prejudice and bias against the one who is delivering the Message, or to be frank, whatever tactic that he can use.

I have preached the Cross all of my life, and have preached it strongly to say the least! However, until the Lord revealed to me the totality of this Message of the Cross as it regards our victory in our everyday walk, I had no knowledge whatsoever of the Cross in this capacity. In fact, in listening on tape and in reading hundreds of Messages and teaching material, I have heard and read so little on this subject, as to be almost nonexistent. In one or two Commentaries, I did see at least the beginning stages of these great Truths which I am attempting to bring to you, and that only in the last few weeks, at least as I dictate these notes. So, this Truth, in fact the most important Truth of all, has been seriously neglected in these last few years.

As simple as it seems to me, I have noticed that it is difficult for some Believers to grasp this of which I speak. I think the major reason is because of Satan stealing it away from their hearts and minds. Jesus referred to this in the *"Parable of the Sower"* (Mat. 13:3-23). That's the reason the Master said, *"Who hath ears to hear, let him hear"* (Mat. 13:9).

## INSTRUCTIONS FROM THE LORD

In the latter part of 1998, the Lord instructed me to teach again Romans, Chapters 6, 7, and 8 over our 90-minute, daily Radio Program. In fact, this Program goes out over all of our Network of Stations and the Internet. Actually, I had already taught these three Chapters in Romans in the first part of 1997.

After I began teaching on these subjects, the Holy Spirit actually told me to continue, which has now been about a year, and which all has been on the Cross.

After about five or six months, I was concerned that the people would be tired of hearing this particular subject; however, after praying about the situation quite a number of times, the Lord spoke to my heart, actually informing me that I was to continue the teaching on the Cross until further notice. This we have done, and I am now beginning to understand why.

Satan fights the reception of this Message to such a degree, attempting to block it out from people's minds, even attempting to hinder their understanding, that these Truths have to be proclaimed over and over again. Of course, the Lord already knew this, and now I'm beginning to see this which the Holy Spirit is doing.

The Truth is, even though one definitely hears this Word with one's ears, the facts are, it has to get down into one's spirit before it can be properly understood. Consequently, there has to be at least a measure of Faith exhibited in this manner, which the Lord

NOTES

has said that He would supply, that is if we will trust Him for this (Rom. 12:3).

## WAKE OR SLEEP

The phrase, *"That, whether we wake or sleep,"* actually has to do with the physical state of one's person at the time of the Resurrection.

As is obvious, Paul continues to address the Rapture of the Church, which he clearly delineated in I Thessalonians 4:13-18. He is stating again that all who are redeemed, dead or alive, will at that time be raptured, which, of course, speaks of the Resurrection.

## BE WITH CHRIST

The phrase, *"We should live together with Him,"* concerns the concluding part of Salvation. Believers are now Washed, Sanctified, and Justified, but will then, and we speak of the Resurrection, be Glorified (I Cor. 6:11; 15:51-57).

That's why Jesus said, *"Because I live, ye shall live also"* (Jn. 14:19). That's why He also said, *"And whosoever liveth and believeth in Me shall never die"* (Jn. 11:26).

## THE RESURRECTION

Paganism was and is without the Resurrection hope (Eph. 2:12; I Thess. 4:13). Greek philosophy taught the *"immortality of the soul,"* the soul being considered Divine; of the body, being matter and, therefore, considered evil, there was no hope.

Paul's proclamation of the Resurrection was ridiculed in Greece (Acts 17:32).

According to Scripture the soul is not Divine, nor is the body evil. Created in God's Image, man was *"very good"* in every aspect of his being (Gen. 1:27, 31; 2:21) and was destined to Eternal Life in body and soul (Gen. 3:22). Even after the Fall man does not need deliverance from the body; he rather needs that his body and soul be delivered from the power of sin and death, which Christ grants to Believers (Jn. 6:40; 11:24-26; I Cor. 15:54-56).

## THE WORK OF GOD AND CHRIST

It is God Who by an almighty creative act raised the dead (Mat. 22:29; I Cor. 6:14; 15:38; II Cor. 1:9; 4:14). This work, however, is mainly accomplished through agents:

Prophets and Apostles (I Ki. 17:17; II Ki. 4:32; Acts 20:10) and particularly through God's Son, Jesus Christ, Who is the Father's unique Agent (Jn. 6:39-40).

He Himself is the Resurrection and the Life (Jn. 11:25). He brought life and immortality to light (II Tim. 1:10) and His Resurrection in glory guarantees that of those who are His (I Cor. 15:20-23, 47-49; I Thess. 4:14). Though Christ as God's Agent will also raise those who lived and died without Him, and we speak of the unsaved, their Resurrection is not the result of His Redemptive Work, nor is it Redemptive in nature. While in fact He will definitely raise them, it will be as their Divinely appointed Judge (Jn. 5:26-30), from Whose Hand each one will receive *"according to what he has done in the body"* (II Cor. 5:10).

This Resurrection, at times referred to as the *"Resurrection of Damnation"* (Jn. 5:29), will take place about 1,000 years after the *"Resurrection of Life"* which we are studying here.

## RESURRECTION IN THE OLD TESTAMENT

The Old Testament contains only a few statements which give clear evidence of an eschatological (Endtime) Resurrection Hope. However, that by no means implies that such a hope was unknown in Israel.

To God's people Israel, the emphasis was upon a long life on Earth (Ex. 20:12) but with a not so clear view of an eternal future for the whole man.

This is because God's Redemptive Work in Christ was then only partially revealed. The full Resurrection Hope could, therefore, not be known nor enjoyed until Christ had conquered death. That is at least one of the reasons, that the Cross is so very, very important!

The true Believers in Israel must have known that their mighty God of Whom Moses sang, *"I kill and I make alive"* (Deut. 32:39), had more in store for them than this life and not only for their souls but also for their bodies, for the two are inseparable according to Old Testament teaching.

Of Abraham, the writer of Hebrews says that *"he considered that God was able to raise men even from the dead"* (Heb. 11:19).

NOTES

As well, it states that the Patriarchs were looking forward to *"the city which hath foundations,"* desiring *"a better country"* than Canaan, and that *"these all died in Faith"* (Heb. 11:8-16).

To these Passages full justice is done only if one regards them as implying the Resurrection Hope however vague in that early stage.

## THE DOCTRINE OF THE RESURRECTION

Christ is to raise and judge all dead. Unequivocally the New Testament teaches the raising of all the dead, those in Christ as well as those without Him, by Jesus Christ Who will judge them according to their works (Jn. 5:28-29; Acts 17:31; Rom. 14:10; II Cor. 5:10; Rev. 11:18; 20:11-15).

The end of God's ways cannot be the intermediate state, in which man exists without his body (Heb. 12:23; Rev. 20:4). Man in his totality was created for eternity, whereas the judgment will be concerned about what everyone has done in the body (II Cor. 5:10); hence a bodily Resurrection, either to Eternal Life or to eternal judgment under the Wrath of God (Mat. 10:28; 25:34; Jn. 3:36; 5:29; Rev. 20:15).

Though Christ as the Divinely appointed Judge (Acts 17:31) will raise all the dead, only the Resurrection of His Believers, to life eternal, is guaranteed by Christ's Resurrection (I Cor. 15:20; I Thess. 4:14).

Since the essence of Scripture is the Gospel of Salvation, little is said in the New Testament about the Resurrection of those without Christ. Only in Revelation, Chapter 20 is this mentioned. All the emphasis, especially in the great Chapter of the Resurrection (I Cor. Chpt. 15) is on that of the Believers.

## THE RESURRECTION BODY — A BODY OF FLESH

Many present-day so-called theologians reject the idea of a Resurrection in a body of flesh, either on so-called scientific grounds, which implies a denial of God's Power (Mk. 12:24), or because they regard the flesh as the source or seat of sin. According to them man will be raised as a spirit, or in an *"angelic,"* immaterial body.

Though in Scripture and particularly in Paul's writings the word *"flesh"* sometimes denotes man's evil nature, nowhere is the flesh-body as such proclaimed evil and the source of sin. Sin is in the heart, the spiritual center of man's personality, which generates the evil (Gen. 8:21; Mk. 7:14; Rom. 2:5).

The flesh-body is an ethically neutral medium which, as far as Believers are concerned, belongs to Christ (I Cor. 6:15), is a temple of the Holy Spirit (I Cor. 6:19), and a means to serve God (Rom. 6:12-13).

That in Scripture the word *"body"* would denote man's *"self"* or *"spiritual personality,"* as some aver, cannot be substantiated. In fact, the Resurrection of the dead in a body of flesh is guaranteed by Jesus' Resurrection in a body of *"flesh and bones,"* with scars of His wounds visible, and capable of being touched and of eating food (Lk. 24:38-43; Acts 10:41).

At His Ascension Jesus did not discard this flesh-body, as is clear from the Scripture (Acts 1:11; Phil. 3:21; Rev. 1:17). Since the resurrected Believers will be like the risen Christ (I Cor. 15:49; Phil. 3:21; I Jn. 3:2), we too will be raised in our bodies of flesh (I Cor. 15:35-42). Only in this way is man saved in his totality, and able to live on a new Earth (Isa. 65:17; 66:22; Mat. 5:5; Rev. 21:1-3).

PARTICULAR SCRIPTURES

There are several Scriptures used by those who deny a coming Resurrection, but on investigation prove no such thing. They are as follows:

Jesus told the Sadducees (Mat. 22:30; Mk. 12:25) that the resurrected Saints will be like Angels. The context, however, makes it clear that the resemblance will lie in the fact that after the Resurrection there will be no marriage. Luke recorded the reason for this change in Luke 20:36: *"They cannot die anymore,"* which means that reproduction is no longer needed to fill the places that have become vacant because of death.

There is no reference here to the nature of the Resurrection body, and the Passages quoted do not even imply that the distinction between male and female will be abolished. In fact, the Scripture plainly says, *"And to every seed his own body"* (I Cor. 15:38).

This means that in the coming Resurrection, the gender will remain as it always has been, as well as the various colors. It doesn't mean that babies will remain babies, or little children accordingly, or the very aged in that condition however.

The Scripture doesn't tell us, at least of which I am aware, as to the status of little babies and little children which have gone on to Heaven, or how they will be changed in the Resurrection. The Scripture just simply tells us, *"But God giveth it a body as it hath pleased Him"* (I Cor. 15:38).

Upon a little baby dying, I cannot conceive of it remaining in that particular state in Heaven until the coming Resurrection. As well, at the Resurrection, I cannot conceive of little babies and little children being given glorified bodies, which will yet have to mature and grow into adulthood in Heaven. So, if my thinking is right, the Resurrection will bring everyone, the young and the old, to a perfect age. And what will that perfect age be?

John said this, *"Beloved, now are we the sons of God, and it doth not yet appear what we shall be: but we know that, when He shall appear, we shall be like Him; for we shall see Him as He is"* (I Jn. 3:2).

If John meant that literally, that means that everyone in the Resurrection will be about 33 years old, for that was the age of Christ when He was crucified and raised from the dead.

A SPIRITUAL BODY?

The Resurrection body is called a *"spiritual body"* (I Cor. 15:44).

This, however, does not mean that it will be a body consisting only of spirit. The statement characterizes the Resurrection body as one completely filled and governed by the Holy Spirit.

Before the Fall of man in the Garden of Eden, every evidence is that Adam was governed completely by his own spirit, of course, moved upon and helped by the Holy Spirit. In other words, his physical body was subservient to his spirit.

It is the spirit of man which communes with God and worships God. After the Fall, man spiritually died, and did so instantly, which means his spirit was cut off from God totally and completely. That being the case, his physical body which is the weakest link

NOTES

in the chain of spirit, soul, and body, became the dominant force, i.e., *"the flesh."*

Even though redeemed man is now *"born again,"* meaning that his spirit once again communes with the Lord and worships Him, still, the physical body, although neutral, presents itself as a powerful force. In fact, it is the physical body which will be *"redeemed"* at the Resurrection (Rom. 8:23). The word *"redeemed"* in Romans 8:23 does not mean that the body is not now saved, for at the Born-Again experience the entire man is saved, even as Paul will reiterate in I Thessalonians 5:23. At the Resurrection, the physical body will then be glorified, completing the Salvation process.

## FLESH AND BLOOD

Another statement by Paul that *"flesh and blood cannot inherit the Kingdom of God"* (I Cor. 15:50) is often considered to exclude the idea of a Resurrection body of flesh. The Apostle, however, teaches something entirely different.

The expression *"flesh and blood"* as used here, never denotes the *"substance"* of the body, but man in his totality as a frail and perishable creature (Mat. 16:17; Gal. 1:16; Eph. 6:12; Heb. 2:14).

It has the same meaning in I Corinthians 15:50, shown by the fact that in the parallel phrase the word *"corruption"* is used, which obviously denotes the whole man in his corruptibility and not the substance of his body.

The entire context shows that man, as a frail, perishable creature, cannot enter God's glorious, Endtime Kingdom. He first must be made immortal, imperishable, powerful, and glorious. That will be done at the Resurrection, when God glorifies the physical body of every Saint of God, both those who have died and those who are alive at that time.

## IDENTITY AND CHANGE

Though the Resurrection body will be essentially identical to the present body in that it is a body of flesh, there will be a tremendous change regarding the conditions of its existence.

Paul emphasized the necessity of such a change for the dead as well as for those who are living when Jesus returns. This change is necessary because the resurrected Believer enters upon a new world of impeccable perfection and Heavenly Glory (I Cor. 15:47-49) like that of Christ (II Cor. 3:18), a glory which will differ in accordance with the individual Believer's dedication to the Lord in this life (Dan. 12:3; I Cor. 3:14-15; II Cor. 9:6).

NOTES

## THE DEGREE OF GLORY ON THE RESURRECTED BODY

The difference then in manifested glory, as it regards individual Believers in the coming Resurrection, will be according to their consecration on Earth. Then, I am definitely positive, many Saints of God of whom the Church as a whole knew little or nothing, will then as Daniel said, *"shine as the brightness of the firmament"* (Dan. 12:3), while some others who were very famous on this Earth, will no doubt, manifest much less glory. To be sure, that will be very interesting. One can well imagine, the glory that will be manifested on Paul, and others like him, in that coming glad day. However, as the song writer says, *"Jesus will outshine them all"* (Rev. 1:12-18).

This very thought should cause the Believer to hunger and thirst after Righteousness, to commit oneself totally to the Lord in every capacity, to draw ever nearer unto Him. What we're speaking of here one must understand, is that which will be eternal. It will not be a transition stage, but rather everlasting. So, what are we saying?

We're saying that this life *here* is what will decide the glory *there*! And to be sure, the Lord Who knows the hearts of all men, and Who does not judge by the seeing of the eye or the hearing of the ear, will most definitely judge Righteous Judgment (Isa. 11:3-5).

Due to this difference of degree regarding manifested glory, we should understand that all Believers will not be the same in that capacity in eternity. What this will entail of course, only God knows; however, of this we can be certain:

Every Saint who has ever lived will be instantly obvious regarding glory, as to the degree of their consecration or the lack thereof, respecting their life on Earth.

Some may ask as to the status of those on Earth who did not have an opportunity to live any life for the Lord, inasmuch as they died in infancy or very soon after coming to Christ?

That being the case, which it definitely is with many, we must fall back on the words of Abraham, *"The Judge of all the earth* (shall) *do right"* (Gen. 18:25).

God, Who has perfect foreknowledge, will of course be able to know what they would have been and what they would have done, and on that basis, will reward accordingly.

As an example Paul said:

*"There are also celestial bodies, and bodies terrestrial: but the glory of the celestial is one, and the glory of the terrestrial is another.*

*"There is one glory of the Sun, and another glory the Moon, and another glory of the Stars: for one star differeth from another star in glory.*

*"So also in the Resurrection of the dead . . . it is raised in glory"* (I Cor. 15:40-44).

(11) "WHEREFORE COMFORT YOURSELVES TOGETHER, AND EDIFY ONE ANOTHER, EVEN AS ALSO YE DO."

A spiritual and intellectual grasp of the provisions Paul has been describing leads to individual as well as collective growth of the Body of Christ. The Apostle is quick to acknowledge progress along this line: *"Just as in fact you are doing."* Yet he also looks forward to even greater attainments (I Thess. 4:1).

The idea of the *"comfort"* relates to that which will happen in the coming Resurrection and through eternity.

## COMFORT

The phrase, *"Wherefore comfort yourselves together,"* presents the same expression as used in I Thessalonians 4:18. In essence, the Apostle is saying that, irrespective as to what might be happening in the world, Believers are to comfort themselves with the Scriptural Promise that we will escape the Wrath of God that will be poured out on this world. The *"comfort"* here entails many things, of which the following are but a few:

1. There is going to be a Rapture of the Church, which will involve every single Believer who has ever lived.
2. Jesus will be the One Who will come back for the Saints, and will do so Personally.
3. The dead in Christ will have the same privileges regarding Resurrection as those who will be alive at that particular time. Of course, as is obvious, and looking down through the many centuries past, most of the Saints have already gone on to be with the Lord, and are now awaiting the coming Resurrection. We who are alive certainly should be doing the same!
4. At that time, every Saint of God will be instantly glorified, which will complete the Salvation process (I Cor. 6:11).
5. The degree of glory, as we have just addressed, will be manifested according to consecration to the Lord regarding our lives on Earth.
6. This glorious state which will take place in the coming Resurrection, will be eternal, i.e., *"everlasting."*

This is why Paul said:

*"But as it is written, Eye hath not seen, nor ear heard, neither have entered into the heart of man, the things which God hath prepared for them that love Him.*

*"But God hath revealed them unto us by His Spirit"* (I Cor. 2:9-10).

## EDIFICATION

The phrase, *"And edify one another, even as also ye do,"* refers to cheering and strengthening one another. Consequently, the question should be asked, if in fact, we do actually follow this admonition as given by the Holy Spirit through Paul.

Is it not true that too often these truths are discussed with only academic or passing interest? At times, this world is *"too much with us."* When the prospect of the Lord's return is a practical aspect of daily living, then this present world — so physically real, so apparently permanent — will slip into its proper perspective.

The Holy Spirit through the Apostle is admonishing us here to talk about these things constantly. We are to look forward to that coming moment, eagerly anticipating its rapture and joy. The Truth is, the more we dwell on these things, even as we have just stated, the less attraction this world has.

As well, when we consider, that what is coming, what is prepared for us, in fact, what Jesus has prepared at such great price, and I refer to the Cross, is so much more wonderful, so much greater, so greater in fact that

NOTES

there is no comparison, and I speak of this present world, that we should eagerly anticipate this coming event.

*"Edify"* in the Greek is *"oikodomeo,"* and means *"to be a house-builder, to construct, to build up."* Consequently, we have here the Holy Spirit telling us, that the discussion, the understanding, the dwelling on these things, will build us up spiritually, which will flow over into the physical, mental, domestical, even material, etc. To be sure, discussing the things of this world, which regrettably we probably do far more than we do the things of which here the Spirit speaks, will bring no edification whatsoever, but rather the very opposite.

The world which looks so real at present, is rather in fact, so transitional, while the things of God, which do not appear real, are in fact, eternal.

It is noteworthy that affection for the Person of the Lord is that which in this Epistle makes His promised Coming so precious to the Christian. To meet Him — to be with Him — rather that the rest, victory, and glory then to be enjoyed by the Believer, is what is here set before the heart. Even though these other things are definitely important, even as we've already attempted to bring out, and even though the joy of being with fellow-Believers is as well emphasized, still, all of those things are not at all given first place. First place goes in its entirety, and by far to the joy of seeing the Lord, being with the Lord, and more particularly, being with Him forever.

Incidentally, in closing the comments on this particular Verse, I think the Holy Spirit through the Apostle is telling us that if we as Believers, will set our minds on the Lord, talk about Him, talk about what He is going to do as it regards Endtime events, and in fact, all that He does, everything else will then go for us in a much better way. Many Christians are suffering nervous disorders, emotional stress, discouragement, even depression, when a simple following of this admonition, would remedy much of this distress, if not all!

(12) "AND WE BESEECH YOU BRETHREN, TO KNOW THEM WHICH LABOUR AMONG YOU, AND ARE OVER YOU IN THE LORD, AND ADMONISH YOU;"

NOTES

Paul will now give a long list of practical principles of daily living, which should be applied to our lives. Even though the statements are very short, even as we shall see, they contain the very ingredients of Christianity.

Heading this list are the exhortations regarding the proper attitude toward leaders in the Church.

It was the responsibility of these leaders to *"stand over"* the rest of the Assembly in the Lord. A secondary sense of *"caring for"* is also involved here. Yet the element of *"caring for"* cannot erode the authority of the Office of the Pastor and the need to *"respect"* the Office. Anarchy is always wrong, particularly among Christians.

Where Believers are united with Christ, respectful submission to Christian leaders is service to the Lord. The leaders were charged with guiding the congregation. They were also to *"admonish"* the congregation, which pertains to correction administered either by word or deed. It implies blame on the part of the one admonished.

Such admonishment, arouses resentment, since discipline is never pleasant. Still the Apostle presents admonition as necessary for the congregation and requires respect for those who are forced to exercise such.

## SPIRITUAL LEADERS

The phrase, *"And we beseech you Brethren, to know them which labour among you,"* contains the beginning of a wealth of information.

*"Know"* in the Greek is *"eido,"* and means *"to behold, to consider, to have knowledge of, to perceive, to be sure, to understand."* It means to know for sure that this particular leader is from the Lord, of the Lord and for the Lord. The Truth is, every Believer is going to follow the Ministry of a Preacher. It is ordained that way in the Plan of God (Eph. 4:11-13). The idea is, that you *"know"* the one you are following, in that you are certain that he is preaching the Gospel, he is anointed by the Holy Spirit, and he has the Mind of God. If in fact, the wrong one is followed, which so often is the case, untold harm will be the result, possibly even the loss of one's soul.

A Church can rise no higher than its leader. While it is certainly true, that some few Believers in the Church can definitely rise higher in a spiritual sense, for the most part, that will not be the case. Whatever type of spirit, of attitude, of direction, of spirituality, that is presented by the Pastor, that is what mostly the Church will be. As should be obvious, this sword has two sides:

A Godly Preacher is one of the greatest blessings to the Church, whether a local Assembly, or the Church as a whole; however, as much of a blessing is the man of God, as detrimental is the one who is a wolf in sheep's clothing (Mat. 7:15-29).

The sad Truth is, that for every one Godly Preacher of the Gospel, there are many more who are the very opposite. That being the case, considering that most Preachers are not Godly, it is not so easy as one would think, to be led to the right one. However, there are Godly Preachers in the land. If the Believer, consequently, will earnestly seek the Lord as it regards those whom they will follow, the Lord without fail, will direct them to the right Church, the right Preacher, etc. However, most Christians I'm afraid, little seek the Lord as it regards these all-important matters, rather making their decision on carnal factors alone.

Also, and which the Believer should think about carefully, *"Satan is a master at getting people to believe that the truly Godly is ungodly, and the ungodly is Godly!"* He does it as *"angel of light"* (II Cor. 11:12-15).

And then again, millions of Christians attend a particular Church simply because of the name on the door. In other words, they attend certain Churches because it is of their Denomination. This means, that their priority is totally wrong. It is the Preacher who stands behind the pulpit which should make the difference. And as well, he is what he is, not because he belongs to a certain Denomination or group, but because of the moving and operation of the Holy Spirit within his heart and life.

## LABOR

Concerning a Godly Pastor or Evangelist, and where the other Offices of Apostle, Prophet, and Teacher, also fall into these areas, the work of the Minister is exactly here what Paul says, *"labour."* In fact, if the spiritual leader conducts himself or herself as one should conduct themselves, it is the hardest work in the world.

NOTES

The responsibility, as should be obvious, is absolutely phenomenal. At times, the weight of such, is almost unbearable, even as brought out in Paul's Epistles on a regular basis.

And then, the true Preacher of the Gospel must seek the Lord constantly, that there will be a moving and operation of the Holy Spirit within his life and ministry, which will be of great blessing to the people. This does not come easily, cheaply, or quickly. It takes a constant seeking of the Lord on behalf of such a man or woman, for these things to be brought about. He is ever conscious of souls and then, after conversion, the care of souls.

I think we can see from Paul's writings, as to what priority ought to be, as it regards Preachers of the Gospel. As it pertains to Pastors, of course, there are many duties involved other than the Preaching and Teaching of the Word. Those duties are extremely important; however, the most important thing by far, is the Word of God that is presented to the people, and more particularly, the leading of the Lord as it regards that Word, and the Anointing of the Holy Spirit upon that Word. Regrettably, many Preachers specialize in other things, with the giving of the Word to the people taking second place, etc. Such an attitude is backwards.

The thing that's going to get Believers through, is not the excellent *"bedside manner"* of the Preacher, or his winsome personality. It is going to be the Word of God which pertains to the way it is presented, and the Anointing and Operation of the Holy Spirit upon that Word. Consequently, the true Preacher of the Gospel, even as we've already stated, must have a strong prayer life, coupled with an astute study of the Word, which will enable the Holy Spirit to perform His work in the Preacher's life, which can then be given to the people. Unfortunately, even as we've stated, this is seldom the case, with other things too often being primary.

## THE FIVEFOLD OFFICES OF THE MINISTRY

Ephesians 4:11 tells us, *"And He gave some, Apostles; and some, Prophets; and some, Evangelists; and some, Pastors and Teachers."*

These are given, *"For the perfecting of the Saints, for the Work of the Ministry, for the edifying of the Body of Christ"* (Eph. 4:12).

*"Over you"* in the Greek is, *"proistamenous,"* and means *"taking the lead, or those who stand in front of you."* In this case, it is speaking of the Pastor of the local Church.

*"In the Lord"* refers to the fact that this individual is called of God, and it is obvious that he or she is called of God.

It also means, that the Lord has not only called this particular individual, but as well, He has put him in this particular place as the Pastor of this local Church, etc. Consequently, this rules out those chosen by men. Of this, we must be very careful.

Satan loves to exert religious authority, and he does so through unconsecrated men. And what do I mean by that?

As should be obvious, there were no religious Denominations in the Early Church. However, I think one can say without fear of contradiction, that the spirit of Denominations or organizations was definitely present in the Early Church. Consequently, as long as the Leadership of particular Denominations conduct themselves according to the Word of God, as it regards Government, the Denomination as an organization, can be a tremendous help to the Work of God all over the world. That is the ideal!

However, too often, these men who have been elected by popular ballot, consider these offices which are not Scriptural, in fact to be Scriptural, and, therefore, to carry spiritual authority. Many of these individuals consequently feel, that whatever they say, must be obeyed, and without question. Such is the ruination of the Church.

While the Church definitely must have organization, as should be obvious, this organization must be kept Scriptural, must be after the Government of God and not the Government of man. The pattern is laid out before us in the Book of Acts and the Epistles. In fact, the Government presented there, is that which was devised by the Holy Spirit, which means that it's God's Way, and it must not be added to or taken from.

## WHAT WAS THE GOVERNMENT OF THE EARLY CHURCH?

First of all, and as stated, there were no religious Denominations or even a headquarters Church which exercised authority. Such did not exist. There definitely was a fellowship of Churches, which of course was alike in Doctrine and principle. As well, there were definitely Churches used by the Holy Spirit as it referred to His Leadership, as was Antioch (Acts 13:1-2).

In fact, the local Church was and should be now, the highest spiritual authority, one might say. In other words, there was no outside spiritual authority which exercised control over the local Church. While advice may be given from other quarters, even as Paul constantly advised the Churches, still, the Church was free to accept or reject that which was offered.

Also, as is very obvious, there definitely was control exercised, but it was always by the Holy Spirit. In other words, Paul and others, always conducted themselves with the idea in mind, that they were undershepherds, and that Christ as the Chief Shepherd is always the Head of the Church, and a very active Head at that! If one studies the Book of Acts and the Epistles of Paul to any degree, all of this becomes quickly obvious. In fact, it must be this way, if the Holy Spirit is to have His Way, and Christ is to serve as *"Head."*

Once again, I emphasize that it's not wrong to have Denominations or to belong to Denominations. Neither is it wrong to have offices in these particular Denominations, even as it refers to organization. Such are necessary; however, it must always be understood, that those particular offices are administrative only, and never fall into the position of the spiritual. The only Spiritual Offices in the Church are that of, *"Apostles, Prophets, Evangelists, Pastors, and Teachers."* Any other offices are man-devised, which means they are not Scriptural at least as far as spiritual authority is concerned.

As well, even though the fivefold Calling definitely has spiritual authority, it is never over people, but always over spirits of darkness, etc. (Eph. 6:11-12). Even Paul did not exercise authority over people. He only *"admonished"* as we shall see!

It should as well be noted, that the titles as used in the New Testament of *"Bishop, Presbyter, Shepherd, Elder, and Pastor,"* are all referring to the Pastor of a local Church. There was no such thing in the Early Church as a *"Bishop"* who was in charge of a number of Churches, or even an area, etc. While that definitely came into being after the Early Church began to apostatize, which was after the passing of the original Apostles, it definitely was not Scriptural, and led ultimately to the Catholic Church. Unfortunately, men love to add to or take away from the Word of God. We must be very careful to obey the Word in every respect. If it is not Scriptural, it should not be heeded or obeyed.

## ADMONISHMENT

The phrase, *"And admonish you,"* presents direction regarding spiritual and moral discipline.

There are three expressions referred to here regarding different functions of the Leaders rather than to three kinds of Church Officers, etc. Early Church organization was relatively uncomplicated (Acts 14:23). Regrettably, it is not the same presently, and because men have left the Word of God.

These leaders apparently guided the organization, managed the funds, and counseled in spiritual matters. Those three expressions are:

1. Labor.
2. Leadership.
3. Love.

If the Pastor truly loves his people, he will not be a men pleaser, but will definitely admonish them when needed. In other words, he will love them enough to admonish them.

It is not pleasant to be admonished or to have to admonish.

*"Admonish"* in the Greek is, *"noutheteo,"* and means *"to put in mind, to caution or reprove gently. It is a mild rebuke or warning."*

It is not pleasant for a Preacher to have to do that, as should be obvious; however, the Preacher who refuses to do such, especially when he sees glaring inconsistencies and spiritual problems, is definitely not obeying the Lord. This is a part of the Calling, and if this part is not engaged when needed, then we fail the Lord, and we fail the people over whom we have been placed in charge. Once again, we come back to the statement of *"love."*

If a Preacher truly loves his people, truly cares for them, truly is concerned about their spiritual welfare, he will definitely admonish them when needed. He will do so kindly, gently, and lovingly, but it definitely will be done.

NOTES

(13) "AND TO ESTEEM THEM VERY HIGHLY IN LOVE FOR THEIR WORK'S SAKE. AND BE AT PEACE AMONG YOURSELVES."

Another part of Paul's *"requests"* regarding Leadership is that Leaders be held *"in highest regard in love."* It actually means *"consider them worthy of being loved."*

Rulers in the local assembly must be held *"in the highest regard"* and given wholehearted support, and this in a spirit of *"love."* As suitable reason for this high appreciation is *"their work,"* and being called *"of the Lord."*

As well, leaders were to guard against abusing their authority, which meaning is carried in the last phrase of this Verse.

## TO ESTEEM VERY HIGHLY

The phrase, *"And to esteem them very highly in love for their work's sake,"* carries more reference to the work they do, than to the person in question. If one does the Work of the Lord, and truly does that Work, which means they are called to do that Work, for that sake, they are to be esteemed very highly.

While all Believers are slaves of the Lord, and Preachers more than all, even as Paul constantly brought out, still, it is to be ever considered as to Whom we belong. This is very important! When one touches a man or woman of God in a negative sense, one in essence is touching the Lord. Three things are here said:

1. Preachers, and we speak of God-called Preachers, should be esteemed very highly.
2. They should be loved greatly.
3. All of this is for their *"Work's sake,"* which pertains to the Call of God on their lives.

It is the same as showing respect to the Ambassador of a particular country. The way the Ambassador is treated, is the way the country is treated which he represents. In fact, that's the reason that Ambassadors in most nations of the world, are given immunity from certain standards respecting the host country. Unfortunately, at times that immunity is abused; nevertheless, it is still given, because of all the implications involved.

When dealing with a Preacher of the Gospel, all of these things must be kept in mind.

Of course, he or she is human like anyone else; nevertheless, they are Ambassadors of the Lord Jesus Christ, and as such, must always be respected accordingly.

For many, many years, Frances and I traveled from Church to Church in Evangelistic Work. In fact, that was all that Donnie knew for the formative years of his life.

I noticed that Churches which love their Pastor, treated him grandly, were concerned about him, and showed that love and concern, were Churches which were blessed greatly. Conversely, I noticed that Churches that treated their Pastor as a *"hired hand,"* meaning they could hire him and fire him at will, were not blessed at all. They were always in a state of turmoil, changing Pastors about like people would change shoes.

## UNSCRIPTURAL GOVERNMENT

For the most part, I think that the majority of the modern Church has slipped into an unscriptural form of government, as it regards their local situation. Far too often, Deacon Boards run the Church. Perhaps, at least for the most of them, that is not their intention, but that's pretty well what it's come to, simply because of really not knowing the Scriptural pattern.

In the Book of Acts and the Epistles, which must be our Standard for all things regarding the Work of God, we do not find Deacon Boards in the realm of spiritual leadership apart from the Pastor of the local Church. While they definitely are to be involved in spiritual leadership, it is to be in the form of helping the Pastor carry out his duties in every capacity, at least where they are able to do so. We find this in Acts Chapter 6, where it seems that the Office of the Deacon was instituted by the Holy Spirit. Even though this designation of Deacons is not given to these men selected here, I personally think the Scripture is clear that this is actually what they were.

In I Timothy Chapter 3, we find that the qualities of both Pastors (Bishops) and Deacons, to be very similar. So, what actually are the duties of Deacons?

Except by implication, the Word of God does not specify; however, the implication is, that the Deacons should do all they can to help the Pastor in every manner possible. They should seek to help him carry out his burden for the Church, and that means to stand behind him with their strength, support, and prayers, doing all within their power to carry forth the Work of God.

NOTES

As far as actual duties are concerned, they should help pray for the sick, visit the sick, help take care of all the many duties of ushering in the Church, plus the simple operation of getting things done, whatever those things might be. They should help with busing, if there is busing, maintenance, if it lies within their power to do so. In other words, anything, that helps the local Assembly to carry forth its duties.

Regarding decisions to be made concerning the borrowing of money, the construction of buildings, etc., Deacons of course, should have a great say in all of this, giving all of it prayerful attention and tendering all the responsibility they know toward this all-important task.

## THE VISION

Most of the time, it is the Pastor who has the burden and vision respecting the Church regarding the construction of new buildings, or whatever is needed. Deacons are to look at this very closely, pray about it extensively, and unless they personally see something extremely detrimental in such a direction, they should stand behind the Pastor in these efforts.

If they see something which they feel is unwise, it is their duty to call such to the attention of the Pastor. If the Pastor insists upon going ahead anyway, in other words claiming what he is doing is right, and the Deacon sincerely thinks it isn't, the Deacon should remove himself from the situation. It would even be better for him to go to another Church if at all possible.

If that is not possible, and he is forced to take a stand, he must be very careful about what he does, that it not hurt the Church more than it helps the Church. Only total consecration to the Lord, and dedication to His Work, with the entirety of the situation soaked in prayer, will bring such a position out to a successful conclusion. So, the Deacon must examine his own heart at all times, as should be obvious.

As well, if the Deacon feels that any particular course is not wise, or even unscriptural, and after examining his own heart he feels that he has no ulterior motives, he should voice his concern to the Pastor. If the Pastor continues to feel that such a course is right, and Scriptural, in most circumstances the Deacon should acquiesce and give his full support to the Pastor, despite his concern. The Deacon should understand, that the Pastor of the local Church is the highest spiritual authority in that particular Church, and that this Office must be respected accordingly at all times. That by no means is meant to claim that the Pastor is always right. In fact, sometimes he isn't.

If the Deacon feels strongly about the matter, whatever the matter might be, as it regards the wisdom of such a direction, and he feels he cannot conscientiously support the Pastor in this endeavor, he should follow his conscience, but only after much prayer. Even then, he must be very careful how he addresses the situation, that he does not cause more problems in the Church, than the help he is supposed to provide.

As to what course he should then take, no definitive direction can be laid down, for each situation would have to stand on its own merit or lack thereof. As we have stated, he must always keep in mind the dignity and authority of the Office of the Pastor as the highest Spiritual Leadership in the local Church. This I'm afraid, is what many modern Deacons tend to forget.

## UNSCRIPTURAL GOVERNMENT

I think the reason for this lies in the realm of the corruption of Church Government as held by many Denominations. Much, if not most, of the Leadership in Denominations hold the Office of Pastor in the local Church as somewhat less than the Biblical Standard requires. Their idea seems to be, at least in most cases, *"Preachers come and go,"* and are, therefore, not to be taken too seriously. In fact, if the issue were pressed, I think that Denominational Leadership would probably hold the Office of the Deacon in even higher regard than that of the Pastor. Whether they admit it or not, their actions lean strongly in that direction. As a result, this spirit filters down into the local Church, which as well causes many Deacon Boards to treat the Office of the Pastor accordingly. Such direction cannot help but hurt the local Church.

NOTES

In fact, the Office of the Deacon is a very holy Office, and should always be looked at accordingly. But at the same time, and as stated, it must understand that the Office of the Pastor must never be abrogated in the sense of spiritual authority. But yet, that authority, even as the authority of the entirety of the fivefold Calling, is to always be subject to the Scriptures. If the Word of God is violated by anyone holding true spiritual offices, their direction must never be followed. The Word of God takes precedent at all times and in all cases.

Paul said, *"For they that have used the Office of a Deacon well purchase to themselves a good degree, and great boldness in the Faith which is in Christ Jesus"* (I Tim. 3:13).

## PEACE

The phrase, *"And be at peace among yourselves,"* proclaims the esteem just mentioned as helping to produce such peace. The words *"among yourselves"* in the Greek strongly suggest that the imperative was directed to Leaders and followers alike. The responsibility for sanctified relationships rests upon both.

Pastors are not always, as one suspects might have been the case at Thessalonica, as skilled and tactful as they might be. Some understanding of the burdens of leadership however, mixed with esteem based on Christian love, would resolve most of the friction occasioned by the mistakes and the criticism of such leaders. Robertson remarks: *"We need wise Leadership today, but still more wise following. An army of Captains and Colonels never won a battle."*

Even though this statement concerning *"peace"* may seem to be somewhat simplistic; however, there is probably nothing more important in the local Church. Nothing is more frustrating than an atmosphere of dissension, quarreling, and murmuring (criticism that is said under one's breath). God is able to give Leaders Grace despite the lack of peace and unity among their people. But so much more can be done when people are in one accord (Horton).

(14) "NOW WE EXHORT YOU, BRETHREN, WARN THEM THAT ARE UNRULY, COMFORT THE FEEBLEMINDED, SUPPORT THE WEAK, BE PATIENT TOWARD ALL MEN."

If it is to be noticed, when Paul began the previous statement he did so by using the Word *"We beseech you."* Here he begins by using the phrase, *"We exhort you,"* which in essence says, *"We urge you,"* which is more authoritative than his previous *"We beseech."*

What follows, at least through Verse 22, are some 14 commands applicable to all Christians. They deal with about everything one could think.

WE EXHORT YOU

The phrase, *"Now we exhort you, Brethren,"* as just stated, carries a much stronger authority than the previous admonition. The significant thing about this admonition is, that obligation is laid on the whole Church. It is not just the Leaders who are to warn, encourage, support, and restrain from retaliation. These words are incumbent upon all!

By the use of the word *"Brethren,"* many things are to be understood.

First of all, if we are in fact *"Brethren,"* which we definitely are in the Lord, we should adhere to the old adage which refers to family relationships, *"Blood is thicker than water."* In this case, it is the Blood of Christ, which has been applied to the hearts and lives of all Believers, making us one in Christ.

And yet, it is as well to be understood, that even though family ties in the natural create a definite bond, still, greater hatred can be built up in this context than even that which is outside those ties. It is the same with Christianity!

Whereas normal family ties can only go so far, the Family of God is something else altogether. While relationship is the same, the Family of God has the Holy Spirit to help us; consequently, there is no excuse for quarrels among and between Believers.

Second, understanding that we are Ambassadors for Christ in this world, if we cannot get along between ourselves, how in the world can we expect the unsaved to be impressed by that which we profess. In other words, inasmuch as we are *"Brethren,"* members of the Family of God, we are honor-bound, duty-bound, to conduct ourselves accordingly.

NOTES

THE UNRULY

The phrase, *"Warn them that are unruly,"* speaks of those who leave the ranks.

*"Unruly"* or *"disorderly"* was originally a military term expressing the character of those soldiers who would not keep rank. In other words they were out of order, troublemakers, causing problems!

How did they do this?

It really doesn't matter as to how it was done, only that it was done. It can be done through gossip, meddling in other people's business, refusing to do their part, etc.

*"Warn them"* is the same as *"admonish."*

Going back to the military, if an army is undisciplined, it's not going to win any battles, as should be obvious. It is the same with the Church, hence the Holy Spirit using this terminology. So the Holy Spirit means the following:

If a soldier is constantly causing trouble, which of course affects others, that soldier will be first warned. If he insists on continuing in such a direction, he might even be warned a second time; however, if the problem persists, he will be arrested and thrown into the stockade for a period of time. If that does not remedy the situation, he will ultimately be given a dishonorable discharge, or even worse.

If the Holy Spirit gave this type of admonition, and He definitely did, then He means for us to understand what He is saying.

A Godly Pastor never enjoys putting anyone out of the Church. But if the *"unruly"* will not change despite repeated warnings, even as the Holy Spirit through Paul here insists, sometimes, such drastic action as excommunication from the local Body is necessary.

That is not to mean that the individual cannot go elsewhere and continue to serve the Lord; however, whatever problems they've had which have caused their difficulties, to be sure, those problems will be taken with them, with the situation more than likely continuing wherever they go.

FEEBLEMINDED

The phrase, *"Comfort the feebleminded,"* probably should have been translated *"Comfort the fainthearted,"* for that's what the Greek word *"oligopsuchos"* means. It refers to those who grow discouraged and, therefore, lose heart in the midst of the conflict, whatever that conflict might be.

Having Faith in God, and, therefore, trusting Him as to all circumstances, we should never become fainthearted or discouraged; however, perhaps all of us at one time or the other do succumb to this difficulty. Consequently, in such circumstances, the person is to be encouraged, strengthened, lifted up, helped, and all of that is done, by pointing out the Promises of the Word of God, as it regards any situation.

There is actually no reason, however, for any Christian to ever get discouraged. The Lord guides and controls all things. While men rule, God overrules, and we can be certain, that He Who notes every sparrow's fall, and numbers the very hairs of our heads, can easily do whatever needs to be done.

While Satan definitely does cause problems at times, and great problems at that, still, we must understand that he can only do what the Lord allows him to do (Job Chpts. 1-2). In fact, every Scriptural indication is, that he has to seek permission from the Lord for whatever he does, and is even then given strict guidelines which without fail he must follow.

Understanding that, we should realize that we are always under the watchful care of our Heavenly Father. We are His Children, members of His Family, who He loves so much, for whom He paid a terrible price on the Cross for our Redemption and relationship.

Even though He does watch over us very carefully, He still gives us an amazing amount of latitude. In fact, He allows us to even become a part of this great work in carrying out His Will on Earth. But still, He is always the Captain, and of that we are certainly thankful. Understanding that, as stated, we should not become discouraged but always trusting in Him, which He strongly desires that we do.

## WEAK

The phrase, *"Support the weak,"* refers to those, who do not have proper understanding of the Cross of Christ, and what it means to their everyday walk before God. Consequently, attempting to walk in victory outside of those parameters, they meet only with defeat.

NOTES

We who know God's prescribed order of victory, which is the Cross of Christ, and Faith in that Finished Work, which always guarantees the help of the Holy Spirit, should support these individuals, by informing them of their prerogative in Christ. This is what Paul was talking about in Galatians 6:1.

Weak Christians are not to be thrown out of the Church. They are to be told the reason they are weak, and how that victory is obtained in Christ. Once again, it is an explanation of the Cross and all it affords.

## PATIENCE

The phrase, *"Be patient toward all men,"* refers to all the categories just mentioned. No matter how strong we might presently be, we must always remember that the Lord in getting us to this place, has been very patient with us. We are to show the same toward others.

I have noticed in explaining the great Victory of the Cross, that it is not always understood at first. In fact, it is seldom understood at first, with repeated efforts required. Consequently, patience toward others is definitely required on our part.

It is a wonderful and glorious privilege to know and understand the rudiments of what Christ has done for us at the Cross and in His Resurrection; however, none of us have come to this place easily. I think of the patience which the Lord has shown me, and I must realize that such longsuffering on His part is so extraordinary that it beggars description. Why did it take so long for me to learn? Why couldn't this great Truth have been given and grasped sooner?

And yet I know and realize, that ever how long it has taken, that the fault is definitely not that of the Lord's, but mine altogether. And as such, the Lord had to show continued patience toward me, which He always did, and without reproval. How I will ever thank Him for that, and in fact, I still must have the continued blessing of His patience directed toward me. Knowing and understanding that, and in fact, knowing it so graphically, makes it much easier to show patience toward others.

(15) "SEE THAT NONE RENDER EVIL FOR EVIL UNTO ANY MAN; BUT EVER FOLLOW THAT WHICH IS GOOD, BOTH AMONG YOURSELVES, AND TO ALL MEN."

The natural tendency to retaliate and inflict injury for a wrong suffered must be strongly resisted, no matter what the injury.

Apparently the Christian stand against retaliation crystallized very early, no doubt being formulated from Principles established by Christ in His Sermon on the Mount (Mat. 5:38-42). Jesus refuted a false inference drawn from Exodus 21:23-24 (Lev. 24:19-20; Deut. 19:21). *"An eye for an eye, and a tooth for a tooth"* was originally intended to restrain people from going beyond equal retaliation in punishment for social wrongs against the community. However, the Scribes had distorted the Commandment's purpose by using it to justify personal revenge. What had been given as restrictive Law had through human traditions been transformed into a permissive rule. In speaking out against this tradition, Jesus emphatically set the tone for His followers in forbidding personal revenge altogether.

In place of wrong, injury, or harm dictated by a vengeful spirit, Christians must diligently endeavor to produce what is intrinsically beneficial to others, whether other Christians or unbelievers. The seriousness of the abuse suffered is no issue.

Some Thessalonians doubtless had been victims of unjustified harsh treatment, but regardless of this, a positive Christian response is the only suitable recourse. The welfare of the offender must be the prime objective (Thomas).

## DO UNTO OTHERS AS YOU WOULD HAVE THEM DO UNTO YOU

The phrase, *"See that none render evil for evil unto any man,"* presents Christianity as the only system of such noble practice. The spirit of the world, and in fact, all religions in one way or the other, is to *"render evil for evil."*

Denney says that *"Revenge is the most natural and distinctive of vices . . . It is the one which most easily passes itself off as a virtue."*

This Law, that is if one is to refer to this given by Paul as a Law, is positive, and is universally binding. The moment we feel ourselves acting from a desire to *"return evil for evil,"* that moment we are acting wrong.

It may be right to defend our lives, and the lives of our friends; to seek the protection of the Law for our persons, reputation, or property, against those who would wrong us; to repel the assaults of calumniators and slanderers; but in no case should the motive be to do them wrong for the evil which they have done us. In fact, Paul sought the aid of the legal jurisprudence of Caesar to protect himself against the Jews who were trying to kill him (Acts 25:10-11).

And yet, for people who have seriously wronged us, and have not repented of these deeds, while we must certainly forgive them, and do so immediately, this doesn't mean that fellowship can be enjoined. In fact, unless the thing is made right, no fellowship can be had with such individuals.

If we are to notice, when Joseph recognized his Brothers who had come to Egypt to purchase grain during a time of famine (they did not recognize him), he did not jump into their arms, or even reveal himself to them. These men had previously been murderers at heart, and Joseph wanted to know if they had changed, before he would reveal himself. Consequently, he tested them greatly over a period of several months, which testing determined that they had changed, and then, and only then, did he reveal himself to them (Gen. Chpts. 42-45).

When it comes to revenge, this prerogative is always that which belongs to the Lord. In other words, He has said, *"Recompense to no man evil for evil . . . Avenge not yourselves, but rather give place unto wrath: for it is written, vengeance is Mine; I will repay, saith the Lord."*

He then said, *"Therefore if thine enemy hunger, feed him; if he thirst, give him drink . . . Be not overcome of evil, but overcome evil with good"* (Rom. 12:17-21).

The reason is simple; no Believer is morally qualified to render punishment to another. That must be left in God's Hands. Conversely, we are to always take the position, of rendering good for evil.

## THAT WHICH IS GOOD

The phrase, *"But ever follow that which is good, both among yourselves, and to all*

NOTES

*men,"* clearly spells out the direction we should follow. As well, this direction leaves no space for wiggle room. We are to render good to all men, irrespective to whom they might be, and to what they have done, at least as it lies within our power.

Of course, the Truth is, one cannot do these things, cannot be what the Lord requires us to be, without His help. Nevertheless, we are always promised that help, which will without doubt be forthcoming, if we make the effort toward carrying out that which is commanded of us. The Lord always increases Faith to those who set about on the road of Faith.

If one is to notice, He said *"Toward all men."* This means that there is not to be one standard of morals towards the Brethren and another towards the world.

Like the prohibition of fornication, abstinence from revenge is practically a new thought for the Greeks of that day, among whom feuds were frequent and undying. Regrettably, for all outside of the Lord, it is the same presently.

The Holy Spirit demands this, because the Lord conducts Himself in exactly that same manner toward the human race, and despite the fact, that most care not for Him at all, and in fact, work judiciously against Him. Nevertheless, *"The Lord is good!"*

(16) "REJOICE EVERMORE."

The Holy Spirit here through the Apostle, means exactly what He says. We are to *"rejoice evermore."* In fact, we have every reason to do such!

The Lord has saved us from eternal darkness, has given us His Holy Spirit Who abides with us unfailingly, has been so good to us, so merciful to us, so gracious to us, that our thoughts and attitudes are to always be in the realm of *"rejoicing."*

As well, even if we are having difficulties, we should rejoice in the fact that the Lord is coming soon, and that which awaits us, will see no difficulties or problems of any nature. In fact, that is in essence what the entirety of this Epistle is all about. So, rejoicing of a consequence, is always in order.

As well, rejoicing in the Lord, increases one's Faith in God, and one's trust in the Lord, for the simple reason, that it is impossible for one to rejoice and doubt at the same

NOTES

time. So, rejoicing in the Lord is an excellent prescription for discouragement, disconcertment, discontentment, and all similar things, which means that this bubbling spirit flows over into our emotions, and in fact the entirety of our being.

If in fact, all Christians obeyed this stipulation, there would be much less sickness and much less emotional disturbance.

Therefore, in these two words *"Rejoice evermore,"* we find the prescription for physical health, mental health, and spiritual health.

(17) "PRAY WITHOUT CEASING."

This admonition doesn't mean, as should be obvious, that we are to be on our knees without ceasing, but that we should be in a spirit of prayer unceasingly. In other words, we should pray about everything, which means to submit everything to the Lord for leading, guidance, and direction. In fact, it is probably in the area of prayer that the Holy Spirit helps us more so than any other manner (Rom. 8:26-27).

Considering that most Christians regrettably, don't pray at all, means that a great part of the help which the Holy Spirit can give, is in fact, not given. Most Christians do not understand the value of prayer, which means that they do not understand that this is God's Way of doing so many things for us. Without prayer, there can be no proper communion with the Lord, which means that relationship is greatly hindered. Consequently, that being the case, spiritual stagnation is the result, or worse!

Without a proper prayer life, there is no Spiritual Growth, which means that the Believer is not going much of anywhere with the Lord. To have a proper prayer life opens the door to all types of wonderful things, hence the Apostle saying, *"Pray without ceasing."*

(18) "IN EVERY THING GIVE THANKS: FOR THIS IS THE WILL OF GOD IN CHRIST JESUS CONCERNING YOU."

A final member of this triplet (rejoicing, prayer, and giving thanks) for personal development, is *"give thanks in all circumstances."* This means, that no combination of happenings can be termed *"bad"* for a Christian because of God's constant superintendence (Rom 8:28). We must always recognize that seeming aggravations are but a temporary part of a larger plan for our spiritual well-being. Out of this perspective we can always discern a cause for thanks. In fact, failure to do this is a symptom of unbelief (Rom. 1:21).

*"For this is God's Will for you in Christ Jesus"* justifies all three brief commands. This means that true victories in life are won by Christians who are joyful, prayerful, and thankful (Thomas).

NOTES

### THE GIVING OF THANKS

The phrase, *"In every thing give thanks,"* doesn't mean *"for everything,"* but rather *"in everything."*

The idea here presented by the Holy Spirit through the Apostle, has to do with negative things that come our way, which pertain to all types of circumstances and difficulties. To be sure, the Believer is definitely not immune from problems and hindrances, some being very severe. So, the idea that we can reach some type of spiritual nirvana, where there will be no more problems or difficulties, at least this side of the Resurrection, presents a false idea. Such isn't, and such is not to be!

The idea is, irrespective of the negative things which might happen to us, we are to continue to give thanks to the Lord, and for many and varied reasons.

First of all, despite the difficulties, we have so many more things which are good which are taking place in our lives, and all given to us and caused by the Lord, that the positive far, far outweighs the negative.

As well, we will find as Christians, when comparing ourselves with those in the world who do not know the Lord and in fact do not serve Him, that our lives are far more peaceful, far more productive, and far more blessed than our worldly counterparts.

Therefore, no matter what happens, we still can thank the Lord, and thank Him grandly, because He has saved us, given us Eternal Life, brought us from darkness to Light, and made us joint heirs with Himself. As well, we know that whatever this life holds, it is only temporary, and that grand and glorious things await all who have placed their trust in Christ.

### THE WILL OF GOD

The phrase, *"For this is the Will of God in Christ Jesus concerning you,"* refers to *"rejoicing evermore, praying without ceasing, and in everything giving thanks."* Knowing this is the *"Will of God"* we should be diligent in obeying these precepts.

God by the Gift of His Son has laid us under the obligation of perpetual thanksgiving. Our whole lives ought to be one continued Thank-Offering for all the Blessings of Redemption.

The short phrase, *"In Christ Jesus,"* portrays the parameters through which all of the great things of God come to us. It speaks of what Jesus did at the Cross and in His Resurrection.

### THE CROSS AND THE MIND-SET OF PAUL

If we do not properly understand the mind-set of the Apostle, then we will have an improper understanding of what he is saying. For instance, and even as we have already mentioned, when he uses the phrase as he does here *"in Christ Jesus,"* he is speaking of what Jesus did at the Cross, this great Finished Work, and everything which pertains to the Atonement. When Paul mentions Faith, he is speaking of Faith in this great Work. When he talks about Grace, it is with the understanding that Grace comes solely and completely through the Cross of Christ. In other words, the Cross made Grace possible.

The Apostle doesn't explain this every single time, because if he had, the Bible would be three feet thick.

For instance, he said, *"For Christ sent me not to baptize, but to preach the Gospel: not with wisdom of words, lest the Cross of Christ should be made of none effect"* (I Cor. 1:17).

This tells us in no uncertain terms, that the *"Cross of Christ"* is where Salvation is found, where Victory is found, where Healing is found, in other words, where everything is found as it pertains to God. So, when we read the Epistles of Paul, we should always read them with this in mind. If we do, his meaning about everything will become much more clear.

The problem is, a great part of the modern Church doesn't even believe in the Cross of Christ. And even the part which does believe in the Cross, limits it pretty well to the initial Salvation experience, not understanding at all, the part the Cross plays in our everyday living for God. In fact, there is absolutely nothing we have from the Lord, do for the Lord, or that pertains to the Lord, but that it comes totally through the Cross. The problem of the Church, is its making the Cross of Christ of noneffect, exactly as Paul states here.

The great Plan of God as it refers to Redemption, is little understood by most Christians. While those who are truly saved definitely believe in the Cross, for that's the only way they can be saved; still, the Cross, at least in the understanding of most, doesn't stand out in their thinking. It's just sort of a part the entirety of the mix concerning Christ. To be frank, I would suspect that most Christians give a great deal more thought to His Miracles than they do the Cross. In fact, the Cross is openly repudiated in many Charismatic circles, claiming that it was the worst defeat that Christianity has ever known, etc. For anyone to think such a thing, shows a total lack of knowledge as it regards Redemption and the Atonement. In fact, such thinking portrays a total misunderstanding altogether of the Plan of God regarding Redemption. To misunderstand other things is one thing; however, to misunderstand something about the Cross of Christ, is serious indeed! To be sure, everything that Christ did was of the utmost importance; however, it was the Cross and the Cross alone, which brought Redemption to dying humanity. In this great Sacrifice is our Salvation, Justification, Sanctification, Divine Healing, and in fact, prosperity and blessing of every sort. It all comes through the Cross, or it doesn't come at all!

To be what one ought to be in Christ, to receive from Christ what one ought to receive, necessitates a proper understanding of the Cross of Christ. The Believer must understand, that this is the very purpose for which Jesus came. This is the reason that God became flesh and was born of the Virgin Mary. He came to die on a Cross.

This is the reason for His Perfect Life in every respect, He must provide a Perfect Sacrifice, with the giving of His human body, which He did on the Cross. As well, His Miracles attested to the fact that He definitely was the Son of God, because as Nicodemus said, *"For no man can do these miracles that thou doest, except God be with Him"* (Jn. 3:2).

NOTES

In other words, it was not just another man dying on the Cross, it was the Son of the Living God.

Understanding and knowing that, the Believer must realize, that all that he has comes through what Christ did at the Cross. He must understand also, that the benefits of the Cross will actually never cease, and because the Shed Blood of Jesus Christ, is the seal of this Everlasting Covenant (Col. 1:14; Heb. 13:20).

Understanding that, the Believer should anchor his Faith in the Cross, which God intends, considering that this is where the price was paid, and in fact the price that was paid. The object of one's Faith is so very, very important, actually the single most important thing there is as it regards the Child of God (Gal. 6:14).

Considering that the Finished Work of Christ constitutes the parameters under which and by which the Holy Spirit works, should tell us something (Rom. 8:1-2). As Believers, we must have His help, leading, and guidance in all things. And to be sure, we definitely must have His great Power. In fact, we can have all that He has, but only according to our Faith in the Cross of Christ. He will not function otherwise!

(19) "QUENCH NOT THE SPIRIT."

As is obvious, Paul is speaking of the Holy Spirit Who abides within our hearts and lives, and is present in order to carry out the Will of God, which refers to leading and direction as it regards every single Believer. In other words, God has a perfect plan, tailor-made for each individual, from the moment they give their heart to Christ and on through the entirety of each life.

The great hindrance to that is self-will, carnality, the flesh, self-righteousness, with basically all of these designations meaning the same thing — self-will instead of God's Will.

Understanding that every single individual is different, and accordingly that God's Will for each life is different, still, many things are the same. The greatest reason for self-will or the flesh, etc., in most lives I think, is not actually intentional. While of course, it definitely would be intentional with some, I think for the most, they simply don't know God's prescribed order by which the Holy Spirit faithfully abides, and they try within their own abilities and efforts, although very religious, to do what in fact only the Holy Spirit can do; consequently, they *"quench the Spirit,"* i.e., *"which means to extinguish the Spirit."* In other words, the track on which we are going, is not the track on which He is going. He will not change, because He cannot change.

On what track is He going?

NOTES

## THE WAY OF THE SPIRIT

As I have said several times, when we as Believers think of Faith, or Grace, or Justification, or Sanctification, etc., we should at the same time think of the Cross. In fact, all of these great attributes of God, are so closely intertwined with the Cross, as to virtually make these words synonymous with the Cross. In other words, when one says *"Faith"* one is at the same time saying the *"Cross!"*

It is the identical same thing with the Holy Spirit. Of course, the Holy Spirit is not an attribute of God, He is God; nevertheless, He works so closely within the confines of the Finished Work of Christ, carries out His duties so much within the realm of that Sacrifice, adheres so totally to this which Jesus did at the Cross, that I think we would do well, when we think of the Holy Spirit that we at the same time think of the Cross.

To show how closely tied the Holy Spirit is to the Finished Work of Christ, which as I have previously stated one could even refer to as the *"Constitution of Christianity,"* before the Cross, the Holy Spirit could not come into the heart and life of the Believer to abide (Jn. 14:17). At the Cross, Jesus paid the terrible sin debt of man owed to God, which atoned for all sin, thereby wiping the slate totally and completely clean, at least for those who would place their Faith and Trust in Christ, and what He did at the Cross (Jn. 3:16; Rev. 22:17). So, the Cross and the Resurrection made it possible for the Justification process to be completed, thereby making it possible for the Holy Spirit to come into our hearts and lives and abide (Gal. 3:14).

That's the reason that every Believer should avail himself of every single aid that comes his way enabling him to learn more about the Cross of Christ. In view of that, I would strongly urge the Reader to secure all of our Teaching Series on the Cross of Christ, of which presently there are approximately 20 or more of these sets. Each Series or set, contains six cassette tapes, with about nine hours of teaching.

In fact, there is absolutely nothing in one's life that's more important than learning this great Truth, and learning all that one can learn in respect to this which is the key to all things. In fact, it is literally impossible for one to exhaust this of which Christ has done at the Cross on our behalf.

Please do not misunderstand the following; however, as Paul addressed the Churches in Galatia by saying *"O foolish Galatians"* (Gal. 3:1-4), my thoughts run parallel as it concerns most modern-day Christians. I would not place you the Reader in that category, simply because the very fact of your obtaining this Commentary tells me that you are hungry for God, and want to learn more about His Word. And if you will heed these things we're saying concerning the Cross of Christ, you will observe your life being gloriously and wondrously changed by the Power of God, in fact, a change for the better which will actually never end. In other words, it just keeps getting better and better in every capacity.

And yet so few Christians will bother to take advantage of this which is the single most important thing in their lives, with in fact, nothing else even remotely coming close to this as it regards importance.

The Way of the Cross, is the Way of the Holy Spirit, and the Way of the Holy Spirit, is the Way of the Cross. To fail to understand that, is to quench the Spirit, which means you have extinguished His efforts on your behalf, which also means you are doomed to failure just as sure as I dictate these notes. God has only one way of Victory, not five, three, or even two, only one! That one way is the Way of the Cross.

(20) "DESPISE NOT PROPHESYINGS."

Why would the Holy Spirit through the Apostle make this statement?

The purpose of the Gift of Prophecy, which is one of the nine Gifts of the Spirit (I Cor. 12:8-10), is for *"edification, exhortation, and comfort"* (I Cor. 14:3). As such, and as should be obvious, it is a great Blessing to the Church as a whole, and to individual Believers.

However, this Gift has been abused, and in fact, has probably been abused more than any other of the Gifts of the Spirit.

How?

*"Despise"* in the Greek is *"exoutheneo,"* and means *"contemptible, least esteemed, set at nought."*

Many people attempt to use (misuse) this Gift, by giving direction to people, which the Holy Spirit has never intended. This Gift, as stated, is to *"edify, exhort, and comfort."* There is nothing in those three words that lends credence to direction or the charting of a course.

While the Holy Spirit at times will definitely verify a course or direction that He has already given, He will never initiate direction or the course by this method. By that I mean the following:

Untold numbers of people have had someone to *"prophesy"* over them, giving them direction, telling them to do certain things, of which they have had no previous knowledge. As stated, the Holy Spirit at times may definitely do such, but it will only be after He has first given such direction to the individual in question.

There are many illustrations I could give, but the following will suffice:

A particular family came to Baton Rouge from a foreign country. To make the story very brief, they allowed that they had come here because an individual had prophesied over them, telling them this was the thing to do. So, they sold everything they had, and came, despite the fact that immigration laws are very strict in this capacity as it regards entrance into the United States from a foreign country.

The upshot is, they ultimately were forced to return to their native country, having pretty well lost everything they had. This is what I mean about the abuse of this gift.

Did the Lord tell this family to move to Baton Rouge? Obviously He didn't! So, they were very foolish to base their actions on this so-called *"prophesy"* which in reality was no prophesy at all, but rather something out of one's own mind.

Suffering at the hands of such, one can well understand how some would *"despise prophesying."* And yet, we must not deny

NOTES

the real and genuine simply because there are counterfeits.

(21) "PROVE ALL THINGS; HOLD FAST THAT WHICH IS GOOD."

To balance the two prohibitions, Paul stipulates that all Charismatic manifestations be tested with a view to accepting what is valid and disallowing what is not.

The mere claim to inspiration was and is not a sufficient guarantee, because inspirations were known at times to come from below as well as from above (I Cor. 12:2).

Some have found in these words of Paul an illusion to a saying of Jesus preserved by a number of Church Fathers, including Clement of Alexandria and Origen. Origen wrote, claiming these words to be from Christ, *"Be ye approved moneychangers."* To this Clement adds a thought about moneychangers, *"who reject much, but retain the good."*

Followers were thus figuratively warned against accepting false prophets.

## PROVE ALL THINGS

The phrase, *"Prove all things,"* ties in exactly with that which we have just stated regarding the previous Verse. In other words, the Apostle is saying, that when prophecies are given, they should be put to the test. And what is that test?

The first question which must be asked always, and about all things: *"Is it Scriptural?"* However, the Reader must understand, *"Just because something is not unscriptural, does not necessarily mean that it is actually Scriptural."*

By that I mean, that Satan inspires many things which aren't necessarily unscriptural, but at the same time, they definitely aren't Scriptural. Let me give an example:

When Paul and Silas were led by the Lord to go to Philippi to plant a Church, some days or weeks after arriving there, the Scriptural account gives the following:

There was a girl who was possessed by a *"spirit of divination"* who began to follow Paul and others with him, saying, *"These men are the servants of the Most High God, which shew unto us the Way of Salvation"* (Acts 16:16-17).

What this girl was saying was not unscriptural, and in fact was true; however,

NOTES

at the same time, it definitely was not Scriptural, in that the inspiration came not from the Lord but from Satan. Consequently, Paul cast this spirit out of the girl (Acts 16:18).

As we have previously stated, the Lord is not the only One Who gives inspiration, with Satan following suit oftentimes. If the Believer is close to the Lord, it will quickly become obvious as to the source of what is being offered.

The idea of *"proving all things,"* is that nothing is to be accepted at face value. In fact, and as we have often said, *"Satan is a master at making that which is not of God seem to be of God, and that which is of God, seem to be not of God!"* His business is subterfuge, chicanery, trickery, fakery, and deception. As an *"angel of light"* he is a master at this effort, and causes many Christians to go astray, by believing that which they think is of the Lord, and because it appears to be of the Lord, but actually isn't (II Cor. 11:12-15).

HOLD THE GOOD

The phrase, *"Hold fast that which is good,"* refers to the sifting process of accepting that which is definitely of the Lord, and rejecting that which isn't!

These short Verses tell us in no uncertain terms, that Satan will make every effort to counterfeit the genuine. To be sure, his counterfeits are so close to the original, that it takes one who truly loves the Lord, is truly following the Lord, is truly seeking to know and understand God's Word, to tell the difference. That's the reason it is absolutely imperative for the Believer to be totally consecrated to the Lord. Otherwise, one is vulnerable to deception by Satan, and most probably will be deceived!

As would be obvious, anything and everything that is of the Lord is *"good,"* which refers to the fact, that it is for our benefit, our edification, our comfort, and our blessing.

I am grieved when I see Believers failing to heed this which is said by the Apostle to *"prove all things,"* and thereby accepting that which is *"not good."* I know what the end result will be.

Satan doesn't lead people astray for the mere pursuit of the exercise. He does so in order that he may *"steal, kill, and destroy"* (Jn. 10:10).

If the Believer will understand his place and position in the great Finished Work of Christ, will keep his Faith in the Cross, which gives the Holy Spirit the latitude to do great things in one's life, one need never fear going astray or accepting that which is false. Once again, I come back to the premise, that the Believer must know and understand his position *"in Christ,"* which can only be understood by what Jesus did at the Cross on our behalf. This is the foundation of Christianity, the foundation of knowing Christ, the foundation of all that we are in Christ.

(22) "ABSTAIN FROM ALL APPEARANCE OF EVIL."

While the Apostle is addressing himself to that which parades itself under the guise of being *"of God,"* he is at the same time speaking of every single thing that is evil, irrespective of what it is, where it is, how it is, or who it is.

*"Abstain"* in the Greek is *"apechomai,"* and means *"to hold oneself off, to be distant."*

*"Appearance"* in the Greek is *"eidos,"* and means *"fashion, shape, sight, form, view."* It also means *"to understand that which one is observing."*

*"Evil"* in the Greek is *"poneros,"* and means *"hurtful, degeneracy, derelict, vicious, malice, grievous, harm, lewd, wicked."*

The thought is to shun evil wherever it appears. It is a sign of robust spiritual health to have a fear of and a shrinking from all that would grieve our Lord, to obediently separate oneself from whatever the Spirit reveals as wrong.

The result of shunning the appearance of evil, is a longing for the good, a hungering and thirsting after Righteousness (Mat. 5:6).

The idea is, that we shrink back not only from evil itself, but from that which even seems to be wrong. There are many things which are known to be wrong. They are positively forbidden by the Laws of Heaven, and the world concurs in the sentiment that they are wicked, i.e., *"murder, hatred, racism, drunkenness, drug addiction, etc."*

But there are also many things about which there may be some reasonable doubt. It is not easy to determine in the case what is right or wrong. The subject has not been fully examined, or the question of its morality may be so difficult to settle, that the mind may be nearly or quite balanced in regard to it.

The safe and proper rule is to lean always to the side of Holiness. In these instances, at least if this advice is followed, it may be certain that there will be no sin committed by abstaining, and there definitely may be sin committed if we indulge.

## IS IT THE WILL OF GOD?

The Christian makes a mistake when he begins to ask, *"Is this sin?"* or *"Is that sin?" "Is it right to do that?" "Is it wrong to do that?"*

Such an attitude in spirit is very similar to the Pharisees and Scribes of old, who tried to come up to the very edge of the Law, but not break the Law. For a Christian to be constantly asking these type of questions, could show that they are wanting to do something that may not be right. In other words, they are trying to see how close to the Law they can come, without actually breaking it, exactly as the Pharisees of old.

There shouldn't be an attitude in us as Believers, to want to do anything that would even remotely seem to be wrong. As Paul said, we must *"abstain from the very appearance of evil."*

The question that Christians ought always to ask is, *"Is this the Will of God for me?"* The Holy Spirit wants to lead us and guide us in all things that we do. To be sure, there are many things which may not be sin within themselves, but which may not be the Will of God for us. We should always want the Will of God, for this is the best way, the happiest way, the most joyful way, the most fulfilling way. Anything else is a poor, poor second, if that!

## A PERSONAL EXAMPLE

The year was 1958 if I remember correctly. Frances and I had just started in Evangelistic Work. Donnie was four years old.

To say the least, our beginning days were very humble. Preachers were not flocking all over us attempting to book us for meetings, and money was in very short supply, but yet this is what God had told us to do.

NOTES

The day in question was a Sunday. Actually it was early Sunday afternoon. We were having that day what was referred to then as a *"dinner-on-the-ground."* Actually, we were immediately behind the little Church, where I was then conducting a meeting.

In fact, this Church was very, very small, with only about 25 or 30 in attendance that day.

While this fellowship was taking place, I looked up to see my Uncle driving up in a brand-new Cadillac. He was the Father of my first cousin, Jerry Lee Lewis. Jerry at that particular time was vying with Elvis Presley for the number one spot in Rock-'n'-Roll.

My Uncle spotted me instantly, and walked over with a big smile on his face.

He was a tall, angular man, about 6'2".

His first words were, that is if I remember correctly, *"Jimmy, I have great news for you."* He paused for a few moments and then continued:

*"Sam Phillips has sent for you. He wants you to be the very first artist in the new Gospel line which Sun Records is beginning."*

He then went on to say, *"In two weeks you can buy a new car."* He paused again!

He looked over at my car and said, *"Son, you need a new car!"*

And he was right, the one Frances and I owned, had seen better days.

He was very excited about the news he had brought, and others were who had overheard him. To be sure, I was as well.

I opened my mouth to tell him that I was ready to go now, when the Holy Spirit within my heart said, *"No, you can't go!"*

I'm sure on my face I must have looked startled, because my Uncle stared at me for just a few moments.

When I didn't speak, he said, *"Jimmy, did you hear what I said?"*

Oh yes, I had heard him, but I had also heard the Holy Spirit.

I had already opened my mouth to tell him I was ready, when in mid thought I had to stop and say, *"Uncle Elmo, I'm sorry I can't go."*

If I remember the thoughts and words that came that day of so long ago, I began to apologize to him.

I remember him answering, and saying, *"But Jimmy, it's Gospel music, and there could be nothing wrong with that."*

He was right, there was nothing wrong with that; however, it would have been wrong for me, because the Holy Spirit had said *"No!"*

As the tears filled my eyes, I then answered him, saying, *"Uncle Elmo I know that. Please understand how grateful I am for your kindness; however, I cannot tell you why I can't go, because I don't really know myself; I just can't go."*

I'll never forget my Uncle looking at me for a few moments and saying nothing, and then finally that tall man answered and said, *"Jimmy, I believe I do understand, and I respect your answer."*

He turned and walked away, getting in that new Cadillac and driving off. I watched him disappear down the road, and then I overheard a lady nearby say:

*"Did you hear what he just did?" And then she added, "He turned down that offer!"*

I excused myself from those standing nearby, and walked in the back door to the little Church. I found a small broom and mop closet, walked into this little dusty space and closed the door.

I stood there for a period of time saying nothing, and then finally, *"Why Lord?"*

I then added, *"Why couldn't I go and take this offer? It is Gospel music, and You know how much we need the money?"*

Then the Lord spoke to my heart. To be sure, His Words were very few, saying only, *"Trust Me!"*

That's all it was, *"Trust Me!"*

However, it was enough. I stepped outside that closet, knowing that I had the Mind of God and that was all that mattered.

LOOKING BACK

As I dictate these notes on November 16th, 1999, it has been over 40 years ago since that time. To be sure, trusting the Lord that day, and ever after, has been the greatest thing I ever did.

He knew what He had in store for me. He knew what He was going to do.

To make the story very brief, He helped us to sell over 15,000,000 Recordings all over the world. We did it without signing up with any company, strictly according to what He told us to do.

NOTES

He was and is my arranger, my promoter, my distributor, in effect, my everything.

This is what I mean by having the Will of God. It's not exactly what one can do and cannot do, but rather, *"Is this the Will of God for my life?"*

(23) "AND THE VERY GOD OF PEACE SANCTIFY YOU WHOLLY; AND I PRAY GOD YOUR WHOLE SPIRIT AND SOUL AND BODY BE PRESERVED BLAMELESS UNTO THE COMING OF OUR LORD JESUS CHRIST."

In this one Verse of Scripture, Paul addresses several things:

1. Sanctification.
2. The whole man.
3. Holiness.
4. The Rapture of the Church.

SANCTIFICATION

The phrase, *"And the very God of Peace sanctify you wholly,"* presents that which only God can do.

The *"Sanctification"* of which Paul speaks here, is *"progressive Sanctification."* As we have previously explained, when the individual comes to Christ, he is immediately given a position of Sanctification, which means that the war between himself and God has been stopped, with peace declared. This comes about because of what Jesus did at the Cross, and one's Faith in that Finished Work. All sin has been washed away and atoned, and done so by the Precious Blood of Jesus Christ.

The idea is, as Paul here states the case, as the Believer has *"positional Sanctification,"* he is to now go forward in *"conditional or Progressive Sanctification."* Consequently, the *"Peace"* of which is spoken here, concerns the Peace of Progressive Sanctification.

What do we mean by that?

As we said at the beginning, only God can sanctify the individual. But yet, we Christians over and over again, fall into the trap of trying to sanctify ourselves. We trust the Lord for Salvation, but we trust ourselves for Sanctification. The sadness is, that we don't really know that we're doing this in this manner, but ignorance has never brought us victory (Gal. 3:1-3).

## HOW DOES GOD SANCTIFY US?

We are told here by Paul that the Lord definitely does sanctify us, but the great question is, how does He do this thing?

I suppose that many Christians just somehow think it is an automatic process. But yet, most don't see the results of this automatic process within their lives, and the reason is, it is not being done.

The Sanctification process of the Believer, which is the development of Righteousness and Holiness within our lives, actually, Christlikeness, is brought about totally and completely by the Holy Spirit (Rom. 8:29); however, there is a manner and a way in which He does all of this, and in fact, the only way in which this is done.

The Believer can walk in Victory, experiencing Spiritual Growth in the Lord, only by one method. That method is the Cross. Let the Reader understand, that if any other way is attempted, any other direction is tried, there will be no Sanctification. This progressive work is carried out by the Holy Spirit only according to what Jesus did at the Cross. And let us explain that:

Believers can no more sanctify themselves, than sinners can save themselves. Unfortunately, many sinners think they can save themselves, and many Christians think they can sanctify themselves. The success in either direction is zero.

The power of sin is too strong, and the flesh is too weak to carry out this which must be done. That's the reason that Jesus said, *"Watch and pray, that ye enter not into temptation: the spirit* (spirit of man) *indeed is willing, but the flesh is weak"* (Mat. 26:41).

## THE FLESH

Paul oftentimes used the term *"the flesh"* in describing this situation, actually the same word as used by Christ. What did they mean by *"flesh"*?

Without going into an involved explanation, if one will remember the following, it will explain what the flesh actually is.

The flesh is any effort we make in order to be an overcomer, or be righteous, or holy, outside of Faith in the Cross. And it doesn't really matter what it is, what type of effort it might be, or how religious it might be. If it's outside of the Cross of Christ, it must be labeled as *"the flesh"* (Rom. 8:8). It refers to self-efforts, which means the individual is not trusting Christ but rather himself. This confuses many Christians, because the things they are doing in order to bring about Sanctification and Christlikeness, are within themselves normally very spiritual things, and, therefore, very legitimate in their own right. So, inasmuch as what is being done is good, whatever it might be, such as fasting, witnessing, etc., it is automatically thought that such constitutes the trusting of Christ.

It doesn't!

## WHAT DOES IT MEAN TO TRUST CHRIST?

Almost every Christian in the world, that is if they are truly saved, concludes themselves as *"trusting Christ."* And of course, in a sense they are. One cannot be saved unless one is truly trusting Christ.

However, trusting Christ for Salvation, is totally different than trusting Christ for Sanctification. In fact, most Christians while truly trusting Christ as it regards their Salvation, are in fact, not trusting Him as it regards their Sanctification. The Truth is, most Christians don't have the slightest idea as to what trusting Christ actually means as it refers to one's Sanctification. If they've heard anything about it at all, it's only been something that nebulous, which gives them no explanation whatsoever.

Trusting Christ for Sanctification requires an even greater involvement, a greater understanding, actually, a far greater understanding of the Finished Work of Christ, than it does regarding one's initial Salvation experience. To be frank, the sinner doesn't have to understand much of anything as it regards being saved, only that he believes in Christ and what Christ did at the Cross, and accepts the Lord as Saviour. That's about it! The Holy Spirit doesn't require more, because it's actually impossible for the unsaved individual to understand more than that. In fact, the Holy Spirit has to help him understand even that.

However, once the person comes to Christ, the Lord expects the Believer to study the Word, to know the Word, in fact, to make the Word a part of his everyday life. To say it another way, the Holy Spirit expects us to know a little something about what we have in Christ.

THAT WHICH YOU MUST KNOW

Paul gave the explanation of what the Believer is in Christ in the Sixth Chapter of Romans. Even though the entirety of this Chapter addresses itself to this all-important subject, Verses 1-6 give the ingredients.

First of all, when the believing sinner comes to Christ, he is literally *"Baptized into His* (Christ's) *Death"* (Rom. 6:3).

This is not speaking of Water Baptism, but rather the Crucifixion of Christ. I have used the word *"literally,"* because in the Mind of God that's exactly what it is.

When Jesus died on the Cross, He died as our Substitute and our Representative Man. It was all done for us and not at all for Himself. When He died, He paid the terrible sin debt owed by man to God, thereby, atoning for all sin. Inasmuch as sin is Satan's legal claim upon humanity, the Evil One lost his claim at that point, at least for those who will believe (Jn. 3:16).

Upon simple Faith in this which Christ did, the Lord reckons the individual as literally being Baptized into the Death of Christ.

The Crucifixion of Christ, which of course exhibits His Death, satisfied all the claims of God against sinful, wicked humanity. It wiped the slate clean, leaving nothing owing by the believing sinner. It is all in Christ. In other words, the Lord as our Representative Man did for us what we could not do for ourselves. As one African said, *"I should have hung there myself, but He took my place."*

That's exactly what happened! He took our place.

Faith in Him, and what He did there, reckons in the Eyes and Mind of God all His benefits to accrue to me and to you. In other words, the Lord now looks at me as absolutely perfect, simply because of what Christ has done, and because the debt has been paid.

Christ was then buried (placed in a tomb) and this is very important also (Rom. 6:4). This Fourth Verse says that *"We are buried with Him by Baptism into Death."* Once again, we are not speaking of Water Baptism, but rather the actual, literal Death and Burial of Christ.

NOTES

The Burial of Christ is important, and more particularly, our being buried with Him, simply because it refers to all the past life, past iniquities, sins, depravity, rebellion against God, ad nauseam!

Once again, Christ did all of this as our Substitute and our Representative Man.

However, Christ did not stay in the tomb, but *"was raised up from the dead by the Glory of the Father"* (Rom. 6:4).

When He was raised from the dead, the Scripture says, *"Even so we also,"* which puts us in the same category as His Death and Burial. In other words, when He was raised from the dead, we were in Him, and were raised from the dead as well, to *"walk in newness of life."* We were *"planted together in the likeness of His Death, and we also* (are) *in the likeness of His Resurrection"* (Rom. 6:4-5).

Now Paul says, *"Knowing this* (that which God expects us to know, even as I have stated), *that our old man* (what we once were before Christ) *is crucified with Him, that the body of sin might be destroyed* (all the old life is gone and past), *that henceforth we should not serve sin"* (Rom. 6:6).

This Sixth Verse proclaims our Sanctification.

The Believer is to know these things we have just said, and in knowing them, is to place his Faith in this which has been done, which carries over even unto the present, and actually will carry forth forever. This is called *"The Finished Work of Christ."* Inasmuch as it is a Finished Work, that means that we do not have to do anything else, and in fact, if we attempt to do anything else to bring forth Sanctification (Victory), we are in effect insulting Christ. That should be obvious! (Heb. 9:28).

All we have to do is understand this, place our Faith in this, knowing that the Victory has already been won in totality, and then the Holy Spirit will come in to work for us and do the things which only He can do, in bringing about Sanctification and Christlikeness.

THE HOLY SPIRIT

As we said at the beginning of this statement respecting Sanctification, the Holy Spirit is the only One Who can carry out this process. This is what Paul says so graphically in Romans, Chapter 8.

He tells us, *"There is therefore now no condemnation to them which are in Christ Jesus* (we've just explained that to you), *who walk not after the flesh* (by one's own efforts), *but after the Spirit* (the Holy Spirit)."

He then said, *"For the Law* (this is a Law of God which cannot be broken) *of the Spirit* (the Law by which the Holy Spirit works) *of Life* (power which gives us Victory) *in Christ Jesus* (meaning that this Law is actually the Finished Work of Christ) *hath made me free from the Law of sin and death"* (Rom. 8:1-2).

These two Scriptures, plus the balance of the Eighth Chapter of Romans, plainly tell us, the manner in which the Holy Spirit works within our hearts and lives. As we've already stated, He always works within the boundaries of what Christ did at the Cross, as it refers to the Atonement. Inasmuch as Jesus there paid it all, the Holy Spirit will not honor our own personal efforts in this regard. In other words, He will not help us to make the attempt to sanctify ourselves. And to be sure, an attempt is all it's going to be, because no Victory will be achieved in this way (Rom. 4:4).

All the Holy Spirit wants you to do, is to simply understand these things we have just taught you regarding what Jesus did for you at the Cross and in His Resurrection. He wants you to know and understand your part in all of this, even as we have attempted to show you in very simple terms.

Once you know this, you are to place your Faith in this, and in nothing else. That's exactly what Paul was talking about when he said, *"Abraham believed God, and it was counted unto him for Righteousness"* (Rom. 4:3).

Believe what?

Believed that God would send a Redeemer into this world in order to save mankind, and would do so, by dying for lost humanity (Gen. 22:13-14). Actually, Abraham knew that God would give His Son to bring this thing about, and he knew that to do so, God would have to become Man, hence his own personal involvement in this in bringing forth the Promised Seed, but he didn't know that Christ would die on a Cross (Rom. 4:18). The knowledge of the Cross would be given to Moses (Num., Chpt. 21).

Once you the Believer put your Faith in the Cross of Christ, exactly as Abraham did,

NOTES

believing that in this, you will have Victory over every power of darkness, the Holy Spirit will then help you, and in fact, this is the only way He will help you. He works strictly, even as we've said, from your Faith respecting the Finished Work of Christ.

If we attempt to do anything else to bring about this Victory, as more than likely all of us have done at one time or the other, we only succeed in *"frustrating the Grace of God"* (Gal. 2:20-21).

THE GRACE OF GOD

The Grace of God is something that every Believer must have constantly. In fact, we are *"saved by Grace through Faith"* (Eph. 2:8).

So, what is the Grace of God?

The Grace of God is simply the means by which the Goodness of God is extended to those who are not worthy of such. In fact, the qualifications for being a recipient of the Grace of God, is to be disqualified, and know it. In other words, we do not merit these good things He gives us, cannot merit them, and in fact will never be able to merit them. The very moment we attempt to do something to bring about our Sanctification, other than having Faith in the Cross of Christ, we are in essence trying to earn this which God gives, which then says that we do merit it, which stops the Grace of God. That's why Paul said, *"Now to him that worketh* (tries to earn something from God) *is the reward not reckoned of Grace, but of debt* (in other words, God owes this to me because of some type of work I have done)" (Rom. 4:4).

God will not respond favorably to such, and in fact, such an effort on our part angers Him (Rom. 8:8).

Most Christians have precious little of the Grace of God working in their lives, simply because they don't know these things of which we are attempting to bring to you; therefore, they are doing the very thing they shouldn't do, which frustrates the Grace of God, which means that they're not going to receive this which they desire, i.e., *"Victory!"*

The only way to keep the Grace of God coming to you the Believer, is to continue to have Faith in the Cross of Christ. God has always had Grace. He doesn't have more

Grace under the New Covenant than He did under the Old Covenant.

The difference is, due to what Jesus did at the Cross, the Grace of God can flow much more freely to believing sinners and to Christians than before the Cross. In other words, the Cross opened the door to a free-flowing of the Grace of God, at least to those who will believe. In fact, the Cross did more than just open the door, it kicked the thing down, leaving the great Word, *"Whosoever will, let him take the Water of Life freely"* (Rev. 22:17).

What I'm teaching you here can change your life, and change it in such a way that it will almost be as though you are *"Born-Again!"* If you will heed the Word of God, and as we have attempted to explain it to you, and believe with all your heart, you will see a change in your life, that is so glorious and wonderful, that it will absolutely defy description. It is tragic when so many Christians are living so far below their Spiritual privileges in Christ. And please believe me, I know what that means.

I have walked this path, exactly as Paul did in Romans, Chapter 7. I know what it is to cry, *"O wretched man that I am, Who shall deliver me from the body of this death?"* (Rom. 7:24). I know what it is to try, and to try so hard, and still fail. And I also know what Paul said, *"The Law of the Spirit of Life in Christ Jesus hath made me free from the Law of sin and death"* (Rom. 8:2).

I sought the Lord until this answer came, and when it came, it totally revolutionized my life. In fact, this Revelation, this Victory, this great Word of God, just keeps enlarging day-by-day. It will do the same for you!

## DOESN'T THE CHURCH KNOW THIS?

The Truth is, the far greater majority of the Church doesn't know this. In the last several decades, the Church has been moved so far away from the Cross, that it anymore little knows its privileges in Christ. We have been inundated with teaching on Faith in the last few years, but sadly and regrettably, it has not been Faith in the Cross, but Faith in something else entirely. To prove my point think carefully about the following:

The Faith which has been taught in the last several decades, has been Faith that reaps things, i.e., *"money!"* The Truth is, no one received any money from this kind of Faith, except the Preachers. In fact, it has just about wrecked the Church. The sadness is, it doesn't know that it's wrecked, thinking rather that it is *"rich, and increased with goods, and has need of nothing."* It doesn't know that in reality it is *"wretched, miserable, poor, blind, and naked"* (Rev. 3:17).

Faith in the Cross of Christ generates Righteousness and Holiness, i.e., *"Christlikeness,"* in the heart and life of the Believer, which is the intention and work of the Holy Spirit. I would trust that the Reader can see the vast difference.

The Church has heard more about Faith in the last several decades, than it has in the entirety of its previous existence put together; however, it has been Faith in the wrong thing, and to be sure, if it's not Faith in the Cross of Christ, it is wrong, irrespective of its object.

The terrible Truth is, that the modern Church, at least for the most part, does not know how to have Victory, to walk in Victory, or anything about Victory. The failure rate among Preachers is absolutely awful, which means that it is even worse as it regards the Laity.

Yes, there definitely are exceptions to this, but as a whole, it is exactly as I'm saying.

The only remedy is the Cross of Christ! And when I say the only remedy, I mean the only remedy. There is no other, and because there doesn't need to be another.

## REPETITION

I'm sure the Reader by now can see that I have taken and do take every opportunity at my disposal in comment on the Scriptures, to portray the Cross of Christ. I am doing this deliberately, even pushing it to the limit, even to the point of saying the same thing over and over again in different ways. I'm doing this simply because, this of which we are teaching, is the single most important thing there is to you the Believer. As Salvation is the single most important thing for the unredeemed, Sanctification is the most important thing for those who know Christ.

The results of not knowing this of which we speak, is a repeat of Romans, Chapter 7. As someone has well said, *"If we do not heed the lessons of history, we are apt to repeat them."*

NOTES

That's the reason that I have gone into detail concerning this all-important subject, attempting to address it from every angle I can. Sometimes it is hard to understand spiritual things, even by Christians. Satan takes every opportunity to deceive us, and to hinder us from hearing and understanding the Truth. But if the heart is sincere before God, these Truths which we have given and are giving to you, will be understood, because the Holy Spirit will see to it that they are understood.

The point I wish to make is this:

If in the study of this material, you feel that we're being overly repetitive, and it tends to be of little interest to you, then I would have to say that you little understand this of which we are saying. If you properly understand it, meaning it has been revealed to your heart by the Holy Spirit, even as all Truth must be revealed, then you will read what we say with great joy, and in fact, will not be able to get enough of this *"Truth"* which will make you free (Jn. 8:32).

And please allow me to warn all who read these words:

To hear this Truth and to reject it, will not leave the person as they have been. To reject the Light which God gives, and this definitely is Light, and I actually believe the greatest Light of all, will mean not only losing this which you could have had, but also what little you do have. One might say that is a Law of the Word of God (Mat. 25:29).

## SPIRIT, SOUL, AND BODY

The phrase, *"And I pray God your whole spirit and soul and body,"* proclaims the make-up of the whole man.

From this Passage and others similar, we know that man was created spirit, soul, and body. Actually the true person, which is incidentally eternal, is the spirit and the soul. The body, which Paul describes as a tent or tabernacle, is actually a covering for the true person (II Cor. 5:1). However, this is not meant to say that the body is insignificant even though it is the weakest link of man's triune being. That will be rectified in the coming Resurrection, when the body will be redeemed, i.e., *"changed into a body of immortality"* (Rom. 8:23; I Cor. 15:51-57).

NOTES

The triune part of man, or *"parts"* one might say works in harmony and according to the following:

1. The spirit of man: This part of man deals with the spirit world. In fact, all true worship of God must come from this part of man. Jesus said, *"God is a Spirit: and they that worship Him must worship Him in spirit* (by their human spirit as moved upon by the Holy Spirit) *and in Truth* (according to the Truth of the Word of God)" (Jn. 4:24). Unsaved man cannot worship God in any capacity, because he is spiritually dead. He must be Born-Again in order to have communion with his Maker (Jn. 3:3).

The spirit and the soul of man are different. While both are immortal, the spirit of man is made up of the intellect, will, mind, and conscience. In other words, the spirit is the part of man which *"knows"* (I Cor. 2:11). The soul of man concerns passions and feelings (Job 14:22).

2. The soul: The soul of man is the person or personality, and that which addresses itself through the physical body, hence man being called *"a living soul"* (Gen. 2:7).

One can say that the soul is the part of man which *"feels,"* hence the passions of a man (Job 14:22).

3. The physical body: The physical body which harbors the five senses, addresses itself to the world. As stated, it is the tent or tabernacle of the soul and the spirit. Whereas the soul and the spirit are immortal (will never die), the physical body is very much mortal, and made that way because of original sin. As Paul said, this present physical body is *"dissolving"* (II Cor. 5:1). In the Resurrection it will be given glorified form, which will again make it immortal, as before the Fall.

The physical body being the weakest link in this three part chain one might say, of spirit, soul, and body, it is the part of man through which Satan attempts to steal, kill, and destroy (Jn. 10:10). However, the physical body is not necessarily wicked within itself or necessarily holy. In fact it is neutral. But being weak, it presents the greatest problem to the being of man. In fact, the Sanctification of the physical body, which makes it possible for it to yield in all senses to Righteousness, can be made so only by the Holy

Spirit (Rom. 6:13; 8:1-5).

THE DOMINION OF MAN

One can say, I think, without fear of contradiction, that when God created man, man was His highest form of creation, even higher than the Angels.

Psalms 8:4-6 says, *"What is man that You are mindful of him? And the son of man, that You visit him?*

*"For You have made him a little lower than the angels, and have crowned him with glory and honor.*

*"You made him to have dominion over the works of Your hands, and have put all things under his feet."*

Incidentally, the Hebrew word translated *"angels"* in Psalms 8:5 is *"Elohim,"* which should have been translated *"God"* or *"Godhead."* This means that God originally created man even higher than the Angels.

However, Adam fell because of sin, and was made subject to death, and all that death entails — the specimen of humanity which we presently see. But Christ, as the Last Adam, has redeemed man from this fallen position, and has raised us up to sit with Him in Heavenly Places (Eph. 2:6-7; 3:8-11).

THE WHOLE MAN

Paul's statement here concerning the Sanctification of the *"spirit and soul and body,"* shoots down the theory propagated by some, that the soul and the spirit are saved but not the body, or as taught by some, the spirit is saved and not the soul and the body, which are being saved, etc. None of that is correct.

When an individual sins, the entirety of man sins, spirit, soul, and body. When a person is saved, the entirety of the individual is saved, spirit, soul, and body. As well, the Sanctification process, as is glaringly evident here, involves equally, spirit, soul, and body, hence the Holy Spirit using the words through Paul, *"wholly,"* and *"whole."*

BLAMELESS

The phrase, *"Be preserved blameless,"* presents this cleansing as reaching every part of man's nature: his affections, his will, his imagination, the springs of his motive-life. His body is included as the temple of the Holy Spirit (I Cor. 6:19) and as the vehicle and instrument of personal life (Rom. 6:12-13, 19).

NOTES

As we have stated, there is no way that man can bring about this process within his own abilities, not even the Godliest among us. Paul couldn't do it, even as the Seventh Chapter of Romans bears out.

As well, no Church can do this thing, no set of rules and regulations, not even manifestations of the Holy Spirit, as grand and glorious as they might be.

The only way the Sanctification process can work in the heart and life of the Believer, is by Faith in what Jesus did at the Cross and in His Resurrection. The Believer as we have said repeatedly, is to have Faith in that, and I speak of the Finished Work of Christ, His great Sacrificial Offering of Himself, through which the Holy Spirit works.

As the sinner believed Christ as it regards the initial Salvation experience, the Believer is to continue to put and keep his Faith in that great Finished Work, which enables the Holy Spirit to carry out the task of perfecting Christlikeness in our hearts and lives. We use the term *"Sanctification process,"* because it definitely is a process.

This means that what is to be done, is not done overnight, which means it's not done quickly.

WHY IS SANCTIFICATION NOT A QUICK PROCESS?

That Sanctification is a process, which within itself refers to a time span, is not the fault of the Holy Spirit, but rather the individual.

As we've already stated, the weakest link in this process is the human body, and that's why the process takes as long as it does. Once again, we go back to the Words of Christ, *"The spirit* (spirit of man) *indeed is willing, but the flesh is weak"* (Mat. 26:41).

The process is slowed up dramatically so, and even stopped altogether or near so, by the Believer not understanding the manner in which the process is to work. In fact, this is the biggest cause of all types of problems in the heart and life of the Believer.

Even when the Believer knows and understands the process according to Romans, Chapters 6 and 8, due to the weakness of the flesh, there are still difficulties. That's the reason that Jesus told us that the Cross had to be taken up *"daily"* in our following of Him (Lk. 9:23-24). It is as if Faith has to be renewed even on a daily basis in the Finished Work of Christ.

Why does the Lord demand such on a *"daily"* basis?

The self-will and pride factors in human beings, even the Godliest, are such an ever present danger, that if a daily reminder is not enjoined regarding our total dependence on what Christ did at the Cross, we will quickly lose sight of the Source of our life and victory in Christ.

When Jesus spoke of Himself as being *"meek and lowly in heart,"* He was striking at the very heart of the problem (Mat. 11:28-30). Of course, it was not a problem with Him at all, simply because He was *"meek and lowly"* at all times. Unfortunately, none of us can say that about ourselves, and because it would not be true about ourselves. But yet, this is that toward which we must strive, and which is the very heart of the Sanctification matter.

WHAT DOES IT MEAN TO BE BLAMELESS?

First of all, the world and even the Church has its own definition and criteria as it regards being *"blameless"*; however, the Church's criteria often is not the same as that of God's.

To be blameless before God, which is what the Spirit through Paul is here addressing, is actually twofold:

1. It refers to putting total dependence in what Jesus did at the Cross, understanding that we cannot make ourselves blameless. This is true Faith, because the object of such Faith is as it ought to be — the Cross of Christ. The Scripture says, *"Abraham believed God, and God counted it to him for Righteousness,"* which can be translated into *"blamelessness"* (Rom. 4:3).

This means that Abraham received this *"blamelessness"* by Faith, which refers to his Faith in the coming Redeemer, and what He would do in His Death and Resurrection to deliver humanity and not at all by works of any nature.

2. While the above is actually the *"blamelessness"* which God recognizes, and does not denote spiritual perfection; still, this Faith — Faith in the Finished Work of Christ — will ultimately play out to blamelessness in our everyday walk before God, which is of course, the intention of the Spirit.

While the Bible does not teach sinless perfection, it does teach that sin will not have dominion over the Believer, that is, if the Believer has as the true object of his Faith, the Finished Work of Christ (Rom. 6:14).

NOTES

THE RAPTURE OF THE CHURCH

The phrase, *"Unto the Coming of our Lord Jesus Christ,"* refers to the Rapture. At that time, every Saint of God will be instantly changed by the Power of God, all being given a Glorified Body (I Cor. 15:51-57).

The implication of this last phrase is strong indeed! It refers to the fact, that the individual must be continuing in the Faith up until the time of death or the Rapture, in order to be saved. This shoots down the erroneous doctrine of unconditional eternal security.

The entire basis of Salvation is predicated on one's Faith and Trust in Christ. If one stops trusting Christ, one forfeits one's Salvation. It cannot be any other way.

While Salvation is definitely not based on the degree of our victorious walk or the lack of such, it definitely is based on our Faith in Christ, and actually our continued Faith in Christ. The Faith that one had in Christ ten years ago, or even last year, will not suffice for the present. Faith is to continue until the *"Coming of the Lord,"* which it surely shall if one dies in the Lord, which Paul has already addressed.

(24) "FAITHFUL IS HE THAT CALLETH YOU, WHO ALSO WILL DO IT."

One who asks God for something can anticipate the fulfillment of his request because of God's character: *"The One Who called you is faithful."* He Who issues an effectual call can be absolutely relied on to carry out His call, including among other things the Sanctification and preservation spoken of in the previous Verse. Faithfulness is a characteristic of God, which means you can depend on Him to do what He has said that He will do.

However, there is a part that man plays, in having Faith in God relative to what has been spoken.

## GOD IS FAITHFUL

The phrase, *"Faithful is He that calleth you,"* refers to the fact that one can be doubly assured that God will do exactly what He has said He will do, if man will only have Faith in that which the Lord has done on man's behalf. The Lord doesn't require much from us. He requires no works whatsoever, no deeds whatsoever, no particular acts whatsoever. He only requires Faith in Him, and more particularly, in what Jesus did at the Cross.

I stress this point, simply because the problem is never God as should be obvious, but always man. God is faithful, and it is up to us to be faithful.

## HOW CAN MAN BE FAITHFUL?

The faithfulness demanded on the part of man, presents itself as a simple situation. It is not difficult nor complex. It is only that man have Faith in Christ, and more particularly, what Christ did at the Cross and in His Resurrection. As well, his Faith must remain in the Cross, understanding that this is the Source, this which Jesus has done on our behalf and for us, of all blessings.

That's all that God requires, and if man does this, man is deemed to be faithful.

However, Satan fights this as he fights nothing else. In fact, every attack by Satan against the individual Believer, whether it's in the realm of the physical, the financial, the domestical, the mental, or the spiritual, is for one purpose only, and that is to destroy our Faith, or at least seriously weaken our Faith. And when we say *"our Faith,"* we are speaking of Faith in the Finished Work of Christ.

God is faithful, if we will be faithful in this of which we have just stated.

## THE CALL

The Lord has called us from something (spiritual darkness), to something (spiritual Light). In this Call to the Light, which is Christ Jesus, He has called us as well to be Holy, i.e., *"Sanctified!"* We must remember this.

NOTES

The Lord saved us, not merely that we not be eternally lost, but that we should be made into the Image of the Heavenly (Rom. 8:29; I Cor. 15:49; Col. 3:10). We are to be Christlike.

Consequently, this is what the Holy Spirit works toward constantly in our lives, and that which He will do, that is if we cooperate with Him respecting our Faith, etc.

## THE HOLY SPIRIT WILL DO IT

The phrase, *"Who also will do it,"* refers to the fact that it will be done if we cooperate with Him.

This Sanctification does not rest in man's powers, struggles, achievements, or even his consecration of himself. It is God *"Who will do it."* And this assurance is based upon the Character of God. He is faithful. He will do what He says He will do, and His purpose in calling men is that they may be holy (Eph. 1:4; I Thess. 2:12; 4:3, 7; II Thess. 2:13-14).

So, if we cooperate with the Holy Spirit, in the realm of placing our Faith in the Finished Work of Christ as it regards this all-important Work in our lives, we can be assured the Holy Spirit will sanctify us, which means we will be *"blameless"* in the sight of God. It really doesn't matter what our personality quirks might be, what other weaknesses there might be, what difficulties or detriments there might be. Irrespective, the Holy Spirit can definitely carry out what is needed to be done, and bring all to a successful, victorious conclusion.

But again, I emphasize that He does not do this automatically, and that's what confuses many Christians. They think it's just automatically done. It's not!

And then again, when Believers are Baptized with the Holy Spirit with the evidence of speaking with other Tongues, many of these think, as I once thought, this guarantees the process. Again, it doesn't!

While the Baptism with the Holy Spirit definitely does give the Spirit of God greater access to the Believer, still, Faith in the Cross which is demanded of every Believer, continues to be demanded. Irrespective of Gifts from God, and how glorious and wonderful they might be, and irrespective as to how much they might help us, still, Faith in the

Finished Work of Christ is never placed on hold. It is demanded of all, and at all times.

If the Spirit Baptized Believer doesn't exhibit proper Faith in the Cross of Christ, he will experience failure just as surely as the Believer who is not Spirit Baptized.

This of which we speak, Faith in the Sacrificial Offering of Christ, is demanded at all times, and is demanded of everyone. This is the very bedrock, the foundation, the center, and circumference of all that God has done for us through Jesus Christ. This is the very reason why He came. To redeem mankind, Salvation could not be spoken into existence. The price had to be paid, and that price was the shedding of His Own Precious Blood on the Cross of Calvary. That's where Satan was totally defeated, and defeated by Christ settling the sin debt owed to God, which atoned for all sin, and thereby destroyed Satan's legal right to hold man in captivity. Sin is the legal claim that Satan has on humanity, but with sin removed, which Jesus did at the Cross, Satan has no more claim.

So, everything was done there for us, and it was all done because of us. In other words, the very reason that Jesus Christ came to this world, was to die on a Cross, and liberate fallen humanity. That's the only way it could be done, at least the only way that we know of as human beings. This we do know, this is the way that God did do this great thing!

## THE PROBLEM WITH MODERN CHRISTIANS

Most Christians don't have the slightest idea as to the great significance of the Cross of Christ. These things we've been saying for the last several pages, are totally foreign to most modern Believers. It's not taught behind most pulpits; consequently, it is not believed, or even known or understood by most Christians. Consequently, Satan has been very successful in steering Christians away from their true foundation to other things, which can never bring victory.

Everything is in the Cross! And when I say everything, I mean everything! All of history strained toward the Cross or strains back to the Cross. The Cross of Christ, which of course also presupposes His Resurrection and even His Exaltation, is the intersection

NOTES

of humanity. Everything converges on the Cross. This is the Plan of God, even as it begins in Genesis, Chapter 4 with Abel offering up the Sacrificial Lamb, which was symbolic of The Lamb of God Who was to come (Jn. 1:29).

While all Christians believe in the Cross, at least if they are a true Christian, most don't have the slightest idea as to the part it plays in the entirety of their Christian experience. In fact, they park the Cross at their initial Salvation experience, and then go on to other things. The trouble with that is, there are no other things.

The Cross is the treasure house of God's store and blessings for the whole of humanity.

Under the old economy of God, the only thing that made it possible for man to approach God, was the blood that was applied to the Mercy Seat of the Ark of the Covenant, situated in the Holy of Holies of the Tabernacle or Temple. That was Israel's Salvation and victory. Everything, all the Blessings, all the miracles, all the protection, all the good things, all centered up totally and completely on the Blood that was poured out upon that Mercy Seat.

What does the Reader think that this Blood represented?

The Blood came from the slain Lamb, which was a symbol or a type of the Son of God Who was to come.

If that in type was Israel's center of communion with God, surely we can understand that the Cross of Christ, of which these other things were but symbols, is the center of all that we have and are in Christ presently (Jn. 3:16; Rom. 3:26; 5:8; 6:2-6; 8:1-2, 11; 10:9-10, 13; I Cor. 1:18; 2:2; Gal. 6:14).

(25) "BRETHREN, PRAY FOR US."

The great Apostle was ever humbly conscious of his own weakness in himself (I Cor. 2:1-5) and his need for supernatural assistance (Rom. 15:30; Eph. 6:19; Phil. 1:19; Col. 4:3). The request reinforced mutual fellowship and confidence. It also serves as a reminder to us to pray habitually for our spiritual leaders.

Paul was always conscious that the Work of God must be done through a united body of Believers with each contributing the Gifts which the Holy Spirit distributes as He wills (I Cor. 12:11).

NOTES

As a Minister of the Gospel, the Lord has called me for a particular task. But yet, I cannot do this thing, unless I have the help of fellow Believers. I must have their prayers and I must have their financial support, at least for the type of Ministry God has called us to carry out.

Of the two, prayer and financial support, the prayer is by far the most important. The struggle is always a spiritual struggle. While other struggles may commence, it is always because of the spiritual struggle, which can only be addressed in prayer and by having Faith in God. So, that's the reason that I plead with all Believers over whom we might have even some small influence. Pray for us.

(26) "GREET ALL THE BRETHREN WITH AN HOLY KISS."

If it is to be noticed, the Apostle said *"an holy kiss."* It is to be remembered that Judas gave Christ a kiss, but it definitely was not holy.

A kiss on the cheek was an Eastern custom of those days. Our custom now, is to shake hands or to embrace.

This has to do with the Family of God. The moment a person comes to Christ, they enter into this great Family, all because of the bond ties of Jesus Christ. He has made us *"one!"* It is the greatest Family in the world, despite the problems and difficulties.

(27) "I CHARGE YOU BY THE LORD THAT THIS EPISTLE BE READ UNTO ALL THE HOLY BRETHREN."

Very probably Paul sensed the far-reaching import of the teaching of this Epistle and its binding authority as part of the Canon of Scripture (I Cor. 14:37). Whatever the case, this charge has implications of Divine punishment for failure to comply. The first recipients of the Letter, probably the Church Leaders, were bound under oath *"to have this Letter read to all the Brothers."*

Obviously it was to be read aloud. Under restrictions of limited educational privilege, not all participants then in Christian circles were able to read for themselves. The further limitation of insufficient copies and expense of writing materials prohibited distribution to all.

The only solution was to give the Epistle a place in public worship alongside the Old Testament Scripture, the consequence of which would eventually be recognition of its authority, as an inspired Epistle or Book, in which it was, and was included in the Canon of Scripture, which we now know as the *"New Testament."*

## A CHARGE

The phrase, *"I charge you by the Lord,"* in effect says in the Greek, *"I put you under oath by the Lord."* It is equivalent to binding a person by an oath. This is in essence a military command, and is meant to be obeyed.

The phrase *"by the Lord,"* not only proclaims the significance of what is being said, but as well implies, that the Holy Spirit had told Paul to do this thing — demand that this Epistle be read to *"all the Holy Brethren."*

As well, the Reader must understand, that this charge not only included the Thessalonians, but every single Believer and for all time. Also, it extends to every other Book in the Bible, and in fact the entirety of the Word of God. This must be understood!

In those days, as stated, all did not have the privilege of being able to read, with education being limited; however, while that problem still exists in some measure presently, it is only in small measure. Most people now can read. Consequently, as a Believer you must read the Bible. You must read it with an open heart, an open spirit, with a thirsty soul. As well, it must be read habitually, even on a daily basis.

Jesus said, *"Man shall not live by bread alone, but by every Word that proceedeth out of the Mouth of God"* (Mat. 4:4).

Notice that He said, *"every Word that proceedeth out of the Mouth of God,"* which includes the entirety of the Bible. That means that every single part of the Bible is necessary, and should be given equal attention.

It also means, that as much as we guarantee ourselves a daily supply of physical bread, we are to treat the Word of God in the same manner as it regards our spiritual man. In other words, if we're going to partake of physical food each day, we definitely must partake of the Word of God each day as well.

I suppose I have read the Bible completely through nearly 50 times or more. There is no way that I have proper vocabulary to express my love for the Word of God. In fact, every single Victory which has been brought my way by the Lord, has without exception, come through the Word of God.

It is absolutely impossible to exhaust the Word, inasmuch, as it is the Word of God. This means one might say, that it is in effect a *"living thing!"* Inasmuch as it is that, it is totally unlike any of the world's literature, historical narratives, novels, or anything else put in written form. The Bible, which is the Word of God, is unique within itself.

## THIS EPISTLE

The phrase, *"That this Epistle be read,"* was demanded for many and obvious reasons. First of all, it is the Word of God; second, it was desperately needed by all the hearers.

The method in those days, was for one to stand in front of the people, and read aloud the article or item in question. During the course of the reading, people were allowed to interrupt and ask questions, if they so desired. Consequently, the reading of the Epistle would not only have answered many questions, but would have engaged the listeners into a learning process, which was the intention of the Holy Spirit all along.

On the day this Epistle arrived, and it is not known as to who delivered it, I know it was warmly received by the Elders at Thessalonica. The Church was new and the converts as well; consequently, they were desirous of learning all they could about the Lord, and there was no greater Teacher than the Apostle Paul.

At the earliest convenience, the people were called together, with the news no doubt buzzing that an Epistle had been received from Paul.

As the crowd, and it was probably small, gathered round the one who had been selected to read the Epistle, there was anticipation in the air. You could feel it in the very excitement of the people. What would the great Apostle say to them?

Even though they could not have known it then, but still the fact remains, that the day or night that this Brother stood before them to read this Letter, he was holding in his hand the very first Epistle of the New Covenant. The significance of this moment was of such import as to defy all description.

NOTES

As the individual who is to read the Text unfolds the Scroll, and begins to read, *"Paul, and Silvanus, and Timotheus, unto the Church of the Thessalonians, which is in God the Father and in the Lord Jesus Christ,"* he was reading the first Words ever penned regarding all that Jesus did respecting man's Salvation, as it pertains to the great Work and Plan of God. As well, this was the first Church to which an Epistle would be sent.

The world would not have noticed this event, and Rome even if it had known of this particular time, would have given it no notice at all; however, in the eyes of God, Whose eyes alone really matter, this was the single most important thing happening in the world of that day.

As this man (or woman) began to read, I can imagine a holy hush as it settled over the ones who had gathered. They could sense it was something special. Every word was savored, relished, and digested. I know that they sensed the Presence of God, whether they knew and understood the significance of this moment or not.

If this was done at evening, I suspect that it was the early morning hours before they broke up. They would have discussed the Text, asking questions, even stopping to pray about certain phrases, wanting the exact meaning, and the Holy Spirit would not have disappointed them.

When they would have left that night, that is if it was night, they would have left refreshed, encouraged, strengthened, and lifted up. They had heard the Word of God, and it had been such a blessing to their souls.

Those who had questions in their minds regarding the passing of loved ones, as to what would happen to them in the coming Rapture, now had their questions answered. There was a deep peace that filled their souls as a result of what the Holy Spirit through the Apostle had said.

But is it any different now! The Word of God continues to have the same effect. It blesses, it strengthens, it encourages! So, we continue in the long train from these Thessalonians.

## HOLY BRETHREN

The phrase, *"Unto all the Holy Brethren,"* presents that which is very interesting.

It is significant that Paul says *"all the Brethren,"* and more significant still, that he says *"all the Holy Brethren."* He has written frankly about their needs, but all are Brethren, and not even the weakest are to be left out of his fellowship. The idea is this:

The Lord, Who paid such a price for our souls, regards every single Believer, weak or strong, as *"holy."* Even though He does this from a position of Divine Love, and because of the great price that He has paid for our Redemption, still, we must never take this for granted. This confidence placed in us, and confidence it is, should inspire us to live up to His expectations. Especially considering what He has done for us, the least we can do, is to try to be what He wants us to be.

To be sure, that which He desires, is for our good and our pleasure and our joy and our happiness, a million times over. Considering that and understanding that, we should rise to the level which He desires.

(28) "THE GRACE OF OUR LORD JESUS CHRIST BE WITH YOU. AMEN."

The distinctive farewell of the Apostle was always built around his favorite concept, Grace, which replaced the usual farewell of the time (Acts 15:29).

This trait is distinctive in his Epistles whether the benediction be longer (II Cor. 13:13) or shorter (Col. 4:18; I Tim. 6:21; II Tim. 4:22; Titus 3:15).

The primacy of Grace resulting from the saving Work of *"our Lord Jesus Christ"* was a constant theme as the Apostle sought the welfare of those he served (Thomas).

GRACE

The phrase, *"The Grace of our Lord Jesus Christ,"* presents the Goodness of Christ evidenced in the tremendous price He paid on our behalf in order that we might have Redemption. Consequently, we must never forget, that this Grace did come at tremendous price, even as stated. We refer to the Cross, and all of its terrible implications, but yet, that which opened the door to Eternal Life.

Paul was referred to as the *"Apostle of Grace."* This referred to the fact that he taught, and because the Holy Spirit desired that he do so, that Salvation is always by Grace through Faith (Eph. 2:8). Because it is of Grace, it is a *"Gift of God."* And yet, we must not forget, that this great Gift cannot be received, unless we evidence Faith in that which made it all possible — the Cross of Christ!

NOTES

THIS GRACE IS FOR YOU

The phrase, *"Be with you,"* refers to the greatest single thing that could ever happen to anyone at any time and at any place. If one has the Grace of the Lord Jesus Christ, one has Salvation, one has Eternal Life. As stated, there is nothing greater, nothing more wonderful, nothing more eternal. It is all of Christ that it may be all of Grace!

AMEN

The Epistle is closed with this word which means *"True"* or *"Truth."*

As we have repeatedly stated, the Bible is the only revealed Truth in the world today, and in fact ever has been.

It is November 17, 1999, as I conclude our efforts respecting this Commentary on this First Epistle of Paul the Apostle to the Thessalonians. What an honor it has been to engage in this effort, in fact, what an honor it is to have anything to do with the Word of God in any capacity.

If our efforts fall out to any strength and blessing to you, then all the Praise goes to the Lord. And as I have said previously, if the study of this material blesses you even half as much as it has me in its preparation, then you will be blessed.

Thank you for being a part of our efforts for the Cause of Christ.

*"I serve a risen Saviour, He's in the world today,*
*"I know that He is living, whatever men may say;*
*"I see His hand of mercy, I hear His voice of cheer,*
*"And just the time I need Him He's always near."*

*"In all the world around me I see His loving care,*
*"And tho' my heart grows weary, I never will despair;*
*"I know that He is leading thro' all the stormy blast,*

*"The day of His appearing will come at last."*

*"Rejoice, rejoice, O Christian, lift up your voice and sing,*
*"Eternal Hallelujahs to Jesus Christ the King!*
*"The Hope of all who seek Him, the Help of all Who find,*
*"None other is so loving, so good and kind."*

*CHORUS:*

*"He lives, He lives, Christ Jesus lives today.*
*"He walks with me and talks with me along life's narrow way.*
*"He lives, salvation to impart;*
*"You ask me how I know He lives?*
*"He lives within my heart."*

NOTES

# THE BOOK OF II THESSALONIANS

NOTES

## THE INTRODUCTION TO THE SECOND EPISTLE OF PAUL TO THE THESSALONIANS

It is November 18, 1999 as I begin work on the Commentary of II Thessalonians. It's a beautiful day outside, with not a cloud in the sky, with the temperature hovering at about 70 degrees.

In attempting to write these Commentaries with the telephone ringing, it seems every other minute, and with every other type of interruption, I find myself praying that somehow the Lord will help me to find a cohesive element, hopefully inspired by the Spirit, which will put it all together in the right fashion.

But at the same time, how so much I enjoy our labor of love as it regards this effort, and what a privilege it is to be able to study the Word of God in this fashion. I think I can say without any fear of contradiction that there has never been anything in my life that has fallen out to such Spiritual Growth as the writing of these Commentaries. Of course, I am speaking of my own personal Spiritual Growth. The amazing thing about the Word of God is, the impossibility exhausting its potential. The more that one studies its precepts, the more it takes on a life of its own, and almost grows before one's eyes. For sure it grows in one's heart. I only pray that you the Reader, will be blessed in the study of this material, as I am in attempting to formulate its pages. I know that you are a student of the Word, or you would not have secured this Volume. I don't believe you will be disappointed!

### THE CROSS OF CHRIST

Sometime in 1996 the Lord began to give me a Revelation regarding the Cross, the great Finished Work of Christ. I say *"began,"* because that Revelation continues even unto this hour. If the Reader will notice (in fact, how can you not help but notice), you will find that I take every opportunity presented to extol the virtues of the great Cross of Christ, i.e., *"the Finished Work."* Even more than that, I believe this Revelation which the Lord has given unto me, is going to fall out to a victorious conclusion in the hearts and lives of millions. I do not think I exaggerate!

As well, I believe this which the Spirit has given us, will take you the Reader to a deeper depth and a higher height in this great Substitutionary Offering of Christ, and what it all means, than you have ever previously known or even thought possible. Again, I do not feel that I exaggerate!

I have felt led of the Lord to address this subject in every way possible, hopefully that it may get down into your spirit, and thereby, perfect its great work.

The answer to every question, the solution to every problem, the highway to every victory, is found in the Cross of Christ, i.e., *"the Atonement."*

As Fanny Crosby said, that great Spirit-inspired songwriter of so many years ago: *"This is my story, this is my song!"*

### THE OCCASION OF THIS EPISTLE

The persons to whom this Epistle was written were *"the Church of the Thessalonians,"* or the Christian converts in the city of Thessalonica. We have already discussed this in our introduction to I Thessalonians, so we will not cover that ground again.

In order to understand this Second Epistle, we must endeavor to ascertain the condition of the Thessalonian Church when the Apostle wrote to them. Paul had been compelled to leave the Thessalonians only partially instructed in Christianity; consequently, they were defective both in the knowledge of its Doctrines and in the practice of its precepts. He had written them an Epistle to correct abuses and to supply what was lacking in their Faith (I Thess. 3:10). However, he was to learn that there were other problems there as well, hence the Second Epistle.

The Apostle had received a good report regarding the Thessalonians, but still there were some erroneous views concerning the Advent of Christ. He had addressed these issues to a certain extent in his First Epistle, but it seems that more instruction was needed.

## THE COMING OF THE LORD

The Lord Jesus Christ had left the world about 20 years before. He had promised to return at an uncertain date, and, therefore, nothing was more natural than the Church in general expecting His immediate return. Various circumstances, both in the Church and in the world, it seems, had heightened this expectation. Consequently, such a view of an immediate Advent had taken possession of the minds of the Thessalonian converts.

Their anxiety for the loss of their deceased relatives, who, they thought, would lose all the benefits occurring at the Advent, had indeed been assuaged by the former Epistle, but the expectation of the immediacy of the Advent itself had grown in strength.

The Thessalonians, it would seem, from misapprehending some Passages of Paul's First Epistle, considered that the Day of Christ was at hand. It would also seem, that mistaken and enthusiastic Teachers had also nourished this deception by appealing to visions and to the traditionary sayings of the Apostle; and it would even appear that an Epistle had been forged in the name of the Apostle, which further exacerbated the problem.

The consequence was that many of the Thessalonians were neglecting their secular business and living idle and useless lives, conceiving that there was no point in laboring in a world which was so soon to be destroyed, or of performing the duties belonging to a state of things which was so soon to terminate.

NOTES

Their only duty they felt, was to be in readiness for the immediate Coming of their Lord.

## PARTIALLY RIGHT

While they were certainly right in remaining in a state of readiness for the Coming of the Lord, they were wrong as it regarded their attitude and action.

Accordingly the design of the Apostle, in writing this Epistle, was to correct the error which the Thessalonians entertained concerning the immediate Advent, and to rectify those abuses to which that error had given rise.

The main object of the Apostle was to warn the Thessalonians, and all others as well, against thinking that the Day of the Lord was then imminent. The Apostle reminds them of his former instructions on this point, and tells them that a series of events — the manifestation and destruction of the Man of Sin — must first intervene.

*"Now we beseech you concerning the Advent of our Lord Jesus Christ and our gathering together unto Him, that ye be not soon shaken in your mind, or be troubled, neither by spirit, nor by word, nor by letter as from us, as that the Day of the Lord is at hand"* (II Thess. 2:1-2).

And along with this correction of error, was the correction of the disorders occasioned by it.

## THE DATE OF THE WRITING OF THIS EPISTLE

It is most probable that II Thessalonians was written very shortly after the writing of I Thessalonians. Silas and Timothy, as in the First Epistle, join with Paul in the salutation, and were consequently still in his company when he wrote this Epistle. It was probably written at Corinth.

But when Paul left Corinth, we are not informed that these two fellowworkers accompanied him (Acts 17:8); nor, from what appears, were they ever afterwards both together with him. Timothy, we are informed, rejoined Paul at Ephesus (Acts 19:22); but there is no further mention of Silas in the Acts of the Apostles.

Consequently, the date of the writing was probably in or near A.D. 53 (Gloag).

THE BREVITY OF THIS LETTER

Even though short, the Holy Spirit through Paul gives us an amazing amount of information regarding Endtime events.

For instance, he tells us in the Second Chapter that the Church must be raptured away, before the Man of Sin can be revealed. In that Chapter, he also reveals the great Apostasy which will grip the Church at this particular time. In fact, the Church has already entered this Apostasy of which the Apostle spoke. Understanding that, we must realize exactly how close it is to the Rapture of the Church, and the fulfillment of Endtime events, as predicted by the Prophets of old. We are living on the very threshold of these things they said, and which the Apostle details, throwing even more light on the subject. We had best take heed and great heed at that!

THE SECOND EPISTLE

I Thessalonians is believed by most Scholars to be the First Epistle penned by the great Apostle. Consequently, due to the fact that this Epistle was written so near the First, it is more than likely his Second.

This is extremely important in that these two Epistles are the beginning of instructions as it regards the New Covenant as it was given to Paul. The Apostle wrote 14 Epistles, that is if he actually wrote the Book of Hebrews, which I personally believe he did. Each Letter, for that's what they were, constitutes that which was inspired by the Holy Spirit, which means it is error free, and provides teaching and instruction peculiar to that particular Epistle, but yet complimentary of all the others.

Even though the entirety of the Word of God, all the way from Genesis through the Book of Revelation, falls into the same category, still, I think I can say without any fear of contradiction or exaggeration, that the 14 Epistles written by Paul more than any other, serve as the foundation of that which we commonly refer to as *"Western Civilization."* The Jew from Tarsus, more than any other man I think, laid the groundwork for the propagation of the Message of Jesus Christ and what He did for us at the Cross and in His Resurrection, which in effect, is the New Covenant. In fact, it was to Paul to whom the New Covenant was given.

NOTES

OF VITAL INTEREST TO YOU

Although brief, I think the prophetic content of this short Epistle is going to prove immensely interesting and helpful to you concerning Endtime events. Consider the following:

At the end of two Millenniums or one Millennium, the Lord has always done something great toward the advancement of the Salvation Message.

At the end of two Millenniums, the great Word of Justification by Faith was given to Abraham.

One Millennium from that, the Lord told David that the Messiah would come through his lineage.

One Millennium from David, Christ was born.

We are now at the end of two Millenniums from the time of Christ, which has been the age of the Church. This means that something grand and glorious is about to happen, and to be sure, very, very soon! This means that the Rapture of the Church is very near, which Paul outlines in the Second Chapter of this short Epistle. It's all there, and if you are interested in Endtime events, as I know you are, this Epistle is going to prove to be tremendously instructive and informative to you.

Thank you for sharing our efforts.

Jimmy Swaggart

CHAPTER 1

(1) "PAUL, AND SILVANUS, AND TIMOTHEUS, UNTO THE CHURCH OF THE THESSALONIANS IN GOD OUR FATHER AND THE LORD JESUS CHRIST:"

After a period of probably several months, new reports from Thessalonica reached Paul while he and his missionary party were still in Corinth. These reports were such as to lead him to write a second Epistle. Conditions reflected in II Thessalonians are similar to those in the first Letter, though in some ways problems had become worse. In the second Letter he sent to the Thessalonian Church Paul provides solutions for a new set of circumstances (Thomas).

PAUL, SILAS, AND TIMOTHY

The phrase, *"Paul, and Silvanus, and Timotheus,"* presents the same salutation, at least at the beginning, as the First Epistle. So, the two are still with Paul, but as stated, this will not be for long, with both shortly going elsewhere, and Silas not actually being mentioned again (Acts 18:5). Silas was mentioned in II Corinthians 1:19, which was written some eight to ten years after II Thessalonians, but only with reference back to the time at Corinth.

What a privilege it was for these men to have the opportunity of association with Paul. Not only would an account of their Ministries be given on the pages of the Word of God, at least to a certain extent, but how much they must have learned in being with the great Apostle. Of course, the Holy Spirit put all of this together, but I wonder how much they knew and understood of the great significance of this moment while they were living it!

For them to have the privilege and opportunity to be there, at least when some of these things were happening, and especially to be mentioned in connection with Paul, would mean they would go down in history as some of the most famous individuals who have ever lived. In fact, I think it can be easily said and without any fear of contradiction, that their names, along with others of that period, have been read and mentioned more than any other person in history. I'm not sure that would have mattered that much to them, but it has happened anyway!

As well, at least in the spiritual sense, these men had to have been heavyweights in their own right. I don't think it could have been otherwise. The Holy Spirit selected them for this task. Also, there is every evidence that Timothy picked up the torch when Paul was later called home to Glory. As well, Peter mentioned Silas as being with him, whose First Epistle was written about a year later than Paul's First Epistle to the Corinthians.

NOTES

So it seems when Silas left Paul at Corinth, quite possibly he went to be with Simon Peter at Babylon (I Pet. 5:12-13).

In the realm of the New Covenant that was given to Paul, which was the Message of the Cross and gave to the world Salvation by Grace through Faith, the Lord also gave to the Apostle tremendous insight into coming, Endtime events, regarding the Church. In fact, the greater bulk of this short Epistle will deal with these events, actually shedding more light on this particular subject than perhaps any other effort.

THE CHURCH OF THE THESSALONIANS

The phrase, *"Unto the Church of the Thessalonians,"* presents Paul's second Epistle, not only to these particular Believers, but as well, the second one he had ever written, at least as far as we know. As I mentioned in the closing remarks concerning the previous Epistle, what an honor it was for this Church to be the recipient of the first two Epistles written by Paul, which would constitute the Word of God. I doubt very seriously at the time they understood the significance of all of this, and quite possibly it would have been beyond the scope of anyone's thinking at that particular time. How so honored and blessed they were, and yet the only thing on their minds as it regards the Work of the Lord it seems, was an explanation as it concerned the Coming of the Lord.

This should be a lesson to us as to how important anything and everything is as it pertains to the Work of God. At that particular time in history, Nero was the leader of the Roman Empire. It had stretched its tentacles over much of the world of that day. In fact, it was the greatest empire the world had ever known, at least up to then, and would survive for several more centuries. But yet in the Mind of God, the single most important thing on Earth at that time, was not the happenings of Caesar, or the Senate at Rome, or the pushing of mighty Roman Armies into the enlarging of the Empire, but rather this little obscure group of people in the city of Thessalonica who had recently accepted Christ. That was the single most important thing that was taking place in the world of that day, at least in the eyes of God,

Whose eyes Alone actually matter! It is the same presently:

The world takes little or no notice at all as it regards the Work of God; however, this is by far the most important thing happening in the world today. Hollywood holds no attraction for the Lord of Glory, and neither does the leadership of mighty nations, even this great United States of America, with the exception as to how it impacts His Work on Earth.

But of course, the world cannot see that, simply because the world has no interest in that. In fact, it doesn't even know or understand what it does see as it regards this of which we speak. Consequently, the great question is, *"Do Believers actually see the Work of God as they should?"*

## GOD OUR FATHER AND THE LORD JESUS CHRIST

The phrase, *"In God our Father and the Lord Jesus Christ,"* proclaims coequally the Source of Grace and Peace, as being the Father and Christ. However, the Father has done all of this through Christ, by what He did at the Cross and in His Resurrection.

Actually, the Name *"Lord Jesus Christ"* is the Resurrection Name of our Lord. *"Lord"* stands for Deity, *"Jesus"* stands for Saviour, and *"Christ"* stands for the Messiah, the Anointed One, the Incarnation.

Once the Believer understands the Cross, the entirety of the Word of God takes on a brand-new meaning. In other words, we understand what is being said, why it is being said, and how it is being said. Paul being the one to whom the New Covenant was given, or at least its meaning as carried out by Christ, will have a heavier flavor in his writings than the other Apostles, although all that they write and say, complement grandly this which he writes.

God is our Father, inasmuch as we have been adopted into the Family of God. Hence we can now call Him *"Father"* (Rom. 8:15); however, this could not have been done unless Jesus had gone to the Cross and settled the terrible sin debt owed to God by man. In other words, Jesus did for us, what we could not do for ourselves. In fact, the Cross was the very reason that God became man, and came to this Earth. The Cross was ever before

NOTES

Him, illustrating the fact, that the Cross is the central purpose, the focus point, the foundation of all that we are in Christ, have in Christ, and shall be in Christ.

## THE CROSS AND THE MODERN CHURCH

In the minds of most Christians, the Cross is merely an incident in the midst of all the other great things Christ did. In fact, many in the Charismatic community, refer to the Cross as the greatest defeat that Heaven ever knew.

Such a statement is not only wrong, but actually borders on the very edge of blasphemy. It shows a terrible misunderstanding of the Atonement, which characterizes the very purpose of God.

Actually, the Church is pretty well divided into three camps:

1. A great segment of the Church places Christ and all that He did at the Cross in a subsidiary role, if at all, rather majoring in *"the ethics of Christianity."* Consequently, it is a Christianity which for the most part, whether it realizes it or not, denies Christ and all that He has done. There is no Salvation in this false way, and to be sure, there are no ethics either. It is impossible to hold to any kind of ethic, without the power of the Holy Spirit. And to be sure, the Holy Spirit will have nothing to do with a mere philosophy of Christianity, which ignores the Finished Work of Christ. In fact, the Cross of Christ is an offense to this segment of the Church (Gal. 5:11; I Pet. 2:8).

2. A large segment of the Church believes in the Cross of Christ, but limits it to the initial Salvation experience, having little or no understanding at all the part the Cross plays in our everyday living before God. The Cross is not central in their thinking, with it only a part of the mix as it regards Christ.

Such thinking by and large, includes most Pentecostals, Fundamentalists, and Charismatics. In fact, many Charismatics deny the veracity of the Cross, which means they are preaching *"another Jesus, another spirit, and another gospel"* (II Cor. 11:4).

Although this group is certainly saved, even with many being Baptized with the Holy Spirit, most do not walk in victory, because victory cannot be obtained and held, unless one has a proper understanding of the Cross of Christ.

3. There are a few in the Church who definitely do understand the meaning of the Cross of Christ, and what it affords for the Child of God. They understand the Cross to be central in the great Work of God, actually towards that which all history strains, the very purpose of God, and that which has made everything possible.

We understand that the solution to every problem, the answer to every question, is found in the Cross of Christ, i.e., *"the Finished Work of Christ."*

Consequently, we place our Faith totally and completely in that Finished Work, which guarantees the help of the Holy Spirit, which guarantees victory in our everyday living and life (Rom. 8:1-2).

However, even though this number is few who properly understand the Finished Work of Christ, it is in fact growing everyday.

That's the reason I plead with you, that is if it's at all possible, that you get these Commentaries into the hands of as many people as possible, and especially Preachers. The Church must return to the Cross of Christ.

Martin Luther the great Reformer stated, that the Reformation which in fact changed the world, could be summed up as to how one viewed the Cross of Christ. Does one see that, the Substitutionary Offering of Christ, as the central core of one's Salvation and Victory, or does one look to other things? That's the great question, and that's always been the great question.

(2) "GRACE UNTO YOU, AND PEACE, FROM GOD OUR FATHER AND THE LORD JESUS CHRIST."

Comparable phrases identifying the Sources of *"Grace and Peace"* occur in all other Pauline superscriptions.

The words make explicit what is already implicit, that God is ultimately the only Source of Grace and Peace.

Two persons of the Godhead are specified: the Father and the Son. Considering that the Holy Spirit inspired Paul to write these words, we have here the entirety of the Trinity.

To Paul, Jesus was Deity in the fullest sense. This is the only justification for placing His Name beside the Father's as Coauthor of the unmerited favor and harmonious relationship pronounced in this greeting.

NOTES

## GRACE UNTO YOU

The phrase, *"Grace unto you,"* pronounces the manner in which God deals with the human race. Grace is the means by which the Goodness of God is extended to Believers who do not, and in fact, cannot merit such. It is granted to all on the basis of the great Sacrifice of Christ. In other words, the Cross of Christ is what makes the Grace of God possible. All that God requires of Believers, is to place their Faith in what Christ did at the Cross and in His Resurrection, understanding that this is the Source of all Blessings, and Grace will always be forthcoming in an unending stream.

God has always had Grace, i.e., *"the desire to bestow good things upon Believers."* However, due to man's sin, God has always been very limited as to what He could do in this respect. However the Cross changed all of that.

The Cross paid the terrible sin debt owed by man to God, which atoned for all sin, past, present, and future, at least for those who will believe (Jn. 3:16), which now makes it possible for God to issue forth a constant river of good things to those who trust and believe Him.

However, the Believer must ever understand, that all of this was made possible by what Jesus did at the Cross, and, therefore, our Faith must always be in that great Substitutionary Work. In fact, if one's Faith is not placed squarely in the Cross of Christ as it regards all things, simply because the Cross made all good things possible, the Believer will succeed only in frustrating the Grace of God (Gal. 2:20-21). This means that Faith outside of the Cross of Christ, stops the flow of Grace, which guarantees that the Christian is going to be a defeated Christian, irrespective as to what he might do otherwise.

To keep the flow of Grace coming in an uninterrupted stream so to speak, one must ever understand the means by which this Grace comes. It is not solely because of the Goodness of God, because God has always been good. As well, it hasn't been because of a lack of desire on His part to do good things for those who trust Him, for He has always had that desire.

It is the Cross which made and makes all of this possible.

NOTES

### HOW DID THE CROSS MAKE IT POSSIBLE?

The Fall of Adam and Eve, our first parents, in the Garden of Eden, was of far greater magnitude than any of us will ever know. The main problem was that the disobedience to God, the terrible sin that was committed, of necessity, cut, so to speak, the spiritual umbilical cord from God to Adam. As a result, Adam is now devoid of all spirituality, i.e., *"spiritually dead."* In the place of the Divine nature which Adam and Eve had before the Fall, the sin nature now rules.

This sin nature, which simply refers to man gravitating toward that which is wicked and evil, and on a constant basis, is the reason that modern psychology can never hope to address this subject, at least with any positive results. Man's entire being is taken over by the powers of darkness, which means he gravitates toward that which is wrong because he has no contact with his Maker. Consequently, his every thought is sin, his every action is sin, his every direction is sin, and in fact all he does constitutes sin. In Truth, man can do no other, can be no other, can have no other way, but this way of *"stealing, killing and destroying"* (Jn. 10:10).

This is the cause of all war, man's inhumanity to man, sickness, disease, affliction, loneliness, crime, etc.

### A THRICE HOLY GOD

Due to the Fall, and what it did to man, incidentally, God's choicest creation, a thrice holy God cannot associate with man. In fact, if he did in any capacity, man would automatically die (Rev. 4:8).

To give man some means of communication with Him, and even communion in a limited sense, from the very outset of the Fall, the Sacrifices of particular animals were instituted. We find this in Genesis, Chapter 4 in the episode of Cain and Abel. In these Sacrifices, the Lord made it clear that they were but symbols of One Who was to come, Who would redeem fallen humanity. This in essence, was a Covenant which God made with Adam.

In fact, when Cain was born, Eve said, *"I have gotten a man from the Lord"* (Gen. 4:1). The title *"Lord"* insinuates Covenant God, which means that Eve thought that Cain was the coming Redeemer, Who would get them out of this terrible dilemma. Unfortunately, he wasn't! He was instead a murderer.

Some time later, when *"Seth"* was born, Eve had lost Faith, saying *"For God, hath appointed me another seed instead of Abel, whom Cain slew"* (Gen. 4:25). Had she continued to have Faith in the Covenant, she would have continued to use the title *"Lord,"* but instead, she uses the title *"God,"* which signifies that she no longer believes in the Covenant.

In fact, Seth was actually the one through whose lineage, the Messiah, the Redeemer, would actually come (Lk. 3:38).

During all of this time, God was the same then as He is now. In other words, His goodness, i.e., *"Grace,"* is no different now than then. The Sacrifices were a stopgap measure, but the blood of bulls and goats could not take away sins (Heb. 10:4). Consequently, and as stated, God was limited as to what He could do regarding the human race. A thrice holy God, cannot have communion with sinful men. Whereas communion with God brings life to the Believer, such would bring death to the unbeliever, if carried out in the same capacity.

As one looks at the Old Testament, one sees a river of blood, which was spilled from the slit throats of untold millions of particular animals such as lambs, goats, rams, etc. All of this typifies the Cross, and in no uncertain terms. If we do not see this, do not understand this, do not comprehend this, then we are completely misreading the Word of God.

Some may blanch at the thought of all of these animals being slaughtered; however, such portrays the Holiness of God, and the sinfulness of man. It also portrays the Love of God, in trying to reach humanity, which He ultimately did through the Death and Resurrection of His Only Son (Jn. 3:16).

During all of these times, God was no less merciful, no less full of Grace, no less good, no less compassionate than He is now.

When Jesus finally came, Who would fulfill all the prophecies, and actually be the great Sacrifice, which would put away all other Sacrifices, then and only then, could the matter be settled.

The blood of bulls and goats could not take away sins, but the Sacrifice of Christ, in the pouring out of His Own Life's Blood, could, and in fact, did take away sin, and in totality (Jn. 1:29). Inasmuch as the Cross of Christ, which was an absolute necessity, if God was to have fellowship with man, and man have fellowship with God, had to be carried out, then it is incumbent upon Believers to understand that the Cross of Christ is the central core of Redemption.

The sin debt being removed by what Jesus did there, the door was then opened that God could have fellowship with man, and extend to him all the graces of Heaven.

THE RENT VEIL

In the Tabernacle and Temple of old, there was a Veil which separated the Holy Place from the Holy of Holies. The Holy of Holies is where God dwelt between the Mercy Seat and the Cherubim. Into this Sacred Place no one could enter, except the High Priest and only once a year, and then only with blood, the blood of a slain animal, which was to be applied to the Mercy Seat (Ex. 26:31-33; Lev. 16:2-6; Heb. 10:19-20).

When Jesus died on the Cross, the Scripture says, *"And, behold, the Veil of the Temple was rent in twain from the top to the bottom"* (Mat. 27:51).

Josephus the Jewish Historian, said that this *"Veil"* weighed some 2,000 pounds, was 4" thick, and that 4 yoke of Oxen could not pull it apart. But when Jesus died, the thing rent or tore from the top to the bottom, as if God ripped it asunder with His Hands, opening up the Holy of Holies, which means total access to Him, by *"Whosoever will"* (Rev. 22:17).

The Death of Jesus, which is blatantly obvious, made all of this possible. The sin debt now being paid, the Way to God has been opened up, which is all made possible by the Cross. This is the reason that the Cross was a necessity, and actually, the very Center and Core of man's Redemption, and, therefore, man's Faith.

NOTES

Again I state, the Cross made it all possible!

PEACE

The phrase, *"And Peace,"* represents that which is the fruit of Grace. When man believes God for Salvation, which means that he accepts what Jesus did at the Cross on his behalf, the enmity caused by sin, being removed, *"Peace"* between God and man is now restored. In other words, the war caused by sin, is over, and man has made Peace with God. That is what is referred to as *"Justifying Peace."*

However, Paul is not speaking here of Justifying Peace, but rather *"Sanctifying Peace,"* which is very similar to Justifying Peace, but which most Christians have great difficulty in understanding.

As the sinner believes Christ for his Salvation, thereby gaining Justifying Peace, the Christian is to likewise trust the Lord and what He did at the Cross for his Victory, which is *"Sanctifying Peace."*

As stated, there is a perpetual war going on between unconverted man and God, caused by man's sin. While that war ceases upon conversion, another war begins in the heart and life of the Believer between the flesh and the Spirit. As someone has said, Justification is the Holy Spirit fighting *"for"* us, while Sanctification is the Holy Spirit, fighting *"in"* us.

The problem is, we want to fight this war ourselves, which means we are not depending on what Christ did at the Cross, which frustrates the Grace of God, and as well, denies the help of the Holy Spirit. As a result, the Saint although definitely having *"Justifying Peace,"* does not have *"Sanctifying Peace,"* which makes life miserable, to say the least!

In fact, as Paul uses both words *"Grace"* and *"Peace,"* he is speaking of *"Sanctifying Grace"* and *"Sanctifying Peace."*

The only way that the Saint of God can have Sanctifying Grace, is to place his Faith in what Christ did at the Cross, which then opens the channel of God's Grace, which comes to us in an unceasing flow, guaranteeing *"Justifying Peace."* Conversely, if we attempt to sanctify ourselves, as most Christians attempt to do, our efforts frustrate the Grace of God, which as well, destroys our Sanctifying Peace (Gal. 2:20-21).

This is what I meant by the Believer understanding the Cross. Once this is understood, then every word in the Bible takes on a brand-new meaning, with the entire content becoming clear as it regards its direction. Everything in the Word of God is tied to the Cross of Christ. If we fail to understand that, or attempt to go beyond the Cross, we lose our way with God, because the Cross of Christ is the only way to God (Ex. 12:12).

### THE FATHER AND CHRIST

The phrase, *"From God our Father and the Lord Jesus Christ,"* proclaims to us the results of the previous Verse.

If one is to notice, the Church, i.e., *"Believers,"* is *"in"* God our Father and the Lord Jesus Christ. This is done through what Christ did at the Cross, and our Faith in that (Rom. 6:2-6). As a result of being *"in Christ,"* certain things come to Believers *"from"* God our Father and the Lord Jesus Christ. In this case, *"Sanctifying Grace and Sanctifying Peace."*

(3) "WE ARE BOUND TO THANK GOD ALWAYS FOR YOU, BRETHREN, AS IT IS MEET, BECAUSE THAT YOUR FAITH GROWETH EXCEEDINGLY, AND THE CHARITY OF EVERY ONE OF YOU ALL TOWARD EACH OTHER ABOUNDETH;"

As is his practice in every Epistle but Galatians, Paul begins his remarks by thanking God for the spiritual progress of those to whom he is writing. Here his appreciation is marked by a feature found nowhere else except later in this same Epistle — he was obligated to express gratitude for what God had done in their lives. *"We ought"* appears only here and in II Thessalonians 2:13 in connection with his thanksgiving and gives a glimpse into how Paul conceived of his duty to God.

This unusual reference to responsibility, thought by some to be prompted by the Readers' remarkable progress or by a special need among them, should be limited to a special personal duty to God (Rom. 1:14; I Cor. 9:16-17), because the Greek verb (*"ought"* as in the original Text), implies an exclusive personal responsibility.

NOTES

Paul never ceased feeling a compulsion to give gratitude to God for what Christ had done. This refers to the Cross!

### THANKFULNESS TO GOD

The phrase, *"We are bound to thank God always for you, Brethren,"* refers to a positive debt incurred, which it would be a dishonesty not to pay. As usual, Paul commends their strengths first of all, before addressing their problems.

*"Bound"* in the Greek is *"opheilo,"* and means *"to be under an obligation to do a thing, to be indebted, to be a debtor."*

As stated, this refers to what God has done for the Thessalonians, and as a matter of fact for the entirety of the human race, in giving His Only Son as a Sacrifice for sin, which made it possible for mankind to be saved. Understanding that as we should, that is if we do, causes a perpetual thanksgiving to God to come from our hearts, as it regards this great Work. Again, we come back to the Cross.

If we properly understand the Cross, the price paid there, at least as far as a human being can understand such, such praises and thanksgiving will be constant. To realize who we were, sinners without God and without hope, doomed to an eternal hell forever and forever, and that God through the giving of His Son, the Lord Jesus Christ, saved us from all of this and as well gave us Eternal Life, how can we not help but praise Him! Again we emphasize, the Cross was the center of all this, the means by which it was all done, the actual ingredient of Redemption.

Of course, when we speak of the Cross, we are not speaking of a wooden beam, but rather what Jesus did on that Cross in order to redeem lost humanity.

If we do not understand the Cross in this fashion, there will be little praise to God solicited from the heart, with spiritual conceit, and self-righteousness being the result. That means that if you the Reader do not have a compulsion in your heart to constantly thank God for this great Salvation afforded you, you have an improper understanding of the Cross!

### NECESSARY

The phrase, *"As it is meet,"* means that it is right and proper in the circumstances of the case. In other words, this is the proper thing to do, and we speak of constant thanksgiving to God for what Jesus did, which makes possible all the grand things the Thessalonians have, as well as all other Believers, and for all time.

In fact, much of our praying should be made up of thanksgiving to the Lord for this great Salvation afforded to us, and at such great price! Because it's so important, please allow me to state the case again.

If we do not feel a constant compulsion to praise the Lord, and more specifically, to praise Him for saving our souls, understanding the great price that was paid in order that all of this might be done, then this shows that we do not have a proper understanding of that price, i.e., *"the Cross."* In fact, the Holy Spirit will constantly remind us of our need to praise the Lord in this respect, that is if our Faith is properly centered on the Finished Work of Christ.

When John had his great vision of the Throne of God, the Scripture says, *"And I beheld, and lo, in the midst of the Throne, and of the four Living creatures, and in the midst of the Elders, stood a Lamb as it had been slain"* (Rev. 5:6).

As is obvious in this Vision, even as the Fourth Chapter grandly proclaims, worship is the theme. We find here, in the very midst of all that is happening, the Holy Spirit proclaiming the fact, that all of this is made possible, at least as far as the redeemed are concerned, by the *"slain Lamb."* This must never be forgotten, and in fact, cannot be forgotten, if we properly understand the meaning of the *"slain Lamb."*

## FAITH

The phrase, *"Because that your Faith groweth exceedingly,"* presents a significant commentary on Christian growth.

*"Growth"* in the Greek is *"huperauxano,"* and means *"to abound beyond measure; to grow exceedingly healthy and fruitful, as a good tree planted in good soil."* Significant also is the fact that such growth took place at a time of tribulation, even as the next Verse proclaims.

The Apostle was no doubt overjoyed at this report Timothy had brought him. Due to not having the opportunity to spend the time there he needed to spend, he was concerned that the Thessalonians would not be properly grounded in the Faith. However, his fears are laid to rest, as Timothy explained to him how that they had not only maintained their Faith, but had in fact, experienced a growth in Faith.

NOTES

## GROWING FAITH

The Scripture plainly says, *"So then Faith cometh by hearing, and hearing by the Word of God"* (Rom. 10:17).

As should be obvious, the more that one hears the Word, studies the Word, learns to trust the Word, the more that Faith will increase. However, when Paul mentions here the growing of the Faith of these Thessalonians, what exactly did he mean?

In the last several decades, the Church has had more teaching on Faith than possibly the balance of its existence all put together. Most of this teaching has been wrong, and has led the Church down a primrose path, with the end result now little more than mere *"greed."* In other words, the so-called Faith Message has pretty well degenerated into the *"money gospel!"* There once was great emphasis on healing, but even that has pretty well fallen by the wayside. While Divine Healing is definitely a Biblical Doctrine, the manner in which it was being taught, was wrong. The idea was, according to your level of Faith, you can receive healing for anything. And if the person was not healed, then the blame was laid on them as not having enough Faith, etc. There is nothing in the Word of God to substantiate such thinking. While the Lord definitely heals, to be sure, He is not sitting up in Heaven waiting for somebody's Faith to rise to a certain level before He will give them this which they so desperately need. To be frank, such thinking is silly!

The major reason that the modern Faith Message was and is wrong, is because the object of its Faith wasn't and isn't right. The object must always be the Finished Work of Christ, to which the Word of God points to constantly.

To attempt to take a particular Scripture such as Mark 11:24, and then to force God into some type of activity because of our

NOTES

claiming certain things, is not Faith, and above all, it is not Faith in the Word. It's merely an effort to manipulate the Word of God, which of course the Lord will never allow.

While these great Promises in the Word of God are definitely real and real for us today, the secret is, that we want what He wants us to have, no more, no less! It must always be, *"Not my will, but Thine, be done"* (Lk. 22:42).

Of course, as we know and understand, when Jesus uttered those words, He was in the Garden, and it was only hours before His Crucifixion. Actually, He was speaking of the coming Crucifixion.

THE CORRECT OBJECT OF FAITH

The type of Faith which Paul was speaking about as it regarded the Thessalonians, was Faith in the Finished Work of Christ, i.e., *"the Substitutionary Sacrifice, the Atonement."* In fact, our understanding of the Word of God must be in this capacity, or else it will be an imperfect understanding.

The story of the Bible, which of course is the Word of God, is that of man's Redemption. In fact, John said, *"In the beginning was the Word, and the Word was with God, and the Word was God"* (Jn. 1:1).

Of course, as is obvious, the Holy Spirit through John, is here making Christ and the Word one and the same.

Then it tells us, *"And the Word* (Christ) *was made flesh, and dwelt among us"* (Jn. 1:14).

Of course, He became flesh for one purpose, and that was to die on the Cross. Inasmuch as God cannot die, He would have to become flesh in order to do so, which He did! In other words, this was the very purpose and reason for His becoming *"flesh."*

Then the Scripture says, *"The next day John seeth Jesus coming unto Him, and saith, Behold the Lamb of God, which taketh away the sin of the world"* (Jn. 1:29).

Here in plain terminology, we have the reason as to why the Word was made flesh, and the purpose intended. It was to redeem lost humanity, which demanded the Death of Christ on the Cross, which alone would satisfy Heavenly Justice. In fact, this has been in the Mind of God from eternity past (I Pet. 1:18-21).

The point I'm attempting to make is, that when we say that we have *"Faith in the Word,"* we must at the same time understand, that the Word constantly, continually, absolutely, in fact, as straight as an arrow, always points towards the Cross of Christ. So, if one says they're having Faith in the Word, and they do not understand that the Word and the Cross are one and the same, then they really do not have proper Faith in the Word.

In fact, the biggest sin of the Church is attempting to manipulate the Word of God. And what do I mean by that?

MANIPULATION OF THE WORD

This is exactly what Satan did in the temptation of Christ in the wilderness (Mat. Chpt. 4). Without going into detail, to be sure, Satan used the Word, and to be sure again, it was not merely that he twisted it somewhat, but rather, that he was trying to get Christ to use the Word for His Own purposes, instead of the Will of God. That was the great effort of Satan.

Most Christians miss this as it regards the temptation in the wilderness. They think it only pertains to Satan misquoting the Word, which He did do; however, that was not the main problem.

The main problem, as stated, and which is so very, very serious, was to get Jesus to use the Word in a way it was never meant to be used, and that is to satisfy one's own desires. The very Ministry and Message of Christ, the very Life and Living of Christ, was to obey the Father in every capacity and at all times. So, Jesus did nothing except the Father told him to do such. In other words, He never used His great power one single time, on His Own behalf.

That is a far cry from the modern Faith Message, of which the very thrust is total self-will, with the Will of God being totally ignored. There could be no greater sin!

So when one claims to understand the Word of God, their understanding must be in the realm of the Word and the Cross being one and the same. Consequently, when words like *"Faith," "Grace," "Righteousness,"* and *"Sanctification,"* etc., are spoken by Paul, these words must always be in connection with the Cross. Everything comes through the Cross of Christ, and of course I'm speaking of all that we receive from God. If man doesn't understand that, then he doesn't understand anything about God or His Plan of Redemption, or the Word of God for that matter!

The Faith of these Thessalonians was growing, because of them anchoring their belief in totality in the Finished Work of Christ. As it regards the growth of our Faith, it is the same principle now as then.

## LOVE

The phrase, *"And the charity of every one of you all toward each other aboundeth,"* speaks of love and should have been translated accordingly.

Actually, *"Faith"* and *"Love"* contain in themselves the whole of the Christian Life; Faith is its commencement, its source; love is not only its outcome, its spiritual action, but its completion; the climax of the Christian life is to be made perfect in love.

*"Toward each other"* presents the first hallmark of Christianity, that we love the Brethren. This means that love is not a mere general affection, but is to be specially manifested *"toward each Believer."* As well, the word *"aboundeth"* means that it is to ever increase in intensity.

If one does not love fellow Christians, and express that love accordingly, then how can he love those who are not Christians? As well, love not expressed, is not really love, but only cheap theatrics.

Once again, and even at the risk of being overly repetitious, I must emphasize the fact that if one does not have a proper understanding of the Cross, what Jesus did there, what it all means to the Believer, then one cannot properly grow in Faith or love. The end of everything as it pertains to God's dealings with man, is the Cross of Christ. So, we must understand everything centering up in the Atonement.

That means that we do not properly understand Faith, Love, Sanctification, or anything else for that matter as it pertains to the Lord, unless we understand that all of these attributes and complements center up in the Cross.

The Cross of Christ is the epitome of Faith, in that God had Faith that men would respond to the Cross as it refers to Redemption. As well, love centers up in the Cross as the greatest demonstration of such the world has ever known. Sanctification falls into the same category, in that Christ set Himself apart unto God for the very purpose of offering Himself as a Sacrifice. As well, the Cross and the Resurrection, are the means by which Justification is effected in the heart and life of the Believer. Grace can only be extended to mankind, as Faith is exhibited in the Cross, which makes Grace possible. As well, the Cross is the very means of reconciliation and forgiveness.

Coming to the Holy Spirit, He is able to abide within our hearts and lives, simply because of what Jesus did at the Cross in paying the terrible sin debt. Therefore, His power expended within our hearts and lives, is done so strictly on the merits of the Finished Work of Christ, and our Faith in that great Work (Rom. 8:1-2).

As it pertains to Divine Healing, the Scripture plainly says, *"By Whose stripes ye were healed"* (I Pet. 2:24), which speaks of a part of the Crucifixion process.

## WHERE IS THE MODERN CHURCH?

To be sure, the far greater majority is not anchored in the Cross of Christ by any means. In fact, the modern Church little knows where it is, and that's because it has lost track of where it's been.

If it's of God, it was raised up as a result of Faith in the Cross of Christ, and what He did there, which serves as the foundation of all that we are in the Lord. But the Church has drifted from that. Of course, there is an exception here and there, and thank God for that. However, those exceptions are rare!

Much of the Charismatic world has opted totally for the *"money gospel,"* which in fact is *"another gospel,"* which means, it is no gospel at all. In fact, that particular direction, is no more than a *"scam,"* or a *"con job."* In secular society, people get put in jail for such blatant fabrications.

In the Pentecostal variety, of which I am associated, they are chasing all over the world looking for manifestations and signs, in the final analysis, with very little being actually done.

NOTES

The Denominational Church world has for all practical purposes totally and completely denied the Holy Spirit, which leaves them with nothing but a man-devised, man-operated system, which of course, God cannot bless. That means, that even though there is a mountain of religious machinery at work in these particular circles, which speaks of great activity, in fact, there is almost nothing being done for the Lord.

As stated, there is an exception here and there, and for that we are grateful; however, for the most part it is as I have said.

In fact, the Church has entered into the final great apostasy, actually, the time of the Laodicean Church so to speak, and in that capacity, things will not get better (Rev. 3:14-22).

Irrespective of these problems, the Lord has always had a Remnant who have believed Him, trusted in Him, and have followed Him with all their love and attention. As I have previously said, I believe the dividing line between the Apostate Church and the Godly Remnant is going to be, and in fact already is, the Cross of Christ. However, in Truth, the Cross has always been the dividing line. It was with Cain and Abel, and it has been that way ever since. We look to the Cross and live, even as did the Israelites in the wilderness when they were bitten by serpents, or we look elsewhere and die.

Those who put their Faith and Trust in Christ and what He did at the Cross and in His Resurrection, are going to be mightily and gloriously used of God. This and this alone, is the True Church (Mat. 16:15-19).

## TAKING UP THE CROSS DAILY

This matter of the Cross is of such consequence, that Jesus said, *"If any man will come after Me, let him deny himself* (quit trying to sanctify self with self), *and take up his Cross daily, and follow Me"* (Lk. 9:23).

Most Christians completely misunderstand this Passage. They know that Jesus said it, and they also know that it includes everyone, *"any man!"* In other words, all who follow Christ, and without exception, must take up the Cross, and not only take it up, but do so on a *"daily"* basis.

However, they think that this refers to *"suffering"*; therefore, they draw back from what Jesus said here, missing the whole point entirely.

To be sure, suffering and even great suffering was carried out on the Cross, and was done so by Christ; however, He is not speaking here of us dying on a Cross, but rather understanding the following:

1. As stated, every single thing we receive from the Lord, comes through the Cross, and without exception.

2. Not only is Salvation for the sinner guaranteed in the Cross, but as well, Victory for the Believer. In fact, there is Victory in no other source.

3. Understanding that, we are to place our Faith in this which Jesus has done for us, and keep our Faith there.

4. We are to do this even on a *"daily"* basis, which is somewhat like the Manna which fell from Heaven, while the Children of Israel were in the wilderness. It is almost like renewing one's Faith each and every day, as we look to the Cross of Christ for what we need, understanding that it was there that Jesus paid the price for all things.

5. Taking up the Cross, and taking it up daily, refers to the Believer knowing and understanding that all his benefits come from the Cross. It means that we look to this great Finished Work of Christ for all things, i.e., *"all that we need!"* In fact, that's really the whole idea of Jesus' statement. As stated, He's not referring to people suffering as most Christians think, but rather enjoying the benefits for which He paid such a price.

So, instead of this Passage as given by Christ being something foreboding and dreadful, it is really the very opposite. Bearing the Cross, and doing so on a daily basis, is the most thrilling and wonderful exercise or experience in which one could ever begin to engage. This is the secret of all Living and all Life.

As well, when Jesus said *"Deny himself,"* He's not speaking of asceticism, which is a denial of all things which are pleasurable, etc. The Church got into that in the Dark Ages, and some are still in it presently.

No, that's not what it means!

For us to deny ourselves, simply refers to the fact that we are not to try to do what Christ has already done, and which in fact we cannot do no matter how hard we try. Unredeemed

NOTES

man's biggest problem is his attempt to save himself, and the Christians' biggest problem, is the attempt to sanctify himself. It is the old problem of *"self!"*

Self is not to be destroyed, because in fact we are a *"self."* Self is to be properly hidden in Christ, which Paul outlined in Romans 6:2-6, where he referred to the person literally being Baptized into Jesus' Death, which also includes His Burial and Resurrection. We can also add the Exaltation to that (Eph. 2:6).

Our biggest problem is self. That is what Jesus was speaking about when He said, *"For whosoever will save his life shall lose it* (shall seek to gain these things by self-effort)*: but whosoever will lose his life for My sake, the same shall save it* (will lose self in Christ)*"* (Lk. 9:24).

SUFFERING

Stop and think a moment, if Jesus had meant that we need to suffer in order to live for Him, as most Christians think, this would be saying that what He did at the Cross was not enough, and we have to add our suffering to His Work. Such is preposterous!

But that's exactly what most Christians think. Any poor soul who has to go through a particular problem of some difficulty, is looked at as *"bearing the Cross."* The common retort to that is, *"I pray that the Lord never asks me to do such a thing."*

None of that is correct. While there definitely are problems at times, it has nothing to do with bearing the Cross.

The Work of Christ is a *"Finished Work!"* That means there is nothing else that needs to be added and in fact, there is nothing else which can be added. He has done it all. Actually, the Holy Spirit calls it the *"Everlasting Covenant,"* meaning that it will never have to be amended or replaced (Heb. 13:20). So, the very idea that we think we can do something that will aid the process of Redemption or Victory in any way, is an insult to Christ of the highest proportions.

Under the old economy of God, and I refer to the Mosaic Law, the duties of the Priests never ended. Consequently, even though there were other types of sacred furniture and utensils in the Tabernacle and Temple, there was no chair. This meant, that the work of the Priests continued, simply because more and more Sacrifices always had to be offered. The blood of bulls and goats could not take away sin, only cover it.

However, when Christ completed His Work on the Cross and the Resurrection, He went back to the Father and *"sat down on the Right Hand of the Majesty on High"* (Heb. 1:3).

This meant, that His Work was complete, it was total, and in fact, so complete and so total, even as previously stated, that it will never have to be amended or replaced. It is the *"Everlasting Covenant."*

All that God demands of us, is Faith in this which He has done (Eph. 2:8-9). He wants no more, no less! Just Faith in what He has done.

It seems so simple, but yet it's so difficult for us to do. We keep trying to insert *"self"* into the picture, attempting to sanctify ourselves, attempting to bring about in our lives, that which the Holy Spirit Alone can do. And to be sure, everything He does is done squarely on what Christ did in the Atonement. That is His legal boundaries. He will not overstep those boundaries, and if we step outside of them, which we always do when we attempt to insert self, He will not afford us His help. It always must be *"in Christ"* (Rom. 8:1-2), which refers to what He did at the Cross and the Resurrection.

(4) "SO THAT WE OURSELVES GLORY IN YOU IN THE CHURCHES OF GOD FOR YOUR PATIENCE AND FAITH IN ALL YOUR PERSECUTIONS AND TRIBULATIONS THAT YE ENDURE:"

Paul in essence is saying, that in his visits to other Churches, he boasts of the perseverance and Faith of the Thessalonians.

The Apostle relating this to the Thessalonians, was meant to encourage all of the Believers, but more particularly, those who felt inferior because of failures (I Thess. 5:14). The Apostle speaks to this discouragement when he says, *"As far as we are concerned your progress has been tremendous, so much so that we boast about it to other Churches."* The Churches to which Paul had boasted were probably more widespread and in the vicinity of Corinth.

Churches everywhere had heard this report. This did not necessarily include every single Church of course, but represents a rela-

NOTES

tively widespread dissemination of the news (Thomas).

GLORY IN YOU

The phrase, *"So that we ourselves glory in you in the Churches of God,"* presents to us several things:

1. The persecutions Paul mentioned in the last phrase of this Verse, must have been more severe than appears on the surface. Unbelieving Jews assaulted them because of their Christian Testimony. Unbelieving Gentiles joined in with persistent persecution, which could have taken any turn and probably did. For them to have left one heathen temple and gone to another, would have excited no reproach whatsoever. But to accept Christ, and to leave these heathen temples altogether, of course arouses the ire of Satan. As well, the Jews knew exactly why they were joining in the persecution. They hated Christ! However, the Gentiles would have known nothing about Christ, so their hatred or opposition, would strictly have been yielding themselves as a tool of Satan, even though they would not have understood such. Of course, all fall into that category; however, with some, even many, it is done unwittingly.

2. The Spiritual Growth of the Thessalonians had been gained without the help of Godly Teachers. Of course, Paul had grounded them adequately, but his time there had been so short, that much had been left unsaid and undone. So, their growth was even more remarkable!

3. We learn from this that all victories were reported in the various Churches, which created a bond of unity and love, with the Thessalonians being the topic at this particular time. Of course, news did not travel so fast in those days, but when it was received, it was spread abroad among all the followers of Christ, concerning whatever good things had happened. In the face of such persecution, and considering they were all relatively new converts and especially, that they had very little leadership at this time, their Spiritual Growth is all the more remarkable and worthy of such testimony.

4. Is it possible that all similar advances on Earth, are heralded in the portals of Glory as well?

NOTES

PATIENCE AND FAITH

The phrase, *"For your Patience and Faith,"* refers to *"steadfastness,"* and the fact they were able to endure because their Faith was in God and His Promises.

What do we mean by that?

The Thessalonians were not looking at their circumstances, whatever those circumstances may have been, but rather to God and His Promises. As well, this was not a momentary thing, but rather a *"steadfastness,"* i.e., *"patience."*

The idea is, *"Lord you will lead us through, You will help us to overcome, You will help us to remain faithful, despite the circumstances and variances of life."*

The Believer must understand, that the persecutions and tribulations of the next phrase, even though engineered by Satan, were in fact, allowed by God. To be sure, He will allow Satan only a certain amount of latitude (Job Chpts. 1-2), and even though Satan of course means it for our harm, the Lord means it for our good.

In a sense, every single Believer is in the same position as the spies of old (Num. Chpt. 13).

Ten of these spies saw the walled cities and the giants, while two of the spies, Joshua and Caleb saw the Promises of God (Num. 13:30-33).

Unfortunately, the majority of the people of Israel listened to the spies of doubt and unbelief rather than Joshua and Caleb, which consigned them to several more decades of wilderness problems, while all the time they could have been in the land of Canaan.

ONCE AGAIN I COME BACK TO THE CROSS

In the last 30 or 40 years of the 20th Century, the Church has had the great Promises of the Bible held up as a potential for every Believer, and rightly so. I speak of Promises such as Matthew 21:22; Mark 11:24; John 14:14; 15:7, etc. However, for the most part the Church has attempted to use these Promises somewhat as a magic wand or talisman, which of course, the Lord can never honor.

The main reason that He will not honor or respect such Faith or even His Promises when used in such a manner, is because they have been moved outside of the Cross. These Promises are definitely real, just as real today as when they were uttered nearly 2,000 years ago; however, all the Promises of God, in fact, the entirety of the Word from Genesis through Revelation, are all centered up in Christ, Who is centered up in the Cross.

A proper understanding of the Cross of Christ, which means to give it the priority which it certainly has in the Scriptures, is to guarantee the Will of God in every facet of life. However, when the Cross of Christ, which of course is the Finished Work of Christ, the great Atonement, is placed in a subsidiary role, that is if given any place at all, the whole belief system becomes suspect and in fact, is in error.

As we've already stated, we cannot really understand words like *"Patience," "Faith,"* or *"Grace,"* etc., unless we understand these words in connection with the Cross of Christ. Everything must be tied to His Finished Work, for it is there that Redemption was purchased, which includes the entirety of the manner in which God deals with man, and man deals with God.

## LET'S LOOK AT A PERFECT EXAMPLE

When the Children of Israel came back to the Promised Land after their dispersion in Babylon, they met a nation that was totally destroyed, with its cities razed to the ground.

In the midst of this ruin, the first thing that normally would have been done, would be the building of a wall around Jerusalem for protection, etc. However, that was not what the Holy Spirit told them to do. They were told first of all to build an *"Altar"* (Ezra 3:1-3).

Instructed by the Scriptures, they offered up the Burnt-Offerings and the Sin-Offerings, both of course, types of Christ and what He would do at a future day on the Cross, and thus publicly confess themselves to be guilty sinners, and that only by the shedding of Atoning Blood could they be forgiven and brought back to God.

Dread of the surrounding nations did not cause them to seek safety in walls and battlements, but in Burnt-Offerings and Sin Sacrifices. They, in effect, and in spirit, sought refuge in a Crucified Saviour.

NOTES

Does the Reader understand the great significance of all this? As well, let not the Reader think that this may have been the case under the old economy of God, but has been changed at present. While to be sure, it has to a great deal definitely been changed, but not by God, but rather by an unbelieving Church.

Man's problem today is sin, exactly as it has always been man's problem. As well, there is only one solution for sin, and that is the Shed Blood of the Lamb. It was the case then, hence the Sacrifices, and it is the case now, hence the great Sacrifice of Christ, which will never need to be repeated.

## PAUL AND THE THESSALONIANS

Paul's Message to the Thessalonians was Jesus Christ and Him crucified (I Cor. 2:2). He wasn't able to stay there long enough to properly ground them in all the great rudiments of the Faith, but he gave them an excellent foundation, the foundation of the Cross.

This was Paul's Message, which becomes very obvious, at least to anyone who honestly reads his Epistles. As well, this was all orchestrated by the Holy Spirit, even down to every single word written by the Apostle, as with all the writers of the Bible.

Paul said, *"For Christ sent me not to baptize, but to preach the Gospel"* (I Cor. 1:17).

Now of course we must ask the question as to what is the Gospel?

Of course, we know the meaning of the word *"Gospel,"* is *"Good News"*; however, what is that good news?

The Apostle went on to say, *"Not with wisdom of words, lest the Cross of Christ should be made of none effect"* (I Cor. 1:17).

Then the Apostle tells us that the *"preaching of the Cross,"* is the Gospel (I Cor. 1:18).

Consequently, if one is not *"preaching the Cross,"* then one is not preaching the Gospel, which means he or she is preaching *"another gospel"* (II Cor. 11:4).

How much is the Cross being preached presently? Of course, some few Preachers definitely are preaching the Cross; however, that number is few and far between; consequently, the Church is by and large a failing Church, instead of a victorious Church. Inasmuch as there can be no real Faith without a proper understanding of the Cross, which means there can be no real victory in the life of the Saint, this puts the modern Church in a precarious situation, simply because most of the Church is not preaching the Cross at all.

For all practical purposes, the leadership of most of the modern Pentecostal Denominations, at least in the United States and Canada, has opted for the psychological way, which means they have rejected the Cross of Christ. One cannot have it both ways, considering that each cancels out the other. Even though I would rather believe that this has been done because of an ignorance of the Word, I am very concerned, however, that it has rather been done because of unbelief. The more I study this subject, the more I must come to the conclusion that it can only be done through unbelief, at least as far as such leadership is concerned.

That means that these men simply do not believe that what Jesus did at the Cross and in His Resurrection presents the answer, and in fact, the only answer for hurting humanity. They simply no more believe that Faith in what Christ did there sets the captive free, which means that drunkards can be made sober, harlots can be made holy, bondages of darkness can be broken, lives can be totally and miraculously changed by the Power of God, and in fact, can be changed only in this manner.

Again I emphasize, one cannot have it both ways. One either believes or one doesn't believe. If one doesn't believe, one resorts to the humanistic way of the world, which is the psychological way.

## THE QUANDARY OF THE MODERN CHURCH

This of which I've said mostly pertains to so-called leadership. (Actually, in the Mind of God, these individuals are not spiritual leaders. Being elected to an administrative office by popular ballot, does not at all constitute spiritual leadership. While some of these individuals may definitely fall into the category of spiritual leadership simply because they have one of the fivefold Callings, Eph. 4:11, their being elected by popular ballot to an administrative office, in no way enhances their original Calling by God.)

NOTES

Irrespective of all of this, much of the Church looks to these individuals as spiritual leadership, whether they are or not. Consequently, they are swayed in one way or the other by the direction taken by these individuals. If the leadership opts for the psychological way, most of the laity in these respective Denominations do the same. Conversely, if the leadership follows the Word of God as it regards the Cross of Christ, the rank and file so to speak, for the most part will do the same.

As I have said in previous comments, and will continue to say, the Cross of Christ is going to be, and in fact already is, the dividing line between the Apostate Church and the True Church. It really has always been that way; however, I think now it is going to become much more pointed, meaning that this Truth is going to be made so clear to the Church, that it will have to be purposely accepted or purposely rejected.

## PERSECUTIONS AND TRIBULATIONS

The phrase, *"In all your persecutions and tribulations that ye endure,"* suggests continued and repeated sufferings which were still going on.

From Acts 17:5, 13 and I Thessalonians 2:14 we learn that the Thessalonians had suffered much persecution from the Jews and from their own countrymen, but being fully persuaded of the Gospel, and having the actual power of it working in their lives, they would not turn aside from it. In fact, persecution has never actually hurt the True Church and never will.

*"Persecution"* in the Greek is *"diogmos,"* and means *"to pursue, to follow, to press forward."* In other words, the persecution was active and planned and then pursued with vigor.

*"Tribulations"* in the Greek is *"thlipsesin,"* and means *"affliction."*

The difference between the two words *"persecutions and tribulations"* is, that while *"tribulation"* is quite general, and implies no personal enmities, *"persecution"* means that a certain set of persons were organizing certain active measures for the annoyance or hurt of the Church. Such persecution was still being *"endured"* when the Letter was written.

Their poor hearts and their false teachers would demand the visible intervention on Earth of the Lord to rescue them from their tormentors, but the Apostolic Doctrine of the Rapture formed a sure basis for both Faith and Patience. Faith believes He will come, and Patience waits for His Coming.

(5) "WHICH IS A MANIFEST TOKEN OF THE RIGHTEOUS JUDGMENT OF GOD, THAT YE MAY BE COUNTED WORTHY OF THE KINGDOM OF GOD, FOR WHICH YE ALSO SUFFER:"

This subject of persecution and affliction naturally raises the question of justice and fair play. Why would God allow such, especially considering that these were His people who were being persecuted?

THE RIGHTEOUS JUDGMENT OF GOD

The phrase, *"Which is a manifest token of the Righteous Judgment of God,"* presents the general sense that there would be a future Judgment, when the Righteous who were persecuted would be rewarded, and the wicked who persecuted them would be punished. The manner in which they bore their trials was an indication, also, of what the result would be in regard to them. Their Patience and Faith under persecutions were constantly showing that they would *"be counted worthy of the Kingdom of God,"* for which they were called to suffer.

The sense of this phrase is, that the endurance of affliction, in a proper manner, by the Righteous, is a proof that there will be Righteous Judgment of God at the last day.

The gist is, that it is guaranteed that this Judgment is coming, and as well, it will be a *"Righteous Judgment,"* which guarantees that nothing will be overlooked.

As the Scripture says here, every single Judgment ordained by God can be said to be *"Righteous."* It is *"Righteous"* simply because it is *"right."* The world has been so psychologized in the last few decades, that it anymore little expects a coming Judgment, if at all! The Bible declares man to be personally responsible for his actions, while humanistic psychology claims that outside forces are responsible. The Bible declares man to be inherently evil, therefore, needing to be *"Born-Again,"* while humanistic psychology claims that man is inherently good.

NOTES

So, the idea that man one day is going to face a Judgment, and a Judgment by God at that, is little believed at all. Irrespective, that Righteous Judgment is coming.

It is called the *"Great White Throne Judgment,"* and will take place at the end of the thousand year reign of Christ, which will include the second Resurrection of Damnation (Rev. Chpt. 20). There the books will be opened, and man will give account. He will not be able to refute anything, as the entirety of his actions on Earth, which includes the ill-treatment of the Thessalonians, plus all others serving God, have been and are being recorded for all to see.

This tells us that at least a part of this Righteous Judgment will be based on the treatment of Believers by unbelievers. While the Lord definitely does take vengeance now, to be sure, the totality of such vengeance will be carried out at that Judgment.

WORTHY OF THE KINGDOM OF GOD

The phrase, *"That ye may be counted worthy of the Kingdom of God,"* is not meant to imply that persecution and tribulations make one worthy, for they don't! No personal merit accrues from suffering as such, although God uses it in the refining of our souls through Grace. Consequently, the phrase could possibly be translated in this manner; *"God purposes to account His Children worthy of the Kingdom of God, for which they also suffer"* (Acts 5:41; I Pet. 4:12-16). The *"Kingdom"* seems here to be thought of in its future aspect.

The moral argument in this Passage turns two ways:

1. The Righteous Judgment of God is shown in sustaining and justifying His persecuted people now.

2. God's *"Righteous Judgment"* is shown in punishing the wicked and rewarding the faithful in a future reckoning.

It might be said in this manner; *"Our steadfastness in suffering is seen as proof of our true Faith* (and also as evidence of the awful moral state of the world)." The suffering of Believers for Christ's sake is also a guarantee of future Judgment; in a moral universe there must necessarily be a rectifying of life's injustices. It is assumed that the Readers will agree with the basic principle of reward and punishment, which without fail, will be handed out to all concerned at that coming day, both the Righteous and the unrighteous. Such will take place for the Child of God at the *"Judgment Seat of Christ."* This will not be a Judgment of sins, for that was handled at the Cross, but rather of one's works. As well, punishment, will consist of the lack of reward, and no more, because Jesus took our punishment on the Cross.

However, as this *"Righteous Judgment"* speaks to the unsaved, it points to the coming *"Great White Throne Judgment"* (Rev. Chpt. 20). It will be reversed there.

The only *"reward"* then given to the unsaved (for no saved will be there), will be the fact of less punishment as it regards degree, but not duration, for whatever punishment is meted out, will last forever (Lk. 12:47-48).

To deny all of this is to be plunged into a moral chaos, which of course God cannot abide.

Thus we have in this Passage, continuing through Verse 10, *"The Judgment of God"*:

1. The moral basis of Judgment (II Thess. 1:5-7).
2. The time and the circumstances of the Judgment (II Thess. 1:7).
3. The basis and the nature of punishment (II Thess. 1:8-9).
4. The basis and the nature of reward (II Thess. 1:10).

TO SUFFER

The phrase, *"For which ye also suffer,"* refers to something which is a given concerning true Christianity.

In his last Epistle shortly before his death, Paul wrote to Timothy, *"That they may also obtain the Salvation which is in Christ Jesus with eternal glory."* Then he added, *"It is a faithful saying: For if we be dead with Him* (having been baptized into His Death) (Rom. 6:3)*, we shall also live with Him* (having been raised with Him in His Resurrection) (Rom. 6:4-5): *if we suffer* (endure)*, we shall also reign with Him"* (II Tim. 2:10-12).

Thus, whether Christians suffer physically or not, the important thing is to endure. This means that Believers are to stand their ground when others are fleeing, to hold out when others are giving in, to remain steadfast to the end whatever others do (Horton).

Once again, it is not the suffering or even the enduring which sanctifies the Child of God, that being accomplished only by one's Faith in the Finished Work of Christ, by which the Holy Spirit carries out this great work. It simply means, even as we have said, that God allows so much suffering for each individual in one form or the other, that we might learn obedience.

The Scripture plainly says of Christ, *"Though He were a Son, yet learned He obedience by the things which He suffered"* (Heb. 5:8).

This doesn't mean that he learned to *"be"* obedient, for had that been the case, it would have meant that He had been disobedient, which of course never happened.

The idea is, that Christ as a Man, *"The Man Christ Jesus,"* learned through suffering to trust the Father in all things.

Suffering is allowed by God as it regards His Children, that we might learn even as Christ did, Who is our Example.

Of course, the great difference in us and Christ is, He was never disobedient, while we have been disobedient many times. And at least some of the suffering we engage, is because of our disobedience. The idea is, *"I don't want to go through that again, so I must learn the 'why' and 'what!'"*

As this *"obedience"* ever pointed Christ toward the Cross, which was the object all along, it points us to the same direction. It is always *"The Cross!" "The Cross!" "The Cross!"*

(6) "SEEING IT IS A RIGHTEOUS THING WITH GOD TO RECOMPENSE TRIBULATION TO THEM THAT TROUBLE YOU;"

It is here stated how God will pay back those responsible for troubling Christians. They will be repaid proportionately for the suffering they have caused God's people. This is only right (*"just"*) in God's eyes and is the reason this future Judgment is called *"Righteous."*

To be sure, even as the Apostle outlines in the following Verses, this *"Righteous Judgment"* will come at the conclusion of all things; however, it must also be ever understood that *"God is angry with the wicked*

NOTES

*every day"* (Ps. 7:11), and *"The arms of the wicked shall be broken"* (Ps. 37:17). No one, but no one, gets anything by God.

WHAT ABOUT CHRISTIANS WHO HINDER OTHER CHRISTIANS?

Unfortunately, that is often the case. It's bad enough to be opposed by the evil spirits of darkness along with the system of this world, but to have Believers who claim to be serving the same Lord and working for the same cause to also oppose you, and at times even strongly so, presents the worst cut of all.

It is said of Christ regarding Judas, *"Yea, Mine Own familiar friend, in whom I trusted, which did eat of My bread, hath lifted up his heel against Me"* (Ps. 41:9).

Of course we know that is an extreme case; however, any Christian who opposes a true Christian in any manner, is definitely functioning in the spirit of Judas, which is a dangerous thing indeed!

This doesn't refer to correction which at times is needed. I'm speaking of opposition, in other words, trying to do one harm and hurt, irrespective of the excuses given.

Of course the question begs to be asked and answered, *"How can one who claims to be of Christ, at the same time oppose, and even greatly so, that which is of Christ?"* There are two answers to that question:

1. Deception: Even Christians, and at times even good Christians, can momentarily be deceived. Notice I said *"momentarily!"* If they truly know and love the Lord, the Holy Spirit will ultimately be able to get them onto the right path. If after the Holy Spirit's prodding, they refuse to obey, then their situation can become spiritually dire, even as it has with many. To sin against light is the worst sin of all.

However, circumstances at times can be so arranged by Satan, that it is at times very difficult to see through the surface problems to the real Truth. The Crucifixion of Christ is an excellent example:

Even though Jesus plainly told His Disciples, that He would be killed and rise again the third day (Mat. 16:21-23), when that actual time came, it was so horrifying, so gruesome, so seemingly final, that not a single Disciple believed that He was actually going to rise from the dead. The circumstances and the surface situation were so obvious and final, that the Disciples could not work their way through this horror!

Even though my own personal situation is no comparison to that, still, the principle is the same. It has been very hard for the Church, even those who are Godly, to see through the surface problems, and know exactly what the Holy Spirit is doing. No, I'm not even remotely suggesting that the Holy Spirit has anything at all to do with wrongdoing, but I am definitely saying that He, at times, does use such, to bring about a desired conclusion.

An excellent example is the terrible situation in which David found himself, when he numbered Israel without paying the proper ransom tax as demanded by the Law of Moses, which had to do with Redemption (II Sam. Chpt. 24).

Many people overlook this, simply because they do not understand the gravity of David's sin at this time; however, I remind the Reader, that 70,000 men died as a result of the plague which followed as a result of this sin. So that tells us it was bad indeed!

However, out of this horror, the Lord gave David, and in fact, all of Israel, a demonstration of the Cross, by fire coming from Heaven to devour the Sacrifice which was offered at that time to appease the terrible situation (I Chron. 21:26).

As well, out of this came the site where the Temple would be built by Solomon, because that's where the Sacrifice was instructed to be offered, and where the fire fell (II Sam. 24:16-25).

To be sure, this is a very expensive way to come to the realization of the Will and Revelation of God; unfortunately, that's the route that most of us seemingly have to take.

The Holy Spirit has already begun portraying to the Church that which only He can do, as it regards the veracity of our personal Ministry. As the proof becomes more and more undeniable that we are of God, and not only of God, but with a worldwide Work for God remaining to be done, which in fact has already begun, Believers are going to have to make a decision. And to be frank, that

NOTES

decision is not going to so much be Jimmy Swaggart, as it is the Cross of Christ.

However, is it too much to say that to reject one is to reject the other? To be sure, it was that way with Paul; to reject Paul was to reject Grace, and to reject Grace was to reject Paul. Of course, when one says *"Grace,"* one is at the same time saying *"the Cross!"*

2. Paul referred to some of these people as *"false Brethren"* (II Cor. 11:26).

This means they were not even saved, despite their profession! It is the same with many modern Christians, and that would go for many so-called Religious Leaders!

Despite their claims, a lot of these people simply do not know the Lord. They are like the Pharisees of old; consequently, they will not change!

Of course, only the Lord can make that judgment. It is not up to us to do so! And yet, with some of these individuals, I think it is so obvious, even as it was with Paul, that they must be labeled as *"false Brethren,"* meaning that they are not really brothers in the Lord, but something else entirely.

## A RIGHTEOUS THING

The phrase, *"Seeing it is a righteous thing with God,"* doesn't mean that maybe it might be or maybe it isn't, but rather an assumption which is beyond dispute.

*"With God"* is literally in the Greek *"by the side of God,"* and so *"from God's standpoint."* In other words, He is the One Who determines what is *"Righteous"* and what isn't *"Righteous."* Man doesn't make that determination, because man is not qualified to make that determination. That's the reason, that no Believer is to ever attempt to revenge himself on others. It is always to be left in the hands of God (Rom. 12:17-21).

Jesus said, and He meant every word of it, *"Judge not, that ye be not judged.*

*"For with what judgment ye judge, ye shall be judged: And with what measure ye mete, it shall be measured to you again."*

He then said, *"And why beholdest thou the mote that is in thy Brother's eye, but considerest not the beam that is in thine own eye?"*

He then said, *"Thou hypocrite . . ."* (Mat. 7:1-5).

NOTES

Understanding, that every single derogatory thing that we do to someone else, and in whatever capacity, is going to come back to us as well, should give us pause! As well, the scenario can be turned around, in that all the good that we do to others, will definitely be returned to us, which should make us want to follow that course. Jesus said, and plainly, *"Thy Father which seeth in secret Himself shall reward thee openly"* (Mat. 6:4).

## THE RECOMPENSE OF TRIBULATION

The phrase, *"To recompense tribulation to them that trouble you,"* presents a two-fold meaning:

1. Of course, it refers to the coming Judgment of which the next Verses proclaim, which will address itself to the entirety of the world, and in fact, every unsaved person who has ever lived. There's a reckoning day coming for all things, for all people, for all situations, and all circumstances. To be sure, the One Who notes every sparrow's fall, who numbers the hairs on the heads of all people, will exact a total account. It cannot be otherwise! And I speak of the *"Great White Throne Judgment"* (Rev. 20:11-13).

God's Laws were not given in order to be ignored or wantonly broken. As well, irrespective as to whether men believe in God or not, irrespective as to whether they believe the Bible or not, all to be sure, will give account to the Word of God, and in every respect.

Some may think that because they are Moslem, or Buddhist, etc., that this absolves them of giving account; however, it absolves them of nothing!

As we've previously stated, the world has been so psychologized in the last several decades, that the idea of a coming Judgment is scoffed at; nevertheless, irrespective of the lies of men, judgment is coming, and of that all can be certain.

2. It should be understood, that not only is there a coming judgment for those who would hinder the Work of God or the people of God, there is judgment in this life as well (Mat. 7:1-2). Ananias and Sapphira and their judgment as recorded in Acts Chapter 5, is but one example. In fact, there are countless people presently who are sick or who die prematurely, because they seek to hinder the

people of God in some way. Only the Lord knows the financial reverses occasioned by such, and many other types of problems which could be named.

With most of these individuals, and to be sure the number is large, it is not known exactly as to the cause of their problems, at least as far as outward observance is concerned; however, if the Truth be known, for many the cause is the Judgment of God.

As well, this would apply far more stringently to those who claim to know the Lord, but yet set themselves to hinder the Work of God in some fashion, which always falls out to hindering those who are truly called of God. It is for certain that the unsaved will fall into such a category, but I am persuaded that judgment upon those who claim to know the Lord, but yet seek to hinder His Work, are dealt with far more severely.

Paul suffered much at the hands of those in the world, in other words those who didn't know the Lord; however, the greatest hindrance to his work and his person, was by those who did claim to know the Lord, whether national Israel, or those in the Church who opposed his Doctrine of Grace. I cannot but believe that their judgment was more severe.

At the same time, this doesn't mean that everyone who has problems, is having these problems simply because of these things we have mentioned. For instance, Paul had all types of problems, but it certainly wasn't because he had opposed the Work of God, but rather the very opposite. In other words, his problems came because of doing the Will of God, not opposing the Will of God!

## THE PRICE THAT WAS PAID

I think the average Christian little knows or understands the love that God has for His Children. If He loves the world, and by that we mean the unredeemed world, enough to send His Only Son to die for this unredeemed world, then think how much He must love those who have made Him the Lord of their lives. In fact, I don't think any of us know or properly understand the depth or the degree of that love, and in fact I'm not sure it's possible to understand it.

Irrespective, considering that we were bought at such a price, it should be understandable at least somewhat to all of us, as to how much disfavor the Lord looks upon those who would hinder or hurt His Children. Considering the price that He paid for our Redemption, considering what it all means, should give us an idea as to His feelings for those who call upon His Name. So, when He speaks of those who trouble the Child of God, and in any way we might quickly add, it is not with Grace that He speaks. This must be clearly understood! It is with Judgment that He thus speaks.

NOTES

(7) "AND TO YOU WHO ARE TROUBLED REST WITH US, WHEN THE LORD JESUS SHALL BE REVEALED FROM HEAVEN WITH HIS MIGHTY ANGELS,"

The idea here is twofold:

First of all, the Lord is saying that the trouble is soon going to be over. It refers to the time when the Saint dies, or else at the Rapture of the Church, which is yet to come. In either case, the Saint will be at *"rest!"*

Second, the Lord is coming back to the Earth, which speaks of the Second Coming. It will actually be during the time of the Battle of Armageddon, when the Lord Jesus will be revealed Personally to culminate with vengeance the *"everlasting destruction"* and exclusion from the Lord's Presence and Glory.

## REST WITH US

The phrase, *"And to you who are troubled rest with us,"* refers to a personal guarantee by the Holy Spirit, that this time of *"rest"* from all problems, all troubles, and all difficulties, is definitely coming.

Even though the Saint will not enjoy reading these words, the Truth is, the *"trouble"* will continue until we die, or the Rapture takes place. As Believers, we are in an alien society. In other words, as Believers this society is alien to us, and will remain that way until the very end. The idea, that Christianity is going to gradually take over the entirety of the world, which will bring back Christ, is totally unscriptural. To be sure, a change is coming, but it's going to be exactly as Paul says in the next Scripture, *"in flaming fire."* As stated, this refers to the Second Coming of the Lord, when to be sure, all enemies will then be put down and forever, but it will be a very violent time, and not at all like some of the modern prognosticators attempt to tell us.

To try to change society is a fruitless task, but yet that's what the Church has attempted to do in the last several decades. Instead of changing society, society has succeeded in changing the Church, and that is catastrophic!

So, the animosity, the anger, and contention translating into *"trouble,"* will continue until the Rapture of the Church. To be frank, after the Rapture, when millions will give their hearts and lives to Christ, the *"trouble"* will actually intensify, with untold numbers forced to give their lives for the Cause of Christ (Rev. 7:14).

THE LORD JESUS WILL BE REVEALED FROM HEAVEN

The phrase, *"When the Lord Jesus shall be revealed from Heaven with His mighty Angels,"* refers to the Second Coming.

As we've already stated, this will be a cataclysmic event, in fact, the most striking event the world has ever known. To properly describe the Second Coming of the Lord, even the most ardent Bible Scholar would be hard put to do so. It will be so striking, so powerful, so absolutely all-encompassing, even as Paul here describes!

THE SECOND ADVENT OF CHRIST

As we've already stated, the Second Advent refers to the Second Coming of Christ. At that time, every Believer who has ever lived will come with Him. It will be the time when the Lord will come back to this Earth to take possession of that which is rightfully His. In fact, He will rule and reign from Jerusalem, with the knowledge of the Lord at that particular time covering the entirety of the Earth as the waters cover the sea (Hab. 2:14). Every Saint of God, with all having Glorified Bodies, will help Him rule and reign. It will be a time of unprecedented peace and prosperity. It is called the *"Kingdom Age."*

THE CROSS HAS MADE IT ALL POSSIBLE

What Jesus did at the Cross is so all-encompassing, so total, so complete, that nothing was left undone, hence it being referred to as *"The Finished Work."* At the present time, even though everything that Adam lost in the Fall has been addressed in the Cross, still, we presently only have a portion of that which Jesus has done.

NOTES

Concerning this, Paul said, *"And not only they* (the Creation and all it entails), *but ourselves also* (refers to Believers), *which have the Firstfruits of the Spirit* (even though Jesus at the Cross addressed every single thing lost in the Fall, we only have a part of that possession now, with the balance coming at the Resurrection), *even we ourselves groan within ourselves* (proclaims the obvious fact that all Jesus paid for in the Atonement has not yet been fully realized), *waiting for the Adoption* (should be translated *'waiting for the fulfillment of the process, which Adoption into the family of God guarantees'), to wit, the Redemption of our body"* (the glorifying of our physical body that will take place at the Resurrection [Rom. 8:23]).

So, presently we only have the *"Firstfruits"* of what Jesus did at the Cross. At the Resurrection, the balance of the benefits of the Atonement will be given to us, which will include Glorified Bodies, and being in the Presence of Christ forever and forever.

THE SECOND COMING

The Second Coming is but another stage in the great Plan of God, all made possible, as stated, by the Cross. While it will be our Lord's Second Coming, with all its attendant power, prestige, and glory, which will be unlike anything the world has ever known before, every Saint of God who has ever lived will be with Him, and will have the privilege of enjoying the glory of that coming time. Incidentally, it will take place in the very midst of the Battle of Armageddon, when the Antichrist will be bearing down upon Israel, with these beleaguered people on the very edge of annihilation.

Actually, that will be the intention of the Antichrist — to completely annihilate Israel, thereby doing what Haman, Herod, and Hitler could not do. But for the coming of the Lord, he would succeed. But he will not succeed, because the Lord hasn't forgotten the Promises that He has made to the Patriarchs, Prophets, and Apostles of old. God never fails on His Promises; they always, without exception, come to pass. However, and as we have just stated, it is the Cross which has made all of these Promises possible. To be sure, God has the power to do anything; however, His Nature, because of His Holiness, will not allow Him to do certain things.

For instance, God could not merely make a decree that the terrible blight of sin be eradicated. While He had the power to do such, His perfectly righteous Nature, as stated, would not allow such. He had to pay the price for sin, and pay it in full. This was done at the Cross, and only at the Cross.

THE ANGELS OF HIS POWER

The phrase, *"His mighty Angels,"* which in the Greek, actually says *"the Angels of His Power,"* indicates to us that Angels are part of God's power over the vast creations. The true Angels help God maintain order over others who are now in rebellion with Satan (Dan. 10:11-21; Eph. 3:9-10; 6:12; Rev. 12:7-12).

So this tells us at the Second Coming, when the Lord comes back to Earth, He will have with Him, not only every Saint of God who has ever lived, but as well, at least a great number of His Mighty Angels, making this the greatest invasion the world has ever known (Rev. Chpt. 19).

THE DESCENT FROM HEAVEN

Our Lord describes this great event in Matthew 24:27-31, and John in Revelation 19:11-16. It occurs at the close of the second half of Daniel's Seventieth Week, or in effect at the close of the Great Tribulation. John describes our Lord as coming out of an opened Heaven riding on a white horse. He comes as a Warrior to judge and make war. On His Head are many crowns. The Greek word here for crowns is *"diadema."*

Trench describes this crown as a white linen band or fillet encircling the brow, an insignia of royalty. He says, *"The diadem strictly was a different thing from what a crown now is or was, and it was no other than a fillet of silk, or linen, or some such thing. Nor appears it that any other kind of crown was used for a royal ensign, except only in some kingdoms of Asia, but this kind of crown, until the beginning of Christianity in the Roman Empire."*

NOTES

Commenting on Revelation 19:12, he says, *"In this last Verse it is sublimely said of Him Who is King of kings and Lord of lords, that 'on His head were many crowns'; an expression with all its magnificence, difficult to realize, so long as we picture to our mind's eye such 'crowns' as at present monarchs wear, but intelligible at once, when we contemplate them as 'diadems,' that is, narrow crowns encircling the brow."*

DIADEMS

*"These many 'diadems' will then be tokens of the many royalties — of Heaven, of earth and of hell (Phil. 2:10) — which are His; royalties once usurped or assailed by the Great Red Dragon, the usurper of Christ's dignities and honors, Who has therefore His Own seven diadems as well (Rev. 13:1), but now openly and forever assumed by Him Whose rightfully they are."*

In relation to the Millennial Kingdom which is about to come, these diadems represent our Lord's rule over all of the kings and other rulers who will retain their local self-governments under the supervision of the King of kings during the thousand years of His reign as world dictator.

As someone has well said, the greatest form of government in the world is that of a dictatorship, providing one can find a good dictator. But of course, that has been impossible up to the time of Christ. But with Christ, the world will find a Dictator Who is benevolent, kind, gracious, and Who of course will judge accordingly.

A VESTURE DIPPED IN BLOOD

John says that Christ will be clothed with a vesture dipped in blood (Rev. 19:13).

This refers to the price He paid at the Cross of Calvary in order that mankind might be saved. It is to never be forgotten, but rather held up as the ensign or banner of Redemption, and to be held up forever and forever!

At this time, every Saint of God who has ever lived will be with Christ, coming back with Him to rule and reign on this Earth for 1,000 years, and then to go into the renewed Earth forever and forever (Rev. Chpts. 21-22). However, it is to be ever understood, that all of this that we Saints have, the blessing, the association, the environment, the privilege, the greatness, grandeur, and glory, all are because of what He did at that Cross now some 2,000 years ago.

A *"vesture"* is a robe, and here speaks of the end of this robe dipped in blood. It is a robe no doubt, that is snow white; however, dipped in blood, it will be fringed with red.

The Scripture says that this *"vesture"* is *"dipped in blood."* The word *"dipped"* in the Greek is *"bapto,"* a word often used of the act of dying cloth, and the very word from which we get our word *"baptism."*

Some expositors claim that this vesture dipped in blood is meant to describe our Lord's clothing in anticipation of the Battle of Armageddon where His Robe will be stained with the blood of the soldiers of the Antichrist, spattered on Him in the midst of that terrible carnage.

I don't think so!

Even though He will definitely be the great Victor concerning that Battle, the description given in Revelation, Chapter 19 all supports the contention as to Who He actually is, which of course presupposes what He will do. The vesture dipped in blood symbolizes what He did at the Cross in order that man might be redeemed.

The great armies out of Heaven, the Holy Angels and the Saints from Adam to the Rapture, all resplendent with an enswathement of glory, follow Him. He comes to smite the nations and rule them with a rod of iron, an absolute Dictator, however, all wise as stated, and benevolent. Only the Personal Presence of our great God and Saviour Jesus Christ will solve the Earth's situation and bring peace and blessing to its inhabitants. And this will be accomplished only by force, and not at all by political means, as many in the modern Church contend.

Daniel said, *"Thou sawest till that a stone was cut out without hands, which smote the image upon his feet that were of iron and clay, and break them to pieces . . . and became like the chaff of the summer threshing-floors; and the wind carried them away, that no place was found for them: and the stone that smote the image became a great mountain, and filled the whole earth"* (Dan. 2:34-35).

NOTES

That *"Stone"* is Christ. The *"image"* represents the nations of the world. The stone breaking these images all to pieces, represents the Second Coming of the Lord, even as John portrays in Revelation, Chapter 19. As is obvious, this coming and takeover of the world, which will definitely happen, will be by force and not by any other means.

## A DESCRIPTION OF THE SECOND COMING

Our Lord describes His Coming to the Earth in the words, *"As the lightning cometh out of the east, and shineth even to the west, so shall also the Coming of the Son of Man be"* (Mat. 24:27).

He will descend with the swiftness of lightning. According to some Bible Scholars, Heaven is at least 2,932,848,000,000,000,000,000 miles from the Earth. As is obvious, if that is correct, it is outside this particular universe.

Lucifer said, *"I will exalt my throne above the stars of God."* He also said, *"I will sit in the sides of the north"* (Isa. 14:13).

Astronomy has discovered stars whose light has taken 500 million years to reach this Earth, this light traveling at the speed of 186,000 miles per second. With this information, mathematics will give one the distance of Heaven from the Earth.

The Lord Jesus will come with the speed of lightning. Furthermore, His Coming will be with the brilliance of a lightning flash and against the dark background of a darkened Sun, Moon, and Stars. Our Lord says, *"The Sun shall be darkened, and the Moon shall not give her light, and the Stars shall fall from Heaven."*

The Greek word for a *"Star"* is *"aster,"* used of stars, also of shooting stars or meteors.

Here we have a rain of meteors falling on the Earth. John predicts this same thing in the Sixth Seal (Rev. 6:12-13), *"The Sun became black as sackcloth of hair, and the Moon became blood, and the Stars* (meteors) *of Heaven fell unto the earth."* When our Lord comes to the Earth with the Angels and the Saints in one great blaze of glory, it will be to an Earth that is somewhat darkened, and even out of a darkened sky. He describes this as the *"sign of the Son of Man in Heaven."*

NOTES

## A SIGN FROM HEAVEN

The word *"sign"* in the Greek is *"semeion,"* the word used of a miracle which purpose it is to attest the Divine Source of the Message delivered by the one performing the miracle. Here it is a miracle whose merciful purpose is to prove to the Earth-dwellers that the One coming from Heaven is indeed the Son of God Who should be received with joy.

But the human race, seeing this wonderful spectacle in the skies and realizing who is coming shall mourn. The word is *"kopto,"* which means *"to beat one's breast in grief."* John says, *"All kindreds of the earth shall wail because of Him"* (Rev. 1:7). The same word is used. It is a wail of anger, of grief that He is coming, a wail of resentment, of frustration.

## THE ARRIVAL ON EARTH

Zechariah tells us that the first place our Lord's blessed feet will touch will be the Mount of Olives (Zech. 14:4). He ascended from the Mount of Olives (Acts 1:9-12). The Angels promised His return in the same manner in which He ascended, a visible, bodily return.

His contact with this Earth will touch off an earthquake, supernaturally timed and caused, and an earthquake different from any earthquake that ever shook this Earth. Its center will be the Mount of Olives.

At this place it will be just violent enough to break that mountain into two parts, but not strong enough to level it to the ground (Zech. 14:4-5), and it increases in violence as it spreads. This could possibly be the same earthquake referred to in the Seventh Trumpet (Rev. 11:13-19) where one-tenth of Jerusalem is destroyed, the same earthquake of the Seventh Vial (Rev. 16:17-20), where the city of Babylon, commercial metropolis of the Antichrist is destroyed, and the near mountains and islands are obliterated.

Babylon, suddenly leveled to the ground by this earthquake, the Earth under the city and surrounding it filled with rich oil deposits opened up and set on fire from the burning city, is described by John in Revelation Chapter 18:9-11. The whole Earth *"shall bewail her and lament for her, when they shall see the smoke of her burning. She shall be utterly burned with fire . . . in one hour is thy judgment come . . . Thus with violence shall that great city Babylon be thrown down, and shall be found no more at all."*

Quite possibly, the whole Earth watching what will happen to rebuilt Babylon, will be by Television.

Such are some of the descriptive touches John gives us of the future destruction of this rebuilt city of Babylon.

## THE BATTLE OF ARMAGEDDON

With his kingdom ruined, Europe crippled by this earthquake, the Mediterranean a Sea of blood, the inhabitants tortured by the noisome sore, scorched with the heat of the Sun, in agony because of the plague of darkness, with nothing to drink it seems but blood or else *"bloody water,"* Babylon in ashes, the Antichrist is now faced with a battle, the issue of which is to decide who will be the ruler and god of this Earth, the Lord of Glory or himself!

John tells us that the demons will gather the kings of the whole Earth to the battle (Rev. 16:14-16). Zechariah also informs us that God will gather all nations against Jerusalem to battle (Zech. 14:1).

The apparent contradiction is resolved when we note that God is said to do something which He allows demons or others to do.

The Antichrist will come against Israel, thinking surely to destroy her, having massed forces large enough, he thinks, to accomplish the task. He knows if he can destroy Israel, then the Promises of God are defeated, and in effect, if that happens, he and actually Satan, will have won this deadly conflict of the ages and of all time.

He should be reminded, that there have been many nations and empires which have tried to destroy Israel, but rather have been destroyed themselves. Even though Israel crucified their Messiah and the world's Saviour, still, the Promises in the Word of God are that they will be brought back, and God always keeps His Promises (Rom. Chpt. 11).

## MASADA

Sometime ago while standing on top of the great mountain fortress of Masada, and hearing the guide give an account of what happened there nearly 2,000 years ago, I made a statement to him that took him aback for a few moments.

He was explaining as to how the Romans had built the great Earth embankment to the top of this fortress and thereby ultimately defeated the Jews. In fact, most of the Jews committed suicide, rather than be captured. He was pointing out the still visible traces of the Roman encampment of nearly 2,000 years ago.

When he finished, I said to him and the others who stood nearby, *"But where is Rome today? Her Empire is no more, while Israel once again occupies this country."*

The guide was Jewish, and he stood there for a moment looking at me and said nothing.

When he finally spoke, he said, *"You know, I've never thought of that!"*

That alone is enough to let the world know that the Promises of God are real and in fact, will never be defeated or denied.

In those days of long ago, to use an earthly vernacular, very few people would have bought stock in Israel's future. Rome ruled the world and was all-powerful. However, whatever God has laid His hand on, one can be sure that it will survive. It may have some ups and downs, and there may be some problems, but the end result is going to be positive. It cannot be otherwise!

## THE PLACE OF THE BATTLE

The place of the battle will be Israel.

Zechariah tells us that confusion shall enter the ranks of the armies of the Antichrist as they advance upon Israel. In fact, he will come very close to succeeding, with half of Jerusalem falling to the thrust of his effort (Zech. 14:1-3).

However, as the Lord then comes back, the Spirit of God will cause his soldiers to fight one another, and a plague will cause the flesh of these soldiers to consume away from their skeletons (Zech. 14:12-13).

John tells us that blood shall come out of the winepress (the battlefield) to the horse bridles (Rev. 14:20). Due to the overflowing rain which will take place then, even as Ezekiel prophesied (Ezek. 38:22), it will probably be blood mixed with water, but at any rate turning the water red.

The carnage will be so great that the blood soaked bodies of the soldiers of the Antichrist will be piled upon one another as he hurls his legions into the place of battle. In fact, God will invite the carrion birds of the air to a supper He has prepared for them, even the dead bodies of the soldiers of the Antichrist (Rev. 19:17-18).

NOTES

At that time, the Antichrist and his False Prophet will be thrown alive into Hell. Much of his army will be killed in battle. Satan will be thrown into the Bottomless Pit, and his demons with him. On this devastated Earth filled with unsaved humanity who worshipped the Antichrist and Satan and who opposed the Coming of the Lord of Glory with the same venomous hatred that Satan did, among these the Lord Jesus is now to set up Earth's Golden Age and give the human race one more opportunity to be saved.

However, at this present time, December of 1999, the population of the Earth is approximately six billion people. There is a possibility, that as many as four billion could be killed in the coming seven years of Great Tribulation, which Jesus said would be the worst the Earth has ever known (Mat. 24:21).

The next few Verses of our study in II Thessalonians, will aptly bring this out, even though said in only a few words.

(8) "IN FLAMING FIRE TAKING VENGEANCE ON THEM THAT KNOW NOT GOD, AND THAT OBEY NOT THE GOSPEL OF OUR LORD JESUS CHRIST:"

This of which is said by the Holy Spirit through Paul, has no overtones of selfish vindictiveness of revenge, but proceeds from the Justice of God to accomplish appropriate punishment for criminal offenses.

For a long, long time, Godly people have wondered at the longsuffering of God regarding the wickedness and evil of this Earth. We are here plainly told, that the longsuffering will ultimately be brought to an end. Just as surely as we read these words before us, just as surely this Judgment will come.

## VENGEANCE

The phrase, *"In flaming fire taking vengeance,"* gives us the manner of the Second Coming.

We have in Verses 7 and 8, three phrases giving a brief description of *"The Revelation of Christ"*:

1. The place: From Heaven.
2. The attendant retinue: His Mighty Angels.
3. The manner: in flaming fire.

The picture is notable for its restraint and brevity.

The expression *"taking vengeance"* if not understood correctly, will be negative. However, as in I Thessalonians 4:6, God is the Avenger, the Administrator of moral justice. In other words, *"He will do justice."* To be sure, the judgment will be swift, sure, awful, and terrible; however, it will not be one ounce more than is justified. In fact, one can say with certainty that the judgment will be less than it ought to be.

The *"flaming fire"* mentioned here, is not the fire of Hell, but rather that which will accompany the Lord at the Second Coming. The Prophet Ezekiel said, *"And I will plead against him with pestilence and with blood; and I will rain upon him, and upon his bands, and upon the many people that are with him, an overflowing rain, with great hailstones, fire, and brimstone"* (Ezek. 38:22).

The *"fire and brimstone"* mentioned here, no doubt refers to lightning and burning meteorites which will be hurled from Heaven against the Antichrist and his armies. The Lord has the elements of the heavens at His disposal, and to be sure, those elements will be used at that particular time, and in fact, throughout the Great Tribulation.

As should be obvious, these elements are of far greater destructive power than anything that man could ever have. For instance, the eruption of Mt. St. Helens in Washington State in the mid-80's, was equal to over 10 Atomic Bombs, of the size dropped on Japan in World War II. Actually, in Glacier National Park, the Mountain which blew there several thousands of years ago, was, it is said, a hundred times the blast of Mt. St. Helens. So, we're speaking of force, that has no equal in human terms. In other words, the Antichrist and his armies, no matter how large they are, simply will not have a chance.

## THE DAY OF THE LORD

This term, *"The Day of the Lord,"* is a technical term used by the Old Testament Prophets to designate a certain future period with regard to Israel. It will begin in the coming Great Tribulation, come to a climax at the Second Coming as it regards judgment, but of course, extend through the Millennium, and actually forever. The context in which it is found in the Old Testament defined the term (Isa. 2:12; 13:6, 9; 34:8; Jer. 46:10; Lam. 2:22; Ezek. 13:5; 30:3; Joel 1:15; 2:1; 3:14; Amos 5:18; Obad. vs. 15; Zeph. 1:7-8, 18; 2:2-3; Zech. 14:1; Mal. 4:5).

The character of this period is seen in the following: *"For the Day of the Lord of Hosts shall be upon every one that is proud and lofty, and upon everyone that is lifted up; and he shall be brought low"* (Isa. 2:12).

*"Howl ye; for the Day of the Lord is at hand; it shall come as a destruction from the Almighty.*

*"Behold, the Day of the Lord cometh, cruel both with wrath and fierce anger, to lay the land desolate: and He shall destroy the sinners thereof out of it.*

*"For the Stars of Heaven and the constellations thereof shall not give their light: the Sun shall be darkened in his going forth, and the Moon shall not cause her light to shine"* (Isa. 13:6, 9-10).

The prediction of the darkening of the Sun and Moon fixes the Day of the Lord as the Great Tribulation Period, for these things are to take place at that time (Mat. 24:29; Rev. 6:12; 8:12). In the context of this mention of the Day of the Lord is the prediction of the destruction of the city of Babylon (Rev. 13:19-22). *"Alas for the day! For the Day of the Lord is at hand, and as a destruction from the Almighty shall it come"* (Joel 1:15).

*"Multitudes, multitudes in the valley of decision: for the Day of the Lord is near in the valley of decision"* (Joel 3:14).

In this context we have, *"For, behold, in those days, and in that time, when I shall bring again the captivity of Judah and Jerusalem,*

*"I will gather all nations and will bring them down into the valley of Jehoshaphat, and will plead with them there for My people and for My heritage Israel, whom they have scattered among the nations and parted My land"* (Joel 3:1-2).

## THE BATTLE OF ARMAGEDDON

This is not a prediction of the captivities and the restoration under the Medo-Persian

NOTES

Empire, but of the worldwide dispersion, A.D. 70, the regathering at a yet future date (the Day of the Lord), and the Battle of Armageddon. The context of Zechariah 14:1, *"Behold the Day of the Lord cometh,"* includes the following:

1. The gathering of all nations against Jerusalem by God, the taking of the city, the return of the Lord to the Mount of Olives, which is also pictured in Revelation 19:11-16 and Matthew 24:27-30.

2. The earthquake which synchronizes with the earthquake at the end of the Great Tribulation (Rev. 6:12; 11:13; 16:18).

3. The assumption of the Earth ruled by the Lord Jesus.

In Malachi 4:5 we have, *"Behold, I will send you Elijah the Prophet before the coming of the great and dreadful Day of the Lord."* In the context we have, *"For behold, the day cometh, that shall burn as an oven; and all the proud, yea, and all that do wickedly, shall be stubble: and the day that cometh shall burn them up, saith the Lord of Hosts, that it shall leave them neither root nor branch"* (Mal. 4:1), and then comes the prediction of the second Advent in the words, *"But unto you that fear My Name shall the Sun of Righteousness arise with healing in His wings"* (Mal. 4:2).

EVENTS IN THE DAY OF THE LORD

From the foregoing, the following things should be clear:

1. The Day of the Lord has to do with the nation Israel, not with the Church, which latter was unknown to the Old Testament Prophets. Peter says that they searched their writings in vain in an effort to discover what would take place between the Cross and the Millennium (I Pet. 1:10-12). Paul tells us that the fact that Jew and Gentile would someday be one body was unknown until it was revealed to him (Eph. 3:4-7).

2. The period designated by the term *"Day of the Lord"* is still future.

3. The character of the period is one of judgment upon Israel because of its sin.

4. It refers to the period beginning with the Great Tribulation, since events predicted by the Old Testament Prophets are those which John predicts in connection with the period of the time spoken of in Revelation, Chapters 6-19, a period of unexampled trouble which will take place after the Church is caught out, and which is designated by the term, *"the Great Tribulation"* (Rev. 7:14), but will extend into the Millennium and actually forever. It is the time when the Lord will rule!

5. It is the time of the coming to Earth of the Messiah in Judgment. Hence, it cannot refer to the First Advent, since He came in humiliation and offered Himself as the Sacrifice for sin, but rather to the *"Second Advent"* i.e., *"The Second Coming."*

Some of the references to the Day of the Lord in the Old Testament have a fulfillment in the past, and are precursors of the Day of the Lord to follow. Yet the complete fulfillment in the case of the use of the term mostly, still awaits a future day.

THE DAY OF CHRIST

Paul, in II Thessalonians Chapter 1 is seeking to comfort the Saints in that local Church who were being persecuted for their Christian testimony and were enduring tribulation.

These tribulations were the righteous judgment of God in the form of discipline. Then he tells them that persecutors of the Saints will be punished *"when the Lord Jesus shall be revealed from Heaven with His Mighty Angels,*

*"In flaming fire taking vengeance on them that know not God, and that obey not the Gospel of our Lord Jesus Christ:*

*"Who shall be punished with everlasting destruction from the Presence of the Lord, and from the Glory of His Power;*

*"When He shall come to be glorified in His Saints, and to be admired in all them that believe"* (II Thess. 1:7-10). This is clearly the Second Advent or the *"Day of the Lord."*

The Angels will accompany Him at that time to the Earth. In His Coming from Heaven to Earth He will be glorified in His Saints and admired in all those who believe. But the Saints must be glorified themselves if the people of Earth are to see the reflected glory of the Lord Jesus in them. This implies a previous coming of the Lord Jesus to glorify the living Saints and raise the dead Saints for the purpose of glorifying their bodies restored to them. The fact that He comes from Heaven

NOTES

with them indicates that He had taken them with Him to that place previous to His descent to the Earth, which necessitates His previous coming for them. This is the Rapture of the Church, or as one might refer *"the Day of Christ!"*

John sees the Second Coming in Revelation 19:14, where he says, *"The armies which were in Heaven followed Him upon white horses, clothed in fine linen, white and clean."* These are Saints, not Angels. The fine linen, John speaks of is the Righteousness of the Saints (Rev. 19:8).

Angels do not possess Righteousness. There is a distinction between the Second Coming of the Lord Jesus and His Coming to take His Saints to Heaven, even as we have seen. As well, this is not to be considered as two parts of the Second Coming. The Second Coming is second to the First Coming as recorded in the Gospels. The writer to the Hebrews speaks of this Second Coming in Hebrews 9:28. This is the Second Advent, not His coming into the air to catch out His Church.

The typology here is of the High Priest appearing the first time to Israel at the Brazen Altar to offer the Sacrifice. Then he enters the Holy of Holies to sprinkle the Blood on the Mercy Seat. Following that he comes through the gate of the Court, appearing to Israel a second time, having accomplished Salvation.

So our Lord appeared the first time to Israel, and being rejected, put away sin through His Crucifixion. He is in Heaven now as High Priest. He will come again to Israel in His Second Advent.

But the point is, He comes *"with"* His Saints, which is the Day of the Lord, having previously descended into the atmosphere of the Earth to catch them out, which is the *"Day of Christ!"*

## THE LETTER

These Thessalonian Saints who were the objects of the persecutions of pagan unbelievers and were enduring tribulation, were the recipients of a letter informing them that the Day of the Lord was then present. This letter contained the forged signature of the Apostle Paul (the words in this Text *"Day of Christ"* should have been *"Day of the Lord,"* which are contained in the best Greek Texts).

NOTES

As a result they were shaken in mind and troubled, and for two reasons. If the Day of the Lord was then present, they had missed the Rapture of the Saints, and they were left to undergo the Judgments of the Great Tribulation. The words *"letter as from us"* indicate that a letter had been sent to them to that effect, and with the forged signature of Paul upon it. It is clear from all this that Paul had instructed them as to the Rapture of the Church, which he did in his first Letter to this Church (I Thess. 4:13-18), and that he also had given them the same Old Testament teaching regarding the Day of the Lord and its character.

They were at that time going through a period of tribulation, and the forged letter informed them that this tribulation was the one predicted in the Old Testament. Paul writes to correct this false statement and to assure them that the tribulations they were undergoing were not the ones described in Old Testament writings.

He begs them by the Coming of the Lord Jesus Christ and their gathering together unto Him, not to be troubled by this forged letter stating that they were in the midst of the *"Day of the Lord."* This had not yet happened, and in fact, would not happen until the Rapture of the Church takes place first (II Thess. 2:3-14).

## DECEPTION

Paul says, *"Let no man deceive you by any means because,"* and then comes an ellipsis which is followed by the words *"except there come,"* and he then lists two things which must precede the Day of the Lord. Those two things are *"a falling away"* and *"the revealing of the man of sin."* We will look at the second one first, since it requires but a brief treatment in comparison to the first one.

The word *"reveal"* in the Greek is *"apokalupto,"* which means *"to lay open what has been veiled or covered up."* Paul describes the Antichrist (the man of sin) as he *"who opposeth and exalteth himself above all that is called God, or that is worshiped, so that he as God sitteth in the Temple of God, showing himself that he is God."*

Paul, by the use of *"apokalupto"* refers here, not to the Antichrist's appearance as the benevolent world dictator, but to the disclosure of his true character which will take place in the middle of Daniel's Seventieth Week (Dan. 9:27). He refers to the disclosure of his hidden personality.

The Great Tribulation, or the worst part, is probably the last three and one half years of this seven year period. That, Paul says, cannot come until the Antichrist is revealed in his true identity. Since he was not a world dictator at the time Paul wrote the Thessalonian Letter, and the inhabitants of the Earth still had freedom of worship, the Day of the Lord, as should be obvious, had not yet come.

### A FALLING AWAY

The other thing which Paul says must come before the Great Tribulation is *"a falling away"* (II Thess. 2:3). The Greek word for *"falling away"* is *"apostasia,"* and is preceded by the definite article, which actually says in the Greek *"the falling away,"* which can refer to the last great apostasy of the Church, which in fact, we have presently already entered into.

However, the words *"falling way"* as given in this particular Scripture are the translators' *"interpretation"* of what *"they thought"* the Greek text meant here, not the actual *"translation"* of the Greek word itself.

The root verb of *"falling away"* in the Greek is *"aphistemi"* which means, *"to cause to withdraw, to go away, depart, withdraw from."* In a context where true and false doctrines are in view, it would mean *"to fall away from true doctrine,"* but the additional idea comes from the context, not the verb. No such specification is attached to this word here. The fact that our word *"apostasy"* is the transliteration of the Greek word means nothing except that in a context where a departure from the Faith is in view the verb does have reference to an apostasy, and that the word *"apostasy"* has been invested with that meaning. Considering this, it means that the translation as given in the King James Version is more an *"interpretation"* rather than a *"translation"* of the word. The translators should have translated rather than interpreted the word, and should have allowed the English Reader to make his own interpretation in the light of the context.

NOTES

There is a second meaning to the Greek word *"apostasia,"* which means *"a departure, a disappearance."* The Apostle has just referred to the gathering together of the Saints to the Lord Jesus at His Coming (II Thess. 2:1), which is the departure of the Church from the Earth. In his previous Letter (I Thess. 4:13-18), he had described that event in the words, *"Then we which are alive and remain shall be caught up together with them in the clouds to meet the Lord in the air,"* which involves a departure from the Earth.

### THE RAPTURE OF THE CHURCH

Considering this, and looking closely at the associating Scriptures, what Paul actually said in II Thessalonians 2:3 is, *"Let no man deceive you by any means: for that day shall not come* (Great Tribulation)*, except there come a departure first* (which speaks of the Rapture)*, and that man of sin* (then) *be revealed, the son of perdition."*

Consequently, Paul is here speaking of the departure of the Church which has been holding back the revelation of the Antichrist. All of which means that the Church will be caught out of this Earth before the Antichrist is revealed in his true identity as the one who puts down all forms of religious worship and sets himself up as God to be worshiped.

In fact, he says it again in another way in II Thessalonians 2:7, *"For the mystery of iniquity doth already work: only he* (the Church) *who now letteth* (or hindereth, and in this case hinders the advent of the Antichrist) *will let* (continue to hinder)*, until he* (the Church) *be taken out of the way* (which refers to the Rapture)."

When the Church is taken away, as Paul plainly says in these Verses, the Antichrist will then be revealed, with the Tribulation commencing, which will culminate with the Second Advent of the Lord Jesus. The Great Tribulation Period is *"the Day of the Lord."* His Coming into the air to catch out His Church is *"the Day of Christ."* Paul speaks of the latter in Philippians 1:6 as *"the Day of Christ Jesus."*

Thus, Paul differentiates between the two terms, speaking of *"the Day of the Lord"* as a period of judgment upon the nation Israel, and of *"the Day of Christ,"* a time of rejoicing for the Church at the Rapture, the latter to precede the former.

THEM WHO KNOW NOT GOD

The phrase, *"On them that know not God,"* refers to the world, and actually means *"they do not wish to know Him."* They want and desire their heathen religions or whatever it is they have embraced.

Some years ago we had a lady from India who attended Family Worship Center once or twice. She told someone that she was rejecting Christ and going back to India, where she could be a *"god."* She was referring to all the untold millions of false gods worshiped by most of the population of India, even to the point of individuals becoming *"god!"* In one way or the other, that is the feeling of much of the world. They do not know the Lord because they do not desire the know the Lord.

The root problem in all of this is, that men like their sin. So, they look for some type of religion which will allow them to continue in their sin, and at the same time appease their conscience. In fact, millions in Christianity do the same thing, even as the next phrase proclaims.

A FAILURE TO OBEY THE GOSPEL

The phrase, *"And that obey not the Gospel of our Lord Jesus Christ,"* in effect, proclaims a second group.

This group has heard the Gospel, which means they've been given an opportunity to accept the Gospel, and in fact have accepted portions of the Gospel. However, they do not desire to obey all the Gospel, so they search for a Church which will make them feel comfortable in their present disobedience, of which there are many. As stated, millions in modern Christianity fit this example.

Most people attend a particular Church which in fact is what they are. In other words, the Church teaches what they are, so they have an affinity for that particular Church. This goes for those who are spiritual and those who aren't spiritual.

Of course, there are many Christians who are not living as they ought to live, but want Christ to be the Ruler in their lives; consequently, they find a Church, that is if one is available, which in fact teaches the Truth.

NOTES

Regrettably, this number is very small, but thank God for the few who really do *"hunger and thirst after Righteousness."*

The deceiving of oneself is a favorite pastime of many Christians. They seek to appease their conscience, so they find a Church which fits with their lifestyle. In other words, if they want to continue in a particular type of sin, and do not desire to obey the Lord in all things, they seek out a Church which caters to that which they desire to do. It's not hard at all to find one of such stripe.

The culminating and most grievous sin of all is the rejection of Christ and of God's gracious invitation in His Son (Mk. 12:1-12; Rom. 2:8; 10:16, 21).

All of this comes down to the Cross of Christ, which of course is the Finished Work of Christ, i.e., *"the Atonement."* As we have previously stated, and will continue to state, the Cross of Christ has always been the dividing line between Truth and apostasy. I personally feel that the Cross as the dividing line is going to be more pronounced than ever in these last days. In other words, if the Cross is rejected in any fashion, or ignored, the individual is going to go into apostasy, because there is no place else to go. Therefore, when we speak of *"the Gospel of our Lord Jesus Christ,"* we're speaking of what He did at the Cross on our behalf, in order that we might have Redemption.

THE GREAT PLAN OF GOD

The story of the Bible is the story of the Redemption of man. The manner of that Redemption is the Cross of Christ (I Cor. 1:19; 2:2; Gal. 2:14). In fact, the Cross of Christ as the Plan of God, was instituted in the Mind of God from eternity past, which refers to a time prior to the creation of the Earth (I Pet. 1:18-21).

That being the case, we should, therefore, understand the reason for the Incarnation, i.e., *"God becoming man."* As God He could not die; therefore, in order to die, which had to be done if man was to be redeemed, God would have to become man, hence the Incarnation.

This should tell us that the Cross was the primary objective, the very purpose and reason for the coming of Christ, and the means by which Salvation is afforded. Understanding that, we should realize the great significance of what Christ did there, which means, that the Cross of Christ, which at the same time presupposes His Burial, Resurrection, and Exaltation, is the single most important thing in the great Plan of God. So the following questions must be asked:

Is the Cross of Christ the most important thing in the modern Church?

I think the answer to that is obvious! To the far greater majority of the Church, the Cross is little considered at all, and in many circles even repudiated.

Where the repudiation was once carried out by those referred to as *"Modernists,"* this malady has now spread even to those who claim to be Spirit-filled, i.e., *"Charismatics!"* While all Charismatics definitely do not fall into this category, far too many do.

Even many Pentecostals fit this same characterization, in that the Cross is ignored if not repudiated. It is impossible to embrace humanistic psychology, without at the same time refusing and rejecting the Cross of Christ. One cannot have it both ways. It is either one or the other!

Either Jesus addressed every single problem at the Cross, or else He didn't, and if He didn't, we must seek the help of the likes of Freud, etc.; however, He did address everything at the Cross.

Is the Cross of Christ paramount to you as an individual Believer?

Many Christians have the mistaken idea, that if the leaders of their particular Denomination do a certain thing, they are without question then to follow. Somehow, they think that following these individuals who are so-called leaders absolves them (the laity) of all responsibility. Nothing could be further from the Truth.

It doesn't matter what the Pastor of your Church believes and teaches or the leaders of your particular Fellowship or Denomination. It's what you believe that counts. Whenever you stand before the Lord, you will not be able to use as an excuse the leadership of others. You will have to answer for yourself and yourself totally. So again I ask the question, *"How do you as an individual address the Cross?"*

NOTES

Irrespective as to what others say, the Cross of Christ must be paramount within your heart and life and that refers to totality. In other words, you must understand and believe that every single solution to every single problem is found in the Cross, and the Cross alone!

## WHAT JESUS DID THERE

Everything that Jesus did in His earthly Life and Ministry, was meant to point in its entirety to the Cross. The Cross was ever His destination. In other words, He came for the specific purpose of dying on the Cross, for this was necessary in order to redeem fallen humanity.

This means that He addressed every single problem which mankind might have at the Cross.

How did He do that?

First of all, He had to pay the terrible sin debt owed by man to God. This could be done only by the sacrifice of His life; therefore, He literally offered up Himself as a Sacrifice. That means He was not executed or killed as we think of such, but that He in effect actually offered up Himself. In fact, had He not so desired, no man could have taken His Life from Him.

The sin debt was so huge, so monstrous, so ungodly, that the only thing which would pay this debt was *"a Life"*; however, it had to be a perfect life. Consequently, He had to be virgin born, which He was. Otherwise, He would have been born in original sin as all others.

In His earthly life even as a child growing up, He had to be perfect in word, thought, and deed.

Many argue that it would not have been possible for Him to have sinned; however, there is no Scriptural validation for such thinking. In the first place, He had to be the Second or Last Adam (I Cor. 15:45-50). As the first Adam had the potential to sin, which he did, the Last Adam, the Lord Jesus Christ had to have the same potential, which He did, but of course, did not sin or fail even in the slightest degree.

In fact, in the great Redemption process, God reduced the entirety of Heaven down to *"The Man, Christ Jesus."* In other words, had He in fact failed even in the slightest degree,

Satan could have then claimed the Throne of God, even as he desired and is recorded in Isaiah 14:13. But of course, Christ did not fail at all!

He in effect offered up His physical Body as a Sacrifice, which alone could satisfy the terrible sin debt. Man could not do this thing, because man is ungodly and polluted, therefore, unacceptable! So, God would have to become man, and do for man what man could not do for himself.

Christ as our *"Substitute"* is recorded in Isaiah, Chapter 53. Christ as our *"Representative Man,"* is recorded in Psalm 22.

When Jesus paid the sin debt which He did by dying on the Cross, this destroyed Satan's legal right to humanity, for his legal right was and is sin.

In other words, Satan had a legal right before God to hold sinful man in captivity, literally making man his slave, due to man's fallen condition, i.e., *"sinful condition."* But when Jesus paid the price for man's Redemption, by atoning for all sin, which He did in paying the sin debt through His death, that removed Satan's legal claim; however, for the benefits of this great work to be carried out in one's heart and life, in other words for one to be transferred from the kingdom of darkness to the Kingdom of Light, one must exhibit Faith in this which Jesus did. That's all that God requires, but He definitely does require that (Rom. 10:9-10, 13; Eph. 2:8-9; Rev. 22:17).

When Jesus paid that debt, it addressed every single sin, every single iniquity, every single transgression. Nothing was excluded, with everything included. That's the reason that our victory is found in the Cross, and only in the Cross. Jesus addressed every single problem that one can think of at the Cross, paid the just debt, broke Satan's claim, which sets men free, at least for those who believe (Jn. 3:16).

That means that every single person in this world, for in fact Jesus died for the entirety of the world and for all time, can be free from any and all sin, any and all bondages, totally, absolutely, and completely.

## THE OBJECT OF OUR FAITH

To have this Salvation, this freedom, this victory, one only has to exhibit Faith in what Christ has done. As stated, that's all that God requires (Eph. 2:8-9).

But that means, that having Faith in the Finished Work of Christ for our every need, we cannot have Faith in other things. In other words, our Faith cannot be a divided Faith, must not be a misplaced Faith, but Faith totally and completely in the Atonement. That's where most Christians have their major problem.

Most of Christianity, at least in the last several decades, has not been taught this of which I say; consequently, they have Faith in about everything, instead of the right thing. In fact, there has been more teaching on Faith in the last several decades than all the balance of Christianity put together. The trouble is, most of it has been wrong, simply because it's not been Faith in the Cross.

Faith must always have as its object the Cross of Christ, because that's where the price was paid for everything that man receives from God. Without the Cross of Christ, nothing is received, nothing is had, nothing is obtained, in other words, Jesus is the Door, and according to Exodus 12:13, it is a bloody door, i.e., *"the Cross!"*

Even though the teaching on Faith in the last few decades has been labeled *"Faith in the Word,"* it has actually been anything but that. In effect, it's been a perversion of the Word, with individuals attempting to take certain Scriptures, such as Mark 11:24, claiming whatever they want to claim by using that particular Scripture, which is supposed to move God into some type of action. All of that is foolishness, and as stated, a perversion of the Word, which God will never honor.

Every Promise in the Word of God is predicated totally and completely on the Will of God. That should go without saying; as well, the Word is anchored completely in the Cross, even as the Cross is anchored completely in the Word (Jn. 1:1, 14, 29).

When one begins to understand the veracity of the Cross of Christ, then the entirety of the complexion of the Word of God, which includes the entirety of the Plan of God, takes on a brand-new meaning. That means if one doesn't see the Word through the Cross, then the Word is not properly understood, and, self-will and self-righteousness are always the

NOTES

NOTES

result. To see the Word through the prism of the Cross, sees the entirety of the Plan of God, which then becomes overly obvious. This is God's Way, and any other way spells disaster for the Believer. That's the reason Paul said, *"For many walk, of whom I have told you often, and now tell you even weeping, that they are the enemies of the Cross of Christ."*

He then said, *"Whose end is destruction, whose God is their belly, and whose glory is in their shame, who mind earthly things"* (Phil. 3:18-19).

In essence, *"the Faith"* is *"the Cross,"* as *"the Cross,"* is *"the Faith!"*

## WHY WAS THE CROSS NECESSARY?

In fact, the Cross was absolutely necessary. That means that Jesus could not be stoned to death or die in any other fashion, but of necessity, must die on a Cross.

Paul explains this in Galatians 3:13 by saying, *"Christ hath redeemed us from the curse of the Law, being made a curse for us: for it is written, cursed is every one that hangeth on a tree."*

This Passage was derived from Deuteronomy 21:23.

If an individual committed a crime that was dastardly, the person was to first be stoned to death, and then to show the displeasure of God at such a thing, their body was to *"hang on a tree."* However, it was not to hang there all night, only for a period of time. This would show God's displeasure, in other words, the curse of God upon that particular individual.

Consequently, we're speaking here of the worst types of crimes, the most evil, the most wicked types of sins, whatever they may have been. We speak of cold-blooded murder, or something of that nature.

In essence, the Cross is the same thing as the *"tree."* As well, Jesus, even though dying on a Cross, did not remain on the Cross during the night, but was removed in late afternoon. He died at 3:00 p.m., actually, the time of the evening Sacrifice. Due to the fact that the Passover Sabbath was approaching, which was Thursday at this particular time, His Body was removed not long after His expiration. (This particular Sabbath was not the same as the regular, weekly, Jewish Sabbath, which was Saturday.)

The death of Christ had to be such a death that would atone not only for sin as we think of such, but as well the worst type of sin irrespective as to what it might be. In other words, nothing could be left undone, even the worst of the worst! So, He had to bear the full brunt of the curse of the Law which was death, and the worst type of death at that, which was death upon the tree, i.e., *"the Cross."*

That's the reason we say that Jesus addressed every single, solitary problem that one could ever think of having, when He paid the supreme price on the Cross of Calvary. He left nothing undone which means, as previously stated, that every single individual irrespective of their bondage, can be free and we mean totally free.

## WHAT DO WE MEAN BY *"FREE"*?

The freedom which Christ affords, is totally unlike anything the world has to offer. The following illustration may be of some help:

If a dog has a biting problem, the problem can be curtailed by putting a muzzle on him. In effect, that's all the world can do. That's the very best that Alcoholics Anonymous, or Gamblers Anonymous, etc., can ever hope to do, and that only with a very small number. They can apply a muzzle. However, as should be obvious, the person even though they stopped drinking or gambling, etc., is not really free. The craving is still there. In other words, what causes the problem to start with is still present, hence the individual has to constantly get up the rest of his or her life and say, *"I am John Doe, and I am a recovering alcoholic,"* etc.

When Christ sets an individual free, which He has done with untold millions, He doesn't use a muzzle. Such is no longer necessary.

The freedom that Christ affords, which is gained only by one's Faith in what He did at the Cross, changes totally the nature of the individual in question, with the unholy desire completely removed. This means that to merely stop doing something is not quite enough. The nature of the individual must be changed, and there must be a power introduced into one's life which is greater than the power that has caused the individual to live in bondage. We will address that next.

When Christ gives a person freedom, which He always will do when one properly places their Faith, and irrespective of the problem, the individual then enjoys a freedom that is absolutely unparalleled in the world. The power of the bondage is totally and completely broken, with the craving or ungodly desire no longer present. In effect, what that individual previously was, he no longer is. That goes for the sinner initially coming to Christ, or the Christian obtaining victory. The victory is the same, even as the solution is the same.

That's why Jesus said, *"And ye shall know the Truth* (the Truth of the Cross), *and the Truth shall make you free"* (Jn. 8:32).

## WILL MAKE YOU FREE

If the Reader is to notice, He used the word *"make,"* which implies a process. And what does that mean?

While freedom instantly comes upon proper Faith in the Cross, which gives the Holy Spirit the latitude to work, that doesn't mean that Satan will cease all activity. Even after one receives and understands this great Truth, and then applies it by Faith to his heart and life, in which victory comes immediately, Satan will test one's Faith, and of that, one can be sure. In fact, the Lord allows him certain latitude in this respect (Lk. 22:31-32).

This means that there may be even failure of some sort even after one comes to the realization of this great Truth. So why does that happen?

If in fact it does happen, and more than likely it will, it doesn't mean that this Truth is wrong, but rather that our Faith is weak. We must remember, that we have just begun to believe God in the right way, and there are many things we still don't know about this great path of Victory. Satan takes advantage of this weak Faith, and causes us problems. However, if such a thing does occur, the Believer must ask the Lord to forgive him, which the Lord always will (I Jn. 1:9), and then to show him where he has gone wrong, if in fact that has been the case. The Lord will definitely hear and answer that prayer.

Consequently, the Believer will find himself gradually getting stronger and stronger, with Satan's efforts becoming weaker and weaker. This is why Jesus used the word *"make,"* implying a process.

In fact, the Believer will definitely come to understand that this great work is a process, with the Believer getting stronger and stronger as we go forward in Christ.

However, please do not allow me to sound discouraging. The Truth is, the Spiritual Growth of the Believer, once a proper understanding of the Cross is enjoined, will increase at a pace heretofore unknown. Actually, there cannot be any real growth without a proper understanding of the Cross. When the Cross is properly understood and acted upon, even on a daily basis (Lk. 9:23-24), Spiritual Growth will then take place which will be obviously noticeable in the heart and life of the Believer.

Without this knowledge of the Cross and the acting upon that particular knowledge, if the Believer will be honest with himself, he will have to come to the conclusion that his Spiritual Growth has been very, very slow if any at all. That will change with one's understanding of the Cross and Faith in that great, Finished Work.

I say these things in this manner, because I don't want the Believer to get discouraged. Once this great Truth of the Cross is made real, and once it is accepted in the heart and life of the Believer, the life of that particular person becomes so exciting, so real, so vibrant, that it's almost like one has been Born-Again. In view of that, this living example of the power of Christ within one's life, failure of any nature becomes extremely discouraging. Knowing the weakness of our Faith in the initial stages, I always feel that it is proper to explain this in this manner as it regards the proper Faith walk.

## THE HOLY SPIRIT

The key to everything we are in Christ, everything we have of Christ, and everything we have received from Christ, is the Holy Spirit. When Paul spoke about Jesus being hanged on the tree, he followed that statement by saying, *"That the Blessing of Abraham might come on the Gentiles, through Jesus Christ; that we might receive the Promise of the Spirit through Faith"* (Gal. 3:14).

NOTES

The problem with the Christian is, we think we can sanctify ourselves, which means to bring about Righteousness and Holiness within our hearts and lives according to our own efforts. We probably do not think of it in such crass terms, but that's actually what's being done.

It doesn't work that way!

The Believer has to have the help of the Holy Spirit in every single thing he does. In other words, we are not going to receive anything from the Lord, unless it is given to us through the Ministry, Office, and Person of the Holy Spirit. He Alone is the Executor of all of the Promises and Blessings of God. In fact, He is God!

So, having God literally living within our hearts and lives, understanding that we are actually a temple of the Holy Spirit (I Cor. 3:16), provides a potential that is absolutely extraordinary to say the least. In other words, there is nothing that the Holy Spirit cannot do; however, He is in our hearts and lives for a specific purpose, and that is to make us Christlike. He means to root out every single sin, every single transgression of disobedience, and everything that is contrary to the Will of God, whatever that might be.

So, how does He do all of this?

If that question were to be posed to Christians, I suspect that the answer would be for almost all, *"He just does it!"* Of course, such an answer means that the Believer doesn't have the foggiest notion as to how the Holy Spirit works within our lives.

In fact, those who are associated with Old-line Denominations, which have by and large rejected the Holy Spirit, know almost nothing about the Third Person of the Godhead Who is supposed to live within their hearts and lives. Actually, the far greater majority of these people aren't even saved, so that means the Holy Spirit is not really present at all.

Even for the few who are actually saved, they are taught almost nothing about the Holy Spirit, with Him working precious little in their lives as would be obvious.

Unfortunately, even for those who claim to be Spirit-Baptized, beyond speaking in Tongues, most don't have any idea whatsoever as to how the Holy Spirit performs His work. As stated, most would just simply say *"He just does it!"* So, the upshot of all of this is, that even though the Holy Spirit is definitely present in the hearts and lives of all true Believers, He in fact, is not allowed to do very much within our lives. The reason is simple. Our Faith is misplaced, which in effect, ties His hands.

NOTES

The Holy Spirit demands that the Believer know and understand that the solution to every single problem, the answer to every single question, always and without exception, is found in the Cross of Christ. That's the reason it's so very, very important, that the Believer understand that it is the Cross through which all blessings come.

Upon having and accepting that knowledge, the Holy Spirit demands that Faith be placed in the Cross. This stifles all self-will, and dependence on self (Rom. 8:1-2).

Once the Believer's Faith is properly placed, which of course, refers to the Finished Work of Christ, which refers to what Jesus did at the Cross, the Holy Spirit will then work on our behalf, bringing about all the great things for which Jesus paid such a price. Most Christians don't understand this. In other words, they don't have any idea as to how the Holy Spirit works, why He works, or the manner in which He works. As stated, they just somehow think it's all automatic. It isn't!

As we have previously stated, the Believer must have a greater power evident within his life than the power of sin. And to be sure, sin has a tremendous power, a power in fact of such magnitude, that even God could not speak Redemption into existence, but rather had to come down here and pay a terrible price. So from that, we should understand as to how lethal and deadly that sin actually is. It definitely isn't greater than the Power of God, but it is greater than anything else other than the Power of God.

Consequently, it takes the Power of God to master and overcome sin within our lives, in order that sin not dominate us in any respect (Rom. 6:14). That power is registered in the Holy Spirit; however, He exhibits this power strictly on the basis of what Christ did at the Cross, and our Faith in that Finished Work. He will not work otherwise, which means, if we attempt to sanctify ourselves in any way, He will not work with us, which guarantees our defeat (Rom. 8:2).

Once the Believer begins to understand that all solutions are found in the Cross, and begins to place his Faith in that, the Holy Spirit Who is able to do all things, will begin to go to work in his life, with things which seem to us impossible, whatever they might have been, suddenly being thrown or cast aside, and so easily! What is difficult or even impossible for us, is no problem to Him whatsoever. But if we do not know the manner in which He works, we cannot be the beneficiary of all that He does.

## THE HOLY SPIRIT AND THE LAW

When we say *"Law"* we mean just that; however, we're not speaking of the Law of Moses. We are speaking of *"The Law of the Spirit of Life which is in Christ Jesus"* (Rom. 8:2).

This means that the Holy Spirit works within the boundaries of a specific *"Law!"* And what is this Law?

As we've just quoted, it's the Law which is *"in Christ Jesus."* This refers to what He did at the Cross and in His Resurrection.

So, of what does this Law consist?

The Work of Christ on the Cross was and is a legal work. You remember we stated that Satan's claim upon humanity was a legal claim based upon sin. In other words, sin gives Satan a legal right to place humanity in bondage, which he definitely has done. Jesus took away that claim, by settling the sin debt, which He did with the giving of His Own Life. So, His work was and is a legal work, which Satan must obey.

Instead of going into detail as to what this work included, which to be sure would be a massive account, suffice to say, whatever man needs, and that covers the waterfront to use some street vernacular, it is found in the legal Work of Christ at the Cross. That should be easy to understand!

The Holy Spirit works within those parameters, and exclusively within those parameters. He will not venture outside of this *"Law,"* and for all the obvious reasons.

First of all, He doesn't break the Law, and, second, He doesn't need to. Anything and everything that man needs, is found in the Atonement.

This is why the Holy Spirit gets very upset, and please believe me that is the case, whenever we as Believers venture outside of the Cross, attempting to bring about things we need. What do we mean by that?

NOTES

The only thing that is required of the Believer, is to have Faith in the Cross, meaning that we anchor our Faith in that Finished Work, seeing to it that it is never removed. That's all the Holy Spirit asks of us, which will guarantee His great benefits. In other words, He will guarantee that all the benefits of the Cross become ours, if we will only exhibit Faith in this which Christ has done (Rom. 6:2-6; 8:1-2).

The problem is, most Christians not knowing the Message of the Cross, attempt to bring about the desired results in their lives by efforts and machinations of their own. Almost all the time, these individuals are very sincere, and even very spiritual in the things they attempt to do, but they never achieve the results they desire, with in fact, the situation only resulting in them angering God (Rom. 8:8).

For instance, millions in the Church think if they have a problem, they should get a Preacher to lay hands on them, and this will take care of the problem. The laying on of hands is definitely a Scriptural Doctrine, and should be carried out, however, if in fact, we think we can overcome sin or the Devil in this manner, we will find that we have turned this Doctrine into works, which God cannot honor. That means it doesn't matter if the greatest man of God in the world lays hands on you, if in fact you are trying to gain victory by this method, the results will be zero or less. In other words, you'll find yourself going backwards instead of forward. But this is where much of Christianity presently is.

At this moment, untold thousands of Christians are running all over the world, trying to obtain some particular *"blessing,"* they think can be had in a certain place. Their trip by and large is a waste of time. As one of my associates has said, *"Believers do not need a touch near as much as they need the Truth!"*

While it's very proper for Christians to have hands laid on them, it should always be for the right reason, which is for blessing or healing (Mk. 16:18).

## ERRONEOUS CONCEPTIONS

Back in the late 1980's I had the occasion to speak at length with two of the brightest lights in the Charismatic world. In fact, I hold both of these men in very high regard. We were discussing this very thing, and I speak of having victory, walking in victory, etc.

Both suggested or rather flatly stated, that the only way for this to be done, and we speak of Christians who are having problems, is for hands to be laid on them, and the demons to be rebuked, etc.

Even though I have every confidence that both of these men were very sincere, the Truth is, they were both sincerely wrong.

In fact, were that the case, Jesus would not have had to have come down here and died on a cruel Cross. All He would have had to have done, would be to properly instruct Believer's in the laying on of hands, etc. I'm sorry, but sin is far more powerful than that!

If this is wrong, why would these two men, who in fact are household names, have suggested such?

They suggested such, simply because they didn't know any better. They do not know the Truth of the Message of the Cross; consequently, they have to have some type of answer, which is an answer that will not work.

## DELIVERANCE

The word *"deliverance"* is the great word of Christianity. Notice what Paul said concerning Christ:

*"Who gave Himself for our sins, that He might deliver us from this present evil world, according to the Will of God and our Father"* (Gal. 1:4).

This means that all of mankind is held captive by Satan, which means that one has to be delivered from that power by a greater power, which is what Christ did at the Cross. In fact, the very word *"deliver"* means *"to rescue from something,"* in this case, *"Satan."* It is the release effected by the payment of a ransom, or the required price, which of course refers to Redemption, and the price paid by Christ. However, this price was not paid to Satan, but rather to God, which as stated, destroyed Satan's claim.

In fact, there is nowhere in the Bible that Preachers or anyone for that matter other than the Lord, are told to deliver people. And yet, we have untold numbers of Preachers attempting to do this. As stated, they attempt to deliver people by the laying on of hands, by rebuking Satan, by casting out demons, etc.

NOTES

While in fact, all of these things are very legitimate in their own right, but to be legitimate, they must be used in the manner and way in which the Lord has originally described.

Concerning deliverance, Jesus said, *"The Spirit of the Lord is upon Me, because He hath anointed Me . . . to preach deliverance to the captives"* (Lk. 4:18).

If one is to notice, Jesus said *"to preach deliverance,"* not *"to deliver."* What did He mean by that?

Once again, we go back to the premise that all deliverance is found in the Cross of Christ, and one's Faith in the Cross. In fact, I am preaching deliverance to you even as you read these words.

It refers to telling someone how to be delivered, by them placing their Faith in the Cross of Christ, in which the Holy Spirit will then give them great victory. That's what Jesus meant by *"preaching deliverance."*

Instead, we have far too many Preachers attempting to deliver people by their own efforts, which the Bible does not sanction whatsoever. In fact, all efforts outside of the Cross of Christ constitute the flesh, and greatly anger the Lord (Rom. 8:8). It doesn't matter how spiritual these things may seem to be, and how spiritual we think we are by engaging them, if it's not within the parameters of the Cross of Christ, in which parameters alone the Holy Spirit works, it must be constituted as *"flesh,"* which cannot please God.

Once again we come back to the knowing of Truth which makes us free (Jn. 8:32).

For several hundreds of people to line up, or any number for that matter, and for a Preacher to lay hands on all of these people, may look very dramatic and Faith-filled, but for the most part, there will be very little accomplished by this method. To be sure, there would be much greater blessing in store if the people had a Godly man or woman lay hands on them strictly to bless them, which is totally Scriptural (Gen. 48:14; Num. 8:10; 27:23; Deut. 34:9; Mat. 19:15; Mk. 5:23; 6:2, 5; Lk. 4:40; 13:13; Acts 5:12; 13:3; 14:3; 19:11; 28:8; I Tim. 4:14; II Tim. 1:6; Heb. 6:2). Of course, and as stated, that goes for prayer for the sick also; however, for people to get in a prayer line and have hands laid on them in order for them to get victory over the world, the flesh, and the Devil, is by and large a waste of time. Once again, if such could be done by this method, then Jesus died needlessly on the Cross.

No! It took a terrible death in a terrible place, in order for this great thing to be brought about, and God expects us to recognize that. When we put our Faith in the Finished Work of Christ, the Holy Spirit will then help us, and victory is assured. In fact, that is the only method of victory that God has, because it's the only method that is needed.

### TAKING UP THE CROSS DAILY TO FOLLOW JESUS

Jesus said, *"If any man will come after Me, let him deny himself, and take up his Cross daily, and follow Me"* (Lk. 9:23).

In fact, basically the same thing was also said in Matthew 16:24 and Mark 8:35.

What Jesus says here is very obvious, but yet most Christians totally misunderstand. Most have the idea, that bearing the Cross refers to some terrible type of suffering which comes upon some Christians, with others looking on and saying, *"I pray the Lord never requires such of me!"* etc. Such presents a totally erroneous view of what Jesus means here.

While the Cross definitely did embody terrible suffering, even beyond imagination, it was the suffering which Christ did for us, actually on our behalf. When He spoke of taking up the Cross daily to follow Him, He was not speaking of Christians going through some regimen of suffering as many believe, but rather the very opposite.

He is speaking here of Believers understanding first of all, that all of their blessing and help comes through the Cross, and that God wants us to have all of these benefits, for which Jesus paid such a price. In other words, we are to look to the Cross exclusively. That's what He meant by *"taking up the Cross."*

This means that the obedience of this injunction, is actually the greatest thing that could ever happen to a Believer. Bearing the Cross guarantees one all blessings, all benefits, in fact, everything which Jesus did on that cruel tree. This is the key to all blessings, to all favor from God! That's why Paul said, *"But God forbid that I should glory* (boast), *save in the Cross of our Lord Jesus Christ, by whom the world is crucified unto me, and I unto the world"* (Gal. 6:14).

NOTES

In fact, the Cross is a great reproach to the world and most of the Church. That is sad but true! The reason for this, is because the Cross tells man how wicked he is, and how loving that God is. Man does not want to admit to either! So, the Cross is a reproach to him.

Also, when Jesus said that we must *"deny ourselves,"* He wasn't speaking of asceticism (the denial of all pleasure). He was rather speaking of not trying to obtain by our own efforts what can only be obtained by Faith in the Cross of Christ.

As well, when he said that this must be done *"daily,"* He was speaking of the need to constantly renew one's Faith in the Finished Work of Christ.

Unfortunately, the major problem of man is pride. And whenever Christians began to walk in victory, as they surely shall do whenever they look to the Cross of Christ, there is a tendency in all of us to want to think good of ourselves. Renewing our Faith *"daily"* in the Cross, puts self in its proper place, which is in Christ, knowing that we deserve no credit at all for this victory, but that all credit must go exclusively to Christ.

(9) "WHO SHALL BE PUNISHED WITH EVERLASTING DESTRUCTION FROM THE PRESENCE OF THE LORD, AND FROM THE GLORY OF HIS POWER;"

The consequences of permanent separation from God come out forcibly in the phrase *"from the Presence of the Lord."* Banishment, actually, from the Lord's Presence is what Jesus taught about punishment (Mat. 7:23; 8:12; 22:13; 25:30; Lk. 13:27). Words cannot adequately express the misery of this eternal condition. On the other hand, those in Christ can anticipate the very opposite: *"We will be with the Lord forever"* (I Thess. 4:17).

Some have questions whether the parallel phrase, *"from the majesty of His Power,"* can likewise signify separation. If *"majesty"* is a visible manifestation proceeding from His Power, there is no problem in understanding how this expression describes the anguish of separation. Instead of enjoying that glory or majesty, such will never be known by those destined to everlasting punishment.

EVERLASTING DESTRUCTION

The phrase, *"Who shall be punished with everlasting destruction,"* means exactly what it says.

The Greek for *"punished"* is *"dike,"* and means *"justice."*

*"Destruction"* in the Greek is *"olethros,"* and means *"ruin or undoing."*

The idea is, whatever it is that causes the destruction or ruin is eternal. It is not annihilation as is clear from the words which follow and which expand the thought. The punishment means to be banished *"from the Presence of the Lord, and from the glory of His Power."*

The nature of the punishment is unending separation from the Face of the Lord, and thus from every good. It is the exact opposite of the estate of the redeemed, whose eternal bliss is found in the Presence of Christ. These words are filled with infinite sadness almost too terrible to contemplate. And yet the fate of the wicked is, at the most, only the fulfillment of the choice of those who will not have Christ to reign in their lives.

Denney speaks of the finality of the Gospel: *"Obey, and you enter into a Light in which there is no darkness at all: disobey, and you pass eventually into a darkness in which there is no Light at all . . . It is not a question of less or more, of sooner or later, of better or worse; what is at stake in our attitude to the Gospel is life or death, Heaven or hell, the outer darkness or the Glory of Christ."*

God's action in allowing His people to be persecuted, and in permitting the existence of their persecutors, had a double purpose: A. To test the fitness of His people for government; and, B. To manifest the fitness of their persecutors for judgment.

The being *"counted worthy"* of II Thessalonians 1:5, 11 does not support the Doctrine of Salvation by merit, for here it is not a question of Salvation but of participation in government; and also it was not a question of the making themselves worthy, but of God counting them to be so. It was a question of sharing in *"this calling."*

NOTES

God has long patience, but at the appointed time He will recompense tribulation to the troublers of His people, while to His troubled people He will recompense rest, which of course will take place at death or the Rapture of the Church.

The punishment of the rebels and persecutors will be everlasting destruction — as stated, not everlasting annihilation, for these terms destroy one another. God is a consuming fire, and the Lord Jesus Christ is God; hence the statements of Verses 8 and 9.

Until that desired day dawns, the followers of the Lord Christ are to expect nothing but persecution from the world (Williams).

THAT WHICH IS TO COME

When one begins to comprehend the magnitude of this of which we are discussing, it becomes staggering in concept. In fact, anything which is branded as *"eternal"* takes on brand-new proportions.

The *"eternity"* considered, takes on two aspects, one of eternal Light and the other of eternal darkness; however, even that is a gross understatement. With this glorious *"Light"* which is all ensconced in Christ, comes Eternal Life, the glory of His Presence forever, and the privilege of living in the New Jerusalem, forever and forever. We're speaking of something, which John the Beloved describes graphically in the last two Chapters of Revelation, which description to be sure, completely boggles the mind.

On the other hand, to be eternally lost, which means to be banished from the Presence of God forever and forever, also draws to itself eternal perdition or hellfire. In other words, every unsaved person who has ever lived, which refers to all who would not make Christ their Lord and Saviour, will burn in Hell forever and forever. I realize this is blunt, but it happens to be the Truth (Rev. 21:8).

Understanding this of which we have said, and knowing that it is true, but yet, most of the population of the world, and for all time, completely ignores this which is proclaimed in the Word of God, thereby facing eternity in unbelief. In other words, they die without God! That means that the far greater majority of the population of humanity even from the beginning of time, are at this moment in eternal Hell. They will be released from this place only one time, and that is to stand at the Great White Throne Judgment, where they will then be banished to the Lake of Fire, there to burn forever and forever (Rev. 20:10-15).

The Truth is, most people in the world actually believe there is a God; however, being unsaved and, therefore, having absolutely no Spiritual Life whatsoever, their idea of God is grossly skewed, actually preposterous! Their major response to eternity or, life after death, is, *"If there is anything out there, then I think I'm prepared for whatever it is!"*

Their judgment is based on *"good deeds"* vs. *"bad deeds!"* But of course, none of that carries any weight with God whatsoever.

So that means that almost all of humanity dies lost. In fact, the Scripture plainly says, *"For wide is the gate, and broad is the way that leadeth to destruction, and many there be which go in thereat."*

Christ then said, *"Because strait is the gate, and narrow is the way, which leadeth unto life, and few there be that find it"* (Mat. 7:13-14).

The Lord then gave the great warning concerning *"false prophets,"* and how they are to be recognized as it regards *"good fruit"* or the lack of such (Mat. 7:15-29).

This tells us that most of the people have died eternally lost because they followed spiritual leaders, Preachers, etc., who were *"false!"* That should be a very sobering thought! Actually, it applies to all the religions of the world, plus that which we refer to as *"Christianity."*

## CAN A LOVING GOD CONDEMN A SOUL TO HELL FOREVER AND FOREVER, AND JUSTIFY HIMSELF IN DOING SO?

The heading I have just given is the title of a Message I have preached quite a number of times down through the years. It's a very sobering thought!

When we speak of souls being banished into eternal Hell forever and forever, that causes any serious thinking individual to shrink back in horror. The first response is that a loving God could not do such a thing. Punishing the unredeemed for a period of time is one thing, but forever and forever is something else again! And yet, that's exactly the way it is.

NOTES

First of all, God definitely is loving, kind, benevolent, compassionate, and longsuffering. As well, and at the same time, He is definitely justified in the action that will be taken concerning *"everlasting destruction"* even as Paul said in the Passage of our study.

How is that so?

Men are condemned to eternal Hell not so much for what they are, although that definitely does enter into the picture, but for the most part, that they have rejected God's solution, Who is Jesus Christ, and the Redemption afforded by Him through His Death on the Cross and Resurrection (Jn. 3:16; Rom. 10:9-10, 13).

When one considers the price that Heaven has paid for the Redemption of man, and of course, we speak of God becoming man, and suffering the horrible humiliation of dying on the Cross solely for the Redemption of lost humanity, understanding that, we must come to the conclusion that God is perfectly just in the action taken concerning the eternal destiny of the lost.

Being *"saved"* or *"lost,"* is of far greater magnitude than the words themselves imply.

Sin is the ruination of all that is good. It is the blight of the universe, the blight of eternity. It is the damnation of mankind, and the very reason that Jesus had to die on the Cross. In other words, the death He died, proclaims to us the magnitude of the reason He had to die. Considering that God Who is almighty, and could speak worlds into existence, but could not speak Redemption into existence, lets us know the magnitude of this situation.

To be *"saved"* means to be *"born again"* which is demanded of mankind. This is the only way the sin question can be handled. As well, to be *"born again"* one must accept Christ and what He did at the Cross, which alone brings Salvation. Only the Death and Resurrection of Christ, and Faith in that which He did, can change mankind, which is demanded by God, and rightly so! It is all in Christ, and it is all in what He did at the Cross and in His Resurrection. That's the reason the Cross is so very, very important! (I Cor. 1:18; 2:2). Man cannot be in the Presence of God without being cleansed by the Precious Blood of Jesus Christ, which is all done by Faith in what Christ did at the Cross

(Eph. 2:8-9). In other words, God cannot tolerate sin in any capacity.

That means, that all who do not know God, which means they have not accepted Christ, must be quarantined forever and forever, because of the terrible malady of sin that they carry within themselves. The place of this quarantine will be the *"Lake of Fire"* (Rev. 20:10-15).

Considering all the pain, death, dying, sickness, and sorrow which sin has caused in this world, for God to allow even one individual filled with sin, which means they have rejected Christ, into the realm of the Righteous, would be the most beastly thing that one could ever begin to imagine. Once again, Heaven would soon be turned into a hell, and all of creation would be thrown back again into the horrible problem that has existed now for thousands of years, filling the Earth with blood, and which has already been addressed at such great price.

Yes, even having an elementary understanding of the situation, one must immediately come to the conclusion that a loving God can definitely condemn a rebellious soul to Hell and burn him there forever and forever, and justify Himself in doing so.

## THE PRESENCE OF THE LORD

The phrase, *"From the presence of the Lord,"* says far more than meets the eye.

All life comes from God. This means that this *"Life"* energizes the entirety of creation, even though most of mankind does not live for God, and in fact has no Spiritual Life whatsoever. Still, whether the unredeemed realize it or not, they draw sustenance from God every single moment of their lives. His *"Presence"* sustains the Earth, holds back the powers of darkness, keeps Satan at bay, and makes it possible for humanity to live, even though most live in rebellion against Him.

In the coming eternal banishment, this life-giving *"Presence"* of God will no longer be present. To be sure, unredeemed man presently has no idea as to his dependence on God, even as he denies Him. It is certain that he will know when this *"Presence"* is removed, and removed it will be at that coming dark day.

If the Gospel, as conceived in the New Testament, has any character at all, it has the character of finality. It is God's last word to men. And the consequences of accepting or rejecting are final; it opens no prospect beyond life on the one hand, or death on the other, which are the results of obedience or disobedience.

NOTES

## THE GLORY OF HIS POWER

The phrase, *"And from the Glory of His Power,"* presents words filled with such infinite sadness as to be almost too terrible to contemplate.

The *"Glory of the Power of God"* stands ready to deliver any soul in sin, and no matter how deep that sin may be, if they will only say yes to Christ. He can save! He can deliver! And He does so majestically!

When the eternal soul, however, is banished into eternal Hell forever and forever, the Presence of God will no longer shine forth in that place, and as well, there will be no *"Glory of His Power"* to deliver. To be sure, the eternal souls in eternal Hell, will scream forever and forever for deliverance, but it's a prayer that will never be answered, and because second, fifth, and tenth chances are all on this side of the grave. As stated, the Gospel of Christ is God's last Word to men.

Going back to the words *"everlasting destruction,"* some false cults have put a false interpretation on these words and similar, claiming that the coming punishment of lost souls is not eternal. This matter is serious enough, that I think it would be profitable for us to look at the subject more closely.

## CONCERNING ANNIHILATION

One of the most whimsical and foolish delusions which Satan in recent years has palmed off on some shallow-thinking Christians is the heresy that the souls of the wicked are to be annihilated. Strangely enough, this error was never known among the ancient heathens, who believed, even before they knew anything about the Bible, that the souls of the good and bad both exist forever.

There is no darkness like that which comes from rejected Light. The rejection of the plain teachings of God's Word has brought forth greater infidels than the heathen ever knew, and more heresies than the ancients ever dreamed of.

This notion of the annihilation of the wicked is propagated by putting a false meaning upon the Bible words *"destruction"* and *"punishment."* The word *"destroy"* does not mean to annihilate, but to wreck, ruin, render utterly useless for the purpose for which it was made.

The words *"everlasting destruction," "everlasting punishment"* are perverted into meaning annihilation. If the wicked are to be annihilated and their punishment will not be everlasting, then their destruction will not be *"everlasting."* In fact, the everlastingness of punishment is put opposite the everlastingness of reward; and if it does not mean everlasting in the one case, neither does it mean that in the other.

Again, the word *"death"* is perverted into meaning annihilation. But the term *"death"* is the opposite of *"life,"* and not the opposite of existence. Life and death are opposite; existence and nonexistence are opposite; and it is false reason to take the opposite of life and make it mean the opposite of something else.

We know in the realm of nature and of mind, that death is not annihilation. A piece of plank is dead; it was once a living tree, full of life, and the life has now left it; but it still exists.

A dead human body still exists, with all its members and organs, though the life has left it; yet not one particle is annihilated. And in the realm of the mind, Satan and evil spirits are dead in sin — they are separated from the True Life of God, which is Love; and yet they exist. And just as truly and as rationally as demons have an existence, who are separated from the Life of God, so the souls of the wicked will exist forever, though dead in sin.

This is implied in the Words of Jesus, when He shall say: *"Depart from Me, ye cursed, into Hell, prepared for the Devil and his angels* (Mat. 25:41). These very words imply that the wicked exist coextensively with Satan and fallen angels.

## NOTHING WILL EVER BE ANNIHILATED

Again, there is not a single hint in the whole realm of matter of all kinds that anything will ever be annihilated. The Holy Spirit says, in Eccl. 3:14: *"I know that whatsoever God doeth, it shall be forever; nothing can be put to it, nor anything taken from it, and God doeth it that men should fear before Him."*

This statement covers the whole extent of creation. There is no sign that any atom of matter has ever been annihilated. Created substances can undergo a thousand changes — solids become liquids, liquids solids, gasses turn into rocks, and rocks into vapor — and yet there is no trace in the history of the world of anything like annihilation. And so in the human mind; we may forget millions of things, but under certain mental conditions, every event in our past can be recalled to the recollection.

This delusion of annihilation bears upon its very face the handiwork of the Devil; it is just the Doctrine that will suit the wicked — give them license to live as they please in this life, with the hope of plunging into nonexistence when they leave this world.

No Christian can entertain an error like this without weakening the Spiritual Life, for all error is poison to the soul. Yet there are many people who fancy they can walk in communion with the Holy Spirit, and yet drink down this heresy that is afloat in the world. Some professed Christians fancy that they are more merciful than the Lord, and they think it will help out the Doctrine of Divine Mercy to accept such errors.

But we must be careful how we accept the Doctrine of Mercy from the Devil, for that's exactly where this doctrine of annihilation comes from, for it is his aim to turn every Truth of the Word of God into a lie. And if he can get people to believe his lie, he will damn their souls (Watson).

(10) "WHEN HE SHALL COME TO BE GLORIFIED IN HIS SAINTS, AND TO BE ADMIRED IN ALL THEM THAT BELIEVE (BECAUSE OUR TESTIMONY AMONG YOU WAS BELIEVED) IN THAT DAY."

This Passage pertains to the Second Coming, when all the Saints come back with Christ to this Earth, at which time Christ will set up His earthly Kingdom. He will do so in splendor and glory, along with force and might. The Saints at that time, will look upon Him with wonder and admiration, as should be obvious!

To be sure, the world that will greet Christ at that time, will be a world in chaos. It will

NOTES

have undergone some seven years of judgment and war such as it has never previously known and will never know again (Mat. 24:21). And the area from which Christ will reign, which will be Jerusalem and the Middle East, will be the most severely destroyed of all; consequently, a gargantuan construction program will begin, with Jerusalem becoming the capital of the entirety of the world, and Christ becoming its King. That's why the Holy Spirit through John said, *"And He* (Jesus) *hath on His vesture and on His thigh a name written, KING OF KINGS, AND LORD OF LORDS"* (Rev. 19:16). It will be the beginning of the thousand year reign of Christ, along with all His Saints, which will transform the world into a Garden of Eden, unlike anything it has ever known before. Consequently, the *"admiration"* will be abundant!

GLORIFIED IN HIS SAINTS

The phrase, *"When He shall come to be glorified in His Saints,"* means that Christ will be the Center and Focal Point of all. His Glory, His Attributes, His Blessedness will be seen in the persons of the Saints, who are also described as *"them that believe."* This means that our characters, like mirrors, will reflect or reproduce His Glory. This awe-inspiring Revelation will be the cause of thanksgiving and rejoicing.

It will not be the Holy Angels who will glorify Him, but holy men whom He has redeemed with His Blood. Christ will be glorified in his Saints, inasmuch as our glory is the result of His sufferings and death, and our holiness is the reflection of His Holiness.

*"Glorified"* in the Greek is *"endoxadzo,"* and means *"to adorn with glory."* It refers to His Glory seen in the Blessings conferred upon Saints as the eternal rulers of the universe and as the heirs of all things.

IN ALL THAT BELIEVE

The phrase, *"And to be admired in all them that believe,"* refers to being made marvelous in all them that believe. The general idea here is twofold:

1. Christ will be so glorious, so wonderful, so magnificent in all aspects of His Person, whether in the realm of government,

NOTES

power, creative ability, or whatever one can think, that His rulership, for He will be the Ruler of the entirety of the world, will be a wonder to the entirety of mankind, generating admiration by all. For the first time in human history, the nations will be at peace, because the Prince of Peace is ruling. There will be equity, fairness, and justice for all. As well, the curse on the Earth will be lifted, with even the deserts becoming a verdant garden. Industry will produce implements of peace and welfare for humanity instead of weapons of war. In fact, there will be so much as it regards *"plenty"* that no person in the world will do without anything that is necessary. Isaiah said, *"In that day shall the Branch of the Lord be beautiful and glorious, and the fruit of the earth shall be excellent and comely for them that are escaped of Israel"* (Isa. 4:2). That *"Branch"* is Christ.

Isaiah also said, *"Of the increase of His Government and Peace there shall be no end, upon the Throne of David, and upon His Kingdom, to order it, and to establish it with judgment and with justice from henceforth even forever. The zeal of the Lord of Hosts will perform this"* (Isa. 9:7).

In fact, we could continue on with page after page of the wonders and excitement which will take place during this coming, glorious, Kingdom Age, when Christ will rule supremely over the Earth, along with all the Saints of God who have ever lived, with Israel then rightfully in her place. However, suffice to say, this coming day will be glorious to say the least, and its advent is near at hand.

2. Not only will Christ be manifested in a glorious manner, however, the source of His highest triumphs will be what is seen in the Glorified Saints. His main honor, when He returns to the world, will not be the outward splendors which will attend His Coming, nor the Angels who will accompany Him, nor the manifestation of His Power over the elements, but rather the Church which He has redeemed. It will then be seen that He is worthy of universal admiration, and because He has redeemed the Church. And how will that be?

1. For having conceived the Plan of redeeming lost humanity.

2. For being willing to become Incarnate, and to die to save us.

3. For the defense of His Church in all its persecutions and trials.

4. For raising His people from the dead, as it regards the great Resurrection.

5. For the virtues and graces which we will exhibit in that day and forever.

THE HONOR OF CHRIST AND HIS CHURCH

This appropriate honor of Christ in the Church has never yet been fully seen. His people on Earth, have, in general, most imperfectly reflected His Image. We have, in general, been comparatively few in number, and scattered upon the Earth. We have been poor and despised. Often we have been persecuted, and regarded as the *"filth of the world and the offscouring of all things."* The honors of this world, as are painfully obvious, have been withheld from us. The great have regarded it as no honor to be identified with the Church, and of course we speak of the True Church, and the proud have been ashamed to be enrolled among the followers of the Lord.

In this coming Kingdom Age all this will be changed, and the assembled Church will show to admiring worlds how great and glorious is its Redeemer, and how glorious was the Work of Redemption.

THE TESTIMONY

The phrase, *"Because our testimony among you was believed,"* refers to the entirety of the Gospel of Christ.

Twice in this one Verse, Paul uses the word *"believe"* or *"believed."* Believe what? one might quickly ask!

Of course, the instant retort is, that we believe the Gospel of Christ, i.e., *"believe in Christ."*

However, what does it actually mean to believe in Christ?

As we have said in other ways, whenever the words *"believe"* or *"Faith"* are used, or any other similar type words, it always refers to believing what Christ did at the Cross on our behalf, and the accomplishment of His Resurrection. This always must be the center point or focal point of our belief or Faith. Just to believe in Christ is not enough. In fact, Satan believes in Christ, but he certainly isn't saved, and in fact never will be.

NOTES

The idea is, that we as Believers focus our Faith on what Christ did at the Cross on our behalf. All Faith must anchor in that, or else it will not be Faith which God will recognize. Once our Faith is properly anchored in the Cross of Christ, i.e., *"the Finished Work of Christ,"* i.e., *"the Atonement,"* then all other things which pertain to the Lord, will stream from that on our behalf.

Again, as we've said repeatedly, all of the things that we receive from the Lord, and in whatever capacity, must come through the Person and Office of the Holy Spirit. He Alone makes real to us all that Jesus did in the Atonement, i.e., *"in His Work on the Cross."*

Several things must always be done as it regards our walk with the Lord. Some of them are as follows:

1. God operates strictly from the principle of Faith.

2. All Faith must be anchored strictly in the Cross of Christ, in other words, what He did there for lost humanity.

3. Whatever we may call it, it is not Faith unless it's anchored in the Cross.

4. We must understand that in the Cross is the answer and solution to every single thing we might need. Christ overlooked nothing in His Great Work accomplished there. Consequently, the Cross is the place to which we are to look, and from which we are to receive (I Cor. 1:18; 2:2; Gal. 6:14).

5. The moment the Believer comes to Christ, the Holy Spirit takes up His abode within the heart and life in the Child of God; consequently, the Believer actually has God living within Him, with His heart and life actually serving as the temple of God (I Cor. 3:16).

6. The Holy Spirit works exclusively from the Finished Work of Christ, in other words, according to what Christ did at the Cross, and in His Resurrection. It is called, *"The Law of the Spirit of Life in Christ Jesus"* (Rom. 8:2). In other words, the Holy Spirit guarantees us all that Christ did for us at the Cross, but He demands that we have Faith in this Great Finished Work at all times.

7. These things we have said concerning Faith, the Cross, and the Holy Spirit, constitute

the only source of Victory and Life for the Child of God.

THE COMING DAY

The phrase, *"In that day,"* refers to the coming Kingdom Age, but actually speaks of forever.

As someone has said, *"The Saints have no past, and the Devil has no future."*

The Saint should always keep his eyes on the coming of *"that Day!"* Paul said, *"If in this life only we have hope in Christ, we are of all men most miserable"* (I Cor. 15:19).

This is at least one of the reasons that this modern Gospel, which I refer to as the *"greed gospel,"* is so unscriptural and, therefore, wrong. Its total emphasis is on the here and now, with almost no thought whatsoever as it regards this *"coming Day."* The Truth is, they are selling out cheap, simply because many souls will be lost in the pursuit of *"greedy gain!"*

The idea of the True Gospel of Jesus Christ is, that there are difficulties and problems now, as are overly obvious; however, this life is not the reward, but actually only the *"school time"* one might say. Consequently, whatever problems we might have now, whatever our lot might be, it is only for a short duration, for there is coming a *"great day,"* of which the Bible plainly tells us, that is going to be wonderful and glorious to say the least! As a result, we must never allow in any way our eyes to become fastened onto the present problems. As well, we must not allow in any way our affections to be anchored at this present time in this present world.

Whether our time now is good or bad, whether it is hard or easy, whether it is short or long, this is not where it is. Our hope is totally in Christ and what He has prepared for us, and to be sure, it will be glorious!

Paul said, *"But as it is written, Eye hath not seen, nor ear heard, neither hath entered into the heart of man, the things which God hath prepared for them that love Him.*

*"But God hath revealed them unto us by His Spirit"* (I Cor. 2:9-10).

(11) "WHEREFORE ALSO WE PRAY ALWAYS FOR YOU, THAT OUR GOD WOULD COUNT YOU WORTHY OF THIS CALLING, AND FULFILL ALL THE GOOD PLEASURE OF HIS GOODNESS, AND THE WORK OF FAITH WITH POWER:"

NOTES

Even though this Verse is filled with glorious Promises, it is also replete with a veiled warning. In other words, Saints can drift from the Promises of God, and in fact, cease to believe, and thereby lose their way. Were that not true, this prayer by the Apostle, would be a fruitless exercise.

PRAYER

The phrase, *"Wherefore also we pray always for you,"* presents the idea that the hope of Believers cannot be realized except through supernatural help. We should read those words, very, very carefully! Thus, the Apostle passes naturally to prayer.

We see again the stress and reliance on intercessory prayer. Paul's prayer is fourfold, and includes the next Verse:

1. That God would count them worthy of the eternal calling.
2. That God would fulfill all His pleasure of goodness in them.
3. That God would fulfill in them the Work of Faith with power.
4. That Christ and Saints may be glorified in each other by Grace.

Sadly and regrettably, the modern Church is not a praying Church. In fact, one of the Prophecies given at the turn of the Twentieth Century was, *"In the last days My people will praise Me to Whom they no longer pray."*

It is impossible for a Believer to have any type of communion with the Lord, any type of relationship with the Lord, without at the same time having a prayer life of some nature. If in fact that is true, and it definitely is, then this means that most modern Christians have little or no relationship with the Lord whatsoever. As stated, most Christians simply don't pray!

Admittedly, prayer is hard work, but at the same time, it is the most rewarding exercise in which one could ever begin to engage.

As I have said repeatedly in these Volumes, in late 1991, the Lord instructed me to begin two Prayer Meetings a day. I will admit, that before this particular time, incidently a time of tremendous difficulty and problem for myself personally and this Ministry, I would have thought that a bit much. In fact,

I have always had a strong prayer life, even from the time of a child; however, the Lord knew that the coming years (from late 1991), would be extremely difficult and stressful. Consequently, I would need these times each day before Him, which would give me strength and power, which it most definitely has. In fact, we continue this regimen unto this very hour, and in fact, will continue it until the Coming of the Lord.

As I dictate these notes, it is December 4, 1999. Consequently, some eight years have passed since that particular time. Along with the difficulties, and there have been many, at the same time, as a result of these constant Prayer Meetings, the Lord has made Himself so very real unto me and in a way that I have never known previously. In fact, He has taken me to greater spiritual heights than I've ever known before. In the midst of this, He has given me the great Revelation of the Cross, which to be sure has completely revolutionized my life, and I also believe will be of tremendous benefit to the Church as a whole, even on a worldwide basis. I do not believe that any of this would have happened, had it not been for these Prayer Meetings which the Lord told me to engage.

I am not saying by this that all Believers should have two Prayer Meetings a day, but I am saying that every Believer should have a strong prayer life. I think both Christ and Paul set for us the examples of this, and I might quickly add, if Christ needed a strong prayer life, where does that leave us! (Mat. 14:23; 26:36, 41; Mk. 6:46; 14:32, 38; Lk. 6:12; 9:28; Jn. 14:16; 16:26; 17:9, 15, 20).

## COUNT YOU WORTHY OF THIS CALLING

The phrase, *"That our God would count you worthy of this calling,"* presents the fact that it is holy character as evidence of saving Faith which will qualify men on *"that day."* In the most fundamental sense the Christian hope is in the merit and worthiness of another, that is, Christ. However, the idea is, that if we are properly in Christ, such will be reflected in our lives regarding holy living.

Unless it is mere rhetoric, which it definitely isn't, this prayer implies the possibility of the called ones being counted unworthy at the last. Bicknell says, *"Paul certainly held that Believers might cease to believe for whatever reason, thereby falling from Grace, and then be proved unworthy of their calling."*

NOTES

*"Worthy"* in the Greek is *"axioo,"* and means *"to deem entitled or fit, deserving, or suitable."* If language means anything, this means that some will definitely not be counted *"worthy,"* or *"suitable!"*

*"Calling"* in the Greek is *"klesis,"* and means *"an invitation."* Consequently, it can refer to the past, or rather conversion (I Cor. 1:26), or also to future blessedness (Phil. 3:14), which it does here!

## HOW IS ONE MADE WORTHY?

First of all, we readily know that it is impossible for anyone to make themselves worthy. Paul plainly said, *"For by Grace* (the goodness of God) *are ye saved through Faith* (Faith in what Christ did at the Cross on our behalf)*; and that not of yourselves* (nothing we can do)*: it is the Gift of God* (and a gift must be simply received. It cannot be earned. If so, it's not a gift)*:*

*"Not of works, lest any man should boast"* (Eph. 2:8-9).

In fact, the great sin of the world is their attempt to make themselves worthy by various different types of efforts. Also, it is the great sin of the Church, in attempting to sanctify ourselves, which we can no more do, than the sinner can save himself.

So, we know that it is impossible for any human being to be worthy before God, at least within himself, irrespective as to what one might do. How then can one be made worthy?

As in the Scripture we have just quoted, one is made worthy, and completely worthy at that, by simply exhibiting Faith in what Christ did at the Cross on our behalf. When this is done, the Righteousness of Christ, which is the only Righteousness that God will recognize, instantly becomes ours (Rom. 4:3).

At that moment, the moment of Salvation, the believing sinner is not only made Righteous, but also is blessed with the advent of the Holy Spirit within his life (Gal. 3:14). Naturally, the Spirit of God is present within our lives to carry out a particular work. That work is, that we might be made Christlike in our *"walk,"* exactly as we have been made Righteous by our *"Faith."*

However, as should be obvious, this *"worthiness"* can be lost, if two things are engaged:

1. If the Believer takes the attitude that sin is of little consequence, and, therefore, one can live in sin and at the same time have Salvation, he will soon find himself with a hardened heart, because hardness is the result of sin. The Scripture plainly says, *"Take heed, Brethren* (Paul is here speaking to Believers), *lest there be in any of you an evil heart of unbelief, in departing from the Living God.*

*"But exhort one another daily, while it is called today; lest any of you be hardened through the deceitfulness of sin."*

He then said, *"For we are made partakers of Christ, if we hold the beginning of our confidence steadfast unto the end"* (Heb. 3:12-14).

Once again, if language means anything, this tells us that Believers can quit believing, i.e., *"quit believing God's Way and insert instead their own way,"* and thereby be eternally lost.

2. As we are saved by Faith, we are also kept by Faith. This of course, refers to Faith in the Cross of Christ. If the Believer shifts his trust from the Cross to other things, and continues in that mode, which will always take the individual downward in a spiritual sense, if that fruitless direction is not changed, the individual can and will be lost.

Salvation is based totally on trust in Christ, and that means trust in what He did at the Cross on our behalf. If that trust is transferred to other things, once again, Paul plainly says, *"If they* (Christians) *shall fall away* (fall away from trust in Christ), *to renew them again unto repentance* (is impossible)*; seeing they crucify to themselves the Son of God afresh, and put Him to an open shame"* (Heb. 6:6).

Paul is not saying here that a backslider cannot come back to Christ, or that one cannot repent and be restored. He is saying, that if one comes to the place of rejecting Christ and what He did at the Cross, that there is no way for that person to repent, because repentance is always based upon a return to the Finished Work of Christ. Otherwise, it's repentance which God will not recognize, seeing that such an effort makes a mockery of the Crucifixion of the Son of God, as should be obvious!

NOTES

Unfortunately, there are millions of professing Christians presently, who make no attempt to live for God, but openly live a life of sin, and think they are saved, simply because someone told them that once they received Christ, they can never lose Christ, no matter what they do.

In fact, many of these people have never truly been saved to begin with, but some of them truly have. Regrettably, they have chosen to believe a lie, and a lie has never saved anyone. If they continue in that particular mode of unbelief, they will die eternally lost, even as Paul says here!

THE PLEASURE OF HIS GOODNESS

The phrase, *"And fulfill all the good pleasure of His goodness,"* refers to all the wonderful things the Holy Spirit desires to do for us, and in fact will do for us, if we will only cooperate with Him.

*"His"* was inserted by the translators, with the Text originally reading, *"And fulfill all the good pleasure of goodness."*

*"Goodness"* is listed as the Fruit of the Holy Spirit (Gal. 5:22). The desire or resolve for it is implanted by the Spirit. But resolve after uprightness in heart and life, although definitely necessary, is still not good enough within itself. Paul here prays for the realization, which the next phrase tells us how this goodness can be brought about.

As well, if one is to notice, the word *"all"* is used, referring to the fact, that the Holy Spirit wants and desires that we have His complete work, which is *"His good pleasure."* This means that He is pleased, and pleased grandly so, whenever these great attributes are *"fulfilled"* in our lives.

As should be obvious, this Work of the Spirit, as it refers to the goodness of God being perfected within our lives, lends toward the *"worthiness of this calling."*

So what happens, if this is not done?

Of course, only the Lord can judge each and every individual. Thankfully, He judges the heart rather than the actions. To be sure, His Judgment is always perfect and pure, for He alone can see into the heart of man.

The Bible does not teach sinless perfection, but it does teach that sin will not have dominion over us, that is if we truly trust in

Christ and what He did at the Cross (Rom. 6:14). To be sure, the struggle between the flesh and the Spirit which commences at Salvation, and intensifies at the Baptism with the Holy Spirit, will in fact, never end until we die, or until the coming Rapture.

So we're not speaking here of the cessation of struggle. In fact, all Believers are at particular stages in their Spiritual Growth. These stages of course, do not have anything to do with our Salvation, but rather our Sanctification.

Let's look now at the manner in which this great work of Sanctification, for this is actually of what Paul is addressing, can be carried out in our lives.

## FAITH AND POWER

The phrase, *"And the Work of Faith with power,"* refers to the completion of every work which Faith begins. Only *"with Power,"* the Power of Divine Grace that is, is fulfillment possible. In other words, only God can do this, but He definitely can do it, and definitely will do it, if we will only cooperate with Him.

Taking Verse 11 as a whole, one senses the urgency not only of present holiness of heart, but also of continuous progress and growth in both the inward and outward aspects of this life of Holiness in Christ.

*"Work"* in the Greek is *"ergon,"* and means *"deed, doing, labor."* However, this *"deed, doing, and labor"* is not to be on our part, but rather is on the part of the Holy Spirit. In other words, it is *"His Work,"* which is being carried out within our hearts and lives, and not *"our work!"*

In fact, this is the area of greatest conflict for the Child of God. We try to make this our work, which means we are attempting to sanctify ourselves, which of course, is a fruitless task. It is not only fruitless, it also angers God, because in effect, these particular efforts, which all of us have engaged at one time or the other, are an insult to the great Finished Work of Christ (Rom. 8:8).

We might quickly add, that the *"work"* in which the Holy Spirit is engaged, can be brought about within our lives, only according to our Faith in the great Finished Work of Christ. In other words, this *"work"* of the Holy Spirit is predicated totally upon the

NOTES

*"work"* carried out by Christ at the Cross and in His Resurrection.

## FAITH

The *"work"* here mentioned, is that which true Faith produces, and what do we mean by that?

The *"Faith"* here mentioned, is the Faith which the Believer must have in what Christ did at the Cross. This means that every single thing we need, everything we must have, all the blessings, all the necessary strength and power, all the Righteousness, all the Sanctification as well as Salvation, and in every capacity, are found in the Cross of Christ, i.e., *"the Finished Work of Christ."* So, when we speak of *"Faith"* we must understand that it's Faith in this of what Christ has done on our behalf. In other words, He did all of this for us, and not at all for Himself.

This means that the Believer does not really have to do anything toward this great project within his heart and life, except evidence Faith in the Cross, and thereby, keep his Faith in the Cross.

This sounds very easy, but in fact, it is the area that Satan seeks to hinder the most. In other words, he will attempt to shift your Faith from this great Work of Christ, to your own efforts and works. To be sure, these things to which you are shifted are most of the time very holy and righteous within their own right. Consequently, they deceive us. And what do I mean by that?

I'm speaking of good things within our lives, such as prayer, fasting, witnessing, the giving of money to the Cause of Christ, manifestations of the Spirit, etc. All of these things we have named, are very good in their own way and right, and should be engaged by Christians constantly; however, if we think by the doing of these things, that we earn merit or worthiness with God, we then turn them into works, which God can never honor. Satan knows this, and constantly seeks to push us in these directions. He knows we will not find any victory there whatsoever.

Now please understand, we are not meaning by these statements, that Christians should quit praying or fasting, or giving to the Work of God or witnessing, etc., not at all! We are merely saying that we must not turn these things into works, which can be done, and in fact are done constantly.

Whether we realize it or not, any trust, Faith, or confidence, that we might place in anything, other than the Finished Work of Christ, no matter how good these things might be in their own way, does nothing but frustrate the Grace of God within our lives (Gal. 2:20-21).

It is obvious that Paul is here speaking of Sanctification; consequently, he is speaking of victory over the world, the flesh, and the Devil. There is only one way this can be obtained, only one manner in which it can be produced, only one method by which this victory is available, and that is through what Christ did at the Cross. Consequently, our Faith must rest in that and that alone, because it is in that and that alone, in which the Holy Spirit works. As stated, all of this is a Work of the Spirit, meaning that we cannot do it ourselves, even though we are Believers, and that He works exclusively from the foundation, principle, and parameters of the great Atonement of Christ carried out at the Cross. These are the legal boundaries in which He works, and if we go outside of those boundaries, which we always do, if we place trust in anything except Christ and the Cross, we succeed only in tying His hands.

Does the Reader understand what we are saying?

Because this is so very, very important, please allow me to use an example, which in fact, I have already used. But due to the significance of all this, it describes what I'm trying to say, very aptly, and serves as an excellent example.

NOTES

### THE FAMILY CURSE

Without going into detail, there are some Preachers who teach that problems in the lives of Believers are at times caused by *"a family curse."* They derive this from Deuteronomy 5:9 where it says, *"Visiting the iniquity of the fathers upon the children unto the third and fourth generation of them that hate Me."* Of course, it is speaking of great sins committed, which the previous Verse explains.

However, if one is to notice, there is a qualifier on this which says, *"them that hate Me."* In other words, if that particular family continues to transgress the Word of God, which in effect says that they hate God, this curse will be visited upon succeeding generations.

But it also says, *"And showing mercy unto thousands of them that love Me and keep My Commandments"* (Deut. 5:10).

The moment that any member of any family comes to Christ, no matter what others did in the past, that curse is broken for that individual totally and completely, and is greatly lessened for the entire family (Acts 16:31). Paul plainly said, *"If any man* (and it means any man) *be in Christ, he is a new creature: old things are passed away; behold, all things are become new"* (II Cor. 5:17).

What kind of Salvation would it be, for God to continue to hang around the neck of one of His Children, a particular curse instituted generations back? But yet, many Christians believe this foolishness, traveling hundreds of miles to have some Preacher lay hands on them, in order to rebuke the family curse. Such efforts on both the part of the individual and the Preacher (but moreso on the Preacher), are an insult to Christ and what He did at the Cross on our behalf.

This is actually saying that Christ did not finish the Work at the Cross, and has to have this particular arrangement carried out before the person can have full Victory and Salvation. I would hope the Reader can see how wrong this is, but yet, untold thousands of Christians believe this lie, and a lie it is.

Jesus said, *"Ye shall know the Truth, and the Truth shall make you free"* (Jn. 8:32). I think it should be obvious, that a *"lie"* cannot set us free, and this *"family curse"* thing as it regards Believers, is definitely a lie.

However, I have used this as an example, to show how our Faith can be taken away from the Cross of Christ, placed in something else, which might look good on the surface, and because of Scriptural ignorance may be accepted; however, such things will never bring any satisfaction or victory of any nature.

To be sure, there are all types of curses on the human race, including families, and of every despicable description; however, upon coming to Christ, all of those curses in totality are completely broken. And if there are continuing problems, it is because we as Believers do not understand the part the Cross plays in our continued living for God. Satan takes full advantage of ignorance as should be obvious. And to be sure, if the Believer does not properly understand this great route to Victory which is the Cross, and his Faith in that great Finished Work, there are going to be problems, and even severe problems at that. In fact, Paul gives us his own experience in this realm in Romans Chapter 7. However, the Lord gave him the answer to this dilemma, which he gave us in Romans Chapters 6 and 8.

## POWER

The *"power"* is always found in the Holy Spirit (Acts 1:8). Of course, His Power is almighty, meaning that He can do anything, because He is God. The question is, how can I get Him to use His great power on my behalf, in order that this great work of Faith be carried out within my life, which will *"fulfill all the good pleasure of His goodness"*?

He tells us in Romans 8:2: The Holy Spirit through Paul said, *"For the Law of the Spirit* (the Law by which the Holy Spirit works) *of Life* (that for which we seek) *in Christ Jesus* (meaning, that all of this is in what Christ did at the Cross) *hath made me free from the law of sin and death."*

So, what is this *"Law"*?

It simply means, as we have already stated, that the Holy Spirit works within the parameters of what Christ did at the Cross and in His Resurrection. Of course, this would also include His Exaltation (Rom. 6:2-6; Eph. 2:6).

As Believers, we are to have Faith in this which Christ has done on our behalf, and we speak of the Cross, understanding that this is the Source of all Salvation, Sanctification, Healing, Blessings, Prosperity, and Power; in other words, everything!

When we place our Faith in this, understand that this is totally the Source of all that we ask and seek, the Holy Spirit will then use His Mighty Power on our behalf. He will not do so, irrespective that He is present within our hearts and lives, if our Faith is not properly placed. That's where the power

NOTES

is, and that's why the Holy Spirit through Paul used this phrase in this particular Verse in this manner, *"and the Work of Faith with power."*

## WHY IS POWER NEEDED?

When we consider that we are now in Christ, and that we are new creations, which means that we are not what we once were, and that Satan no longer has a hold on us, why do we now need Power?

While we are all of these things, this doesn't mean that Satan is going to cease in his activities against us. And to be sure, Satan definitely does have power, despite what some Preachers say! As well, this power is greater than any willpower that we may personally have. This means, that within ourselves, according to our own strength and ability, even though we are Believers, we still cannot overcome Satan. The power that he brings against us, is beyond our scope of operation or even understanding for that matter. So, that means if we are trying to oppose him within our own strength, we are sure to fail!

Of course, almost every Christian, if not all, would claim that they are not opposing Satan by their own strength or machinations, but through and by the Power of God, etc. Christians throw around the Name of Jesus, thinking that this is going to scare Satan, or else we engage in other efforts whatever they might be, all the time thinking that this means our dependence is on the Lord.

The Truth is, none of these things we do, constitutes any dependence on God whatsoever. Irrespective of the terminology we use, or how loud or boisterous we might be, it is still only personal strength on which we are depending, which guarantees failure, despite all the loud bravado, etc.

In the last few decades, Christians have learned to lie to themselves. We boast about our great victory, when in Truth, we are not walking in victory. Of course, some few definitely are, but that number is small indeed! The majority of Christians today, and because they have been taught wrong, are not living in victory, not walking in victory, and in fact do not enjoy Victory in the Lord.

Why?

We are trying to oppose the Evil One within our own strength, and his power is too great for us. Of course we won't admit that, shouting loudly as to how great we are in Christ, etc. The Truth is otherwise!

The Lord does not expect us to oppose Satan within our own strength, having provided all that we need in the Finished Work of Christ. The problem is, most Christians have no idea as to the part the Cross plays in their everyday living after their conversion experience. In other words, they think the Cross pertains only to their initial Salvation experience, with it then being left behind, with them going on to better and greater things. In fact, in many modern Charismatic circles, the Cross is looked at as a defeat instead of victory, which borders on blasphemy. Nevertheless, that's what they are being taught! Consequently, they are doomed to defeat even before they begin.

The facts are, that the Cross of Christ plays just as much a part in our everyday walk before God, which constitutes our living and our victory, even as it did in our initial Salvation experience. We must understand that and believe that. That's why Paul said, *"For the preaching of the Cross is to them that perish foolishness; but unto us which are saved it is the Power of God"* (I Cor. 1:18).

As we've already stated, this great *"Power of God"* which comes through our Faith in the Cross, is in fact, ensconced in the Holy Spirit. As Believers, all we have to do is to understand where our victory is, and I speak of the Cross of Christ. It is there that Jesus defeated every power of darkness, atoned for all sin, satisfied the claims of Heavenly Justice, and thereby made it possible upon Faith, for believing sinners to have the Righteousness of Christ. In the Cross of Christ is all Life, all Victory, and all the attributes of God given to us on behalf of Christ.

We must understand that and have Faith in that, and never depart from that. Then the Holy Spirit will exert His Mighty Power on our behalf, and at all times, with Victory in our hearts and lives assured, even on a daily basis (Lk. 9:23).

Without the Power of the Holy Spirit exhibited on our behalf, no Believer can walk in victory, simply because we are no match for Satan. This great Power will be manifested within us and for us, if we will only exhibit Faith in the Finished Work of Christ, and continue to do so each and every day of our lives (Lk. 9:23).

NOTES

(12) "THAT THE NAME OF OUR LORD JESUS CHRIST MAY BE GLORIFIED IN YOU, AND YE IN HIM, ACCORDING TO THE GRACE OF OUR GOD AND THE LORD JESUS CHRIST."

Here Paul states the purpose of his prayer — the glorification of Christ in Believers and they in Him (Isa. 66:5). This is an intermediate step toward the final recognition of the Lord's Own Worthiness and Majesty and the Saints' participation in these things with Him. *"Name"* is a reference to the Dignity, Majesty, and Power of the Lord's revealed Character.

## CHRIST GLORIFIED IN BELIEVERS

The phrase, *"That the Name of our Lord Jesus Christ may be glorified in you,"* presents the object of the Holy Spirit, in other words, that which He is carrying out within our hearts and lives.

How can this be done?

*"Name,"* as in Old Testament usage, signifies not just identity but the revealed character of the Person. Due to the way this is given, it refers to Christ's Redemptive Work.

*"Lord"* refers to Deity, meaning that Jesus is God!

*"Jesus"* refers to *"Saviour,"* meaning that He is our Redeemer.

*"Christ"* refers to the Anointed One, referring to what He was anointed to do, i.e., *"The Spirit of the Lord is upon Me, because He hath anointed Me to preach the Gospel to the poor; He hath sent Me to heal the brokenhearted, to preach deliverance to the captives, and recovering of sight to the blind, to set at liberty them that are bruised, to preach the acceptable year of the Lord"* (Lk. 4:18-19).

All of this refers to what His Work at the Cross would bring about. So, *"The Name of our Lord Jesus Christ may be glorified in us,"* only as we understand His Redemptive Work on the Cross, place our Faith in that, which allows the Holy Spirit to bring about the benefits of the Cross within our lives. It can be done no other way!

NOTES

### DOES THE READER THINK THAT I STRESS THE CROSS TOO MUCH?

The Truth is, I don't stress it enough. The Truth is, it would be impossible to stress it too much.

Every single thing from God to man comes through the Cross of Christ. Every single thing from man to God, goes through the Cross, or else it is not accepted by God. If Jesus had not gone to the Cross on our behalf, His Virgin Birth, His spotless, pure Life, His miracles, His healings, in fact, all that He did, would have been totally in vain. While all of these things were necessary and definitely played their part, it was the Cross of Christ which effected the Redemption of lost and dying humanity. That's the reason that all Faith must center up in the Cross and thereby spring from that Finished Work. It's the only basis on which the Holy Spirit will work, and because it is the great Plan of God for the human race (I Pet. 1:18-20).

### IN HIM

The phrase, *"And ye in Him,"* in effect echoes the Words of Christ when He said, *"At that day* (after the Cross when the Holy Spirit would come) *ye shall know that I am in My Father, and ye in Me, and I in you"* (Jn. 14:20).

We can be glorified in Him only on one basis, and that is the basis of our Faith in His glorious, Finished Work. Faith in Jesus alone is not really enough. It must be Faith in what He did at the Cross on our behalf (Jn. 3:16).

This is what Jesus told Nicodemus: *"And as Moses lifted up the serpent in the wilderness, even so must the Son of Man be lifted up* (lifted up on the Cross)*:*

*"That whosoever believeth in Him* (believes in what He did at the Cross on our behalf) *should not perish, but have Eternal Life"* (Jn. 3:14-15).

How much clearer can it be!

Only in this manner can the Name of the Lord be glorified in us, and us in Him.

### THE NAME OF JESUS

Incidently, the Name of Jesus is effective not at all as some type of magic talisman, but only in the realm of what He did regarding His Finished Work on the Cross. His Name as *"Saviour,"* is glorified only in this regard and in this respect. This is what causes Satan to fear Christ so very, very much!

When Satan hears the Name of Jesus, and he knows that the Saint has Faith in that Name, according to the great Work carried out at the Cross, which spells Satan's defeat, he automatically retreats. However, he will retreat on that basis and that basis only!

Unfortunately, millions of Christians fling about the Name of Jesus, thinking it carries some type of magic power, or by the mere fact of us saying it, that it will produce some type of effect in the spirit world. It will definitely do just that, but only if we understand what the Name actually means.

As stated, it actually means *"Saviour,"* which refers to what Jesus did at the Cross, where Satan was totally and completely defeated. Unfortunately, most Christians do not think of the Name of Jesus in that respect, therefore, Christ is not glorified within them, simply because He can be glorified in us only according to our understanding of His great Atonement.

### THE GRACE OF GOD

The phrase, *"According to the Grace of our God and the Lord Jesus Christ,"* simply means that all of these good things, these wonderful things, these miraculous things, these eternal things, all made possible by the Cross, are freely given to us by the means of Grace.

Grace is not an act, but rather a *"means."* It simply means, that all the things that we receive from the Lord, and that means everything, is simply because of His goodness. Grace is the means by which that goodness is extended to us. It means we don't deserve it, and in fact could never deserve it, but that all is simply a *"Gift of God!"*

The word *"Grace"* immediately closes the door to all works on our part. It means that if we attempt to institute any type of works, which in effect says within themselves that we are trying to earn these things which God will only release as a Gift, that we succeed only in nullifying these Gifts. As the Apostle said, all of this is *"according to Grace,"* which means it's not according to our works or personal merit.

As well, we must understand, that the Grace of God is extended to man only through the

Cross of Christ. God has always had Grace. In fact, He doesn't have anymore Grace today, than He did 5,000 years ago. He is however, able to extend Grace far more liberally now, simply because of what Jesus did at the Cross. The Cross opened the door, in a way that it had never been opened before. To be frank, it not only opened the door, it kicked the thing down. That's the reason that the Holy Spirit can now say, *"And whosoever will, let him take the water of life freely"* (Rev. 22:17).

As well, if it is to be noticed, this Grace proceeds from Both *"God and the Lord Jesus Christ."*

*"Come, Thou Fount of every blessing,*
*tune my heart to sing Thy Grace;*
*"Streams of Mercy, never ceasing, call*
*for songs of loudest praise.*
*"Teach me some melodious sonnet,*
*sung by flaming tongues above;*
*"Praise the Mount! I'm fixed upon it,*
*Mount of Thy Redeeming Love."*

*"Here I raise my sign of victory; hither*
*by Thy help I'm come;*
*"And I know, by Thy good pleasure,*
*safely to arrive at home.*
*"Jesus sought me when a stranger,*
*wandering from the fold of God;*
*"He, to rescue me from danger,*
*Interposed His Precious Blood."*

*"O to Grace how great a debtor, daily*
*I'm constrained to be!*
*"Let Thy Goodness, like a fetter, bind*
*my wandering heart to Thee;*
*"Prone to wander, Lord, I feel it, prone*
*to leave the God I love;*
*"Here's my heart, O take and seal it,*
*seal it for Thy Courts above."*

## CHAPTER 2

(1) "NOW WE BESEECH YOU, BRETHREN, BY THE COMING OF OUR LORD JESUS CHRIST, AND BY OUR GATHERING TOGETHER UNTO HIM,"

Problems had arisen among the Thessalonian Christians which made it necessary for Paul to take corrective measures in this Second Epistle. In the First Letter, he had instructed them in the comforting and inspiring Truth of the Lord's Coming and the *"gathering together"* of all the Saints to be with Him. In some way, however, the error was spreading that Paul taught that the Day of the Lord was already present. This seems to have produced a foment of excitement and alarm, as well as a disorderly movement on the part of some who had stopped regular work to await Christ's return. In this Passage Paul deals correctively with this matter; in Chapter 3 he deals with the disorderly faction.

Farfetched theories, date setting, and fanatical movements have tended, in all periods of the Church's history, to discredit the Truth about Christ's return. Those who *"love His appearing"* (II Tim. 4:8) will not permit these things to obscure the *"Blessed Hope"* (Titus 2:13).

It will be helpful, in interpreting these Passages, to keep in mind the general background.

The little Christian community at Thessalonica is passing through tribulation. There is no assurance of speedy release from suffering. But the Message is that God is on the Throne; assurance is given that future triumph for Christ and those who are Christ's is certain. Chapter 1 has pointed out that God is a Righteous Judge governing a moral universe. Chapter 2 will outline the defeat of evil powers at their very worst, and the fulfillment of God's lofty purpose for the Church (Airhart).

### BESEECH YOU

The phrase, *"Now we beseech you, Brethren,"* presents the Apostle beginning with a familiar phrase.

By the use of the word *"Brethren"* we know that Paul is speaking to Believers. Having at once quieted their hearts as to their present sufferings, the Apostle now proceeds to prove to them that *"the Day of the Lord"* with its terrors and judgments had not yet arrived. He had told them in his First Epistle (I Thess. 5:4) that they should be raptured to Heaven prior to those Judgments, and that when the Lord Jesus Christ appeared to execute these

NOTES

Judgments, they would appear with Him (Col. 3:4; I Thess. 3:13).

As well, the Apostle not at all talks down to these young converts in Christ, but rather appeals to them as an equal by using the familiar phrase *"we beseech you!"* There are several reasons for this:

First of all, that's the nature of the Apostle, and I speak of humility. It should be the nature of all Believers.

As well, he is not allowed by the Holy Spirit to lord it over these Saints, even though he is the great Apostle, and they are but new converts. There is no place in the Work of God for such attitude or action, which so often characterizes, sadly and regrettably, the modern Church.

Third, the Apostle is looking forward to their Spiritual Growth, to when they will be equal with him as far as the Knowledge of the Word is concerned, which will be produced by their Christlikeness. Of course, the Truth is, that most of these Saints would never reach that particular state, if any; however, the Apostle, and because he has Faith, will treat them as though this is actually the case.

## THE COMING OF THE LORD

The phrase, *"By the Coming of our Lord Jesus Christ,"* refers, in a sense, to both Comings. We speak of the Rapture of the Church, and also of the Second Coming.

As we said in Commentary on I Thessalonians, there is no reason that the Rapture of the Church and the Second Coming of our Lord should be confused. They are two distinct Comings and, in a sense, do not relate to each other. In fact, the two Comings are separated by at least seven years, and possibly even more.

## OUR GATHERING TOGETHER

The phrase, *"And by our gathering together unto Him,"* refers solely to the Rapture of the Church.

The Greek word *"episunagogue,"* translated *"gathering together"* occurs only once again in the New Testament, where it is used with reference to the assembling of Christians for worship (Heb. 10:35). Here it is used with reference to the assembling

NOTES

of Believers to Christ, when He shall be revealed from Heaven. It is the time of the great Resurrection, when the dead in Christ shall be raised, and those in Christ who are alive will be gloriously changed (I Cor. 15:51-57).

## THE RAPTURE OF THE CHURCH

Writing to the Thessalonian Saints (I Thess. 4:13-18) who were mourning the loss of loved ones who had gone to be with Christ, he comforts them with the knowledge that they will see them again when the Lord Jesus comes for His Own. He tells them that in view of the fact that they believe that Jesus died and rose again, He would bring these loved ones from Heaven with Him as He comes into the atmosphere of this Earth to take the living Saints with Him to Heaven.

Then Paul informs them that the Saints living at the time of the Rapture will not precede the dead Saints in the glorification of their bodies, for the latter will receive their bodies back glorified, and then the living shall have their bodies changed in a moment (I Cor. 15:52).

The word *"moment"* in the Greek is *"atomos"* from the Greek *"temno"* which means *"to cut,"* which when put together means, *"That which cannot be cut in two or divided."* We get our word *"atom"* from this Greek word.

The change will take place in an instant of time so small that it cannot be divided, an atomic moment, so to speak. What an experience it will be for the Saints living on Earth when Jesus comes!

The change over from a mortal to an immortal body, from a body clothed with man-made garments to a body clothed with an enswathement of glory produced from within, from one indwelt by the sinful nature to one without it, from a body in which there is blood to one without blood, from a body in which there may be imperfections and disease to one in which these things are not present, and in fact will never again be present, from a body all tired out to one in which there will be inexhaustible supplies of energy to serve the Living God for all eternity, from a face wrinkled and lined with sin to a face in which the beauty of Jesus shines untrammelled by the marks which sin leaves upon our faces now, from a mind broken down by 6,000 years of human sin to a mind clear and powerful to think God's thoughts after Him. What a change an atomic second will make when Jesus comes for us!

One can only shout *"Hallelujah!"*

HOW CLOSE WILL CHRIST COME TO THIS EARTH AT THE TIME OF THE RAPTURE?

We who are alive when He comes will meet Him in the air.

There are two Greek words for *"air."* They are *"aither"* and *"aer."*

A Greek could stand on Mount Olympus, the highest mountain in Greece and point upward saying, *"aither."* This would refer to the upper, rarefied atmosphere above the mountaintops, extending on up into the heavens.

Pointing downward he would say *"aer,"* which refers to the lower, denser atmosphere below the tops of the mountains, at least that particular mountain. The Holy Spirit led Paul to use the Greek word *"aer"* (I Thess. 4:17). This means that our Lord when coming for His Church will descend to a point below the mountaintops of this Earth, but will not in fact touch the Earth.

Mount Olympus is slightly above 6,000 feet in altitude. This means that Jesus will come anywhere between approximately 6,000 and several hundred feet to this Earth at the time of the Rapture.

THE CLOUDS

All the Resurrected Saints will be caught up together *"in the clouds."* However, there is no definite article in the Greek Text. It simply says we shall be caught up *"in clouds,"* which actually means, *"clouds of Saints."*

The same Greek word for *"clouds"* is used in Hebrews 12:1 in the phrase, *"Wherefore seeing we also are compassed about with so great a cloud of witnesses."* The writer is thinking of the thousands of people in the Greek Stadium surrounding the Athletes. The word is also used in the Greek classics of a cloud of foot soldiers.

What a spectacle that will be, large groups of Saints, their bodies glorified, clothed with an enswathement of Glory shining with a Heavenly radiance, arising in great masses to Heaven!

NOTES

CAUGHT UP

The words *"caught up"* as given in I Thessalonians 4:17 are the translation of the Greek word *"harpazo,"* which in its several meanings throws a flood of light upon this glorious Event. We have already given these meanings in Commentary on I Thessalonians, and will not repeat them here. Suffice to say, the word is used of Divine Power transferring a person marvelously and swiftly from one place to another.

Ever how far Heaven is from Earth, we will be transported there with the speed of *"thought."* It will be one moment on Earth, and the next moment in Heaven.

The Great Saviour from Heaven will claim His Body, the Church, and will eagerly take the Church with Him to Heaven. Such is the Rapture in brief.

That which will follow the Rapture, which we will study, will be Daniel's Seventieth Week portraying the reign of the Antichrist and the Great Tribulation. But before that period of some seven years comes, the Saints will have been caught up to be with the Lord. There is no prophecy unfulfilled that would withhold His Coming for the Church. In fact, the departure of the Church could occur at any moment.

(2) "THAT YE BE NOT SOON SHAKEN IN MIND, OR BE TROUBLED, NEITHER BY SPIRIT, NOR BY WORD, NOR BY LETTER AS FROM US, AS THAT THE DAY OF CHRIST IS AT HAND."

We find from this Verse, that the Thessalonians were shaken in mind and troubled, for false doctrine always has a tendency to do this. For if the Day of the Lord had already set in, the Apostle's teaching about the hope of the Rapture was false, and if he erred on so important a matter, what security had they that his Gospel was infallible?

If these two Epistles be read together it will appear that the Teachers who confused and mistaught the Thessalonians were Jewish Believers. Their hopes were set upon the return of the Messiah to the Earth and the setting up of His Kingdom at Jerusalem. They still had not shaken the idea of the immediate restoration of the Kingdom to Israel, which Jesus had plainly told them to put aside (Acts 1:6-7).

Hearing all of this, the Thessalonians surmised that those who had fallen asleep in Christ would consequently miss that Kingdom. In fact, Paul in his First Epistle had used the word *"we"*; therefore, these Teachers could argue that he and Silas and Timothy (II Thess. 2:2) expected that Event in their lifetime; therefore, it must be near at hand, and that of necessity, the *"Day of the Lord"* had already begun.

That Day, as predicted in Isaiah, Chapter 13; Joel, Chapter 2; Amos, Chapter 5; etc., was to be a day of darkness and unparalleled terror, to be immediately succeeded by the appearing of the Messiah in His Glory.

The sufferings that the Thessalonians were enduring at the time supported such teaching. However, what they failed to realize, was that their views were all earthly, and, therefore, did not match up with the Prophecies.

Paul reminds them that the *"Day of the Lord"* will be brought about by the appearing of the Antichrist and the False Prophet (II Thess. 2:3, 9), and prior to that, the Thessalonian Believers, along with every other Believer, both living and dead would be caught away from the Earth to meet the Lord in the air, there to be with Him, and then to come back with Him at the Second Coming.

The Thessalonians appear to have lost the hope of this Rapture, even as many at present have. Nevertheless, it is going to happen just as surely as the Word of God is True, for the teaching of the Rapture is the Word of God.

## DO NOT BE TROUBLED

The phrase, *"That ye be not soon shaken in mind, or be troubled, neither by spirit, nor by word, nor by letter as from us,"* presents several means by which a false message could come, and no doubt did.

Several things are said here:

1. False doctrine which of course is a false way, always causes one to be shaken in mind. In other words, there is an unsettled feeling, an unsettled spirit, which robs one of peace.

The Greek word used here signifies properly, that one is moved as a wave of the Sea or tossed upon the waves as is a vessel in a storm (Mat. 11:7; 24:29; Lk. 6:38; Acts 6:31; Heb. 12:26).

NOTES

The Word of God correctly interpreted, and applied to our hearts and lives, always produces peace. There may be a storm whirling around us, but inwardly there is peace. It is only when we misinterpret the Word, or leave the Word through self-will, that consternation arises.

Since late 1991 I have had occasion to prove this over and over. The Lord had spoken to my heart, and had done so in a graphic way that left absolutely no doubt, that I was to continue ministering, in other words, I was to do exactly what He told me to do and not listen to man. As well, and as I've already related, He told me to begin two Prayer Meetings a day, which we immediately instituted.

To be sure, the Church world (not Family Worship Center) was demanding the very opposite. In fact, they were doing all within their power to silence my voice. They didn't want me preaching the Gospel, and the reason was very simple. They didn't like what I preached, because I opposed strongly many of the ways in which the Church was heading, which Message incidently, proved to be exactly right.

Irrespective of the outward storm, which in fact blew as I had never known before, there was an inward peace that never left and remains unto this day, and in fact is greater than ever. I knew I was in the Will of God and despite what man said, that was all that mattered.

To be sure, I was shaken in many ways, but not *"in mind."* I knew what the Lord had said, and I knew I was attempting to follow Him as closely as possible, therefore, my mind has never been shaken at all.

2. A wrong direction will not only produce a disquietment of mind, it will also bring on an agitation, i.e., *"trouble!"*

*"Troubled"* in the Greek is *"threomai,"* and means *"to clamor, to frighten, to wail."* This portrays the degree of the *"shaken mind."*

3. Neither by spirit: This could well refer to a pretended message by Tongues and Interpretation or Prophecy or Revelation. In effect, the Apostle is saying that it doesn't matter how many of these supposed Messages come forth, which proclaim other than the Truth, they are not to be heeded. That simply tells us, that the Gifts were abused, which they are often done! Of course, the question

must quickly be asked as to the spiritual state of the individuals being used accordingly.

The immediate answer is that they are not right with God. In Truth, there is definitely a possibility that these individuals were truly given these Gifts by the Lord to begin with, and were used by Him in some capacity for a time; however, at some point the individual strayed from the right way of the Lord, and continued to use the Gifts, but of course, without the sanction or moving of the Holy Spirit. In other words, what they were now saying was out of their own minds.

These individuals, whomever they might have been, can make things right with God, and be rightly used of the Lord once again; however, it would require repentance and a return to dependence on the Lord and a complete disavowal of self-will. Unfortunately, many do not return to the right way.

In the last several decades, much harm has been done in the Church because of this very thing. The gifts have been misused and abused by many, which always causes problems and difficulties, because some immature Christians, even as these in Thessalonica, think it's actually from God and take it to heart. Some even base their lives or actions or decisions on such, which always leads to great difficulties and problems.

The Reader should always remember, that the Gifts are always to be judged according to Scripturality (I Cor. 14:29).

As well, Believers are never to be led by the Gifts, unless the Lord has first spoken to them concerning the question at hand.

4. Nor by Word: This would concern those who claimed to have a *"word from the Lord,"* concerning this particular situation regarding the Rapture and the Second Coming, which did not agree with Paul's teaching. In essence, the Apostle is saying that this so-called *"word,"* is not from God, is, therefore, not Scriptural, and must be ignored.

5. Nor by letter as from us: This evidently refers to a letter which had been written by someone concerning these events, who had forged Paul's name to the script.

THE DAY OF CHRIST

The phrase, *"As that the Day of Christ is at hand,"* probably should have been translated *"the Day of the Lord,"* for it seems the latter is given in the best Manuscripts.

NOTES

As we have previously stated, the *"Day of Christ,"* refers to the Rapture of the Church, while the *"Day of the Lord"* refers to all events after the Rapture.

Even though the Rapture will be mentioned in the balance of this Chapter, still, the major thrust concerns the Second Coming, and those things which will take place preceding that great Event, as it concerns the Great Tribulation.

The whole idea of this Chapter concerns the return of the Messiah to the Earth and the setting up of His Kingdom at Jerusalem. Paul is now giving some instructions as to when this will happen, or in other words, the things which must take place before it can happen.

(3) "LET NO MAN DECEIVE YOU BY ANY MEANS: FOR THAT DAY SHALL NOT COME, EXCEPT THERE COME A FALLING AWAY FIRST, AND THAT MAN OF SIN BE REVEALED, THE SON OF PERDITION;"

In essence, the Apostle is saying that the Day of the Lord had not yet arrived, and in fact would not arrive, until two conspicuous phenomena would be brought to pass. Those two things are: A. The Rapture of the Church; and, B. The appearance of the Man of Sin, the Beast, i.e., *"the Antichrist!"* Inasmuch as these two things had not yet taken place, despite the persecution and tribulation that the Thessalonians were even then experiencing, the *"Day of the Lord"* had not yet arrived. I might quickly add, that as such applied then, it also applies now.

DECEPTION

The phrase, *"Let no man deceive you by any means,"* concerns the purpose of this Epistle. It was to calm Believers and assure them that the *"Day of the Lord"* had not yet come; the Rapture of the Church and the Antichrist, as stated, must take place first, before the Second Coming.

It is ironical, the Thessalonians were thinking that the Second Coming could take place at any hour, while the modern Church little thinks He is coming at all. The deception is clear in either case, just the same!

While the *"Day of the Lord"* will actually commence after the Rapture of the Church, which will include the Great Tribulation, the Second Coming, and then the Millennium; still, the part of the Day of the Lord of which the Apostle is speaking here to the Thessalonians, at least in order to answer their question, concerns only the Second Coming.

Were it not possible to deceive and to be deceived, the Holy Spirit through the Apostle would not have made this statement. In fact, deception is one of, if not Satan's greatest weapon. The Truth is, most all the world presently is deceived, and in fact most all the world has always been deceived. Every unsaved person is deceived to such an extent that the situation is malignant. They have believed a lie, simply because the entire fabric of Satan's work and existence is based on a lie (Jn. 8:44-45).

Actually, many Christians are also deceived. For instance, untold millions have been deceived as it regards the Baptism with the Holy Spirit. They have been told that such is not for today, etc., and they have believed this lie.

Others have been told they can live in sin, and still maintain the Grace of God, and, therefore, be saved. In fact, the list of ways of deception is almost endless.

## DECEPTION

In order to deceive, Satan caters to the selfish desires on the part of the individual. Of course, he most of the time cloaks his intentions with high sounding religious phraseology, but the Truth is, he is catering to the base elements of the human heart.

For instance, the modern *"money gospel"* is but one example. It caters to man's greed, of which all of us seem to have at least a modicum of this evil. Another example took place in the early 1990's. The Church was going to usher in the Millennium by electing good men and women to public office, therefore, accomplishing this feat by political means. However, this didn't pan out too well as is now obvious. Nevertheless, at the time it was a heady thing, and because it catered to man's pride.

So, Satan's efforts are mostly centered up in the catering to both passion and pride. In fact, the two often overlap. This brings us to the *"Tree of the Knowledge of Good and Evil"* (Gen. 2:17). As is obvious, there is a *"good"* side to this tree (good in man's eyes), and an *"evil"* side. It is very obvious as to what the evil is, with even the unredeemed world opposing this particular direction. This speaks of murder, drunkenness, drug addiction, jealousy, envy, hatred, racism, etc. However, the good side is something else altogether.

The good side speaks of man's efforts to save himself, all the religions of the world, the distortion of Christianity by removing it from the foundation principle of *"Jesus Christ and Him Crucified"* (I Cor. 2:2). It is even more deadly than the evil side, simply because the evil is obvious, while the good is not obvious at all. Probably one could say without fear of contradiction, that the good side of this tree, has destroyed more people than even the evil side of the tree. Even though deception springs from both, the deception ensconced in the so-called good, is of far greater power.

## THE MEANS OF DECEPTION

While there are many means, the basic thruway on which Satan brings about his desired end, is ignorance of the Word of God. Of course, I'm speaking now of Believers. To whatever degree of ignorance of the Word characterizes any Believer, to that degree will the individual be deceived in some manner. Now what we've just said is very important, so important in fact, that I want to say it again:

The Word of God is Truth (Jn. 17:17). It alone is our road map, our guide, our direction. The Holy Spirit functions totally and entirely from the premise of the Word. And He Himself of course, also is Truth (I Jn. 5:6).

To whatever part of the Word we do not know, and especially as it regards the great foundational Doctrines, to that degree Satan to be sure is going to cause us great problems. The situation becomes even worse, when we realize that there is no excuse for not knowing the Word.

The sad fact is, far too many Christians leave it up to their Pastor, or someone else to do their spiritual thinking for them. If they like the man (or woman) they simply believe whatever they are told.

Even if the man or woman is Godly, and even if they have a great understanding of the

NOTES

Word, still, while those who sit under such a Ministry will definitely be blessed and blessed greatly, still, this in no way absolves anyone of the responsibility of learning the Word themselves. So, the greatest cause of spiritual deception is either the Believer not knowing the Word of God, or else not wanting to follow the Word of God, therefore, twisting it in order to make it fit their own perverted desires. Either way, *"ignorance or perversion,"* will lead to nothing but disaster.

## DEPARTURE

The phrase, *"For that day shall not come, except there come a falling away first,"* should have actually been translated, *"For that day shall not come, except there come a departure first."*

As we've already discussed in previous Commentary, many, if not most, Greek Scholars agree that the proper translation of the Greek word *"apostasia,"* as used here, should be *"departure"* instead of *"falling away."* In fact, the following Scholars, and I speak of those who translated the Word of God before the King James Version, and who were given up to be some of the best, understood this Greek word to mean *"a departure"* at least, as it is used here: Tyndale (1534), Coverdale (1535), The Geneva Bible (1537), Cranmer (1539), and Beza (1565), using it accordingly in their translations.

While it is true that the Greek word *"apostasia"* was used at times both in classical and common Greek in the sense of a defection, a revolt, in a religious sense a rebellion against God, and of the act we today call apostasy, which is a departure from Truth. But these are acquired meanings of the word from the context in which they are found, not the original, basic, literal meaning, and should not be imposed upon the word where the context does not qualify the word by these meanings, even as it doesn't here.

With the pure translation of the word before us now, the next step is to ascertain from the context, that to which this departure refers. Paul is speaking of two things, first of all, the Rapture of the Church, and then the Great Tribulation characterized by the advent of the Man of Sin. The Apostle has just referred to the gathering together of the Saints to the Lord Jesus at the Rapture (II Thess. 2:1), so now he continues with his teaching in the same vein, which throws added light on the subject. So, the meaning of the word here as stated, should not have been *"falling away"* but rather *"departure,"* and speaking of the Rapture.

Leaving that and going to another subject, perhaps it would be wise to look at the word *"day"* as it was used here by the King James Translators. Inasmuch as Paul is speaking of this coming time, in other words, when these things will happen, perhaps it would be helpful to look at the word *"day"* a little closer!

## DAY

The word *"day"* as used in the Bible and otherwise for that matter, is commonplace. But it is also a surprising key to the uniqueness of the Bible's view of time. And it is a key to help us see how freely and purposely God intervenes in history.

Looking at it first from the perspective of the Old Testament, we find that the Hebrew word *"yom"* best communicates the Old Testament concept of time. *"Yom"* is translated *"day," "time,"* or *"year,"* and can express either a point in time or a period of time, for instance the phrase, *"during those days."* Specifically, *"yom"* can stand for the following:

1. The daylight hours.
2. A 24-hour period.
3. An undetermined period of time encompassing months or years or even centuries.
4. A particular point in time.

## THE MANNER OF EXPLANATION

The word is theologically important in at least three ways:

1. First, *"yom"* is linked with the Bible's unique concept of time, which has become that of the Western world through our Judeo-Christian heritage.

In the ancient Near East, however, the myths that provided a framework for life envisioned time as a cycle. There was a repeated yearly cycle, and life's meaning was sought in the repeated rounds of the seasons, marked by winter's death and spring's rebirth.

The Hebrew concept, expressed in the Old Testament, is a dramatic contrast to that of the surrounding nations. In Scripture, time is not viewed as a cycle but as a line, springing from a definite beginning (Creation) and moving toward a Divinely revealed and purposed end. Scripture sees the meaning of the universe and of our lives as outside the repetitive patterns that mark human experience. The meaning of it all is in the sweep of a history that had a definite beginning and will have a promised end.

2. We find a distinct relationship also, between time (history) and God. God, the Ancient of Days, stands outside time. He existed before time; He is both Creator and Shaper of time's flow.

3. The phrase *"the Day of the Lord"* or *"that day"* is often used by the Prophets to indicate a period of time during which God Personally intervenes in history to carry out some specific aspect of His Plan.

## THE SEVEN DAYS OF CREATION

There have been disagreements giving rise to a range of meanings as it regards the Hebrew word *"yom,"* as it pertains to the seven days of Creation in Genesis Chapter 1 and going into the first few Verses of Genesis Chapter Chapter 2.

It is my contention that the argument is sealed in that Moses was speaking of a literal 24-hour day, by Him repeatedly using the phrase *"evening and morning"* to define this Hebrew word *"yom."*

Even as with Greek words, to properly define Hebrew words which can have several meanings, one must look at the associating texts, in other words, what the writer is speaking about at the particular time. Every indication is, and as stated, Moses was speaking here of literal 24-hour days, meaning that the Lord brought the Earth back to a habitable state in five literal 24-hour days, made man on the sixth day, and then rested on the Seventh (Gen. 1:5, 8, 13, 19, 23-27; 2:1-3).

In fact, the Lord did not actually create the Earth at this particular time, that already having been done in the dateless past. What He did was to bring that which had already been created, as stated, to a habitable state. How long the original creation took, and exactly when it took place, the Bible does not actually say.

NOTES

At the same time, as it regards the five days of bringing the Earth back to a proper state, there is geological evidence, in fact, tremendous amounts of such evidence, that this was done in a very short period of time.

## THE DAY OF THE LORD

The theologically significant phrases *"the Day of the Lord"* and *"that day"* occur often in the Prophets. They usually identify events that take place at history's end (Isa. 7:18-25). The key to understanding the phrases is to note that they always identify a span of time during which God Personally intervenes in history, directly or indirectly, to accomplish some specific aspect of His Plan.

What events do Old Testament Prophets most often link to these phrases?

Briefly, the Day of the Lord is seen as a day of terror, during which Israel would be invaded and purged with an awful destruction. Amos warned those of his day who hoped God would intervene soon: *"Woe to you who long for the Day of the Lord! Why do you long for the Day of the Lord? That Day will be darkness and not light"* (Amos 5:18).

Zephaniah adds, *"The great Day of the Lord is near — near and coming quickly. Listen! The cry on the Day of the Lord will be bitter, the shouting of the warrior will be there. That Day will be a Day of wrath, a Day of distress and anguish, a Day of trouble and ruin, a Day of darkness and gloom, a Day of clouds and blackness"* (Zeph. 1:14-15).

The dark terror of Divine Judgment was to be poured out on unbelieving Israel (Isa. Chpt. 22; Jer. 30:1-17; Joel Chpts. 1-2; Amos Chpt. 5; Zeph. Chpt. 1) and on the unbelieving peoples of the world (Ezek. 38-39; Zech. Chpt. 14).

But Judgment is not the only aspect of that Day. When God intervenes in history, He will also deliver the remnant of Israel, bring about a national conversion, forgive sins, and restore His people to the land promised Abraham (Isa. 10:27; Jer. 30:19-31:40; Mic. Chpt. 4; Zech. Chpt. 13).

And what will be the outcome of the *"Day of the Lord"*? *"The arrogance of man will be brought low and the pride of men humbled; the Lord Alone will be exalted in that Day"* (Isa. 2:17).

## THE NEW TESTAMENT EXPLANATION

The Greek word *"hemera"* is used to indicate literal days and may also be extended to indicate indeterminate periods of time, exactly as the Hebrew word *"yom"* in the Old Testament.

Naturally, the Gospels used the word *"Day"* in the Old Testament sense of *"that day"* to indicate Endtime Judgment and the return of Jesus (Mat. 7:22; Mk. 13:32; Lk. 17:31).

When using the word *"Day"* in an eschatological (Endtime) since, the Epistles tend to identify particular aspects of the Endtime. Thus, the writers speak of the *"Day of Wrath"* (Rom. 2:5; Rev. 6:17), the *"Day of Judgment"* (II Pet. 2:9; 3:7), the *"Day of Redemption"* (Eph. 4:30), the *"Day of the Lord"* (I Thess. 5:2; II Pet. 3:10), the *"Day of Christ"* (Phil. 1:6, 10; 2:16), the *"Great Day of God"* (Rev. 16:14), and the *"Day God visits"* His people (I Pet. 2:12).

## THE LAST DAYS

A number of Passages in the New Testament seem to suggest that the writer and readers were then living in the *"last Days"* (Acts 2:17-18; 3:24; II Tim. 3:1; Heb. 1:2; II Pet. 3:3; I Jn. 2:18). What did the writers mean?

The concept that we live in history's final day is not to say that the eschatological (Endtime) period that marks history's end has come. Instead, the writers view history as a process that will culminate in *"that Day,"* and they view this present age as the final moment before the intended climax.

John sees principles of evil at work now that will be given full reign in the end period (I Jn. 2:18). A hostility to Truth will prevail at history's end and is incipient at this very moment (II Tim. 3:1-13).

The distinctive difference between these Days and the Day of the Lord, in which God's purposes are drawn together and brought to their conclusion, is this: Our age, which began with the Resurrection of Jesus, is the last great historical epoch before God's final intervention.

Consequently, as the term *"the last Days"* is used, it actually began as stated, at the Resurrection of Christ, and more specifically on the *"Day of Pentecost,"* which incidently, was both a 24-hour day and a period of time which has extended even to this very moment. The period from then until now, actually constitutes *"the last Days,"* and because as stated, it is the last great historical epoch before God's final intervention. So, one might say that at this moment, we are now living in the last of the last days, and to be more specific, possibly even the last hours of the last of the last days.

In view of this, as Peter reminds us, we live in a very temporary universe, one that is about to be destroyed. How should we then live?

We need to *"live holy and Godly lives, as* (we) *look forward to the Day of God and pray for the hastening of its coming.*

*"While that Day will bring about the destruction of the Heavens by fire and that the elements will then melt with a fervent heat, still, in keeping with His Promises we are looking forward to a new Heaven and a new earth, the eternal home of Righteousness"* (II Pet. 3:11-13).

## THE REVELATION OF THE MAN OF SIN

The phrase, *"And that man of sin be revealed,"* pertains to the Antichrist. Incidently, as should be obvious, the Antichrist is not a system, a nation, an ethnic group, or anything of that nature. We're speaking here of an individual, a man. Actually the Greek article is used here in both cases actually saying, *"the man of the sin."* So we're speaking here of a specific man and of a specific sin, that man being the Antichrist and that sin being the consummate rebellion against Christ.

This man will be so wicked that, bad as other men are, wickedness should be his mark by which he is distinguished from all others; a man who belongs to sin, in whom the ideal of sin has become realized and incarnate.

What kind of sin will be most prominent in him is not expressed in the word itself; but the context points clearly to that which is, in fact, the crowning sin — spiritual pride and rebellious arrogancy (Eph. 6:12); all against Christ and the Cross.

## THE SIN

As stated, this is *"the sin,"* and does not speak necessarily of the great vices of the age of which are so clearly defined as sin.

NOTES

However, even though these things definitely are sin, and wicked sin at that, there is a sin which is worse.

*"The sin"* began with Cain, attempting to offer up sacrifices to God other than that which represented Christ and Him Crucified (Gen. Chpt. 4; I Cor. 2:2). That is *"the sin,"* and in fact, has always been *"the sin!"*

This sin, which characterizes most Churches and all the religions of the world, constitutes the highest rebellion against God's great Plan of Redemption, which was brought about, and in fact could only be brought about, through the Death and Resurrection of Jesus Christ, God's Only Son.

The Antichrist, however, is going to take this sin to a level as it has not been known previously. He will refine its terrible direction down to the last degree, pointing to a salvation outside of Christ and Him Crucified. Due to having the help of the False Prophet in the performing of miracles, he will be able to convince much of the world. His rise to power will be extremely religious, in fact, far more religious than any dictator who has ever preceded him.

Consequently, it should readily be known, that any and all deviations from *"Christ and Him Crucified,"* as it refers to Salvation, or anything else for that matter that pertains to God, are functioning in the spirit of the Antichrist. That's why John the Beloved said, *"Little children, it is the last time* (last days and the spirit of the last days)*: and as ye have heard that antichrist shall come, even now are there many antichrists; whereby we know that it is the last time"* (I Jn. 2:18).

John was saying the same thing I have just said, that all who point to a proposed salvation other than *"Christ and Him Crucified,"* are functioning in the spirit of *"the Antichrist."* In fact, that's the reason he is referred to as *"Antichrist,"* is because he will oppose the Salvation afforded at the Cross.

He also said, *"And this is that spirit of antichrist, whereof ye have heard that it should come; and even now already is it in the world"* (I Jn. 4:3).

If this spirit of the Antichrist, this rejection of Christ and more particularly, the Cross of Christ, was in the world in John's day, and it definitely was, it should be understood that this problem is even more pronounced at present, and because we're living in the very last of the last days, which is leading to the rise of *"the man of the sin."*

NOTES

As I have been saying in this Volume, the line between the True Church and the apostate Church, is the Cross of Christ. As also stated, it has always been that; however, I personally feel that it will be more pronounced now than ever.

I do not know how much the Reader is aware of present happenings in the modern Church, but suffice to say, the situation is already acute.

There was a time that only the Modernists denied the basic fundamentals of the Faith, actually giving no credence to the Cross of Christ whatsoever. While these continue in that vein, they have been joined by many in the modern Charismatic community, who claim to be Spirit-filled, etc.

Many of these have so denied the Cross, calling it a place and time of weakness and defeat, that they will not sing any songs whatsoever concerning the Cross or the Blood, etc. I think many of these people give little credence even to the part the Cross plays in their initial Salvation experience. In fact, I know they give it no credence whatsoever.

They are able to disguise their teaching and thinking on this very important subject, by high sounding religious phraseology, and by claiming to believe in all the other great fundamentals of the Faith; however, I must warn the Reader, that if our thinking is confused as it regards the Cross of Christ, it will be confused as it regards everything else respecting Christ. Consequently, that which we're speaking of here is very, very serious! In fact, the attacks upon the Cross are going to become more and more pronounced, and for the following reason:

The entirety of the Plan of God is wrapped up in the great, Vicarious, Sacrificial Offering of Christ in the giving of Himself on the Cross for dying, lost humanity. In fact, this is the story and one might say, the entirety of the story of the entirety of the Bible. It's the foundation of all that God has done, is doing, and shall do. So, an attack upon the Cross, is an attack upon the very foundation

NOTES

of Christianity. As stated, this is *"the sin"* and more particularly *"the sin"* of *"the man of the sin."*

THE SON OF PERDITION

The phrase, *"The son of perdition,"* literally means *"son of destruction."* Some have taken this Passage, as given by Paul, and tied it with John 17:12, making Judas the incarnated Antichrist. While Judas was definitely antichrist, as are most of the world for that matter, still, Jesus wasn't meaning that Judas would be raised from the dead and thereby become the incarnated Antichrist.

The two, Judas and the Antichrist, actually have no relationship with each other. Judas was born, lived, and died nearly 2,000 years ago. The Antichrist, while possibly being alive at present, will not make his debut until after the Rapture of the Church. While Judas destroyed himself, and the Antichrist will do likewise, all brought about by the rejection of Christ, still, that's where the similarity ends. In fact, the Antichrist will not be a reincarnation of any man who has previously lived, but will be whatever he is in his own right.

He is called *"the man of sin"* because he will be the embodiment of rebellion against the true way of Salvation, which is Faith in Christ and the Cross (I Cor. 1:18; 2:2).

THE RISE OF THE ANTICHRIST

The world stage is presently being set for the advent of the Antichrist. In fact, it began in 1948, when Israel became a nation again after some 1,900 years of wanderings as outcasts all over the world. Even in the midst of much controversy and opposition, with almost the entirety of the world against them, they have carved out a nation that is powerful far beyond its size and scope.

The opposition has come mostly from the Muslim world, with the Palestinian problem seeming to have no solution. The entirety of the Middle East is a powder keg, and the fuse is already lit. It is the flashpoint of the world, and made so by the Muslim threat and their hatred of Israel.

Even though the land area of the State of Israel comprises less than 1/10 of 1% of all the land area occupied by the Arabs, the Arabs want that 1/10 of 1% also. As well, they are not satisfied with the Palestinians having a State within the State of Israel, but rather they desire every Jew to be annihilated and Israel to be made extinct. That is their goal!

Neither the United States nor any other nation has been able to solve this problem. The problem, in fact, gets thornier all the time. However, the Antichrist will literally make his debut by solving this problem. He will somehow appease both the Jews and the Muslims, making the Jews think that he is the long awaited Messiah. They will actually announce to the entirety of the world that Jesus Christ has now been proved to be the Impostor they claimed He was, and the Antichrist will be heralded far and wide as the real Messiah, or so they think!

Jesus actually predicted this. He said, *"I am come in My Father's Name, and you received Me not: if another shall come in his own name, him you will receive"* (Jn. 5:43).

The Antichrist will go so far as to sign a seven-year nonaggression pact with Israel, guaranteeing their protection. To be sure, the world will rejoice. All of this will take place very soon after the Rapture; however, Israel will be rudely awakened when the Antichrist throws off this pretense, attacking them, with Israel being defeated for the first time since becoming a nation in 1948. Thus, will arise the *"man of sin,"* who will do all within his power to destroy Israel; but he will be stopped by the Second Coming.

THE SEVENTIETH WEEK OF DANIEL

The Book of Daniel and the Book of Revelation go hand in hand respecting the interpretation of Bible Prophecy concerning the Endtime. In fact, I think it's not possible for one to understand the Book of Revelation, unless one first has an understanding of the Book of Daniel. Consequently, I would strongly advise the Reader to secure for yourself our Commentary on Ezekiel and Daniel (Vol. 5).

As the Christ of God dominates the scene in the Gospel narratives, so the Antichrist of Satan is the moving figure in the seven year period known as the Seventieth Week of Daniel. Before discussing the events which comprise this period, it will be well to consider briefly the character, purpose, and identity of that sinister figure who will soon move into the theater of human activity.

## THE CHARACTER OF THE ANTICHRIST

The Name *"Christ"* is the English spelling of the Greek Name *"Christos"* which means *"The Anointed."* When we speak of the Christ of God we refer to the Lord Jesus, very God of very God, God the Son Incarnate in human form, the One Who by His substitutionary death on the Cross paid the penalty of human sin and thus made a way for a Righteous God to offer Salvation to a believing sinner on the basis of justice satisfied.

The prefixed preposition to *"Christ"* in the name *"Antichrist"* is *"anti,"* which means either *"instead of"* or *"against,"* depending upon the context in which it is found. A study of the contexts in which the name occurs leads one to the conclusion that the meaning in this case is *"against,"* which means that the Antichrist is one who will come, and who will be against Christ.

The Antichrist will be so opposed to Christ, that he will at the same time be totally opposed to the Word of God altogether. As well, he will hate all types of worship, even erroneous worship, if it is not worship of him solely.

He will seek to establish his throne, and his own twisted religion.

God's great Truth is that in Christ God is man, and he will substitute for that his own lie, that in him (the Antichrist) man is God. However, this has been the spirit of the world all along, even from the time of the Fall in the Garden of Eden.

He will not call himself the Christ, for he will be filled with the deadliest hate against the Name and Offices, as against the whole spirit and temper, of Jesus of Nazareth, the Exalted King of Glory. But, inasmuch as no one can resist the Truth by a mere negation, he must offer and propose something positive in the room of that Faith which he will assail and endeavor utterly to abolish. And thus we may certainly conclude that the final Antichrist will reveal himself to the world — for he too will have his *"apokalupsis* (revelation)*"* (II Thess. 2:3-8), his *"parousia* (coming)*"* (II Thess. 2:9) — as, in a sense, its Messiah; not, indeed, as the Messiah of Prophecy, the Messiah of God, but still as the world's Saviour; as one who will bless the many who will obey him, giving to them the full enjoyment of a present material Earth, instead of a distant, shadowy, and uncertain Heaven; abolishing those troublesome distinctions now the fruitful sources of so much disquietude of bridging men of so many enjoyments, between the True Church presently and the world, between the Spirit and the flesh, between Holiness and sin, between good and evil.

NOTES

To be frank, the modern *"money gospel,"* carries the same spirit as the future Antichrist will carry, because this spirit comes from the same source, Satan. The present *"money gospel"* places all of its emphasis on the *"here and now,"* belittling and confusing the *"there and then,"* i.e., *"Heaven."* The only difference is, the modern *"money gospel"* parrots or *"uses"* the Word of God in its twisted version, while the Antichrist, of course, will totally deny the Word in every respect. Nevertheless, the spirit that characterizes this so-called modern gospel, is the same spirit that will characterize the Antichrist, and in fact, is a precursor of that false one who is to come. As well, the spirit of modern Denominationalism falls into the same category, even as it places its emphasis on its particular *"Church"* instead of Christ. All of this is very subtle, in fact at the same time claiming Christ; however, the tip-off is in the emphasis. In other words, what does a particular Ministry or Church emphasize? Or one might ask, *"Where is the greatest emphasis?"* Is it on Christ or something else? Or to ask it in another way, *"Does Christ have to share the emphasis with other things?"*

The coming Antichrist will present himself to the world as the true center of its hopes, as the satisfier of its needs and healer of all its hurts, with in fact, Israel at the outset, claiming him to be their long awaited Messiah. They will be in for a rude awakening!

## THE PURPOSE OF THE ANTICHRIST

We go back now to the time when nothing existed apart from the Triune God, Father, Son, and Holy Spirit. The sons of God (Gen. 6:2; Job 1:6; 38:7), the Angels were the first moral intelligences God created, at least of which we are aware. They antedate the created universe, for they shouted for joy at the splendor of the new creation (Job 38:4-7).

Among them was the supreme Angel, Lucifer, mightiest in power and wisdom, most glorious in beauty. Ezekiel said of him, *"Thou sealest up the sum, full of wisdom, and perfect in beauty."* He was placed in the Eden of the first perfect Earth of Genesis 1:1, with a twofold office and responsibility as the Anointed of God, a Priest in His Sanctuary, and as a King (Isa. 14:12-17; Ezek. 28:12-19).

As Priest and King, he had the responsibility of directing the Earth inhabitants in their worship of God, and of ruling over them. The predication of a pre-Adamic race is a logical necessity when we regard Lucifer as Priest and King, which he was under God.

Sin entered his heart when he declared in his purpose to exalt his throne which God had given him upon Earth, above God's throne, and to take the place of God receiving the worship of the pre-Adamic race (Isa. 14:12-17). The Earth creatures at that time, whoever and whatever they were, to whom he ministered followed him into this sin of rebellion. The Judgment of God fell in the form of banishment from the Earth and the rendering of the Earth and its planetary heavens a chaos, as recorded in Genesis 1:2, (*"And the earth became without form and void"*).

From that time on to the present, Satan and the pre-Adamic race, which the latter we recognize today as the demons, have never ceased in their efforts to regain dominion over this Earth. From the fact that the demons of the Gospel narratives never have rest unless they are within a physical body, either that of a human being or an animal, the inference is clear that at one time they had physical bodies. And the only place in the category of created moral intelligences where we can put these demons is right here, the disembodied beings of the race of creatures over which Lucifer ruled before his fall.

Science has demonstrated the great age of the universe at many millions of years. If that is in fact correct, and there is no Biblical evidence that it isn't, in all this time Satan and his demons (the principalities of Eph. 6:12), have nurtured a growing intensity of hatred toward God and a determination to dethrone Him as the God of the Heavens and of all creation, to be worshiped.

NOTES

### MAN — A SUPERIOR CREATION?

With the restoration of the Earth to a perfect state again and the placing of man upon it, as recorded in Genesis, Chapters 1 and 2, Satan and his demons recognized the fact that they were being supplanted by a race of superior beings, in fact, a new creation of God — man (Gen. 1:3-2:25).

Before the Fall, there is every evidence, that man was originally created higher even than the Angels.

At the temptation, Adam hands the scepter of the Earth back to Satan, and the latter becomes god of this world (II Cor. 4:4). Satan and his demons appropriate the lower atmosphere around this Earth as their point of attack upon a fallen race of creatures, the purpose of which is to enthrone Satan on this Earth again as the god whom the human race worships. He has succeeded to the extent that he has his throne on Earth (Rev. 2:13 *"seat,"* which in the Greek is *"throne"*). However, whereas humanity as a whole (with the exception of the saved) serves him, yet it worships many gods. Even though this false worship is directed by himself, it is still not that which he desires, desiring rather to centralize all this worship in himself. This he will do in the Antichrist.

### THE FIRST HALF OF THE COMING GREAT TRIBULATION

Daniel, in 9:24-27, speaks of a period of 70 weeks or 70 sevens of years, 490 years, during which certain things will take place with reference to God's Chosen People, the Jewish nation, this period being divided into: 49 years during which time Jerusalem was to be rebuilt after the dispersion (the fulfillment recorded in Ezra and Nehemiah); 434 years, after which time the Jewish Messiah was to come (fulfilled in the Incarnation of Christ); and, the last period which is seven years.

With the Crucifixion of the Messiah by Israel and Israel's consequent destruction by the Romans, and their dispersion over the then-known world, God's prophetic clock with regard to Israel stopped running. In other words, the seven year period is still future. That which has come between the First Advent of the Messiah and the yet future Seventieth Week (a week of years) of Daniel is the Church Age of which the Old Testament Prophets knew nothing. They saw the mountain peaks of Prophecy in a straight line with no valleys between. We, from our perspective, see them broadside, and can, therefore, see the length of time intervening between the fulfillment of the various predictions.

In Daniel 9:26, Daniel speaks of the destruction of Jerusalem by the Romans, which took place in A.D. 70. The nation being destroyed, there is a silence in the Bible concerning Israel, which lasted for about 1,900 years. In 1948, Israel in fulfillment of Bible Prophecy, once again became a nation. However, one might say that she became a nation only in part, not having all the land as promised to them by God through Abraham, that part being occupied by the Arabs, and neither do they occupy the Temple Mount, that being occupied by the Moslems as well.

Daniel 9:27 begins with the words, *"And he* (the Antichrist) *shall confirm the covenant with many for one week* (seven years)*,"* which actually starts the clock running again for Israel. This speaks of the Antichrist making a Covenant with Israel guaranteeing their protection, a Covenant which is supposed to last for seven years. So, as stated, we have a silence between Daniel 9:26 and 9:27, due to the fact that Israel was not then a nation.

This Covenant which the Antichrist will make with Israel will no doubt be many faceted, but will definitely be one of religious toleration of the Temple worship in Jerusalem, even as the balance of Verse 27 bears out. In other words, Israel is going to somehow rebuild her Temple, and no doubt on the same spot where the Moslem Dome of the Rock presently stands — or else right beside it.

Daniel speaks of the Antichrist as standing in the Holy of Holies of the Temple in Jerusalem, thus causing the Sacrifice and oblation to cease. Paul speaking of this same ruler as *"the man of sin,"* says that he as God sits in the Temple at Jerusalem. John, in his first Letter (I Jn. 2:18), refers to this same person as the Antichrist, and predicts his coming.

NOTES

Thus, the distinctive mark of the seven year period is a period of time in which the Antichrist makes a treaty of religious toleration with the Jewish nation, a period which is divided into two parts of three and one half years each by the Antichrist's violation of the treaty *"in the midst of the week."*

These two parts of the Coming Great Tribulation could be poles apart in their character. The first it seems will be a period of worldwide peace and prosperity, a peace and prosperity incidently brought on and maintained by the Antichrist in the first three and one half years of this treaty.

The second or the last half, will be a period of unexampled tribulation from two sources, God and the Antichrist, and is properly designated *"the Great Tribulation"* (Mat. 24:21).

Let's look first of all at the first three and one half year period.

## THE ENTRANCE OF THE ANTICHRIST

That which prepares for the Seventieth Week is, of course, the appearance of the Antichrist on Earth. John records this momentous event in the words, *"And I saw when the Lamb opened one of the seven seals, and I heard one of the four living creatures saying, as it were the noise of thunder, be coming"* (Rev. 6:1).

The words *"and see"* are not in the best Greek Texts. (Nestle puts them in the apparatus below his Greek Text, which means that in the judgment of this textual critic, these words were not in the original Manuscript which left the hands of John.)

The living creature is an angelic being, the representative of God. The words *"be coming"* were not addressed to John. He was on Patmos and under the complete control of the Holy Spirit in order that He might give him the contents of the Book of Revelation. He testifies (Rev. 1:10) that he *"became in the Spirit on the Lord's Day,"* not *"was in the Spirit."* The phrase *"was in the Spirit"* would describe the usual *"relative control"* of the Spirit over John.

It actually means that John came under the *"absolute control"* of the Spirit for the period of the Visions given him, which are recorded in the Book of Revelation. Peter had a like experience on the housetop of Simon the tanner. Luke called it a trance.

The words, *"Be coming,"* were not addressed to John. He did not need the loudness of a thunderclap to hear the Angel. That thunderous voice was given to announce the advent of the Antichrist.

This tells us that events on Earth, at least of any magnitude, take place only after the go ahead is given in Heaven. In other words, and as should be obvious, God controls all. Men at times think they rule, but God overrules. They come and they go, but only according to the Plan of God. God being God, He can do these things without infringing upon the free moral agency of man.

## ANTICHRIST — THE EMPEROR OF A REVISED ROMAN EMPIRE

The next thing John saw was a rider on a white horse, who is the Antichrist, in the guise of a peaceful warrior. He has no arrows although he does have a bow. This means that his manner of approach will be one of peace and friendship. A crown will be given to him. It is a conqueror's crown (Stephanos). He is now the Wild Beast of Revelation 17:8, having seven heads, which pertain to the seven spirits of the Empires which have once oppressed Israel, even up unto the time of the ten nations which we will address next. Those seven are: Egypt, Assyria, Babylon, Medo-Persia, Greece, Rome, and the ten nations which will persecute Israel immediately before and during the beginning of the Great Tribulation.

The *"ten horns"* represent those ten nations which are yet to come about. There we have the Revised Roman Empire with the Antichrist at its head. We say *"Revised"* simply because it will be different than the original Roman Empire. For instance, Rome will not be the capital of this new confederation, but rather Babylon, at least at the beginning. And there we have the fulfillment of Daniel's Visions of the successive Gentile world Empires.

In the image vision of the Second Chapter of Daniel we see their outward glory, but only those which pertained from Daniel's day onward. In other words, the first two, Egypt and Assyria, are not shown on this image regarding the dream given to Nebuchadnezzar.

NOTES

On this image as given in the dream, we see the outward glory of these respective empires. Babylon was represented as the head of gold; Medo-Persia by the breast and arms of silver; the Grecian Empire represented by the belly and thighs of brass; Rome was represented by the legs of iron, with Revised Rome, which is yet to come, represented by the feet of iron and clay.

The Lord gave Daniel the same vision as He had given to Nebuchadnezzar, as is recorded in Daniel, Chapter 7; however, we see here the actual spirit of these Empires. Babylon in this vision was represented by the Lion, Medo-Persia by the bear, the Grecian Empire represented by the leopard, and the indescribable beast represented Rome. The ten horns represent the Revised Empire which is yet to come. These will be made up of a confederation of ten kings under the Antichrist.

## HOW HE COMES TO THE THRONE

We will look behind the scenes of all this for a moment. It is a matter of Biblical record that Satan and his demons are the motivating factors backing the destinies of the nations of this world. In fact, Satan offered world domination over the nations to our Lord as a reward for worshipping him, and Jesus did not dispute his claim to ownership. In fact, he moves the nations around according to his will as a man moves checkers on a checkerboard, and all to one end, his own incarnation in the Antichrist as the sole object of worship. His demons and fallen angels carry out his will. Daniel speaks of the great fallen angel who was deputed by Satan to direct the destinies of Persia (Dan. 10:13). John speaks of demons gathering the kings of the Earth to the Battle of Armageddon (Rev. 16:13-14).

In the last half of the Twentieth Century, the world has seen a surge forward respecting the religion of Islam. Of course, Satan is the instigator of that religion as well as all religions. But Islam is the most militant, and that which straddles the Middle East, and is the contesting force against Israel. In fact, militant Moslems have sworn Israel's destruction, which they seek to carry out on a continuous basis. As would be obvious, they also hate America, because they credit this nation with using its might and power to back up Israel. In fact, the United States straddles the fence so to speak in attempting to placate both the Arabs and Israel. As a point of interest, the United States grants Israel approximately four billion dollars in grants and aid, while doing the same with Egypt.

In the early part of the last half of the decade of the 1990's, Israel signed a peace treaty with the Palestinians. It is an attempt to try to solve an almost impossible situation. In fact, there has been more violence since the treaty was signed than before. The reasons are obvious, strong elements among both the Palestinians and the Israelis do not want the treaty to succeed, hence their opposition. In fact, there is little evidence from a Scriptural point of view that it will succeed, with the problems there continuing to increase. This we do know, the nations of the world are presently being jockeyed into position by Satan, and allowed by the Lord, for the advent of the Antichrist. We are that close!

Exactly as to how this will be done, we are not told.

PREDICTIONS!

As I dictate these notes, I have before me predictions made by Bible Scholars in the middle of the Twentieth Century. Most of these individuals, could only see Russian Communism as the prime shaker and mover during the Endtimes; however, as we all now know, Russian Communism is no more. So, that means their predictions were unscriptural!

Considering these things, I think it is unwise to attempt to point out as to exactly how all of this is going to be done, except to say, that it is going to be done, whatever method is used. Of this we can be sure, events from the time of World War II unto the present, have all been pieces on this great checkerboard, which are falling into place, with the situation speeding up dramatically with the formation of Israel as a nation in 1948, which was a direct fulfillment of Bible Prophecy.

The Church is coming down to the very close of its time and age. We are expecting the Rapture at any time! The next Millennium will see Israel completely restored as the lead nation in the world under Christ, Who will reign Personally from Jerusalem.

NOTES

But before that moment comes, the Rapture must take place, followed by the seven year Great Tribulation, which we are here discussing. In other words, Satan is about to make his final and greatest thrust of all, that for which he has been working toward from the very beginning.

Many would ask the question as to the thoughts and ideas of the Evil One. Does he think he can really win in this conflict? Does he think he can actually overthrow God?

Yes, he does! He is deceived just the same as all the billions of his duped followers. He knows the Bible, but he does not believe the Bible. He actually thinks that he will win this conflict, despite the great defeat he suffered at the Cross of Calvary.

To win this victory, he will seek to destroy Israel, for if these people can be destroyed, which in fact he has attempted to do many times in the past, then the entirety of the great Plan of God falls down. So, it will be in that direction that he will make his major thrust, hence, the Battle of Armageddon, as it is described in Ezekiel, Chapters 38 and 39.

So again I emphasize, how all of the nations of the world will be moved into position for the advent of the Antichrist, with all the necessary events brought to pass, I cannot tell, and I don't think any other Bible Teacher can either. Suffice to say, it will be done!

PEACE!

Gaining ascendancy as a problem solver, the Antichrist will assume the role of a benevolent despot, providing peace and a period of prosperity, which will lull the world to sleep.

This Peace is spoken of in Revelation 6:4. The rider on the red horse is the Antichrist about to wage war. The Greek reads, *"It was given to him to take the peace from the earth."* The definite article *"the"* appears in the Greek Text, and is all-important. It points out a *"particular peace."*

It indicates that this peace does not pertain to merely a part of the Earth, but in fact for the entirety of the Earth. This is the peace which will characterize the first three and one half years of the Seventieth Week of Daniel. Paul speaks of this peace in I Thessalonians 5:1-3.

Writing to Christians he says, *"But of the times and seasons, Brethren, ye have no need that I write unto you.*

*"For yourselves know perfectly that the Day of the Lord so cometh as a thief in the night.*

*"For when they shall say, Peace and safety, then sudden destruction cometh upon them."*

The *"Day of the Lord"* is the Great Tribulation, the last three and one half years of Daniel's Seventieth Week. With it comes the cessation of this false peace and the terrors of the Tribulation.

The act which will take peace from the Earth, will be his causing the Sacrifice and oblation in the Jerusalem Temple to cease. At the same time, he will declare war on Israel, turning against all forms of religion, demanding that all the people of the world, at least all those over whom he has control, worship him and him only. This is when Israel will be rudely awakened as to the true colors of this man of sin. He will not be their Messiah, but actually their destroyer, or at least he will seek to do that. This is what Jesus was meaning when He said, *"I am come in My Father's Name, and ye receive Me not: if another* (the Antichrist) *shall come in his own name, him ye will receive"* (Jn. 5:43).

Israel will realize what a mistake she has made! Now, the last three and one half years of the Great Tribulation, will begin the worst time of terror that the world has ever known. Jesus said of this time, *"For then shall be great tribulation, such as was not since the beginning of the world to this time, no, nor ever shall be.*

*"And except those days should be shortened, there should no flesh be saved: but for the elect's sake* (Israel) *those days shall be shortened"* (Mat. 24:21-22).

## THE REBUILDING OF BABYLON

The first three and one half years of the Great Tribulation will be marked by unexampled prosperity. As stated, this is represented by the Antichrist on the white horse (Rev. 6:2). Trade and commerce will flourish during this time, with the Antichrist's genius in the realm of world commerce seen

NOTES

in his rebuilding the ancient city of Babylon on the banks of the Euphrates. It will be his commercial metropolis of the world. Where it all began, is where it all will end.

Right in the midst of the rich oil country of the lower Mesopotamian Valley, he will rear this city of skyscrapers.

Isaiah's prediction of the destruction of the city of Babylon includes the necessity of it being rebuilt (Isa. 13:17-22). The following facts make this imperative:

1. The prediction of its destruction is in a context of the Day of the Lord (Isa. 13:9-10). One can take this prediction out of its context and make it apply to the capture of Babylon by the Medes and Persians. But that is not correct Bible exegesis. The Day of the Lord is the Great Tribulation Period. The functional disturbances of the heavenly bodies at that time (Isa. 13:10) are the same as in Revelation 6:12-13; 8:12; and both Scriptures refer to the same period.

2. Isaiah states that Babylon will resemble the cities of Sodom and Gomorrah in their destruction. These cities were burnt to the ground by fire and brimstone. The history of the city of Babylon discloses the fact that when the Persian General Cyrus in 541 B.C. took it, no destruction resulted. It was captured by the strategy of diverting the Euphrates River which ran through the city.

Cyrus then marched his soldiers over the dry riverbed through the riverbank gates which had been carelessly left open during the drunken orgy of Belshazzar. To be destroyed as Sodom and Gomorrah were destroyed, the city needs to be rebuilt.

3. The Prophet says that after its destruction it will never be inhabited. Clarence Larkin in his book *"The Book of Revelation"* is authority for the statement that the site of ancient Babylon has always been inhabited since its capture; consequently, what has happened to Babylon in the past, has not fulfilled the Prophecies. He gives the following details to substantiate his assertion.

## BABYLON THE CITY

After its capture by the Medes and Persians in October of 539 B.C., the city revolted against Darius Hystaspis and was taken by strategy. This took place in 516 B.C. Xerxes, about 478 B.C., plundered the great Temple of Baal at Babylon.

Alexander the Great in 331 B.C. marched against the city, but the citizens threw open the gates and received him with acclamations. After the death of Alexander, Seleucus, one of his generals, ambitious to build a capital for himself, founded Seleucia in the neighborhood of Babylon and gradually drew off the inhabitants of Babylon. This was in 293 B.C. Strabo, who died in A.D. 25, speaks of the city as being to a great extent deserted.

However, the Jews left from the captivity still lived there in large numbers. In A.D. 60 Simon Peter was working among them, for he wrote his first Letter (I Pet. 5:13) from that place. Theodoric, about the middle of the Fifth Century speaks of Babylon inhabited only by Jews. These still had three Jewish universities there and in the last year of the First Century issued the Babylonian Talmud.

In A.D. 917 Ibu Hankel mentions Babylon as an insignificant village, but still in existence. In A.D. 1000 it seems to have grown into a town of some importance, for it was known as the *"Two Mosques."* Shortly after this it was enlarged and fortified and called *"Hilla."* In A.D. 1898 Hilla contained about 10,000 inhabitants and was surrounded by fertile lands. Date groves stretched along the banks of the Euphrates River. Certainly, the prophecy of Isaiah has not yet been fulfilled which says, *"It shall never be inhabited."*

## THE DESTRUCTION OF BABYLON

John, in Revelation, Chapter 18, describes the rich commercial city of Babylon, and its destruction by earthquake and fire, and the consequent weeping and mourning all over the Earth over its destruction, which later takes place at the close of the Great Tribulation.

As well, Zechariah predicts that the center of commercial activity of the Earth will finally be located at Babylon. In his vision of the *"Ephah"* which is the symbol of commerce, he states that it was lifted up from the land of Palestine and carried by two stork-winged women to the land of Shinar (Babylon) *"to build it an house in the land of Shinar: and it shall be established, and set there upon her own base"* (Zech. 5:5-11).

NOTES

Now, it will take considerable time to swing the center of commercial activity of the Earth from such places as New York, Chicago, London, San Francisco, and Tokyo, and to build a city such as is described in Revelation Chapter 18. All of which indicates that the establishment of the city of Babylon as the Antichrist's commercial metropolis of the world must take place at least some years before Daniel's Seventieth Week begins. This fact also gives us some indication as to the time of the Great Tribulation.

The Rapture of the Church can occur at any moment. There is no unfulfilled prophecy that would withhold the Coming of the Lord Jesus for His Church. But there is now only the beginning of a swing to the East regarding commercial activity, and especially oil, with some talk as well of the rebuilding of Babylon by Saddam Hussein, which means we're closer to the fulfillment of Bible Prophecy concerning the rebuilding of the city, whoever in fact actually does build it.

## RELIGIOUS TOLERATION UNDER THE ANTICHRIST

In the first three and one half years of the Tribulation which will be mostly a time of peace, there will be religious toleration by the Antichrist.

During this particular time, the Jewish remnant of 144,000 Jews sovereignly chosen to Salvation for a special Ministry during this three and one half year period (Rev. 7:1-8), will preach the Gospel of the Kingdom at least to Israel and maybe to the ends of the Earth, and then will be raptured (Rev. 14:1).

This Gospel will be the same Message which John the Baptist and the Messiah preached (Mat. 3:1-2; 9:35), announcing the Coming of the Messiah to establish the earthly kingdom of Israel and offering Salvation from sin through this same Messiah.

In the time of the Antichrist the Message that will be given by these 144,000 Jews among other things, will announce the Second Advent of the Messiah to become ruler over Israel and the Gentile nations, and in fact the entirety of the world, and to offer Salvation through His Precious Blood.

It seems that the Antichrist will do nothing about this during that particular time.

NOTES

As a result, Gentiles and Jews from every nation (John says, *"a great multitude which no man could number, of all nations, and kindreds, and people, and tongues"*) will accept the Message and be saved (Rev. 7:9-17).

## THE ANTICHRIST DESTROYS ALL RELIGIOUS WORSHIP

That which divides the seven year period into two parts of three and one half years is Daniel's statement that *"In the midst of the week he* (Antichrist) *will cause the sacrifice and oblation to cease, and for the overspreading of abominations he shall make it desolate"* (Dan. 9:27).

Abruptly, the Antichrist terminates the treaty of religious toleration he made with Israel and displays his true character, not that of a friend of the Jewish people, but their bitter enemy.

He follows the precedent of Antiochus Epiphanes of Syria, 175 B.C., who profaned the Jewish Temple and sacrificed a sow on the Brazen Altar, and enters the Holy of Holies of the Jerusalem Temple as the sign that the Temple has been terminated. Our Lord speaks of this in Matthew 24:15-16 when He warns Israel, *"When ye therefore shall see the abomination of desolation spoken of by Daniel the Prophet standing in the Holy Place . . . Then let them which be in Judea flee into the mountains."*

Paul speaks of the same action in II Thessalonians 2:4 where he speaks of the Antichrist *"who . . . as God sitteth in the Temple of God, showing himself that he is God."* Here we have the beginning of the destruction of all forms of religion on the face of the Earth with the Antichrist instead deifying himself.

The occasion of this act and its motivation will be the casting out of Satan and his demons from the place of access to God's Throne and from their kingdom in the atmosphere of this Earth. John speaks of this in Revelation 12:7-12.

Michael and other Angels, no doubt under Michael, will forcibly eject them. Satan at once starts to persecute Israel, and God protects His chosen people in a specially reserved hiding place for about three and one half years, the last half of this seven year period (Rev. 12:13-17). This fixes the ejection of Satan to this Earth as occurring in the middle of the Great Tribulation, at the same time that the Antichrist turns against Israel and deifies himself. Incidently, Israel will flee at that time to the forsaken city of Petra.

The result will be the Rapture or possibly the martyrdom of the 144,000 of Israel who during the first half of the week preached the Gospel of the Kingdom to the ends of the Earth. These are seen in Heaven in Revelation 14:1-5. More than likely their converts will likewise be martyred. These are seen also in Heaven (Rev. 7:9-17) and are described by John as having come out of the Great Tribulation.

The Antichrist will now set about to take over the entirety of the world, for that will be his goal. In the areas which he dominates, he will demand worship, with miracles performed by his False Prophet, all the while setting himself up as god.

During this time in his efforts to conquer the world, the Scripture says that *"tidings out of the East and out of the North shall trouble him: therefore he shall go forth with great fury to destroy, and utterly to make away many"* (Dan. 11:44).

At this time he will probably defeat Russia as well as Germany and then also Japan and China, etc.

At this time, he will leave off in his efforts to destroy Israel, with them by and large having fled Jerusalem and the nation of Israel, where they will be kept by the Lord in Petra (Ps. 60:6-12; Isa. 26:20; 63:1; Ezek. 20:33; Dan. 11:41; Hos. 2:14; Mat. 24:16; Rev. Chpt. 12).

Now will begin the most horrible spectacle of judgment the world will have ever known.

## THE JUDGMENTS OF GOD

We turn now to the operations of God with respect to those activities and the apostasy of the human race. These are in the form of Judgments directed chiefly against the throne of the Antichrist and the territory of the Revised Roman Empire, which will include the Middle East and Western Europe.

The purpose of these Judgments is to bring men to repentance concerning their sins of idolatry, demon worship, murders, sorceries, fornications, and thefts, but which will have, sadly and regrettably, little effect (Rev. 9:20). Even in the midst of God's Judgments there is mercy, but little appreciated we might quickly add!

In the midst of the Antichrist's kingdom, hail and fire mingled with blood will destroy at least one third of Europe's forests and all standing food crops. Then, a meteor will fall into the Mediterranean Sea, and one third of the Sea becomes blood, one third of its marine life dies, and one third of the commercial and Naval vessels will be sunk. Following close on the heels of that Judgment, a meteor poisons one third of the fresh water supply of Europe, and many will die from drinking this poisoned water (Rev. 8:7-11). Note, if you will, the Mercy of God in the midst of these Judgments. There is not a complete destruction, but only one third.

Then the Bottomless Pit is opened, and the imprisoned demons are let loose upon the inhabitants of the Earth. They are forbidden to touch those who have the seal of God in their foreheads, and ordered to torment those who do not. The demons are forbidden to kill them, but commanded to torment them. The torment inflicted will be so severe that those who are subject to it will seek to escape its pain by suicide. But try as they will, they will not be able to die (Rev. 9:1-12).

Following this, a superhuman army of demon horsemen, 200,000,000 strong, will kill one third of the Earth's population (Rev. 9:13-21). However, more than likely, these spirit horsemen will not be seen, only the effects of what they do. Then those who receive the mark of the Beast are afflicted with a *"noisome and grievous sore"* (Rev. 16:2).

At that time, the heat of the sun will be intensified, so intensified in fact that men will be scorched. However, instead of bringing them to repentance, the result will be that they will blaspheme God even more. Finally, a plague of darkness, which will seem to have some type of pain-causing effect, will cause men to literally gnaw their tongues as a counterirritation in an attempt to alleviate the pain caused by the darkness.

Before closing this discussion of the Seventieth Week of Daniel, it will be well to ask ourselves, just how close is this period to the times in which we are now living? In fact, the Rapture of the Church may occur at any moment. However, the Seventieth Week of Daniel cannot actually come for a considerable length of time as of yet.

NOTES

The commercial city of Babylon which is to be destroyed in that period is not yet in existence. The Jewish Temple in Jerusalem which the Antichrist will violate in the middle of that period is not now in existence. The ten horned kingdom which we might refer to as the Revised Roman Empire with the Antichrist at its head must come into existence as well before the seven year period, for him to make a seven year pact with the Jews and others for this particular period.

Irrespective as to how all of this will come about, and come about it shall, as stated, the Rapture cannot be very long into the future. As a Child of God, our foremost concern should be that we're walking close to the Lord, ever drawing nearer to Him, that we might be ready at that moment.

Unfortunately, as Peter prophesied, *"Knowing this first, that there shall come in the last days scoffers, walking after their own lusts,*

*"And saying, where is the Promise of His Coming? For since the fathers fell asleep, all things continue as they were from the beginning of the creation."*

And then Peter said, *"The Lord is not slack concerning His Promise, as some men count slackness; but is longsuffering to us-ward, not willing that any should perish, but that all should come to repentance"* (II Pet. 3:3-4, 9).

This is the time of repentance; tomorrow there may be no time.

(4) "WHO OPPOSETH AND EXALTETH HIMSELF ABOVE ALL THAT IS CALLED GOD, OR THAT IS WORSHIPPED; SO THAT HE AS GOD SITTETH IN THE TEMPLE OF GOD, SHEWING HIMSELF THAT HE IS GOD."

This pertains to the mid-point of the Great Tribulation, when the Antichrist will show his true colors. He will at that time declare war upon Israel, actually moving his headquarters from the newly built city of Babylon to Jerusalem, at least the religious part of his headquarters. As well, he will direct a determined opposition to the True God which will be a leading feature of this apostasy. He will occupy the Holy of Holies in the Temple, and demand worship that is due God alone. Of course, this is the Jewish Temple which will be rebuilt in Jerusalem in the near future.

Some deny that this is an actual person, but rather a spirit or a particular movement, etc. However, every indication in the Word of God points to the fact that this will be a man, a man incidently, who might even be alive at this present time as a boy or in his teens.

THE EXALTING OF HIMSELF

The phrase, *"Who opposeth and exalteth himself above all that is called God,"* pertains to his declaration of himself as deity. In effect, he challenges God, exalts himself above all elements of worship in any capacity even to the True God, recklessly and blasphemously claiming deity for himself. This is the fulfillment of the Prophecies given by Daniel in Chapters 7 and 8 of his great Book.

This sin is not original, actually characterizing the entirety of the human race who rebels against God, at least in some measure. In fact, Satan's original sin, for he was the one who originated this sin, was the attempt to become God which the human race should worship. To be sure, the Evil One is not an atheist even though he is responsible for atheism in the world and every other lie that is told. Lucifer who is now Satan, was originally created by God as the strongest, most powerful, and most beautiful Angel possibly ever created. In fact, he served God in Righteousness and Holiness for an undetermined period of time. So, he full well knows God, and in fact, all about his Creator. He knows so much in fact, that in his evil rebellion, he wants to be God; consequently, this spirit of Satan imbues itself more or less in all his followers. The idea here is, that the Antichrist will take this spirit to a deeper depth and higher height than any other human being has ever done previously. He will do two things:

OPPOSE GOD

Of course, the question must first be asked as to how an individual can actually oppose God.

In reality as far as hurt and damage are concerned, there is really very little anyone can do. God is all in all, the Creator of the ages, far above the ability of man to cause Him difficulties of any nature; however, man can oppose God, even as man does constantly, by opposing God's Word, His Plan, and in effect, all that God does through His Son, the Lord Jesus Christ, respecting Salvation along with the Work of the Holy Spirit. Man opposes God by opposing God's Way. That *"Way"* is Christ! So, most of the opposing down through the ages has been against Christ, Who is the only Way to the Father, and in fact the only Way of Salvation, which He carried out through the Cross.

Man cannot get at God except through Christ, and cannot really get at Christ, except through those who follow and serve Christ. So, the opposition is really against God's people.

The Antichrist will take this one step further or one might say, will refine the process, at that time by opposing all who follow Christ, but at the same time opposing Israel. It is ironical, the Antichrist will oppose Christ and Israel opposes Christ also. But yet, Satan knowing the Promises of God as it regards Israel, and their restoration, knows if he can take them out, the entirety of the Plan of God then falls to the ground. God's Word cannot be denied. If any of His Word fails, in essence, all of it fails, hence Jesus saying, *"Heaven and earth shall pass away, but My Words shall not pass away"* (Mat. 24:35).

The greatest opposition down through the many centuries has been the opposition against God's Plan of Salvation through His Son, the Lord Jesus Christ, through what He did at the Cross. So, the greatest opposition has been against this Plan, i.e., *"the Cross!"* It is opposed by the world, and regrettably, by much of the Church.

In fact, this was the greatest center of opposition against Paul in his efforts to establish the Church. His national countrymen, the Jews, hated him because of his proclamation of Christ and Him Crucified. Many in the Church also attempted to add Law to Grace, which in effect would nullify the Cross of Christ. While opposition takes many forms, if one could get to the heart of the matter, it would always be centered up against *"Jesus Christ and Him Crucified."* Man, and

NOTES

especially religious man, is ever trying to add to that great Work, or take from that great Work! Either way, presents a disaster!

## THE EXALTATION OF SELF

Once again, this has been the problem of humanity since the Fall. Self is exalted above God.

Anything we do that adds to the Finished Work of Christ, or takes from the Finished Work of Christ, presents the exaltation of self, which is the greatest sin of all.

While all religion does this, the Catholic Church no doubt fills this position most of all, at least as it pertains to the part of Christianity which is apostate.

This is true of anyone who sets aside Divine Laws; who undertakes to legislate where God only has a right to legislate, and whose legislation is contrary to that of God. Any claim of a dominion over conscience; or any arrangement to set aside the Divine Laws, and to render them as nonapplicable, would correspond with what is implied in this description.

Unfortunately, many Protestant Denominations fall into the same spirit as that of Catholicism, attempting to claim dominion over the conscience. As it regards opposition against God, there is no greater sin. What I'm about to say is going to be strong, and it will offend some people, but it needs to be said simply because it is true.

The most evil thing in the world is not actually that which most people believe to be evil, and I speak of alcohol, drugs, immorality, etc. To be sure, those things are wicked, and in fact, exceedingly wicked; however, there is something far more wicked, and simply because it is far more subtle, actually coming from the *"good side of the Tree of the Knowledge of Good and Evil."* I speak of most religious leadership. I didn't say all, but I do say *"most."*

In fact, there is very little in the world more evil than the leadership of many religious Denominations. This is what crucified Christ. It was not the drunks and the gamblers, etc., as vile as that is, who crucified Christ, but rather the religious leaders of Israel. To be sure, it has not changed from then until now.

NOTES

The sad part is, most of the people who belong to these Denominations have little understanding of this of what I say. They are far removed from the actual happenings; however, to be sure, it ultimately will definitely affect them spiritually and in a very negative way.

Even though I've mentioned Denominations, this of which I speak is really a spirit, which characterizes itself in so-called independent religious circles also. In Truth, there's nothing Scripturally wrong with having a Denomination or being associated with a Denomination. If they are conducted right, they can be a great blessing as a tool for the Work of God. It is only when men try to make something spiritual out of that which is plainly nonspiritual that the harm comes in.

So, I'm not saying that it's wrong to belong to a Denomination, for it isn't. Neither am I saying that institutionalized religion is wrong, simply because it is institutionalized. Neither am I opposing organization, etc. I am rather speaking of the spirit of control which abrogates the Word of God, thereby setting a course that is ungodly, which hinders the Work of God greatly.

To be sure, the Antichrist will take this to a new level. Whereas most of the present self-exaltation continues to *"use"* God in some capacity to further its own ends, he will oppose every facet of the Word of God, of the Plan of God, and actually of anything that pertains to God in any fashion. He will place himself above God in every capacity, actually claiming to be God, even as Paul will say in the last phrase of this Verse. It will be Satan's greatest effort against God, in other words in one fell swoop. He will invest everything into this *"man of sin,"* this *"son of perdition,"* who in effect will try to be the imitation of Christ, even though he will hate Christ, hence called *"the Antichrist."*

## WORSHIP

The phrase, *"Or that is worshiped,"* actually refers to *"an object of worship."* It may be applied to the worship of a heathen divinity, or of the True God. It may also refer to a person, an idol, or a place.

The idea is, the Antichrist will place himself not only above the God of the Heavens, but as well above Mohammed, Buddha, all the Hindu gods, in fact, any and all types of worship to any type of so-called gods, anywhere in the world.

His desire will be to rule the entirety of the world, and have the entirety of the world worshiping him upon pain of death. In other words, worship him or die. While he will succeed in a particular area of the Earth which he has conquered, or at least somewhat, he will not be able to take over the entirety of the world, his efforts being stopped at Armageddon, by the Second Coming of the Lord. Daniel said of him, *"He shall also stand up against the Prince of princes* (against Christ)*; but he shall be broken without hand"* (Dan. 8:25).

## THE TEMPLE OF GOD

The phrase, *"So that he as God sitteth in the Temple of God,"* refers to the Jewish Temple which will be rebuilt one might say, and more than likely in the same place where the Moslem Dome of the Rock now sits, or else immediately beside this edifice. There is plenty of room on the Temple Mount for this to be done; however, I seriously doubt that this will be the case, and I speak of erecting a second structure on the Temple Mount.

It is believed that the Holy of Holies of Solomon's Temple sat immediately over the spot where Abraham was to offer Isaac. In fact, this very spot sits in the middle of the Dome of the Rock, surrounded by a fence.

The Moslems claim Abraham as their father the same as the Jews, but that Ishmael was the promised seed instead of Isaac. Jews and Christians of course, know that Isaac was the one through whom the Seed would come, the Lord Jesus Christ (Gen. 21:12). In other words, Isaac was in the lineage of Christ and not Ishmael who was the son of a bondwoman, therefore, a work of the flesh and not of the Spirit.

Israel as a nation cannot be complete at least in her thinking presently, until the Temple is rebuilt. In fact, her manner of worship completes her nationhood.

But at the same time, we know that Christ has fulfilled all of this, making sacrifices and the keeping of Feast Days, etc., no longer necessary. Israel, having rejected Christ, will once again attempt to reinstitute the sacrificial system. Of course, she must have her Temple in order for the entire Mosaic procedure to be carried out.

NOTES

It is quite probable and almost a guaranteed fact, that the Antichrist will have a great deal to do with Israel actually rebuilding her Temple. The very fact of him being able to do such a thing, that is if in truth he will be actually responsible, will portray a diplomatic ingenuity possessed possibly by no one else in the world. So, if he can bring this about, especially considering the animosity between the Jews and the Moslem Arabs, such will portray genius of unparalleled proportions. In fact, this no doubt will be one reason that Israel will think he is the Messiah, especially considering that he no doubt will be Jewish himself — actually, the Scripture tells us that he will be a Syrian Jew (Dan. Chpt. 11).

Irrespective of the difficulties involved, we definitely do know that this Temple is going to be built, and more than likely and as stated, will be built on the present site of the Moslem Dome of the Rock. What is very difficult for man and even impossible, is of no difficulty for the Lord whatsoever. He can bring about events easily enough, that things can be done previously thought impossible to be done. In fact, if the Antichrist is instrumental in this situation, it will only be because God allows such to be done.

The Antichrist *"sitting in the Temple of God,"* pertains to the prophecy by Daniel when he said, *"And he* (the Antichrist) *shall confirm the covenant with many for one week* (with Israel and other Nations for seven years)*: and in the midst of the week* (after three and one half years) *he shall cause the sacrifice and the oblation to cease* (will actually declare war on Israel, taking over the Temple, actually making it his religious headquarters), *and for the overspreading of abominations he shall make it desolate* (referring to the stopping of all worship of God in any capacity), *even until the consummation* (for three and one half years, or until the end of the Great Tribulation), *and that determined shall be poured upon the desolate"* referring to his destruction at the Second Coming (Dan. 9:27).

At this particular time, Israel will realize what a fool she has been in believing this man to be the Messiah. He will now show his true colors, and in fact, would completely destroy Israel at this particular time, but for other situations which arise. At any rate, Israel will flee Jerusalem and the nation as a whole, with hundreds of thousands no doubt going to Petra, this ancient city in Jordan, which is now empty, actually encircled by mountains, possibly unlike any other city in the world.

The Antichrist having bigger fish to fry (Dan. 11:44), will go north and east to fight great battles in order to consolidate his kingdom, which will take him the major part of three and one half years. At the first part of this three and one half year period, he will set himself up as god, declaring this Temple as his temple, and demanding worship, which he will receive by his followers. Him *"sitting in the Temple"* refers to him taking over the Temple, making it his religious headquarters, and above all proclaiming himself at that time as *"god."*

THE CLAIM OF DEITY

The phrase, *"Shewing himself that he is God,"* proclaims his announcement of deity as it regards himself.

To be sure, this proclamation will be accompanied by great miracles, carried out by the False Prophet who will even be able to call fire down from Heaven in the sight of men (Rev. 13:11-15).

The Scripture plainly says that the Antichrist and the False Prophet will *"deceive them that dwell on the earth, by the means of those miracles which he had power to do in the sight of the Beast." "The Beast"* refers to the Antichrist (Rev. 13:14).

To be sure, this which will be done at that time will not be some mere slight of hand, but will impress the entirety of the world, and will be powerful beyond belief, designed to deceive, as it shall aptly do.

Due to this powerful manifestation of miracles on the part of the False Prophet, hundreds of millions and possibly even as many as half the population of the world, will actually worship this man as god. There will then be very little restraint, even as Paul will say in later Verses.

(5) "REMEMBER YE NOT, THAT, WHEN I WAS YET WITH YOU, I TOLD YOU THESE THINGS?"

NOTES

Is it possible that a note of impatience may be detected in Paul's question? If the Thessalonian Believers had recalled what Paul had already taught on this particular subject concerning the Rapture, the Second Coming, etc., disturbing elements regarding false teaching and false thinking could have been eliminated.

The Apostle was certain about their previous familiarity with the substance of Verses 3 and 4, because he had personally given them this information.

Why is it that the Truth is so easily forgotten, while error seems to stick like glue?

REMEMBER

The phrase, *"Remember ye not,"* in effect answers itself, at least for many in the Church in Thessalonica. The Truth is, they didn't remember these things Paul had already told them, or else they had come to the place that they really didn't believe the things he had said, and due to the error which was being fed them.

What we're seeing here is without a doubt, the greatest problem in the Church presently, even as it always has been. I speak of false doctrine pushing out that which is true and Biblical, with the true not being remembered or else rejected.

We have two factors here:

1. When these Truths were given by Paul to these people, they should have done exactly what the Lord told Joshua to do. His word was clear and concise:

*"This Book of the Law shall not depart out of thy mouth* (in other words, talk about it continuously)*; but thou shalt meditate therein day and night, that thou mayest observe to do according to all that is written therein: for then thou shall make thy way prosperous, and then thou shall have good success"* (Josh. 1:8).

Even though the Lord was then speaking of the Law of Moses, while what Paul was giving was the New Covenant; still, the principle is the same.

If all Christians everywhere, would get the Truth and hold to the Truth, and do so by discussing it constantly, even meditating on it day and night, to be sure the Truth would not only be preserved, but the Lord would even add to what was already given.

The Believer should understand, that the Word of God is our very life. It is our all in all, our past, our present, and our future. There is nothing, but nothing, that is even remotely as important as the Word of God and more particularly, that Word applied to our lives.

2. Even though false doctrine always has a powerful pull simply because of evil spirits which are fomenting its fabrications, still, the Truth has greater power, even far greater power, simply because the Holy Spirit superintends Truth (Jn. 16:13). However, if we are not properly addressing Truth as we should, and I speak of the instruction given in point one, the power of false doctrine will definitely take its deadly toll. The Holy Spirit does all He can to ward off these things, but if our knowledge of the Truth is skimpy at best, He has very little to work on in our lives. Regrettably, that's the case with most Christians!

### THE PRESENCE OF PAUL

The phrase, *"That, when I was yet with you,"* presents a privilege and opportunity given to the Thessalonians that not many folk would ever have. Think of the privilege of being able to sit under the Ministry of Paul! Even though it was only for a short time, he was able to impart to them that which no other man in the world could have given them. The reason is simple, and is not meant at all to take away from the original Twelve or anyone else, but it was to Paul that the New Covenant was given; consequently, he had more knowledge in this capacity than any other man alive at that time.

So the point I'm making is, there was no excuse for the Thessalonians allowing false doctrine to come in. It is one thing not to know the Truth, but it's something else altogether to have the privilege of the Truth, but to let it slip. The Scripture says concerning this, *"Therefore we ought to give the more earnest heed to the things which we have heard, lest at any time we should let them slip"* (Heb. 2:1).

It is my personal belief that Paul wrote Hebrews. And if that is the case, he no doubt had in mind the many times that this very thing had happened — Saints had simply let the Word slip out of their grasp.

NOTES

### THE MESSAGE THAT PAUL PREACHED

The phrase, *"I told you these things,"* completes the question concerning their remembering.

As we said at the outset of our Commentary on I Thessalonians, Paul was not able to stay as long as he desired in Thessalonica, due to problems which arose in the city which forced him to leave; however, to be sure, he made the most of what time he did have.

The evidence is clear here that he dealt with them quite extensively concerning Endtime happenings; consequently, he is calling it to their remembrance.

Paul had no doubt studied Daniel extensively and minutely. As well, the Lord gave him even more insight regarding Endtime matters, which he gives to us in this Chapter. However, by Paul making this statement, it is obvious that he covered all the great Doctrines of the Faith while with the Thessalonians, plus prophetic events, showing us how important these things actually are. Paul knew that these things would be many centuries coming to pass, but still, it was important that the Thessalonians know the entirety of the great Plan of God. They were pulled away from these Truths only because of listening to false teachers.

(6) "AND NOW YE KNOW WHAT WITHHOLDETH THAT HE MIGHT BE REVEALED IN HIS TIME."

The Apostle now gives us more details as it concerns this coming time which incidently, is presently upon us. When Paul uttered these words under the leading of the Holy Spirit, the Church was in its founding stages. But yet the Holy Spirit through the Apostle, now tells us what is going to happen in the last of the last days.

Daniel did not reveal anything about the Church, because his prophecies did not pertain to the Church, only about Israel. The Holy Spirit, however, now gives us the role of the Church as it concerns these Endtime things.

### THAT WHICH RESTRAINS

The phrase, *"And now ye know what withholdeth,"* speaks of the Church. Before we go into detail, please allow me to say, that if the Thessalonians could then know, surely we can now know, especially considering that the fulfillment of all of these things is at hand.

Paul is speaking about the Second Coming of the Lord which will be the time when He will set up His Kingdom on Earth. He is telling the Thessalonians that several things must take place before this can come about. Those things are:

1. The Rapture of the Church: As we've already explained, Verse 3 should have been translated, *"For that day* (the Second Coming) *shall not come, except there come a departure first* (for this is what the Greek word here actually means), *and* (then) *that man of sin be revealed, the son of perdition* (the Antichrist)."

2. A short period of time after the Rapture, and it's not certain as to how long this period of time will be, maybe even several years, the Antichrist will make his debut, which Paul proclaims in both Verses 3 and 4, as well as through Verse 12 of this Chapter.

3. After these things, the Second Coming will take place, actually at the very conclusion of the Great Tribulation during the Battle of Armageddon (Rev. Chpt. 19). At that time, Christ will set up His Kingdom on Earth, with Satan locked away in the Bottomless Pit, along with all his demon spirits, etc. (Rev. 20:1-3).

## WHAT IS THIS GREAT RESTRAINER OF LAWLESSNESS OF WHICH PAUL SPEAKS HERE?

Concerning that which hinders or restrains, and we are speaking of the hindering of sin and the restraining of sin, there has been some confusion as to what this really is.

Many have claimed that Paul is speaking here of the Holy Spirit, actually claiming that He will be taken out of the world at the time of the Rapture; however, this is incorrect, inasmuch as the Holy Spirit is God. As such, He is everywhere.

Beside that, on the Day of Pentecost, Peter, quoting the Prophet Joel, said, *"And on My servants and on My handmaidens I will pour out in those days of My Spirit; and they shall prophesy:*

*"And I will show wonders in Heaven above, and signs in the Earth beneath; blood, and fire, and vapor of smoke:*

*"The sun shall be turned into darkness, and the moon into blood, before that great and notable day of the Lord come:*

*"And it shall come to pass, that whosoever shall call on the Name of the Lord shall be saved"* (Acts 2:18-21).

This Passage plainly tells us that great numbers of people will be saved in the coming Great Tribulation, which these Verses portray. To be sure, no one can be saved without the convicting and regenerating Power of the Holy Spirit (Jn., Chpt. 3). So, the idea that the Holy Spirit is going to be taken out of the world at the Rapture of the Church has no validity in Scripture.

## THE CHURCH

Actually, it is the Church here of which Paul speaks. The Church is that which will *"withhold."* The word *"withhold"* in the Greek is *"katecho,"* which means *"to hold down."* In other words, it is the True Church (not the apostate Church) which holds down sin in the world. When the True Church is gone in the Rapture, then the Antichrist will *"be revealed."*

Jesus plainly stated, *"you are ye"* speaking of Believers, *are the salt of the earth* (that which preserves)."

He also said, *"Ye are the light of the world"* (Mat. 5:13-14).

Consequently, when both the preservative and the illumination are removed from this Earth, one can well imagine what it will be like.

## THE MANNER IN WHICH THE CHURCH SERVES THIS PURPOSE

The Lord Jesus Christ, or actually what He has done as it regards the Cross and the Resurrection, is the Bearer and the Cause of all good things on this Earth. In other words, every single good thing that's happened in this world, and irrespective as to what it might be, the cause and effect can be laid at the feet of our Lord and Saviour, Jesus Christ. However, all of this is carried out through Believers who have given their hearts to Christ, and Who lives within us through the Person of the Holy Spirit (Jn. 14:17, 20). Consequently,

NOTES

the only Righteousness, Godliness, and Holiness in this world, is that which resides in Believers through Christ and Christ Alone! Due to the great significance of what we're saying, I want to say it again so as the Reader will have no misunderstanding.

Most Believers do not fully understand the degree of the Righteousness of Christ.

For the first 1,600 years after the Fall in the Garden of Eden, the Bible records only two individuals who served the Lord in Faith and Righteousness. I speak of the time up to Noah, but not including at this moment that particular Patriarch. Those two individuals were Abel and Enoch. While there certainly may have been others, these are the only two recorded. As we all know, Abel was murdered, and I feel that if Enoch had not been translated, he would have been murdered as well. In fact, during that some 1,600 years, the Scripture says, *"The wickedness of man was great in the earth and every imagination of the thoughts of his heart was only evil continually."*

It then says, *"And it repented the Lord that He had made man on the earth, and it grieved Him at His heart"* (Gen. 6:5-6).

This tells us how wicked that particular time was, and it was wicked simply because there was no *"salt"* or *"light"* in the world. Due to reasons I will not now address, God has always worked through intermediaries, in other words, through men and women. However, He can only work through those who will believe and obey Him. As stated, during that particular time it is recorded that only two men actually did believe and obey Him, hence the terrible wickedness in the Earth.

Noah found Grace in the sight of the Lord because it said, *"Noah walked with God"* (Gen. 6:8-10). Consequently, he and his family were spared in the Flood, with actually the entirety of the human race starting all over again in the lineage of Noah's three sons (Gen. 9:25-27).

Up until the time of Abraham, which was some 400 years after the Flood, there is no record as to who lived for God and who didn't. In fact, the evil once again became very pronounced as mankind began to multiply (Gen. Chpts. 10-11).

NOTES

There are some who believe that Shem is actually the one who witnessed to Abraham resulting in his Salvation one might say. Some also think that Shem and Melchizedek are one and the same; however, even though that possibility exists, there's no real Scriptural proof of such. However, we do know that Shem lived to be about 600 years old, actually still being alive the first 75 years of Abraham's life (Gen. 11:10-32). Another word about that:

When you read in the first nine Chapters of Genesis of these individuals living extremely long lives, with Methuselah living the longest of all, some 969 years, this is actually how long they lived. In other words, you're not reading fables. The reason is according to the following:

Man was originally created by God to live forever. In fact, he was so wondrously and gloriously created, that even as powerful as sin actually was and is, it took nearly a thousand years to finally wear down this marvelous specimen and then to kill him. If one is to notice as one reads deeper into Genesis, the life span slowly gets shorter and shorter, until finally it is about 70 years or less. Even with all of our vaunted science presently, the situation, at least on a worldwide basis, has not changed much from the 70 year cycle.

Moses wrote in the Ninetieth Psalm, *"For all our days are passed away in Thy wrath: we spend our years as a tale that is told.*

*"The days of our years are threescore years and ten* (70)*; and if by reason of strength they be fourscore years* (80)*, yet is their strength, labor and sorrow; for it is soon cut off, and we fly away"* (Ps. 90:9-10).

At the Resurrection this will all be changed, with the possession of Eternal Life which every Believer now has, then becoming a practical experience. That's why Jesus said, *"I am the Resurrection, and the Life: he that believeth in Me, though he were dead, yet shall he live:*

*"And whosoever liveth and believeth in Me shall never die"* (Jn. 11:25-26).

## ABRAHAM

Abraham was then called by God (Gen. Chpt. 12), from whose loins and Sarah's womb would come a people, the Jews, who would believe God and be the salt and light in the world. In fact, during Israel's time, they were the only people on Earth who were living for God, and in fact, only some of them. In the world outside of Israel, death reigned, with all manner of wickedness and sin, resulting in pain, torture, and an unimaginable negative lifestyle. In fact, there was no freedom, with the strong pushing down the weak, with life being very cheap.

The purpose of Israel was to bring Christ into the world which they did. And then from His great Work at the Cross and the Resurrection, the Church was brought about in order to touch the entirety of the nations of the world, which it has more or less.

So, every iota of good in this world, is because of Jesus Christ, which translates into those who serve and follow Him. Of course, the major universities of the great nations of the world would never agree to such a thing, considering that they think they fill that role, with Politicians thinking the same of themselves, etc. Nevertheless, the real cause of all freedom, all prosperity, all good things, is Jesus Christ, Who proclaims His Way by the Power of the Holy Spirit, through Believers all over the world.

While men might build mighty kingdoms without God, without God they cannot bring about Righteousness. The Scripture plainly says, *"Righteousness exalteth a nation: but sin is a reproach to any people"* (Prov. 14:34).

Righteousness can only be obtained through the Lord, for within himself, man has no Righteousness. Consequently, when the Church is taken out of this world, even though there will definitely be other people saved during the Great Tribulation, still, that number will be small by comparison to the millions who presently know Christ. With the Church gone, and of course I speak of the True Church, all Righteousness will be taken out of the world. This will leave nothing but spiritual darkness, which will set the stage for the rise of the Antichrist. In other words, with no restraints left, the way of Righteousness will be gone, with nothing left but wickedness and evil. It will not be a pleasant time to say the least!

## THE REVELATION OF THE ANTICHRIST

The phrase, *"That he might be revealed in his time,"* speaks entirely of the Antichrist. *"His time"* will be after the Rapture of the Church, as Paul plainly states in Verses 3 and 7.

Some Preachers desire to have the Church play a great role in the coming Tribulation; however, if one studies Daniel, there is no place in his Prophecies for the Church, simply because Daniel's Seventieth Week, is the concluding seven years of the 490 year Prophecy regarding Israel by that Statesman (Dan. 9:24-27). These were particular times of God's dealings with Israel after the Babylonian dispersion, with 69 of these weeks, or 483 years concluding with the destruction of Jerusalem in A.D. 70, leaving one remaining week of years, i.e., *"seven years."* That seven years will be taken up in the coming Great Tribulation, and has absolutely nothing to do with the Church, but altogether concerns itself with Israel. So, to attempt to insert the Church into this seven year period of time, especially considering the Prophecies of Daniel and Paul, does great violence to the Scriptures. In fact, the age of the Church will conclude with the Rapture, which will take place before this seven year period begins. To fail to understand that, is a failure to understand the clear and plain Prophecies of Daniel as they concern Israel.

The Church has no place in the Promises and Prophecies concerning the restoration of Israel, even as the Prophecies concerning the Restoration of Israel have no place in the Church. Israel's time was not the time of the Church, and the time of the Church is not the time of Israel. While Jews can definitely be a part of the Church, even as many now are, still, for the most part the Jews have rejected Christ and continue to do so. That will be remedied with the Second Coming.

In fact, the Church and all who died in the Faith before the Church, will be included in the First Resurrection, and will come back with Christ at the Second Coming (Rev. Chpt. 19). All of these, which will include every Born-Again person who has ever lived, even all the way back to Abel, will help Christ administer the affairs of this Earth and the universe forever; however, that will be somewhat different and apart from national Israel, which will have then accepted Christ, and once again be restored as the leading nation in the world. This will be in the coming Kingdom Age.

NOTES

No, there is no indication in Scripture whatsoever that the Church will go through any part of the coming Great Tribulation, with in fact, every Scripture militating against this.

It is the business of the Church to be looking at this time for the Rapture. This should be our interest, our concern, and our observation. In other words, the Church, and of course I speak of the True Church, is getting ready to leave this world. Regrettably, many in the modern Church don't think so, and don't even believe in the Rapture. They have set their affections on the things of this world, hence the modern *"money gospel,"* etc.

But the True Church must not be deterred by false doctrine or the siren call of false prophets, but rather must be *"listening"* for the Trump and *"looking"* for the Saviour.

(7) "FOR THE MYSTERY OF INIQUITY DOTH ALREADY WORK: ONLY HE WHO NOW LETTETH WILL LET, UNTIL HE BE TAKEN OUT OF THE WAY."

In this particular Passage, Paul once again proclaims the Rapture of the Church. In interpreting these Scriptures, one must first of all get the general idea of the entirety of the subject matter.

As we've already stated, the subject matter is the Second Coming of the Lord, with Him setting up His earthly Kingdom at Jerusalem. The Thessalonians had become confused due to false doctrine which had come into their ranks, etc.

First of all, they thought all of this was to take place immediately, with Paul clearing the record that it was not going to happen then. Second, they were concerned that those who had recently died, would miss out on this great coming event of the Lord's Reign.

Paul addresses all of this in both Epistles, by telling them that the dead in Christ will in fact be raised (I Thess. 4:13-18). He now sets the record straight by telling them when all of these things are going to take place, in other words the times of the end.

Of course, he gave no dates because such would have been unscriptural. In fact, he did not even know himself when these times would come. But he did know, as given to him by the Holy Spirit, that two things must come about before the Second Coming. Those two things are: A. The Rapture; and, B. The advent of the man of sin, the Antichrist.

NOTES

## THE MYSTERY OF INIQUITY

The phrase, *"For the mystery of iniquity doth already work,"* concerns the advent of false teaching by false teachers.

*"Mystery"* denotes something which was previously unknown or secret before it is revealed. So also one of the names of Babylon, the seat of the Antichrist's power is *"Mystery"* (Rev. 17:3).

*"Iniquity"* means *"lawlessness,"* but lawlessness in a particular way. It refers to going outside the Law of God, which means outside of His Word.

Even at the time the Apostle was writing these words, the seeds of apostasy were already being sown by false teachers, etc. The leaven of lawlessness (a repudiation of the Word of God) was fermenting inside Christianity. In other words, the foundations of a false Christianity were even then being laid.

Thus, the Apostle warned the Ephesians that false teachers would arise among themselves; to Timothy he writes of those perilous times which were even then present; and, in his Epistles, mention is made of false practices and doctrines, such as the worship of Angels, abstinence from meats, bodily mortifications, and the honor conferred on celibacy.

So also John the Beloved, in his First Epistle, refers to this working of Antichrist power when he says, *"Little Children, it is the last time* (during the Endtime)*: and as ye have heard that Antichrist shall come, even now are there many Antichrists.*

*"Every spirit that confesseth not that Jesus Christ is come in the flesh is not of God: and this is that spirit of Antichrist, whereof ye have heard that it should come; and even now already is it in the world"* (I Jn. 2:18; 4:3).

Even though Paul did not go into detail, John did! Jesus came in the flesh for the particular purpose of going to the Cross, which alone could redeem lost humanity. So, what Paul and John both are actually saying is, that this mystery of iniquity begins with a departure from the Cross.

## THE CROSS OF CHRIST

I believe I can say without any fear of Scriptural contradiction, that all departure from Truth into error, or all going into apostasy, which is a departure from Truth, begins with the forsaking of the Cross of Christ as the only way of Salvation (I Cor. 1:18; 2:2). Consequently, Satan fights the Cross as he fights nothing else.

Inasmuch as the Cross is the place of all victory, or else one might say, the great Act of Christ in the giving of Himself, this great Sacrifice affords us everything that we have in the Lord (Gal. 1:4). If in fact, everything comes to us through the Sacrificial, Atoning Work of Christ on the Cross, which of course includes His Resurrection, Ascension, and Exaltation, then it stands to reason, that a departure from this, and I speak of this Finished Work, is a departure from Truth.

In seeking the Lord for several years, and earnestly so I might quickly add, as to the secret of victorious, overcoming Christian living, when the answer did come, and come it did, I was led to the Cross. The Holy Spirit took me to Romans, Chapter 6, which spells out succinctly the place and position of the Believer in Christ, in which is our total victory. Of course, Romans, Chapter 8 adds greatly to this, with even Romans, Chapter 7 playing its part. He led me to that Chapter, and then plainly spoke to my heart saying, *"The answer which you seek is found totally and completely in the Cross."*

I cannot even begin to relate to you as to how I felt when this great Truth was revealed to me. He then showed me that inasmuch as this is true, my Faith must anchor itself in the Cross, i.e., *"this great, Finished Work of Christ"* (Rom. 6:2-6).

He then showed me that once my Faith is in the Cross, understanding that this is where all victory was won and all victory is obtained, that the Holy Spirit will then help me do all the things which need to be done (Rom. 8:1-2).

Even though the totality is very complicated, still, the fundamentals of this are very simple. To reiterate:

1. The answer to every question and the solution to every problem is found in the Cross of Christ.

2. Understanding that, our Faith must rest in the Cross, this Finished Work of Christ. This means that the Cross, or more particularly what Jesus did there, must ever be the object of our Faith.

NOTES

3. When the object of our Faith is the Cross, and remains the Cross, even as it must, the Holy Spirit, Who always works within the parameters of the Atonement, i.e., *"the Finished Work of Christ,"* will then work, and work mightily upon our behalf.

### THAT WHICH HAS BEEN TAUGHT

Upon coming to Christ as a child, I was taught in our Church that the Cross and Faith in the Cross were an absolute necessity for one to be saved. Even though the sinner may not understand much of anything about Christ and the Cross, still, he must believe that Jesus died for him, and upon that confession, even in a limited way, Salvation will be the instant result (Rom. 10:9-10, 13; Eph. 2:8-9). However, I was taught nothing as to the validity of the Cross of Christ as it concerns our daily living for the Lord.

Consequently, I preached the Cross strongly as it regards the sinner coming to Christ, and by the Grace of God saw hundreds of thousands brought to a saving knowledge of Jesus Christ. With the help of the Lord, I resisted strongly the efforts of Modernism to demean the Cross, as it regards the Salvation of the lost. As stated, God honored our efforts respecting this Message of Redemption.

Even though I was taught this great Subject very succinctly, and preached it in the same manner, as stated, I was taught almost nothing as it concerns the place of the Cross in our everyday living before God. In fact, almost the entirety of the Church world fell into this same error. Almost nothing was taught anyone as to how to live a victorious, overcoming, Christian life.

We Pentecostals thought and taught that the Baptism with the Holy Spirit with the evidence of speaking with other Tongues, guaranteed this victorious life. In fact, that's what I preached.

While the Baptism with the Holy Spirit definitely does have a great bearing regarding everything that happens to the Child of God, the Truth is, that within itself is not the cause or the route of Victory. In other words, the mere fact of being Baptized with the Holy Spirit guarantees no victory at all, only the potential of Victory.

NOTES

As a result of this error, I saw as much failure in the Pentecostal camp, as I did in the non-Pentecostal camp. In fact, I knew what failure was first-hand, and that despite the fact of trying everything within one's power not to fail.

Much of the non-Pentecostal world, in attempting to address this problem, which of course is distasteful at best, simply came to the conclusion that one must sin a little bit everyday, etc. Of course, Paul very succinctly addressed this in Romans 6:1-2 by saying, *"Shall we continue in sin, that Grace may abound?"*

His answer was instant, *"God forbid!"* So, we know that way is wrong.

While we Pentecostals didn't teach that, what we were in fact teaching was just as wrong. The teaching was much to the effect, *"Salvation by Faith, and Sanctification by self."* And so we piled up rules one on top of the other, thinking somehow, that would perform the task. It only succeeded in making it worse.

We Pentecostals have a bad habit of lying to ourselves. We have the Baptism with the Holy Spirit, or at least we claim to have; therefore, we are to be some type of superhuman, spiritual giants. So we cover up what is really happening, making the facade of proposed victory larger and larger, while inside there is actually very little victory.

## DESPERATION GENERALLY PRECEDES REVELATION

In observing all of this, and sincerely attempting to find an answer, the Lord has to allow, at times, one to come to the point of desperation, before the Revelation can be given.

Why?

I'm not sure I have the answer to that question. Perhaps it's pride! Perhaps the problems are far deeper than we realize! At any rate, if we are truly sincere before the Lord, He will allow events to transpire which will bring us to the place of desperation. We then know that we have to find an answer. That's what happened to Jimmy Swaggart.

It's not very pleasant to have the entirety of the world laughing at you, and even almost all of the Church following suit. It's not very pleasant being called a *"hypocrite,"* among many other choice names I might quickly add. It's not very pleasant having people think the very worst of you, when you know in your heart, you're doing your very best to live as close to God as you know how.

At such a moment, you will either sink or swim, live or die! That's what I mean by desperation. There must be an answer, and by the Grace of God I set out to find that answer.

To be sure, it didn't come quickly. That's what I mean by layer after layer in which the Holy Spirit must peel back in order to get at the Truth. In other words, most of the time, and perhaps all of the time, the situation is far worse than we realize, which means that it's only the Lord Who can handle such a thing.

This desperation came in October of 1991. I began to cry to the Lord at that time, even as I had never sought His Face before. To be sure, I've always had a strong prayer life; however, there is a difference in a prayer life of communion and petition and a prayer life of communion and desperation.

If I remember correctly, it was sometime in the early part of 1997 that the Lord began to speak to my heart regarding the answer for which I had so long sought. The Revelation began to come, and it was the Revelation of the Cross, exactly as I have just attempted to give to you in brief. To say that it revolutionized my life, would be a gross understatement. In fact, everything has changed, and I mean everything.

I know what it is to experience the words and position of which Paul spoke when he said, *"O wretched man that I am! Who shall deliver me from the body of this death?"*

I also now know what he means when he said, *"There is therefore now no condemnation to them which are in Christ Jesus, who walk not after the flesh, but after the Spirit"* (Rom. 7:24; 8:1). It is in the latter in which I presently live.

As the Lord has opened up this Revelation, He has helped me to see everything in a different perspective. In other words, I now see everything in the parameters of the Cross of Christ, and I mean everything!

So, when Paul spoke of the *"mystery of iniquity,"* in the Greek Text he used the definite article actually saying, *"the mystery of the iniquity."* So it's not just sin or lawlessness of which he is speaking, but rather a particular sin, a particular iniquity or lawlessness.

If *"the Faith"* pertains to the great Sacrifice, and it definitely does, then *"the iniquity"* pertains to a departure from *"the Faith."*

NOTES

### THE MARCH OF THE CHURCH

Not long after the time of Paul, the Church began to go into apostasy. It did not do so quickly, but little by little it departed from the Cross of Christ, and did so in many and varied ways.

The Cross of Christ, and Faith in that great Sacrifice, constitute the entirety of the embodiment of Salvation, and all that it means to be in Christ. A departure from that, constitutes *"the iniquity."* That departure may come in different ways, but the end result is the same — destruction.

The way it came about in the Early Church, or rather ultimately did after several centuries, was that men were taught to look to the Church for Salvation, instead of the Cross. This led to the Government of God being abrogated, with man setting up his own government, which led to the Catholic Church, and the advent of Popes and Priests, with all its attendant false doctrine and denial of the Faith.

It is pretty much the same presently! Religious men attempt to get their followers to look to the Church, to themselves, or even to particular doctrines — anything but the Cross. That is the great iniquity, which means that the Cross is the dividing line between Truth and error, between Salvation and apostasy.

So, if it was already at work in Paul's day, in which it definitely was, then the situation is even worse presently.

### WHAT THE LORD SPOKE TO MY HEART IN EARLY 1992

In seeking His Face regarding our own personal situation as well as the Work of God, the Lord moved that morning in a powerful way. If I remember correctly, it was in January.

In this time of a great moving of the Holy Spirit, the Lord spoke to my heart that morning saying, *"You have asked me to heal your Ministry, and that I will do; however, I actually have to heal the entirety of the Church."*

He then spoke to my heart some things which I do not feel at liberty to relate; however, suffice to say, He has healed this Ministry and is healing this Ministry. By that I mean, what the Lord has done, has to now be disseminated among the people, which is being done at this very moment. However, the healing of the Church is something else altogether, but yet it relates strongly to the things I have just said.

I believe that the Revelation which the Lord has given us concerning the Cross, and especially considering what it's done for me personally and for this Ministry, is going to play a great part also in the healing of the Church, and of course I'm speaking of the True Church. I personally believe that the Lord is also calling others in this same capacity. But I stress the fact, the Cross is going to be, and in fact is, the dividing line. To reject it is to reject Christ. To accept what He did at the Cross, which has also been the foundation of the Church, is to accept Christ and all He has done. So, what we are speaking about here is not something that has just happened, but in fact has always been the manner and the way in which God has dealt with the human race. In other words, it has always been the Cross, even as it is now the Cross. To repudiate that, is to repudiate God and His Word.

In view of that, I believe the Lord is once again about to open up both Television and Radio to us in a greater way than ever, that this Message of the Cross may be spread over the entirety of the Earth. To be sure, whatever He wants, is what we want. No more, no less!

### THE RAPTURE

The phrase, *"Only He who now letteth will let, until he be taken out of the way,"* speaks of the Rapture of the Church, and coincides with the statement in Verse 3 as we have previously stated, which should have been translated, *"For that day shall not come* (the Second Coming of the Lord)*, except there come a departure first."*

The pronoun *"he"* confuses some people.

In Verses 4 and 6, the pronoun *"he"* refers to the Antichrist, while in Verse 7 *"he"* refers to the Church.

The idea is, that the Church (the True Church) will continue to hinder lawlessness until the Rapture. And then the Antichrist will be revealed.

This is conclusive proof that the Rapture takes place before Daniel's Seventieth Week and the Tribulation of Revelation 6:1-19:21.

According to Daniel 9:27, the Antichrist will be here for at least seven years, for he makes a seven year covenant with Israel. If he is here for seven years, which will be the last seven years of this age, and if he who hinders lawlessness refers to the Church and is taken out of the way before he comes, then the Rapture will take place before the last seven years of this age and before the Antichrist comes at the beginning of those seven years.

As we've already stated, this last seven years is the fulfillment of the Prophecy given by Daniel concerning God dealing with Israel for seventy weeks of years (Dan. 9:24). As also stated, 483 of those years have already been fulfilled and concluded with the destruction of Jerusalem by Titus in A.D. 70. The only thing that remains regarding Israel is this last seven year period, which pertains to Israel only, and has nothing to do with the Church (Dan. 9:27).

Preachers are constantly trying to force the Church into the coming Great Tribulation, or else they deny the Tribulation altogether, claiming that all of that was fulfilled in A.D. 70.

While that time definitely was important, for it signaled the conclusion of the Sixty-ninth Week of years; however, there was no Antichrist at that time who made a seven year covenant with Israel concluding the prophecy of Daniel regarding his Seventieth Week (Dan. 9:24). That is yet to come, and will take place in the coming Tribulation (Dan. 9:27), which will be followed by the Second Coming of the Lord, which didn't take place in A.D. 70 either (Rev. Chpt. 19).

As well, the Church wasn't *"taken out of the way"* in A.D. 70, as it will be in the Rapture.

The question should be asked, *"Taken out of the way of what?"*

Paul is here discussing the rise of the Antichrist, and he is referring to the Church which is the great hinderer of lawlessness, but when it is taken out of the way, will leave the way open for the Antichrist to be revealed.

NOTES

THE CROSS OF CHRIST

To which I have briefly alluded, I personally believe that the Lord, through the Person, Power, and Agency of the Holy Spirit, is attempting to bring the Church back to the Cross. The Cross alone can get the Church ready for the Rapture. In truth, the Cross is definitely not something new, having been the foundation of Faith even from the very beginning. During Old Testament times, Believers looked forward to a prophetic Jesus, Who would redeem mankind, and do so by the Cross, typified by the Sacrifices. Presently, we look back on a historical Jesus, Who has effected Redemption by going to the Cross, meaning that it is now a *"Finished Work."*

The only requirement for being ready for the Rapture is to be *"in Christ"*; however, there are millions presently in the modern Church who aren't even saved. In other words, they've never been Born-Again. They are religious, but lost! The only way these untold millions can be made to see their lost condition is for the Cross to be preached.

This is the reason that Paul said, *"We preach Christ Crucified"* (I Cor. 1:23).

He also said, *"Christ sent me not to baptize, but to preach the Gospel, not with wisdom of words, lest the Cross of Christ be made of none effect"* (I Cor. 1:17).

In this very Passage, we are told exactly what the Gospel really is. It is Jesus and what He has done for us at the Cross.

(8) "AND THEN SHALL THAT WICKED BE REVEALED, WHOM THE LORD SHALL CONSUME WITH THE SPIRIT OF HIS MOUTH, AND SHALL DESTROY WITH THE BRIGHTNESS OF HIS COMING:"

Paul deals with three things in this Verse:

1. The Rise of the Antichrist.
2. The Second Coming of the Lord, which of course is different than the Rapture of the Church.
3. The Manner of that Coming.

The idea is, that the Antichrist will have such power that the nations of the world will not be able to stop him in his quest for world dominion, as well as his claims of deity. He will be invested with the powers of darkness as no other man in history has ever been invested, even though there have been many forerunners, etc. However, and to be sure, the Lord will be able to take him out, and will do so at the Battle of Armageddon, when Israel is on the very verge of destruction.

### THE REVELATION OF THE WICKED ONE

The phrase, *"And then shall that wicked be revealed,"* refers to the Antichrist making his debut after the Rapture of the Church.

To refresh the memory of the Reader, there's nothing in Scripture that says the great seven year Tribulation will begin immediately after the Rapture. In fact, the Scripture says the opposite.

First of all, the word *"revealed"* in the Greek is *"apokalupto,"* and means *"to take off the cover, to disclose."* This actually refers to his signing the seven year pact with Israel (Dan. 9:27; Mat. 24:15-31).

It should be obvious that the Antichrist will have to rise to power before this seven year pact is signed. So, there will probably be a period of time, maybe even several years after the Rapture of the Church, before this seven year period commences.

With the Church gone, which is the great restrainer of evil, and again we speak of the True Church, the way will be prepared for *"that Wicked"* to be revealed.

Even though I personally believe that the translation of Verse 3 is incorrect in the King James, and should have been translated *"departure"* instead of *"falling away"*; still, the Bible definitely teaches a *"falling away"* in the last days concerning the Church. Paul plainly said to Timothy, *"Now the Spirit speaketh expressly,* (in no uncertain terms), *that in the latter times* (the days in which we now live) *some shall depart from the Faith* (from the Cross), *giving heed to seducing spirits, and doctrines of devils"* (I Tim. 4:1).

As well, this great apostasy, which means a falling away from Truth, and more particularly, from *"the Truth,"* which refers to the great Salvation Message of the Cross of Christ, is already upon us, and is growing in intensity. It is the apostasy of the last day, the last age, in fact, the last days of the Church. Jesus personally predicted this concerning His warning to the Church of Laodicea.

NOTES

His exact Words were, *"I know thy works, that thou art neither cold nor hot: I would thou wert cold or hot.*

*"So then because thou art lukewarm, and neither cold nor hot, I will spew thee out of My mouth.*

*"Because thou sayest, I am rich, and increased with goods, and have need of nothing; and knowest not that thou art wretched, and miserable, and poor, and blind, and naked"* (Rev. 3:14-17).

This describes the present Church perfectly.

But again, I warn the Reader, that this great iniquity of which is spoken here, this falling away from *"the Truth,"* concerns itself with a specific act. That specific act is the departure from the Cross of Christ to other things, which characterizes the present Church.

Many in the modern Church have abandoned the Biblical way of Salvation and Victory over sin, by embracing humanistic psychology. One cannot have it both ways: Either Christ paid the price at Calvary's Cross, there addressing Himself to every single solitary sin and bondage, and, therefore, is able to deliver us (Gal. 1:4), or else He didn't, and we need to resort to Freud. One cannot have it both ways, inasmuch as each cancels out the other.

It is tragic, but the Leadership of the two largest Pentecostal Denominations in the world, the Assemblies of God and the Church of God, have both opted in no uncertain terms for the psychological way. Of course, it is my prayer that such will change; however, as far as I can see, the situation has not improved but has actually worsened in the decade of the 1990's.

Most reading these words may not consider this to be very significant; however, if anyone would think such a thing it only shows that they little know their Bibles or for that matter, the rudiments of humanistic psychology.

You're now reading why the Leadership of these Denominations, plus others we haven't named, so strongly resent Jimmy Swaggart. They may claim other things, but the fact is they do not desire anyone to call attention to the error and gross error at that, of their particular course and direction. The Truth is, they have tried everything in their power to silence my voice, but by the Grace of God they have not been successful. I realize that most think it is other things; however, those *"other things"* as distasteful as they may have been, were only an excuse not the actual reason. I have given you the reason.

The Leadership of these Denominations, at least in the United States and Canada, plus most all other institutionalized religion as well as the independent variety, have departed from the Cross of Christ, thereby opting for the psychological way or whatever. But irrespective as to what way it might be, if the Cross is forsaken, is diminished, is not held up as the answer to the ills of man, whatever other way that has been chosen that way is the way of destruction. The Scripture plainly says, *"There is a way which seemeth right unto a man, but the end thereof are the ways of death"* (Prov. 14:12).

THE TRUE CHURCH

This is the reason I keep using the phrase *"the True Church!"* To be sure, there is an apostate Church, which is far larger than the True Church and in fact, always has been. In fact, the line is not easily drawn between these two Churches, with both at times being intermingled. In other words, there are Godly Preachers and people in the Denominations I've just mentioned, etc. Nevertheless, I personally feel that the Holy Spirit is drawing a line between the two, and that line is the Cross of Christ. In fact, and even as we've already stated, that has always been the line between the true and the false. But I feel that the Holy Spirit is going to make that line more and more obvious. I believe as well, that this Ministry will have a part in being used by the Lord in the drawing or the marking out of this line, i.e., *"the Cross of Christ!"*

The Scripture does teach a great harvest of souls in the last days I believe, but it doesn't actually teach a Revival, at least on a wholesale scale. Revival as the Reader knows, speaks of the Church coming back to the Cross. While many will do this, for the Lord still has many who haven't bowed the knee to Baal, the majority in fact will not embrace the Cross of Christ, but will rather go in other directions.

NOTES

This means that this present apostasy which characterizes the modern Church is not going to diminish, but rather deepen. It is the preparation for the Antichrist.

Y2K

It is Sunday Morning about 6 a.m., December, 1999 as I dictate these notes; however, it will be in the new Millennium when you read them.

The sheer fact that God has done something powerful and wonderful regarding Salvation every two Millenniums or one Millennium, should at this time give us pause for reflection, especially considering that we're entering the seventh Millennium of the creation of man.

Two Millenniums after the Fall, God called Abraham out of Ur of the Chaldees, fleshing out the great Salvation Message, by explaining to him Justification by Faith (Gen. 15:6). One Millennium, or about a thousand years later, God took another step forward in this great Revelation, by telling David that it would be through his family that the Redeemer would come (II Sam. Chpt. 7). One Millennium later, Jesus came. The two Millenniums which followed, which brings us up to this present hour, have been the age of the Church. If God holds to His pattern, which I know that He shall, another great event is about to take place, and that great event is the close of the Church Age, which is the Rapture.

Considering these things, one would think that Preachers would be extolling the Church to get ready for the Rapture, or at least to get closer to God. But instead what message has been proclaimed as it regards this new Millennium?

People are being told to stock up on water, certain types of food, to draw their money out of the banks, etc. In other words, there has been almost nothing said as it regards the things of which I speak, but rather this foolishness which I have just mentioned. That should tell you the Reader, as to what condition the modern Church now finds itself. In other words, the apostasy has already set in, and in fact is obvious to all, except the blind!

Two things are about to be revealed:

1. The first will be the Revelation of Jesus Christ to His Church, at least to those who are ready, which we refer to as the Rapture (I Thess. 4:13-18).

2. The Antichrist will then be revealed, which Paul is graphically describing here.

So the great question must be asked, as to which Revelation you are anticipating.

In Truth, many in the modern Church are denying both, claiming that the world is getting better and better, and that Christianity will ultimately come to terms with the other religions of the world, with all embracing each other, etc. It doesn't take much spirituality to see through that foolishness; however, such is regrettably believed by many.

However, as is overly obvious, and as stated, Paul is proclaiming two Revelations in this Chapter. How many presently are actually anticipating the Revelation of Christ to His Church in the Rapture? Of course, the Lord Alone knows the answer to that question. But if indications are reliable, not many presently are looking for that particular Revelation. And as well, most in the modern Church have little interest in the Revelation of the second factor as well. Most are so caught up with the present times, so lulled to sleep by the spirit of the world, or so geared toward the *"get rich gospel,"* that they have little interest in any Rapture or Endtime events in any fashion. In other words, most modern Christians are simply uninterested in the things of which we speak here. Thank God a few are, but that few is small in number.

THE SPIRIT OF HIS MOUTH

The phrase, *"Whom the Lord shall consume with the Spirit of His Mouth,"* should be translated *"the Breath of His Mouth."*

The Prophet Isaiah said, *"He shall smite the earth with the rod of His Mouth, and with the Breath of His Lips shall He slay the wicked"* (Isa. 11:4).

This refers to what will go out of His Mouth at that time, or which He speaks. In Revelation 1:16; 19:15, 21, it is said of the Redeemer that *"a sharp twoedged sword goeth out of His Mouth."* It means that what He speaks is like a sharp sword. It will cut deep; it will lay open the heart; it will destroy his enemies.

NOTES

Of course, the One referred to here, is the Lord Jesus Christ. He is the One Who spoke creation into existence, which is proclaimed in the First Chapter of Genesis, by the Scripture some ten times saying *"and God said"* (Gen. 1:3, 6, 9, 11, 14, 20, 24, 26, 28-29).

The day of sin and rebellion against God is over. Jesus will come back, speaking the great Word which will bring to bear all of His Power against the Antichrist and his armies and Satan in general. The Scripture says, *"A fiery stream issued and came forth from before Him: thousand thousands ministered unto Him, and ten thousand times ten thousand stood before Him: the Judgment was set, and the Books were opened.*

*"I beheld then because of the voice of the great words which the horn* (Antichrist) *spake: I beheld even till the Beast was slain, and his body destroyed, and given to the burning flame"* (Dan. 7:10-11).

We're speaking here of power beyond the concept of the mind of man. Ezekiel describes the Second Coming:

*"And I will plead against him* (the Antichrist) *with pestilence and with blood; and I will rain upon him, and upon his bands, and upon the many people that are with him, an overflowing rain, and great hailstones, fire, and brimstone.*

*"Thus will I magnify Myself, and sanctify Myself; and I will be known in the eyes of many nations, and they shall know that I am the Lord"* (Ezek. 38:22-23).

THE BRIGHTNESS OF HIS COMING

The phrase, *"And shall destroy with the brightness of His Coming,"* tells us that the Second Coming will not be a silent or secret affair, but in fact, will be the most dramatic event in human history, and actually a thousand times over.

Jesus foretold this in Matthew, Chapter 24. He said, *"Wherefore if they shall say unto you, behold, He is in the desert* (speaking of Christ)*; go not forth: behold, He is in the secret chambers; believe it not"* (Mat. 24:26).

In effect, He is saying that the Second Coming is going to be done in such a manner that the world will know beyond the shadow of a doubt, that it is Christ. In other words, Jesus is saying, that when He actually does come

NOTES

back the Second Time, it will be with such power and glory, such wonder and splendor, such display of His Person, that no one in the world will have any doubt as to Who He is, or what has happened. He said:

*"For as the lightning cometh out of the east, and shineth even unto the west; so shall also the Coming of the Son of Man be"* (Mat. 24:27).

He then said, *"Immediately after the tribulation of those days shall the Sun be darkened, and the Moon shall not give her light, and the Stars shall fall from heaven, and the powers of the heavens shall be shaken:*

*"And then shall appear the sign of the Son of Man in Heaven: and then shall all the tribes of the earth mourn, and they shall see the Son of Man coming in the clouds of Heaven with power and great glory"* (Mat. 24:29-30).

This doesn't necessarily mean that the Sun or the Moon will actually burn out, but that His Coming will be with such brightness, splendor, and magnificence, that these planetary bodies will seem insignificant as it regards the giving of their light.

It should be understood, that when the Second Coming takes place, with Christ actually coming down to Jerusalem, and more particularly, the Mount of Olives (Acts 1:9-11), part of the world will be in the night hours with the other part in the daylight hours; however, it will make no difference at that time, for the brightness of His Coming will illuminate the entirety of the heavens, and, therefore, the entirety of the Earth.

As well, His Coming will be accompanied by the greatest display of *"shooting stars,"* that the heavens have ever seen. If it can be imagined as to the largest fireworks display that one has ever seen, and then magnify that a million times, or even a billion times over, one could get some comprehension of what's going to happen at that time.

In fact, this will be a display of joy by the creation, of the Lord's return, with the overthrowing of all sin and shame. Paul spoke of this when he said, *"For we know that the whole creation groaneth and travaileth in pain together until now,"* in other words, waiting for this coming event (Rom. 8:22).

The King is returning, and above that, the *"King of kings, and Lord of lords,"* even as John describes in Revelation, Chapter 19. And as well, every Saint of God who has ever lived, even beginning with Abel, up unto that present time will be with Him. John said, *"And the armies* (Saints of God) *which were in Heaven followed Him upon white horses, clothed in fine linen, white and clean"* (Rev. 19:14).

It is only the Saints of God who are described as wearing such. It pertains to Righteousness, even the Righteousness of Christ, which was purchased with His Own, Precious Blood. So once again, even at the Second Coming, we come back to the Cross. In fact, the Cross will never be forgotten, always held up by God as the means of man's Redemption. Even in the final Chapter of Revelation which describes the coming perfect Earth and perfect age, which incidently will last forever, the Scripture says, *"And there shall be no more curse: but the Throne of God and of the Lamb shall be in it; and His servants shall serve Him:*

*"And they shall see His Face; and His Name shall be in their foreheads.*

*"And there shall be no night there; and they need no candle, neither light of the Sun; for the Lord God giveth them Light: and they shall reign forever and ever"* (Rev. 22:3-5).

The designation *"Lamb"* is used here, signifying that Jesus will be thought of as such forever and forever, because He is the One Who by His Sacrificial, Atoning Death on the Cross of Calvary, satisfied and lifted the terrible curse brought on by sin. Paul said, *"Christ hath redeemed us from the curse of the Law, being made a curse for us . . . That the Blessing of Abraham might come on the Gentiles, through Jesus Christ* (through what He did)*; that we might receive the Promise of the Spirit through Faith"* (Gal. 3:13-14).

(9) "EVEN HIM, WHOSE COMING IS AFTER THE WORKING OF SATAN WITH ALL POWER AND SIGNS AND LYING WONDERS,"

Now the Spirit through Paul brings us back to the advent of the Antichrist, and the manner in which he will make his great rise to power. As should be obvious, his rise will be moreso religious than anything else, even as Revelation 6:1-2 bears out.

## THE ANTICHRIST

The short phrase, *"Even him,"* reverts back to *"that Wicked,"* i.e., *"the Antichrist,"* after speaking about the Coming of Christ.

As should be overly obvious in the Scripture, the Antichrist is a man. He is not a spirit, even though he will be possessed by many demon spirits. As well, this is not a system, even though he will bring about a system of evil and wickedness such as the world has never known before. As well, the Antichrist will not be a government as some teach, even though he will seek to subvert all government on Earth, attempting to bring it all under himself.

To the extent as to who he is, and what he will do, such cannot be now known, even as we've already addressed, until the Church, the great restrainer of evil, has been taken out of the world. As an example, let's look at modern day Israel.

America in a sense has pledged protection for the tiny State of Israel, even though there is no formal agreement. To protect our oil interests thereby placating the Arabs, the United States has no formal agreement of protection with Israel. But yet, America has stood solidly behind this tiny nation, doing so in a de facto sort of way. This nation has taken this course despite the fact that there are powerful factors in this country who are bitterly opposed to Israel. The reason this Government does this, is because of the tens of millions of Born-Again Christians in this nation. Knowing and understanding the Bible, true Christians understand the place of Israel in Bible Prophecy.

In 1987, I received word from someone in Washington (I don't remember who), stating that I might be called to testify before Congress as to why the United States should continue to protect Israel, etc. That call did not come, with the hearings canceled, or else they were held and I was out of the country in Crusades, therefore, unable to attend. I don't remember which happened, but I think it was one or the other. Nevertheless, that gives you a picture of this of which I speak.

Whenever all true Christians are taken out of this nation, and every other nation in the world for that matter, Israel will be left without a friend. Even though she does not quite understand such at present, her only real friends today are those who truly follow Jesus Christ. It is ironical, the Prophecy of Noah so long, long ago has come to pass in totality.

NOTES

He said in that short Prophecy, *"Blessed be the Lord God of Shem* (the son of Noah from whom the Jews sprang)*; and Canaan shall be his servant* (this was another son of Noah whose lineage occupied Canaan, and who ultimately served Israel)."

Noah went on to say, *"God shall enlarge Japheth* (another son of Noah, from whom sprang the Europeans, i.e., *'occupants of the United States, plus some of the yellow race.'* Their blessings are here predicted, which have totally come to pass)*, and he* (Japheth) *shall dwell in the tents of Shem* (meaning that the great Blessing promised to Israel would be forfeited due to their rejection of the Blessing, the Lord Jesus Christ, but Who would be embraced by the descendants of Japheth, therefore, *'dwelling in the tents of Shem,'* which Shem alone should have enjoyed)." However, it didn't say that those tents would be destroyed, but only that the descendants of Japheth would occupy that tent of Blessing with Shem. In fact, the Blessing will ultimately come back to Shem, even as the Prophets of old predicted, and Paul mentioned in Romans, Chapter 11 (Gen. 9:25-27).

The Antichrist will attempt to destroy that *"tent,"* but he will not be successful, even as all those before him were not successful. In fact, history is replete with efforts of evil men to destroy Israel, the latest being the worst of all, the terrible Holocaust under demon possessed Hitler. But yet, the next Holocaust which is shortly to come, and there is definitely going to be one more, will be worse even than that attempted by the Nazis.

## AFTER THE WORKING OF SATAN

The phrase, *"Whose coming is after the working of Satan,"* means that Satan is his sponsor, in fact, investing more into this man, than he has ever invested in any other. This will be Satan's swan song, his final effort, actually his greatest effort.

The word *"coming"* used here to describe him, is in the Greek, *"parousia,"* even the same as the word *"coming"* as it describes the Second Coming of the Lord in Verse 8. Having assured his readers of the Lawless One's doom, Paul now resumes direct description of him. The parallels with the Person and Work of Christ are apparent and intentional.

The Lawless One also has his *"parousia,"* even as the Lord of Glory will have His *"Parousia."*

This *"coming"* at the first, even as we have already stated, will be peaceful. John mentions him as having a bow, which means to be armed for war, but having no arrows (Rev. 6:2). In fact, Daniel prophesied that *"by peace* (he) *shall destroy many,"* meaning, that he will lull the world to sleep and especially Israel, as to his true intentions, claiming peace while all the time preparing for war (Dan. 9:25).

This *"coming"* of the Antichrist, as should be overly obvious, is something that has been foretold for at least 3,500 years, that is if the Ninety-first Psalm was actually written by Moses, as many believe it was (Ps. 91:13-15). Of course, in the Mind of God this has always been known.

*"The working of Satan"* refers to *"the energy of Satan"*; that is, the energetic or efficient operation of Satan.

The word rendered *"after,"* does not here refer to time, but is a preposition, meaning *"according to, in conformity with."*

The system over which the Antichrist presides is originated by Satan, and sustained by those things which he alone can perform.

On the word *"Satan,"* the idea is, that it will be under the direction and control of this great enemy of God, and that the things on which it will rely for support can be traced to his agency. In all the pretended miracles to which it will appeal, there would be nothing which Satan could not accomplish.

As is known and understood, Satan is the archenemy of God, once the mighty Angel Lucifer, originally created by God, who served God in Righteousness and Holiness for an undetermined period of time. In fact, there is some evidence, that he was the most beautiful, the most wise, and the most powerful Angel ever created by God, so powerful in fact, that when he fell, he drew away one third of the angels with him in his rebellion. When this rebellion occurred, we are not told, but we definitely know that it occurred before the creation of man. Actually, the great chaos stipulated between Genesis 1:1 and 1:2, is no doubt the time of this terrible origination of evil. That conflict has raged until now, filling the Earth with graves, bringing untold misery, heartache, and sorrow. To be sure, that day is soon over!

NOTES

The Evil One (Satan) is only a few short years from being locked in the Bottomless Pit, where he will remain until loosed for a short period of time, and then will be consigned to the Lake of Fire forever and forever (Rev. Chpt. 20).

SATAN AND THE WORLD

These things of which we speak, the world cannot see. In fact, much of the world doesn't even believe there is one called Satan, but yet, they are at a loss as to properly defining the meaning of the word *"evil."*

All who are unsaved are spiritually dead, and, consequently, cannot understand these things of which we speak. So, the far greater majority do not believe there is a fallen angel by the name of *"Satan,"* who heads up this kingdom of darkness, despite the fact, that his handiwork of death and destruction is erupting all around us and constantly.

POWER, SIGNS, AND LYING WONDERS

The phrase, *"With all power and signs and lying wonders,"* proclaims the fact that his rise to power, at least in the beginning, will be moreso religious than anything else. This will be necessary for many reasons, but above all to deceive Israel, which he will grandly do.

Israel will actually think he is the Messiah, which he wants them to think, and which he at the outset will declare himself to be. The Truth is, he hates God and especially, the Lord Jesus Christ, and in the midst of his seven year reign, will show himself as to what he really is. At that time, he will attack Israel, breaking his covenant with them, which will be the first defeat Israel has suffered since becoming a nation again in 1948.

The three following nouns which also characterized Christ's Ministry, will characterize the ministry of this Evil One as well, at least in some ways: *"power"* is the suggestion of a supernatural force. *"Signs"* attests to miracles pointing beyond themselves, in other words, to prove a point. *"Wonders"* refers to *"marvels."* As stated, the parallels with the Person and Work of Christ are apparent and intentional.

NOTES

However, the word *"lying"* in the Greek actually should be before all three words — *"lying power," "lying signs"* and *"lying wonders!"*

However, the Reader must understand, that the word *"lying"* as used here, does not necessarily mean that these things are mere trickery. It rather means that the origination of these things is from the great liar himself, Satan, and designed to deceive, even as the next Verse proclaims. Actually, it will be the *"False Prophet"* who will perform these miracles (Rev. 13:11-18).

By claiming to be the Messiah of Israel, the Antichrist even at the outset will claim deity, but at the mid-point of that time period, he will no longer declare himself to be the Messiah of God, but actually God in his own right. In other words, he truly hates God and His Son, the Lord Jesus Christ, and every other pretended deity for that matter, setting himself up solely as *"God!"*

While *"power, signs, and wonders"* are Biblical, that is if carried out in the realm of the Name of Jesus, i.e., *"Righteousness,"* they are to never serve as the cause of foundation of Faith. The foundation of Faith must ever be the Word of God, i.e., *"the Atonement, the Finished Work of Christ."* That's why Jesus related the incident of the rich man in Hell pleading with Abraham to send Lazarus from the dead back to the Earth, in order to testify to his five brothers.

*"Abraham saith unto him, they have Moses and the Prophets; let them hear them.*

*"And he said, Nay, Father Abraham: but if one went unto them from the dead, they will repent.*

*"And He said unto him, if they hear not Moses and the Prophets, neither will they be persuaded, though one rose from the dead"* (Lk. 16:27-31).

All of us want the *"power, signs, and wonders,"* that is, if they are truly from God, but the object of our Faith must never be these things, for Satan can definitely duplicate them as portrayed here, but rather our Faith must ever be in the Cross of Christ.

## THE LAST DAYS

In this terrible apostasy which has even now begun to come upon the Church, the way is being prepared for the advent of the Antichrist, and that within the Church, i.e., *"the Apostate Church."* If one is to notice, this thrust which has already begun, is centered up moreso in those who claim to be Baptized with the Holy Spirit, than anyone else. In fact, many of these people may have actually been saved and Baptized with the Holy Spirit at one time, but have since forsaken the Truth, and are now being used by Satan, but in ways that so closely resemble the Lord, that it is difficult for Believers to ascertain that what is being done is actually real or not!

Satan as a *"roaring lion"* is very dangerous (I Pet. 5:8); as a wolf in sheep's clothing, he is even more dangerous (Mat. 7:15-20). But as an *"angel of light,"* he is the most dangerous of all (II Cor. 11:14). That's how the Antichrist and the False Prophet will make their debut at the beginning, and it is the same presently with those who claim to be performing miracles, but to those who truly know the Word of God, it is obvious that whatever is being done is not Scriptural, therefore, not of God!

## LYING WONDERS

I am thinking now of a particular so-called Ministry, which is greatly influencing the modern Church, and I especially speak of the Pentecostal and Charismatic varieties.

The earmarks of a true, Biblical Ministry do not characterize themselves in this effort; therefore, despite the fact of it looking and sounding so much like God, I must come to the conclusion that it is not of God.

Jesus plainly said, *"Ye shall know them by their fruits"* (Mat. 7:20). He spoke of *"good fruit"* and He also spoke of *"bad fruit."*

For instance, in this particular Ministry of which I speak, despite all the great claims of it being of God, there is almost no one being saved in these meetings. In fact, to my knowledge, very little effort, if any, is even made for people to come to Christ. In other words, that is given little priority, if any priority at all.

Also, there are precious few, if any, Baptized with the Holy Spirit. In fact, the Word of God is preached almost not at all, which means the pattern laid down in the Book of Acts is totally ignored.

The entirety of the effort, and I do not believe I exaggerate when I use the word *"entirety,"* is made up of *"power, signs, and wonders."* Should we not say, *"lying power, lying signs, and lying wonders!"* The people come to see the show, and they are not disappointed! That's what they want, so that's what they get!

As I've said in earlier Commentary, the Church *"has"* what the Church *"is!"*

All types of *"healings"* and *"miracles"* are claimed in abundance, even to the raising of the dead. But the Truth is, these healings cannot be found, at least healings which can be substantiated.

As well, the association of this particular Ministry of which I speak, and which there are many imitators, with a certain so-called Christian Television Network, further emphasizes that of which I speak. It is my personal belief that this Network is doing more to hurt the true Work of God than anything else in the world today. It is fastly shoving the Church, or greatly helping to do so, toward spiritual oblivion. In fact, this certain Ministry in question, is so intertwined with this Network, that one upholds the other. My contention is, that one cannot be of God and at the same time, function in this capacity.

I do not mean to speak negatively of all those who minister over that Network, unless in fact, they are not allowed to preach what they know they ought to preach. But I do greatly oppose those who seek to perpetuate this gargantuan evil, and a gargantuan evil it is!

I believe that any Preacher should proclaim the Word of God wherever the door is opened; however, if restrictions are placed upon that presentation, then it should be obvious that the Message is compromised.

Having said that, I have come to the place that I believe that anyone who ministers over that Network, has already compromised their Message, or they wouldn't be there to begin with.

At this point, some would claim that I should name these individuals or this Network, etc. Actually, it's not the people who I oppose, but rather that which is being done. For the Believer who reads these words to know of particular individuals is of little consequence. The idea is, that you recognize the false message which is being presented, whoever or whatever the bearer of that message!

NOTES

Again I warn the Reader, that we're living in the last of the last days. What we're speaking of here is serious, in fact, very serious! I am very sorry if some people do not like what I say, or if they greatly oppose my person. I do not enjoy that; however, the plaudits of the people are not my business, but rather to hear from Heaven and to deliver that which I have heard. In Truth, I am a *"watchman,"* exactly as every Preacher ought to be a *"watchman"* (Isa. 21:11; Ezek. 3:17; 33:7).

I believe in miracles! I believe that God still performs miracles today. In fact, I believe that He is constantly performing miracles on our behalf, but yet, and as stated, this must never be the criteria or foundation of our Faith, but rather the Word of God.

Let's see what the Word actually does say about *"signs, wonders, and miracles."*

### MIRACLES IN THE BIBLE

Scripture never relates miracles hesitantly. There have been many miracles worked in the world by God down through the centuries, as should be obvious. Consequently, it is fascinating to discover the situation in which these particular miracles were worked, and what they are intended to teach us.

Again I want to emphasize, I believe that God is a God of miracles, that He still performs miracles today, and in fact, that He is performing miracles constantly on our behalf, even though at times, we may not be aware of all the things which are being done.

### A PERSONAL EXAMPLE

Sometime back in writing the notes for one of the Commentaries, and if I remember correctly, it was one of the Gospels, the Spirit of the Lord I believe, spoke to my heart respecting this particular subject.

Any person who is truly Born-Again, and who truly has a relationship with Christ, and who truly seeks His Face, which refers to His leading and guidance, definitely has the Lord working for him constantly.

As the Lord spoke to me that morning, He said, I believe, *"Every time you petition*

*Me for certain situations, I always have to perform a number of miracles in order for this thing to be brought about. You may not see what is being done, nor may you have any knowledge of what is being done; nevertheless, every answer to prayer includes miracles in one fashion or the other, whether observed or not!"*

From that moment, I have looked at *"miracles"* in an entirely different light, and I pray that you will as well.

## THE OLD TESTAMENT

Three different Hebrew words are closely associated with miracles. *"Pala"* is used 70 times in the Old Testament, and means *"to be marvelous or wonderful."* The root usually refers to God's acts, either in shaping the universe or acting in history on behalf of His people. The word focuses on people's reaction when they are confronted by a miracle. The Believer sees the Power of God, as God invades time and space to do something wonderful, in fact, too wonderful for humans to duplicate.

Another Hebrew word *"Mopet"* occurs some 36 times and also means *"wonder," "miracle"* or *"sign."* It is used to recall God's acts in Egypt (Ex. 4:21; 7:3, 9) and the punishments and provision that testified to His perpetual care of Israel throughout her history (Deut. 6:22; 7:19-24).

Another Hebrew word *"ot"* means *"sign."* Of all the related Hebrew words, it has the widest range of meaning, but in almost all of its approximately 80 occurrences it clearly means *"miraculous sign."* Each plague inflicted on Egypt is described as an *"ot,"* as are the continuing acts of God for Israel in their travels (Deut. 4:34; II Ki. 20:9; Isa. 38:7).

## THE MESSAGE OF MIRACLES

As the Hebrew word *"pala"* indicates, miracles are intended to have an impact on the observer. They create a sense of awe and wonder, a sense of the inescapability of God as an active force within the world of time and space.

We gain insight into the impact of miracles by noting four results of the ten plagues in Egypt. First, the plagues focused Israel's Faith; for from that time on, God was identified with these acts performed on behalf of His people (Ex. 6:7). God exercised His Power to fulfill His ancient Covenant Promises to the children of Abraham, which He always does respecting anything He has ever promised.

Two other purposes are seen in the fact that it would be through the plagues that the Egyptians not only would be confronted with the knowledge of Who Jehovah is, but also would allow Israel to leave Egypt (Ex. 7:5).

## LORD

Fourth, the plagues served as a judgment on the gods of Egypt (Ex. 12:12). The powerlessness of human religious invention would be displayed as the Living God exercised His Power.

Each of these purposes is clearly linked with God's Revelation of His Nature. The false images of Believer and unbeliever alike are shattered as God steps from the mysterious beyond to enter our here and now. The God of miracles must be responded to and not ignored, for the God of Scripture is no Being of tenuous spirituality Whose influence is limited to a mystic, immaterial setting.

For Believers, this affirmation of God's reality and power is comforting, and the Psalms constantly call on worshippers to remember and tell of His Works. As David expressed it, *"Tell of all His wonderful acts.*

*"Remember the wonders He has done, His miracles"* and *"Declare . . . His marvelous deeds among all people"* (I Chron. 16:9, 12, 24). In other words, God can be counted on by His people.

## MIRACLES IN THE NEW TESTAMENT

A number of Greek words are associated with New Testament miracles. Each is linked with acts that clearly violated what the people of the New Testament understood of natural law. Each produced wonder and the compelling conviction that the supernatural had been confronted.

The Greek word *"Dynamis"* is often translated *"miracle."* It is from a root meaning *"power"* and emphasizes the miracle as a spontaneous expression of God's elemental power.

NOTES

Another Greek word *"Semeion"* used some 77 times in the New Testament, indicates *"sign."* Its basic meaning is that of an authenticating mark or token. When it refers to a miraculous sign (Jn. 2:11; Acts 4:16, 22; I Cor. 1:22), it emphasizes the authenticating aspect of the miracle as an indication that supernatural power is involved.

*"Teras"* is another Greek word used some 16 times in the New Testament, but is used only in the phrase *"signs and wonders."*

Another Greek word *"ergon"* is used, and clearly means *"miracle,"* but sometimes is translated *"work"* (Jn. 7:3; 10:25, 32).

AMAZING

The New Testament, particularly the Gospels, describes many miracles. These were performed by Jesus or by His followers. They are distinctive in several ways.

First, New Testament miracles are never associated with spells or incantations. Jesus simply spoke or gestured, and the work (miracle) was done. The power was in Jesus, not in a formula for magical control of the supernatural.

Second, the miracles of Christ were never performed to punish. Rather, Jesus' miracles were performed to rescue human beings from physical and spiritual forces that bound them. The Gospel associated with Jesus is truly good news for humanity.

Third, in every way the miracles provide testimony to Jesus' supernatural power and authority, and they witnessed to His ultimate victory. The Kingdom over which He rules will come at last, for neither hunger, sickness, madness, death, nor demon can stand against Jesus. All fall back before Him. Because Jesus will return, the ultimate fate of all of man's enemies is sealed.

THE INTENDED MESSAGE

The essential message of miracles is sketched above. God has shown us His power and has proved that His power will be used to benefit us. We can trust Jesus fully. He is able, and He wills only our good.

But there was also a perhaps surprising contemporary Message to be found in Miracles. Jesus was authenticated to follower and enemy alike as God's Perfect Man. Yet the reaction of each group was different.

NOTES

His Disciples saw in the miracles Jesus' Glory, and they *"put their Faith in Him"* (Jn. 2:11). But His enemies did not do so.

Both Nicodemus (Jn. 3:2) and the man born blind (Jn. 9:33) recognize and state that God must be enabling Jesus to do miracles, but the Pharisees did not see and neither would they admit this to be the case (Mat. 12:24; Jn. 9:34). This is reminiscent of Pharaoh; he was evidently convinced but not converted by the plagues on Egypt (Ex. 12:31).

The New Testament speaks of a future burst of apparent miracles. I speak now of the Passage of our study, this Second Chapter of II Thessalonians. As history nears its end, God's final enemy will appear with *"all kinds of counterfeit miracles, signs, and wonders."* These will deceive *"those who are perishing,"* not those whose Faith is anchored rather in the *"Living and Written Word of God."*

THE LESSON TO BE LEARNED

It is hardly surprising that the Bible's stories of miracles do not produce Faith today in those who are unwilling to accept Scripture's testimony about Jesus. It is Faith in the Word, and more particularly, the Word as it relates to the Finished Work of Christ, which brings us to Scripture's Vision of God, as One Who towers above the *"natural law."* In other words, the unconverted cannot rise above that natural law simply because they do not know God.

When God is seen as He really is, which can only be done by Believers, miracles, while they produce praise and wonder, hardly seems strange at all. We believe in a God who performs miracles; consequently, we expect miracles, and are not surprised when they happen. Because as the little chorus says, *"That's the kind of God that I serve!"*

As well, we must not allow the false, in other words, the counterfeit, to turn our eyes away from spiritual reality, and that reality is, God is a God of might and miracles.

In fact, the Bible opens with miracles, continues with miracles, and presents the God of miracles, at least for those who will believe (Mk. 9:23).

(10 "AND WITH ALL DECEIVABLENESS OF UNRIGHTEOUSNESS IN THEM THAT

PERISH; BECAUSE THEY RECEIVED NOT THE LOVE OF THE TRUTH, THAT THEY MIGHT BE SAVED."

The motivation of the Lawless One is to deceive. It is the nature of unrighteousness to palm itself off as Righteousness. This means that *"those who are perishing"* will be particularly vulnerable to trickery. Not only will they confuse unrighteousness with Righteousness; they will also attribute Deity to this Lawless One.

As we shall see, their blindness is a self-imposed blindness because of a prior refusal to *"love the Truth and so be saved."* Such people lack a positive committal to the Gospel. And to be sure, this is just as blamable as indifference or even antagonism toward the Truth. The right choice always brings people Salvation and deliverance; however, as deception deepens in the Church presently, such only serves to pave the way for the devices of the Lawless One. And this is what I want the Reader to understand:

The great deception which the Antichrist will foster off on the entirety of the world but especially the Jews, claiming to be the Messiah, which at first Israel will accept, is already being prepared by the spirit of deception even at this present time.

## DECEPTION

The phrase, *"And with all deceivableness of unrighteousness in them that perish,"* refers to the fact that *"all lying powers and lying signs and lying wonders,"* will be used to deceive the world.

The idea here isn't that millions will perish because they believe the Antichrist, but rather, that they have forsaken the Truth, and inasmuch as they have charted this course of their own volition, the Lord will allow the Evil One to produce results which will accelerate the slide downward; however, it must be remembered that the *"perishing"* of these hundreds of millions, even as it has always been in the past and even now at the present, is because of a decision these particular individuals have already made. The idea is:

For those who will Righteousness, God sees to the matter that Righteousness comes to the person (Mat. 5:6). But for those who

NOTES

will or desire unrighteousness, the Lord wills such to them.

That's the reason we have repeatedly stated that *"the Church has what the Church is!"*

## THE DECEPTION OF UNRIGHTEOUSNESS

All sin, i.e., *"unrighteousness,"* has and contains a form of deception. In other words, the very fact of sin is deception itself. The whole thing is deception, meant and intended to deceive the unwary one. But the Truth is, man cannot be deceived, unless man desires to be deceived. In other words, and as we've already stated, the individual purposely and with design, wills in his heart to go in a direction that is not of God. When this happens, whether it is with the unbeliever or the so-called Believer, in effect one might say, God will honor their desire. He will permit things to happen that accelerates their slide downward, which only increases the deception, and because this is what they want and desire.

It must be remembered here, that even though this deception in the coming Great Tribulation, and especially the first half, will engulf the entirety of the world in some measure, that in reality, it is a religious deception. However, in one sense, all deception is spiritual in one way or the other, whether the person is an unbeliever or a Believer.

The Church presently is being prepared for one of two things:

1. For those who want and desire the True Ways of God, a true relationship with the Lord, the glory, Grace, and power of God, in other words, for the Lord to rule their lives, the Holy Spirit is preparing such individuals in the Church for a greater moving and operation of the Holy Spirit. Unfortunately, that number is few.

2. A great part of the Church doesn't want to live and abide by the Word of God. In other words, the Word is not their criteria, but rather other things. They want their sin and Salvation at the same time. They are deceived, and in Truth, their deception is becoming deeper with each passing day.

Inasmuch as that is what they want, that is what they will get, and in fact is what they are getting presently.

In the late 1980's the Church in glaring visibility in effect stated that they did not want the Salvation of souls, the deliverance of men and women from the bondages of darkness, the Baptism with the Holy Spirit, but rather something else. They have received that *"something else!"*

Consequently, the Church presently runs after fads and manifestations, which claim to be of the Spirit, but most of the time are totally of the flesh, i.e., *"the Devil."* As a result, people are *"barking like dogs"* and claiming this to be a Work of the Spirit, while others *"roar like lions,"* claiming the same thing accordingly. Others *"laugh"* for protracted periods of time, claiming this to be a Work of the Spirit, when the Truth is, most in the modern Church have absolutely no idea as to what is truly of the Spirit and what isn't! At the present, untold thousands are going to huge meetings to *"see the show!"*

It seems to make no difference to these people that precious few people are saved if any, that precious few are Baptized with the Holy Spirit, if any, that precious few are truly delivered from the terrible bondages of darkness, if any, that precious few people are truly healed, if any, despite the wild claims! They just want to see another rabbit pulled out of the hat, all cloaked in a claim of the moving and operation of the Holy Spirit.

It's bad enough to lie, but it's worse yet to attempt to make the Holy Spirit a part of such a lie. Such is extremely dangerous, but yet, those deceived have no knowledge that their slow drift with the current is steadily gathering speed, with the falls just ahead!

This Verse is actually speaking of the energizing by Satan of *"counterfeit miracles"* to be performed by the Antichrist. The Greek word for *"deceivableness"* is *"apate."* This means that the miracles will be real; their purpose will be to deceive the observer.

## THE POWERS OF SUGGESTION OR THE POWERS OF DARKNESS?

In the last few months (as I dictate these notes) I have received a number of letters plus firsthand reports, concerning a particular so-called Evangelist, and the proposed *"miracles"* in his meetings, or proposed demonstrations of the power of God, etc. Almost all of these reports were the same.

NOTES

They basically stated that what was being done was not merely the power of suggestion, but rather something else altogether. They declared that it definitely was not God, but at the same time, power was definitely being exhibited in some fashion. In other words, the demonstrations were not counterfeit, but rather real, actually meant by Satan to deceive the people. The power being demonstrated belonged to him and not to God. And yet, the largest coliseums in the nation are packed to capacity with those who claim to be saved and baptized with the Holy Spirit, and for the most part, believing that all that is being done is of God.

Consequently, the question must be asked as to the spiritual condition of all of these thousands of people. How can so many actually be deceived, if in fact, these demonstrations actually aren't of God?

In fact, some few aren't deceived, and they correctly discern the spirits for what they actually are, i.e., *"spirits of darkness!"* However, that number is few.

If in fact this of which we speak actually is not of God, what will happen to the people who believe that it is?

Anyone who believes that something is of God when it actually isn't, or conversely, who believes that something isn't of God when it actually is, only shows the true state of their heart. As previously stated, they could not be deceived if their hearts were truly right with God.

Does this mean they aren't saved?

To be frank, most of these individuals actually aren't saved. But then some are; however, they are extremely weak in a spiritual sense, and if in fact, they continue in that direction, they will ultimately lose their way altogether. In fact, this is the very purpose of Satan.

He desires to make the unsaved think they are saved, and to drag those who are truly saved away from their position in Christ, which he succeeds in doing many times. That is the entirety of the purpose of deception. It is to make people think something which is wrong.

However, if a person is truly following the Lord, which means to be truly led by the Holy

Spirit, without fail, that person need not fear, because they definitely will be led into all Truth and not error (Jn. 16:13).

In such a case, does the so-called Preacher or the Evangelist know that he (or she) is actually being used by the Devil, and what they're doing is not of God?

No! In almost all cases, the Preacher is deceived as well, actually believing that what is happening is of God, when in Scriptural reality it isn't. Once again, that's the basic form of deception.

Deception is far more powerful, when the perpetrator of such actually believes what he is proclaiming and doing. Such an effort is far more convincing than the efforts of those who are merely attempting to perpetuate a scam. Nevertheless, the individual believing that what he is doing is of God, in no way makes it actually of God.

The criteria is not the fact that we believe, but the fact of what we believe. In other words, *"is it Scriptural?"*

The next Phrase in this Tenth Verse, tells us why these things happen.

THE TRUTH

The phrase, *"Because they received not the love of the Truth, that they might be saved,"* proclaims here a specific type of Truth.

The wording here proclaims that it is not ignorance or misunderstanding of the Truth, but rather inhospitality toward the Truth — in other words, a refusal to welcome and accept it (I Thess. 1:6; 2:13). The problem is moral, actually a matter of choice.

The clear implication is *"that God had sent them the power to create in them the love of the Truth, but that they had willfully refused to receive it or cooperate with it."* That's what I meant by stating that in the late 1980's the Church as a whole, in effect, stated by their actions, that they did not desire the Truth, and, therefore, the decade of the 1990's has seen the Church receiving what it wanted and desired, which has been fakery and trickery, which means that the Church as a whole has never been in worse shape spiritually than now.

It is not only the Truth (the saving Truth as embodied in the Person of Christ) that is offered to men, but also the gracious ability to appreciate, to embrace, and to love the Truth. But in *"the perishing"* all this is rejected, and what they reject is their only hope of Salvation.

NOTES

THE LORD JESUS CHRIST AND THE CROSS

To come down to the bottom line, what is being rejected here is the Truth of the Cross, for the Truth of the Cross is the only manner in which men can be saved. The Church presently desires Christ without a Cross. They love the Jesus of the Virgin Birth, the Jesus of miracles, the Jesus of great healings, the Jesus Who multiplies the loaves and the fishes, but they are like the crowds who left Christ, when they were told that in order to be saved they must *"eat His flesh and drink His Blood"* (Jn. 6:53).

Of course, Jesus wasn't speaking of His flesh literally being eaten or His blood literally being drunk, but was rather expressing His soon coming Sacrificial, death at Calvary. Paul explained this in Romans 6:2-6. The Jews wanted the Jesus of the miracles, but not the Jesus of the Cross. Paul labeled this as *"another Jesus . . . another spirit . . . and another gospel"* (II Cor. 11:4).

If it is to be noticed, the Greek Text carries the definite article actually saying *"the Truth,"* specifying a particular Truth. This Truth is *"Jesus Christ and Him Crucified"* (I Cor. 2:2). It is this Truth, the Truth of the Cross, which is being rejected.

Although Satan may cloak the situation in various different ways, the facts are, that the Church either accepts the Cross of Christ, which is the Plan of God as it regards the Salvation of humanity and the victory of the Saint, or else they reject the Cross of Christ in favor of other things, whatever those other things might be! Let's look at this more closely:

As we've stated, Satan cloaks all of this to keep people from actually seeing what is really taking place.

For instance, and as we've already addressed, the modern Church, and especially the Pentecostal and Charismatic varieties, for the most part, has totally embraced humanistic psychology as the answer to the ills of man. For instance, if a Preacher who is ordained with the Assemblies of God has any type of problem, before he can be reinstated into that particular Denomination, it is required of him that he undergo psychological counseling. While most of the laity knows nothing about these things, to be sure, they will ultimately feel its affects, whether they understand why or not. In other words, the spiritual coldness and deadness which ultimately filters down to the local levels, naturally affects the laity, but most of the time they don't know why.

Were one to ask the Leaders of the Assemblies of God or the Church of God, the two largest Pentecostal Denominations, as to their thoughts regarding the Cross of Christ, one would probably receive a very positive answer. So, as I have stated, it is all cloaked with an emphasis on other things, when in reality, it is the Cross of Christ which is either being accepted or rejected.

To continue to use humanistic psychology as an example, it is impossible for one to accept that particular lie, and the Cross at the same time. Each cancels out the other. If one accepts the psychological route, whether one understands so or not, one has rejected the Cross. At the same time, if one accepts the Cross of Christ as the answer to the ills of humanity, one at the same time is rejecting humanistic psychology, whether they understand it or not.

It is the great contest between God's Way, which is the Cross, and which has always been the Cross, versus man's way, which takes many forms, and which actually originates with Satan himself.

Let's forget humanistic psychology for the moment and look at other things:

THE HOLY SPIRIT

If Believers are truly led by the Spirit, which of course the Spirit seeks to do at all times, that is to lead the Saint, He will always lead the Saint to the Cross. The reason is simple! This is where the price was paid for all Salvation and all Victory. Consequently, this is the way and means through which the Spirit works as it regards the Saint of God (Rom. 8:2). Actually, the entirety of the Eighth Chapter of Romans, proclaims the dynamics of the Holy Spirit as it regards the Victory and Sanctification of the Saint of God.

NOTES

If one is to notice, Paul over and over again used the phrase *"in Christ,"* specifying the Believer's position in his Lord. *"In Christ"* refers totally and completely to what Christ did at the Cross on our behalf, and how that our Faith places us in Him concerning this great Sacrifice which resulted in total and complete Salvation and Victory. However, it is the Holy Spirit Who makes all of these things possible in the heart and life of the Saint as to what Jesus did in the Atonement, all on our behalf. But the Spirit requires one thing on the part of the Saint:

He requires that we have Faith in the Cross of Christ, in other words, that our Faith totally and completely rests in this great Finished Work. This is the secret to all victory. If the Saint has misplaced Faith, which most have, the Holy Spirit simply cannot work in that capacity. While He remains in the heart and life of the Believer, as A.W. Tozer said, *"We clip His wings."* He demands that we have Faith in the great Sacrifice of Christ, and then He guarantees us His excellent work on our behalf, which always garners Victory for the Child of God.

One cannot have Faith in the Cross of Christ and humanistic psychology at the same time, or anything else for that matter.

So, that's why I say that *"the Truth,"* speaks of a specific Truth, and as the Bible uses the phrase, it speaks of the great Atoning Work of the Cross of Christ. Please allow me to say it again:

The dividing line for the True Church and the apostate Church is the Cross of Christ, even as it always has been. It began with Cain and Abel and has continued unto this very hour.

Do you the Reader understand and accept the veracity of the Cross of Christ as the foundation of all that God has done and is doing for the human race, or do you place it in a subsidiary role, if any role at all?

To be blunt, your answer to that question will decide whether you perish or not!

THE LOVE OF THE TRUTH

I want this phrase *"the love of the Truth"* to be looked at closely. What exactly does it mean? It is the Holy Spirit Who gave these words to Paul; consequently, they are very important.

So, we are speaking here not only of *"the Truth,"* but as well *"the love of the Truth."*

Let me explain:

If one truly understands the Cross of Christ, truly understands that this is where the totality of man's Salvation was affected, which also includes and totally so, the Victory and Sanctification of the Saint, one will have a great love for this Truth. In other words, one cannot get enough of hearing about it, talking about it, and reading about it, even as you are now reading these words.

If in fact one brushes this aside, having little desire to hear this great Truth but rather something else, then one does not have a love for this Truth. For instance, there are thousands of Churches which dot the landscape, whose primary message is not the Cross of Christ, but something else altogether. Thousands of these Churches specialize in the *"greed gospel,"* in other words, their message makes money the priority. The dangling carrot of riches is held before the suckers, and suckers they are, with the only one getting rich being the Preacher. As should be obvious, the Cross plays no part at all in such a gospel; consequently, there is no love for this Truth in those parameters.

The same can go for humanistic psychology. For the Preachers who have embraced this error, these *"high things which exalt themselves above the Knowledge of God,"* they have no desire to hear the Message of the Cross. As a result, they would have no love for this Truth.

One might ask oneself the question as to exactly how many Churches really do love this Truth. The facts are, not many! Paul referred to such as *"enemies of the Cross of Christ"* (Phil. 3:18).

He also said, *"But God forbid that I should glory* (boast), *save in the Cross of our Lord Jesus Christ, by Whom the world is crucified unto me, and I unto the world"* (Gal. 6:14).

I must quickly ask, is your boast in the Cross? Does the Church you attend boast in the Cross? Or does it boast of something else entirely?

## SALVATION

This of which we speak is not a periphery Doctrine, but rather the foundation of Christianity. In other words, if one does not have a proper understanding of *"the Truth,"* which understanding will always generate a *"love of the Truth,"* one's Salvation is literally at stake. Consequently, what we're speaking about here, is of the utmost importance!

Satan doesn't really care where you place your Faith, or how much Faith you might have, just as long as it is in something else other than the Finished Work of Christ. In other words, the sky is the limit as it regards your Faith, just so it's not in the Cross. That means that he will fight this Message of the Cross as he fights nothing else because he knows that in the Cross is all Salvation, all Victory, all Healing, all Prosperity, and all Sanctification. In other words, everything is found in the great Sacrifice of Christ.

So what we're speaking of here is not something which is optional. We're speaking of the very foundation of the Faith, that which guarantees your Salvation and your Victory in the Lord, which means this is the single most important subject in the world.

Peter said, *"Neither is there Salvation in any other* (speaking of Jesus)*: for there is none other Name under Heaven given among men, whereby we must be saved"* (Acts 4:12).

He is speaking here of the Name of Jesus, as is obvious! But what does the Name *"Jesus"* mean?

It means *"Saviour,"* which speaks of what He did on the Cross in order that we might be saved.

This is the Truth which you must love, and in fact, about which you must seek to learn more and more. If a love for this Truth is not had, and I mean in the capacity of which I have spoken, then the Believer should *"examine himself, whether ye be in the Faith"* (II Cor. 13:5).

Once again, *"the Faith"* speaks of the great Sacrifice of Christ, the great Atonement of Christ, where Jesus purchased man's Redemption by the spilling of His Own, Precious Blood, which delivered us from the powers of darkness and gave to us Eternal Life. That is *"the Faith!"* (Jn. 3:16; Gal. 1:4).

In this Tenth Verse of II Thessalonians, Paul is obviously speaking of the coming Great Tribulation, and the untold millions who will accept the Antichrist; however, the

NOTES

spirit of the Antichrist is already in the world and in the Church, even as we have attempted to bring out. I have done my best and am doing my best, that the Reader understand that these matters are not only that which will happen in a coming day, but are actually taking place at this very moment in the hearts and lives of untold millions. This *"deceivableness of unrighteousness"* is already at work, as it always has been, but now I think, on a more accelerated basis. As well, more and more the Holy Spirit is drawing the line, which is the Cross of Christ, i.e., *"the Truth,"* as the crossover. Accept it and be saved; reject it and be lost!

(11) "AND FOR THIS CAUSE GOD SHALL SEND THEM STRONG DELUSION, THAT THEY SHOULD BELIEVE A LIE:"

By covering again the same ground in Verses 11 and 12 as in Verses 9 and 10, Paul reemphasizes the fate of rejecters of the Truth and adds more information about them. Already he has shown Satan's part in getting them to believe lies and bewildering them with deceitful measures and he has shown their refusal to love the Truth. Because they deliberately reject God, He Himself will send them a powerful delusion so that they will believe *"the lie,"* for that is actually the way it is said in the Greek Text.

This *"working of error"* will be supernatural in character so as to prove irresistible to rebellious humanity. *"Powerful delusion"* is another way of referring to *"the lie"* and deceit already predicted.

If one does not believe *"the Truth"* the only alternative is *"the lie!"* In fact, this Scripture is emphatic in the understanding that God will see to it that what the person wants is what the person gets. If they want *"the Truth,"* they will get the Truth. If they want *"the lie,"* they will get the lie!

## THIS CAUSE

The phrase, *"And for this cause,"* refers back to the last phrase of the Tenth Verse. It is *"the Truth"* which is *"the Cross,"* of which the Holy Spirit through the Apostle speaks here. This is where one's Faith must be centered. If that is rejected, the end result is destruction, for it can only be destruction, since God only has One Way of Salvation.

NOTES

The Lord said through the Prophet Jeremiah, *"And ye shall seek Me, and find Me, when ye shall search for Me with all your heart."*

He then said, *"And I will be found of you, saith the Lord: and I will turn away your captivity"* (Jer. 29:13-14).

There is no way I can properly relate what these Passages just quoted mean to me. In October of 1991, I set about to do exactly this which the Spirit said through the Prophet. I believed His Word, and even though the answer did not come quickly, it did come. And when it came, it was the most revolutionary thing that I have ever experienced.

I set out to find the answer as to the *"how"* of the victorious walk of the Child of God. Where is the Victory? How is there Victory? Wondrously and gloriously, the Lord showed me that all victory, all answers, all solutions, are found in totality, in the Cross of Christ. It's what He did there, and did totally and completely on our behalf.

Despite Jesus being God, despite being Virgin born, despite His miracles, etc., had He not gone to the Cross, man could not have been redeemed, could not have been saved. It was only the blood which was applied to the doorposts of the homes of the Children of Israel in Egypt, which effected their Salvation. To be sure, the Lord had performed miracle after miracle in previous months, demanding that Pharaoh let His people go. Although the miracles were very important, and were definitely from God, they effected no deliverance.

It was only when the Lamb was slain and its blood spilled and applied as directed by the Lord, that guaranteed deliverance of the Children of Israel. It was on this basis that God performed the greatest miracle of all, taking out the firstborn in every home in Egypt, even of the beasts, which hit at the very heart of Pharaoh and Egypt as a whole. As well, such action totally smashed the religious beliefs of Egypt, as it respected the afterlife. They believed that all lived on in the continued lives of the firstborn. In other words, if the firstborn in any family had a long and prosperous life, this guaranteed the afterlife of the mother and the father, as well as all the siblings.

By the slaying of the lamb, the Lord would show Egypt that Salvation was definitely in the firstborn, but not in each family, only in the Firstborn of God. That *"Firstborn"* is Jesus! And ironically enough, it not only has to do with Jesus being the Firstborn as it regards the Incarnation and, therefore, the True Man after Whom all are to follow, but as well, that Jesus is also the Creator or Originator of Salvation, by being the means through which Salvation is brought about as it regards the Cross of Calvary and His Resurrection (Col. 1:18-19).

The application of the Blood in Egypt, and Faith in that process, guaranteed the deliverance of the Children of Israel, which was symbolic or typical of the Shed Blood of the Lamb, i.e., *"Jesus Christ,"* and our Faith in the Atoning Work, which guarantees us Salvation.

DESPERATION AND REVELATION

The Lord showed me that not only was the Salvation of all mankind found in the Cross and only in the Cross, which necessitates one's Faith in that Finished Work, but as well, all Victory and Sanctification for the Child of God. In other words, everything that the Child of God needs, and that means everything, is found in the Cross, and only in the Cross. My desperation resulted in Revelation, for which we will always give God the Praise and the Glory.

As the Lord revealed this to me, and actually continues to add to that Revelation even unto this hour, I came to realize that most of the Church has little or no understanding as it regards the Cross. Those who truly love the Lord definitely do believe in the Cross of Christ, and they understand the part the Cross plays in one's initial Salvation experience; however, thereafter, and I speak of one's walk before God, having victory over the world, the flesh, and the Devil, the Church, at least for the most part, has absolutely no knowledge or understanding as it regards this all-important work. In other words, as important is the Cross in the initial Salvation experience, as important is the Cross in our daily walk before God. This is the answer, and the only answer, for all Victory, all overcoming of sin, all Sanctification, etc.

NOTES

As a result of the Church having little knowledge of this of which I speak, most Christians are not living a victorious life. While they love the Lord, and I speak of those who are truly saved of course, inasmuch as this Truth has not been taught them, most are struggling trying to accomplish themselves what only the Holy Spirit can accomplish and bring about. In fact, such an existence, is a miserable existence, but regrettably and sadly, the existence in which most Christians now find themselves.

THE PROCLAMATION OF THIS WORD

I know what this great Truth, in fact *"the Truth,"* has meant to me personally. I know how it has changed my life. I also know, that the Lord intends for us to proclaim this Message to the entirety of the Church all over the world. My Ministry is not only to get people saved, but it's also to proclaim the way of Victory to the Church, and this we must do.

As Paul requested the Readers of His Epistles to pray for him, I implore you to do the same for this Evangelist. Pray that I will always do God's Will, that selfish motives will never be the energy of this Preacher, and above all that we may walk softly before the Lord at all times. Pray that the Lord will help us, that the Gospel may have free course, in other words, that we might get it to as many people as possible throughout the entirety of this world.

For some eight years now, the Holy Spirit has poured through me the need for a greater working and manifestation of His Power and leading in my own heart and life. I have sought His Face constantly in this regard. In fact, as I dictate these notes, I have just come back from our morning Prayer Meeting (Dec. 13, 1999), and the Lord moved in a mighty way in this very respect.

It was as if I could see and feel the pain of the lost. It was as if I could feel their helplessness, their imprisonment in darkness. Of course, the unsaved do not know the Lord in any capacity. Being spiritually dead, they have absolutely no feeling or understanding as it regards God or His Word. It remains for the Word of God to be delivered to them, and for the Holy Spirit to move mightily upon that Word and upon that sinner with conviction, before they can come to a knowledge of Christ. Only then can those terrible bondages of darkness be broken. Isaiah said it well:

*"To open the blind eyes* (spiritually blind), *to bring out the prisoners from the prison* (all unsaved are in bondage), *and them that sit in darkness out of the prison house"* (Isa. 42:7).

In fact, we are seeing God move in great ways; however, what I want to see, what I believe the Spirit is telling me that we will see, so far eclipses that which we have seen in the past, as to be of no comparison. I cannot believe the Holy Spirit has moved upon my heart as He has in these last few years, and continues to do so at this very moment, without bringing to fruition that which I have sensed and felt so strongly. In fact, I have already begun to sense a heavier Anointing of the Holy Spirit in our Ministry than ever before. I believe it's going to grow in intensity with the results being, great numbers of people being brought to Christ, as well as great numbers of Believers learning the source of their Victory, which is the Cross of Christ and their Faith in that Source. So I ask you to continue to pray for us, please!

NOTES

## A STRONG DELUSION

The phrase, *"God shall send them strong delusion,"* refers to what we have just said. If one doesn't want *"the Truth,"* God will see to it that one receives a *"delusion,"* i.e., *"a working of error."* One might say that this is a terrible combination when God and Satan are agreed to deceive a man! And yet, God uses Satan constantly to achieve His (God's) Own purposes.

These words are not a mere assertion of judicial permission, but of actual retribution. It is the ordinance of God that the wicked by their wicked actions fall into greater wickedness, and that sin is thus punished by sin; and what is an ordinance of God is appointed by God Himself, which means, that it is inviolable, i.e., *"secure from assault or trespass."*

Concerning this delusion, Bruce says that *"a power is set in operation within them which makes them prone to embrace error."*

Some may blanch at the idea of God being the One Who is instrumental in this delusion. Does that make Him then, the Author of falsehood? Can He intend anyone to believe a lie, and especially a lie with such terrific consequences, as is here in view?

The opening words *"for this cause"* supply the answer to these questions.

The idea of delusion does not begin with God, but rather with the individual. It is what they want, meaning they have purposely and with deliberation, turned their back upon the Truth, even after the Truth is presented to them. In view of that, which has characterized untold millions, even billions, down through history, God simply makes it possible for them to have what they demand to have — a delusion.

## THE LIE

The phrase, *"That they should believe a lie,"* actually should have been translated, *"that they should believe the lie."* The Greek Text has the definite article *"the lie,"* which refers to a specific lie. The idea is this:

Irrespective as to what direction it might take, this lie centers up in a rejection of the Cross of Christ, which is God's only method of Salvation. In effect, they will say that they do not believe in the Cross, but rather choose another way, which of course is a delusion, i.e., *"the lie."*

During the coming Great Tribulation the deception that will envelop the entirety of the Earth, will not really be any different than now, except it will be far more powerful. *"The Truth"* has always been the same, which is the Cross of Christ as it regards the Salvation of humanity, and *"the lie"* has always been the same, which is a rejection of that Truth, rather opting for something else. In other words, as *"the Truth"* has been operative in the world from the very beginning (Gen. Chpt. 4), *"the lie"* has been operative as well. In fact, this was the scene and the cause of the first murder, as Cain murdered his brother Abel. God had given *"the Truth,"* which at that time centered up in the Sacrifice of an innocent victim, a lamb of the flock, which would symbolize the coming Redeemer. Abel offered that Sacrifice and was accepted by God, as all will be accepted who offer the same Sacrifice, i.e., *"Faith in the Crucifixion and Resurrection of Christ."*

Cain had instead offered the fruit of his own hands, the work of his own effort, stubbornly refusing to offer the Sacrifice as commanded by God, which God could not accept. In anger, Cain murdered his brother, and the animosity has continued from then until now. As stated, it has always been *"the Truth"* versus *"the lie."* The only difference in now and the coming Tribulation, is that the entire spectrum of all these things of which we speak, will be much more pronounced. In fact, the entirety of the world has either gone to Heaven or Hell, according to their acceptance or rejection of *"the Truth."* While there is only one Truth, there are many lies! It is whatever Satan can get anyone to believe.

WHAT CAUSES A PERSON TO BELIEVE *"THE LIE"*?

As stated, to believe *"the lie"* one first has to hear and reject *"the Truth."* Why would anyone do that?

I suppose the answer is as multifaceted as the number of people of which we speak. Self-will plays perhaps the greatest part in all deception. In other words, there has to be something in someone's heart, something which is evil, which causes the rejection of *"the Truth,"* and the acceptance of *"the lie!"* Deception has no chance with a pure heart. Hence, the Scripture says, *"Blessed are the pure in heart: for they shall see God"* (Mat. 5:8).

One might say that the struggle between humanity and God has always been self-will versus God's Will. This was the characterizing feature of Christ. His entire life was the Will of God, which it had to be in order for Him to be the perfect Sacrifice, and as well, to be the perfect example for all who would look to Him.

Most pass off Christ carrying out the Will of God with a wave of the hand. They reason that He was and is God, so the carrying out of the Will of God was not difficult for Him at all. In fact, many Preachers claim that He could not do otherwise. The Truth is different:

For Christ to be the Second and, therefore, the Last Adam, He had to have the same capacity as the first Adam. In other words, it definitely was possible for Him to fail. Were this not possible, He could not have been our Representative Man, i.e., *"the Last Adam."*

NOTES

He properly set the example for us, by finding and carrying out the Will of the Father in all things. That and that alone is our example.

The Scripture says concerning the Will of God which pertains to self-will, *"Take heed, Brethren, lest there be in any of you an evil heart of unbelief, in departing from the Living God"* (Heb. 3:12).

(12) "THAT THEY ALL MIGHT BE DAMNED WHO BELIEVED NOT THE TRUTH, BUT HAD PLEASURE IN UNRIGHTEOUSNESS."

There is an awful finality about this Verse. It is straightforward in its proclamation, leaving no room for side issues. In other words, one is either lost or saved. There is no middle ground.

The ultimate consequences for them who obey not God will be condemnation. Failing to appropriate the Truth of the Gospel, they willingly choose wickedness instead. Consequently, they cannot blame circumstances. Retrospect will show their own wrongly directed personal delight to be the cause of God's adverse judgment against them.

This speaks of a coming Judgment which unfortunately, most of the world denies. In effect, the world has been so psychologized, which teaches that man is not personally responsible, but that the cause of his aberrations lies outside of himself, that the idea of a coming personal judgment is denied. But make no mistake about it, denial or not, the judgment is coming.

THE BELIEVING OF THE TRUTH

The phrase, *"That they all might be damned who believed not the Truth,"* refers as we have been stating, to a specific Truth, of which the Word of God constantly projects, which is the Cross of Christ and the Salvation contained therein.

There are three stages in the descent of such people which will take them into final perdition:

1. *"Because they received not the love of the Truth"* (II Thess. 2:10).

Having the power to choose and to welcome the Truth, and we speak of the Truth of the Cross, they voluntarily reject it.

It is not that the Truth was not or is not presented to them, but that in fact it is presented and rejected. Actually, this is where most of the world stands presently.

2. Having rejected the Truth, they *"believe a lie."* They have lost the ability to tell the difference between Truth and error. They are described in Isaiah 5:20: *"Woe unto them that call evil good, and good evil; that put darkness for light, and light for darkness; they put bitter for sweet, and sweet for bitter!"* They now approve of, and delight in, wickedness.

3. Consequently, the only alternative now is the inevitable Judgment of God. Going back to what we have previously said, irrespective that man doesn't believe in a coming Judgment, that he claims of himself to not be responsible, that Judgment is coming. Furthermore, it will be *"the Judgment"* (Rev. 20:11-15).

*"The Judgment"* will come because of *"the unrighteousness,"* because of rejecting *"the Truth,"* which speaks of *"the Cross."* In other words, this Judgment will be held strictly because of man's rejection of God's only Plan for Salvation, the Cross of Christ.

We see in this God working, not arbitrarily, but through moral Law, to accomplish His Righteous purposes. The Hebrew thought-pattern is to bypass secondary causes and describe all that happens to the direct activity of God, which is correct (Ex. 9:7, 12; II Chron. 18:22). Our own tendency is often the opposite: to exalt a so-called impersonal law, which of course, is a law of our own making, which God will not honor.

Of course the moral law is not self-operating; it is rather God's method with men.

The point is that God does not act capriciously in sending a deluding influence upon Truth-despisers. The universe is a moral cosmos (an orderly harmonious systematic arrangement) rather than a moral chaos. The result of willful spurning of Light is to come to a state where darkness is no longer distinguishable from Light, and thus to come to final ruin. This Passage should be compared with Romans 1:18-32.

In fact, this entire section (II Thess. 2:1-12) offers remarkable insights into the Ways of God with men, as well as the character of sin and of the unregenerated human heart. Consequently, one might roughly outline the Passage as follows:

NOTES

1. The Christian hope, or Christian stability (vss. 1-2).
2. The culmination of evil, or sin unmasked (vss. 3-5).
3. The restraining power, or the Divine purpose (vss. 6-7).
4. The final counterfeit, or sin's deceitfulness (vss. 9-11).
5. The Christian's security, or love of the Truth (vs. 10).
6. The certain judgment, or the wages of sin (vss. 11-12).

## THE TERRIBLE EFFECT OF SIN

A German Saint was dying. He was asked the question as to what he had learned in the many years of his Christian experience. His answer was somewhat revealing:

*"I have learned how awful that sin actually is,"* he said!

That's the problem with the human race, it has no idea as to the horror of sin, even though its evidence is all around us. Being spiritually dead, they cannot understand its ruin and eternal judgment.

Unfortunately, the Church is not too far behind in its evaluation of this terrible malady that has slaughtered every single human being who has ever lived, with the exception of those of us who are presently alive, but to be sure are dying as well. It has filled the Earth with blood, with war, with sorrow, sickness, and heartache.

Some may take me to task for saying that the Church doesn't properly understand the terrible awfulness of sin; however, my statement is made on the following basis:

If the Church properly understood the horror of sin, it would not continue to project its worthless remedies as it regards this monster. It would understand fully and totally, that sin is so awful, so horrible, so terrible, that even God could not speak or decree this monster out of existence, even though He could make worlds by the simple Word of His Mouth. Instead, He had to become man, come down to this Earth, and die on a Cross in order to remedy the horror of this situation.

We must understand, that when we say that God cannot do something, considering that He is Almighty, then we must understand how severe the situation actually is.

God could not speak Redemption into existence, even though He had the power to speak everything else into existence.

We can only understand the magnitude of the horror of sin, by trying to grasp the Truth of the price that was paid to break the grip of this monster on the human race.

Considering that, how dare we promote some flimsy excuse, claiming such to be a remedy for sin, and I speak of symbolic Church ordinances, or even the Church itself, or our pitiful rules and regulations! There is only one thing that cleanses from sin, and in fact cleanses from all sin, and that is *"the Blood of Jesus Christ"* (I Jn. 1:7).

## THE CROSS OF CHRIST

The longer I live for God, the more I parrot the words of the dying German Saint. More and more, I have come to see the awfulness of sin, the awfulness of its impact, the awfulness of its eternal consequence, so much so in fact, that I literally tremble at the thought of sinful failure. I believe that the Revelation which God has given me of the Cross, this great Finished Work of Christ, this great Atonement, this Vicarious, Efficacious, Offering of Himself on that cruel tree, has at the same time increased in my spirit a hatred and fear of sin such as I have never had before.

The Grace of God which comes through the Cross, has not had the effect of causing sin to be taken lightly by any means, but rather the very opposite! The Truth is, I don't think that most of the Church understands the horror of sin, or the effectiveness of the Cross. In fact, the two go hand in hand.

How can we understand the Power of the Cross (I Cor. 1:18), and at the same time promote humanistic psychology as the answer to the ills of man? How can we understand the Power of the Cross, and at the same time claim that some pitiful, pathetic organization such as the Church as an earthly institution can absolve men from sin and make them holy? If we understood the power and necessity of the Cross, how in the world could we project some symbolic ordinance, such as Water Baptism as having power to wash away men's sins? No wonder the Prophet Isaiah said:

*"But we are all as an unclean thing, and all our righteousnesses are as filthy rags; and we all do fade as a leaf; and our iniquities, like the wind, have taken us away"* (Isa. 64:6).

NOTES

## THE REMEDY

Thank God, there is a remedy! However, that remedy is not with man, from man, of man, or in man. In fact, it is not of this Earth at all, but altogether from Heaven, and altogether through what God did to redeem this lost race, and I speak of His Only Son going to the Cross and thereby, satisfying the terrible sin debt against humanity. The Old Testament addresses this problem in countless ways. But perhaps the following, is one of its most graphic portrayals:

Toward the end of David's life and reign, he determined to number Israel, or in other words, to take a census of the fighting men of Israel. I will not take the time here to go into detail as to the circumstances that led up to this situation, but will rather portray its results.

Taking a census seemed to be a harmless thing; however, God had said in the Mosaic Law, that if a census was taken, all who are 20 years old and above . . . shall give half a shekel as Atonement money. This no doubt was silver, as silver is symbolic of Redemption. The Scripture says that this was to be done *"to make an Atonement for your souls."* It was to be *"a ransom for his soul unto the Lord"* (Ex. 30:11-16). This Atonement money was to be used in the service of the Tabernacle.

Why was this so important?

Israel was to ever understand, that her Salvation, her protection, and her prosperity, all depended on the *"Shed Blood of the Lamb"* (Ex. 12:13).

In fact, it is the same today with the modern Church, and in fact, always has been.

David ignored this plain Scriptural command, numbering Israel without obeying the Lord in this matter; consequently, what he did in essence said, *"Our dependence is in our strength of arms, and not in God."* It is doubtful that David actually thought this; however, to be lax about this matter, was to be lax in the most important thing of all; I speak of the Cross of Christ, for that's what this half shekel of Atonement money actually symbolized.

To be brief, the Judgment was swift and sure. Seventy thousand men were stricken down with a plague in Israel. To be sure, the cause of this plague was not only David's ignoring of the Law of God, and more particularly, the failure to understand Israel's strength, which was the Blood of the Lamb, but also that Israel had gone into idolatry (II Sam. 24:1). Irrespective, whether idolatry or David ignoring the Atonement money, their sin, as is all sin, centered up in a denial of the Cross of Christ.

### WAS NOT GOD CRUEL IN SUCH SWIFT AND TERRIBLE JUDGMENT?

God would have been cruel not to have done such a thing.

The real sin here, was the ignoring of God's solution for this terrible problem, which is the Cross of Christ, which was symbolized in many things, in this case the half shekel of Atonement money. The other things such as idolatry, or what David did, were merely a result of *"the sin,"* the denial of the Cross, which is the sin of the human race, and in fact always has been. Let the Reader properly understand that:

*"The sin"* is the denial of the Cross, which always results in all type of works of the flesh. To be sure, these *"works of the flesh"* take on all type of transgressions and infractions (Gal. 5:19-21).

The ignoring of the Cross, the denial of the Cross, the placing of the Cross in a subordinate position, has always been, and is the great sin of humanity. If the Cross is properly understood, in other words given its rightful place, with Faith there properly placed, all the other sin problems will take care of themselves. The Cross is the only solution for sin, and man's great sin is the ignoring or the denial of that solution.

So, it was not a matter of God pouring out Judgment upon Israel and whether He was justified in doing so, there was no choice in the matter. To ignore the Cross, gives Satan a latitude to make his claims of destruction, which to be sure, he always does.

*"The Law of the Spirit of Life in Christ Jesus,"* which refers to the Cross of Christ, i.e., *"the Atonement,"* was made by God. In other words, this is a Law of God, made by God and upheld by God. If we ignore this Law, which speaks of the Finished Work of

NOTES

Christ as the solution for all sin, we do so at our peril. There can only be judgment, even as we're studying in this Second Chapter of II Thessalonians.

To ignore the Cross breaks and insults the Law of God, which can only be visited with punishment, but at the same time with God showing David and the leaders of Israel the remedy for this situation.

Through the Prophet Gad, David was told to *"rear an Altar* (a type of the Cross of Christ) *unto the Lord in the threshingfloor of Araunah the Jebusite"* (II Sam. 24:18).

This David did, *"offering Burnt Offerings and Peace Offerings to the Lord"* (II Sam. 24:25).

The *"Burnt Offering"* was to be consumed totally on the Altar, with the exception of its skin. It was sometimes referred to as the *"Whole Burnt Offering."* It symbolized God giving His all, which referred to the giving of His Only Begotten Son in Sacrifice, in order to atone for sin respecting dying, lost humanity.

The *"Peace Offering"* was offered in conjunction with the *"Burnt Offering."* Only a part of it was to be burnt on the Altar, with another part given to the Priests which they could take for their families, and another part taken and eaten by the Offerer. The meal or feast which was to be eaten in a certain way, would typify communion with God now restored, as a result of the Burnt-Offering now offered or Sin-Offering, etc.

Whether these Peace-Offerings were carried out in this particular manner at this time by David, we are not told. In fact, due to the urgency of the situation, the Peace-Offering may have been burned on the Altar in totality, exactly as the Burnt-Offering. If that actually did happen in that manner, it would have been the intent which would have been recognized by God.

Of course, all of this symbolized the Redeemer Who was to come, Who Alone is the Salvation for lost humanity, and more specifically, by what He did on the Cross.

Incidently, the Scripture says that when David built the Altar unto the Lord on this particular spot (the threshingfloor of Araunah the Jebusite, where the Temple would later be built), and offered up *"Burnt Offerings and Peace Offerings, and called upon the Lord,"* that, *"He* (God) *answered him from Heaven by fire upon the Altar of Burnt Offering"* (I Chron. 21:26).

In other words, God sent a lightning bolt of fire out of Heaven onto this Altar, consuming the Sacrifices, which portrayed God sending His Judgment upon His Own Son, rather than on sinful men, but only, if men place their Faith in this Atoning Work.

The Bible says that when this was done, *"So the Lord was entreated for the land, and the plague was stayed from Israel"* (II Sam. 24:25).

## THE CROSS AND TOTAL DESTRUCTION

The only thing that holds back total destruction for humanity is the Cross of Christ. Sin has such a power, that without the Grace of God coming through the Cross, which it always does, and in fact the only way it can come, the world would have been destroyed a long time ago.

God has no choice but to put down sin and iniquity. The great ameliorating factor in all of this is the Cross. In other words, even as the Lord typified by sending fire from Heaven upon the Sacrifice in the presence of David and others, Jesus took the Judgment, in fact, the smiting of God, in our place and in our stead (Isa. 53:4).

The Cross of Christ is the only thing that has stood, and does stand, between God and the destruction of the entirety of humanity. That's how important the Cross actually is! One need only look back to the time of the Flood, which took place about 1,600 years after Adam, to see the dire peril of the human race. While the Sacrificial system was instituted at the very beginning as we see in Genesis, Chapter 4, still, there were so few people who followed the Lord during that particular time, that it resulted in the Flood which was an absolute necessity. Even after the Flood, at times entire tribes of people had to be completely taken out because sin had reached such a state that it threatened the entirety of civilization.

One Archeologist, who incidently did not profess Christ, at least of which I am aware, made the following statement:

*"The God of the Old Testament Who gave instructions for entire tribes to be wiped out, did future generations an incalculable service by doing this."*

NOTES

He went on to relate as to how their excavations had shown certain things which were totally destructive, such as incest — and incest on a wholesale scale. As well, bestiality (sex with animals) was practiced in the same fashion. Homosexuality was rampant as well!

What this would have produced in succeeding generations, would have been wholesale mental and physical perversions.

The world has known a modicum of true civilization, only with the spread of the Gospel, i.e., *"the effects of the Cross."* Other than that, it would have been doomed a long time ago. That's how important the Cross has been and is for the entirety of humanity. And yet the Church doesn't seem to realize the significance of this of which we speak.

## PLEASURE IN UNRIGHTEOUSNESS

The phrase, *"But had pleasure in unrighteousness,"* refers to a perversion of the moral nature. This means that their want of Faith arose, not from any defect in their understanding, but from the perversion of their moral nature, meaning not only total depravity, which in fact is the condition of all the unsaved, but rather a taking of this totally depraved nature to its furthest extent of depravity.

The Greek has the definite article which actually says, *"the unrighteousness,"* which specifies a particular unrighteousness. It is really referring to the results of a rejection of the Cross of Christ.

The great sin of man, even as we've already stated, is the rejection of God's solution to the sin problem which is the Cross, which always results in sins of the flesh of some nature. It's impossible to be otherwise. The mistake the Church makes is, that it addresses the symptom too often rather than the cause. Consequently, it succeeds in doing little more than the world, which means to put a muzzle on someone when the situation gets out of hand. That's not the answer!

The person is in the state they are in, whether saved or unsaved, because they have failed to function according to God's prescribed order. A failure to do that always leads to continued failure in every respect. God's prescribed order is the Cross of Christ, which is of course the Finished Work, in which all must place their Faith, whether for the initial experience of Salvation, or for victory after one has been saved. A failure to do that, guarantees one being eternally lost, that is if they are unsaved, or continued spiritual failure if one is saved. Either way, the Cross is the answer, and the only answer.

Hence, *"the unrighteousness"* specifies exactly that which is being addressed, i.e., *"a rejection of God's manner of Salvation and Victory, which is the Cross of Christ."*

(13) "BUT WE ARE BOUND TO GIVE THANKS ALWAY TO GOD FOR YOU, BRETHREN BELOVED OF THE LORD, BECAUSE GOD HATH FROM THE BEGINNING CHOSEN YOU TO SALVATION THROUGH SANCTIFICATION OF THE SPIRIT AND BELIEF OF THE TRUTH:"

The words *"chosen"* or *"predestination"* or *"foreknowledge,"* although different, actually come from the same root. The following will help the Reader to properly understand these terms.

Whenever these words are used in Scripture, it is always speaking about *"what"* is being chosen, predestined, or foreknown, rather than *"who!"*

For instance in this particular Verse, the Holy Spirit through the Apostle is not saying who is chosen here, but rather what. In other words, for those who freely accept Christ, which means to accept Him of their own free will, which all have that privilege, they are chosen to have Salvation *"through Sanctification of the Spirit and belief of the Truth."* In other words, the manner in which they are to be saved is that which is chosen and not the individuals themselves.

Satan has been very successful in twisting certain words in the Bible, such as these which we are now addressing. Consequently, many people believe that they are predestined by God to be lost, and there's nothing they can do about it, while others believe they are predestined to be saved, and no matter what they do or how wicked it is, they are saved and will remain so, all because they are predestined, etc. None of that is the Truth.

The *"who"* and *"what"* of Salvation is found in the most oft quoted Scripture in the Bible, John 3:16. It says:

NOTES

*"For God so loved the world* (that means the entirety of the world) *that He gave His only Begotten Son* (gave Him for the entirety of the world), *that whosoever* (that means anyone in the world) *believeth in Him should not perish but have everlasting life."*

How much clearer could it be!

## THE GIVING OF THANKS

The phrase, *"But we are bound to give thanks always to God for you,"* refers to those who did not succumb to the lie of Satan, but in fact *"received the love of the Truth,"* i.e., *"Christ and Him Crucified."*

The preceding Verses have traced the dreadful picture of the mystery of lawlessness and of the power of evil at work in the world. It is enough to make the heart tremble, which it actually has as I have attempted Commentary on those Verses. But despite all of this, Paul engages in thanksgiving as it regards these Thessalonians who have given their hearts and lives to the Lord Jesus Christ.

The manner in which Paul frames his words in this Scripture and those following tells us that Salvation is no afterthought with God, nor is He surprised by the forces of evil. God plans, not man's ruin, but his Salvation, and this from the beginning, having foreknown man's plight. Paul rejoices that God has indeed elected men to Salvation, actually, *"Before the foundation of the world"* (Eph. 1:4). This election is simply all those who of their own free will place their trust in Christ.

The force of this Truth upon the Thessalonians is that since they have now trusted in Christ they are caught up in God's eternal purpose and loving provision, and, therefore, need have no fear, proclaiming what *"chosen"* or *"election"* actually means. There is no suggestion here of an unconditional election; indeed, the succeeding expressions indicate quite the opposite. It is not *"who"* as stated, that is actually chosen or elected for Salvation, but rather the *"manner"* in which Salvation comes and is carried out, after one freely accepts Christ. There is no room for human merit or boasting, only Faith.

The idea of this first phrase is, that despite all the powers of darkness, despite the subterfuge, the deception, the sin, and the iniquity, all fostered by Satan, still, God has people who love Him and are serving Him. Paul is thanking the Lord for this.

*"Bound"* in the Greek is *"opheilo,"* and means *"to be under obligation, in which the carrying out of this obligation will bring benefit, gain, advantage, and profit."* This simply says that the Lord will bless us for praying for other Believers, but it goes further than that.

Giving thanks to God for the Salvation of others, even as Paul proclaims here, makes a statement to the spirit world, both darkness and light. The Holy Spirit desires this, because it makes a statement. It says, and which we should understand as Believers, that despite all the powers of darkness, that Satan does not take best, cannot take best, and in fact despite all his efforts otherwise, many people are truthfully and honestly serving God.

This is in line with the preceding Verses which tell us how awful that sin is, how powerful that sin is, and how destructive that this dread malady actually is. But despite that, there are many who are serving God, and for this Paul gives thanks, and which we as well should give thanks also, and constantly!

## BELOVED OF THE LORD

The phrase, *"Brethren beloved of the Lord,"* carries within its meaning, all that the Lord has done to provide Salvation for lost souls. Considering the tremendous price that has been paid, one can at least somewhat conceive of the worth of that which has been purchased, in this case, eternal souls. Consequently, considering the price which proclaims the worth, each and every soul who accepts the Lord is greatly *"beloved."*

*"Beloved"* in the Greek is *"agapao,"* and means *"the God-kind of love, or else to love as only God can love, in fact, so much, that He would give His Only Son for the one so loved."*

## CHOSEN FOR SALVATION

The phrase, *"Because God hath from the beginning chosen you to Salvation through Sanctification of the Spirit and belief of the Truth,"* as already stated, concerns itself not with the *"who"* of Salvation, in other words who will be saved, but rather the *"manner"* of Salvation, or rather how one is to be saved.

What is that manner?

1. Sanctification of the Spirit: Sanctification refers to a cleansing for the purpose of separating one unto God from a profane, secular, and carnal use. As Believers are separated from these things, they are at the same time separated *"to"* a sacred and spiritual use.

This can only be done by the Holy Spirit, and not by man at all. Actually it is the first work of the Spirit in the Salvation process. Upon Faith in the Finished Work of Christ, the believing sinner is first of all *"washed,"* which is a part of the Sanctification process, which then qualifies a person to be set apart exclusively unto God (I Cor. 6:11).

This *"washing"* incidently has nothing to do with Water Baptism, but is rather a work of Faith, as one is actually washed in the Blood, which means to accept what Christ did at Calvary on our behalf.

2. Belief of the Truth: Once again, we come back to *"the Truth,"* i.e., *"Salvation by Grace through Faith in the Cross of Christ"* (Eph. 2:8-9). When one believes in what Christ did at the Cross, thereby accepting Him as Lord and Saviour of one's life, Sanctification by the Spirit begins immediately.

In this statement as given by Paul, however, there is an added thought that must be brought out, and which is so very important for the Child of God. What we've said thus far, pertains to the sinner coming to Christ; however, the following pertains to the Christian.

## PROGRESSIVE SANCTIFICATION

The moment the believing sinner comes to Christ he is instantly *"washed, Sanctified, and Justified"* (I Cor. 6:11). As we've already stated, it is all done by the Holy Spirit, which guarantees a perfect Sanctification, which is the only kind that God can accept. That is one's position in Christ, which never changes; however, the practical aspect of one's Sanctification is something else altogether.

It is somewhat like a man or woman who is inducted into the Armed Forces. When he or she raises his or her hand and pledges to protect the nation, etc., at that moment, the swearing in, he or she is in the Armed Forces.

NOTES

In fact, they'll never be more a soldier or sailor, even if they climb the ranks to that of General or Admiral, etc.

But the Truth is, even though that person is a soldier or sailor immediately upon induction, they have to immediately go into training, because if not, and war is engaged, they could get themselves killed and others as well.

It is the same with the Christian. At the moment of Salvation, one is just as saved as they will ever be; however, much training is now required to make that person actually into the Christian soldier which God requires them to be. The major difference in induction into God's Army and a secular army is, there may or may not be a war as it regards the secular army, while with the Christian, war is declared the moment they accept Christ, and continues all the days of their life. So, the Holy Spirit sets about to train the Christian, which is not difficult, except for our own proclivity to try to train ourselves.

Paul addressed this in Ephesians Chapter 1. Whereas the *"manner"* of Salvation is proclaimed in the Verse of our study, the *"purpose"* of Salvation is given to us in the Ephesian Letter. Paul said, *"According as He hath chosen us in Him before the foundation of the world, that we should be holy and without blame before Him in love"* (Eph. 1:4).

Once again we have the word *"chosen,"* but here as stated, it gives the purpose. The Holy Spirit intends to develop holiness and blamelessness within our lives, all *"in love,"* all spelling out *"Christlikeness!"*

Our major problem is as Christians, instead of allowing the Holy Spirit to work out the Sanctification process, and a process it is, we attempt to do it ourselves, which always brings on spiritual disaster of one sort or the other. In fact, the Sanctification of self by self is the great effort of the Church, but one always doomed to failure.

The Sanctification process is not that much different from the Salvation process. As the believing sinner trusts Christ and what He did at the Cross in order to be saved, the believing Christian is to continue to do the same as it regards Sanctification.

As we've previously stated, and will even continue to state, the Believer must understand that every single thing he needs and in whatever capacity, is found totally and completely in what Christ did at the Cross, and in His Resurrection. In fact, absolutely nothing was left unaddressed and unattended. His Work was and is truly a Finished Work. So, if the Believer is having problems with cigarettes, with lustful thoughts, with uncontrollable temper, with gambling, with jealousy, etc., the answer to that problem is found in the Cross, and the Cross alone. The Believer can attempt to get victory in a thousand other ways, all seeming to be good on the surface, but will find that no positive results are effected, but rather the opposite.

Understanding that all solutions are in the Cross, the Believer must place his Faith in the Cross exclusively. He must believe that what Jesus did there was done solely for him, and that what Jesus did solved every problem. If he doesn't believe that, then he's in trouble!

If he places his Faith in the Cross, in other words ever making the Cross the object of his Faith, and keeping his Faith in that Finished Work, the Holy Spirit will then work on his behalf, doing all the things in his life which are needed (Rom. 8:1-2).

Now this doesn't mean that Satan will cease all activity against such a Christian. He will continue to test our Faith, to try to hinder us, and above all to hinder the Sanctification process; however, if our Faith is properly placed in the Cross, and remains in the Cross, the Holy Spirit to be sure, will get the work done.

If one is to notice, Paul said *"the belief of the Truth,"* meaning that one can believe wrong things, which in fact most of the world does and even the Church. It should be obvious, that what we believe is so very, very important. As someone has said, *"We do what we do because we believe what we believe."*

You the Reader should ask yourself as to what you are believing. Are you believing the Truth, or only part Truth, or perhaps not any Truth at all? Nothing is more important than this of which the Apostle speaks; consequently, nothing should be more important to us as well!

(14) "WHEREUNTO HE CALLED YOU BY OUR GOSPEL, TO THE OBTAINING OF THE GLORY OF OUR LORD JESUS CHRIST."

The phrase *"by our Gospel"* proclaims several Truths to us, which of course tells us

NOTES

several things. The amazing thing about a proper understanding of the Cross is, that it opens up the Word of God as nothing else. In fact, I feel it's very near impossible for one to properly and fully understand the Word, unless one has a proper understanding of the Cross. Considering that the entirety of the Word is centered up in this great Plan of God, it stands to reason if the Cross of Christ is properly understood, then all the other pieces will tend to fall into place.

CALLED

The phrase, *"Whereunto He called you,"* in effect presents the two sides in the matter of Salvation. The initiative and the power are God's; the necessary response is man's. God's Grace neither overwhelms nor cancels man's responsibility. Salvation is a moral matter and, therefore, real choice is involved.

*"Call"* or *"called"* is a common word, used in both Testaments in common ways. But as with many other common terms, Scripture often lifts such a word beyond the ordinary. Both Testaments invest this simple word and the ideas it conveys with special significance when it is used to describe our relationship with the Lord.

THE OLD TESTAMENT

*"You are no longer to call her Sarai,"* God told Abraham (Gen. 17:15). Abraham's wife's name was changed to Sarah, which means *"Princess."*

The naming and renaming of things, places, and persons is seen often in the Old Testament (Gen. 1:5, 8, 10; 31:48-49; Ex. 15:23).

Such activity is always significant, for to the Hebrews a name was more than a label. A name was an identifier, expressing significant information about a quality or characteristic of the thing named. This thought is carried over into the New Testament.

Jesus angrily drove the merchants out of the Temple Court, saying, *"My House will be called a house of prayer"* (Mk. 11:17). The very nature of the Temple, expressed in the name *"house of prayer,"* was violated by those who bought and sold there in flagrant disregard of the sanctity of the Temple.

Similarly, Luke 1:32 reports that Jesus is to be *"called the Son of the Most High."* This is a strong statement of Jesus' essential Deity. The Name affirms His identity.

NOTES

It is also likely that in Old Testament usage the right to a name implies at least a limited authority over that which is named. God, by right of creation, assigned names to His works (Gen. Chpt. 1). Adam, given dominion over God's creation, was permitted to name the animals (Gen. 2:19) and his wife (Gen. 3:20). God reassured Israel, *"I have called you by name; you are Mine"* (Isa. 43:1).

The Lord created, formed, and redeemed Israel and has sealed the relationship by calling Israel by name. He claims Israel as His Own and asserts His sovereign care over them, even as He has called us to belong to Him (Rom. 1:6).

CALLED TO A TASK

The common Christian notion of a *"calling"* is expressed in the Old Testament. The leaders of the Tribes of Israel were *"appointed,"* literally, *"called"* as it regarded their roles (Num. 1:16).

The story of Isaiah's commissioning (Isa. 6:1-8) is just one example that, in the Bible, God set individuals aside for specific tasks. And Paul clearly expresses this conviction: He sees himself as one *"called to be an Apostle and, therefore, set apart"* (Rom. 1:1; I Cor. 1:1).

CALLING ON GOD

The Old Testament often uses this phrase (Gen. 4:26; I Ki. 18:24; Ps. 4:3; 18:3; 53:4). Such a call always expects a response. To call on God is to ask and even expect God to act.

It is significant that most often when Old Testament Believers called on the Name of the Lord, they were in a desperate situation in which only God could help. How good it is to know that God invites us to turn to Him in the day of trouble and gives us His Promise: *"Call upon Me in the day of trouble; I will deliver you, and you will honor Me"* (Ps. 50:15).

THE NEW TESTAMENT

There is a significant shift in root meanings between the Hebrew and Greek terms. The Old Testament word *"call"* or *"calling"* emphasizes the utterance or the Message. The

New Testament emphasizes the intent: to call is to speak to a person with the purpose of bringing him or her nearer. The nearness may be physical (Jesus *"called the crowd to Him,"* Mk. 8:34) or relational (*"those who are called to belong to Jesus Christ,"* Rom. 1:6).

Despite the shift in emphasis from the Hebrew meaning to the Greek, as it regards the root, *"called"* is used in the New Testament with all the commonplace meanings of our language and with the special meanings — naming, calling to a task, and calling on God — noted in the Old Testament. What is especially significant for us is that the New Testament lifts the concept of calling out of both commonplace and Old Testament contexts. In the Epistles, God's Call is transformed into a technical theological term.

NOTES

## GOD'S CALL IN THE GOSPELS

The idea of *"call,"* when involving communication of a message, has always carried significant implications. A call is issued by a person of higher rank to those of lesser rank (Gen. 24:58; Ex. 1:18; 12:21). Thus, a call is something more than an invitation: it is a command and requires a decision by the ones called.

The called are to hear and respond. Yet, to call does not assure a favorable response, or even a response at all. Human beings can ignore or reject even the Call of God, which regrettably and sadly, most do!

The freedom to reject is illustrated in Old Testament history and is seen clearly in some of the Gospel parables. Jesus told of a wedding banquet prepared by a king for his son (Mat. 22:2-10). The king's servants invited (called) the intended guests. But when those invited refused to come, the king turned to the streets to find the crowds that were needed to fill the wedding hall. The same story is repeated in Luke 14:16-24, with the same lesson taught. Those who are called but refuse the invitation will be excluded from the final celebration of Redemption.

In the Gospels, then, *"call"* is often used in the sense of invitation, with the response of the invited being uncertain. Indeed, Matthew 22:14 says that *"many are invited* (called), *but few are chosen* (few choose to favorably respond)." The invitation is broad and inclusive. But few respond as stated! Not all accept the invitation that God extends to us in Jesus.

But to those who respond favorably to God's Call, what is received is of such magnitude, such Grace, such glory, and even such eternal consequence, that to refuse such a Call is the highest insult that one could ever tender toward God. Consequently, there is nothing left but eternal darkness.

## OUR GOSPEL

The phrase, *"By our Gospel,"* tells us several things:

1. Paul was given the New Covenant, which actually defined what Jesus carried out at the Cross and in His Resurrection. Consequently, that is the Gospel of which he speaks.

2. The *"Gospel"* in which Christ gave to Paul, is the only Gospel there is. In fact, the Apostle stated, *"But though we, or an Angel from Heaven, preach any other Gospel unto you than that which we have preached unto you, let him be accursed"* (Gal. 1:8).

In fact, he plainly stated, and was inspired by the Holy Spirit to do so, that there was no such thing as *"another Gospel,"* and if it was, it was a spurious gospel which would save no one.

3. This *"Gospel"* which Paul proclaimed, is the Gospel of *"Jesus Christ and Him Crucified"* (I Cor. 2:2). It is the Gospel of the Cross, and there is no other.

4. Paul used the term *"our Gospel,"* simply because others were attempting to bring in other gospels. In fact, that problem persists even unto this present hour. However, let the Reader ever understand, there is only *"One Lord, One Faith and One Baptism"* (Eph. 4:5).

*"One Lord"* speaks of course of Christ, Who gave Himself on the Cross in order to redeem lost humanity.

*"One Faith"* refers to *"the Faith,"* which is that which Christ did regarding His Great Sacrifice, in which the Believer is to have Faith.

*"One Baptism"* refers to the believing sinner upon Faith being baptized into the death of Christ (Rom. 6:3). It has nothing to do with Water Baptism.

5. This great *"Call"* cannot come to the unredeemed, unless the True Gospel in some

manner is given to them. It doesn't have to be much given, even only a few words, with the Holy Spirit quickening such to the heart, but at least some Gospel is demanded. The implication is, that the *"Call"* cannot come, unless the Gospel is first offered in some manner.

6. Understanding this, it is our duty as Believers to take this Gospel to a hurting world. God has done His Part in the giving of His Only Son for our Redemption. It's up to us now to do our part, in taking this Gospel to all of mankind.

So, the question should be asked, *"Are you doing your part in this all-important task?"*

THE OBTAINING OF THE GLORY

The phrase, *"To the obtaining of the Glory of our Lord Jesus Christ,"* pertains to the wonder and splendor which comes with Salvation, and only by *"our Lord Jesus Christ."*

It is clear that our Salvation is rooted in Love, planned in eternity, initiated in time, and consummated in glory. Essentially, Salvation is all of Grace, since it is originated in God's loving choice, wrought through the Power of God's Spirit, bestowed by answering God's Call, and perfected in the Glory of God's Son (Airhart).

The *"obtaining of the Glory,"* refers to splendor, magnificence, wonder, in fact, such magnificence as to defy all description. The idea is, that each and every Saint will partake of this same glory as the Saviour in Heaven. What a Gift is this glorious Salvation!

To be endowed with and to share the Glory of their Lord was what the Thessalonians were to expect, and all other Believers as well, and not the terrors of the Day of the Lord, of which Paul has been describing.

So, there we have it in juxtaposition: *"The Glory of the Lord"* or the terrors of *"the Day of the Lord!"*

(15) "THEREFORE, BRETHREN, STAND FAST, AND HOLD THE TRADITIONS WHICH YE HAVE BEEN TAUGHT, WHETHER BY WORD, OR OUR EPISTLE."

The idea of this Passage is that the Thessalonians, and all other Believers for that matter, not listen to false doctrine, which in effect is anything which contradicts that taught by Paul. Satan through his emissaries, sometimes even well-meaning Christians, is continually attempting to insert leaven into the purity of the Gospel. He does so in varied ways, and is always subtle in his approach, but sadly and regrettably, very successful.

NOTES

However, let it ever be understood, that no one escapes the results of false doctrine, which always will cause tremendous problems in the heart and life of the Believer — problems incidently, which will always take a deadly toll.

STAND FAST

The phrase, *"Therefore, Brethren, stand fast,"* refers to standing fast in the Gospel that Paul had preached unto them, not allowing anything to come in and subvert this great Truth, which in fact, is *"the Truth!"* The very words *"stand fast"* imply that the Believer will definitely be assailed.

This is basically what Paul had told the Ephesians when he said, *"Wherefore take unto you the whole armor of God, that ye may be able to withstand in the evil day, and having done all, to stand.*

*"Stand therefore, having your loins girt about with Truth . . ."* (Eph. 6:13-14). The idea is this:

God has allotted every Believer a particular Life, Ministry, and Message. The Holy Spirit has planned the description for each Believer. Whatever Satan does, whatever the power of his attacks, we are not to give ground one inch. In other words, we are to stand firm, to stand our ground, not allowing the Evil One to take one iota of this which God has given unto us. To be sure, he will make every effort to rob us of this which is so wonderful and glorious, and which belongs exclusively to us, bought and paid for by the Precious Blood of Jesus Christ. Nothing must be surrendered by the Child of God, nothing must be compromised!

HOW CAN ONE BE ASSURED OF VICTORY?

If the Believer attempts to *"stand fast"* within himself, after his own strength and ability, or by his own machinations, to be sure, he will not succeed. Even though Paul addresses this here only in a very limited way, he is actually speaking of our Sanctification.

The problem with too many modern Christians is, they want all type of Blessings from

God, almost all in the financial and physical sense, while ignoring the Sanctification process. Such is not to be! The chief Ministry of the Holy Spirit is to make you and me Christlike. That's His task, and, therefore, must come first. To be sure, all of these other things will be added, but only if we seek first the Kingdom of God.

Having established that fact, we must look at God's formula one might say, for being able to properly *"stand fast in the Lord."* Every Believer desires to do this, in other words to be a Champion, and that's exactly what the Lord wants us to be.

Once again we go back to the Cross. That's where the answer is, as that's where the answer has always been.

Even at the risk of being overly repetitive, please allow me to once again say, that we must understand that all the answers which we seek, all the solutions which we desire, all are found, and without exception, in the great Sacrifice of Christ at the Cross. Everything we need was carried out there, and that means everything.

Understanding that, we must place our Faith in the Cross of Christ, believing that whatever we need to properly *"stand fast"* in the Lord, is found there. It was done only for us, and it stands to reason, that the Lord wants us to have all that He has done, especially considering the tremendous price that has been paid.

The only way that one can properly *"stand fast"* is by the help of the Holy Spirit. As we've said many times, that help is not automatic, but yet it's not difficult to have. It only awaits us properly placing our Faith in the Cross, and that's not hard to do. To be sure, when our Faith is properly placed, in other words the object of our Faith is the Cross which it must be, then the Holy Spirit will help us do whatever needs to be done. And of this we can be certain:

The Holy Spirit is God; consequently, He is Almighty and all-knowing, and He can do anything which needs to be done. In other words, all Believers have within them the Living God, Who is up to any task. But we must never forget, that He always works within the parameters of the Finished Work of Christ. In other words, everything is *"in Christ"* (Rom. 8:2). That's why He demands our Faith to be properly placed.

NOTES

## OUR FAITH

The Scripture plainly says that we are *"saved by Grace through Faith. It is the Gift of God"* (Eph. 2:8-9). Faith is the great ingredient through which the Lord works. In fact, it is the only way in which He works with us. He doesn't demand much, but He does demand that we have Faith.

What does that mean?

It simply means to believe Him.

However, we may again ask the question, *"Believe in Him for what or how?"*

The Truth is, everyone in the world has Faith in something; however, only a few truly have Faith in God; nevertheless, the whole world has Faith in some manner, but it's not Faith which God will honor. What we want to know and have, is the type of Faith which God desires, and which He will honor, and in fact, will always honor.

I suppose there has been more teaching on Faith in the last few decades than all the balance of the history of the Church put together. But yet, I think there is less true Faith presently than ever before.

Why?

Most of the teaching on Faith has had the wrong object in mind. It's been Faith in our Faith, or else a better way to say it, *"Faith in the Word."* That sounds very spiritual, and in fact is spiritual, if it's properly understood. The trouble is, most don't really know what they're saying.

When one says *"Faith in the Word,"* most of the time the thought is that we choose a particular Scripture, a Scripture incidently which fits something that we want, and then try to force God to move or act according to us quoting this Scripture over and over again, or something of that nature.

That's not Faith! In fact, such efforts are really little better than the Eastern Cult religions reciting something over and over again.

Others have been taught and, therefore, think, that by merely pointing out some particular Scripture such as Mark 11:24, and thereby claiming whatever it is they think it says, that such acclamation or recognition is Faith and will, therefore, move God to do what we want. In other words, the Scripture says so, I believe it, and, therefore, I'm going to have what I want.

If one is to notice, almost all of this is what we want, with little thought as to what God wants. Such is not only selfish but downright dangerous. In fact, God is not going to honor such requests, because it's not proper Faith. Because Scriptures are used, does not at all mean they are used properly. In other words, the mere fact of Scriptures being brought into play means little or nothing. In fact, it might mean much, but not necessarily so.

This type of Faith is not really in the Word of God despite certain Scriptures being used, but is actually in ourselves; consequently, it is doomed from the start!

First of all, it's not hard to have Faith. As we've stated, everyone has Faith in something and to be sure, every single Christian has Faith in God. They couldn't be saved if they didn't!

So the great question or problem is not in having Faith, but rather *"the object of our Faith."* That's where the problem is.

It does no good for a Christian to attempt to build up his Faith, or increase his Faith, or to get more Faith, if his Faith is in the wrong object. And that's the place and position of most Christians. They do not know what the object of their Faith is to be.

If asked such a question, they would probably say *"The object of my Faith must be the Word of God,"* which we've already addressed, or just plain *"God!"*

All of that is well and good, but it really does not say anything. In fact, it does say much and even very much if the person understands what the Word of God actually is and Who and What God actually is.

The story of the Bible is the Redemption of lost humanity. The Plan of God is the Salvation of lost humanity; consequently, that being the case, and it is, it all centers up on the Cross of Christ. That is the great intersection of history, the great intersection of humanity, and the great intersection of Salvation. That's where the price was paid, that's where man's Salvation was and is effected. And that goes for everything else that man receives from the Lord, irrespective as to what it might be.

NOTES

So, understanding this, our Faith must always be anchored in the Cross of Christ. This must be the object of our Faith, and this alone!

### WHY THE CROSS?

The Cross is the means by which God has redeemed humanity through His Son, the Lord Jesus Christ. Christ offered up Himself on the Cross, which paid the terrible sin debt owed by man to God. He became our Substitute and our Representative Man. It was there that the great Work was carried out and accomplished and in totality I might quickly add!

So when the Bible speaks of Faith, it is actually always speaking of Faith in what God did through His Son Jesus Christ at the Cross. As horrible as it was, this was demanded by God, and I speak of the death of Christ on the Cross, that is if the sin debt was to be satisfied, which within itself would break the grip of Satan on humanity. The Cross was the means by which this was done.

That's why all of history strains toward the Cross, and by history I'm referring to Biblical history. And of course, as Biblical history goes, so goes secular history.

As well, as history strained toward the Cross, it also strains from the Cross. This means that the Cross was not an accident or an incident, but rather the Plan of God, and the only Plan which would bring about Salvation for lost, dying humanity. Therefore, the Cross of Christ is the single most important factor in the great Plan of God, actually the very center and core of God's Plan for lost humanity. In fact, the Cross was ever before Christ, for this was the reason, the very reason, for which He came.

If you were to be saved and to receive this glorious Redemption, which opens up the door of Heaven to all who are so privileged, then the Cross was an absolute necessity. That's why it must ever be the object of your Faith, and as well, the means by which the Holy Spirit fills our hearts and lives, and works on our behalf (Rom. Chpt. 8).

Faith in that and that alone, can help you to *"stand fast."* Inasmuch as every Believer has Faith, or else you couldn't be saved, this means that every single Believer and irrespective as to whom you might be, can *"stand fast!"* Just anchor your Faith in the Cross of

Christ, leave it there, refuse to allow it to be moved, believe the Promises of God, and you will find the Holy Spirit in this respect wondrously and gloriously helping you, and in ways you never dreamed possible. You standing alone, no matter how strong you might think you are, is no match for the Devil. You standing in the Power of the Holy Spirit, with your Faith anchored in all that Jesus has done for us at the Cross, is not only a match for Satan, but more than a match, *"more than a conqueror through Him Who has loved us."*

TRADITIONS

The phrase, *"And hold the traditions which you have been taught,"* refer to what is given or handed over to one. For example, precepts or Doctrines handed down by Moses and the Prophets, either in writing or orally, are traditions. In I Corinthians 11:23 and 15:3, Paul uses the same concept.

It is the origin of traditions which establishes their value or lack thereof (Mk. 7:8; Col. 2:6-8). Paul's teaching is not self-originated, as are many traditions.

If a tradition doesn't square perfectly with the Word of God, it is to be abandoned. The equation (to be equal) of human commentary with Divine Revelation was condemned by the Lord. By such tradition the Word of God was *"transgressed"* or *"made of none effect"* (Mat. 15:3, 6; Mk. 7:8-9, 13). In fact, many, if not most, of the doctrines taught by the Jews during the time of Christ were merely traditions which were *"the commandments of men,"* which means they did not coincide with the Word of God, and as stated, were roundly condemned by our Lord (Mat. 15:9; Mk. 7:6-7).

Regrettably, tradition which does not square with the Word of God continues to plague the modern Church.

Some years ago, a particular Leader of a major Pentecostal Denomination made a statement to me, which was patently unscriptural. He was older than I so I couched my words very carefully.

Very kindly I said to him, *"My Brother, what you're saying isn't Scriptural!"*

I remember him stuttering for a few moments, and then finally saying *"But that's our tradition!"*

NOTES

In other words, I suppose it did not matter to him that it wasn't Scriptural. In fact, most modern Churches, and I speak of Denominations, are operated solely on the premise of their Constitution, Bylaws, and tradition. The Word of God is little consulted, if at all! The Brother who answered my question, to whom I have just referred, that is if the tone of his voice was any indication, didn't even think of consulting the Word of God about the matter. He operated, as almost all in these particular positions do, solely from tradition, which much, if not most, of the time is contrary to the Word of God. Whenever Denominations stop consulting the Word of God, and rather make up their own rules as they go along, they have just destroyed themselves, at least as it regards usefulness for the Kingdom of God. They may continue to be big and rich, but as far as spiritual effectiveness is concerned, that door is closed.

David bringing the Ark into Jerusalem should be a graphic lesson for all. The Scripture says regarding this event, *"And David consulted with the captains of thousands and hundreds, and with every leader"* (I Chron. 13:1).

But David didn't consult with the Lord, didn't consult with God's Word, and death was the result (I Chron. 13:7-10).

They attempted to bring the Ark of God into Jerusalem on a *"new cart,"* when this was not God's Way. It was rather to be carried *"on the shoulders of Priests"* (Num. 7:9).

The Priests were types of Christ, meaning that the Power and Glory of God could come to sinful humanity only through the atoning Work of the Lord Jesus Christ, of which the Priests, as we have stated, were types.

As well, David in this first attempt to bring in the Ark, ignored the Sacrifices, which evidently the Lord told him to definitely include when he finally did bring the Ark into Jerusalem several months later (II Sam. 6:13). Israel was to ever know, as the Church must ever know, that all that we are and all that we have, resides on the foundation of the Shed Blood of the Lamb. It is only through the Sacrifice of Christ, of which the Old Testament Sacrifices were types, that we are able to receive anything from the Lord. The Cross of Christ is ever the centerpiece of all that we are.

NOTES

## DEATH

Many may read the account of Uzzah who put his hand against the Ark in order to steady it, and was promptly stricken dead, and think that such is not possible now. In Truth, it is not only possible now, but in fact happens far more often. Most don't understand that, thinking this is the day of Grace in which God has suspended all Judgment. Actually, the opposite is the Truth (II Sam. 6:6-7).

The Holy Spirit through Paul as the Apostle ministered at Athens said, *"And the times of this ignorance* (Old Testament) *God winked at; but now* (this age of Grace) *commandeth all men every where to repent"* (Acts 17:30).

In this age of Grace which is due to the Cross, the Light of the Gospel has spread all over the world; consequently, God requires much more now than He did in Old Testament times, when there was little Light. So, what am I saying?

I am saying that Doctors may put on the death certificate certain things, or others may refer to it as an *"accident,"* but if the Truth be known, much of this of which I speak, and I speak primarily of professing Christians, is the Judgment of God.

When Christians ignore the Word of God rather holding to their own traditions, they are flirting with Judgment, as should be obvious. Look at what happened to Israel!

They refused the True Gospel of Jesus Christ rather holding to their own traditions and they got exactly what they demanded.

They wanted and demanded a Messiah who would follow the military route, instead of the path of Redemption. As stated, they got exactly what they wanted.

According to their tradition they attempted to usurp authority over Rome, which resulted in Israel being destroyed as a nation in A.D. 70.

The tradition of which Paul speaks here, held true to the Word of God. He was merely telling them, don't forget what I've told you, but rather hold to it fast. Any other type of tradition must be rejected!

## BY WORD

The phrase, *"Whether by word,"* refers to what they had heard Paul teach and preach in former days, and they were to talk this, to repeat this, to discuss this over and over.

The pronoun *"our"* in the Greek Text belongs to *"word"* as well as *"Epistle."* It could be translated, *"whether by word or Epistle of ours."*

By the use of the pronoun *"our"* he was telling the Thessalonians that they must not listen to any gospel, any other word or message, which did not coincide with his.

Was Paul evidencing an improper spirit as it regards this situation?

Most definitely not!

What we're speaking of here is of far greater dimension than mere preference. We're speaking of the eternal souls of men. And to be sure, Satan does everything within his power to drag Believers away from the True Gospel. He too often succeeds. Of course, Paul knew all of this. He also knew how vulnerable that new converts were and are, consequently, his consternation is evidenced in his First Epistle. He was jealous that these people would retain the True Word of God they had heard from him. He knew what would happen to them should they embrace false teaching. In fact, the very reason for both Epistles, was to set straight false teaching that had crept into their midst.

## WHAT WOULD PAUL'S POSITION PRESENTLY BE REGARDING FALSE DOCTRINE?

I do not think the Apostle would have been too well liked at all by modern Preachers. In fact, I think he would be greatly opposed.

Why?

I cannot conceivably see how that Paul could observe humanistic psychology coming into the Church and not raise his voice against this evil. As well, I cannot see him standing by and saying nothing while the *"greed gospel"* takes its deadly toll. Also, considering how strongly that Paul promoted the Holy Spirit, and rightly so, I feel he would have voiced great disapproval regarding the manner of the modern Church either in ignoring the Spirit, or making a mockery of the Spirit as it regards all types of foolishness.

No, if you have studied Paul as I have studied this Apostle, I think you would come to the conclusion as well that he would not have been a very popular man in the modern Church, should he have lived at this present time. In fact, he wasn't very popular in his day either.

When we think of Paul, we think of the great Apostle, perhaps the greatest example for Christ that the world has ever known; however, he wasn't looked at in that manner too very much during his time. Don't misunderstand, the original twelve Apostles loved Paul dearly, and there is every evidence that they worked with him greatly so; however, there were others in the Church of that day who were greatly antagonized by him regarding his stand as it concerned the great Message of Grace. They wanted to insert Law with Grace, which of course would have destroyed the Message, but which Paul firmly resisted and rightly so. If it is to be noticed, almost all of his Epistles are written in a corrective mode, and for all the obvious reasons.

This we do know, untold millions are now thankful and shall yet be thankful that the great Apostle stood his ground. As well, in eternity future, there will be untold millions who will be thankful that some of us presently stood our ground!

OUR EPISTLE

The phrase, *"Or our Epistle,"* proclaims several things:

1. He is speaking of both First and Second Thessalonians.

2. The Apostle knew that these Letters were actually the Word of God, hence the reason for this injunction.

3. Once again, in view of the fact that the Thessalonians had received at least one letter by someone who had forged Paul's name, he desires to make certain that it is only his Epistles to which they will look.

(16) "NOW OUR LORD JESUS CHRIST HIMSELF, AND GOD, EVEN OUR FATHER, WHICH HATH LOVED US, AND HATH GIVEN US EVERLASTING CONSOLATION AND GOOD HOPE THROUGH GRACE,"

While this could be concluded as a prayer, it is I think, more than that. It is the Holy Spirit through the Apostle telling the Thessalonians, and all other Believers as well, and for all time, that the things spoken here, are given to all Believers by God our Father, and the Lord Jesus Christ. And if by chance we think we do not have these Graces, we should then check our Faith, and more particularly, the object of our Faith.

If we limit both of these Verses to merely a prayer, we then limit the Promises of God, which we dare not do. And to be sure, they are given in the form of a Promise and not merely a prayer, even though as prayer it does not take away from the veracity of what is said.

NOTES

OUR LORD JESUS CHRIST

The phrase, *"Now our Lord Jesus Christ Himself,"* proclaims the Apostle giving the Resurrection Name of our Lord, and by the use of the pronoun *"Himself,"* specifying His Personal involvement.

*"Lord"* refers to Deity; *"Jesus"* refers to Saviour; *"Christ"* refers to *"Anointed."*

*"Himself"* refers to Personal involvement, which Christ always does through the Person and Office of the Holy Spirit, Who resides in the hearts and lives of Believers. This involves relationship, which Christ desires to have and which in fact, He must have with the Believer, if all of these things mentioned here are to be made real in one's life. Of course, if there is no relationship or else it breaks down, such is never done on the part of Christ but always on the part of the Believer.

I know I can say without any fear of contradiction, that it is impossible for the Believer to have any type of relationship with Christ, unless one has a proper prayer life. Nothing can take the place of prayer, which in a sense should be mostly praise, worship, and communion. Of course, petition is involved, but only in part.

And yet we sadly realize, that most Christians don't have much of a prayer life at all, which means they have little or no relationship with Christ, which is a loss of incalculable proportions.

A PERSONAL EXPERIENCE

My day began yesterday at 4:30 a.m. At a little bit after 6 p.m. it was time to get ready for Prayer Meeting. After about 12 hours in the office, I was so tired I could hardly put one foot ahead of the other, and to be sure, had I listened to the tiredness of my physical body, I simply would not have gone.

However, had I not gone, and I'm very glad I can say that I've not allowed physical tiredness to keep me home even one single night for the last eight years, at least that I can remember, I would have missed out on a tremendous blessing.

Sometimes it's hard to pray and it seems like little progress is made; however, at other times, it seems as though all of Heaven breaks through and that which the Lord does for the soul is beyond compare. To be frank, there is no way that words can describe this of which I speak.

I had been seeking the Lord quite extensively about something which was and is very important to the Work of God, and last night, I believe I was able to get through about the matter. The Spirit of God moved mightily and helped me to pray as I had not previously been able to do so. I have every confidence that I will see a positive reaction very shortly.

However, this which I've just mentioned is one thing, but the relationship which is established in this manner, and can only be established in this manner, is beyond price. To say that it's worth the small effort which we put forth would be the understatement of all time.

## GOD THE FATHER

The phrase, *"And God, even our Father,"* once again refers to relationship, and that which alone can be if one is Born-Again. While God is the Creator of all things, He is the Father of only those who have made Jesus Christ the Lord of their lives through the Born-Again experience (Jn. 3:3). In fact, there is no privilege higher than the privilege of being able to say, *"Our Father which art in Heaven."*

## WHO HATH LOVED US

The phrase, *"Which hath loved us,"* presents a statement that cannot be questioned. The reason is, as it always has been and always shall be, that God gave His Son Who sacrificed Himself, that we might be saved. That was a gift of love that is absolutely beyond compare, in fact to such a degree, that there is no vocabulary that could properly express this of which we speak.

NOTES

*"Herein is love, not that we loved God, but that He loved us, and sent His Son to be the propitiation for our sins."* Once again, the Cross is in view, even as the Cross is ever in view.

In fact, I personally think that one cannot really have an understanding of the word *"love,"* unless that word is first of all and immediately linked with what Christ did for us on the Cross. To try to understand the Love of God apart from the Cross is an impossible task. So, whatever conclusion we derive from the definition, our thinking must always go to the Cross and must always remain with the Cross.

## STATEMENT OVER OUR RADIO PROGRAM

We have a 90-minute *"live"* Radio Program at 7 a.m. Tuesday through Friday, over our SonLife Radio Network. Actually, the Program is on seven days a week, and repeated at 7 p.m., with the extra times being re-airings.

In 1997, I taught several Series on the Cross of Christ, I suppose lasting several months; however, in the early Spring of 1999, I felt that the Lord instructed me to teach these Series on the Cross again, and I'm speaking primarily of Romans, Chapters 6, 7, and 8, as well as other salient Chapters concerning the Cross, and to continue doing so until further notice, which we have done. As I dictate these notes, it is December 15, 1999, and we will continue teaching this subject until the Lord says otherwise.

At any rate, on the Program this morning, one of my associates asked me a particular question concerning the Cross. I will not go into the entirety of the answer, but only this particular part. He asked about my understanding of the Bible since the Revelation of the Cross. My answer was as follows:

The great words and terms of the Bible such as *"Faith," "Love," "Grace," "Justification," "Reconciliation," "Righteousness," "Sanctification,"* etc., cannot be properly understood unless one properly understands the Cross. I realize that some may blanch at that statement; however, it is only when the Cross is properly understood, that one can look back and see the deficiency of previous understanding. Before then it would be difficult to explain this of which I say.

When we begin to understand that everything we have from the Lord, and irrespective as to what it might be, is given to us totally and completely according to what Jesus did at the Cross, and that without the Cross, those things could not have been given or received, then we're beginning to understand the Word of God.

At the same time, I am convinced that one cannot really understand this of which I say, or at least properly understand it, unless it is revealed to him by the Holy Spirit; however, the Holy Spirit will definitely do this if the Believer's heart is right, because it is His business to *"guide into all Truth"* (Jn. 16:13-15).

It is my belief, and I have come to this by Revelation, that if one's understanding of the Cross of Christ is deficient, then one's understanding concerning everything else about the Word of God will be deficient as well! I realize that is a strong statement, but I believe it to be true. If the Cross of Christ is the foundation of the Faith, and it definitely is, then it stands to reason that everything must be built upon that particular foundation. In fact, this is what Jesus was speaking about when He gave forth the teaching of the *"wise man* (who), *built his house upon a rock."*

He then said, *"And the rain descended, and the floods came, and the winds blew, and beat upon that house; and it fell not: for it was founded upon a rock"* (Mat. 7:24-25).

He then related to the house which was built upon the sand, and how that *"it fell, and great was the fall of it"* (Mat. 7:27).

The Rock is Christ Jesus, and more particularly, what Christ Jesus did at the Cross. Everything else is *"sand,"* and irrespective as to how pretty the house might be, and how much men may admire it at the beginning, to be sure, ultimately the storms will come, and to be sure again, that house will fall. It is only the Gospel which is built upon the Cross of Christ which will stand.

## EVERLASTING CONSOLATION

The phrase, *"And hath given us everlasting consolation,"* actually refers to *"comfort."* Both *"consolation"* and *"comfort"* are from the same Greek word (parakaleo) and suggests the work of the Holy Spirit, Who is the Comforter. The meaning is encouragement and strengthening more than comfort in the ordinary English sense. This consolation (encouragement) is everlasting because it originates in God's eternal purpose; it is everpresent, and is unfailing for the future.

*"Loved us"* and *"hath given us"* bring to mind John 3:16. They suggest the Work of Christ in His Atoning Death as well as the Gift of the Spirit to the Church.

## HOPE THROUGH GRACE

The phrase, *"And good hope through Grace,"* presents a glorious future for the Child of God, which comes to us through the Grace of God, which is made possible by the Cross of Christ. All our hope is based on the continuance of the spiritual strength imparted by the Father through the Son and the Spirit.

However, the Reader must understand, that all of this is made possible, our present Salvation, and future glory, by what Christ did at the Cross and in His Resurrection. In other words, each of these words, whether *"Hope"* or *"Grace,"* or anything else for that matter as it pertains to the Lord, has attached to it a tremendous price tag; however, the price was paid fully, totally, and completely, by the Lord Jesus Christ.

## GRACE

Many Bible Scholars attempt to make *"Grace"* the foundation of all that we are in Christ. Such an effort constitutes an erroneous understanding of the concept of Grace. Grace is not the foundation, but rather the Cross. While it is true that the Grace of God made the Cross possible, it is only by the Cross, that Grace can be extended to believing souls. It is the Cross on which and through which all Blessings come.

(17) "COMFORT YOUR HEARTS, AND STABLISH YOU IN EVERY GOOD WORD AND WORK."

Several things are presented here:

1. Comfort.
2. To establish.
3. The Word of God.
4. The Work of God.

## COMFORT

The phrase, *"Comfort your hearts,"* refers of course to the Work of the Holy Spirit.

This *"comfort"* does not proclaim the cessation of tribulation or difficulties, but rather encouragement, strength, and comfort in the midst of these difficulties and problems.

The Thessalonians were then undergoing tribulation, but there is no Promise here of these things being lifted.

Why?

Unfortunately, it seems that we need a certain amount of adversity, even though we don't like the adversity. Ever mindful of our growth, the Holy Spirit allows Satan a certain amount of latitude. This keeps us praying and trusting the Lord, while at the same time, the Holy Spirit gives *"comfort."*

TO BE ESTABLISHED

The phrase, *"And stablish you in every good word and work,"* concerns itself with a twofold thrust:

The Child of God is to be established in the Word of God, which foundation is, as we've already stated, the Cross of Christ. This means that a proper understanding of the Atonement, i.e., *"the Finished Work of Christ,"* is an absolute necessity, if we are to be properly established in the Word. This means that the Believer must understand that the key to all victorious living, all overcoming power, is found in the Cross, exactly as Saving Grace is found in the Cross for the sinner who is coming initially to be saved.

To be properly established in the Word of God, will at the same time bring forth success and victory in the *"Work of God."*

*"He was wounded for our transgressions,*
*"He bore our sins in His Body on the Tree;*
*"For our guilt He gave us peace, from our bondage gave us release,*
*"And with His stripes, and with His stripes, and with His stripes our souls are healed."*

*"He was numbered among transgressors,*
*"We did esteem Him forsaken by His God;*
*"As our Sacrifice He died, that the Law be satisfied,*
*"And all our sin, and all our sin, and all our sin was laid on Him."*

NOTES

*"We had wandered, we all had wandered far from the fold of the Shepherd of the sheep;*
*"But He sought us where we were, on the mountains black and bleak,*
*"And brought us home, and brought us home, and brought us safely home to God."*

*"Who can number His generation? Who shall declare all the triumphs of His Cross?*
*"Millions, dead, now live again, myriads follow in His train!*
*"Victorious Lord, victorious Lord, victorious Lord and coming King!"*

CHAPTER 3

(1) "FINALLY, BRETHREN, PRAY FOR US, THAT THE WORD OF THE LORD MAY HAVE FREE COURSE, AND BE GLORIFIED, EVEN AS IT IS WITH YOU:"

Endtime matters were Paul's main concern in writing this Epistle. *"Finally"* indicates that these have in the main been dealt with. Yet an important and related matter needs to be discussed before the Letter ends. Before discussing it, Paul makes one of his typical requests for prayer (Rom. 15:30-31; Eph. 6:18-19; Col. 4:3; I Thess. 5:25; Phile. vs. 22).

The Word of the Lord spreading rapidly and unhindered, does not apply to isolated victories or a single great triumph but to a continuing progress.

PRAY FOR US

The phrase, *"Finally, Brethren, pray for us,"* proclaims several things:

1. As should be obvious by now, the Apostle had a strong prayer life, which without, no Believer can have a proper relationship with the Lord. And as well, let it be clearly said, that Preachers who little pray, little see anything done for God. And the tragedy is, the far greater majority of Preachers have no prayer life at all. Actually, the number who do exercise this privilege and this absolute necessity, is so small as to be almost nonexistent.

2. We note in this request, the humility of the Apostle. Think about it a moment:

Here is the man to whom the Lord gave the New Covenant, which is the proclamation of what Jesus did at the Cross and in His Resurrection. Consequently, we are speaking of the single most important thing on the face of the Earth, and actually the most important thing a thousand times over. In reality, there is no way that human vocabulary could properly express the significance of this of which we speak. As well, the Apostle was given the responsibility of being the *"Masterbuilder"* of the Church. And yet, he would ask these Thessalonians as well as all others to whom he ministered, to pray for him. Also, we must understand that the Holy Spirit sanctioned this.

And yet, why would this be strange?

In reality, it's not strange! It appears strange only because of the pompous attitude of many modern Preachers who think themselves above the lowly prayers of lowly Saints. Need I say more!

3. By Paul asking these Thessalonians to pray for him, who obviously were new converts, which means they had little grasp of the deep things of the Lord, yet, shows us the tremendous value of prayer. The Apostle wanted to teach and in fact, did teach, these new converts the privilege they had in taking everything to the Lord in prayer. We must not allow this lesson to be lost on us.

4. In bringing us into the Kingdom, the Lord gives all Saints an amazing degree of share in the carrying out of the great Work of God. What do we mean by that?

We are expected to do our part in the taking of the Gospel to the world, which falls into two categories:

A. We must take the Gospel to the world, and all Saints are to have a part in this responsibility by the giving of their financial resources to get this great Work done.

B. The second category is the privilege of prayer. Through prayer, the Holy Spirit gives leading and direction to the Saint, as to what and whom he should support respecting this all-important task of World Evangelism. As well, the Holy Spirit moves upon Saints to pray not only for particular Preachers who are carrying out this great Work, but as well for certain areas of the world regarding Evangelism. In other words, the Holy Spirit moves upon Saints to pray about certain things, which to be frank, will little be brought to pass, if the Saints fall down in this all-important responsibility.

NOTES

We make a great mistake if we think that the taking of the Gospel to the world is strictly a business matter, etc. While of course, the Work of God does contain business activities, its greater thrust, however, is always in the spiritual realm. This means, that this all-important task of World Evangelism, actually the single most important thing in the world, cannot be carried out by ordinary business means, as corporations run their affairs, etc. It is carried out in fact, by the Holy Spirit moving upon Saints of God all over the world in prayer, as it regards a burden for a certain place, or a particular situation.

If the Saints fall down in this task, the Work of God suffers immeasurably, and because we are not carrying out our part of this great responsibility. To be sure, the Holy Spirit will never fail in His part, but the trouble is the Church in carrying out its part, as the trouble is always in the Church.

## THE SHARING OF RESPONSIBILITY

Unfortunately, most Saints have been led to believe, that whatever God is going to do, He just does it, and simply because He is God. That's not the way it works!

To be sure, the Lord doesn't need us at all; however, in view of the fact that we are being trained for leadership and rulership which will extend forever, He has given us, as stated, a share in this responsibility. And if we let down on our part, the Work of God suffers greatly, eternal souls are eternally lost, and the hurt is unimaginable regarding degree.

As the Spirit of God begins to move as it regards the taking of the Light to certain parts of the world, He at the same time begins to move upon particular Preachers and particular Saints as it regards this all-important task. He calls Preachers to do certain things, and He calls Saints to help them carry it out, and above all to intercede in prayer regarding what is to be done. The Saint will sense this burden, and will sense it in a way that is unmistakable.

As the Saint begins to pray, rather begins to intercede on behalf of this which is directed by the Holy Spirit, things begin to happen in the spirit world. The powers of darkness seeking to hinder this which the Lord is about to do, or rather seeks to do, are driven back, making it possible for the Work of God to be carried out.

But what happens if the Saints fall down in their duty?

If that happens, and regrettably it happens all too often, the work simply does not get done. Lives are not changed and souls are not saved, all because we didn't do our part.

So, we make a great mistake if we feel that whatever is to be done, God will do it, irrespective as to what we do, and because He is all-powerful and able to do all things. While He definitely is all of these things, still, and as plainly stated, He has given us a share in all of this, and for many and varied reasons. It's up to us not to fail.

The tragedy is, at this moment (as I dictate these notes), and I speak of the final hours of the Twentieth Century and the Sixth Millennium, the Church for the most part, little prays at all. In the last several decades, doctrines have been strongly promoted which bypasses prayer and bypasses the Cross. I speak of doctrines such as *"the confession message,"* or the *"Faith message,"* which in reality is little Faith at all! Actually, these doctrines militate against prayer, claiming that the constant seeking of God shows a lack of Faith, and as well shows that something is wrong, in which nothing can be wrong as it regards the new creation man, so they teach!

Of course, such foolishness shows a total lack of understanding as it regards what prayer actually is. I'll ask the Reader this question:

You have the choice of believing Paul or else the pap produced by much of this so-called modern Faith message. Which will you believe?

## THE UNHINDERED WORD OF GOD

The phrase, *"That the Word of the Lord may have free course,"* is without a doubt, one of the single most important requests that any man could ever make.

NOTES

The Apostle is asking the Saints to pray for him, as it regards his efforts in the proclamation of the Gospel of Christ. He was commissioned by the Lord to take this great Word to the Gentiles, and actually as stated, to establish the Church. He knew that Satan would seek to use every tactic at his disposal to hinder the spread of the Gospel, whether by using Rome, or misguided Christians. Unfortunately, the misguided Christians tended to cause more problems possibly than Rome. So, the Apostle was asking for prayer, that the efforts of the Evil One in this regard would be thwarted, with the Gospel freely going forward.

It should be understood, that Satan's greatest efforts are in the area of hinderance of the Gospel, and to do so any way he can. This is priority with him, and for all the obvious reasons. The Gospel pushes back darkness, robs Satan of his followers, thwarts his plans for the deepening of sin and transgression, pushes back demon spirits in their efforts to steal, kill, and to destroy — in other words, the Gospel of Jesus Christ is Satan's greatest enemy.

## THAT WHICH SATAN USES THE MOST IN SEEKING TO HINDER THE GOSPEL

Without a doubt, and hands down, he uses the Church to carry out his perfidious efforts moreso than anything else. Now that may come as a shock!

It is the duty of the Church to take the Gospel to the world (Mk. 16:15). But ironically enough, it is the Church who hinders this process more than anything else in the world. Of course, the Church which obeys this Command of our Lord is the True Church, while that which hinders and opposes is the Apostate Church. Unfortunately, many Christians cannot tell the difference!

Some of the ways this is done is according to the following:

1. Denominations for the most part love and demand control. They take this control so far, that they abrogate the Headship of Christ, with their efforts becoming man-devised and man-led. Consequently, little or nothing, at least in this mode, is done for God.

In fact, some Denominations began according to the Ways and the Word of the Lord, and for awhile, contributed greatly to the Work of God all over the world. But then little by little most lose their way with control becoming more and more pronounced, which of course, the Holy Spirit cannot abide. What they cannot control they attempt to destroy.

2. False doctrine introduced as *"leaven,"* also takes its deadly toll. Almost all the time, when false doctrine is presented and accepted, the first thing that falls by the wayside is World Evangelism. Almost all false doctrine centers up on the individual, and because of its selfish mode. The True Spirit of Christ centers up on others, while false doctrine centers up on self.

3. Satan is a master at getting people to believe that what is actually of God, isn't, and what isn't of God, is! So, many in the Church come to the place that they are actually supporting the work of Satan. But simply because he has come as an angel of light, they are not aware that it is Satan (II Cor. 11:12-15). In fact, I would say, and I do have some experience, that at least 90% of all the money given and the efforts made toward the Gospel of Jesus Christ, and its spread to others, actually goes to the work of Satan instead. In other words, it is money given to those who are not truly preaching the Gospel, who are not right with the Lord, who are not following the Lord, and many times, who are not even called by God.

The tragedy of all of this is, that people give their money to that which they are, and I'm speaking of that which is in the spiritual sense. What do I mean by that?

Flesh attracts flesh, just as the Holy Spirit attracts the Holy Spirit one might say. Unfortunately, and despite the fact that the Church is larger numerically than it's ever been before in its history, there are probably less people truly filled with the Spirit and led by the Spirit, than ever before in history. Consequently, that which is not of God, will be financed and promoted.

## THE GLORIFIED WORD

The phrase, *"And be glorified,"* refers to coming out to its full glory which speaks of positive effect in people's lives.

*"Glorified"* in the Greek is *"doxadzo,"* and means *"to be made glorious"* (II Cor. 3:10).

NOTES

In fact, there is nothing more glorious in the world than a life which has been changed by the Gospel of Jesus Christ, brought from darkness to Light, brought from slavery to freedom, brought from sin to Salvation, brought from sickness to health, brought from a drain on society to a blessing to society. In fact I think one can say that this is the greatest miracle known to humanity. It is truly *"glorious!"*

## THE CROSS AND THE WORD OF THE LORD

Paul's Message, or rather *"the Word of the Lord,"* was *"Jesus Christ and Him Crucified"* (I Cor. 2:2). So, if we think of the Word of the Lord as anything other than the preaching of the Cross, then it's not the Word of the Lord (I Cor. 1:18).

In fact if that is true, and it definitely is, then that means there's not much Word of the Lord presently being preached.

There are many Preachers who don't even believe in the Cross of Christ, therefore, do not preach it at all.

There are others who do believe in the Cross of Christ, or at least one might say they don't not believe it; however, they little preach it, if at all, simply because of knowing little or nothing about that for which the Cross stands.

There are other Preachers who understand the Cross of Christ as it regards the initial Salvation experience, and preach it accordingly, but that's as far as they go. Consequently they get people saved, which is wonderful and glorious, but they don't have much of a Message as it regards Christian growth.

There are a few Preachers who know and understand the veracity of the Cross in its totality, even as Paul proclaimed this great Message, who preach the Cross as it regards the initial Salvation experience for the sinner coming to Christ, and also preach the Cross as it regards our everyday Walk before God. Regrettably, these Preachers are as scarce as the proverbial hen's teeth. So, we have a lot of people who have genuinely come to Christ, but are not living victorious, Christian lives, simply because they are not given this Truth of the Cross.

## WHAT IS THE TRUTH OF THE CROSS?

To begin with, the Truth of the Cross is the *"Power of God"* (I Cor. 1:18), and second, it is the *"Wisdom of God"* (I Cor. 1:24).

These two words *"Power"* and *"Wisdom,"* in the briefest of brevity explain the Cross in totality.

In Truth, both *"Power"* and *"Wisdom"* are derived from the Holy Spirit. The Cross within itself contains no Power or Wisdom, as should be obvious. But the facts are, the Cross makes possible the advent of the Holy Spirit in the hearts and lives of Believers, who has all power and all wisdom, etc.

To be saved, all the sinner has to do is simply believe in Christ, accept Him as one's Saviour, and as well what He did on the Cross on our behalf (Jn. 3:16). When this happens, a legal work is carried out and completed in Heaven making it possible for the sinner to be cleansed and washed from all sin, actually done so, due to the fact that Jesus shed His Life's Blood which atoned for all sin.

To be sure, there is Power needed in all of this, which is always furnished by the Holy Spirit. In fact, the Holy Spirit functions in every single part of any and all things done by the Godhead on Earth. The Holy Spirit anoints the Word as it is preached, convicts the sinner as it regards the Word, and then gives the sinner Faith to believe the Word, that is if the sinner wills to do so (Rev. 22:17). Due to the power of sin, and the prison in which the sinner is locked (Isa. 42:7), there has to be power expended to set the captive free, which is furnished by the Holy Spirit.

The Wisdom of God pertains not only to all the things being done and carried out, but to the overall Plan of God as well.

The sinner coming to Christ is one thing; however, for that sinner who is now a new creature in Christ to live a Godly life, is something else altogether. It takes the Power of God for this to be brought about, and for this Power to be manifested, one has to function according to the *"Wisdom of God."* The Wisdom of God is this:

## THE WISDOM OF GOD

The Believer must understand that everything he needs is found in the Cross of Christ, or rather what Christ did at the Cross on our behalf and in His Resurrection. If the Believer looks elsewhere, there will be no victory. This is a part of the great Wisdom of God, which is the Plan of God.

Once the Believer looks to the Cross instead of himself or anything else for that matter, thereby placing his Faith in this which Christ has done on our behalf, which again is the *"Wisdom of God,"* the Holy Spirit can then work on his behalf.

The Holy Spirit has the Power to do anything, simply because He is God. What we want, is for Him to use that Power on our behalf.

Let the Believer understand, that just because he speaks in tongues doesn't mean that the Power is expended on his behalf, not at all! In fact, he can even have Gifts of the Spirit, and see mighty things done for God in other ways, and still not live and walk in victory himself, and simply because he doesn't know how to use his Faith, which will open the door for the Spirit of God to do what only He can do.

I realize the statement we've just made might be somewhat shocking to many Christians, but the Truth is, it is happening everyday. Let's look at it closer.

## BEING USED OF GOD

Most Believers think that if a Preacher, or anyone for that matter is being used of God, that means that they are walking totally and completely in victory. If they find out they aren't, they tend to want to crucify the individual, etc.

The Truth is, that most of the Preachers presently being used of God, some few being used greatly so, are in fact, not walking in Victory at all themselves. That may come as a shock, but it is true.

The only way that any Believer, Preachers included, can walk in victory, is to have a proper understanding of the Cross, evidencing Faith in that Finished Work, which will guarantee the help of the Holy Spirit, which will then guarantee Victory. Only in this way can Victory be had and Victory be kept. Unfortunately, there's not one Preacher out of 10,000 who knows and understands this of which I have just said. Consequently, there is no personal victory within their lives.

Now what does that mean?

NOTES

It means that in some way, and in some fashion, sin is dominating them. It may be one of the vices such as alcohol, drugs, immorality of some stripe, gambling, etc., or it may be one of the sins of pride such as jealousy, envy, a lack of humility, arrogance, greed, etc. But to be sure, in some way, in some fashion, sin is dominating that person (Rom. 6:14).

Most of the time, sins of pride in these individuals, whatever it might be, are little held against the individual by their followers. While some few Believers can see these sins, or the result of these sins, most can't; however, if it's sins of passion which overtake the Preacher, and in whatever manner, and these things are found out, most of the time, the followers of this particular Preacher will now be just as negative toward him as they had previously been positive.

While of course, God alone knows the hearts of these Preachers, whomever they might be, more than likely, most of them are struggling and fighting in the realm of these situations, and especially if it's sins of passion; however, despite their struggling to overcome, they always lose. There is simply no way they can come out with victory in the manner in which they are addressing the situation. Consequently, when they are found out, they are accused most often of being a hypocrite, of being a fake, etc. None of that is true! The Truth is, they just simply don't know God's prescribed order of Victory.

## THE WRONG THINKING OF THE CHURCH

The Church too often comes to these conclusions, simply because they have no idea as to the Victory process as laid out in the Scriptures. As well, they have a completely erroneous concept of Preachers of the Gospel.

First of all, and especially if the Preacher is being used of God, they think that Preacher is above all of these powers of darkness, etc. Never mind, that their followers are mostly living lives of spiritual failure, they look up to their hero, thinking, that even though they (the Laity) don't have much victory, their hero does. So it becomes a situation almost of *"idol worship!"* But woe unto that hero, if he fails in any way, or at least, the people find out about the failure. As stated, as much as they have previously idolized this individual, they will now literally hate him, and in fact, will do all they can to facilitate the destruction process. Denominational leadership, usually jealous of one being used of God, will then join in the process as well, that is if the Preacher is unfortunate enough to be a part of that particular group, whatever it is!

The whole thing, the Preacher, the Laity, the Church as a whole, mostly functions in an unscriptural way, which always comes out to very negative results.

NOTES

## PUNISHMENT

The Church takes the position that if a sin is committed, and especially by Preachers, the Preacher must be punished. They operate from the theory that the sin was committed because the person desired to do such a thing, whatever it may have been.

Constantly the statement is made, *"Sin is a choice,"* and of course if that is correct, all the person has to do is to choose not to do it, and if in fact, he chooses to do something that's wrong, that means he's evil or whatever, and deserves punishment.

Scripturally, the entire premise is totally wrong.

While of course, we cannot answer for all people; we can answer for most.

It is true that sin is a choice, but not in the way that most think. The choice is in the realm of going God's Way, or another way, *not* as to whether one commits a certain sin or not. Let us explain that:

## THE POWER OF CHOICE

While it is true that everyone has the power of choice, that power is not what most people think it is. It is *not "Do I commit this sin or do I not commit this sin!"* It is rather, and I speak of Believers *"Do I go God's Way, or do I go another way."* That's where the power of choice is, and that only.

What is God's Way?

God's Way is the Way of the Cross, which means that the Believer has the choice of trusting in what Christ did at the Cross on his behalf, which will guarantee victory if he places his Faith in that Finished Work. That's where the choice is, and that's only where the choice is.

NOTES

If the Believer has no knowledge of this of which we speak, which regrettably most don't, he is going to make a choice in other directions which guarantees defeat. In other words, it doesn't matter how hard he tries not to fail, in some way, he is going to fail. And if it happens to be one of the sins of passion, and the failure is found out, he can expect nothing but destruction from the Church. It's sad but true!

If the Believer knows and understands the Cross of Christ, and his part in that great Sacrifice, then he definitely does have the power of choice as it regards committing sin, etc., but only if his Faith is properly placed in the Cross of Christ.

No Believer, that is if he is a true Believer, wants to sin. He has the Divine Nature within him, and the thoughts of sin are abhorrent.

The trouble is, the Church has had so little teaching on the Cross in the last few decades, that it has little knowledge, if any at all, as it regards the great Finished Work of Christ, and especially as it pertains to the Believer. As we've said many times, the Church pretty well understands the role of the Cross as it regards the initial Salvation experience, but that's about as far as it goes. So, having an erroneous concept of failure and victory, they take the position, that if someone does something wrong, it is because they desired to do that, and, therefore, they must be punished. That's totally wrong!

What good would it have done to have punished Paul when he was in the state described in Romans, Chapter 7? The man was trying with everything within himself to bring about victory, but to no avail. To punish him on top of that, would have been adding insult to injury. No, that's not the answer at all, and in fact, to do such a thing makes the people doing the punishing commit a worse sin, than the sin for which the individual is being punished. As well, no Christian is morally qualified to punish another Christian.

The answer is in Galatians 6:1. When the Christian does something wrong, 99 times out of 100, the wrongdoing is committed because they do not understand God's prescribed order of Victory, which is the Cross. Consequently, they are to be taught that which is right, and then immediately restored to where they had formerly been. There certainly may be some circumstances to where that would not be desirable, but in most it would.

With most Christians, a proper explanation of the Cross, and their part in that great Finished Work, at least as it regards their walk before the Lord, will solve the problem.

And yet, I'm sure there are some who do not fit this mold, but rather desire to do certain things which are wrong, and of course, which are detrimental to the Cause of Christ. In such a case, such persons need to be disfellowshipped (I Cor., Chpt. 5).

THE OVERRIDING OF THE WILL

Romans, Chapter 7 gives us a description of the Believer who is trying to walk the road of Victory by his own ability and machinations, which always fail. This is the description of the Christian who does not know his place in Christ, and the victory afforded by the Cross. In fact, Romans, Chapter 7 is the story of Paul after his Salvation experience on the road to Damascus, and him being Baptized with the Holy Spirit, but not yet knowing the way of victory as it pertains to the Cross. Consequently, he attempted to bring about this victory by his own efforts, but of course was not able to do so, as no one is able to do so.

Concerning the will, or willpower, he said, *"For I know that in me* (that is, in my flesh,) *dwelleth no good thing: for to will* (willpower) *is present with me; but how to perform that which is good I find not"* (Rom. 7:18).

Even though many Christians have problems believing this; nevertheless, it is true! If the Believer does not have his Faith properly placed in the Finished Work of Christ and keeps it there, which allows the Holy Spirit to then help him, which guarantees Victory, that Believer is going to fail. In other words, despite his willpower, and all of his efforts, Satan is simply going to override his will. It's given to us in black and white in Romans, Chapter 7, and shouldn't be too difficult to understand. As I've stated, the Believer definitely does have a choice, which means that his will can definitely bring about a certain positive result, and I speak of the choice of going God's Way, which is the Way of the Cross. But that's where his will or willpower begins and ends. We must understand that, but regrettably, most Christians don't understand that, because they've been taught all type of wrong things. To the degree that we vary from the Word of God, to that degree will we suffer harm or do harm. Regrettably, many, if not most, Denominations have little interest whatsoever in abiding by the Scriptures, and unfortunately, that goes for most Independent organizations also. They rather make up their own rules as they go along.

But for the individual who wants to abide by the Word of God, and who desires to have all that Christ has afforded by His Sacrificial, atoning Work on the Cross, then there is abundant good news. The Believer can walk in victory, can be an overcomer, can have all that God has promised, but only if we go His Way, i.e., *"the Way of the Word of God,"* i.e., *"the Way of the Cross"* (Gal. 6:14).

### CHANGED LIVES

The phrase, *"Even as it is with you,"* refers to two things:

1. The Apostle Paul had been, and still was, their Teacher, their Preacher, their Evangelist, actually their Father in the Lord; consequently, the Gospel definitely had free course with them, with the Apostle giving them the Word of God in its entirety, and without the Word being compromised to any degree.

2. As a result, the Word had been *"glorified,"* within their lives, which refers to it carrying out its glorious work, thereby making these new converts at Thessalonica, into strong Saints.

(2) "AND THAT WE MAY BE DELIVERED FROM UNREASONABLE AND WICKED MEN: FOR ALL MEN HAVE NOT FAITH."

This Passage is startling, but cues us in to the greatest weapon used by the Evil One.

By the manner in which Paul speaks of *"the Faith,"* we know that he's speaking here of professing Christians. These are Christians who are loaded down with self-will, who have rejected the Cross of Christ, which regrettably also characterizes the far greater majority of the modern Church.

Most of the Churches of Paul's day were in fact planted by the Apostle; consequently, virtually all of the people in these Churches had heard the True Gospel. But yet, there were some who came in such as the Judiazers, who definitely had rejected the Cross, and more particularly, the Christ of the Cross, rather proclaiming *"another Jesus."* Actually, this was the same Jesus, but proclaimed in a different way.

NOTES

### UNREASONABLE AND WICKED MEN

The phrase, *"And that we may be delivered from unreasonable and wicked men,"* can only be understood as to whom these individuals might be, by linking the last phrase of this Verse concerning Faith with the first phrase.

The word *"unreasonable"* means *"absurd or out of place, amiss."*

*"Wicked men"* refers to those with bad aims and purposes. They are sometimes well-meaning but misguided.

These individuals, whomever they may have been, had not the right view of things; and probably does not refer so much to their being positively wicked or malicious, as *"to their putting things out of their proper place."* They gave an undue prominence to certain things, and less importance to others than they deserved. They had a distorted view of the Word of God, which presented a constant obstruction to the True Gospel.

### THE FAITH

The phrase, *"For all men have not Faith,"* should have been translated, *"For all men have not the Faith,"* for it refers to a specific type of Faith, i.e., *"Faith in Christ and His Finished Work accomplished at the Cross."*

Had Paul been speaking here of rank sinners, he would not have mentioned the word Faith, and especially *"the Faith,"* simply because it is a given that the unsaved do not have *"the Faith,"* or any type of Faith for that matter as it refers to God. Being spiritually dead, Faith in the Word of God, has no meaning for the unsaved.

So, Paul is speaking here of so-called Believers in the Church, who had their eyes fixed on religious beliefs which did not coincide with *"the Faith,"* i.e., *"the Cross of Christ."*

Such individuals cause terrible problems in the Church, simply because their doctrine is wrong, it being a doctrine of works, etc. Paul calls them *"unreasonable and wicked,"* showing us what he thinks of those, or rather what the Holy Spirit thinks of those, who have repudiated the Cross of Christ; as strong as the warning was then, as strong must be the warning presently!

These individuals are addressed in this manner because of several reasons. The following are some:

1. They have purposely rejected the Cross of Christ, substituting other things in its place.

2. Purposely rejecting it, means they also oppose it, and to the point of bodily harm if necessary, concerning those who preach the Cross. To be frank, the modern varieties would do the same if the law of the land permitted such.

3. Any doctrine which does not stream directly from the Cross, is listed here by Paul as *"wicked!"* The idea is: A. To try to live and be as one ought to outside of the Cross, is without fail going to produce wickedness in the heart and life of any individual who attempts such a course; and, B. Anything which is proposed as the Way of the Lord outside of the Cross is labeled as *"wicked!"* In fact, this is the great sin of man, attempting to save oneself outside of trusting in Christ and the Cross, or attempting to live the Christian Life by means and ways other than the Cross of Christ (Rom. 8:8).

*"The Faith"* always refers to *"Jesus Christ and Him Crucified"* (I Cor. 2:2). By Paul using the definite article *"the"* in the Greek, proclaims to us that the Holy Spirit is saying this is the only Faith, and anything else that proposes itself to be Faith, is not recognized by the Lord. Consequently, this puts the modern Church into serious circumstances, for the Cross plays little part in today's modern Gospel.

(3) "BUT THE LORD IS FAITHFUL, WHO SHALL STABLISH YOU, AND KEEP YOU FROM EVIL."

The appeal here is away from man to the Faithfulness of God, a familiar expression with Paul (I Cor. 1:9; 10:13; I Thess. 5:24).

In Verse 3, Paul shifts back abruptly from a request for himself to concern for his Readers. They needed to be guarded from the Evil One, whose strategy included both deception as *"an angel of light"* (II Cor. 11:14) and the pressure of persecution as *"a roaring lion"* (I Pet. 5:8).

NOTES

## THE LORD IS FAITHFUL

The phrase, *"But the Lord is Faithful,"* presents the appeal to the revealed character of God, despite all the outward appearances or circumstances which militate against Faith, which is one of the basic characteristics of the Thessalonian Letters. This is equally true of the teaching on either moral matters or future events. The Faithfulness of God — this is the soul's anchor in the storm and in the darkness. In other words, God can be depended on. Though men cannot be trusted, God is faithful to His Promises and His Purposes. He may always be confided in; and when men are unbelieving, perverse, unkind, and disposed to do us wrong, we may go to Him, and we shall always find in Him One in Whom we may confide and trust.

Once again, this phrase *"But the Lord is faithful,"* harks back to the previous Verse, and lends credence to the fact that Paul is there speaking of those in the Church who were not faithful, because they would not subscribe to *"the Faith,"* i.e., *"the Cross."*

## THE CHILDREN OF ISRAEL IN THE WILDERNESS

The Lord took the Children of Israel through the wilderness after leaving Egypt, in order to teach them specific lessons. They could have gone another way; however, He wanted them to be placed in a position to where they had to trust Him exclusively. There were no bakeries in the wilderness, little pasture for the flocks in the wilderness if any, and many times even no water. So, they had to trust God for everything, and they proved that He was faithful. In other words, He could set a table in the wilderness, which He did!

That Israel had to remain there for nearly 40 years was their fault and not God's. He only intended for them to stay in the wilderness for about a year at the most.

Believers have to learn that the Lord is Faithful, because at the outset, Believers have a tendency to want to trust other men. To be frank, Preachers are the worst of all concerning this. They look to other men to get them places to preach, other men to provide Churches for them, etc. This can never be pleasing to God.

He wants us to look to Him, and through experience come to the knowledge that He is Faithful. By that we mean the following:

As stated, man most of the time isn't faithful; in fact, only a few actually are. So, as Believers, while we love all the Brethren, we must learn to put our trust totally and completely in God, and not man. Man will fail you, whereas God will never fail.

### A PERSONAL EXPERIENCE

Since late 1991, Jimmy Swaggart Ministries has had to learn to trust God exclusively and totally for anything and everything. All other means of existence, of sustenance, of provision in totality, were cut off. In other words, we could expect no help from man, be it those in the world or those in the Church. To be frank, those in the Church world, at least almost all, were doing everything they could to completely silence this Ministry. They did not succeed, but it was not for lack of trying.

This meant that we have had to trust God for every single thing, and that includes the finances, Ministry, to open doors for Missions projects, in other words, everything!

We have learned that the Lord is faithful, and we have learned it by experience, which is the greatest education of all. To be sure, there have been times that I didn't know how we would make it, but every single time the Lord has always provided. He just keeps working miracle after miracle, showing, just as He did so long ago with Israel, that He definitely can set a table in the wilderness. Again I emphasize, *"The Lord is Faithful!"*

In all of this, I have learned to look to Him exclusively, to depend on Him exclusively, to look to man not at all, but only to the Lord. To be sure, we love the Brethren, and it hurts when they seek to hinder the Work of God, or make attempts to keep us from carrying out the Call of God on our lives. But I've learned to place them in the Hands of the Lord and let the Lord take care of the situation. Again, He is Faithful!

### THE ESTABLISHMENT OF FAITH

The phrase, *"Who shall stablish you,"* refers to what the Lord will do in our lives, if we will only give Him latitude.

NOTES

The establishing of which Paul speaks here, concerns *"the Faith."* In other words, He will establish us in the Faith, which has to do with the Cross of Christ, which of course is the Finished Work. We will learn in being established, that the solution to every problem is in the Cross, the answer to every question is in the Cross, and the meeting of every need is in the Cross! When the Believer is thus established, he will truly know what is *"More Abundant Life"* (Jn. 10:10), and the *"Rest"* promised by Christ Jesus upon coming to Him (Mat. 11:28-30).

Being established accordingly, creates an assurance in the heart and life of such a Believer. It is the greatest life there is, the most rewarding life. This is what Christianity actually is, and keeps one shouting the victory, irrespective of the persecution or difficulties otherwise.

Beginning sometime in 1997, the Lord began to open up to me the great Revelation of the Cross. From that time on, this Revelation has continued, and along with that has come a *"joy unspeakable and full of glory."* So, this of which I say, I have lived; consequently, I know what I'm talking about, having literally proved the Word of God.

### PROTECTION FROM EVIL

The phrase, *"And keep you from evil,"* refers to the only way that one can be kept from evil, which refers to being established in *"the Faith!"*

Several translations have *"the Evil One"*; however, it really doesn't matter! The Cross of Christ, and one's Faith in the Cross, guarantees the help of the Holy Spirit, and protects the Believer from both the Evil One and his evil, i.e., *"evil designs."*

(4) "AND WE HAVE CONFIDENCE IN THE LORD TOUCHING YOU, THAT YE BOTH DO AND WILL DO THE THINGS WHICH WE COMMAND YOU."

Confidence in the Lord's Faithfulness leads to an expression of confidence in the Readers, who belong to the Lord.

*"Confidence in the Lord about you"* is an expression which puts rather concisely the Divine and human factors involved in the successful work of the Church. Confidence, in this matter, is not in the Lord Alone irrespective of human cooperation. Certainly, confidence

ought not to be in people alone. Rather, confidence of success is well-founded when men keep themselves in the Hands of the Lord, and when the Lord is permitted to work through obedient human channels (Airhart).

## CONFIDENCE IN THE LORD CONCERNING YOU

The phrase, *"And we have confidence in the Lord touching you,"* proclaims the obedience of the Thessalonians which flowed from the Grace of Christ; it was in consequence of the communication of the influences of the Holy Spirit that they were enabled to make progress and to persevere in the Christian life. This idea is this:

The Thessalonians were properly grounded in *"the Faith,"* i.e., *"the Cross,"* thereby established and protected from the Evil One; therefore, Paul definitely could express confidence in them, because they were on the right road to victory and Spiritual Growth. Outside of the Cross there is no confidence; in the Cross, there is all confidence! *"In the Lord"* qualifies this statement.

Of course, even as we have stated, his confidence in the Thessalonians was not in their own ability or strength, but rather *"in the Lord."* However, it must be understood, that millions claim to be in the Lord, while living a life of spiritual failure all the time; consequently, the idea is:

While many Believers are definitely *"in the Lord,"* that is if they're truly Born-Again, they definitely aren't reaping the results of their position in Christ, but rather the opposite. While they are saved, there is no victory, and because their Faith is misplaced.

Of course, when Paul speaks of someone being *"in the Lord,"* he is meaning that they firmly understand their place and position in Christ, which means that they know and realize that all things come from and through the Cross of Christ. Consequently, they are to ever evidence Faith in that Finished Work, and then they can expect the help of the Holy Spirit, Who is able to keep any and all Saints walking in total and perpetual victory.

## A SCRIPTURAL AND SPIRITUAL CHARGE

The phrase, *"That ye both do and will do the things which we command you,"* presents

NOTES

the fact and even the Truth, that growth in Grace, constancy, and steadfastness of purpose can be realized only as Believers maintain an attitude of obedience toward God, actually, an attitude that is motivated by a love for Him that transcends all other objects of affection.

God Alone can give proper direction to our course, a course incidently that will involve, whether we like it or not, further opposition and persecutions and maybe even sufferings, and thus further growth in patience and Grace.

The word translated *"command"* is a strong expression, commonly used of military orders. The same term is used in Verses 6, 10, and 12. Paul is tactfully preparing the Readers for the disciplinary measures which will follow.

It must always be understood, that the Word of God does not contain suggestions, but as far as we are concerned, whether it is issued in the form of a command or not, it definitely in our minds must be a command to us. What Paul was talking about with the Thessalonians, and all others for that matter, is the Word of God, so it must be heeded and followed in this spirit.

Paul knew that what he was giving them was the Word, and if obeyed, would result in tremendous Spiritual Growth and constant victory. If disobeyed, the opposite would be the result, hence the Apostle using such terminology as *"command!"*

## THESE COMMANDS AND THE CROSS

In all of these terms used by the Apostle such as *"in the Lord,"* or *"command,"* etc., as well as all the great words of the Faith such as Grace, Love, etc., all and without exception, lead straight to the Cross. As I've said several times already, when we use these terms, we are at the same time speaking of the Cross, and when we mention the Cross, we are at the same time using these terms, whatever they might be. The Reader understanding that, will find the Word of God much easier to comprehend, actually explaining itself.

It is true that the Apostle doesn't mention the Cross every time he mentions these particulars, and for several reasons. First of all, should he have done such a thing, the Bible would have been six feet thick. As well, there is another reason which carries much more weight:

Every single thing that Paul wrote, as well as every other writer in the Bible, was inspired by the Holy Spirit. In other words, they said exactly what the Holy Spirit wanted them to say, even down to the very word.

In studying the Bible all of my life, I noticed a long time ago, that the Holy Spirit will oftentimes veil things to where the mere surface attention does not bring out the actual Truth contained therein. In other words, we have to dig!

Paul said, *"In Whom* (Christ) *are hid all the treasures of wisdom and knowledge"* (Col. 2:3).

This means that these particular treasures are not on the surface, but are rather somewhat hidden, which requires, as stated, that we dig for these things, etc.

Once the Believer sees the Cross, understands the Cross, which actually means to understand the Plan of God, then the Believer will see the Cross in every single thing that's said and done respecting the Word of God. While it's not all the time on the surface, even as we are addressing here, it is nevertheless there!

(5) "AND THE LORD DIRECT YOUR HEARTS INTO THE LOVE OF GOD, AND INTO THE PATIENT WAITING FOR CHRIST."

The help of the Lord of course, is indispensable as it regards our daily victory. Paul has complimented the Thessalonians, but that does not imply that they are self-sufficient.

Consequently, two particulars are presented in this Verse:

1. The realization and understanding that we are in need of God's help constantly. Inasmuch as God is Love, and desires to do good things for us, it is not difficult to obtain His help, providing we understand one thing:

We must never forget that all of the help we receive, all of the sustenance obtained, all of the Blessings which follow, all and without exception come through what Jesus did at the Cross and in His Resurrection. We are to look to the Cross constantly, ever having Faith in that Finished Work, realizing our own insufficiency and total insufficiency at that, which will guarantee the help of the Holy Spirit. This is the secret of victorious, overcoming, powerful Christian living.

2. The patient waiting for Christ, does not refer to the coming Rapture, but rather that our Faith is not to waiver in times of difficulties regarding particulars, but that we are to have confidence that in His time, He will do that which we need, whatever that need might be.

NOTES

There is stress here on the primacy of the heart life of Christians. The emphatic language suggests that it is vitally important, which should be obvious, for God to be in control of our hearts.

Getting back to our waiting on Christ, we must ever understand, that He is never late while at the same time, He is never early. His timing is just as important as that which He will do, when the time arrives, whatever it might be.

## THE DIRECTION OF THE LORD

The phrase, *"And the Lord direct your hearts into the Love of God,"* tells us that the Lord wants total control within our lives, but it is control which must be freely given by ourselves to Him, for He will never take it by force.

As well, we must understand, that everything He does for us, with us, to us, or in any capacity for that matter, is strictly done by His Love. In other words, He has nothing but Love for us, and all His dealings with us, are done strictly from the basis of the Love of God, and from no other principle. Of course, all of this is done through the Person, Agency, Office, and Power of the Holy Spirit, Who abides within us (Jn. 14:16).

As we've said time and time again, the Holy Spirit works within our hearts and lives strictly according to the parameters of what Jesus did on the Cross and in His Resurrection. That always is His sphere of operation; however, it is imperative, that we freely and willingly give the Spirit control of our lives. To be sure He wants that control, and in fact, cannot do near for us what He desires to do, as stated, unless He has that control. But it's control which we must freely give Him. He always functions as a perfect gentleman within our hearts and lives.

It is somewhat as if He is a visitor, and then it's up to us, to make Him feel at home, by desiring strongly that He take control. This is the manner in which the Lord directs our lives, that is if we will allow Him to do so.

NOTES

A PERSONAL EXPERIENCE

I can remember the very first time I ever even heard anything about the Holy Spirit. I was eight years old. In fact, I hadn't even known before then that there was a Holy Spirit; however, from that moment forward, and I will not take the time to go into the detail as to how I heard, I have had a hunger for the Spirit of God within my heart. Actually, I was Baptized with the Holy Spirit with the evidence of speaking with other Tongues just a few weeks later.

I have watched Him work within my life from then until now in amazing ways, letting me know day-by-day, just how important He really is to all that I am and all that I do.

And yet, from the time that the Lord began to give me the Revelation of the Cross, which if I remember correctly, began sometime in early 1997, from then until now (December of 1999), I think I have learned more about the Holy Spirit than all my previous experience put together. It is like a proper understanding of the Cross has opened up an understanding of the Holy Spirit, even as it has in everything else pertaining to the Word of God, and more particularly, His Person.

In fact, one cannot really learn about Christ without the direction of the Holy Spirit, and one cannot learn about the Holy Spirit without a proper understanding of the Cross.

A.W. Tozer said, *"If we do not properly understand the Cross of Christ and our place and part in that great Finished Work, we clip the wings of the Holy Spirit,"* or words to that effect.

THE HEART

As we've explained previously, the Holy Spirit uses the term *"the heart,"* as it refers to man, to describe the very depths of one's being. It speaks of one's passions, feelings, will, intellect, even the soul and the spirit, and more particularly the soul and the spirit. It has nothing to do with the heart as a physical organ as we think of such.

Consequently, it is from the heart that control which the Holy Spirit desires must be given.

This is the reason Salvation cannot be merely an intellectual affair, even though it definitely does affect the intellect, Salvation of necessity must begin in the heart, which refers to the depth of one's very being.

This was typified under the old Mosaic Law, by the *"Whole Burnt-Offering."* The entirety of the animal except for its skin, was to be offered up on the Altar, specifying that God gives His all for us, which in fact He did, in the Sacrifice of His Son and our Saviour, the Lord Jesus Christ. The Whole Burnt-Offering also specified, that inasmuch as the Lord has given His all for us, we are in turn, to give our all to Him, i.e., *"the heart!"*

THE LOVE OF GOD

Man almost all of the time operates from the position of greed, selfishness, personal ambition, etc. It is pretty much from the position, *"do it unto him before he does it unto you!"*

Someone has well said, that too often the friends we have are such because of what we can do *for* them or *to* them. That's a sad state of affairs, but regrettably, it is the Truth.

Of course, that is the way man operates and not God. He functions entirely from the premise of Love. Man was created not out of need, but from the principal of love; consequently, man has been redeemed in the same way. This actually means, that every single thing that God does, and that speaks of His creation of all things, His dealings with man, in fact all that He does in every capacity, is without exception, done from the principal of love. Even the Judgment of God which at times must be brought into play, is done from love, and love totally. It is difficult for sinful man to see this, actually it is impossible! In fact, everything that unredeemed man looks at, he looks at with a jaundiced eye, which colors everything he sees in terms of greed, selfishness, etc.

After the believing sinner comes to Christ, while his understanding of God instantly changes because of the Divine Nature that is now within him, still, he (the Believer) must learn to function from an entirely different manner than he has previously known . . . from the basis of love. The following will hopefully help us to understand this a little better:

1. The first thing the Believer must understand is, even as we have just stated, that God functions totally and completely from

the principal of love. In fact, *"God is Love,"* which is somewhat difficult for us to understand. We as Believers have love, but that is a far cry from actually *"being love,"* which God is! However, the idea is, that the Love of God becomes so much a part of us, that we actually become love as well. While it is true that we can never come up to His level as should be obvious, still, this should be our motivation and goal.

2. In view of what we have just said, we must understand that everything that God does *with us* and for us, is totally from the basis of love, and nothing else. He has no ulterior motives! Once we understand this, and function ourselves totally from this premise, we will truly begin to see God as our *"Heavenly Father."*

3. The cause of fear in the heart of the Child of God, is because of an imperfect love toward our Heavenly Father. John plainly said, *"There is no fear in love; but perfect love casteth out fear: because fear hath torment. He that feareth is not made perfect in love"* (I Jn. 4:18). The idea is this:

If we properly understand just how much that God loves us, and that our love is complete in Him, we will automatically know that first of all nothing can happen to us without His direct approval, etc. We do not belong to Satan, and he has no control over us and in fact, he has nothing to say about what happens to us in any capacity. We are strictly in the domain of the Heavenly Father, and we must understand that.

Consequently, if our love for God is as it ought to be, we will ever know that He has nothing but good for us, and is working everything toward our good, and will allow nothing to happen to us but that it is ultimately good. Consequently, *"perfect love casteth out fear."*

4. Unless we understand the Cross of Christ, thereby placing all our Faith in that great Finished Work, understanding that this was the greatest display of love the world has ever known, we cannot really grow in love toward the Lord. The Cross of Christ is the foundation of such love, which means that the Love of God within our hearts and lives is predicated totally upon our understanding of the Cross and our place in that Finished Work.

NOTES

In fact, a proper understanding of the Cross is an absolute necessity as it regards anything we are in the Lord, or receive from the Lord.

Does the Reader understand this?

PATIENT WAITING

The phrase, *"And into the patient waiting for Christ,"* pertains to our waiting for Him to rectify the situation, whatever the situation might be.

In the case of the Thessalonians, they were undergoing severe persecution. Knowing that God can do anything, and can do so immediately as He so desires, the great question always is, even as it must have been with the Thessalonians, why doesn't the Lord stop or change this situation of persecution now? The Holy Spirit through Paul is here telling us that we should *"patiently wait for Christ,"* which as stated, teaches us many things.

Believers must be brought to the understanding that our petitions to the Lord regarding Him doing any number of things, must of necessity involve everything instead of merely our own desires. In other words, when we ask the Lord to do something, most of the time we think only of ourselves. We have need of Him doing certain things as it affects us. However we must ever understand, that the help that the Lord gives us is always designed with two things in mind:

1. Everything is for our good, even the delay.

2. Oftentimes, answers to prayer on our behalf involves others being affected. The Lord loves these people as well, and of course, will do nothing to harm them. Therefore, at times an answer must be delayed on their account.

3. As we grow in the Lord, we must come to the place that we petition Him on the basis of His Divine Plan. In other words, we want the overall good of everything, exactly as He does, hence our petition being offered in this respect. Then we patiently wait for Him, knowing that His timing is just as important as all other things He does.

As well, our waiting on the Lord is never wasted time. In the meantime, He draws us closer to Him, teaches us patience, increases our Faith, and renews our strength (Isa. 40:31).

(6) "NOW WE COMMAND YOU, BRETHREN, IN THE NAME OF OUR LORD JESUS CHRIST THAT YE WITHDRAW YOURSELVES FROM EVERY BROTHER THAT WALKETH DISORDERLY, AND NOT AFTER THE TRADITION WHICH HE RECEIVED OF US."

Paul now comes to practical Christianity. The things we claim as from the Lord, as it regards Salvation, Redemption, etc., if not played out in our lives, is a glaring testimony to the fact that actually these great attributes aren't present. In other words, the individual is professing but not actually possessing.

WE COMMAND YOU

The phrase, *"Now we command you, Brethren, in the Name of our Lord Jesus Christ,"* does not present itself as a Preacher demanding or commanding certain things, but rather the Apostle saying, that what he is telling the people is *"the Word of God."* As such, it should always be a command to us, in whatever capacity it might be. This is the idea of the statement.

Much space in this Letter is given to dealing with the disorderly and idle Brethren in the Church. This indicates that the problem had grown more serious than at the time of the writing of the first Letter, in which relatively little space was given to this (I Thess. 4:11-12; 5:14). Evidently the idlers had failed to heed the first Letter. Stronger measures are, therefore, to be taken.

In fact, *"In the Name of our Lord Jesus Christ,"* as used here, means *"by the authority of Jesus Christ."* Paul thus commands the Church who are addressed as *"Brethren."* The command is authoritative, and yet the appeal is that of a Brother to his Brethren.

WHAT THE SCRIPTURES MEAN BY THE TERM *"CHURCH!"*

When most people think of Church, they think of a particular Denomination, or the Church where they attend, or the Church on the corner, etc.

None of that is what the Scripture refers to when the word *"Church"* is used, or even the word *"Brethren,"* which Paul uses here in addressing the Church.

It is unfortunate, but even most Spirit-filled people think of the Church in the wrong

NOTES

terms. They almost always equate it with some type of Denomination or at least a fellowship of some kind. When this is done, spiritual authority is always misplaced. In other words, Believers will grant spiritual authority to democratically elected administrators in the Church, or to some self-appointed individual. In fact, there has been so little teaching on this subject, that most Believers hardly even know what the Church is anymore. Particular Denominations claim they are *"the Church,"* with evidently some people believing it or they could not continue the charade.

When the term *"Church,"* or any similar term such as *"Brethren"* are used in the Bible, it is simply referring to individuals who have been *"called out of the world,"* and *"called unto God,"* i.e., *"born again!"* (Jn. 3:3). It is never referring to a Denomination, to a particular institution, or anything of such nature. So, the spiritual authority claimed by Denominations, or self-appointed individuals, carry no Scriptural validity, and are to be ignored. Christ is the *"Head"* of the Church and not man. The Holy Spirit is the One Who carries out the commands of Christ in every respect, all designed to bring about the *"Will of God"* in the hearts and lives of individual members of this great *"Church,"* i.e., *"Body of Christ"* (Rom. 8:26-27).

Millions of Christians have it in their minds, that if some Leader in a Denomination or Fellowship of some kind, who has been elected by popular ballot issues forth some type of command, that it must be obeyed without question.

Not only are such commands not to be obeyed, they are more than all just simply to be ignored. While we as Believers are to love all people, and especially those in the Church, still, we are not to obey that which is unscriptural. The Word of God is to always be the criteria for all things. And there is no place in the Word that gives anyone spiritual authority who has in fact taken on himself that authority, which means it's not granted by Scripture.

WHAT CONSTITUTES LEADERSHIP IN THE CHURCH?

As we have stated, Christ is always the *"Head"* of the Church, and the Holy Spirit is the One Who always carries out the commands of Christ, and does so in every respect. So, the Believer is to earnestly seek the Lord at all times, asking the leadership of the Holy Spirit in all things (Jn. 16:13).

One of the major reasons that unscriptural men in unscriptural positions, occupying unscriptural offices, can do these things, is simply because most Christians little seek the Lord respecting guidance and leading, but rather leave it up to someone else. In fact, it is much easier to leave it up to someone else, at least in the short run. To be sure, to do such in the long run, will cause spiritual wreckage in many lives.

Second, the Pastor of the Local Church is to be looked at as spiritual authority, providing that what he is preaching and teaching is Scriptural. Once again, everything is to be judged according to the Word of God. If anyone steps outside the boundaries of Scripture, they are not to be obeyed, as ought to be obvious. The sadness is, most Believers have no idea as to what is Scriptural or not Scriptural. Sadly, when the Church gets in this condition, it is on the verge of self-destruction, at least from a spiritual viewpoint.

The Local Church as spiritual authority, and more particularly the Pastor of that Church, has its foundation in the entirety of the Book of Acts and the Epistles. As well, when Jesus gave His Messages to the seven Churches of Asia, those Messages were more to the point sent to the Pastors of those particular Churches (Rev. 2:1, etc.). This shows us where the authority is ensconced at least where the Local Church is concerned, but once again, everything must be predicated on the Scripturality of each situation. Obedience is never to be enjoined regarding that which is unscriptural.

Other than the Pastor of the Local Church, spiritual authority is of course given as well to all the fivefold Callings of *"Apostles, Prophets, Evangelists, Pastors, and Teachers"* (Eph. 4:11). However, when we speak of spiritual authority, we must always understand, that this is never over other human beings, but rather over evil spirits in the world as it regards all the powers of darkness (Eph. 6:11-18).

If one is to notice, the type of spiritual authority claimed by Denominational Leaders, etc., is always over other people. It is virtually never over evil spirits of darkness, which are the real cause of problems in the Church.

When it comes to Leadership as far as Doctrine is concerned which of course charts the course for the Church, and which as well must always be Scriptural, such Leadership is always ensconced in *"Apostles."* In other words, the thrust of the Church will always come through these whom God has called in a special way respecting a special Message for the Church, which gives it leadership and direction. Of course, the Church is not forced to heed this which the Holy Spirit gives, but can reject that which the Spirit is saying to the Churches; however, as should be obvious, such will always be done with great spiritual peril in the offing (Rev. 2:7, etc.).

Direction for the Church as it regards Leadership and Doctrine, is never given through Educators, Administrators, Denominational Leaders, or self-appointed Bishops, etc., but always by *"Apostles."* We find this in the entirety of the Book of Acts and in the Epistles.

As well, Apostles are called by God, and not elected by popular ballot. This means that someone being elected to some particular religious, administrative office, in no way means that they are an Apostle, or in fact, that they have any type of spiritual authority whatsoever, which in fact, they don't!

That doesn't mean that those offices are wrong! In fact, they aren't wrong, that is if they are understood in their correct perspective. The Church needs Administration and, therefore, to carry out such, it needs Administrators. But we're not to confuse that with spiritual authority, or even spiritual leadership.

The Lord does not operate His Work as a democracy. Actually, He doesn't function at all like earthly governments, etc. Unfortunately, the Church far too often seeks to do just that, i.e., *"operate like the world!"* In fact, *"improper Church Government"* has been the cause of most spiritual declension down through the ages. It has brought more harm to the Church than anything else that Satan has proposed. Men love to wield authority, and religious men most of all. They are not content to let the Lord be the *"Head"*

NOTES

of His Church, but rather treat Him as a passive Head. Also, in such an atmosphere, the Holy Spirit is able to function little, if any at all; consequently, most all activity carried out in that which we refer to as *"Church,"* is not of God, which means it was not originated by the Holy Spirit, which means it is man-devised. Therefore, the Holy Spirit can have nothing to do with this which functions in this manner. The Spirit can bless only that which the Spirit originates and carries out. Regrettably, there aren't very many Preachers of the Gospel, or Laity for that matter, who will seek the Lord in such a fashion. But thank God for the few who do, for they are the ones who impact the entirety of the world, with all the religious machinery which fills the land, affecting the world not at all!

### THOSE WHO WALK DISORDERLY

The phrase, *"That ye withdraw yourselves from every Brother that walketh disorderly,"* refers to those who will not heed the Word of God, as given by the Apostle Paul, even as the next phrase proclaims.

The phrase *"that ye withdraw yourselves"* presents a nautical expression, which means *"shorten the sails."* Metaphorically it means to keep out of the way, to withdraw, and rather to withdraw fellowship. There is no allusion to excommunication.

*"That walketh disorderly,"* literally means, *"to walk out of the ranks of the Word of God."*

Due perhaps to excitement about the Coming of the Lord (or whatever), the disorderly Brethren were loafing, refusing to work, turning from their duties, and accepting no responsibility. This probably led to meddlesome conduct and even dependence on others for support.

The Church is a social fellowship as well as a spiritual fellowship, and must bear responsibility for the conduct of its members. It cannot be indifferent to these unruly Brethren. In order to preserve Christian standards, the disorderly must be made to feel the pressure of Christian sentiment against their irresponsible conduct.

For instance, the Church is to avoid close company with such loafers in order to shame them. As stated, excommunication or total ostracism are not to be contemplated, but rather a social aloofness which will indicate that a standard has been raised, and that to violate it invites the rebuke of the Church.

NOTES

When the Brother or Sister begins to show responsibility in that they are mending their ways, they are to be welcomed back into fellowship and made to feel welcome.

As this would direct itself to loafers, of which we will say more in a moment, it also should be carried out with regard to any type of situation. If there are Christians who are living in sin, and refuse to repent, the Scripture plainly says that we must disfellowship these people (I Cor. Chpt. 5). If they do repent, and there is evidence of that repentance, which is not hard to ascertain, they are to be instantly restored, even as I Corinthians, Chapter 2 brings out.

To be sure, there may definitely be some situations which would arise, which are very severe in nature, for example as child molestation. If that, God forbid, would be the case, and even if there is adequate repentance, due to the fact that others could possibly be harmed, even little children, it would not be wise to restore that individual immediately to a position of leadership of any nature. Common sense would dictate such a course as should be obvious.

While not many situations of this nature would arise, due to fallen man living in a fallen world, it is wise to expect anything, and to do our very best to prepare for the same. If we seek to follow the Word in all accounts, to be sure, the Holy Spirit will give us guidance in all things (Jn. 16:13).

### INSTRUCTIONS RECEIVED FROM US

The phrase, *"And not after the tradition which he received of us,"* refers to instructions already given by Paul, which in effect, had been given to him by the Holy Spirit. Consequently, they were binding, inasmuch as they were from God, and were, therefore, *"The Word of God."*

The Apostle is saying that these individuals, whomever they were, who were conducting themselves in a disorderly fashion, knew better, for these very matters had been discussed by Paul when he was there, and mention had been made in the previous Epistle (I Thessalonians).

This shows by the word *"tradition"* the Apostle did not mean *"unwritten doctrines"* handed down from one to another, as normally this word means. He is meaning, that this is what the Lord had given him, and he had given it to the Church at Thessalonica, and furthermore, it worked, even as the Word of God always works, and should be practiced.

(7) "FOR YOURSELVES KNOW HOW YE OUGHT TO FOLLOW US: FOR WE BEHAVED NOT OURSELVES DISORDERLY AMONG YOU;"

Paul calls attention here to his own example, and the Holy Spirit allowed him to do such.

We should be able to do so accordingly, but only if our example measures up.

The Apostle was not an idler. His Readers could verify this claim (*"you yourselves know,"* I Thess. 2:1; 3:3; 4:2; 5:2). In fact, in imitating Paul, they would be imitating the Lord Himself (I Thess. 1:6) because Paul's life was so carefully patterned after his Lord's. He did not loaf at Thessalonica, nor depend on others.

Paul did not have to exert himself so tirelessly. As an Apostle, he had *"the right to such help"* (I Cor. 9:4; I Thess. 2:7). He decided, however, to forego this privilege and leave an example for them to imitate.

## TO FOLLOW PAUL

The phrase, *"For yourselves know how ye ought to follow us,"* was said by the Apostle for several different reasons. *"Follow"* in the Greek is *"mineomai,"* and means *"to imitate."* Some of these reasons are as follows:

1. The Word of the Lord: Paul had been given the New Covenant, which actually proclaims that for which Jesus died. Consequently, more than anyone in the world at that time, he knew the Way of Salvation.

To be sure, Peter, John, and others, definitely preached Jesus, which of course upon acceptance by believing sinners meant Salvation; however, even though they knew that even greater than Paul due to having spent some three and one half years personally with Christ, still, when it came to the rudiments of Sanctification, which Paul is actually discussing here, in this they deferred to him.

I don't want the Reader to think that all other Apostles other than Paul were lightweights, for that definitely was not the case at all! In fact, these other men were mightily used of God as ought to be obvious, still, it was to Paul to whom the New Covenant was given; consequently, he was the only one at the beginning, who knew all its ramifications. That's the reason he did his very best to train men like Timothy, Silas, etc.

2. The Apostle definitely wasn't being egotistical by using the phrase *"follow me."* The simple Truth was, he knew the way; consequently, it would have been wrong for him to have said otherwise.

3. False apostles and false teachers were constantly rearing their heads trying to draw people away after themselves, which continues unto this hour. As I've said many times, Satan is a master at getting people to believe that *"what is of God isn't, and what isn't of God is!"* Of course, he does so by deception. And to be sure, if that problem was rampant then, hence Paul admonishing the Thessalonians to follow him, to be sure, the problem is acute presently.

## HOW DOES THE BELIEVER KNOW WHAT IS RIGHT?

As we've said previously, all false apostles appeal to baser desires in the hearts and lives of Believers. One of the favorite ways presently is to appeal to greed. In other words, the people are told, if they will give so much money to this particular Preacher, that the Lord will grandly regard them with many times more than what they have given. It's all cloaked with many Scriptures, twisted I might quickly add, which makes it seem right to the unwary soul. As well, it seems that all of us have at least, in some ways, a modicum of greed in our hearts; consequently, the ground seems to always be fertile there, at least to a certain extent.

And then false teachers, and I speak of those who have an agenda in mind other than the proper spiritual development of the Believer, appeal as stated, to baser instincts. In other words, people are told as to how much their talents and abilities are overlooked, while at the same time, the false teacher subtly discounts the true man of God. It's all very subtle, very slick, and loaded with Scriptures, and most of the time with a few prophetic words thrown in, even as Paul addressed in Verse 2 of the previous Chapter.

Irrespective of the tact taken, there has to be something ill-conceived in the heart of the individual, before the false teacher can pull them aside. If the Believer is humble before the Lord, and is daily seeking the Lord asking for leading and guidance by the Holy Spirit, ever watchful for the wiles of the Evil One, seeking his best to know the Word and follow the Word, there is no danger of that person being led astray. Unfortunately, not very many fall into that category.

False teachers desire to pull away individuals from the True Way of Christ, to other ways, basically for two reasons:

1. They want to control people; however, they want to control people for various reasons, with the greatest reason of all being the carrying out of their agenda, whatever that agenda might be.
2. Money: Somewhere behind it all, one will always find money to be the culprit. That's why Paul also said, *"the love of money is the root of all evil"* (I Tim. 6:10).

### BEHAVIOR

The phrase, *"For we behaved not ourselves disorderly among you,"* means that he did not get out of his rank or post of duty, but kept his place and discharged his duties at all times and places as a true and tried soldier of Jesus Christ.

*"Disorderly"* in the Greek is *"ataktos,"* and means *"out of order, not in order of battle, not at one's post of duty, undisciplined, irregular, lawless, and, therefore, disorderly."*

Paul could make this bold command because he was *"imitating Jesus."* He said in another place, *"Be ye followers* (imitators) *of me, even as I also am of Christ"* (I Cor. 11:1). As long as we know Christ, are doing our level best to imitate Him, and are sure of such within our hearts, then and only then, could we make such a statement as Paul makes here.

The word *"disorderly"* as used here by the Apostle actually cuts two ways: A. The opposite of disorderly is a sanctified life, in other words, that sin has no dominion over the individual (Rom. 6:14); and, B. It speaks of the way in which one lives regarding their duties, which we will study in the next Verse.

NOTES

(8) "NEITHER DID WE EAT ANY MAN'S BREAD FOR NOUGHT; BUT WROUGHT WITH LABOUR AND TRAVAIL NIGHT AND DAY, THAT WE MIGHT NOT BE CHARGEABLE TO ANY OF YOU:"

Now we come to the practical applications of Christianity. What the Apostle will say here ought to be read and reread by all Believers, and for each word to be taken to heart.

If Christianity doesn't affect in a positive way one's responsibilities, one's duties, one's actions, in other words, practical Christian living, then it's not much Christianity. In other words, the person needs to go back and read the Word again, and apply it to himself.

### PAUL WAS NO SPONGER

The phrase, *"Neither did we eat any man's bread for nought,"* means that the Apostle didn't make himself a burden to others. Let's look at actually what was happening here:

When Paul went into a new area to build a Church, he would immediately secure gainful employment for himself, most of the time as a repairer of tents, etc. Every Jewish Father was obligated to teach their sons a trade, irrespective as to how wealthy they might have been. This was a part of their culture. Evidently, the craft of tent repairing or tentmaking, was the trade which had been taught Paul when he was a boy. Even though it was what we might presently call *"minimum wage work,"* that was the way he supported himself in these places.

After a period of time people would begin to be saved with a Church being formed; however, the Apostle continued to support himself in this manner, at least in part for the following reasons:

Almost all of these people who would come to Christ were Gentiles, which means they had formerly been idol worshippers. Almost every city had several major, heathen temples, of which to at least one, most every Gentile was a devotee. The priests of these heathen temples, used every ploy they could to wheedle money out of their followers. Paul wanted to set an example, that the Gospel of Christ was not in any way similar to the heathen practices. So he supported himself!

This didn't mean that it was wrong for Preachers to be supported. Actually, the

Apostle did receive offerings for particular projects, even extensively so (II Cor. Chpts. 8-9). As well, Churches at times would send him support, which he gladly accepted (Phil. 4:14-19). It is the *"example"* of which the Apostle was always concerned, even as the next Verse proclaims.

## LABOR

The phrase, *"But wrought with labor and travail night and day,"* proclaims that which the Thessalonians knew to be true. Why is he hitting this so strongly?

Evidently there were idlers and loafers in the Church at Thessalonica, as regrettably there are in many Churches, who sponged off other people, refusing to work and earn their own living. So Paul is here addressing the situation, and will address it very strongly as we will later see.

There are several things that every Christian is honor-bound to do, at least as it regards everyday living. The following are some of those things:

1. The word of a Believer ought to be his bond. In other words, you can depend on what he says. If he says he will be there at 7 p.m., he will be there at 7 p.m.
2. The Believer does not lie. Even if it hurts him, he will tell the Truth.
3. The Believer will earn his own way, even as Paul is addressing here. He will not sponge off others. In other words, he will not try to borrow money from other people, nor constantly hint, or in fact, hint at all, regarding his particular needs. He will take these needs to the Lord, and to the Lord only!
4. He will give his employer a good day's work. He will not loaf on the job; he will not take opportunities to gab to others about things which do not pertain to his employment, thereby robbing his employer of work he is being paid to do. The boss doesn't have to constantly look over his shoulder, but can be confident that he is attending to his duties.
5. He will not concern himself with other people's affairs. In other words, he will keep his nose out of other people's business, attending to his own, which should be enough to keep him occupied.
6. If he owes money to anyone, he will pay the money on time. If something happens that's not his fault, in which he does not have the money at that particular time, he will go to the party involved and explain his situation. He will never ignore rightful obligations.
7. He will have a good disposition at all times, never sour and morose, but always rejoicing in the Lord, in order to set a good example of what Christ means to the heart.
8. He will be perfectly honest in all matters, and that means to the Internal Revenue, as well as to the employer for whom he works, or any and all others for that matter. A lie to the I.R.S. in the eyes of God, is just as much a lie as a lie to one's Mother! Honesty covers all territory. It means honesty in all things, to which the Believer will definitely subscribe.
9. He will put Christ first in all things, with the Lord ever serving as his example. In doing so, he will also serve as an example to others. That is the general idea in all of this which Paul is saying.

NOTES

## CHARGEABLE TO ANY OF YOU

The phrase, *"That we might not be chargeable to any of you,"* refers to the fact that the Apostle, nor any in his party, allowed themselves to be a burden to any of the people at Thessalonica, or anywhere else for that matter.

The Apostle said almost the same thing in his First Epistle, expressed in almost similar terms: *"For ye remember, Brethren, our labor and travail; for laboring night and day, because we would not be chargeable unto any of you, we preached unto you the Gospel of God"* (I Thess. 2:9).

Why the repetition?

Any time the Holy Spirit says something, of course it is very important. Any time He repeats the admonition, it is of extreme importance; consequently, we should be made to realize by this repetition, as to how important all of this in the eyes of God, as it regards followers of the Lord.

We represent Jesus Christ. We are His Ambassadors. As such, we are to conduct ourselves accordingly at all times. In other words, the Believer is always on duty which means He is never off duty. Every word we say, every step we take, every action on our part, even every thought we think, is to always be done with the idea in mind, that we are representing Christ, and as such, we must seek to be a true Representative. Nothing is more important! If we will ask the Holy Spirit to help us in this endeavor, to be sure, He definitely shall!

(9) "NOT BECAUSE WE HAVE NOT POWER, BUT TO MAKE OURSELVES AN ENSAMPLE UNTO YOU TO FOLLOW US."

In this one short Scripture we have several great Truths.

If the Christian reads over all of these things and little comprehends their vast significance, the Christian is greatly shortchanging himself. These words were given to us for a purpose. The Holy Spirit desires, even demands, that we heed these admonitions, understanding, that all of this is not only for the good of Christ, but specifically for our own good as well!

## THE POWER

The phrase, *"Not because we have not power,"* refers to the fact that he was a Preacher of the Gospel, and more than that, an Apostle. By saying that he did not want to be a burden to them, Paul did not mean to give the impression that the work of the Ministry should not be supported financially. He had the power (the authority and the right) to ask them to give him all the support he needed. But he waived that right, and for the reasons we have previously mentioned. In fact, he insists upon the right of support in his First Epistle to the Corinthians (I Cor. 9:1-18).

## AN EXAMPLE

The phrase, *"But to make ourselves an example unto you to follow us,"* presents that which should be the criteria for every Child of God. We should want to be, and strive to be, an example of Righteousness, practical duty, responsibility, and lifestyle, in fact, in any and all things, because everything we do as Believers portrays Christ, whether poorly or the opposite. So, the question we should always ask ourselves is, *"Am I a proper example as it regards Christ and all His Work?"*

In fact, and as stated, Christ is the perfect example; however, He serves as that example only through His followers. If we serve Him badly, it as should be obvious, reflects on Him poorly. I think we don't think upon this often enough.

NOTES

The idea of this Text is, that if people wanted to truly follow the Lord, wanted to truly serve God, they would also at the same time, desire to follow Paul. Otherwise, they would look in other directions. It is the same presently.

## OBSERVATION

It's not really very difficult to ascertain the lifestyle of any Preacher. What kind of prayer life does he have? That's not difficult to determine. If he truly has a prayer life, in some way that will be obvious. What about his attitude and spirit? Certainly, that shouldn't be difficult to ascertain!

Is he truly anointed when he preaches? However, that's not so easy to detect. In fact, it would be very easy, if all Believers knew what the Anointing was; but I'm concerned that many don't know. So they mistake for the Anointing, that which in reality is not the Anointing but actually the flesh.

Is he a proper student of the Word? As a Preacher of the Gospel, the Word should be the primary love of his life. If that is the case, that will portray itself as well.

Are souls saved under his Ministry? Are Believers Baptized with the Holy Spirit? Are the sick at times truly healed? Are people delivered by the Power of God under his Ministry?

Of course, these results would vary, but if the Gospel is truly being preached and lived we might quickly add, at least some of these results will be obvious.

I'm saying these things, simply because every Believer in the world is going to follow some Preacher. Even though this is not the primary subject matter of which Paul relates here, it does enter into these things which he says. The Lord has set in the Church *"Apostles, Prophets, Evangelists, Pastors, and Teachers"* (Eph. 4:11).

This is all done *"For the perfecting of the Saints, for the work of the Ministry, for the edifying of the Body of Christ"* (Eph. 4:12).

Regrettably, all of these who claim to be such, actually aren't, and as well, some who have definitely been called of God, are not conducting themselves presently as they should. So, the Believer must look very carefully as to the Preacher he follows. Much is at stake, as should be obvious.

(10) "FOR EVEN WHEN WE WERE WITH YOU, THIS WE COMMANDED YOU, THAT IF ANY WOULD NOT WORK, NEITHER SHOULD HE EAT."

Paul reinforces his example by this definite command. From a very early time, denying food to the lazy was a traditional form of discipline in the Church.

As stated, and as is obvious here, the Apostle comes down hard, or rather the Holy Spirit through him, as it regards laziness.

Coming up as a child, my parents taught me that laziness was at least one of the worst sins that there could be. Consequently, I was raised with that in mind, and to be sure, in doing the Work of the Lord it has done me in good stead.

THIS WE COMMANDED YOU

The phrase, *"For even when we were with you, this we commanded you,"* concerns itself with the idea that this question had come up previously. Unfortunately, this is a problem that seems to stay with the Church. There are always loafers, idlers, in other words, those who want something for nothing. Some people have the ridiculous idea, that if they are a Christian, that someone ought to take care of them. However, the Apostle even in his blunt way, will address this problem head-on, and leave absolutely no room for doubt as to what he is saying.

WON'T WORK, DON'T EAT!

The phrase, *"That if any would not work, neither should he eat,"* tells us two things:

1. If a person is lazy, then let them do without, even down to the place of not having anything to eat.

2. If a person in fact is lazy, then it's wrong to give to a person of this nature.

The law laid down here by the Apostle extends to all who are able to work for a living, but who will not do such, consequently binding us to *"not"* contribute to their support if they will not labor for it. And when we say *"work,"* it means anything that they are physically capable of doing.

There are some people who are always claiming they're willing to work, but they are too good to do manual labor. That would not have worked at all with Paul, considering that's exactly what he did to support himself, dirty, manual labor in the repairing of tents, etc. As well, what he did, and to which we have already alluded, was labor that would have garnered no more than what we refer to presently as *"minimum wages."* So, the idea that one considered oneself too good to do certain jobs, would not have set well with the Apostle, as I think is here overly obvious!

It's amazing as to the lengths to which some people will go, in order not to have to work. Their back is bad, or the sun is too hot, or they are trained for more responsible things, etc.

Here at the Church (Family Worship Center), even as most Churches, we have people coming by quite often who want a handout. We solved that problem a long time ago by telling them, that if they will work two or three hours, or whatever is called for, we will pay them. Almost all the time, this settles the question, with them not being able to do so!

Once again we come back to Paul's terse statement, *"that if any man would not work, neither should he eat."*

As well, *"hard luck stories"* abound of every description. I've even had people to come into our prayer meetings, people incidently with whom I was not acquainted, who would pray loudly and voice their needs accordingly, all the time working a ploy to get somebody to give them money.

I remember on one occasion, we had an individual who was a stranger to us who came into one of the prayer meetings and began to pray loudly about his truck needing a new transmission. I listened to this for a few moments and then went over to him, quietly suggesting that perhaps it might be better for him to do his praying elsewhere. As he drove away I noticed that his transmission seemed to be working pretty well.

True Christians have big hearts, at least most! Consequently, they want to help people, but to help someone who will not help themselves, is not really helping them, but only hurting them. If we'll follow the Scriptures regarding this situation, and of course anything else for that matter, it will come out right.

NOTES

(11) "FOR WE HEAR THAT THERE ARE SOME WHICH WALK AMONG YOU DISORDERLY, WORKING NOT AT ALL, BUT ARE BUSYBODIES."

The Apostle not only gives command as to what should be done with these particular type of individuals, but as well, adds another reflection as to what they are.

Most of the time, people do things because that's what they are. That wouldn't hold true in all cases, but it definitely does I think, in many, if not most.

DISORDERLY

The phrase, *"For we hear that there are some which walk among you disorderly,"* means the same thing as in Verse 7.

The English word *"disorderly"* as we've already stated, means *"unruly,"* among other things. But none of these meanings exactly fit the Greek word of which it is the translation. The proper use of the Greek word is clearly seen in an early account of a father who apprenticed his son to a weaver for one year. The contract provided for the details of food and clothing for the period of apprenticeship. Then the contract stated if there were any days on which the boy failed to attend or *"played truant,"* the father must see that the boy report for work an equivalent number of days after the apprenticeship was over.

The word translated *"disorderly"* is the Greek word in the contract which means *"to play truant."*

These Thessalonian Saints were playing truant from their daily employment. The occasion for this is suggested in the context where Paul says, *"The Lord direct your hearts into the Love of God, and the patient waiting for Christ."* The doctrine of the immanent return of the Lord Jesus for His Church was firmly believed in this Church. The Saints looked from day-to-day for that event.

Some argued, of course wrongly, that if the Lord might come the next day, there was no need for earning one's daily bread. But Paul, who had taught them this great Truth of the immanency of the Lord's return, and whose expectation was just as intense as that of the Thessalonian Saints, calls their attention to the fact that he worked for his daily bread in order that he might not be obligated to anyone for support. His rule was that if anyone did not work, he should not eat. He defines, as the next phrase says, what he means by *"disorderly"* in the words *"working not at all."* Thus, the context agrees with the First Century usage of the word, *"to play truant."*

NOTES

DATE SETTING AND CREDIT CARD SCAMS

Back in the early 1990's or late 1980's, whichever, many in the Church fell for the prediction that the Rapture of the Church would take place on a particular day. A Preacher had made this prediction based on some of the Jewish Feast Days, etc.

Regrettably, despite the fact of such a conclusion being totally unscriptural (Acts 1:6-7), he wrote a small booklet on the subject, which as stated, was believed by many.

Consequently, inasmuch as the Lord was going to rapture away His Church on this particular day, many Christians filled their Credit Cards up to the limit under the guise that the amount didn't matter simply because they would be gone.

In the first place, it's a mystery to me as to how someone could be anxiously looking for the Lord's return, and at the same time, planning fraud by intentionally attempting to cheat Credit Card Companies in this manner! While it is certainly true that there will be many Credit Card accounts unpaid when the Rapture actually does take place, still, that will not be an intentional thing, true Believers not knowing when the Lord is to return. But to purposely plan something of this nature, is almost incomprehensible as it regards someone who refers to themselves as a *"Christian!"*

When it comes to Sanctification, which refers to our lives being cleaned up, which means that we stop lying, stop cheating, stop defrauding people, etc., in other words, we provide things honest in the sight of all men, most Christians have little idea as to what you're talking about. I suppose that's at least one of the reasons that the *"Cross,"* which is the ways and means by which the Sanctification process is brought about, is not such an interesting subject.

Concerning people who conduct themselves accordingly, and make no effort to change, I seriously doubt as to them truly knowing the Lord. I think they have made a profession, but there is really no possession of true Salvation. The very work and business of the Holy Spirit is to bring the individual in line with Christlikeness. To be sure, if He is present, even though there will certainly be struggles, and there may even be some things which are very difficult to overcome, with the time span even being long, still, He ultimately will succeed in what He has been sent to do.

It's not difficult to observe the working of the Holy Spirit in one's life, that is if one has any contact with a particular person very much at all. There are signs; however, if there is no evidence whatsoever of such, that's a pretty good sign that the individual is really not even saved.

A REFUSAL TO WORK

The phrase, *"Working not at all,"* means they are sponging off of others.

Everyone has to eat, sleep, and wear clothes. Consequently, there has to be at least some money coming in for these things to be purchased, etc. So that means, that one must hold some type of employment, whatever it might be. As well, if a man or woman has a family to support, the obligations become much more obvious. That's the reason that Paul also said, *"But if any provide not for his own, and especially for those of his own house, he hath denied the Faith, and is worse than an infidel"* (I Tim. 5:8).

Again, I think it's fairly obvious, that the Apostle didn't have much patience with loafers! And neither do I!

BUSYBODIES

The phrase, *"But are busybodies,"* refers to meddling in that which does not pertain to them, meddling in the affairs of others.

These are *"busybodies instead of busy."* In the Greek there is a play on words: literally, *"not working, but working around,"* i.e., *"being unprofitably employed."*

Of these people, Robertson says, *"These theological deadbeats were too pious to work, but perfectly willing to eat at the hands of their neighbors, while they piddled and frittered away the time in idleness."* There is hardly a more damaging influence in the

NOTES

Church than the gossiping tongue of an idle or footloose member.

As someone has said, these types of people are busy with what is not their business.

(12) "NOW THEM THAT ARE SUCH WE COMMAND AND EXHORT BY OUR LORD JESUS CHRIST, THAT WITH QUIETNESS THEY WORK, AND EAT THEIR OWN BREAD."

Whenever this Epistle was read to the Assembly, as it was commanded to be done, and with such people present, I wonder what were their thoughts?

Of course, the ideal is, that these problems never arise to begin with; however, the perfect Church does not yet exist; consequently, there are problems and which must be addressed. Paul was very straightforward as is painfully obvious here, but at the same time I feel, continued to use tact. He wanted the message to be plain and clear, therefore, understood without difficulty; therefore, he had to say the things he said in the way and manner in which they were said.

In preaching the Gospel for many, many years, I have noticed that people will throw something over their shoulder as not referring to them, if they have the slightest excuse to do so; consequently, the Preacher, that is if he is to follow the Lord, has to say something plain and clear enough to where there is no doubt as to what is being said, but at the same time be as tactful as possible. This is a fine line, and not so easy to carry out.

BY OUR LORD JESUS CHRIST

The phrase, *"Now them that are such we command and exhort by our Lord Jesus Christ,"* refers to the Apostle having the Mind of the Lord and, therefore, the authority of the Lord Jesus Christ in making these statements. Consequently, the hearers or Readers must understand that what they are hearing is not merely the advice of a Preacher, but rather the Word of the Lord. Consequently, it is binding on all, which means if ignored, will always bring about serious consequences.

In fact, this which we have just said applies not only to these present words by Paul, but actually to the entirety of the Word of God. Inasmuch as it is the *"Word,"* it means that whatever is said is right and true, and definitely meant by the Lord to be followed with all responsibility. In fact, there is nothing more important!

In respect to this, the Apostle could say *"we command,"* and because by Whose authority this is being said. While the statement is strong, one must as well understand, that the type of people to whom this is being said would understand no other type of terminology.

WORK

The phrase, *"That with quietness they work, and eat their own bread,"* tells us several things:

1. Quit being busybodies, attempting to meddle in other people's affairs. *"Quietness"* means that we tend to our own business.

2. They were to work at some task, and, therefore, not be idle. This means that there is always something we can do, even though it may not be the task for which we are trained, or the job which we would like. But if we have to, we'll take whatever job comes our way. Once again, if the Apostle was not ashamed to labor at repairing tents, which was the most menial of menial labor, then surely others should not be ashamed to do whatever needs to be done if necessity arises.

3. Eating their own bread, means they did not eat the bread of others for which they did not labor. This is certainly not meaning that it's wrong to invite someone over for a meal, or to accept if an invitation is extended. It is speaking solely of sponging off others. This must cease!

(13) "BUT YE, BRETHREN, BE NOT WEARY IN WELL DOING."

Having outlined and undergirded the necessary disciplinary action, Paul turns again to address the Church as a whole in order to safeguard the entire situation. There are always risks in the administration of Church discipline, no matter how necessary the action is. One danger is that the spirit of those administering the discipline may be less than Christlike. Another is that the discipline may fail in its purpose, and may drive away rather than save those for whom Christ died.

WELL DOING

The idea is, while Believers are to refuse to support those who are busybodies and lazy, still, those who are truly in need should not be forgotten (Gal. 6:9).

NOTES

There are some people who definitely need help, and through no fault of their own. These individuals should be helped, with a Christlike love and concern.

At times, people fall into negative circumstances through no fault of their own. They are not lazy, not busybodies, not shiftless, but for whatever reason, something has happened adverse, which has thrown them into difficult straits. One must remember, that during those days there was no social security net from the Government of any nature. Whatever problems individuals had, whether through old age, or other situations, loved ones had to take care of the individuals, or the Church in some cases. And of course when this happened, they were given by the Church tasks to perform.

The idea in all of this is that it's a privilege to be permitted to do good. It is the great distinguishing characteristic of God that He always does good. It was that which marked the Character of the Redeemer, that He *"went about doing good"*; and whenever God gives us the opportunity and the means of doing good, it should be to us an occasion of special thanksgiving. Of this opportunity, we should never grow *"weary!"* The reason should be obvious:

Where the need is obvious and legitimate, we should be quick to respond at least to the extent that we are able to do so, and because the Lord has been so very, very good to all of us. Among all the other reasons, that is at least the primary reason why we should conduct ourselves accordingly. Considering His goodness to us, and knowing how much we depend on Him for that goodness to continue by His Grace, how can we do less for others, when the need truly arises!

(14) "AND IF ANY MAN OBEY NOT OUR WORD BY THIS EPISTLE, NOTE THAT MAN, AND HAVE NO COMPANY WITH HIM, THAT HE MAY BE ASHAMED."

Then there was only one Church in the city, and disciplinary action of the nature which Paul demands, could be effective. Presently, as is obvious, there are many Churches in any given city, at least in most places; consequently, such an individual, that is if he so desires, simply moves to another Church in which he continues his activities. In fact, such activities are not isolated but actually continue on a regular basis by such individuals.

Irrespective, the Word of the Lord as given here by Paul, is to always be carried out by any local Church regarding these types of situations. Whatever the offending party does is one thing; however, it is up to sincere Believers to make every attempt to follow the Word, not only concerning situations of this nature, but everything else as well!

BY THIS EPISTLE

The phrase, *"And if any man obey not our word by this Epistle,"* notes several things:

1. Despite oft repeated warnings and teachings contained in this Letter and in the First Epistle, as well as in Paul's personal Ministry, there is the possibility that some will refuse to obey. In view of that, we are not speaking here of a case of misunderstanding, but of flagrant self-will. Consequently, steps regarding discipline now must be taken.

2. Obedience of the Word of God is actually what is at stake here. The Bible is our road map, our guide, in effect our leadership. It was given by the Lord to show man how to live. To disobey, especially when the right way is clear and plain, shows a complete disregard for the Word of God, when in reality, obedience should be the hallmark of every Believer, i.e., *"to seek to do everything according to what the Word of God shows and tells us to do."*

3. When Paul used the words *"this Epistle,"* of course he was speaking of the Book or Letter we now refer to as II Thessalonians. As well, by these words, and others given in this Letter, he is claiming inspiration, meaning that this Epistle is the Word of God, the same as Genesis, Exodus, etc. Consequently, for anyone to deny its precepts, is to deny the Word of God.

No doubt, some would attempt to do just that, in effect claiming that these were merely Paul's thoughts only, but to such thinkers, he serves notice and in no uncertain terms, that *"this Epistle"* is in fact, the Word of God.

DISCIPLINE

The phrase, *"Note that man, and have no company with him, that he may be ashamed,"* doesn't actually speak of excommunication, but rather a withdrawal of fellowship within the Local Body. From the wording given, it seems as if he was still allowed to come to the Services, but would not be included in any of the particular happenings of the Church, such as the *"Love Feasts,"* which then characterized many of the Assemblies.

The idea is, that such action by the entire Assembly would make him ashamed, with him then mending his ways. However, let it be understood, even as the next Verse proclaims, that all of this action was to be taken in order to bring the individual back into the fold, and not otherwise. In fact, all the discipline that the Lord exercises on anyone is always for the purpose of restoration and not otherwise.

Once the individual begins to obey the Word of God, and it will be very obvious when that happens, this means that the situation is now resolved, and no further action is to be taken. Punishment for the sake of punishment is nowhere enjoined in the Bible, at least by those who claim to follow the Lord. In the first place, no Believer is morally qualified to punish another Believer, that being left in the hands of God.

When it comes to more serious offenses, such as the incest of I Corinthians, Chapter 5, if the individual refuses to repent, he or she is to be excommunicated from the Church. And what does that mean?

It is actually simple. As stated, they are to be given every opportunity to repent and to come in line with the Word of God, but if they refuse, or else the evidence is otherwise, they are to be told they are not welcome anymore in that particular Church.

Whatever the sin is, that is one thing; however, the action to be taken, that is if adverse action needs to be taken, is not nearly so much for the sin involved, as for the refusal to obey the Word of God regarding repentance. In other words, the individual in essence says, *"I'm going to do what I want to do, irrespective as to what anyone else says, etc."* In such a case, there is nothing left but the expelling of that individual from the Local Body.

If the individual truly repents, and such a position is not difficult to detect, according to II Corinthians, Chapter 2, the person is to be reinstated in the Church, with the Church

NOTES

forgiving him or her for the particular violation of the Word.

## SIN, FORGIVENESS, AND THE CROSS

While it probably can be said, that self-will is always involved in some way in all failure, for the most part I think, most Christians fall into sin simply because they do not know or understand God's prescribed order of Victory. In other words, Satan attacks them in a particular way, and they oppose him in all the wrong ways, which means they are destined for failure in some manner. Sometimes that failure manifests itself in particular vices or at other times in other ways; nevertheless, without following God's prescribed order of Victory, there is no way the Believer can be an overcomer.

While I'm sure there are some Christians who want to do certain wrong things irrespective as to what the Word of God or anyone else might say, I personally think that the far greater majority do not fall into that category. They get into trouble simply because they do not know or understand God's Way. Unfortunately, the Way of the Cross, for this is that of which we speak, is not too very much preached behind most modern pulpits. Consequently, the very Way and Manner for which Jesus died, which is to give us Salvation and Sanctification, is in some way ignored. While most Preachers who truly believe the Bible know and understand the Cross as it regards the initial Salvation experience, and the necessity of the believing sinner's Faith in that Finished Work, they little understand the part the Cross plays in the Sanctification process. Consequently, Believers are left to struggle on their own, trying one method after another to find victory, with none producing the right results.

So, with most Believers who go astray, the answer to that individual is to explain to them God's correct method of Victory, which is found in the Cross of Christ, which will generally handle the situation in totality, that is if the person is sincere about walking clean before the Lord.

To punish such a person does not do any good, as should be obvious. The person has failed because they do not know God's Way of Victory over sin. In fact, many of these people struggle greatly not to fail, in fact, doing all within their power to overcome; however, irrespective of their efforts, irrespective or their willpower, irrespective or their desire to do right, if they do not follow that which is given to us in the Word of God as it regards walking in victory, they will fail just as sure as their name is what it is. So, why would one want to punish such a person? The failure within itself has been of such magnitude that it almost kills the individual, and to add punishment to that, shows a total lacking of knowledge as it regards the entire Plan of God regarding Salvation and our living for Him. Understanding this, what Christian would be so crass to think they are morally qualified to punish anyone! (James 4:12). Unfortunately, there are some Religious Leaders who do think they are so qualified. They seem to think that *"group decision"* legalizes or justifies their action. Again, there's nothing in the Word of God to substantiate such thinking. In fact, and even as we've already stated several times, the Local Church is the highest spiritual authority according to the Word of God, and nothing must abrogate that particular authority. While outside advice and counsel can certainly be given, the final decision, with no force or threat from outside forces leveled against that decision, is always to be from the Local Church, regarding problems in that Church. Even then, it must be according to the Word of God. The Word is always the criteria in all things.

## WHAT DO WE MEAN BY EXPLAINING THE CROSS?

The fundamental or criteria for understanding the Message of the Cross, is found in Romans, Chapters 6 and 8. Romans, Chapter 6 tells us how that we were baptized into His Death at His Crucifixion. And please understand, that is not speaking of Water Baptism, but that which actually takes place in the Mind of God whenever the believing sinner evidences Faith in Christ and what He did at the Cross (Rom. 6:3).

That means that God awards the believing sinner all that Christ did at the Cross, which refers to the total sin debt being paid, which destroyed Satan's legal claim upon

NOTES

NOTES

humanity, at least for those who will believe (Jn. 3:16).

The believing sinner is at that time placed *"in Christ,"* which means that everything that Christ did at the Atonement, now becomes ours.

Christ was then buried, and we are buried with Him. He was then raised from the dead, and we were raised with Him in newness of life, all of this by simple Faith in these things which He did (Rom. 6:3-6). As well, Paul also said that Christ now is exalted by the Right Hand of the Father, with every Saint of God also in a sense exalted with Him (Eph. 2:6). The idea is, that we were placed *"in Christ"* by the simple exhibition of our Faith toward Him, which in the Mind of God makes us literally the beneficiary of our great Benefactor, the Lord Jesus Christ.

All of it was done at the Cross, which refers to our Sanctification, our Justification, our Reconciliation, forgiveness of all sin, and in fact, every single benefit of which one can think including all Victory.

Now that we have come to Christ, we are to understand that all of this great Victory was won at the Cross; consequently, our Faith is to ever be in that great Finished Work, understanding that this is the place that our Victory was won and where our Victory is maintained.

Now enters Romans, Chapter 8 which shows us the dynamics or the Work of the Holy Spirit within our lives.

Upon conversion, the Holy Spirit comes into the heart and life of every Believer. At that time, the Believer is to ask the Lord for the Baptism with the Holy Spirit, which the Lord will definitely give, and which is always accompanied by the speaking with other Tongues (Acts 2:4). In fact, this is not a suggestion, but rather a command (Acts 1:4).

Even though the Holy Spirit definitely comes into every heart at conversion, that is totally different than the Baptism with the Holy Spirit, which the latter always follows conversion, but only if the Saint asks the Lord for this great Gift. In other words, it's not automatic as many teach, but rather a Gift that is separate and different than the initial conversion experience. It doesn't make one more saved, but it definitely does give one more power, which is desperately needed by the Child of God (Acts 1:8).

In fact, without the Baptism with the Holy Spirit, just about everything is shut off as it regards our walk with God. If one looks at the particular Denominations who have rejected the Baptism with the Holy Spirit with the evidence of speaking with other Tongues, one will find that the Holy Spirit is little relied upon at all. In fact, He for all practical purposes, is totally ignored in these circles. Consequently, just about everything that's done in those circles is strictly man-devised and man-directed, which means that almost nothing is done for God. In fact, every single thing done for the Lord on this Earth, even though carried out by Man (Eph. 4:11-13), must originate with the Holy Spirit, be empowered by the Holy Spirit, and be carried out by the Holy Spirit.

However, just because individuals are in fact Baptized with the Holy Spirit, this in no way guarantees that the Holy Spirit will do all these grand and glorious things. The potential is there, but if the Believer attempts to function outside of the parameters of the Finished Work of Christ, which pertains to what Jesus did at the Cross, then the Holy Spirit simply will not help. The Holy Spirit doesn't demand much, but He does demand the following:

He demands first of all, that the Believer understand, that every single thing that we need as a Christian is found in what Christ did at the Cross. We must not go outside of that great, Finished Work.

In view of that, the Holy Spirit demands that we have Faith in that great Sacrifice, and that we have Faith exclusively in that great Sacrifice.

Then and only then, will the Holy Spirit work on our behalf (Rom. 8:1-8).

## WHAT DO WE MEAN BY FUNCTIONING OUTSIDE THE PARAMETERS OF THE CROSS OF CHRIST?

It means anything other than simple Faith in the Cross. For instance, there are many Believers who think that their source of Victory lies within them fasting one or two days a month, etc. While fasting is definitely Scriptural, that is not the source of Victory.

Other Christians believe if they give so much money to the Work of the Lord, or pray so much each day, or witness to so many souls each week, this will guarantee victory, or whatever it is they seek.

At this particular time, which is the beginning of the new Millennium, untold thousands of Christians are running all over the world looking for a Preacher who they think God is using, who will lay hands on them, and then their problems are solved, or they will be drawn closer to God, or they will get victory over sin, etc.

While all of these things we have mentioned are definitely Scriptural, and should be a part and parcel of the Believer's lifestyle, still, if we attempt to do these things in the manner that I have mentioned, we turn it into law, which means we have shifted our Faith from the Finished Work of Christ, to our own efforts. And even though these efforts may be in good things even as we've mentioned, still, such constitutes misplaced Faith. In other words, if I have Faith that some Preacher can lay hands on me, and that will constitute my victory over sin or whatever, I have then taken my Faith from where it rightly belongs, which is the Cross of Christ, and placed it in something else, which God can never honor, which means that the Holy Spirit will not give me that for which I seek. In fact, He might bless the person, simply because the laying on of hands is definitely Scriptural. In fact, the laying on of hands, even as we've already stated, has to do with *"blessing"* and *"Divine Healing."* When we go beyond that, thinking that such brings about victory over sin, or whatever in other directions, God simply will not honor that, because we have taken our Faith away from the Finished Work of Christ, and placed it elsewhere.

These things fool us, because they actually are Scriptural in their own right, but the Truth is, we have just shifted our Faith from its rightful place in the Cross, to other things. That's where we go wrong, and that's why we fail!

There are untold numbers of Christians who are prayed for by someone, and they actually are blessed by the Lord at that particular time. And then they are more confused than ever when some days or weeks

NOTES

later, the problem returns, whatever the problem might be. So what do they do then?

Some try to find another Preacher, while others simply refuse to face up to the Truth, with others getting discouraged and quitting altogether.

The situation is as one of my associates said, *"You don't need a touch nearly as much as you need the Truth!"*

POSITION AND ACTIVITY

All of these things we have mentioned refer to *"activity."* The Truth is, all that God has for us, whether it is Righteousness, Justification, Sanctification, Reconciliation, Blessing, Grace, Love, Faith, etc., is ours because of what Jesus did at the Cross, which refers to *"position."* In other words, all of these things are ours because of our position in Christ.

Instead, we think they come about because of our *"activity,"* which is not the case, and actually has the opposite effect. In other words, the more active we are in trying to bring these things about, the further away we are driven from their actual realization.

The moment the believing sinner comes to Christ, all of these things mentioned plus some we have not mentioned are instantly his. They are his not because he has worked for them, or has earned them, or merits them in any way, but simply because of what Christ did at the Cross and in His Resurrection, and our Faith in that. We're automatically placed by God *"in Christ,"* which guarantees us all of these things.

However, due to wrong teaching, after becoming a Christian, we tend to think that we now have to earn the things mentioned, or else we get involved in something as I've already mentioned, and according to our activity we become Righteous, or whatever! None of that is correct.

While true Faith definitely always produces activity, activity will never produce Faith. That is given by God (Rom. 12:3), strictly because of our being in Christ, which refers to our Faith in what Christ has done. It is the same with Grace, Love, Power, Righteousness, etc. Those things are not activities but rather a *"position,"* which speaks of our *"position in Christ,"* which came about because of our Faith in what Christ did at the Cross.

Holiness falls into the same category, as well as Sanctification. Much of the Church world thinks of Salvation by Faith, but Sanctification by self. And if you fail to sanctify yourself, they will come down on you like dark on midnight. The Truth is, no one can sanctify themselves, no matter how hard they try. So what happens?

We have a Church full of hypocrites and liars! I realize that's strong, but it happens to be the Truth.

People are taught to confess that which they really do not have. And to be sure, unless your Faith is properly placed, you cannot have that which the Lord has promised (Jn. 10:10). Christians by the millions are claiming victory which they do not have, because they've been taught to confess things which do not exist, at least in their lives. While confession is definitely important, lying is never right.

It is proper to confess one's victory and overcoming strength, which is actually what the Child of God should do, and do constantly; however, such is to be done only because of what Christ has done for us at the Cross and our Faith in that. Then the confession is right, but only then (Rom. 6:11).

### LET'S LOOK AT FAITH FOR A MOMENT!

Faith is the great principle through which God deals with the human race. Almost every Christian knows that. However, that's about all that most know.

If asked to explain it, most would not know what to say or how to explain it, except to say *"It means to have Faith in God," or "Faith in the Word of God,"* etc. Those things certainly are correct, but in reality they don't actually say much.

When we speak of having Faith in the Word, most Christians think that means to simply find a Scripture that fits their problem, and then recite it over and over again, believing that somehow this is going to move God to action. Really that's not Faith, and in fact, it's not so much removed from the Eastern cult religions of simply repeating things over and over, etc.

As stated, the Truth is, most of the modern Church has little understanding of what Faith actually is, despite the fact, that there has been more teaching on Faith in the last several decades than probably all the balance of history put together.

NOTES

When the Scripture speaks of Faith, it must always be understood, that it's speaking of Faith in the Cross, which refers to the Finished Work of Christ. If that is not understood, then the person doesn't really know what Biblical Faith actually is.

The story of the Bible is the story of man's creation (Gen. Chpts. 1-2), man's Fall (Gen. Chpt. 3), and man's Redemption (Gen. Chpt. 4 through the rest of the Bible). So, if that much of the Bible is given over to man's Redemption, we must ask the question as to how man has been redeemed.

Of course we know that man has been redeemed by God giving His Only Son to die on the Cross (I Cor. 2:2). So, when the Bible speaks of Faith, it is really speaking of *"the Faith,"* which actually refers to what Christ did at the Cross and in His Resurrection, on behalf of dying, lost humanity.

So, if the Christian doesn't understand that Faith is always to be directed toward the Cross, then the Christian doesn't really understand what Faith actually is, and will have a terrible time trying to live as one ought to live for the Lord.

When Faith is mentioned, it is always to be mentioned in connection with the Cross. It is always to be in the Cross, understanding that from this great Finished Work, every single benefit comes to the Child of God, and in fact, comes no other way. Any other way that man projects, is an insult to the integrity of God, and the great Sacrifice of Christ, which of necessity, angers God, as should be obvious (Rom. 8:8).

So, getting back to our original subject, most Believers fail the Lord, simply because they do not understand their place and position in Christ, as it relates to the Cross and all that Christ did there. If this is properly explained to them, most will then begin to walk in victory; however, it is literally impossible for the Believer to have victory as he ought to have, without understanding the Message of the Cross.

(15) "YET COUNT HIM NOT AS AN ENEMY, BUT ADMONISH HIM AS A BROTHER."

*"Attitude"* is what is here in question; however, it is the attitude of strong Believers toward the erring Brother or Sister which is in view.

As someone has well said, *"Two wrongs don't make a right."* Someone doing wrong, even as Paul addresses here, in no way gives license to other Believers to do wrong toward that individual. So, the Church must be very careful as to its attitude, its spirit, and actually the steps taken toward the person in question.

### ENEMY?

The phrase, *"Yet count him not as an enemy,"* means to not count him outside of Christ, but only as an erring Brother, which means he's going in the wrong direction.

This shows the true spirit in which discipline is to be administered. We are not to deal with the individual as an adversary over whom we are to seek to gain a victory, but as an erring Brother — a Brother still, though he errs.

There is a great danger that when we undertake the work of discipline we shall forget that he who is the subject of it is a Brother, and that we shall regard and treat him as an enemy. Such regrettably, is human nature. We set ourselves in array against him. We cut him off as one who is unworthy to walk with us. We triumph over him, and consider him at once as an enemy of the Church, and as having lost all claim to its sympathies. We abandon him to the tender mercies of a cold and unfeeling world, and let him take his course.

Perhaps we follow him with anathemas, which means that we hope that bad things happen to him, and hold him up as unworthy the confidence of mankind.

I realize these words we have just said are biting, cutting, and cruel; but yet, I am afraid that much of the Church operates accordingly.

As someone has said, *"the World is slow to forgive and the Church forgives not at all!"* What a travesty, at least, if it is true, and it definitely is with many!

### WHAT SHOULD BE OUR ATTITUDE AND DISPOSITION IN SUCH A SITUATION?

First of all, we should always remember that at times we have done wrong ourselves; consequently, we've had to go to the Lord begging and pleading for His Mercy, Grace, and forgiveness. And how did He forgive us?

Did He chide us? Reprimand us? Put us on probation? Treat us as a less Christian from then on? I think we all know the answer to that. No! The Lord never conducted Himself toward us in that fashion; consequently, even though always opposing sin of every stripe, we should ever love the sinner, doing everything within our power to bring them back.

In view of that, we should ask ourselves the question, is what I'm doing helping him or hurting him?

We must remember that the individual involved here, has openly rejected the Word of the Lord. In other words, he has stated that he is not going to obey what Paul has said, and for any variety of reasons. This puts him in a rebellious, offending, disobedient role, as should be obvious.

Now considering that, we can take the attitude that inasmuch as he has done this, then we should act toward him in a very harsh manner, because we are justified in doing so.

No we aren't! That's the spirit of this entire statement as given by Paul. We are never justified in acting wrong ourselves, irrespective as to what the respective individual might have done. We are to always conduct ourselves toward an erring Brother, irrespective of his present situation, as the Lord conducts Himself toward us. As stated, we are to never condone sin in any fashion. But at the same time, every effort we make, must always be in the capacity of bringing the Brother back, and never driving him further away.

### SELF-RIGHTEOUSNESS

In all of this, self-righteousness can raise its ugly head. If that in fact is the case, the attitude will always be one of harshness and censure toward the individual in question. In fact, self-righteousness justifies itself by putting down others. Somehow it makes the person feel that they are hard on sin if they are hard on the sinner. Unfortunately, they will succeed in getting much, if not most, of the Church to agree with them in their harsh actions.

So, when a Believer conducts himself in the very opposite manner as demanded here

NOTES

by Paul, for the command as given by the Apostle extends to the Church as well as to the offender, the one doing the correcting, if he isn't careful, can find himself committing a worse sin than the one he is correcting (II Cor. 2:8-9).

## ADMONISHING A BROTHER

The phrase, *"But admonish him as a Brother,"* refers to the fact that we're not to forget that this individual is our brother or Sister in the Lord. As such, we are to treat them accordingly.

We are to never forget, that not only is every single Believer our Brother and our Sister, but as well, that person belongs to the Lord, in essence, Christ died for them, just as He died for us. In other words, considering that this individual is the property of the Lord, we should conduct ourselves toward him or her in that fashion.

This means that our actions will be based on love. It doesn't mean that we condone sin, for love cannot condone sin, considering that this terrible blight is the destruction of all that is good. Every Christian must always take a firm stand against sin of any nature. But at the same time, we must be very kind and considerate, at least as far as is possible, toward the sinner.

The Word of God is clear in all of these matters. So there is no room for misunderstanding regarding these things. If there is sincere repentance on the part of the individual, which will be quickly obvious, that person is to be restored to fellowship, totally and completely. There is no such thing as probation with the Lord. If someone thinks that, would they be so kind as to point it out in Scripture. They can't, because it doesn't exist.

If a person will not repent, in other words they insist upon continuing in their wrong direction, they are to be disfellowshipped as Paul proclaims here, and if the sin is of a certain magnitude, they are to be excommunicated from the Church. But even after such is done, that is if it needs to be done, and there is evidence ultimately of repentance on the part of the individual, they are to be accepted back into the Church and restored to their rightful place.

NOTES

However, even though severe steps have to be taken in some cases, still, everything must be done on the basis of hopefully bringing the Brother or Sister back to the Lord. Nothing is ever to be done in the realm of punishment, or with the idea in mind, *"If you don't do what I tell you to do, we will banish you for life,"* etc. The criteria is to always be the Word of God, not what some man says, etc.

There should not be any room for misunderstanding, with the Word of God being very clear on this subject (I Cor. Chpt. 5; II Cor. Chpt. 2; II Thess. Chpt. 3).

(16) "NOW THE LORD OF PEACE HIMSELF GIVE YOU PEACE ALWAYS BY ALL MEANS. THE LORD BE WITH YOU ALL."

This statement by Paul recognizes that ultimately God Alone can bring about compliance with what Paul has asked of his Readers. *"Yet without the Lord's help all your efforts will be in vain"* is the thought behind this petition. *"The Lord of Peace"* Alone can make harmony among Believers a reality. While this is, first and foremost, Peace with God, it provides the ground for Believers' Peace with one another (Eph. 2:14-18; I Thess. 5:23).

*"At all times"* asks that there be no break in the flow of Christ's Peace (Jn. 14:27; 16:33; Col. 3:15); *"in every way"* asks that the prevalence of Peace continue no matter what the outward circumstances.

*"The Lord be with all of you"* requests what was previously guaranteed for Christians. His Promise never to leave or forsake His Own provides the assurances of this (Heb. 13:5).

## PEACE

The phrase, *"Now the Lord of Peace Himself give you Peace always by all means,"* presents a beautiful conclusion, even though there have been several rather stormy and stern Passages in this Letter. Of course, this is the way that the Lord works. He admonishes, even as He did here through Paul, but He always closes His remarks with hope and the Promise of great Blessing, which lets us know that His admonition is always for our good and never otherwise.

Peace is God's Gift through Grace, and the Gift is given only in Christ. In fact, *"the Lord of Peace"* is Christ (Jn. 14:27).

In this statement, Paul sees Christ's Peace as completely satisfying. It is continual and adequate; it is not dependent upon changing circumstances. Paul has in mind the needs of the Readers, and Christ's Peace is the answer.

They are suffering persecution and some may be martyred; some are mourning their dead; they are troubled by thoughts of the Lord's return; they are acquainted with the *"mystery of iniquity"*; some are fainthearted; they also, even as we have been addressing, are having internal problems of discipline. And yet, knowing these circumstances, Paul prays for the Peace which only Christ can give.

There is really nothing greater for the well-being of the Believer than the Peace of God promised here. In fact, I personally believe that many illnesses and sickness are caused by a lack of Peace in the heart and life of the Believer. Of course, it is not possible for the unsaved to have the Peace of God, so they have no protection whatsoever against these things which are very negative. But that is not so with the Child of God.

And yet, if it were not possible for Christians to lack this Peace, in other words, if it was an automatic thing with all Believers, and for all time, then Paul would not have made this statement. The Truth is, it's quite possible for a Believer not to enjoy the Peace of God as one should.

Seeing how important this is, I think the following will be of great help to you the Reader.

## THE CROSS OF CHRIST GUARANTEES THE PEACE OF GOD

In fact, it's not possible for the Believer to have the Peace of God, and a continuing peace at that, unless the Believer understands the Message of the Cross, and places their Faith in a continuing basis in that Finished Work. The sadness is, many Christians don't really know or understand what the Peace of God is at least in the sense of Sanctification, for this is what Paul is addressing. The simple reason is, they've never really had this Peace; therefore, they don't actually know what they are missing. In fact, if they were asked, they would immediately claim the Peace of God, even though they really do not have such within their lives. How do I know this?

NOTES

First of all, there is a great difference in the Peace which God gives to all Believers at conversion, which in fact all Believers readily have, which itself provides an assurance and security, than the Sanctifying Peace of which Paul speaks here. They are two different things altogether.

Every single Believer in the world, and irrespective of their consecration or Sanctification, enjoys *"Justifying Peace"*; however, only a few Christians truly have *"Sanctifying Peace,"* and that's what we are addressing here.

I know what I'm talking about, at least on a personal basis, because the situation of which I have described concerning not knowing what this Peace actually is, is where I once was. Please believe me, in attempting to sanctify oneself, there is no *"Sanctifying Peace,"* but rather the very opposite. And the tragedy is, probably about 98 percent of the Christians who are attempting to sanctify themselves, which means by their own efforts, etc., don't really know or understand that this is actually the case. They think that whatever is being done, is all in the Lord, etc. Never mind the fact that they are failing in some way, and doing so constantly, they just work harder and harder, try harder and harder, involve themselves in more and more religious activity, with all of this effort making them believe that they're doing exactly what the Lord wants. Please believe me they aren't!

It may come somewhat as a shock to read these words which say that there are some Christians, in fact, probably most Christians, who have never really enjoyed *"Sanctifying Peace,"* in fact, the very thing which Paul addresses here. That doesn't mean they aren't saved, and it doesn't even really mean they aren't close to the Lord. It just means, that they aren't enjoying what they actually are in Christ, but rather, are attempting to bring about within their lives what only the Holy Spirit can actually do.

Religion is a frightsome business! It is all involved in activity, do more! Do more! Do more! We never quite seem to understand that whatever it is we're trying to do, which we cannot do anyway, Jesus has in fact, already done!

If you the Believer will simply understand that your *"Sanctifying peace"* is in the Cross of Christ, meaning that it's in His Finished Work, in other words, that provision was made in the Atonement for this very thing, and you will put your Faith totally in that Finished Work, then the Holy Spirit will guarantee you this glorious, wonderful, *"Sanctifying Peace."* And please believe me, once you have it, and most certainly some few of you actually do, then you will know exactly this of which I speak. And I might quickly add:

If you have to ask, *"Do I have it?"*, that's a sure sign that you don't!

This is the *"More Abundant Life,"* of which Jesus spoke (Jn. 10:10). This is the *"Rest"* which He promised (Mat. 11:28-30).

When I didn't have it, even though I thought I had it, presents the case of most modern Christians. However, when I truly did have it, and continue to have it unto this hour, and will have it by the Grace of God forever, I now know that I didn't have it during those years that I thought I had it, if you will permit this play on words.

The things of God cannot be compared with the things of the world; consequently, a personal experience is demanded of all Believers regarding any and all things given to us by the Lord. In other words, someone else cannot receive on your behalf what you only can receive for yourself. So, there's no way that one can really know or understand the great and wonderful things the Lord has for him, until those things are received. All are received, by one placing their Faith totally and completely in the Cross of Christ, looking to that Finished Work for these great and beautiful Blessings.

## THE PRESENCE OF THE LORD

The phrase, *"The Lord be with you all,"* means that all can have this *"Sanctifying Peace,"* and in fact, the pronoun *"all"* includes even the offending ones whom Paul has been addressing.

To be sure, they cannot have any *"Sanctifying Peace,"* as long as they're in a state of rebellion; however, if they will get things right with the Lord, obey the Word of God, even as the Holy Spirit has given through Paul, they too can enjoy these great things given by the Lord, as a result of what He did at the Cross.

NOTES

Actually, the Lord never penalizes an individual, by withholding Blessings from them, irrespective of what they've done in the past, if they will only straighten up at the present and start to walk with the Lord. In fact, that is the very premise of true Christianity. As I've already stated, God has no one on probation. As well, there is no such thing as second class or third class Christians with the Lord.

There is definitely such a thing as disobedient and rebellious Christians, which of course, forfeits many things from the Lord, as should be obvious. However, the moment that person straightens up, and begins to obey the Word, even as we have stated, that person can then begin to flow in the Blessings of God and without restraint.

Unfortunately, many Christians love to put other Christians into some type of second class position, but not the Lord! Thankfully and gratefully, it is the Lord Who counts, and not man, whatever man might say or do.

(17) "THE SALUTATION OF PAUL WITH MINE OWN HAND, WHICH IS THE TOKEN IN EVERY EPISTLE: SO I WRITE."

It seems that Paul was dictating this Letter to a Scribe up to this particular Verse of Scripture. At this point he took the pen into his own hand to add a closing greeting.

Though he undoubtedly did this quite frequently, he has called attention to it only here, in I Corinthians 16:21, and in Colossians 4:18.

Apparently Paul followed this practice consistently, expecting Churches where he had served to recall his distinctive handwriting. It was particularly needed in this Epistle as a deterrent against any future attempt to forge a letter in his name (II Thess. 2:2).

## HIS OWN HANDWRITING

The phrase, *"The salutation of Paul with mine own hand,"* would have been a distinctive signature of the Apostle easily recognizable by all who knew Paul. In other words, they recognized his handwriting.

Everyone has a particular manner and style of writing, at least those who do write, such as myself, etc. Paul evidently dictated to a Scribe, with him then adding the benediction in his own handwriting. This seemed to have been the way that he was most comfortable in the writing of his Letters. This means that he did not actually pen the Letters, but the words were his.

I write in much the same way, except I dictate into a dictaphone, with it then transcribed by a secretary. There possibly may be better ways of writing, but this suits my purpose and helps me to get a lot of work done very speedily.

In fact, I can type very well, and could easily use a computer, just as Paul could write very well also; however, it is faster for me this way, even as it was no doubt faster for Paul in the manner in which he wrote his Letters.

And please understand, in comparing writing styles, I am in no way attempting to compare what Paul wrote with that which I write. He was inspired by the Holy Spirit to write these Letters which we have in the New Testament, which means that the Holy Spirit intended for it to be the Word of God. Of course, my efforts, as all others, amount to far less, as should be obvious.

Also, Paul wrote a number of other Epistles which were no doubt extremely helpful, but were not inspired by the Holy Spirit, which would somewhat fall into the category of the efforts made by the rest of us.

EVERY EPISTLE

The phrase, *"Which is the token in every Epistle,"* presents the Apostle saying that this is his style. That is, this signature is a *"sign"* or *"proof"* of the genuineness of the Epistle.

His Letters to the Thessalonians being his first, and being conscious that they would be followed by others equally inspired, and which would be addressed to other Churches, it was reasonable and needful that he should guarantee their authenticity by a token.

MANNER OF WRITING

The phrase, *"So I write,"* proves the authenticity of the Letter, which as stated, those who knew Paul could easily recognize.

It might be quickly added, that these words written by the Apostle Paul, which was the beginning of the New Covenant to the Church, even as it was given to Paul by the Holy Spirit, was and is, beyond the shadow of a doubt, the single most important documents in the history of mankind. Of course, when I say this I am not placing Paul's Letters as more important than the balance of the Word of God. It all falls into the same category, the Holy Spirit being the Author, irrespective as to the Scribe.

NOTES

It is amazing the manner in which the Lord used human instrumentation to bring forth His Word. And despite this human instrumentation there is no contradiction or error, even though the Word of God was some 1,600 years in being written. So, when Paul said, *"So I write,"* it was far more than a mere benediction, but rather the greatest words that anyone would ever read, in effect, *"Words of Life."*

(18) "THE GRACE OF OUR LORD JESUS CHRIST BE WITH YOU ALL. AMEN."

The signature closing phrase of all Paul's Epistles, *"The Grace of our Lord Jesus Christ be with all of you"* or an equivalent is found at the close of all his writings. This means that not only did Paul sign his name at the end of these Epistles, but as well, he wrote these particular closing words in every case.

The present benediction agrees verbatim with that of I Thessalonians 5:28 except for the *"all"* added here. Significantly, no one was excluded in this Church, not even those he had rebuked at various points. As stated, all of this which God gives can be theirs as well, if they will only follow closely the Lord and obey His Word.

Of course, that applies to all of us as well!

GRACE

The phrase, *"The Grace of our Lord Jesus Christ be with you all,"* presents not only the Apostles signature Blessing, but that of the Holy Spirit as well.

*"Grace"* is preeminently a Pauline word; it is found alike in the salutations with which Paul addresses his Churches, and in the benedictions with which he bids them farewell; it is the beginning and the end of His Gospel; the element in which we Christians live, and move, and have our being. Thankfully, he excludes, as stated, no one from this Blessing; not even those who have been walking disorderly, that is, if they will only begin to obey the Word.

NOTES

If we had imagination enough to bring vividly before us the condition of any of these early Churches, we would see how much is involved in a blessing like this, and what sublime confidence it displays in the goodness and Faithfulness of our Lord. The Thessalonians, a few months ago, had been heathens; they had known nothing of God and His Son; they are at present living still in the midst of a heathen population, under the pressure of heathen influences both in thought and conduct, beset by numberless temptations; and if they were mindful of the life from which they had come forth, they were not without opportunity to return.

Paul would willingly have stayed with them to be their Pastor and Teacher, their guide and their defender, but his Missionary calling made this impossible. After the merest introduction to the Gospel, and to the new life to which it calls those who receive it, they had to be left to themselves. Who should keep them from falling? Who should open their eyes to understand the ideal which the Christian is summoned to work out in his life?

Amid their many enemies, where could they look for a sufficient and ever-present ally? The Apostle answers these questions when he writes, *"The Grace of our Lord Jesus Christ be with you all."* Although he has left them, they are not really alone. The Love of God, which visited them at first uncalled, will be with them still, to perfect the work it has begun. It will guard them behind and before; it will be a Sun and a Shield to them, a Light and a defense.

In all their temptations, and all their sufferings, in all their moral perplexities, in all their despondencies, it will be sufficient for them. There is not any kind of help which a Christian needs which is not to be found in the Grace of our Lord Jesus Christ, which comes to us through the Cross, which tells us of the great price that He has paid, that we might have all of these great and wonderful things.

THE INFORMATION FIRST GIVEN

It is amazing that in the very first Epistles written by Paul, as designed by the Holy Spirit, that information concerning the coming Rapture and last day events would be given, and in fact, given with such clarity. It is obvious as to the significance of all of this, considering the place and position given by the Spirit of God.

In essence, the Spirit of God is telling us the end from the beginning and the beginning from the end. The Word of God does not leave people hanging. It is definite, secure, forthwith, and forthright. It tells us where we have been, where we are, and where we are going. As stated, nothing else in the world can even remotely touch that.

The Holy Spirit did not broach the great subject of the Rapture in I Thessalonians, along with other tremendous Revelations of the Endtime in II Thessalonians, without purpose. He wanted the Thessalonians to understand this of which is coming, and to understand it in no uncertain terms. He wants the same for all Believers presently as well! Consequently, if we treat lightly these glorious Revelations, then we treat lightly the Spirit of God.

To understand that these things uttered by Paul so long, long ago, are now about to come to pass, and in fact definitely will come to pass in this particular Millennium, should sober us, and cause us to want to draw ever closer to our Lord. In fact, that is the intention of the Holy Spirit, whether speaking to the Thessalonians so long ago, or us presently — for us to ever draw closer to God.

THE FIRST EPISTLES

While the Church at Thessalonica was not the first one planted by Paul or others for that matter, it was the first one, as far as we know, to receive an Epistle which would be labeled as *"the Word of God."* Consequently, this handful of men and women in Thessalonica were privileged to say the least!

The Church as a whole, and I speak of the Church on a worldwide basis, is much older now than when these first two Epistles were written. Time has taught her many things; but yet it is the same Holy Spirit, Who is working diligently to prepare us for the great events of which Paul here so grandly speaks.

And yet through it all, it is *"Grace"* that shines like a beacon of light that 2,000 years have not extinguished and in fact cannot extinguish, with it growing even brighter with each passing day.

And in all of this, and I speak of what we have in Christ, this great Salvation, this wonderful assurance of Eternal Life, all in totality have come by and through the Cross of Christ and at such great price. God has always been a God of Grace. He did not suddenly become this 2,000 years ago. But it was the Cross which made it possible for Him to open the flood gates, in order that His Grace may pour out like a river to undeserving souls. He only asks that we simply *"believe,"* and by believing, I refer to *"believing in what Jesus did at the Cross and in His Resurrection, all on our behalf."*

AMEN

*"Truth."*

It is 3:35 p.m., December 21, 1999, as I conclude our remarks regarding Paul's Second Epistle to the Thessalonians. How I thank the Lord for the privilege of being able to study this great Epistle and to place on paper the thoughts of my heart.

I have grown immeasurably in this writing effort, and I would pray in your study of this material, that this would be your experience as well. What an honor to have the privilege of studying the Word of God, and what an honor to be able to learn some things about the Word of God. To understand that it is absolutely inexhaustible only makes it more desirable. Who can plumb the extent of its depths, or climb the scales of its heights? None ever have, and none ever will!

Thank you for purchasing this Volume, or perhaps it was given to you by a friend. At any rate, we're very glad to have you as a partner in our efforts to hopefully open up the Word of God to a greater extent. If in fact we have been successful in doing this, thereby strengthening you in your Christian walk, then all of our efforts have been worthwhile. In any case, the Blessings are all of the Lord, and we give Him all praise and all glory.

Jimmy Swaggart

*"We've a story to tell the nations*
*"That shall turn their heads to right;*
*"A song that shall conquer evil*
*"A story of Peace and Light."*

NOTES

*"We've a Message to give to the nations,*
*"That the Lord Who reigneth above*
*"Hath sent His Son to save us,*
*"And show us that God is Love."*

# INDEX

The index is listed according to subjects. The treatment may include a complete dissertation or no more than a paragraph. But hopefully it will provide some help.

As well, even though extended treatment of a subject may not be carried in this Commentary, one of the other Commentaries may well include the desired material.

# For all information concerning the *Jimmy Swaggart Bible Commentary,* please request a Gift Catalog.

You may inquire by using Books of the Bible.

- Genesis (639 pages) (11-201)
- Exodus (639 pages) (11-202)
- Leviticus (435 pages) (11-203)
- Numbers<br>Deuteronomy (493 pages) (11-204)
- Joshua<br>Judges<br>Ruth (329 pages) (11-205)
- I Samuel<br>II Samuel (528 pages) (11-206)
- I Kings<br>II Kings (560 pages) (11-207)
- I Chronicles<br>II Chronicles (528 pages) (11-226)
- Ezra<br>Nehemiah<br>Esther (288 pages) (11-208)
- Job (320 pages) (11-225)
- Psalms (688 pages) (11-216)
- Proverbs (320 pages) (11-227)
- Ecclesiastes<br>Song Of Solomon<br>*(will be ready Summer 2012)* (11-228)
- Isaiah (688 pages) (11-220)
- Jeremiah<br>Lamentations (456 pages) (11-070)
- Ezekiel (508 pages) (11-223)
- Daniel (403 pages) (11-224)
- Matthew (625 pages) (11-073)
- Mark (606 pages) (11-074)
- Luke (626 pages) (11-075)
- John (532 pages) (11-076)
- Acts (697 pages) (11-077)
- Romans (536 pages) (11-078)
- I Corinthians (632 pages) (11-079)
- II Corinthians (589 pages) (11-080)
- Galatians (478 pages) (11-081)
- Ephesians (550 pages) (11-082)
- Philippians (476 pages) (11-083)
- Colossians (374 pages) (11-084)
- I Thessalonians<br>II Thessalonians (498 pages) (11-085)
- I Timothy<br>II Timothy<br>Titus<br>Philemon (687 pages) (11-086)
- Hebrews (831 pages) (11-087)
- James<br>I Peter<br>II Peter (730 pages) (11-088)
- I John<br>II John<br>III John<br>Jude (377 pages) (11-089)
- Revelation (602 pages) (11-090)

For telephone orders you may call 1-800-288-8350 with bankcard information. All Baton Rouge residents please use (225) 768-7000. For mail orders send to:

Jimmy Swaggart Ministries<br>P.O. Box 262550<br>Baton Rouge, LA 70826-2550

---

Visit our website: www.jsm.org

NOTES

# NOTES

# NOTES

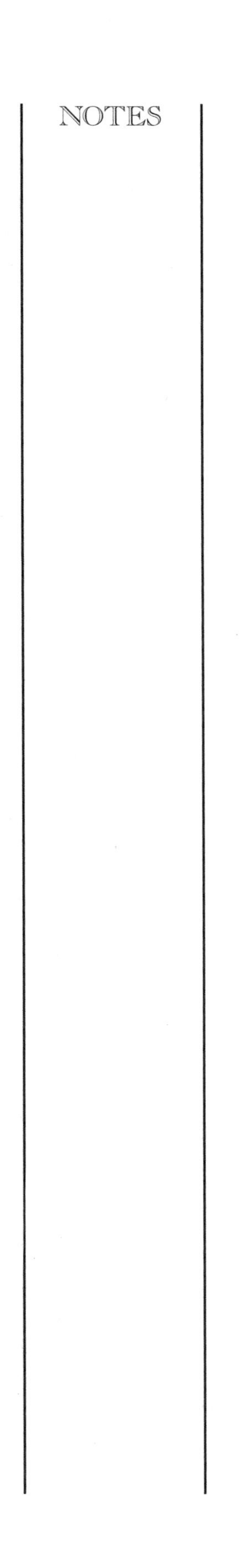
NOTES

NOTES

NOTES

NOTES